ANCIENT IRAN AND ITS NEIGHBOURS

LOCAL DEVELOPMENTS AND LONG-RANGE INTERACTIONS IN THE FOURTH MILLENNIUM BC

ANCIENT IRAN AND ITS NEIGHBOURS

LOCAL DEVELOPMENTS AND LONG-RANGE INTERACTIONS IN THE FOURTH MILLENNIUM BC

EDITED BY CAMERON A. PETRIE

With contributions by
John R. Alden, Hajar Askari, Hossein Azizi Kharanaghi, Rachel Ballantyne,
Gian Luca Bonora, Jacob Dahl, Morteza Djamali, Hassan Fazeli, Barbara Helwing, Vanessa M. A. Heyvaert,
Kristen Hopper, Matthew Jones, Carla Lancelotti, Marjan Mashkour, Roger Matthews, Bernadette McCall,
Benjamin Mutin, Dariosh Norolahie, Cameron A. Petrie, Holly Pittman, Susan Pollock, Daniel T. Potts,
Mitchell Rothman, Alireza Sardari, Lora Stevens, Christopher P. Thornton,
Hamid Reza Valipour, Massimo Vidale, Lloyd Weeks, Tony J. Wilkinson and Henry T. Wright

BIPS

The British Institute of Persian Studies

BRITISH INSTITUTE OF PERSIAN STUDIES
ARCHAEOLOGICAL MONOGRAPHS SERIES III

OXBOW BOOKS
Oxford and Oakville

Published by
Oxbow Books, Oxford, UK

© Oxbow Books and the individual authors, 2013

ISBN 978-1-78297-227-3

This book is available direct from:

Oxbow Books, Oxford, UK
(Phone: 01865-241249; Fax: 01865-794449)

and

The David Brown Book Company
PO Box 511, Oakville, CT 06779, USA
(Phone: 860-945-9329; Fax: 860-945-9468)

or from our website

www.oxbowbooks.com

Cover images:
Front: image of the southern part of the Iranian Plateau and its neighbouring regions in winter.
Back: image of the northern part of the Iranian Plateau and its neighbouring regions in winter.

Both images were generated using NASA Blue Marble: Next Generation satellite imagery, originally produced Reto Stöckli and obtained from NASA's Earth Observatory (NASA Goddard Space Flight Center)
See: http://earthobservatory.nasa.gov/Features/BlueMarble/

Images prepared by C. A. Petrie

A CIP record for this book is available from the British Library

Printed and bound in Great Britain by
Short Run Press, Exeter

CONTENTS

Technologies of craft and administration

Synthesis and discussion

Appendices

Abbreviations

AJA	*American Journal of Archaeology*
AMI	*Archaeologische Mitteilungen aus Iran*
AMIT	Archaeologische Mitteilungen aus Iran und Turan
BaM	*Baghdader Mitteilungen*
Bib Or	*Bibliotheca Orientalis*
ANES	*Ancient Near Eastern Studies*
CDAFI	*Cahiers de la Délégation Archéologique Française en Iran*
CHIr	*Cambridge History of Iran*
EIr	*Encyclopaedia Iranica*
EW	*East and West*, New Series
IA	*Iranica Antiqua*
ICHTO	Iranian Cultural Heritage and Tourism Organisation
JAOS	*Journal of the American Oriental Society*
JCS	*Journal of Cuneiform Studies*
JFA	*Journal of Field Archaeology*
JNES	*Journal of Near Eastern Studies*
JRAS	*Journal of the Royal Asiatic Society*
RA	*Revue d'Assyriologie*

CONTRIBUTORS

JOHN ALDEN
Museum of Anthropology
University of Michigan
Ann Arbor, MI, USA
jralden@umich.edu

HAJAR ASKARI
Sasanian Research Foundation of Fars
Shiraz, Iran

MOHAMMAD HOSSEIN AZIZI KHARANAGHI
University of Tehran
Tehran, Iran

RACHEL BALLANTYNE
McDonald Institute for Archaeological Research
University of Cambridge
Cambridge, UK
rmb51@cam.ac.uk

MANUEL BERBERIAN
Ocean County College
Toms River, NJ, USA
manuel.berberian@gmail.com

GIAN-LUCA BONORA
"L.N. Gumilev" Eurasian National Univeristy
ul. Munaytpasova 5, 010000, Astana, Kazakhstan
gianluca.bonora6@unibo.it

JACOB L. DAHL
Faculty of Oriental Studies
University of Oxford
Oxford, UK
jacob.dahl@orinst.ox.ac.uk

FRANÇOIS DESSET
Archéologies et Sciences de l'Antiquité (UMR7041)
Maison Archéologie & Ethnologie
Paris, France
francois.desset@wanadoo.fr

MORTEZA DJAMALI
Institut Méditerranéen d'Ecologie et de Paléoécologie
UMR CNRS
Aix-en Provence, France

HASSAN FAZELI NASHLI
University of Tehran
Tehran, Iran
hfazelin@ut.ac.ir

BARBARA HELWING
German Archaeological Institute
Eurasia Department
Berlin, Germany
Barbara.Helwing@dainst.de

VANESSA M. A. HEYVAERT
Royal Belgian Institute of Natural Sciences
OD Earth and History of Life
Geological Survey of Belgium
Brussels, Belgium
vanessa.heyvaert@naturalsciences.be

KRISTIN HOPPER
Department of Archaeology
Durham University
Durham, UK
k.a.hopper@durham.ac.uk

MATTHEW JONES
School of Geography
University of Nottingham,
Nottingham, UK
matthew.jones@nottingham.ac.uk

CARLA LANCELOTTI
IMF-CSIC
c/Egipciaques, 15
08001 Barcelona
carla.lancelotti@imf.csic.es

MARJAN MASHKOUR
CNRS / MNHN
UMR 7209, Archéozoologie, Archéobotanique
Dept EGB- Case postale 56
55 rue Buffon
75005 Paris, France
janmash2000@yahoo.com

Roger Matthews
Department of Archaeology
University of Reading
Reading, UK
r.j.matthews@reading.ac.uk

Bernadette McCall
Department of Archaeology
University of Sydney
Sydney, Australia
Bernadette.McCall@sydney.edu.au

Benjamin Mutin
Peabody Museum of Archaeology and Ethnology
Harvard University, 11 Divinity Avenue
Cambridge, MA 02138
USA
benmutin@gmail.com

Dariush Noorollahi
School of Geography
Islamic Azad University of Khorramabad, Iran

Cameron Petrie
Department of Archaeology and Anthropology
University of Cambridge
Cambridge, UK
cap59@cam.ac.uk

Holly Pittman
History of Art
University of Pennsylvania
Philadelphia, PA, USA
hpittman@sas.upenn.edu

Susan Pollock
Institut für Vorderasiatische Archäologie
Freie Universität
Berlin, Germany
spollock@zedat.fu-berlin.de

Daniel T. Potts
Institute for the Study of the Ancient World
New York University
New York City, NY, USA
daniel.potts@nyu.edu

Mitchell S. Rothman
Department of Anthropology
Widener University
Chester, PA, USA
msrothman@widener.edu

Alireza Sardari
Iranian Center for Archaeological Research (ICAR)
National museum, Imam Khomeini street
Tehran
sardary@yahoo.com

Lora Stevens
Department of Geological Sciences
California State University
Long Beach, CA, USA

Christopher P. Thornton
Asian Section
University of Pennsylvania Museum
3260 South St
Philadelphia, PA 19104
cpt2@sas.upenn.edu

Hamid Reza Valipour
Department of Archaeology
Faculty of letters and Humanities
Shahid Beheshti University

Massimo Vidale
Department of Cultural Heritage
University of Padua
Padova, Italy
massimo.vidale@unipd.it

Lloyd Weeks
Department of Archaeology
University of Nottingham
Nottingham, UK
Lloyd.Weeks@nottingham.ac.uk

Tony Wilkinson
Department of Archaeology
Durham University
Durham, UK
t.j.wilkinson@durham.ac.uk

Henry, T. Wright
Department of Anthropology
University of Michigan
Ann Arbor, MI, USA
hwright@umich.edu

ACKNOWLEDGEMENTS

This volume is the product of a group effort by a collection of committed colleagues, and the helpful assistance of some key allies and critical friends. As is discussed in more detail in the introduction, this volume developed out of the papers given at a workshop on Iran in the fourth millennium BC that was held in Cambridge in June 2009. The workshop was made possible by grants kindly provided by the British Institute of Persian Studies, the Ancient India and Iran Trust, and the McDonald Institute for Archaeological Research. The production of this volume has been supported financially by the British Institute of Persian Studies, the McDonald Institute for Archaeological Research, and Trinity College Cambridge. I would like to take this opportunity to thank all the authors who have contributed to this volume. Without exception they met the deadlines that were imposed, and tolerated the often excessive levels of comments that came back to them from the editor. From my perspective as editor, they made the process of putting together the volume as pleasant as is reasonably possible. I would also like to thank those authors who reviewed the initial drafts of the papers presented here. Most read one of the other papers in the volume and several read more than one. In addition, I would like to thank Dan Potts, Christopher Thornton, Augusta McMahon and especially Lloyd Weeks, whose support has made this volume possible. I would especially like to thank Helen Knox for her diligent and precise copy-editing, which has resulted in a much cleaner series of documents than would have been possible if it had only been left up to the authors and editor. I would also like to thank Clare Litt, Val Lamb, Sam McLeod and all those at Oxbow who have helped produce such a handsome volume in double-quick time. Lastly, I would like to thank my family, Sophie, Cleo and Stella, for putting up with me while producing this book. I would like to dedicate it to the present and future archaeologists of Iran.

Cameron A. Petrie, Cambridge, January 2013

1. ANCIENT IRAN AND ITS NEIGHBOURS: THE STATE OF PLAY

Cameron A. Petrie

Introduction

The fourth millennium BC was as a critical period of socio-economic and political transformation in many parts of ancient Western Asia, including the different regions that make up the Iranian Plateau and its surrounding mountain and piedmont zones (Fig. 1.1). It is well known that this protracted period witnessed the appearance of the world's earliest urban centres, hierarchical administrative structures, and writing systems. These developments are all indicative of significant changes in socio-political structures that have been interpreted as evidence for the rise of early states (e.g. Wright and Johnson 1975, 1985; Wright 1977, 1978, 1998), and related processes of interaction, particularly trade (e.g. Algaze 1993, 2005b, 2007, 2008). Initially these transformations were seen as the product of a particularly focused period of increasing complexity at the end of the fourth millennium BC, but they are now seen as being embedded in longer-term processes that began in the later fifth millennium BC, and continued through the fourth and into the early third millennium BC. Iran was an important player in the inter-regional dynamics of socio-economic contact and the medium- to long-range trade in raw materials and finished items throughout this period.

The primary focus of investigations into the processes of socio-economic and political transformation during the fourth millennium BC has traditionally been ancient south Mesopotamia, although for various reasons much of the focus has now shifted to the regions to its north and north-west. In the minds of many scholars, archaeology in modern Iran has been in stasis since the late 1970s, and there has been little development in thinking about the local contexts of the ancient populations of Iran and how they interacted with the populations of Mesopotamia and other areas. After several decades of limited activity, however, Iranian archaeology

experienced a period of resurgence in the 2000s. Sites excavated in the early twentieth century have now been re-evaluated, the reassessment of incompletely studied material from sites excavated in the 1960s and 1970s has commenced, and new survey and excavation projects are filling gaps in knowledge and coverage. Taken together, new research in Iran and in several neighbouring countries has dramatically expanded our knowledge and understanding of local developments on the Iranian Plateau and of long-range interactions during the critical period of the fourth millennium BC.

The workshop entitled Ancient Iran and Its Neighbours: Local Developments and Long-Range Interactions in the Fourth Millennium BC (Fig. 1.2) and the resultant volume which bears the same name, developed from the desire to bring the results of this new (and renewed) research in Iran together in one place. Furthermore, it was an attempt to contextualise the archaeology of what is perhaps more correctly referred to as the Iranian Plateau and its surrounding mountain and piedmont zones, in relation to broader debates about socio-economic and political developments in Western Asia.

This volume presents 20 papers from world experts and specialists of the archaeology of Ancient Iran and its neighbours during the fourth millennium BC, and endeavours to outline the current state of research and highlight some clear objectives for future research. This introductory chapter lays out the *raison d'être* for the volume, by introducing the archaeology of Western Asia and particularly the Iranian Plateau and its mountain and piedmont zones in the fourth millennium BC. In doing so, it outlines the major interpretive models that have been proposed to assess the archaeology of this period. It will also introduce the format and details of the Ancient Iran and Its Neighbours workshop and the papers that were presented there, and outline the

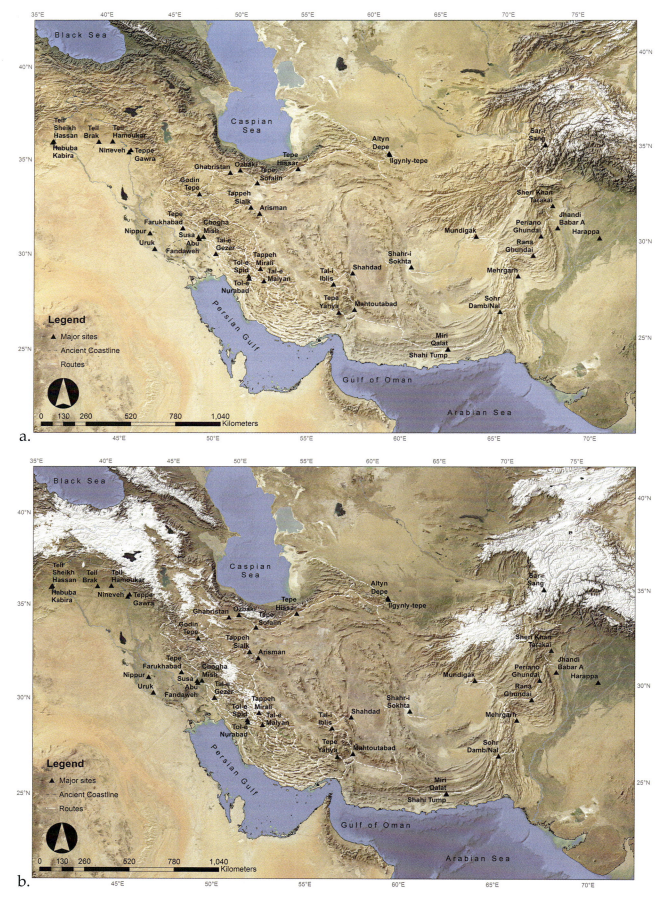

Figure 1.1. a. Summer 2004. b. Winter 2004. NASA Blue Marble image of the Iranian Plateau and its related mountains and piedmonts, with the location of major settled intermontane valleys and alluvial plains indicated by black triangles, and the routes between them and across the plateau indicated in white. NASA Blue Marble: Next Generation satellite imagery was produced by Reto Stöckli and obtained from NASA's Earth Observatory (NASA Goddard Space Flight Center). See: http://earthobservatory. nasa.gov/Features/BlueMarble.

Figure 1.2. Participants of the Ancient Iran and Its Neighbours workshop. 1. Barbara Helwing, 2. John Alden, 3. Cameron Petrie, 4. Tony Wilkinson, 5. Holly Pittman, 6. Kristin Hopper, 7. Enrico Agnolin, 8. Mitchell Rothman, 9. Roger Matthews, 10. Wendy Matthews, 11. François Desset, 12. Jacob Dahl, 13. Helen Taylor, 14. Jenny Marshall, 15. Lisa-Marie Shillito Roberts, 16. Augusta McMahon, 17. Salaam al-Kuntar, 18. Guillermo Algaze, 19. Joan Oates, 20. Reinhard Bernbeck, 21. David Wengrow, 22. Lloyd Weeks, 23. Lars Røgenes, 24. Susan Pollock, 25. Matthew Jones, 26. Vanessa Heyvaert, 27. Jane McIntosh, 28. Benjamin Mutin, 29. Margareta Tengberg, 30. Jérôme-F. Haquet, 31. Carla Lancelotti. Absent – Massimo Vidale, Marjan Mashkour.

fundamental themes and issues that frame the papers presented in this volume. At the outset, however, it is important to comment on some of the terminology that pervades the papers that follow, introduce the relevant geography of the Iranian Plateau and its neighbouring areas, and highlight some of the limitations in approach and coverage.

Terminology

What do we mean by Iran?

In this volume, there is a degree of looseness in the use of the term "Iran". In general, when authors refer to the archaeology of Iran, they are writing about the archaeology of the modern state of Iran. In geographical terms, however, they are also typically writing about the archaeology of the Iranian Plateau and its associated mountains and piedmont zones. The Iranian Plateau and its mountains and piedmonts combine to form one of the dominant geographical features of Western Asia, consisting of a number of major mountain ranges, alluvial plains and fans, intermontane valleys, and desert areas (Fig. 1.1). Taken as a whole, the Iranian Plateau is the key geographical unit that links Western Asia to the South Asian subcontinent, and the various regions of Central Asia, but not all of the Iranian Plateau lies within the bounds of modern Iran. It stretches across parts of Afghanistan, Pakistan, and Turkmenistan, and if the definition were pushed, it could also include parts of north-eastern Iraq. In many ways the Iranian Plateau and its mountains and piedmonts are a logical unit of study, and it is this broader definition that is implied in the use of the name "Iran" in the title of this volume and the papers that it includes.

As Pollock (this volume) points out, it is important not to let modern political boundaries structure our thinking about the past. While most of the contributions focus primarily on archaeological sites within the borders of modern Iran, many of the papers make reference to the archaeology of what are effectively the "neighbouring" regions referred to in the title of the volume (e.g. Hopper and Wilkinson; Wright; Rothman; Thornton; Pittman). In the case of the papers by Mutin and by Bonora and Vidale, there is also explicit coverage of the archaeology of regions outside the borders of modern Iran. Nevertheless, as will be discussed further below, it must be acknowledged that the coverage of the archaeology of the Iranian Plateau and its mountains and piedmonts in the fourth millennium BC is only partially complete. There are areas that have been investigated but are not discussed here, and many areas contain archaeological secrets that are yet to be revealed.

Uruk *and* Proto-Elamite

Since they first began being used in 1930, the terms *'Ubaid, Uruk*, and *Jemdat Nasr* have been multivalent. Although they were effectively derived from the names of type-sites in Mesopotamia, these terms have been used as descriptive labels for pottery types and assemblages, specific archaeological strata, chronological periods, shared material culture, and in the case of *Uruk* and *Jemdat Nasr*, inscribed tablets and proto-writing (Potts 1986: 20–22; also Weeks *et al.* 2010). The term *Proto-Elamite* was introduced earlier (Scheil 1905), and has a more complicated history (see Potts 1999: 71; Abdi 2003). Although initially used to refer to the earliest inscribed tablets recovered at Susa, *Proto-Elamite* is a term that is now similarly multivalent, and is used to refer to pottery types, archaeological strata, a chronological period, distinctive material culture, and inscribed tablets and proto-writing (Abdi 2003; Helwing 2004: 46). Unlike the Mesopotamia-derived terms, however, the term *Proto-Elamite* also carries linguistic connotations. Potts (1999: 71–79) has pointed out that the term is a misnomer, as it implies an evolutionary connection to later *Elamite* languages and scripts that cannot be demonstrated (see Dahl 2009, 2012).

The terms *Uruk* and *Proto-Elamite* are used liberally in the papers that follow, as are references to a wide range of chronological phases whose names are often region-specific. In general there is a degree of consistency and clarity in the use of these terms, although there is variation in several elements, including the chronological spans that are presented. To aid comprehension of what are in many instances regional or even site-specific terminologies, the chronological correlations between these different phases are summarised in Figure 1.3. No attempt has been made to cleanse and/or systematise the views, chronology, or terminology used by the various authors, other than to ensure that the use of terminology is clarified where necessary. As is inevitable, differences of opinion emerge in the following pages.

The Iranian Plateau and its mountains and piedmonts

The geography, climate, and resources of the Iranian plateau will be briefly introduced to outline the spatial and environmental context for the discussion that follows of the broader theoretical background to the archaeology of Western Asia and Iran in the fourth millennium BC.

Geography, environment, and climate

The broad geographical expanse of the Iranian Plateau and its mountains and piedmonts have

Year BC	Period	Susiana	Deh Luran	Central Western Zagros	Central Plateau	Margiana	Fars	Fasa/Darab	Kerman	Daulatabad/Soghun	Seistan	Makran
5000	Neolithic	E Susiana	Sabz / Khazineh	Godin XI	Sialk I.3-5 / L Neolithic II	M Djeitun	Shamsabad	Late Neolithic	Iblis 0/I?	Yahya VII		
	Early Chalcolithic	M Susiana	Mehmeh / Bayat	Godin X/Dalma	E Trans Chalcolithic	L Djeitun	E Bakun		Iblis I	Yahya VI		Period I
4500		L Susiana/Susa I	Farukh	Godin IX/She Gabi	L Trans Chalcolithic	Pre Chalco Anau IA	M Bakun	Chalco.	E Iblis II	Yahya VC / Yahya VB		
				Godin VIII	E Chalco		L Bakun		L Iblis II	Yahya VA		Period II
4000	Late Chalcolithic	Terminal Susiana	Post Farukh	Godin VII / Godin VI:3	Sialk III.4-5 M Chalco	E Chalco NMG I	Lapui	Lapui/ Vakilabad	Iblis III			
		Susa II	E Uruk / M Uruk	Godin VI:2	Sialk III.6-7 L Chalco	M Chalco NMG II	Initial/E Banesh / E-M Ban.		Iblis IV	GAP		Period IIA
3500		A.I.17/17X	L Uruk	Godin VI:1	Sialk IV.1	L Chalco NMG III	L-M Banesh	Unknown	Iblis V?	Yahya IVC	Period 1	Period IIIB
3000		Proto-Elamite/ Susa III	Jemdet Nasr		E Bronze I Sialk IV.2				Iblis VI?			
	Bronze Age	Susa IV	E Dynastic	Godin IV	E Bronze II	NMG IV	L Banesh			GAP	Period II	Period IIIC
2500				Godin III.6			GAP?					

Figure 1.3. *Comparative chronological chart for the regions of ancient Iran and its neighbours.*

several distinctive features, zones, and regions (Fig. 1.1; Fisher 1968; Harrison 1968). Starting from the west, the Zagros Mountains demarcate one arm of the "Fertile Crescent", stretching in a general south-easterly orientation from the Taurus range in the north to the head of the Persian Gulf and then further to the south-east and east, where they line the northern coast of the Persian Gulf and the Gulf of Oman. The lowland piedmont zones to the west of the Zagros Mountains develop into relatively steep uplands comprising ranks of high ridges that are separated by either narrow linear valleys or intermontane valleys and plains. Narrow shores or small plains that lie along a rugged coastal strip mark the coastal regions along the northern shore of the Persian Gulf, and there are narrow valleys and intermontane plains behind the adjacent foothills and the parallel ridges. The ridges at the south-eastern end of the Zagros are more widely spaced, and the intermontane valleys and plains are typically broader than those in the western Zagros. The ridges at the eastern end of the Zagros join the north–south oriented Qā'in-Bīrjand highlands, which link with the Alborz Mountains and the Kopet Dag to the north. Much of the centre of the plateau is either mountainous or is dominated by various deserts, such as the Dasht-e Kavir, Dasht-e Lut, and Sistan Basin, while the Qā'in-Bīrjand highlands separate the Dasht-e Lut from the Sistan Basin. Further to the south-east lie the serried ridges of Makran and Pakistani Baluchistan, which bend to the north and link up with the Suleiman Ranges, which make up the extreme eastern edge of the greater plateau. These areas are also characterised by ridges of different heights and intermontane valleys. The north-eastern part of the plateau, which lies in northern Afghanistan, is made up of the Hindu Kush, which is separated from Makran by the Helmand desert basin. The mountains of the Hindu Kush are particularly high and many areas are difficult to traverse. To their north are the alluvial basin of Bactria and the desert oases of Margiana that lie out in the Kara Kum Desert. To the west of the Hindu Kush and north of the Qā'in-Bīrjand highlands lie the series of ranges and intermontane valleys that make up the Kopet Dag, and to the north of the Kopet Dag lie the piedmonts and alluvial fans at the southern edge of the Kara Kum Desert. The western end of the Kopet Dag joins with the northern uplands of the Alborz Mountains, which are relatively narrow but particularly steep. At their western end, the Alborz Mountains link up with the Zagros ranges and are located to the south of the Caucasus Mountains.

This extensive geographical expanse encompasses a considerable variety of environmental and climatic zones (Ganji 1968). In general the environment of the mountain zones reflects their altitude, and the Zagros, Alborz, Hindu Kush, and Suleiman Mountains all have markedly higher levels of annual precipitation than the areas of the central and more southern part of the plateau, which are all significantly more arid, particularly the desert areas of the Central Plateau (Ganji 1968). Within individual areas, there is also seasonal variation in temperature and vegetation cover, with the highland areas being marked by humid or semi-humid forests, while the more arid zones have steppe or desert vegetation (Bobek 1968).

Settlement and natural resources

Within this varied range of environments there are regions in most parts of the plateau and the adjacent piedmont areas that are suitable for human occupation. Sedentary settlement in different parts of the plateau is typically limited to the piedmonts, alluvial plains, and valleys that have both adequate water resources and sufficient areas of arable land. Only a limited number of areas were suitable for extensive and intensive settlement in the past, and these are irregularly distributed (de Miroschedji 2003; Petrie *et al.* 2009).

The Iranian Plateau also hosts a diverse range of natural resources that were important for the populations of greater Western Asia (Potts 1999; Algaze 2008; Wengrow 2010). Perhaps the most significant of these in the fourth millennium BC were woods of numerous types (e.g. Potts 1999: table 2.9); stone, including a range of precious and semi-precious types (Potts 1999: table 2.6), particularly lapis lazuli; and metals, including lead, silver, and perhaps most importantly copper, which played a key role throughout late prehistory and was sourced from outcrops in different locations on the Central Plateau (Bazin and Hubner 1969; Pigott 1999a, 1999b; Pigott *et al.* 2003; Thornton 2009; Weeks 2012, 2013; also Algaze 2008: 95).

Georgina Herrmann's (1968) study of early lapis trade still stands as one of the most authoritative works on the topic. Despite claims that there was a lapis source in the Chagai Hills in Pakistani Baluchistan (e.g. Jarrige 1988: 28; Jarrige and Hassan 1989: 160–62; Casanova 1992), it is now clear that there was only one primary (and viable) source for lapis in ancient Western Asia. That source was the Šar-i Sang area of Badakhshan in the far north-eastern part of the plateau, on the northern side of the Hindu Kush in northern Afghanistan (Law 2011: 528–43).

Wood was available from a variety of different sources on the plateau, but was most widespread throughout the western parts of the Zagros and the Alborz, which are the most temperate (Bobek 1968). In contrast, metal sources were relatively abundant on the Central Plateau, including the major sources at Anarak and Veshnoveh, and other sources near Qazvin and in Kerman (Algaze 1993; 2005b: fig. 35; Pigott 1999a, 1999b; Pigott *et al.* 2003; Frame 2004; Weeks 2008, 2012).

Routes of passage and routes of interaction

Within the highlands in particular, but also in many of the arid regions, communication and interaction is made possible by paths, tracks, and passes of differing length, which make use of oases, plains, and intermontane valleys of varying width, and also narrow geological faults and passes. These routes provide access between different regions, and enable people to traverse the plateau in different directions, along specific corridors. These routes of passage make up networks of interaction and communication that were (and are) used by people moving between lowland and highland areas and across the interior of the Plateau, and within each of these zones (Fig. 1.1a–1.1b). Some parts of the plateau are affected by snowfall in the winter, while others are arid and lack reliable sources of water (Fig. 1.1a–1.1b). It is likely that the distinctive topography of the Iranian Plateau and its mountain and piedmont zones imposed specific constraints on human movement and behaviour throughout later prehistory and subsequent periods, including its key role in the various Silk Routes that ultimately linked the Far East with Western Asia and Europe. While human traction was undoubtedly one of the most important elements of mobility and transport during the fourth millennium BC and inevitably served to limit movement, it is important to point out that by the late fourth millennium BC, there is clear evidence that pack donkeys and wheeled carts were in use on the Iranian Plateau (Sherratt 1997; Wright 2001), which inevitably played an important role in increasing the pace and volume of various interactive processes.

The possible routes via which lapis travelled from its source to Mesopotamia (and also Egypt) were long and relatively difficult, either traversing substantial parts of the greater Iranian Plateau, or crossing the Hindu Kush and moving down the Indus River and thence via the Persian Gulf. Although there is clear evidence for connections between Mesopotamia and the Persian Gulf during the fifth and third millennia BC, there is an absence of evidence for such connections during the fourth millennium BC, and also relatively little lapis. The toponym Dilmun, however, which is the name for Bahrain and the adjacent area of Saudi Arabia, appears in the third millennium BC (Potts 2009b: 30–31). Parker and Goudie (2007) have suggested that the early urbanism in the late fourth millennium BC was concurrent with a localised phase of high aridity in the Persian Gulf, and referred to this period as "the Dark Millennium" (also Uerpmann 2003; Wengrow 2010: 64–65). On the basis of current evidence, therefore, it is most likely that during the fourth millennium BC overland routes were being used for trade and communication in preference to the Persian Gulf.

Using least-cost path modelling, T. C. Wilkinson (2012) has shown that the lowest-cost route in terms of geographical difficulty actually skirts the northern edge of the plateau and follows the Caspian Sea coast before crossing the Alborz where it meets the northern Zagros and Taurus ranges. The extensive evidence for lapis exploitation at Tepe Hissar during the fourth millennium BC (*Period II*; Tosi 1984, 1989; Thornton *et al.*, this volume), however, suggests that at least some of the stone was carried via the plateau during that period. If so, it probably skirted the Hindu Kush and Kopet Dag piedmont before crossing the Kopet Dag or the Alborz, and proceeded along the southern side of the Alborz along the edge of the Central Plateau and thence through one of the passes in the Zagros to Mesopotamia. All possible routes across the plateau necessitate at least skirting the edge of the Central Plateau, followed by passage across one of the many passes of the Zagros Mountains and into the lowlands, thus linking many of the geographically distinct regions that lie in different parts of the plateau (Fig. 1.1). Wengrow (2010: 37) has proposed that these lapis routes were the "channels along which meanings and values spread between otherwise disparate groups".

The routes along which wood and metals moved across and subsequently left the plateau were inevitably shorter than those used for lapis, but all would have required the use of many of the same passes through the Zagros Mountains. As in the case of lapis lazuli, the routes via which wood and metals moved were also networks that both facilitated and constrained the spread of meanings and values, and ideas, technologies and, inevitably, people.

Limitations and caveats

Issues of approach

The fourth millennium BC poses a specific set of methodological problems for scholars, as it sits at the very transition between the prehistoric and (proto-) historic periods in ancient Western Asia. While the preceding millennia are marked by a number of clear transformations in socio-economic behaviour, they are clearly prehistoric, as is much of the fourth millennium itself. Approaches to archaeological research and particularly the theorisation of the socio-economic dynamics that were in play thus inevitably operate within the scope of what can feasibly be discussed in such prehistoric contexts. By *c.* 3300–3100 BC, however, we reach a transition point after which begins a protracted period marked by the increasing use of texts and associated administrative paraphernalia to record a wide range of information. While the fourth millennium BC as a whole is marked by tantalising evidence for transformations in socio-economic organisation, and the operation of trading and interaction systems in various regions, the precocious textual materials only provide information about a diverse yet relatively limited range of "things"

Cameron A. Petrie

(e.g. places, animals, plants, manufactured products, literature, and designations; Englund 1998a). This contrasts sharply with the evidence from the mid-third millennium BC onwards in Mesopotamia and many of the neighbouring regions, where there is an "embarrassment of riches" in terms of the range and diversity of the textual sources that exist and inform us about socio-economic, religious, and political activities (e.g. Postgate 1994; Kuhrt 1997; Potts 1997; Van De Mieroop 2004, 2006). Given that there is clear evidence of cultural continuity from the fourth into the third millennium and beyond in many of the regions where early texts were used, particularly in Mesopotamia (Algaze 2008, 2012), there has been an inevitable temptation to draw on the textual resources of the later periods to frame explanations and draw analogies for the types of activities (socio-economic, religious, and/or political) occurring during the fourth millennium BC. This approach has been particularly prevalent when trying to understand the economics of long-range interaction in the fourth millennium BC (e.g. Algaze 2001a, 2001b, 2005a, 2008, 2012). There has also been a tendency to draw on a range of ethnographic analogies to frame explanations, particularly those related to the behaviour of nomads and/or mobile groups. This approach has been used to understand both the groups that are referred to in the third millennium BC and later who operate beyond the bounds of urban societies, and to speculate on their fifth- and fourth-millennium BC predecessors (e.g. Barnard and Wendrich 2008; Alizadeh 2010). The scholars drawing these analogies are cognizant of and clearly acknowledge the limitations of such approaches, and several reviewers of these works have questioned the appropriateness of their use (e.g. Postgate 1996; McMahon 2010; Potts 2008; Weeks 2013), but the models that derive from such analogies stand in the literature. Our understanding of the fourth millennium BC is thus inevitably left with instances where hypotheses are qualified as "possible", rather than the "likely" or "probable" that we would no doubt prefer, but it is precisely these attempts to speculate on the range of possible explanations that stimulate further research.

Coverage

The Iranian Plateau is an enormous geographical entity that crosses the borders of a number of modern states, which lie in a part of the world that has seen varying degrees of political unrest since the 1970s. As a result, many areas on the plateau have not yet been investigated systematically, and there are many areas where a basic awareness of the archaeological record exists, but few excavations. There is also the added complication that research in different areas

has been carried out by archaeologists in different eras, coming from very different research traditions.

The workshop from which this volume derives aspired to be as representative as possible in terms of participants, and in many ways that aim was achieved. Not everyone that was invited could attend, however, and sadly too few papers by Iranian scholars were presented. Circumstances beyond their control meant that none of the invited Iranian scholars were able to attend the workshop in the first place and only a small number of those who were intending to come were able to submit papers for this volume; nonetheless, the papers that were submitted make a profoundly important contribution to it.

Many of the papers discuss survey and excavations conducted before the Iranian revolution (e.g. Wright; Rothman; Thorton; Alden; Pittman; Matthews; Dahl *et al.*). The intervening period highlighted the fact that there were considerable gaps in our knowledge and several of the papers present the results of more recent excavation in regions that had not previously been investigated in detail (e.g. Helwing; Fazeli *et al.*; Petrie *et al.*; Sardari; Vidale and Desset). Inevitably there remain gaps in our knowledge, and these will only be filled by new programmes of question-oriented fieldwork and research (see Petrie, this volume: Conclusion).

Investigating Western Asia and Iran in the fourth millennium BC

Given its strategic geographical location and the richness of its raw material resources, it was perhaps inevitable that the peoples of the Iranian Plateau became important agents in a range of socio-economic and political processes throughout the late prehistoric and early historic periods. This is particularly true for the fourth millennium BC. When attempting to situate fourth-millennium BC Iran in a broader archaeological discourse relevant to this period, however, one finds it unavoidable to focus on other areas. This is partly because ancient Mesopotamia and the greater Fertile Crescent have been the axis around which much of our thinking about ancient Western Asia has rotated. For the fourth millennium BC, this point is particularly emphasised by the virtual deluge of books, journal articles, and volumes of collected papers that have appeared since the 1980s dealing with the *Uruk* period. This wealth of publications has made it hard to escape the intense focus on the developments that took place in Mesopotamia and the consideration of the impact that these developments had on neighbouring regions. Furthermore, it has hindered scholars' ability to determine whether these developments might have been taking place independently in those neighbouring regions.

The "Uruk expansion" and the "Uruk World System"

In Mesopotamia and many of the surrounding regions, the term *Uruk* had been used to refer to the entirety of the fourth millennium BC since 1930 (Frankfort 1932; Perkins 1949; see Potts 1986). Our understanding of what has since been referred to as the "Uruk phenomenon" (e.g. Collins 2001), however, increased exponentially from the 1960s onwards, thanks to surveys conducted around the type-site of Uruk/Warka by Adams and Nissen (1972), the characterisation and analysis of the *Uruk* material repertoire by Nissen (e.g. 1988, 2002; also Sürenhagen 1986, 1987), the detailed survey of the surface at Uruk itself (Finkbeiner 1991), and a number of significant rescue and non-rescue excavations in various regions in north Mesopotamia (e.g. Strommenger 1980). Although awareness of this important period grew progressively, it was Guillermo Algaze's identification of an "Uruk Expansion" (1989), and his provocative proposal of the existence of an "Uruk World System" (1993, 2005b) that proved to be the primary catalyst for an ongoing academic debate about the nature of early complexity and the dynamics of contact, interaction, and influence.

Algaze applied the principles of economic anthropology to the interpretation of the *Uruk* period, particularly in terms of understanding socio-economic processes and the nature and development of early complexity and urbanism in southern Mesopotamia. Although his arguments have gone through several iterations and reformulations, at its heart Algaze's primary proposition is that the Mesopotamian "core" came to dominate its less economically advantaged and developed "periphery" (Algaze 1989, 1993, 2001a, 2005a, 2005b, 2007, 2008, 2012). Although such a statement inevitably simplifies an elegant and nuanced set of models, they all posit the existence of an asymmetrical relationship that sees a level of southern Mesopotamian "influence" on its surrounding regions.

In Algaze's initial conception (1993, 2005b), the dominance of southern Mesopotamia saw phases of colonisation and the establishment of colonies in the form of "enclaves", "stations", and "outposts" (Algaze 1993; 2005b: 13). Although much of this has since been challenged and in some ways superseded, the interpretation of the situation in Iran has largely remained static. Algaze (e.g. 1989, 2008) has long considered trade to be the critical (and previously under-appreciated) factor in the development of urbanism and complexity in both southern Mesopotamia and the surrounding regions. The lack of a range of raw materials on the Mesopotamian alluvium and their presence in the surrounding regions meant that from the time of the earliest settlement on the plains, exchange and trade provided Mesopotamia with a variety of exotic or at least

otherwise unavailable raw materials, particularly specific types of stone, wood, and metals (see Potts 1997).

In his seminal volume *The Uruk World System*, Algaze (1993; 2005b: 2) suggested that periods of centralisation and coherence on the alluvium were, "preceded by an increase in resource procurement activities and were generally followed by more or less successful processes of expansion that can be interpreted as attempts to control the critical routes through which flowed the needed resources". He argued that the elaboration of socio-economic differentiation and the transition to urbanism in Mesopotamia during the mid-fourth millennium BC resulted in increased demand for prestige raw materials and goods (i.e. metals, lumber, and semi-precious stones) that were unavailable in the lowlands (Algaze 1993, 2005b). This demand in turn led to the progressive development of a system of implanting "enclaves", "stations", and "outposts" to facilitate the supply of raw materials and finished items from the areas surrounding the alluvium (Algaze 1993; 2005b: 23, 46–60). The differentiation of each type of colony settlement is based on its size and local context, with *enclaves* being large central settlements at strategic nodes along lines of communication in the north that were surrounded by a cluster of smaller dependent villages; *stations* being small settlements which lay on waterways and supported communication and interaction with enclaves; and *outposts* being small isolated settlements located at important points on the overland communication routes in the Zagros and the Taurus.

The identification of interaction and influence during the *Uruk* period is primarily based on the appearance of a range of specific material culture items, primarily ceramic vessels (e.g. bevel-rim bowls, jars with drooping spouts, jars with incised shoulder decoration) outside the area of the Mesopotamian alluvium from where they originated. Assessing the distribution patterns of this material, Algaze (1993, 2005b) delineated two distinct dynamics of interaction between Mesopotamia and the Iranian Plateau and its western piedmont. In Susiana, in lowland south-west Iran, there is evidence of the widespread adoption of Mesopotamian-style material culture, and also ultimately administrative practices, during the *Susa II* period, which spans much of the fourth millennium BC. Algaze (1993; 2005b: 16) argued that this evidence was indicative of a deliberate colonisation of Susiana by people from Mesopotamia for the purpose of acquiring and holding land, effectively making it an eastern extension of the Mesopotamian alluvium (Algaze 1993; 2005b: 113; also Amiet 1979). In Algaze's formulation, this annexation of what is effectively one of the piedmonts of the Iranian Plateau apparently preceded the more formal phase of deliberate resource procurement. This latter period saw expansion from centres in southern Mesopotamia to places like Nineveh and Tell Brak and from there to the Balikh Valley, and the subsequent consolidation of these areas through the foundation of enclaves, stations, and possibly outposts further north into the highlands (Algaze 1993; 2005b: 110ff.). While lowland Susiana appears to have been colonised in some fashion, there is also clear evidence for the presence of ostensibly Mesopotamian pottery at sites in the Iranian highlands such as Godin Tepe in the Central Western Zagros, and Tappeh Sialk on the Central Plateau. Algaze (1993; 2005b: 62–63) suggested that these later occupations were representative of "outposts" of the colonial system, although he did not specify whether this process was operating from Mesopotamia or Susiana. Earlier, Weiss and Young (1975) had claimed that Godin Tepe was an outpost of Susa, as Susa is far closer to Godin Tepe and Tappeh Sialk than those settlements are to lower Mesopotamia.

In his initial formulation, Algaze (1993; 2005b: 107) proposed that the *Uruk* expansion was a likely catalyst for the "growth of complex, differentiated, and independent socio-political systems across some portions of the periphery", and made reference to the development of the "Proto-Elamite state" or "Proto-Elamite polity" on the Iranian Plateau in this context. In this formulation, long-distance resource acquisition and related interaction thus accounts for development in both core and periphery, and it is perhaps unsurprising that such a provocative claim was not widely accepted by those working in the periphery.

Reorienting thinking on the "Uruk expansion"

Algaze's proposal of an "Uruk World System" has unquestionably been the catalyst for an unresolved debate about the fundamental intra- and interregional relationships that existed before, during, and after the development of the earliest urbanised settlements in ancient Western Asia (e.g. Lupton 1996; Stein 1999a, 1999b, 2005; Rothman 2001a; Collins 2001; Postgate 2002; Butterlin 2003). To some extent, the intensity and orientation of the debate is due to the significant reorientation that has occurred in the locus of fieldwork in the Near East. The intensification of interest in the *Uruk* period has paradoxically coincided with the cessation of archaeological fieldwork in Iraq, which has in turn contributed to an increase of attention on the archaeology of eastern Syria and south-east Turkey.

The increase in work "outside" southern Mesopotamia has also been accompanied by improvements in archaeological research methods and recovery strategies, and an abundance of well-analysed and dated material from these regions has now been generated. In contrast, there has been virtually no new information from the traditional Mesopotamian heartland (Nissen 2001, 2002). Research in areas traditionally considered peripheral to southern Mesopotamia has revealed a range of evidence for the local dynamics that preceded, accompanied, and succeeded the protracted phase of *Uruk* contact. This evidence has been used to critique Algaze's model, support the formulation of alternative hypotheses that seek to de-emphasise the role of interregional interaction in socio-economic development, and highlight the likelihood that the periphery might have seen a range of independent developments. These alternate views are presented in detail in several volumes (e.g. Stein 1999b; Rothman 2001a; Postgate 2002; Butterlin 2003; Frangipane 2007), and the salient arguments will be outlined here.

Part of the reaction to Algaze's "Uruk World System" model derives from the critique of the world-system model as initially defined by Wallerstein (1974; see also Kohl 1978, 1989), particularly the assumptions that: a) the dominance of the core means that the periphery is passive; b) core-periphery relationships were exploitative and unequal exchange comes to structure the political economy of the periphery; and c) long-distance exchange is a prime mover of social change (Stein 1999a: 16–26; after Wolf 1982; Curtin 1984; Schortman and Urban 1994). Despite these problems, Stein (1999a: 27–43) has pointed out that archaeologists have used the world-system model extensively as an interpretative tool, even though there have been questions about the suitability of the concept of a world-system to describe pre- or non-capitalist systems. He has also recognised that for world-system models to conform to ancient contexts, substantial modifications to the original definition are required (Stein 1999a: 27–43). For example, Stein (1999a: 35) points out that several examples of trade relationships in ancient Western Asia, such as that between Mesopotamia and the entities of Dilmun, Magan, and Meluhha in the third millennium BC, are more likely to have involved relationships of interdependence rather than core-controlled asymmetric exchange.

In looking at the fourth millennium BC, it has been noted that there was significant socio-economic development in "peripheral" areas before the period of *Uruk* "contact", and populations in Anatolia and Iran were controlling sources of raw materials and producing technologically advanced products, suggesting that there was a degree of technological parity (Lupton 1996; Stein 1999a: 112–16). Stein (1999a: 46–64) has proposed two complementary models of inter-regional exchange as alternatives to the world-system models generally, but also more specifically as alternatives to Algaze's world-systems model for fourth-millennium BC Mesopotamia (Stein 1999a: 82–169). The model of trade diasporas recognises variation in power relations, and suggests that foreigners endeavoured to act as trade specialists who, while maintaining their distinctive cultural identity, did not dominate the hosts in enclaves or colonies. Communication and transport were so difficult that centralised state institutions were incapable of providing physical or economic security to the agents in long-distance interaction, and foreigners were present at the behest of the local ruling elite, suggesting that a reciprocal or mutually exploitative relationship was in operation (Lupton 1996: 68; Stein 1999a: 46–48). Stein (1999a: 99–100) argues that settlements like Godin Tepe and Hacınebi may conform well to this trade diaspora model.

This model can co-exist with a model of distance parity, which suggests that there was a distance-related decay in the power that could be exerted by core states (Stein 1999a: 62–64). Building on Mann's (1986) four overlapping sources of social power (ideological, economic, military, and political), Stein (1999a: 55–57) argues that economic power can be derived from the distribution of natural resources, the inter-regional balance of population, technological advantage – particularly the organisational component – and political organisation in the form of complex, stratified, and integrated societies. It is not easy to exert power across space to influence distant centres or polities, however, and maintaining power in this fashion is expensive due to the cost of transport in human, animal, and material terms (Stein 1999a: 57–59). As such, the ability of the core to exercise power diminishes over distance, so relations become increasingly symmetrical with greater distance, including the decline/reduction/ restriction of control over: 1) inter-regional exchange; 2) the importance of long-distance relative to local exchange; 3) the trade of bulk goods in contrast to prestige goods; 4) economic pressures towards specialised production of goods for export; 5) influence of core elites on periphery elites; and 6) the ability of the core to exert military, economic, or political control, and the degree to which the process of interaction impacts upon the socio-economic and political organisation of the periphery (Stein 1999a: 62–64). Stein (1999a: 114) argues that the vast distances between Uruk and the highland sources of wood and copper in Anatolia and the Iranian Plateau, which could only be reached by travelling up-stream and up-hill, would undoubtedly have constrained the power and coercive force that could be exerted from southern Mesopotamia.

Other alternate perspectives have also been presented, including those outlined in volumes edited by Rothman (2001a) and Postgate (2002). Rothman (2001b: 6) has highlighted the fact that although Algaze's initial formulation argued that development in the north was catalysed by contact with the south, by the end of the 1990s there was evidence for social hierarchy and the development of control mechanisms at various sites, including

Arslan Tepe, Hacınebi, and Tepe Gawra, before the appearance of evidence for increased cultural contact (see Frangipane 2001, 2007; Stein 1999b, 2001; Rothman and Peasnall 1999; Rothman 2001c, 2002).

The range of criticisms levelled at different elements of Algaze's model is broad. Wright (2001) notes that an increase in the number and resolution of the radiocarbon dates from the northern regions shows that the process of *Uruk* interaction was much more protracted than previously thought, potentially lasting up to 600 years (also Wright and Rupley 2001).[1] Frangipane (2001, 2002) questions the degree to which elites, technology, production, and trade, as evidenced at Arslantepe, were influenced by the south, and sees most developments as the product of local dynamics. Stein (2001, 2005) reiterates his view that there was a measurable decline in the level of control that was possible over increasing distances. Schwartz (2001) questions whether the *Uruk* colony settlements in the north, such as Habuba Kabira and Jebel Aruda, were actually involved in trade and suggests that they were colonies of settlers (see Rothman 2001b). One of the key points in several papers in the Rothman volume (Rothman 2001b, 2001c; Frangipane 2001; Stein 2001; Pittman 2001) relates to the significance that can be gleaned from the presence of south Mesopotamian-styled artefacts and technologies – in Rothman's words (2001b: 21) "asking whether the appearance of these artifacts represents colonization by Southerners, trade or emulation". Inevitably the meaning and significance of introduced or adopted elements changes over time, and may also be variable between regions, settlements, or even different locations within one settlement. Rothman (2001b: 24) stresses that, while there is evidence of increased levels of contact between various regions and southern Mesopotamia, increased interaction along regional interaction networks, and the possible migration of populations to the north, it is unlikely that this can be explained by "any single factor or cause", and he also noted that there is little agreement on a range of factors.

While Stein's alternative models certainly have potential, Rothman (2001a) and Postgate's (2002) volumes highlight the fact that there is a richness and level of nuance to the reading of the northern evidence that is lacking in the interpretation of the situation in the Iranian Plateau and its mountains and piedmonts. As acknowledged by Stein (1999a: 102, 115), both his and Algaze's models have generally focused on *Uruk*– related settlements rather than the local societies of the regions in which those sites appear, and have been formulated with limited consideration of the local non-*Uruk* contexts. The latest insights into the local pre-*Uruk* contexts on the plains of north Syria dramatically alter our basic understanding of the evolution of urbanism, and show the potential for challenging some of the long-held fundamental tenets of Mesopotamian archaeology. For instance, there is now evidence from Tell Brak (Oates *et al.* 2007; Ur *et al.* 2007, 2011; McMahon *et al.* 2007) and Tell Hamoukar (Gibson *et al.* 2002; Ur 2011; al-Kuntar and Abu Jayyab in press) of large urban-scale sites in the north, with a distinctive northern character, before any trace of *Uruk* influence, and potentially before urban centres had developed in the south.

"The Mesopotamian Advantage" and "The Sumerian Take-off"

Although Algaze found himself, to use his own words, "eating a lot of crow" (Wilford 2000) in the wake of the range and wealth of new evidence from south-east Turkey and eastern Syria, he has steadfastly continued to develop his interpretive models to take account of these new findings. This has seen him shift his focus to dynamics in the south, incorporating the results of new investigations into the environment of southern Mesopotamia (e.g. Pournelle 2003, 2012; Lawler 2011; Hritz *et al.* 2012; Hritz and Pournelle in press). As with his world-system model, his new formulations ("The Mesopotamian Advantage" [2001a] and "The Sumerian Take-off" [2005a, 2007, 2008]) are provocative and encourage debate.

The key tenets of Algaze's more recent formulations are that the rise of complexity in southern Mesopotamia was a synergy that resulted from the material advantages afforded by the region, including: a) a density and variety of subsistence resources; b) the ability to obtain higher and more reliable yields; and c) a more efficient transport system based on riverine transport (Algaze 2001a: 200–04; 2005a; 2007: 362–65; 2008: 40–63, 123–27). The technological and social developments that ultimately grew out of these material advantages, which Algaze calls "ideational" technologies or "technologies of the intellect" (i.e. mass production of standardised commodities, organisation and control of dependent labour, information processing, and record keeping), resulted in economic advantage for southern Mesopotamia through asymmetrical exchange based on the low-cost production of luxury textiles and the advantages of import substitution, which both led to "multiplier effects" (Algaze 2001a: 207–09; 2005a; 2007; 2008: 64–92, 127–39). He sees this as a multi-stage process beginning with trade in specialised commodities between the nascent centres of the southern alluvium (*Early Uruk*?), followed by a phase of competitive emulation between the centres and import substitution of certain items (e.g. clay sickles for flint tools; *Middle Uruk*), before a phase of extensive external trade involving outposts at strategic locations (*Middle* and *Late Uruk*; Algaze 2001a: 207; 2005a; 2007: 353–54). In this new model the flag appears to follow trade, and the latter stage particularly resembles key aspects of the *Uruk* world-system model (see above),

although Algaze (2005a; 2007: 355; 2008: 77) also sees this final stage as representing a shift in approaches to metals, such that the cities of southern Mesopotamia were no longer simply consumers, but became value-added producers who used imported ingots and perhaps ores.

For Algaze (2008: 156) "trade was the key transformative agent in the crystallisation of early Sumerian urban societies", and he sees it not as the product of complexity, but a key driving element in the process. The supply of exotics by trade was used by elites to mark, legitimise, and expand their unequal access to resources and power, and was critical for major initiatives such as the elaborate temple building projects seen at Uruk (Algaze 2001: 208; 2001a; 2005a; 2007; 2008: 93–99). In his comment on Algaze's (2001a) paper, Lamberg-Karlovsky (2001) emphasises the importance of the supernatural and the fact that the elites in early Mesopotamia were in control of divinely sanctioned socio-economic structures, and this element invariably demands further consideration. Wengrow (2010: 29–30) has emphasised that the unusual materials obtained through trade were not "exotica", but were important elements in a social system that is able to acquire and deploy these resources as what he calls "markers of distinction". They take the form of currency, and are signs of sacred power that elites use to maintain their special relationship with the gods, thereby legitimating the hierarchical social structures (Wengrow 2010: 29–30). Algaze, however, also acknowledges that at present the evidence is equivocal, and it is unclear whether trade is a cause or a consequence—his belief in the primacy of trade is in his words, "more a proclamation of faith than a conclusion made necessary by evidence at hand" but one that is "based instead on my explicit theoretical orientation concerning the root forces that generally underlie endogenous urban processes" (Algaze 2008: 156). Until detailed excavations are carried out at relevant sites in southern Mesopotamia and in the surrounding regions, we will be left with more questions.

Various studies have also shown that early texts almost exclusively deal with local matters (e.g. Damerow and Englund 1989; Englund 1998b), and there is no textual information from the fourth or early third millennia BC on long-distance trade. While the texts do not address many things that are evident in later periods, as Algaze (2005a; 2008: 77) has pointed out, they do list metals and metal objects, and also stone beads, including the signs for lapis lazuli, which translate to "beads of the mountain" (Englund 1998a: 98). As Wengrow (2010: 27) has pointed out, the early texts do not reveal anything about how the technology of writing, its learning or transmission within and between societies, but there was clearly an organised scribal tradition that facilitated this process (Damerow 2006; Dahl *et al.*, this volume).

Although initially advocating the chronological primacy of developments in southern Mesopotamia (Algaze 2001a: 200), Algaze now acknowledges that cities developed early in the north (Algaze 2008: 117–22). Primacy in terms of scale, density, and complexity of settlements still sits in the south, however, with its larger sites, agglomerations of settlements, and clearer signs of settlement and socio-economic hierarchies (Algaze 2001a: 209–10; 2005a; 2007: 358–62; 2008: 102–21), but as McMahon has pointed out (2010: 135), the evidence is heterogeneous and the differences between the developments in the south and the north are marked, which makes it difficult to draw comparisons.

Alongside Algaze's evolving thoughts on development in Mesopotamia, there has also been a range of other views put forward about processes and dynamics. For instance, Collins (2001) has argued that the *Uruk expansion* saw the spread of a social ideology (i.e. management, administration, trade, economy, urbanisation, warfare, and religion). Gosden (2004: 53) has presented an overtly post-colonial view in arguing that the *Uruk* expansion saw the creation of a shared cultural milieu or *koine* in which there were many participants and all of them had influence. If Mesopotamia was at all central then its importance was due to the special depth and potency that it had in relations with the divine (Gosden 2004: 53). Within this shared cultural milieu, Gosden (2004: 53) argues that the use of bevel-rim bowls, numerical tablets, and ultimately proto-writing saw the progressive objectification of people and things, where the material world was divided into quantities that had set values, and that the *Uruk* expansion saw the dispersal of this phenomenon. This sentiment is echoed and expanded by Wengrow (2010: 80) who asks, "why would products manufactured in southern Mesopotamia have been especially desirable in the first place?" and suggests that it is potentially an outgrowth of the move towards measurement and standardisation, which led to the beginnings of the branding of commodities that may have been regarded as sacred in nature by both those in southern Mesopotamia and elsewhere (Wengrow 2010: 81–87). None of these views supplant those outlined by Algaze.

In an important instance of reflexivity, Algaze spends some time considering the limitations of the available evidence and positing a way forward for future research (Algaze 2008: 151–65), and as this volume will show, many of these issues are also relevant to the discussion of the archaeology of the Iranian Plateau and its mountains and piedmonts. For example, Algaze (2008: 151–65) highlights the need for the consideration of various types of agency, and also the need for material evidence for palaeoenvironment, trade, households and property, palaeozoology, mortuary evidence, chronology, and the nature of *Early Uruk* occupation in southern Mesopotamia. Disappointingly, this list covers a very wide range of archaeological evidence types, suggesting that there is a considerable amount of work to be done. All of these categories can only be properly investigated through new excavations and surveys on the ground.

Research on Iran in the fourth millennium BC

As will be apparent from the above review, archaeological sites in Iran are typically deemed to have played an important role in the fourth millennium BC, and the settlement patterns of Susiana and the distinctive occupation at Godin Tepe are used by various scholars as clear case studies for dynamics of colonisation (e.g. Amiet 1979; Algaze 1993; 2001a; 2005b: 11–18, 53–57, 62–63; Potts 1999; Stein 1999a; Gosden 2004). The evidence from these regions is no doubt compelling, but the evidence for contact with Mesopotamia in the pre-enclave occupation levels at Godin Tepe (Badler 2002; Rothman and Badler 2011) and the appearance of bevel-rim bowls and other *Uruk* ceramic forms in otherwise local assemblages at sites like Ghabristan (Majidzadeh 1977, 1981, 2008), Tappeh Sialk (Ghirshman 1938; Helwing 2004), Tal-e Kureh (Alden 1979, 2003), and possibly even Tal-i Iblis (Caldwell 1967), has not been discussed with any robustness or chronological precision. Taking Rothman's (2001b: 21) line, we might rightly ask, "does this material represent colonization, trade or emulation?" The significance of the bevel-rim bowl has been discussed from an Iranian perspective (e.g. Beale 1978; Potts 2009a), and it is likely that there will be many possible explanations to explain the appearance of any one vessel form across a large area.

The lack of information referred to by Stein (1999a) about local non-*Uruk* contexts in areas that are peripheral to Mesopotamia is particularly true for the Zagros and areas further to the east into which the proposed *Uruk* enclaves/way stations were implanted. In fact, with relatively few exceptions (e.g. Wright 1998; Potts 1999; Pittman 2001; Matthews and Fazeli 2004; Helwing 2005a, 2005b), the nature of cultural interaction between Mesopotamia and its neighbours in the fourth millennium BC has not focused on the Zagros and the Iranian Plateau and their mountain and piedmont areas in any great detail. When the plateau is discussed, it is invariably from a Mesopotamian perspective, and as Potts (2004: 24–25) has noted, there has been a tendency to present simplistic impressions of the archaeological circumstances in the various regions of the plateau. Furthermore, the dynamic that develops in Susiana and in the highlands during the *Proto-Elamite* or *Susa III* periods and how it relates to the *Uruk* phenomenon has also largely been left out of consideration in most of the discussion of the *Uruk* phenomenon itself (see below).

The proposed *Uruk* colonisation of Susiana and the precise motivations for this process are an interesting case in point. While Wright and Johnson used the evidence from Susiana in several seminal volumes and papers to discuss the evolution of early states (e.g. Johnson 1973; Wright and Johnson 1975, 1985; Wright 1977, 1978, 1987, 1998), the nature of the relationship between the centres that develop in Susiana (Susa and Chogha Mish) and those of Mesopotamia is rarely articulated. Algaze initially suggested (1993; 2005b: 16) that Susiana was colonised in the form of a political takeover, but Potts (1999: 59–67) has pointed out that Susiana shows evidence for the use of a relatively small selection of the numerical systems found at Uruk, and used this to support his suggestion that the colonisation of Susiana was not politically motivated, but was effected through a more informal infiltration of Uruk/southern Mesopotamians (Potts 1999: 67). Alizadeh (2010: 370) prefers the term migration for explaining this process. It is notable that Johnson (1973) showed that this colonisation is likely to have occurred during the *Early* and *Middle Uruk* periods, rather than the *Late Uruk*.

As Algaze (2001a, 2005a, 2007, 2008; see above) has pointed out, there are fundamental differences in scale between the urban behemoth at Uruk and the notably smaller centres at Susa and Chogha Mish, so there were inevitably differences between the two regions in the operations, motivations, and structures. How are we then to conceptualise the early to mid-fourth-millennium BC developments in Susiana? Were these developments the result of processes simply taking place in an extension of Mesopotamia, or were they related to, yet distinct from, those processes happening in Mesopotamia?

It is also notable that while there have been important publications that have taken reflective approaches to look from the "periphery" of east Turkey (e.g. Stein 1999a; Frangipane 2007), this has not yet happened for Iran. For instance, it might be argued that the preferential distribution of desirable raw materials in the highlands of the Iranian Plateau gave that region a fundamental source of economic power, and this was perhaps enhanced by the possession of the technological knowledge to exploit these resources, particularly copper. Precisely how this potential for economic power and technological knowledge played out in the interaction between different populations in the highlands, and between those groups and the inhabitants of the lowlands of Mesopotamia, has not been clearly articulated.

The lack of integration of Iranian material into broader theoretical debates relating to the fourth millennium BC is in some respects a product of the cessation of archaeological field research in Iran immediately after the revolution of 1979. Many of the more important sites excavated in the 1970s remained largely unpublished, and the fact that many

of the scholars engaged in the discussion of the *Uruk* phenomenon were not specialists in the archaeology of Iran was undoubtedly a contributing factor.

In the 1960s and 1970s Iranian prehistory was intensively investigated by Iranian and non-Iranian scholars, leading to the discovery of a number of fourth- and early third-millennium BC occupation phases at sites in lowland Khuzestan, the intermontane valleys of the Central Western Zagros, the highlands of Fars, in various locations on the Central Plateau, as well as areas to the south-east in Kerman and the Helmand Basin in Seistan. Also at this time, new soundings were excavated at Susa and Tappeh Hissar, which had both been excavated with basic methods in the late nineteenth and/or early twentieth century, with the aim of clarifying certain phases of their chronology (e.g. Le Brun 1971; Dyson and Howard 1989; Dyson 1987). These reinterpreted sequences, combined with the data from excavations at sites such as Godin Tepe and Tepe Yahya made it clear that there is a great deal of regional diversity in the cultural assemblages of the early to mid-fourth millennium BC (see Voigt and Dyson 1992), which reflects a degree of continuity from the fifth millennium BC (e.g. Weeks *et al.* 2010; Petrie 2013). The regional diversity evident between *c.* 4000 and 3500 BC appears to persist throughout the rest of the millennium, but there are a number of overt changes to the dynamic that are of profound significance. Of particular interest is the clear evidence that there were two separate phases during the mid- to late fourth millennium BC, each characterised by the widely dispersed use of clay tablets: the earlier Mesopotamian-influenced *Uruk* or *Susa II* phase; and the *Proto-Elamite* or *Susa III* phase, which appears to be more specifically related to the Iranian Plateau, and is believed to continue into the early third millennium BC (e.g. Damerow and Englund 1989; Potts 1999).

After an extended period of limited fieldwork and related research, there has now been more than a decade of new archaeological research in Iran. This resurgence in research activity has seen surveys and excavations undertaken in regions and at sites that had not previously been investigated. In addition, projects focused on reconsidering sites excavated in the early twentieth century have commenced, most notably Tappeh Sialk (Malek Shahmirzadeh 2002, 2003, 2004, 2006a, 2006b), and there have been moves to reassess incompletely studied material from several pre-revolution excavations at sites including Godin Tepe (Gopnik and Rothman 2011), Tappeh Hissar (Thornton 2009), and Tal-e Ghazir (Tall-e Gezer; Alizadeh, in preparation). One of the collateral benefits of all this work is that we now have new or reinterpreted information about the fourth millennium BC from many parts of the plateau, and a considerable range of this material is discussed in this volume. It is becoming increasingly apparent that there was more regional diversity in Iran than similarity, but an up-to-date assessment of the local developments and long-range interactions that operated across the Iranian Plateau and its mountains and piedmonts throughout the fourth millennium BC has not previously been attempted.

Those working on the archaeology of Iran during the fourth millennium BC find themselves in a challenging position. The evidence for the precocious developments that took place in south and north Mesopotamia during this period suggests that the developments on the plateau were subordinate to those in the lowland areas to the west, and this has played out in the way the fourth millennium BC has been discussed more generally. This volume seeks to challenge this subordinate position, and to present and discuss the evidence from the Iranian Plateau and its mountains and piedmonts on its own terms. By its very nature, the Iranian Plateau is invariably more complex and varied than the alluvial plains of Mesopotamia. While alluvial plains and intermontane valleys exist in profusion in the mountains and on the plateau, they are restricted in size, and thus the size of concentrated population agglomerations is limited. The plateau as a whole is also enormous and spans a wide variety of climatic, environmental, and vegetation zones, requiring varying approaches to subsistence. While important natural resources are available, in most instances they had to be moved over considerable distances. To understand the nature of local developments and long-range interactions operating both within Iran and between Iran and its neighbours during this period, it is essential to consider the archaeological evidence from the plateau as a whole. It is also important to assess the dynamics operating when there was clear evidence for more formalised linkages between populations for the first time, during the so-called *Proto-Elamite* period.

Defining the **Proto-Elamite** *"phenomenon"*

At the end of the fourth millennium BC, the piedmonts and highlands at the western end of the Iranian Plateau and a large area of the plateau proper saw the adoption of distinctive material culture that falls under the name *Proto-Elamite*, including a range of ceramic forms (e.g. bevel-rim bowls, nose-lugged bichrome jars), seals, sealings, and distinctive inscribed tablets that display a writing system related to, yet distinct from, the *Uruk* Mesopotamian system (Damerow and Englund 1989; Englund 1998a, 1998b; Damerow 2006). As Englund (1998b) has noted, *Proto-Elamite* documents are distinct in that they are written in a linear script with linear syntax, tablets begin rather than end with a colophon, headings do not contain numerical notations and entries include an ideogram and then a numerical notation rather than the reverse. These elements suggest that *Proto-Elamite* was a bookkeeping system

rather than the recording of spoken language, and that it post-dated proto-cuneiform (Englund 1998b). *Proto-Elamite* tablets have now been found at sites ranging in size from 2 to 50 ha in Susiana (Susa; Le Brun 1971, 1978; Le Brun and Vallat 1978), Ram Hormuz (Tall-e Gezer; Whitcomb 1971; Alizadeh, in preparation), the southern Zagros (Tal-e Malyan; Nicholas 1990; Sumner 1988, 2003), Kerman (Tepe Yahya; Potts 2001), and Seistan (Shahr-e Sokhta; Amiet and Tosi 1978) (see Dahl *et al.*, this volume), as well as various locations on the Central Plateau, including the Qazvin (Ozbaki; Majidzadeh n.d., 2001, 2003) and Tehran Plains (Tepe Sofalin; Hessari and Akbari 2007) and Kashan (Tappeh Sialk; Ghirshman 1938).

There have been several wide-ranging discussions of the dynamics and significance of the *Proto-Elamite* phenomenon (e.g. Potts 1977, 1999; Lamberg-Karlovsky 1978, 2012; Alden 1982; Sumner 1986), but it is clear that terminological and conceptual problems abound. For instance, Potts (1999: 71–79; also Whitcomb 1971: 65–66) has pointed out that the term *Proto-Elamite* is a misnomer when used to describe the texts, in that they appear to have originated at Susa but are not precursors to the later *Old Elamite*, so he has advocated the use of the term *Susa III*. Caldwell (1967: 21–26; 1968: 178, 182–83) suggested that the *Iblis IV*-period occupation at Tal-i Iblis was part of a *Jemdet Nasr oikoumenê*, which existed during the late fourth millennium BC and broadly paralleled the earlier *'Ubaid oikoumenê* of the mid-fifth millennium BC. The focus of the plateau *oikoumenê* was shifted from the Mesopotamian *Jemdet Nasr* to the *Proto-Elamite* by Whitcomb (1971: 2–3, 60–73) in his discussion of the *Proto-Elamite* from the viewpoint of the material discovered at Tall-e Gezer, and he actually suggested that these comprised two overlapping *oikoumenês*. Potts (1977) subsequently argued that the word *oikoumenê* implies diffusion and influence, and suggested that the notion of a horizon style, i.e. a trait (or traits) that cross-cuts and ties regional sequences, is more relevant, and advocated the use of the term "universe" to characterise the *Proto-Elamite* phenomenon. While reaffirming the relevance of the concept of a horizon style, Abdi (2003: 150) has noted that how and why this material was dispersed is still unresolved. The phrase *Proto-Elamite* phenomenon will be used here, as it is deliberately vague and ambiguous, reflecting the lack of a unifying and consensual model.

While *Proto-Elamite* cultural material is widely distributed, it is not entirely homogeneous, and it typically appears nested in some way within a local material culture assemblage (e.g. Potts 1977). This local context has not been fully explored. Furthermore, what the *Proto-Elamite* phenomenon actually represents, precisely how it operated within Iran, and how (and if) it interleaved with the contemporaneous situation in Mesopotamia (*Late Uruk? Jemdat Nasr?*), are processes that have not been comprehensively reconsidered in the wake of the Mesopotamia-related theoretical discussions put forward in the 1990s and 2000s.

Several factors have complicated our comprehension of the late fourth millennium BC in Iran. For a country of Iran's size, there is always going to be a problem of coverage, and this has been emphasised by the fact that excavations and surveys in previously unexplored regions continue to throw up surprises (e.g. Maral Tepe at Ozbaki, Majidzadeh n.d.). Some critical sequences such as the Operation ABC deposits at Tal-e Malyan have only lately been published (Sumner 2003). Also, much of the evidence from critical sites such as Godin Tepe, Tappeh Hissar, and Tall-e Gezer was long left unpublished, and only recently has work begun on investigating and publishing this material systematically (e.g. Gopnik and Rothman 2011; Thornton 2009; Alizadeh, in preparation). In addition to this, the *Proto-Elamite* script languished for some time, although recent systematic work (e.g. Dahl 2005a, 2005b, 2009, 2012) is bringing exciting insights into the world's second oldest writing system (Dahl *et al.*, this volume).

There is a range of factors that need to be considered when trying to comprehend the *Proto-Elamite* phenomenon, including geography, chronology, the mechanisms of contact and interaction, and the inherent socio-economic and potentially even political dynamics that underlie the process. The complex geography of the Iranian Plateau and its mountains and piedmonts has led to a number of specific approaches to interpreting the dynamics of the fourth millennium BC, particularly the *Proto-Elamite* phenomenon. Geographically the lowland plains of Khuzestan lie adjacent, and are broadly similar, to the alluvial plains of southern Mesopotamia, but the two are geographically distinct and watered by different hydrological regimes (Tigris-Euphrates versus the Karun-Karkheh). Furthermore, Khuzestan and southern Mesopotamia appear to have been separated by the headwaters of the Persian Gulf throughout the fifth and fourth millennia BC (Sanlaville 2002; Sanlaville and Dalongeville 2005; Heyvaert and Baeteman 2007; Walstra *et al.* 2010, 2011; Lawler 2011; Hritz *et al.* 2012; Hritz and Pournelle, in press). This has implications for the nature of contact between the two regions and also the nature of interaction between highland Iran, lowland Iran, and Mesopotamia. Importantly, it appears that the only methods of direct contact between the area around Uruk and that around Susa would either have involved a circuitous overland route to the north from Uruk and thence east via Deh Luran, or a more direct route by boat.

Another key element that has been problematic is the evidence for absolute chronologies. Dyson (1987), Voigt and Dyson (1992), and Helwing (2005a) have all outlined cogent relative chronological sequences that highlight what appear to be the temporal linkages

between the various sites that present *Proto-Elamite* material, but questions have been raised about our capacity actually to situate this material in absolute time (Petrie in press). There has been a general lack of reliable dates from canonical sites such as Susa, and some of the radiocarbon dates that are available from critical sites such as Tal-e Kureh are imprecise to the point of being unusable. Radiocarbon dating is also particularly perilous for the period between *c.* 3400 and 2900 cal. BC as there is a large plateau in the calibration curve at this point (Petrie in press; Dahl *et al.*, this volume). Unfortunately, this span covers the date range of both the *Late Uruk* and the *Jemdet Nasr* periods in Mesopotamia, the *Susa II/ Late Uruk* (Acropole I.22–18), the *Susa II/III Transition* (Acropole I.17–17X/17Ax), and the *Susa III/Proto-Elamite* (Acropole I.16–14B) occupations at Susa; *Godin VI:1*, *Sialk IV₁–IV₂*, *Period IVC2* at Tepe Yahya, and the entirety of the *Middle Banesh* occupation at Tal-e Malyan and other sites in Fars. As such, it completely straddles the two key periods related to the earliest texts in Western Asia. Furthermore, Wright and Rupley's (2001) reanalysis of the radiocarbon dates for fourth millennium BC Mesopotamia and its neighbouring regions drew attention to a potentially interesting factor related to the radiocarbon dates for the *Middle Banesh/Proto-Elamite* Tal-e Malyan. There are no radiocarbon determinations for the *Early Middle Banesh* period occupation at Tal-e Qarib, but at first glance the ranges of the *Late Middle Banesh* dates from Tal-e Malyan are virtually identical to those from *Late Uruk* Godin (Wright and Rupley 2001: figs. 3.1–3.3). Furthermore, the ranges of these *Proto-Elamite* Tal-e Malyan dates are earlier that the *Late Uruk* date ranges from Habuba Kabira and Arslantepe VIA, the former of which is supposed to represent the final florescence of *Late Uruk* expansion/ colonisation (cf. Wright and Rupley 2001: figs 3.1– 3.3). While there are good grounds to differentiate between different phases on the basis of the presence and absence of a particular type of material culture, the existence of the plateau in the calibration curve makes it almost impossible to differentiate between these phases using absolute dates without high-quality well-stratified radiocarbon determinations that are subjected to Bayesian statistical analysis. This fundamental problem emphasises the importance of establishing well-stratified local chronologies for the fourth millennium BC before we go too far in drawing relative parallels across long distances.

While the geography and chronology clearly create practical issues that need to be thought through, there are also conceptual issues that must be considered, and there remains no consensual view. At various points, the *Proto-Elamite* phenomenon was regarded as an eastern extension of the Mesopotamian/*Jemdet Nasr oikumenê* (e.g. Whitcomb 1971: 3), and one that was broadly contemporaneous with the *Jemdat*

Nasr period (see Abdi 2003). As noted above, Potts (1977) suggested that the *Proto-Elamite* phenomenon encapsulated a "universe", which he argued was marked by participation in directed activities such as commodities trade and exchange, and was being managed by elites at Tal-e Malyan or Susa. Lamberg-Karlovsky (1978: 116) subsequently proposed that a *Proto-Elamite* state formed in Susiana and subsequently expanded its reach across the plateau to control distant populations and economically valuable resources. This would have involved some degree of population movement and resulted in the acculturation of local populations in a process of internationalism that saw a formalisation of both economic and political interaction between the centres in different regions (Lamberg-Karlovsky 1978: 116–19; see also Abdi 2003). Amiet (1979) suggested that the *Proto-Elamite/Susa III* period represented a shift in the dynamic in south-west Iran, where the Mesopotamian influence of the *Susa II/Uruk* period retracted, and Susiana became linked with the highland areas of Fars, particularly Tal-e Malyan and the Kur River Basin. Alden (1982) presented a very different model of this process, maintaining that the *Proto-Elamite* period was marked by a clear change in the economic relationships between the parts of the plateau that had economic resources, and Mesopotamia. In Alden's view (1982: 613, 622–24), *Proto-Elamite* populations had economic motives and became engaged in wholesale and retail trade mechanisms—acting as middle-men between the highland sources of raw materials and finished goods and the transhipment centre of Susa, which in turn acted as a port of trade with Mesopotamia. Alden (1982: 621) regarded the *Proto-Elamite* population in highland Fars as immigrants from Susiana (possibly Chogha Mish via Izeh) who merged with the local population, although he does also entertain the possibility that they might have come from somewhere else on the Iranian Plateau. He suggested four factors which may have caused this movement: 1) population growth in the nuclear region; 2) an attempt by lowland populations to extract tribute from highland populations; 3) military and/or political pressures forcing migration from the lowlands; or 4) an attempt by lowland populations to control the supply of highland exotics; he clearly favours the latter proposal (Alden 1982: 621–22), but he (Alden 1982: 624) also ultimately regards the *Proto-Elamite* script and the phenomenon generally as emanating from highland Fars. Although Alden's models were subject to a range of criticisms (see comments, Alden 1982), it is notable that Amiet has argued that this period sees an annexation of Susiana by the highland polity centred at Tal-e Malyan (Amiet 1993); and although Sumner has pointed out that the issue is still open to question, he appears to favour the latter suggestion (Sumner 2003: 113). In contrast, Potts (1999: 83) has cogently argued that

Susa was the "centre at which the Susa III writing system developed".

Sumner (1986; see Alden, this volume) took a different interpretative tack in attempting to conceptualise the origins of the highland centre of Tal-e Malyan and its relationship with lowland Susiana. As Alden reiterates in detail in his contribution to this volume, Sumner proposed, with considerable speculation, that the rise of the *Proto-Elamite* phenomenon was closely connected to the transition to mobile pastoralism as a result of a progressive agricultural crisis (Sumner 1986: 207). Although he acknowledges that the evidence is largely circumstantial (Sumner 2003: 113), he (Sumner 1986: 207) hypothesised that the success of the transition to herding resulted in overgrazing of local pastures, the shift to full-time pastoral nomadism, and resultant conflict between settled farmers and nomads. This in turn led to a situation where villagers obtained protection from tribal leaders, who settled and attracted craftsmen and markets to their village headquarters (e.g. Tal-e Qarib; Sumner 1986: 208–09; see Alden, this volume). Sumner was keen to emphasise that the combination of Tal-e Malyan's size, the growth in craft production, the use of tablets, glyptic, and the mobilisation of wealth indicates that *Middle Banesh*-period Tal-e Malyan was engaged in "political and commercial events played out on a larger stage, for greater stakes" (Sumner 1986: 209). Alizadeh (2010) has recently argued for the critical role played by nomadic populations in the fourth millennium BC.

Several other interpretations of the *Proto-Elamite* phenomenon have been outlined, and range from Algaze's (2001a: 200) suggestion that the *Proto-Elamite* "state" developed as a reaction to the rise of Sumerian complexity, to Helwing's (2004, 2005a) proposal that the appearance of *Proto-Elamite* material culture, particularly the administrative apparatus, was the product of a gradual process that culminated in the rise of a distinctive highland political entity.

Why the *Proto-Elamite* phenomenon broke down is also relatively poorly understood. Although there is evidence that the occupied area at Tal-e Malyan decreased, it was during this period that the fortification wall was constructed around the site, suggesting that the site remained populous for at least some of the *Late Banesh* period (Sumner 2003: 117). Alden has suggested that the apparent drop in population at the site of Tal-e Malyan and the hinterland sites may represent an exodus of the *Late Middle* phase immigrants either into the highland regions or back into the lowlands of Khuzistan (Alden 1979: 169). Lamberg-Karlovsky (2001: 221; 2003) has suggested that the disappearance of the *Proto-Elamite* script was an instance of writing as a practice being rejected, and in suggesting that this was a conscious act, asks, "what was the reason for it?" The answer is at present unclear, but the *Proto-Elamite/Susa III* script effectively ceased to exist, and there is an 800-year gap in the use of texts on the plateau (Dahl 2009). In many ways, the reasons for the decline of the *Proto-Elamite* phenomenon are dependent upon the explanation of the phenomenon as a whole.

The degree to which the demise of the *Proto-Elamite* phenomenon can be seen as a decline or a collapse, however, is questionable. For example, until relatively recently it has been strongly emphasised that it was highly likely there was a chronological hiatus in the Kur River Basin between the *Banesh* and the subsequent *Kaftari* period of occupation (*c.* 28/2600–2200 BC – e.g. Sumner 1988: 315–16, 317; 2003: 53–55). The publication of the results from the H5 sounding (Miller and Sumner 2004), and the newly excavated H1s sounding (Alden *et al.* 2005) at Tal-e Malyan, however, indicate that there is evidence for continued occupation at the site between the two periods, even if there is a decline in the sedentary population of the Kur River Basin between *c.* 2800 and 2200 BC (Miller and Sumner 2004: 87–88). The exploration in the Mamasani region thus far shows that there is a protracted gap in settled occupation in that region during much of the third millennium BC (Petrie *et al.* 2009). There is, however, evidence for the *Proto-Elamite* occupation at Susa continuing into the *Early Dynastic* period (Dittman 1986), although the degree to which there is an overlap, and its duration, is unclear. Therefore, while the texts ceased to be used, and presumably the administrative structures that they represented broke down, occupation at many of the key sites did not cease.

This extended review, it is hoped, shows that there is an abundance of relevant issues related to the archaeology of the Iranian Plateau and its mountain and piedmont zones that are worthy of careful exploration and consideration, and provides a very protracted introduction to the rationale for the Ancient Iran and Its Neighbours workshop and the volume that you are now reading. In the following sections, the details of the workshop and the volume will be outlined, and the specific themes of the volume will be introduced.

Ancient Iran and Its Neighbours

The workshop

Following discussions with colleagues during 2007 and 2008, it was decided to hold a workshop on Iran in the fourth millennium BC in Cambridge in 2009. From the outset, this event was intended to be medium-sized, including approximately 30 invited attendees and open to all interested parties. By keeping numbers small, it was hoped that there would be active discussions between scholars closely familiar with the material being reviewed.

The Ancient Iran and Its Neighbours workshop was eventually held at the McDonald Institute for Archaeological Research on 26–28 June 2009, and was largely made possible by grants kindly provided by the British Institute of Persian Studies, the Ancient India and Iran Trust, and the McDonald Institute for Archaeological Research.

The workshop was divided into themed sessions, spread over three days, and included papers on geography and climate, regional settlement dynamics, bioarchaeology, region and/or site-specific case studies, and a range of specific material culture/ technology-based studies. Presenters were asked to focus on both material remains and the overarching dynamics that link material assemblages together in order to gain insight into relations between populations. Presenters were also asked to pay some attention to issues of relative and absolute chronology, and to present new radiocarbon data if such were available. Each day of the workshop concluded with sessions that reviewed the papers presented, and attempted a broad synthesis of the data, including discussion of broader theoretical approaches that might be used to explain some of the patterns of social, economic, and political behaviour that were being observed. The presentations and ensuing discussions were recorded and transcribed, and these transcriptions are also included in the volume.

All presenters and many of those who were unable to attend were asked to submit papers for the present volume. With relatively few exceptions, everyone who presented a paper at the workshop either submitted or contributed to a paper. The workshop unfortunately coincided with a period of social unrest in Iran, and this meant that most of the Iranian scholars who had planned to attend were unable to travel. Several of these colleagues were able to send papers and these were presented; many of these contributions were also submitted as papers for the volume (see below).

The volume

This volume presents revised versions of the majority of the papers that were presented at the workshop. In general the coverage is chronologically broad, and most regions of the greater Iranian Plateau and its mountains and piedmonts are at least referred to and many are discussed in detail. There are papers discussing Susiana (Wright), the Central Western Zagros (Rothman), and the Central Plateau (Helwing; Fazeli *et al.*; Thornton), as well as the Kopet Dag piedmont zones (Bonora and Vidale). There are also papers discussing different parts of Fars (Sardari; Petrie *et al.*; Alden) as well as Kerman (Vidale and Desset), and the areas of Iranian and Pakistani Baluchistan (Mutin). Some papers take a more holistic view, including a review of the environmental and climatic evidence (Jones *et al.*) and an assessment of the dynamics of long-term settlement shifts (Hopper and Wilkinson), as well as papers on metallurgy (Weeks), sealing and its associated iconography (Pittman), two papers dealing with the issue of writing systems and administration (Matthews; Dahl *et al.*), and an overview paper discussing issues of scale, difference, and mobility (Pollock).

There are some obvious gaps, most notably the area at the far north-east of the plateau, in the Hindu Kush and the northern part of the Suleiman Mountains, where there has been very little archaeological research into the fourth millennium BC and no recent work. There are areas such as Shushtar and Ram Hormuz that have been discussed in recent publications (Moghaddam 2012) or are soon to be discussed in forthcoming volumes (Alizadeh, in preparation) by colleagues who were unable to attend the workshop. We know next to nothing about the fourth-millennium BC occupation on the northern coast of the Persian Gulf. Research has shown that there is fifth-millennium BC occupation in various locations (e.g. Carter *et al.* 2006; Askari Chaverdi *et al.* 2008), but the region has not been explored in sufficient depth to identify the presence of any fourth-millennium pottery, which is largely unpainted and invariably more difficult to spot than the painted ceramics of the *Early Chalcolithic*. One region that has been explored, but which is not covered explicitly, is the zone of northern Baluchistan and the southern part of Khybur Pakhtunkhwa, which lies at the western edge of modern Pakistan. A recent volume (Petrie 2010) has discussed the archaeology of this region in great detail, and makes explicit linkages to the fourth-millennium archaeology of the Kopet Dag piedmont and central Baluchistan, which are both reviewed in this volume (Bonora and Vidale; Mutin); it was decided to encourage readers to defer to that publication.

The authors who have contributed have each dealt with a range of themes, including:

- Environment, landscape and spatial scale
- Chronology and issues of temporal scale
- Local developments and regional diversity
- Technology and transmission
- Long- and short-range interaction and manifestations of trade
- Power, control, negotiation, conflict and violence

The papers themselves and the way that they deal with these themes will not be discussed in detail here. Rather, in the concluding chapter, the significant conclusions of the papers will be brought together into a broad synthesis that aims to highlight the emerging paradigms that are shaping our understanding of the fourth millennium BC in Iran, and to establish an agenda for future work.

Note
1   Rothman's volume (2001) made a specific attempt to outline a regional chronological framework for the *Late Chalcolithic*, and advocated the use of a universal terminology for the period (i.e. LC 1–LC 5).

Bibliography

Abdi, K. 2003. "From Écriture to Civilisation: Changing Paradigms of Proto-Elamite Archaeology", in Miller, N. F. and Abdi, K. (eds), *Yeki bud, yeki nabud: Essays on the Archaeology of Iran in Honor of William M. Sumner*, 48, Cotsen Institute of Archaeology, University of California, Los Angeles: 140–51.

Adams, R. McC., and Nissen, H. J. 1972. *The Uruk Countryside: The Natural Setting of Urban Societies*, University of Chicago Press, Chicago.

Alden, J. R. 1979. *Regional Economic Organization in Banesh Period Iran*, unpublished Ph.D. dissertation, Department of Anthropology, University of Michigan, Ann Arbor.

Alden, J. R. 1982. "Marketplace Exchange as Indirect Distribution: An Iranian Example", in Ericson, J. and Earle, T. (eds), *Contexts for Prehistoric Exchange*, Academic, New York: 83–101.

Alden, J. R. 2003. "Excavations at Tal-e Kureh. Appendix D", in Sumner, W. M. (ed.), *Malyan Excavation Reports, Volume III: Proto-Elamite Civilization in the Land of Anshan*, University of Pennsylvania Museum, Philadelphia: 187–98.

Alden, J. R., Abdi, K., Azadi, A., Beckman, G. and Pittman, H. 2005. "Fars Archaeological Project 2004: excavation at Tal-e Malyan", *Iran* 43: 39–47.

Algaze, G. 1989. "The Uruk Expansion: cross-cultural exchange in early Mesopotamian Civilisation", *Current Anthropology* 30: 571–608.

Algaze, G. 1993. *The Uruk World System: The Dynamics of Expansion of Early Mesopotamian Civilisation*, 1st edition, University of Chicago Press, Chicago.

Algaze, G. 2001a. "Initial social complexity in southwestern Asia: the Mesopotamian Advantage", *Current Anthropology* 43: 199–233.

Algaze, G. 2001b. "The prehistory of imperialism: the case for Uruk period Mesopotamia", in Rothman 2001a: 27–83.

Algaze, G. 2005a. "The Sumerian Takeoff", *Structure and Dynamics: eJournal of Anthropological and Related Sciences*, http://escholarship.org/uc/item/76r673km (accessed 30 December 2012).

Algaze, G. 2005b. *The Uruk World System: The Dynamics of Expansion of Early Mesopotamian Civilisation*, 2nd revised edition, University of Chicago Press, Chicago.

Algaze, G. 2007. "The Sumerian Takeoff", in Stone, E. C. (ed.), *Settlement and Society: Essays Dedicated to Robert McCormick Adams*, Cotsen Institute of Archaeology, University of California, Los Angeles: 343–68.

Algaze, G. 2008. *Ancient Mesopotamia at the Dawn of Civilisation: The Evolution of an Urban Landscape*, University of Chicago Press, Chicago.

Algaze, G. 2012. "The end of prehistory and the Uruk period", in Crawford, H. (ed.), *The Sumerian World*, Routledge, Oxford: 68–94.

Alizadeh, A. 2010. "The rise of the highland Elamite state in southwestern Iran 'Enclosed' or Enclosing Nomadism?", *Current Anthropology* 51 (3): 353–83.

Alizadeh, A. ed. in preparation. *Ancient Settlement Patterns and Cultures in the Ram Hormuz Plain, Southwestern Iran: Excavations at Tall-e Geser and Regional Survey in the Ram Hormuz Area*, Oriental Institute Publications 140, Oriental Institute, Chicago.

Amiet, P. 1979. "Archaeological discontinuity and ethnicity duality in Elam", *Antiquity* 53: 195–204.

Amiet, P. 1993. "The period of Irano-Mesopotamian contacts 3500–1600 BC", in Curtis, J. E. (ed.), *Early Mesopotamia and Iran: Contact and Conflict 3500–1600 BC*, British Museum Press, London: 23–30.

Amiet, P. and Tosi, M. 1978. "Phase 10 at Shahr-i Sokhta: excavations in Square XDV and the late 4th millennium B.C. assemblage of Sistan", *East and West* 28: 9–31.

Askari Chaverdi, A., Petrie, C. A. and Taylor, H. 2008. "Early village settlements on the Persian Gulf littoral: revisiting Tol-e Pir and the Galehdār Valley", *Iran* 46: 21–42.

Badler, V. R. 2002. "A Chronology of Uruk Artefacts from Godin Tepe in Central Western Iran and Its Implications for the Interrelationships Between the Local and Foreign Cultures", in Postgate, J. N. (ed.), *Artefacts of Complexity: Tracking the Uruk in the Near East, British School of Archaeology in Iraq*, Aris and Philips, Oxford: 79–110.

Barnard, H. and Wendrich, W. eds 2008. *The Archaeology of Mobility: Old World and New World Nomadism*, Cotsen Advanced Seminars, Cotsen Institute of Archaeology, University of California, Los Angeles.

Bazin, D. and Hübner, H. 1969. *Copper Deposits in Iran: Geological Survey of Iran*, Report 13, Geological Survey of Iran, Tehran.

Beale, T. W. 1978. "Bevelled rim bowls and their implications for change and economic organisation in the later fourth millennium B.C.", *JNES* 37: 289–313.

Bobek, H. 1968. "Vegetation", *CHIr* 1: 280–93.

Butterlin, P. 2003. *Les Temps Proto-Urbains de Mésopotamie*, CNRS Éditions, Paris.

Caldwell, J. R. ed. 1967. *Investigations at Tal-i Iblis, Illinois State Museum Preliminary Reports*, Vol. 9, Illinois State Museum Society, Springfield.

Caldwell, J. R. 1968. "Pottery and the cultural history of the Iranian Plateau", *JNES* 27: 178–83.

Carter R. A., Challis, K., Priestman, S. M. N. and Tofighian, H. 2006. "The Bushehr Hinterland: results of the first season of the Iranian-British Archaeological Survey of Bushehr Province, November–December 2004", *Iran* 44: 63–103.

Casanova, M. 1992. "The sources of lapis-lazuli found in Iran", in Jarrige, C. (ed.), *South Asian Archaeology 1989*, Prehistory Press, Madison: 49–56.

Collins, P. 2001. *The Uruk Phenomenon: the Role of Social Ideology in the Expansion of the Uruk Culture during the Fourth Millennium BC*, British Archaeological Reports 900, Archaeopress, Oxford.

Curtin, P. 1984. *Cross-cultural trade in World History*, Cambridge University Press, Cambridge.

Dahl, J. 2005a. "Animal husbandry in Susa during the Proto-Elamite period", *Studi Micenei ed Egeo-Anatolici* 47: 81–134.

Dahl, J. 2005b. "Complex graphemes in Proto-Elamite", *Cuneiform Digital Library Journal* 2005/3: 1–15. http://cdli.ucla.edu/pubs/cdlj/2005/cdlj2005_003.html (accessed 30 December 2012).

Dahl, J. 2009. "Early writing in Iran: a reappraisal", *Iran* 47: 23–32.

Dahl, J. 2012. "The marks of early writing", *Iran* 50: 1–12.

Damerow, P. 2006. "The origins of writing as a problem of historical epistemology", *Cuneiform Digital Library Journal*, 2006, http://cdli.ucla.edu/pubs/cdlj/2006/cdlj2006_001.pdf (accessed 23 December 2012).

Damerow, P. and Englund, R. K. 1989. *The Proto-Elamite texts from Tepe Yahya*, Peabody Museum of Archaeology and Ethnology, Harvard University, Cambridge, MA.

Dittmann, R. 1986. "Susa in the Proto-Elamite period and annotations on the painted pottery of Proto-Elamite Khuzestan", in Finkbeiner, U. and Röllig, W. (eds), *Ğamdat Nasr: Period or regional style?*, TAVO Beiheft B 62, Wiesbaden: 171–98.

Dyson Jr., R. H. 1987. "The relative and absolute chronology of Hissar II and the Proto-Elamite horizon of northern Iran", in Aurenche, O., Evin, J. and Hours, F. (eds), *Chronologies in the Near East*, BAR International Series 379, Archaeopress, Oxford: 647–78.

Dyson Jr., R. H. and Howard, S. M. eds 1989. *Tappeh Hesar: Reports of the Restudy Project, 1976*, Case Editrice le Lettere, Florence.

Englund, R. K. 1998a. "Texts from the Late Uruk Period", in Attinger, P. and Wäfler, M. (eds), *Späturuk–Zeit und frühdynastische Zeit*, OBO 160/1, Göttingen: 15–233.

Englund, R. K. 1998b. "Elam iii. Proto-Elamite", *EIr* VIII (Fasc. 3): 325–30.

Finkbeiner, U. 1991. *Uruk. Kampagne 35–37, 1982–84: die archäologische Oberflächenuntersuchung (Survey)*, Phillip von Zabern, Berlin.

Fisher, W. B. "Physical geography", *CHIr* 1: 3–110.

Frame, L. D. 2004. *Investigations at Tal-i Iblis: Evidence for Copper Smelting During the Chalcolithic Period*, unpublished B.Sc. dissertation, Dept. of Materials Science and Engineering, Massachusetts Institute of Technology, Cambridge, MA.

Frangipane, M. 2001. "Centralization processes in Greater Mesopotamia: Uruk 'Expansion' as the culmination of an early system of intra-regional relations", in Rothman 2001a: 307–48.

Frangipane, M. 2002. "'Non-Uruk' developments and Uruk-linked features on the Northern borders of Greater Mesopotamia", in Postgate, J. N. (ed.), *Artefacts of Complexity: Tracking the Uruk in the Ancient Near East*, British School of Archaeology in Iraq, Cambridge University Press, Cambridge: 123–48.

Frangipane, M. ed. 2007. *Arslantepe Cretulae: an Early Centralised Administrative System Before Writing*, Università di Roma "La Sapienza", Rome.

Frankfort, H. 1932. *Archaeology and the Sumerian Problem*, Studies in Ancient Oriental Civilisation 4, Oriental Institute of the University of Chicago, Chicago.

Ganji, M. H. 1968. "Climate", *CHIr* 1: 212–49.

Ghirshman, R. 1938. *Fouilles de Sialk*, Musée du Louvre, Département des antiquités orientales, Série Archéologique 4, Geuthner, Paris.

Gibson, McG., Maktash, M., Franke, J. A., Al-Azm, A., Sanders, J. C., Wilkinson, T. J., Reichel, C., Ur, J., Sanders, P., Salameh, A., Hritz, C., Watkins, B. and Kattab, M. 2002. "First Season of Syrian-American investigations at Hamoukar – Hasekeh Province", *Iraq* 64: 45–68.

Gopnik, H. and Rothman, M. eds 2011. *On the High Road: The History of Godin Tepe, Iran*, Royal Ontario Museum/Mazda Press, Toronto.

Gosden, C. 2004. *Archaeology and Colonialism*, Cambridge University Press, Cambridge.

Harrison, J. V. 1968. "Geology", *CHIr* 1: 111–85.

Helwing, B. 2004. "Tracking the Proto-Elamite on the Central Iranian Plateau", in Malek Shahmirzadeh, S. (ed.), *The Potters of Sialk: Sialk Reconsideration Project Report 3*, Archaeological Reports Monograph Series 5, Iranian Center for Archaeological Research, Tehran: 46–58.

Helwing, B. 2005a. "Early complexity in highland Iran: recent archaeological research into the Chalcolithic of Iran", *TÜBA-AR* 8: 39–60.

Helwing, B. 2005b. "Long distance relations of the Iranian highland sites during the late Chalcolithic period: new evidence from the Joint Iranian-German excavations at Arisman", in Franke-Vogt, U. and Weisshaar, H-J. (eds), *South Asian Archaeology 2003*, Forschungen zur Archäologie aussereuropäischer Kulturen, Linden Soft, Aachen: 171–78.

Herrmann, G. 1968. "Lapis lazuli: the early phases of its trade", *Iraq* 30 (1): 21–57.

Hessari, M. and Akbari, H. 2007. "The preliminary excavation report on Sofalin mound in Pishva", *The 9th Annual Congress [meeting] of the Iranian Archaeologists*, Volume 1, Iranian Cultural Heritage, Tourism and Handicraft Organization, Tehran: 131–64.

Heyvaert, V. M. A. and Baeteman, C. 2007. "Holocene sedimentary evolution and palaeocoastlines of the Lower Khuzestan plain (southwest Iran)", *Marine Geology* 224: 83–108.

Hritz, C. and Pournelle, J. in press. "Feeding history: deltaic resilience, inherited practice, and millennial-scale sustainability in an urbanized landscape" in Goldstein, D. (ed*.), From Field to Table: Historical Ecology of Regional Subsistence Strategies*, University of South Carolina Press, Columbia.

Hritz, C., Pournelle, J. and Smith, J. 2012. "Revisiting the Sealands: report of preliminary ground reconnaissance in the Hammar District, Dhi Qar and Basra Governorates, Iraq", *Iraq* 74: 37–49.

Jarrige, J-F. 1988. *Les Cités oubliées de l'Indus*, Musée National des Arts Asiatiques Guimet, Paris.

Jarrige, J-F. and Hassan, M. U. 1989. "Funerary complexes in Baluchistan at the end of the third millennium in the light of recent discoveries at Mehrgarh and Quetta", in Frifelt, K. and Sørenson, P. (eds), *South Asian Archaeology 1985*, Curzon Press, London: 150–66.

Johnson, G. A. 1973. *Local Exchange and Early State Development in Southwestern Iran*, Archaeological Papers, 51, Museum of Anthropology, University of Michigan, Ann Arbor.

Kohl, P. 1978. "The balance of trade in southwestern Asia in the mid-third millennium B.C.", *Current Anthropology* 19 (3): 463–93.

Kohl, P. 1989. "The use and abuse of world systems theory", in Lamberg-Karlovsky, C. C. (ed.), *Archaeological Thought in America*, Cambridge University Press, Cambridge: 218–40.

Kuhrt, A. 1997. *The Ancient Near East c. 3000–330 BC*, Routledge, Oxford.

al-Kuntar, S. and Abu Jayyab, A. K. in press. "The Political Economy of the Upper Khabur in the Late Chalcolithic 1–2: Ceramic mass-production, standardisation and specialisation", in McMahon, A., Crawford, H. and Postgate, J. N. (eds), *Preludes to Urbanism: Studies in the Late Chalcolithic of Mesopotamia in Honour of Joan Oates*, Cambridge, McDonald Institute Monographs: PAGES.

Lamberg-Karlovsky, C. C. 1978. "The Proto-Elamites on the Iranian Plateau", *Antiquity* 52: 114–20.

Lamberg-Karlovsky, C.C. 2001. "Comment on 'Initial social complexity in southwestern Asia: the Mesopotamian Advantage'", *Current Anthropology* 43: 220–21.

Lamberg-Karlovsky, C. C. 2003. "To write or not to write" in Potts, T., Roaf, M. and Stein, D. (eds), *Culture Through Objects: Ancient Near Eastern Studies in Honour of P.R.S. Moorey*, Griffith Institute, Oxford: 59–75.

Lamberg-Karlovsky, C. C. 2012. "Iran and its neighbors", in Crawford, H. (ed.), *The Sumerian World*, Routledge, Oxford: 559–78.

Law, R. 2011. *Inter-regional Interaction and Urbanism in the Ancient Indus Valley: A Geological Provenience Study of Harappa's Rock and Mineral Assemblage*, Occasional Paper 11, Linguistics, Archaeology and the Human Past, Research Institute for Humanity and Nature, Kyoto, Japan.

Lawler, A. 2011. "Did the first cities grow from marshes?", *Science* 331 (14 January): 141.

Le Brun, A. 1971. "Recherches Stratigraphiques à l'Acropole de Suse, 1969–1971", *CDAFI* 1: 163–217.

Le Brun, A. 1978. "Le Niveau 17B de L'Acropole de Suse (campagne de 1972)", *CDAFI* 9: 57–154.

Le Brun, A. and Vallat, F. 1978. "L'origine de l'écriture à Suse", *CDAFI* 8: 11–59.

Lupton, A. 1996. *Stability and Change: Socio-Political Developments in North Mesopotamia and South-East Anatolia*, BAR International Series 627, Archaeopress, Oxford.

McMahon, A. 2010. "Review of *Ancient Mesopotamia at the Dawn of Civilisation: The Evolution of an Urban Landscape*, by Guillermo Algaze", *Cambridge Archaeology Journal* 20 (1): 134–35.

McMahon, A., Oates, J., al-Quntar, S., Charles, M., Colantoni, C., Hald, M. M., Karsgaard, P., Khalidi, L., Soltysiak, A., Stone, A. and Weber, J. 2007. "Excavations at Tell Brak 2006–2007", *Iraq* 69: 145–71.

Majidzadeh, Y. n.d. *Ozbaki*, Iranian Center for Archaeological Research, Tehran.

Majidzadeh, Y. 1977. *Tepe Zagheh: A Sixth Millennium B.C. Village in the Qazvin Plain of the Central Iranian Plateau*, unpublished Ph.D. dissertation, Department of Anthropology, University of Pennsylvania.

Majidzadeh, Y. 1981. "Sialk III and the pottery sequence at Tepe Ghabristan, the coherence of the cultures of the Central Iranian Plateau", *Iran* 19: 141–46.

Majidzadeh, Y. 2001. "Les Fouilles d'Ozbaki (Iran). Campagnes 1998–2000", *Paléorient* 27(1): 141–45.

Majidzadeh, Y. 2003. *The Third Season of Excavations at Ozbaki*, Iranian Center for Archaeological Research and Iranian Cultural Heritage Organisation, Tehran.

Majidzadeh, Y. 2008. *Excavation at Tape Ghabrestan, Iran*, IsIAo, Rome.

Malek Shahmirzadeh, S. (ed.) 2002. *The Ziggurat of Sialk: Sialk Reconsideration Project Report 1*, Iranian Cultural Heritage Organisation, Tehran.

Malek Shahmirzadeh, S. (ed.) 2003. *The Silversmiths of Sialk: Sialk Reconsideration Project Report 2*, Iranian Cultural Heritage Organisation, Tehran.

Malek Shahmirzadeh, S. ed. 2004. *The Potters of Sialk: Sialk Reconsideration Project Report 3*, Archaeological Reports Monograph Series 5, Iranian Center for Archaeological Research, Tehran.

Malek Shahmirzadeh, S. ed. 2006a. *The Fishermen of Sialk: Sialk Reconsideration Project Report 4*, Archaeological Reports Monograph Series 7, Iranian Center for Archaeological Research, Tehran.

Malek Shahmirzadeh, S. ed. 2006b. *Sialk the Oldest Fortified Village of Iran: Sialk Reconsideration Project Final Report*, Archaeological Reports Monograph Series, Iranian Center for Archaeological Research, Tehran.

Mann, M. 1986. *The Source of Social Power: A History of Power from the Beginning to A.D. 1760*, Cambridge University Press, Cambridge.

Matthews, R. and Fazeli, H. 2004. "Copper and complexity: Iran and Mesopotamia in the fourth millennium B.C.", *Iran* 42: 61–75.

Miller, N. F. and Sumner, W.M. 2004. "The Banesh-Kaftari interface: the view from Operation H5, Malyan", *Iran* 42: 77–89.

Miroschedji, P. de 2003. "Susa and the Highlands: Major Trends in the History of Elamite Civilisation", in Miller, N. F. and Abdi, K. (eds), *Yeki bud, yeki nabud: Essays on the Archaeology of Iran in Honor of William M. Sumner*, Cotsen Institute of Archaeology Monograph No. 48, Cotsen Institute of Archaeology, Los Angeles: 17–38.

Moghaddam, A. 2012. *Later Village Period Settlement Development in the Karun River Basin, Upper Khuzestan Plain, Greater Susiana, Iran*, BAR International Series 2347, Archaeopress, Oxford.

Nicholas, I. M. 1990. *The Proto-Elamite Settlement at TUV*, Malyan Excavation Reports, III, University of Pennsylvania Museum of Archaeology and Anthropology, Philadelphia.

Nissen, H. J. 1988. *The Early History of the Ancient Near East, 9000–2000 BC*, University of Chicago, Chicago.

Nissen, H. J. 2001. "Cultural and political networks in the ancient Near East during the fourth and third millennia B.C.", in Rothman 2001a: 149–79.

Nissen, H. J. 2002. "Uruk: key site of the period and key site of the problem", in Postgate, J.N. (ed.), *Artefacts of Complexity: Tracking the Uruk in the Ancient Near East*, British School of Archaeology in Iraq, Cambridge University Press, Cambridge: 1–16.

Oates, J., McMahon, A., Karsgaard, P., al-Quntar, S. and Ur, J. 2007. "Early Mesopotamian urbanism: a view from the north", *Antiquity* 81: 585–600.

Parker, A. G. and Goudie, A. 2007. "Development of the Bronze Age landscape in the southeastern Arabian Gulf: new evidence from a buried shell midden in the eastern extremity of the Rub' al-Khali desert, Emirate of Ras al-Khaimah", *Arabian Archaeology and Epigraphy* 18 (2): 132–38.

Perkins, A. L. 1949. *The Comparative Archaeology of Early Mesopotamia*, Studies in Ancient Oriental Civilisation 25, Oriental Institute of the University of Chicago, Chicago.

Petrie, C. A. ed. 2010. *Sheri Khan Tarakai and early village life in north-west Pakistan*, Bannu Archaeological Project Monographs, Vol. 1, Oxbow Books, Oxford.

Petrie, C. A. in press. "Iran and Uruk Mesopotamia: chronologies and connections in the 4th millennium BC", in McMahon, A., Crawford, H. and Postgate, J. N. (eds), *Preludes to Urbanism: Studies in the Late Chalcolithic of Mesopotamia in Honour of Joan Oates*, Cambridge, McDonald Institute Monographs.

Petrie, C. A. 2013. "The Chalcolithic of south Iran", in Potts, D. T. (ed.), *Oxford Handbook of Iranian Archaeology*, Oxford University Press, Oxford: 121–59.

Petrie, C. A., Weeks, L. R., Potts, D. T. and Roustaei, K. 2009. "Perspectives on the Cultural Sequence of Mamasani", in Potts, D. T., Roustaei K., Petrie, C. A. and Weeks, L. R. (eds), *The Mamasani Archaeological Project Stage One: A report on the first two seasons of the ICAR – University of Sydney Joint Expedition to the Mamasani District, Fars Province, Iran*, 2nd edition, BAR International Series 2044, Archaeopress, Oxford: 169–96.

Pigott, V. C. 1999a. "The development of metal production on the Iranian Plateau: an archaeometallurgical perspective", in Pigott, V. C. (ed.), *The Archaeometallurgy of the Asian Old World*, University Museum monograph 89, University Museum symposium series vol. 7, MASCA research papers in science and archaeology vol. 16, University Museum, University of Pennsylvania, Philadelphia: 73–106.

Pigott, V. C. 1999b. "A heartland of metallurgy: Neolithic/Chalcolithic metallurgical origins on the Iranian Plateau", in Hauptmann, A., Pernicka, E., Rehren, T. and Yalçin, Ü. (eds), *The Beginnings of Metallurgy*, Der Anschnitt Beiheft 9, Deutsches Bergbau-Museum, Bochum: 107–20.

Pigott, V. C., Rogers, H. C. and Nash, S. K. 2003. "Archaeometallurgical investigations at Malyan: the evidence for tin-bronze in the Kaftari phase", in Miller, N. F. and Abdi, K. (eds), *Yeki Bud, Yeki Nabud. Essays on the Archaeology Iran in Honor of William M. Sumner*, Cotsen Institute of Archaeology Monograph No. 48, Cotsen Institute of Archaeology, Los Angeles: 161–76.

Pittman, H. 2001. "Mesopotamian intraregional relations reflected through glyptic evidence in the Late Chalcolithic 1–5 periods", in Rothman 2001a: 403–43.

Postgate, J. N. 1994. *Early Mesopotamia: Society and Economy at the Dawn of History*, Routledge, London.

Postgate, J. N. 1996. "Review of Algaze, G. 1993. *The Uruk World System: The Dynamics of Expansion of Early Mesopotamian Civilisation*, 1st edition, University of Chicago Press, Chicago", *JAOS* 116 (1): 147–148.

Postgate, J. N. ed. 2002. *Artefacts of Complexity: Tracking the Uruk in the Ancient Near East*, British School of Archaeology in Iraq, Cambridge University Press, Cambridge.

Potts, D. T. 1977. "Tepe Yahya and the end of the 4th millennium on the Iranian Plateau", in Deshayes, J. (ed.), *Le Plateau Iranien et l'Asie Centrale des origines à la conquête islamique*, Centre National de la Recherche Scientifique, Paris: 23–31.

Potts, D. T. 1986. "A contribution to the history of the term 'Ǧamdat Naṣr'", in Finkbeiner, U. and Röllig, W. (eds), *Ǧamdat Naṣr: Period or Regional Style? Papers given at a Symposium Held in Tübingen, November 1983*, Beihefte zum Tubinger Atlas des Vorderen Orients, Reihe B. (Geisteswissenschaften) Nr. 62, Dr. Ludwig Reichert Verlag, Wiesbaden: 17–32.

Potts, D. T. 1997. *Mesopotamian Civilisation: The Material Foundations*, Cornell University Press, Ithaca, NY.

Potts, D. T. 1999. *The Archaeology of Elam: Formation and Transformation of an Ancient Iranian State*, Cambridge World Archaeology, Cambridge University Press, Cambridge.

Potts, D. T. 2001. *Excavations at Tepe Yahya, Iran 1967–1975: The Third Millennium*, American School of Prehistoric Research Bulletin, 45, Peabody Museum of Archaeology and Ethnology, Harvard University, Cambridge.

Potts, D. T. 2004. "The Uruk Explosion: more heat than light?", *The Review of Archaeology* 25 (2): 19–28.

Potts, D. T. 2008. "Review: Alizadeh, A., *et al.* The Origins of State Organisations in Prehistoric Highland Fars, Southern Iran. Excavations at Tal-e Bakun", *Bibliotheca Orientalis* VXV.1–2: 195–206.

Potts, D. T. 2009a. "Bevel-rim bowls and bakeries: Evidence and explanations from Iran and the Indo-Iranian Borderlands", *JCS* 61 (1): 1–23.

Potts, D. T. 2009b. "The archaeology and early history of the Persian Gulf", in Potter, L. G. (ed.), *The Persian Gulf in History*, Palgrave Macmillan, London: 27–56.

Pournelle, J. 2003. *Marshland of Cities: Deltaic Landscapes and the Evolution of Early Mesopotamian Civilisation*, unpublished Ph.D. dissertation, University of California, San Diego.

Pournelle, J. 2012. "Physical geography", in Crawford, H. (ed.), *The Sumerian World*, Routledge, Oxford: 13–32.

Rothman, M. S. ed. 2001a. *Uruk Mesopotamia and Its Neighbours: Cross-Cultural Interactions in the Era of State Formation*, SAR Press, Santa Fe.

Rothman, M. S. 2001b. "The local and the regional: an introduction", in Rothman 2001a: 3–26.

Rothman, M. S. 2001c. "The Tigris piedmont, eastern Jazira and highland western Iran in the fourth millennium BC", in Rothman 2001a: 349–401.

Rothman, M. S. and Badler, V. 2011. "Contact and development in Godin Period VI", in Gopnik, H. and Rothman, M. (eds), *On the High Road: The History of Godin Tepe, Iran*, Royal Ontario Museum/Mazda Press, Toronto: 67–137.

Rothman, M. S. and Peasnall, B. 1999. "Societal evolution in small, pre-state centres and polities: the example of Tepe Gawra in northern Mesopotamia", in Stein, G. (ed.), "Special Issue: L'expansion urukéenne: perspectives septentrionales vues à partir de Hacınebi, Hassek Höyük et Gawra", *Paléorient* 25 (1): 101–14.

Sanlaville, P. 2002. "The deltaic complex of the Lower Mesopotamian Plain and its evolution through millennia", in Nicholson, E. and Clark, P. (eds), *The Iraqi Marshlands. A Human and Environmental Study*, Politico's Publishing, London: 133–50.

Sanlaville, P. and Dalongeville, R. 2005. "L'évolution des espaces littoraux du Golfe Persique et du Golfe d'Oman depuis la phase finale de la transgression post-glaciaire", *Paléorient* 31 (1): 9–26.

Scheil, V. 1905. *Documents archaïques en écriture proto–élamite*, MDP 6, E. Leroux, Paris.

Schortman, E. M. and Urban, P. A. 1994. "Living on the edge: core/periphery relations in ancient southeastern Mesoamerica", *Current Anthropology* 35 (4): 401–30.

Schwartz, G. M. 2001. "Syria and the Uruk expansion", in Rothman 2001a: 233–64.

Sherratt, A. 1997. *Economy and Society in Prehistoric Europe*, Edinburgh University Press, Edinburgh.

Stein, G. 1999a. *Rethinking World-Systems: Diasporas, Colonies, and Interaction in Uruk Mesopotamia*, University of Arizona Press, Tuscon.

Stein, G. ed. 1999b. "Special Issue: L'expansion urukéenne: perspectives septentrionales vues à partir de Hacınebi, Hassek Höyük et Gawra", *Paléorient* 25 (1): 11–22.

Stein, G. 2001. "Indigenous social complexity at Hacınebi (Turkey) and the organisation of Uruk colonial contact", in Rothman 2001a: 265–306.

Stein, G. 2005. "The political economy of Mesopotamian colonial encounters", in Stein, G. (ed.), *The Archaeology of Colonial Encounters: Comparative Perspectives*, SAR Press, San Diego: 143–71.

Strommenger, E. 1980. *Habuba Kabira: Eine Stadt vor 5000 Jahren*, Phillip von Zabern, Mainz-am-Rhein.

Sumner, W. M. 1986. "Proto-Elamite Civilisation in Fars", in Finkbeiner, U. and Röllig, W. (eds), *Ğamdat Naṣr: Period or Regional Style? Papers given at a Symposium Held in Tübingen, November 1983*, Beihelfte zum Tubinger Atlas des Vorderen Irients, Reihe B. (Geisteswissenschaften) Nr. 62, Dr. Ludwig Reichert Verlag, Wiesbaden: 199–211.

Sumner, W. M. 1988. "Maljan, Tall-e (Anšan)", *Reallexikon der Assyriologie* 7: 306–20.

Sumner, W. M. 2003. *Early Urban Life in the Land of Anshan: Excavations at Tal-e Malyan in the Highlands of Iran*, University of Pennsylvania Museum of Archaeology and Anthropology, Philadelphia.

Sürenhagen, D. 1986. "Archaische Keramik aus Uruk Warka. Erster teil: Die Keramik der Schichten XVI–VI aus der Sondagen 'Tiefschnitt' und Sagengraben in Eanna", *Baghdader Mitteilungen* 17: 7–95.

Sürenhagen, D. 1987. "Archaische Keramik aus Uruk Warka", *BaM* 18: 1–92.

Thornton, C. P. 2009. *The Chalcolithic and Early Bronze Age Metallurgy of Tepe Hissar, Northeast Iran: A Challenge to the "Levantine Paradigm"*, unpublished Ph.D. dissertation, Department of Anthropology, University of Pennsylvania.

Tosi, M. 1984. "The notion of craft specialization and its representation in the archaeological record of early states in the Turanian Basin", in Spriggs, M. (ed.), *Marxist Perspectives in Archaeology*, Cambridge University Press, Cambridge: 22–52.

Tosi, M. 1989. "The distribution of industrial debris on the surface of Tappeh Hesar as an indication of activity areas", in Dyson, R. H. and Howard, S. M. (eds), *Tappeh Hesar: Reports of the Restudy Project, 1976*, Case Editrice le Lettere, Florence: 13–24.

Uerpmann, M. 2003. "The Dark Millennium: remarks on the final stone age in the Emirates and Oman", in Potts, D. T., al-Naboodah, H. and Hellyer, P. (eds), *Archaeology of the United Arab Emirates*, Trident, London: 73–81.

Ur, J. A. 2011. *Tell Hamoukar, Volume 1. Urbanism and Cultural Landscapes in Northeastern Syria: The Tell Hamoukar Survey, 1999–2001*, Oriental Institute Publication 137, Oriental Institute, Chicago.

Ur, J. A., Karsgaard, P. and Oates, J. 2007. "Early urban development in the Near East", *Science* 317: 1188.

Ur, J., Karsgaard, P. and Oates, J. 2011. "The spatial dimensions of early Mesopotamian urbanism: the Tell Brak suburban survey 2003–2006", *Iraq* 73: 1–20.

Van De Mieroop, M. 2004. *A History of the Ancient Near East ca. 3000–323 BC*, 1st edition, Blackwells, Oxford.

Van De Mieroop, M. 2006. *A History of the Ancient Near East ca. 3000–323 BC*, 2nd edition, Blackwells, Oxford.

Voigt, M. and Dyson Jr., R. H. 1992. "Chronology of Iran, ca. 8000–2000 B.C.", in Ehrich, R. W. (ed.), *Chronologies of Old World Archaeology*, Vols. I–II, Chicago, Chicago University Press: 122–78; 125–53.

Wallerstein, E. 1974. *The Modern World System*, Academic Press, New York.

Walstra, J., Heyvaert, V. M. A. and Verkinderen, P. 2010. "Assessing human impact on fan development using satellite images: a case-study from Lower Khuzestan (SW Iran)", *Geodinamica Acta* 23: 267–85.

Walstra, J., Heyvaert, V. M. A. & Verkinderen, P. 2011. "Mapping the alluvial landscapes of Lower Khuzestan (SW Iran)", in Smith, M. J., Paron, P. and Griffith, J. S. (eds), *Geomorphological Mapping: a Professional Handbook of Techniques and Applications*, Elsevier, Amsterdam: 551–75.

Weeks, L. R. 2008. "The 2007 early Iranian metallurgy workshop at the University of Nottingham", *Iran* 46: 335–345.

Weeks, L. R. 2012. "Metals", in Potts, D.T. (ed.), *A Companion to the Archaeology of the Ancient Near East*, Wiley-Blackwells, Oxford: 295–316.

Weeks, L. R. 2013. "The development and expansion of a Neolithic way of life", in Potts, D. T. (ed.), *Oxford Handbook of Iranian Archaeology*, Oxford University Press, Oxford: 49–74.

Weeks, L., Petrie, C. A. and Potts, D. T. 2010. "'Ubaid-related-related? The 'black-on-buff' ceramic traditions of highland southwest Iran", in Carter, R. A and Philip, G. (eds), *Beyond the 'Ubaid, Transformation and Integration in the Late Prehistoric Societies of the Middle East*, Studies in Ancient Oriental Civilization Series, Oriental Institute of the University of Chicago, Chicago: 247–78.

Weiss, H. and Young, T. C. 1975. "The Merchants of Susa Godin V and Plateau-Lowland Relations in the Late Fourth Millennium B.C.", *Iran* 13: 1–17.

Wengrow, D. 2010. *What Makes Civilization?* Oxford University Press, Oxford.

Whitcomb, D. S. 1971. *The Proto-Elamite Period at Tall-i Ghazir, Iran*, unpublished B.A. thesis, Emory University, Athens, GA.

Wilford, J. N. 2000. "Ruins alter ideas of how civilization spread", *New York Times*, published May 23 2000, http://www.nytimes.com/2000/05/23/science/ruins-alter-ideas-of-how-civilization-spread.html (accessed 26 January 2013).

Wilkinson, T. C. 2012. *Tying the Threads of Eurasia: Trans-regional Routes and Material Flows in eastern Anatolia and western Central Asia, c. 3000–1500 BC*, unpublished Ph.D. thesis, University of Sheffield, Sheffield.

Wolf, E. 1982. *Europe and the People Without History*, University of California Press, Berkeley.

Wright, H. T. 1977. "Recent research on the origin of the state", *Annual Review of Anthropology* 6: 379–97.

Wright, H. T. 1978. "Toward an explanation of the origin of the state", in Cohen, R. and Service, R. (eds), *The Origin of the State: the Anthropology of Political Evolution*, Institute for the Study of Human Issues, Philadelphia: 49–68.

Wright, H. T. 1987. "The Susiana hinterlands during the era of primary state formation," in Hole, F. (ed.), *Archaeological Perspectives on Western Iran*, Smithsonian Institution Press, Washington: 141–55.

Wright, H. T. 1998. "Uruk states in southwestern Iran", in Feinman, G. M. and Marcus, J. (eds), *Archaic States*, SAR, San Diego: 173–97.

Wright, H.T. 2001. "Cultural action in the Uruk world", in Rothman 2001a: 123–47.

Wright, H. T. and Johnson, G. A. 1975. "Population, exchange, and early state formation in southwestern Iran", *American Anthropologist* 77: 267–89.

Wright, H. T. and Johnson, G. A. 1985. "Regional perspectives on southwest Iranian state development", *Paléorient* 11 (2): 25–30.

Wright, H. T. and Rupley, E. S. A. 2001. "Calibrated radiocarbon age determinations of Uruk-related assemblages", in Rothman 2001a: 85–122.

2. MID-HOLOCENE ENVIRONMENTAL AND CLIMATIC CHANGE IN IRAN

Matthew Jones, Morteza Djamali, Lora Stevens, Vanessa Heyvaert, Hajar Askari, Dariush Noorollahi and Lloyd Weeks

Introduction

Past climate and environmental change is of long-standing and fundamental interest to archaeologists. A number of recent syntheses have examined the role of climate change and environmental modification in understanding the rise, spread, and in some instances collapse of early complex societies across south-west Asia (e.g. Staubwasser and Weiss 2006). In an Iranian context, various scholars have highlighted the role of human-environment interactions in the expansion of Neolithic communities, in the growth and decline of Chalcolithic pastoral societies, and for the development of the first urban societies (e.g. Hole 1994, 1998; Henricksen 1985; Miller and Kimiae 2006). Here we review proxy evidence of climatic and environmental conditions to provide an independent background to societal development in Iran during the fourth millennium BC. To put the fourth millennium BC (i.e. 5000 to 6000 years BP) into a long-term context, we look at the evidence for climate and environmental change from the early to mid-Holocene (*c.* 10000 to 2000 years BP). Antecedent conditions are particularly useful in framing the magnitude and rapidity of climatic changes. As continuous records of change are relatively scarce from Iran itself and those that are available have limited spatial extent, we also draw on records from wider south-west Asia.

The fourth millennium BC sits at a key transition in global climate from an early Holocene "optimum", when northern hemisphere temperatures and Indian Ocean monsoon (IOM) rainfall were highest *c.* 8 kyr BP (e.g. Chen *et al.* 2008), to a late Holocene climate state (Fig. 2.1). This transition saw a southward shift in the mean position of the Inter-tropical Convergence Zone (ITCZ) during boreal summer and a weakening of the Indian monsoon, among other

changes worldwide (Wanner *et al.* 2008). Globally, the nature of this transition appears to have varied between proxy record location, with some recording a gradual change in climate that follows the trend of waning summer insolation forcing (Fig. 2.1), e.g. the precipitation record of southern Oman speleothems (Fleitmann *et al.* 2003). Other sites experienced an apparently sudden and dramatic shift in conditions, e.g. the Saharan dust record marking the end of the African Humid Period at 5500 yr BP (deMenocal *et al.* 2000). The type of transition (gradual or abrupt) is intrinsically linked to the characteristics of the archive, the climate proxy, and its location, as well as the nature of the climate change itself. For example, the latter, more abrupt change in Saharan dust may reflect the sensitivity of the specific core location to a gradually southward-moving climate front, rather than a sudden change for an entire region, a hypothesis supported by the south- and eastward migration of people out of sub-tropical Africa at this time (Kuper and Kröpelin 2006). The timing of abrupt mid-Holocene shifts also varies spatially. Whereas the increase in Saharan dust occurred at around 5.5 kyr BP, the major decrease in IOM rainfall recorded in the northern Oman speleothem records occurred at around 6.3 kyr BP (Fleitmann *et al.* 2007).

In addition to longer millennial-scale shifts, there are a number of short-term climatic events, which may have had an impact across different parts of the region. During the fourth millennium BC, a pronounced event at 5.2 kyr BP, clearly evident in the Soreq speleothem record (Bar Matthews *et al.* 1997), has been potentially linked to drought in other regional records, including those from Iran (Staubwasser and Weiss 2006).

The timing and nature of these climate shifts have potentially important implications for societies both

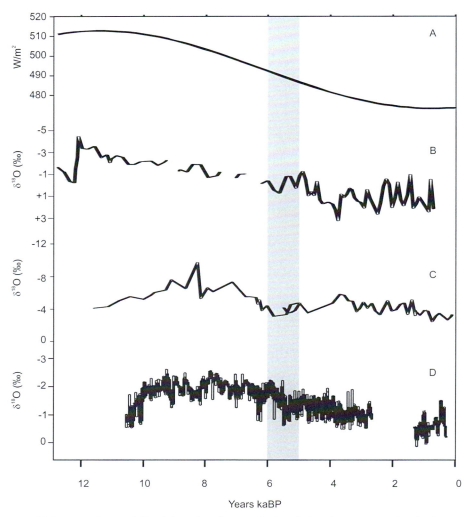

Figure 2.1. Long-term Holocene climate shifts driven by changes in insolation (A, summer insolation at 30°N; Berger and Loutre 1991). Records shown are from Eski Acigol, Turkey (B; Roberts et al. 2001), Zeribar, Iran (C; Stevens et al. 2006) and Qunf Cave, Oman (D; Fleitmann et al. 2003). The fourth millennium BC is highlighted.

within and adjacent to the region in which climatic change has been identified. The fact that these shifts occurred in different places at different times probably created a complex climatic landscape in which early societies had to exist. This potential spatial variability highlights the importance of increasing the density of robustly dated records of past climates from across the entire region of investigation, and cautions against the over-interpretation of local conditions from reconstructions that may be hundreds of kilometres away from the site of interest in a different climatic regime.

Climate and environment in Iran today

To place past changes in perspective and better understand possible controls on regional climate systems, it is important to consider the environmental and climatic settings in present-day Iran. These

patterns have been reviewed by several authors (e.g. Alijani and Harman 1985; Ghasemi and Khalili 2008) and are thus only outlined here. In general, Iran is semi-arid to arid, with mean annual precipitation less than 250 mm. The climate over the majority of the Iranian plateau is of Mediterranean-type, although with stronger continentality compared to the Mediterranean Basin. Precipitation occurs mainly during the winter months due to depressions originating from the Mediterranean and North Atlantic, which move westwards towards the continental interior of the Near East (Alijani and Harman 1985). During spring, humid air masses coming from the Mediterranean Sea follow a storm track that passes over the Black Sea and absorbs more moisture, causing rainstorms in the northern half of Iran (Stevens *et al.* 2001). The southern half of Iran is mainly deprived of this precipitation and remains dominated by winter precipitation (Razei *et al.* 2008). The southern Caspian shoreline also sees significant amounts of autumn precipitation, driven by the locally available moisture source (Khalili 1973). In the far south of Iran, rainfall today is only slightly affected by the Indian summer monsoon, although this system may have had a more significant impact on past Iranian precipitation. Today, the IOM has the most impact on Iranian climate through its control on the degree of subtropical high-pressure subsidence responsible for the dry summer conditions in most regions of Iran (Djamali *et al.* 2010).

Biogeographically, Iran is situated between Euro-Siberian (northern), Irano-Turanian (the majority of the country's surface), and Saharo-Sindian (southern) floristic regions (Zohary 1973). The Zagros Mountains in western Iran are covered by open deciduous oak woodlands and pistachio/almond scrubs. Vegetation in the central Iranian plateau is mainly composed of *Artemisia* steppes in well-drained areas and diversified halophytic communities dominated by Chenopodiaceae in the saline plains. The northern slopes of the Alborz Mountains in the south Caspian region contain a temperate to subtropical humid forest with many relict species. In southern Iran, east of the Zagros, pseudo-savanna vegetation containing many Saharo-Sindian elements is similar to the subtropical vegetation of Africa and Arabia.

Evidence of Holocene climate and environmental change from Iran

Lake records

The most complete records of Holocene environmental and climate change in Iran come from lake cores from the north-west Zagros, i.e. Lakes Urmia (e.g. Bottema 1986), Zeribar, and Mirabad (e.g. van Zeist and Bottema 1977; Stevens *et al.* 2001, 2006; Griffiths *et al.* 2001). Significant traces of large-scale anthropogenic activities in the pollen diagrams of Iran so far published seem only to appear from *c.* 3500 years ago (Iron Age), potentially resulting from the spectacular expansion of agricultural and fruit growing activities during the reign of the Achaemenid (550–330 BC) and Sassanian (AD 224–642) empires (Djamali *et al.* 2009). These alterations in vegetation are due to increasing socio-economic and political stability as well as the development of irrigation techniques (e.g. Goblot 1979; Malekzadeh 2007). Current evidence therefore suggests pollen records during the fourth millennium BC are more likely to represent changes in environment or climate, rather than anthropogenic influences, although this must be taken with our own caveat regarding palaeo-environment over-interpretation from spatially disparate records. The Urmia, Zeribar, and Mirabad records indicate that during the middle part of the Holocene, the landscapes of western and

north-western Iran were already dominated by open deciduous oak woodlands and pistachio/almond scrub in the Zagros Mountains and by juniper woodlands in the Azerbaijan area (e.g. Bottema 1986; Djamali *et al.* 2008).

Both the pollen and oxygen isotope records from Zeribar and Mirabad display mid-Holocene environmental shifts (Stevens *et al.* 2006). The percentage of oak pollen recorded at the two sites rises from around 10 to 50% between 7000 and 6000 years BP (Fig. 2.2). This change is associated with a gradual shift to more positive oxygen isotope values in Zeribar over the same time period (Stevens *et al.* 2001), but a more rapid shift, around 5800 years BP in the Mirabad record (Stevens *et al.* 2006). A fourth-millennium BC drought is suggested by the poor preservation of pollen in one sample at Mirabad, marking a potential desiccation event. This event is accompanied by an increase in oxygen isotope values, also constrained by a single point but coincident in timing with the 5.2 kyr BP event (Stevens *et al.* 2006). Current sampling resolution and dating control from Iranian records make it difficult to engage robustly with debates around the regional extent, and nature, of "events" at 4.2 and 5.2 kyr BP.

Although Iranian and European late-glacial and Holocene vegetation development show many similarities, they are different in that during the early Holocene, the forest expansion in Iran did not occur until *c.* 6500 years ago with an apparent delay of several thousand years after the start of the Holocene (Roberts 2002). The reasons for the delayed post-glacial expansion of oak, in particular, in the Near East and the associated regional shift to more positive lake oxygen isotope values remain under debate (e.g. Djamali *et al.* 2010; Jones and Roberts 2008).

Recently the delayed early Holocene re-expansion of trees in the Zagros/Anti-Taurus Mountains has been related to a long-distance forcing effect of Indian summer monsoon intensification (Djamali *et al.* 2010). The pollen evidence suggests that in the Zagros Mountains the mid-Holocene is manifested by more humid conditions favouring the maximum expansion of oak woodlands in north-west Iran and south-east Anatolia (van Zeist and Bottema 1977; Wick *et al.* 2003; Wasylikowa *et al.* 2006). Stevens *et al.* (2001, 2006) explain the shift to more positive oxygen isotope ratios in the Zeribar and Mirabad lake records during the same period as a move to more spring-dominated precipitation, as well as an overall increase in moisture.

Clear evidence of changing lake levels in some of the larger basins around the Iranian plateau, including the Caspian Sea in the north (e.g. Hoogendoorn *et al.* 2005) and the Sistan basin in the south-east (Huntington 1905), has been recognised for some time. Rychagov (1997) shows that there was a highstand of the Caspian Sea halfway through the fourth millennium

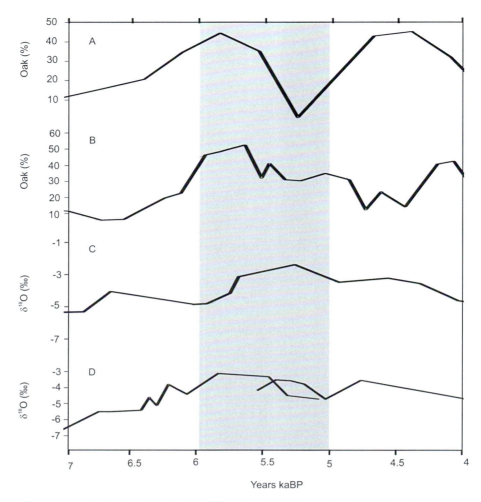

Figure 2.2. Detailed proxy records during the fourth millennium BC in Iran. A and B show the percentage of oak pollen at Mirabad and Zeribar respectively (Van Zeist and Bottema 1977). C and D show the δ¹⁸O records from the same records (Stevens et al. 2006). The fourth millennium BC is highlighted; there is a clear drop in oak around 5.2 kyr BP, associated with desiccation at the site and the most positive oxygen isotope values, which may mark the regional 5.2 kyr BP drought.

BC, one of a series of oscillations superimposed on an overall trend of lake level fall post-7 kyr BP. Kakroodi *et al.* (2012) demonstrate similar patterns of change from the south-east Caspian shoreline in northern Iran for the period post-5 kyr BP. Former lake basins exist south and west of Shiraz, which marks the southern edge of naturally open water bodies in the region today, with lakes such as Muharlou and Parishan. These former water bodies may hold key information about the timing of previous wetter periods and the former extent of summer monsoonal rains from the south or Mediterranean winter storms south through the Zagros.

Geomorphology and tectonics

In addition to climatic information, geomorphological data – e.g. fluvial deposits (Kehl *et al.* 2009), which are also partially driven by human and tectonic activity,

can lead to important information about landscape development in and around archaeological sites. Given the acknowledged changes in climate, sea level, vegetation, and tectonic and anthropogenic activities, significant changes in landform probably occurred across Iran during the Holocene, and early societies are likely to have lived in landscapes that looked somewhat different to the ones we see today.

The mountain ranges in the north and west of Iran provide a ready source of material to erode and therefore substantial thicknesses of Quaternary sediments have accumulated in river valleys and on the central arid plain (Brookes 1982). Little work has been done at the level of detail required or with suitable dating control, in order to examine landscape variability within the Holocene. Most significant changes in river geomorphology are thought to date to the last glacial period (Beaumont 1972) or to the period between the last glacial and the early Holocene, when gravels were deposited, and the mid-Holocene, which is marked by deposition of sands and silts. There appears to be a gap in deposition for much of the Holocene in fluvial sequences across the region (Brookes 1982) with incision dominating (Rigot 2010). The pattern of changing deposition may also be due to tectonics (Regard *et al.* 2006) or to landscape stability, as more stable, vegetated areas reduce the amount of material available for erosion. This, combined with the continued uplift of the mountain regions, would have led to periods of river erosion rather than deposition. Kehl *et al.* (2009) suggest that the Kur River, near Shiraz, was incising from about 10-yr BP with the development of Holocene soils in the alluvium. Rigot (2010) describes early Holocene deposition in the Tang-i Bulaghi plain (Fars Province) between 9000 and 8000 yr BP, followed by erosion by the Poulvar River. Late Holocene deposition, after 2000 yrs BP, is thought to be associated with increased farming in the region, as well as a more humid climate. Recent multidisciplinary research in Lower Khuzestan has also suggested late Holocene change due to human impact, with the rapid deposition of alluvial fans from *c.* 2500 cal BP as a result of successive avulsions and the construction of extensive irrigation canal networks during the Sasanian period (Heyvaert 2007; Walstra *et al.* 2010, 2011).

Sea-level change

Coastal areas are likely to have been significantly affected by global sea-level changes during the Holocene as well as tectonic activity, leading to relative sea-level changes along the Iranian coast (e.g. Pirazzoli 1998; Preusser *et al.* 2003; Pirazzoli *et al.* 2004). The Persian Gulf was completely dry during the Last Glacial Maximum and became drowned again during the early Holocene global sea-level rise around 10 kyr BP (Uchupi *et al.* 1999).

Since the early nineteenth century, historians and geomorphologists have debated the position of the Persian Gulf shoreline in the Arvand Rud region as a result of the post-glacial sea-level rise (e.g. Beke 1835; Lees and Falcon 1952; Sanlaville and Dalongeville 2005). Recently, a large-scale palaeogeographical reconstruction of the Lower Khuzestan plain and the northern extension of the Persian Gulf has been made for different time slices between 8000 and 450 cal BP (Baeteman *et al.* 2004; Heyvaert 2007; Heyvaert and Baeteman 2007). During the early and middle Holocene, the Lower Khuzestan plain was a low-energy tidal embayment under estuarine conditions. The rapid relative sea-level rise in the early Holocene forced the coastline to transgress swiftly across the shelf. The drowning of what was probably the antecedent valley of the Arvand Rud resulted in the development of extended tidal flats. A deceleration of the relative sea-level rise after *c.* 5500 cal BP, associated

with more arid conditions, allowed coastal sabkhas to extend and aggrade while the position of the coastline remained relatively stable. A retreat of the sea has also been reported from the Hormoz Strait area at *c.* 5 kyr BP (e.g. Bruthans *et al.* 2006) suggesting that the fourth millennium BC was a period of significant coastal change in parts of Iran. Continued deceleration of the relative sea-level rise, and human activity as described above, initiated the progradation of the coastline from *c.* 2500 cal BP in the Lower Khuzestan plain (Heyvaert 2007; Heyvaert and Baeteman 2007).

Evidence of change from the wider region

There are significant shifts evident in climate proxy records from across the region between 7000 and 5000 years BP associated with the decrease in solar insolation following the Holocene climatic optimum as discussed in the introduction. These post-climatic optimum changes are not always smooth, with some locations showing a rapid, threshold response and variations in the timing of shifts. West of Iran, significant shifts in most of the records from the Levant occur around 7000 years BP with rapid decreases in Dead Sea lake levels (e.g. Migowski *et al.* 2006) and increases in speleothem oxygen isotope ratios (e.g. Bar-Matthews *et al.* 1997). Gradual shifts occur, however, between 7000 and 5000 years BP, in proxy records from the Red Sea and Negev desert (Robinson *et al.* 2006). To the south of Iran speleothem records from southern Oman show gradual changes during the mid-Holocene, but rapid shifts to drier climates at 6300 years BP in the north (Fleitmann *et al.* 2007). The lake record from Awafi, eastern Arabia, also suggests a southward shift of the Indian summer monsoon at this time as here, as well as at many of the other Arabian sites, lakes dried out around 6000 years BP (Parker *et al.* 2004).

To analyse the spatial and temporal variability in mid-Holocene climate changes in Iran and the surrounding region we have taken 14 key terrestrial records of hydrological change through the early and mid-Holocene (Table 2.1) and produced semi-quantified records of wetness for each site. The Holocene range of each proxy at each site was given a scale of 1 (driest) to 10 (wettest) and the "wetness" at each site was compiled into maps at 1000-year time steps between 8000 and 3000 years BP to examine regional patterns (Fig. 2.3).

There are clearly concerns with using different proxies, as each proxy has its own sensitivities and thresholds to moisture balance. Furthermore, the determination of "wet" from different authors is clearly subjective, and it is often difficult to interpret what different proxies or different authors mean. Increased wetness may mean increased rainfall, increased effective rainfall (i.e. evaporation vs.

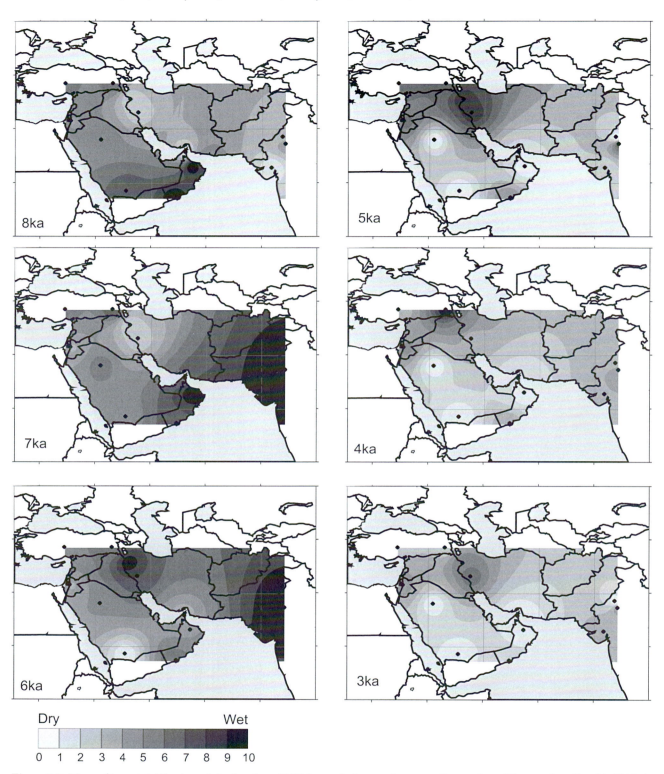

Figure 2.3. Maps of terrestrial "wetness" during the mid-Holocene in Iran and surrounding regions. Sites used are listed in Table 1.

precipitation), and/or increased humidity, and may be annual or seasonal in different records. It is also likely that the controls on "wetness" at a given site will change with time or at different timescales, adding another level of complexity to the interpretation.

The careful interpretation of each proxy at each site is therefore important before robust conclusions can be drawn. Here, we assume that controls on wetness remain constant for our chosen proxies in each archive during the Holocene (Table 2.1).

Table 2.1. Sites and proxies used in the development of "wetness" maps (Fig. 2.3).

Site	Proxy	Definition of "wet"	Reference
Dead Sea	Lake Level	High = wet	Migowski et al. 2006
Awafi	Na:Ti	High = wet	Parker et al. 2006
Lunkaransar	Lake Level	High = wet	Prasad and Enzel 2006
Didwana	Lake Level	High = wet	Prasad and Enzel 2006
Nal Sarova	Lake Level	High = wet	Prasad and Enzel 2006
Hoti Cave	$\delta^{18}O$	Negative = wet	Fleitmann et al. 2007
Qunf Cave	$\delta^{18}O$	Negative = wet	Fleitmann et al. 2007
Lake Zeribar	% Oak	High = wet	Van Zeist and Bottema 1977
Lake Mirabad	% Oak	High = wet	Van Zeist and Bottema 1977
Lake Mundafan	Lake Level	High = wet	McClure 1976
Soreq Cave	$\delta^{18}O$	Negative = wet	Bar-Matthews et al. 1997
Lake Van	Humidity (from $\delta^{18}O$)	High = wet	Lemcke and Sturm 1997
Eski Acigol	$\delta^{18}O$	Negative = wet	Roberts et al. 2001
An-Nafud	Lake level	High = wet	COHMAP Members 1994

The resulting map shows that in general the region got drier from a maximum wetness between 7 and 6 kyr BP, as monsoon rains moved south and became reduced in intensity in the south-east of the region, and North Atlantic sourced rains were reduced in the north-west of the region. Iran, sitting in between these two systems and with the least number of proxy records, is currently difficult to fit into this pattern. Given the data available from Mirabad and Zeribar it looks as though Iran follows patterns more similar to those to the east, rather than to the south or west. Chen et al. (2008) showed that proxies from arid Central Asia, in contrast to the moisture history of the region dominated by the Asian summer monsoon, describe low effective moisture in the early Holocene and highest "wetness" during the mid-Holocene.

Although we have not used every available reconstruction in this analysis, the maps highlight the areas of severe data shortage, especially in present-day eastern Iran, Afghanistan and Pakistan. This limits the usefulness of such an analysis in terms of prediction or projection of conditions between palaeoclimate records, as we have discussed above, but is of great use in identifying areas for future work and understanding the limitations of our knowledge. It also highlights the difficulties of comprehending the past climate in the region between the Mediterranean and the IOM, where, in both regions there are more data points and patterns of change are relatively well established (e.g. Roberts et al. 2008).

Summary

The fourth millennium BC sits at the end of a global climate reorganisation following the Holocene climatic optimum. The speed and timing of the shift from early to late Holocene climatic settings appears to have varied across the region. At higher temporal resolutions there are currently no local records from Iran that can look at centennial-scale climatic change within the fourth millennium BC in detail, and this is an important area for future research, especially to confirm the local impact of the 5.2 kyr and 4.2 kyr events. New sites, or new higher-resolution proxy and dating analyses from known sites are required.

The complex interplay between people, climate, landscape stability, and tectonics during much of the Holocene in Iran and its location at the crossroads between different cultural and climatic influences, make this information difficult to obtain. There is a need to think carefully about how to unpick the different forcing mechanisms from natural and archaeological archives and a clear need for multidisciplinary programmes to take this work forward.

Bibliography

Alijani, B. and Harman, J. R. 1985. "Synoptic climatology of precipitation in Iran", Annals of the Association of American Geographers 75: 404–16.

Baeteman, C., Dupin, L. and Heyvaert, V. M. A. 2004. "The Persian Gulf shorelines and the Karkheh, Karun, and Jarrahi Rivers: a geo-archaeological approach. First Progress Report. 1. Geo-Environmental Investigation", Akkadica 125: 155–215.

Bar-Matthews, M., Ayalon, A. and Kaufman, A. 1997. "Late Quaternary paleoclimate in the eastern Mediterranean region from stable isotope analysis of speleothems at Soreq Cave, Israel", Quaternary Research 47: 155–68.

Beaumont, P. 1972. "Alluvial fans along the southern foothills of the Elburz Mountains, Iran", *Palaeogeography, Palaeoclimatology, Palaeoecology* 12: 251–73.

Beke, C. T. 1835. "On the geological evidence of the advance of the land at the head of the Persian Gulf", *Philosophical Magazine Series 3* 7(37): 40–46.

Berger, A. and Loutre, M. F. 1991. "Insolation values for the climate of the last 10 million years", *Quaternary Sciences Reviews* 10: 297–317.

Bottema, S. 1986. "A late Quaternary pollen diagram from Lake Urmia (northwestern Iran)", *Review of Palaeobotany and Palynology* 47: 241–61.

Brookes, I. A. 1982. "Geomorphologic evidence for climatic change in Iran during the last 20,000 years", in Blintliff, J. L. and van Zeist, W. (eds), *Paleoclimates, paloenvironments and human communities in the eastern Mediterranean region in later prehistory,* BAR International Series 133: 191–228.

Bruthans, J., Filippi, M., Geršl, M., Zare, M., Melková, J., Pazdur, A. and Bosák, P. 2006. "Holocene marine terraces on two salt diapirs in the Persian Gulf, Iran: age, depositional history and uplift rates", *Journal of Quaternary Science* 21: 843–57.

Chen, F., Yu, Z., Yang, M., Ito, E., Wang, S., Madsen, D. B., Huang, X., Zhao, Y., Sato, T., Birks, H. J. B., Boomer, I., Chen, J., An, C. and Wünnemann, B. 2008. "Holocene moisture evolution in arid central Asia and its out-of-phase relationship with Asian monsoon history", *Quaternary Science Reviews* 27: 351–64.

COHMAP Members. 1994. Oxford Lake Levels Database. IGBP PAGES/World Data Center-A for Paleoclimatology Data Contribution Series # 94-028. NOAA/NGDC Paleoclimatology Program, Boulder CO, USA.

deMenocal, P., Ortiz, J., Guilderson, T., Adkins, J., Sarnthein, M., Baker, L. and Yarusinsky, M. 2000. "Abrupt onset and termination of the African Humid Period: rapid climate responses to gradual insolation forcing", *Quaternary Science Reviews* 19: 347–61.

Djamali, M., de Beaulieu, J. L., Miller, N. F., Andrieu-Ponel, V., Ponel, P., Lak, R., Sadeddin, N., Akhani, H., and Fazeli, H. 2009. "Vegetation history of the SE section of the Zagros Mountains during the last five millennia; a pollen record from the Maharlou Lake, Fars Province, Iran", *Vegetation History and Archaeobotany* 18: 123–36.

Djamali, M., de Beaulieu, J. L., Shah-Hosseini, M., Andrieu-Ponel, V., Ponel, P., Amini, A., Akhani, H., Leroy, S. A. G., Stevens, L., Lahijam, H. and Brewer, S. 2008. "A late Pleistocene long pollen record from Lake Urmia, NW Iran", *Quaternary Research* 69: 413–20.

Djamali, M., Akhani, H., Andrieu-Ponel, V., Braconnot, P., Brewer, S., de Beaulieu, J. L., Fleitmann, D., Fleury, J., Gasse, F., Guibal, F., Jackson, S. T., Lezine, A. M., Medail, F., Ponel, P., Roberts, N. and Stevens, L. 2010. "Indian Summer Monsoon variations could have affected the early-Holocene woodland expansion in the Near East", *Holocene* 20: 813–20.

Fleitmann, D., Burns, S. J., Mudelsee, M., Neff, U., Kramers, J., Mangini, A. and Matter, A. 2003. "Holocene forcing of the Indian monsoon recorded in a stalactite from southern Oman", *Science* 300: 1737–39.

Fleitmann, D., Burns, S. J., Mangini, A., Mudelsee, M., Kramers, J., Villa, I., Neff, U., Al-Subbary, A. A., Buettner, A., Hippler, D. and Matter, A. 2007. "Holocene ITCZ and Indian monsoon dynamics recorded in stalagmites from Oman and Yemen (Socotra)", *Quaternary Science Reviews* 26: 170–88.

Ghasemi, A. R. and Khalili, D. 2008. "The association between regional and global atmospheric patterns and winter precipitation in Iran", *Atmospheric Research* 88: 116–33.

Goblot, H. 1979. *Les Qanats, une technique d'acquisition de l'eau.* Mouton/École des hautes études en sciences sociales, Paris, The Hague.

Griffiths, H. I., Schwalb, A. and Stevens, L. R. 2001. "Environmental change in southwestern Iran: the Holocene ostracod fauna of Lake Mirabad", *Holocene* 11(6): 757–64.

Henricksen, E. 1985. "The early development of pastoralism in the central Zagros highlands (Luristan)", *Iranica Antiqua* 20: 1–42.

Heyvaert, V. M. A. 2007. *Fluvial Sedimentation, Sea-level History and Anthropogenic Impact in the Great Mesopotamian plain: A new Holocene Record,* unpublished Ph.D. thesis, Vrije Universiteit Brussel, Brussels.

Heyvaert, V. M. A. and Baeteman, C. 2007. "Holocene sedimentary evolution and palaeocoastlines of the Lower Khuzestan plain (southwest Iran)", *Marine Geology* 224: 83–108.

Hole, F. 1994. "Environmental instabilities and urban origins", in Stein, G. and Rothman, M. (eds), *Chiefdoms and Early States in the Near East; the Organizational Dynamics of Complexity,* Prehistory Press, Madison. Monographs in World Archaeology No. 18: 121–51.

Hole, F. 1998. "The Spread of Agriculture to the Eastern Arc of the Fertile Crescent: Food for the Herders", in Damania, A. B., Valkoun, J., Willcox, G. and Qualset, C. O. (eds), *The Origins of Agriculture and Crop Domestication,* International Center for Agricultural Research in the Dry Areas, Aleppo: 83–92.

Hoogendoorn, R. M., Boels, J. F., Kroonenberg, S. B., Simmons, M. D., Aliyeva, E., Babazadeh, A. D. and Huseynov, D. 2005. "Development of the Kura delta, Azerbaijan; a record of Holocene Caspian sea-level changes", *Marine Geology* 222–223: 359–80.

Huntington, E. 1905. "The Basin of Eastern Persia and Seistan", in Pumpelly, R. W. (ed.), *Explorations in Turkestan.* Carnegie Institute Washington DC, Publ. 26: 219–316.

Jones, M. D. and Roberts, C. N. 2008. "Interpreting lake isotope records of Holocene environmental change in the Eastern Mediterranean", *Quaternary International* 181: 32–38.

Kakroodi, A. A., Kroonenberg, S. B., Hoogendoorn, R. M., Mohammd Khani, H., Yamani, M., Ghassemi, M. R. and Lahijani, H. A. K. 2012. "Rapid Holocene sea-level changes along the Iranian Caspian coast", *Quaternary International* 263: 93–103.

Kehl, M., Frechen, M. and Skowronek, A. 2009. "Nature and age of Late Quaternary basin fill deposits in the Basin of Persepolis/Southern Iran", *Quaternary International* 196: 57–70.

Khalili, A. 1973. "Precipitation patterns of Central Elburz", *Theoretical and Applied Climatology* 21: 215–32.

Kuper, R. and Kröpelin, S. 2006. "Climate-Controlled Holocene Occupation in the Sahara: Motor of Africa's Evolution", *Science* 313(5788): 803–07.

Lees, G. M. and Falcon, N. L. 1952. "The geographical history of the Mesopotamian plains", *Geographical Journal* 118: 24–39.

Lemcke, G. and Sturm, M. 1997. "δ¹⁸O and trace element measurements as proxy for the reconstruction of climate changes at Lake Van (Turkey): preliminary results", in Dalfes, N. D. (ed.), *Third Millennium BC Climate Change and Old World Collapse*. NATO ASI Series: 653–78.

McClure, H. A. 1976. "Radiocarbon chronology of late Quaternary lakes in the Arabian Desert", *Nature* 411: 290–93.

Malekzadeh, M. J. 2007. "Dams of the ancient city of Istakhr", in Emami, K., Alyasein, A., Karimian Sardashti, N., Shayan, N., Ehsani, M., Meschi, M. (eds), *Proceedings of the International History Seminar on Irrigation and Drainage*, Iranian Ministry of Energy, Tehran: 121–25.

Migowski, C., Stein, M., Prasad, S., Negendank, J. F. W. and Agnon, A. 2006. "Holocene climate variability and cultural evolution in the Near East from the Dead Sea sedimentary record", *Quaternary Research* 66(3): 421–31.

Miller, N. and Kimiae, M. 2006. "Some plant remains from the 2004 excavations of Tall-e Mushki, Tall-e Jari A and B, and Tall-e Bakun A and B", in Alizadeh, A. (ed.), *The Origins of State Organizations in Prehistoric Highland Fars, Southern Iran: Excavations at Tall-e Bakun*. OIP 128, Chicago: 107–18.

Parker, A. G., Goudie, A. S., Stokes, S., White, K., Hodson, M. J., Manning, M. and Kennet, D. 2006. "A record of Holocene climate change from lake geochemical analyses in southeastern Arabia", *Quaternary Research* 66: 465–76.

Parker, A. G., Eckersley, L., Smith, M. M., Goudie, A. S., Stokes, S., Ward, S., White, K. and Hodson, M. J. 2004. "Holocene vegetation dynamics in the northeastern Rub' al-khali desert, Arabian Peninsula: a phytolith, pollen and carbon isotope study", *Journal of Quaternary Science* 19: 665–76.

Pirazzoli, P. A. 1998. "A comparison between postglacial isostatic predictions and late Holocene sea-level field data from Mediterranean and Iranian coastal areas", *GeoResearch Forum*, Vol. 3–4. Trans Tech Publications, Switzerland: 401–20.

Pirazzoli, P. A., Reyss, J.-L., Fontugne, M., Haghipour, A., Hilgers, A., Kasper, H. U., Nazari, H., Preusser, F., Radtke, U. 2004. "Quaternary coral-reef terraces from Kish and Qeshm Islands, Persian Gulf: new radiometric ages and tectonic implications", *Quaternary International* 120: 15–27.

Prasad, S. and Enzel, Y. 2006. "Holocene paleoclimates of India", *Quaternary Research* 66(3): 442–53.

Preusser, F., Radtke, U., Fontugne, M., Haghipour, A., Hilgers, A., Kasper, H. U., Nazari, H. and Pirazzoli, P. A. 2003. "ESR dating of raised coral reefs from Kish Island, Persian Gulf", *Quaternary Science Reviews* 22: 1317–22.

Raziei, T., Bordi, I. and Pereira, L. S. 2008. "A precipitation-based regionalization for Western Iran and regional drought variability", *Hydrology and Earth System Sciences Discussions* 5: 2133–67.

Regard, V., Bellier, O., Braucher, R., Gasse, F., Bourlès, D., Mercier, J., Thomas, J.-C., Abbassi, M. R., Shabanian, E. and Soleymani, S. 2006. "10Be dating of alluvial deposits from southeastern Iran (the Hormoz Strait area)", *Palaeogeography, Palaeoclimatology, Palaeoecology* 242: 36–53.

Rigot, J.-B. 2010. "Dynamique de la rivière Poulvar et morphogénèse de la plaine de Tang-i Bulaghi (Fars, Iran) à l'Holocène. Premiers résultats", *Géomorphologie* 1: 57–72.

Roberts, N. 2002. "Did prehistoric landscape management retard the post-glacial spread of woodland in Southwest Asia?", *Antiquity* 76(294): 1002–10.

Roberts, N., Reed, J. M., Leng, M. J., Kuzucuoglu, C., Fontugne, M., Bertaux, J., Woldring, H., Bottema, S., Black, S., Hunt, E. and Karabiyikoglu, M. 2001. "The tempo of Holocene climatic change in the eastern Mediterranean region: new high-resolution crater-lake sediment data from central Turkey", *Holocene* 11: 721–36.

Roberts, N., Jones, M. D., Benkaddour, A., Eastwood, W. J., Filippi, M. L., Frogley, M. R., Lamb, H. F., Leng, M. J., Reed, J. M., Stein, M., Stevens, L., Valero-Garces, B. and Zanchetta, G. 2008. "Stable isotope records of Late Quaternary climate and hydrology from Mediterranean lakes: the ISOMED synthesis", *Quaternary Science Reviews* 27: 2426–41.

Robinson, S. A., Black, S., Sellwood, B. W. and Valdes, P. J. 2006. "A review of palaeoclimates and palaeoenvironments in the Levant and Eastern Mediterranean from 25,000 to 5000 years BP: setting the environmental background for the evolution of human civilisation", *Quaternary Science Reviews* 25: 1517–41.

Rychagov, G. I. 1997. "Holocene oscillations of the Caspian Sea, and forecasts based on palaeogeographical reconstructions", *Quaternary International* 41–42: 167–72.

Sanlaville, P. and Dalongeville, R. 2005. "L'évolution des espaces littoraux du Golfe Persique et du Golfe d'Oman depuis la phase finale de la transgression post-glaciaire", *Paléorient* 31: 9–26.

Staubwasser, M. and Weiss, H. 2006. "Holocene climate and cultural evolution in late prehistoric-early historic West Asia", *Quaternary Research* 66: 372–87.

Stevens, L. R., Wright Jr., H. E. and Ito, E. 2001. "Proposed changes in seasonality of climate during the Late-glacial and Holocene at Lake Zeribar, Iran", *The Holocene* 11: 747–56.

Stevens, L. R., Ito, E., Schwalb, A. and Wright, H. E. 2006. "Timing of atmospheric precipitation in the Zagros Mountains inferred from a multi-proxy record from Lake Mirabad, Iran", *Quaternary Research* 66: 494–500.

Uchupi, E., Swift, S. A. and Ross, D. A. 1999. "Late Quaternary stratigraphy, Paleoclimate and neotectonism of the Persian (Arabian) Gulf region", *Marine Geology* 160: 1–23.

Van Zeist, W. and Bottema, S. 1977. "Palynological investigations in western Iran", *Palaeohistoria* 19: 19–85.

Walstra, J., Heyvaert, V. M. A. and Verkinderen, P. 2010. "Assessing human impact on fan development using satellite images: a case-study from Lower Khuzestan (SW Iran)", *Geodinamica Acta* 23: 267–85.

Walstra, J., Heyvaert, V. M. A. and Verkinderen, P. 2011. "Mapping the alluvial landscapes of Lower Khuzestan (SW Iran)", in Smith, M. J., Paron, P. and Griffith, J. S. (eds), *Geomorphological mapping: a professional handbook of techniques and applications*, Elsevier, Amsterdam: 551–75.

Wanner, H., Beer, J., Bütikofer, J., Crowley, T. J., Cubasch, U., Flückiger, J., Goosse, H., Grosjean, M., Joos, F., Kaplan, J. O., Küttel, M., Müller, S. A., Prentice, I. C., Solomina, O., Stocker, T. S., Tarasov, P., Wagner, M. and Widmann, M. 2008. "Mid- to Late Holocene climate change: an overview", *Quaternary Science Reviews* 27 (19–20): 1791–1828.

Wasylikowa, K., Witkowski, A., Walanus, A., Hutorowicz, A., Alexandrowicz, S. W. and Langer, J. L. 2006. "Palaeolimnology of Lake Zeribar, Iran, and its climatic implications", *Quaternary Research* 66 (3): 477–93.

Wick, L., Lemcke, G. and Sturm, M. 2003. "Evidence of Late-glacial and Holocene climatic change and human impact in eastern Anatolia: high-resolution pollen, charcoal, isotopic and geochemical records from the laminated sediments of Lake Van, Turkey", *Holocene* 13 (5): 665–75.

Zohary, M. 1973. *Geobotanical foundations of the Middle East*. Gustav Fischer Verlag, Stuttgart.

3. POPULATION AND SETTLEMENT TRENDS IN SOUTH-WEST IRAN AND NEIGHBOURING AREAS

Kristen Hopper and T. J. Wilkinson

Introduction

This paper examines how settlement data obtained from archaeological survey can be used to estimate population trends at regional and interregional levels. Long-term settlement trends spanning the fifth–third millennia BC are discussed for several key regions representing both highland and lowland environments in south-west Iran and the neighbouring regions. These data are compared and considered in conjunction with topics such as settlement dispersal and agglomeration, changes in subsistence strategies, and demographic factors. The limitations of such an analysis, as defined by different survey methodologies, data manipulation, and data comparability are also reviewed. The considerable time span addressed in this paper will focus on broad trends of settlement rather than discussions of brief chronological phases. While such debates are integral to the study of highland/lowland interaction, as well as to the development of early villages and state formation, the goal of this paper is to view each of these major and minor developments in the context of the *longue durée*.

Within south-west Iran, archaeological survey is well developed thanks to the pioneering work of Robert McCormick Adams (1962) over fifty years ago, as well as a florescence of surveys in the two decades that followed (e.g. Hole 1969; Johnson 1973; Levine and McDonald 1977; Miroschedji 1981; Neely and Wright 1994; Schacht 1976; Sumner 1972; Wright 1969, 1979; Wright and Carter 2003; Zagarell 1982). Methodological and theoretical approaches to survey and settlement pattern analysis have taken many forms. A number of the surveys conducted in Iran during the 1960s and 1970s involved problem-oriented frameworks that aimed at answering questions related to early agriculture, early state formation, and urbanisation, or with a period-specific focus (i.e. Hole 1977; Hole *et al.* 1969; Johnson 1973). A long-

term view of settlement trends was also utilised by several projects and integrated into studies of regional population dynamics (e.g. Adams 1962; Sumner 1972, 1990a). Study and restudy of ceramic assemblages has also been fundamental in enabling inferences to be made about population trends, and these data have been successfully integrated with other sources of evidence (Alizadeh 1992; Kouchoukos 1998). The data gathered from these surveys provides an excellent record for comparison of long-term population and settlement trends. This paper is intended to be a preliminary synthesis that makes use of the material available to present results that, rather than being solely quantitative, are also qualitative. At the outset we emphasise that any study of long-term trends in settlement and population will be, at best, approximate. Nevertheless, we feel that the existing data sets should be harnessed to determine to what degree they provide a coherent picture (see also Hopper 2007).

Study areas

South-west Iran encompasses the low-lying alluvial plains of Khuzestan, a substantial portion of the Zagros Mountains, and the foothills in-between, each representing a diverse, but interrelated environmental setting for human settlement that is crucial to understanding the socio-cultural, political, and economic development of the region (Fig. 3.1). Khuzestan, and in particular the Susiana Plain, has been chosen as our starting point because of the rich archaeological record that has been recorded by numerous surveys. We compare this to settlement records from the neighbouring Deh Luran and Ram Hormuz plains to establish a baseline trend for the lowland regions. This picture is then compared to settlement trends occurring in the Kur River Basin in Fars, and the Islamabad Plain in Kermanshah within

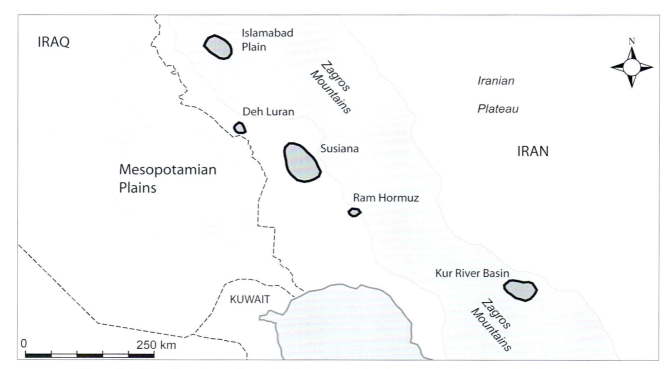

Figure 3.1. Map of south-west Iran and Mesopotamia showing survey regions mentioned in the text.

the Central Zagros Mountain zone. Beyond south-west Iran, we produce an index of interregional population and settlement by comparing gross trends from the Susiana plain with those of southern Mesopotamia. In order to maintain a manageable data set, the scope of this project did not move beyond these specific survey areas. The last few years, however, have seen further surveys conducted in several regions of south-west Iran, including the Mamasani Project in Fars and the surveys conducted by Moghaddam and Miri in the Mianab Plain and the "Eastern Corridor", which have provided data that could enhance any future analysis of this topic (Moghaddam and Miri 2003, 2007; Zeidi *et al.* 2009; McCall 2009).

The concept of a highland/lowland dichotomy is well established within the literature, and has mainly focused upon the two major regions of the Susiana Plain and the Kur River Basin, which were the foci of the major polities centred on Susa and Anshan (Tal-e Malyan) in the third and second millennia BC (Carter and Stolper 1984: 1–4; Miroschedji 2003). The varied environment of south-west Iran lends itself to different types of land use, and both sedentary and mobile modes of subsistence. The lowland plains and intermontane valleys make up the majority of agriculturally productive areas, which, along with the slopes and foothills, are also good for pasturage. Seasonal movement between the uplands and lowlands by mobile pastoralists and semi-sedentary groups has been observed in many ethnographic studies (e.g. Barth 1965; Beck

1986). While it has been proposed that analogous behaviour took place in prehistory (Alizadeh 2010), the applicability of the mobility model has also been questioned (Potts 2008; Weeks *et al.* 2010; Petrie 2011). The potential for transhumant movement throughout this landscape reminds us that the Khuzestan plains and the Zagros mountain chain should not be seen as a strictly dichotomous set of environments, but as complementary ones linked by networks through which the movement of people, materials, and ideas can occur (Adams 1962: 110; Alizadeh 2010).

Preservation and loss of settlement data

Some geoarchaeological studies of Iran have provided a bleak view of the preservation of the ancient settlement record, suggesting that so much of the record has been buried that reconstructed settlement trends can be meaningless (Brookes *et al.* 1982). Many of the early geoarchaeological studies, however, were based on a limited number of sections and minimal control from air photos or satellite imagery, and thus do not indicate the complexities of valley fill development. Elsewhere in the Near East, alluvial plains such as in the Amuq Plain of southern Turkey, the Khuzestan Plains of Iran, and the Balikh Valley of Syria, have been shown to consist of a mosaic of areas obscured by sedimentation, alternating with various "windows" characterised by little sedimentation and maximum visibility (Kouchoukos 1998; Wilkinson 2003; Casana and Wilkinson 2005).

Therefore, although the settlement record will be obscured in some areas of active sedimentation, elsewhere the settlement record will remain visible (although still biased by various factors). In the context of the present paper it is important to appreciate that where prehistoric settlement has been preserved, later settlement will probably also be preserved. Nevertheless, in most cases, there will also be a bias that results in the earlier settlements being less evident than those of later date because of the tendency of later archaeological levels to obscure those of earlier date.

In the context of south-west Iran, Kouchoukos has demonstrated that within the Khuzestan plain the majority of prehistoric sites were preserved on the older alluvial sediments that made up only *c*. one third of the area of the plain (see below; Kouchoukos 1998; Kouchoukos and Hole 2003). For the same region, when the elevation of the base of tell strata is compared to the level of the surrounding ground surface it is possible to estimate the amounts of Holocene sedimentation. One such area of lower sedimentation and enhanced site visibility has been revealed around the site of Choga Mish and neighbouring parts of the eastern Susiana plain. Elsewhere in the Upper Khuzestan Plains, sedimentation consisted not only of alluvial deposits, but also included irrigation sediments that accumulated as a result of the discharge of sediment-rich waters onto irrigated fields, especially during the last few thousand years. Such deposits mapped by the *FAO Khuzestan Soil Survey Project*, together with a small number of field sections (Spence 1956: soil map of the Dezful area), suggest that prehistoric sites have been preferentially obscured by both irrigated

and alluvial sediments in the northernmost plain over the areas further south towards the Haft Tepe ridge.

In the south-eastern Khuzestan plain, low-energy mountain fringe alluvial fan development has obscured a number of prehistoric sites that were then re-exposed by the rejuvenation of wadi systems caused by the construction of a major Sasanian canal system, and the subsequent avulsion of the Karun River along the Gar Gar channel (Alizadeh *et al.* 2004; Lees and Falcon 1952; Moghaddam and Miri 2003, 2007). In terms of population dynamics, these exposures are important not only for demonstrating the existence of a buried prehistoric landscape, but also because some of these sites may have been occupied by mobile pastoral communities (Alizadeh *et al.* 2004; Alizadeh 2010).

A model of sedimentary accumulation devised by Mike Kirkby (1977: 280–83) has now been supplemented by data from a 2002 field project (Alizadeh *et al.* 2004) (Fig. 3.2) to show that the sedimentary levels from the Dar Khazineh area to the south-east of Shushtar fall roughly in line with those obtained in the 1970s. Rather than sedimentation terminating at around 2000 BC as suggested by Kirkby, however, the accumulation of irrigation sediments on the older plain surfaces has resulted in further sedimentation of 1–3 m (Alizadeh *et al.* 2004: 78–79).

Unfortunately, even less is known about the spatial pattern of sedimentation in the Kur River Basin, but the large amount of prehistoric settlement remaining demonstrates that there has been a significant amount of site survival (Sumner 1990a). This inference is supported by geomorphological studies of dated sediment-soil sequences that demonstrate that the

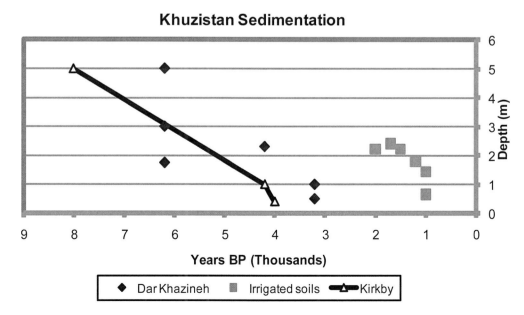

Figure 3.2. A model of sedimentary accumulation devised by Mike Kirkby (1977: 280–83) has now been supplemented by data from a 2002 field project (Alizadeh et al. 2004).

plains consist of silt and clay fluvial and aeolian sediments (loess) with associated lake deposits and palaeosols, the upper layers of which were deposited in the late Pleistocene and early Holocene (Kehl *et al.* 2009: fig. 8). With the exception of a lower terrace formed during the mid- to late Holocene, the depth of mid- to late Holocene sediment on the plains is less than 2 m, suggesting that the archaeological record at the time of survey was relatively complete.

The situation in south-west Iran, noted above, can be compared with that in both southern and northern Mesopotamia:

• In southern Mesopotamia, alluvial and irrigation sediments form a deep carpet over the landscape

in the northern plains and Diyala region, whereas further south, such sedimentation declines significantly. In addition, extensive areas of aeolian activity and lower alluvial deposition occur in sedimentary windows where sites are less likely to be deeply buried, and might even be raised on pedestals above the plain (Wilkinson 2003: 80–82).

• In contrast, in rain-fed upper Mesopotamia ribbons of sedimentary deposition obscure settlements along the main river channels, but much of the plain and undulating steppe consist of broad areas of minimal deposition upon which the archaeological record remains well preserved. The contrasts between all three areas are summarised in Figures 3.3 and 3.4.

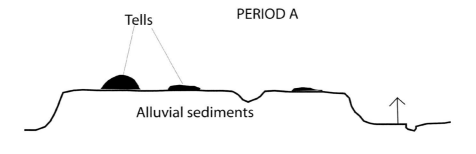

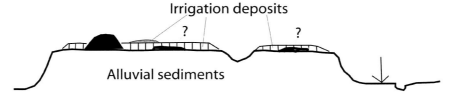

Figure 3.3. Khuzestan sedimentary model.

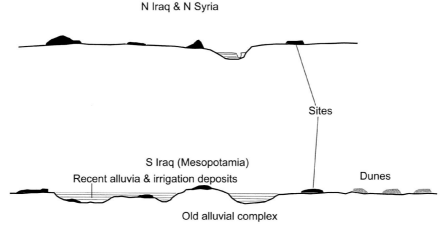

Figure 3.4. Mesopotamian alluvial model.

Overall, given the prevailing uncertainties, it is best to see the remaining patterns of prehistoric settlement as representing a minimal figure that provides a sample of the total site count. The question we therefore have to ask of the existing patterns is whether they provide a consistent and coherent record of settlement through time.

The survey data

In order to compare settlement trends from a range of survey areas it is advisable to use a common variable. In this case we have chosen to use aggregate occupied area and the total number of sites occupied in each phase. This made the comparison of different data sets easier and remains closest to the raw data. In this way we are able to focus on robust trends that fall within an acceptable margin of variation.

When considering the issue of contemporaneity of settlement occupation (e.g. Weiss 1977; Schacht 1981, 1984; Sumner 1990b) one cannot assume that all the sites attributed to a specific period were occupied at the same time, especially when dealing with phases that last several hundred years. A number of ways of standardising data have been suggested: these include Dewar's (1991) contemporaneity algorithm, which has previously been applied to data from the Susiana and Deh Luran plains (Neely and Wright 1994: 200–11, fig. VI.1; Kouchoukos 1998: table 3.9, fig. 3.13a; Kouchoukos and Hole 2003: 58–59). This algorithm provides an estimate of the number of sites that may have been occupied at any one time in a particular period by assessing the degree of continuity of occupation at individual settlements, but it is still not possible to know precisely which sites were occupied in the relevant sub-period. For this paper we have chosen to employ the raw data, rather than those processed according to the Dewar method (1991), but in future we intend to employ a temporal model that allows for comparison between archaeological phases of different lengths (Wilkinson *et al.* 2012).

Estimates of population density can also be made to provide an estimate of the total number of people occupying that region. Population densities are derived for settlements by an assumed relationship between population and habitation space (Kramer 1982; Sumner 1989) and within Near Eastern archaeology the application of population densities ranging from 100–200 people per hectare of site area are relatively common (although higher estimates are also feasible, see Postgate 1994). These densities are attested by ethnographic research for communities in Iran and throughout the Middle East (Adams 1965: 24; Johnson 1973: 66; Kramer 1980; Sumner 1989), but it would be simplistic to assume that a blanket density is appropriate for each household in a community or each community in a region. A relative rise or fall in the aggregate occupied area can potentially tell us more about population trends than absolute figures. Similarly, synchronous or asynchronous population or settlement trends can provide an estimate of population flux over the *longue durée*.

Finally, the use of several independent chronologies for Susiana and numerous comparative chronologies for south-west Iran means that it is difficult to compare data sets in an unbiased way, although recent approaches to temporal modelling are now able to resolve this dilemma (Lawrence 2012). Comparative chronologies produce parallel developments in adjacent regions based on ceramic similarities, but we must question whether or not we can truly compare data dependent on chronologies, rather than chronological data. For this reason it is necessary to test the sensitivity of the data to chronological variation, and this approach highlights the reliability of gross trends. If we look at the amount of aggregate occupied area for each period in two or more different periodisations for the same region (Fig. 3.5), and a similar outcome is produced, then it can be argued that the pattern is relatively robust. In the present study, each data set was placed into the most up-to-date relative/absolute chronology (at the time of the study) for that region. When compared, this approach pinpoints potentially problematic differences in timing for the beginning, end, and length of periods. Even with variation in timings, however, the scale of the study has allowed us to step back and look at the overall picture. Ultimately, the magnitude of difference or similarity between the settlement curves over the long term is the most telling and reliable factor.

Population and settlement trends in Khuzestan

The aggregate occupied area through time for the Susiana plain is indicated in Figure 3.5. The first series is a combination of several different period specific surveys: firstly, of the *Village* period survey by Frank Hole, reanalysed by Nicholas Kouchoukos (1998); secondly, the *Uruk* period survey by Gregory Johnson (1973); and finally the *Susa III* period survey by John Alden (1987). The second series consists entirely of the curve published by Pierre de Miroschedji (2003: 21, fig. 2.2, 2.3). The remainder of the time span covered in this analysis (i.e. after the *Susa III* period) is represented here solely by de Miroschedji's population curve.

While there is slight variation in the timing and magnitude of settlement increases and decreases in the fifth–mid-third millennia BC, three robust, overarching trends are clearly visible. Initially, a period of growth and slight decline is apparent in the fifth to the early fourth millennium BC. This is followed by a significant decrease in settled population in the mid- to late fourth millennium, which continues through to the early third millennium BC. This decrease is placed into further context by the massive increase in aggregate occupied area that followed after the early third millennium BC.

Surveys of the neighbouring Deh Luran plain by Neely and Wright (1994), and the Ram Hormuz Plain by Wright and Carter (2003) can be used to demonstrate whether or not there are synchronous trends at the greater regional level. If the aggregate occupied area through time is compared for the Susiana, Deh Luran, and Ram Hormuz plains, it is evident that the sixth and first half of the fifth millennium BC were a period of growth followed by general stability in populations, as is implied by the aggregate occupied hectares (Fig. 3.6). Both the Ram

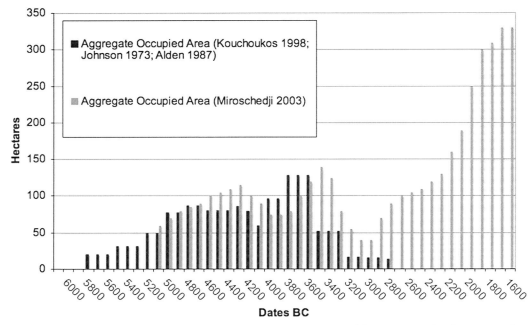

Figure 3.5. Aggregate occupied area for the Susiana Plain (data from Johnson 1973; Alden 1987; Kouchoukos 1998; Miroschedji 2003).

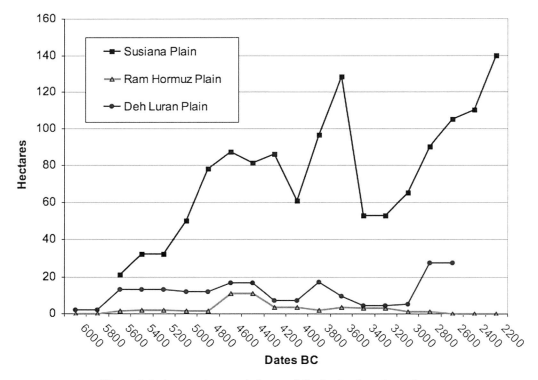

Figure 3.6. Aggregate occupied area of the lowland study regions.

Hormuz and the Deh Luran data show an increase in aggregate occupied hectares contemporary with a decrease in the total number of sites, which indicates settlement agglomeration.

The substantial increase in population on the Susiana plain during this period could be an indication of a greater number of births over deaths, migration from other regions, or a product of an incomplete archaeological record (with the earliest sites being buried under later occupation). In addition, geomorphological processes such as aggradation, as well as sedimentation caused by agricultural intensification and irrigation (Spence 1956), could have reduced the number of prehistoric sites. Nicholas Kouchoukos (1998: 93–100; also Kouchoukos and Hole 2003: 56–57, fig. 5.3) used geomorphological maps of the Susiana plain to estimate the number of sites of the village period (*c.* 6000–4000 BC) that may have been lost due to their location within areas of alluviation and associated erosion (i.e. within "new alluvium"), as compared to the number of sites on "old alluvium". He took the number of sites recorded on the old alluvium as compared to the young alluvium and estimated that there may be 30% more sites than have been recovered (Kouchoukos 1998). As noted above the presence of significant deposits of irrigation sediments will compound this loss of prehistoric sites.

Furthermore, changes in the physical landscape of the Upper Khuzestan plains may have resulted in the settled area of the fifth millennium BC being underestimated, as already discussed (see *Study areas* above; Alizadeh *et al.* 2004). The effects of the above-mentioned processes will be greatest during the earliest periods, and must be borne in mind when we observe the substantial increases in population and settlement trends.

The *Early* and *Middle Uruk* phases represent the peak of aggregate occupied area in the *Uruk* period for the Susiana, Ram Hormuz, and Deh Luran Plains and the similarity of the trends in these areas is reflected in Figure 3.6 in the period between 3900 and 3400 BC. The tendency towards settlement agglomeration continues through the *Uruk* phase in the lowland plains. In Susiana, according to Johnson's (1973) data from the *Terminal Susa A* to the *Uruk* phases, the aggregate occupied hectares are higher than the number of sites, and even when in the *Late Uruk* phase there is a marked decrease in permanent settlement, the amount of aggregate occupied hectares is almost four times the number of sites, indicating that population is sparse but concentrated into larger settlements (see Fig. 3.7).

After a zenith in sedentary settlement on the Susiana and Deh Luran plains, the later fourth millennium saw a decrease in settled population (Johnson 1973; Wright and Johnson 1985: 29). In Susiana, the aggregate occupied hectares decrease to less than half and the total number of sites to

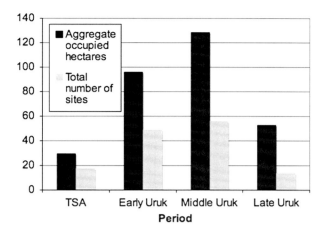

Figure 3.7. The relationship between the aggregate occupied area and the number of sites in the Uruk period; these appear to indicate settlement agglomeration.

less than a third. In the following *Susa III* period, Alden's (1987: fig. 39) data indicates there are very few sedentary sites and overall a very low population, with the eastern and northern parts of the plain being abandoned at this time. Despite a very low proposed population, the pattern of settlement still tends to be nucleated.

It is possible that the eastern portion of the plain was being utilised by mobile groups, as has been suggested by Alizadeh (2008: 26), and that the remaining sedentary population retreated towards Susa, as they may have done previously during the sedentary population decline in the *Late Susiana* phase (Alizadeh 1992: 57; Hole 1987a; 1987b: 85), but other factors may have contributed to this empty landscape. For example, soil and irrigation reports from the *FAO Khuzestan Soil Survey Project* (Spence 1956) indicate that areas in the northern parts of the plain were subject to sedimentation from later irrigation systems, and that these deposits may have obscured the settlement pattern.

Comparative settlement trends in south-west Iran – highlands and lowlands

Settlement trends in the lowlands are now compared to trends occurring in the upland regions of the Zagros Mountains, namely in the Kur River Basin surveyed by William Sumner (1972, 1990b, 2003) and the Islamabad Plain surveyed by Kamyar Abdi (2002, 2003). The stability and instability of the pattern over the long term is especially important to this comparison. The aggregate occupied area of each of the study regions over time is illustrated in Figure 3.8, which highlights three broad trends: 1) a period of regional growth; 2) a decline in settlement in the era that followed; and 3) a surge in settled populations in the lowlands of south-west Iran.

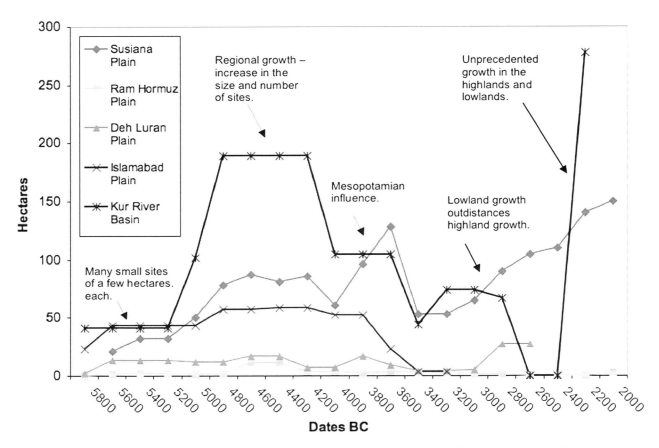

Figure 3.8. Interregional population trends in south-west Iran – Susiana (Alden 1987; Johnson 1973; Kouchoukos 1998; Miroschedji 2003; Schacht 1987); Deh Luran (Neely and Wright 1994); Ram Hormuz (Wright and Carter 2003); Islamabad Plain (Abdi 2002); Kur River Basin (Sumner 1990b, 1994).

Regional growth

In south-west Iran, what had been a phase of dispersed agricultural villages in the sixth millennium developed and grew to reach a peak in the mid-fifth millennium BC. This peak coincided with a trend towards settlement agglomeration, as indicated by a decrease in the total number of sites, but an increase in the average size of sites in both the highlands and lowlands. Furthermore, similarities between pottery styles in the majority of the study regions indicate that there was apparently more interaction between the highlands and lowlands in the later fifth millennium onwards, suggesting an increase in movement between regions (Voigt and Dyson 1992; Petrie 2011), possibly facilitated by transhumance and mobile groups (Alizadeh 1992: 56, 2006: 18; Voigt and Dyson 1992; Abdi 2002: 181).

Settlement decline potentially associated with Mesopotamian growth

Towards the end of the fifth millennium and during part of the fourth millennium BC, there appears to have been a decline in all of the regional populations

in south-west Iran. On the other hand, the early fourth millennium witnessed major growth on the lowland plains of Mesopotamia and the crystallisation of the agglomeration trend, whereas there was a decrease in sedentary settlement in the highlands. Increases in settled population in southern Mesopotamia at this time would have required a great influx of people from other regions and these population fluxes could have contributed to the settlement decline in south-west Iran (see Adams 1981: 60, 69–70). In addition to population flux outside south-west Iran in the fourth millennium BC, this decline may have resulted from disparities between the number of births and deaths, or changes in subsistence strategies, although it is unlikely that they could account for such major differences between regions.

Lowland growth and sedentary population increase

From the mid-fourth to the mid-third millennium, one can discern different settlement trajectories in the Kur River Basin and the lowlands. The previously perceived complete desertion of the landscape by sedentary populations in the Kur River Basin in the mid-third millennium BC, however, may no longer hold true. Recent work has indicated that a small but continuous population occupied the site of Tal-e Malyan throughout this period and future research may continue to amend this reading of the settlement record (Alden *et al.* 2005; Miller and Sumner 2004). Overall, the magnitude of the increase of settlement in the Susiana and Deh Luran plains beginning in the mid-fourth until the third millennium BC is notable and was substantially greater than that of the Kur River Basin. At the time of writing there was no data available for the Islamabad Plain beyond the second quarter of the third millennium BC, allowing no further elucidation of the general situation in the highland plains during this period. On the basis of the available evidence, it thus appears that in the later third millennium BC, unprecedented population growth coupled with settlement nucleation occurred in both the highlands and lowlands.

Susiana and Mesopotamia

Comparison of settlement trends in south-west Iran with those in southern Mesopotamia enables us better to understand population flux and interaction between these regions. Adams's (1981) surveys of lower Mesopotamia, which he broke down into a Northern Enclave (the Nippur/Adab area), and a Southern Enclave (Uruk area), provide settlement data that can be compared with that from the Susiana plain. The aggregate occupied area for the above-mentioned survey areas between the fifth and third millennia BC is

illustrated in Figure 3.9 (note that Upper Mesopotamia-Northern Mesopotamia on Fig. 3.9 is simply used as a yardstick; it is not discussed in this analysis).

Throughout the fifth millennium BC, local cultural traditions dominated, and towards the latter half of the millennium we see increased interaction between highland and lowland areas in south-west Iran, manifested in similar pottery traditions (Alizadeh 1992; Abdi 2003; Sumner 2003). It appears that there was less interaction between Mesopotamia proper and the regions of south-west Iran under consideration until the *Later Susiana* period (*Late Ubaid* in Mesopotamia). As in south-west Iran, Mesopotamia appears to have undergone regional growth throughout the course of the fifth millennium BC, but the magnitude and configuration of this development was unique to each region.

The *Uruk* period (starting at around the beginning of the fourth millennium BC) represents a clearly defined phase of cultural interaction between Mesopotamia and south-west Iran, in both the lowlands and highlands of the Central Western Zagros (Young 1969; Johnson 1973; Henrickson 1994; Pollock 2001; Miroschedji 2003; Algaze 2004). Adams (1981: 60, 69–70) has suggested that the dramatic growth at the beginning of the *Uruk* phase in Mesopotamia required massive immigration and/or sedentarisation of mobile populations on top of general population growth, after which the population and urban growth of Mesopotamia was far above that of south-west Iran. The significant difference in the total settled area in Mesopotamia and south-west Iran becomes apparent during this time, and it is evident that the aggregate

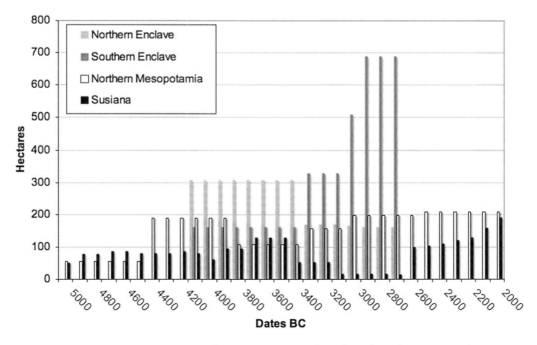

Figure 3.9. Aggregate occupied area – Susiana and north and south Mesopotamia.

occupied area in southern and northern Mesopotamia is significantly higher than the Susiana plain (Fig. 3.9; also Wright, this volume). Hole (1987b: 85) has argued that the *Late Susiana* (*Susa A*) population decline is linked to an increase in Mesopotamian populations in the *Early* to *Late Uruk*. This hinges on the assumption that the *Uruk* phase began earlier in Mesopotamia than in Iran. Notably, in the data from both the Susiana (Johnson 1973) and Ram Hormuz (Wright and Carter 2003) plains, the apex of *Uruk* period growth occurred in the *Middle Uruk* period, which is slightly later than the initial increase in southern Mesopotamia, possibly indicating further movement within the Uruk "world". The increases in settlement on the Khuzestan plains, however, follow a decrease in the preceding period, which differs from the situation in Mesopotamia (Adams 1981: 70). This reinforces the notion that Mesopotamian growth may have been at the expense of population in south-west Iran in the late fifth millennium BC.

It has also been suggested that there was a population migration from the northern Mesopotamian plains to further south in southern Mesopotamia by the *Late Uruk* phase, but this cannot account for all of the population that would appear to have abandoned the northern region (Adams 1981: 70). Pollock's (2001: 212–13) reanalysis of the data from the *Heartland of Cities* surveys using Dewar's algorithm suggests that the decrease in population in the northern Mesopotamian plains was not so marked, and this has implications for movement beyond the Uruk heartland. She suggested that instabilities in southern Mesopotamia made it more likely for people to migrate from there to the "peripheries" in order to escape, but equally that northern Mesopotamian population levels could have remained low because they were constantly losing population (Pollock 2001: 220).

To summarise, one of the more pronounced trends in the survey data is that the *Middle* and *Late Uruk* decline in aggregate occupied area in Susiana and the Deh Luran plains beginning around 3600 BC, followed by a decline in the Islamabad Plain and the Kur River Basin around 3500 BC, corresponds to the major growth of settlement in Mesopotamia (Figs 3.8 and 3.9). This implies a significant flux of population from Iran into Mesopotamia, although the actual mechanism behind such a shift remains elusive.

The decline in settled area during the *Susa III* phase (early third millennium BC) on the Susiana plain mirrors a substantial increase in the aggregate occupied area and large settlements that occurred in southern Mesopotamia especially around Uruk in the *Early Dynastic* phase (Adams 1981: 90; Johnson 1973).

Further comparisons can be drawn if we take the amount of settled hectares per square kilometre of the surveyed area, forming a proxy for settlement density (Fig. 3.10). While there is no available data to compare settlement density throughout the *Village Period*, around 4000 BC it does appear that the density of settlement in the Uruk area was only slightly greater than that estimated for the Susiana plain. Adams (1981: 60) noted that "there is little reason to doubt that at least the sedentary part of the population was larger and more dense in parts of Khuzestan during much of the *Susiana* sequence than it was anywhere in southern Mesopotamia during roughly the same interval". The distinctive trend apparent in the analysis of the total amount of settled area (Fig. 3.9), however, is again apparent when we compare the rise in the density of settlement in the Southern Enclave (Uruk area) – as well as Northern Mesopotamia – relative to the dip in settled area in Susiana in the later fourth millennium BC.

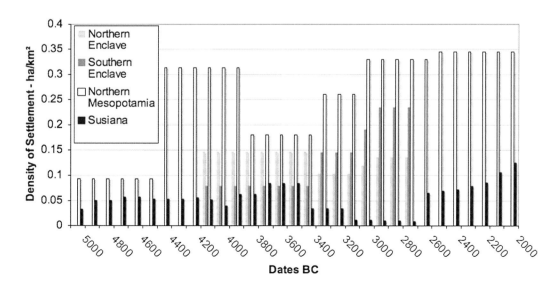

Figure 3.10. Density of settlement in Mesopotamia and Susiana.

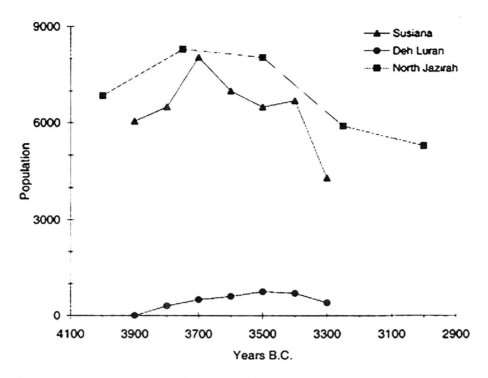

Figure 3.11. Population estimates for Susiana, Deh Luran, and North Jazira (Kouchoukos 1998: fig. 5.9; after Wilkinson and Tucker 1995).

The above is only an interim statement because absolute population densities produce other figures. If we simply look at the relative differences they produce, however, there are alternative interpretations for the density of settlement (i.e. Kouchoukos's [1998: fig. 5.9] population estimates based on a population density in persons per hectare – see Fig. 3.11). Consequently, the question becomes, is the processed data more relevant for interpreting long-term interregional population trends or does the raw data (or as close to it as we can get to it) provide a better approximation?

Discussion and conclusions – long-term settlement dynamics

Survey data from the Susiana plain and lowland Khuzestan provides a record of settlement and population that can be compared with similar data from the highlands of south-west Iran and northern and southern Mesopotamia to chart long-term trends throughout the region. What is most important about these comparisons is not the actual number of settlements or aggregate occupied area, but the relative difference between the peaks and troughs in settlement. The sixth and early fifth millennia BC are times of both growth and stability in the highlands and lowlands of south-west Iran. This trend may partly result from environmental and geomorphological factors, because the earliest settlement may have

been buried by sedimentation and later occupation. Increased contact between highland and lowland regions is evident by the similarity in pottery styles. The end of the fifth and the early fourth millennium BC see a decline in regional population and the subsequent *Uruk* phase indicates a rise in population and sedentary settlement in Mesopotamia, followed shortly thereafter by a rise in population on the Khuzestan plains.

Population trends depend on demographic factors such as birth rates and death rates, together with shifts in subsistence and other economic strategies. Potentially of significance also are population fluxes between regions, specifically in the form of movements of mobile pastoralists. All of the above play a role in the resultant population level. The understanding of archaeological population levels is made more difficult by the incompleteness of the archaeological record and the lack of written records, especially for the prehistoric periods. Growth in settled area and number of settlements – as seen in the sixth and fifth millennia BC throughout south-west Iran – must, in part, result from natural population growth caused by a higher birth over death rate. Neolithic populations in general experienced a rapid rate of population growth at the transition to sedentary farming communities, a growth rate that was probably maintained in later periods as well (Hassan 1981: 234). It is also likely that in early urban conditions, not only was the birth rate not substantially raised, but also death rates were high due to the incidence of infectious diseases and poor public health. If constant immigration did not occur, it would be unlikely that early urban populations would be able to sustain such a high population level (Hassan 1981: 235). It is therefore likely that mass movements of people were a key factor in phases like the *Uruk* in south-west Iran and Mesopotamia. Specifically, the late fourth-millennium BC population decline in western Iran and the complementary growth in Mesopotamia (above and on Figs 3.8 and 3.9) implies that settlement growth and urbanisation in Mesopotamia were perhaps at least partially fuelled by such a movement of population. Migration (or perhaps the less directional "population flux") should be considered as one of several factors accounting for the increase in population experienced at this time and in the *Susa III, Early Dynastic,* and *Kaftari* phases in different parts of south-west Iran (i.e. Adams 1981; Pollock 2001; Sumner 1986, 1990b).

It has been suggested that sedentary populations lack the mobility and group flexibility that provide coping mechanisms to enable such communities to deal with times of stress (Hassan 1981: 253). This may also explain why, in times when sedentary populations declined, as during the *Late Uruk* and *Early Susa III* period on the Susiana, Deh Luran, and Ram Hormuz plains, there was a general tendency for settlement agglomeration to continue. In other words the higher social organisation in larger centres and the lower level of group flexibility perhaps pre-empted a shift to a more mobile lifestyle.

Adams (1966: 58) has put forward the notion of population reservoirs to account for the flow of population between urban, rural, and mobile sectors. This would imply that there were "reservoirs" of population in each different subsistence group that are fluid enough to fill deficits in the rural, urban, or nomadic sectors. Such sectors would, in turn, also have been linked by complex physical, cultural, social, and political networks. In addition, all populations can exhibit differences in birth and death rates, which cumulatively can result in significant differences in the overall population. Unless such differences are significant, however, they are unlikely to account for some of the major disparities observed in the regional archaeological records.

On the other hand, processes of sedentarisation and nomadisation may greatly affect regional and interregional population dynamics and the ability to understand these interactions is hampered by the invisibility of segments of the population in the archaeological record.

One possibility that may explain regional settlement disparities involves the concept of "desettlement" as coined by Alizadeh (2010: 372). This refers to the process "in which a large portion of the population does not leave a region permanently but reverts to a life of pastoral nomadism without leaving much archaeological evidence behind." Such a process would fit some of the circumstances indicated in the population trends, and furthermore the more general model of Alizadeh, in which mobile highland pastoralists were able to dominate the lowlands, both numerically and in terms of the power relationships, might also provide a general mechanism for population flux between regions. Furthermore, specific times of minimal sedentary population such as the *Susa III* period, which were discussed earlier in terms of geomorphological processes that may have obscured the settlement record, can possibly be explained further by "desettlement". This episode may not just represent an absence of sedentary settlement, but rather that a region could still have been utilised for both grazing and cultivation by "mobile agropastoralists" who were not necessarily living on the plain (Alizadeh 2010: 372).

As Petrie (2011: 169; also Weeks *et al.* 2010) has suggested, however, whereas mobility is integral to explaining the movement of ideas and things, in prehistory, "the way that mobility is manifested is very significant". Seasonal mobility, transhumance or the movement of people through social and cultural factors (i.e. marriage), and economic factors (trade and exchange) may also have contributed to the trends discussed above.

Overall, the raw data on settlement trends in south-west Iran and neighbouring regions demonstrates regional disparities that are sufficiently substantial to invite explanation, not simply on a case-by-case basis but according to a broader model of population dynamics. Although the long-term population trends of south-west Iran, with its geographical dichotomy into highlands and lowlands, would display greater harmony if we had the ability to view the entire range of this constantly changing population (including the elusive mobile groups), it has been a productive exercise to take the data at face value, because they imply that ancient populations in western Iran and Mesopotamia were remarkably dynamic, a situation which accords well with recent data from the arid margins of Syria (Geyer *et al.* 2006; Wilkinson *et al.* 2012).

Bibliography

Abdi, K. 2002. *Strategies of Herding: Pastoralism in the Middle Chalcolithic Period of the West Central Zagros Mountains*, unpublished Ph.D. dissertation, Museum of Anthropology, University of Michigan, Ann Arbor.

Abdi, K. 2003. "The early development of pastoralism in the central Zagros mountains", *Journal of World Prehistory* 17(4): 395–448.

Adams, R. M. 1962. "Agriculture and early urban life in southwestern Iran", *Science* 136(3511): 109–22.

Adams, R. M. 1965. *Land behind Baghdad: A History of Settlement on the Diyala Plains*, University of Chicago Press, Chicago, London.

Adams, R. M. 1966. *The Evolution of Urban Society*, Aldine Publishing Company, Chicago.

Adams, R. M. 1981. *Heartland of Cities: Surveys of Ancient Settlement and Land Use on the Central Floodplain of the Euphrates*, University of Chicago Press, Chicago.

Alden, J. R. 1987. "The Susa III Period", in Hole, F. (ed.), *The Archaeology of Western Iran: Settlement and Society from Prehistory to the Islamic Conquest*, Smithsonian Institution Press, Washington, D.C.: 157–70.

Alden, J. R., Abdi, K., Azadi, A., Beckman, G. and Pittman, H. 2005. "Fars Archaeology Project 2004: excavations at Tal-e Malyan", *Iran* 43: 39–47.

Algaze, G. 2004. *The Uruk World System: the Dynamics of Expansion of Early Mesopotamian Civilization*, University of Chicago Press, Chicago.

Alizadeh, A. 1992. *Prehistoric Settlement Patterns and Culture in Susiana, southwestern Iran: the Analysis of the F.G.L. Gremliza Survey Collection*, Museum of Anthropology, University of Michigan, Ann Arbor.

Alizadeh, A. 2006. *The Origins of State Organizations in Prehistoric Highland Fars, southern Iran: Excavations at Tall-e Bakun*, The Oriental Institute of the University of Chicago, Chicago.

Alizadeh, A. 2008. *Chogha Mish II: The Development of a Prehistoric Regional Center in Lowland Susiana, Southwestern Iran*, The Oriental Institute of the University of Chicago, Chicago.

Alizadeh, A. 2010. "The rise of the highland Elamite state in southwestern Iran: "enclosed" or enclosing nomadism", *Current Anthropology* 51.3: 353–383.

Alizadeh, A., Kouchoukos, N., Wilkinson, T. J., Bauer, A. M., and Mashkour, M. 2004. "Human-environment interactions on the upper Khuzestan plains, southwest Iran: recent investigations", *Paléorient* 30(1): 69–88.

Barth, F. 1965. *Nomads of South Persia*, Allen and Unwin Ltd, London.

Beck, L. 1986. *The Qashqa'i of Iran*, Yale University Press, New Haven.

Brookes, I. A., Levine, L. D. and Dennell, R. W. 1982. "Alluvial sequence in central west Iran and implications for archaeological survey", *Journal of Field Archaeology* 9(3): 285–99.

Carter, E. and Stolper, M. W. 1984. *Elam: surveys of political history and archaeology*, University of California Press, Berkeley.

Casana, J. J. and Wilkinson, T. J. 2005. "Settlement and Landscapes in the Amuq Region", in Yener, K. A. (ed.), *The Archaeology of the Amuq Plain*, Oriental Institute Publications, Chicago 131: 25–65, 203–80.

Dewar, R. E. 1991. "Incorporating variation in occupation span into settlement-pattern analysis", *American Antiquity* 56(4): 604–20.

Geyer, B., Besançon, J. and Rousset, M. O. 2006. Les peuplements anciens, in Jaubert, R. and Geyer, B. (eds), *Les marges arides du croissanrt fertile. Peuplements, exploitation et contrôle des ressources en Syrie du Nord*, Maison de l'Orient et de la Méditerranée – Jean Pouilloux, Lyon 43: 55–69.

Hassan, F. A. 1981. *Demographic Archaeology*, Academic Press, New York.

Henrickson, E. F. 1994. "Outer limits: settlement and economic strategies in the central Zagros highlands during the Uruk era", in Rothman, M. S. and Stein, G. (eds), *Chiefdoms and Early States in the Near East: the Organizational Dynamics of Complexity*, Prehistory Press, Madison: 85–102.

Hole, F. 1969. "Report on the survey of Upper Khuzistan", in Hole, F. (ed.), *Preliminary Reports on the Rice University Khuzistan Project*, Department of Anthropology, Rice University, Houston.

Hole, F. 1977. *Studies in the Archeological History of the Deh Luran Plain: The Excavation of Chagha Sefid*, Museum of Anthropology, University of Michigan, Ann Arbor.

Hole, F. 1987a. "Archaeology of the Village Period", in Hole, F. (ed.), *The Archaeology of Western Iran: Settlement and Society from Prehistory to the Islamic Conquest*, Smithsonian Institution Press, Washington, D.C.: 29–78.

Hole, F. 1987b. "Settlement and society in the Village Period", in Hole, F. (ed.), *The Archaeology of Western Iran: Settlement and Society from Prehistory to the Islamic Conquest*, Smithsonian Institution Press, Washington, D.C.: 79–106.

Hole, F., Flannery, K. V. and Neely, J. A. 1969. *Prehistory and Human Ecology of the Deh Luran Plain: An Early Village Sequence from Khuzistan, Iran*, Museum of Anthropology, University of Michigan, Ann Arbor.

Hopper, K. 2007. *Long-term Population Dynamics in Southwest Iran*, unpublished M.A. thesis, Department of Archaeology, Durham University, Durham.

Johnson, G. A. 1973. *Local Exchange and Early State Development in Southwestern Iran*, Museum of Anthropology, University of Michigan, Ann Arbor.

Kehl, M., Frechen, M. and Skowronek, A. 2009. "Nature and age of Late Quaternary basin fill deposits in the Basin of Persepolis: Southern Iran", *Quaternary International* 196: 57–70.

Kirkby, M. J. 1977. "Land and water resources of the Deh Luran and Khuzestan Plains. Appendix I", in Hole, F. (ed.), *Studies in the Archaeological History of the Deh Luran Plain: The Excavation of Chogha Sefid*. Memoirs of the Museum of Anthropology, University of Michigan no. 9, Ann Arbor: 251–88.

Kouchoukos, N. 1998. *Landscape and Social Change in Late Prehistoric Mesopotamia*, unpublished Ph.D. dissertation, Yale University, New Haven.

Kouchoukos, N. and Hole, F. 2003. "Changing Estimates of Susiana's Prehistoric Settlement", in Miller, N. F. and Abdi, K. (eds), *Yeki bud, yeki nabud: Essays on the Archaeology of Iran in Honor of William M. Sumner*, Cotsen Institute of Archaeology, University of California, Los Angeles: 53–59.

Kramer, C. 1980. "Estimating Prehistoric Populations", in Barrelet, M-T. (ed.), *L'archéologie de l'Iraq du début de l'époque néolithique à 333 avant notre ère: perspectives et limites de l'interprétation anthropologique des documents*, Colloques internationaux du CNRS 580, Paris: 315–34.

Kramer, C. 1982. *Village Ethnoarchaeology: Rural Iran in Archaeological Perspective*, Academic Press, New York.

Lawrence, D. 2012. *Early Urbanism in the northern Fertile Crescent: Regional Settlement Trajectories and Millennial Landscape Change*, unpublished Ph.D. thesis, Department of Archaeology, Durham University, Durham.

Lees, G. M. and Falcon, N. L. 1952. "The geographical history of the Mesopotamian plains", *Geographical Journal* 118 (1): 24–39.

Levine, L. D. and McDonald, M. M. 1977. "The Neolithic and Chalcolithic periods in the Mahidasht", *Iran* 15: 39–50.

McCall, B. 2009. *The Mamasani Archaeological Survey: Long Term Settlement Patterns in the Mamasani District of the Zagros Mountains, Fars Province, Iran*, unpublished Ph.D. thesis, University of Sydney.

Miller, N. F. and Sumner, W. M. 2004. "The Banesh-Kaftari Interface: The View from Operation H5, Malyan", *Iran* 42: 77–90.

Miroschedji, P. de 1981. "Prospections archéologiques au Khuzistan en 1977", *CDAFI* 12: 169–92.

Miroschedji, P. de 2003. "Susa and the highlands: major trends in the history of Elamite civilization", in Miller, N.F. and Abdi, K. (eds), *Yeki bud, yeki nabud: Essays on the Archaeology of Iran in Honor of William M. Sumner*, Cotsen Institute or Archaeology, University of California, Los Angeles: 17–38.

Moghaddam, A. and Miri, N. 2003. "Archaeological research in the Mianab Plain of lowland Susiana, southwestern Iran", *Iran* 41: 99–137.

Moghaddam, A. and Miri, N. 2007. "Archaeological surveys in the 'eastern corridor', south-western Iran", *Iran* 45: 23–55.

Neely, J. A. and Wright, H. T. 1994. *Early settlement and irrigation on the Deh Luran Plain: village and early state societies in southwestern Iran*, Museum of Anthropology, University of Michigan, Ann Arbor.

Petrie, C. A. 2011. "'Culture', innovation and interaction across southern Iran from the Neolithic to the Bronze Age (6500–3000 BC)", in Roberts, B. and Vander Linden, M. (eds), *Investigating Archaeological Cultures: material culture, variability and transmission*, Springer, New York: 151–82.

Pollock, S. 2001. "The Uruk period in southern Mesopotamia", in Rothman, M. S. (ed.), *Uruk Mesopotamia and Its Neighbors: Cross-Cultural Interactions in the Era of State Formation*, School of American Research Press, Sante Fe: 181–232.

Postgate, J. N. 1994. *Early Mesopotamia: Society and Economy at the Dawn of History*. Routledge, London.

Potts, D. T. 2008. "Review of A. Alizadeh, The origins of state organizations in prehistoric highland Fars", *Bibliotheca Orientalis* 65: 195–206.

Schacht, R. M. 1976. "Some notes on the development of rural settlement on the Susiana Plain", in Bagherzadeh, F. (ed.), *Proceedings of the IVth annual symposium on archaeological research in Iran: 3rd–8th November 1975*, Iranian Centre for Archaeological Research, Tehran: 446–62.

Schacht, R. M. 1981. "Estimating past population trends", *Annual Review of Anthropology* 10: 119–40.

Schacht, R. M. 1984. "The contemporaneity Problem", *American Antiquity* 49(4): 678–95.

Schacht, R. M. 1987. "Early historic cultures", in Hole, F. (ed.), *The Archaeology of Western Iran: Settlement and Society from Prehistory to the Islamic Conquest*, Smithsonian Institution Press, Washington, D.C.: 171–203.

Spence, C. C. 1956. *Report to the Government of Iran on farming potentials for irrigation in Khuzistan*, ed. F.A.O. F.A.O., Rome.

Sumner, W. M. 1972. *Cultural Development in the Kur River Basin, Iran: An Archaeological Analysis of Settlement Patterns*, unpublished Ph.D. dissertation, Department of Anthropology, University of Pennsylvania, Philadelphia.

Sumner, W. M. 1986. "Proto-Elamite Civilization in Fars", in Finkbeiner, U. and Röllig, W. (eds), *Ğamdat Naṣr: Period or Regional Style?*, Ludwig Reichert Verlag, Tübingen: 199–211.

Sumner, W. M. 1989. "Population and settlement area: an example from Iran", *American Anthropologist* 91(3): 631–41.

Sumner, W. M. 1990a. "Full-coverage Regional Archaeological Survey in the Near East: An Example from Iran", in Fish, S. K. and Kowalewski, S. A. (eds), *The Archaeology of Regions: A Case for Full-coverage Survey*, Smithsonian Institution Press, Washington, D.C.: 87–115.

Sumner, W. M. 1990b. "An archaeological estimate of population trends since 6000 BC in the Kur River Basin, Fars Province, Iran", in Taddei, M. (ed.), *South Asian Archaeology 1987*, Istituto Italiano per il Medio ed Estremo Oriente, Venice: 3–16.

Sumner, W. M. 1994. "The evolution of tribal society in the southern Zagros Mountains, Iran", in Stein, G. J. and Rothman, M. S. (eds), *Chiefdoms and Early States in Near East: The Organizational Dynamics of Complexity*, Monographs in World Archaeology 18, Madison: 47–66.

Sumner, W. M. 2003. *Early Urban Life in the Land of Anshan: Excavations at Tal-e Malyan in the Highlands of Iran*, Museum of Archaeology and Anthropology, University of Pennsylvania, Philadelphia.

Voigt, M. M. and Dyson, R. H. 1992. "The Chronology of Iran, ca. 8000–2000 B.C.", in Ehrich, R. W. (ed.), *Chronologies in Old World Archaeology*, University of Chicago Press, Chicago: I: 122–78, II: 125–53.

Weeks, L., Petrie, C. A. and Potts, D. T. 2010. "'Ubaid-related-related? The 'black-on-buff' ceramic traditions of highland southwest Iran", in Carter, R. A and Philip, G. (eds), *Beyond the 'Ubaid, Transformation and Integration in the Late Prehistoric Societies of the Middle East*. Studies in Ancient Oriental Civilization Series. Oriental Institute, University of Chicago, Chicago: 247–78.

Weiss, H. 1977. "Periodization, Population and Early State Formation in Khuzistan", in Levine, L. D. and Young, T. C. (eds), *Mountains and Lowlands: Essays in the Archaeology of Greater Mesopotamia*, Undena Publications, Malibu: 347–69.

Wilkinson, T. J. 2003. *Archaeological Landscapes of the Near East*, University of Arizona Press, Tucson.

Wilkinson, T.J. and Tucker, D. J. 1995. *Settlement Development in the North Jazira: A Study of the Archaeological Landscape*, British School of Archaeology in Iraq and the Department of Antiquities and Heritage, Baghdad.

Wilkinson, T. J., Galiatsatos, N., Lawrence, D., Ricci, A., Dunford, R. and Philip, G. 2012. "Late Chalcolithic and Early Bronze Age landscapes of settlement and mobility in the Middle Euphrates: a reassessment", *Levant* 44: 139–85.

Wright, H. T. 1969. *Archaeological Survey in the Areas of Ram Hormuz, Shushtar and Gutwand*, Museum of Anthropology, University of Michigan, Ann Arbor.

Wright, H. T. 1979. *Archaeological investigations in northeastern Xuzestan, 1976*, Museum of Anthropology, University of Michigan, Ann Arbor.

Wright, H. T. and Carter, E. 2003. "Archaeological Survey on the Western Ram Hormuz Plain 1969", in Abdi, K. and Miller, N. F. (eds), *Yeki bud, yeki nabud: Essays on the Archaeology of Iran in Honor of William M. Sumner*, Cotsen Institute of Archaeology, Los Angeles: 61–82.

Wright, H. T. and Johnson, G. A. 1985. "Regional Perspectives on Southwest Iranian State Development", *Paléorient* 11(2): 25–30.

Young Jr., T. C., 1969. *Excavations at Godin Tepe: First Progress Report*, Royal Ontario Museum, Toronto.

Zagarell, A. 1982. *The Prehistory of the Northeast Bahtiyari Mountains, Iran: The Rise of a Highland Way of Life*, Kommission bei Ludwig Reichert Verlag, Wiesbaden.

Zeidi, M., McCall, B. and Khosrowzadeh, A. 2009. "Survey of Dasht-e Rostam-e Yek and Dasht -e Rostam-e Do", in Potts, D. T., Roustaei, K., Petrie, C. A. and Weeks, L. R. (eds), *The Mamasani Archaeological Project Stage One: A report on the first two seasons of the ICAR – University of Sydney Joint Expedition to the Mamasani District, Fars Province, Iran*, Archaeopress, Oxford: 147–68.

4. A BRIDGE BETWEEN WORLDS: SOUTH-WESTERN IRAN DURING THE FOURTH MILLENNIUM BC

Henry T. Wright

Introduction

During the last century, advances in archaeological methods have given researchers a completely different view of pre- and proto-historic cultural developments. Better stratigraphic and architectural excavation techniques, more sophisticated regional survey strategies, better approaches to contextual studies, and increasingly precise methods of absolute dating have swept away the vision of slow, steady increases in the complexity of early civilisations. Archaeologists now realise that, like the historic societies long known from the textual record, there was a mosaic of different kinds of pre- and proto-historic formations emerging and disappearing with startling rapidity. This contribution looks at one part of the great cultural mosaic of south-west Asia – south-western Iran, a bridge between the Mesopotamian alluvium and the mountain ranges and inner basins of Iran – from the end of the fifth to the middle of the fourth millennium BC. This period encompasses key steps in the development of specialised hierarchical control – the first emergence of what have been traditionally termed "states" – and the study of the south-western Iranian region helps us better to understand the processes of earliest state formation in a broader trans-regional perspective.

South-western Iran is relatively rich in natural resources. The front ranges and foothills of the central Zagros Mountains to the north and east have resources of stones, woods, and summer pasturage. The alluvial fans have permanent streams providing rich soil and water for permanent agriculture and pasture. The often saline and poorly watered alluvial steppes to the south-west provide winter pasture (Fig. 4.1). This alluvial desert and the marshes of the major rivers buffer south-western Iran from alluvial Mesopotamia in what is today southern Iraq, while the high Zagros buffer it from the interior plateau of Iran. There were numerous passable routes across these difficult borderlands, however, and nomads, traders, armies, and refugees were long able to move from region to region.

The cultural centre of south-western Iran throughout most of the time from the later fifth millennium BC to the end of the first millennium AD was a town called Shushun in earliest texts (Vallat 1980), Susa in classical times, and Shush today. This town gave its name to the region of Shushen, Susiana in classical times, and today the central portion of Khuzestan. In the following discussion, for four successive periods, I will first focus on the regional economy and settlement around Susa, then discuss related centres to the west and east in south-western Iran and beyond.

South-western Iran at the end of the fifth millennium BC

From approximately 4300 to 4150 BC, Susa was the centre of the rich *Suse Phase* polity, which had an organised network of smaller centres and villages whose elites participated in an elaborate display of iconography (Amiet 1972; Hole 1983; Wright 1994). By the end of the fifth millennium BC, however, this region was facing the consequences of the decline of this polity in a time of less rainfall and probably also a time of conflict with polities in alluvial Mesopotamia to the south-west (Neely and Wright 1994: 172; Wright 1994: 79). Although the ceramics is use after 4150 BC (Fig. 4.2) were technically some of the best made in the region, and were being made using fifth-millennium potting techniques and continuing the use of earlier vessel shapes, for the most part they ceased to manifest the elaborate *Suse Phase* symbolism. Diagnostic among these are flat-lipped basins with thumb-impressed strips below the rim (Fig. 4.2/f–i), large jars with very everted rims (Fig. 4.2/n–o), and fine jars or beakers (Fig. 4.2/j).[1] These characteristic plain ceramics were recognised by Robert Dyson (1966: 315–36) in his 1954 sounding at Susa, and by Joseph Caldwell (1968: figs

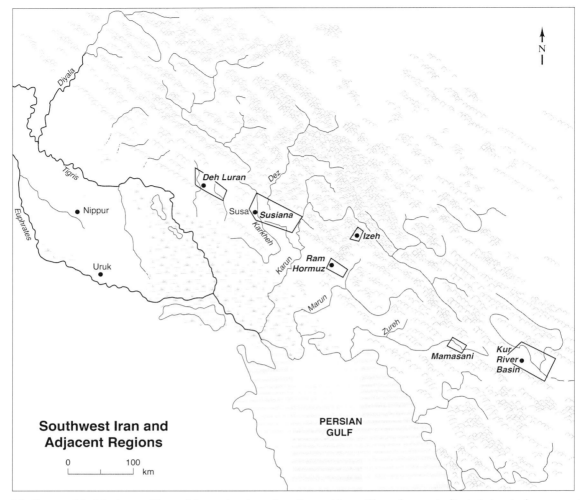

Figure 4.1. Geographical features of lower Mesopotamia and south-west Iran. The polygons indicate intensively surveyed areas. The large black dots mark major sites with fourth millennium BC occupation.

7–10) in his analysis of the 1948–49 excavations at Tal-e Ghazir. None of these samples, however, are large or have very good context, and only scraps of architecture, craft debris, food remains, or other artefacts were reported. We are indebted to Gregory Johnson's study of what he termed the *Terminal Suse A Phase*, as well as of the subsequent *Uruk* phases for key regional evidence (Johnson 1973). I suggest a date for the *Terminal Suse Phase* of 4150–4000 BC, concordant with *Post Ubaid* and *Early Uruk* dates from Upper Mesopotamia (Wright and Rupley 2001: 97–100).

During this time, Susa was still the only definite small centre on the northern Susiana Plain. Current evidence suggests that the entire Acropole mound was occupied, with settlement covering at least 10 ha. On 16 other sites, the sherd distribution is limited, suggesting occupation at each covered 1 ha or less (Fig. 4.3) The maximum total occupied area was thus about 30 ha (Johnson 1973: 87, fig. 15) and Robert M. Schacht (1980: 791) estimated a population of 5600 people, about one third of estimates during the preceding *Suse Phase*. Johnson (1973: 87–90) noted that these settlements were

distributed in a least three linear groups, suggesting orientation along natural or artificial watercourses, as one would expect in times of diminished rainfall.

The *Terminal Suse Phase* assemblage does not occur west of the Susiana Plain. There is only one possible late fifth-millennium BC site on the Deh Luran Plain, 110 km west-north-west of Susa, the village site of Sargarab (DL-169 in Neely and Wright 1994: 130–38). This settlement of small houses, courtyards, and terraces covers about 0.7 ha and has nearby check dams for rain-fed fields as well as small canals perhaps to water orchards. It has a ceramic assemblage whose closest relations are with the ceramics of northern Zagros and upper Mesopotamia with their vegetal and crushed calcite tempers (Figs. 4.4–4.5). Among the distinctive forms are tapered rim bowls (Figs. 4.4/b, 4.5/c), large bowls or basins, often with beaded rims and thumb-impressed strips (Figs. 4.4/f–j, 4.5/a), necked jars with round or ledge rims (Fig. 4.5/d–h, i–j), fine jars or beakers (Fig. 4.5/b) and flat-bottomed trays, perhaps bread moulds (Fig. 4.5/l). Some vessels on this ware have red slips, and

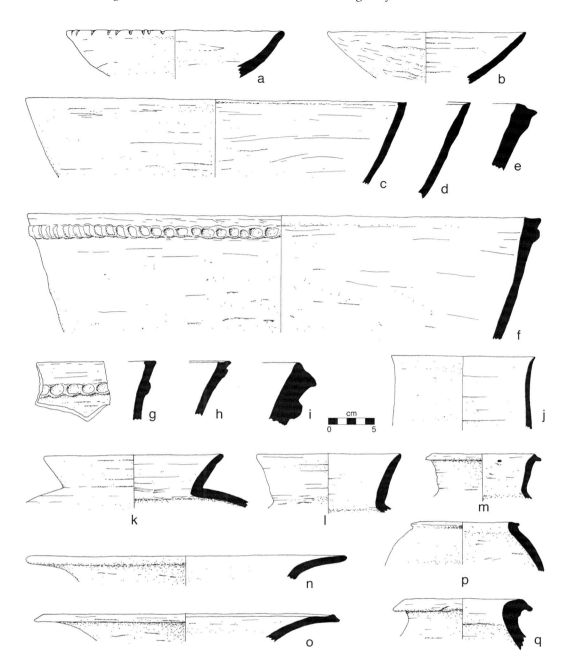

Figure 4.2. Terminal Suse Phase *ceramics from Site KS-269 on the Susiana Plain (after Wright* et al. *1975: Fig. 9).* **a.** *Round lip bowl with lip hatching. No visible inclusions. Dm 22. Reddish yellow (7.5Y 6/5) body.* **b.** *Round lip bowl. Trace of fine sand and calcite inclusions. Dm 20. Reddish yellow (7.5YR 7/5) body.* **c.** *Flat lip basin. Trace of fine sand and calcite inclusions. Dm c. 40. Yellow (10YR 8/5) body.* **d.** *Round lip basin. No visible Inclusions. Dm c. 40. Pale yellow (2.5Y 8/3) body.* **e.** *Flat lip basin. No visible Inclusions. Dm c. 58. Very pale brown (10YR 8/3) body.* **f.** *Flat lip basin with thumb-impressed appliqué strip. No visible inclusions. Dm c. 55. Pale yellow (2.5Y 7/3) body.* **g.** *Flat lip basin with thumb-impressed appliqué strip. No visible inclusions. Dm c. 60. Very pale brown (10YR 7/4) body.* **h.** *Flat lip basin with thumb-impressed appliqué strip. No visible inclusions. Dm c. 38. Reddish yellow (7.5YR 7/5) body.* **i.** *Flat lip basin with thumb-impressed appliqué strip. No visible inclusions. Dm c. 52. Reddish yellow (7.5YR 8/5) body.* **j.** *Fine beaker. No visible inclusions. Dm 15. Very pale brown (10YR 8/4) body.* **k.** *Flared neck jar. No visible inclusions. Dm 18. Light Red (2.5YR 6/6) body.* **l.** *Flared neck jar. No visible inclusions. Dm 15. Pink (7.5YR 7/4) body.* **m.** *Ledge rim jar. No visible inclusions. Dm 12. Pink (5YR 8/4) body.* **n.** *Very flared jar with round lip. No visible inclusions. Dm 34. Pale brown (2.5Y 7/3) body* **o.** *Very flared jar with concave lip. No visible inclusions. Dm 32. Reddish-yellow (5YR 7/6) body.* **p.** *Neckless ledge rim jar. No visible inclusions. Dm 11. Reddish yellow (7.5YR 8/5) body.* **q.** *Ledge rim jar. No visible inclusions. Dm 14. Very pale brown (10YR 8/3) body.*

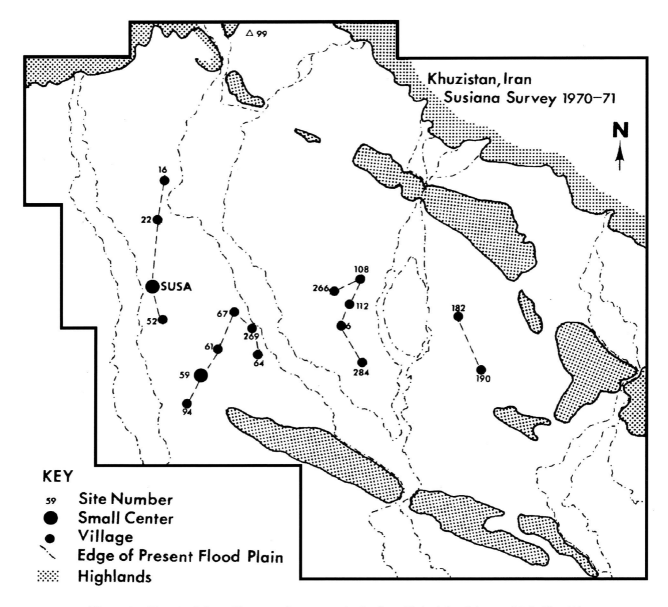

Figure 4.3. Terminal Suse Phase *settlement on the Susiana Plain (after Johnson 1973: Fig. 15).*

some have painted horizontal bands. Another ceramic ware of northern affinity has coarse angular calcite inclusions; this is used exclusively to make large globular hole-mouth jars with thickened rims (Fig. 4.5g). There is, in contrast, one unmistakable sand-tempered *Terminal Suse Phase* basin rim (Fig. 4.4/e) and two sand-tempered ledge rim jars (Fig. 4.5/k) of *Early Uruk* affinity, indicating contact between these different ceramic traditions.

In contrast, sites on the lower alluvium of the Tigris and Euphrates to the south-west exhibit a different ceramic style, a *Terminal 'Ubaid* assemblage, although it is placed in the *Early Uruk* period by some (Adams and Nissen 1972: 99–100). The technology and forms of these vessels are similar to those of *Late 'Ubaid* ceramics, but lack painted decoration

except on a few small jar necks and shoulders. It seems that the factors which led *Terminal Suse Phase* potters to cease painting their pottery might have also motivated *'Ubaid* potters as well. In contrast to south-western Iran, however, Adams (1981: 60–75, fig. 11) has demonstrated that there were more and much larger sites in Mesopotamia, particularly in the area east of Nippur. The largest of these, Tell Al-Hayyad, covered almost 50 ha (Adams 1981: 280, figs 11, 13, 14). It would not be surprising if this dense settlement network had impacts on the much smaller centres and settlement systems in south-western Iran. Among the possible motivations are conflict over interstitial areas of pasturage and marshland between lower Mesopotamia and Susiana, or competition over access to highland raw materials. However, these were relatively small populations, marsh and pasture areas were vast, and the demand for highland resources would have been small.

East of the Susiana Plain during this period, scattered occupation is attested. On the Ram Hormuz Plain 110 km from Susa, occupation is known only from the high central mound of Tal-e Ghazir (Caldwell 1968: 350, figs 7–10). In the mountains to the north and north-east, survey has recorded a large campsite with *Terminal Suse Phase* sherds on the plain of Qaleh Tol,

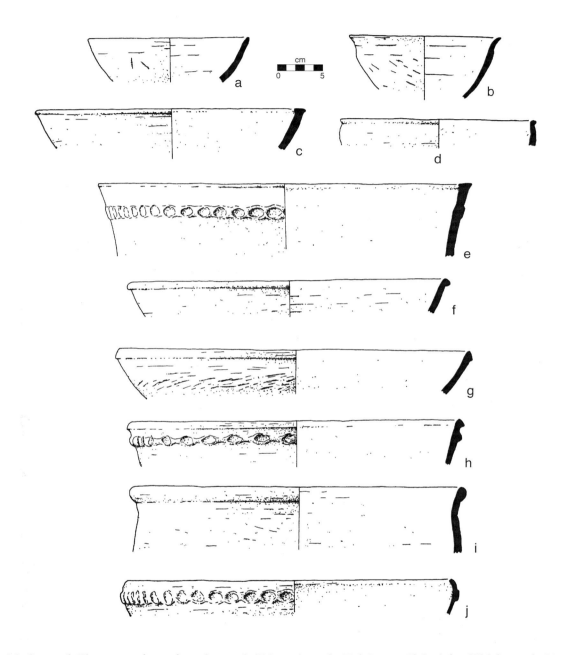

Figure 4.4. Sargarab Phase open forms from Sargarab (DL-169) on the Deh Luran Plain (after Wright et al. 1975: fig. 7; Neely and Wright 1994: figs. IV.44–IV.46). **a.** *Round lip bowl. Vegetal and calcite inclusions. Dm 20. Red (2.5YR 5/8) body.* **b.** *Tapered rim bowl. Vegetal and calcite inclusions. Dm 18. Pinkish white (7.5YR8/2) body.* **c.** *Flat lip bowl. Vegetal and calcite inclusions. Dm 37. Reddish yellow3 (7.5YR 6/8) body.* **d.** *Beaded rim incurved bowl. Vegetal and calcite inclusions. Dm 22. Red 10R 4/5) body.* **e.** *Large basin with thumb-impressed appliqué strip. Fine sand and vegetal inclusions. Dm 47. Pale yellow (2.5Y 8/3) body.* **f.** *Beaded rim bowl. Vegetal and calcite inclusions. Dm 40. White (5Y 8/1) body.* **g.** *Large beaded rim bowl. Vegetal and calcite inclusions. Dm 52. Reddish brown (5YR 5/5) body.* **h.** *Large beaded rim bowl with thumb-impressed appliqué strip. Vegetal and calcite inclusions. Dm 50. Weak red (10R 5/2) body.* **i.** *Large beaded rim bowl. Vegetal and calcite inclusions. Dm 50. Very pale brown (10R 7/4) body.* **j.** *Large incurved bowl with thumb-impressed appliqué strip. Vegetal and calcite inclusions. Dm 46. Yellowish brown (10YR 5/7) body.*

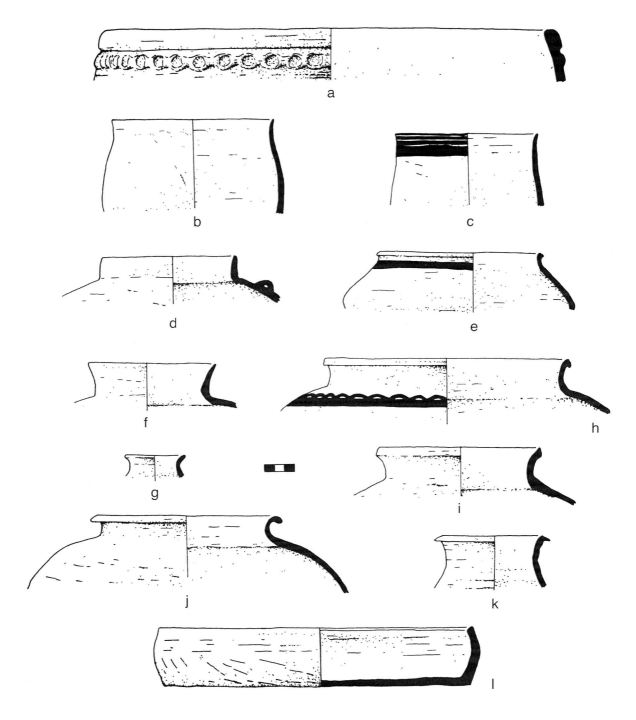

Figure 4.5. Sargarab Phase jars from Sargarab (DL 169) on the Deh Luran Plain (Wright et al. *1975: fig. 8; Neely and Wright 1994: figs. IV.44–IV.46).* **a.** *Large beaded rim incurved basin with thumb-impressed appliqué strip. Vegetal and calcite inclusions. Dm 50. Reddish yellow (7.5YR 6/8) body.* **b.** *Fine beaker. Vegetal and calcite inclusions. Dm 19. White (5Y 8/1) body.* **c.** *Tapered rim bowl. Vegetal and calcite inclusions. Dm 18. Light grey (5Y 6/1) body. Reddish brown (5YR 4/2) painted rim bands.* **d.** *Straight neck jar with oval lug. Vegetal and calcite inclusions. Dm 13. Light reddish brown (2.5YR 6/5) body.* **e.** *Neckless beaded lip jar. Vegetal and calcite inclusions. Dm 15. Pale brown (10YR 6/3) body. Reddish brown (2.5YR 5.4) slip. Dark greyish brown (5YR 4/2) painted rim bands.* **f.** *Round lip, flared neck jar. Vegetal and calcite inclusions. Dm 12. Dark grey (5YR 4/1) body.* **g.** *Hole mouth jar. Coarse angular calcite inclusions. Dm 25. Reddish yellow (5YR 6/6) body.* **h.** *Beaded lip, flared neck jar with painted shoulder band. Vegetal and calcite inclusions. Dm 24. Light reddish brown (5YR 6/4) body, dark grey (10YR 4/1) painted shoulder bands.* **i.** *Beaded lip, flared neck jar. Vegetal and calcite inclusions. Dm 23. Pale red (2.5YR 7/3) body.* **j.** *Beaded lip, flared neck jar. Vegetal and calcite inclusions. Dm 17. Light red (2.5YR 6/5) body.* **k.** *Ledge rim, flared neck jar. Fine sand inclusions. Dm 12. Pinkish white (5Y 8/2) body.* **l.** *Small tray. Vegetal and calcite inclusions. Dm c. 35. Pale brown (10YR 6/3) body.*

50 km north-east of Ghazir (Wright 1987: 144), and two small village sites on the plain of Izeh (Shahideh 1979: 54). These sites are in parts of the plains that are without summer water supplies, and may be the sites of transhumant pastoralists. Farther east, in the large and high Kur River Basin of southern Iran (Sumner 1988, also 1994), small early *Lapui Phase* centres and villages flourished, but there are no indications of stylistic similarities to Susiana at this time. In the smaller plains of Mamasani, which lies 90 km west-north-west of the Kur River Basin, excavation at Tol-e Spid (Petrie *et al.* 2009: 93–95, 101–05, 124, figs 4.50–4.59) and Nurabad (Weeks *et al.* 2009: 36, 49–53, figs 3.99–3.102), has documented few similarities to *Terminal Suse Phase* assemblages. Definitively early *Lapui* layers, however, have not yet been reported (see Petrie *et al.*, this volume). Similarly, there is little evidence from surface survey of material with relations to the *Terminal Suse Phase* (McCall 2009).

In sum, during the late fifth millennium BC, in contrast to lower Mesopotamia, the world of south-western and southern Iran was one of relatively isolated clusters of relatively small settlements. The assemblages of domestic technology were local developments, with little evidence of exchange between Lower Mesopotamia, south-western Iran, and southern Iran. There were few larger emergent primate centres and little evidence of settlement hierarchy, as one would expect if developed control hierarchies were operating (Fig. 4.6).

South-western Iran at the beginning of the fourth millennium BC

A nadir in Susiana settlement was reached about 4000 BC when even the Acropole of Susa was abandoned, and the walls of mud-brick buildings were eroded to mere stubs, an erosive process which takes about 50 years in this area. When the Acropole was reoccupied, a new ceramic assemblage, defining an *Early Uruk Phase* was in use (Fig 4.7).[2] There are some forms used before, such as simple bowls (Fig. 4.7/d–f), flat

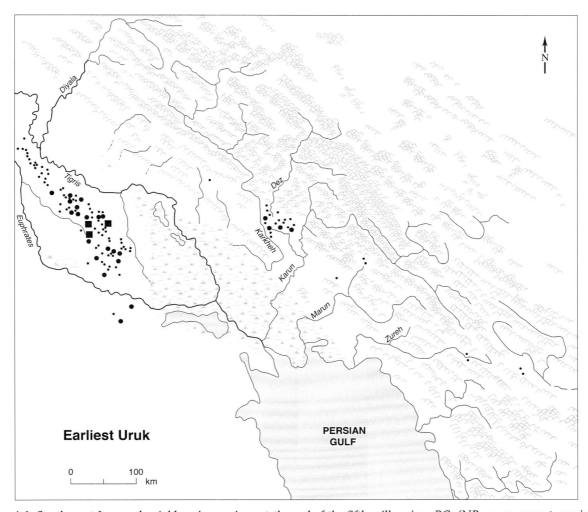

Figure 4.6. South-west Iran and neighbouring regions at the end of the fifth millennium BC. (NB: as we cannot consistently separate the earlier and later Early Uruk occupations on the sites surveyed in lower Mesopotamia, we show the same generalized Early Uruk distribution on both Fig. 4.6 and 4.9).

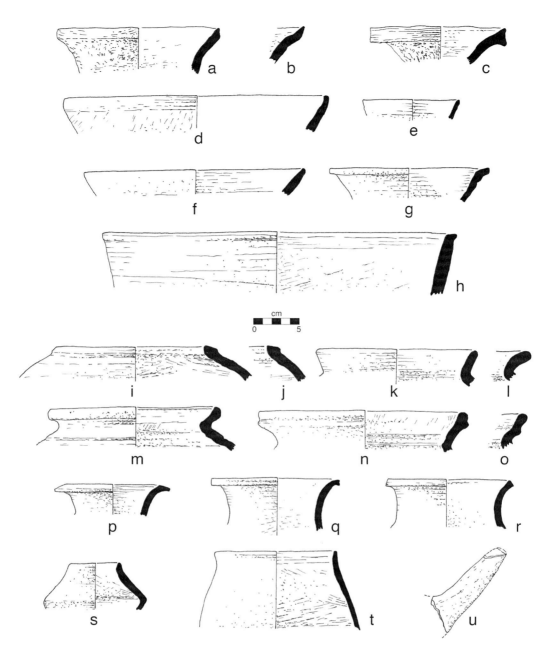

Figure 4.7. Early Uruk vessels from Suse Acropole III on the Susiana Plain. **a.** *Rough tapered rim bowl (layer 7, 003.01), trace vegetal inclusions. Dm 17. Light red (2.5YR 6/5) body.* **b.** *Rough tapered rim bowl (layer 11, 006.01), vegetal inclusions. Dm 18. Very pale brown (10YR 7/4) body.* **c.** *Rough bevel-rim bowl (layer 10, 005.09), vegetal inclusions. Dm 14. Reddish yellow (5YR 7/6) body.* **d.** *Round lip bowl (layer 11, 006.03), trace vegetal inclusions. Dm c. 29. Light yellowish brown (10YR 6/4) body.* **e.** *Round lip bowl (layer 7, 003.06), coarse sand inclusions. Dm 10. Reddish yellow (5YR 6/6) body.* **f.** *Round lip bowl (layer 9, 1144.05), trace fine sand. Dm 23. Very pale brown (10YR 8/4) body.* **g.** *Beaded rim bowl (layer 7, 1114.14), trace medium sand and vegetal inclusions. Dm 17. Light red (2.5YR 6/6) body.* **h.** *Large flat lip basin (Layer 10, 005.08), trace fine sand inclusions. Dm 35. Very pale brown (10YR 8/4) body.* **i.** *Hole mouth jar (layer 7, 1113.02), coarse sand and vegetal inclusions. Dm 15. Reddish yellow (5YR 8/6) body.* **j.** *Hole mouth jar (layer 7, 1123.02), coarse sand. Dm 15. Pink (7.5YR 7/4) body.* **k.** *Heavy round lip jar (layer 7, 1079.04), fine sand. Dm 15. Reddish yellow (7.5YR 8/4) body.* **l.** *Heavy round lip jar (layer 7, 1136.02), trace fine sand and vegetal inclusions. Dm 25. Reddish yellow (7.5YR 8/4) body.* **m.** *Grooved round lip jar (layer 7, 1114.08, Dm 18), Trace fine sand and vegetal inclusions, Dm 14. Pink (7.5YR 8/4) body.* **n.** *High band rim jar (layer 9, 1144.04). Dm 26. White (10YR 8/3) body.* **o.** *High band rim jar (layer 10, 1149.01). Dm 14. White (10YR 8/3) body.* **p.** *Ledge rim jar (layer 7, 1079.05, Dm 12), medium sand and vegetal inclusions. Dm 8. White (2.5Y 8/2) body.* **q.** *Flared expanded jar (layer 11, 006-02), trace vegetal inclusions. Dm 13. White (7.5YR 8/3) body.* **r.** *Flared expanded jar (layer 11, 006-01), trace vegetal and calcite inclusions. Dm 13. Pink (5YR 7/3) body.* **s.** *Small fine beaker (layer 7, 1079.03), medium sand inclusions. Dm 5. White (2.5Y 9/2) body.* **t.** *Fine beaker (layer 10, 1011.49), trace vegetal inclusions. Dm 13. Light brownish grey (2.5Y 6/2) body.* **u.** *Straight spout (layer 7, 008.05), coarse sand inclusions. Very pale brown (2.5Y 8/3) body.*

lip basins (Fig. 4.7/h), fine jars or beakers (Fig. 4.7/s–t), and flared neck jars with round lips. Among the many new forms are mould-made tapered rim bowls (so-called "proto-bevel-rim bowls") (Fig. 4.7/a–b), and at the end of the period the first bevel-rim bowls (Fig. 4.7/c), both on rough vegetally tempered ware appear. Carinated and beaded rim (Fig. 4.7/g) bowls also occur. Common earlier in the period are heavy hole mouth jars without necks but with ledge rims, usually of a coarser ware (Fig. 4.7/i–j), and later in the period are low necked jars with heavy rounded lips, often with a groove on the inside of the neck (Fig. 4.7/k–m). Jars with high band rims, also usually with a groove on the inside of the neck (Fig. 4.7/n–o) are common. Flared neck jars with flattened expanded rims (Fig. 4.7/q–r) and ledge rims (Fig. 4.7/p) often with straight spouts (Fig. 4.7/u) were important throughout the period. These new forms have affinities with both the *Terminal 'Ubaid* assemblages of lower Mesopotamia and the *Late Chalcolithic 2* of Upper Mesopotamia (Rothman 2001). I now tentatively date this period on the Susiana Plain between 4000 and 3800 BC (Wright and Rupley 2001: 120).

Survey evidence shows the southern part of the upper Susiana plain was densely settled during the *Early Uruk* period (Fig. 4.8; also Johnson 1973: 90–92, fig. 16), with small centres from 3–5 ha at Susa, Abu Fanduweh (KS-59; 12 km south-east of Susa),[3] KS-79 (12 km east-south-east of Abu Fanduweh), and Deh No (KS-120; 12 km east of KS-79) and 45 other village sites, covering a total of 95 ha. Late in this phase, Susa emerges as the major centre, covering at least 12 ha. Assuming a population density of 115–150 people per hectare, population could have reached up to 11,000–14,000 people for the later *Early Uruk* period. A large village site (KS-76) was tested by Johnson (1987) and produced evidence of substantial herding of cows as well as some sheep, goat, and pigs (Mudar 1988). Domestic wheat is attested in flotation samples from *Early Uruk* deposits at Susa (Miller, personal communication). Using local traditional grain productivities for the area, Johnson (1973: 95–98) has shown that all settlements, including the expanded centre of Susa, had enough nearby land to have been self-sufficient in grain. Given the limited evidence available in 1973, Johnson was unwilling to

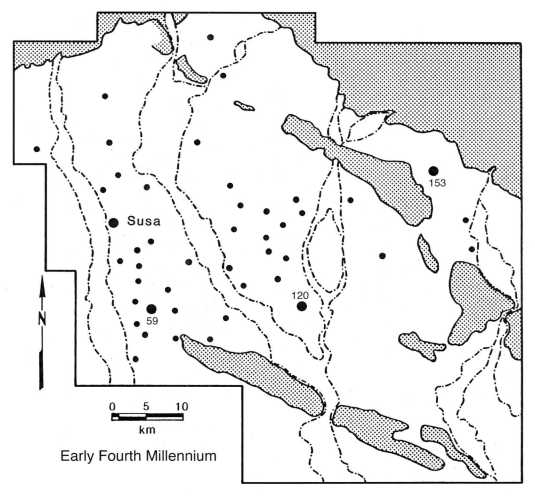

Figure 4.8. Early Uruk *settlement on the Susiana Plain (after Johnson 1973: fig. 16).*

characterise the socio-political organisation during the *Early Uruk* period on the Susiana plain.

We now have some additional insight from Susa itself and from reconsideration of the survey evidence. Stève and Gasche (1971) have shown that the public area in the centre of the Acropole was in use at this time, but the architecture was poorly preserved. Preliminary excavations in 1978 on the northern Acropole (Wright 1985: 729–31) revealed parts of an architectural complex lacking domestic features, but with parched wheat, counters, and an unfinished stamp seal in the latest *Early Uruk* layer. It is likely this was part of a grain storage facility, but its precise institutional context is difficult to assess. In a reconsideration of the survey data, Johnson (1987) demonstrated that the south-western plain around Susa and Abu Fanduweh had a regular spatial structure, that the distribution of ceramic variants could be related to the influence of the large settlements on nearby villages, and that the larger centre at Susa had far higher densities of discarded mass-produced bowls than the villages, suggesting greater control of labour in the centre. Although we lack the seals and sealings in contexts that would help us directly to document the developing control apparatus, it is likely that political figures at Susa were building a state during the later *Early Uruk* period (Wright 1998).

To the west of the Susiana Plain on the Deh Luran Plain, there was a local development during the *Early Uruk* period which continued to use the Sargarab ceramics related to the Zagros and Upper Mesopotamia, but with the addition of early variants of mass-produced bowls and some sand-tempered *Early Uruk* vessel forms. At the north-west end of the plain, there was an *Early Uruk* centre of 8 ha (Neely and Wright 1994: 156–59), fed by a substantial canal 8.5 km long (Neely 1994: 189) and with seven nearby smaller settlements. There are also three scattered smaller settlements to the south-east. Stone footings exposed by erosion on two sites indicate that there were many open spaces and thus, based on roofed space, only about 115 people per hectare of settlement. Taking into account this lower population density, the seven sites dating to the earlier sub-phase of the *Early Uruk* covered 14 ha and had up to 1500 inhabitants; and the five sites dating to the later sub-phase of the *Early Uruk* tightly clustered in the west part of the plain, covered 11 ha and had up to 1300 inhabitants (Neely and Wright 1994: 173–75). Taking into account the movement of settlement during the period, however, Robert Dewar (1994: 207–08) estimated a mean settled population of only 600 people at any point during this phase. While we have little evidence of the social or political organisation of Deh Luran communities at this time, we can infer a small local hierarchically organised settlement group in an uneasy existence between much larger neighbours to the south-west and south-east.

In the lower alluvium of the Tigris and Euphrates, to the south-west of Susiana, stratigraphic excavations are surprisingly few and poorly reported. Based on survey collections, however, ceramic styles appear to be similar to those of Susa during this period (Adams and Nissen 1972: 99–100). Settlement patterns (Adams and Nissen 1972; Adams 1981) show continued high density of settlement along the Tigris and Euphrates channels between Nippur and Uruk (Fig. 4.9). Using Dewar's (1994) method to measure the abandonment and foundation of settlements during a time period, Pollock (1999: 52–75, table 3.1) has estimated 169 ha of simultaneously occupied *Early Uruk* – in the broadest sense – settlement. Assuming a low density of 115–150 people per hectare[4] this would indicate an average settled population of 19,400–25,300 people, almost twice as much as is estimated for the northern Susiana Plain.

To the east of the central Susiana Plain on the Ram Hormuz plain, occupation continued on the small, high central mound of Tal-e Ghazir. Substantial mud-brick walls and pottery similar to that of Susa was recovered (Caldwell 1968: 350, figs 11–14), but no additional sites are known. In the mountains 75 km north-east of Tal-e Ghazir on the plain of Izeh (Wright 1979: 59–60) there is one large centre of 9.6 ha and one large village site of 3.1 ha with ceramics also similar to those of Susa. The centre, Tepe Zabarjad, could have been watered by a permanent spring on the south side of the plain, but the village is on the northern part of the plain, which has no summer water supply, and was probably used primarily in the winter by people who would have been transhumant pastoralists during the summer. The winter population of this plain could have been as high as 1600 people.

Farther east, the contemporary *Lapui* population of the Kur River Basin followed their own local development, showing little relation to those of Susiana (Alden 2003; Sumner 1988; see Petrie *et al.*, this volume; Sardari, this volume). There were four small centres with *Lapui* ceramics evenly spaced across the basin ranging between 2.5 and 4 ha in size. Scattered around them were at least 65 smaller sites, each covering about 1 ha. Sumner (1988), arguing that his survey did not examine every mound and is thus not comparable to those in Susiana, does not offer a site area estimate, but clearly *Lapui* settlement was comparable in terms of density to that of the upper Susiana Plain, with evident settlement hierarchy, although without a known emergent larger centre similar to contemporary Susa. The ceramics are exclusively of local plain burnished wares, with only generic similarities to ceramics in the lowlands. In the northern part of nearby Mamasani, *Lapui* ceramics are found on the thoroughly surveyed Dasht-i Rostam plain. There were 11 small settlements, of which the largest in the centre of the richest agricultural land,

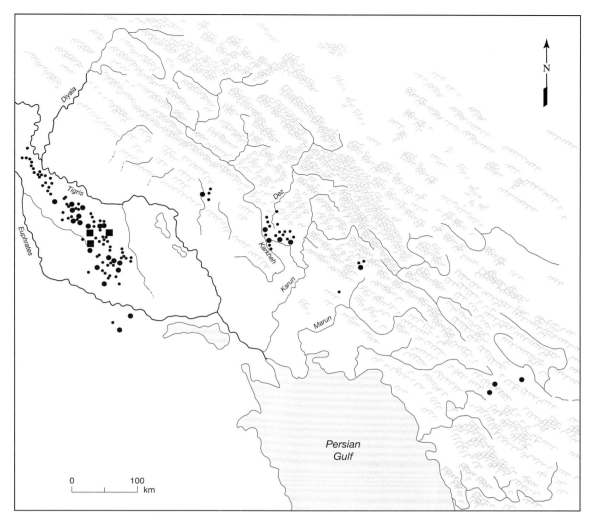

Figure 4.9. South-west Iran and neighbouring regions at the beginning of the fourth millennium BC. (NB: as we cannot consistently separate the earlier and later Early Uruk *occupations on the sites surveyed in lower Mesopotamia, we show the same generalized* Early Uruk *distribution on both Fig. 4.6 and 4.9).*

Tol-e Spid, may have reached 2.1 ha (Petrie *et al.* 2009; McCall 2009: 216, fig. 9.4; see Petrie *et al.*, this volume). The late *Lapui* layers of Nurabad in the southern part of Mamasani have yielded a few ceramic forms similar to *Early Uruk* in south-west Iran and both upper and lower Mesopotamia beyond (Weeks *et al.* 2009: 50–51, fig. 3–100: TNP871 and fig. 3–101: TNP 808), but these are few in comparison with many *Lapui* vessel fragments.

Having reviewed the evidence from the better-known component areas of the region of south-western and southern Iran, we are now in a position to address broader questions of trans-regional interaction during the early fourth millennium (Fig. 4.10).

First, what was the relation between the large early Uruk formations of nearby alluvial Mesopotamia and south-western Iran? Although the main land route between Susiana and lower Mesopotamia ran through Deh Luran, the tiny population in Deh Luran,

clustered in the far west of the plain, could not block access to central Susiana. The population around Susa, however, rapidly recovered from its nadir at the end of the *Terminal Suse Phase*. Its domestic ceramics had elements of the *Suse Phase* tradition and of *Early Uruk* ceramics derived from 'Ubaid traditions on the alluvium. Was this indicative of an introduced population, derived from lower Mesopotamia, as some have suggested (Algaze 1993: 13–17; 2008: xiv)? It could also represent a synthetic population – partly local and partly immigrant from lower Mesopotamia, developing in opposition to competitors to the south-west. Or it could simply have been a local population interacting with those to the south-west. With little evidence beyond the bare skeleton of surveyed settlements and ceramics, lacking even an adequate absolute chronology in either south-west Iran or lower Mesopotamia, we cannot be certain. What is clear is that our approximate estimates for the number of

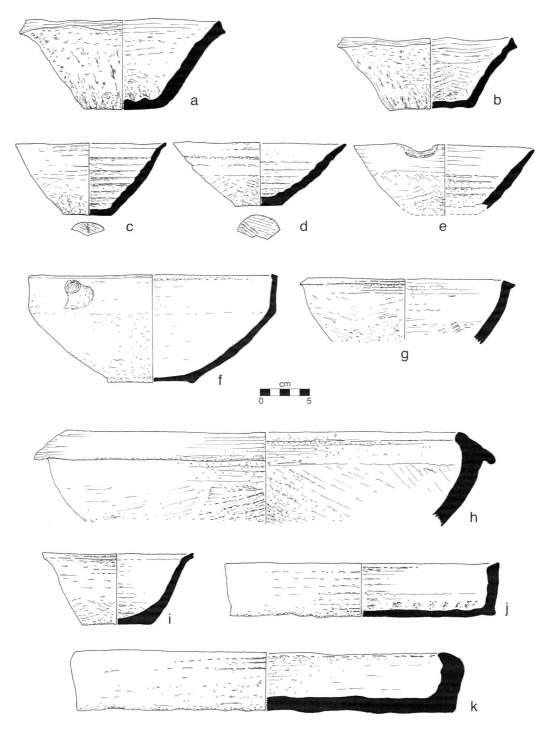

Figure 4.10. Middle Uruk *open forms from Tepe Sharafabad on the Susiana Plain.*[6] **a.** *Rough ware bevel-rim bowl (Uruk Dump, layers 2–5 in intrusive pit, 0065b), vegetal inclusions. Dm 19. Ht 9. Reddish yellow (7.5YR 6/5) body.* **b.** *Rough ware bevel-rim bowl (Uruk Pit, layers 22–24, 0252c), vegetal inclusions. Dm 18. Ht 7. Reddish yellow (5Y 8/3) body.* **c.** *Conical cup (Uruk Pit, layer 9, 0191.11), trace fine sand. Dm 14. Ht 7. White (10YR 8/2) body. Note knife-cut base.* **d.** *Conical cup (Uruk Pit, layers 6–10, 0027.31), trace calcite and vegetal inclusions. Dm 16. Ht. 6. Pink (7.5YR 8/4) body. Note knife-cut base.* **e.** *Conical cup (Uruk Pit, layer 8, 0235.15), trace vegetal inclusions. Dm 15. Pale yellow (5Y 8/3) body. Note lip spout. Base reconstructed.* **f.** *Flat lip carinated bowl with conical spout (Uruk Dump layers 2–5 in intrusive pit, 0065), trace fine sand. Dm 24.* **g.** *Bevel-lip bowl (Uruk Dump West, layer 7, 0101.29), fine calcite inclusions. Dm 20. Ht 5.5.* **h.** *Ledge-rim basin (Uruk Pit, layers 22–24, 0252.11), coarse sand and calcite. Dm 38. Pink (7.5YR 7/4) body.* **i.** *Ledge rim cup (Uruk Pit, layers 19–24, 111.14), no visible inclusions. Dm 14. Ht c. 7. Reddish yellow (7.5YR 7/6) body. Burnished interior and rim.* **j.** *Tray (Uruk Dump West, layer s 2–5 in intrusive pit, 0065.93), medium sand vegetal inclusions. Dm c. 26. Very pale brown (10YR 7/4) body.* **k.** *Tray (Uruk Pit, layers 5–10, 0008,22), vegetal inclusions. Dm c. 38, probably oval. Pink (7.5YR 7/4) body.*

people in the core of lower Mesopotamia are much higher than those for the Susiana Plain.

Second, what is the relation between south-western Iran and populations in the mountains and basins of the Iranian plateau to the north-east? Isolated settlements in areas relatively close to Susa, such as Ram Hormuz and Izeh, are large and/or located on high defensible mounds, often an indication of unsettled conditions. There is indirect evidence of transhumant pastoralists. On the high plains of the southern Zagros and southern Iran there is little evidence of interaction with the centres of population in Susiana and Mesopotamia. Few ceramics or other items showing relation to *Early Uruk* Susiana have been reported on *Lapui* sites. Ceramics strikingly similar to *Lapui* ware are known from some *Suse Phase* sites (e.g Dollfus 1971: fig. 19, pl. VIII: 15; Le Brun 1971: fig. 38:5), significantly earlier than the *Early Uruk* period. It seems likely that these similarities result from interaction between fifth-millennium BC Susiana and some still unknown highland pottery tradition. There is no evidence of *Lapui* material in the few well-reported *Early Uruk* sites in Susiana. At present it appears that highland southern Iran and lowland south-eastern Iran had few if any relations during the early fourth millennium BC.

South-western Iran in the middle of the fourth millennium BC

Whatever their genesis, *Middle* and *Late Uruk* settlements on the Susiana Plain are part of the *Uruk* world from 3800 to *c.* 3150 BC. The excavation evidence is better than for earlier periods (Stève and Gasche 1971; LeBrun 1971, 1981, 1985; Delougaz and Kantor 1996; Alizadeh 2008). This evidence shows that the changes in architecture, ceramics, seals, and other aspects of record keeping parallel those in lower Mesopotamia proper. The record is biased toward the later part of this time span, however, and generally lacks extensive architectural exposures, especially of public buildings. In spite of the greater amount of reported work, those who work in Susiana are not in agreement regarding even some key aspects of the frames of reference. I will focus these remarks on the organisation of settlement networks, economies, and control apparatuses during the earlier part of this six-century time span, here termed the *Middle Uruk* period. A sample from the small site of Sharafabad dating to the end of the *Middle Uruk Phase* (Wright *et al.* 1981, 1989) illustrates this development (Figs. 4.10–4.11).[5] The ceramics of this period are a development from *Early Uruk* ceramics. There are a number of distinct manufacturing sequences or *chaînes opératoires* involving different clay mixtures and different production approaches (Van der Leeuw 1994). Simplifying Van der Leeuw's analysis, the major sequences are: (1) rough mould-made ware, (2) fine sandy and (3) coarse sandy wares, patch and ring-built

ware finished on a turntable, and (4) fine ware thrown on a fast wheel.

Rough ware was used primarily for the mass production of mould-made "bevel-rim bowls" (Le Brun 1980; Goulder 2010) (Fig. 4.10/a–b), which developed from the *Early Uruk* tapered rim bowl, and dominates all *Middle* (and *Late*) *Uruk* assemblages. Rough ware was also used for later *Middle* (and *Late*) *Uruk* thickened rounded rim trays (Fig. 4.10/l). Both may have been used in bread baking.

Fine sandy ware was used for similar open forms to those made previously, such as simple bowls and carinated bowls (Fig. 4.10/f). During this period there were also various ledge rim bowls. A small red burnished variant is illustrated (Fig. 4.10/i). Also attested are the bevel-lip bowls with obliquely cut rims (Fig. 4.10/g), which predominated in *Late Uruk* times. Restricted or closed vessel forms used before include jars with straight neck variants with flattened rims (Fig. 4.11/i). Flared neck jars with expanded flattened lips have differentiated into a larger heavy form with an expanded rim (Fig. 4.11/f) and a smaller thin vessel form (Fig. 4.11/g) and the high band rim jar evolved into a heavy form in which the band rim has been pressed down to the shoulder (Fig. 4.11/h). A rare ledge rim form with burnished red slip occurred (Fig. 4.11/k). A rare fine sandy grey ware ledge rim jar was burnished and fired under reducing conditions (Fig 4.11/i).

Coarse sandy ware was used for large ledge rim basins (Fig. 4.10/h). It was also used for straight flat rim trays (Fig. 4.10/l) earlier in the *Middle Uruk* period (Fig. 4.10/j). Among the closed jar farms, coarse sandy ware was used for larger flared round lip jars (Fig. 4.11/a) and also for some of the smaller round bodied jars with strap handles (Fig. 4.11/e). Both of these jar forms show evidence of direct use over fires.

The predominant fine ware forms of this period were conical cups with knife-cut bases (Fig. 4.10/c–e) (rather than the string-cut bases common in *Late Uruk* times and later), but there were also a few small jars (Fig. 4.11/b) which were made on a fast wheel, presaging extensive use of this method to produce jars and bottles during the *Late Uruk* Phase.

Middle Uruk jars exhibit a limited range of plastic decoration. This includes punctuates (Fig 4.11/i, k), reserve slip decoration (Fig. 4.11/g), shoulder grooves, incised cross-hatched bands (Fig. 4.11/i) (though few of the elaborated bands with cross-hatched triangles common in *Late Uruk* south-western Iran), or small nose lugs (Fig. 4.11/i, j). Conical spouts, either short (Fig. 4.11/h) or long (Fig. 4.11/g), were common on such jars throughout this period. Some longer conical spouts on small plain jars are slightly curved, and these developed into droop spouts on bottles in the succeeding *Late Uruk* period. I now tentatively date this period on the Susiana Plain between 3800 and 3400 BC (Wright and Rupley 2001: 121).

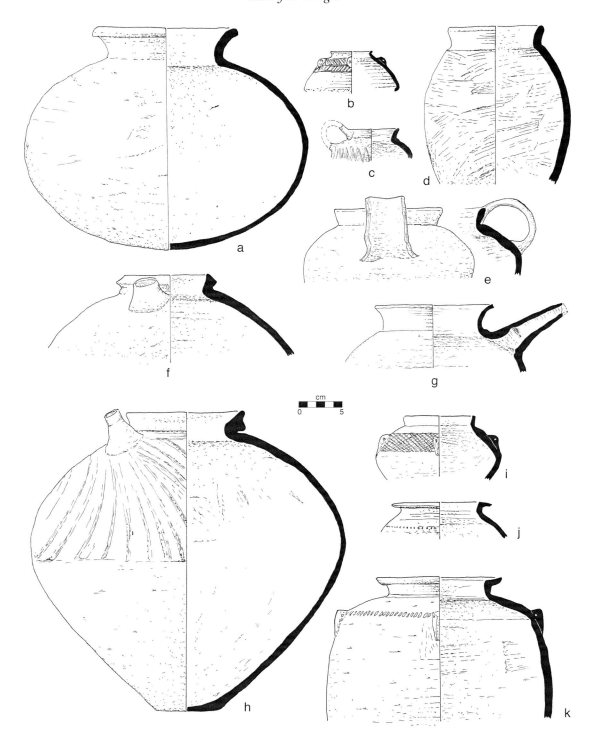

Figure 4.11. Middle Uruk *closed forms from Tepe Sharafabad on the Susiana Plain.* **a.** *Heavy round lip jar (Uruk Dump East, layer 2, 0014.01).* **b.** *Small round lip jar with nose lugs and incised band (Uruk Pit, layers 22–25, 0136.05).* **c.** *Small globular round lip jar with strap handle rocker decoration (Uruk Pit, layers 22–25, 0136.05).* **d.** *Heavy round lip jar (Uruk Pit, layer 8, 0190.11).* **e.** *Globular round lip jar with strap handle (Uruk Pit, layer 11, 0193.06), 15% medium sand inclusions. Dm 12. Light grey (2.5Y 7/1) body.* **f.** *Heavy expanded rim jar with spout (Uruk Pit, layers 14–22, 0087).* **g.** *Fine expanded rim jar with spout (Uruk Pit, layer 9, 0191.04), trace of vegetal inclusions. Dm 13. White (5y 8/3) body.* **h.** *Low expanded band rim jar with conical spout and reserve slip decoration (Uruk Rooms, Layer 7, 0095.010), 5% medium sand inclusions. Dm 13. Pale brown (10YR 7/4) body.* **i.** *Small flat lip jar with nose lugs and incised band (Uruk Dump, layers 2–5 in intrusive pit 0065.x), trace of fine sand. Dm 8. White (2.5 Y 8/2) body.* **j.** *Ledge rim grey ware jar with punctate band (Uruk Pit, layers 25–26, 0253.32), trace of fine calcite inclusions. Dm 11. Grey (10YR 5/1) body, burnished exterior.* **k.** *Ledge rim jar with nose lugs and punctate (Uruk Pit, layers 8–14, 0045.07), 10% medium sand inclusions. Dm 14. Pink (5YR 7/4) body, red (2.5YR 4/6) slip.*

During *Middle Uruk* times the Upper Susiana Plain was prosperous (Fig. 4.12; Johnson 1973: 101–07, fig. 19). Both the higher Acropole and lower Apadana of Susa appear to have been completely occupied, increasing the size of the centre to at least 25 ha. Two other centres – long-established Abu Fanduweh and more recently resettled Chogha Mish – share the upper town/lower town structure with Susa and are thought to have covered about 10 ha during this time span. Thick deposits of *Late Uruk* debris cover *Middle Uruk* layers at both sites, however, the areas of occupation cannot be precisely measured, and Abbas Alizadeh (2008, personal communication) questions whether these sites were occupied during *Middle Uruk* times at all. Smaller than these major sites are four centres, ranging from 3.5 to 6.5 ha in size. Smaller yet are two discrete groupings, 17 sites ranging from 1.5 to 3.0 ha, and 30 that are less that 1.5 ha (Johnson 1973: 74–79). These sites cover 127 ha, and assuming a population density of 115–150 people per hectare, population could have reached up to 14,000–19,000 people during the *Middle Uruk* period. The excavations at Sharafabad (Wright *et al.* 1981) and other sites (Mudar 1988) show

that wheat, barley, lentils, and flax were cultivated; sheep, goat, and a few cows were herded; and pigs were either kept or hunted. Using local traditional grain productivities for the area, Johnson (1973: 96–98) argued that during the *Middle Uruk* period the large centre of Susa would no longer have been self-sufficient in grain, and therefore would have had to obtain grain from other nearby settlements. In addition to the agricultural economy, the craft economy is relatively well understood. There is evidence of *Middle Uruk* potting installations at various centres (Johnson 1973: 107) and indications of distribution networks for pottery (Johnson 1973: 113–27), and chert blade manufacturing areas in some rural villages (Johnson 1973: 109), but not others (Pollock 2008). In general, the complexity of technologies such as wheels and moulds for potting and levers for making blades, as well as the precise standardisation of pottery attributes, ground stone vessels and tools, and recording systems argues for defined crafts reproduced by systems of apprenticeship (Wright 2001: 134–39). There is evidence for both balanced economic exchange and tribute extraction (Wright 2001: 141–43).

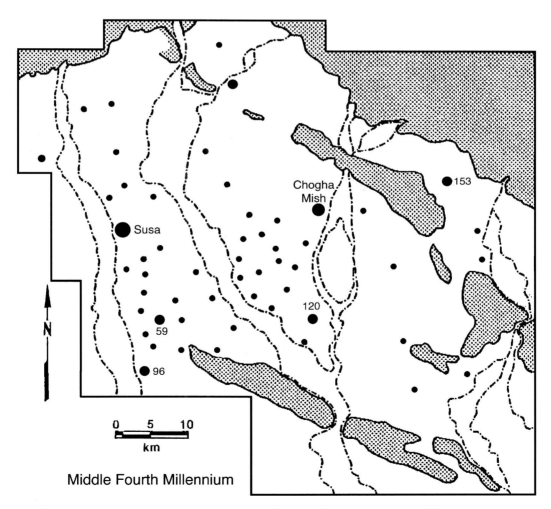

Figure 4.12. Middle Uruk *settlement on the Susiana Plain (after Johnson 1973: fig. 19).*

There is some direct evidence for systems of control on the upper Susiana plain. Except perhaps for a large tripartite building at Chogha Mish (Alizadeh 2008), we have no well-preserved public architecture from this period. Alas, this building had relatively few items on its floor from which one might infer the activities performed there. One small rural site and the larger centres of Susa and Chogha Mish, however, have produced objects sealed with both cylinder and stamp seals which imply both hierarchical and lateral relations (Wright *et al.* 1981). At the small rural centre of Sharafabad there were both modest residences and an elaborate building decorated with clay cone mosaic (Wright *et al.* 1981: 268–69). Locally resident figures in authority sealed jars and bales with stamp seals and closed storehouse doors with stamp seals. Goods in jars and bales with non-local cylinder seal impressions were locally distributed. Summary statistics on goods or labour were recorded using counters and wrapped in spherical envelopes of clay (Wright *et al.* 1981: 277–81). Finished "bullae" with *Middle Uruk* seal impressions have been found at both Susa (Amiet 1972) and Chogha Mish (Delougaz and Kantor 1996), although none have seal impressions identical to those from Sharafabad. This recording system required local figures and sites like Sharafabad and receiving officials at centres such as Susa or Chogha Mish. The fact that the envelope could be broken and the counters checked further implies higher-level adjudicating officials. We can also infer a higher-level authority, which would set policy and appoint officials. The authority, decision-making, and control indicated by these administrative artefacts alone implies that, internally specialised and hierarchical control apparatuses – the essential feature on a state – were active on the Susiana Plain.

Deh Luran, which was both a producer of useful materials such as bitumen, flint, other stones, and goat hair and a transit point halfway between Susa and the Uruk centres of the alluvium, was also prosperous during *Middle Uruk* times. During the *Middle Uruk* period, new villages were established in the central plain and the established *Early Uruk* centre to the west was abandoned, and centrally located Tepe Farukhabad began to grow (Neely and Wright 1994: 175–76; Wright 1981: 181–84). The local *Early Uruk* tradition of ceramics with vegetal and calcite inclusions continued, but sand-tempered *Middle Uruk* jars and cups appear and bevel-rim bowls are common (Wright 1981: 169). The excavations here revealed not only domestic buildings and features and modest burials, but mother-of-pearl inlay (Wright 1981: 162, fig. 75j, pl. 19a), carnelian beads, and a spherical envelope with impressions of both cylinder and stamp seals (Wright 1981: 156, 162, fig. 75d, pl. 16e), indicating people of importance were present and concerned with control of the local movement of goods or labour. This evidence implies a small local enclave prospering from local production and exchange with larger *Middle Uruk* enclaves to the south and east.

It is not surprising that this prosperous period saw continued relations with the valleys of the high Zagros and perhaps even with the southern Iranian plateau. Small centres on the Ram Hormuz and Izeh plains probably continued. The route between the Susiana Plain and Ram Hormuz had *Middle Uruk* sites, and Tal-e Ghazir probably continued to be a local center on the Ram Hormuz Plain (Moghaddam and Miri 2007). In Izeh, only the 3 ha centre of Tepe Sabzali Zabarjad (Wright 1979) continued to be occupied during *Middle Uruk* times. Limited excavation shows that this isolated centre manufactured its own ceramics in *Middle Uruk* styles, distinguished by limestone inclusions, but was supported by goods – specifically sand-tempered ceramics and stone stools – and animals, including substantial proportions of cows from outside (Redding 1979), presumably the Susiana Plain. Ceramics also show relations with the *Initial Banesh Phase* of the Marv Dasht, as discussed below.

In the high valleys of the southern Zagros and the adjacent interior plateaux in Fars, *Lapui* traditions continued through most of the time period when *Middle Uruk* flourished in many parts of the lowlands. In the Mamasani area 380 km east-south-east of Susa, from the well-excavated and well-dated deep sequence at Tol-e Spid, several vessels from the end of this time period, for example an out-turned ledge-rim jar from latest *Lapui* layer 20 (Petrie *et al.* 2009: fig. 4.57, TS 1961) and a large bevel-rim bowl from *Transitional Lapui/Banesh* phase 19 (Petrie *et al.* 2009: fig. 4.60, TS 1933) duplicate examples from Zabarajad on the Izeh Plain (Wright 1979: fig. 32, table 10: 01106, 01406). In the Kur River Basin, multiple surveys record a range of small settlements whose location indicates dry farming, limited irrigation using springs, and indirectly widespread pastoralism. The surviving settlement distribution shows little evidence of hierarchy. During a small stratigraphic excavation at Tal-e Kureh, Alden (2003: 187–98, D2–D8) recovered an *Initial Banesh* assemblage in layers 8 and 9 dated to about 3400 BC, among which were a number of bevel-rim bowl sherds and an out-turned ledge-rim jar with grit inclusions (Alden 2003: fig. D5:5) similar to examples from Izeh and Tol-e Spid. Also, there are a ledge-rim bowl (Alden 2003: fig. D5:1) and a bevel-lip bowl (Alden 2003: fig. D4:13), both of a fine sandy fabric. These important collections appear to have been lost when the excavation headquarters at Malyan were destroyed during the 1980s (Sumner, personal communication), thus we cannot restudy them, but the use of radically different fabrics suggests at least three different manufacturing sequences (*chaîne opératoire*): (1) rough mould made ware, (2) gritty or sandy ware, and (3) fine ware. Potts (2009) has cogently argued that bevel-rim bowls indicate shared methods of food preparation rather than any generalised cultural relationship. The widely shared small jars and bowls, however, are unlikely to be tied to a specific cuisine. The presence of a minority of *Uruk*-related vessel forms and manufacturing sequences in a context of a majority of ceramics derived from local *Lapui* ware at the moment in which ceramic manufacturing becomes important at Tal-e Kureh, suggests a movement of lowland potters and their craft techniques rather than of whole communities. These shared ceramic forms may presage the emergence of the developed *Banesh* phase ceramics, which represent a synthesis of *Lapui* and *Uruk* elements. Arguments about the social and political structure of the Kur River Basin during the *Late Lapui* or *Initial Banesh* periods (Sumner 1988; Alizadeh 2010; Alden, this volume) cannot be resolved with the available limited record. In order to assess the organization of the social formations in the southern highlands of Iran we need extensive sampling of architecture and features in different kinds of settlement.

Having reviewed the evidence from portions of south-western and southern Iran, we can address broader questions of trans-regional interaction during the middle of the fourth millennium (Fig. 4.13).

First, although the settlement network on the Susiana Plain is larger and well organised, it is likely that the settlements and networks of nearby alluvial Mesopotamia were even larger. We cannot quantitatively assess *Middle Uruk* settlement and degree of organisation in Mesopotamia proper, however, because of dense later debris and the limited knowledge of *Middle Uruk* ceramic indicators in that region.

Second, the smaller valleys of the Middle Zagros foothills within 150 km of Susa are closely related to Susa. Some areas, such as Izeh, are more closely related, perhaps frontier outposts. Others, such as Deh Luran, may have been more independent but still had economic linkages.

Third, the evidence of relations between the lowland Susiana plains and Mesopotamia on the one

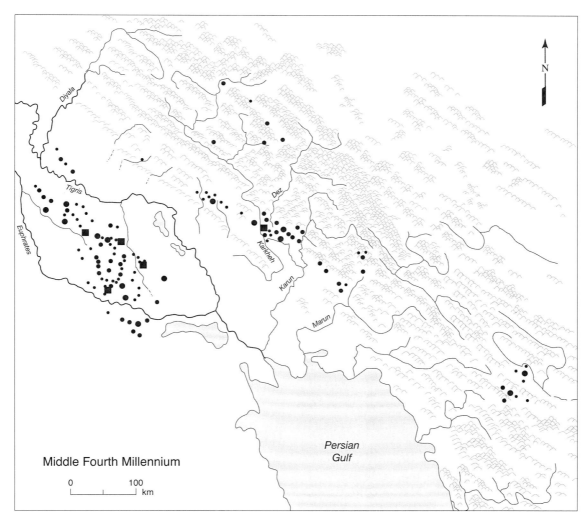

Figure 4.13. South-west Iran and neighbouring regions at the mid-fourth millennium BC. (NB: the recognition of Middle Uruk *occupations on the sites surveyed in lower Mesopotamia is very tentative).*

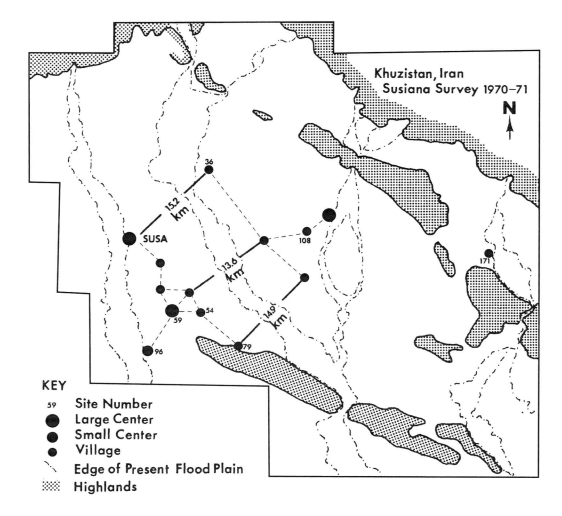

Figure 4.15. Late Uruk *settlement on the Susiana Plain (after Johnson 1973: fig. 32)*

longer visible (Alizadeh *et al.* 2004). In addition, the areas between the larger plains, with smaller valleys and uplands require survey and excavation if we are to resolve the questions raised regarding the role of nomads in cultural change in south-western Iran (Abdi 2003; Alizadeh 2010; Wright 1987). This requires different kinds of survey and excavation programs, focused on ephemeral features, animal remains, and limited artefact inventories (Hole 1980). For both the plains and the uplands, integrated palaeo-ecological approaches can provide documentation of climate and biology that we never dreamed was possible (Djamali *et al.* 2009; Stevens *et al.* 2001).

B. New excavations: the late fifth- and fourth-millennium BC samples discussed here are almost all small samples from tiny excavations. Most of the excavations of the 1970s were well done, but many of the samples are no longer available for restudy. We need larger excavations undertaken with the exacting standards of the teams of Jean Perrot at Susa and William Sumner at Tal-e Malyan, from which samples are carefully conserved for reanalysis as our insight and technical methods improve.

C. Absolute dating: methods for age determinations have greatly improved since the 1970s. Radiocarbon dating is more precise and possible problems are better understood. Furthermore, we have other dating methods such as thermo-luminescence and optically stimulated luminescence that can be used independently to check radiocarbon dating. These methods, however, are unlikely to reduce the error range of dates to less than a century. More precise methods, such as dendro-chronology, will be needed if we are ever to monitor economic and political processes believed to have been important in the past.

D. New technical studies: physio-chemical methods for assessing the sources of stones, clays, and other materials or the methods used to manufacture metal items are now well established. Isotopic and organic chemical methods are just beginning to have impacts. The microscopic analysis of use-traces is increasingly applied. Determining past usage from the analysis of residues in ceramics and on the working edges of tools, and the life histories of people and their animals from isotopic and related studies (Bocherens *et al.* 2000) is just beginning. Studies of ancient DNA from remains from ancient Iran are still in the future. All these approaches require that archaeologists carefully recover the required samples and send them to appropriate laboratories.

None of these new (and often expensive) approaches, however, will help us to understand past cultural processes, unless we think imaginatively and clearly about history and culture and ask useful questions. Few projects both carefully designed and methodologically innovative have been attempted and brought to final publication anywhere in south-west Asia. For the fourth millennium BC, the Arslantepe project (Frangipane 2007) stands as an example of clear thought and imaginative use of a diversity of methods we should all emulate.

Notes

1   No well-preserved *Terminal Suse Phase* localities have been excavated and reported, so a surface collection from KS-269, a small unnamed site without later occupation (Wright *et al.* 1975: 137–39, 143, 147) is used to exemplify these ceramics. Inclusions have been geologically identified under low magnification; Diameters in centimetres are approximated with a concentric circle chart, and colours are taken with a Munsell colour chart just under the exterior surface. Mr. Munsell's un-imaginative colour terminology has been followed.

2   These ceramic observations and those illustrated on Figure 4.7 are from the author's Acropole III sounding, initiated under the aegis of the Délégation Archéologique Française en Iran during the autumn of 1978, but so far not completed (Wright 1985).

3   It is notable, however, that there are few *Early Uruk* sherds in the surface collections, and recent excavations by Abbas Alizadeh (personal communication) have found no *in situ Early Uruk* ceramics.

4   This is an assumption fraught with difficulties (see Postgate 1994 for a very guarded view), and which ignores people living in nomad camps.

5   The illustrated *Middle Uruk* ceramics, to be discussed at length in the forthcoming monograph on the 1971 excavations at Tepe Sharafabad, are identified by locus and specimen numbers detailed in this forthcoming text. The "Uruk Dump" loci, stratified deposits east and west of a large wall, have parallels with *Early Uruk* ceramics and are thought to be earlier. The "Uruk Pit" loci, a stratified deposit covering two and a half years (Wright *et al.* 1981), have some features that presage *Late Uruk* ceramics and are thought to be later. The collections are housed in the University of Michigan Museum of Anthropology.

6   The *Late Uruk* pottery illustrations are based on sherds housed in the University of Michigan Museum of Anthropology, as indicated by the five digit UMMA numbers.

Bibliography

Abdi, Kamyar. 2003. "The Early Development of Pastoralism in the Central Zagros Mountains" *Journal of World Prehistory* 17: 395–448.

Adams, R. McC. 1981. *The Heartland of Cities*, University of Chicago Press, Chicago.

Adams, R. McC. and Nissen, H. J. 1972. *The Uruk Countryside*, University of Chicago Press, Chicago.

Alden, J. R. 1982. "Trade and Politics in Proto-Elamite Iran", *Current Anthropology* 23: 613–640.

Alden, J. R. 2003. "Excavations at Tal-e Kureh" in Sumner, W. M. (ed.), *Early Urban Life in the Land of Anshan*, University Museum of Archaeology and Anthropology, Philadelphia: 187–98.

Algaze, G. 1993. *The Uruk World System*, University of Chicago Press, Chicago.

Algaze, G. 2008. *Ancient Mesopotamia at the Dawn of Civilization*, University of Chicago Press, Chicago.

Alizadeh, A. 2008. *Chogha Mish II: Final Report on the Last Six Seasons of Excavation, 1972–1978*, David Brown Books, Oakville.

Alizadeh, A. 2010. "The rise of the Elamite state in southwestern Iran: 'Enclosed' or enclosing nomadism", *Current Anthropology* 51/3: 353–83.

Alizadeh, A., Kouchoukos, N. J., Wilkinson, T. J., Bauer, A. and Mashkour, M. 2004. "Human-environment interactions on the upper Khuzestan plains, Southwest Iran", *Paléorient* 30: 69–88.

Amiet, P. 1972. "La glyptique susienne des origines à l'époque des Perses achéménides", Mémoires de la Délégation Archéologique en Iran XLIII, Paul Geuthner, Paris.

Bocherens, H., Mashkour, M. and Billiou, D. 2000. "Palaeoenvironmental and archaeological implications of isotopic analyses (13C, 15N) from Neolithic to present in Qazvin Plain (Iran)", *Environmental Archaeology* 5: 1–19.

Caldwell, J. R. 1968. "Tell-i Ghazir", in *Reallexikon der Assyriologie und Vorderasiatische Archeologie* III: 349–55.

Dahl, J. L. 2009. "Early writing in Iran: a re-appraisal", *Iran* 7: 23–31

Damerow, P. and Englund R. K. 1989. *The Proto-Elamite Texts from Tepe Yahya*, Bulletin 39: American School of Prehistoric Research, Peabody Museum of Archaeology and Ethnology, Cambridge MA.

Delougaz, P. and Kantor, H. J. 1996. *Chogha Mish Volume I: The First Five Seasons of Excavations 1961–1971*, edited by Alizadeh, A., Oriental Institute Publications 101, Oriental Institute, Chicago.

Dewar, R. E. 1994. "Changing Population Patterns during the Early Phases of Occupation on the Deh Luran Plain", in Neely, J. A. and Wright, H. T. (eds), *Early Settlement and Irrigation on the Deh Luran Plain: Village and Early State Societies in South-western Iran*, Technical Report of the University of Michigan Museum of Anthropology No. 26, Ann Arbor: 200–11.

Dollfus, G. 1971. «Les fouilles à Djaffarabad de 1969 à 1971», *CDAFI* 1 : 17–81.

Djmali, M., Beaulieu, J-L., Miller, N. F., Andrieu-Ponel, V., Ponel, P., Lak, R., Sadeddin, N., Akhani, H. and Fazeli, H. 2009. "Vegetation history of the SE section of the Zagros Mountains during the last five millennia; a pollen record from the Maharlou Lake, Fars Province, Iran, *Vegetation, History and Archaeobotany* 18/1: 123–36.

Dyson, R. H. 1966. *Excavations on the Acropole of Susa and the Problems of Susa A, B, and C,* Ph.D. dissertation, Harvard University.

Frangipane, M. ed. 2007. *Arslantepe-cretulae: An Early Centralised Administrative System Before Writing,* Università di Roma "La Sapienza", Dipartimento di Scienze Storiche Archeologiche e Antropologiche dell'Antichità, Rome.

Goulder, J. 2010. "Administrators' bread: an experiment-based re-assessment of the functional and cultural role of the Uruk bevel-rim bowl", *Antiquity* 84: 351–62.

Hole, F. 1980. "The Prehistory of herding: some suggestions from ethnography". in Barrelet, M. T. (ed.), *L'Archéologie de L'Iraq du début de l'époque néolithique a 333 avant notre ère,* Editions de la Centre Nationale de la Recherche Scientifique, Paris: 119–30.

Hole, F. 1983. "Symbols of religion and social organization at Susa", in Young Jr, T. C., Smith, P. E. L. and Mortensen, P. (eds), *The Hilly Flanks and Beyond,* Studies in Ancient Oriental Civilization No. 36, the Oriental Institute of the University of Chicago, Chicago: 313–33.

Johnson, G. A. 1973. *Local Exchange and Early State Development in South-western Iran,* Anthropological Paper of the Museum of Anthropology, University of Michigan No. 51, Ann Arbor.

Johnson, G. A. 1976. "Early State Organization in South-western Iran", in Bagherzadeh, F. (ed.), *Proceedings of the IVth Annual Symposium on Archaeological Research in Iran,* Centre for Archaeological Research in Iran, Tehran: 190–224.

Johnson, G. A. 1987. "The changing organization of Uruk administration on the Susiana Plain", in Hole, F. (ed.), *The Archaeology of Western Iran,* Smithsonian Institution Press, Washington DC: 107–140.

Johnson, G. A. 1989. "Late Uruk in Greater Mesopotamia: expansion or collapse?", *Origini* 14: 595–611.

Le Brun, A. 1971. "Recherches stratigraphiques à l'acropole de Suse, 1969–71", *CDAFI* I: 163–216.

Le Brun, A. 1978. "Le Niveau 17B de L'Acropole de Suse (Campagne de 1972)", *CDAFI* 9: 57–154.

Le Brun, A. 1980. "Les écuelles grossières: état de la question", in Barrelet, M. T. (ed.), *L'archéologie de l'Iraq,* Éditions du Centre National de la Recherche Scientifique, Paris: 59–70.

Le Brun, A. 1985. "Le Niveau 18 de l'Acropole de Suse: mémoire d'argile, mémoire du temps», *Paléorient* 11/2: 31–36.

McCall, B. 2009. *The Mamasani Archaeological Survey: Long Term Settlement Patterns in the Mamasani District of the Zagros Mountains, Fars Province, Iran,* unpublished Ph.D. thesis, University of Sydney.

Moghaddam, A. and Miri, N. 2007. "Archaeological surveys in the "Eastern Corridor", South-western Iran", *Iran* 45: 23–55.

Mudar, K. 1988. "The effects of context on bone assemblages: examples from the Uruk Period in South-western Iran", *Paléorient* 14: 151–68.

Neely, J. A. 1994. "Changing Water management and Irrigation during the early phases of occupation on the Deh Luran Plain", in Neely, J. A. and Wright, H. T. (eds), *Early Settlement and Irrigation on the Deh Luran Plain: Village and Early State Societies in South-western Iran,* Technical Report of the University of Michigan Museum of Anthropology No. 26, Ann Arbor: 183–200.

Neely, J. A. and Wright, H. T. 1994. *Early Settlement and Irrigation on the Deh Luran Plain: Village and Early State Societies in South-western Iran,* Technical Report of the University of Michigan Museum of Anthropology No. 26, Ann Arbor.

Petrie, C. A., Asgari-Chaverdi, A. and Seyedin, M. 2009. "Excavations at Tol-e Spid" in Potts, D. T., Roustaei, K., Petrie, C. A. and Weeks, L. R. (eds), *The Mamasani Archaeological Project Stage One: A report on the first two seasons of the ICAR – University of Sydney Joint Expedition to the Mamasani District, Fars Province, Iran,* Archaeopress, Oxford: 89–134.

Pittman, H. 1994. *The glazed steatite glyptic style: the structure and function of an image system in the administration of protoliterate Mesopotamia,* D. Reimer, Berlin.

Pollock, S. M. 1999. *Ancient Mesopotamia: The Eden that Never Was,* Cambridge University Press, Cambridge.

Pollock, S. M. 2008. "Rubbish, routines, and practice: chipped stone blades from Uruk Period Sharafabad, Iran", *Iran* 46: 43–66.

Postgate, J. N. 1994. "How Many Sumerians per hectare?", *Cambridge Archaeological Journal* 4: 47–65.

Potts, D. T. 2001. *Excavations at Tepe Yahya, Iran 1967–1975: the Third Millennium,* American School of Prehistoric Research Bulletin 45, Peabody Museum of Archaeology and Ethnology, Cambridge, Mass.

Potts, D. T. 2009. "Bevel-Rim Bowls and Bakeries: Evidence and Explanations from Iran and the Indo-Iranian Borderlands", *JCS* 61: 1–23.

Redding, R. W. 1979. "Faunal Remains from Tappeh Zabarjad" in Wright, H. T. (ed.), *Archaeological Investigations in Northeastern Xuzestan, 1976,* University of Michigan Museum of Anthropology Technical Report No. 10, Ann Arbor: 87–93.

Rothman, M. ed. 2001. *Uruk Mesopotamia and Its Neighbors,* School of American Research, Santa Fe.

Sajjadi, M. 1979. "The Proto-Elamite period on the Izeh Plain" in Wright, H. T. (ed.), *Archaeological Investigations in Northeastern Xuzestan, 1976,* University of Michigan, Museum of Anthropology Technical Report No. 10, Ann Arbor: 93–98.

Schacht, R. 1980. "Two models of population growth", *American Anthropologist* 82: 782–798.

Shahideh, E. 1979. "The Susiana period on the Izeh Plain" in Wright, H. T. (ed.), *Archaeological Investigations in Northeastern Xuzestan, 1976,* University of Michigan, Museum of Anthropology Technical Report No. 10, Ann Arbor: 50–58.

Stève, M-J. and Gasche, H. 1971. *L'Acropole de Suse: Nouvelles Fouilles,* MDAI XLVI, Brill, Leiden/Geuthner, Paris.

Stevens, L. R., Ito, E., Schwalb, A. and Wright Jr, H. E. 2006. "Timing of atmospheric precipitation in the Zagros Mountains inferred from a multi-proxy record from Lake Mirabad, Iran", *Quaternary Research* 66: 494–500.

Stolper, M. W. 1985. "Proto-Elamite texts from Tall-i Malyan" *Kadmos* 24: 1–12.

Sumner, W. M. 1988. "Prelude to proto-Elamite Anshan: the Lapui Phase", *IA* 23: 23–44.

Sumner, W. M. 1994. "The evolution of tribal society in the southern Zagros mountains, Iran" in Stein, G. and Rothman, M. (eds), *Chiefdoms and Early States in the Near East,* Prehistory Press, Madison: 47–65.

Sumner, W. M. 2003. *Early Urban Life in the Land of Anshan: Excavations at Tal-e Malyan in the Highlands of Iran,* Malyan

Excavation Reports Vol. III, Philadelphia, University of Pennsylvania Museum.

Vallat, F. 1978. "Les documents épigraphiques de l'Acropole (1969–71", *CDAFI* 1: 235–245.

Vallat, F. 1980. *Suse et l'Elam*, Éditions de l'Association pour la Diffusion de la Pensée Française, Paris.

Van der Leeuw, S. E. 1994. "The pottery from a Middle-Uruk dump at Tepe Sharafabad, Iran. A technological study", in Binder, D. and Courtin, J. (eds), *Terre cuite et société: la céramique, document technique, économique, culturel. Actes des XIV rencontres internationales d'archéologie et d'histoire d'Antibes, 21–23 octobre 1993*. Éditions APDCA, Juan- les-Pins: 269–301.

Weeks, L. R., Alizadeh, K. S., Niakan, L., Alamdari, K., Khosrowzadeh, A. and Zeidi, M. 2009. "Excavations at Tol-e Nurabad" in Potts, D. T., Roustaei, K., Petrie, C. A. and Weeks, L. R. (eds), *The Mamasani Archaeological Project Stage One: A report on the first two seasons of the ICAR – University of Sydney Joint Expedition to the Mamasani District, Fars Province, Iran*, Archaeopress, Oxford: 31–88.

Wright, H. T. 1979. "The Uruk Period on the Izeh Plain and Excavations at Tappeh Zabarjad", in Wright, H. T. (ed.), *Archaeological Investigations in Northeastern Xuzestan, 1976*, University of Michigan Museum of Anthropology Technical Report No. 10, Ann Arbor: 59–87.

Wright, H. T. ed. 1981. *An Early Town on the Deh Luran Plain: Excavations at Tepe Farukhabad*, Memoir No. 13, Museum of Anthropology, University of Michigan, Ann Arbor.

Wright, H. T. 1985. "Excavations of IVth Millennium levels on the Northern Acropolis of Suse, 1978", *National Geographic Research Reports* 21: 725–34.

Wright, H. T. 1987. "The Susiana hinterlands during the era of primary state formation," in Hole, F. (ed.), *Archaeological Perspectives on Western Iran*, Smithsonian Institution Press, Washington: 141–55.

Wright, H. T. 1994. "Pre-state political formations", in Stein, G. and Rothman, M. (eds), *Chiefdoms and Early States in the Near East*, Prehistory Press, Madison: 67–84 [Reprinted with correction from Earle, T. K. (ed.), 1982. *The Evolution of Complex Societies: The Harry Hojier Lectures for 1982*, Undena Press, Malibu].

Wright, H. T. 1998. "Uruk States in south-western Iran", in Feinman, G. and Marcus, J. (eds), *Archaic States*, School of American Research Press, Santa Fe: 171–97.

Wright, H. T. 2001. "Cultural action in the Uruk world", in Rothman, M. (ed.), *Uruk Mesopotamia and Its Neighbours*, School of American Research, Santa Fe: 123–47.

Wright, H. T. and Rupley, E. S. A. 2001. "Calibrated radiocarbon age determinations of Uruk-related assemblages", in Rothman, M. (ed.). *Uruk Mesopotamia and Its Neighbours*, School of American Research, Santa Fe: 85–122.

Wright, H. T., Redding, R. and Miller, N. 1981. "Time and process in an Uruk rural community", Barrelet, M-T. (ed.), *L'Archéologie de l'Iraq*, Colloque International 560 du Centre National de la Recherche Scientifique, Paris: 265–89.

Wright, H. T., Redding, R. and Pollock, S. M. 1989. "Monitoring interannual variability: an example from the period of early state development in southwestern Iran", in O'Shea, J. and Halstead, P. (eds), *Bad Year Economics*, Cambridge University Press, Cambridge: 106–13.

Wright, H. T., Neely, J. A., Johnson, G. A. and Speth, J. D. 1975. "Early fourth millennium developments in southwestern Iran", *Iran* XIII: 129–47.

5. INTERPRETING THE ROLE OF GODIN TEPE IN THE "URUK EXPANSION"

Mitchell S. Rothman

Introduction

Two themes have dominated the scholarly discussion of what has been described as Greater Mesopotamia in the fourth millennium BC. One is the origin of complexity, often framed as the origin of the state, the other is the nature of interactions across the region; specifically, how exchange relationships affected the evolutionary trajectory of societies in a number of ecologically distinct, geographically separate areas within the Greater Mesopotamian region. That region, in addition to the alluvium of southern Iraq and south-western Iran, includes south-eastern and eastern Turkey, western Iran, North Syria, and northern Iraq; that is, areas traversed by the Tigris and Euphrates Rivers and their tributaries (Fig. 5.1).

The first theme primarily found its inspiration in the work of Henry Wright and his students (Wright H. T. 1977, 1994, 1998; Wright H. T. and Johnson 1975; Johnson 1973; see Rothman 2004). The latter resulted from a theory propounded by Guillermo Algaze, first in his Ph.D. dissertation (1986), then in a series of books and articles (1989, 1993, 2001, 2005, 2008; see Rothman 2001; Wright 1995).

The artefactual pattern that underlies Algaze's theory is easy to describe. A distinctive artefactual corpus, associated with the *Uruk* culture phenomenon, dominated the alluvial plains of southern Iraq and south-western Iran (Fig. 5.2). The societies in the north and east of Greater Mesopotamia had styles of artefacts, especially pottery, collectively called *Late Chalcolithic*, which were clearly different from those of the *Uruk*. After approximately 3600 BC, southern *Uruk* pottery styles began to appear in an area from the northern steppes into the lower mountain ranges of the Taurus and Zagros, at local *Late Chalcolithic* sites. *Late Uruk* or *LC5* sites like Habuba Kabira and Jebel Aruda, built in previously underpopulated areas of North Syria, were uniformly *Uruk* in terms of their material cultural assemblage. Northern sites with

Uruk pottery appeared to be located in a dendritic pattern along one of two major north–south routes following the beds of the Euphrates and Tigris rivers. Therefore, Algaze interprets sites both newly founded and pre-existing with significant *Uruk* pottery as part of an "Uruk expansion" network of trade. The assumption is that the highly developed city states of southern Mesopotamia set up colonies or, at more remote places in the resource-extracting areas, outposts to trade for or take the raw materials needed for the purposes of these otherwise resource-poor southern states.

Algaze (2008: 95) lists as fourth-millennium trade items "(1) pine used as roofing timber; (2) copper, silver, lead, and gold used as tools, weapons, and jewelery […]; (3) precious stones such as lapis, carnelian, agate, chalcedony, amazonite, amethyst, aragonite, and jasper […]; (4) semi-precious stones such as chlorite, obsidian, rock crystal, quartz, alabaster, gypsum, marble, diorite, serpentine, and bituminous limestone […]; (5) common stones such as basalt, flint, and obsidian […]; (6) bitumen […]; and (7) valuable liquids such as wine." Some believe that in the fourth millennium BC wool appropriate for spinning into yarn was not grown on every variety of sheep. Highland sheep had longer strands of wool appropriate for weaving and therefore wool might also have been imported into the south (Anthony 2007: 60ff.). This is especially important, because one of the proposed trade goods manufactured in large, specialised workshops in the south was a particularly fine wool cloth (Algaze 1993). Wine, which apparently originated in the South Caucasus, was evidenced in a number of sites including Godin Tepe.

This argument is essentially about the movement of goods and how they affected the economy and, based on that, the socio-political organisation and identities of peoples in different environmental and geographical nature of the broader region (see Petrie

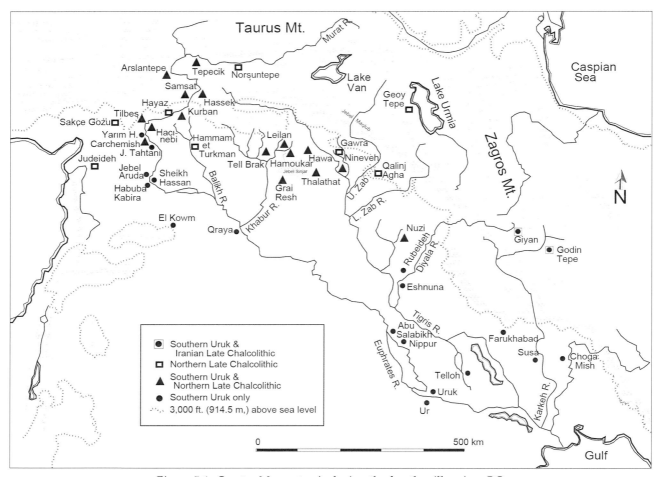

Figure 5.1. Greater Mesopotamia during the fourth millennium BC.

Introduction for a discussion of the geography). The emphasis in this chapter will be largely on those aspects as they relate to a site in the central western Zagros, Godin Tepe. The natural environment of agricultural production and the topography of this region are also essential factors. The societies of the southern alluvium were in need of resources, because that area is basically a silt-filled basin formed by run-off from the Tigris and Euphrates rivers. The northern steppe and especially the two adjoining mountain fronts are essentially different. They consist of mountain valleys and piedmont plains. Their agriculture was supported by rainfall, not irrigation as in the south, but arable land within those valleys was at a premium. This limited the potential size of population, and the potential for surplus production, which are both important factors in a number of schemes of cultural evolution (Rothman 1994; Sanders *et al.* 1979).

In addition, as Algaze (2008) has argued, transportation – in the case of the southern alluvium via easy, efficient canal routes – is one key to economic development and, coupled with that, social elaboration. The same can be said for the proposed *Uruk* expansion. Stein (1999b) has proposed that the distance needed

to travel for trade limited the control possible by southern bureaucrats, but ease and cost of transport are equally important. Arslantepe and the northern steppe were prominent in the *Early Uruk* expansion, as were Habuba Kabira and Jebel Aruda in the later phases, in part because of the ease of transport down the Euphrates River. Rowton (1967) located the source of large logs for southern construction in this northern area for this very reason. The central western Zagros is another matter altogether. As Xenophon and other generals who sought to conquer or pass through this area lamented, it is hard to cross even in the most propitious season (Rothman 2011a). In the winter snows it is all but impossible. The reason southern Mesopotamians established a more intense interaction with the central western Zagros later than with the Upper Euphrates Basin may well be transport issues. So, too, the resources tapped from the central western Zagros must have been more limited in physical size. Large wine jugs or wooden logs are likely to have been too difficult and costly to transport. Metal ores, wool, and precious and semi-precious stones may thus have been more practical. These highland Iranian areas may equally have served as transport depots for goods coming from even farther away, such as lapis

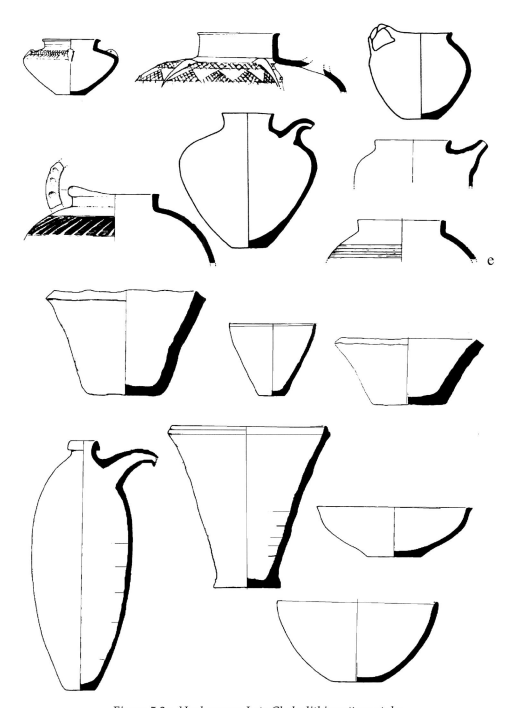

Figure 5.2a. Uruk versus Late Chalcolithic pottery styles.

lazuli, only found in Badakshan, Afghanistan, whose transport routes passed through these highland areas. Herrmann (1968) writes that the lapis trade in the earlier parts of the fourth millennium BC passed through the north piedmont at sites such as Tepe Gawra, but shifted south through Susa, which would require a central Zagros route.

The cities of the southern alluvium grew, as Algaze now argues (2008), because of the production and exchange of finished products, first locally and then regionally. Older exchange networks no longer sufficed. Those older networks are usually described as down-the-line exchange (Renfrew 1977; Renfrew *et al.* 1969), in which people nearest the source extract material, retain some raw materials and pass some on to nearby settlements. The people at those secondary sites save a percentage of what is now a smaller amount, and pass some on to their closest neighbours. As one goes farther down the line from the source area ever decreasing amounts of the particular material

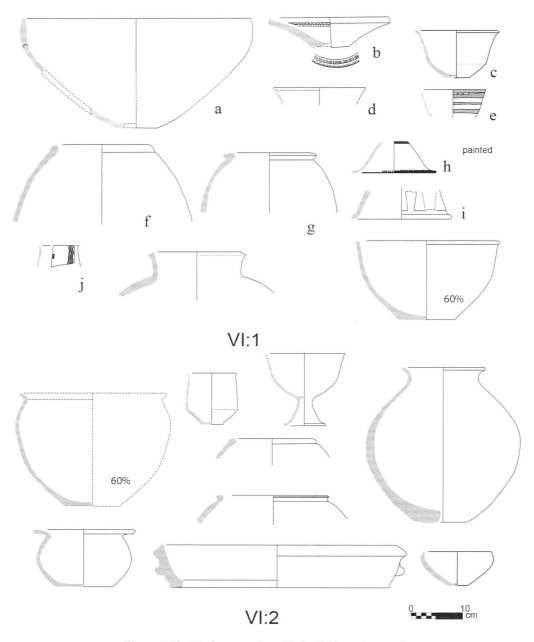

VI:1

VI:2

Figure 5.2b. Uruk versus Late Chalcolithic pottery styles.

are found. Algaze proposes that the trading system called the *Uruk expansion* represents direct interaction with the resource extracting areas with the aim of capturing larger quantities of material for direct transport to the ultimate destination, one of the city states of the south. Algaze (1993, 2008) has argued that these colonies and outposts were operated by people who came from the south.

In this explanatory model, Godin Tepe should be one of the outposts. This multi-period site sits at the centre of the Kangavar Valley in central western Iran, astride one of the "choke points" on the main north–south Zagros intermontane route. This same route would later constitute a section of the Great Silk Route. With its unique oval enclosure at the high point of the mound, Godin Tepe is one of a small number of extensively excavated sites with significant fourth-millennium BC deposits in the central western Zagros. The others are Baba Jan and Tepe Giyan. The former has little to report on the period, and the latter suffered much damage over the last century. Whereas Tepe Giyan's seals and sealings represent stylistic connections within the Zagros and onto the north-east piedmont of modern Iraq, their full context is missing (Caldwell 1976). Godin Tepe, on the other hand, had numerical tablets, seals, and Uruk pottery types that would seem to link it to the southern Mesopotamian world.

Algaze (1993: 53ff.) classifies Godin Tepe as an Uruk outpost. As he writes (1993: 53):

"the site is strategically located in the southeastern corner of the Kangavar Valley, near a natural entrance cut by the Gamas Ab River. On the highest point, a small fortified outpost of the Uruk Period (Godin V [*sic* VI:1]) has been excavated. Surrounding this fort was a larger indigenous settlement (Godin VI [*sic* VI:1]). The fort itself was built in non-Uruk style that conformed to local highland canons, and a significant proportion of pottery contained within was also of local style and manufacture (about 50%). Nevertheless, a wide range of typical Uruk artefacts was found within the structure…. These intrusive elements and the commanding position of the fortified structure in which they were found have been interpreted to signify the presence of actual foreigners at the site, presumed to be merchants from Susa by the excavators (Weiss and Young 1975)…What is unquestionable is that whoever held the fort at the very top of the Godin mound controlled also an important link along the Khorasan Road, which allowed access from the Diyala Valley into the Iranian central plateau and points east."

After completing the reanalysis and publication of Godin Tepe (Rothman and Badler 2011) the questions being asked here, and also by Matthews in the current volume are, was the Oval Compound occupied by foreigners and what was its function? Was it a production, storage or military stronghold? Furthermore, it is important to consider what this says about the *Uruk expansion* in general and about Godin Tepe in particular.

T. Cuyler Young found Godin Tepe during a survey in 1961, and his primary interest in digging the site was the Iron Age levels (Gopnik 2011). His first sounding in 1965 (Operation B), however, revealed the sites' deep history (Young and Levine 1969, 1974). Near the end of the season in 1971, Young's team uncovered the northern edge of the Oval Compound (hereafter 'Oval') in what was then called period V. The Oval yielded some artefacts clearly of the lowland Uruk tradition among many artefacts associated with the highland zone. The final 1973 season was dedicated to clearing the Oval and rather quickly digging two deeper soundings: XYZ near the north wall of the Oval compound; and the Brick Kiln Cut down the slope of the mound. From these sounding operations it became clear that Godin had a much deeper history than even the 1965 trenches had revealed.

Periodisation

The dating and nomenclature of the fourth-millennium BC levels at Godin has changed considerably over time. The initial attempt was based on the 1965 Area B sounding when Young (2004), by his own admission, made the mistake of believing the local VI pottery ended when he found some typical *Uruk* pottery. Various graduate students worked on different levels of the site, and Virginia Badler (2002) created

a relative chronology based on the 1965 sounding. As I "lived" with the field notes during their reanalysis for the final publication, the flaws in the excavation and recording became quite clear. Elevations were rarely taken and most times natural strata were not followed; rather, absolute "spits" or trenches dug parallel or perpendicular to walls to varying depths made it impossible to verify whether Badler's seriation was plausible. For example, she makes distinctions between levels, such as 19, 20, and 21. In parts of the sounding these were stratigraphically distinct. In other parts they were not, and levels were often assigned *ex post facto*, even though sherds from all three 'strata' were stored as one unit in the same bag. When Virginia Badler, Cuyler Young, and I began to plan the Godin VI/IV volume that became part of the final book and web archive (Gopnik and Rothman 2011), the rational answer was clear. The beginning of the fourth millennium BC was level VII by relative chronology, and level VI began not long after, distinguished from VII by the percentages of painted wares. In Godin VI, painted pottery all but disappeared. Fast wheel pottery techniques represented by string-cut bases and *Uruk* trays began to appear before buildings were enclosed by the Oval's wall (Rothman and Badler 2011). When the buildings were surrounded by the Oval's wall, functional types were replaced by either new local forms or lowland *Uruk* shapes and wares. Logic told us that dividing Godin VI into three levels made sense: Godin VI:3, the continuation of VII; Godin VI:2, before the oval wall was built when some lowland *Uruk* types appeared; and Godin VI:1, the period when the Oval was walled and many more *Uruk* types appeared (Young 2004; Rothman and Badler 2011). Badler continues to argue for a VI:1A and B in the Oval. In her favour, there was evidence of the blocking-off of some doorways and the building of a wall in the courtyard, whose shape and purpose is nonetheless hard to explain. In my opinion, however, sorting out the relative position of associated floors is all but impossible. There remain no clear criteria for drawing reliable conclusions about what should be in A and what in B across the Oval.

Theories of occupation of the Oval

In 1975, Young and his then student assistant, Harvey Weiss, wrote an article entitled, "Merchants of Susa: Godin V and plateau-lowland relations in the late fourth millennium B.C.". In it they claimed that the Oval was a colony of lowland traders from Susa. In a sense they presaged the theories of Algaze, quoted above. Badler (2002) called it a fort for local people, based on the presence of weapons in the Oval and because of its thick walls.

If we are to answer questions as to what the functions of the Oval were and who occupied it, we first have to examine the evidence for the nature of the interaction with lowland polities. This is at the heart of Algaze's model. His assumption, and the assumption of World Systems theorists in general, is that the societies of the core controlled the behaviour of the peripheries. Furthermore, the so-called peripheral societies theoretically lack any centralised institutions of their own. In fact, analytically they are not independent societies at all: "the fundamental unit of social change is the world-system and not the society" (Hall and Chase-Dunn 1996: 11–12).

Other societies in the Mesopotamian periphery contradict this idea. For example, Arslantepe (Frangipane 2007) not only had developed very sophisticated redistributive networks with centralised control, but the long evolutionary pathways leading to this societal level were apparent before any evidence of significant contact with the Mesopotamian south. Other societies of the *LC/Uruk* period show similar developments, such as at Tepe Gawra (Rothman 2002) and Hacınebi (Stein 1999a).

The focus here is the pottery, seals, and sealings (see also Matthews, this volume). If there was enough contact to have affected the highland sites significantly, we should see it archaeologically and be able to trace its routes. The heart of such an analysis is style and organisational technology. In our effort to distance ourselves from a simple "pots equal people" formulation that typified an older culture of historical archaeology, we have at times thrown the metaphorical baby out with the bathwater. In the ancient, as in the modern world symbols encoded in style are meaningful indicators of common identity, the intensity of intra-group interaction, and the nature of cross-cultural contact. From flags to dress and household goods to public symbols, groups distinguish themselves from one another by use of artefact style, and ethnic behaviours like food choice and preparation. At the same time, the globalisation of the world shows the adoption of "foreign" symbols – British china in colonial India, or Western business suits in Nigeria – sometimes as markers of status, at times necessities of doing business.

The case of the third-millennium BC *Ninevite V* is illustrative. As the older *Uruk* system declined, nascent leadership groups in the so-called periphery regrouped into new polities. In the *Ninevite V* area, initially this change was marked by a readoption of *'Ubaid*-style painted designs in contrast to the western *Plain Simple Wares*, *Scarlet Wares* of the Iran-Iraq front, *Jezirah painted ware*, and *Jemdet Nasr ware* (Rothman and Fuensanta 2003). The fourth millennium BC contained the seeds of the local developments in the third millennium BC; it is exemplified by a series of style zones of this period. Already mentioned were the *Uruk* and *Late Chalcolithic*, but the *Late Chalcolithic*

is far from uniform. Northern Mesopotamia tended to be split into eastern and western zones, and again into mountain and lowland zones (Rothman 2001).

In the central western Zagros, the local pottery traditions are called Godin VI after the terminology used for the Godin and Kangavar survey. Godin VI:2, when a very limited number of *Uruk* techniques were used and *Uruk* pottery types (bevel-rim bowls, string-cut bases, and *Uruk* trays) were present, has a number of parallels in the area that place it in the Santa Fe LC 3 and 4 periods (Rothman 2001; Rothman and Badler 2011: 90–91). Local Godin VI pottery has a considerable distribution in the area of Kangavar, Hamadan, Malayer, and Nehavand (see Fig. 5.3). E. Henrickson (1994) calls the related material in the western Zagros *Attenuated VI*. As evidenced in the following Godin IV period, there are some forms of cultural borders between the Mahidasht Valley to the west and Fars Province some distance to the south-east (Levine and Young 1986). When mapped, finds of clearly *Uruk* pottery styles in the highlands of the central western Zagros follow the established routes up the Diyala River through the Mahidasht to Kangavar. It is also possible that they came via the Susiana Plains up the Karkeh River or some similar route (Fig. 5.3). I would propose that the logic behind this pattern is that contacts with the southern alluvium did not represent a widespread interaction of high- and lowland, but a directed route towards resource areas along the precursors of the Great Silk Road. In this respect, Algaze's idea that contact in Iran represented trade may be valid.

His ideas about Godin Tepe representing a southern outpost manned by southerners are, however, not supported. The pottery tested using instrumental neutron activation analysis (Blackman 2011) were all made of local clays, and the style of these *Uruk* pieces have local Godin VI elements, indicating that they were made by a local *Uruk* potter or, more likely, were copies made by a local potter. Badler (2002) has pointed out that the cooking pots in the Oval were of local highland style. This contrasts with the trading group at Hacınebi (Stein 1999a, 1999b), where *Uruk* cooking pots and butchering techniques were used. The ceramic evidence therefore suggests that there is no direct evidence of a physical presence of southern people in any significant numbers at Godin. To that extent I agree with Matthews' assessment (this volume) that the Oval was utilised by local people. As you will read below, however, there are some ways in which I disagree with Matthews, particularly with regard to seals and sealings. In any case, the conclusion that southerners did not live in the Oval undercuts Algaze's hypothesis that Godin Tepe was an outpost of a southern city state in which the southern administrators lived.

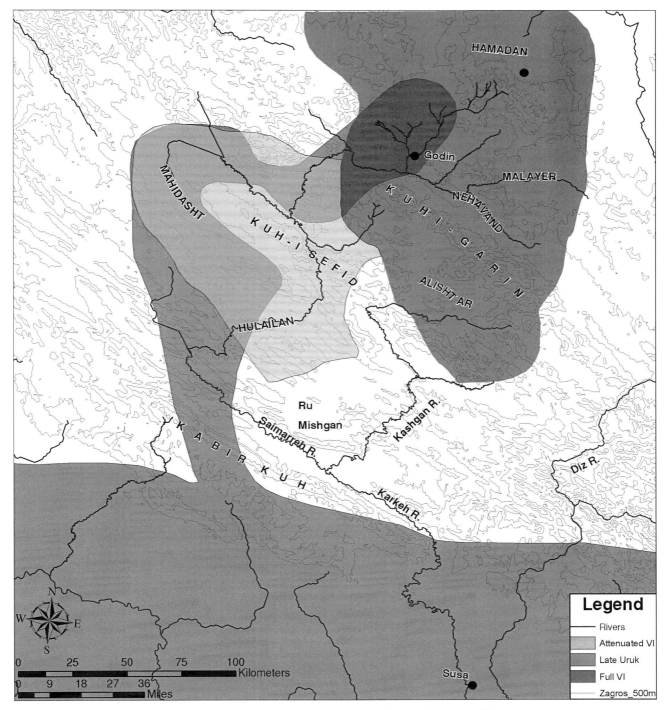

Figure 5.3. Distribution of pottery styles in the central western Zagros.

The Oval

The latest and most important set of buildings in use during Godin VI are those within the Oval's wall (Figs 5.4 and 5.5; Rothman and Badler 2011). This compound consists of a group of structures around a central courtyard placed at what would have been the high point of the mound. The compound encompasses an area of approximately 560 m² of a 15 ha mound surface (or 5.6%). The structures within the wall can be divided into separate buildings composed of adjoining rooms. The Oval was ultimately abandoned and what remained was preserved in fairly good context. Area 21 and room 22 in the north-east corner of the compound were burned.

The Oval contained a series of structures. Most prominent was the Northern Building (rooms 14–20). The remainder included a second not completely excavated building in the east (rooms 22–23), three sealed rooms on the west (rooms 10, 12, and 13), a small building in the south-west (room 6), and an entrance in the south (rooms 2–4). A number of rooms including the north-west corner of the northern building (room 14) were cut away by the construction of the Oval's wall, suggesting therefore that some of the buildings inside it predate the wall. There are three triangular rooms (rooms 5, 10, and 13) that accommodate the curve of the oval wall, which suggests that these rooms were built after the wall. The overall impression is that the builders of the Oval were taking advantage of the limited space available. At the southern end of the Oval, based on the way this additional structure appears to block one side of the entrance door, there may have been an unroofed enclosure, perhaps even for animals. Near the end of the occupation of the Oval, the doorways to rooms 2, 10, 12, and 13 were sealed. The excavators recovered most of the tablets in the Northern Building and the southern entrance rooms.

All of the buildings within the Oval share certain features. Four of the rectangular rooms have interior niches on their long walls (rooms 2, 6, 18, and 22),

and one of these rooms (room 6) also has interior niches on its short walls. Ethnographic parallels suggest that these niches might have been used as storage shelves. Of the 13 completely excavated rooms in the Oval, only five have hearths on their initial floors. Three of the hearths (rooms 17, 18, and 19) are heating fireplaces, while two (rooms 5 and 6) were constructed as cooking hearths, complete with griddles. These may represent living as opposed to storage or public rooms.

The southernmost set of buildings forms an entrance. Visitors or residents would have entered through room 4. One interpretation of where the tablets were concentrated is that material sealed or noted on tablets would have been carried through the gate and checked in with the guard, who would deposit it for future audits on a shelving unit in room 3. Room 5 might have been where guards stayed and possibly cooked meals while on duty. The purpose of room 2 with its bin and remains of a wine jar and eating vessels is not clear. It was closed off near the end of the Oval occupation.

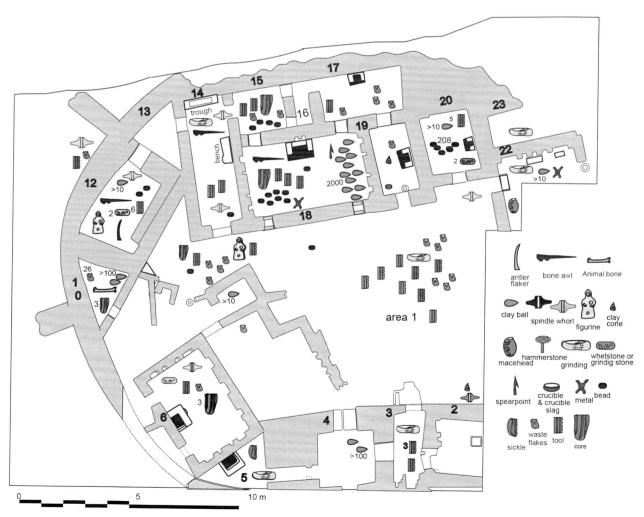

Figure 5.4. Distribution of artefacts in the Godin Oval.

The building most likely to have had a special function is the Northern Building, which consisted of rooms 14–19 and possibly 20 (Figs. 5.4–5.5). The main room, 18, cannot be approached directly from the courtyard. Its two openings to the courtyard are windows, and a visitor would have entered through room 14 or 19 and then gone through room 15 or 17. A deep trough in the rear of room 14 contained 10 discarded tablets, and five tablets lay beside the trough in room 15. The excavators recovered charred lentils near a bench. Room 15 also has a small curtain wall. It creates area 16, which is less than 1 m wide; too small to be a working space, it was possibly a newel wall for a staircase to a second floor over rooms 15 and 17. Against the eastern window of room 18 were a number of large pots, apparently smashed as walls fell in after abandonment. Around them were 1759 small, unfired clay balls and some scattered grain. The room yielded additional groups of less than 100 unfired clay balls, each recovered from the entrance,

room 4, and from room 10. Unbaked clay balls have many uses, including as bobbins or loom weights for weaving, and as clay blanks for softening and then shaping into sealings or tablets. Their association with a metal spear and a mace head in room 22, however, implies that they may have been used as weapons (Rothman and Badler 2011: 99). Rooms 18, 17, and 19 contained large hearths. This is an unusually large number of hearths, which perhaps suggests that this building served a different function than a normal house. Signs of domestic activity did exist, however, including 14 beads, two bone tools, two stone spindle whorls for making yarn, a ground stone quern, two lithic cores (for making blades or used secondarily as a large grinder or hammer), and some blades and flakes.

The pottery from room 18, aside from the storage jars apparently containing the clay balls, consisted of sherds from a set of eating vessels. For Godin VI.1 the small bowl, bevel-rim bowl, and eating tray

Figure 5.5. Distribution of pottery types in the Godin Oval.

appear to constitute an eating set. The bevel-rim bowl replaced an in-turned rim bowl of the previous period. The excavators recovered many fewer bevel-rim bowls than are typically found in LC5 southern Mesopotamian sites, where they appear to have been throwaway ration bowls. Here they are part of an eating set and are of a slightly higher quality than the southern Mesopotamian ones. The great benefit of the southern versions is that they do not need to have been made by skilled potters. Similar sets were recovered in rooms 14, 15, and 18, and the open area 1. Additional sherds found in these areas were parts of serving and storage vessels. Although the hearths are forms that are not usually classified as cooking hearths, a number of sherds classified by Badler as cooking vessels, based on their ware, lay on the floor of the Northern Building.

A person could only enter rooms 13 and 12 from room 14 of the Northern Building. Room 12 had unusually thick walls, which Badler (2002) has previously interpreted as evidence of a safe storeroom. Its contents do indicate that it was a special function room, lacking any potsherds in good context, but with a variety of tools: spindle whorls, beads, a bone awl and horn flaker, a grinding tool, a few clay balls, and a figurine of a woman. This suggests that it was a workroom rather than a storeroom. The presence of three broken sealings implies that materials for the workshop were controlled and accounted for by some local functionary.

In the final days of the Oval's occupation room 10 appears to have been used as a place to deposit trash. Its contents include a blank tablet, an unsealed tablet with three incised wedges, a sealing, an abundance of pottery sherds, several clay balls, a flint core, and many lithic flakes. Also, most of the limited quantities of animal bones found within the Oval were recovered from this room: 11 fragments from cattle, 32 from sheep or goats, and one from a red deer (Crabtree 2011). At the south-western side of the Oval, room 6 appears to constitute a residence. Excavators found the only two cooking hearths in this area, but unfortunately this area was excavated even more quickly than much of the rest of the compound and its finds are badly mixed. Serving bowls, a spindle whorl, a grinder, a quern, lithic tools, and one of the only sickles recovered from the Oval also remained in reasonably good context in this area.

The remaining areas are either only partially excavated or poorly understood. The rooms on the eastern side of the Oval were beyond the baulks. Room 22 had charred grains and legumes on its floor, whether for household stores or part of a larger storeroom for a larger population we cannot know. One possible material stored there was dung for fuel, as barley, wheat, lentil, and weed remains are a typical diet for village sheep and goats. Excavators found a quern, a mace head, a few clay balls, a metal chisel, a sealed numeric tablet, and eating and serving vessels in rooms 22 and 23. Room 20, a thick-walled room separated from all other buildings, yielded one spectacular find (now in Tehran): a necklace of 208 black and 2 white stone beads. The other remains, a hearth, sherds of a wine jar, grinding stones, and lithic blades do not imply any particular set of activities. The artefacts from the open courtyard were mostly lithic blades, flakes and cores, and pottery of the same types as in the rooms, as well as tablets near the entrance to room 14.

Christopher Edens (2002) published a study of the lithics of Godin VI and concluded that there were two lithic industries. One was a flake industry, where flakes were roughly removed from pebbles of chert or flint. They were used as rough cutting implements or were more finely chipped into points, scrapers, or blades. The other industry used much more carefully prepared cores from which finer bifacial Canaanean-type blades were struck. No Canaanean-type blade cores were identified from Godin VI, although excavators did discover some in the following level IV, which was dominated by Kura Araxes people (Rothman 2011b). Edens therefore concluded that the bifacial blades were made elsewhere in the highlands and exchanged with the residents of Godin VI. Similar specialised blade-making workshops have been identified in south-eastern Turkey from the fourth and third millennia BC at Değirmentepe and Titriş Hoyuk. The presence of crucible fragments indicate that a fairly sophisticated metallurgical technology was in use at Godin VI:1 (Frame 2011). At the same time, evidence of metal smelting at Seh Gabi in the *Middle Chalcolithic* period indicates that metallurgy was an old craft in the Kangavar Valley (Hamlin (Kramer) 1974).

Residents of the Oval

The residents of the Oval were apparently locals who lived in the Oval and oversaw a number of possible activities. These include some craft, military, and administrative activities. The tablets (Matthews, this volume) appear to record, among other possibilities, local staple resources being moved into the Oval, audited and possibly stored there. A group with at least coordinating authority would have used it.

What would one expect if Godin were occupied by lowland people? At Habuba Kabira and Jebel Aruda in northern Syria the occupants of newly founded colonies of southern people used the full range of *Uruk* pottery types. Their architecture followed the southern alluvial architectural plans. At Hacınebi, a site in south-eastern Turkey in which a colony of lowland people lived side by side with a local *Late Chalcolithic* population, southern residents also had a full set of *Uruk* pottery types and sealings. They even used the inefficient clay sickles typical of the south, despite being near many good sources of chipping stone. Arslantepe on the Upper Euphrates, on the other hand, was a site that had developed significant administrative and economic centralisation before the *Uruk* expansion (Frangipane and Palmieri 1983; Frangipane 1993, 1994, 1997, 2001, 2007). The excavators found locally made copies of *Uruk* types, although they are a minority (not more than 30%) of all pottery types, and many retained distinctly northern features. A full corpus of *Uruk* types was not present. Similar patterns existed in the Oval at Godin. Outside the Oval in the area of the Brick Kiln Cut (Fig. 5.6) contemporaneous buildings had a few *Uruk* types, but mostly local Godin VI wares, as well as farming and domestic tools. Most of the animal remains from Godin VI phase were found there as well. Crabtree's (2011) analysis of the age of butchering revealed a distribution not of nomadic pastoralists, who preserve their capital and emphasise milk or wool over early butchering. In general it is not a pattern for wool. She describes it as the sort of herding strategy for provisioning a town with meat

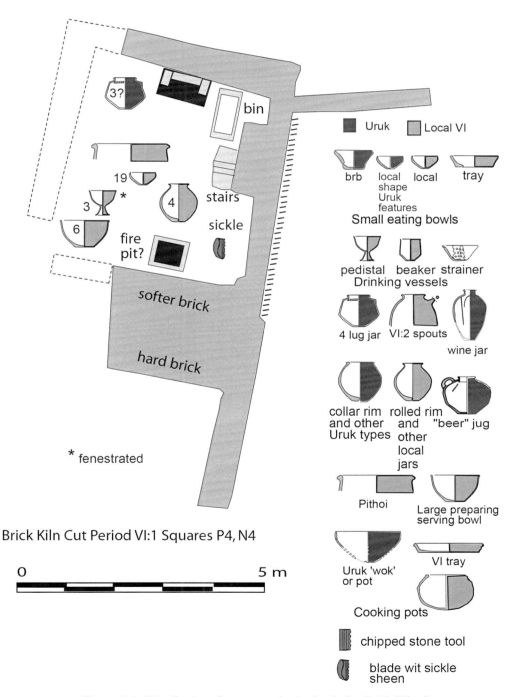

Figure 5.6. *Distribution of pottery styles in the Godin Brick Kiln Cut.*

(Crabtree 2011). Because few animal bones came from the Oval itself, one cannot say whether the Brick Kiln Cut bones were specifically for residents or occupants of the Oval, or for the site in general. What is critical here is that the pattern one would tend to expect for a village or other primary agriculture-producing site appears not to exist here. What the tablets and activities we can document show is that Godin Tepe, certainly by VI:1, had some special functions.

Kangavar survey

A possible central role for Godin Tepe during Period VI can be inferred from the site's place in the settlement pattern of the Kangavar Valley (Fig. 5.7). Godin was by no means an isolated settlement but was part of a local settlement system and connected to larger networks of interaction with the broader *Uruk* and highland worlds. As we saw by mapping the spread of *Uruk* types, that connection followed the "high road".

The settlement data from Period VI paint an interesting picture of what Godin's role might

have been. The problem we face in assessing these settlement data is that only very general ceramic types were collected to date sites. We can distinguish Period VI from Period IV or VII pottery, and we can tell if the presence of bevel-rim bowls places settlement sometime after 3600 and before 3050 BC. In that long span of time, however, individual mounds could have been occupied, abandoned, and reoccupied many times. Within those limits, what settlement data appear to tell us is that Godin was the centre of the Kangavar Valley system in Period VI. The valley is divided into three quite distinct ecological niches: the flood plain, the Velishgird uplands, and the Kangavar hill country. From the time that Godin VII and VI:3 pottery was used, the number and occupied area of mounds increased dramatically (Young 2004). Most of this increase was in the well-watered flood plain (6% of sites and 70% of total occupied area). The settlements in the flood plain clustered toward the south-east. In the Velishgird uplands settlements clustered near the main branch of the Gamas Ab River. As it is less effective for agriculture, the Kangavar hill country has fewer and more scattered sites. Godin surveyors

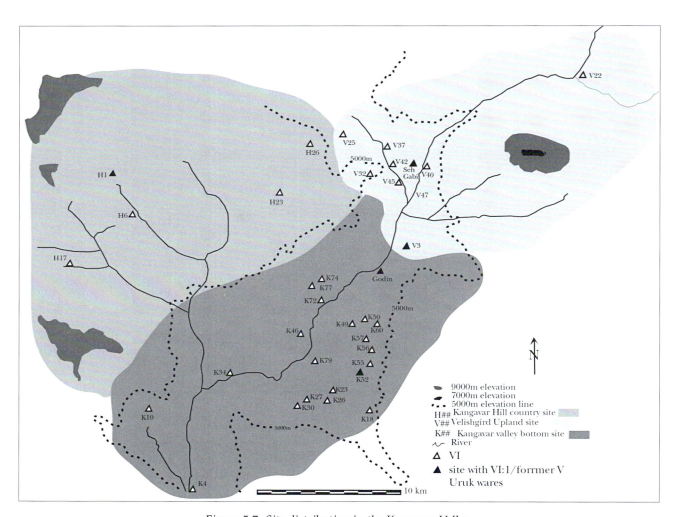

Figure 5.7. Site distribution in the Kangavar Valley.

collected *Uruk* pottery (bevel-rim bowls) from four sites. With the exception of the nearby site labelled V3, the sites with bevel-rim bowls tended to be in the middle of clusters of village sites, perhaps indicating secondary control points (Young 2004). Seh Gabi in the uplands and K52 in the plain are equidistant from Godin, at approximately 4.5 km distance. The one site with bevel-rim bowls in the Velishgird uplands is 20 km away at the head of one tributary of the Gamas Ab. Godin Tepe's central geographic position at the intersection of these two zones makes it a natural place to control the flow of goods. In particular, the increase in occupation of the best agricultural land raises the possibility that the function of Godin as a centre would involve collecting surplus grain either to feed dependants for their public works or as a hedge against bad agricultural years. This is also indicated by a few of the tablets found at the site, as Matthews argues (this volume).

Godin then would find its best analogy with a site such as Arslantepe (Frangipane and Palmieri 1983; Frangipane 1993, 1994, 1997, 2000, 2007) or Tepe Gawra (Rothman 2002). That is to say, it was a small centre in a society that was becoming more socially and politically complex over a long period, from the *Middle Chalcolithic* onwards. Such control as was being exerted was based primarily on exploitation of local resources. The Oval in this analogy was much less elaborated (i.e. less complex) than the temple/palace compound at Arslantepe. We simply do not have enough information on the site outside the Oval to specify whether the group inside were more powerful than the population at large. The Oval was certainly symbolic of a central role for the site. A comparison with Tepe Gawra XII and XIAB may be useful in this regard. In Gawra XII, the population began an engagement with larger networks through craft production and exchange. The systems of control represented by seals and their sealings were elaborated to some degree, but they do not indicate a central authority (Rothman 2001). Rather, they indicate a series of competing and cooperating extended family groups, each with craft and exchange functions, each receiving exotic goods such as lapis lazuli and obsidian. Agriculturally they created a central silo, controlled by sealings. This opening of their interaction sphere ended with the destruction of the site and the deaths of many residents. After the site was quickly reoccupied, residents built a fortress, the Round House, with storage facilities, guard rooms, etc. Craft production did not occur in the Round House, but in certain ways it mirrors the Oval in function.

What distinguishes late fifth- to early fourth-millennium BC Tepe Gawra from late fourth-millennium BC Godin Tepe is the clear evidence of contact with southern Mesopotamians. We do not know exactly which materials were shipped into the south or returned to the mountains and in general, it is unusual in this prehistoric period to know for certain which goods were being moved. We know, however, that exotic materials arrived in the southern alluvium, and we know that these materials existed in the so-called periphery or were transported through it. Without trace analysis like G. Wright's work on obsidian (1969) or obvious materials like lapis lazuli, however, we really cannot specify what was being traded. If it were wool or animals, we would have no record of their existence. The distribution of *Uruk*-style pottery described above indicates the contact, and the details of the Oval indicate developments contemporaneous with the contact.

Seals, tablets, and the nature of highland-lowland interaction at Godin

What may give us a bit more insight into the correlation of contact and development are the tablets and their seal designs (see Pittman 2001, 2011). So far, Matthews (this volume) and I agree, but I cannot believe that exchange was not a major part of the function of Godin and a key to why they built the Oval wall. The key to understanding the connection with *Uruk* societies, either in southern Mesopotamia or south-western Iran may be the seals and sealings (Fig. 5.8). All the Mesopotamian city states and the colony sites, such as Habuba Kabira, yielded numerous seals and sealings. Sealings were used in antiquity to control the movement of goods (Rothman 1994). A cloth or hide was placed over the openings of the vessel and string was tied tightly around it, before clean clay was placed over the knot and stamped or rolled with a seal that, it is generally acknowledged, identified which individuals or offices had access to the sealed goods (e.g. Frangipane 2007). Logically, we assume that when containers arrived at their destination authorised persons would break the seal open to access their contents. Tablets were normally used to record goods not easily stored in small containers, such as animals or large quantities of grain. They were sealed to represent the shipping authority. One would expect however, many clay sealings to be found at the place where goods were destined, and seals where they were dispatched. The exception would be storerooms that were controlled by authorities with their seals of office, but no door sealings were found at Godin.

The majority of seal impressions recovered from Godin were on tablets. As Pittman (2011: 114) writes, "Both functionally and iconographically all the seals impressed on the Godin tablets and container sealings are closely comparable to ones found either at Uruk or at Susa in levels that can be dated to level 17 of the Acropolis sounding (LC 5, see Rothman and Badler 2011, table 4.1: 70). They are in fact so similar that they must have been made in the same workshop."

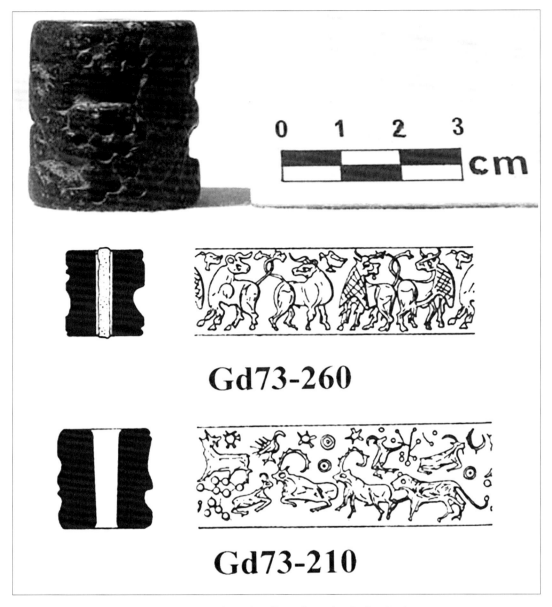

Figure 5.8. Seals and sealings from the Godin Oval.

The only seal recovered from Godin VI (Gd 73-260), a cylinder, came from the Oval courtyard area. Another cylinder seal (Gd 73-210) was found built into a brick of Godin Period IV:1b. It was probably accidentally included in the brick when the clay for its manufacture was dug from the earlier Period VI levels. The question raised by these seals and the sealings on tablets is, where did they come from? A neutron activation analysis of clays from the tablets, now in Tehran, would answer that question with regard to the sealings. One might ask why tablets were used for recording grain, when sealed sacks would be easy enough to use. Similarly, why would a purely local system of staple extraction and

storage by a local leadership organisation require a recording system as sophisticated as tablets? The sophisticated seal designs on the two seals would rather suggest that the destination of sealed items should be somewhere where the authority of the designs would be recognised, that is, the lowlands. Alternatively, the seals themselves could be gifts from the lowlands to persons recognised as some sort of shipping agent.

Were this cylinder seal from the south, it opens a line of inquiry into the nature of the relationship between what I argue are local coordinators or comptrollers and foreign traders or administrators. I do not say leaders, because in my opinion Godin

Tepe lies evolutionarily between the true leaders of Arslantepe and the coordinating mechanisms from Tepe Gawra XX/XIAB. One might then ask why local persons would want to engage in an exchange relationship with foreigners. Gosden (2004: 31) presents an interesting perspective on how to view the relationships inherent between the Godin Tepe residents and southern authorities/traders:

> "The middle ground was created through a mutually beneficial exploration of differences in the form of sociability on all sides the values so produced.... The middle ground [...] by definition was one of mediation. The middle ground was composed of a series of links between individuals [....], who could act as representatives of their group. No decisions or links were binding without gifts, and gifts had to be culturally appropriate, appealing to the values of both sides."

If we could show that the occupants of the Ovals were of higher rank – although in truth we cannot – one could readily see in this relationship a pathway to further control and eventually authority, like that of the rulers of Arslantepe. We are left with more questions than our data permit us to answer adequately.

Conclusions

What then do we make of this? I do think that Algaze (1993) is right in saying that the initial impetus for the inter-regional trading network was from southern Mesopotamia. I agree that it was a formal system with recording methods shared among participants to the degree they needed one. I agree that the transport systems as well as irrigation agriculture on flat alluvial plains did give the south a head start that continued into the third millennium BC. I believe that Adams's (1981) idea that the challenge of unreliable yields and the resulting central role of storage and control of a dense population against jealous neighbours were factors in impelling administrative and political development, but this reconstruction requires some direct influence on trading partners in the distant mountains. Whether those traders or administrators were in control of trade, as Algaze proposes, or required entire colonies to control that trade is less clear. That there was someone from the south in place in the highlands, perhaps more to negotiate terms of trade and to mark the destination with the southern system of marking seals, seems plausible.

To my mind, the logic of the World Systems models stifles our understanding of these subtleties of ancient reality. I think we must be precise with our terms. Hacınebi having a district, or a colony, of traders, does not mean that we are seeing a classic colonial economic empire à la England and India or the pre-Revolutionary Americas, nor can we presume that the colonists were under direct control of the home country.

I do not see that because the southerners had advantages, what Algaze calls Mesopotamia's "take-off", this necessarily means that their neighbours were incapable. I think that we are really talking about agency here, people with goals, plans, stratagems, and, of course, unintended consequences. If we want to take this as our model, we need to reject the pre-packaged World Systems modelling, which like Soviet Marxist archaeology concentrates on looking for data to validate what is already believed. I think we need to look at each ancient societal system from its own point of view, its own potentials and circumstances, rather than blend it into a World System or necessarily an assessment of which is better and which worse. We need fewer examples from the Akkadian or the Ur III periods and an assessment of different types of data. As Vitelli (1999) writes about ceramic studies, we need to look up, not back, if this is what we want to discover. The ancients were certainly not aware of a goal for their evolutionary pathway. Whatever they were doing or planning was certainly based on their current conditions and situation.

We need less "either-or" thinking, less Algaze is right or wrong. The debate about the *Uruk expansion* reminds me of the early days of the New Archaeology, when the big question was whether change resulted from diffusion and migration or independent invention. Of course, we know now that it can and often is a complex interplay of all three. So, was Algaze right about Godin? The answer is in some ways yes and in others no. To me, the evidence shows clearly that there was contact between Mesopotamia and central western Iran. If you were trying to get a reliable supply at a negotiated exchange rate, wouldn't you have someone pick the material and seal the outgoing package? Wouldn't you want to develop the abilities and then reward good suppliers? Is Matthews right as well? Again, I would say he is partly correct. A local strategy would be the most reliable, but as Blanton *et al.* (1996) argue, one of the possible pathways to greater control and rank is to emphasise one's role in wider exchange networks outside one's local social system. One has to remember that in southern Mesopotamia and in the highlands, these political systems were just developing. Such leadership organisations as existed were no doubt experimenters rather than groups in command of completely articulated systems.

There are a few things I believe we know based on the analysis of Godin VI. There was contact between southern Mesopotamia and the central western Zagros. Based on the resources the south lacked, to some degree this contact involved the movement of goods from the mountains to the lowlands. Furthermore, we can say with some confidence that Godin Tepe was a kind of small centre in its area, based on its location and institutions like the one represented by the Oval. What we cannot conclusively say is what the traded materials were. Equally, except for the one tablet with the grain sign and a part of a room with grain and lentil on the floor, we cannot say what goods were being circulated in the local settlement system. We also do not know how the centre at Godin Tepe was organised, whether there were individuals or groups promoted to leadership status, and whether that status represented a coordinating role or an authoritative one. I believe we can say that the occupants of the Oval were not from the south, although the possibility of a southern administrator or trader being present is plausible. So, to me, Godin Tepe remains somewhat of a mystery, one which future work in the central western Zagros may help us to unravel.

Bibliography

Adams, R. Mc. 1981. *Heartland of Cities*, University of Chicago Press, Chicago.

Algaze, G. 1986. *Mesopotamian Expansion and Its Consequences: Informal Empire in the Late Fourth Millennium BC*, Ph.D. dissertation, Oriental Institute, University of Chicago.

Algaze, G. 1989. "The Uruk Expansion: Cross-cultural Exchange in Early Mesopotamian Civilization", *Current Anthropology* 30: 571–608.

Algaze, G. 1993. *Uruk World System*, University of Chicago Press, Chicago (1st edition).

Algaze, G. 2001. "The Prehistory of Imperialism: The Case of Uruk Period Mesopotamia", in Rothman, M. (ed.), *Uruk Mesopotamia and its Neighbors: Cross-cultural Interactions in the Era of State Formation*, SAR Press, Santa Fe: 27–84.

Algaze, G. 2005. *Uruk World System*, University of Chicago Press, Chicago (2nd edition).

Algaze, G. 2008. *Ancient Mesopotamia at the Dawn of Civilization*, University of Chicago Press, Chicago.

Anthony, D. 2007. *The Horse, the Wheel, and Language*, Princeton University Press, Princeton.

Badler, V. R. 2002. "A Chronology of Uruk Artefacts from Godin Tepe in Central Western Iran and Its Implications for the Interrelationships Between the Local and Foreign Cultures", in Postgate, J. N. (ed.), *Artefacts of Complexity: Tracking the Uruk in the Near East*, British School of Archaeology in Iraq, Aris and Philips, Oxford: 79–110.

Blackman, M. J. 2011. "Chemical Characterization of Godin VI Ceramics by Instrumental Neutron Activation Analysis", in Gopnik and Rothman 2011: 111–12.

Blanton, R., Feinman, G., Kowalewski, S. and Peregrine, P. 1996. "A dual-processual theory for the evolution of Mesoamerican Civilization", *Current Anthropology* 37(1): 1–14.

Caldwell, D. 1976. "The early glyptic of Gawra, Giyan, and Susa, and the development of long distance trade", *Orientalia* 45(3): 227–50.

Crabtree, 2011. "The animal bone from Godin Period VI", in Gopnik and Rothman 2011: 109.

Edens, C. 2002. "Small things forgotten? Continuity among change at Godin Tepe", *Iranica Antiqua* 37: 31–46.

Frame, L. 2011. "Metallurgy of Godin VI", in Gopnik and Rothman 2011: 105.

Frangipane, M. 1993. "Local components in the development of centralized societies in Syro-Anatolian regions", in Frangipane, M., Hauptmann, H., Liverani, M., Matthiae, P. and Mellink, M. (eds), *Between the Rivers and over the Mountain*, Universita di Roma "La Sapienza", Rome: 133–61.

Frangipane, M. 1994. "The record function of clay sealings in early administrative systems as seen from Arslantepe-Malatya", in Ferioli, P., Fiandra, E., Fissore, G. and Frangipane, M. (eds), *Archives Before Writing*, Scriptorium, Rome: 125–37.

Frangipane, M. 1997. "A 4th millennium temple/palace complex at Arslantepe-Malatya", *Paléorient* 23/1: 45–73.

Frangipane, M. 2000. "The Late Chalcolithic/EB I sequence at Arslantepe", in Marro, C. and Hauptmann, H. (eds), *Chronologies de Pays du Caucase et de L'Euphrate aux IVe–IIIe Millénaires*, De Boccard, Paris: 439–72.

Frangipane, M. 2001. "Centralization processes in Greater Mesopotamia: Uruk "Expansion" as the culmination of an early system of intra-regional relations", in Rothman, M. (ed.), *Uruk Mesopotamia and its Neighbors: Cross-cultural Interactions in the Era of State Formation*, SAR Press, Santa Fe: 307–48.

Frangipane, M. ed. 2007. *Arslantepe Cretulae: an Early Centralised Administrative System Before Writing*, Università di Roma "La Sapienza", Rome.

Frangipane, M. and Palmieri, A. 1983. "A protourban centre of the Late Uruk period", *Origini* 12: 287–454.

Gopnik, H. 2011. "History of the excavations at Godin Tepe", in Gopnik and Rothman 2011: 5–19.

Gopnik, H. and Rothman, M. 2011. *On the High Road: The History of Godin Tepe, Iran*, Royal Ontario Museum/Mazda Press, Toronto.

Gosden, C. 2004. *Archaeology and Colonialism*, CUP, Cambridge.

Hall, T. and Chase-Dunn, C. 1996. "Comparing World-Systems: concepts and hypotheses, in Peregrine, P. and Feinman, G. (eds), *Pre-Columbian World Systems*, Prehistory Press, Madison: 11–25.

Hamlin (Kramer), C. 1974. "Seh gabi", *Archaeology* 27: 274–77.

Henrickson, E. F. 1994. "The outer limits: settlement and economic strategies in the Central Zagros highlands during the Uruk Era", in Stein, G., and Rothman, M. (eds), *Chiefdoms and Early States in the Near East: The Organizational Dynamics of Complexity*, Prehistory Press, Madison: 85–102.

Herrmann, G. 1968. "Lapis lazuli: early phases of its trade", *Iraq* 30(1): 21–57.

Johnson, G. 1973. *Local Exchange and State Development in Southwest Iran*, Anthropological Papers of the Museum of Anthropology 51, University of Michigan, Ann Arbor.

Levine, L. and Young Jr., T. C. 1986. "A summary of the ceramic assemblages of the central western Zagros from the Neolithic to the third millennium B.C.", in Huot, J. H. (ed.), *Préhistoire de la Mésopotamie*, Éditions du CNRS, Paris: 15–53.

Pittman, H. 2001. "Intra-regional relations reflected through glyptic evidence", in Rothman, M. (ed.), *Uruk Mesopotamia and its Neighbors: Cross-cultural Interactions in the Era of State Formation*, SAR Press, Santa Fe: 403–44.

Pittman, H. 2011. "The seals of Godin VI", in Gopnik and Rothman 2011: 113–15.

Renfrew, C. 1977. "Alternative models for exchange and spatial distribution", in Earle, T. and Ericson, J. (eds), *Exchange Systems in Prehistory*, Academic Press, New York: 71–90.

Renfrew, C., Dixon, J. E. and Cann, J. R. 1969. "Further Analysis of Near Eastern Obsidians", *Proceedings of the Prehistoric Society* 34: 319–31.

Rothman, M. S. 1994. "Sealings as a control mechanism in prehistory: Tepe Gawra XI, X, and VIII", in Stein, G. and Rothman, M.S. (eds), *Chiefdoms and Early States in the Near East*, Prehistory Press, Madison: 103–20.

Rothman, M. S. ed. 2001. *Uruk Mesopotamia and its Neighbors: Cross-cultural Interactions in the Era of State Formation*, SAR Press, Santa Fe.

Rothman, M. S. 2002. *Tepe Gawra: the Evolution of a Small, Prehistoric Center in Northern Iraq*, The University of Pennsylvania Museum Publications, Philadelphia.

Rothman, M. S. 2004. "Studying the development of complex society: Mesopotamia in the late fifth and fourth Millennia BC", *Journal of Archaeological Research* 12(1): 75–119.

Rothman, M. S. 2011a. "The environment of Godin Tepe IV", in Gopnik and Rothman 2011: 49–65.

Rothman, M. S. 2011b. "Migration and resettlement: Godin Period", in Gopnik and Rothman 2011: 138–206.

Rothman, M. S. and Badler, V. 2011. "Contact and development in Godin Period VI", in Gopnik, H. and Rothman, M. 2011: 67–137.

Rothman, M. S. and Fuensanta, J. 2003. "The Archaeology of the Early Bronze I and II Periods in Southeastern Turkey and North Syria", in Özdogan, M., Hauptmann, H. and Basgelen, N. (eds), *Köyden Kente Dogu'da Ilk Yerleimler*, Arkeoloji ve Sanat Yayınları, Istanbul: 583–622.

Rowton, M. 1967. "The woodlands of ancient western Asia", *JNES* 26: 261–77.

Sander, W. T., Parsons, J. and Santley, R. S. 1979. *The Basin of Mexico: Ecological Processes in the Evolution of a Civilization*, Academic Press, New York.

Stein, G. ed. 1999a. "The Uruk expansion: northern perspectives from Hacınebi, Hassek Höyük and Gawra", *Paléorient* 25(1): 7–172.

Stein, G. 1999b. *Rethinking World-Systems: Diasporas, Colonies, and Interacton in Uruk Mesopotamia*, University of Arizona Press, Tucson.

Vitelli, K. 1999. "'Looking up' at early ceramics in Greece", in Skibol, J. and Feinman, G. (eds), *Pottery and People*, University of Utah Press, Salt Lake City: 184–98.

Weiss, H. and Young, T. C. 1975. "The Merchants of Susa Godin V and Plateau-Lowland Relations in the Late Fourth Millennium B.C.", *Iran* 13: 1–17.

Wright, G. 1969. *Obsidian Analysis and Prehistoric Near East Trade: 7500 to 3500 B.C.*, Museum of Anthropology Anthropological Papers 37, Ann Arbor.

Wright, H. T. 1977. "Toward an explanation of the origin of the state", in Hill, J. (ed.), *Explanation of Prehistoric Change*, University of New Mexico Press, Albuquerque: 215–30.

Wright, H. T. 1994. "Prestate political formations", in Stein, G. and Rothman, M. S. (eds), *Chiefdoms and Early States in the Near East*, Prehistory Press, Madison: 67–84.

Wright, H. T. 1995. "Review, of Algaze, Uruk World Systems", *American Anthropologist* 97: 151–52.

Wright, H. T. 1998. "Uruk states in southwestern Iran", in Feinman, G. and Marcus, J. (eds), *Archaic States*, School of American Research, Santa Fe: 173–98.

Wright, H. T. and Johnson, G. 1975. "Population, exchange and early state formation in south western Iran", *American Anthropologist* 77: 267–91.

Young, T. C. 2004. "The Kangavar Survey, periods VI to IV", in Sagona, A. (ed.), *A View from the Highlands: Archaeological Studies in Honour of Charles Burney*, Peeters, Herent, Belgium: 645–60.

Young, T. C. and Levine, L. 1969. *Excavations of the Godin Project: Second Progress Report*, Occasional Paper 17 of the Royal Ontario Museum, Toronto.

Young, T. C. and Levine, L. 1974. *Excavations of the Godin Project: Second Progress Report*, Occasional Paper 26 of the Royal Ontario Museum, Toronto.

6. SOME THOUGHTS ON THE MODE OF CULTURE CHANGE IN THE FOURTH MILLENNIUM BC IRANIAN HIGHLANDS

Barbara Helwing

Introduction

The first complex urban societies of highland Iran appear some time in the second half of the fourth millennium BC, during the so-called *Proto-Elamite* period. According to current archaeological tradition, the term "Proto-Elamite" can be used to refer to a chronological period, a set of shared material culture, and/or a shared script or language. These attributes, however, do not allow a closely circumscribed social unit, culture, or even a political or ethnic group to be defined (although the use of the same script over a large area indicates that at least a related sign system or language was used). Most archaeologists are aware of this problem and are thus cautious when talking about a "Proto-Elamite phenomenon", "horizon", or even a period.

The term "Proto-Elamite" originally referred to a script found on a group of clay tablets excavated at Susa (then known as "Anshanite"; Scheil 1905) in the late nineteenth century. At this time, the newly discovered writing system was assumed to be the predecessor of second-millennium BC Elamite, which it is not. Stratigraphically controlled excavations at Susa in the 1960s–1970s allowed the archaeological context of the so-called *Proto-Elamite* tablets to be established and revealed that they first appeared in the Acropolis I from level 16 upwards (Le Brun 1971; see Dahl *et al.*, this volume). Further tablets have since been found in small numbers at Tepe Yahya (Phase IVC; Damerow and Englund 1989), Tal-e Malyan (*Late* and *Middle Banesh* phases; Stolper 1985), and Tappeh Sialk, which yielded one such tablet (assigned to Sialk Period IV2; Ghirshman 1938).

Archaeologists have also used the term "Proto-Elamite" more broadly to refer to a shared set of material cultural traits, which includes ceramic vessel types and distinctive types of numerical tablets (e.g.

Alden 1982; Abdi 2003). Under this archaeological definition, the *Proto-Elamite* period/phase begins around 3300 BC with the appearance of numerical tablets, which is earlier than the philologically defined period. The real script only appears in the latter part of the period.

The known *Proto-Elamite* centres had substantial populations and were characterised by an urban-style architectural layout that included large-scale buildings of presumably administrative function. At Tal-e Malyan there is evidence for the specialised, mass-production of everyday goods, such as pottery, which was created in standardised forms using the fast wheel (Alden 1979, 1982, this volume; Nicholas 1990; Sumner 2003). An incipient administration made use of cylinder seals and clay tablets to record economic transactions, a process that culminated during the latter half of this period with the additional use of written texts.

Key features of the *Proto-Elamite* period—an urban lifestyle, including the division of labour and complex administration—are also characteristic of other early states, such as that which emerged during the first half of the fourth millennium BC in the Mesopotamian lowlands. As one of the earliest excavated examples, the city of Uruk still stands as an icon for early state formation in lowland Mesopotamia and is often regarded as the centre of this development (e.g. Nissen 2002). Urban settlement, public institutions such as temples, and an advanced administration culminating in the invention of writing, are among its major attributes. The results of archaeological investigation at Uruk have at the same time shaped our expectations regarding what such an urban centre or early state should look like.

The emergence of comparable urbanisation in Iran during the *Proto-Elamite* period is therefore often regarded as being modelled on, and influenced by, the Uruk prototype. Whether this influence was realised through long-distance trade (e.g. Alden 1982), the emulation of cultural models (e.g. Schortman and Urban 1994), a true colonisation of the Mesopotamian "periphery" (e.g. Algaze 1993; Lamberg-Karlovsky 1978), or a secondary state formation remains a matter of lively debate (see Stein 1999; Petrie Introduction, this volume). There is currently little consensus concerning the appearance of the "Proto-Elamite phenomenon" in Iran. This suite of cultural material and the underlying dynamics that link diverse areas across Iran seem to occur suddenly, after an interruption or even collapse of ongoing occupation, displaying a remarkably uniform appearance over a large area of the highlands. Whether, and to what extent, external factors contributed to these sudden changes remain so far unanswered questions. Such an abrupt cultural change requires explanation, prompting questions such as: why did it happen? Can we identify any triggers that led to this rapid change? Were the changes induced from within or from the outside – and if the latter, to what extent was the Uruk model transferred to the Iranian settlements?

This paper aims to take a closer look at the dynamics behind the seemingly sudden appearance of *Proto-Elamite* urban settlements in the Iranian highlands. The study is based on data from recent excavations at the site of Arisman, on the southern fringe of the central Iranian desert, the Dasht-e Kavir. As with other Iranian sites, the transition to the *Proto-Elamite* appears to be rapid and disruptive here. The observations yielded from this recent research will be discussed within the wider geographical and chronological context, following the major cultural developments in the Iranian highlands and in the alluvial lowlands of Mesopotamia throughout the fourth millennium BC. Such a broad perspective is necessary in order to identify potential predecessors and prototypes of the late fourth-millennium BC *Proto-Elamite* phenomenon.

The earlier fourth millennium BC

Based on our current knowledge, pre-*Proto-Elamite* Iran appears largely as a culturally fragmented landscape. This fragmentation is overcome only with the integration of these diverse landscapes into the wider realm of supra-regional trade relations around the middle of the fourth millennium BC and the subsequent emergence of the *Proto-Elamite* complex in central and southern Iran, while the north-west underwent different developments. Discussion of pre-*Proto-Elamite* Iran will thus be structured according to the regional variation observed.

Khuzestan and the plains below the Zagros foothills

The Khuzestan lowlands appear to have experienced significant influence from southern Mesopotamia during the first half of the fourth millennium BC. This followed a little-known and poorly dated period of occupation towards the end of the fifth millennium BC, when the two larger centres of Choga Mish (Delougaz and Kantor 1996) and Abu Fanduweh (Alizadeh, in prep.) prospered while Susa apparently lay abandoned. The resettling of Susa (Acropolis I excavation, layer 22–17; Le Brun 1978b, 180–185, figs 31–32 for layer 18; Wright, this volume) and the Susiana plain during the fourth millennium BC involved the imitation of architecture and material culture typical of *Uruk* sites in Mesopotamia, albeit with a reduced cultural repertoire compared to the Mesopotamian model. For example, the Susian scribes only used six notation systems, whereas a total of 13 models are currently known from Uruk (Potts 1999: 58–61). Nevertheless, tripartite architecture constructed from standardised bricks, the mass production of typical *Uruk* pottery types, cylinder seals, and other evidence indicate that the Khuzestan lowlands can be considered an integral part of the *Uruk* world during the earlier half of the fourth millennium BC. This characterisation does not, however, imply any assertion regarding political relations at this time.

This notion of full inclusion into an *Uruk*-related world equally applies to some of the smaller plains located along the foothills of the Zagros Mountains, such as the "Eastern Plain" and the Ram Hormuz Plain (Moghaddam 2012; Wright and Carter 2003; Alizadeh, in prep.), as well. Bevel-rim bowls, *leitfossil* of the *Uruk* period, are not only attested, but were certainly being produced locally in some sites, as is evident from misshapen charges from ceramic kilns excavated at Choga Mish and Abu Chizan (Delougaz and Kantor 1996: 29 pl. 11, C; Moghaddam 2012: 127–28, fig. 5.26,27). However, the assemblages also contain other materials, such as *Lapui*-type ceramics, which are attested, for example, at Tal-e Geser (Alizadeh, in prep.), and some of the *Uruk*-related material seems to have been imported to sites on the margins of the Khuzestan Plain, also attested at Tal-e Geser (Alden *et al.*, in prep.).

Southern Iran

Southern Iran is home to the least-known cultural complex of the earlier fourth millennium BC, which is known as the *Lapui* period and is characterised by a grit-tempered red burnished ware. *Lapui* ceramics appear to have been in use at least between 3900 and 3500 BC (Petrie *et al.*, this volume) and are known from Tal-e Nokhodi (Goff 1963, 1964) and Tal-e Bakun (Bakun period V; Langsdorff and McCown 1942) and were defined as a period marker by both L. Vanden Berghe (1954) and later W.M. Sumner in his Kur River Basin survey (Sumner 1988: 24). *Lapui* pottery has been recently identified in stratified deposits at the two Mamasani sites, particularly Tol-e Spid (Petrie *et al.* 2009; also Petrie *et al.*, this volume). Recent excavations conducted at Tappe Mehr Ali (Sardari Zarchi and Razai 2008; Sardari, this volume) in northern Fars have yielded the extensive exposure of *Lapui* architecture. With the exception of pottery, however, we still lack sufficient excavated evidence to describe the way of life at this time (Petrie *et al.*, this volume; see Sardari, this volume). The *Lapui* period seems partly to overlap with the *Middle Uruk* period, as is evidenced by the co-occurrence of red burnished *Lapui* ware and bevel-rim bowls at Tol-e Spid (Petrie *et al.* 2009: 129).

Moving further south-east from Fars, a red ceramic with sparse painting represents the post-Bakun development in the restricted area of the Fasa Valley in the earlier fourth millennium BC. This material, called Vakilabad pottery (Kerner 1993), seems to have been coeval with the *Lapui* period.

Central Iran

In the first half of the fourth millennium BC, central highland Iran maintained a lifestyle based on village communities, which used painted pottery developed out of older, fifth-millennium BC prototypes. This pottery tradition illustrates the rather conservative character of the pottery production techniques employed on the Central Plateau, in contrast to the other groups presented below. This process was first observed in period III at Tappeh Sialk (4100–3400 BC; Nokandeh 2010: 75–77). Sialk III communities seem to have enjoyed relative stability and prosperity, as indicated by the prolonged occupation sequences that reach as much as 8 m at Tappeh Sialk (Ghirshman 1938; Nokandeh 2002). The Sialk III community experimented with copper smelting and the processing of silver (Pernicka 2004). During the later phases of Sialk III, contact with the Mesopotamian *Uruk* world is attested through the selective borrowing of specific pottery types such as bevel-rim bowls, nose-lugged jars, and spouted vessels (Amiet 1985). One possible reason for this contact may have been the demand for metal by lowland communities (including Susa etc.; Matthews and Fazeli 2004). It seems, however, that this contact between the late Sialk III communities and the *Uruk* world had only a limited effect on the internal organisation of the highland communities. No evidence for subsequent differentiation within the settlements in terms of architecture or burial practices has been found to date.

South-eastern Iran

During the earlier fourth millennium BC, sites in south-eastern Iran faintly mirror post-*Bakun* cultural developments in Fars, but the scanty evidence for the moment precludes daring overall interpretations. The two major reference sites are Tal-e Iblis in the Bardsir Plain (Caldwell and Malek Shahmirzadi 1966; Caldwell 1967) and Tepe Yahya in the Soghun Valley (Beale 1986a; Potts 2001; also Petrie 2013). The two sites are about 250 km apart, but they share some major characteristics.[1] The architectural record for the earlier fourth millennium BC shows a continuous transformation from multi-room buildings to individual houses at both locations and at both sites, the sequences are interrupted towards the middle of the fourth millennium BC. Furthermore, a certain amount of Fars-related material is observed in both locations, such as painted black-on-buff wares and some *Lapui*-related material (Sumner 1988: 28–29) besides an otherwise distinct assemblage of black-on-red painted ceramics (for Tepe Yahya, see Beale 1986b; for Tal-e Iblis, see Chase *et al.* 1967). Examples of bevel-rim bowls indicating contacts with a larger world appear at Tal-e Iblis together with the characteristic painted *Aliabad* wares, and are observed in a flat zone about 180 m south-west of the main mound within an assemblage otherwise typical for Sialk IV (Chase *et al.* 1967). At Tepe Yahya, bevel-rim bowls occur in phase IVC (Beale 1978; Potts 2001).

Recent rescue work at the badly damaged site of Mahtoutabad, next to Jiroft, has now provided some additional evidence for the dating of the south-east Iranian sequence, although architectural remains and small-scale craft activities were recorded only to a minor extent in phase Mahtoutabad I (Vidale and Desset, this volume). Mahtoutabad I and II refer to the late fifth–early fourth millennium BC; Mahtoutabad II is correlated with Iblis IV and *Aliabad*, and material for a later occupation with obvious relations to *Uruk/Jemdet Nasr* is known only from secondary deposits (Vidale and Desset, this volume).

Despite the patchy evidence, the overall impression of early fourth-millennium BC developments in south-eastern Iran is that of a region remotely related to developments elsewhere in the highlands of inner Iran. After a continuous development towards increased differentiation as visible in the architectural record, the region seems to have become briefly integrated into the wider world of supra-regional trade around the mid-fourth millennium BC.

North-western Iran

North-western Iran belongs to a different cultural sphere that extended from northern Syria to eastern Anatolia and across to north-western Iran and the southern parts of Azerbaijan, with local variation occurring. Important sites dating to the early fourth millennium BC have been excavated in both Iran (Geoy Tappe) and Iraq (Tepe Gawra), and this phase of occupation correlates with the LC2-4 periods at Tepe Gawra (Wright and Rupley 2001; Rothman 2002; Butterlin 2009). Characteristic features include pottery vessels made from chaff-tempered coarse wares (CFW), produced at least partly on the wheel and fired at low temperatures. Regional varieties of this CFW horizon can be further distinguished. For example, evidence from northern Syria indicates that CFW assemblages correlate with the post-*Ubaid* emergence of urban centres such as Tell Hamoukar (Reichel 2002) and Tell Brak (McMahon and Oates 2007; Oates *et al.* 2007), which were involved in long-distance relations for the procurement of raw material such as obsidian and metal. Recently, evidence for warfare was uncovered at both Tell Brak (McMahon and Oates 2007; Oates *et al.* 2007) and Hamoukar (Reichel 2006), adding to the picture of an elitist and highly competitive society. These Syrian centres, in contradiction with the *Uruk*-centric model from around 3800 BC, transformed into epigones of a new system of centralised society. In eastern Anatolia, Arslantepe (Frangipane 2004) and Norşuntepe (Hauptmann 1979; Gülçur 2000) seem to represent comparable localised centres, with good evidence for specialised architecture and centralised control of storage linked to redistribution (at least for specific purposes). Evidence from the north-east of the CFW koiné is based on patchy evidence from Tilkitepe in Turkey (Korfmann 1982), Geoytepe in Iran (Burton Brown 1951), and Leilatepe in Azerbaijan (Narimanov *et al.* 2007). One feature unifying these north-eastern sites is the use of pottery with hastily applied paint. In Iran, there are more sites besides Geoytepe characterised by this CFW, but none of these have yet been excavated (Kroll 1990). To the south-east, CFW is found as far as Choga Mish in the Khuzestan plain, where it appears as part of an otherwise strongly *Uruk*-related assemblage (Alizadeh 2008).

Summarising the earlier fourth millennium BC

The macro-complexes just identified as characteristic of the first half of the fourth millennium BC differ from each other in terms of both material culture and life ways. Most noticeable are the changes in approaches to pottery production: many complexes follow on from earlier traditions of painted wares that employed a rich repertoire of motifs and used firing temperatures of up to 1100°C, but only the communities in central and south-eastern Iran and in the Fasa Valley continued this tradition of painted wares well into the fourth millennium BC. Hence they appear somewhat "conservative", although towards the very end of the Sialk III period new tools such as turning devices were also employed in these regions (Petrie 2011). The north-west Iranian/Gawra-related group switched to chaff-faced wares. These could be fired at much lower temperatures and thus may have been employed to save fuel. Painting was almost completely abandoned or was only applied in a hasty fashion. In contrast to the painted and chaff-tempered wares are the southern Iranian *Lapui* ceramics that were still fired at high temperatures, but the fine varieties have a red slipped shiny surface and sharply accentuated shapes, indicating a new fashion in tableware.

Contact with the *Uruk* world

All of these different traditions, manifest in the varying pottery styles, were influenced to some degree by contact with the Mesopotamian *Uruk* world at some point before 3500 BC. This impact is reflected by innovations in material culture alongside the usual local assemblages. For example, some pottery *leitfossils* such as bevel-rim bowls, spouted vessels, and nose-lugged jars, which relate to specific consumption practices, were now also found in the Iranian highlands as were occasional seals and tokens (e.g. Tappeh Sialk, Godin Tepe, Tol-e Spid, Tal-e Kureh). The latter relate to the *Uruk* administrative sphere, but we have no information as to how they were used in the highlands. The impact of these innovations and the types of changes they manifest vary from location to location, with a tendency to diminish with increasing distance from the lowlands. Periods VII and VI at the western Iranian site of Godin Tepe, for example, are characterised by the simultaneous use of two types of material culture; the local painted wares of the Sialk III tradition and the establishment of a building area in the centre of the mound with a largely *Uruk* influenced pottery and glyptic assemblage (Rothman and Badler 2011; Rothman, this volume; Matthews, this volume). In the sites of the Central Plateau, a few *Uruk*-influenced pottery vessels occurred at Tappeh Sialk and Arisman, but based on the fabrics observed at Arisman they appear to have been locally produced (Boroffka R. and Parzinger 2011: 109, 129, 131; Helwing 2011b: 213). There also appears to be a relatively weak impact on the CFW horizon and the *Lapui* complex. There is, however, no evidence to suggest that the adoption of these new *Uruk*-related forms resulted in any significant impact on the way of life in these Iranian communities, although it has been suggested that the adoption of bevel-rim bowls may have been related to culinary changes (e.g. Potts 2009).

Profound changes during the later fourth millennium BC

Profound and rapid change occurred some time during the second half of the fourth millennium BC with the appearance of the "Proto-Elamite phenomenon".

Proto-Elamite sites seem to appear almost concurrently over a large area and share a remarkably uniform appearance in terms of architecture, pottery, and administrative artefacts. They link the culturally fragmented landscape of the highlands with standardised assemblages of architecture and pottery modelled on, but not identical to, *Uruk* prototypes.

Proto-Elamite remains were excavated at several localities in highland Iran, although only a few of them yielded a stratigraphic sequence (Table 6.1). Susa in Khuzestan and Tappeh Sialk in the highlands have the longest chronological sequences and are therefore the major reference sites. A similarly long sequence also appears to be present at Tal-e Geser (Caldwell 1968; Whitcomb 1971; Alizadeh, in prep.).[2] It is assumed for Susa that a transitional period between the *Uruk*-related and *Proto-Elamite* phases possibly existed, which is, however, not attested in the known archaeological sequence, but reconstructed from fill layers (Susa Acropole I, 17–16 transition = Acropole I, 17Ax; Le Brun 1971: 210; Dittmann 1986a: 171; 1986b: 133–42, 296–97).[3] At Tappeh Sialk, Period III.7 ended in a conflagration and the *Proto-Elamite* occupation followed after an unknown period of time (Ghirshman 1938; Helwing 2004). In the Mamasani region, the Tol-e Spid sounding yielded a sequence covering the *Lapui* period in levels 31–20, and level 19 is considered to comprise the transition to the *Banesh* period (Petrie *et al.* 2009, this volume); given the small size of the sounding and the large time span covered as indicated by the calibrated radiocarbon dates, I consider that an uninterrupted sequence covering the transition from *Lapui* to *Early Banesh* existed in the excavated area of Tol-e Spid is highly unlikely.

Other major sites with *Proto-Elamite* layers appear to have been newly founded settlements. Tal-e Malyan (Sumner 1986, 1988, 2003; Alden, this volume) was established on previously unsettled ground during the *Middle Banesh* period and the period IVC occupation at Tepe Yahya (Potts 2001) was established on top of a settlement that had been abandoned for

several centuries. Tal-e Iblis (Chase *et al.* 1967) and Mahtoutabad (Vidale and Desset, this volume) both yielded *Proto-Elamite*-related ceramic inventories only, without architectural contexts, from areas slightly away from the main site, as if there could have been newly founded occupations on clean ground.[4] In summary, none of these sites provide robust data for a real transitional phase (Alden, this volume). How then, can this break in the archaeological sequence be explained?

Theorising gaps and rapid culture change

Change is a continual experience in human life. It can take place in a slow or rapid fashion, smoothly or violently, induced from the outside or the inside, but no matter how it occurs, it shapes all of our lives. Although the time span of a human life may not be sufficiently long enough for individuals to be aware of ongoing slow change, changes may become obvious after their occurrence. Archaeology takes a long-term perspective, tracing history's *longue durée*. Continuous and rapid change may therefore appear condensed and initially difficult to differentiate, but careful analysis of the relevant settlement stratigraphies holds the key to identifying both slow and rapid change.

A variety of change that appears rapidly and abruptly and affects all spheres of life—population, institutions, administration, economy, and so on—is often described as collapse.[5] Reasons are manifold, and collapse can be induced by internal or external factors, or by a combination of both. An abrupt replacement of the existing order induced by a new, outside factor could be, for example, a military conquest and subsequent colonisation. Rapid change could equally be brought about by the breakdown of an existing system prompted by internal factors such as mismanagement of resources, social upheaval, and many others. Obviously, the most usual form would be a combination of internal and external factors—weak systems fall prey to internal turmoil or external challenges much more easily than stable systems.

Table 6.1. Chronological chart showing fourth-millennium BC settlement sequences in Iran.

est. years BC	Susa acr. I	Malyan	Yahya	Sialk	Arisman
2800	14B	Late Middle Banesh		IV2	Graveyard C
3100	16				
3100		Middle Banesh	IVC2	IV1	Settlement C
		Relocation or lower layer?			Slag heaps
3400	17A(x)gap?		gap	gap	Relocation
3400	17	Tal-e Kureh			
"Late Uruk"				III6–7	Settlement B
3600	18				

A collapse scenario, however, cannot explain what comes afterwards. Investigation into post-collapse scenarios has only recently become a field of archaeological inquiry. Previously, gaps were not really fully acknowledged or were simply given the label "Dark Age". Understanding the aftermath of collapse requires a clear view of the pattern of change: what is it that actually changes, and what stays the same? This needs to be clarified before approaching the question posed here: what happened and what happened afterwards?

Tainter's (1999) exemplary study (summarised in Table 6.2) of post-collapse periods emphasises reduced complexity as one major characteristic. He proposes that the archaeological record might be characterised as follows: the settled population can be expected to decline to a certain degree, a pattern that would be best evident from settlement size and density patterns. The previously existing social order would become disrupted, manifested in the archaeological record as traces of more or less violent events, such as destruction layers in settlements and evidence such as the desecration of monuments or memorials, or through abandonment of settled places and areas. The emerging new social order would be structured according to much simpler principles than the previous one. The failure of centralised power would result in territorial and political fragmentation, providing scope for formerly less complex communities on the periphery of the previous central power to become more complex themselves, enforcing further regional differentiation. Literate civilisations might furthermore react by creating a specific post-collapse mythology that preserves a memory of previous glory through a utopia of a heroic or a golden age, unreachable at present. This mythology steps into the gap left by the disruption of great traditions, such as monumental architecture and art.

There are, however, no rules as to the length of time such post-collapse conditions endure. Depending on the forces to organise a recovery, the resources available and, possibly, examples of more successful

societies, a failed system may recover quickly. It is my hypothesis here that during the transition from the *Late Chalcolithic*, the Iranian highlands was in loose and possibly indirect contact with the wider world of *Uruk* Mesopotamia. A short-term collapse of the *Uruk* dynamic was followed by a quick renewal of order through the emulation of a complex society model as it had been established previously at Uruk, and possibly at Susa and other *Uruk*-related centres. According to Tainter's model, a power vacuum situation in the centre of an integrated system allows previously peripheral areas to establish themselves as more complex entities. The foundation of a few large *Proto-Elamite* urban sites, at the expense of small rural settlements that were characteristic of the *Late Chalcolithic* landscapes in Iran, would manifest the successful remodelling of a new complex and integrated world.

Rapid culture change in the Iranian highlands?

As noted above, evidence dating to the beginning of the second half of the fourth millennium BC reveals the decline and abrupt end of occupation at most relevant sites before the onset of the *Proto-Elamite*. At Susa, layer Acropole I.16, followed a period of unknown length during which this specific area of the site at least seems to have been deserted (Acropole I.17X – see above). At Tappeh Sialk, layers representing a conflagration seal the end of Sialk III occupation. Tal-e Malyan and Tepe Yahya, both later to become major *Proto-Elamite* centres in the southern Iranian highlands, possessed no known settlements at this time. All of this evidence indicates that a period of abandonment or reduced settlement activity preceded *Proto-Elamite* occupation at major sites. If change had been externally induced, for example by a military conquest or colonisation, it might be assumed that settlement sequences would have been established anew directly after destruction. The hiatus in occupation at many settlements therefore suggests a

Table 6.2. Archaeologically visible markers of post-collapse development (after Tainter 1999).

Historical pattern	Archaeological record
Population decline	Settlement size and density; possibly no settlements at all
Disruption of social order	Destruction layers; rededication of monuments
Simplification of social structures	Archaeological record more ephemeral in general; lack of central institutions; decline in complexity visible, e.g. in burial rites
Territorial and political fragmentation	Material culture should reflect regional particularities
Increasing regional differences in reaction to a decrease in centralisation	
Increase in complexity in previously less complex regions	Visible only with supra-regional data: all evidence regarding complexity, in relation to previous centre

system failure caused by internal rather than external factors, followed by a period representing very little integration. A profound internal reorganisation only took place subsequently. The application of Tainter's criteria (Table 6.3) allows us to characterise the abrupt cultural change evident in the transition to the *Proto-Elamite* period more precisely as collapse and post-collapse development, as will be further elaborated below. The population appears to have declined and the complex social order dissolved; destruction layers are followed by indices of simpler societal reorganisation; and in addition, there is evidence for cultural fragmentation in previously central regions that may have allowed formerly peripheral regions to adopt a new role as a central authority.

Presentation of new data: the Arisman excavations

The prehistoric site of Arisman (Vatandoust *et al.* 2011)[6] is located about 60 km south-east of Tappeh Sialk and has extensive evidence for copper- and silver-processing. The maximum height of the cultural layers is 1.6 m. It lies at the foot of the Karkas Mountains on a gravel fan within a narrow stretch of watered land, on the southern edge of the Dasht-e Kavir. Due to spatial shifts in occupation over time, the site extends over an area of more than 1 km², but not all of this was occupied at the same time. As a consequence, no settlement mound ever formed.

Excavations were carried out in five different areas, labelled A to E. Areas B and C yielded evidence of domestic houses and workshops and Area B evidence of the mid-fourth millennium BC. Area C dated to the late fourth to early third millennium, i.e. the *Proto-Elamite* period. Both areas are about 400 m apart, indicating a shift in settled space. Areas A, D, and E were slag heaps related to metal processing.

Arisman in the earlier fourth millennium BC

The oldest excavated structure at Arisman is a one-room *pisé* house with a hearth in Area B (Boroffka N. *et al.* 2011). This is overlain by a sequence of rubble layers, with pottery kilns of the Sialk III period dug into the debris. The material culture from these deposits indicates a date late in the Sialk III sequence—more precisely the final phase of the Sialk III$_{6-7}$ period (Parzinger 2011: 132–36). During this time, Arisman metal production thrived: copper was extracted through crucible smelting in pit furnaces, shaft-hole axes were cast in single-valve moulds, silver was refined through cupellation (Helwing 2011d). Some gold scrap was also found, all indicating a period of experimentation with various metals. The metallurgical production documented at the site is by no means unique. Shaft-hole axes were also produced contemporaneously at Ghabrestan (Majidzadeh 1979) and probably also at Ma'morin (Mehr Kian, personal communication). Finished shaft-hole axes are found at Susa, unfortunately not in well-documented contexts, but two are reported in relation to the Susa I graves found below the *massif funéraire* (Tallon 1987; Helwing, in prep.).

The radiocarbon dates for Area B span the period 4050–3400 BC, with the earliest readings far outside the overall range of the Sialk III period (Görsdorf 2011). Since the Sialk III material assemblage at Arisman looks largely uniform and matches the Sialk III$_{6-7}$ final phase (Boroffka R. and Parzinger 2011; Parzinger 2011), it is probable that the old readings for the Sialk III contexts should be regarded as outliers caused by the use of old wood (Helwing 2011a).

Indications of contact between the population of Arisman Area B and those of the lowlands of Khuzestan or Mesopotamia are sparse, but unequivocal. A conical clay object found in Area B is clearly a token

Table 6.3. *Changes in the archaeological record correlating with the beginning of the* Proto-Elamite *period, sorted according to lowland sites (Susa, left column) and highland sites (right column).*

Lowlands/Khuzestan	*Highlands*
Decrease in settled area	Decrease in settled area in relation to concentration of population in few large places
Urban planning continues	Urban planning is new
Standardised building materials continue	Standardised bricks are new
Not enough evidence for craft production excavated in Susa	New organisation of craft production
Administration was previously established and continues	Not enough evidence to evaluate administration system
Burials are new and were not attested in the Susa acr. I, 22–18 levels	Burials already in late Sialk III
Silver is used, but no evidence for processing	Silver cupellation continues
Pottery corpus includes Uruk-related types	Pottery corpus includes Uruk-related types

(Helwing 2011c: 269, fig. 44, fig. 94.358). Bevel-rim bowls occur in small quantities; spouted bottles are attested, and nose-lugs are known, although on vessel shapes that do not compare with the lowland ones (Boroffka R. and Parzinger 2011). A small amount of burnished grey ware also recalls lowland prototypes. If we compare these artefacts with material from the lowlands, counterparts can be found in the *Middle Uruk*/proto-literate assemblages of Susa, Choga Mish, and Uruk among others (cf. ceramic assemblages in Le Brun 1978b: fig. 32; Delougaz and Kantor 1996: pls. 17–28; Sürenhagen 1986).

Arisman in the *Proto-Elamite* period

The *Proto-Elamite* Area C occupation (Chegini *et al.* 2011) consists of a planned urban domestic quarter with houses constructed in regular lots along an alleyway. Standardised bricks resembling *riemchen* were used.

Although the site is flat with a maximum of 1.6 m of preserved cultural layers, we were able to identify a sequence of eight archaeological phases. Three of these, Phases 6, 4, and 3, correspond to periods of relatively long use. Phase 6 was the major occupation period. Most the rooms—as far as were preserved—seem to have been in use for some time, as evidenced by several phases of floor replastering. In Phase 4 the ruins were reused for workshops. These were open-air, although probably sheltered from the wind. Even before the construction of the houses, the area had served a similar purpose, with pit furnaces for copper smelting.

Following this usage of the abandoned houses as an open-air workshop, the area temporarily fell into disuse. Phase 3 corresponds to a late *Proto-Elamite* graveyard, dug into the house ruins. Both infants and adults were found buried in jars. Some of these burials contained copper bracelets and black and white stone beads. Some finer items such as two cylinder seals and a silver pendant were found immediately below the surface and seem to have originated from burials that had been located higher up, and were destroyed by erosion. According to the radiocarbon dates, the period covered by Area C occupation is limited to the second half of the fourth millennium BC, roughly 3350–3100 BC (Helwing 2011a).

Changes evident between occupations in Arisman B and C

Arisman fits the known *Proto-Elamite* settlement pattern for the Central Iranian Plateau perfectly, almost mirroring the Tappeh Sialk sequence (Ghirshman 1938; Helwing 2004). The relocation of the settlement from Area B to C occurred at a time when other highland sites were abandoned and reorganised. The *Proto-Elamite* occupation – houses, workshops, and the later graveyard – differs in many respects from the earlier Area B occupation. Most important is a total change in architectural design, from single-room *pisé* constructions to urban-planned quarters using standardised *riemchen*-like bricks.

Settlement patterns reveal an important change as well. The survey of the Arisman hinterland yielded evidence for eight sites dating to the Sialk III period (Chegini and Helwing 2011b). Three of these may have been smelting sites, but the remaining five were settlements. For the *Proto-Elamite* period, however, only one site is attested: Arisman. This was by now much larger than any of the recorded Sialk III sites.

The *Proto-Elamite* period also witnessed the introduction of new copper-processing technology. Furnace smelting was now used instead of the crucible smelting practised during the late Sialk III period (Helwing 2011d). One technology that did not change, however, was the extraction of silver using cupellation, which was a technique extensively attested in Area B (Helwing 2011d). The burial customs of the Sialk III period are only poorly known. In Arisman Area B, burials occurred with very few grave-goods within the garbage layers of the Area B workshops. Burials rich in offerings only became common during the developed *Proto-Elamite* period, to which phase the extensive graveyard of Area C Phase 3 dates.

Evidence for Sialk III administrative activity is restricted to a single token, found in Area B. By contrast, the Area C graveyard dating to the later *Proto-Elamite* period yielded cylinder seals of various types well known from other *Proto-Elamite* sites.

Pottery technology completely transformed between the two phases, from the largely handmade painted ceramics of Sialk III to wheel-turned mass-produced wares (Helwing 2011b). Significantly, although there was extensive change in the way work was organised, continuity is still evident in the use of specific shapes and functional classes of pottery vessels. All of the pottery forms that continue belong to a previous *Uruk*-related repertoire – bevel-rim bowls, nose lugged jars, spouted vessels, and carinated beakers (Helwing 2011b). It goes without saying that this set of pottery forms probably relates to specific habits of consumption.

In summary, Arisman thus provides evidence for profound change in settlement patterns, layout and architecture, and for the organisation of labour through the large-scale usage of copper-smelting furnaces and the standardisation of pottery production in the mid- to late fourth millennium BC. Evidence for administration and burial customs is limited by the small-scale exposure, so any generalisations may be premature. At the same time, continuity is still evident: from the persistence of specialised technology such as silver cupellation; and from the continued use of a select repertoire of pottery vessels.

Comparison of Arisman evidence with highland and lowland reference sites

A comparison of the Arisman evidence with that from Tappeh Sialk, as the highland reference site for Arisman, and with Susa, as the lowland counterpoint, reveals the following pattern: in the lowlands, a slight settlement decrease can be observed in the area around Susa (Wright 1987: 145; Alden 1987), alongside obvious continuity in urban planning and the use of standardised building materials. In the highlands around Tappeh Sialk, the settled area seems to have decreased as well, since preliminary survey (Danti 2006) did not reveal a second *Proto-Elamite* site in the neighbourhood. This is comparable to the pattern visible around Arisman, where a major population concentration is also documented in a single place (Chegini and Helwing 2011). The introduction of standardised bricks and urban layout, in contrast to the *Uruk*-influenced lowlands,[7] was accomplished on the Central Iranian Plateau only after the beginning of the *Proto-Elamite* period.

With regard to craft production, the lowlands have yielded very little archaeological evidence. In the highlands, however, a significant change in the organisation of craft production can be identified,[8] be it in the introduction of the potter's wheel or smelting furnace technology.

Administrative technology was already well established in the lowlands during the mid-fourth millennium BC (Le Brun 1978a, 1990; Vallat 1971, 1978). Evidence from the highland sites is meagre, but at Tappeh Sialk, seals dating to Period III have been found (Nokandeh 2010: 123, pl. 99.55–56). At Arisman, administrative technology is well attested through seals used in the later *Proto-Elamite* period, but any predecessors remain elusive but for the single, aforementioned token.

The same warning regarding the ambiguities of archaeological record applies to burials. While these are lacking at Susa, they occur at Tappeh Sialk in the late III period (Ghirshman 1938: 43–44, pl. 351–3). At Arisman, jar burials appear to be a new trait of the later *Proto-Elamite* period but earlier, less well-furnished burials are also attested in Area B (Boroffka N. *et al.* 2011: 35, figs 14, 15).

Alongside these indicators for potentially rapid change, there exist hints at continuity in certain types of craft production, including metal and pottery. Silver cupellation technology is clearly a continuous trait at both Tappeh Sialk and Arisman (Pernicka 2004), while corresponding evidence is lacking from the lowland site of Susa. With regard to pottery, the persistence of *Uruk*-derived shapes is attested both at Susa (Le Brun 1971, 1978b) and in the highlands in Arisman (Fig. 6.1), while at the same time the previous Sialk III-related shapes went out of use.

Matching archaeological evidence and theoretical models

The change evident in the highlands indicates a significant increase in complexity with the onset of the *Proto-Elamite* period, while at the same time continuity in a few selected traits is visible. When compared to the criteria defined by Tainter (1999; see above), it becomes clear that this pattern is consistent with his observations on post-collapse developments in formerly peripheral regions. According to this model, the beginning of the *Proto-Elamite* period would not represent the result of an external system imposed onto unsuspecting indigenous people; rather, a model known to the communities in the highlands through previous contacts with *Uruk* Mesopotamia and/or Khuzestan, which was emulated according to the needs and traditions of the highland communities, and then developed further and refined at a moment when the lowland centre of gravity became less influential. In such a scenario, the exemplar model existed previously, but it was not until a vacuum occurred in the lowland centre(s) that the elites of the highland communities could exert their authority. An increase in social complexity is evidenced in the *Proto-Elamite* archaeological record by indications of specialised labour, administration, and differentiation in burials goods. The emulation of earlier, *Uruk*-related social models is also an integral feature. The new elites that took advantage of the situation were crucial to the reorganisation of Iranian highland communities into urbanised societies that relied to a large extent on the exploitation of local raw materials for external trade. The centralised urban settlement of *Proto-Elamite* Arisman, specialising largely in craft production, could only flourish after a shift of influence and power in the lowlands created the opportunity for these new developments.

Notes

1   It remains difficult to relate these stratigraphic sequences in terms of absolute chronology. While the Tepe Yahya stratigraphic sequence refers to well-observed building layers, the Tal-e Iblis sequence is composed of observations from different trenches dug partly in artificial units.

2   The site was excavated in the 1940s and is currently under reinvestigation by Abbas Alizadeh (personal communication).

3   Dittman (1986a: 171) has doubts that a real hiatus existed in Susa (see Dahl *et al.* this volume).

4   It is probably no coincidence that also in other areas of western Asia, settlements of the "Late Uruk" period are occasionally founded at a distance from older mounded settlement sites; examples for this can be Habuba Kabira South (Strommenger 1980) or Tepecik on the Upper Euphrates (Esin 1976, 1982); these sites tend to be under-represented in survey records, as was observed also e.g. in the Syrian Jazirah (Ur and Wilkinson 2008).

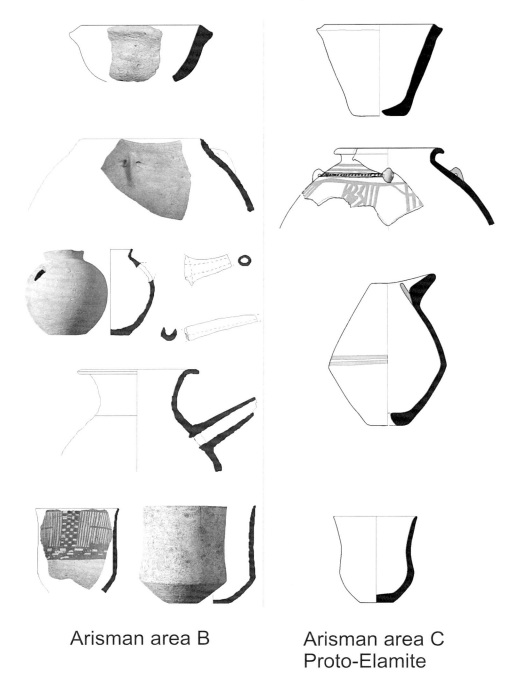

Arisman area B

Arisman area C
Proto-Elamite

Figure 6.1. Arisman. Continuity of pottery production according to pottery types of the Late Chalcolithic *(area B, left column) and the* Proto-Elamite *(area C, right column) period (area B after Boroffka R. and Parzinger 2011: nos. 578, 380, 474–76, 354, 128, 24; area C after Helwing 2011b).*

5   Collapse scenarios as models in archaeological explanation have been formulated since the 1980s by various scholars, among others Joseph Tainter (1988) and Norman Yoffee and G. L. Cowgill (1988) and will not be repeated here; the parallel transition from a centralised to a less complex organisation that occurs around 3000 BC in eastern Anatolian Arslantepe has recently been equally interpreted as a collapse scenario, see Frangipane 2009.

6   Work was carried out in a joint effort between the Iranian Cultural Heritage Organization, the Geological Survey of Iran, the German Archaeological Institute, the German Mining Museum, Bochum, and the Technical University Freiberg, between 2000 and 2004. I would like to thank all contributors and team members for their support and unfailing commitment to the project.

7   At Susa, the earliest appearance of *riemchen*-type bricks is documented in layer 18 of the Acropolis I sounding, see Le Brun 1978b: 180.

8   Also emphasised, through different reasons, by Fazeli *et al.* 2007; Nokandeh 2010.

Bibliography

Abdi, K. 2003. "From Ecriture to Civilisation: Changing Paradigms of Proto-Elamite Archaeology", in Miller, N. F. and Abdi, K. (eds), *Yeki bud, yeki nabud: Essays on the Archaeology of Iran in Honor of William M. Sumner*, Cotsen Institute of Archaeology, University of California, Los Angeles: 140–151.

Alden, J. R. 1982. "Trade and politics in Proto-Elamite Iran", *Current Anthropology* 23: 613–40.

Alden, J. R. 1987. "The Susa III period", in Hole, F. (ed.), *The Archaeology of Western Iran*, The Smithsonian Institution, Washington, London: 157–70.

Alden, J. R., Minc, L. and Alizadeh, A. in preparation. "Appendix A. INAA analysis of ceramics from three Iranian sites: compositional signatures and evidence for ceramic exchange as seen from Tall-e Geser", in Alizadeh, A. (ed.), *Ancient Settlement Patterns and Cultures in the Ram Hormuz Plain, Southwestern Iran: Excavations at Tall-e Geser and Regional Survey in the Ram Hormuz Area*, Oriental Institute Publications 140, Oriental Institute, Chicago.

Algaze, G. 1993. *The Uruk World System: The Dynamics of Expansion of Early Mesopotamian Civilization*, University of Chicago Press, Chicago.

Alizadeh, A. 2008. *Choga Mish II. A Prehistoric Regional Center in lowland Susiana, southwestern Iran. Final report on the last six seasons, 1972–1978*. Oriental Institute Publications 130, Oriental Institute, Chicago.

Alizadeh, A. ed. in preparation. *Ancient Settlement Patterns and Cultures in the Ram Hormuz Plain, Southwestern Iran: Excavations at Tall-e Geser and Regional Survey in the Ram Hormuz Area*, Oriental Institute Publications 140, Oriental Institute, Chicago.

Amiet, P. 1985. "La période IV de Tépé Sialk reconsidérée", in Huot, J-L., Yon, M. and Calvet, Y. (eds), *De l'Indus aux Balkans. Recueil à la mémoire de Jean Deshayes*, Maison de l'Orient, Paris: 293–312.

Beale, T. W. 1978. "Bevelled rim bowls and their implications for change and economic organization in the later fourth Millennium B.C.", *JNES* 37: 289–313.

Beale, T. W. 1986a. *Excavations at Tepe Yahya, Iran, 1967–1975: The Early Periods*, Bulletin of the American School of Prehistoric Research 38, Harvard University Press, Cambridge, MA.

Beale, T. W. 1986b. "The ceramics", in Beale, T. W. and Lamberg-Karlovsky, C. C. (eds), *Excavations at Tepe Yahya, Iran 1967–1975: The Early Periods*, Bulletin of the American School of Prehistoric Research 38, Harvard University Press, Cambridge, MA: 39–90.

Boroffka, R. and Parzinger, H. 2011. "Pottery of the Sialk III period", in Vatandoust *et al.* 2011: 98–193.

Boroffka, N., Chegini, N. N. and Parzinger, H. 2011. "Excavations at Arisman, Area B", in Vatandoust *et al.* 2011: 28–39.

Burton Brown, T. 1951. *Excavations in Azarbaijan, 1948*, John Murray, London.

Butterlin, P. ed. 2009. À propos de *Tepe Gawra, le monde proto-urbain de Mésopotamie*, Subartu 23, Brepols, Turnhout.

Caldwell, J. R. ed. 1967. *Investigations at Tal-i-Iblis*, Illinois State Museum Society, Springfield.

Caldwell, J. R. 1968. "Ghazir, Tell-i", in *Reallexikon der Assyriologie* 3: 348–55.

Caldwell, J. R. and Malek Shahmirzadi, S. 1966. *Tal-i-Iblis. The Kerman Range and the Beginning of Smelting*, Illinois State Museum, Springfield.

Chase, D., Caldwell, J. R. and Fehérvári, I. 1967. "The Iblis sequence and the exploration of excavation areas A, C, and E", in Caldwell, J. R. (ed.), *Investigations at Tal-i-Iblis*, Illinois State Museum Society, Springfield: 111–201.

Chegini, N. N., Fahimi, H. And Helwing, B. 2011. "Excavations in Arisman, Area C", in Vatandoust *et al.* 2011: 40–68.

Chegini, N. N. and Helwing, B. 2011. "Archaeological survey in the hinterland of Arisman and Kāšān", in Vatandoust *et al.* 2011: 421–83.

Damerow, P. and Englund, R. 1989. *The Proto-Elamite Texts from Tepe Yahya*. Bulletin of the American School of Prehistoric Research 39, Cambridge MA.

Danti, M. D. 2006 (1384). "The Sialk regional archaeological survey 2005 Sialk Reconsideration Project", in Malek Shahmirzadi, S. (ed.), *The Fishermen of Sialk: Sialk Reconsideration Project, Report 4*, Archaeological Report Monograph Series 7, Iranian Cultural Heritage Organisation, Tehran: 67–78.

Delougaz, P. and Kantor, H. J. 1996. *Choga Mish. Vol. 1. The first five seasons of excavations, 1961–1971*, edited by Alizadeh, A., Oriental Institute Publication 101, Oriental Institute, Chicago.

Dittmann, R. 1986a. "Susa in the Proto-Elamite Period and Annotations on the Painted Pottery of Proto-Elamite Khuzestan", in Finkbeiner, U. and Röllig, W. (eds), *Gamdat Nasr: Period or Regional Style*, Beihefte zum Tübinger Atlas des Vorderen Orients, Reihe B (Geisteswissenschaften), vol. 62, Dr. Ludwig Reichert Verlag, Wiesbaden: 171–98.

Dittmann, R. 1986b. *Betrachtungen zur Frühzeit des Südwest-Iran. Regionale Entwicklungen vom 6. bis zum frühen 3. vorchristlichen Jahrtausend*, Berliner Beiträge zum Vorderen Orient 4, Dietrich Reimer Verlag, Berlin.

Esin, U. 1976. "Tepecik Excavations, 1972", in *Keban Project 1972 Activities*, Keban Project Publications, Series I, Turkish Historical Society Press, Ankara: 109–17.

Esin, U. 1982. "Tepecik Excavations, 1974", in *Keban Project 1974 Activities*, Keban Project Publications, Series I, Turkish Historical Society Press, Ankara: 95–118.

Fazeli, H., Coningham, R. A. E., Young, R. L., Gillmore, G. K., Maghsoudi, M. and Raza, H. 2007. "Socio-economic transformations in the Tehran Plain: Final season of settlement survey and excavations at Tepe Pardis", *Iran* 45: 267–86.

Frangipane, M. ed. 2004. *Alle origine del potere. Arslantepe, La collina dei leoni*, Milan.

Frangipane, M. 2009. "Rise and collapse of the Late Uruk centres in Upper Mesopotamia and Eastern Anatolia", *Scienze dell'antichità* 15: 15–31.

Ghirshman, R. 1938. *Fouilles de Sialk, près de Kashan 1933, 1934, 1937 (I)*, Geuthner, Paris.

Goff, C. 1963. "Excavations at Tall-i Nokhodi", *Iran* 1: 43–70.

Goff, C. 1964. "Excavations at Tall-i Nokhodi, 1962", *Iran* 2: 41–52.

Görsdorf, J. 2011. «Radiocarbon datings», in Vatandoust *et al.* 2011: 370–374.

Gülçur, S. 2000. "Norşuntepe: Die chalkolithische Keramik (Elazig/Ostanatolien)", in Marro, C. and Hauptmann, H. (eds.), *Chronologies des Pays du Caucase et de l'Euphrate aux IVe–IIIe Millénaires*, Varia Anatolica, vol. 11, D'Istanbul, I.F.d.E.A., general editor, De Boccard, Paris: 375–418.

Hauptmann, H. 1979. "Kalkolitik Çağdan İlk Tunç Çağının bitimine kadar Norşuntepe'de yerleşmenin gelişime", in

Kurumu, T. T. (ed.), *VIII. Türk Tarih Kongresi*, Türk Tarih Kurumudan Yayınları, vol. IX, 8, Kurumu, T.T., general editor, Türk Tarih Kurumu, Ankara: 55–63.

Helwing, B. 2004. "Tracking the Proto-Elamite on the Central Iranian Plateau", in Malek Shahmirzadi, S. (ed.), *The potters of Sialk*, Sialk Reconsideration Project, Report 3, Iranian Cultural Heritage Organisation, Tehran: 45–58.

Helwing, B. 2011a. "Archaeological comments on the radiocarbon datings", in Vatandoust *et al.* 2011: 374–75.

Helwing, B. 2011b, "Proto-Elamite pottery from areas A, C, D and E", in Vatandoust *et al.* 2011: 194–251.

Helwing, B. 2011c. "The small finds from Arisman", in Vatandoust *et al.* 2011: 254–327.

Helwing, B. 2011d. "Conclusions: The Arisman copper production in a wider context", in Vatandoust *et al.* 2011: 523–31.

Helwing, B. in preparation. "Trade in metals in Iran and the neighboring areas, a reflection based on results of the excavations at Arisman (Iran)", in Casanova, M. and Law, R. (eds), *South Asian Archaeology 2007*, Conference Proceedings, SAA Ravenna 2007, "The lapis lazuli road", Archaeopress, Oxford.

Kerner, S. 1993. *Vakilabad-Keramik*. Berliner Beiträge zum Vorderen Orient 13, Dietrich Reimer, Berlin.

Korfmann, M. 1982. *Tilkitepe. Die ersten Ansätze prähistorischer Forschung in der östlichen Türkei*, Istanbuler Mitteilungen, Beiheft 26, Wasmuth, Tübingen.

Kroll, S. 1990. "Der Kultepe bei Marand. Eine chalkolithische Siedlung in Iranisch–Azarbaidjan", *AMIT* 23: 59–72.

Lamberg-Karlovsky, C. C. 1978. "The Proto-Elamites on the Iranian Plateau", *Antiquity* 52: 114–20.

Langsdorff, A. and McCown, D. E. 1942. *Tall-i Bakun A: Season of 1932*, Oriental Institute Publications 54, University of Chicago Press, Chicago.

Le Brun, A. 1971. "Recherches stratigraphiques à l'acropole de Suse, 1969–1971", *CDAFI* 1: 163–216.

Le Brun, A. 1978a. "La Glyptique du niveau 17B de l'acropole (campagne de 1972)", *CDAFI* 8: 61–79.

Le Brun, A. 1978b. "Suse, Chantier 'Acropole 1'", *Paléorient* 4: 177–92.

Le Brun, A. 1990. "Les document économiques du niveau 18 de l'acropole de Suse et leurs modes de groupement", in Vallat, J-F. (ed.), *Contribution à l'histoire de l'Iran. Mélanges offerts à Jean Perrot*, Recherche sur les civilisations, Paris: 1–14.

McMahon, A. and Oates, J. 2007. "Excavations at Tell Brak 2006–2007", *Iraq* 69: 145–71.

Majidzadeh, Y. 1979. "An early prehistoric coppersmith workshop at Tepe Ghabristan", in *Akten des VII. Internationalen Kongresses für Iranische Kunst und Archäologie, Munich, 1976*. Archäologische Mitteilungen aus Iran, suppl. 6, DAI, Berlin: 82–92.

Matthews, R. and Fazeli, H. 2004. "Copper and complexity: Iran and Mesopotamia in the fourth millennium B.C.", *Iran* 42: 61–75.

Moghaddam, A. 2012. *Later Village Period Settlement Development in the Karun River Basin, Upper Khuzestan Plain, Greater Susiana, Iran*, BAR International Series 2347, Archaeopress, Oxford.

Narimanov, I. H., Akhundov, T.I. and Aliyev, N. H. 2007. *Leylatepe. Settlement, tradition, a stage in ethnocultural history of South Caucasus*, National Academy of Sciences of Azerbaijan, The Institute of Archaeology and Ethnography, Baku.

Nicholas, I. M. 1990. *The Proto-Elamite Settlement at TUV*, Malyan Excavation Reports I, University of Pennsylvania Museum of Archaeology and Anthropology, Philadelphia.

Nissen, H. J. 2002. "Uruk: Key site of the period and key site of the problem", in Postgate, N. (ed.), *Artefacts of complexity. Tracking the Uruk in the Near East*, BSAI, Aris and Phillips Ltd, Warminster: 1–16.

Nokandeh, J. 2002. "Gozaresh-e layeh negari-e boresh-e alef dar tappeh-e jonoubi-ye Sialk" (in persian), in Malek Shahmirzadi, S. (ed.), *The Ziggurat of Sialk*, Sialk Reconsideration Project, Report, vol. 1, Iranian Cultural Heritage Organization, Tehran: 55–84.

Nokandeh, J. 2010. *Neue Untersuchungen zur Sialk III-Periode im zentraliranischen Hochland: auf der Grundlage der Ergebnisse des „Sialk Reconsideration Project"*, unpublished Ph.D. dissertation, Freie Universität Berlin.

Oates, J., McMahon, A., Karsgaard, P., Al Quntar, S. and Ur, J. 2007. "Early Mesopotamian urbanism: A new view from the north", *Antiquity* 81(313): 585–600.

Parzinger, H. 2011. "Sialk III pottery from Area B. Sialk III pottery chronology", in Vatandoust *et al.* 2011: 128–43.

Pernicka, E. 2004. "Kupfer und Silber in Arisman und Tappeh Sialk und die frühe Metallurgie in Iran", in Stöllner, T., Slotta, R. and Vatandoust, A. (eds), *Persiens antike Pracht*, Deutsches Bergbau-Museum, Bochum: 232–39.

Petrie, C. A. 2011. "'Culture', innovation and interaction across southern Iran from the Neolithic to the Bronze Age (c. 6500–3000 BC)", in Roberts, B. and Vander Linden, M. (eds.), *Investigating Archaeological Cultures: Material Culture, Variability and Transmission*, Springer, New York.

Petrie C. A. 2013. "The Chalcolithic of south Iran", in Potts, D.T. (ed.), *Oxford Handbook of Iranian Archaeology*, OUP, Oxford: 120–58.

Petrie, C. A., Asgari Chaverdi, A. and Seyedin, M. 2009. "Excavations at Tol-e Spid", in Potts, D. T., Roustaie, K., Petrie, C. A. and Weeks, L. (eds), *The Mamasani Archaeological Project Stage One. A report on the first two seasons of the ICAR – University of Sydney expedition to the Mamasani District, Fars Province, Iran*, BAR International Series 2044, Archaeopress, Oxford: 89–134.

Potts, D. T. 1999. *The Archaeology of Elam: Formation and Transformation of an Ancient Iranian State*, Cambridge World Archaeology, Cambridge University Press, Cambridge.

Potts, D. T. 2001. *Excavations at Tepe Yahya, Iran, 1967–1975: The Third Millennium*, Bulletin of the American School of Prehistoric Research 45, Peabody Museum of Archaeology and Ethnology, Harvard University, Cambridge MA

Potts, D. T. 2009. "Bevel-rim bowls and bakeries: Evidence and explanations from Iran and the Indo-Iranian borderlands", *JCS* 61(2): 1–23.

Reichel, C. 2002. "Administrative complexity in Syria during the 4th millennium B.C. – the seals and sealings from Tell Hamoukar", *Akkadica* 123: 35–56.

Reichel, C. 2006. "Urbanism and warfare – the 2005 Hamoukar, Syria, excavations", *Oriental Institute News and Notes*: 1–11.

Rothman, M. S. 2002. *Tepe Gawra: The evolution of a small prehistoric center in Northern Iraq*, University Museum Monographs 112, University of Pennsylvania, Museum of Archaeology and Anthropology, Philadelphia.

Rothman, M. S. and Badler, V. 2011. "Contact and development in Godin Period VI", in Gopnik, H. and Rothman, M. (eds), *On the High Road: The History of Godin Tepe, Iran*, Royal Ontario Museum/Mazda Press, Toronto: 67–137.

Sardari Zarchi, A. and Razai, A. 2008. "Gozaresh-e moghadamati-ye kawosh-haye bastanshenasi, nejat bakhshi, Tappe Mehr 'Ali (Eqlid, Fars)", *Tabestan va payiz 1385*, Internal report, submitted to Iranian Center for Archaeological Research (in Persian).

Scheil, V. 1905. *Documents en écriture proto-élamite*, Mémoires de la Mission archéologique en Perse 6, Paris.

Schortman, E. and Urban, P. 1994. "Living on the edge: core-periphery relations in ancient southeastern Mesoamerica", *Current Anthropology* 35: 401–30.

Stein, G. J. 1999. "Material Culture and Social Identity: the Evidence for a 4th Millennium BC Mesopotamian Uruk Colony at Hacinebi, Turkey", *Paléorient* 25(1): 11–22.

Stolper, M. W. 1985. "Proto-Elamite texts from Tall-i Malyan", *Kadmos* 24(1): 1–12.

Strommenger, E. 1980. *Habuba Kabira. Eine Stadt vor 5000 Jahren, Ausgrabungen der Deutschen Orient-Gesellschaft am Euphrat in Habuba Kabira – Syrien*, Philipp von Zabern, Mainz-am-Rhein.

Sumner, W. M. 1986. "Proto-Elamite Civilization in Fars", in Finkbeiner, U. and Röllig, W. (eds), *Gamdat Nasr: Period or Regional Style*, Beihefte zum Tübinger Atlas des Vorderen Orients, Reihe B (Geisteswissenschaften), vol. 62, Dr. Ludwig Reichert Verlag, Wiesbaden: 199–211.

Sumner, W. M. 1988. "Prelude to Proto-Elamite Anshan: The Lapui phase", *Iranica Antiqua* 23: 23–43.

Sürenhagen, D. 1986. "Archaische Keramik aus Uruk-Warka. Erster Teil: Die Keramik der Schichten XVI–VI aus den Sondagen 'Tiefschnitt' und 'Sägegraben' in Eanna", *Baghdader Mitteilungen* 17: 7–95.

Sumner, W. M. 2003. *Early Urban Life in the Land of Anshan: Excavations at Tal-e Malyan in the Highlands of Iran*, Malyan Excavations Reports III, University Museum Monograph, 113, University of Pennsylvania Museum of Archaeology and Anthropology, Pennsylvania.

Tainter, J. A. 1988. *The Collapse of Complex Societies*, New Studies in Archaeology, Cambridge University Press, Cambridge.

Tainter, J. 1999. "Post-collapse societies", in Barker, G. (ed.), *Companion Encyclopedia of Archaeology*, Routledge, London, New York: 988–1030.

Tallon, F. 1987. *Métallurgie Susienne I. De la fondation de Suse au XVIIIe avant J.-C.*, Notes et Documents des Musées de France 15, Éditions de la Réunion des musées nationaux, Paris.

Ur, J. A. and Wilkinson, T. J. 2008. "Settlement and economic landscapes of Tell Beydar and its hinterland", in Lebeau, M. and Suleiman, A. (eds), *Beydar Studies 1*, Subartu, Brepols, Turnhout: 305–27.

Vallat, F. 1971. "Les documents épigraphiques de l'acropole (1969–1971)", *CDAFI* 1: 235–45.

Vallat, F. 1978. "Le matériel épigraphique des couches 18 à 14 de l'acropole", *Paléorient* 4: 193–96.

Vanden Berghe, L. 1954. *Archaeologische navorsingen in de omstreken von Persepolis*, Jaarbericht ex Oriente Lux 13: 394–408.

Vatandoust, A., Parzinger, H. and Helwing, B. eds 2011. *Early mining and metallurgy on the Central Iranian Plateau. Report on the first five years of research of the Joint Iranian-German Research Project*, Archäologie in Iran und Turan 9, Philip von Zabern, Mainz-am-Rhein.

Whitcomb, D. S. 1971. *The Proto-Elamite Period at Tall-i Ghazir, Iran*, B.A., Emory University, Athens, Georgia.

Wright, H. T. 1987. "Susiana Hinterlands during the era of primary state formation", in Hole, F. (ed.), *The Archaeology of Western Iran*, Smithsonian Series in Archaeological Inquiry, Washington DC, London: 141–55.

Wright, H. T. and Carter, E. 2003. "Archaeological survey on the Western Ram Hormuz Plain", in Miller, N. F. and Abdi, K. (eds), *Yeki Bud, Yeki Nabud: essays on the archaeology of Iran in honor of William M. Sumner*, Cotsen Institute of Archaeology at UCLA, Los Angeles: 60–82.

Wright, H. T. and Rupley, E. S. A. 2001. "Calibrated radiocarbon age determinations of Uruk-related assemblages", in Rothman, M. S. (ed.), *Uruk Mesopotamia and its Neighbors: Cross-Cultural Interaction and its Consequences in the Era of State Formation*, School of American Research Press, Santa Fe: 85–122.

Yoffee, N. and Cowgill, G. L. 1988. *The Collapse of Ancient States and Civilisations*, Tucson University of Arizona Press, Tucson.

7. THE *LATE CHALCOLITHIC* AND *EARLY BRONZE AGE* IN THE QAZVIN AND TEHRAN PLAINS: A CHRONOLOGICAL PERSPECTIVE

Hassan Fazeli Nashli, Hamid Reza Valipour and Mohammad Hossein Azizi Kharanaghi

Introduction

The Tehran and Qazvin plains are well suited for studying the rise and decline of cultural complexity from the sixth up to the start of the third millennium BC. The two plains are located on the southern side of the central Alburz Mountains and archaeologically have been defined as part of the north Central Plateau of Iran (Voigt and Dyson 1992). Chronologically, the fourth millennium BC of the north central plateau has been subdivided into the *Middle Chalcolithic* (*c.* 4000–3700 BC), *Late Chalcolithic* (*c.* 3700–3400 BC), and *Early Bronze Age I* (3400–2900 BC) periods (Fazeli *et al.* 2005; Pollard *et al.* 2012). Within the first half of the fourth millennium BC, most settlements of the north Central Plateau and north-east of Iran display similar cultural materials while during the second half of the fourth millennium BC the degree of cultural uniformity changed within the above regions (see Thornton, this volume). Within the Qazvin Plain cultural affiliation shifts to the central Zagros and north-west Iran after 3400 BC. Survey and excavations within the Tehran, Kashan, Qom, and Arisman plains reveal that the *Sialk III$_{6-7}$* ceramics ceased being used around 3400 BC and were replaced by *Proto-Elamite* cultural material after 3300 BC. The chronological framework of such cultural subdivision, based on the recent archaeological investigations at the most important sites in the north Central Plateau of Iran, allows the proposal of a medium date for the start and end of each period within the different sites (see Table 7.1).

The *Late Chalcolithic* period, which is referred to as *Sialk III$_{6-7}$* on the north Central Plateau, ended around 3400 BC. This date can be confirmed by the recent radiocarbon results acquired from the excavated sites of Tepe Ghabristan, Tappeh Sialk South, Arisman, and Qoli Darvish (Pollard *et al.* 2012). As mentioned above, within the two regions from 3400 to 2900 BC we see the appearance of two different cultural assemblages, the so-called Proto-*Elamite/proto-literate* and the *Kura-Araxes*. Therefore, the terminology of *Early Bronze Age I* will be used here to label the period from 3400 to 2900 BC in north central Iran.

Chronology of the fourth and the early third millennia BC: general information and absolute chronology

The most important fourth-millennium BC sites on the Tehran plain include Tepe Sadeghabadi, Tepe Shoqali, Mafin Abad, Maymoon Abad, Tepe Cheshmeh-Ali, Tepe Sofalin, Tepe Pardis, and Ahmadabad Kozegaran (Fig. 7.1). Eric Schmidt's unpublished ceramic collection from Tepe Cheshmeh-Ali, which is now housed in the University of Pennsylvania Museum of Archaeology and Anthropology and the Oriental Institute of the University of Chicago, includes a range of remarkable ceramics of the *Middle Chalcolithic* period and some sherds of the *Late Chalcolithic* period (Matney *et al.*, forthcoming). During the renewed excavation of Tepe Cheshmeh-Ali in 1997 no archaeological evidence was found for the *Middle* or *Late Chalcolithic* periods (Fazeli *et al.* 2004), suggesting that the cultural layers of these periods were disturbed after the 1930s. Evidence of the *Middle* and *Late Chalcolithic* periods was documented on the surface at Tepe Pardis, but during the excavation of the site in 2004 no cultural layers from either period were recovered, suggesting that cultural material of the fourth millennium BC was cut and disturbed

Table 7.1. Modelled transition dates for each site on the Central Plateau (cal. BC).

Cultural Period	Tepe Chahar Boneh	Tepe Ebrahim Abad	Tepe Zagheh	Tepe Ghabristan	Tepe Sagz Abad	Tepe Shizar	Arisman	Sialk N	Sialk S	Tepe Qoli Darvish	Cheshmeh-Ali	Tepe Pardis
Iron Age Iron Age I					*End 980* Start 1450	*Start 1700*				Start 1528		*Start 1536*
Late Bronze Age					End 1450 *Start 1780*	*End 1700*				End 1681		
Middle Bronze Age										End 1857		
Bronze Age EB II Kura-Araxes 2900–2000										Start 2088		
EB I Proto-literate 3400–2900						*Start 2970*	Start 3280		Start 3150	End 3002		
Late (LC) 3700–3400				*End 2700* Start 3780	End 3540 Start 3670	End 3940	End 3480					
Chalcolithic Middle (MC) 4000–3700				End 3780 Start 3940					End 3814 Start 3940			End 3333
Early (EC) 4300–4000				End 3940 Start 4390					End 3940			Start 4756
Late (TC II) 4600–4300		*End 5000*	End 4320								*End 4691*	End 4756
Transitional Chalcolithic Early (TC I) 5200–4600		Start 5120	Start 5380					Start 5145			Start 5167	Start 5102
Late Neolithic Late (LN II) 5600–5200	*End 5220* Start 5320	End 5120 *Start 5530*						End 5249 Start 5376				End 5102
Early (LN I) 6000–5600	End 5670 Start 6010							End 5715				

during the Parthian period (Coningham *et al.* 2004). In contrast, recent excavation at Tepe Shoqali indicates occupation history from the fifth to the fourth millennium BC (Hessari and Aliyari 2007), but in general there is a lack of clear excavated evidence for the *Late Chalcolithic* on the Tehran plain. Settlement survey data indicates that there was a reduction of site numbers on the Tehran plain from the *Late Chalcolithic* period onwards. The maximum site size during the *Chalcolithic* was 7 ha, suggesting that there were no large agglomerations of settled population during this period (Fazeli 2001). The settlements are located close to the riverbanks or springs, which helped villagers to access direct water resources. Some have only one phase of occupation, but most have multiple cultural phases.

The only excavated *Bronze Age I* (*Sialk IV, Proto-Elamite/proto-literate*) site of the Tehran plain is Tepe Sofalin, situated 1000 m above sea level (Hessari and Akbari 2007). The site is located to the north of the city of Pishva, very close to the borderlands of the central desert. While most *Chalcolithic* sites are located close to water sources and in areas suitable for agriculture and cultivation, Tepe Sofalin is located on the hilly flanks at the border of the plain and the desert, although it has been noted that the site sits adjacent to a large alluvial fan (Dahl *et al.*, this volume). During the first season in 2006, six trenches were opened, including three of 3 × 3 m, and one each of 4 × 4 m, 5 × 5 m, and 10 × 10 m. The 2006 season and later excavations

did not expose any evidence of architectural remains.

During the late fourth and the early third millennia BC, the size appears to have extended horizontally across an area of *c.* 15 ha, but this may not be an accurate indication of site size. The depth of archaeological layers of the site is less than 2 m, similar to the depth of occupation at Arisman (Helwing 2005b, this volume). *Chalcolithic* sites on the Iranian Central Plateau can typically be defined as tell sites with archaeological deposits ranging in depth from 5 to 12 m. Tepe Sofalin is clearly a different type of site, with a short period of occupation and no architecture exposed in the limited excavations.[1] Despite a lack of evidence for architectural remains or rich cultural layers at Tepe Sofalin, the ceramics of the mid- to late fourth millennium BC consist of so-called *Proto-Elamite* period forms. In addition, a large and important corpus of administrative material has been found together with the pottery at Tepe Sofalin, including a clay bulla and numerical and *Proto-Elamite* tablets. It is likely that the site was occupied for a short period of time, *c.* 200 years.

With regard to the chronology of the second half of the fourth millennium BC, it should be mentioned that the *Late Chalcolithic* and *Early Bronze Age* sites of the Tehran plain do not yet have any radiocarbon dates. As will be described below, the latest radiocarbon date from the *Late Chalcolithic* (*Sialk III$_{6-7}$*) at Tepe Sagzabad falls before *c.* 3550 BC. By looking at the radiocarbon results from Tepe Qoli

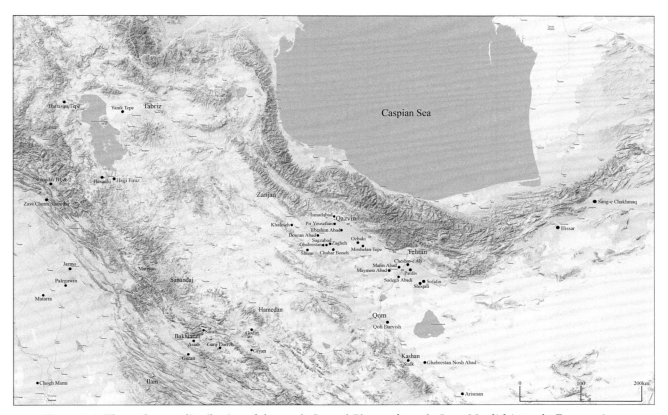

Figure 7.1. The settlement distribution of the north Central Plateau from the Late Neolithic to the Bronze Age.

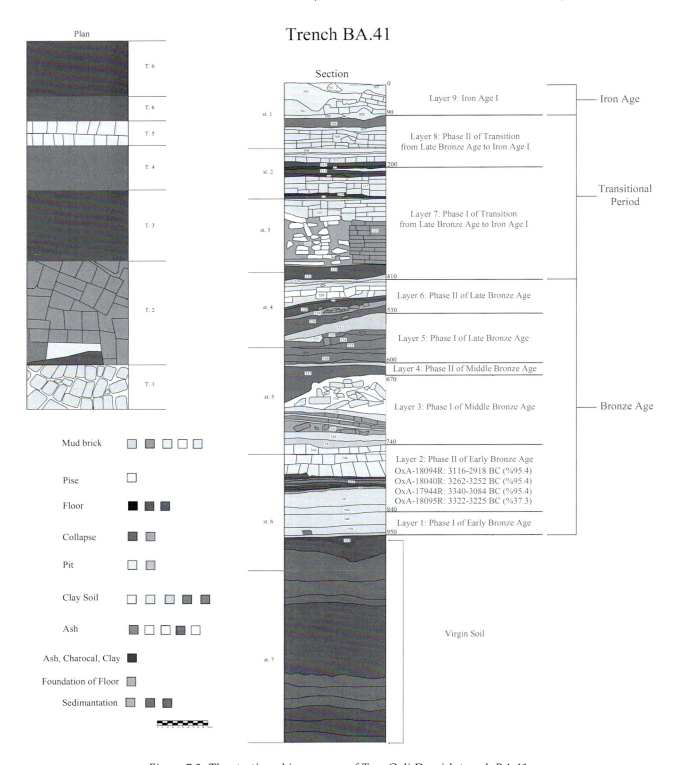

Figure 7.2. The stratigraphic sequence of Tepe Qoli Darvish trench BA.41.

Darvish (Fig. 7.2; Sarlak 2011), Tappeh Sialk South (Fig. 7.3; Nokandeh 2010), and Arisman (Helwing, this volume), however, it is possible to propose an approximate date for Tepe Sofalin. At Qoli Darvish, the *Early Bronze Age I* is defined by both *Proto-Elamite* ceramics and tablets, although the latter are very few in number. The calibration of four radiocarbon dates

from the single layer of trench BA.41 (layer 2 from the bottom) indicates a time period ranging between 3182 and 3035 cal. BC at 68%. Recent work on the Proto-Elamite tablets from Tepe Sofalin (Dahl *et al.*, this volume) indicates that the tablets are primarily comparable with the late *Proto-Elamite* tablets from Susa (except TSF 11). If we accept the radiocarbon

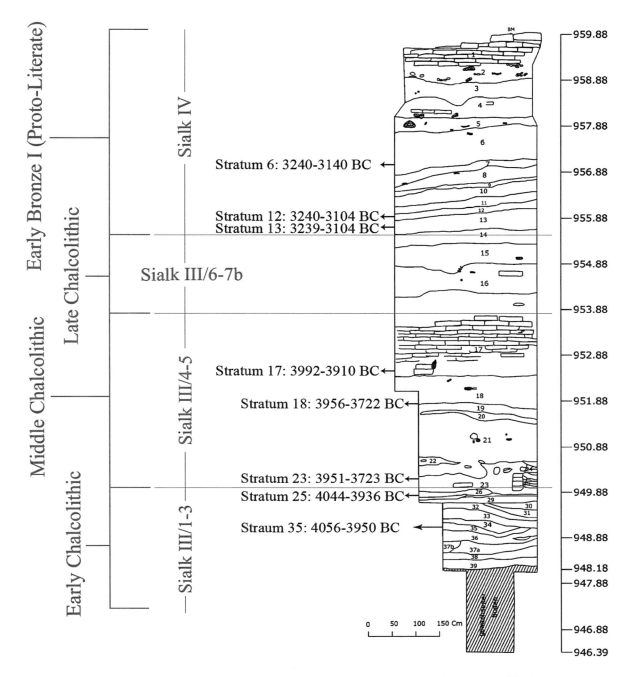

Section of Trench E1 (Nokandeh, 2010: 49, Abb. 6)

Figure 7.3. The stratigraphic sequences of Tappeh Sialk South trench E1.

date of Qoli Darvish and Dahl *et al.*'s correlation, then Tepe Sofalin potentially dates to the latest phase of the fourth millennium BC, *c.* 3100–2900 BC. Helwing has also categorised Tappeh Sialk *Period IV*$_2$ and Arisman area A and C as dating to the *Proto-Elamite* period, between 3100 and 2900 BC (Helwing 2006). Recent research carried out at Tappeh Sialk South reveals the *Late Chalcolithic* period with date ranges of 3710–3490 BC and 3760–3510 BC, indicating that the *Late Chalcolithic* period ended by *c.* 3500 BC. The

radiocarbon dates from Tappeh Sialk *Period IV* are as follows:

Trench E, level 6	3240–3104 cal. BC
Trench E, level 12	3240–3104 cal. BC
Trench E, level 13	3239–3104 cal. BC
(*Nokhandeh 2010*).	

These dates are very close to the radiocarbon results of Tepe Qoli Darvish, and indicate that the beginning of *Proto-Elamite* occupation around Kashan and Tehran started in *c.* 3250 BC (but see Dahl *et al.*, this volume). Information about the *Late Middle Chalcolithic* (4000–3700 BC), *Late Chalcolithic* (3700–3400 BC), *Early Bronze Age I* (3400–2900 BC), and *Early Bronze Age II/Kura-Araxes* (2900–2200 BC) on the Qazvin plain comes from excavations at four sites: Tepe Shizar, Tepe Ghabristan, Tepe Sagzabad, and Tepe Ismailabad, as well as a settlement survey undertaken in 2003 (Fazeli and Abbasnegad 2005). There is clear evidence for *Kura-Araxes* (*EBAII*), *Late Bronze*, and *Iron Age* ceramics from the surface of sites such as Duranabad and Pir Yousefin (Fazeli 2004) but in general, the evidence for the *Bronze Age* is limited and we suggest that the majority of the ceramics belong to the *Middle Bronze Age*. In contrast to the Tehran plain, however, for the Qazvin plain there are more secure data for the fourth millennium BC from large horizontal excavations, including stratigraphic information and radiocarbon dates. Nonetheless, as seen on the Tehran plain, after the second half of the fourth millennium BC most of the settlements of the Qazvin plain were abandoned. Occupation appears to have continued on the hilly flanks that border the Qazvin plain, but there are different settlement types and archaeological materials to those seen on the plains. Sites such as Tepe Shizar and Tepe Ismailabad are situated in areas more suitable for dry farming and also for the grazing of animals, while sites on the plains were more suitable for larger populations and agriculture based on irrigation. Recent palaeo-environmental studies (Schmidt *et al.* 2011; Maghsoudi *et al.* n.d.) within the Qazvin plain indicate that human population settled an area in order to access fresh water and appropriate soil for cultivation, making pottery and other activities. These studies also reveal that the migration of channels across the alluvial fan had affected the settlement abandonments of prehistoric communities of the Qazvin plain.

The most important settlement with fourth-millennium BC occupation on the Qazvin plain is Tepe Ghabristan with evidence for up to 700 years of occupation during the *Early*, *Middle*, and *Late Chalcolithic* periods (Fazeli *et al.* 2005). In the early 1970s E. O. Negahban, then director of the Institute of Archaeology, University of Tehran, instigated excavations at the sites of Zagheh, Ghabristan, and Sagzabad as part of a long-term project of archaeological research in the Qazvin plain that continued until 1979. At Ghabristan, several trenches were investigated, exposing 19 archaeological levels that corresponded to four cultural periods: Archaic, *Early*, *Middle*, and *Late Plateau* periods (Negahban 1973). Level 19 was the lowest level reached and was situated just above virgin soil, but no stratigraphic sequence was ever published and the chronology was established predominantly on ceramic evidence (see Fazeli *et al.* 2005). In order to understand the chronology and estimate the size of Tepe Ghabristan 11 trenches were opened during renewed excavations in 2002. Six trenches were exposed in the northern, southern, and western areas of the mound and a further five in the central region, close to the previously excavated area (Fazeli *et al.* 2005). Trenches in the northern and western sections contain natural clay deposits and graves dated to the first millennium BC. The two trenches in the south revealed only *Late Chalcolithic* materials, consisting mostly of the remains of a kiln and finds related to craft production. Only the five trenches in the central area covered the three main phases of *Early*, *Middle*, and *Late Chalcolithic* periods. All of the excavated areas so far appear to have exposed industrial areas.

Seven samples for radiocarbon dating were taken from Trench L34 (Fig. 7.4) to enable the re-evaluation of the chronology of Tepe Ghabristan (Fazeli *et al.* 2005). Trench L34 was 2 × 5 m at the surface and

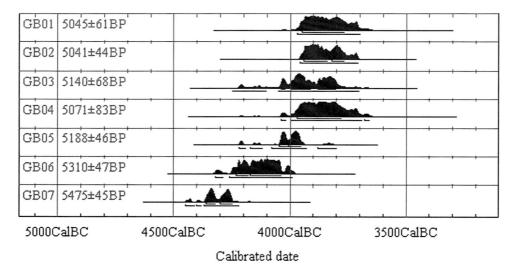

Figure 7.4. Radiocarbon dates of Tepe Ghabristan: trench L34.

reduced to 2 × 2 m at a depth of 2 m. Virgin soil was reached 5.3 m below ground surface, and an area of 4 × 2 m was exposed. A total of 18 separate layers comprising 29 contexts were identified. The two uppermost *Late Chalcolithic* layers were disturbed by illegal excavations. The first undisturbed layer was context 5, at a depth of 113 cm. A pit containing bone needles, stone tools and flakes, fragments of figurines, and round clay objects was exposed in context 8, and a further pit was revealed in context 11, where stone and copper tools, slag, and a microblade were found. Subsequent contexts contained walls, floors, and ovens. These recent excavations demonstrated that the beginning of the *Middle Chalcolithic* period at Tepe Ghabristan began *c.* 4000 BC and ended *c.* 3700 BC (Fazeli *et al.* 2005). On the basis of the 2002 excavations it was not possible to establish when the site was abandoned, but recent excavation at Tepe Sagzabad in 2008 has presented new and secure evidence for the *Late Chalcolithic* period.

The likelihood that Tepe Ghabristan was extensively occupied during the *Late Chalcolithic* period across an area of more than 15 ha is supported by the recent excavations at Tepe Sagzabad. Sagzabad is located 200 m east of Tepe Ghabristan and is approximately 12 ha in size, although most of this appears to be *Bronze* and *Iron Age* in date. The site has 10 m of archaeological deposits of which 5 are located under the modern ground surface. Unfortunately the site was very badly damaged both before and after the 1970s, and at present there is no unaffected area

suitable for horizontal excavation. For chronological purposes the team opened four vertical 2 × 2 m trenches at Tepe Sagzabad in 2008 in order to re-evaluate the chronology of the site (Fazeli *et al.* 2011). In trench IV (the south-west of the site) the team found evidence of *Late Chalcolithic* period occupation. Absolute dates from the two lower layers are 3760–3640 BC (context 4026) and 3650–3520 BC (context 4027) (Table 7.2). Also in 2008, a trench was opened in the garden situated between the two sites of Sagzabad and Tepe Ghabristan (95 m west of Tepe Sagzabad), which penetrated to a depth of 5.70 m below the ground surface. The layers in the uppermost 4 m contained only natural river sediments, but below this, between 40 and 50 cm of *Late Chalcolithic* period cultural materials consisting of animal bones and a variety of ceramics such as string-cut bases, buff ware (painted and unpainted), and bevel-rim bowls were recorded. During the 2009 excavation season, a 6 x 5 m trench was opened at Sagzabad close to trench IV to access more secure data for the *Chalcolithic* period. Of the 29 contexts exposed, 12 contained *Late Chalcolithic* ceramics, but only the lowest layer was not disturbed. The most recent excavations at Tepe Sagzabad support the theory that Tepe Ghabristan was abandoned *c.* 3550 BC when its size extended across more than 15 ha. The Sagzabad region was not reoccupied until around 1700 BC. The radiocarbon dates from the Tepe Sagzabad excavations indicate a *c.* 1700-year gap between the *Late Chalcolithic* period and the *Iron Age* occupation.

Table 7.2. Calibrated and modelled dates for Tepe Sagzabad based on archaeological period, including dates from Gif-sur-Yvette (Pollard et al. *2012).*

Sample no.	Trench	Context	Phase	Material	δ¹³C	¹⁴C age	Error	Range (2σ 95.4%)
Gif-10350	O XXI/2	L XIII		bone	-18.0	2950	40	1070–900 BC
Gif-10349	N XXI/2	L IX		bone	-19.2	2945	45	1300–930 BC
Gif-10348	A	LXXIV		bone	-18.0	2915	60	1300–1010 BC
Gif-10347	A	L XXX		bone	-19.6	2820	30	1300–1030 BC
OxA-20663	II	2006	IA I	charcoal	-23.7	2912	31	1250–1010 BC
OxA-20661	II	2008	IA I	charcoal	-25.6	2935	29	1260–1040 BC
OxA-20662	II	2015	IA I	charcoal	-22.6	3041	30	1410–1210 BC
OxA-20548	II	2017	IA I	charcoal	-25.7	3082	32	1425–1270 BC
OxA-20547	II	2022	IA I	charcoal	-25.9	3162	34	1500–1330 BC
OxA-20660	IV	4004	IA I	charcoal	-23.3	3021	28	1390–1130 BC
OxA-20658	IV	4010	IA I	charcoal	-26.5	2990	29	1370–1130 BC
OxA-20738	II	2034	LBA	charcoal	-23.9	3362	34	1740–1535 BC
OxA-20546	IV	4016	LBA	charcoal	-23.1	3225	30	1610–1430 BC
OxA-20659	IV	4026	LC	charcoal	-26.5	4909	33	3760–3640 BC
OxA-20657	IV	4027	LC	charcoal	-24.2	4791	32	3650–3520 BC

The two other excavated sites of the Qazvin plain, Tepe Ismailabad and Tepe Shizar, are both small sites located in the highland/mountainous region to the north of the Qazvin plain that is more suitable for grazing of animals/transhumant life and agriculture. Tepe Ismailabad is located to the north-west of the present city of Qazvin and is 100 × 70 m in size and has 4.50 m of archaeological deposits. The upper layers present evidence of *Early Bronze Age* while the lower layers consist of materials of the *Late Chalcolithic* period.

Tepe Shizar is a mound 19 m high located in a mountainous area, geographically a corridor valley linking the Central Plateau with the central western Zagros Mountains. A stratigraphic trench was opened in the site in 2006, and although 17 m of cultural deposits were excavated, the team could not reach virgin soil (Valipour 2006). A total of 52 contexts were recorded in trench I and 53 contexts in trench II. Based on radiocarbon dating and relative chronology, trench I covers the two main periods of *Bronze* and *Iron Age* occupation. Trench I produced only one *Bronze Age* date, 2570–2350 BC from context 1047 (Table 7.3). The latest radiocarbon dates from trench II2 are *Bronze Age* in date, spanning 2870–2620 BC (context 2034) and 2880–2620 BC (context 2013). Due to a lack of charcoal samples, however, the team could not date the whole sequence (Table 7.3). For example, there are no radiocarbon dates for the period between 3800 and 2890 BC, but based on the presence of *Early Bronze Age II* and *Middle Bronze Age/Kura-Araxes* ceramic types in burnished grey wares and red-slipped wares at the site there was

continuity of occupation throughout this period. The cultural materials from trench II at Tepe Shizar span the *Late Chalcolithic* and *Middle Bronze Ages*. In the lower layers of Tepe Shizar, *Dalma*-type ceramics were also recorded. This type of ceramic compares with that seen at Tepe Soha Chai in Zanjan, where it is dated between 4200 and 4000 BC. As we will see later in this paper we suggest the *Kura-Araxes* period at Tepe Shizar possibly started during the *Early Bronze Age II* period with no evidence of *Early Bronze Age I*, but we need larger excavations at the site to demonstrate exactly when this phase began.

By comparing the radiocarbon dates of Tepe Ghabristan and Shaizar it appears that there was a gap in settled occupation between 3550 and 1700 BC. In the hilly flanks and mountainous area there is short gap between *c.* 3500 and 2900 BC when *Kura-Araxes* cultural material appears.

Relative chronology and cultural interaction: a view from the ceramic evidence

During the *Middle* and *Late Chalcolithic* periods and the *Bronze Age*, a variety of painted and unpainted ceramics were recorded at various sites in the Tehran and Qazvin plains, which are significant for the study of the degree of cultural interaction through time and space and also for investigating questions regarding relative chronology. It seems that distinctive intercultural relationships within the Central Plateau started in the second half of the sixth millennium BC (Fazeli *et al.* 2009). The widespread distribution

Table 7.3. *Calibrated and modelled dates from Tepe Shizar assuming a single sequence from Trench II to Trench I (Pollard* et al. *2012).*

Sample no.	Trench	Context	Phase	Material	δ13C	14C age	Error	Range (2σ 95.4%)
OxA-18106	I	1002	IAI	charcoal	-20.2	2836	28	1110–910 BC
OxA-18107	I	1007	IAI	charcoal	-24.6	2925	28	1260–1020 BC
OxA-18108	I	1008	IAI	charcoal	-21.8	3034	27	1395–1210 BC
OxA-18201	I	1016	IAI	charcoal	-24.7	3333	29	1690–1530 BC
OxA-18202	I	1021	LBA	charcoal	-23.9	3334	30	1690–1525 BC
OxA-18109	I	1029	LBA	charcoal	-24.0	3467	29	1880–1690 BC
OxA-18110	I	1047	EBA	charcoal	-21.9	3961	30	2570–2350 BC
OxA-18255	II	2013	EBA	charcoal	-24.2	4143	35	2880–2620 BC
OxA-18203	II	2017	EBA	charcoal	-22.8	4106	32	2870–2505 BC
OxA-18204	II	2031	EBA	charcoal	-24.9	4174	33	2890–2630 BC
OxA-18205	II	2034	EBA	charcoal	-25.7	4137	32	2870–2620 BC
OxA-18206	II	2048	M & LC	charcoal	-24.8	5123	32	3990–3800 BC
OxA-18207	II	2048	M & LC	charcoal	-24.9	5127	32	4030–3800 BC
OxA-18334	II	2050	M & LC	charcoal	-25.4	5152	32	4040–3810 BC
OxA-18208	II	2051	M & LC	charcoal	-25.3	5184	33	4050–3950 BC

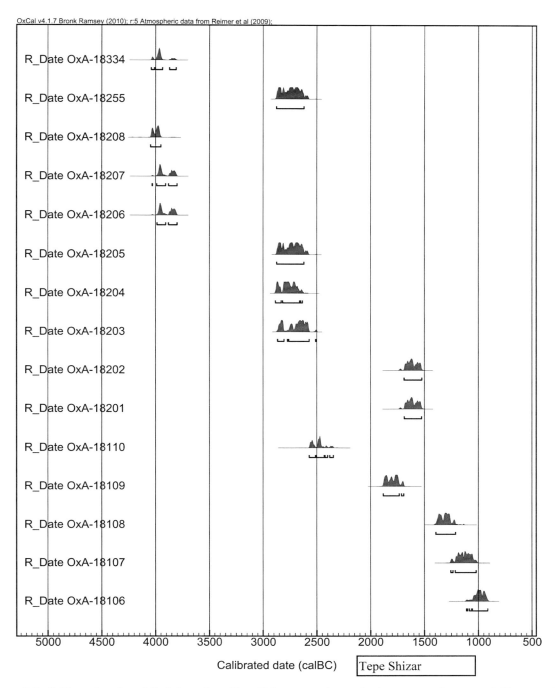

Figure 7.5. Calibrated and modelled dates from Tepe Shizar assuming a single sequence from trench II to trench I.

of *Sialk I* buff ware ceramics at settlements on the Tehran, Kashan, and Qazvin plains indicates a degree of interaction between the inhabitants of these plains during the second half of the sixth millennium BC. The fifth millennium BC saw the importation of raw materials and finished products such as turquoise, agate, carnelian, shells, as well as differentiation in mortuary practices, ritual activities, specialisation in craft production, long-distance trade, and intra-settlement relationship (Fazeli and Abbasnegad 2005). From the current data it seems that ranked societies

emerged on the Iranian Central Plateau during the fifth millennium BC, and continued in the fourth millennium BC (Helwing 2005a; Matthews and Fazeli 2004).

The ceramic evidence then suggests that from 3700 to 3400 BC some form of cultural relationships was established between the Iranian Central Plateau, central Zagros, south-western Iran, and Mesopotamia. During the *Bronze Age I* period there appear to have been new dynamics in play. The northern parts of the Central Plateau appear to be linked to northwest

Iran, as indicated by the appearance of *Kura-Araxes* ceramics, and to southwest Iran, as indicated by the appearance of *Proto-Elamite* material. In order to understand the nature and chronology of these dynamics on the north Central Plateau, we have classified the ceramics of the two plains into four major categories:

1. Ceramics that can be characterised as typical of the Iranian Central Plateau occurred mostly between 3700 and 3400 BC;
2. *Uruk* Mesopotamian types/initial *Proto-Elamite* (probably occurred between 3400 and 3150);[2]
3. *Proto-Elamite* occurred mostly between *c.* between 3150–2900.
4. *Kura-Araxes* types found after *c.* 3000 BC.

Middle Chalcolithic *period*

Archaeological evidence indicates that, from 5200 BC onwards ceramics were produced in workshop areas outside domestic spaces within the Qazvin and the Tehran plains in sites such as Tepe Zagheh and Tepe Pardis (Wong *et al.* 2010). Specialisation and centralisation of ceramic production is one of the main characteristics of the *Transitional Chalcolithic* period. The level of socio-economic differentiation established during the fifth millennium BC became more complex during the fourth millennium BC through the production of metal and ceramics in workshops at Tepe Ghabristan, which were spread across an area nearly 4 ha in size. A number of specific technological innovations in ceramic production are very characteristic of the *Middle Chalcolithic* period, including the use of the wheel and the firing of a variety of ceramic vessels in large kilns (Fig. 7.6).

The *Middle Chalcolithic* period is characterised by both red and cream/buff fabric ceramics, which have been described in detail by Majidzadeh (2008), who classified the period as *Ghabristan II*. The majority of the *Middle Chalcolithic* ceramics consists of, a) fine painted pottery; and b) crusted ware. The painted groups can be subdivided into the three groups: very fine, fine, and thick wares (Fazeli 2007).

FINE PAINTED WARE: The well-burnished painted fine wares were made with the use of a fast wheel and were fired in kilns at a high temperature (Wong 2008). Both organic and inorganic temper was used to prepare the clay and the finished ceramics were covered with a fine wash slip. The majority of fine painted wares consists of, 1) tall bowls with open rim and concave base; 2) bowls with trumpet base; and 3) small open bowls (Fig. 7.7). These forms are found widely distributed at sites including Tepe Ghabristan (Fazeli 2007), Tappeh Sialk (Ghirshman 1939), Tepe Cheshmeh-Ali (archive of the Pennsylvania Museum, Oriental Institute of the University of Chicago), Mafinabad, and Sadeghabadi (Fazeli 2001).

Approximately two-thirds of the exterior of these bowls was carefully decorated with geometric, plant, and animal designs. In general there is an increased range of designs in this period, which includes geometric motifs such as hatched bands, hour-glasses, alternately inverted filled triangles, parallel wavy bands with vertical hatching, combs and unilateral ladders, and representational motifs such as animals, birds, and plants. Spiral plants, both plain and decorated, and goats with decoration between the horn and body are also characteristic of this period (Fig. 7.8).

CRUSTED PAINTED WARES: based on the technology and the quality of firing, crusted painted wares can be divided into types: 1) wheel-made painted storage jars with the temper of organic materials, which are well fired; 2) handmade red storage jars tempered with organic material, which are low-fired (Fig. 7.9). From a technological point of view, usually the lower parts are made by sequential slab and the upper part is made

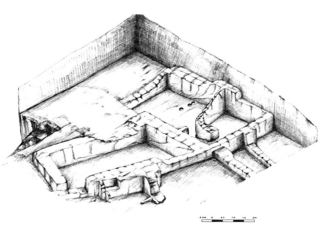

Figure 7.6. Three-dimensional plan of the Middle Chalcolithic *period ceramic kilns at Tepe Ghabristan.*

Figure 7.7. Examples of the three major fine painted ware of Tepe Ghabristan (from left to right): 1) tall bowls with open rim; 2) bowls with trumpet base; and 3) small open bowls.

Figure 7.8. Different motifs on Middle Chalcolithic pottery from Tepe Ghabristan.

Figure 7.9. Crusted painted wares: 1) wheel-made painted storage jar; 2) handmade red storage jar.

by coil techniques. The wheel-made large jars were fired while it seems the handmade vessels were fired in open kilns at a lower temperature. The wheel-made ceramics have simple everted rims and the upper part of the ceramic is painted with simple horizontal lines. About two-thirds of the storage jars have a cylindrical body and a sharp carination at the join with the small base. The surface is covered with a thick layer of slip. It is likely that many examples of these storage vessels were sunk and/or fixed in the floor. The whole surface of the handmade red storage jars was painted elaborately with both geometrical and animal designs such as the goat and snake. For example in Figure 7.9 (at right), three snakes are vertically depicted on the neck, and horizontal hatched motifs were added into the large goat with horns turned to the back. This indicates high investment of time on the production of even the crusted ware.

GREY WARE: the fourth-millennium BC grey ware of the Qazvin plain is different from the contemporary *Uruk*-type grey ware of Mesopotamia in respect of manufacturing technology, form, and decoration (Fig. 7.10). Burnished grey ware, initially thought by Majidzadeh (2008) to be restricted to Ghabristan, has since been found at other sites such as Ismailabad in Qazvin in a recent survey, and also at Tepe Ozbaki (Majidzadeh 2001: 143) and in Tappeh Sialk *Period III$_{6-7}$* (Nokandeh 2010). This is a handmade ceramic of dark grey to black fabric with a high proportion of organic material for temper; it is also slipped and highly burnished on both surfaces. The grey ware is either plain or decorated with incised motifs of parallel lines and diagonal or horizontal hatched alternating upright and inverted triangles with shared borders (Majidzadeh 2008). Grey fabric sherds are present in small numbers in the lower levels of the *Middle Chalcolithic* period and steadily increase through the *Late Chalcolithic*. Light-brown fabric ceramics, which in all other respects are similar to the grey ware, including the incised decoration, have also been recovered. This variety has been mentioned by Majidzadeh who considered it to be

of the same ceramic tradition. It is possible that these are examples of grey ware vessels that were not fired properly – i.e. too much oxygen came into the kiln, so they fired brown instead of grey. Majidzadeh (1977: 191–94; 1981) attributed the occurrence of the grey ware to the migration or invasion of new people from outside the Central Plateau. Grey ware is present in small numbers in the early *Middle Chalcolithic* levels, however, and its production increases in the later *Middle Chalcolithic* and the *Late Chalcolithic* levels, providing evidence of a very gradual introduction and increasing use of grey ware over time. Such a pattern indicates an internal innovation rather than a sudden introduction by an unknown conquering people. The so-called "grey ware", therefore, should be seen as an innovation that took place within the north-western Central Plateau tradition rather than as a result of migration. Furthermore, there is no parallel in either forms or decoration in the *Kura-Araxes* region or Mesopotamia in this period.

SIMPLE BUFF WARE: this buff ware was made by sequential technique and used large organic materials for temper. These ceramics were fired at a relatively low temperature and appear to have been used for cooking. Simple shallow buff ware vessels have flat bases with vertical rims and a cylindrical body. At Tepe Ghabristan one simple cylindrical flat base with a height of 12 cm was found (Fig. 7.11/1).

SIMPLE RED WARE: simple red ware is very similar to buff ware and its only difference is its colour. This handmade ware was covered with a thick layer of slip and fired at a relatively low temperature. Vessel forms consist of open bowls with concave base that appear in both large and small sizes (Fig. 7.11/2).

Late Chalcolithic *period*

The *Late Chalcolithic* period is characterised by increased interaction between the Iranian Central Plateau, the central Zagros, and Mesopotamia as attested by the presence of painted buff ware, string-cut bases, and bevel-rim bowls. Except for Arisman,

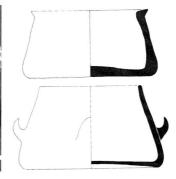

Figure 7.10. Tepe Ghabristan grey ware samples.

most of the information for this period comes from surface data and vertical excavation.

BUFF WARE: very fine wheel-made painted and unpainted buff and/or very pinkish ware has frequently been recovered from the *Late Chalcolithic* period deposits at sites such as Tepe Ghabristan (Fig. 7.12 and 7.13), Tepe Maymoonabad, Arisman, and Tappeh Sialk. Common forms include vertical and inverted-rim hemispherical bowls of shallow to medium depth, some with a pedestal base painted with rows of animal decoration such as leopards, goats with S-shaped horns, and cups and open bowls with concave and oblique walls, incurving and flared rims, and flat base. A thin wash is typically present on both surfaces. Temper consists mainly of inorganic material and the clay appears well

Figure 7.11. (1) Simple buff ware and (2) simple red ware from Tepe Ghabristan.

Figure 7.12. Painted buff ware from Tepe Sagzabad.

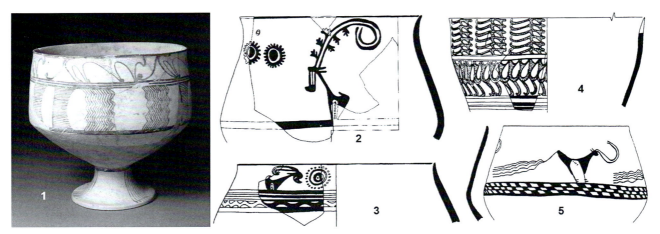

Figure 7.13. Painted buff ware from different sites: 1), 2), 3) and 4) from Tappeh Sialk Period III6–7; 5) from Godin Tepe.

Figure 7.14. String-cut bases from Tepe Maymoonabad.

levigated. Most motifs consist of geometric designs but stylised animals such as goats, leopards, cattle, and birds were found in abundance.

The presence of some of the typical Iranian Central Plateau ceramics such as buff wares at sites such as Godin Tepe(Rothman and Badler 2011; Rothman, this volume) indicates that a degree of interaction and communication had been established with the central western Zagros during the second half of the fourth millennium BC.

STRING-CUT BASES: very few samples of string-cut bases were recovered from Tepe Ghabristan during the excavations in 2006 from the disturbed layers above the *Middle Chalcolithic* layers. String-cut bases were found in *Late Chalcolithic* period deposits, however, at Tepe Maymoon Abad on the Tehran plain (Fig. 7.14). Use of the wheel indicates a specific skill level and also attempts to reduce the amount of time spent on ceramic production. The vessel must first be thrown enough to be quite symmetrical (Badler 2002). Unfortunately the small number of string-cut bases on the two plains does not permit analysis of the shapes and forms, but they all appear to come from small bowls.

BEVEL-RIM BOWLS: during the *Late Chalcolithic* period there was a change in the choice of physical characteristics of the ceramics that were utilised on the Tehran and Qazvin plains, as attested by the adoption of coarse ceramics such as bevel-rim bowls. The bevel-rim bowl is the most obvious example of utilitarian coarse ceramics found in the *Late Chalcolithic* sites of Ghabristan (Fig. 7.15), Maymoonabad, Cheshmeh-Ali, and Tappeh Sialk III$_{6-7}$. At Tepe Ghabristan, 50 bevel-rim bowl fragments were found in the workshop areas, and small numbers have also been recorded at other *Chalcolithic* sites (Potts 2009; see also Mayyas *et al.* 2012). Bevel-rim bowls have a widespread distribution during the fourth millennium BC in the Near East, especially in Mesopotamia, Iran, and Anatolia (e.g. Millard 1988; Nissen 1988; Algaze 1989; Buccellati 1990; Stein and Misir 1994; Brown D. 2000; Matthews and Fazeli 2004; see particularly the review by Potts 2009).

Many authors have considered the purpose of these bowls depending on their production characteristics, abundance, standard size, and presence in specific archaeological contexts, particularly alongside symbolic or administrative artefacts (Adams 1960: 9;

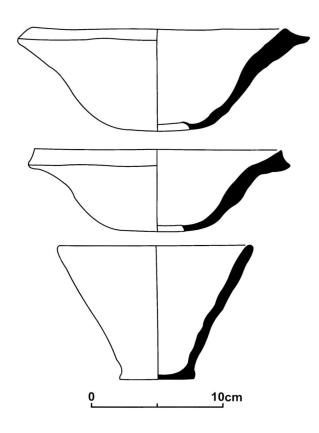

Figure 7.15: Bevel-rim bowls from Tepe Ghabristan (Majidzadeh 2008).

0   10cm

Nissen 1970: 137; Beale 1978; Millard 1988; Buccellati 1990; Algaze 1993; Nissen *et al.* 1993: 14, 70). In terms of function, there is a range of evidence that suggests that bevel-rim bowls were used as bread containers or/and moulds for baking bread (Millard 1988; also Potts 2009; Goulder 2010).

Early Bronze Age I

As was explained earlier, the two sites of Tepe Shizar and Ismailabad represent the cultural periods of the early third millennium BC and so far there is archaeological evidence to fill the gap from 3550 to 2900 BC within the region. There was also a hiatus in occupation at Tepe Ghabristan and Sagzabad from 3500 to 1700 BC. The *Kura-Araxes* material culture is distributed across a vast area, stretching from the Caucasus, across northern Mesopotamia and into the central Zagros (Young 1966; Burney and Laing 1971; Kiguradze and Sagona 2003; Rothman and Kozbe 1997; Kushnareva 1997; Rothman and Badler 2011). In the north-west of Iran sites such as Tepe Baroj (Alizadeh and Azarnoush 2002), Goy Tepe K1-2 (Brown 1951), Geglar Tepe B, Yanik I–II (Burney 1962, 1964), and Haftavan Tepe VII–VIII (Burney 1970, 1973, 1975) have evidence of *Kura-Araxes* material

culture. The chronology of the *Kura-Araxes* period has been divided into 3500–3000 BC for the *Early* (KA I), 3000–2700 BC for the *Middle* (KA II), and 2700–2200 BC for the *Late Kura-Araxes* (KA III) periods (Peasnall and Rothman 1999; Rothman and Kozbe 1997). The appearance of *Kura-Araxes* material in the central western Zagros is seen at sites such as Godin IV (Young and Levine 1974; Rothman 2011, this volume) and third-millennium BC Tepe Gurabin, which appears to correspond to the *Kura-Araxes II* period. As we will see below, the *Early Bronze Age II/Kura-Araxes* ceramics of Tepe Shizar belong to a period ranging from *c.* 3000 to 2700 BC. At Tepe Shizar on the Qazvin plain, four main categories of pottery were recorded:

1. Red pottery (simple and painted);
2. Buff pottery (simple and painted);
3. Grey ware;
4. *Kura-Araxes* type.

RED WARE: Simple red ceramics are covered with red slip on the surface with a buff and red colour core. The surfaces of some sherds have traces of smoke, which indicates that they were used for cooking. The ceramics are well fired and have inorganic materials used for temper. Forms include bowls, jars, and plates. Most of the vessel forms are small or large bowls. The large bowl forms have open mouths and the body varies from hemispherical to vertical. Small bowls include open forms with concave base and everted rim. Some small bowls have a carination on the body. Large bowls have flat bases and some have a carination on the body. Small storage jars have a hemispherical body with everted rim. One sample has a handle comparable in form to some from the *Kura-Araxes* assemblages (Fig. 7.16). Only three painted black-on-red sherds were found, which are technologically very similar to the simple red types, and come from small bowls painted with simple geometric designs (Fig. 7.17).

BUFF WARE: simple buff wares were recorded in trench I, and very few samples came from trench II. As far as the technology is concerned there is differentiation in the manufacture of the ceramics from the beginning to the end of the use of this type of ceramic. The pottery of trench I has a thick layer of buff slip and is not considered to be fine ware. The simple buff wares of trench I are handmade, well fired, and the temper is of organic materials. Forms consist of closed rim bowls and beakers (Fig. 7.18). The simple buff wares of trench II have both organic and inorganic temper with a thick slip, and can be classified as fine wares. Both wheel-made and handmade techniques were used in the production process. Large jars and bowls are the main group of forms found in trench II (Fig. 7.19). Painted buff wares were found in both trenches but did not consistently occur in all layers. The colour of the paint is usually brown but very rarely black was also used. Common designs consist of horizontal

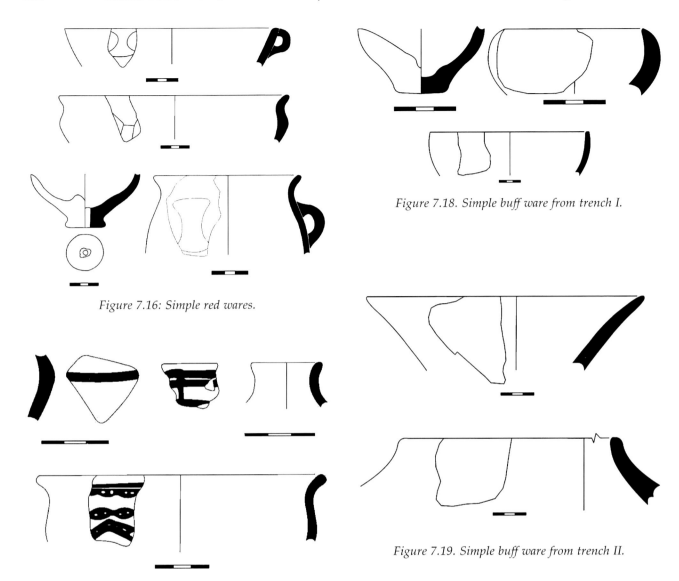

Figure 7.16: Simple red wares.

Figure 7.17. Painted red wares.

Figure 7.18. Simple buff ware from trench I.

Figure 7.19. Simple buff ware from trench II.

and vertical geometric lines. Usually most of the paint was applied on the exterior surface, but very rarely on the inside of the vessels. Most of the painted buff fragments were body sherds, making it very difficult to comment about the range of forms, although some belong to small bowls with vertical body and everted rim (Figs 7.20–7.21). The painted buff vessels were wheel-made and decorated with geometric designs.

GREY WARE: this type of pottery was only found in trench I and consists of very dark to light grey fabric that in some cases has a red core. The ceramics are well fired, and organic temper was used for both handmade and wheel-made vessels. Some sherds were also burnished and there are both simple and painted wares. Forms consist of jars and bowls. Bowls appear in two sizes, small and large. Small bowls have an S-shaped body, although there are also open bowls and some with a hemispherical

body. Large bowls have a flat base, and close to the rim it flares out from the hemisperical body (Fig. 7.22).

KURA-ARAXES CERAMICS: the burnished fine black *Kura-Araxes* ceramics are one of the important groups of Tepe Shizar (Fig. 7.23), which technologically can be compared with the material from other contemporary sites in the central Zagros of Iran. The *Kura-Araxes* wares consist of both simple and painted groups. Engraved and painted decoration was applied mostly in the upper parts of vessels close to the neck and consist of horizontal zigzags, points, and sun-like shapes, etc. Forms consist of bowls, jars, and beakers and some have handles with a flat base. The ceramics of Tepe Shizar can be compared with the site of Tepe Gourab in Malyer and also with Tepe Doranabad on the Qazvin plain (Fazeli and Abbasnegad 2005).

Figure 7.20. Painted buff ware from trench I.

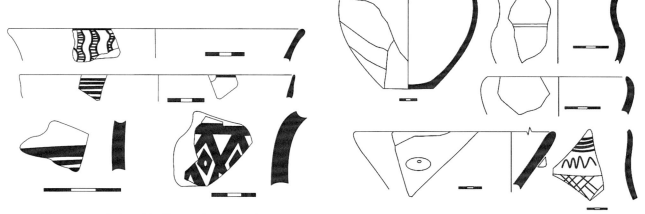

Figure 7.21. Painted buff ware from trench II.

Figure 7.22. Grey ware ceramics.

Figure 7.23. The Kura-Araxes ceramics from Tepe Shizar.

Proto-Elamite ceramics: Hessari's recent publication indicates the following pottery types in Tepe Sofalin (Fig. 7.24; Hessari and Akbari 2007). A similar ceramics assemblage was also found at Qoli Darvish (Fig. 7.25), Tappeh Sialk, and Arisman. Most of the ceramics from Tepe Sofalin are comparable with those of the above-mentioned sites and consist of:

1. Bevel-rim bowls;
2. Pedestal-based goblets;
3. Banesh trays (*Uruk* tray);
4. Hole-mouth wares;
5. Drooping spout wares;
6. Everted wares;
7. Folded wares;
8. Ledge rim ware (Hessari 2011).

The waste materials, slag, and kiln remains from the site also indicate local production of *Proto-Elamite* ceramics. Administrative artefacts from the site include tokens with the different shapes ranging from simple spheres to cones, rectangles, triangles, bi-conoids, and even jugs and animals. One example of a clay bulla was also found, bearing the impression of a cylinder seal, revealing administrative activities. Dahl *et al.*'s (this volume) analysis of the *Proto-Elamite* tablets found at Tepe Sofalin reveals similarities to the tablets from Susa, and Dahl *et al.* suggest that there were links between the two settlements during the *Proto-Elamite* period.

Conclusion

A long history of occupation on the plains to the south of the Alburz Mountains is demonstrated in Table 7.1. Chronological studies within the above regions started in the 1930s with the excavation of Tepe Hissar (Schmidt 1937) and have continued up to the present (e.g. Sarlak 2011; Vatandoust *et al.* 2011). Such studies indicate that agricultural village societies first appeared on the north Central Plateau around *c.* 6000 BC. In chronological terms, the beginning of the settled occupation up to the end of the *Bronze Age* can be summarised as follows:

1. Gap in occupation at the *Neolithic* sites of Chahar Boneh;
2. It is clear that there is a gap in occupation at many settlements on the Qazvin, Tehran, and Kashan plains during the fifth millennium BC. For example, there is a large gap between the two settlements of Tappeh Sialk North and Tappeh Sialk South of at least 600 years. Such an interruption occurred in many settlements of the Qazvin plain (Fazeli *et al.* 2005, 2009; Pollard *et al.*, 2012). For instance, Tappeh Sialk North was abandoned at *c.* 4900 BC and from then until 4600 BC there is a period of alluvial sedimentation which may be associated with the cause of site abandonment;
3. As discussed above, there is little persistence in settlement occupation on the Tehran and Qazvin plains during the fourth and third millennia BC. There is a gap in occupation of up to 1700 years at large settlements, *c.* 1700–1800, such as Tepe Ghabristan (*Late Chalcolithic*) and Tepe Sagzabad (*Late Bronze Age*). No strong archaeological evidence supports the continuity of occupation in other parts of the plain, although there is some evidence that small-scale occupation continued in the hilly flanks, but with some interruption. Tepe Shizar is one example in which even in the mountainous area there is a gap from *c.* 3500 to 2900 BC.
4. In 2011 the site of Maymoonabad was excavated under the direction of Rohollah Yousefi mainly for

chronological purposes. His excavation indicates that, while some parts of the site are represented with 6 m of *Sialk III$_{6-7}$* ceramics, other parts show less than 2 m of *Uruk* cultural materials and architecture (Yousefi, personal communication), which is similar to the sequence seen at Arisman, where there was a sudden shift in the location of the settlement between the two periods (Helwing, this volume). Helwing (2006) also proposed the terminology of a *Proto-Elamite* transitional period (3400–3100 BC) parallel with the cultural layers of Tepe Maymoonabad.

5. Related to the beginning of the *Proto-Elamite* within the Central Plateau, although Arisman somehow fills the gap between the *Late Chalcolithic* and *Early Bronze Age 1*, there is a gap in occupation of around 300 to 200 years in many settlements. In some settlements there is evidence of a short period of *Proto-Elamite*, but there is no archaeological information from *c.* 2900 to 1700 BC in the Qazvin, Tehran, Kashan, and Qom plains.

More archaeological evidence is needed to establish whether there was some type of economic crisis or whether socio-political factors caused the abandonment of sites, or even whether environmental factors caused system change. The recent palaeo-environmental studies within the Kashan plain (Simpson and Kouramps *et al.* in press), the Tehran plain (Gilmore *et al.* 2007), and the Qazvin plain (Schmidt *et al.* 2011) support the theory that environmental factors such as Holocene climate change and environmental catastrophes such as earthquakes, floods, and volcanoes may have caused changes in cultural behaviour, social complexity, and human settlement patterns (e.g. Berberian and Yeats 2001; Haug *et al.* 2003; Brooks 2006; Staubwasser and Weiss 2006; Kaniewski *et al.* 2008). Many settlements in Iran, including sites on the Iranian Central Plateau, are situated on active alluvial fans, which pose flood and sediment inundation hazards, but provide fertile soils for agriculture. Furthermore, many settlements are situated close to active faults, which are sources of large earthquakes but also provide conduits for water, thus justifying the so-called "fatal attraction" of humans to earthquake-prone locations (Jackson 2006; Schmidt *et al.* 2011). We hope that by combining archaeological, climatological, and geological studies in the region in the future, it will be possible to present a better understanding of the human past in this part of Iran.

Acknowledgements

The authors are grateful to Drs Hessari and Yousefi who gave us their unpublished data from the two sites of Sofalin and Tepe Maymoonabad.

Notes

1   In the 2011 season of excavation the excavators of Tepe Sofalin found evidence of architectural remains (Hessari, personal communication).

2   The information about the settlement history of the Central Iranian Plateau between 3400 and 3150 BC is not exactly clear. In 2011 Rohollah Yousefi excavated Maymoonabad and of the two trenches excavated by him, one revealed cultural materials belonging to the *Sialk III$_{6-7}$* period and the second trench provided information on *Uruk* materials. Therefore, by ^{14}C date of the site and publication of the excavation report, they probably date to the end of the *Late Chalcolithic* period and the beginning of the *Proto-Elamite*.

Bibliography

Adams, R. M. 1960. "The origin of cities", *Scientific American* 203(3): 153–68.

Algaze, G. 1989. "The Uruk expansion: cross-cultural exchange in Early Mesopotamian civilization", *Current Anthropology* 30: 571–608.

Algaze, G. 1993. *The Uruk World System: The Dynamics of Expansion of Early Mesopotamian Civilization*, University of Chicago Press, Chicago.

Alizadeh, M. and Azarnoosh, M. 2002. "Tepe Baroj systematic survey, Sampling methods and results of statistical studies", *Journal of Archaeology and Art History* 33: 16–33.

Badler, V. R. 2002. "Chronology of Uruk artefacts from Godin Tepe in Central Western Iran and implications for the interrelationships between the local and foreign cultures", in Postgate, J. N. (ed.), *Artefacts of Complexity, Tracking the Uruk in the East*, vol. 5, Iraq Archaeological Reports, British School of Archaeology in Iraq, London: 79–109.

Beale, T. W. 1978. "Bevelled rim bowls and their implications for change and economic organization in the later fourth millennium B.C.", *JNES* 37: 289–313.

Berberian, M. and Yeats, R. S. 2001. "Contribution of archaeological data to studies of earthquake history in the Iranian Plateau", *Journal of Structural Geology* 23(2–3): 563–84.

Brooks, N. 2006. "Cultural responses to aridity in the Middle Holocene and increased social complexity", *Quaternary International* 151: 29–49.

Brown, B. T. 1951. *Excavations in Azerbaijan, 1948*, J. Murray, London.

Brown, D. 2000. "The cuneiform conception of celestial space and time", *Cambridge Archaeological Journal* 10(1): 103–22.

Buccellati, G. 1990. "Salt at the dawn of history: the case of the bevelled-rim bowls", in Matthiae, P., van Loon, M. and Weiss, H. (eds.), *Resurrecting the Past: A Joint Tribute to Adnan Bounni*, Nederlands Instituutvor het NabijeOosten, Leiden: 17–40.

Burney, C. A. 1962. "Excavation at Yanik Tepe, Azerbaijan, 1961", *Iraq* 24: 134–52.

Burney, C. A. 1964. "Excavations at Yanik Tepe, Azerbaidjan, 1962: third preliminary report", *Iraq* 26: 54–62.

Burney, C. A. 1970. "Excavations at Haftavan Tepe 1968: first preliminary report", *Iran* 8: 157–72.

Burney, C. A. 1973. "Excavations at Haftavan Tepe 1971: third preliminary report", *Iran* 11: 153–72.

Burney, C. A. 1975. "Excavations at Haftavan Tepe 1973: fourth preliminary report", *Iran* 13: 149–64.

Burney, C. and Lang, D. 1971. *The Peoples of the Hills, Ancient and Ararat Caucasus*, Weidenfeld and Nicholson, London.

Coningham, R.A.E., Fazeli, N.H., Young, R. and Donahue, R. 2004. "Location, location, location: a pilot survey of the Tehran plain in 2003", *Iran* 42: 1–12.

Fazeli, H. 2001. *Social complexity and craft specialisation in the late Neolithic and Early Chalcolithic period in the Central Plateau of Iran*, unpublished Ph.D. dissertation, University of Bradford.

Fazeli, N. H. 2004. *The Archaeology of the Qazvin Plain from the Sixth to the First Millennium BC*, University of Tehran Press, Tehran.

Fazeli, N. H. ed. 2007. *Socioeconomic Transformation of the Qazvin Plain, Excavation of Tepe Ghabristan, Season III*, Iranian Center for Archaeological Research, Tehran.

Fazeli, N. H. and Abbasnegad, R. S. 2005. "Social Transformation and International interaction in the Qazvin Plain during the 5th, 4th and 3th millennia B.C.", *AMIT* 37: 7–26.

Fazeli, N. H., Coningham, R. A. E. and Batt, C. M. 2004. "Cheshmeh-Ali revisited: towards an absolute dating of the Late Neolithic and Chalcolithic of Iran's Tehran Plain", *Iran* 42: 13–23.

Fazeli, N. H., Wong, E. and Potts, D. T. 2005. "The Qazvin Plain revisited: a reappraisal of the chronology of north western Central Plateau, Iran in the 6th to the 4th millennium BC", *Ancient Near Eastern Studies* 42: 3–82.

Fazeli, N. H., Darabi, H., Naseri, R. and Fallahian, Y. 2011. "Relative and absolute dating of Tepe Sagzabad, Qazvin plain", *Journal of Archaeological Research* 3: 133–58 (in Persian).

Fazeli, N. H., Beshkani, A., Markosian, A., Ilkani, H. and Young, R. 2009. "The Neolithic to Chalcolithic transition in the Qazvin Plain, Iran: chronology and subsistence strategies", *AMIT* 41: 1–21.

Ghirshman, R. 1939. *Fouilles de Sialk*, Volume I, Geuthner, Paris.

Gilmore, G. K., Coningham, R. A. E., Young, R., Fazeli, N. H., Rushworth, G., Donhworth, G., Batt, G. 2007. "Holocene alluvial sediments of the Tehran Plain: sedimentation and archaeological site visibility", in Willson, L., Dickinson, P. and Jeandron, J. (eds), *Reconstructing Human-Landscape Interactions*, Cambridge Scholars, Newcastle: 37–67.

Goulder, J. 2010. "Administrators' bread: an experiment-based re-assessment of the functional and cultural role of the Uruk bevel-rim bowl", *Antiquity* 84 (324): 351–62.

Haug, G. H., Gunther, D., Peterson, L. C., Sigman, D. M., Hughen, K. A. and Aeschlimann, B. 2003. "Climate and the collapse of Maya civilization", *Science* 299 (5613): 1731–35.

Helwing, B. 2005a. "Early mining and metallurgy on the western Iranian Plateau: first results of the Iranian-German archaeological research at Arisman, 2000–2004", *AMIT* 37: 423–34.

Helwing, B. 2005b. "Long-distance relations of the Iranian Highlands sites during the Late Chalcolithic Period: new evidence from the joint Iranian-German excavations at Arisman, Prov, Isfahan, Iran", in Franke-Vogt, U. and Weisshaar, H-J. (eds), *South Asian Archaeology 2003*, FAAK Band 1, Aachen: 171–78.

Helwing, B. 2006. "The rise and fall of Bronze Age centers around the Central Iranian Desert – a comparison of Tappe Hesar II and Arisman", *AMIT*: 35–48.

Hessari, M. 2011. "New evidence of the emergence of complex societies on the central Iranian plateau", *Iranian Journal of Archaeological Studies* 1.2: 35–48.

Hessari, M. and Akbari, H. 2007. "The preliminary excavation report on Sofalin mound in Pishva", *The 9th Annual Congress [meeting] of the Iranian Archaeologists*, Volume 1, Iranian Cultural Heritage, Tourism and Handicraft Organization, Tehran: 131–64.

Hessari, M. and Aliyari, M. A. 2007. "The report of stratigraphy at Shoghali mound in Pishva", *The 9th Annual Congress [meeting] of the Iranian Archaeologists*, Volume 1, Iranian Cultural Heritage, Tourism and Handicraft Organization, Tehran: 165–200.

Jackson, J. 2006. "Fatal attraction: living with earthquakes, the growth of villages into megacities, and earthquake vulnerability in the modern world", *Philosophical Transactions of the Royal Society A – Mathematical Physical and Engineering Sciences* 364 (1845): 1911–25.

Kaniewski, D., Paulissen, E., Van Campo, E., Al-Maqdissi, M., Bretschneider, J. and Van Lerberghe, K. 2008. "Middle East coastal ecosystem response to middle-to-late Holocene abrupt climate changes", *Proceedings of the National Academy of Sciences* 105 (37): 13941–46.

Kiguradze, T. and Sagona, A. 2003. "On the origins of the Kura-Araxes cultural complex", in Smith, A. and Rubinson, K. (eds), *Archaeology in the Borderlands*, Costin Institute of Archaeology, Los Angeles: 38–94.

Kourampas, N; Simpson, I. A. Fazeli Nashli, H. Manual, M. Coningham, R. in press. "Sediments, Soils and Livelihood in a Late Neolithic Village on the Iranian Plateau: Tepe Sialk", in Matthews, R. and Fazeli Nashli, H. (eds), *The Neolithization of Iran, the formation of Neolithic societies*, Oxbow and BANEA, Oxford.

Kushnareva, Kh. K. 1997. *The Southern Caucasus Prehistory, Stages of Cultural and Socioeconomic Development from the Eighth to the Second Millennium BC*, translated by H. N. Michael, University Museum of Pennsylvania, Philadelphia.

Maghsoudi, M., Simpson, I., A. Kourampas, A. and Fazeli, N. A. n.d. *Effect of Environmental Condition on Settlement Formation in Qazvin Plain-Iran.*

Majidzadeh, Y. 1977. *Tepe Zagheh: A Sixth Millennium B.C. Village in the Qazvin Plain of the Central Iranian Plateau*, unpublished Ph.D. dissertation, Department of Anthropology, University of Pennsylvania.

Majidzadeh, Y. 1981. "Sialk III and the pottery sequence at Tepe Ghabristan, the coherence of the cultures of the Central Iranian Plateau", *Iran* 19: 141–146.

Majidzadeh, Y. 2001. "Les Fouilles d'Ozbaki (Iran). Campagnes 1998–2000", *Paléorient* 27(1): 141–45.

Majidzadeh, Y. 2008. *Excavation at Tape Ghabrestan, Iran*, IsIAo, Rome.

Matney, T., Thornton, C., Fazeli, N. H., and Pittman, H. forthcoming. *The Schmidt Expedition to Cheshmeh Ali, Iran, 1934–1936*, University of Pennsylvania Museum of Archaeology and Anthropology, Philadelphia.

Matthews, R. and Fazeli, N. H. 2004. "Copper and complexity: Iran and Mesopotamia in the fourth millennium BC", *Iran* 42: 61–75.

Mayyas, A., Stern, B., Gillmore, G., Coningham, R. A. E. and Fazeli, N. H. 2012. "Beeswax preserved in a Late Chalcolithic Bevelled-rim bowl from the Tehran Plain, Iran", *Iran* 50: 13–25.

Millard, A. R. 1988. "The bevelled-rim bowls: their purpose and significance", *Iraq* 50: 49–57.

Negahban, E. O. 1973. "Preliminary Report on the Excavation of Sagzabad", *Marlik* 1: 1–19 (in Persian).

Nissen, H. J. 1970. "Grabunge in den Quadraten K/L XII in Uruk-Warka", *BaM* 5: 101–91.

Nissen, H. J. 1988. *The Early History of the Ancient Near East, 9000–2000 B.C.*, University of Chicago, Chicago.

Nissen, H., Damerow, P. and Englund, R. K. 1993. *Archaic Bookkeeping: Early Writing and Techniques of Economic Administration in the Ancient Near East*, University of Chicago Press, Chicago.

Nokandeh, G. 2010. *Neue Untersuchungen zur Sialk III-Periode im zentraliranischen Hochland : auf der Grundlage der Ergebnisse des, Sialk Reconsideration Project*, unpublished Ph.D. dissertation, Verlag im Internet GmbH, Berlin.

Peasnall, B. and Rothman, M. S. 1999. "Societal evolution of small, pre-state centers and polities: the example of Tepe Gawra in Northern Mesopotamia", *Paléorient* 25(1): 101–14.

Pollard, A. M., Davoudi, H., Mostafapour, I., Valipour, H. R., and Fazeli, N. H. 2012. "A new radiocarbon chronology for the Late Neolithic to Iron Age on the Qazvin Plain, Iran", *International Journal of Humanities of the Islamic Republic of Iran* 19.3: 1–41.

Potts, D. T. 2009. "Bevel-rim bowls and bakeries: evidence and explanations from Iran and the Indo-Iranian borderlands", *JCS* 61: 1–23.

Rothman, M. S. 2011. "The environment of Godin Tepe IV", in Gopnik, H. and Rothman, M. (eds), *On the High Road: The History of Godin Tepe, Iran*, Royal Ontario Museum/ Mazda Press, Toronto: 49–65.

Rothman, M. and Kozbe, G. 1997. "Muş in the early Bronze Age", *AS* 45: 105–26.

Rothman, M. S. and Badler, V. 2011. "Contact and development in Godin Period VI", in Gopnik, H. and Rothman, M. (eds), *On the High Road: The History of Godin Tepe, Iran*, Royal Ontario Museum/Mazda Press, Toronto: 67–137.

Sarlak, S. 2011. *Archaeology and History of Qom*, Shakes Publisher, Tehran.

Schmidt, A., Quigley, M., Fattahi, M., Aziz, G., Maghsoudi, M. and Fazeli, N. H. 2011. "Holocene settlement shifts and palaeoenvironments on the Central Iranian Plateau: investigating linked systems", *The Holocene* 21(4): 583–95.

Schmidt, E. F. 1937. *Excavation at Tepe Hissar, Damaghan, 1931–1933*, University of Pennsylvania Press for the University Museum. Pennsylvania.

Simpson, I. and Kouramps, N. n.d. *A Late Neolithic Landscape of Settlement and Farming on the Iranian Plateau, Preliminary insights from thin section micro morphology of mound and mound-fringing deposits at Tepe Sialk North, Kashan, central Iran.*

Staubwasser, M. and Weiss, H. 2006. "Holocene climate and cultural evolution in late prehistoric-early historic West Asia: an introduction", *Quaternary Research* 66(3): 372–87.

Stein, G. J. and Misir, A. 1994. "Hacinebi excavations, 1992", *Kazi Sonuclari Toplantisi* 15: 131–52.

Valipour, H. R. 2006. *Preliminary Report of Excavation at Tepe Shizar, First Season*, Archive Iranian Center for Archaeological Research, Tehran.

Vatandoust, A., Parzinger, H. and Helwing, B. eds 2011. *Early mining and metallurgy on the Central Iranian Plateau. Report on the first five years of research of the Joint Iranian-German Research Project*, Archäologie in Iran und Turan 9, Philip von Zabern, Mainz-am-Rhein.

Voigt, M. and Dyson Jr., R. H. 1992. "The chronology of Iran, ca. 8000–2000 B.C.", in Erich, R. W. (ed.), *Chronologies in Old World Archaeology*, 3rd Edition, 2 Volumes, University of Chicago Press, Chicago: 78–96.

Wong, E. H. Y. 2008. *Ceramic Characterization and Inter-site Relationships in the Northwestern Central Plateau, Iran, in the Late Neolithic to the Bronze Age*, unpublished Ph.D. dissertation, University of Sydney.

Wong, E. H. Y., Petrie, C. A. and Fazeli, N. H. 2010. "Cheshmeh-Ali Ware: a petrographic and geochemical study of Transitional Chalcolithic Period ceramic industry on the north Central Plateau of Iran", *Iran* 48: 1–13.

Young Jr., T. C. 1966. "Survey in Western Iran, 1961", *JNES* 24(4): 228–39.

Young Jr., T. C. and Levine, L. 1974. *Excavation of the Godin project: second progress report*, Occasional Papers, no. 26, Royal Ontario Museum, Toronto.

8. TEPE HISSAR AND THE FOURTH MILLENNIUM BC OF NORTH-EASTERN IRAN

C. P. Thornton, A. Gürsan-Salzmann and R. H. Dyson Jr.

Introduction

It has long been recognised that north-eastern Iran was an important frontier zone between the oasis settlements of Central Asia and the Iranian Plateau in late prehistory (e.g. Sarianidi 1971; Tosi 1973–74; Kohl 1984; Cleuziou 1986). The important regional divide between the western and eastern halves of north-eastern Iran (e.g. Biscione 1981), whereby the material culture of eastern Mazandaran, Semnan, and

Golestan is entirely different from the contemporary material culture of Khorassan, is similarly well established (Fig. 8.1). As Emran Garajian (personal communication) has suggested, the regions around Sari, Damghan, and Gorgan up to the Sumbar Valley of western Turkmenistan should be thought of as the eastern frontier of northern Iran, while northern and eastern Khorassan should be considered the northern frontier of eastern Iran. Although our archaeological

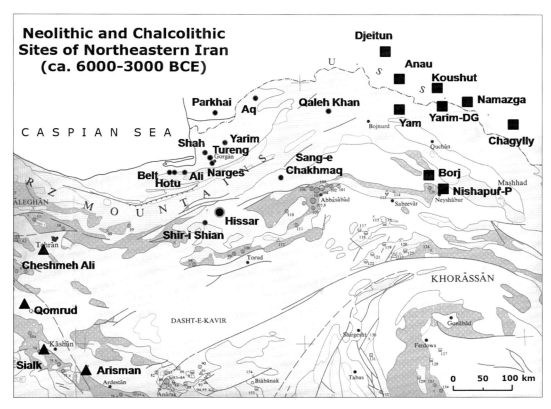

Figure 8.1. Map of late prehistoric sites in north-eastern Iran, showing the relationship between Sialk-sequence sites of north Central Iran (triangles), Hissar-related sites of north-eastern Iran (circles), and Namazga-sequence sites of Central Asia (squares) (adapted from Bazin and Hübner 1969: pl. XXV).

knowledge of much of Khorassan is quite limited (e.g. Gropp 1995), with the possible exception of the Atrek Valley (Kohl and Heskel 1980; Ricciardi 1980; Kohl *et al.* 1982), recent exploration and excavation in this region by Iranian scholars has done little to change this model of a divided frontier zone in the late prehistory of north-eastern Iran (e.g. Garajian 2006; Vahdati 2010; see also Azarnoush and Helwing 2005).

In studying the fourth millennium BC of north-eastern Iran, the "divided frontier" model is certainly appropriate. To the east, sites display ceramics and small finds entirely at home in Central Asian settlements of the Namazga culture (periods II–III). To the west, sites display ceramics and small finds more closely related to those of the central Iranian Plateau (Sialk III period) than to their neighbours to the east. Indeed, while north-eastern Iranian potters to the west gradually transitioned into a grey ware tradition over the span of the fourth millennium BC, those to the east stayed "faithful" to the Namazga painted pottery tradition, adopting grey wares only in the Namazga IV period of the third millennium BC (Hiebert and Dyson 2002: 120).

A full review of the fourth millennium BC in north-eastern Iran is well beyond the scope of this paper, but we present below the revised stratigraphic and ceramic sequence of Tepe Hissar. By far the most famous prehistoric site in this region, Tepe Hissar provides a nearly unbroken archaeological sequence from the late fifth until the early second millennium BC. In this paper, we focus on the data retrieved by the 1976 Restudy Project, which provides the only radiocarbon-based ceramic sequence for the fourth millennium BC of north-eastern Iran.

Tepe Hissar: background

The prehistoric mound of Tepe Hissar (or "Tappeh Hesar"), located just outside the modern city of Damghan in north-eastern Iran, was first systematically excavated in 1931–32 and 1932–33 by Erich F. Schmidt under the auspices of the University of Pennsylvania Museum (Schmidt 1933, 1937) (Fig. 8.2). The site was then re-examined in the 1970s by the Hesar Restudy Project, which was an international team under the co-direction of Robert H. Dyson Jr. and Maurizio Tosi (e.g. Bulgarelli 1974; Dyson 1977; Dyson and Howard 1989; Gürsan-Salzmann 2007). Although Schmidt was a good excavator (for his day) who took meticulous notes, he later abandoned his stratigraphic field assessment in favour of a typological sequence based on ceramics from the 1,637 intramural burials found at the site (Schmidt 1937: 301). Thus, his "Hissar I" period, generally found in the earliest strata, denoted graves containing only painted pottery. His "Hissar III" period, which was generally found in the later strata, denoted graves containing mostly burnished grey pottery, while his "Hissar II" period denoted

any graves containing both painted and grey wares. Stratigraphic levels were then labelled I, II, or III (with sub-phases A, B, C) based on the graves, which were often presumed to have been dug under the floors of houses.

Needless to say, this scheme is problematic, due mainly to three key assumptions made by Schmidt (1937: 319). First, he proposed that grey wares completely replaced painted wares, which we now know they did not. Second, he assumed that if the inhabitants of Tepe Hissar at a particular period used two types of pottery, then both would be represented in the graves of that period, which we now know they were not. Finally, and most egregiously, Schmidt assumed that graves belonged to the floors directly above them (Schmidt 1937: 67). In fact, as shown by the 1976 Hesar Restudy Project, graves were generally dug into the ruins of abandoned houses, often several metres below the contemporary surface. Thus, while the general sequence of Hissar I–III has some archaeological reality, the details of Schmidt's arbitrary assignment of periods to specific architectural and mortuary remains requires extensive revision.

The 1976 Hesar Restudy Project was meant to solve many of the problems inherent in Schmidt's periodisation (Dyson 1977). Excavations on the Main Mound (Howard 1989), the North Flat (Dyson and Remsen 1989), the South Hill (Tosi and Bulgarelli 1989), and The Twins (Biscione, unpublished) established the first radiocarbon-dated stratigraphic sequence at Tepe Hissar (*c.* 4300–1800 BC). In addition, surface survey work and limited horizontal excavation on the Main Mound, the North Flat, and the South Hill provided a better understanding of various industries and crafts carried out at the site (Bulgarelli 1973, 1974, 1979; Tosi 1984, 1989; Pigott *et al.* 1982; Pigott 1989). Furthermore, Susan Howard's unpublished dissertation research on the ceramics from the Main Mound disproved many of Schmidt's assumptions about the transition from painted pottery to grey wares (see Dyson 1985).

Because these areas of Tepe Hissar were studied separately, however, there remained a need for a final integration of the stratigraphic sequence of the site, most especially of the different terminologies chosen by Dyson for the North Flat (phases A–D), by Tosi for the South Hill (phases 1–8), by Howard and Pigott for the Main Mound (stages A–F), and by Dyson (1987) for the Hissar II period (*Early, Middle,* and *Late Hissar II*). Through re-examination of the original field notes from 1976, Thornton and Dyson were able to work out an integrated stratigraphic sequence for the Main Mound and North Flat (Table 8.1; see Thornton 2009). In addition, Gürsan-Salzmann has been studying these two areas of the site using Schmidt's original field notes and the results of the 1976 Hesar Restudy Project. A critical part of her research has been

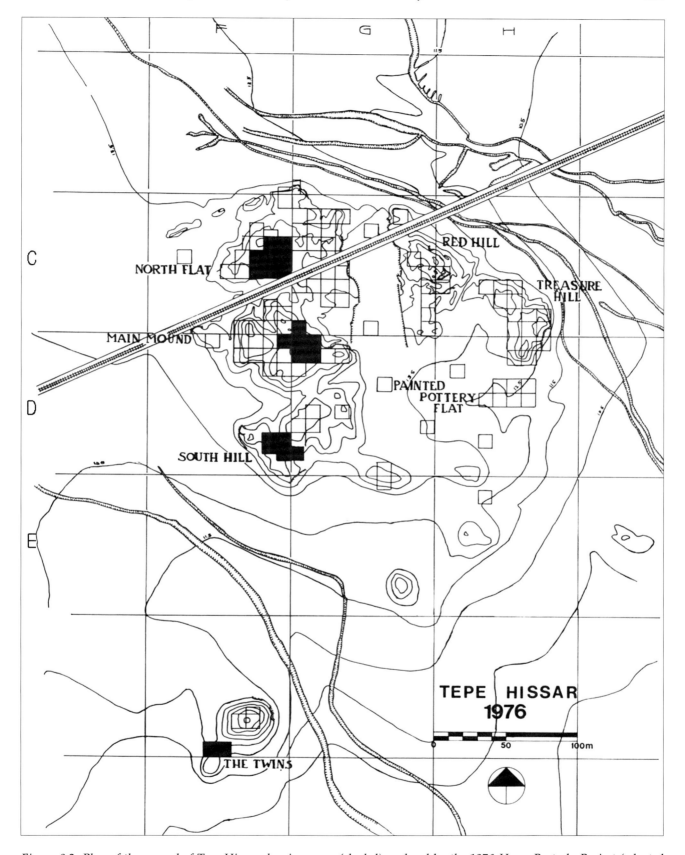

Figure 8.2. Plan of the mound of Tepe Hissar showing areas (shaded) explored by the 1976 Hesar Restudy Project (adapted from Dyson and Howard 1989: fig. 4).

Table 8.1. A reference chart detailing the new phases in the Tepe Hissar sequence and their correlates from both the 1930s and 1970s excavations.

				North Flat			Main Mound		
Phase	*Dyson 1987*	*Schmidt 1937*	*Date Range*	*Context*	*Dyson Term*	*DF09*	*Context*	*Howard Term*	
A		IIIC	2200–1800 BCE	Schmidt CF 39 kiln	Phase A	P 1–4		Stage A	
B		IIIB	2500–2200 BCE	Burned Bldg CF 46–7 + 56	Phase B	P 5–8?	DG 20 ovens	Stage B	
						P lot 9		Stage C1	
C		IIIA	2900–2500 BCE	"diagonal wall" CF 58 B1	Phase C	P 10–11		Stage C2	
							Walls 40-41		
D-C Trans	Late His II	late IIB	3100–2900 BCE	CF 58 2+3	Phase C	P 12–14			
								Stage D1	
D	Mid His II	IIB	3350–3100 BCE	CF 48 /14/ CF 57	Phase C	P 15–17 Bldg 1 (upper)	Buildings 2–3	Stage D2 Stage D3	
E-D Trans	---	early IIB	c. 3400 BCE	CF 48 'wall 9' CF57 TT 'lot 0'	Phase D	Bldg 1 (lower)	/10/ 28 + 33 /14/ 29 + 42	Stage E1	
E	Early His II	IIA	3650–3400 BCE	CF 57 TT 1–3	Phase D	DS 3–8	---	Stage E2–E3	
F-E Trans		IC/IIA	c. 3700 BCE			DS 9–14	---	Stage F1–F2	
				CF57 Schmidt					
F		IC	3900–3700 BCE			DS 15–16	---	Stage F3	

the compilation of a ceramic database from the excavations in these two areas (both the 1930s and 1976 excavations) in order to look at changing styles and forms over the fourth and third millennia BC (Gürsan-Salzmann, forthcoming). These ceramic data, in combination with the new stratigraphic assessment, provide a controlled archaeological sequence for the fourth millennium BC that will be useful in assessing and redating both Schmidt's unpublished burial assemblages at Tepe Hissar and also excavations at other sites in north-eastern Iran.

Tepe Hissar: new phasing and key ceramic types

The revised sequence for the fourth and third millennia BC at Tepe Hissar presented here removes any confusion caused by the 1976 terminology.[1] A number of so-called "transitional phases" have been inserted into the sequence, which serves two purposes. First, it alleviates a few of the mistakes made by the 1976

excavators when they published their results over a decade after leaving the field.[2] Second, it emphasises the general continuity seen in the ceramic corpus over time despite changes in painted motifs, forms, and frequency of ware types (see Gürsan-Salzmann, forthcoming). It should be noted, however, that the ceramic sequence detailed below is based *only* on the 1976 excavations, which were extremely limited in size. Thus, this sequence is meant to be preliminary and must await Gürsan-Salzmann's forthcoming volume for finalisation.

The Main Mound has the most complete sequence at the site, based on the Deep Sounding excavated by Pigott, the Pinnacle baulk excavated by Howard, and the areas north of "Building 3" (areas /10/ and /14/) in which Howard excavated the stratum between the top of the Deep Sounding and the bottom of the Pinnacle baulk (Fig. 8.3). The third-millennium BC levels of the Pinnacle, however, were extremely limited in size relative to the broad horizontal area explored by Dyson on the North Flat (Dyson and Remsen 1989),

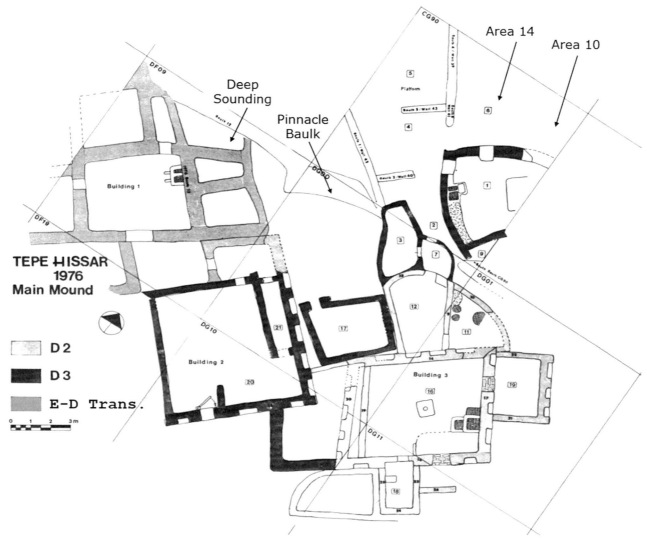

Figure 8.3. A corrected plan of the Main Mound excavations of Susan Howard and Vincent Pigott (adapted from Howard 1989: fig. 10).

just as the "test trench" excavated by Dyson into fourth-millennium BC strata on the North Flat must be viewed in relation to the much broader exposure on the Main Mound (Fig. 8.4; Table 8.2). The excavations on the South Hill carried out by Tosi and Bulgarelli (1989) are also important for discussions of the fourth millennium BC at Tepe Hissar, but unfortunately the dating of this sequence remains uncertain and must await further study (see Thornton, in press).

The earliest period reached by the 1976 restudy team was at the bottom of the Deep Sounding on the Main Mound and is called in our new terminology "Phase F" (Fig. 8.5). This period, dated somewhat arbitrarily to the early fourth millennium BC following Dyson (1991) and Voigt and Dyson (1992), had very limited horizontal exposure (1 × 1 m). Even so, Pigott found evidence of steatite working at this depth as well as a small number of grey ware sherds among the unpainted coarse wares and the geometric and

linear patterned black-on-buff and black-on-red painted vessels (unpublished field notes). Of the unpainted coarse wares, the presence of coarse orange ceramics tempered with copper slag – what Howard called "utility ware" (see Dyson 1985) – is particularly interesting. All of this evidence suggests that even in the early fourth millennium BC, Tepe Hissar was a production site for a wide range of crafts.

The "F–E Transitional Phase" just above these levels in the Deep Sounding contained ceramics very similar to those of Phase F, although the ceramic forms and geometric/linear painted motifs are slightly more complicated (e.g. "checkerboard" patterns) (Fig. 8.6). Many of these motifs are similar to those found on ceramics from Tappeh Sialk III_{5-6} (e.g. Ghirshman 1938: pl. XIV).[3] Also appearing for the first time at Tepe Hissar, at least in Pigott's limited sequence, are zoomorphic motifs, most notably the "felines" (e.g. spotted leopards) so indicative of Schmidt's Hissar

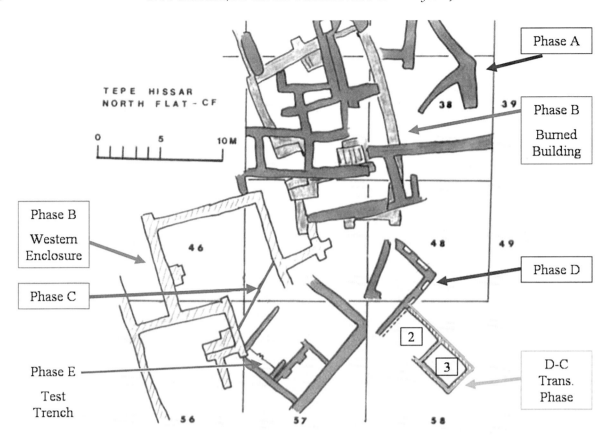

Figure 8.4. An annotated plan of the North Flat excavations of Robert H. Dyson Jr. (adapted from Dyson and Remsen 1989: fig. 13).

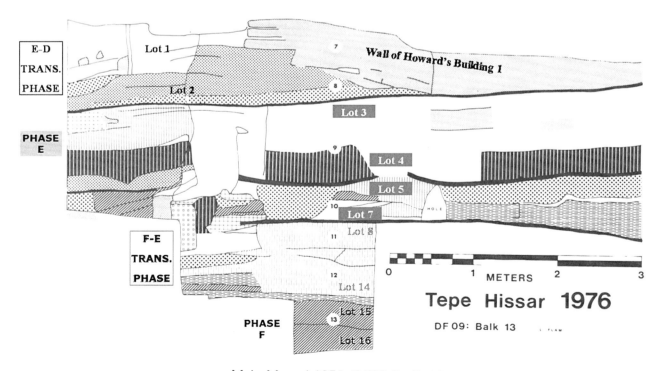

Main Mound 1976: DF09 Baulk 13

Figure 8.5. An annotated section of the Deep Sounding on the Main Mound (adapted from Howard 1989: fig. 4).

Table 8.2. A list of radiocarbon dates from Tepe Hissar related to the fourth-millennium sequence (adapted from Dyson and Lawn 1989)

Sample #	C14 date	Context	Schmidt Period	Phase	Date Range (2-sigma)
P-2615	4350±50 bp	NF CF58 Burned Rooms	Hissar II	D-C Transitional Phase	3099–2888 cal BC
P-2617	4420±50 bp	NF CF37 below BB	Hissar II	Phase D?	3328–2916 cal BC
P-2619	4830±60 bp	NF CF57 test trench lot 3	Hissar IC/IIA	Phase E	3737–3506 cal BC
P-2621	4550±70 bp	MM Bldg 3 Area 2, lot 23	Hissar II	Phase D	3393–3025 cal BC
P-2622	5060±320 bp	MM DF09 DS-12	Hissar IC/IIA	F-E Transitional Phase	4534–3029 cal BC
P-2623	5200±70 bp	NF CF57 SW corner lowest	Hissar IC/IIA	Phase F?	4237–3918 cal BC
P-2698	4280±70 bp	NF CF58 Burned Rooms	Hissar II	D-C Transitional Phase	3089–2659 cal BC
P-2699	4410±60 bp	NF CF57 SW corner niche	Hissar II	Phase D	3329–2908 cal BC
P-2700	4370±70 bp	NF CF58 Burned Rooms	Hissar II	D-C Transitional Phase	3135–2884 cal BC
P-2703	4270±60 bp	NF CF37-38 below BB	Hissar II	Phase D?	3031–2664 cal BC
P-2704	4340±60 bp	NF CF57 NW corner	Hissar II	D-C Transitional Phase	3113–2872 cal BC
P-2706	4240±70 bp	NF CF58 Burned Rooms	Hissar II	D-C Transitional Phase	3010–2616 cal BC
P-2707	4530±60 bp	MM Bldg 3 kiln 3, lot 35	Hissar II	Phase D	3375–3023 cal BC
P-2708	4440±50 bp	MM Bldg 3 Rm 11, lot 31	Hissar II	Phase D	3331–2937 cal BC
P-2709	4540±60 bp	MM Bldg 3 Rm 1, lot 11	Hissar II	Phase D	3379–3033 cal BC
P-2710	4380±70 bp	MM Bldg 3 Rm 7, lot 37	Hissar II	Phase D	3328–2890 cal BC
P-2711	4570±60 bp	MM Bldg 3 Rm 3, lot 35	Hissar II	Phase D	3397–3092 cal BC
P-2760	4530±50 bp	MM CG90 P-15	Hissar II	Phase D	3369–3076 cal BC
P-2774	5750±60 bp	MM DF09 DS-5	Hissar IC/IIA	Phase E	4730–4466 cal BC

All samples were wood charcoal.
Dates calibrated using Calib 5.01 (Reimer *et al.* 2004 calibration)
"P-..." numbers come from PENN XXII in Hurst and Lawn 1984

IC phase (Fig. 8.6). Although the "ibex" motifs of Schmidt's Period IC do not appear in the Deep Sounding sequence until the following Phase E, this is probably a product of the limited exposure and not a reality of the ceramic sequence.

Phase E can be subdivided (based on floors found in the top levels of the Deep Sounding) to an earlier ("E2") and a later ("E1") sub-phase. In the earlier sub-phase, significant evidence of steatite and calcite working was found among painted buff-slipped pottery often bearing zoomorphic motifs like the felines from the previous phase. Large striped triangles were often painted "hanging" from the rim on many red-slipped vessels of this period. By the later sub-phase, the elaborate zoomorphic motifs had given way to more abstract designs, such as the "long-necked gazelles" (of Schmidt's Period IIA) and the combination of hatched circles with rows of alternating triangles (of Schmidt's Period IIB). The latter motif, which continues into the following "E–D Transitional Period," has good parallels with ceramics from Sialk III$_7$ (e.g. Ghirshman 1938: pl. LXXII no. 38). The bottom of Dyson's test trench on the North Flat (P-2619), which provided a radiocarbon date with a 2-sigma range of 3740–3500 cal. BC, contained similar ceramics to those found in Phase E levels on the Main Mound.

The E–D Transitional Phase separates the top of the Deep Sounding from the bottom of the Pinnacle on the Main Mound, and is only known from the small excavations in areas /10/ and /14/ carried out by Howard (unpublished field notes) (Fig. 8.7). Two major changes occurred in this period. First, buttressing started to appear on the mud-brick architecture of the time – this is a feature that becomes ubiquitous in the following Phase D (see Dyson 1987: 659). Second, grey wares became more common than painted wares (especially painted buff wares) for the first time. Certain painted motifs, such as hatched circles (often without alternating triangles), continue well into Phase D levels, while others, such as hanging striped triangles and zoomorphic images, disappear during the E–D Transitional Phase. New painted motifs such as the "opposed tongues" appear at the very beginning of Phase D (Howard's "Stage D3"), while imported Caspian Black-on-Red Ware from the Gorgan Plain first appears in E–D Transitional Phase levels (*c.* 3400 BC).

At the same time, grey ware forms and decorations became much more elaborate in the E–D Transitional Phase or in early Phase D (Fig. 8.8). Burnishing, incising, grooves/ridges make up the range of decorations on grey ware vessels of this period.[4] Tall

Hissar II: Painted Motifs

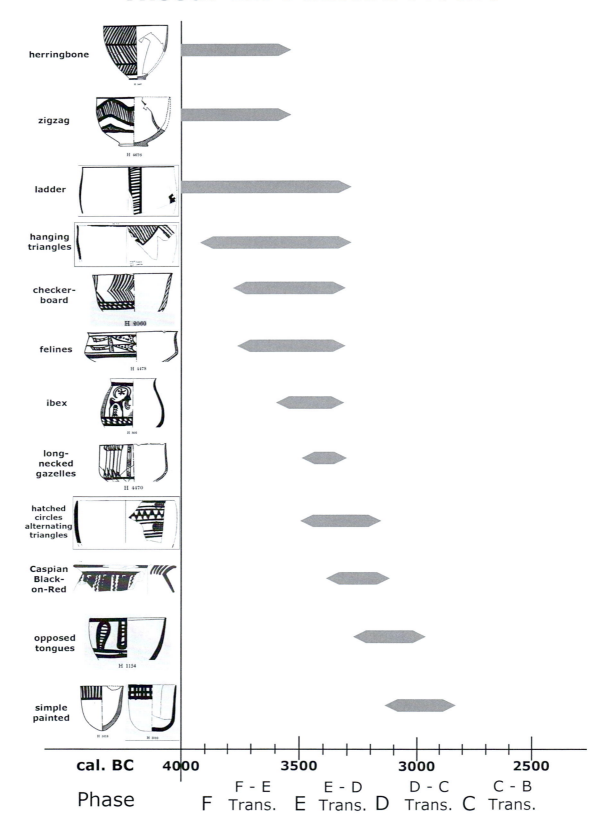

Figure 8.6. A chronological chart showing the sequence of certain painted motifs on Tepe Hissar ceramics over the fourth millennium BC.

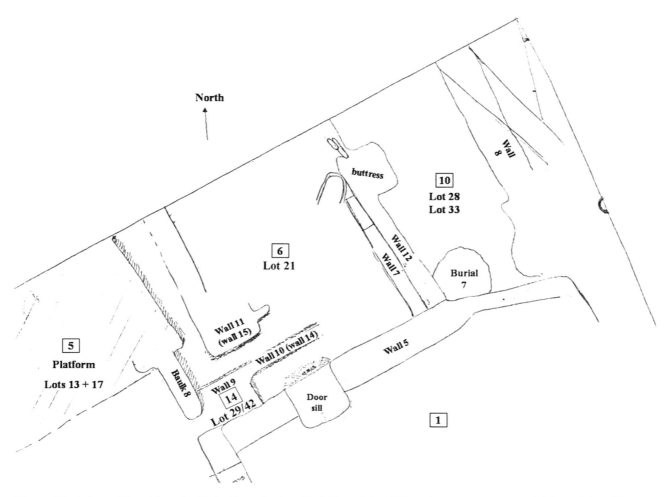

Figure 8.7. A plan of Area 10 on the Main Mound, where E–D Transitional Phase layers were excavated (adapted from Howard, unpublished field notes).

sharply carinated pedestalled vessels, which had first appeared in the E–D Transitional Phase, became de rigueur in Phase D (although less sharply carinated) (Fig. 8.8/C1, C2). The grey wares themselves become finer and "clinkier" in Phase D, some even achieving a "metallic" semblance. Unpainted coarse wares (including "utility wares") continued unabated from earlier periods, although several sub-types (e.g. storage jars with rail rims and "braziers") appear for the first time in the E–D Transitional Phase and continue into Phase D. The most notable coarse wares that appear in Phase D and continue into the proceeding phase are the chaff-tempered flat trays (called "clay pans" in Tosi and Bulgarelli 1989: fig. 3) – a point we will return to below.

The D–C Transitional Phase is known from the Pinnacle baulk on the Main Mound, but most especially from the two burned rooms on the North Flat excavated by Hasan Tala'i and Heydeh Biscione (née Eqbal) in Schmidt's trench CF 58 (see Dyson and

Remsen 1989: 99–105). These two rooms produced four radiocarbon dates typical of what Dyson (1987) called the "Late Hissar II" period (*c.* 3100–2900 BC [P-2615, 2698, 2700, 2706]). While many ceramic forms continue from Phase D (such as the simple bowls and goblets with linear or hatched designs painted on the rim, or the coarse ware pots with pierced vertical lug handles), new forms appeared in this period that prelude the Hissar III pottery tradition of the third millennium BC. Notable forms of this type include jars with trough spouts, grey ware bottles/pitchers (Fig. 8.8/E2), and beakers (Fig. 8.8/D2). Pattern-burnishing (in cross-hatched and herringbone patterns), which appeared infrequently in Phase D, became common in the D–C Transitional Phase, as did grey "stoneware", distinguished by its thickness, light grey colour, and high firing. At the same time, the more "Gorgan"-style decorations on grey wares (e.g. incising, ridges) became less common in this later period.

Hissar II: Grey Ware Forms

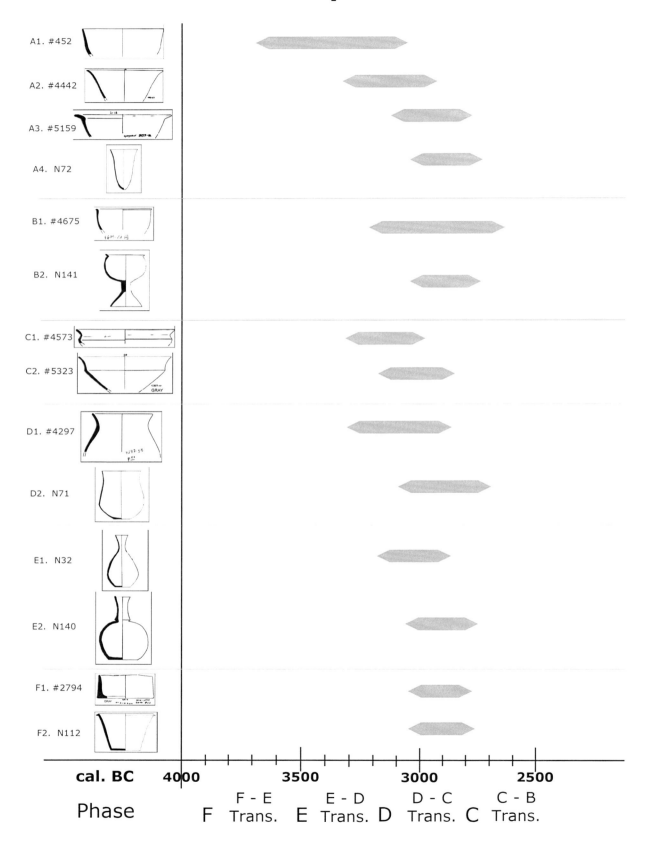

Figure 8.8. A chronological chart showing the evolution of certain grey ware forms over the fourth millennium BC.

Discussion

In a recent paper comparing the fourth-millennium BC Tepe Hissar sequence with her work at Arisman in north-central Iran, Helwing (2006) noted how Tepe Hissar's sphere of cultural affiliation shifts over this era. From *c.* 4000–3500 BC, much of the material culture from Tepe Hissar (particularly the ceramics, but also the architecture and technological practices) shows strong similarities to sites in the west, such as Tappeh Sialk and Arisman. Between 3500 and 3000 BC, this sphere of influence shifts to the north and east, with Tepe Hissar material culture showing stronger connections to the Gorgan and sites in southern Turkmenistan (Helwing 2006: 44–45). Unfortunately, Helwing did not know of our recent research into the Tepe Hissar sequence (discussed above), and thus there are a number of outdated assumptions about Tepe Hissar in her paper. Furthermore, as discussed in our introduction to this paper, the connections between Tepe Hissar and the Namazga sequence sites of southern Turkmenistan and north-eastern Iran are practically non-existent until well into the third millennium BC (i.e. after the Hissar II period). Her general observations about Tepe Hissar's changing "cultural orientation" from west to north/north-east, however, are entirely accurate.

What could have caused such a dramatic shift in Tepe Hissar's cultural orientation in the middle of the fourth millennium BC? It is fairly clear that the sites of the Gorgan Valley fluoresced around this time, becoming important centres by the early third millennium BC. It is unclear, however, whether they arose *before* the cultural shift at Tepe Hissar (thereby perhaps contributing to the change) or *because of* Tepe Hissar's reorientation towards the north. Indeed, it was in the second half of the fourth millennium BC that Tepe Hissar's metallurgical production and lapidary work (particularly with lapis lazuli) became large-scale and centrally organised, leading to greater social differentiation (as seen in the appearance of "elite" burials) and more overall wealth within the settlement. Perhaps the resource-poor lowland sites of the Gorgan became the major consumers of Tepe Hissar's manufactured products, drastically reducing the need for the craftspeople of Tepe Hissar to trade their products further to the west. Or perhaps the trade routes to the west collapsed (Helwing, this volume), leading the craft producers of Tepe Hissar to find markets to the north. Only future study of the Gorgan Valley sites will be able to answer such questions.

At around the same time that Tepe Hissar began to focus northwards, the sites of north-central Iran (Qazvin, Tehran, and Kashan Plains) began to show stronger connections to the south-western Iranian sphere, culminating with their inclusion in the early *Proto-Elamite* horizon of the Sialk IV$_1$ period (*c.* 3400

BC) (see Alden 1982; Helwing 2004, this volume). With the exception of a few unusual artefacts, such as the glazed steatite cylinder seal (H 693) from insecure contexts at Tepe Hissar (Dyson and Harris 1986), there is almost no evidence for contact with the *Late Uruk* or *Proto-Elamite* horizons in north-eastern Iran (Dyson 1987). This is surprising, given the strong evidence for *Late Uruk* and *Proto-Elamite* influence in north-central Iran, south-eastern Iran, and even as far east as Pakistani Makran if we speak only of bevel-rim bowls (e.g. Lamberg-Karlovsky 1978; Potts 2009). Were the people using *Late Uruk* or *Proto-Elamite* material and who colonised important sites such as Tepe Yahya, Sofalin, and Godin Tepe, just not interested in Tepe Hissar, or were they simply unable to assert any real authority over the people of this distant region?

There are no easy answers to this question. Further research into the chronological sequence and, indeed, directionality of so-called *Proto-Elamite* features across the Iranian Plateau is needed to resolve many of the ongoing debates in the literature (e.g. *cf.* Helwing 2004 to Petrie in press), but our reassessment of the 1976 Hissar sequence and ceramics provides a few points of interest related to this topic. For example, there is the almost ubiquitous appearance of chaff-tempered trays in Phase D and D–C Transitional Phase contexts at Tepe Hissar, as well as grey ware imitations in the D–C Transitional Phase (see Fig. 8.8/F1). These trays have obvious parallels with *Late Uruk*/early *Proto-Elamite* low-sided trays known from the Oval Enclosure at Godin Tepe, *Middle Banesh* Tal-e Malyan, Tal-e Ghazir levels 36–37, Sialk III$_7$–Sialk IV levels in north Central Iran, and many other contemporaneous sites (see Helwing 2004). The appearance of trough spouts at Tepe Hissar, albeit in burnished grey wares, is another sign of influence from, or at least connection with, the west but the complete absence of bevel-rim bowls (BRBs) at this site or, indeed, from north-eastern Iran *in toto*, requires explanation. To this end, the single example of what appears to be an imitation BRB made in chaff-tempered grey ware (H76-N112 from CF58/3/; see Fig. 8.8/F2) from a D–C Transitional Phase context on the North Flat is quite striking.

Conclusion

The fourth millennium BC of north-eastern Iran was a period of complex interactions on both a regional and a supra-regional level. For reasons that are not well explained, this frontier zone was divided between east and west for most of late prehistory, with sites to the east showing greater affinities to their northern and southern neighbours, while sites to the west showed stronger connections to their western neighbours. As seen from the sequence at Tepe Hissar, however, these cultural orientations were not writ in stone, but highly dynamic interactions prone to change due to varying economic and political situations. For example, as north-central Iran became absorbed into the *Late Uruk/Proto-Elamite* sphere of influence in the second half of the fourth millennium BC, Tepe Hissar reoriented itself (or was reoriented) to the north and north-east. With large amounts of lapis lazuli coming in from the east (despite limited cultural connections) and with new potential markets in the resource-poor lowlands of the Gorgan Valley and the Kopet Dagh piedmont, the inhabitants of Tepe Hissar may have consciously preserved their political independence from the *Proto-Elamites* by making themselves economically self-sufficient. Unconsciously, however, they seem to have adopted certain cultural markers used by their western neighbours, including distinct pottery types and even proto-literate counting tablets (Tosi and Bulgarelli 1989: fig. 5). While the exact mechanisms of such a transfer are not yet understood, we hope that the revised ceramic and stratigraphic sequence from Tepe Hissar presented here will provide new insight into the complex local dynamics that underscore larger patterns in the cultural milieu.

Notes

1   For example, Dyson and Remsen's "Phase D" on the North Flat was assigned without attempting to correlate with Howard and Pigott's "Stage D" on the Main Mound. Upon reassessment of the 1976 field records, it became apparent that "Phase D" and "Stage D" were not actually contemporaneous.

2   For example, when Howard returned to her field notes to reconstruct the sequence of the Main Mound, she wrongly assumed that the top of the Deep Sounding (dug into "Building 1") was even with the bottom of the Pinnacle (standing on the surface associated with "Building 2"). In fact, the floor of Building 1 was almost 1 m below the floor of Building 2.

3   The absolute dating of the Sialk sequence is still a matter of some contention. For example, Fazeli *et al.* (2005: 78) date Sialk III_6 to *c.* 3700 BC based on their work in the Qazvin Plain, while Helwing (2006: 36) dates the same phase to *c.* 3900 BC based on her work in the Kashan Plain. In his recent review of the fourth millennium in Iran, Petrie (in press/2013) agrees with Fazeli and dates Sialk III_6 to *c.* 3650 BC. It is hoped that new excavations at Tappeh Sialk by Dr Fazeli and his team will provide tighter stratigraphic control of this important ceramic sequence.

4   Although proper studies of the Gorgan Plain ceramics have not been carried out (see Cleuziou 1986, 1991), Thornton's personal observations of the Tureng, Shah, Yarim, and Narges Tepe collections suggest that incised, bossed, and ridged grey ware vessels are much more common on the Gorgan Plain than at Tepe Hissar. Thus, the occasional appearance of these types at Hissar along with Caspian Black-on-Red ware between 3400 and 3000 BC may suggest that such grey wares were brought to Hissar from the lowland sites to the north.

Bibliography

Alden, J. R. 1982. "Trade and politics in Proto-Elamite Iran", *Current Anthropology* 23(6): 613–40.

Azarnoush, M. and Helwing, B. 2005. "Recent archaeological research in Iran – prehistory to Iron Age", *AMIT* 37: 189–246.

Bazin, D. and Hübner, H. 1969. *Copper Deposits in Iran*, Report 13, Geological Survey of Iran, Tehran.

Biscione, R. 1981. "Centre and periphery in late protohistoric Turan: the settlement pattern", in Hartel, H. (ed.), *South Asian Archaeology 1979*, Dietrich Reimer Verlag, Berlin: 203–13.

Bulgarelli, G. M. 1973. "Tepe Hissar", *Iran* 11: 206.

Bulgarelli, G. M. 1974. "Tepe Hissar. Preliminary report on a surface survey, August 1972", *East and West* 24: 15–27.

Bulgarelli, G. M. 1979. "The lithic industry of Tepe Hissar at the light of recent excavation", in Taddei, M. (ed.), *South Asian Archaeology 1977*, Istituto Universitario Orientale, Naples: 39–54.

Cleuziou, S. 1986. "Tureng Tepe and burnished grey ware: a question of 'frontier'?" *Oriens Antiquus* XXV: 221–56.

Cleuziou, S. 1991. "Ceramics IX: The Bronze Age in Northeastern Persia", *EIr* 5(3): 297–300.

Dyson Jr., R. H. 1977. "Tepe Hissar, Iran, revisited", *Archaeology* 30(6): 418–20.

Dyson Jr., R. H. 1985. "Comments on Hissar Painted Ware", in Huot, J-L., Yon, M. and Calvet, Y. (eds), *De l'Indus aux Balkans: recueil à la mémoire de Jean Deshayes,* Recherche sur les civilisations, Paris: 337–46.

Dyson Jr., R. H. 1987. "The relative and absolute chronology of Hissar II and the Proto-Elamite horizon of northern Iran", in Aurenche, O., Evin, J. and Hours, F. (eds), *Chronologies in the Near East*, BAR International Series 379, Archaeopress, Oxford: 647–78.

Dyson Jr., R. H. 1991. "Ceramics: Neolithic period through Bronze Age in northeastern and north-central Persia", *EIr* 5(3): 266–75.

Dyson Jr., R. H. and Harris, M. V. 1986. "The archaeological context of cylinder seals excavated on the Iranian Plateau", in Kelly-Buccellati, M. (ed.), *Insight Through Images: Studies in Honor of Edith Porada*, Bibliotheca Mesopotamica 21, Undena Publications, Malibu, CA: 79–110.

Dyson Jr., R. H. and Howard, S. M. eds 1989. *Tappeh Hesar: Reports of the Restudy Project, 1976*, Case Editrice le Lettere, Florence.

Dyson Jr., R. H. and Lawn, B. 1989. "Key stratigraphic and radiocarbon elements for the 1976 Hissar sequence", in Dyson and Howard 1989: 143.

Dyson Jr., R. H. and Remsen, W. C. 1989. "Observations on architecture and stratigraphy at Tappeh Hesar", in Dyson and Howard 1989: 69–110.

Fazeli, H., Wong, E. H. and Potts, D. T. 2005. "The Qazvin Plain revisited: a reappraisal of the chronology of northwestern Central Plateau, Iran, in the 6th to the 4th millennium BC", *ANES* 42: 3–82.

Garajian, O. 2006. "Some traces of Turkmenistan prehistoric cultures in Khorasan Province in Iran", in Zare, S. (ed.), *The Second Symposium of Iranian Young Archaeologists, Iran – Tehran*, ICHTO, Tehran: 69–98.

Ghirshman, R. 1938. *Fouilles de Sialk, vol. 1*, Librairie Orientaliste Paul Geuthner, Paris.

Gropp, G. 1995. *Archäologische Forschungen in Khorasan, Iran*, Beihefte zum Tübinger Atlas des Vorderen Orients Nr. 84, Dr. Ludwig Reichert Verlag, Wiesbaden.

Gürsan-Salzmann, A. 2007. *Exploring Iran: The Photography of Erich F. Schmidt, 1930–1940*, University of Pennsylvania Museum, Philadelphia.

Gürsan-Salzmann, A. forthcoming. *Chronology at the Crossroads of Western Asia: Bronze Age Ceramic Sequence from Tepe Hissar, Iran*, University of Pennsylvania Museum, Philadelphia.

Helwing, B. 2004. "Tracking the Proto-Elamite on the Central Iranian Plateau", in Malek Shahmirzadi, S. (ed.), *The Potters of Sialk*, Iranian Center for Archaeological Research, Tehran: 45–58.

Helwing, B. 2006. "The rise and fall of Bronze Age centers around the Central Iranian Desert – a comparison of Tappe Hesar II and Arisman", *AMIT* 38: 35–48.

Hiebert, F. T. and Dyson Jr., R. H. 2002. "Prehistoric Nishapur and the frontier between Central Asia and Iran", *IA* 37: 113–50.

Howard, S. M. 1989. "The stratigraphic sequence of the Main Mound at Tappeh Hesar, 1976", in Dyson and Howard 1989: 55–68.

Kohl, P. L. 1984. "Prehistoric 'Turan' and Southern Turkmenia: the problem of cultural diversity", in Lal, B. B. and Gupta, S. P. (eds), *Frontiers of the Indus Civilization*, Books & Books, Indian Archaeology Society, New Delhi: 321–31.

Kohl, P. L. and Heskel, D. 1980. "Archaeological reconnaissance in the Darreh Gaz plain: A short report", *Iran* 18: 160–72.

Kohl, P. L., Biscione, R. and Ingraham, M. L. 1982. "Implications of recent evidence for the prehistory of northeastern Iran and southwestern Turkmenistan", *IA* 17: 1–20.

Lamberg-Karlovsky, C. C. 1978. "The Proto-Elamites on the Iranian Plateau", *Antiquity* 52: 114–20.

Petrie, C. A. in press. "Iran and Uruk Mesopotamia: chronologies and connections in the 4th millennium BC", in McMahon, A., Crawford, H. and Postgate, J. N. (eds), *Preludes to Urbanism: Studies in the Late Chalcolithic of Mesopotamia in Honour of Joan Oates*, McDonald Institute Monographs, Cambridge.

Pigott, V. C. 1989. "Archaeo-metallurgical investigations at Bronze Age Tappeh Hesar, 1976", in Dyson and Howard 1989: 25–34.

Pigott, V. C., Howard, S. M. and Epstein, S. M. 1982. "Pyrotechnology and culture change at Bronze Age Tepe Hissar (Iran)", in Wertime, T. A. and Wertime, S. F. (eds), *Early Pyrotechnology: The Evolution of the First Fire-Using Industries*, Smithsonian Institute Press, Washington DC: 215–36.

Potts, D. T. 2009. "Bevel-rim bowls and bakeries: Evidence and explanations from Iran and the Indo-Iranian borderlands", *JCS* 61: 1–23.

Ricciardi, R. V. 1980. "Archaeological survey in the upper Atrek Valley (Khorassan, Iran): Preliminary Report", *Mesopotamia (Torino)* 15: 51–72.

Sarianidi, V. 1971. "Southern Turkmenia and Northern Iran: Ties and differences in very ancient times", *East and West* 21(3–4): 291–310.

Schmidt, E. F. 1933. *Tepe Hissar Excavations 1931*, The Museum Journal, v. 23.4, University Museum, Philadelphia.

Schmidt, E. F. 1937. *Excavations at Tepe Hissar: Damghan*, University Museum, Philadelphia.

Thornton, C. P. 2009. *The Chalcolithic and Early Bronze Age Metallurgy of Tepe Hissar, Northeast Iran: A Challenge to the "Levantine Paradigm"*, unpublished Ph.D. dissertation, Department of Anthropology, University of Pennsylvania.

Thornton, C. P. in press. "A return to the South Hill of Tepe Hissar, Iran", in Cerasetti, B. and Lamberg-Karlovsky, C. C. (eds), *My Life is Like the Summer Rose: Maurizio Tosi e L'Archeologia Come Modo di Vita*, BAR International Series, Archaeopress, Oxford.

Tosi, M. 1973–74. "The northeastern frontier of the Ancient Near East", *Mesopotamia (Torino)* 8–9: 21–76.

Tosi, M. 1984. "The notion of craft specialization and its representation in the archaeological record of early states in the Turanian Basin", in Spriggs, M. (ed.), *Marxist Perspectives in Archaeology*, Cambridge University Press, Cambridge: 22–52.

Tosi, M. 1989. "The distribution of industrial debris on the surface of Tappeh Hesar as an indication of activity areas", in Dyson and Howard 1989: 13–24.

Tosi, M. and Bulgarelli, G. M. 1989. "The Stratigraphic Sequence of Squares DF 88/89 on South Hill, Tappeh Hesar", in Dyson and Howard 1989: 35–53.

Vahdati, A. A. 2010. "Tepe Pahlavan: A Neolithic-Chalcolithic site in the Jajarm Plain, North-eastern Iran", *IA* 45: 7–30.

Voigt, M. M. and Dyson, R. H. J. 1992. "The chronology of Iran, ca. 8000–2000", in Ehrich, R. W. (ed.), *Chronologies in Old World Archaeology*, University of Chicago Press, Chicago: 122–78.

9. THE *MIDDLE CHALCOLITHIC* IN SOUTHERN TURKMENISTAN AND THE ARCHAEOLOGICAL RECORD OF ILGYNLY-DEPE

Gian Luca Bonora and Massimo Vidale

Introduction

This paper presents a general review of the *Middle Chalcolithic* (or *Namazga II* period) of southern Turkmenistan (*c.* from the middle to the late fourth millennium BC), including periodisation and absolute chronology. An inventory of the known sites shows the rise along the piedmont of the first early towns, imposing themselves upon networks of minor rural sites. At the same time, a small number of centres in the ecologically constrained endoreic delta of the Tedjen River were fortified with defensive walls and round angular towers at a surprisingly early date. Ilgynly-depe, in the Chaacha-Meana district of the piedmont strip, shows not only fully developed crafts (pottery production, metallurgy, stone working, perhaps textiles manufacturing), but also the first hints of long-distance trade. A complex symbolic apparatus (wall paintings, formal seats, copper artefacts, stone sculptures, and terracotta figurines) appeared in special rooms, some of which might have been planned and used as steam baths or hammams rather than – as more commonly proposed – cultic buildings. We will review the research at Ilgynly-depe and also the *Middle Chalcolithic* funerary record of the region. Contrary to the traditional Soviet idea of *Chalcolithic* or "Aeneolithic" egalitarian tribal communities suddenly transformed into city states by a secondary urban revolution in the second half of the third millennium BC, early urban growth and social stratification processes were already active 1000 years before.

Contextualising southern Turkmenistan in the fourth millennium BC

Many assume that the prehistoric societies of southern Turkmenistan represented the "north-eastern periphery of the Near East Civilization" (Tosi 1973–1974), as along the Kopet Dag piedmont the original knowledge of farming and herding would have been partly borrowed from the south-western Iranian Plateau (Harris and Gosden 1996; Harris 2010).

The local prehistoric communities, however, can hardly be imagined as passive recipients of cultural innovation from their southern and western neighbours. Ceramics and inscribed documents of the *Uruk* and *Proto-Elamite* phenomena, identified to the south-east up to the foot of the first mountain chains of Iranian Baluchistan (Lamberg Karlovsky 1978; Potts 2001; Vidale and Desset, this volume) were never found beyond the Kopet Dag (Hiebert 2002: 35). The economic interests and associated ideological values at the root of the fast spreading *Uruk* and *Proto-Elamite* phenomena "clashed" here with a highly structured and quite different social world, the result of at least 3000 years of selective pressure and local evolution. The communities of the region, since the beginning of farming and sedentary life around 6000 BC, evolved into independent hierarchical social organisations, even if affected and partially transformed by contacts and exchanges with their neighbours. During the *Neolithic* and *Chalcolithic*, cultural and economic relationships between southern Turkmenistan and the northern fringe of the Iranian Plateau recall a core-periphery model of interaction, but the process was soon intensified by the fast development of metallurgy and other industrial sectors. At the same time, the prehistoric societies of these two cultural worlds seem to have given rise to a series of discrete, highly fluid political entities, each having something both to offer and to gain from exchange and communication. Southern Turkmenistan was not at the periphery of early agriculture and cattle-breeding foci farther west, but was an integral and leading partner within a much wider south-west Asian cultural interactive sphere from the ninth to the fourth millennium BC."

After a constellation of unstable agro-pastoral settlements became widely established from the Levant to the northern and eastern margins of the Iranian Plateau, and far eastwards, the fourth millennium BC was an epoch of significant change and development across the Iranian Plateau and the surrounding regions."

In the *Chalcolithic*, the piedmont plain north of the Kopet Dag mountain ridge – stretching in what is today southern Turkmenistan from the shores of the Caspian Sea to the lower Tedjen River valley (Fig. 9.1) – hosted a succession of increasingly sophisticated and complex communities, living in populated villages and farming their land by means of artificial irrigation. People exploited two millennia of cumulative skill in farming and husbandry within severely constrained and demanding ecosystems, and interacted with the local nomadic communities. They also produced and used handmade and wheel-thrown pottery, knapped flint and ground stone, and cast lead, silver, gold, and copper alloys. A substantial and developed metallurgy – considering the local absence of important ore sources – was carried out

both within individual dwellings in larger centres and in less important specialised independent sites (Thornton 2009, 2010). Although settlement systems mostly developed in a discontinuous fashion, regional uniformities in the forms and styles of pottery are evidence of intimate and resilient modes of communication across time and space.

In the last centuries of the *Chalcolithic* (*c.* 3300–3000 BC), while a large area of the central and western Iranian Plateau was variously affected by the so-called "Uruk" and "Proto-Elamite" expansions, in southern Turkmenistan local evolutionary processes gave birth to independent large-scale early urban communities (Namazga-depe, Kara-depe, Altyn-depe, Ilgynly-depe, and Geoksyur 1). Forty years of Russian excavations at Altyn-depe and other sites, from the Kopet Dag to the edge of the Kara Kum desert, revealed high levels of social complexity (defensive walls and monumental gates, and the emergence of different specialised crafts, partially centralised in the early urban compounds). In the *Middle Chalcolithic* layers at Ilgynly-depe, the local metallurgy provides an early example of technical sophistication and widespread consumption of valuable copper goods (Masson 1962: table X, 23; Solovyova *et al.* 1994: figs 3.4, 3.6, 4.1; Berezkin and Solovyova 1998: 93).

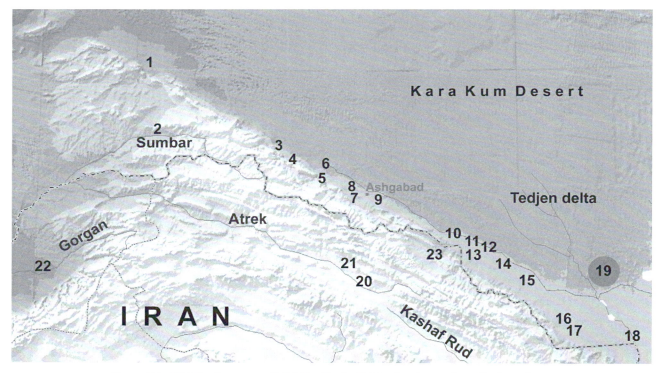

Figure 9.1. Distribution map of Middle Chalcolithic *sites in southern Turkmenistan.*
Key: 1 = Chinghiz-depe; 2 = Parkhay II; 3 = Gievdzhik-depe; 4 = Til'kin-depe; 5 = Gavych-depe; 6 = Suncha-depe; 7 = Ekin-depe; 8 = Ak-depe; 9 = Anau north; 10 = Kara-depe; 11 = Elen-depe; 12 = Jassy-depe; 13 = Namazga-depe and Gara-depe; 14 = Sermancha-depe; 15 = Ulug-depe; 16 = Altyn-depe; 17 = Ilgynly-depe; 18 = Serakhs site; 19 = sites of the "Geoksyur oasis": Geoksyur 1, Akcha-depe, Aina-depe, Jalangach-depe, Geoksyur 7, Geoksyur 9, Mullali-depe, and Chong-depe; 20 = Tepe Yam; 21 = Tepe Shirvan; 22 = Yarim Tepe (on the Gorgan plain); 23 = Yarim Tepe (on the Darreh Gaz plain).

Although such craft systems mainly exploited local resources, new archaeometric studies and sourcing of stone and metal base materials will reveal, in future, more complex patterns of medium- and long-range procurement and trade. The first beads and pendants in turquoise and lapis lazuli show direct or indirect links with the Kara Kum desert fringe or the north-eastern Iranian Plateau, the Hindukush valleys, and the Badakshan region of eastern Afghanistan (Kurbansakhatov 1987: 91, fig. 44.1; Masson 1962: 8, 22, table X.3). The range of such connections is shown by the discovery of red *Spondylus* shell beads, coming from the shores of the Mediterranean or the Persian Gulf, in graves dated to the *Transitional Chalcolithic* of the plains (early fourth millennium BC), in northern-central Iran (Fazeli and Vidale, ongoing research). Terracotta model wheels, in this period, demonstrate the spreading of wagons drawn by camels, wild equids, or oxen (Kurbansakhatov 1987: fig. 44, 17; Sarianidi 1960: 273, table VII, 16 and 17; Khlopin 1969: table VII, 45 and 17, table XXIII, 8 and 9, table XXVI, 48–50; see also Kircho 2009 for an updated review of wheeled transport in south-western Central Asia).

We must also mention the enigmatic "weights" or *gyr* with handle in polished stone from Anau north, Kara-depe, and Ilgynly-depe (Masson 1960: 354, fig. 12 and 451, table XXXII, 1, 4; 1962: table XI, 10–3; Korobkova and Sharovskaja 1994: 27–30; Hiebert 2003: fig. 7.15), which might have been used in the production of textiles, possibly kilims or carpets.[1] Examples of these dating to the fourth millennium BC have also been found at Sheri Khan Tarakai in north-west Pakistan (Knox *et al.* 2010: 222–24, fig. 7.50–7.54). The new technological and demographic realities demanded a growing investment in domestic and early urban administration, as demonstrated by stamp seals and unbaked clay sealings at Kara-depe, Geoksyur 1, and Altyn-depe (Masson 1960; Sarianidi 1965; Kircho 1990; Masson and Kircho 2008: pl. 119, 1–2; pl. 145, 13–21, pl. 168) as well as at Ilgynly-depe (unpublished surface find, 1999: Bonora *et al.*, in press). Special constructions interpreted as "shrines" or "sanctuaries" were attached to multi-roomed seats of extended families, linked to each other by kinship and tribal ties. Some rooms had special round "hearth-altars", wall paintings, and coloured benches, with valuable or symbolic artefacts scattered on the floors (Kircho 2007: 194–96).

Chronology and periodisation

The *Chalcolithic* in southern Turkmenistan is traditionally divided into three phases, *Early*, *Middle*, and *Late* periods. In the archaeological literature of Middle Asia, such three-tiered subdivision is also known as *Namazga I, II*, and *III* (hereafter *NMG I, II*, and *III*), after the work of B. A. Kuftin (1956) at the largest known prehistoric settlement, Namazga-

depe near Kaakha. These periods at Namazga-depe, however, were established through rough artificial cuts, about 0.5m thick, recording general changes in the ceramics, matched by changes in architecture. The paradigm widely popularised by V. M. Masson and V. I. Sarianidi (1972) was that in the second half of the third millennium BC in the *NMG V* period (in Mesopotamian terms, from the late *Early Dynastic* period to the *Ur III* state), a secondary "urban evolution", described in strictly Childeian terms, affected the southern agricultural societies of Turkmenistan. Dramatic changes included a sudden and sharp class differentiation, a vertical growth of the craft sectors, a subdivision of the towns or cities into neatly segregated functional and residential sectors, and an incipient invention of a "proto-writing" system on cultic terracotta figurines (Masson and Sarianidi 1972).

Until approximately the 1990s, the *NMG I* period was dated to the fifth millennium BC, *NMG II* to the first half of the fourth millennium BC, and *NMG III* to the second half of the fourth millennium BC (Kuftin 1956; Masson 1956a, 1962, 1982; Masson and Sarianidi 1972; Khlopin 1969; Kohl 1984). Recently, F. T. Hiebert and K. Kurbansakhatov's excavation at Anau north, with new radiocarbon dates (Hiebert 2003), a reanalysis of the prehistoric complexes along the Kopet Dag also carried out by Hiebert (2002), and the long-standing work at Altyn-depe and Ilgynly-depe by V. M. Masson, L. Kircho, Ju. Berezkin, and N. Solovyova, similarly supported by new radiocarbon dates (Berezkin 1993; Masson and Berezkin 2005; Masson and Kircho 2008), produced a slightly modified and more refined chronology. The piedmont was not a compact cultural entity, as suggested by the generic term "Namazga Civilisation". Its western, central, and eastern sectors experienced their own trajectory of cultural development, distinguished by shared traits but also by totally original features. The chronological sequence presently available is detailed in Table 9.1.

The alternate use, in both Russian and English archaeological literature, of the terms "Chalcolithic" (a word frequently used in the archaeology of the Ancient Near East) and "Aeneolithic" (more common, together with "Copper age" in the archaeology of south-eastern Europe) for indicating the same evolutionary stages, is rather confusing. Although in this paper we have adopted the first label, the two terms are synonyms.

Ceramic classes and cultural areas of the mid-fourth millennium BC

Ak-depe, near Ashgabad, is – together with the graveyard of Parkhay II (see below) – one of the few sites of southern Turkmenistan documenting for the middle phase of the *Chalcolithic* the stratigraphic

Table 9.1. The emerging chronological framework for the Chalcolithic period along the Kopet Dagh piedmont (modified after Hiebert 2002, 2003). SWT, in the western region, stands for "south-western Turkmenistan"; here the chronology is based on I. N. Khlopin's research (1997, 2002) on the graveyards of the Sumbar valley.

Period	Western region	Central region	South-eastern region	Absolute chronology
Pre-Chalcolithic		Anau 1A or KD 4		c. 4500–4000 BC
Early Chalcolithic	SWT VII period	NMG I or KD 5	Dashlidji period	c. 4000–3500 BC
Middle Chalcolithic	SWT VI period	NMG II or late KD 5– early KD 6	Jalangach period	c. 3500–3200 BC
Late Chalcolithic	Late Chalcolithic or SWT V period	NMG III or late KD 6	Geoksyur period	c. 3200–2800 BC

association of bichrome painted pottery (red or brown/black on buff or reddish ware) and grey wares, whose evolution and diffusion can be followed until the *Iron Age*. Here only the 13th layer contained *NMG II – late KD 5* and *early KD 6* – materials, but the exposure was quite limited. The distribution of grey and other well-recognised wares of the *Chalcolithic* period shows a first regionalisation process. In fact, already around the middle of the fourth millennium BC, the piedmont of western Turkmenistan was part of a "grey ware province" (Fig. 9.2/A) stretching into the Gorgan Plain and northern Iran.

It is well known (Masson 1962; Khlopin 1969; Kohl 1984) that the geographic distribution of the main ceramic classes points to a threefold geographical division, with: i) a polychrome red- and brown-on-buff ware in the piedmont strip (firstly appearing in the central piedmont zone at Kara-depe and Namazga-depe) (Fig. 9.2/B); ii) a monochrome black-on-red ware in the eastern piedmont and in the Geoksyur deltaic area (Fig. 9.2/C); and iii) (as already stated) painted wares associated with grey wares in the western piedmont (Fig. 9.2/A). The grey wares of north-eastern Iran and south-western Central Asia in the *Chalcolithic* and *Bronze Age* periods are described as handmade ceramics of dark grey to black fabric, with a high proportion of sand, gypsum, and grog tempers, and more rarely grass or chaff inclusions, fired at high temperatures in strongly reducing atmospheres. The surface is slipped reddish grey to black and often highly burnished. It is either plain or decorated with incised motifs of parallel lines and diagonally or horizontally hatched, alternating upright and inverted triangles with shared borders (Sarianidi 1976; Kircho 1999). Grey fabric sherds are present in small amounts from the lowermost levels of many *Middle Chalcolithic* sites, but later increase. They have been found in large numbers in the *Late Chalcolithic* layers of south-western

Turkmenistan and the nearby regions, where as a result of increased interaction, growing social complexity, and specialisation processes, these grey wares became more homogeneous across the region and finally exhibited increased uniformity in colour, forms, and decoration (Khlopin 1997). Similar grey wares are well documented in the Gorgan plain of north-eastern Iran[2] and in north-central Iran (on the Tehran, Qazvin, and Kashan plains),[3] while in the central and eastern piedmont and in the Geoksyur area this particular *Middle Chalcolithic* ceramic is limited to a few types. The *Middle Chalcolithic* layers of Altyn-depe, where grey or blackish vessels were probably imported from south-western Turkmenistan or the north-central Iranian Plateau, or were local imitations, include hemispherical bowls, biconical pots, and vessels with a sub-cylindrical neck (Masson and Kircho 2008: pls. 6A, 15; 6B, 20; 7V, 17; 50B, 27; 51V, 27). At Kara-depe, two grey ware sherds were dated to the first phase of the *Middle Chalcolithic* (Masson 1960, 1962).

Y. Majidzadeh and other scholars, linking pots and peoples, viewed these or similar grey wares of the northern Iranian plains as evidence of the migration or invasion of new ethnic groups from south-western Central Asia (Majidzadeh 1978, 1981). Today, new discoveries in the north-central Iranian Plateau suggest a very gradual introduction of these wares, followed by internal innovation.

This ceramic "family" has no direct parallels in the surrounding regions (Transcaucasia and Mesopotamia) during this or the preceding periods. As the making of thin-walled vessels, fired in reducing atmospheres to the edge of sintering, may have mirrored a parallel diffusion – among the elites – of prestigious and costly metallic vessels, some grey wares could have been skeuomorphs. At any rate, such technical evolution should be considered a side effect of a growing social hierarchy and social display.

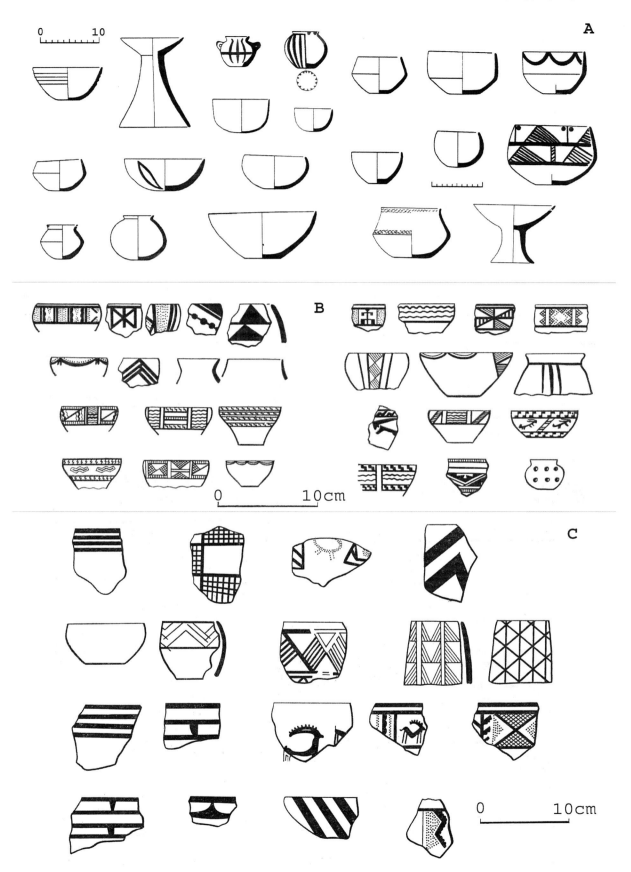

Figure 9.2. Main ceramic classes of the Middle Chalcolithic *in southern Turkmenistan:* **A.** *painted wares associated with grey wares in the western piedmont;* **B.** *polychrome red and brown on buff ware in the piedmont strip (first appearing in the central piedmont zone at Kara-depe and Namazga-depe);* **C.** *monochrome black-on-red wares, common in the eastern piedmont and in the Geoksyur deltaic area.*

Ecological background and early technologies of ancient farming

In prehistoric southern Turkmenistan, rain-fed cultivation of cereals was impossible, as it is at present. For P. Dolukhanov (1981: 375) the seasonal moisture regime of the *Neolithic* and *Chalcolithic* periods did not differ significantly from that of today, even if in the past annual precipitation was greater and spring floods more substantial. The earliest cultivators of the Djeitun *Neolithic* (*c.* 6000–5000 BC) depended on irrigation and/or groundwater in order to ripen the crops. Intensive research at Djeitun (Lisizyna 1965, 1969, 1978; Harris and Gosden 1996; Harris *et al.* 1996; Harris 2010) confirmed this hypothesis. Agriculture with artificial irrigation was also possible where the extensive alluvial clay formations (*takyrs*) border the southern edge of the Kara Kum desert, on the northern edge of terminal run-offs from the Kopet Dag (Harlan and Pasquereau 1969).

Palaeobotanical remains from *Neolithic* contexts at Djeitun, Chopan-depe, Bami, and Chagylly-depe (Lisizyna 1978; Zohary 1989: 359–62; 1996) indirectly confirm that small-scale irrigation in the *Neolithic* allowed the cultivation of domesticated einkorn and emmer wheat (*Triticum monococcum* and *Triticum dicoccum*) and six-row barley (*Hordeum sativum*, in both varieties: naked- and hulled-grain). Moreover, two "stone hoes" found at Chakmakli-depe and dated back to the *Anau IA* pre-*Chalcolithic* period (Berdyev 1968a), would have been well suited to cut irrigation channels and diverting watercourses. Similar tools were discovered at Tappeh Sialk I (Ghirshman 1938). A triangular cross-section channel (1 m in width and 0.24 m in depth) was dated to the *Chalcolithic* (*c.* 5200–4700 BC) at Tepe Pardis, in the Tehran plains. It may be the earliest example of artificial water management in Iran and the surrounding areas. Its antiquity is supported by a series of radiocarbon dates, associated ceramic sherds, and correlation with late *Neolithic-Transitional Chalcolithic* levels (Coningham *et al.* 2006; Fazeli *et al.* 2007; Gillmore *et al.* 2009).

In the following *Chalcolithic*, experienced farmers exploited land surfaces already improved by intensive agricultural cycles, and periodically refreshed by seasonal, small-scale floods. Irrigation agriculture was developed farther east, on the clay and silt plains of the Tedjen River delta. At Geoksyur 1 (Lisizyna 1965, 1972, 1981), a network of canals drew water from the main deltaic branches and associated reservoirs and discharged it near the settlement, where the crop fields were managed. Three parallel canals merged almost at right angles from an ancient silted river, and side canals or *arykhs* branched off from the three canals at various distances. A small water reservoir filled by a ditch was discovered near Mullali-depe or Geoksyur 4, dated back to the end of the fourth millennium BC (Lisizyna 1965: 107–13). Intensive artificial irrigation in the ecologically constrained deltaic area of the

Tedjen might have temporarily granted a noticeable economic surplus to the local groups, but at the same time required the early defensive systems of sites such as Mullali-depe and Jalangach-depe (Fig. 9.3) (among others, Hiebert 2002: 36). Resource concentration and ecological circumscription in the Tedjen delta might be at the root of a diverging pattern of early urban development (after Carneiro 1970).

The Meana-Chaacha region of southern Turkmenistan is named after two streams called Meana-chay and Chaacha-chay. These streams experienced a shift from an eastern or south-eastern direction to a northern or north-western trend (Marcolongo and Mozzi 1997: 49–61), with important consequences on the local settlement patterns (see below). A buried irrigation canal, probably dug in prehistoric times to divert the water of the palaeo-Tedjen River, is best preserved between the two courses, 3–4 km north-east of Ilgynly-depe and more than 5 km east of Altyn-depe.

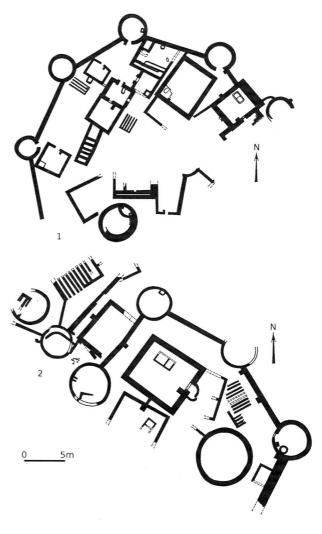

Figure 9.3. Early defensive systems in the Middle Chalcolithic sites of the Geoksyur area (Mullali-depe and Jalangach-depe).

Settlements of the Middle Chalcolithic in southern Turkmenistan and the surrounding regions

The documentation of the *Middle Chalcolithic* period (*NMG II* or *late KD 5* and *early KD 6* in the piedmont plain, see Table 9.1) is much more complete than the preceding *Early Chalcolithic*, dated to the first half of the fourth millennium BC. Extensive excavations were carried out in some sites of the piedmont plain and of the Geoksyur oasis, i.e. Kara-depe, Jalangach-depe, Akcha-depe, Mullali-depe, and to a lesser extent also at Altyn-depe. This allows a more reliable reconstruction of the cultural and socio-technological developments of the middle and second half of the fourth millennium BC (Table 9.2).

A general reconstruction of the stratigraphic sequence obtained from many excavations and test trenches at Altyn-depe was first attempted by V. M. Masson in the late 1970s, and later developed by L. Kircho and V. A. Alekshin (Masson 1977, 1981, 1988; Masson and Berezkin 2005; Masson and Kircho

2008). All tested contexts had *Jalangach*-type painted ceramics and distinctive unpainted red-slipped wares. These ceramics are typical of the *Middle Chalcolithic* of the central region of the piedmont of the Kopet Dag (Masson 1962: 14; 1989: 29; Kircho 1999: 60–64; see above), but are scantily represented in the Geoksyur region (Khlopin 1969: 27, 29). The unpainted red-slipped ware is very close to the pottery of south-western Iran of the *Lapui* phase, dated to the first half of the fourth millennium BC (Sumner 1988). Russian archaeologists concluded that the mound was not fully occupied in the *Early Chalcolithic* and that in the following *Middle Chalcolithic* its settlement area (and possibly its population) was doubled.

NMG II layers were also unearthed in the imposing settlement of Ulug-depe, the site with the longest stratigraphical sequence in Central Asia: from the *Chalcolithic* to the *Achaemenid* period. Ulug-depe is located about 45–50 km north-west of Altyn-depe and Ilgynly-depe, very close to the mosque of the modern city of Dushak. V.I. Sarianidi, between

Table 9.2. Settlements in southern Turkmenistan and the nearby regions in the Middle Chalcolithic *by contexts and (for the few published sites with specific information) their extent on the surface.*

Name	Location	Mid-Chalcolithic layers or finds	Extension in ha	Main bibliographic references
Chingiz-depe	South-western Turkmenistan, west of Kyzyl Arvat	Red-slipped pottery of *NMG II* type		Berdyev 1971: 11
Parkhay II	South-western Turkmenistan, Sumbar valley	About 33 collective graves with *NMG II* material culture		Khlopin 1981, 1997, 2002
Gievdzhik-depe	South-western Turkmenistan, Geok-depe area	In the upper levels		Korobkova 1972
Til'kin-depe	South-western Turkmenistan, Geok-depe area	*NMG II* pottery recorded in the upper layers.		Khlopin 1963: 8 Masson 1962: 8
Gavych-depe	South-western Turkmenistan, Geok-depe area	*NMG II* pottery recorded		Berdyev 1976: 14; Masson 1982: 30
Suncha-depe	South-western Turkmenistan, Geok-depe area.	*NMG II* pottery recorded		Masson 1982: 30
Ekin-depe	Southern Turkmenistan, Ashgabad area	*NMG II* pottery recorded	12–20 ha.	Ganjalin 1956; Khlopin 1963: 8
Ak-depe	Southern Turkmenistan, Ashgabad area	Layer Ak depe II (T: *c.* 7 m)		Durdyev 1959; Masson 1966
		13th horizon		Kircho 1999
Anau north	Southern Turkmenistan, Ashgabad area	Layers 4–2 (*Anau II A* phase)		Pumpelly 1908; Erschov 1956; Hiebert 2003
Kara-depe	Southern Turkmenistan, central Etek	Levels 15–9 (or 10) in sounding 1 (T: *c.* 3 m); levels 17–14 in sounding 2 (T: *c.* 2 m); horizons Kara 6–2 in exc. 1 (T: *c.* 5 m).	Probably between 8 and 14 ha.	Masson 1962, 1982; Hiebert 2002
Elen-depe	Southern Turkmenistan, central Etek	Seven horizons (from II to VIII) (T: 6.5 m)		Shchetenko 1968: 18, 21–24; Masson 1982: 30

crafts or artistic skill (Berezkin 1989, 1992; Berezkin and Solovyova 1998; Solovyova 2000, 2012), not fully reflected in the production of domestic pottery. Most of the vessels, in fact, are unpainted with a buff or reddish surface with dark patches due to uneven firing. Painted pottery is similar to that of Altyn-depe: open bowls and cups painted with parallel blackish lines below the rim and large storage jars bearing chevron-like or schematic vegetal motives. Some fine polychrome sherds, in black and red, were perhaps imported from the Akhal region of southern Turkmenistan, between Anau and Namazga-depe, including Kara-depe.

The bulk of faunal remains belongs to domestic sheep, goats and bovines, and wild half-asses, suggesting that animal breeding and farming coexisted with hunting (Dolukhanov 1981; Kasparov 1989, 1994a, 2006). At Ilgynly-depe the wild half-ass or onager (*Equus hemionus kulan*) accounts for about 15% of the total, while in the *Mesolithic-Neolithic* layers at Djebel and Dam Dam Chesme, bones of this animal are absent or extremely rare. In *Neolithic* Djeitun, onager or kulan bones are absent, and at Chagylly-depe and Chopan-depe they are still very scarce, suggesting that the systematic hunting of these animals was a *Chalcolithic* innovation (Berdyev 1966: 27; Kasparov 1994b: 148). At Ilgynly-depe sheep bones are about 64% of the total capriovines vs. 36% of goats. Domestic dogs were possibly used for hunting or pastoral purposes (Kasparov 1996, 2006). Palaeobotanical materials include charred cereal seeds (mainly wheat and barley) and large amounts of charcoal, showing the exploitation of wetter environments than contemporary ones.

Excavations 1, 4, and 5 exposed the remains of mud-brick domestic and residential complexes with the richly decorated rooms mentioned above, interpreted by the excavators as "sanctuaries" (Fig. 9.6). The identification was supported by benches painted red, first constructed with wooden planks and later plastered; floors and walls painted black; low altars or fireplaces, oval in plan; clay tables and chairs, common in the earlier *Middle Chalcolithic* layers; rows of standardised containers sunk into the floors, almost always along the walls of the rooms; and elaborate wall paintings, preserved in the lower portion of the walls, with snakes, trees, dots, and geometric patterns. Big clay *bucrania* decorated with snakes in relief were discovered in level 5. Many anthropomorphic and zoomorphic statuettes completed the inventories of such rooms. These "shrines" were approximately square in plan with an average floor space of 60 m² (Berezkin 1989; Berezkin and Solovyova 1998; Masson *et al.* 1994). The excellent maps made by the Russian archaeological team (Masson *et al.* 1994; Solovyova *et al.* 1994; Solovyova 2000) show large dumps of sherds and burnt pebbles cracked by firing near these buildings.

Wall paintings in similar buildings were found in four other sites (Pessedjik-depe,[8] Jassy-depe,[9] Sermancha-depe,[10] and Anau[11]). The earliest "shrine" with painted walls in Middle Asia, however, was discovered in the Qazvin plain at Tepe Zagheh (Negahban 1979).[12] This north-central Iranian "sanctuary" is noticeable because of its size (117 m²), platforms or benches built as seats along the walls, a central fireplace, mountain goat skulls and horns mounted on the walls over the benches, and a large number of clay figurines found on the floor. Other buildings with peculiar architectural features, larger than the more common living structures, were found in nearly all the Geoksyur *NMG II* sites. Their distinguishing features are a topographical position near the centre of the settlements, a raised podium or altar in the centre of the room, and platforms or benches along the massive walls. Corners are oriented towards the cardinal points, and their stratigraphical continuity across several living phases confirms an important symbolic function. The most relevant of these constructions are room 1 of Jalangach-depe, room 7 at Mullali-depe, room 5 at Akcha-depe, and room III.1 at Aina-depe (Khlopin 1964). Although some of these rooms may share the functions and symbolic meanings of the "sanctuaries" of Ilgynly-depe, the complex wall paintings of the latter site are unique. Moreover, while the small surviving portions of wall paintings from other agricultural sites, regardless of the subject, were decorated with simple monochrome or polychrome paintings, those of Ilgynly-depe were made with a peculiar "graffito" technique.

According to the Russian excavators, the excellent preservation of the wall paintings of Ilgynly-depe is explained by a ritual process of abandonment of the painted rooms (e.g. Berezkin 1992; Masson *et al.* 1994; Solovyova 2011, 2012). Constructions would have been deliberately burnt and filled in when they went out of use, abandoning large numbers of objects inside. These include unbroken copper tools and many stone implements, among which there were about 70 stone mortars, some with a zoomorphic shape; many animal figurines and no less than 700 terracotta female figurines in unbaked clay; several complete anthropomorphic statues and two dozen in fragments. These buildings also contained equipment for daily use, such as terracotta spindle-whorls, and several wheel-shaped ceramic objects – mentioned above – probably parts of models of cartwheels (Kircho 2009: fig. 1); flint or chert tools; grinding stones; tools for manufacturing metal and stone objects; many small finds in other materials (leather, wood, pigments, and others); and bone awls. From the "sanctuary" of layer IV (Excavation 5), the Russian archaeologists also uncovered disarticulated bones of children and adults as well as two complete infant skeletons laid in an unusual stretched position (Masson *et al.* 1994).

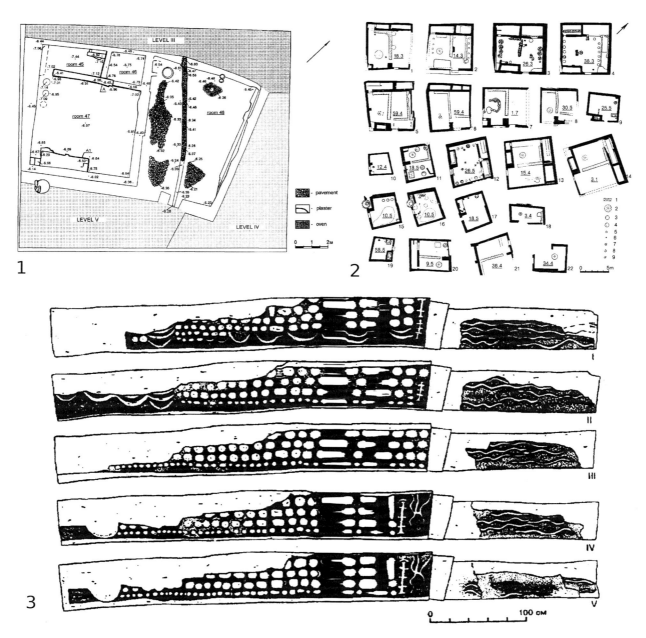

Figure 9.6. "Sanctuaries" at Ilgynly-depe: complex of rooms 45–48 (1) and typology of the square rooms with rows of jars sunk into the ground, benches, and "altars" (2). These structures, with distinctive paintings on the wall (3), might also be interpreted as hammams or special rooms for steam baths (see text).

Some anthropomorphic statues, similar in style to the clay figurines (see below) were made of sandstone (Korobkova 1987; Masson and Korobkova 1989) (Fig. 9.7). A stone human head had ochre stains in the mouth, while another human face decorated the side of a heavy stone container. These statues, like the numerous stone vases found in the dig, were locally manufactured. In fact, unfinished stone objects, production rejects, and waste still visible on the surface of the site are evidence that Ilgynly-depe was at the time an important stone-working centre.

Ilgynly-depe is very rich in copper artefacts and tools (Solovyova *et al.* 1994), the majority of which were found either on the floors of the so-called "sanctuaries" or in the adjacent rooms and open spaces. Such copper tools and ornaments include no less than 90 blades, and chisels, spear points, awls, rods with a thickened, flattened, or broken end, the double-spiral-shaped head of a pin, pipes and rolled beads, sheets, a shaft-hole axe-adze (the earliest so far in the ancient Near East and Middle Asia), and a round mirror. In spite of the hundreds of copper

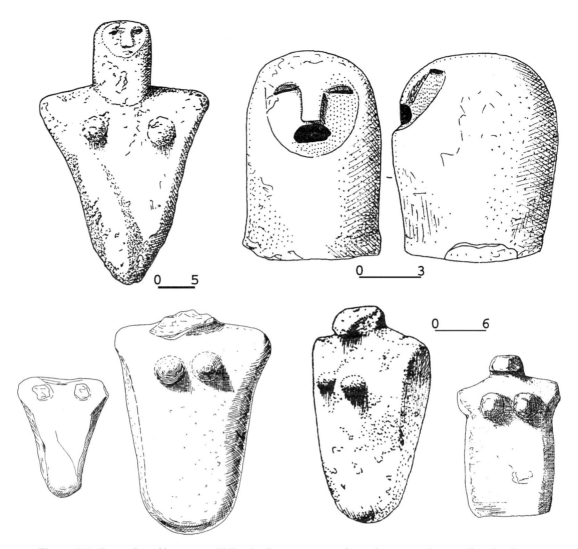

Figure 9.7. Examples of large to middle-sized stone statues from the excavations at Ilgynly-depe.

artefacts found in the excavated trenches and on the surface, the Russians found no slag, crucible fragments, or other pyrotechnological indicators, and considered Ilgynly-depe as a copper-consuming settlement, not involved in metallurgical processing.

The *Middle Chalcolithic* anthropomorphic and zoomorphic figurines (Masson and Korobkova 1989) are perhaps evidence of an aspect of the spiritual life of the settlement (Khlobystina 1977; Antonova and Sarianidi 1990; Solovyova 2005). The most common type is a female image, sitting or rarely standing, with legs, large breasts, a slender neck, and a head covered with a small cap (cf. Sheri Khan Tarakai in Pakistan; Knox *et al.* 2010). Most of these statuettes were found in pieces; they were tempered with chaff and slipped in red or yellowish hues. Some figurines bear painted necklaces, while a few others have a straight line descending from the necklace and passing between the breasts. Other lines are painted on the upper parts of the arms and might represent

bracelets. The largest figurine shows odd painted motives on the hips (comb-shaped patterns, simple and double lines, zigzag, nets, and sun motives with a point in the centre). Zoomorphic figurines are rather schematic, but represent mostly bulls (Kasparov 2000, 2001). Some portrayed goats, wild half-asses (onagers), and dogs.

Ilgynly-depe: new topography and surface studies

In spring 1999, an Italian team and N. Solovyova, Director of the Russian Expedition to Ilgynly-depe, carried out a new topographical plan of Ilgynly-depe during a two-week campaign (Figs 9.4–9.5; see also Salvatori *et al.* 2009: fig. 2). The team mapped the contemporary mound surface reconstructing in detail the shape of the mound and its dynamics of spatial occupation, recording the old Russian trenches, testing the possible evidence of craft activity areas, and studying the local polished stone industry visible on the surface (copper and lead-related artefacts, finished and unfinished stone vessels, grinding stones, pestles, mortars, hollowed and grooved stones perhaps used as weights, rings, and various types of rough-outs; Fig. 9.8). Topographic recording was complemented by pictures taken with a camera suspended on a kite. The new topographic plan shows that the site covers approximately 17 ha and rises to about 14 m above the contemporary surrounding alluvial plain. It extends from north-east to south-west for *c.* 497 m and from north-west to south-east for *c.* 482 m. The perimeter of the settlement is 1520 m.

The search for craft activity areas revealed hundreds of terracotta spindle-whorls of variable size, suggesting that the site had concentrated important spinning and perhaps weaving activities. Also found near the top of the mound was a cluster of metallurgical indicators including tiny slag pieces, copper prills, and fragments of finished objects among which were copper sheets, rods, nails and beads, and a set of lead-like lumps (Salvatori *et al.* 2009). This is the only copper processing area so far discovered in a *Chalcolithic* site of southern Turkmenistan, and demonstrates for certain that some previous ideas (i.e. the absence of metallurgy in the ancient

Figure 9.8. Ilgynly-depe, surface survey. Stone artefacts identified and collected on the surface. Key: A, H, L = different types of stone vessels; B = stone ring; C, F = unfinished stone vessels; D, E = grooved weights; G, I, J, K = possible door sockets.

settlement) were wrong. A crucible fragment, possibly used for melting a polymetallic compound, was found at another point of the mound. Subsequent archaeometric studies revealed that the melting of copper and leaded copper for casting, the fabrication of copper beads by rolling specially prepared flat preforms into cylinder-like pieces, and the forging of short nails with a thick and enlarged head, possibly used for tapestry and wooden furniture, were all being carried out. In contrast, the smelting of copper-bearing ores is not on record; the settlement must therefore have imported semi-finished copper lumps or ingots. Notably, one object had been cast with a lost-wax process. Even more interestingly, the lead-like lumps turned out to be litharge fragments, possibly a by-product of a silver-refining technology.

Besides copper beads, already known from the Russian excavations, the finding of a silver bead and another one in gold suggests that the inhabitants of the centre might have been fully aware of the symbolic implications of ornaments made of the three metals and the involved hierarchy of value and status. With the exception of a few silver beads from Altyn-depe such beads in precious metals were not found in the contemporary graves, where the ornaments are mostly in stones such as gypsum, limestone, carnelian, agate, and others.[13]

The "sanctuaries" as hammams

Were the rooms or "sanctuaries" of Ilgynly-depe abandoned with their precious furnishings, to be ritually destroyed by fire because they were sacred? This is not impossible, but this interpretation (Berezkin 1989, 1992; Masson *et al.* 1994) is difficult to accept, as the deliberate firing of whole buildings, in the heart of a closely packed lattice of domestic dwellings, would have been quite a dangerous undertaking. Even assuming, however, that the abandonment process was entirely dictated by unfathomable ritual reasons, what was the purpose of the rows of ceramic storage jars aligned along the walls? Why were only these special rooms provided with wooden and plaster benches? Why were large amounts of fired sherds and pebbles dumped outside these buildings?

We would like to consider the possibility that these units were hammams, rooms for hot steam baths – in other words, saunas. In Central Asia, Iran, and in many other regions of the Near East and Middle Asia, hot steam is the most common and least expensive medium for personal cleaning and body care. Furthermore, hammams have long been important places for relaxing and socialising (Figs 9.9–9.10). The inhabitants of Ilgynly-depe collected pebbles and potsherds, heated them red-hot, and placed them in rows of jars filled with water on the raised benches or "altars" and along the walls of these rooms. The jars would have thus produced hot steam, while people could sit on the benches, meet, and chat. At the same time hospitality might have had an important ethical value and could have been used as an efficient political strategy. In such socialisation contexts, wall paintings and other symbolic media would have conveyed important ideological messages, re-enforcing the social identities of the groups who owned or managed the bathhouses. The pebbles and cracked rocks used for producing steam would later have been discarded in the dumps beside the house.

Some of the most schematic anthropomorphic figurines found in the destruction layers of these rooms and in other excavated contexts, although generically described by the excavators as "limestone" artefacts, are often made with very coarse-grained, possibly volcanic stones (e.g. Solovyova 2005: nos 550–551, 556–559, 565–567, 569–570). A class of similar, possible anthropomorphic stone artefacts at Shahr-i Sokhta, was described as "volcanic rock polishers" or "reddish-to-black vacuolar basalt polishers". They have been interpreted by M. Tosi (quoted in Ciarla 1981: figs 10, 11, p. 53) as tools for polishing alabaster vessels, but this functional association is doubtful, because such "tools" and stone vessel waste were never found in the same contexts. Similar rocks, in particular vacuolar basalts, are used today in Iranian hammams to scrape the skin, most often on the soles of the feet (Figs 9.9–9.10), and we should consider the possibility that at least some of the "figurines" of Ilgynly-depe were used as skin-scrapers in the daily activities of the bathhouses.

While this interpretation does not preclude a ritual or cultic use of the rooms, their firing in some cases might have been accidental, as a consequence of the intensive use of fuel and fire to heat the stones and sherds. The loss and scattering of many valuable artefacts might have been the result of random processes, and not necessarily of an intentional ritual behaviour. This functional hypothesis, however, does not fully explain some peculiar architectural features (such as the recesses and apparently closed cubicles of these constructions), nor the periodic discovery of human skeletal remains in the ruins. While this difficult question remains fully open to speculation, in our conclusions (see below) we venture to propose some possible socio-political implications of the new interpretation.

Graveyards and burial practices

The *Chalcolithic* and *Bronze Age* graveyard of Parkhay II was discovered in 1977 in the Sumbar valley, on the edge of the modern village of Kara-Kala,[14] in the province of Kyzyl Arvat (Khlopin 1981, 1997, 2002). It contained 273 collective and individual burials, no less than 33 of which date back to the *Middle Chalcolithic* period. The Parkhay II graveyard[15] is

Figure 9.9. Leisure time and socialization activities in a traditional hammam in Iran. An attendant washing and cleaning a visitor: personal cleaning may express hierarchic or power relationships. Note the use of textiles, costly metal objects and, at far right, a plate containing rounded rubbing stones in vacuolar basalt for scraping the skin. Life-sized wax models in a traditional hammam in Iran (in the hammam museum at the Kerman bazaar, Iran).

Figure 9.10. Use of rounded rubbing stones in vacuolar basalt for scraping the soles of the feet, life-sized wax models in a traditional hammam in Iran (picture taken in the hammam museum at the Kerman bazaar, Iran).

unique in the archaeological funerary inventory of the whole of Middle Asia, first because the graves are not disturbed, covered, or interspaced with residential or special-function buildings,[16] and second because – mostly in the *Chalcolithic*, but also in the following *Early Bronze Age* – tombs are collective, with primary and secondary burials. The number of individual graves becomes noticeable only from the *Middle Bronze Age* onwards, while in the *Chalcolithic* and in the *Early Bronze Age* their percentage remains very low. Third, this cemetery is the only one to have collective burials already in the *Early* and *Middle Chalcolithic* periods,[17] confirming that the plains and intermontane valleys of south-western Turkmenistan were a distinct cultural region divided into several socio-political or cultural areas. The intermediate, central position of the Sumbar valley was optimal for spurring autonomous cultural innovation. Four other graveyards in this south-western region (Parkhay I, Sumbar I, Sumbar II, and Yangi Q'ala), which were not intermingled either with residential or with utilitarian buildings, show a clear-cut cultural and ritual distance from the prevailing proto-historic funerary traditions of Middle Asia. All the burials in the four latter-mentioned cemeteries, however, date to the *Late Bronze Age* (Ganjalin 1956; Khlopina 1981; Khlopin 1986).

Some child burials at Anau north, Kara-depe, and Altyn-depe are as wealthy as adult ones, if not wealthier. In the largest settlement of the Meana-Chaacha region, Altyn-depe, the individual burials[18] of the *Middle* and *Late Chalcolithic* periods so far excavated amount to 24 graves, 14 of which belong to children and infants. Only two of the 10 adult burials contained a few grave-goods (nos 199 and 278). One of the 14 child graves (no. 725) had a rich funerary inventory,[19] while another (no. 911) contained a few objects.[20] The other 12 child and infant burials had no grave offerings.

The picture of inequality provided by the graves of Altyn-depe seems fully confirmed at Kara-depe. In this site one of the few *Early Chalcolithic* graves, no. 28,[21] was uncovered during Excavation 1 (Masson 1960). In the layers of the *Middle Chalcolithic* period at Kara-depe 62 individuals burials were excavated, about 57% of which had no furnishings near or above the skeleton. Of the adult graves 43% contain only ceramics (with the exceptions of graves 31[22] and 32[23]). The record of wealthy child burials is more substantial (graves 34, 41, 54, 55, 57, 72, and 75[24]). In the following *Late Chalcolithic*, the percentage of graves with offered goods increases to 64%. One of the *Middle Chalcolithic* graves, no. 31, was very richly furnished, but due to the bad preservation of the skeleton it is not known whether it was a child or not. Besides burials with copper and bone artefacts and necklace and bracelet beads, graves with pottery vessels in grey-blackish ware, placed near the legs or

the skull, are more common. In general, there is no apparent correlation between funerary wealth, sex, and/or age of the deceased.

During the 1904 excavations at Anau north by R. Pumpelly and L. Warner, and those in 1978–1982 by K. Kurbansakhatov and F. T. Hiebert, a total of 23 burials were discovered within the settlement area. The earliest graves (1 and 2) were ascribed to the *Anau IA* proto-*Chalcolithic* period. Eight burials[25] (3 to 10) are dated to the *Early Chalcolithic*.

There were 13 burials in the *Middle Chalcolithic* levels at Anau, nine from the *Anau IIA* layers and four, all containing children, from the *Anau IIB* layers. As at Kara-depe, some were found surrounded by mud-brick enclosures. The furnishings were scarce and had few ceramic vessels, but often contained beads. Grave no. 17, according to Hiebert (2003: 123), or no. 9, according to Masson (1962: 8), had no less than 1066 small beads in a whitish stone, found near the pelvis of a child and decorating the girdle or other garment; and grave 6, excavated by K. Kurbansakhatov, contained a child provided with several hundred small and larger beads made of limestone, probably sewn to the dress or funerary shroud (Hiebert 2003: 120). Thus the funerary record of Anau north, as far as child burials are concerned, is consistent with Altyn-depe and Kara-depe.

At Namazga-depe, information on the *Chalcolithic* graves is very scanty and uninformative.[26] At Ilgynly-depe 88 *Chalcolithic* burials were found. The graves, hosting individuals of various age groups, had no furnishings or were supplied with a single ceramic container. Most were individual tombs and many were secondary burials. A collective grave in a round pit, similar to, and probably a prototype of, the later *NMG III* tholos-like graves in mud brick discovered at Altyn-depe and Geoksyur 1, was also found on the western edge of the site (Masson *et al.* 1994).

In short, the *Middle Chalcolithic* communities of the region practised different types of burials. Collective round tombs, with primary and secondary (fractional) burials, are known at Parkay II, in south-western Turkmenistan and, at least in a single instance also at Ilgynly-depe, on the opposite side of the piedmont strip. These collective chambers usually do not stress (at least in terms of grave furnishings) different levels of rank, status, or wealth. They were empty burial chambers used by some families or particular individuals for generations, perhaps as a symbol of the ancient solidarity and kinship ties that kept together the extended families living in the large multi-roomed complexes. At present, the record is so scanty that it is difficult to understand how far the selective geographical distribution of similar graves depends upon idiosyncratic cultural traditions. We witness a marked differentiation in the grave furnishings of children, mainly expressed by the number and quality of the stone beads worn by the deceased or attached to the funerary garments. The impression is that the ideologies prevailing in the period under scrutiny did not favour the representation of social inequality at the funerals of adults, but for some reason this prescription could be ignored when dealing with children. Obviously enough, the richest graves of infants and children suggest that status and differential access to important symbols, made with valuable materials, was inherited or ascribed at birth on kinship or family lines, and not individually achieved in life.

Conclusions

In the *Middle Chalcolithic* or *NMG II* period of southern Turkmenistan, settlement networks took the form of a scatter of small rural villages pivoting on a few larger central towns, spaced with some regularity at distances of 50–70 km or more, from the Kyzyl Arvat region to the Tedjen delta on the southern margin of the Kara Kum desert. These sedentary settlements thrived thanks to skilled agriculture made possible by artificial irrigation, husbandry, and (most probably) carefully maintained strategic alliances and trade links with the local nomadic groups. The noticeable amounts of wild ass bones at Ilgynly-depe might imply not only that hunting in the steppe had become a form of economic intensification, but possibly also that different specialised groups were gradually attracted towards the sphere of early urban economy, and interacted more systematically with its sedentary population.

These early towns (so far we know of seven) were soon able to concentrate and perform important economic, political, and ideological functions. Although palaces and large cultic buildings have so far not been found, in the area watered by the Tedjen delta, polygonal defensive walls and possibly round towers surrounded some relatively large houses, provided with their storage facilities. This suggests that where land and water were abundant but ecologically constrained, the elites had the resources, authority, and power to plan and defend their settlements with medium- to large-scale architectural projects. The absence of similar defensive concerns, or a lower coercive capacity of the elites, might explain the apparent absence of walls and towers in the settlements of the piedmont.

Studies on the material culture and craft systems show a very advanced technical knowledge and efficient networks of procurement and trade of strategic resources. Copper and stones reached sites such as Ilgynly-depe from medium- or long-distance source areas as consignments of raw materials (for stones) or semi-processed ingots (for copper). The smiths of Ilgynly-depe locally manufactured a wide range of tools and ornaments, copper beads among others. While former studies emphasised

a pretended "primitive" character of the *Middle* and *Late Chalcolithic* metallurgy (e.g. suggesting that the forging technology was crude, and all the tools employed were made of stone; Korobkova and Sharovskaja 1994) later studies suggested that metal beads were processed with advanced copper implements. The inventory of metallurgical techniques practised at Ilgynly-depe reveals that the only meaningful innovation of the late third millennium BC was the introduction of tin as an alloying component (Salvatori *et al.* 2009). All the other processes had been developed 1000 years before.

Gold and silver beads were also used (and probably manufactured) in these centres. Silver might have been locally refined from ores such as galena or lead-rich ingots. Agate, carnelian, gypsum, and limestone were extracted and traded from medium-distance source areas. Precious rare materials such as lapis lazuli or exotic shells, traded from remote source areas, also gradually became part of the local ornaments. Indirect evidence (terracotta spindle-whorls and perhaps stone-handled weights) suggests that these central sites were also intensively involved with the textile industry. There is little doubt that the craft industries of the *NMG II* sites were fully equipped to represent the supremacy of the emerging elites, with both rough and subtle distinctions in each instance.

The welfare of a centre like Ilgynly-depe is also reflected in an abundant local production of stone vessels and anthropomorphic statues. Valuable artefacts of this type circulated together with copper items in the so-called "sanctuaries", which we would rather interpret as hammams or steam houses. This identification does not rule out the possibility that these special buildings were the seat of important occasions of socialisation or formal ceremonies, as suggested by the lavish wall paintings. Most, if not all, of the multi-roomed complexes that form the core of the settlement of Ilgynly-depe were provided with one such room. The heads of the families could gather and meet in these rooms and bathe, perhaps with guests, while performing important rituals and discussing the town's matters. In this light, the steam houses could have been used to perform a kind of "diffuse political control", a possible alternative to a one-sided, direct centralisation of decision-making and religious functions – in the same way as other communities of the ancient Near East and Middle Asia. Finally, the funerary rituals on record so far may reflect a contradiction between traditional egalitarian ethics and the drive to display a growing social inequality: funerals of children, perhaps because the latter were not fully developed social *personae*, seem to have been the contexts in which contrasting values and new compelling political issues reached a compromise.

Notes

1 The earliest fragment of a "weight" or *gyr* comes from the upper horizon of Dashly-depe, near Izgant, 30 km west of Ashgabad. According to I. N. Khlopin, this stone object is dated to a late phase of the *Early Chalcolithic* (Khlopin 1963: 9), while according to A. A. Marushchenko to the beginning of the *Middle Chalcolithic* (Kurbansakhatov 1987: 100). V. A. Alekshin proposed that these objects were used as weights, while for A. P. Okladnikov they had a technical role in irrigation, even though their frequency in domestic debris rather suggests household functions. H. Wulff observed the use of similar large stone weights in rug-making in modern Iranian villages (Wulff 1966: 202–04).

2 At Tepe Pardis in the Tehran plains, the first grey-black burnished ware appears in *Late Neolithic* or *Transitional Chalcolithic* horizons (c. 5200–4700 BC, calibrated ^{14}C dates) (Fazeli *et al.* 2010). At Tepe Hissar the first but still scanty evidence of burnished grey ware is found in the *Hissar IA–IB* periods (*Early–Middle Chalcolithic*), while in the next stage, *Hissar IC–IIA* (*Late Chalcolithic*) burnished grey ware bowls on tall pedestal bases, deep bowls with flaring rims, and short- and long-necked bottles are already in use. Coeval to the *Hissar IC–IIA* period are *Tureng IIA* (sondage A, levels 26–20) (Deshayes 1966, 1967), *Yarim Tepe II* (Crawford 1963; Stronach 1972), and *Shah Tepe III* (Arne 1945). There are, however, substantial differences in the grey ware ceramic traditions of the Damghan and Gurgan regions: incised and applied decoration is common in *Tureng IIA* and *Shah III*, but is absent from the grey ware specimens of *Hissar IC–IIA*. Also the repertory of pottery forms is different.

3 Ghabristan, *Period III*, levels 8–7, in the Qazvin plain (Majidzadeh 1978, 1981), Ozbaki, Mehdikani, Mafinabad, Sadeghabed or Sadeghabadi, Chouqali, Cheshmeh Ali, and Mortezagerd in the Tehran plain (Fazeli *et al.* 2005) and Sialk, layer III$_{4–5}$ in the Kashan plain (Ghirshman 1938). See Piller (2003–2004) for a recent study of the grey wares (grouped in Western, Central and Eastern Grey Ware) on the central and northern Iranian plateau during the Bronze Age.

4 The excavations by a French-Turkmen team in the first years of the new millennium did not uncover new *Chalcolithic* layers, as it considered only the stratigraphic horizons already described by Sarianidi (Lecomte *et al.* 2002).

5 Chingiz-depe is 12 km west-north-west of Kyzyl Arvat and 7 km east of Parou. Gievdzhik-depe and Til'kin-depe are located in the Geok-depe region. The first site is 18 km west-north-west of Geok-depe, while the second is 6 km east of the same city. Gavych-depe is located between the mouth of the Chuli gorge and the railway, while Suncha-depe is located 12 km south-east of Bakharden.

6 The correlation between Excavation 3, where six layers were excavated, and Excavation 5, dug to a total depth of 1.5 m, is based on the following identifications: the bottom of layer II = layer IA; the top of layer III = layer IB; the bed of layer III =layer IIA; and layer IV = layer IIB.

7 Some patterns (black parallel lines under the rim) in the *Jalangach* period are shared by the sites of the Geoksyur area as well as by the ceramic repertories of Altyn-depe and Ilgynly depe; see also the collective burials of the *Late Chalcolithic* at Geoksyur, Altyn-depe, and Ilgynly-depe

8 Pessedjik-depe is a *Djeitun* culture *Neolithic* site in the Geok-depe area (Berdyev 1968b, 1976; Lollekova 1978, 1988). It has a 3.5 m cultural deposit dating back to the *Middle Neolithic* (second half of the sixth millennium BC). The uppermost layer has a large structure, room 12, measuring 64 m², with massive walls, an alabaster-plastered floor, and a big hearth-fireplace. It contained no utilitarian finds. In the second building level of this "sanctuary" or "clubhouse", a fresco was found with geometric designs, in black and red on a whitish background, and naturalistic animals. Other fragments of wall paintings were found by O. Lollekova in 1976 on the low parallel walls near room 12.

9 Jassi-depe, a few kilometres north of Namazga-depe in the eastern Akhal region, was excavated by S. E. Erschov and B. A. Kuftin in the 1950s (Erschov 1952; Kuftin 1956). In two rooms (nos. 15 and 16) of a central building interpreted as a "shrine" (33 m²), with corners oriented towards the cardinal points, repainted geometric frescoes were found with lozenges connected end to end, and a series of wooden columns.

10 Sermancha-depe is a small site in the piedmont between Namazga-depe and Ulug-depe, dated to the *Early Chalcolithic*. Also reported on the surface were *NMG II*-related sherds. A wall painting was discovered here in the 1950s (Masson 1956b: 236).

11 The excavations at Anau north – by S. E. Erschov in 1953 (1956: 27), K. Kurbansakhatov in 1977 and 1982 (Hiebert 2003), and F. T. Hiebert in 1997 (Hiebert 2003) – unearthed several wall paintings. The earliest examples were found in Erschov's second architectural level, corresponding to layer 17 of Hiebert's sequence, and dated to the Anau IBI period, an early phase of the *Early Chalcolithic*. Here, room 3, interpreted as a shrine (Masson 1982: 21), had plastered and painted inner walls with stylised checkerboards and triangles. In the architectural levels of the late phase of the *Early Chalcolithic*, equal to layers 9–5 of Hiebert's column, buildings were found whose inner walls were repeatedly painted black, with benches or piers and square-shaped rooms whose interior had been deliberately cleaned and burned (Hiebert 2003). This interpretation was borrowed from what was proposed for the "sanctuaries" of Ilgynly-depe (Berezkin 1992).

12 This construction was dated, after its general archaeological context, between the end of the seventh and the beginning of the sixth millennium BC.

13 All these stones were visually identified.

14 Not far from the Parkhay II cemetery and from Kara-Kala, the site of Parkhay, formed by an outer rock shelter and an inner cave divided into two sectors, yielded a potsherd near the lowermost layer, possibly belonging to the *Chalcolithic*, without specifying whether it belonged to the early, middle, or late phase of the same period (Harris 2010: 109–10).

15 The toponym Parkhay II was for a long time associated only with the *Chalcolithic* and *Bronze Age* graveyard. A residential settlement near the cemetery has been

recorded by the excavator I. N. Khlopin since 1984, but very little information has been published. In the third figure of the second book on Parkhay II, the location of the settlement is marked by a dotted line running a few metres to the west of the cemetery (Khlopin 2002: fig. 3). The settlement extends for 300–400 m to the south-west of the graveyard, covers an area of 5–6 ha, and its surface is covered by *Early Bronze Age* materials. The thickness of the anthropic deposit is more than 4 m and the layers also contain *Late Chalcolithic* ceramics. D. R. Harris tested the settlement, while searching (unsuccessfully) for *Neolithic* deposits beneath the *Chalcolithic* layers (Harris 2010). He described it as 500 × 300 m site, the surface covered with bones and ceramics. In these new accounts, the topography of the Parkhay II site complex (cemetery and settlement) seems very similar to that of Shahr-i Sokhta: in both cases the residential quarters were built near the space for the dead, but the two areas are neatly segregated.

16   The most common prehistoric funerary custom of Middle Asia was to dig the burial pits into the floors of abandoned residential structures, or build mud-brick tombs in abandoned sectors of the ancient settlements (cemetery *intra moenia*). For the exceptional separation of graveyards and settled areas at Parkhai II and Shahr-i Sokhta see previous note.

17   In the *Late Chalcolithic*, the latest centuries of the fourth and the first centuries of the third millennium BC, collective burials appear in several sites, widespread in Middle Asia. There now follows a catalogue of the sites with *Late Chalcolithic* collective burials so far excavated and published. At Tepe Hissar the remains of ten individuals were uncovered in sq. DG 00 while 12 individuals were unearthed in sq. DG 96; both groups were found in *Hissar III* contexts (Schmidt 1933: 440). In 1962 at Kara-depe a mud-brick rectangular structure (2.20 × 2.60 m) was found, built within the courtyard of one of the massive multi-roomed complexes of the uppermost level, dated to the *Late Chalcolithic* (Masson 1964: 3–4). The number of collective graves at Altyn-depe is higher. We start with the grave with individuals 281–282 from layer Altyn 9 (excavation 1; hereafter exc. 1) dated to the *Late Chalcolithic*; another grave with individuals 291–296 and 308 from layer Altyn 10 (exc. 1) also dated to the *Late Chalcolithic*; a grave with individuals 525–528 and 535 from layer Altyn 9 (still from exc. 1); funerary chamber 27 (individuals 683–686) from layer Altyn 8 (exc. 5), possibly a transitional level between the *Late Chalcolithic* and the *Early Bronze Age*; funerary chamber 3 (individuals 738–739 and 795) from layer Altyn 9 (exc. 5); the funerary chamber in courtyard B (individuals 905–910) from layer Altyn 10 (exc. 5); the funerary chamber in courtyard A (individuals 913–918) from layer Altyn 10 (exc. 5) (Masson and Berezkin 2005). Primary and secondary burials were recognised within round- and squarish-shaped buildings, named tholoi by the excavator, at Geoksyur 1: tholoi А, Б, В, Г and Д from the so-called "excavation of the necropolis", tholoi Ш, Ы, З and another (without a name, within room 51) from exc. 2; and tholoi Т, С, Ц, У, Х, Ф, another without a name (north of tholos Ф), Щ and Е from exc. 3.

All these funerary structures are dated to the *Late Chalcolithic* (Sarianidi 1959, 1960, 1965, 1966; Masson 1964). At Mundigak in Afghanistan a certain number of ossuaries were excavated in mound C (Casal 1961: 45–46), while at Shahr-i Sokhta, in the Iranian Sistan, two collective burials were found by the Italian mission: grave GTT 1003 lower layer, and grave HTW 410 (Piperno and Salvatori 1983, 2007; Piperno 1986; Bonora 1998–99; Bonora *et al.* 2000). More recently, other collective burials (1400?, 2000, 2301, 5605, 6009, 6200, 6301, 6514, and 6605?) were found by the Iranian mission headed by M. Sajjadi (2003, 2007; Sajjadi and Casanova 2006). At Sohr Damb, in the Nal valley of eastern Baluchistan, collective burials were dug both by H. Hargreaves in the 1920s (Hargreaves 1929) and more recently by the German project headed by U. Franke-Vogt (2003–2004, 2005). Here the graves with collective fractional burials hosted infants, children, and adults buried together. Single and multiple burials are briefly reported in a destroyed mound, site 131, in the Darra-ye Bolagi area of Fars, Iran (Azarnoush and Helwing 2005: 206, figs 25, 26). As already stated, Altyn-depe has many examples of this funerary practice, the earliest from layers Altyn 10 and 9, the latest moments of the *Late Chalcolithic*, when Ilgynly-depe was already abandoned or was about to be abandoned. A collective grave in this latter site, dated to the middle of the fourth millennium BC (Masson *et al.* 1994), would be extremely relevant – if such a dating can be confirmed – as the earliest grave of this type in south-eastern Turkmenistan, older than those found at Altyn-depe, and a remarkable deviation from the traditional burial customs of Middle Asia. Regretfully, this (possible) collective burial from Ilgynly is not described.

18   The individual graves at Altyn-depe (Masson and Berezkin 2005) are the following: nos. 186, 189, and 190 (exc. 11, arbitrary cut VII, layer Altyn 11 or later); no. 199 (exc. 11, arbitrary cut XVIII, probably the only one of the *Middle Chalcolithic*); no. 278 (exc. 1, layer Altyn 9 or later); no. 284 and 285 (exc. 1, layer Altyn 9); no. 722 and 725 (exc. 15, layer Altyn 10); nos. 735, 822, 823, 824, 825, 835, 838, 838A, 840, 841, 904, 911, 912, and 919 (exc. 5, layer Altyn 9); nos. 925 and 926 (exc. 5, layer Altyn 11).

19   In grave 725, a child of about 8 years old was buried with 11 vessels, 10 beads, and spacer-beads in lapis lazuli, turquoise, agate, and limestone, a spherical-conical "finial" or "globe" in limestone and two female terracotta statuettes, one of which was painted (Masson and Berezkin 2005: 130, pl. 114).

20   Grave 911 contained a 5–6-year-old child, buried with a painted cup and a small pot, an agate spacer-bead, and an anthropomorphic terracotta statuette in a sitting position (Kircho 1994: figs 2, 14, 15; Masson and Berezkin 2005: 144, pl. 145B, 1–4).

21   The grave contained a newborn infant with rich furnishings: a biconic bowl, a painted biconic jar, and 38 beads in pinkish limestone (Masson 1957, 1960, 1962).

22   Possibly a girl, buried with bracelets, a necklace, and the hair decorated with many other stone beads.

23   With a necklace of 32 beads and a bracelet of 11 gypsum beads.

24 Grave 34 contained the remains of a child of about two years, provided with seven beads in a light brown stone and eight in a dark red stone; grave 41 belonged to a child about four years old, on whose neck 62 gypsum flat beads were found; another child of about four years was buried in grave 54, with 92 carnelian beads found near the skull and the neck; a newborn infant in grave 55 had 32 flat beads in a whitish stone on the neck, and 26 flat and two elongated beads in lapis lazuli near the knees; a newborn infant in grave 57 was accompanied by five elongated beads in gypsum; the skeleton in very bad condition of preservation in grave 72 was furnished with 24 flat gypsum beads found near the right wrist; lastly, grave 75 contained a child of about four years with 420 beads in gypsum, one in carnelian, two in lapis lazuli, and six in silver-coated gypsum, all found near the neck and the chest, a bracelet of seven carnelian beads on the left wrist and a second bracelet of seven beads, two of which in carnelian, four in lapis lazuli, and one in silver. Some animal bones were detected on the legs. In this burial cluster, all tombs belonged to layer Kara 2 of exc. 1, with the exception of the last, found in layer Kara 3 of the same trench.

25 The *Early Chalcolithic* graves of Anau north are listed here following F. T. Hiebert's book (2003: 118–126), providing substantial descriptions and useful drawings and pictures of these funerary contexts. Complementary information may be found in I. N. Khlopin 1963: 9–10.

26 In the words of I. N. Khlopin,"...inside layer XXI [of test trench 1], characterised by polychrome pottery sherds typical of the *Middle Chalcolithic* and by other sherds decorated with patterns of the *Early Chalcolithic*, besides some children and infant burials, was a grave containing an adult, whose sex remains undetermined. The body was lying in a crouched position on the right side, with the arms bent at the elbow, the hands in front of the face, and the skull directed towards the east. The funerary inventory was represented by a painted bowl, dated by V. M. Masson to the beginning of the *Middle Chalcolithic*." (Khlopin 1963: 12). This description contradicts a previous statement by V. M. Masson, who had stated that, "...in the layers of the *Middle Chalcolithic* of test trench 1 three adult burials and four containing children were excavated. Two adult burials, from layer XIX, were filled with corpses lying in a flexed position on the right side and the skulls facing towards the south. In front of the face of one of the two skeletons was a bowl. The body in the grave from layer XXI was also lying in a flexed position, but on the left side, with both arms bent at the elbow and the hands in front of the face. The skull, like the other two previously described, was facing towards the south." (Masson 1962: 11). These two descriptions are so contradictory that it is probable that the two authors are describing two different graves from the same archaeological layer, despite the fact that Khlopin quotes Masson's views on the chronology of the tomb. The picture published by Kuftin (1956: 271, fig. 13) seems to confirm Khlopin's description, but the question remains open, because the orientation, eastwards or southwards, is not reported.

Bibliography

Antonova, E. V. and Sarianidi, V. I. 1990. "Die neolitischen, Kupfer- und bronzezeitlichen Statuetten aus Turkmenistan", *Beiträge zur allgemeinen und vergleichenden Archäologie*, Band 9–10: 5–24, tables 1–30.

Arne, T. J. 1945. *Excavations at Shah Tépé, Iran*, Sino-Swedish Expedition, Publication no. 27, Elanders Boktryckeri Aktiebolag, Goteborg.

Azarnoush, M. and Helwing, B. 2005. "Recent archaeological research in Iran – prehistory to Iron Age", *AMIT* 35: 189–246.

Berdyev, O. K. 1966. "Chagylly-depe – noviy pamjatnik neoliticheskoy dzheytunskoy kul'tury", *Material'naja Kul'tura Narodov Sredney Azii i Kazakhstana*, Nauka, Moscow: 3–28.

Berdyev, O. K. 1968a. "Chakmakli-depe – novyi pamjatnik vremeni Anau IA", *Istorija, Arkheologija i Etnografija Srednei Azii*: 26–34.

Berdyev, O. K. 1968b. "Novye raskopki na poselenjakh Pessedzhik-depe i Chakmakli-depe", *KD (Karakumskie Drevnosti)* II: 10–17.

Berdyev, O. K. 1971. "Nekotorye rezul'taty arkheologicheskikh rabot Instituta Istorii im. Sh. Batyrova AN TSSR (1959–1966 gg.)", *Material'naja Kul'tura Turkmenistana*: 7–23.

Berdyev, O. K. 1976. "Material'naja kul'tura Turkmenistana v period neolita i rannego eneolita", *Pervobytniy Turkmenistan*: 11–34.

Berezkin, Ju. E. 1989. "Eneoliticheskie svjatilishcha Ilgynly-depe", *Izvestija Akademi Nauk Turkmenskoy SSR, serija obshchestvennykh nauk* 6: 20–24.

Berezkin, Ju. E. 1992. "Arkhitekturniy kompleks kak ob'ekt ritual'nogo razrushenija", *Izvestija Akademi Nauk Turkmenskoy SSR, serija obshchestvennykh nauk*: 27–34.

Berezkin, Ju. E. 1993. "Radiouglerodnie dati s Ilgynly-depe v Turkmenii", *KSIA (Kratkie Soobshchenija Instituta Arkheologii)* 209: 12–16.

Berezkin, Ju. E. and Solovyova, N. F. 1998. "Paradnye pomeshchenija Ilgynly-depe (predvaritelnaja tipologija)", *Arkheologicheskie Vesti* 5: 86–123.

Bonora, G. L. 1998–1999. *La tomba GTT 1003 di Sahr-i Sokhta e le sepolture del Calcolitico in Asia Media*, unpublished PhD thesis, Università degli Studi di Bologna, Facoltà di Lettere e Filosofia, Bologna.

Bonora, G. L., Domanin, C., Salvatori, S. and Soldini, A. 2000. "The oldest graves of Shahr-i Sokhta graveyard", in Taddei, M. and De Marco, G. (eds), *South Asian Archaeology 1997*, Isiao, serie Orientale, Rome: 485–94.

Bonora, G. L., Vidale, M., Mariottini, M. and Guida, G. in press. "On the use of tokens and seals along the Kopet Dagh piedmont", *Paléorient*.

Carneiro, R. L. 1970. "A theory of the origin of the state", *Science* 169 (3947): 733–38.

Casal, J-M. 1961. *Fouilles de Mundigak*, Mémoires de la Délégation archéologique française en Afghanistan, tome XVIII, 2 vols, Libraire C. Klincksieck, Paris.

Ciarla, R. 1981. "A preliminary analysis of the manufacture of alabaster vessels at Shahr-i Sokhta and Mundigak in the 3rd Millennium B.C.", in Härtel, H. (ed.), *South Asian Archaeology 1979*, Dietrich Reimer Verlag, Berlin: 45–64.

Coningham, R. A. E., Fazeli, H., Young, R. L., Gillmore, G. K., Karimian, H., Magshoudi, M., Donahue, R. E.

and Batt, C. M. 2006. "Socio-economic transformations: settlement survey in the Tehran Plain and excavations at Tepe Pardis", *Iran* 44: 33–62.

Crawford, V. E. 1963. "Beside the Kara Su", *Bulletin of the Metropolitan Museum of Art* (April): 263–73.

Deshayes, J. 1966. "Rapport préliminaire sur les deux premières campagnes de fouilles à Tureng Tépé", *IA* 5: 83–92.

Deshayes, J. 1967. "Céramiques peintes de Turang Tépé", *Iran* 5: 123–31.

Dolukhanov, P. 1981. "The ecological prerequisites for early farming in Southern Turkmenistan", in Kohl, P. L. (ed.), *The Bronze Age Civilization of Central Asia*, M.E. Sharpe, New York: 359–85.

Durdyev, D. 1959. "Itogi polevykh rabot sektora arkheologii Instituta Istorii, Arkheologii i Etnografii AN TSSR 1956–1957 gg.", *Trudy IIAE* V: 7–14.

Erschov, S. E. 1952. "Kholm Jassi-depe", *Izvestija Akademi Nauk TSSR* 6, 1952: PAGES.

Erschov, S. E. 1956. "Severnoy kholm Anau", *Trudy Instituta Istorii, Arkheologii i Etnografii* 2: 24–36.

Fazeli, H., Wong, E. H. and Potts, D. T. 2005. "The Qazvin plain revisited: a reappraisal of the chronology of the northwestern Central Iranian plateau in the 6th to the 4th mill BC", *Ancient Near-Eastern Studies* 42: 3–82.

Fazeli, H., Coningham, R. A. E., Young, R. L., Gillmore, G. K., Maghsoudi, M. and Raza, H. 2007. "Socio-economic transformations in the plain: final season of settlement survey and excavations at Tepe Pardis", *Iran* 45: 267–86.

Fazeli, N. H., Vidale, M., Bianchetti, P., Guida, G. and Coningham, R. A. E. 2010/in press. "The evolution of ceramic manufacturing technology during the Late Neolithic and Transitional Chalcolithic periods at Tepe Pardis, Iran", *AMIT*.

Franke-Vogt, U. 2003–2004. "Sohr Damb/Nal, Baluchistan, Pakistan", *AMIT* 35–36: 83–141.

Franke-Vogt, U. 2005. "Excavations at Sohr Damb/Nal: results of the 2002 and 2004 seasons", Franke-Vogt, U. and Wiesshaar, H-J. (eds), *South Asian Archaeology 2003*, Linden Soft Editions, Aachen: 63–76.

Ganjalin, A. F. 1956. "Pogrebenija epokhi bronzi i selenija Jangi-kala", *TJuTAKE (Trudy Juzhnoy Turkmenistanskoy Arkheologicheskoy Komplekskoy Ekspedizii)* VII: 374–84.

Ganjalin, A. F. 1959. "Ilgynly-depe", *Trudy Instituta Istorii, Arkheologii i Etnografii AN TSSR*, V: 15–29.

Ghirshman, R. 1938. *Fouilles de Sialk*, vol. 1, Musée du Louvre, Département des antiquités orientales, Série Archéologique no. 4, Geuthner, Paris.

Gillmore, G. K., Coningham, R. A. E., Fazeli, H., Young, R. L., Magshoudi, M., Batt, C. M. and Rushworth, G. 2009. "Irrigation on the Tehran Plain, Iran: Tepe Pardis – the site of a possible Neolithic irrigation feature?", *Catena* 78: 285–300.

Hargreaves, H. 1929. *Excavations in Baluchistan 1925, Sampur Damb, Mastung and Sohr Damb, Nal*, Memoirs of the Archaeological Survey of India, no. 35, Government of India, Central Publication Branch, Calcutta.

Harlan, J. R. and Pasquereau, J. 1969. "Décrue agriculture in Mali", *Economic Botany* 23: 70–74.

Harris, D. R. 2010. *Origins of Agriculture in Western Central Asia. An Environmental-Archaeological Study*, University of Pennsylvania Museum of Archaeology and Anthropology, Philadelphia.

Harris, D. R. and Gosden, C. 1996. "The beginnings of agriculture in western Central Asia", in Harris, D.R. (ed.), *The Origins and Spread of Agriculture and Pastoralism in Eurasia*, Smithsonian Institution Press, Washington DC: 370–89.

Harris, D. R., Gosden, C. and Charles, M. P. 1996. "Jeitun: recent excavations at an early Neolithic site in Southern Turkmenistan", *Proceedings of the Prehistoric Society* 62: 423–42.

Hiebert, F. T. 2002. "The Kopet Dag sequence of early villages in Central Asia", *Paléorient* 28 (2): 25–42.

Hiebert, F. T. (with K. Kurbansakhatov) 2003. *A Central Asian Village at the Dawn of Civilization, Excavations at Anau, Turkmenistan*, University of Pennsylvania Museum of Archaeology and Anthropology, Philadelphia.

Hiebert, F. T. and Dyson Jr., R. H. 2002. "Prehistoric Nishapur and the frontier between Central Asia and Iran", *IA* 37: 111–47.

Kasparov, A. K. 1989. "Mlekopitajushchie Eneoliticheskogo poselenija Ilgynly-depe", *Izvestija Akademii Nauk Turkmenskoy SSR, Serija Obshchestvennykh Nauk*, 6: 24–29.

Kasparov, A. K. 1994a. "Patterns in caprine exploitation at Ylgynly-depe, Turkmenistan", *New Archaeological Discoveries in Asiatic Russia and Central Asia*, Institute for the History of Material Culture, Russian Academy of Sciences, St Petersburg: 36–39.

Kasparov, A. K. 1994b. "Environmental conditions and farming strategy of the protohistoric inhabitants of South-Central Asia", *Paléorient* 20 (2): 143–49.

Kasparov, A. K. 1996. "On a Chalcolithic dog from Southern Turkmenia", *Paléorient* 22 (1): 161–67.

Kasparov, A. K. 2000. "Zoomorphical statuettes from Eneolithic layers at Ilgynly-depe and Altyn-depe in South Turkmeniya", in Mashkour, M., Choyke, A. M., Buitenhius, H. and Poplin, F. (eds), *Archaeozoology of the Near East IVB*, ARC Edition, Groeningen: 156–63.

Kasparov, A. K. 2001. "Vozmozhnosti identificazii zoomorfnykh statuetok iz eneoliticheskikh sloev pamyatnikov Ilgynly-depe, Altyn-depe i Kara-depe v yuzhnoy Turkmenii", *Arkheologicheskie Vesti* 8: 99–105.

Kasparov, A. K. 2006. *Skotovodstvo i okhota epokhi neolita – paleometalla v Juzhnom Turkmenistane*, Evropeyskiy Dom, Moscow.

Khlobystina, M. D. 1977. "Malen'kie bogini turkmenskogo eneolita", *Karakumskie Drevnosti* 6: 102–09.

Khlopin, I. N. 1963. *Pamjatniki rannego eneolita Juzhnoy Turkmenii, Eneolit juzhnykh oblastey Sredney Azii*, Svod Arkheologicheskikh Istochnikov, B3–8, Nauka, Moscow/ Leningrad.

Khlopin, I. N. 1964. *Geoksyurskaja gruppa poselenii epokhi eneolita*, Nauka, Moscow/Leningrad.

Khlopin, I. N. 1969. *Pamjatniki razvitogo eneolita Jugo-vostochnoy Turkmenii, Eneolit juzhnykh oblastey Sredney Azii*, Svod Arkheologicheskikh Istochnikov, B3–8, Nauka, Moscow/Leningrad.

Khlopin, I. N. 1981. "The Early Bronze Age cemetery of Parhay II: the first two seasons of excavations: 1977–78", in Kohl, P. L. (ed.), *The Bronze Age Civilization of Central Asia. Recent Soviet Discoveries*, M.E. Sharpe, New York: 3–34.

Khlopin, I. N. 1986. *Jungbronzezeitliche Graberfelder im Sumbar-Tal, Sudest-Turkmenistan*, C.H. Beck, Munich.

Khlopin, I. N. 1997. *Eneolit jugo-zapadnogo Turkmenistana*, Evropeyskiy Dom, St Petersburg.

Khlopin, I. N. 2002. *Epokha Bronzy jugo-zapadnogo Turkmenistana*, Evropeyskiy Dom, St Petersburg.

Khlopina, L. I. 1981. "Namazga-depe and the Late Bronze Age of Southern Turkmenia", in Kohl, P. L. (ed.), *The Bronze Age Civilization of Central Asia. Recent Soviet Discoveries*, M.E. Sharpe, New York: 35–60.

Kircho, L. B. 1990. "Drevneyshie pechati i ikh ottiski iz Altyn-depe", *SA (Sovietskaja Arkheologija)* 3: 176–83.

Kircho, L. B. 1994. "New Studies of the Late Chalcolithic at Altyn-Depe, Turkmenistan", *New Archaeological Discoveries in Asiatic Russia and Central Asia*, St Petersburg: 39–44.

Kircho, L. B. 1999. *K izucheniju pozdnego eneolita Juzhnogo Turkmenistana (osnovy klassifikazii raspisnoy keramiki i neopublikovannye materialy poselenija Ak-depe)*, IIMK RAN, St Petersburg.

Kircho, L. B. 2007. "Drevnie svjazi naselenija Juzhnogo Turkmenistana i doliny Zeravshana (nachalo formirovanija torgovykh putey v Sredney Azii)", *Zapiski IIMK RAN* 2: 193–208.

Kircho, L. B. 2009. "The earliest wheeled transport in Southwestern Central Asia: new finds from Altyn-depe", *Archaeology Ethnology & Anthropology of Eurasia* 37 (1): 25–33.

Knox, J. R., Thomas, K. D., Khan, F. and Petrie, C. A. 2010. "Small finds from Sheri Khan Tarakai", in Petrie, C. A. (ed.). *Sheri Khan Tarakai and early village life in the borderlands of north-west Pakistan*, Bannu Archaeological Project Monographs, vol. 1, Oxbow Books, Oxford: 211–303.

Kohl, P. L. 1984. *Central Asia. From Beginnings to Iron Age, L'Asie Centrale des origines à l'Âge du Fer*, Éditions Recherche sur les Civilisations, Paris.

Kohl, P. L. and Heskel, D. L. 1980. "Archaeological reconnaissance in the Darreh Gaz plain: a short report", *Iran* 18: 160–72.

Kohl, P. L., Biscione, R. and Ingraham, M. L. 1982. "Implications of recent evidence for the prehistory of northeastern Iran and southwestern Turkmenistan", *IA* 17: 1–20.

Korobkova, G. F. 1972. "Poselenie neoliticheskikh zemledel'zev Gievdzhik-depe v juzhnom Turkmenistane", *USA (Uspekhi Sredneaziatskoy Arkheologii)* 3: 71–73.

Korobkova, G. F. 1987. "Izgotovlenie kamennykh statuy na Ilgynly-depe", *Zadachi sovetskoy arkheologii v svete resheniy XXVII s'ezda KPSS*, Nauka, Moscow: PAGES.

Korobkova, G. F. and Sharovskaja, T. A. 1994. "Stone tools from Ylgynly-depe (Turkmenistan): the evidence from use-wear analysis", *New archaeological discoveries in Asiatic Russia and Central Asia*, Institute for the History of Material Culture, Russian Academy of Sciences, St Petersburg: 27–30.

Kuftin, B. A. 1956. "Polevoj otchet: o rabote XIV otrade Ju.T.A.K.E. po izucheniju kul'turi pervobitno-obshchinnich osedlozemledel'cheskich poselenij epochi medi i bronzi v 1952 g.", *TjuTAKE (Trudy Juzhnoy Turkmenistanskoy Arkheologicheskoy Komplekskoy Ekspedizii)*,, tom VII, Nauka, Ashgabad: 260–90.

Kurbansakhatov, K. 1987. *Eneolit Anau*, Ylym, Ashgabad.

Lamberg-Karlovsky, C. C. 1978. "The Proto-Elamites on the Iranian Plateau", *Antiquity* 52: 114–20.

Lecomte, O., Francfort, H. P., Boucharlat, R. and Mamedow, M. 2002. "Recherches archéologiques récentes à Ulug Dépé (Turkménistan)»", *Paléorient* 2: 123–31.

Lisizyna, G. N. 1965. *Oroshaemoe zemledelie epokhi eneolita na juge Turkmenii*, Nauka, Moscow.

Lisizyna, G. N. 1969. "The earliest irrigation in Turkmenistan", *Antiquity* 43 (172): 279–88.

Lisizyna, G. N. 1972. "Istorija oroshaemogo zemledelija v juzhnoy Turkmeniy (rannezemledel'cheskaja epokha)", *USA (Uspekhi Sredneaziatskoy Arkheologii)* I: 11–16.

Lisizyna, G. N. 1978. *Stanovlenie i razvitie oroshaemogo zemledelija v juzhnoy Turkmenii*, Nauka, Moscow.

Lisizyna, G. N. 1981. "The history of irrigation agriculture in Southern Turkmenia", in Kohl, P.L. (ed.), *The Bronze Age Civilization of Central Asia*, M.E. Sharpe, New York: 350–58.

Lollekova, O. 1978. "Neoliticheskoe poselenie Pessedzhik-depe v juzhnom Turkmenistane", *SA (Sovietskaja Arkheologija)* 4: 176–91.

Lollekova, O. 1988. *Lokal'naja variabil'nost' v kul'ture i khozjaystve dzheytunskikh plemen*, Ylym, Ashgabad.

Majidzadeh, Y. 1978. "Corrections of the internal chronology for the Sialk III period on the basis of the pottery sequence at Tepe Gabristan", *Iran* 16: 93–101.

Majidzadeh, Y. 1981. "Sialk III and the pottery sequence at Tepe Ghabristan: the coherence of the cultures of the Central Iranian Plateau", *Iran* 19: 141–46.

Marcolongo, B. and Mozzi, P. 1997. "Osservazioni geoarcheologiche lungo il bordo della catena montuosa dei Kopet Dagh orientali basate sull'uso di immagini satellitari", in Rossi-Osmida, G. (ed.), *Turkmenistan*, Centro Studi Ricerche Ligabue, Venice: 49–62.

Marushchenko, A. A. 1956. "Itogi polevykh arkheologicheskikh rabot 1953 goda Instituta IAE AN TSSR", *Trudy Instituta Istorii, Arkheologii Etnografii* 2: 5–10.

Masson, V. M. 1956a. "Raspisnaja keramika juzhnoy Turkmenii po raskopkam B.A. Kuftina", *TjuTAKE (Trudy Juzhnoy Turkmenistanskoy Arkheologicheskoy Komplekskoy Ekspedizii)*, vol. VII, Nauka, Ashgabad: 291–373.

Masson, V. M. 1956b. "Pervobytnoobshchinnyy stroy na territorii Turkmenii (eneolit, bronzovyy vek i epokha rannego zheleza)", *TjuTAKE (Trudy Juzhnoy Turkmenistanskoy Arkheologicheskoy Komplekskoy Ekspedizii)*, vol. VII, Nauka, Ashgabad: 233–59.

Masson, V. M. 1957. "Jeitun i Kara-depe", *SA (Sovietskaja Arkheologija)* 1: 143–60.

Masson, V. M. 1960. "Kara-depe u Artyka", *TjuTAKE (Trudy Juzhnoy Turkmenistanskoy Arkheologicheskoy Komplekskoy Ekspedizii)*, vol. X, Nauka, Ashgabad: 319–463.

Masson, V. M. 1962. *Pamjatniki razvitogo eneolita jugo-zapadnogo Turkmenii, Eneolit uzhnykh oblastey Sredney Azii*, Svod Arkheologicheskikh Istochnikov, B3–8, part II, Nauka, Moscow/Leningrad.

Masson, V. M. 1964. "Tradicija kollektivnikh pogrebeniy v Eneolite Sredney Azii, Afganistana i Indii", *Kratkie Soobshchenija Instituta Arkheologii* 101: 3–8.

Masson, V. M. 1966. "Raszvet i upadok kul'tury zemledel'zev jugo-zapada", *Srednjaja Azija v epokhu Kamnja i Bronzy*, Moscow/Leningrad: 151–78.

Masson, V. M. 1977. "Altyn-depe v epochu eneolita", *SA (Sovietskaja Arkheologija)* 3: 164–88.

Masson, V. M. 1981. "Altyn-depe during the Aeneolithic period", in Kohl, P. L. (ed.), *The Bronze Age Civilization of Central Asia. Recent Soviet Discoveries*, New York, M.E. Sharpe: 63–95.

Masson, V. M 1982. "Eneolit Sredney Azii", in Masson, V. M. and Merpert, N. Ja. (eds), *Eneolit SSSR, Arkheologija SSSR*, Nauka, Moscow: 26–34.

Masson, V. M. 1988. *Altyn-depe*, translated by H.N. Michael, The University Museum, University of Pennsylvania, Philadelphia.

Masson, V. M. 1989. "Ilgynly-depe – novyy zentr eneoliticheskoy kul'tury juzhnogo Turkmenistana", *Izvestija Akademi Nauk Turkmenskoy SSR, serija obshchestvennykh nauk* 6: 15–20.

Masson, V. M. 1992. "Ilgynly-depe, a new center of early farming culture in South Turkmenia", in Jarrige, C. (ed.), *South Asian Archaeology 1989*, Prehistory Press, Madison: 195–200.

Masson, V. M. and Berezkin Yu. E. eds 2005. *Khronologija epokhi pozdnego eneolita – sredney Bronzy Sredney Azii (pogrebenija Altyn-depe)*, Trudy IIMK RAN, vol. XVI, Nestor-Istorija, St Petersburg.

Masson, V. M. and Kircho, L. B. 2008. "Glava 1. Izuchenie eneoliticheskikh kompleksov Altyn-depe", in Kircho, L. B., Korobkova, G. F. and Masson, V. M. (eds), *Tekhniko-Tekhnologicheskiy potenzial eneoliticheskogo naselenija Altyn-depe kak osnova stanovlenija rannegorodskoy zivilizazii*, Evropeyskiy Dom, St Petersburg: 13–71.

Masson, V. M. and Korobkova, G. F. 1989. "Eneolithic stone sculpture in South Turkmenia", *Antiquity* 63 (238): 62–70.

Masson, V. M. and Sarianidi, V. I. 1972. *Central Asia: Turkmenia before the Achaemenids*, Thames and Hudson, London.

Masson, V. M., Berezkin, Yu. E. and Solovyova, N. F. 1994. "Excavations of houses and sanctuaries at Ylgynly-depe chalcolithic site, Turkmenistan", in Kozintsev, A. G. and Masson, V. M. (eds), *New Archaeological Discoveries in Asiatic Russia and Central Asia*, Institute for the History of Material Culture, Russian Academy of Sciences, St Petersburg: 18–26.

Negahban, E. O. 1979. "A brief report on the painted building of Zaghe (Late 7th–Early 6th millennium BC)", *Paléorient* 5: 239–50.

Piller, C. K. 2003–2004. "Zur Mittelbronzezeit im nördlichen Zentraliran – Die Zentraliranische Graue Ware (Central Grey Ware) als möglich Verbindung zwischen Eastern and Western Grey Ware", *AMIT* 35–36: 143–73.

Piperno, M. 1986. "Aspects of ethnical multiplicity across the Shahr-i Sokhta graveyard", *Oriens Antiquus* 25: 257–70.

Piperno, M. and Salvatori, S. 1983. "Recent results and new perspectives from the research at the graveyard of Shahr-i Sokhta, Sistan, Iran", *Annali dell'Istituto Universitario Orientale* 43 (2): 173–91.

Piperno, M. and Salvatori, S. 2007. *The Shahr-i Sokhta Graveyard (Sistan, Iran) Excavation Campaigns 1972–1978*, IsIAO, Rome.

Potts, D. T. 2001. *Excavations at Tepe Yahya, 1967–1975. The Third Millennium*, Peabody Museum of Anthropology and Ethnology, Harvard University, Cambridge MA.

Pumpelly, R. 1908. *Explorations in Turkestan, Expedition of 1904*, Carnegie Institution of Washington, Washington DC.

Sajjadi, S. M. S. 2003. "Excavations at Shahr-i Sokhta: first preliminary report on the excavations of the graveyard, 1997–2000", *Iran* 41: 21–98.

Sajjadi, S. M. S. 2007. *Excavations at Shahr-e Sukhteh, Graveyard 1997–2000 Preliminary Report 1*, Cultural and Communication Directorate, Central Office of Cultural Affairs, Tehran.

Sajjadi, S. M. S. and Casanova, M. 2006. "Sistan and Baluchistan Project 2005/2006", *Iran* 44: 347–57.

Salvatori, S., Vidale, M., Guida, G. and Masioli, E. 2009. "Ilgynly-depe (Turkmenistan) and the 4th millennium BC metallurgy in Central Asia", *Paléorient* 35 (1): 47–67.

Sarianidi, V. I. 1959. "Novyy tip drevnikh pogrebal'nykh sooruzheniy Juzhnoy Turkmenii", *Sovietskaja Arkheologija* 2: 235–38.

Sarianidi, V. I. 1960. "Eneoliticheskoe poselenie Geoksyur (Rezul'taty rabot 1956–1957 gg.)", *Trudy JuTAKE*, vol. X, Nauka, Ashgabad: 225–318.

Sarianidi, V. I. 1965. *Pamjatniki pozdnego eneolita jugo-vostochnoy Turkmenii, Eneolit juzhnykh oblastey Sredney Azii*, Svod Arkheologicheskikh Istochnikov, B3–8, Nauka, Moscow/Leningrad.

Sarianidi, V. I. 1966. "Raskopki v jugo-vostochnikh Karakumakh v 1964 g.", *Kratkie Soobshchenija Instituta Arkheologii* 108: 89–95.

Sarianidi, V. I. 1969. "Prodolzhenie rabot na Ulug-depe", *AO (Arkheologicheskie Otkrytija) 1968*, Nauka, Moscow: 434–35.

Sarianidi, V. I. 1972. "Raskopki 1970 g. na Ulug-depe", *USA (Uspekhi Sredneaziatskoy Arkheologii)* I: 53–55.

Sarianidi, V. I. 1976. "Material'naja Kul'tura Juzhnogo Turkmenistana v period ranney bronzy", *Pervobytniy Turkmenistan*, Nauka, Ashgabad: 82–111.

Sarianidi, V. I. and Kachuris, K. A. 1968. "Raskopki na Ulug-depe", *AO (Arkheologicheskie Otkrytija) 1967*, Nauka, Moscow: 342–45.

Schmidt, E. F. 1933. *Tepe Hissar: Excavations of 1931, The Joint Expedition to Persia of the University Museum and the Pennsylvania Museum of Art*, University of Pennsylvania Press, Philadelphia.

Shchetenko, A. Ja. 1968. "Raskopki pamjatnikov epokhi eneolita i bronzovogo veka v Kaakhkinskom rayone", *Karakumskie Drevnosti* 1: 18–29.

Solovyova, N. F. 2000. "The wall-painting of Ilgynly-depe", in Taddei, M. and De Marco, G. (eds.), *South Asian Archaeology 1997*, IsIAO, Rome: 453–65.

Solovyova, N. F. 2005. *Chalcolithic Anthropomorphic Figurines from Ilgynly-depe, Southern Turkmenistan. Classification, Analysis and Catalogue*, Archeopress (BAR International Series 1336), Oxford.

Solovyova, N. F. 2011. "Material evidence of ritual activities in the ceremonial complexes at Ilgynly-Depe", in *The Ancient Material Culture of Turkmenistan and its Place in the Development of World Civilization*, Materials of the Scientific International Conference, April 7–8, 2011, Ashgabat: 103–12 (in Russian, Turkmen, and English).

Solovyova, N. F. 2012. "Ilgynly-Depe: New Evidences", in D. Frenez and M. Tosi (eds.), *South Asian Archaeology 2007*, vol. I, Prehistoric Periods, BAR International Series, Archeopress, Oxford: 244–45.

Solovyova, N. F., Yegor'kov, A. N., Galibin, V. A. and Berezkin, Yu. E. 1994. "Metal artifacts from Ylgynly-depe, Turkmenistan", *New archaeological discoveries in Asiatic Russia and Central Asia*, Institute for the History of Material Culture, Russian Academy of Sciences, St Petersburg: 3–36.

Stronach, D. 1972. "Yarim Tepe", in Moorey, P. R. S. (ed.), *Excavations in Iran: the British Contribution*, Organizing Committee of the Sixth International Congress of Iranian Art and Archaeology, Oxford: 21–23.

Sumner, W. M. 1988. "Prelude to Proto-Elamite Anshan: the Lapui phase", *IA* 33: 23–43.

Thornton, C. P. 2009. "The emergence of complex metallurgy on the Iranian Plateau: escaping the Levantine Paradigm", *Journal of World Prehistory* 22: 301–27.

facilitated the delineation of broad patterns of cultural development and interaction. The complex dynamics of the sixth and early to mid-fifth millennia BC have been reviewed extensively (e.g. Alizadeh 2003, 2006, 2008, 2010; Weeks *et al.* 2006, 2010; Petrie *et al.* 2009b; Petrie 2011, 2013; Weeks 2013). The discussion here will focus on the late fifth and fourth millennia BC.

Mamasani is a region of modern Fars province situated approximately 100 km from the western edge of the Kur River Basin, and lies very much towards the Fars end of the 500 km stretch of the Zagros Mountains that separates lowland Susiana from the highland plains (Fig. 10.1). Since 2003 this region has been the focus of an international archaeological research collaboration known as the Mamasani Archaeological Project (hereafter MAP), which has involved Iranian and Australian archaeologists from academic and research institutions in Iran, Australia, and the UK.[1]

Thus far the MAP has published two editions of an edited volume that presents the preliminary results of excavations and surveys conducted in 2003 (Potts and Roustaei 2006; Potts *et al.* 2009c), and a series of preliminary reports and papers that integrate these results with those of subsequent fieldwork carried out between 2007 and 2011 (e.g. Potts *et al.* 2006, 2007, 2009b; Petrie *et al.* 2005, 2007; Asgari *et al.* 2010; Weeks *et al.* 2010; Petrie 2011). A detailed analysis of the survey data and long-term settlement patterns has also been completed (McCall 2009).

It is clear that in the late fifth millennium BC the lowland and highland regions of south-west Iran had begun to develop along related yet distinctive cultural trajectories (Alizadeh 2006, 2010; Weeks *et al.* 2010; Petrie 2011). While populations in both regions appear to have utilised similar subsistence and craft practices, there were clear differences in the types

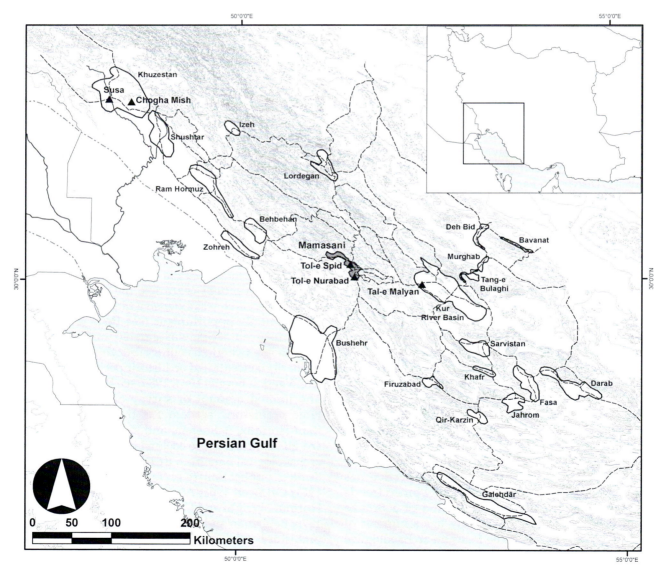

Figure 10.1. Map of south-west Iran, showing the location of Mamasani and other plains and intermontane valleys that have been surveyed archaeologically. Some of the main routes between these areas are shown with a dashed line.

of material culture produced in each, particularly the shapes and decoration used for ceramic vessels and figurines (Weeks *et al.* 2010; Petrie 2011). This distinctiveness appears to have continued during the first half of the fourth millennium BC, and is in many ways intensified. In the lowlands, it is in this *Middle/ Late Uruk* or *Susa II* period that there is evidence for overt interaction between lowland Susiana and southern Mesopotamia (Algaze 1993, 2005, 2008; Potts 1999; Wright, this volume). The material evidence for linkages between these lowland regions does not continue into the highlands, although there are parallels between the early to mid-fourth-millennium BC *Lapui*-period storage vessel forms of highland Fars and those seen in the *Late Bakun* period (Tal-e Bakun A; Langsdorff and McCown 1942: pl. 20) and in Susiana in the earlier *Late Susiana* period (e.g. Susa, Acropole I.27-25; Le Brun 1971: fig. 39; Chogha Mish; Delougaz and Kantor 1996: pl. 162: O-AA; Petrie *et al.* 2009a: 128–29; Wright, this volume). Similarly there is a limited range of material indications of interaction between the lowlands and highlands during the mid-fourth millennium BC, shown in particular by the appearance of examples of bevel-rim bowls at several highland sites (e.g. Tal-e Kureh, Alden 2003a). This evidence for connectivity is relatively limited, however. It was not until the *Proto-Elamite* or *Susa III* period (or "horizon"; cf. Abdi 2003) in the last centuries of the fourth millennium BC that there were clear signs that the highland and lowland regions were interacting more overtly. During this period, populations in the lowlands and highlands utilised a range of similar ceramic vessels and a range of other types of material culture, including tablets inscribed in the *Proto-Elamite* script (Alden 1982, this volume; Potts 1999; Petrie *et al.* 2009b; Dahl *et al.*, this volume). While it is possible to outline this broad developmental sequence, the lack of information about the regions between the highland and lowland extremes of the south-west means that we have limited comprehension of the nuances of the cultural dynamics operating across and also around this region throughout the fourth millennium BC.

This paper will outline the archaeological evidence from Mamasani dated to the late fifth and fourth millennia BC, and attempt to contextualise these results chronologically, spatially, and culturally. It will thus examine local and sub-regional variations in the archaeological record of Fars that speak to the diversity of responses of local communities to changing cultural connections across this period. Particular attention will be given to Mamasani's place in the long-term socio-cultural developments in the greater south-west during this period of later prehistory, and the nature of interaction beyond the Susa-Anshan/highland-lowland axis will also be considered.

The archaeology of Mamasani in the fourth millennium BC

The *Chalcolithic* period (*c.* 4800–3000 BC) in south-west Iran is marked by several distinct socio-economic transformations, and the investigation of these processes has been a major research focus of the MAP's examination of long-term culture change in the Mamasani region. In south-west Iran the protracted *Chalcolithic* period was by no means a homogeneous block, and is traditionally broken up into several phases. The material culture being used in Mamasani during the *Early Chalcolithic* is most akin to that of the *Bakun* phase as known in the Kur River Basin, while that being used in the *Late Chalcolithic* is most akin to that of the *Lapui* and *Banesh* phases in that same region (Petrie *et al.* 2009b; Petrie 2013). This similarity of the Mamasani material to that of the Kur River Basin is telling, and the MAP has deliberately followed the Kur River Basin chronological/cultural terminology (Potts *et al.* 2009a), which will also be followed here. This paper draws on the *Late Chalcolithic* (*Lapui* and *Banesh* period) evidence that has been published (Weeks *et al.* 2009; Petrie *et al.* 2007, 2009a, 2009b) and synthesises it with the results of more recent excavations and analyses.

Chalcolithic occupation in Mamasani has been identified in excavations at two large mound sites and other settlement sites recorded in area surveys (Fig. 10.2). It is presently unclear when the site of Tol-e Spid was first occupied, but excavations have shown that the site preserves an almost continuous sequence of *Late Chalcolithic* occupation that spans from the late fifth to the end of the fourth millennium BC (see below; Petrie *et al.* 2007, 2009a, 2009b). The site of Tol-e Nurabad was first occupied around 6000 BC, and although there are several gaps in the occupation sequence, the site has an important sequence of *Chalcolithic* deposits that span the early, middle, and late fifth, the middle and late fourth, and the early third millennia BC (Weeks *et al.* 2009; see below). In addition to the occupation on these two major mounds, detailed survey of the Dasht-e Rustam Yek and Do plains has identified 14 sites with *Bakun* period occupation, 13 sites with *Lapui* period occupation, and 12 sites with *Banesh* period occupation (McCall 2009; also Zeidi *et al.* 2009; see below).

Tol-e Spid

The mound known as Tol-e Spid stands near the centre of the Dasht-e Rustam-e Yek (Fig. 10.2). The MAP initially carried out excavations at Tol-e Spid over two seasons in 2003, and work continued in early 2007 (Petrie *et al.* 2007, 2009a). In the two initial seasons, a preliminary 2 × 1 m sounding was excavated 10 m down the face of the steep exposed section at the northern side of the site, and this was continued 7 m into the lower part of the mound in

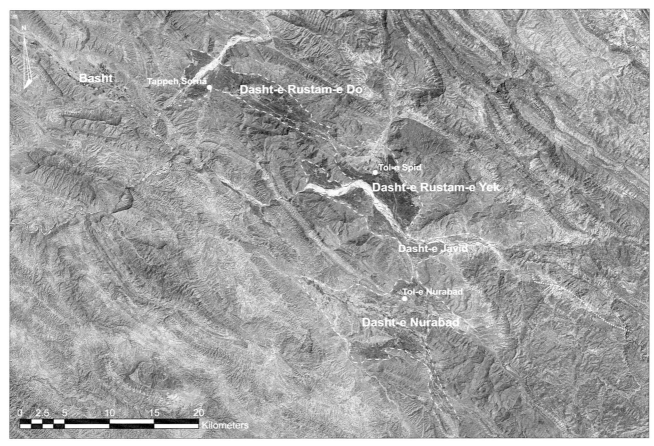

Figure 10.2. Map of Mamasani district, showing the location of the major plains and archaeological sites, including Tol-e Spid and Tol-e Nurabad.

both 2003 and 2007, revealing a protracted (17 m) sequence of both continuous and discontinuous occupation (Petrie *et al.* 2007, 2009a). A hand auger was used to penetrate a further 2 m into the lowermost deposits, as no further excavation was possible in such a confined space. In total, the excavations at Tol-e Spid have revealed evidence for 31 stratified phases of occupation, of which 14 (TS Phases 31–18) appear to date to the fourth millennium BC (Fig. 10.3). Natural soil was not reached, but the lower 7 m of the excavated sequence and the 2 m of deposit penetrated by the auger were characterised by *Banesh* (TS Phase 18), *Transitional Lapui-Banesh* (TS Phase 19), and *Lapui* (TS Phases 20–31) ceramic wares that have traditionally been dated to the fourth millennium BC (see below). Although black-on-buff *Bakun* wares and Neolithic soft ware ceramics were recovered as residual material in various contexts, deposits have not yet been exposed with material from these periods *in situ*. It is important to highlight that the subsequent discussion is based on the results from the 2 × 1 m sounding, and this imposes various fundamental constraints on the interpretations that might be ventured.

The architecture exposed that relates to the early- to mid-fourth millennium BC *Lapui* occupation is characterised by a mixture of river-stone and mud-brick structures, with rounded stones typically being used for wall foundations when they are present, and mud bricks made of clean clay being used for all exposed superstructures (Figs 10.3–10.4; also Petrie *et al.* 2009a: figs 4.12–4.18, 4.21–4.22). In general, the mud-brick walls were preserved to a height of between three and seven courses (e.g. Phases 27 and 23; Fig. 10.3), although there was also one instance of a wall being preserved to 10 courses in height (Phase 20; Fig. 10.3). There is clear evidence that these walls often collapsed (Phases 27 and 30). Not every phase was marked by the exposure of architecture, and there is evidence for individual phases being composed of occupation surfaces and associated hearths (e.g. Phase 25).

The architectural remains exposed in Phases 31–20 make it clear that during the *Lapui* period, Tol-e Spid was occupied and reoccupied successively. There is no evidence that structures or wall stubs were rebuilt and reused in subsequent phases. Rather, the consecutive structural phases were either destroyed through conflagration or levelled by human action (Figs 10.3–10.4). After each such event new buildings appear to have been constructed on different alignments (e.g. Petrie *et al.* 2009a: figs 4.12–4.18, 4.21–4.22).

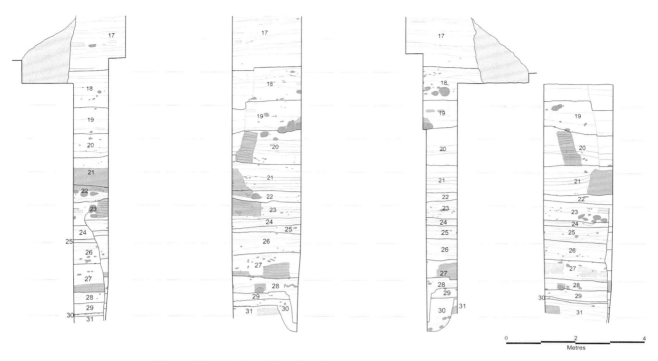

Figure 10.3. Section of fourth-millennium BC deposits at Tol-e Spid.

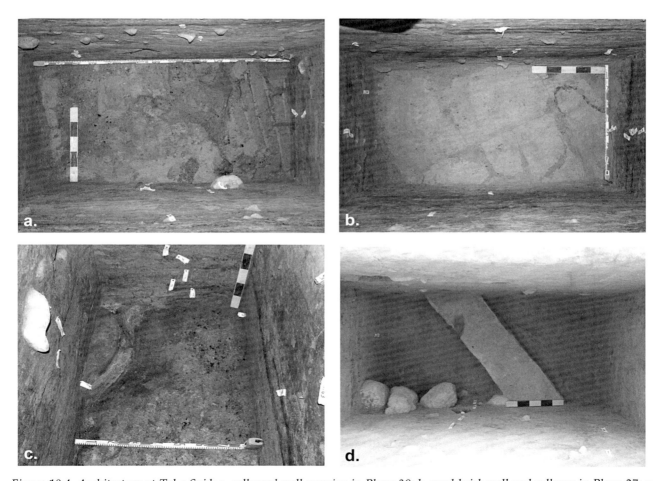

Figure 10.4. Architecture at Tol-e Spid; a. collapsed wall remains in Phase 30; b. mud-brick wall and collapse in Phase 27; c. hearth and floor surface in Phase 25; d. mud-brick wall in Phase 21.

This dynamic suggests that the early to mid-fourth-millennium BC occupation was discontinuous. There was no noticeable build-up of cultural or aeolian deposits between any two phases, however, so it is unlikely that there were dramatic gaps between each structural phase. In several instances, structures built in subsequent phases were built directly above truncated walls and occupation surfaces, suggesting that the occupants of the settlement engaged in frequent rebuilding. Subsequent to the deep sequence of *Lapui* period phases, there are only two occupation phases that date to the *Transitional Lapui-Banesh* and *Banesh* phases of the second half of the fourth millennium BC (Phases 19–18; see below). There is, however, considerable thickness of occupation surfaces in each, perhaps indicating that they built up over an extended period of time.

The limited area exposed in the 2 × 1 m sounding at Tol-e Spid makes it is difficult (and unwise) to draw broader conclusions about the nature of occupation/reoccupation and building/rebuilding at the site during the fourth millennium BC. Based on the evidence in the sounding we can say that within the 500–700 years of *Lapui* period occupation (see below), there were at least 11 separate phases of rebuilding. This implies that individual buildings may have been rebuilt and/or replaced around every 50–60 years. Using Bayesian analytical techniques to calibrate the radiocarbon dates does not result in any greater precision than this. That these structures were not rebuilt using the same wall alignments or the remnants of earlier walls is no doubt significant, and could be interpreted in various ways. In general all of the exposed deposits appear to be related to residential occupation, either in the form of architecture or of living surfaces. The most obvious conclusion is that the precise use of space in this particular part of the settlement appears to have changed relatively frequently, through constant remodelling of buildings or even shifts in property boundaries. Saying anything more about what this pattern represents is beyond the available evidence. That there are only two occupation phases dating to the second half of the fourth millennium BC (*Transitional Lapui-Banesh* and *Banesh* phases) either indicates that these phases of occupation were each of longer duration than the *Lapui* period phases, or that there were periods during the mid- to late fourth millennium BC when this particular part of the site was not being utilised.

The evidence for collapsed structures (e.g. Phases 27 and 30) indicates that buildings were collapsing as a result of deliberate action, abandonment, or because of external forces. During the initial excavation of the Tol-e Spid sounding, the presence of an earthquake fracture was observed, and this is readily visible in the north and south sections (Fig. 10.3; Petrie *et al.* 2009a). A fracture earlier in the sequence was also noted during the second phase of excavations and it was assumed that this was a continuation of the fracture that was initially documented (Petrie *et al.* 2007). Careful examination has indicated, however, that there are almost certainly two earthquake fractures that have affected the fourth-millennium BC sequence at Tol-e Spid, one which occurred between TS Phases 23 and 22, and a second which occurred between TS Phases 18 and 17 (Berberian *et al.* in press/2014). It is also notable that the mud-brick wall exposed in Phase 20 leans to one side (Fig. 10.3), and it is possible that this may have been the result of subsidence and earthquake activity as well.

Mamasani lies astride the north–south Kazerun transverse active fault system, and its valley system appears to have been formed during the longitudinal folding of the Zagros belt (Berberian 1995; Berberian *et al.* in press). It is notable that the first earthquake visible in the Tol-e Spid fourth-millennium BC sequence appears to have been a major event, but one that does not seem to have interrupted the occupation of the settlement. The second earthquake potentially had a far more dramatic impact. It is not clear precisely when this second earthquake occurred, but there appears to be a long gap in occupation, up to 900 years, between Phase 18, which is damaged by the fracture, and Phase 17, which is not (Petrie *et al.* 2009a; Berberian *et al.* in press/2014). It is thus very possible that the end of the *Banesh* period occupation and also the subsequent gap in occupation was provoked by an earthquake. Irrespective of whether an earthquake terminated the fourth-millennium BC occupation at Tol-e Spid, it is clear that seismic activity was a very real concern for the inhabitants of the site, and may have contributed to the need for frequent rebuilding during the early fourth millennium BC.

Tol-e Nurabad

Tol-e Nurabad stands near the centre of the Dasht-e Nurabad, approximately 15 km to the south of Tol-e Spid. The MAP carried out initial excavations at Tol-e Nurabad over two seasons in 2003 (Weeks *et al.* 2009), and further seasons were carried out in December 2008–January 2009 and March 2010. In the two initial seasons, a preliminary 2 × 2 m sounding (Trench A) was excavated 11 m down the face of the steep exposed section at the north-eastern side of the site and was reduced to a 2 × 1 m sounding that was excavated 5 m into the underlying deposits to reach the natural soil (Weeks *et al.* 2009). Approximately 4 m of the Trench A deposits span the mid- to late fourth and early third millennia BC, and comprise eight of the 26 phases of occupation identified (Phases A13–A6; Weeks *et al.* 2009). These phases were characterised by *Late Lapui* (Phases A13–A11), *Transitional Lapui-Banesh* (Phase A10), *Middle Banesh* (Phase A9–A7), and *Late Banesh* (Phase A6) period ceramic wares (see below). Trench C was a 10 × 3 m exposure on an spur of the mound to the west of Trench A, and three of the 10 phases of occupation exposed there appear to date to the fourth millennium BC, on the basis of the presence of *Lapui* (Phases C4–C3) and *Banesh* (Phase C2) period ceramic wares. Trench D was a 10 × 5 m exposure situated just downslope from Trench C that largely comprised Neolithic deposits, but there was a pit (Phase D1) in the upper deposits that contained a mixed assemblage of prehistoric ceramics of *Bakun* to *Kaftari* date, with a small proportion of plain *Lapui* coarse wares and bevel-rim bowls. The 2010 excavations at Tol-e Nurabad concentrated on the Neolithic period deposits of Trench D, and are not relevant to the discussion here.

In comparison to Tol-e Spid, the fourth-millennium BC deposits in Trenches A and C at Tol-e Nurabad contained much less in the way of structural remains, and while numerous floor surfaces were exposed, it appears likely that more informative deposits dating to this period lie elsewhere on the mound. The earliest *Lapui* period deposits exposed in Trench A (Phase A13) were steeply sloping and appear to have been a combination of wash and fill deposits underlying a partially preserved mud-brick wall standing six courses high (Phase A12b). This wall was abutted and overlain by phases of sloping fill deposits (Phases A12a–A11), the uppermost of which appears to mark a transition between the *Lapui* and *Banesh* period deposits (i.e. they are *Transitional Lapui-Banesh*). Phase A10 is composed of a series of floor surfaces, which are covered by a thick layer of packed fill (Phase A9) that is topped by a further sequence of floor surfaces (Phase A8), and which is in turn overlain by a layer of clay containing white cobbles (Phase A7). All of these deposits are characterised by *Middle Banesh* period ceramics (see below). Although strictly lying outside the fourth millennium BC, it is also worth mentioning the fill deposits of Phase A6, which contained *Middle Banesh* pottery alongside a small number of *Late Banesh* sherds. *Late Banesh* pottery sherds were also tentatively identified as residual material in the *Kaftari* period deposits of Phase A5. The fourth-millennium BC deposits preserved in Trench C are even more enigmatic, and are primarily composed of a substantial layer of fill (Phase C4) that was cut by a pit (Phase C3), with both containing *Lapui* period ceramics. These were in turn overlain by deposits of hard-packed fill containing *Middle Banesh* period ceramics (Phase C2) (Petrie *et al.*, in preparation, a).

The limited scale of the excavations makes it difficult to engage in broader discussions about the behaviour of the inhabitants of Tol-e Nurabad during the fourth millennium BC. With the exception of the wall in Phase A12b, the deposits that were exposed appear to relate to open living and/or working surfaces and the intervening fill episodes. While an incautious interpretation might view this as evidence

for ephemeral occupation during the later fourth millennium BC, the depth of deposit in both areas makes it more likely that Trenches A and C have both exposed parts of the site characterised by courtyard working surfaces of some type. Precisely what these surfaces were being used for is as yet unclear. A significant concentration of *Lapui/Banesh* red-slipped wares has been observed on the southern fringes of Tol-e Nurabad, about 200 m south of the excavated trenches, and this provides further evidence of the extent of fourth-millennium BC occupation at the site.

Settlement distribution

In addition to the evidence from the excavations at Tol-e Spid and Tol-e Nurabad, regional survey throughout the Dasht-e Rustam-e Yek and Do plains has revealed fourth-millennium BC occupation on 16 sites (see Table 10.1; McCall 2009; superseding Zeidi *et al.* 2009). Thirteen of these were occupied in the *Lapui* period, 12 were occupied in the *Banesh* period, and nine were occupied in both (see Table 10.1; Fig. 10.5/a–b). It is also worth noting that 14 sites were occupied during the *Bakun* period, and at least five of these were occupied in the *Late Bakun* phase (McCall 2009: table 5.2, 138).

Based on parallels with ceramic material from Tol-e Spid (see below), it appears that five sites were occupied during the *Early Lapui* phase, nine were occupied during the *Middle Lapui* phase, and 11 were occupied during the *Late Lapui* (Table 10.1; McCall 2009: 176–78). The sites with the most protracted occupation were MS 39, MS 43, and MS 51 (Tol-e Spid), and all three were also occupied in the *Late Bakun* period (Table 10.1; McCall 2009: 176–78). The evidence for *Lapui* and *Early Banesh* period occupation at nine sites indicates that there may have been a considerable degree of continuity of settlement location between the two periods (Table 10.1; McCall 2009: 219). Nine sites were occupied during the *Middle Banesh* period, including two that were not occupied in the *Early Banesh* period (Table 10.1; McCall 2009: 220). Only six sites have any evidence for *Late Banesh* occupation, although several of these sites only have one sherd of *Late Banesh* material, including Tol-e Spid (Table 10.1; McCall 2009: 221). Although the evidence is limited, this observation is significant, as this phase of occupation was not preserved in the Tol-e Spid sounding. It would appear that the major *Banesh* period sites were MS 43, MS 47, and MS 51 (Tol-e Spid), with MS 43 and MS 51 both having evidence, at least on the surface, of being occupied in all three sub-phases.

Lapui period settlements were found in both the Dasht-e Rustam-e Yek and Do plains. There were four *Early Lapui* settlements in the Dasht-e Rustam-e Yek as opposed to one in Dasht-e Rustam-e Do. While there were also four settlements in Dasht-e Rustam-e

Table 10.1. Mamasani settlements occupied in the Lapui *and* Banesh *periods*

Site	Early Lapui	Middle Lapui	Late Lapui	Early Banesh	Middle Banesh	Late Banesh
Dasht-e Rustam-e Do						
MS1			X			
MS4		X	X	X	X	
MS8	X	X	X	X	X	
MS11		X	X	X		
MS12			X			X
MS14		X	X	X	X	X
MS18				X	X	X
MS20		X	X	X	X	
MS22					X	
Dasht-e Rustam-e Yek						
MS31	X					
MS36		X				
MS39	X	X	X	X		
MS43	X	X	X	X	X	X
MS45			X			
MS47					X	X
MS51	X	X	X	X	X	X

Yek during both the *Middle* and *Late Lapui* phases, there was a progressive increase in the numbers of settlements in the Dasht-e Rustam-e Do in each of these phases, suggesting an increase in population there during the mid-fourth millennium BC (Table 10.1). In Dasht-e Rustam-e Yek there were three settlements in each of the *Early*, *Middle*, and *Late Banesh* phases, while in the Dasht-e Rustam-e Do there were six settlements in the *Early* and *Middle Banesh* phases and a drop to three in the *Late Banesh*, meaning that it was only in the early third millennium BC that there was an equal number of settlements in the two plains (Table 10.1). The settlement system appears to have been relatively stable during the fourth millennium BC, with a maximum settlement density of between nine and 11 *c.* 1 ha sites, and indications that the beginning and end of the fourth millennium BC saw drops in the overall number of settlements. It is unclear whether this marks a decline in population or the centralisation of the existing population into fewer sites.

Chronology

As Petrie *et al.* (2009b) have noted, there have been a number of outstanding questions relating to the chronology of the *Lapui* and *Banesh* periods in Fars. For example, it has long been supposed that the *Lapui* period spans the first half of the fourth millennium

BC (e.g. Sumner 1988a, 2003; Voigt and Dyson 1992; Alizadeh 2006), but until the excavations at Tol-e Spid, Tol-e Nurabad, and also Tappeh Mehrali (Sardari, this volume), there was relatively little known about the *Lapui* period from excavations. It was thus not possible to confirm its chronological placement. Similarly, there is a lack of clear chronological resolution for the *Banesh* period, in that while there is an abundance of radiocarbon dates for the *Middle Banesh* phase from Tal-e Malyan, the dates for the *Early* and *Late Banesh* phases are of poor quality and there are problems with the radiocarbon calibration curve at the end of the fourth millennium BC, which leave many questions unanswered (Dahl *et al.*, this volume; Petrie in press). Clearly any new dating evidence is likely to be beneficial.

The lower part of the Tol-e Spid sequence (Phases 31–20) is the first protracted sequence of *Lapui* period occupation to have been excavated in Fars. Of the 23 stratified AMS and conventional radiocarbon dates obtained from the entire Tol-e Spid sequence, 15 fall within the late fifth or fourth millennium BC, and nine of these dates are presented for the first time here. Of the 18 stratified AMS and conventional radiocarbon dates from Trench A at Tol-e Nurabad, five fall within the fourth or early third millennium BC (Weeks *et al.* 2009). Although radiocarbon dates from Trench C have been analysed, the dates that should fall in the fourth millennium BC were all modern, while one of

Figure 10.5. a. Lapui *period settlement distribution in Mamasani; b.* Banesh *period settlement distribution in Mamasani.*

the ostensibly fourth-millennium BC Trench A dates was contaminated by bitumen. Taken together, the dates from Tol-e Spid and Tol-e Nurabad make them the best-dated fourth-millennium BC sequences in Fars, and among the best in Iran (Table 10.2, Fig. 10.6).

Of the 20 radiocarbon dates from *Lapui* and *Banesh* period deposits presented in Table 10.2, there is only

one that is problematic. One of the samples from Tol-e Spid (OxA-20003) does not conform at all to the stratigraphic sequence, but while this date is considerably earlier than expected for the deposit from which it originates, it is not at odds with the likelihood that there were earlier, pre-fourth-millennium BC phases of occupation at the site. It

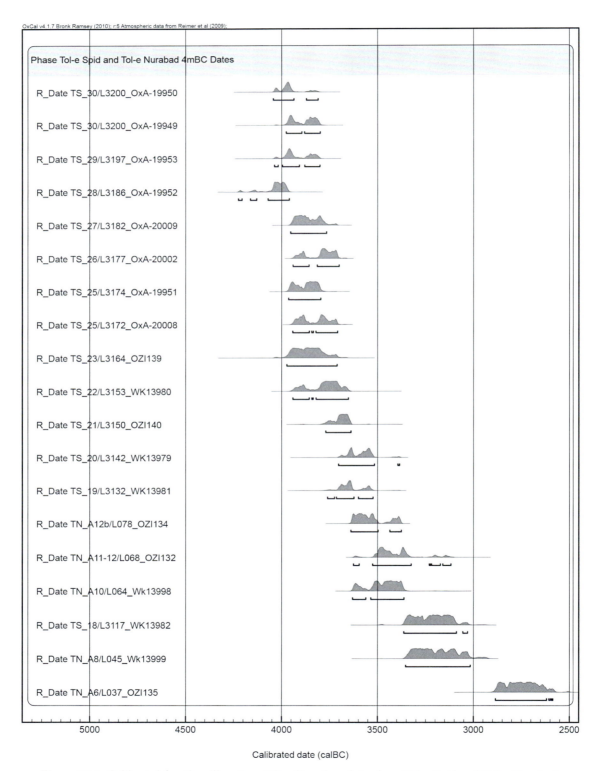

Figure 10.6. Calibrated fourth-millennium BC radiocarbon dates from Tol-e Spid and Tol-e Nurabad.

Table 10.2. Fourth millennium BC radiocarbon dates from Tol-e Spid and Tol-e Nurabad

Tol-e Spid

Phase	Locus	Sample	Material	Taxon	¹⁴C Age BP	Std. Dev. +/-	Cal. Age Probability [95.4% @ (2σ)]	Modelled Cal. Age (2σ)
30	3200	OxA-19950	Charcoal	Capparis	5158	36	4050 (95.4%) 3810BC	4050 (95.4%) 3960BC
30	3200	OxA-19949	Charcoal	Capparis	5112	35	3980 (95.4%) 3790BC	4040 (95.4%) 3950BC
29	3197	OxA-19953	Charred grain	Hordeum + ind.	5134	37	4040 (95.4%) 3800BC	4000 (95.4%) 3940BC
28	3186	OxA-19952	Charred grain	Hordeum	5219	34	4230 (95.4%) 3960BC	3990 (95.4%) 3930BC
27	3183	OxA-20003	Charcoal	Zygophyllum	6072	32	5200 (95.4%) 4850BC	
27	3182	OxA-20009	Charred seeds	Lolium/Festuca	5045	31	3960 (95.4%) 3760BC	3960 (95.4%) 3870BC
26	3177	OxA-20002	Charcoal	Capparis	5002	31	3950 (95.4%) 3700BC	3950 (95.4%) 3830BC
25	3174	OxA-19951	Charred grain	Hordeum + ind.	5087	34	3970 (95.4%) 3790BC	3920 (95.4%) 3790BC
25	3172	OxA-20008	Charred grain	Hordeum + Lens	5018	31	3950 (95.4%) 3700BC	3910 (95.4%) 3750BC
23	3164	OZI139	Charcoal	Indeterminate	5070	60	3980 (95.4%) 3710BC	3870 (95.4%) 3710BC
22	3153	Wk 13980	Charcoal	Indeterminate	4981	51	3940 (21.0%) 3840BC, 3820 (74.4%) 3650BC	3800 (95.4%) 3660BC
21	3150	OZI140	Charcoal	Indeterminate	4910	40	3770 (95.4%) 3630BC	3750 (95.4%) 3640BC
20	3142	Wk 13979	Charcoal	Indeterminate	4821	47	3710 (94.1%) 3510BC, 3400 (1.3%) 3380BC	3700 (95.4%) 3540BC
19	3132	Wk 13981	Charcoal	Indeterminate	4857	48	3760 (70.3%) 3620BC, 3600 (25.1%) 3520BC	3670 (95.4%) 3510BC
18	3117	Wk 13982	Charcoal	Indeterminate	4515	46	3370 (92.7%) 3080BC, 3060 (2.7%) 3030BC	3520 (95.4%) 3200BC

Tol-e Nurabad

Phase	Locus	Sample	Material	Taxon	14C Age BP	Std. Dev. +/-	Cal. Age Probability [95.4% @ (2σ)]
A12b	78	OZI134	Charcoal	Indeterminate	4750	40	3640 (76.2%) 3490BC, 3440 (19.2%) 3370BC
A11–12a	68	OZI132	Charcoal	Indeterminate	4620	50	3650 (84.0%) 3300BC, 3250 (11.4%) 3100BC
A10	64	WK13998	Charcoal	Indeterminate	4682	51	3640 (16.8%) 3550BC, 3540 (78.6%) 3360BC
A8	45	WK13999	Charcoal	Indeterminate	4476	46	3360 (95.4%) 3010BC
A6	37	OZI135	Charcoal	Indeterminate	4160	50	2890 (95.4%) 2580BC

is possible that residual material was redeposited in later phases as a result of a common taphonomic process such as the digging of pits. The remaining dates from the two sites combine to form the most protracted sequence of fourth-millennium BC dates from south-west Iran.

The 13 non-problematic *Lapui* period radiocarbon determinations from Tol-e Spid span an extended period stretching from the very end of the fifth millennium BC to the mid-fourth millennium BC. The recently published radiocarbon dates from Tal-e Bakun A (Periods III and IV) show that the *Late Bakun* deposits at that site date to the mid- to late fifth millennium BC, possibly as late as *c.* 4240 BC (Alizadeh 2006: 120–21), although the most recent/latest *Late Bakun* deposits were not actually sampled. The earliest *Lapui* period radiocarbon date from Tol-e Spid (OxA-19950) has a probability range that extends into the late fifth millennium BC (4050–3810 cal. BC), which indicates that there is some possibility that the *Lapui* period began in the fifth millennium BC, at least in Mamasani. This likelihood is at least partly reinforced by the fact that there are still *Lapui* period deposits below Tol-e Spid Phase 31 (Petrie *et al.* 2007). As such, it is not clear exactly how far the *Lapui* period might extend before 4000 BC. The remaining *Lapui* period radiocarbon determinations from Tol-e Spid span the entirety of the early to mid-fourth millennium BC, and have closely overlapping and non-contradictory probability distributions, affirming that the *Lapui* period extended to around 3500–3400 BC. The one reliable *Lapui* period determination from Tol-e Nurabad (Phase A12b) falls in the mid-fourth millennium BC (3640–3370 cal. BC; Weeks *et al.* 2009: table 3.2), and confirms that the *Lapui* occupation at that site falls in the later part of the period and reinforces the date of the end of the *Lapui* period indicated by the Tol-e Spid determinations. The division of the individual *Lapui* period phases at Tol-e Spid into sub-phases will be discussed below in relation to the ceramic evidence.

Tol-e Spid also has radiocarbon dating evidence for the mid- to late fourth millennium BC, spanning what appear to be *Transitional Lapui-Banesh* (Phase 19; 3760–3520 cal. BC) and *Banesh* (Phase 18; 3370–3030 cal. BC) phases (Table 10.2; Petrie *et al.* 2009a: table 4.4). The range of the Phase 19/*Transitional Lapui-Banesh* date appears to be slightly earlier than expected, and it is statistically identical to the date from Phase 20. It is thus possible that the date comes from residual carbonised material. The limited number of radiocarbon dates means that it is not possible to establish whether there was a gap in the occupation at Tol-e Spid between Phases 19 and 18, although this is a possibility (Table 10.2). On the basis of the radiocarbon dates and also the material remains (see below), the Tol-e Spid *Transitional Lapui-Banesh* phase appears to be at least partly contemporaneous with

Transitional Lapui-Banesh deposits at Tol-e Nurabad (Phases A11–A10, Weeks *et al.* 2009: 76, table 3.2) and the earliest phases at Tal-e Kureh (Stratum 1a-III, Alden 2003a: table D1) in the Kur River Basin. Phase 18 at Tol-e Spid and Phases A9–A7 at Tol-e Nurabad represent the only excavated evidence for *Middle Banesh* period occupation in Fars outside Tal-e Malyan, and the radiocarbon dates (*c.* 3370–3010 cal. BC) conform with what we know from that site. Unfortunately the precision of these dates, and hence their ability to constrain archaeological phases, is limited by the plateau in the radiocarbon calibration curve at the end of the fourth millennium BC (see Dahl *et al.*, this volume). As with the *Middle Banesh* deposits, Tol-e Nurabad Phase A6 is the only *Late Banesh* period occupation to have been identified outside Tal-e Malyan, and the amount of clear *Late Banesh* material at the site is admittedly very limited. The radiocarbon date (OZI135; 2890–2580 cal. BC) from Phase A6 is actually slightly later than the latest *Late Banesh* radiocarbon date from Tal-e Malyan (Sumner 1988b).

In addition to providing insight into the absolute chronology of the archaeological deposits being assessed, analysis of the absolute dating evidence and its relationship to the two earthquake fractures visible in the Tol-e Spid section is also revealing. The first earthquake visible in the sections occurred between Phases 23 and 22 and therefore appears to date *c.* 3850–3680 cal. BC, while the second occurred between Phases 18 and 17, and probably occurred after *c.* 3370–3030 cal. BC (Berberian *et al.* in press/2014). As noted above, it is possible that this latter earthquake terminated the fourth-millennium BC occupation at the site, although it is not possible to say this with any certainty.

Ceramics

The most coherent sequence of *Lapui* period deposits in Mamasani (and Fars) has been exposed at Tol-e Spid, therefore it is logical to use this sequence in an attempt to characterise *Early*, *Middle*, and *Late Lapui* ceramic assemblages, at least as they appear in Mamasani, and to correlate this with the evidence from Tol-e Nurabad. In general, the *Lapui* period material from Mamasani has excellent parallels with surveyed assemblages from sites in the Kur River Basin (Langsdorff and McCown 1942; Sumner 1972, 1988a; Alizadeh 2006; see Petrie *et al.* 2007: fig. 5; 2009a: 101–04, figs 4.50–4.58; Weeks *et al.* 2009: 49–51, figs 3.96–3.99). As noted below, there are differences in the *Banesh* period ceramic forms seen at Tol-e Spid and Tol-e Nurabad, so it is useful to use the evidence from both sites to characterise the *Early*, *Middle*, and *Late Banesh* ceramic assemblages of Mamasani. The *Banesh* period material from Mamasani has excellent parallels with excavated and surveyed assemblages from sites in the Kur River Basin (Sumner 1972, 2003; Alden 1979, 1982, 2003a, 2003b, 2003c; Nicholas 1990; see Petrie *et al.* 2009a: 104–06, figs 4.59–4.66; Weeks *et al.* 2009: 51–54, figs 3.100–3.108).

Vessel form typology

Some apparently residual fragments of *Bakun*-type black-on-buff painted pottery were recovered from Tol-e Spid Phases 31–20, but the majority of the ceramic material was characteristic *Lapui* common ware or red *Lapui* fine ware (Petrie *et al.* 2007; after Sumner 1988a). No examples of the red-slipped buff *Lapui* fine ware were recorded in these deposits, indicating that this type of fine ware only appears in the *Late Lapui* period at Tol-e Spid (Petrie *et al.* 2007: 305; 2009a: 103ff., 129; see Sumner 1988a). A range of fairly standard open and closed vessel types appears to have been used throughout the *Lapui* period, but there is a range of specific morphological and decorative elements which appears in specific sub-phases.

The *Early Lapui* phase ceramic corpus (Fig. 10.7/a) is defined by the ceramics from Tol-e Spid Phases 31–25, which are dominated by vessels produced from a fabric containing grit inclusions (i.e. *Lapui* common ware). There is some evidence for painted decoration, but most vessels have no paint and display signs of surface burnishing. Proportionally there were very few examples of red *Lapui* fine ware in these deposits (<5%). The bowl forms are similar to those seen in other sub-phases, while necked jars typically have upright and out-flaring rims and some hole-mouth jar rims have an overtly flared and pinched rim (Petrie *et al.* 2007: fig. 5).

The *Middle Lapui* ceramic corpus (Fig. 10.7/b) is defined by ceramics from Tol-e Spid Phases 24–21, and is also marked by the dominance of fabrics with grit inclusions. Again there is some evidence for painted decoration, but this is distinct from that seen in the *Early Lapui* deposits (Petrie *et al.* 2009a: pl. 13, figs 4.51), and proportionally there are again very few examples of red *Lapui* fine ware in these deposits (Petrie *et al.* 2009a: 101–03). Bowl forms are similar to those of the *Early Lapui*, but jar forms become more varied, with necked jars appearing in different sizes and with different rim forms, and hole-mouthed jars being simpler (Petrie *et al.* 2009a: figs 4.50–4.56). Pierced lugs are also attested (Petrie *et al.* 2009a: fig. 4.51).

The *Late Lapui* ceramic corpus (Fig. 10.7/c) is defined by ceramics from Tol-e Spid Phase 20, and Tol-e Nurabad Phases A13–A12 and C3–C4. At both sites there is a marked increase in finer vessels, and red-slipped buff *Lapui* fine ware appears for the first time and was used to manufacture a range of familiar *Lapui* period vessel forms (e.g. Petrie *et al.* 2009a: figs 4.57–4.58; Weeks *et al.* 2009: figs 3.97–3.99). There

appears to have been an increase in the frequency of very fine jar rims.

Tol-e Spid Phase 19 and Tol-e Nurabad Phase A11 have been interpreted as representing a *Transitional Lapui-Banesh* phase. These deposits were identified stratigraphically between the *Lapui* and *Banesh* phase deposits and are characterised by a *Lapui*-type ceramic assemblage, including red-slipped buff *Lapui* fine ware vessels, together with vessels that resemble painted *Banesh* wares from the Kur River Basin and a number of non-local forms, including fragments of bevel-rim bowls (Fig. 10.7/d; Petrie *et al.* 2009a: figs 4.59–4.60; Weeks *et al.* 2009: figs 3.100–3.101). This is broadly similar to Alden's characterisation of the *Lapui-Banesh Transition* in the Kur River Basin (Alden, this volume).

In the Kur River Basin, there are two main ceramic fabrics that characterise the *Banesh* period, *Banesh* straw-tempered ware and *Banesh* grit-tempered ware (see Sumner 1972: 43–44; Alden 1979: 211–17; 2003a: 192; this volume). Alden (this volume) has argued that specific vessel forms are characteristic of particular sub-phases: pinched rim bowls with a streak burnish are the most distinctive ceramic indicator of the *Early Banesh*, while chaff-tempered goblets with necked bases and concave chaff-tempered goblet rims denote the *Middle Banesh*, and a range of painting styles and motifs and grooved and impressed deep bowls denote the *Late Banesh*.

Tol-e Nurabad has a more protracted sequence of *Banesh* period deposits (Phases A10–A6) than is evident at Tol-e Spid (Phase 18), so it inevitably lays the best foundation for delineating the composition of the *Banesh* period sub-phase corpora in Mamasani. It is notable, however, that the Mamasani *Banesh* period ceramic material does not neatly follow Alden's scheme for the Kur River Basin. Perhaps the most notable difference between the *Banesh* period ceramics in the two regions is that in Mamasani the red-slipped buff-ware that had first appeared in *Late Lapui* deposits at both Tol-e Spid and Tol-e Nurabad continued to be used in the *Transitional Lapui-Banesh* and throughout the *Banesh* period (Fig. 10.8; Petrie *et al.* 2009a: figs 4.57–4.58; Weeks *et al.* 2009: figs 3.97–3.99). That these red-slipped ware fragments were not residual in the *Banesh* period is emphasised by the fact that many of the vessel forms have good parallels with *Banesh* period forms that typically appear in other wares in the Kur River Basin (Petrie *et al.* 2009a: figs 4.57–4.58; Weeks *et al.* 2009: figs 3.97–3.99).

The evidence for a *Transitional Lapui-Banesh* phase at both Tol-e Spid and Tol-e Nurabad implies that we might expect some *Early Banesh* occupation at both sites and it is likely that Tol-e Nurabad Phase A10 dates to this period given the continued attestation of bevel-rim bowls, but a lack of other chaff-tempered vessel forms (Fig. 10.8a; Weeks *et al.* 2009: 36, figs 3.102–3.103). Tol-e Spid Phase 18 included fragments

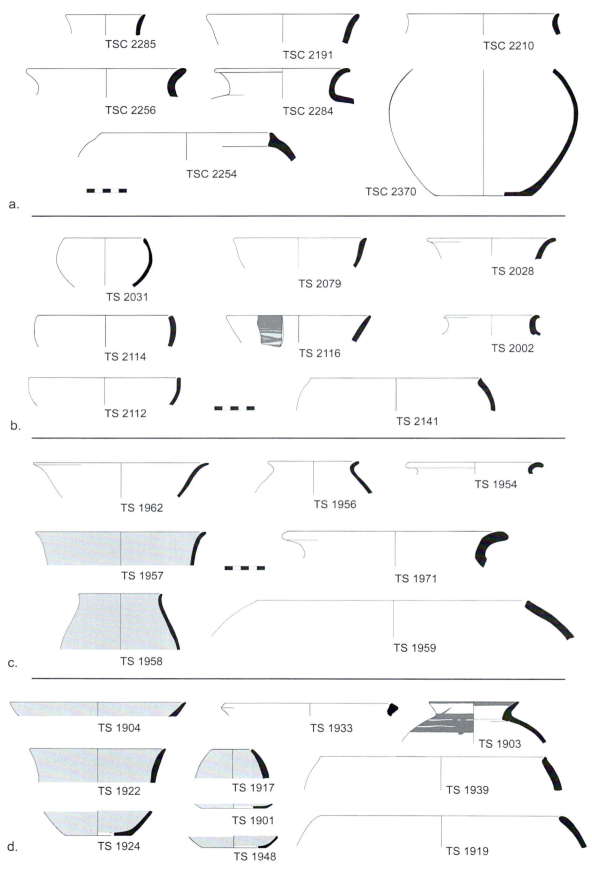

Figure 10.7. Lapui period ceramics from Tol-e Spid: a. Early Lapui; *b.* Middle Lapui; *c.* Late Lapui; *d.* Transitional Lapui-Banesh.

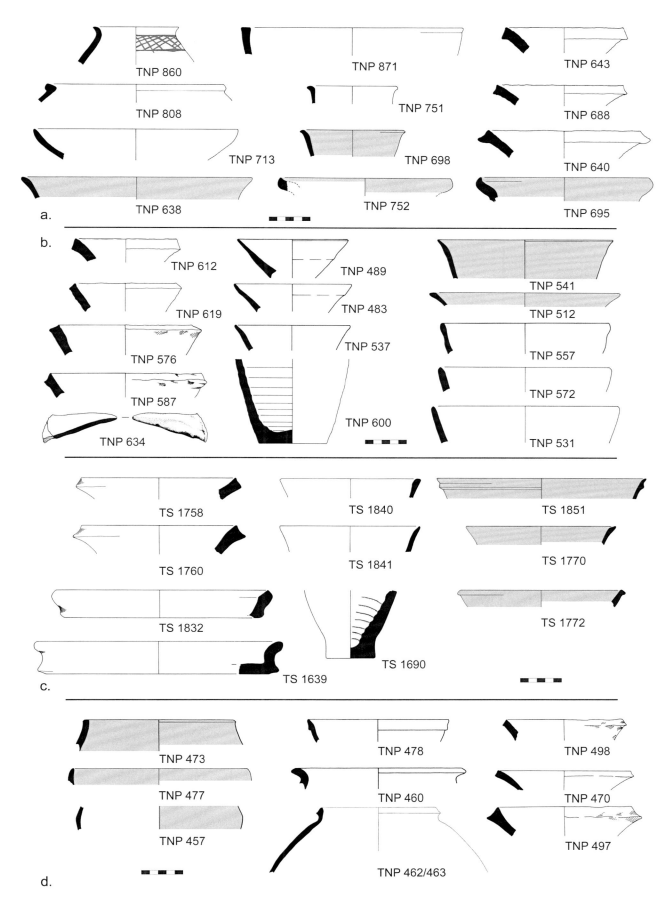

Figure 10.8. Banesh period ceramics from Mamasani: **a.** Early Banesh *(Tol-e Nurabad);* **b.** Middle Banesh *(Tol-e Nurabad);* **c.** Middle Banesh *(Tol-e Spid);* **d.** Late Banesh *(Tol-e Nurabad).*

of pinched rim bowls and chaff-tempered goblets, indicating that there may have been some *Early Banesh* occupation at the site, even if it was not preserved in the sounding (Petrie *et al.* 2009a: fig. 4.63).

The *Middle Banesh* ceramic corpus at both sites (Tol-e Spid Phase 18, Tol-e Nurabad Phases A10–A7 and C2) is more typical, in that a wide range of characteristic grit- and chaff-tempered vessels forms are attested at both sites, including bevel-rim bowls and goblets (Fig. 10.8/b; e.g. Weeks *et al.* 2009: fig. 3.105; Petrie *et al.* 2009a: figs 4.61, 4.63). However, the *Middle Banesh* assemblages at the two sites are not identical. While spouts are present at Tol-e Nurabad (e.g. Weeks *et al.* 2009: fig. 3.105), low-sided trays are not, and while low-sided trays appear in abundance at Tol-e Spid (e.g. Petrie *et al.* 2009a: figs 4.62–4.63), no spouts were recovered there. It is not clear whether this difference reflects variances in function or behaviour between the two sites in the *Middle Banesh* period or is a product of the limited excavated exposures.

There is considerably less evidence for the *Late Banesh* period in Mamasani, so it is inherently difficult to characterise its ceramic corpus. While only one *Late Banesh* sherd was recovered from the surface of Tol-e Spid (McCall 2009: 222), Phase A6 at Tol-e Nurabad contained a small number of fragments of grit-tempered ware with painted decoration, reminiscent of the Kur River Basin *Late Banesh* types (Weeks *et al.* 2009: 54). Possible evidence for *Late Banesh* occupation also appears to come from up to five other sites, although only MS 18 and MS47 produced more than one sherd (McCall 2009: 222) (Fig. 10.8/c).

Evidence for ceramic production

In order to understand the significance of these changes in ceramic wares and vessel forms during the fourth millennium BC, it is useful to consider the evidence for ceramic production and distribution that is encapsulated in the ceramics themselves. There are clearly a number of major changes in the production process during the *Chalcolithic* as a whole, and with the shift from the *Bakun* to the *Lapui* period, we see a complete change in both the types of clays that were being exploited and the approaches to surface decoration to the point where figurative and geometric decoration are virtually abandoned (Sumner 1988a; Blackman 1989). This is all the more marked as it follows the extremely vivid combinations of geometric and figurative motifs used during the *Late Bakun* phase (see Langsdorff and McCown 1942; Alizadeh 2006). The key technological shift in the *Lapui* period seems to be the introduction of the slow wheel, which results in the production of particularly refined rim forms and quite regular circular vessel apertures, which were often lacking in the preceding period. At least in the Mamasani region, a shift from the

production of red fine wares to the production of buff fine wares with a red slip also takes place during the *Lapui* period (see above), but this is the only apparent innovation in the selection and use of clays. With the shift to the *Transitional Lapui-Banesh* (see above) and *Early Banesh* phases, the bevel-rim bowl appears for the first time in the highlands, but this form is one of the only indicators of contact with the lowlands at this time (see above; Alden 1979, 1982, 2003a, this volume). With the *Middle Banesh* phase we see an even more dramatic shift towards simplicity in approaches to decoration and efficiency over refinement in terms of the level of use of mass production. These shifts are seen in the cessation of painted decoration and the use of the fast wheel and moulds to mass-produce vessels. The complete disappearance of painted decoration suggests that potters were choosing different approaches to decoration, although little of this is attested in Mamasani. That the use of this unpainted material became so widespread suggests that this shift was accepted by a population that was either receptive to, or demanding, change. The choice to keep using the red-slipped buff-ware during the *Banesh* period in Mamasani clearly differentiates it from the Kur River Basin in the same period (see above).

Blackman (1989: 104–05, 106) has proposed that the changes in ceramic production observed in the *Lapui* period are unlikely to have been the result of the introduction of new, previously unknown technologies through diffusion, innovation, or migration but are more likely to be the result of cultural responses to changing socio-economic requirements. It is difficult, however, to reconstruct this process using the available survey data from the Kur River Basin. Sumner (1988a) initially suggested that the *Lapui* period marked a drop in the regional population, whereas Alizadeh (2006: 26) has suggested that the *Lapui* period actually saw a population increase. The difference of opinion is a result of the use of different methods for estimating the numbers of settlements during the various sub-phases of the fifth millennium BC, and neither is particularly reliable as they have not incorporated a detailed assessment of the ceramic material collected during the various surveys of the region (Weeks *et al.* 2010). As a result, there is no clear understanding of population dynamics in the early fourth millennium BC in the Kur River Basin, and this makes it inherently difficult to make robust interpretations. The evidence from Mamasani suggests that there was broad continuity in terms of settlement numbers between the *Bakun* and *Lapui* periods (McCall 2009), although a more nuanced analysis shows that there was some reduction in the number of settlements in the *Late Bakun* and *Early Lapui* phases before an increase in the *Middle Lapui* phase that continued into the *Late Lapui* and *Early* and *Middle Banesh* phases (see above, Table 10.1). As pointed out by Blackman, such a pattern need not be explained by migration.

An analysis of the changes in approaches to ceramic production that took place during the fourth millennium BC in the Mamasani region is currently being completed (Petrie *et al.*, in preparation, b), but it is possible to make some preliminary remarks. A combined ICP-AES compositional analysis and petrographic study has been carried out on fourth-millennium BC ceramic fragments from Tol-e Spid, Tol-e Nurabad, and three other settlements in the Dasht-e Rustam-e Yek and Do plains. The petrographic analysis reveals clear differences in composition of fine and coarse ware ceramic fabrics, which is to be expected, but it would appear that the fine ware clays were either deliberately selected because they lacked inclusions or were levigated. A principal component analysis of the ICP-AES data (Fig. 10.9) indicates that the *Lapui* grit-tempered wares found at Tol-e Spid may have been produced using three distinct sources of raw materials, and while some of the samples from Tol-e Nurabad and the other sites fall into these groupings, others do not, suggesting that there may have been more sources exploited by the potters supplying those sites. The *Lapui* fine red and fine red-slipped buff wares appear to have been produced from other distinct sources of raw materials and then distributed to multiple sites in the region. If these distinct sources of raw materials

can be taken as proxies for distinct production locales, it would appear that a relatively elaborate ceramic production and distribution system was in operation in the Mamasani region during the *Lapui* period, with coarse wares being made at multiple locations and often ending up at one settlement, while particular fine wares appear to have been made at specific locations and then distributed to multiple settlements. The complex pattern appears to continue into the *Banesh* period, where some of the coarse and fine ware sources continued to be exploited (Fig. 10.9). It is notable that there is evidence for bevel-rim bowls being produced from yet another source of raw materials and being distributed to both Tol-e Spid and Tol-e Nurabad, which most closely fits the pattern for the production and distribution of fine wares. Notably, the compositional signature for the bevel-rim bowl samples is identical to that for the samples from the vegetal-tempered Neolithic samples analysed for the study.

Bioarchaeological evidence

There has been a great deal of discussion of the developments in subsistence strategies, which may have taken place between the late fifth and early third millennia BC in highland Fars (e.g. Sumner 1986, 1988a; Alizadeh 2006, 2010; Alden, this volume). It must be acknowledged, however, that we continue

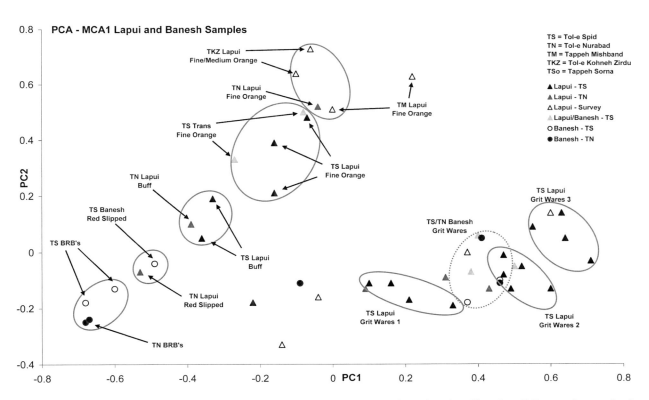

Figure 10.9. Histogram showing results of PCA analysis of ICP-AES data from fourth-millennium BC ceramic samples from sites in Mamasani. Solid ellipses enclose samples of distinctive ware type from different sites. Fine wares align on one axis, at left, and coarse wares cluster at right.

to have little unequivocal information about the nature of the subsistence economy in the *Late Bakun*, *Lapui*, or *Banesh* periods. There is a limited range of bioarchaeological and archaeozoological data available from the Tol-e Nurabad and Tol-e Spid excavations, and although the analysis of this material is currently ongoing, it is possible to make some preliminary observations.

Archaeozoology (M. Mashkour)

Due to the small scale of the excavations that have been undertaken, only limited amounts of faunal remains have been recovered from the excavations at Tol-e Spid and Tol-e Nurabad. Here, the material will be discussed by period rather than by individual phase, with the figures citing NISP data.

During the fourth millennium BC at both sites there was a dominance of caprids (both sheep and goat), and bovids were the next most common species (Mashkour 2009; Mashkour and Sheikhi, in preparation; Mashkour and Mohaseb, in preparation). Suidae represent a relatively minor component of the assemblage and hunting does not appear to have played a major role (Mashkour 2009; Mashkour and Sheikhi, in preparation; Mashkour and Mohaseb, in preparation). This pattern is similar to that seen for the *Bakun* period from Tol-e Nurabad, although it is different to that of the Neolithic, where Caprini almost completely dominate (93.6%) (Mashkour 2009). Although Caprini are consistently more frequent, it is important to point out that in general the proportions of Caprini and *Bos* are almost identical in terms of relative weight, suggesting that they were potentially both equal meat providers (Mashkour and Sheikhi, in preparation; Mashkour and Mohaseb, in preparation). The small size of the assemblages means that we have little knowledge of the nature of herd management and broader subsistence strategies, which might provide some insight into issues related to the role of nomadic pastoralists during this period.

There are some notable differences between the assemblages from the two sites and between the two major fourth-millennium periods. Caprids and bovids almost completely dominate the faunal assemblage at Tol-e Spid during both the *Lapui* and *Banesh* periods (Mashkour 2009: table 5.4a–b; Mashkour and Sheikhi, in preparation), but there is a change in the proportion of the exploitation of Caprini, with the proportion of caprids dropping from 84% to 64% (Mashkour 2009: table 5.4b) between the *Lapui* and *Banesh* periods. Very small numbers of carp and wading birds (heron or egret) were recovered, suggesting that some opportunistic hunting was taking place, but this was not a mainstay of the diet (Mashkour and Sheikhi, in preparation). In Tol-e Nurabad Trench A, there was a minor proportional increase in the use of Caprini between the *Lapui* and *Banesh* periods, from 80% to

89.2% (Mashkour 2009: table 5.2b). In Tol-e Nurabad Trench C, the Caprini proportions remain equal between the periods at 75%, and although Suidae are evident in the *Lapui* period (10%), they are not seen in the *Banesh* period, but there are examples of gazelle bones (Mashkour and Mohaseb, in preparation).

In general the faunal data suggests that the patterns of animal exploitation during the fourth millennium BC remained relatively consistent. As such, there do not appear to have been any major changes in approaches to animal-based subsistence throughout this period in Mamasani.

Palaeo-ethnobotany (R. Ballantyne)

Very limited charred botanical remains were recovered from the 2003 excavations at Tol-e Spid and Tol-e Nurabad. More systematic information is available, however, from the flotation of bulk samples during the 2007 excavations at Tol-e Spid and the 2008–09 excavations in Trench C at Tol-e Nurabad. The Tol-e Nurabad material is currently under analysis, and this summary report presents the 2007 preliminary results from Tol-e Spid.

The charred remains recovered from the earliest *Early Lapui* deposits at Tol-e Spid include small numbers of seeds from economic plants such as barley and flax. Wild plants include *Lolium/Festuca* (rye-grass or fescue) seeds, with lesser amounts of small-seeded legumes, *Galium* (bedstraw) and *Avena* (oats). Material from the later *Early Lapui* deposits includes all these plants and also lentil, bitter vetch, and free-threshing wheat (Table 10.2).

These results compare well with those from Tal-e Bakun A (Miller and Kimiaie 2006), particularly the range of charred wild flora, which are distinct from those reported for the earlier sites of Tall-e Mushki and Tall-e Jari. Despite the very small range of samples at all four sites, the similarity in charred plants between Tol-e Spid and Tal-e Bakun A implies a late fifth- to early fourth-millennium BC regional trend that needs further consideration in terms of land use regimes and on-site activities.

Anthracology (C. Lancelotti)

The analysis of charcoal from Tol-e Spid and Tol-e Nurabad is similarly limited, and the material from Tol-e Nurabad is currently under analysis. The anthracological analysis of material from Tol-e Spid has focused on each of the major *Early Lapui* phases excavated in 2007. The analysis showed a dominance of *Pistacia* (78.4%), and it has been possible to attribute the samples to the species *Pistacia khinjuk* Stocks (Bombay mastic), which is a shrub or tree that can reach 6 m in height and grows on dry rocky soils. *Pistacia* wood is considered a very good fuel source as well as a robust construction timber and its leaves are used as fodder. The second most common species is *Capparis* sp. (caper), a small tree or more commonly a shrub found on dry, salty soils, often in hedges and dry river beds. The fruit is edible in some species and its juice has been used in the past to produce etching on beads in India. All the other species recovered were small shrubs or woody herbs that grow on dry, poor soils. The sample size is too small to convey any information about chronological variations in the environment or in preferential wood use. The results are consistent, however, with previous studies carried out at Tal-e Malyan for the *Banesh* period (Miller 1991).

Discussion and conclusions

The soundings at Tol-e Spid and Tol-e Nurabad and the surveys of Dasht-e Rustam-e Yek and Do have provided important insights into the fourth millennium BC in Mamasani. It is also all too apparent, however, that what we can say is constrained by the size of the exposures at each site and the relatively limited coverage and low intensity of the survey work. Nevertheless, the evidence from Mamasani remains significant for discussions of broader socio-economic developments in fourth-millennium BC south-west Iran.

Tol-e Spid provides the first evidence for protracted occupation throughout the *Lapui* period (i.e. the early to mid-fourth millennium BC) to have yet been excavated and systematically dated in Fars. The Tol-e Spid evidence is complemented and in some ways enhanced by that from Tappeh Mehr Ali (Sardari, this volume), where the sequence contains fewer phases but broader exposures, and includes material such as seals and impressions, which have not yet been found in Mamasani. There is more limited evidence for the *Lapui* period at Tol-e Nurabad, but that evidence also complements that from Tol-e Spid. The excavations of the fourth-millennium BC levels at these three sites have revolutionised our understanding of a period that was previously only understood on the basis of surveys of varying intensities.

It appears that there was a relatively stable settled population in Mamasani during the *Lapui* period, although a raw assessment of the survey data indicates that there was a degree variation in precisely how large this population was and where it was concentrated in the Mamasani region during the *Early*, *Middle*, and *Late* sub-phases. The *Lapui* period population appears to have lived predominantly in village-sized settlements of around 1 ha, sited on pre-existing archaeological mounds, with architecture primarily built of mud brick. The survey revealed no evidence for small sites or scatters on talus slopes, although such sites were not looked for specifically during the survey.

The excavations indicate that Tol-e Spid was likely to have been continuously occupied during the early to mid-fourth millennium BC, although there was clear evidence for continual remodelling and rebuilding of structures. Exactly what the evidence for repeated construction, abandonment/destruction, and rebuilding throughout this period signifies within the context of an overall continuity of material culture will only be revealed through broader exposures in other parts of the site. It is possible that this cycle of building and rebuilding represents seasonal use of the structures, but it is unlikely that substantial mud-brick structures would have been rebuilt and replaced annually. Rather, these structures and mounds like Tol-e Spid and Tol-e Nurabad are almost certainly more representative of a village-based lifestyle that is largely sedentary rather than reflecting a subsistence system based, or at least largely dependent upon, mobile or nomadic pastoralism (cf. Alizadeh 2006, 2010; Alden, this volume; Sumner 1986, 1988a; see Weeks *et al.* 2010; Petrie 2011, 2013). The number of occupation phases and the absolute dates make it possible to suggest that the early to mid-fourth-millennium BC architecture at Tol-e Spid was being renovated and/or rebuilt generationally, approximately every 50–60 years.

The ceramics from Tol-e Spid show that there was development in the assemblage during the early to mid-fourth millennium BC, and it is notable that the red-slipped buff ware only appears during the *Late Lapui* period in Mamasani. It will be important to establish whether this is also true for sites in the Kur River Basin, as it will potentially be possible to differentiate between different phases of *Lapui* occupation at sites identified in previous surveys.

The evidence for *Banesh* period occupation in Mamasani is also significant. There appears to be a considerable degree of continuity in the settled population between the *Lapui* and *Banesh* periods (i.e. across the *Transitional Lapui-Banesh* phase), as indicated by the excavations at Tol-e Spid and Tol-e Nurabad and also by the survey. In several instances there are sites that have evidence for multiple phases of *Lapui* and *Banesh* occupation, although it is important not to assume that there was continuity in occupation in each case. Tol-e Spid and Tol-e Nurabad provide the strongest indications for the existence of a *Transitional Lapui-Banesh* phase, but further excavations and more radiocarbon dates are required fully to understand the nature and timing of this transition.

Various influences appear to have been in play across this transition, particularly as seen in terms of the continuity and evolution of the local ceramic assemblages, but also in terms of what is indicated by the appearance of new types such as the bevel-rim bowl. The evidence for gradual evolution in the ceramic technology within the context of clear evidence for continuity and a degree of conservatism carries the implication that the population in Mamasani remained primarily local, but the appearance of distinctive lowland forms shows that people were exposed to, and receptive of, some elements of external influence. Potts (2009) has argued that the spread of bevel-rim bowls in Iran may be indicative of culinary influence, perhaps in bread making (Goulder 2010). While the adoption of bevel-rim bowls might be indicative of changes in culinary behaviour in Mamasani (cf. Potts 2009), a fuller analysis of vessel use in fourth-millennium BC ceramic assemblages is undoubtedly required, with particular attention being focused on production, distribution, and consumption/use in archaeological contexts that are appropriately detailed.

While the *Banesh* period evidence from Mamasani broadly correlates with that from the Kur River Basin, the continued use of red-slipped buff ware and the production of *Banesh*-type vessel forms in that ware suggests that there were clear differences in ceramic production and taste between the two regions. Thus even within northern Fars, we are not witnessing the homogeneous adoption of specific sets of material behaviours during the different phases of the fourth millennium BC, but local populations may have made choices about the adoption of certain types of material culture and the way that such material was produced. Mamasani and similar regions must be considered on their own terms rather than being grouped together with the Kur River Basin as parts of the highland end of the highland/lowland culture-geographic dichotomy, and this has implications for the way we should conceptualise all regions that might be considered to be "interstitial" or "peripheral".

Although the range of bioarchaeological evidence is limited, it is potentially very interesting. Broad conclusions that incorporate discussion about seasonality and kill-off patterns in animal exploitation will only be possible when analysis of more sizeable faunal corpora has been completed. At this stage, there appears to be no dramatic change in the proportional exploitation of Caprini versus *Bos* between the *Bakun*, *Lapui*, and *Banesh* phases, suggesting that there was no major shift in subsistence strategies during the long *Chalcolithic* period in Mamasani. This evidence should certainly be taken into consideration in the further evolution and reconsideration of models proposing a progressive shift toward mobile pastoralism during the *Chalcolithic* (cf. Alizadeh 2006, 2010; Alden, this volume). The limited palaeoethnobotanical and anthracological evidence similarly shows little change. The data available will likewise benefit from analysis of a larger corpus.

Perhaps most importantly, the evidence for the fourth millennium BC in Mamasani is significant for our understanding of highland societies in Fars and their interaction with populations in the lowlands of the south-west and also with other regions in the highland of southern Iran in this period. During the *Lapui* period or early to mid-fourth millennium BC,

there is only limited evidence for interaction between the highland and lowland regions of south-west Iran. Although there are parallels between some *Lapui* and *Late Susiana* ceramic forms, Mamasani very much appears to be a part of the highland zone, but how similar the behaviour of its inhabitants was to that of the population in the Kur River Basin will only be demonstrated when sites with *Lapui* period occupation are excavated in the region where it was first identified.

Although Mamasani and the Kur River Basin are relatively close together spatially, and the inhabitants of the two regions make use of broadly similar material culture during the fourth millennium BC, it is important to emphasise that there are clear differences between the two regions in terms of settlement trajectories and the associated elements of socio-economic development. As Sumner (1986, 1988b, 2003) and Alden (1979, 1982, this volume) have emphasised, the fourth millennium BC in the Kur River Basin witnessed a series of transformations that resulted in the rise of a highland urban centre and significant evidence for the displacement and possibly also reduction of the settled population, whereas Mamasani has very clear evidence for a high degree of continuity in numbers of settlements and settlement size (McCall 2009; see above), and also the persistence of what appears to be region-specific material culture, particularly the ceramics (see above).

While the *Lapui* period ceramics recovered from survey and excavation in Mamasani are very similar to the *Lapui* survey material from the Kur River Basin (Sumner 1988a) and the material excavated from Tappeh Mehrali in northern Fars (Sardari, this volume), it has long been noted that they also show close affiliation to material from Tepe Yahya (*Lapui*-related ware; Beale 1986: 55–58, figs 4.16–4.17) and Tal-i Iblis (*Bard Sir* red-slipped ware; Beale 1986: 55–58, 85–86) in Kerman (see Petrie 2011, 2013), particularly in some of the open vessel forms and surface finishes. *Lapui*-related red ware vessel forms first appear during *Yahya Period VC* and *Iblis II* (mid-fifth millennium BC), which suggests that the associated technological traditions and innovations related to these wares may have appeared earlier in Kerman than in Fars, and if so, they may have had an eastern origin (Beale 1986: 87; Voigt and Dyson 1992: 145, 149; see also Petrie 2011, 2013). This dynamic is particularly interesting and potentially provocative, as the appearance of *Lapui*-related red ware at Tepe Yahya appears to be contemporaneous with the importation of *Middle Bakun* ceramics from the west (Kamilli and Lamberg-Karlovsky 1979; Beale 1986: 87). As noted above, there are also parallels between some of the *Lapui* period storage vessel types and associated wares seen in the *Late Susiana* period (e.g. Susa, Acropole I.27–25, Le Brun 1971: fig. 39; Chogha Mish, Delougaz and Kantor 1996: pl. 162: O-AA), and similarities also to *Late Bakun* vessels in Fars itself (Tal-e Bakun A, Langsdorff and McCown 1942: pl. 20), so although *Lapui* wares appear to be spatially limited to the highlands and are dominant in Fars during the early to mid-fourth millennium BC, they potentially reflect a range of lowland and highland influences, including important connections to the south-east of the plateau. Although it can be argued that the *Lapui* period developments in ceramic technology took place within a local context (see above; Blackman 1989), it is essential to understand the significance of the potential influences coming from multiple directions elsewhere in southern Iran. Such issues cannot be addressed in Mamasani alone and without doubt, the precise chronological relationships of all the relevant ceramic wares in use across southern Iran during the fourth millennium BC will only be understood after new excavations using high-level stratigraphic and chronological control are carried out. Without clarifying and expanding our knowledge of some of the baseline data, it is potentially unwise to speculate too broadly about the significance of particular cultural dynamics and patterns in the adoption and use of material culture.

During the *Transitional Lapui-Banesh* period in the mid-fourth millennium BC, a number of ceramic indicators provide clear evidence for lowland contact and possible influence in Mamasani, which is also seen at sites like Tal-e Kureh in the Kur River Basin (Alden 1979, 2003a). This lowland material culture appears to have been adopted and assimilated into local assemblages and presumably behaviour patterns. While the appearance of scattered examples of bevel-rim bowls at sites like Tol-e Spid may well be an indication of the spread of culinary practices (cf. Potts 2009), our understanding of the socio-economic and cultural contexts within which these practices were spreading is still poor.

With the *Banesh* period, we see clear evidence for contact and interaction between Mamasani and the Kur River Basin, between the Kur River Basin and places like Arisman (Helwing 2011), and also between these highland regions and the lowlands of Susiana but again, the significance of the dynamic is open to debate and the evidence from Mamasani provides tantalising pieces to the picture. There continue to be considerable differences of opinion with the interpretation of precisely what the *Proto-Elamite* phenomenon actually represented (e.g. Lamberg-Karlovsky 1978; Alden 1982; Potts 1999; Abdi 2003; Butterlin 2003; Helwing, this volume; Alden, this volume). Mamasani was undoubtedly part of the *oikoumene* that appears to have stretched across much of Iran during the *Proto-Elamite* period. There is clear evidence for the use of a range of distinctive ceramic vessel types and administrative technologies in Susiana and in many different parts of the Iranian Plateau, and there are some indications of trade between those regions (e.g. copper axes; cf.

Helwing, this volume). In many ways, however, it is now clear that as our awareness of regions and processes has gradually increased, we are left with more questions about the rationale and nature of the interaction between the populations in the lowland plains, piedmont, and uplands of the Iranian Plateau during the *Proto-Elamite* period (Petrie, this volume: Conclusion).

The evidence from Mamasani reaffirms that the highland regions were not linked as a homogeneous "cultural unit" during the late fourth millennium BC. In all instances, the material culture that is "shared" between regions, such as distinctive vessel forms like bevel-rim bowls and low trays, appears either alongside or nested within a local material culture assemblage. While there are clear similarities in the approaches to administrative technology in many different regions (e.g. Dahl *et al.*, this volume) where tablets are in evidence, they were being used to document local-scale transactions. There may have been culinary influence during this period also (cf. Potts 2009), but such influences were invariably negotiated in distinct ways in different regions. Thus, while it is possible that in the *Proto-Elamite* period we are seeing the long-range diffusion of a range of distinctive and easily recognisable elements of material culture (Abdi's 2003 "horizon"), it might be more appropriate to think of this nested material as a type of veneer that was of varying densities in different regions. The evidence from Mamasani provides an important new instance of a regional dynamic and challenges us to build models that explain this veneer and the various intra- and interregional dynamics that link people at various scales (see Petrie, this volume: Conclusion).

Note
1   The Mamasani Archaeological Project co-directors are D. T. Potts – University of Sydney/ISAW NYU; A. Asgari – Shiraz University; A. Lashkari – ICAR; A. Sardari – Tarbiat Modares University, Tehran; C.A. Petrie – University of Cambridge; and L. Weeks – University of Nottingham.

Bibliography

Abdi, K. 2003. "From Ecriture to Civilisation: Changing Paradigms of Proto-Elamite Archaeology", in Miller and Abdi 2003: 140–51.

Alden, J. R. 1979. *Regional Economic Organisation in Banesh Period Iran*, unpublished Ph.D. thesis, University of Michigan, Ann Arbor.

Alden, J. R. 1982. "Trade and Politics in Proto-Elamite Iran", *Current Anthropology* 23 (6): 613–40.

Alden, J. R. 2003a. "Appendix D – Excavations at Tal-e Kureh", in Sumner, W. M. (ed.), *Early Urban Life in the Land of Anshan: Excavations at Tal-e Malyan in the Highlands of Iran*, Malyan Excavation Reports, III, University of Pennsylvania Museum of Archaeology and Anthropology, Pennsylvania: 187–98, D181–D188.

Alden, J. R. 2003b. "Appendix E – Inventory of Banesh Sites", in Sumner, W. M. (ed.), *Early Urban Life in the Land of Anshan: Excavations at Tal-e Malyan in the Highlands of Iran*, Malyan Excavation Reports, III, University of Pennsylvania Museum of Archaeology and Anthropology, Pennsylvania: 199–204.

Alden, J. R. 2003c. "Sherd Size and the Banesh Phase Occupation in the ABC Operation at Malyan, Iran", in Miller and Abdi 2003: 109–20.

Algaze, G. 1993. *The Uruk World System – The Dynamics of Expansion of Early Mesopotamian Civilisation*, 1st edition, University of Chicago Press, Chicago.

Algaze, G. 2005. *The Uruk World System – The Dynamics of Expansion of Early Mesopotamian Civilisation*, 2nd revised edition, University of Chicago Press, Chicago.

Algaze, G. 2008. *Ancient Mesopotamia at the Dawn of Civilisation: The Evolution of an Urban Landscape*, University of Chicago Press, Chicago.

Alizadeh, A. 2003. *Excavations at the Prehistoric Mound of Chogha Bonut, Khuzestan, Iran: Seasons 1976/77, 1977/78, and 1996*, Oriental Institute Publications 120, Chicago.

Alizadeh, A. 2006. *The Origins of State Organizations in Prehistoric Highland Fars, Southern Iran*, Oriental Institute Publications 128, Chicago.

Alizadeh, A. 2008. *Chogha Mish II. The Development of a Prehistoric Regional Center in Lowland Susiana, Southwest Iran: Final Report on the Last Six Seasons of Excavations 1972–1978*, Oriental Institute Publications 130, Chicago.

Alizadeh, A. 2010. "The rise of the highland Elamite state in southwestern Iran 'Enclosed' or Enclosing Nomadism?", *Current Anthropology* 51 (3): 353–83.

Alizadeh, A. (ed.), in preparation. *Ancient Settlement Patterns and Cultures in the Ram Hormuz Plain, Southwestern Iran: Excavations at Tall-e Geser and Regional Survey in the Ram Hormuz Area*, Oriental Institute Publications 140, Chicago.

Amiet, P. 1979. "Archaeological discontinuity and ethnicity duality in Elam", *Antiquity* 53: 195–204.

Asgari Chaverdi, A., Khosrowzadeh, A., McCall, B., Petrie, C. A., Seyedin, M., Weeks, L. R., and Zeidi, M. 2010. "Archaeological evidence for Achaemenid settlement within the Mamasani Valleys, western Fars, Iran", in Curtis, J. and Simpson, St. J. (eds), *The World of Achaemenid Persia*, I.B. Tauris, London: 287–97.

Beale, T. W. 1986. "The Ceramics", in Beale, T. W. (ed.), *Excavations at Tepe Yahya, Iran 1967–1976: The Early Periods*, American School of Prehistoric Research Bulletin, Volume 38, Peabody Museum of Archaeology and Ethnology, Cambridge, MA: 39–89.

Berberian, M. 1995. "Master 'Blind' thrust faults hidden under the Zagros folds: active basement tectonics and surface morphotectonics", *Tectonophysics* 241: 193–224.

Berberian, M., Petrie, C. A., Potts, D. T., Asgari Chaverdi, A., Dusting, A., Ghāssemi, P., Noruzi, R., Sardari Zarchi, A. and Weeks, L. in press. "Archaeoseismicity of the mounds and monuments along the Kāzerun fault (western Zagros, SW Iranian Plateau) since the Chalcolithic period", *IA 49*.

Blackman, M. J. 1989. "Ceramic technology and problems of social evolution in southwest Iran", in Sayre, E. V., Vandiver, P., Druzik, J. and Stevenson, C. (eds), *Materials Issues in Art and Archaeology: Symposium held April 6–8, Reno, Nevada, U.S.A*, Materials Research Society Symposium Proceedings Volume 123, Materials Research Society, Pittsburgh: 103–08.

Butterlin, P. 2003. *Les temps proto-urbains de Mésopotamie – Contact et acculturation à l'époque d'Uruk au Moyen-Orient*, CNRS Éditions, Paris.

Caldwell, J. R. 1968. "Ghazir, Tell-I", *Reallexikon der Assyriologie und Vorderasiatishcen Archaologie*, Band III, F–G: 348–55.

Carter, E. and Stolper, M. W. 1984. *Elam: Surveys of Political History and Archaeology*, University of California Press, Berkeley.

Delougaz, P. and Kantor, H. J. 1996. *Chogha Mish Volume 1: The First Five Seasons of Excavations 1961–1971*, ed. Alizadeh, A., Oriental Institute Publications 101, Chicago.

Dittmann, R. 1984. *Eine Randebene des Zagros in der Frühzeit: Ergebnisse des Behbehan-Zuhreh Surveys*, Berliner Beiträge zum Vorderen Orient Band 3, Dietrich Riemer Verlag, Berlin.

Goulder, J. 2010. "Administrators' bread: an experiment–based re–assessment of the functional and cultural role of the Uruk bevel–rim bowl", *Antiquity* 84: 351–62.

Helwing, B. 2011. "Proto-Elamite pottery from areas A, C, D and E", in Vatandoust, A., Parzinger, H. and Helwing, B. (eds), *Early mining and metallurgy on the Central Iranian Plateau. Report on the first five years of research of the Joint Iranian-German Research Project*, Archäologie in Iran und Turan 9, Philip von Zabern, Mainz-am-Rhein: 194–251.

Kamilli, D. and Lamberg-Karlovsky, C. C. 1979. "Petrographic and electron microprobe analysis of ceramics from Tepe Yahya, Iran", *Archaeometry* 21 (1): 47–59.

Lamberg-Karlovsky, C. C. 1978. "The Proto-Elamites on the Iranian Plateau", *Antiquity* 52: 114–20.

Langsdorff, A. and McCown, D. E. 1942. *Tall-i-Bakun A: Season of 1932*, Oriental Institute Publications 59, University of Chicago Press, Chicago.

Le Brun, A. 1971. "Recherches Stratigraphiques à l'Acropole de Suse, 1969–1971", *CDAFI* 1: 163–217.

McCall, B. 2009. *The Mamasani Archaeological Survey: long term settlement patterns in the Mamasani district of the Zagros Mountains, Fars Province, Iran*, unpublished Ph.D. thesis, Department of Archaeology, University of Sydney.

Mashkour, M. 2009. "Faunal Remains from Tol-e Nurabad and Tol-e Spid", in Potts *et al.* 2009c: 135–46.

Mashkour, M. and Mohaseb, M. in preparation. "Animal bones from Trenches C and D at Tol-e Nnurabad", in *Mamasani Archaeological Project Stage 2*.

Mashkour, M. and Sheikhi, S. in preparation. "Animal bones from Early Lapui Tol-e Spid", in *Mamasani Archaeological Project Stage 2*.

Miller, N. F. 1991. "Paleoethnobotanical evidence for deforestation in ancient Iran: a case study of urban Malyan", *Journal of Ethnobiology* 5 (1): 1–19.

Miller, N. F. and Abdi, K. eds 2003. *Yeki bud, yeki nabud: Essays on the Archaeology of Iran in Honor of William M. Sumner*, 48, Cotsen Institute of Archaeology, University of California, Los Angeles.

Miller, N. F. and Kimiaie, M. 2006. "Some plant remains from the 2004 excavations of Tall-e Mushki, Tall-e Jari A and B, and Tall-e Bakun A and B", in Alizadeh, A. (ed.), *The Origins of State Organizations in Prehistoric Highland Fars, Southern Iran, Excavations at Tall-e Bakun*, OIP, Chicago: 107–18.

Miroschedji, P. de. 2003. "Susa and the Highlands: Major Trends in the History of Elamite Civilisation", in Miller and Abdi 2003: 17–38.

Marvdasht Plain (Fig. 11.2). The main valleys include Sedeh, Ujan, Bakan, Nemdan, and Eghlid. Some (e.g. the Ujan and Bakan valleys) are flooded during the rainy seasons. This makes them unfavourable for occupation by sedentary societies.

This region belongs administratively to the Eghlid district and, based on nomadic geography, it is referred to as *Sarhad* and has been known as Sarhad-e Char-Dungheh (four areas) in historical sources. According to Farsnameh-e Naseri, these four areas include the plains of Ujan, Khusro Shirin, Khunjasht, and Koshk-e Zard, governed by Qashqai chiefs who were living in the village of Asupas (Husseini and Hassan 1988: 124).

Recent archaeological research in northern Fars

In 2006, Tappeh Mehr Ali was to be submerged by the water rising from the Molla Sadra Dam. The main objective was to excavate the site in order to obtain critical information into the late prehistory of Fars (Figs 11.3–11.4). The site is located in the intermountain plain of Sedeh on the Balengan River, which is a main tributary of the Kur River. Tappeh Mehr Ali covers an area of *c.* 1.2 ha, and is preserved to a height of 12 m above the surrounding plain (Sardari and Rezaei 2007: 158). The site was not previously recorded by Sumner (1972) or Alizadeh (2003).

Tappeh Mehr Ali is much taller than most prehistoric mound sites in Fars, and to gain stratigraphic information two soundings were dug at Mehr Ali and other trenches were also excavated in the central, eastern, and western parts of the mound. Ten occupational phases were identified from one of the stratigraphic soundings, which reveal that the mound was first occupied during the *Early Bakun* period in the early fifth millennium BC and continued to be inhabited until the *Late Bakun* period (Hejebri Nobari *et al.* 2011). The uppermost 6 m of deposits are related to a *Lapui* period occupation, and consist of five separate phases in the stratigraphic sounding.

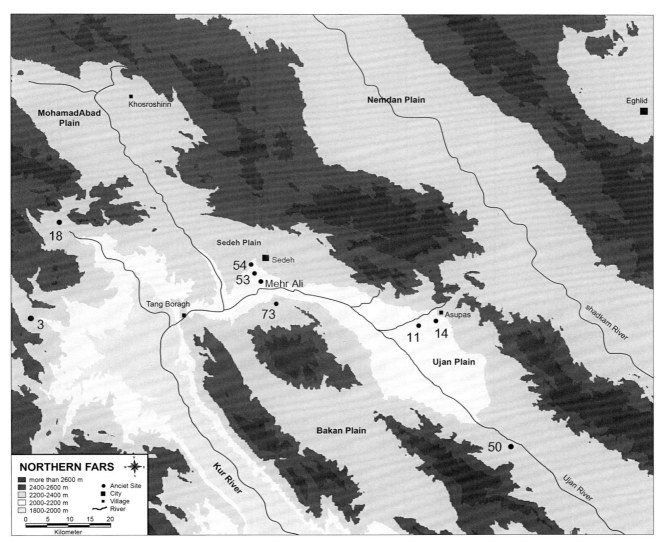

Figure 11.2. Northern Fars with settlement distribution of the Lapui *phase.*

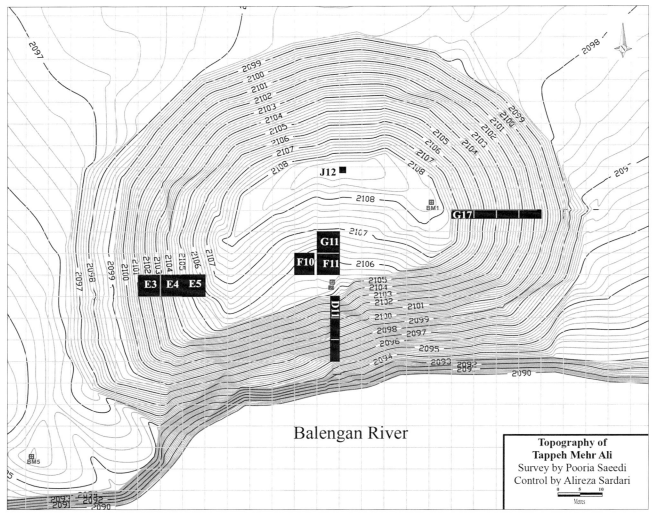

Figure 11.3. Topographic plan of Tappeh Mehr Ali.

Some historical surface remains belonging to the *Achaemenid* and *post-Achaemenid* periods were also identified.

Settlement distribution

In addition to the excavation, an archaeological survey was carried out around Tappeh Mehr Ali in 2006, and some of the surrounding intermountain plains were also surveyed in 2009 by the Eghlid Survey (ES) project. This investigation has the potential to provide a comprehensive impression of the relationship between landscape and settlement patterns, as well as an insight into the intercultural relationships between Tappeh Mehr Ali and other sites in various periods. The survey has so far been carried out in the Sedeh, Ujan, and Khusro Shirin valleys and has resulted in interesting evidence.

During the survey eight *Lapui* sites were identified, and were spatially distributed in the valleys and their flanks (Figs 11.2, 11.5). Based on the survey data, fourth-millennium BC occupation in Eghlid seems

to have been sparse, at least in terms of mounded settlement sites. Of these, none was more than 1 ha in size, although five sites have an elevation of 10 m above the surrounding plain. The Sedeh plain is predominantly an alluvial fan and alluviation by the two rivers has resulted in some extended tracts of land, which are suitable for agriculture. Three of the *Lapui* settlements (ES-54, ES-53, ES-1 [Mehr Ali]) were founded on the river terrace in a linear pattern and it appears that Tappeh Mehr Ali was the largest of these.

There are two other sites, one in the north of the Ujan Plain near the village of Asupas, and the other in the central parts of the Ujan Plain. While the broad and fertile Ujan Plain is suitable for agriculture, today it is flooded during the rainy seasons, which makes it impossible to settle in the flat, lower areas of the plain. Tappeh Asupas, one of the most important sites in the region, had previously been identified and was primarily known because of the discovery of a specific local type of *Lapui* fine ware named Asupas ware (Sumner 1972: 42).

Figure 11. 4. View of Tappeh Mehr Ali from the north.

Figure 11.5. Settlement distribution near Tappeh Mehr Ali.

Two other *Lapui* sites were located on the foothills of the north-western gorge of Tang-e Boragh. In general, four of these settlements were first occupied in the *Lapui* phase while others have continued from the *Late Bakun* phase. Six of the identified settlements date only to the *Late Bakun* period. The settlement numbers may indicate that there was an increase in settlement numbers from the *Bakun* to the *Lapui* period in this region. This pattern has also been observed in the Mamasani region (Zeidi *et al.* 2009: 151; Petrie *et al.* 2009b: 174; McCall 2009) and contrasts with a population decrease in the Kur River Basin (Sumner 1972, 1988, 1990)

Evidence from Tappeh Mehr Ali

Architecture

Deep trench J12 was excavated at the highest point of the mound, and the cultural deposits include 10 levels of occupational deposits from *Middle Bakun* to *Lapui* and historical periods. The *Lapui* occupation comprises six levels of 7 m thickness (Phases 8–3; Fig. 11.6). The remains of five architectural phases were exposed in these levels and make it clear that during the *Lapui* period, Tappeh Mehr Ali was continuously occupied in a pattern of successive structural phases.

Three architectural entities in different phases (Phases 5, 7, 8) all have a similar orientation and were potentially constructed on top of existing or at least partially visible building plans. It is notable that three of these architectural phases consist of mud-brick walls with stone foundations. Similar building techniques were also found in trench D11.

The earliest *Lapui* phase in J12 was dominated by a mud-brick wall (Phase 8), the foundation of which was built using rows of river stones. Some structural remains in the later phases of *Lapui* occupation show a significant gap between layers, pointing to the occurrence of a landslide or seismic disturbance during this period, which has also been observed at Tol-e Spid in Mamasani (Petrie *et al.* 2007, 2009a; Berberian *et al.*, in press). This event appears to have led to a change in the course of the Balengan River to the south of the site, the destruction of southern parts of the mound, and eventually the abandonment of the settlement.

On the central parts of the mound, there is an interesting complex of structures, which were built in several units of different sizes (Figs 11.7–11.8). In the middle of the complex, there is a central room unit larger than the others (locus 68), which is adjoined by six other room units. The mud-brick walls were plastered with gypsum and the floors had been reconstructed several times. Some buildings with various mud-brick walls were found and mud-brick arrangements coloured in brown, dark brown, and green could be taken as an indicator of some kind of wall decoration.

Radiocarbon dating

Five radiocarbon assays analysed at the Waikato laboratory in New Zealand provide an indication of the chronology of the *Lapui* phase occupation at Tappeh Mehr Ali (Fig. 11.9). Of these, three samples came from trench J12, and the earliest came from Locus 42 in Phase 8. The other two samples come from two other trenches and belong to the upper layers of the *Lapui* period.

The overall sequence of stratified radiocarbon dates from Tappeh Mehr Ali provides reliable dates for the beginning of the use of *Lapui* red wares in the north of the Kur River Basin. Phase 8 in trench J12 with abundant *Late Bakun* sherds and some *Lapui* pottery, suggests that it might be a transitional phase from the *Bakun* to the *Lapui* period. The absolute date places this phase within a time span of *c.* 3940–3520 cal BC, which is in agreement with Sumner's relative date for the beginning of the *Lapui* period in the Kur River Basin at around 3900 BC (Sumner 1988: 9). There are, however, radiocarbon dates from Tol-e Spid that indicate that the *Lapui* period in Mamasani may have begun in the late fifth millennium BC (Petrie *et al.*, this volume).

The latest radiocarbon date from trench J12 came from Phase 5 (loc. 25), and spans the period *c.* 3820–3630 BC. The overlying Phase 4 in trench J12 is contemporaneous with Phase 2 in trench F11, which is radiocarbon dated to *c.* 3710–3520 cal BC. The absolute dates suggest that the *Lapui* phase occupation at Mehr Ali continued until around 3500 BC.

Subsistence remains

During excavations at Tappeh Mehr Ali, two fire installations were found – similar to those from *Bakun* period sites such as Tappeh Rahmatabad (Bernbeck *et al.* 2005) and Tall-i Nokhodi (Goff 1963: 45) – which might be called a "complex oven". These two-storey ovens had a firing chamber that separated the fuel from the material to be heated. The smoke and heat did not directly enter the loading chambers of these ovens. The divider between the firing and loading chambers consisted of a flat pebble-covered surface. The function of the ovens most likely seems to have been the processing of agricultural products for easier storage, preservation, and cooking (Fig. 11.10).

Another possible use of the ovens was for the smoking of meat (Bernbeck *et al.* 2005: 98). Quantities of animal bones were discovered close to one of these ovens, potentially indicating that meat might have been prepared for consumption in such a manner.

The faunal assemblage from the site was analysed by Marjan Maskour and Shiva Shaikhi (Shaikhi 2008). The results have provided some evidence about the subsistence strategies of the *Lapui* period occupants at the site, and show that sheep and goat were the most prominent animals (80%) used.

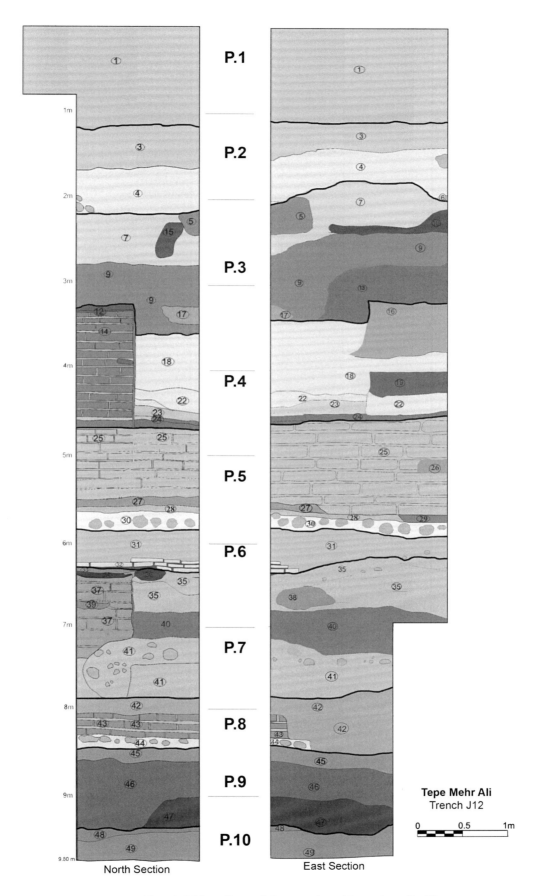

Figure 11.6. Tappeh Mehr Ali trench J12 stratigraphic sections; P= Phase.

Figure 11.7. Central trenches of Tappeh Mehr Ali.

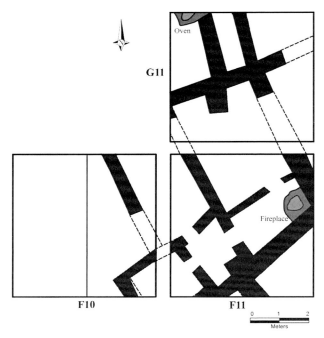

Figure 11.8. Plan of architectural remains of the Lapui occupational phase.

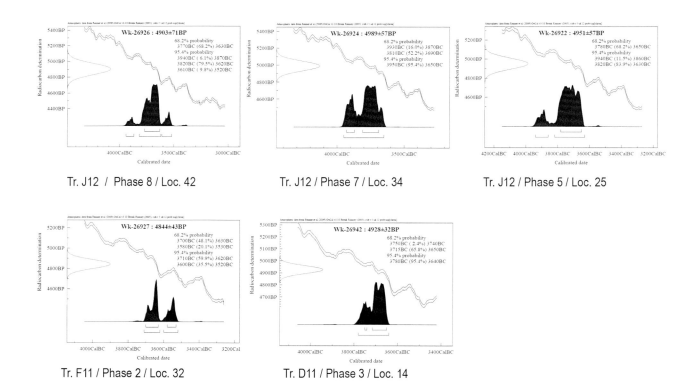

Figure 11.9. Radiocarbon dates from Tappeh Mehr Ali.

Figure 11.10. Two-storey oven in trench J12.

Plant remains, studied by Hengame Ilkhani, have led to interesting results about farming in the *Lapui* and earlier periods. The highest volume of plant remains from the site were broken pieces of almond and pistachio. Today the natural vegetation on the valley floor and slopes to the south-east around the Kur River Basin is pistachio/almond steppe-forest (Miller 1982). As a whole, the proportion of seeds includes 72% almond, 16% pistachio, with cereals only comprising 8% of the assemblage: 4% *triticum aestivum* (bread wheat) and 4% barley. These proportions are steady in all phases from *Middle Bakun* to the *Lapui* periods. Such animal bone and botanical assemblages indicate an agro-pastoral economy emphasising grazing over farming, which can be compared with analyses of the botanical materials from recent excavations at Tal-e Bakun A (Miller and Kimiaie 2006: 113).

Another method applied to interpret subsistence strategies is PIXE (Proton Induced X-ray Emission) analysis of the ancient seeds. In the case of Tappeh Mehr Ali, three samples were analysed by Zahra Mehrabipoor (2010) to measure the density of elements such as iron, calcium, zinc, and others in the seeds. These results show high volumes of calcium, iron, and magnesium in the soil and grains, but low amounts of copper, strontium, and barium. In general, grains

from the site that were consumed by the people of Mehr Ali were of low quality.

Consequently, there is no clear evidence for intensive agriculture from the earliest phases of occupation at the site. It should of course be borne in mind that Tappeh Mehr Ali is geographically placed on a major terrace close to the Balengan River and that some of the surroundings of permanent springs could have been used as suitable locations for agriculture.

Administrative technology

One of the most significant finds from the site was evidence for the use of administrative technologies such as seals and sealings, decorated with geometric designs (Fig. 11.11). A total of five stamp seals and 15 sealings were recovered from trenches in different locations at the settlement. Although they are stylistically akin to seals found at Tal-e Bakun A (Alizadeh 2006), they all belong to the *Lapui* period of occupation and have not been found from earlier phases in Tappeh Mehr Ali.

Two of the seals and six sealings were discovered from trench F11 in the central part of the site. All of the sealings are typical of portable containers such as bags or jars and were presumably meant to

Figure 11.11. Sealings from Tappeh Mehr Ali.

safeguard contents of containers in a warehouse or in preparation for shipping to another location. Sealing of movable objects implies at least some level of socio-economic institutionalisation (Alizadeh 1988, 2006: 87). The material culture from this settlement is the most important *Lapui* period administrative evidence yet discovered in northern Fars, and indicates that there may have been local exchange and regional trade between communities in central Fars.

Conclusion

The evidence presented here clearly does not allow a firm conclusion relating to the nature and evolution of early to mid-fourth-millennium BC settlements in northern Fars. It can be stated, however, that *Lapui* period societies were similar to earlier *Bakun* ones in some respects. Several similarities such as settlement patterns, management mechanisms, subsistence strategies, construction techniques, and other elements appear to indicate a degree of continuity in the socioeconomic system in the transition from the earlier to the later *Chalcolithic* of northern Fars. The

major change appears to have been in approaches to ceramic production, although it is important to note that Blackman (1989) has suggested that the changes in approaches to ceramic production that appear to have occurred between the *Bakun* and *Lapui* period assemblages may well have taken place as a result of local developments.

Although Sumner (1972, 1988) has suggested that there was a decline in settlement numbers in the Kur River Basin during the *Lapui* period, Alizadeh has reanalysed a subset of Sumner's pottery and concluded that the *Lapui* period may actually represent an increase in the settled population or at least an increase in mounded sites (Alizadeh 2006: 50).

The nature of the *Lapui* period subsistence systems in Fars is still open to question. Sumner (1988, 1994) has suggested that as the productivity of fields declined in *Late Bakun* and *Lapui* times, an increased emphasis was put on sheep and goat herding, mainly from sedentary communities located near natural pastures. Sumner believes this system developed in *Late Lapui* times, eventually leading to fully nomadic pastoralism in the subsequent *Banesh* period (Sumner 1986: 207). A large proportion of the faunal remains from Tappeh Mehr Ali indicates that there was a high reliance on pastoral economy in the *Lapui* period, but when one considers the huge accumulations of about 7 m of deposits, it seems likely that some people were still living in villages, producing massive amounts of waste, during the early to mid-fourth millennium BC in northern Fars.

The presence of 7 m of deposit relating to the *Lapui* phases at Tappeh Mehr Ali and also the continuity of occupation from the *Late Bakun* to the *Lapui* period are similar to the deep deposits identified at Tol-e Spid in the Mamasani region (Petrie *et al.* 2007: 307; this volume). The radiocarbon dates from Tappeh Mehr Ali, however, do not confirm Petrie *et al.*'s (2007; this volume) proposal that the *Lapui* period began in the (late) fifth millennium BC.

Northern Fars and the northern peripheries of the Kur River Basin are an attractive place for nomadic people today and may have been so since ancient times, witnessing the movement of large numbers of people semi-annually and/or seasonally. Tappeh Mehr Ali was a settlement occupied in both the *Bakun* and *Lapui* periods, which was situated in a region in northern Fars that appears to have had weakly developed agriculture and an important pastoral economy. This site therefore appears to be a perfect place for establishing whether the beginning of mobile pastoralist modes of life in Fars took place in the *Lapui* period (Sumner 1986) or in earlier phases (Alizadeh 2003, 2006). The evidence for substantial settled occupation at the site throughout the *Lapui* period, however, suggests that there is still much to learn about the subsistence system of this period.

Acknowledgements

The author would like to thank Dr Hassan Fazeli Nashli who has supported the rescue project of Tappeh Mehr Ali. My gratitude also goes to Reinhard Bernbeck, Kamyar Abdi, and Cameron Petrie for reading the preliminary draft of this paper and offering helpful suggestions. Note that any errors in the data and interpretations are entirely mine.

Bibliography

Alden, J. 2003. "Excavations at Tal-e Kureh", in Sumner, W. M. (ed.), *Early Urban Life in the Land of Anshan: Excavations at Tal-e Malyan in the Highlands of Iran*, Malyan Excavations Reports III, University Museum Monograph, 113, University of Pennsylvania Museum of Archaeology and Anthropology, Pennsylvania: D181–D188.

Alizadeh, A. 1988. "Socio–economic complexity in southwestern Iran during the fifth and fourth millennia BC: the evidence from Tall–e Bakun A", *Iran* 26: 17–34.

Alizadeh, A. 2003. "Some observations based on the nomadic character of Fars prehistoric cultural development", in Miller, N. F. and Abdi, K. (eds), *Yeki bud, yeki nabud: Essays on the Archaeology of Iran in Honor of William M. Sumner*, the Cotsen Institute of Archaeology, University of California, Los Angeles: 83–97.

Alizadeh, A. 2006. *The Origins of State Organizations in Prehistoric Highland Fars, Southern Iran, Excavations at Tall-e Bakun*, Oriental Institute Publications, Chicago.

Berberian, M., Petrie, C. A., Potts, D. T., Asgari Chaverdi, A., Dusting, A., Ghāssemi, P. Noruzi, R., Sardari Zarchi, A. and Weeks, L. in press. "Archaeoseismicity of the mounds and monuments along the Kāzerun fault (western Zagros, SW Iranian Plateau) since the Chalcolithic period", *Iranica Antiqua* 49.

Bernbeck, R., Fazeli, H. and Pollock, S. 2005. "Life in a fifth millennium B.C. village: excavations at Rahmatabad, Iran", *Near Eastern Archaeology* 68 (3): 94–105.

Blackman, M. J. 1989. "Ceramic technology and problems of social evolution in southwest Iran", in Sayre, E. V., Vandiver, P., Druzik, J. and Stevenson, C. (eds), *Materials Issues in Art and Archaeology: Symposium held April 6–8, Reno, Nevada, U.S.A.*, Materials Research Society Symposium Proceedings, vol. 123, Pittsburgh: 103–08.

Caldwell, J. R. 1968. "Ghazir, Tell-I", *Reallexikon der Assyriologie und Vorderasiatishcen Archaologie Band III, F–G*: 348–55.

Garrod, O. 1946. "The nomadic tribes of Persia today", *Journal of the Royal Central Asiatic Society* 33: 32–46.

Goff, C. 1963. "Excavations at Tall-i Nokhodi", *Iran* 1: 43–70.

Husseini, F. and Hassan, H. M. 1988. *History of Farsname Naseri*, edited by M. Rastegar Fassaei, Amir Kabir Publishing, Tehran (in Persian).

Langsdorff, A. and McCown, D. E. 1942. *Tall-i-Bakun A: Season of 1932*, Oriental Institute Publications, LIX, University of Chicago Press, Chicago.

McCall, B. 2009. *The Mamasani Archaeological Survey: long term settlement patterns in the Mamasani district of the Zagros Mountains, Fars Province, Iran*, unpublished PhD thesis, Department of Archaeology, University of Sydney.

Mehrabipoor, Z. 2010. *Herbivorous and Nutrition pattern in the life of ancient people of Iran*, unpublished M.A. thesis, Faculty of Humanities, Tarbiat Modares University (in Persian).

Miller, N. F. 1982. *Economy and Environment of Malyan, a Third Millennium B.C. Urban Center in Southern Iran*, Ph.D. dissertation, Department of Anthropology, University of Michigan, University Microfilms, Ann Arbor.

Miller, N. F. and Kimiaie, M. 2006. "Some plant remains from the 2004 excavations of Tall-e Mushki, Tall-e Jari A and B, and Tall-e Bakun A and B", in Alizadeh, A. (ed.), *The Origins of State Organizations in Prehistoric Highland Fars, Southern Iran, Excavations at Tall-e Bakun*, OIP, Chicago: 107–18.

Hejebri Nobari, A., Sardari, A., Fazeli Nashli, H., KhatibShahidi, H. and Rezaei, A. 2011. "Northern Fars during the Bakun period: archaeological evidence from the Eghlid District", *AMIT* 43: 1–22.

Petrie, C. A., Sardari Zarchi, A. and Javanmardzadeh, A. 2007. "Developing societies and economies in 4th millennium B.C. Fars: Further Excavations at Tol-e Spid", *Iran* 45: 301–09.

Petrie, C. A., Asgari Chaverdi, A. and Seyedin, M. 2009a. "Excavations at Tol-e Spid", in Potts *et al*. 2009: 89–134.

Petrie, C. A., Weeks, L. R., Potts, D. T. and Roustaei, K. 2009b. "Perspectives on the Cultural Sequence of Mamasani", in Potts *et al*. 2009: 157–84.

Potts, D. T., Roustaei, K., Alamdari, K., Alizadeh, K., Asgari Chaverdi, A., Khosrowzadeh, A., McCall, B., Niakan, L., Petrie, C. A., Seyedin, M., Weeks, L. R., and Zaidi, M. 2006. "Eight thousand years of history in Fars Province, Iran", *Near Eastern Archaeology* 68/3: 84–92.

Potts, D. T., Roustaei K., Petrie, C. A. and Weeks, L. R. eds 2009. *The Mamasani Archaeological Project Stage One: A report on the first two seasons of the ICAR – University of Sydney Joint Expedition to the Mamasani District, Fars Province, Iran*, BAR International Series 2044, Archaeopress, Oxford.

Sardari, A. and Rezaei, A. 2007. "Report of the Rescue-Archaeological Investigations on the Tappeh Mehr Ali, Eghlid Fars", in *Archaeological Reports*(7): the 9th Annual Symposium on Iranian Archaeology, Iranian Center for Archaeological Research, Tehran, vol. 2: 155–72 (in Persian).

Shaikhi, S. 2008. *Archaeozoological study of the Chalcolithic site of Tepe Mehr Ali Fars, Iran*, unpublished M.A. thesis, Faculty of Literature and Humanities, Tehran University (in Persian).

Sumner, W. M. 1972. *Cultural Development in the Kur River Basin, Iran: an archaeological analysis of settlement patterns*, unpublished Ph.D. thesis, University of Pennsylvania.

Sumner, W. M. 1986. "Proto-Elamite Civilization in Fars", in Finkbeiner, U. and Rolling, W. (eds), *Gamdat Nasr: Period of Regional Style?*, Beihefte Zom Tubinger Atlas des Vorderem Orients 62, Ludwig Reichert, Wiesbaden: 199–211.

Sumner, W. M. 1988. "Prelude to proto-Elamite Anshan: the Lapui Phase", *IA* 23: 23–44.

Sumner, W. M. 1990. "Full-Coverage Regional Archaeological Survey in the Near East: An Example from Iran", in Fish, S. K. and Kowalewski, S. A. (eds), *The Archaeology of Regions: A case for Full-Coverage Survey*, Smithsonian Series in Archaeological Inquiry, Smithsonian Institution Press, Washington DC: 87–115.

Sumner, W. M. 1994. The Evolution of Tribal Society in the Southern Zagros Mountains, Iran, in Stein, G. and Rothman, M. S. (eds), *Chiefdoms and Early States in the Near East: the Organizational Dynamics of Complexity*, 18, Prehistory Press, Monographs in World Archaeology, Madison: 47–65.

Sumner, W. M. 2003. *Early Urban Life in the Land of Anshan: Excavations at Tal-e Malyan in the Highlands of Iran*, Malyan Excavations Reports III, University Museum Monograph, 113, University of Pennsylvania Museum of Archaeology and Anthropology, Pennsylvania.

Voigt, M. and Dyson Jr., R. H. 1992. Chronology of Iran, ca. 8000–2000 B.C., in Ehrich, R. W. (ed.), *Chronologies of Old World Archaeology*, vols. I & II, Chicago University Press, Chicago: 122–78; 125–53.

Weeks, L. R., Alizadeh, K., Niakan, L., Alamdari, K., Khosrowzadeh, A. and Zeidi, M. 2009. "Excavations at Tol-e Nurabad", in Potts *et al.* 2009: 31–99.

Zeidi, M. 2008. "Settlement pattern and population fluctuations of prehistoric to Islamic period in the Upper Kur River Basin (Based on Analyses of Archaeological Material from the 1995 Survey)", *Iranian Journal of Archaeology and History*, vol. 21, no. 2, vol. 22, no. 1: 5–31 (in Persian).

Zeidi, M., McCall, B. and Khosrowzadeh, A. 2009. "Survey of the Dasht-e Rostam-e Yek and Dasht-e Rostam-e Do", in Potts *et al.* 2009: 147–68.

12. THE KUR RIVER BASIN IN THE *PROTO-ELAMITE* ERA – SURFACE SURVEY, SETTLEMENT PATTERNS, AND THE APPEARANCE OF FULL-TIME TRANSHUMANT PASTORAL NOMADISM

John R. Alden

Introduction

At the conference on the *Jemdet Nasr* period held at Tübingen in November 1983, William Sumner presented a paper summarising his views on the economic and political nature of *Proto-Elamite* civilisation in the Kur River Basin of Fars, Iran (Sumner 1986). This paper was filled with intriguing and generally persuasive ideas about the development and organisation of that society, and it reflected Sumner's extensive knowledge of the region developed through years of regional survey and his direction of a five-season excavation programme at the largest *Proto-Elamite* settlement in Iran, Tal-e Malyan.

Looking at settlement data from the Kur River Basin (hereafter KRB), Sumner observed a sustained decline in settlement area within that region from early in the fourth millennium BC (the end of the *Bakun* period) to late in the third millennium BC (the beginning of the *Kaftari* period). He suggested that this pattern was a result of a steady decline in the productivity of the regional agricultural system caused primarily by soil salination. He proposed, however, that the observed decline in archaeological settlement did not necessarily reflect a concomitant decline in regional population. Instead, he argued, this reduction was a result of a gradual transformation of a *Bakun*-era subsistence economy based on irrigation agriculture to a *Banesh* period economy based on pastoral nomadism. In addition, he argued that the ascent of those nomadic groups to political and economic dominance during the *Proto-Elamite* phase resulted in a new and distinctly highland form of political organisation – "a tribal polity...including both sedentary and nomadic elements...sometimes fragmented and sometimes united, under the leadership of tribal khans . . ." (Sumner 1986: 209).

Sumner writes with unusual flair for an academic. Describing the decline of the regional irrigation system during the *Lapui* period, for example, he says, "As time passed it became difficult to muster the necessary communal labor for the annual dam construction and canal cleaning. Eventually the system collapsed; one year the dam was not built, water did not flow to the fields, and the former breadbasket of the valley was virtually deserted" (Sumner 1986: 207). A few paragraphs later, discussing the advent of a tribal-based political organisation, he writes, "The khans settled, each in his village headquarters, for the serious business of dynastic intrigue and political maneuvering." In many ways, his account is so informal that it sometimes reads like a "just-so story".[1]

I do not intend that description as a criticism. Sumner was proposing a model in a way that gave his ideas an immediacy that a more academic presentation would have obscured. But he also wrote informally, I suspect, because he understood that his interpretations were based on impressionistic observation rather than formal analyses of detailed archaeological data. On rereading his paper, I am struck by the limitations of the data available to Sumner when he presented these ideas, and the difficulties those limitations imposed on any attempt to confirm, reject, or refine his hypotheses.

Because there were at the time almost no excavated collections of well-stratified and thoroughly reported material he could use to date his surface collections, Sumner was forced to do his initial analyses using a ceramic typology based largely on surface surveys and a ceramic chronology that divided roughly 5000 years of occupation into a mere seven phases. His reluctance to define subdivisions within these long phases was, he noted in his dissertation, "based entirely on the conviction that meaningful refinements in typology and chronology must be based on evidence from stratified context; such evidence is not available in satisfactory detail for the Kur River sequence" (Sumner 1972: 32).

By 1983 when Sumner presented his Tübingen paper, the situation, at least with regard to the *Banesh* period, had improved. Surface collections from all known *Banesh* occupations in the KRB had been used to divide, at least tentatively, the 600–800-year-long *Banesh* period into five shorter phases (Alden 1979: 47–62). Excavations at Tal-e Malyan – the ancient city of Anshan that during the second millennium BC was one of the twin capitals of ancient Elam – had yielded two large exposures of stratified *Middle Banesh* material from the ABC (Sumner 2003) and TUV (Nicholas 1990) areas and one smaller area of stratified material from the *Late Banesh* phase along the inside of the city wall in grid square BY8 (Sumner 1985). Furthermore, a small sounding at the *Banesh* type site, Tal-e Kureh, provided a stratified sample of material spanning the end of the *Lapui* to the earliest part of the *Banesh* periods (Alden 2003: 187–98). An even smaller sounding in Tal-e Malyan square H5, beneath a sequence of *Kaftari* buildings, yielded a handful of sherds indicating there might have been some occupation at the site in the centuries between the end of the *Banesh* and the beginning of the *Kaftari* periods (Miller and Sumner 2004).

These data, however, were limited in important ways. None of the three large exposures of *Banesh* remains at Tal-e Malyan appeared to represent more than a century or so of occupation. The more limited Tal-e Kureh and H5 soundings did not yield enough pottery to define detailed typological sequences for the eras they had sampled. Only the ABC and TUV sequences overlapped chronologically and in 1983, only the materials from the TUV excavation (Nicholas 1980) and the Tal-e Kureh test (Alden n.d.) had been analysed. In short, there were still major chronological gaps in the excavated *Banesh* ceramic sequence. No *Lapui* period site had been excavated, only one *Banesh* occupation outside Tal-e Malyan had been tested, and there was still a chronological gap of 400–500 years in the KRB settlement record between the end of the *Late Banesh* and the beginning of the *Kaftari*. In addition, a considerable portion of Sumner's KRB survey collections, all of Alden's *Banesh* survey materials, and almost all the ceramics from the Tal-e Malyan excavations, were stored in Iran where they were not accessible for study. Without being able to reference the existing material or revisit the known sites, there was little Sumner could have done systematically to re-evaluate the surface survey data from *Banesh* period sites in the KRB.

While giving full weight to the difficulties Sumner faced, there are two significant omissions in his 1986 paper. First, he does not present phase-by-phase maps of the *Banesh* period settlement system nor explain how he assigned *Banesh* period occupations to specific phases. Thus Sumner's paper describes gross population trends for the KRB, but it does not examine the distribution of that population or look at how that distribution changed through time. Second, the paper does not discuss how existing or potentially available archaeological data might be mustered to support or contradict the ideas it presents about subsistence economy and political organisation.

With regard to the first point, I believe Sumner was unwilling to use the phase-by-phase settlement data from my dissertation for two reasons. First, my procedures for assigning occupational phases to particular sites were not based on the kind of "evidence from stratified context" that he had called for in 1972. Instead, I had used typological associations observed in surface collections and patterns observed in the unpublished material from the Tal-e Malyan excavations to create a rough seriation of *Banesh* ceramics and identify several apparent phase markers found in the surface collections (Alden 1979: 47–59). Second, I think Sumner's respect for academic priorities made him reluctant to publish material that I might eventually want to publish myself. As for not presenting a series of specific consequences that might be expected if his ideas were correct, I believe Sumner intended his Tübingen paper as a first look at a topic he hoped to explore more thoroughly rather than a final word on the subject. In an effort to add flesh to the bones of Sumner's ground-breaking argument, this paper utilises the data from my Ph.D. dissertation and 30 years of hindsight to present a phase-by-phase analysis of *Banesh* period settlement patterns in the KRB and examine the implications of those patterns for various reconstructions of regional economic and political organisation.[2]

Settlement survey in the Kur River Basin

Banesh ceramics were originally identified in the KRB during surface survey, and surface collections are the only data available from all but two of the sites where *Banesh* ceramics have been found. The constraints on using surface collection data to evaluate the extent and chronology of prehistoric settlement are widely recognised, and those who have worked in the KRB are aware of the limitations of the data collected during our various regional surveys. Unfortunately, the irrigable portions of the KRB are presently farmed virtually edge-to-edge and broad swathes of talus slope along the sides of the valley have been cut away to increase the area of tillable land or to remove soil and gravel for road-building or construction. This has the potential to be particularly devastating, as my survey showed that there were numerous sites located along some areas of these talus slopes. The extensive site destruction in this region since Sumner's 1967–1969 survey and the Alden/Jacobs resurveys in 1976 most likely mean that we will never be able to acquire better settlement pattern data from this region. If we wish to examine phase-by-phase changes in settlement types and locations during the *Banesh* period in the KRB, we are forced to use the old survey data.

Sumner carried out an extensive exploratory survey of the KRB during his dissertation research. In 100 days of field survey he visited as many visible mounds in the region as he could reach by "driving down every track as far as possible and walking to every mound sighted," locating a total of 686 sites and identifying 304 sites with pre-Partho-Sasanian occupations (Sumner 1972: 20 and Appendix A). Excluding Tal-e Malyan and Persepolis, he visited 267 pre-Partho-Sasanian sites covering 358 ha, in the main valley of the KRB. He collected purposive samples of sherds from each site, with the aim of acquiring examples of every ware observed, and used these collections to assign periods of occupation to the sites. Although Sumner did not identify the *Banesh* ceramic complex until late in his survey, he subsequently revisited a number of his previously surveyed sites and ultimately found *Banesh* ceramics on 26 sites (see comment in Petrie *et al.* 2009: 195–6 [note 34]). He also noted that, "Most of these [*Banesh*] sites yielded very small sherd collections, often with no more than three or four diagnostic sherds" (Sumner 1972: 42).

Less than a decade later, I carried out an intensive resurvey of *Banesh* sites in the main valley of the KRB, with the aim of breaking the period into sub-phases and using the data on phase-by-phase occupation to reconstruct changing patterns of regional economic organisation (Alden 1979: 34–46). As part of this project, every site where Sumner had identified *Banesh* ceramics was revisited and systematic surface collections were made when later deposits did not overlie *Banesh* remains.

In addition to resurveying sites that yielded *Banesh* material, the Alden survey attempted to evaluate the degree to which Sumner had, a) discovered *Banesh* ceramics on sites where the major occupation was from other periods; and b) discovered sites, particularly un-mounded sites, in various environments within the KRB. This was done by, 1) revisiting and recollecting previously identified sites to look for evidence of minor occupations, including *Banesh* occupations, that might have been missed; and 2) walking or

driving slowly on a motorcycle across selected areas of the valley to see how many previously unidentified sites could be located. The results of these evaluative surveys (reported in Alden 1979: 36–42 and summarised in Petrie *et al.* 2009: 195–96 [note 34]) indicate that the KRB survey data must be interpreted with considerable caution. Given the importance of these data for this paper, it is worth reviewing how the various surveys were conducted, reconsidering how those data are most suitably evaluated, and reformulating the data in what may be more informative ways.

With regard to assessing the success of purposive sampling in identifying secondary occupations on sites, the numbers reported in Alden (1979: 36–37) summarise only the results of my own surveys. Data presented in Alden (1979: table 19 and Appendix B), however, which include site descriptions as well as data from several systematic surveys of later *Qaleh* period sites carried out by Linda Jacobs for her own dissertation research, are more relevant to the question of how many *Banesh* occupations were missed on sites visited during the various KRB surveys. It should be noted that Jacobs and I worked together mapping and collecting many of the sites for our separate dissertation projects. We did part of this work during the 1976 excavation season at Tal-e Malyan, and during that time we talked regularly with Sumner about site locations and material from our surface collections. In addition, during 1976–77 I was able to examine many of Sumner's original survey collections stored in Shiraz, which resulted in several revisions of Sumner's original data (cf. sites 8J8, 9G10, and 9J14 in Alden 1979: Appendix B). This systematic cooperation assuredly helped minimise errors in identifying sites and classifying sherds.

There were important differences between how Sumner made his survey collections and how sites were collected in the Alden and Jacobs surveys. Sumner's samples were all purposive, meaning that he walked across a site and picked up sherds that either distinguished one of his recognised periods or that were distinctive in character but which he did not recognise. The Alden and Jacobs surveys included some purposive samples, but on sites where Sumner had identified major *Banesh* or *Qaleh* occupations, we collected complete surface pick-ups from a stratified random sample of 10 × 10 m squares (Alden 1979: 42–45; Jacobs 1980: 128–31).

Alden and Jacobs together revisited 48 sites Sumner had surveyed – 17 where he had found *Banesh* ceramics and 31 where he had not. Of those 48 sites, there were four (9J4, 9J5, 9J11, and 11K2) where I was reasonably concerned that I may not have visited the same site that Sumner surveyed, and seven (7G5, 8G1, 8G2, 8G5, 8G12, 8G33, and 8G38) that had been severely damaged during the time between Sumner's initial visit and the 1976 resurvey. Subtracting those problematic sites from the resurvey inventory leaves a total of 37 sites that were identified by Sumner and resurveyed in 1976 – a sample of just over 12% of the pre-Partho-Sasanian sites in Sumner's 1972 gazetteer.

Sumner's Appendix A lists occupations as either "major" – where the pottery count for a period exceeds that of other phases "by a large amount" (Sumner 1972: 191) – or "minor". A site could be assigned more than one major period of occupation if its surface assemblage was dominated by roughly equal proportions of pottery from two or more periods, and he was willing to assign a minor occupation on the basis of a single sherd (Sumner 2005). Of the 37 sites that were surveyed more than once, the data from Sumner's survey and the Alden/Jacobs resurveys disagreed on only two of the principal periods of occupation (sites 8F9 and 9G13) – a 5% rate of disagreement. Where we followed Sumner's practice of assigning minor occupations on the basis of a single sherd, however, we failed to identify 18 minor occupations that Sumner had found, identified 24 minor occupations that Sumner had not noted, and agreed on 59 occupations (40 major and 19 minor). Finally, seven of the 24 minor occupations not noted by Sumner were identified from systematic surface collections rather than through purposive sampling.

Since the Sumner and subsequent surveys agreed 95% of the time on the principal occupations of surveyed sites, we can be reasonably confident that if a site with a major *Banesh* occupation was visited, that occupation was recognised. For minor occupations, the level of agreement was much lower. Of a total of 61 minor or secondary occupations from various periods identified on the 37 sites that were surveyed twice, the initial Sumner survey identified 37 (61%) and the resurveys, using both purposive and systematic collections, identified 43 (70%). In short, each single survey failed to identify roughly a third of the known minor occupations on sites in the KRB. Although there are many ways to juggle these numbers, it seems prudent to conclude that the initial

and subsequent surveys of the KRB, taken together, probably identified no more than two-thirds to three-quarters of the minor *Banesh* occupations on known sites in the valley.

To investigate Sumner's rates of site discovery, I resurveyed five areas of the KRB either by walking or careful examination from a slow-moving motorcycle. Three of these areas (two along talus slopes at the valley margins and one in an area where Sumner had found several low mounds with *Banesh* occupations) were selected to examine areas where it seemed likely that *Banesh* occupations had been missed in the initial survey, while the other two were chosen arbitrarily from within the western sector of the KRB where the density of prehistoric settlement was greatest. The results of these surveys are presented in Table 12.1.

There are at least five approaches to interpreting these data. First, the numbers and hectares of new pre-Partho-Sasanian occupations found per square kilometre in the systematic resurveys can be applied to the entire area of Sumner's survey. Second, the resurvey results can be applied to the habitable area of the KRB, i.e. the portion of the valley floor that is neither heavily salinated nor marshy. Third, the ratios of newly discovered to previously discovered occupations in the resurveyed areas can be used to estimate the number and area of undiscovered sites in the area surveyed by Sumner. Fourth, we can apply the rates of site discovery from the resurveys to the western half of the KRB alone, since this was the area that the resurveys actually sampled. Finally, we can divide the resurvey results into two parts, one relating to the rate of discovery of sites on talus slopes around the edges of the KRB and the second involving the rate of site discovery in arable areas of the valley floor, and apply the ratios of site discovery in the resurveys to the two types of habitable area in the western KRB.

My resurveys covered 20.1 km² of arable land and talus slope in the western half of the KRB. Sumner's surveys had identified seven sites totalling 16.9 ha of occupation in that area, and my surveys added 25 new

Table 12.1. Results of KRB systematic site surveys.

	Motorcycle survey	Walking survey	Total
Arbitrary transect	6.6 km² 2 old sites, 2.5 ha 2 new sites, 2.2 ha valley floor survey	2.8 km² 1 old site, 3.6 ha 3 new sites, 0.3 ha (3 new sites are talus) valley and talus survey	9.4 km² 3 old sites, 6.1 ha 5 new sites, 2.5 ha
Selected transect	3.5 km² 2 old sites, 3.4 ha 7 new sites, 4.0 ha valley and talus survey	7.2 km² 2 old sites, 7.4 ha 13 new sites, 3.3 ha (all sites are talus) talus slope survey	10.7 km² 4 old sites, 10.8 ha 20 new sites, 7.3 ha
Total	10.1 km² 4 old sites, 5.9 ha 9 new sites, 6.2 ha	10.0 km² 3 old sites, 11.0 ha 16 new sites, 3.6 ha	20.1 km² 7 old sites, 16.9 ha 25 new sites, 9.8 ha

sites and 9.8 ha of occupied area to the previous totals. I want to emphasise that my surveys focused on areas where Sumner believed he was likely to have missed sites; that most of the sites the resurvey located were either un-mounded or had very low mounds; and that my standards for identifying a scatter of sherds as a "site" were less rigorous than Sumner's. Nevertheless, it is clear that the "driving to every visible mound" survey technique used by Sumner failed to identify a large number of un-mounded sites marked by visible surface sherd scatters.

If the data from Table 12.1 are applied to the full area of the KRB (roughly 2200 km²), then Sumner's survey would appear to have missed around 2740 sites and 1070 ha of occupation from all pre-Partho-Sasanian periods combined. If we assume that there are no sites in the 27% of the KRB that is either marshy or heavily salinated, the initial survey would have missed about 2000 sites and 780 ha of occupation, again from all periods. The third method of estimation, which avoids the problem of using survey data that were not derived from a random sample of the valley surface, applies the ratios of newly discovered to previously discovered site numbers and areas. Sumner (1972: Appendix A) discovered 269 pre-Partho-Sasanian sites covering 548 ha in the main valley of the KRB. With Tal-e Malyan (140 ha) and Persepolis (50 ha) excluded from those totals, his survey identified 267 sites and 358 ha of occupation in that region. If there are 25 new sites and 9.8 ha of new occupation for every seven old sites and 16.9 ha of occupation, then there are about 950 undiscovered sites from all periods, covering a total of 208 ha, in the main valley of the KRB.

Because the systematic resurveys only sampled areas in the western half of the KRB, and because they were divided into talus slope and valley floor resurveys, the fourth approach would be to apply the results of the resurveys only to the areas they were actually sampled – the talus slopes and arable land on the valley floors in the western half of Sumner's survey area. That area, which is roughly the portion of the KRB west of the road from Persepolis through Marv Dasht City and towards Shiraz, includes about 1300 km² of valley floor, 1100 km² of arable land, and 350 linear km of talus slope. Sumner's 1972 gazetteer indicates that, excluding Tal-e Malyan and Persepolis, he found 218 sites covering 275.8 ha in this region. The systematic surveys covered 20.1 km² and roughly 19 linear km of talus slope, and discovered 16 new talus slope sites (3.6 total ha) and nine new valley floor sites (6.2 total ha). If the discovery rates of new sites in the resurveys are applied to the talus slopes and arable area of the valley floor in the western half of the KRB, there would be about 295 talus slope sites (66 ha total area) and 490 sites on the valley floor (340 ha total area) that were not discovered in the initial survey of the western half of the KRB. Finally, if the ratios of newly discovered

to previously discovered talus slope (16:2) and valley floor sites (9:5) are applied to the survey data from the western half of the KRB as estimated by Sumner (1972: figs 18–21), which show approximately 40 talus slope and 178 valley floor sites, then there would be 320 additional talus slope and 320 additional valley floor sites in the western half of the KRB.

To summarise, using various criteria, the Sumner survey may have missed:

ESTIMATE 1: 2740 sites and 1070 ha of occupied area.
ESTIMATE 2: 2000 sites and 780 ha of occupied area.
ESTIMATE 3: 950 sites and 208 ha of occupied area.
ESTIMATE 4: 785 sites and 406 ha from the western half of the KRB.
ESTIMATE 5: 640 sites, 320 talus and 320 valley floor, from the western half of the KRB.

Frankly, I believe that even the most conservative of these procedures overestimates both the number of undiscovered sites and area of unidentified archaeological occupation in the KRB. In my survey I was notably more willing than Sumner to define an occupation on the basis of a very light sherd scatter, and three of the five areas I selected for resurvey were places where I expected, on the basis of conversations with Sumner and the known pattern of *Banesh* occupation, to find a high proportion of undiscovered sites. Consequently, I would not expect the numbers of new sites and occupations identified in my systematic resurveys to be replicated across either the entirety of the KRB or in the sub-regions listed above. Nonetheless, even if there are less than half as many undiscovered sites as the most conservative estimate presented here predicts, there are significant numbers of sites in the KRB that were not identified in the various surveys of the region. The number of unidentified sites could easily be as high as 100% (meaning that the various surveys together have only identified half of the archaeological settlements in the KRB survey region), and if the areas of Persepolis and Tal-e Malyan are included in the total area of pre-Partho-Sasanian occupation in the KRB, the total occupied area in the region could be 50% greater than the area presently identified. In addition, at least a quarter of the minor occupations on known KRB sites have probably not been identified.

The available survey data for the region could thus be missing as many as half of the archaeological occupations in the KRB that were potentially identifiable in 1976. Additional survey would of course be worthwhile but, as noted above, site destruction in the region has been so extensive since the 1970s that the data acquired in the early surveys can never be replicated. Keeping the limitations of these data in mind, I will examine the *Banesh* period settlement data in an effort to elucidate patterns of settlement distribution during the late fourth and early third millennia BC.

Banesh period settlement in the KRB

During the last decade, Sumner collated and combined all available settlement pattern data from the KRB into a single database, the *Kur River Basin Site Gazetteer* (Sumner n.d.). The information in the gazetteer supersedes Sumner's previously published data (Sumner 2003: table 22) and he graciously allowed me to use the information from that gazetteer for this paper. There are several minor differences, however, between the *KRB Gazetteer* data and the data presented in Table 12.2. First, I am reporting my own estimates, as presented in Figures 12.2 and 12.3, for the phase-by-phase occupation at Tal-e Malyan, rather than using the 40 ha listed by Sumner. Second, I have listed 8G35 and 8G38 separately, while Sumner combines them. Table 12.2 includes three sites that yielded no distinctively *Banesh* ceramics but that did have *Asupas* ware, a variety of *Lapui* fine ware that dates to the *Lapui-Banesh Transitional* (Alden 2003: 196), and it includes two sites where *Banesh* occupations were identified by Mohammad Atai' in his recent survey in the KRB (Atai', personal communication). Table 12.2 does not include 18 sites that Sumner designated

as having "Doubtful" *Banesh* occupations or three sites with "Special" occupations. In Sumner's terms, "Doubtful" means the component may be present, but the typological status of the ceramics is problematic; "Special" designates the presence of sherds that may be from a burial or other non-residential use of a site (Sumner n.d.: Key to Inventory Codes). The "Doubtful" and "Special" occupations are, however, shown on Figure 12.1 because they indicate the maximum area in which *Banesh* or possible *Banesh* occupation occurs in the KRB. Phase-by-phase maps of *Banesh* settlement are shown in Figures 12.5–12.8.

Determining phase-by-phase occupations of *Banesh* period sites

In separate attempts to establish phase-by-phase patterns of *Banesh* occupations in the KRB, Sumner (1986: 199; 2003: Appendix E) and I (Alden 1979: Appendix E, 344–53) used different chronological divisions and archaeological criteria to assign site occupations to specific phases of the longer *Banesh* period. In 1978, investigating how *Banesh* period

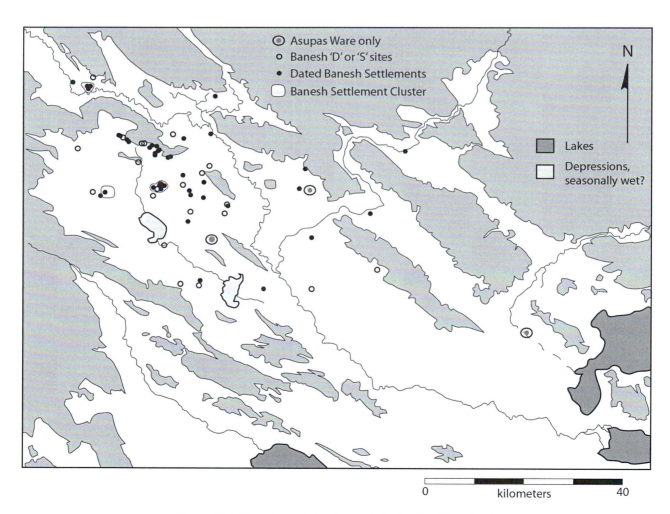

Figure 12.1. Banesh *period settlements in the Kur River Basin.*

Table 12.2. Banesh period occupations in the Kur River Basin, by phase.

Location N	E	Site or cluster name/number	Notes	Banesh area, ha.	L/B Trans.	Early	Mid-	Late
5921	9211	11N6	Asupas		?			
6027	8552	10H7		0.8	0.8			
6012	8680	10I3	*Asupas*	1.2	1.2			
6115	8577	9H21	*Asupas*		?			
6154	8527	9G10		0.3				
6187	8607	Ak Tepe, 5H6		0.8				
6120	8778	9J10		0.8				
6172	8895	T. Kaleh, 9K1		1.2				
6206	8350	T. Malyan suburb		0.5				
6212	8359	T. Malyan, 8F8		50.0		6.0?	50.0	28.0
6221	8472	Qarib cluster, 8G36		0.8				
6225	8456	8G23		1.2			1.2	
6224	8471	Qarib cluster, 8G35	dump*	0.3		0.3		
6225	8472	Qarib cluster, 8G38	w 8G35	2.7		2.7		
6227	8468	Qarib cluster, 8G40		2.0				
6227	8478	Qarib cluster, 8G34	w 8G39	0.7		0.7	0.7	
6229	8473	Qarib cluster, 8G19		0.2		0.2		
6231	8474	Qarib cluster, 8G37	dump	0.1		0.1		
6286	8487	8G5		1.2				
6290	8490	8G2		1.0	1.0	1.0	1.0	
6293	8465	8G1	*Asupas*	1.0	1.0	1.0		1.0
6298	8465	8G42	ceramic	0.8	0.8	0.8		
6204	8563	9H1		0.4				
6208	8532	8G33		1.9				
6217	8529	T. Kaftari, 8G32		0.8				
6237	8564	8H11		1.2	1.2			
6251	8516	8G12		0.8				0.8
6220	8774	8J7	*Asupas*		?			
6223	8751	T. Kamin, 8J4		1.2				
6258	8761	8J2	ceramic	1.2	1.2			1.2
6334	8389	7F8	ceramic	1.0				
6335	8386	T. Kureh, 7F1	*Asupas* ceramic	2.8	2.8	2.8	2.8	2.8
6301	8466	7G15	ceramic	0.4			0.4	0.4
6303	8469	7G7		2.9	2.9	2.9	2.9	
6310	8449	7G12		0.6			0.6	0.6
6312	8463	7G14		0.8				
6314	8454	7G13		0.8				
6322	8407	7G16	trays	0.4			0.4	
6324	8403	7F2		1.2				
6329	8517	7G6		0.8				
6342	8570	T. Shurai	Atai'	1.4				1.4
6307	8965	T. Qasrdasht	Atai'	2.3				
6447	8294	6E1		1.1				
6432	8325	Dorudzan cluster, 6E6		2.0		2.0		

Location		Site or cluster name/number	Notes	Banesh area, ha.	Phases of Banesh occupation, ha.			
N	E				L/B Trans.	Early	Mid-	Late
6437	8323	Dorudzan cluster, 6E3		1.0				
6437	8328	Dorudzan cluster, 6E4		3.6				
6438	8322	Dorudzan cluster, 6E2		0.8				
6418	8581	6H1		1.2	1.2			
		Total sites dated to phase			10	8	9	8
		Estimated size of Tal-e Malyan, ha.			0	6	50	28
		Area of all other sites, ha.			14.1	14.1	10.0	8.2
		Total hectares			14.1	20.1	60.0	36.2

Data from Sumner KRB Gazetteer (June 2009) and Alden 1979
Notes: ceramic=site where grit-tempered ceramics were manufactured
   Atai'= information from M. Atai' survey, personal communication
   Asupas=Asupas ware present
   dump=chaff-tempered ceramic production dump, not an inhabited area
   trays=chaff-tempered Banesh tray production dump, probably an inhabited area
   In total sites counts, a site cluster is counted as a single site

settlement patterns changed through time, I defined five phases of Banesh occupation in the KRB (Initial, Early, Early Middle, Late Middle, and Late) and used specific ceramic markers to assign sites to phases. Five years later, in his Tübingen presentation, Sumner reduced the number of Banesh phases to three (Early, Middle, and Late) and applied unspecified "additional ceramic criteria and less strict rules for assigning surface components to the three sub-phases" (Sumner 1986: 199; 2003: 201). By 1983 he had also been able to confirm, through excavations in 1978 at BY8 (Sumner 1985) and a deep sounding in G5 (Miller and Sumner 2004), that the identification of a Late Banesh phase that I had posited on the basis of surface associations was supported by data from stratified deposits. Finally, while I had left 23 sites, all with very small numbers of Banesh period sherds in their surface collections, without any phase assignment, Sumner distributed those sites proportionally among his three Banesh phases. It must be emphasised that the specific aims of the two studies were behind the different methods each author used, and that those differences reflect pragmatic choices about the interpretation of survey data rather than dogmatic theoretical positions.

In the following sections of this paper, I re-examine the data from my surface collections on Banesh sites in the light of information that has become available since the original analysis was completed (e.g. Sumner 1985, 2003; Nicholas 1990; Abdi 2001; Miller and Sumner 2004; Alden et al. 2005; Alden, in preparation). I continue to define phases of occupation by the presence of chronologically significant ceramic markers, but have reduced the number of phases from five to four, as dividing the Middle Banesh into two parts no longer seems justifiable given the available data from the KRB survey collections. In addition, I

am adding a new settlement type – the site cluster – to my analysis. (The various ceramic wares, types, and variants discussed here are described in Alden 1979: Appendix C; Nicholas 1990: 53–63; and Alden 2003: 190–92.) The dates assigned to the phases are my best approximation of the years that each phase might extend based on general regional parallels, the estimated span of the Banesh, and carbon dates from the Malyan and Tal-e Kureh excavations (Sumner 2003: 51–57). They are only estimations and should be used with caution until more precise dates become available.

Ceramic indicators of occupation during individual phases

Lapui-Banesh Transitional (c. 3500–3400 BC)

This phase combines the Terminal Lapui (TL) and Initial Banesh (IB) phases described in the report on the test excavation at Tal-e Kureh (Alden 2003: 187–98), and is defined by the material from Lots 13–8 (Strata VII–IIIb). While the division between the TL (Lots 13–10) and IB (Lots 9 and 8) made in that report is justifiable on stratigraphic grounds, I have chosen to combine the two phases for the purposes of settlement pattern analysis because, as shown in Table 12.3:

a) Lapui fine ware sherds are common in both TL (46%) and IB (21%) lots, but almost entirely absent in Early Banesh (Lots 7–3; 1%) excavation units;
b) the proportions of Banesh grit and Banesh chaff sherds are generally similar in the TL and IB lots, while roughly twice as frequent in the Early Banesh units;
c) rough slipped ware is much more common in the IB and TL phases than it is in the Early Banesh.

Table 12.3. Ware counts and percentages from the Tal-e Kureh sounding.

	Lapui-Banesh Transitional		Early Banesh
	Lots 13–10	Lots 9–8	Lots 7–3
Lapui fine ware	43 (46%)	13 (21%)	6 (1%)
Rough slipped ware	18 (19%)	24 (38%)	45 (11%)
Banesh grit-tempered	20 (21%)	18 (29%)	245 (58%)
Banesh chaff-tempered	13 (14%)	8 (13%)	123 (29%)
All wares	94	63	419

Data from Alden 2003: table D1

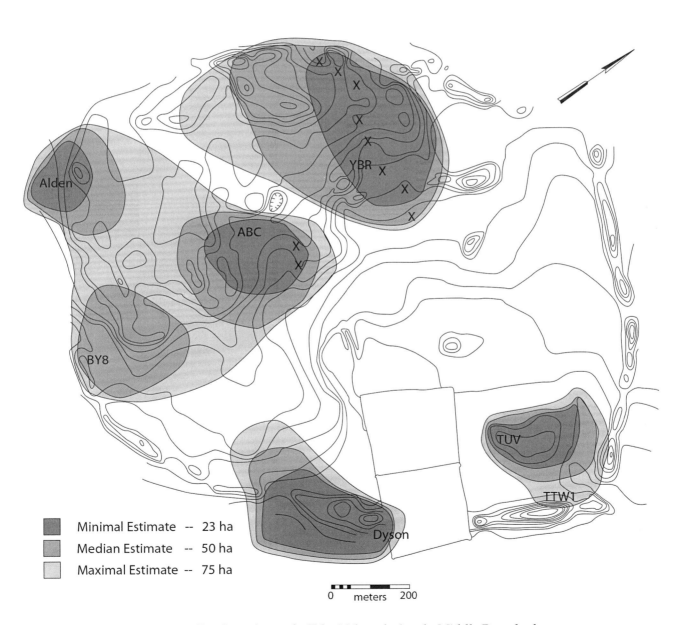

Minimal Estimate -- 23 ha
Median Estimate -- 50 ha
Maximal Estimate -- 75 ha

0   meters   200

Figure 12.2. Site size estimates for Tal-e Malyan during the Middle Banesh *phase.*

Given this division of the Tal-e Kureh strata, I consider the following ceramic types or criteria to be reliable indicators of occupation during the *Lapui-Banesh Transitional*:

a) *Asupas* ware;
b) painted *Lapui* fine ware;
c) bevel-rim trays.

Less positive but still valid criteria include:

d) rough slipped ware;
e) horizontal white painted bands;
f) *Lapui* fine ware carinated bowls, collared neck jars, and bowls with flattened everted rims.

A potentially valid criterion is:

g) bevel-rim bowls in the absence of *Banesh* trays.

Early Banesh (c. 3400–3250 BC)

This phase is defined as the time when Tal-e Kureh was a ceramic production site, which is represented by Lots 7–3 and Strata IIIa–Ib of the Tal-e Kureh sounding (Alden 2003: 195). Given the ceramic distribution observed in this sounding and an analysis of pinched-rim bowl metrics (Alden 1982), I consider the following ceramic types or criteria to be reliable indicators of occupation during the *Early Banesh* phase:

a) pinched-rim bowls with streak burnished red slip.

A potentially valid criterion is:

b) black painted bands on wide horizontal white bands.

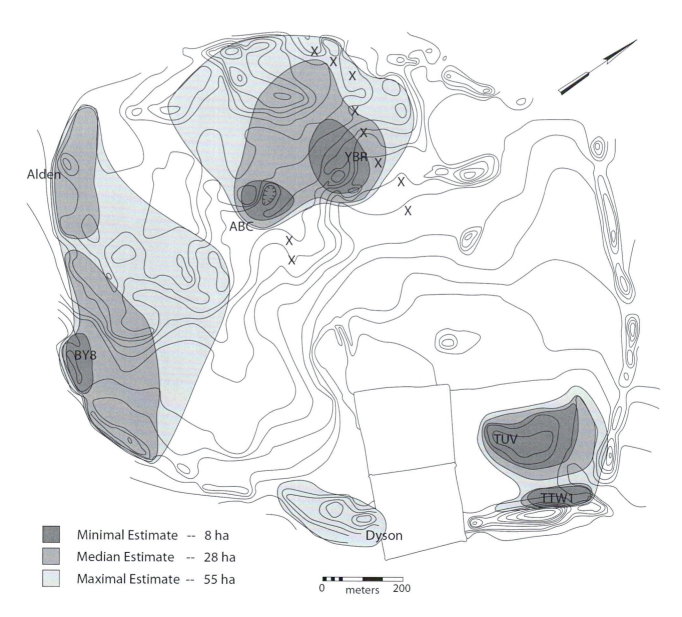

Figure 12.3. Site size estimates for Tal-e Malyan during the Late Banesh *phase.*

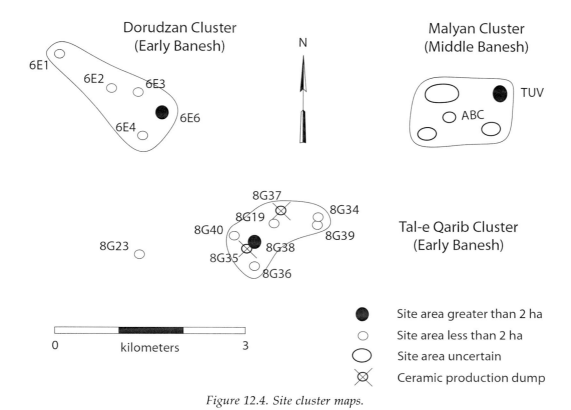

Figure 12.4. *Site cluster maps.*

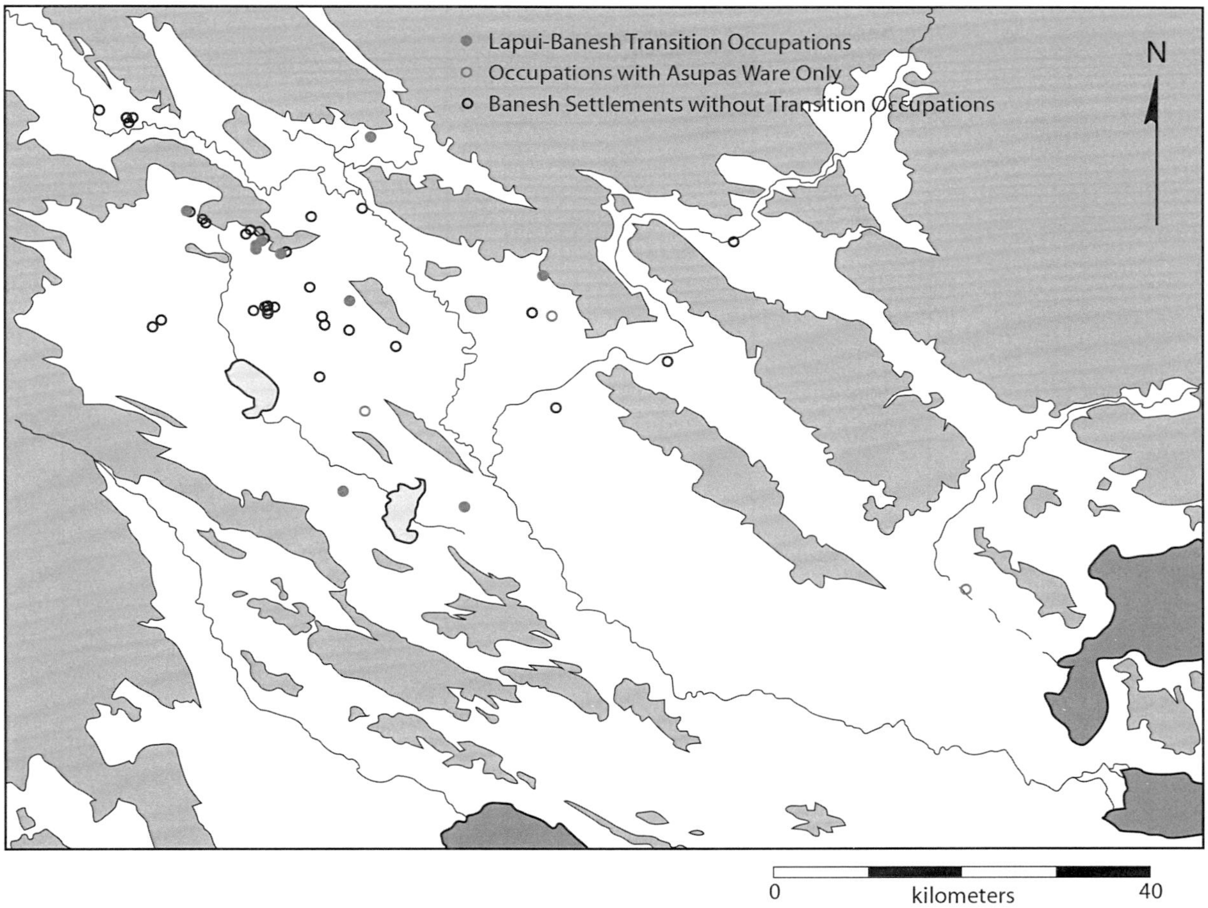

Figure 12.5. Lapui-Banesh Transitional *phase settlement in the Kur River Basin.*

Middle Banesh (c. *3250–2950 BC)*

This phase is defined by the ABC B.L. 2–4 and TUV B.L. 2–3 deposits at Tal-e Malyan. These extensive deposits contained *Proto-Elamite* tablets, exotic small finds, and a wide variety of both chaff- and grit-tempered ceramics. Because neither the ABC nor the TUV reports contain counts of vessel or ware types from the various deposits, and because the illustrated ceramics from these excavations are judgemental samples from the very large volume of excavated material, it should not be assumed that a particular ceramic type or decorative characteristic was absent from these deposits simply because it is not illustrated in the excavation reports.

Fortunately, as the data from systematic surface collections of various *Banesh* sites show (Table 12.4), it seems very likely that chaff-tempered goblets with necked bases and concave goblet rims were only manufactured during the *Middle* and *Late Banesh* phases. No necked goblet bases or concave goblet rims were found in the *Early Banesh* levels at Tal-e Kureh or in the *Early Banesh* chaff-tempered ceramic production dumps at the site of Tal-e Qarib, but both of those varieties were common in the surface collections from

the *Middle/Late Banesh* TUV mound at Tal-e Malyan. Furthermore, the material from the YBR excavations (Alden *et al.* 2005: 42–43) indicates that during that part of the *Late Banesh* phase, necked goblet bases had basal shaving and smoothed concave bases – features not observed in the excavated *Middle Banesh* material. Given these observations, I am treating the presence of the following vessel varieties as reliable indicators of *Middle Banesh* occupation:

a) chaff-tempered goblets with necked bases;
b) concave chaff-tempered goblet rims.

Late Banesh (c. *2950–2700 BC)*

This phase begins sometime after the abandonment of the *Middle Banesh* structures in ABC B.L. 2 and TUV B.L. 2. The *Late Banesh* as known from survey is represented by the material from Site 7G12 (Alden 1979: 52). It is defined by excavated material from BY8 (Sumner 1985) and Layers 13–8 in the TTW1 sounding (Abdi 2001). Representative material also comes from TUV B.L. 1, the 2004 YBR sounding (Alden *et al.* 2005), and surface collections from the TUV mound at Tal-e Malyan. Given the distributions observed in

Table 12.4. *Distribution of chaff-tempered goblet base and rim types.*

Site number	Chaff-tempered goblet bases		Chaff-tempered goblet rims		
	Necked	*Straight*	*Concave*	*All*	*% Concave*
6H1	0	0	0	6	0
7F1 Kureh excav.	0	1	0	14	0
7F1 Kureh surface	0	9	1	28	4%
7G7	8	70	49	511	10%
7G12	1	1	0	0	0
7G15	8	14	0	0	0
7G16	10	4	2	66	3%
8F8a Malyan TUV	11	1	11	50	22%
8G2	6	20	17	176	10%
8G19	0	2	0	0	0
8G23	0	0	1	1	100%
8G34	3	1	0	5	0
8G35 (prod. dump)	0	496	0	803	0
8G36 Qarib	0	6	0	7	0
8G37 (prod. dump)	0	135	0	363	0
8G38 Qarib	0	6	0	6	0
8G39	0	2	0	1	0
8G40	0	0	0	3	0
8G42	0	6	0	0	0
8H11	0	0	0	3	0
8J2	0	0	0	3	0

Data from Alden 1979: table 40

this material, I consider the following ceramic types and criteria to be reliable indications of a *Late Banesh* occupation:

a) maroon on white painting with fine lines;
b) painted triangles filled with diagonal stripes;
c) deep bowls with exterior grooves and impressed rims.

Less positive but still valid criteria include:

d) painted horizontal fine line meanders;
e) small wide-mouth carinated jars with everted rims.

The phase-by-phase occupations that result when these criteria are applied to the ceramic assemblages from *Banesh* sites in the KRB are shown in Table 12.2.

Determining phase-by-phase occupation at Tal-e Malyan

Tal-e Malyan is by far the largest *Banesh* site in the KRB, so reconstructions of the phase-by-phase occupied area in the region will be highly dependent on what is done with this site. The estimated extent of occupation at Tal-e Malyan during the *Middle Banesh* phase is shown in Figure 12.2, which indicates minimal, median, and maximal estimates of occupation of roughly 23, 50, and 75 ha during this era. The minimal estimate is based on data from excavations in the ABC, TUV, BY8, TTW1, and YBR areas; from surface indications of archaeological deposits found in debris around the mouths of *qanat* holes (marked with an X in Figs 12.2 and 12.3); and from observations of *in situ* archaeological material in the edges of eroding areas of the site ("Alden") or areas of modern disturbance ("Dyson", an exposed section cleaning). Surface distributions of *Banesh* sherds were not relied on in these estimates because extensive reworking of *Banesh* deposits during later occupations at Tal-e Malyan have scattered *Banesh* material across the entire site. It should also be noted that the BY8 excavations did not reveal deposits earlier than *Late Banesh*, but also did not reach virgin soil, while in FX106 *Kaftari* deposits rested on virgin soil. The median and maximal estimates of occupied area involve more guesswork, but I am comfortable assigning Tal-e Malyan an estimated size of 50 ha during the *Middle Banesh*, and will use this figure for the analysis presented here.

Given the known exposures of *Late Banesh* deposits in excavation and the relatively limited amount of *Late Banesh* pottery evident on the surface of the site, *Late Banesh* Tal-e Malyan was probably significantly smaller than its *Middle Banesh* predecessor. From the evidence of the BY8 and TTW1 excavations, the city wall appears to have been built at the end of the *Middle Banesh* or the beginning of the *Late Banesh*, and both of these excavations revealed areas of occupation

along the inside of that wall. The TUV mound had *Late Banesh* material both in the uppermost layers of the excavations and across the entire surface of the mound, and there is no overburden at TUV from any post-*Banesh* occupation. Although there is no *Late Banesh* in the ABC excavation, there is *Late Banesh* occupation in the sounding in square H1 and at the bottom of the H5 sounding. Finally, there are at least 2 m of redeposited *Late Banesh* materials at the northern end of the YBR sounding. Neither Sumner (2003: 204) nor I observed *Late Banesh* sherds around the *qanat* holes or in the "Dyson" section on the south side of the road along the south edge of the old walled village, but the possibility that such materials were actually there cannot be discounted. Finally, Sumner noted that at Tal-e Malyan, *Late Banesh* sherds "were rarely found in surface collections except along the north stretch of the city wall, where *Late Banesh* painted sherds are common" (Sumner 2003: 204). Because the contour map of the northern city wall shows no evidence of any adjacent mounding, I have assumed that the *Late Banesh* sherds in the north city wall derive from the material used to build that structure and not from any significant area of ancient occupation. Given these considerations, the minimal, median, and maximal size estimates for Tal-e Malyan during the *Late Banesh* span a particularly wide range – approximately 8, 28, and 55 ha – with the extent of suspected occupation shown in Figure 12.3. The median figure of 28 ha will be used for the analysis presented here.

There are no known *Early Banesh* deposits from any of the Tal-e Malyan excavations, but Sumner found the rim of a pinched-rim bowl in his initial survey of the site and I found a similar rim on the surface of the TUV mound (Alden 1979: tables 41 and 46). In addition, there is at least one rim of a pinched-rim bowl in ABC material archived at the University of Pennsylvania's University Museum from the *Kaftari* trash deposits in ABC. These finds indicate there were at least two areas of *Early Banesh* occupation at Tal-e Malyan, one beneath the TUV mound and another in the vicinity of ABC. In the absence of any data that would indicate the extent of these occupations, I have assigned an area of 6 ha to the *Early Banesh* occupation at Tal-e Malyan, an estimate that I believe is conservative. I have also shown *Early Banesh* Malyan as a possible site cluster on Figure 12.6.

Site clusters as a settlement type

One distinctive feature of the *Banesh* period settlement in the KRB is the presence, during the *Early Banesh*, of at least two site clusters, Dorudzan and Qarib, shown on Figure 12.4. These clusters consist of five or six separate low mounds, between 0.5 and 4 ha in size, scattered across an area of about 1 x 2 km. Each cluster appears to have one larger mound and four

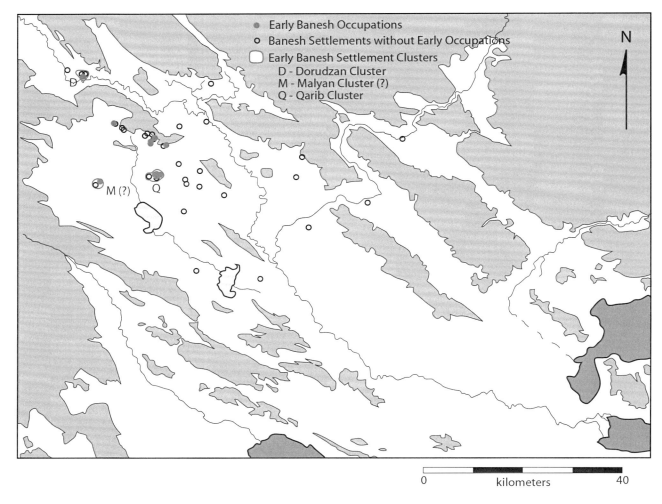

Figure 12.6. Early Banesh *settlement in the Kur River Basin.*

or five smaller ones, and each appears to have a total occupied area in the range of 6 to 8 ha. The mounds of the 6E (Dorudzan) cluster, near the western end of the Dorudzan gorge (Sumner 1972: fig. 14; n.d.), are presently beneath the waters of the Dorudzan dam and I never saw this cluster of sites. The 8G (Qarib) cluster, centred on Tal-e Qarib, was involved in the large-scale production of chaff-tempered ceramics, and also served as the central node in a regional distribution system for pinched-rim bowls (Alden 1979: 87–114; 1982). My reconstruction of the settled area of Tal-e Malyan during the *Middle Banesh*, presented in Figures 12.2 and 12.4, illustrates what appears to be a similar "site cluster" settlement pattern, although the total occupied area of *Middle Banesh* Tal-e Malyan is at least six times larger than the total area of either the *Early Banesh* Dorudzan or Qarib clusters. There were also separate areas of settlement at Tal-e Malyan during the *Late Banesh* but because these are all enclosed within an enormous fortification wall, I believe it is more appropriate to consider them as sectors of a single large settlement

rather than as a cluster of separate but related occupations. In any event, during each phase of the *Banesh* period, the settlement clusters represent the largest concentrations of settled occupation in the KRB.

Phase-by-phase *Banesh* settlement in the KRB

Data on phase-by-phase *Banesh* occupations are listed in Table 12.2, the geographical distribution of settlement is shown in Figures 12.5–12.8, and settlement size distribution is illustrated in Figure 12.9. Although the data must be interpreted with caution, several patterns are clear. First, as shown in Figure 12.1, virtually all known *Banesh* occupation in the KRB is in the western half of the region. Settlements that can be dated to specific phases are relatively dispersed during the *Lapui-Banesh Transitional* phase marking the beginning of the *Banesh* (Fig. 12.5), but in the *Early Banesh* (Fig. 12.6) they become distinctly clustered and *Middle* phase settlements (Fig. 12.7) are

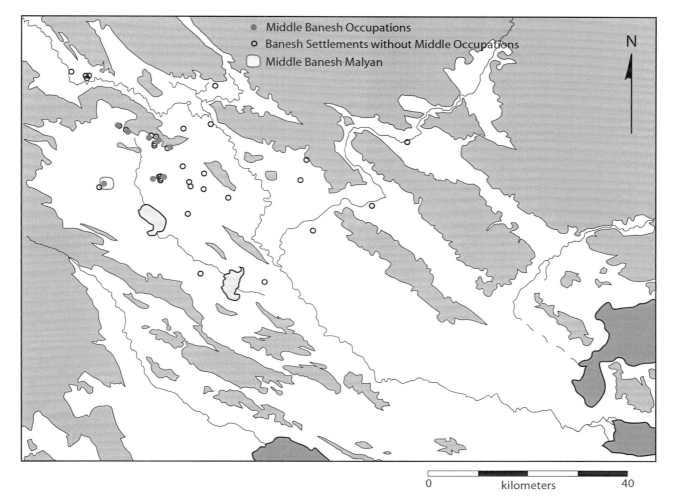

Figure 12.7. Middle Banesh *settlement in the Kur River Basin.*

concentrated in a very limited portion of the region. *Late* phase settlements (Fig. 12.8) are more dispersed and distributed more widely across the valley. Second, looking at either total settlement or phase-by-phase patterns and ignoring Tal-e Malyan, the level of settlement in the KRB is very low throughout the *Banesh* period and, with the exceptions of Tal-e Malyan and the Dorudzan and Qarib clusters, sites are very small. Finally, there are never more than two levels in the site size hierarchy during any phase of *Banesh* occupation in the KRB. Even if only half of all *Banesh* settlements in the KRB have been discovered, it does not appear likely that the basic features of these patterns would change. In particular, I would expect that any undiscovered settlements would be small and located in the western end of the KRB, and would also expect that Tal-e Malyan would still contain more than half of the region's total settled population during the *Middle* and *Late* phases.

The *Lapui-Banesh Transitional* has only 10 positively identified sites, none larger than 3 ha. For the *Early Banesh* there are five small sites and either two or possibly three larger settlement clusters – Dorudzan,

Qarib, and perhaps Tal-e Malyan – covering some 6–8 ha each. The *Middle Banesh* has eight sites of less than 3 ha and the 50 ha city of Tal-e Malyan, while for the *Late Banesh* there are seven sites of less than 3 ha and the 28 ha walled city of Tal-e Malyan. Like the *Early Banesh* settlement clusters, *Middle* and *Late Banesh* settlement at Tal-e Malyan appears to be structured as clusters of neighbouring but separate occupations. Finally, although it is beyond the immediate purview of this paper, it is worth mentioning that during the transitional era between the *Late Banesh* and the *Early Kaftari*, there continues to be some level of occupation at Tal-e Malyan, Tappeh Shurai (M. Atai', personal communication), and site 7G12 (Alden, in preparation). The total settled area in the KRB reaches a minimum during the mid-third millennium BC, but the region is never entirely de-settled.

In the transitional era between *Late Lapui* and *Early Banesh*, the settlement data indicate a relatively simple level of socio-economic organisation. The known sites, with a total area of some 14 ha, are widely dispersed throughout the western half of the KRB. All sites are in the "village-size" category, and there is no evidence

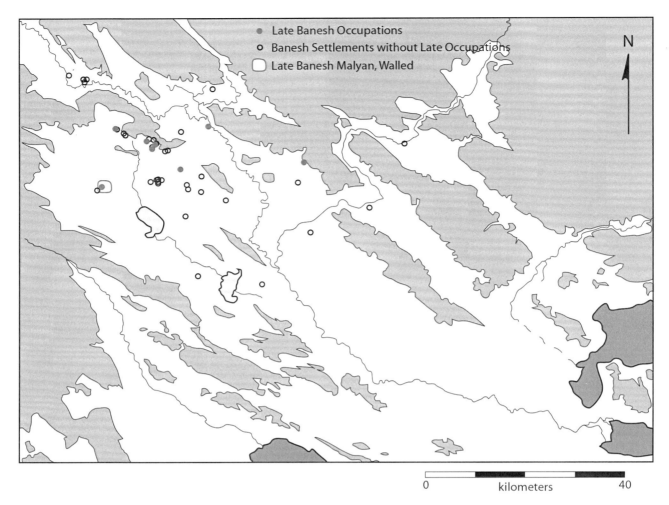

Figure 12.8. Late Banesh *settlement in the Kur River Basin.*

of any settlement at Tal-e Malyan. Although three of these *Lapui-Banesh Transitional* sites – 7F1, 8G42, and 8J2 – have evidence indicating that grit-tempered ceramics were produced there, there are no *Lapui-Banesh Transitional* wasters from any of those sites and the excavation at 7F1 indicates that ceramics were only produced at that site during the *Early Banesh*. In short, during the *Lapui-Banesh Transitional* the settlement pattern and ceramic production data indicate no signs of regional economic integration or political differentiation in the KRB.

During the *Early Banesh*, the total area of known settlement in the KRB increases to 20 ha (14 ha plus a projected 6 ha at Tal-e Malyan) and the settlement pattern changes dramatically. Known settlement, which is limited to the westernmost end of the valley, is distinctly clustered. Definite settlement clusters appear in two well-watered locations in the valley, at Tal-e Qarib and along the Kur River near the western end of the Dorudzan gorge, and a possible third settlement cluster may have been established at Tal-e Malyan. If the various mounds of the Qarib and Dorudzan clusters were all occupied simultaneously,

then both of these clusters would be, like Tal-e Malyan, the size of small towns. During the *Early Banesh*, grit-tempered ceramics were manufactured at Tal-e Kureh, which is almost equidistant between the Dorudzan, Qarib, and Malyan loci, and then distributed from Tal-e Qarib, while enormous quantities of chaff-tempered goblets and trays were being made at Tal-e Qarib (Alden 1982: 91–99). At Qarib, the larger of two dumps of chaff-tempered pottery broken during firing contains an estimated 600,000 kg of ceramics, representing the remains of some half a million chaff-tempered goblets. Even assuming that one in five vessels broke during firing (which is almost certainly an inflated estimate), the material in that one dump alone would indicate that more than two million goblets were manufactured at Tal-e Qarib – enough to supply the entire settled population of the *Early Banesh* KRB with about five chaff-tempered goblets per person per year for 200 years (Alden 1979: 105). In addition, surface finds from Tal-e Qarib include 383 fragments of stone and fine white plaster vessels, which may have been produced at, and were almost certainly distributed from, the Qarib settlement

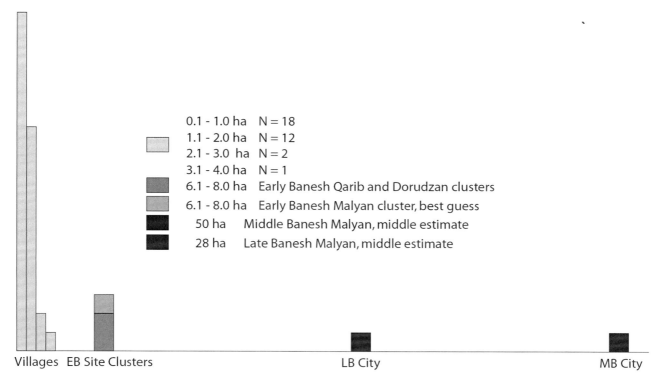

0.1 - 1.0 ha   N = 18
1.1 - 2.0 ha   N = 12
2.1 - 3.0 ha   N = 2
3.1 - 4.0 ha   N = 1
6.1 - 8.0 ha   Early Banesh Qarib and Dorudzan clusters
6.1 - 8.0 ha   Early Banesh Malyan cluster, best guess
  50 ha   Middle Banesh Malyan, middle estimate
  28 ha   Late Banesh Malyan, middle estimate

Villages   EB Site Clusters   LB City   MB City

Figure 12.9. Histogram of Banesh *settlement sizes.*

cluster (Alden 1979: 114–22). Although there is only a two-stage hierarchy of settlement sizes (villages and small town-sized site clusters) evident during this phase, the patterns of ceramic production and distribution and the concentration of stone vessel fragments at Tal-e Qarib indicate a strong degree of regional economic and, more arguably, political integration. It also appears that during the *Early Banesh*, Tal-e Qarib was producing considerably more chaff-tempered pottery than the known settled population of the KRB would consume.

During the *Middle Banesh* phase, the Dorudzan cluster and most of the Qarib cluster appear to have been abandoned. Tal-e Malyan grew into a city of some 50 ha, Tal-e Kureh was still occupied, and there were two small sites along the edge of Kuh-i Kuruni where grit-tempered *Banesh* ceramics (7G15) and *Banesh* trays (7G16) were manufactured. Two of the remaining four sites with known *Middle Banesh* occupations, 7G7 and 8G2, were un-mounded sites with sparse sherd cover along the talus slopes on the southern side of Kuh-i Kuruni. The locations of these talus slope sites, along with the absence of any built-up mounds and the presence of stone alignments that might represent tent sites, led both Sumner and Wright to suggest in conversations that these might represent seasonal encampments of *Banesh*-period pastoralist herders. While I believe such interpretations should be treated cautiously until at least one of these sites has been excavated, the similarities between the KRB talus slope sites

and two excavated sites that have been interpreted as campsites of mobile pastoralists – the *Middle Chalcolithic* site of Tuwah Khoshkeh in the Islamabad Plain of the central Zagros (Abdi *et al.* 2002) and Dar Khazineh, a *Late Susiana 1* and 2 period site in the eastern Susiana Plain (Alizadeh *et al.* 2004) – are certainly supportive of such an interpretation.

There is no evidence of ceramic manufacture at either Tal-e Kureh or Tal-e Qarib during the *Middle Banesh* phase, but the presence of large quantities of chaff-tempered ceramics at Tal-e Malyan (observed by the author in ejecta from *qanat* holes east of the YBR excavation) hint that such ceramics may have been produced at Tal-e Malyan during this era. *Middle Banesh* Tal-e Malyan appears to have retained the structure of neighbouring but separate occupations that distinguish the *Early Banesh* settlement clusters, although on a distinctly larger scale. Building Level 4 in the Tal-e Malyan ABC excavation was delimited by a double wall that may have enclosed the ABC settlement (Sumner 2003: 41) and functioned as a fortification, and the remains of cobblestone foundations observed in an irrigation ditch along the north side of the TUV mound at Tal-e Malyan hint that at some point the TUV mound was also surrounded by a similar double wall (Alden 1979: 195–96, fig. 27). In addition, large stones observed around Operation Z46 and in a collapsed *qanat* some 150 m north of that operation may also represent fortification walls related to individual *Middle Banesh* occupations (Sumner 2003: 204). The *Middle Banesh* site size hierarchy – a large city and a handful of villages, with no small or large towns – is distinctly different from contemporaneous site size hierarchies in agriculturally productive areas of Mesopotamia, and the absence of small settlements within 10 km of the central city is also atypical.

Finally, even without looking at the discoveries from the Tal-e Malyan excavations that were noted by Sumner in his original paper (1986: 204–06) and published in the TUV and ABC excavation reports – discoveries that include an elaborately painted building, large jars decorated with beautifully sculpted reliefs, *Proto-Elamite* tablets, seals, and impressed clay door and jar sealings, and materials such as obsidian, mother-of-pearl, specular hematite, and copper that were acquired from distant sources – the sheer size of Tal-e Malyan makes it clear that it was a dominant centre of economic power and political authority during the *Middle Banesh* phase of the *Proto-Elamite* era.

The *Late Banesh* settlement system, with one city and a handful of small villages, is very similar to that of the *Middle Banesh* phase, although the total estimated area of settlement declines substantially, from 60 ha to about 36 ha. The most significant change is the construction of a massive city wall roughly 5 km long around the complex of occupied areas making up the site of Tal-e Malyan. This wall was far larger and much more massive than the walls around separate areas of the *Middle Banesh* site, and its construction is estimated to have required a minimum of 140,000 person-days of labour for the brickwork alone, or about half a year's work for a crew of 1000 (Sumner 1985: 159). As Sumner notes, a workforce of this size could have been recruited from Tal-e Malyan, but he suggests that if the city's workers were supplemented by members of a nomadic population and the construction was extended over a decade or so, the work could have been done without fundamentally disrupting the annual agricultural cycle. In any event he concludes, "it is clear that local authority was sufficient to direct planning, to assert eminent domain over the required land, to procure materials, to mobilize labor, and to oversee construction" (Sumner 1985: 159) of this enormous project.

The city wall was positioned to surround all settled areas of the *Middle Banesh* city, and it also enclosed over 100 ha of unoccupied area. This pattern has led Sumner and others to speculate that the open area within the wall served as protected space for nomadic groups and their herds to gather and camp during the spring or autumn. Although such a possibility is hard to test for archaeologically, it is certainly plausible and accords with the pattern of autumn nomadic encampments at Tal-e Malyan that we observed while working at the site in the 1970s and in 2004

During the *Late Banesh*, the only known location of ceramic production in the KRB was at site 8J2, the easternmost occupation known for this phase and roughly 40 km from Tal-e Malyan, where grit-tempered ceramics were manufactured. There is, however, some additional information on *Late Banesh* ceramics from an INAA study done in 2008. Seventeen *Late Banesh* grit-tempered sherds from Tal-e Malyan were analysed in an effort to determine if non-local ceramics could be identified in the excavated material from Tal-e Geser, a site in the lowland Ram Hormuz plain about 370 km west-north-west of Tal-e Malyan and 150 km east-south-east of Susa (Alden *et al.*, in press). Unexpectedly, the INAA data showed that four of the 17 samples from Tal-e Malyan (24%) had trace element compositions that aligned with samples from Tal-e Geser, indicating that the sherds from the two sites were presumably manufactured from clays from a single geological region in or near the Ram Hormuz plain (Alden *et al.*, in press: figs A4–A6). Ten of the Tal-e Malyan samples formed a tight cluster with markedly higher concentrations of caesium, aluminium, scandium, tantalum, and thorium; these high-caesium sherds, it is assumed, represent ceramics made from clays from a highland source, presumably somewhere near Tal-e Malyan. Interestingly, none of the sherds in the analysed samples from either Tal-e Geser or Tepe Abu Fanduweh (a large *Uruk* period site on the Susiana Plain near Susa) had trace element signatures similar to the sherds in the high-caesium Tal-e Malyan cluster.

It is important to note that this study only included 82 samples of archaeological ceramics and geological soils, and the sampled ceramics do not represent the full range of material from any of the three sites examined.[3] Nevertheless, these data suggest that during the *Late Banesh* phase, ceramics produced in Ram Hormuz or some nearby district with chemically similar clays were being carried from that region to Tal-e Malyan in the KRB.

Implications for regional economic and political organisation

As stated in the introduction to this paper, Sumner's original statement on the nature of *Proto-Elamite* civilisation in the KRB made two distinct proposals about economic and political organisation during the *Banesh* period. Regarding subsistence economy, he argued that:

> "Proto-Elamite civilization in central Fars was a pastoral nomadic civilization, a tribal society encompassing both tent dwelling pastoralists and sedentary administrators and farmer-craftsmen living at Tal-e Malyan and in its hinterland." (Sumner 1986: 207)

More speculatively, he said that politically:

> "The emerging picture is not of a state level organization as defined by Wright and Johnson (1975), but rather a tribal polity, sometimes fragmented and sometimes united, under the leadership of tribal khans selected from

among competing high ranking lineages. The farmer-craftsmen of Malyan and Qarib functioned within a loosely administered tribal market system to supply both agricultural and craft products to the larger nomadic population, at first within the local region but eventually within the context of interregional competition initiated by the more successful and powerful khans." (Sumner 1986: 209)

The analysis of phase-by-phase settlement patterns presented here is entirely consistent with both Sumner's propositions. It is also consistent with the developmental model of interdependent agricultural villages and mobile pastoralism presented by Alizadeh (2006, 2008, 2010).[4] Most importantly, the settlement data presented here allow developments in *Banesh*-period subsistence economy and political organisation to be linked to specific chronological phases and suggest several refinements to the proposals of Sumner and Alizadeh.

The settlement pattern during the *Lapui-Banesh Transitional* phase has widely dispersed small villages located near springs or small watercourses, and is like the preceding *Lapui* pattern in the KRB (Sumner 1988). This pattern is consistent with a mixed agricultural/pastoral subsistence economy dependent on seasonal rainfall and perhaps some minor small-scale irrigation. The small area of both individual and total regional settlement and the absence of any larger sites or patterns of site clustering suggest that these villages were not incorporated into any sort of hierarchical political organisation. This settlement pattern does not, in my opinion, suggest the presence of full-time nomadic pastoralists during this era.

Early Banesh settlement shows a markedly different pattern. There are two settlement clusters at Dorudzan and Qarib, a small group of un-mounded talus slope sites near large springs that issue from the foot of Kuh-i Kuruni, the Tal-i Kureh grit-tempered ceramic production site, and some sort of small-scale occupation at Tal-e Malyan. The two settlement clusters and the talus slope sites are located in some of the most well-watered locations in the KRB – areas where small-scale irrigation systems could be easily built, where water and good grazing would be available, and in the case of the Qarib cluster, where large quantities of reeds may have been available to use for firing the vast quantities of chaff-tempered pottery that were manufactured in that location.

The apparent abandonment of large areas of the previously occupied portion of the KRB during the *Early Banesh* and the concentration of permanent settlement into the most well-watered areas of the region hint that this may have been a period during which rainfall agriculture became more unreliable (Jones *et al.*, this volume: fig. 2.3). In addition, the Qarib chaff-tempered ceramic production centre was scaled to supply a much larger population than is represented by the 20 ha of archaeologically known

Early Banesh settlement. The presence of a seasonal population of transhumant nomadic pastoralists, spending weeks or months at widely scattered sites throughout the western half of the KRB and using the relatively fragile chaff-tempered goblets and trays produced at Qarib, would explain both the volume of production observed at Qarib and the widespread scatter of sites with only one or two *Banesh* sherds (the "D" and "S" sites shown in Fig. 12.1) across the region.

The *Early Banesh* settlement clusters, as shown in Figure 12.4, appear to represent five or six small groups of people living close to, but spatially separated from, each other. This unusual pattern would be consistent with a society divided into lineage or kin groups, where each group wants to live near, but not together with, the others. On the basis of the changes in the regional settlement pattern observed between the end of the *Lapui* and the *Early Banesh*, on the scale of ceramic production at Tal-e Qarib, and on the spatial patterning in the Qarib and Dorudzan settlement clusters, I propose that these clusters indicate the settlements, either year-round or seasonal, of elements of a tribal society with a subsistence economy based on transhumant pastoral nomadism and settled agriculture supplemented by the kind of opportunistic agriculture practised by ethno-historically known nomadic groups (Alizadeh 2008). I also propose that the *Early Banesh* peoples had a political organisation based on segmentary lineages, and that during this era those lineages were of more or less equal status and power. The loose agglomeration of un-mounded sites with low-density sherd scatters on the talus slopes of Kuh-i Kuruni might represent a similar pattern of clustered and perhaps seasonal occupation. In any event, the *Early Banesh* settlement pattern is in complete accord with Sumner's suggestions about the nature of *Banesh*-era occupation in the KRB. The *Early Banesh* settlement pattern is also conspicuously different from the preceding *Lapui-Banesh Transitional* and subsequent *Kaftari* patterns, and very dissimilar to the *Uruk*-era patterns of settlement distribution and site size hierarchy observed in lowland Khuzistan and neighbouring Mesopotamia (e.g. Johnson 1987; Adams and Nissen 1972).

In the *Middle Banesh* phase, Tal-e Malyan mushroomed to a city of some 50 ha, and the total settled area in the KRB tripled (see Table 12.2). The Dorudzan cluster was apparently abandoned and the Qarib cluster, now only partially occupied, no longer appears to have been involved in ceramic production. Outside Tal-e Malyan, only eight sites totalling 10 ha of occupied area have been identified, and none of those sites are more than 3 ha in size. Furthermore, there is not a single site in the vicinity of Tal-e Malyan that might have produced agricultural products to supplement the agricultural productive capacity of the central city.

Given the estimates used by Sumner (1989) in evaluating the productive capacity of *Kaftari*-era Tal-e Malyan (160 people per ha of settlement, requiring 1.4 ha of land to provide a year's worth of grain for each person, and the capacity to cultivate 4.4 ha per rural person), 2600 of the projected 8000 residents of *Middle Banesh* Tal-e Malyan (roughly speaking, every adult male in the city) would need to be farming all the land within 6 km of the city's boundary to feed a year-round population of 8000. Using Miller's estimate that 2.5 ha of arable land would be required to produce enough grain to feed one person for one year (Miller 1982: 231) and an estimated 160 persons per ha of settlement, the population of *Middle Banesh* Tal-e Malyan would have needed to farm all land within 7 km of the city's boundary to supply the needs of the community. In short, if *Middle Banesh* Tal-e Malyan were occupied all the year round, its residents would have been capable of producing enough grain to feed themselves. Given the assumptions used here, however, it is not easy to see how they could have produced enough grain to provide supplemental sustenance to a large population of mobile pastoralists.

As reconstructed in Figure 12.2, *Middle Banesh* Tal-e Malyan's internal structure looks like a large-scale version of the *Early Banesh* settlement clusters – a series of separate but closely grouped occupational areas. Functionally, the architecture and contents of the ABC and TUV excavations are quite dissimilar, but because these exposures represent only small parts of significantly larger areas of settlement it seems disingenuous to make too much of that pattern. It is worth noting, however, that *Proto-Elamite* tablets are found in both excavations, showing that residents of both areas were keeping records of some kind of generally small-scale economic activity. This indicates that administration and record-keeping at Tal-e Malyan was not limited to large architectural structures like those of ABC or to a single occupational area of the site (Stolper 1985: 12), and hints that the various enclaves of the site may have been "more separate but equal" than hierarchically organised and functionally differentiated. This interpretation is supported by the apparent presence of small-scale fortification walls around both the ABC and TUV occupation areas.

While the settlement structure of *Middle Banesh* Tal-e Malyan is compatible with the segmentary lineage socio-political organisation proposed for the *Early Banesh*, the size and scale of the *Middle Banesh* central settlement is dramatically different. The Qarib and Dorudzan settlement clusters were at best small towns; *Middle Banesh* Tal-e Malyan was not only a city but also "by far the largest inhabited centre in Iran at this time" (Petrie *et al.* 2009: 189). In short, the wealth, power, and influence of the people of Tal-e Malyan increased enormously in the *Middle Banesh*.

Remarkably, there is no indication that this hypertrophic growth in the size of Tal-e Malyan was accompanied by the development of a large-scale irrigation system. The *Middle Banesh* city was not supported by the productive potential of a series of surrounding agricultural settlements, and the city did not serve as a central place providing economic services to a group of subsidiary towns and villages. In fact, the rapid growth and remarkable size of the *Middle Banesh* city in the absence of any significant increase or decrease in the settled population in the remainder of the KRB would be almost impossible to explain without accepting the possibilities that, 1) the city's population grew through the inflow of people who had not previously lived in settled communities within the KRB; and 2) the city was supported by, and provided non-agricultural goods and services to, a large non-resident population of non-settled people, either regionally mobile pastoralists or seasonally transhumant pastoral nomads. Given the limits on the agricultural productivity of the city's population, it also seems plausible that a significant portion of *Middle Banesh* Tal-e Malyan was only occupied seasonally, with lineage members involved in trading, specialised craft production, or political activity arriving in spring and departing in the autumn along with the herds and herders.

How large a pastoral population might the city have served? There is nothing in the settlement data relevant to that question, although it seems likely to me that to support the evident wealth and utilise the apparent capacity for services that a city of Tal-e Malyan's size would provide, the sustained/sustaining transient population would have been more or less comparable in size to the resident population of the city. Would these herders have been seasonally transhumant? Today winters in the KRB are damp and cold and snow is common, and if pastoralists had wintered in the region one assumes they would have built houses for themselves and compounds to shelter their flocks, either within the bounds of Tal-e Malyan or in other settlements in the KRB. No evidence of corrals or shelters for animals was found, however, in the very limited areas of the ABC or TUV excavations and there is no evident increase in the amount of settled area in the rest of the KRB during the *Middle Banesh*. In addition, harvesting and storing fodder for large herds of overwintering sheep and goats, and growing enough grain to feed significant numbers of seasonally resident herders over an entire winter would clearly have strained the productive capacity of Tal-e Malyan's population. Thus, it would appear likely that the proposed population of *Middle Banesh* pastoralists spent spring and autumn in and around the KRB, summer in a highland area with good pasture, and autumn to spring in some warmer and more hospitable region. They would have produced a significant portion of their own grain through the kind of opportunistic agriculture that twentieth-century Iranian pastoral nomads are known to practise (Alizadeh 2006: 35–36). In short, the *Middle Banesh* pastoralists would have been full-time seasonally transhumant pastoral nomads, with a seasonal round similar to that of the nomad groups of the southern Zagros known in the ethnographic record (e.g. Beck 1991, 2003); and like those ethno-historically known tribes, the *Proto-Elamite* nomads would have both utilised and sustained the services of settled populations and large settlements at both ends of their seasonal round.

I would argue that the settlement pattern data presented here can be interpreted as indicating that full-time transhumant nomadic pastoralism first appeared as a fully developed adaptation during the *Early Banesh* period. It is possible that this system had its origins during the *Late Bakun* period of the late fifth to early fourth millennium BC (Alizadeh 2003: 85–86; 2010: 363–65), or that it was adopted from some other region in the Zagros (Abdi 2003). It is easy to imagine, however, how full-time mobile pastoralism might have developed within the KRB. In a process similar to that described by Abdi (2003), during the *Bakun* or *Lapui* periods agricultural villagers in search of better grazing may have moved small herds into the upper reaches of the Kur River drainage during the summer. Then, again seeking better forage, they began moving their animals to a lower region for the winter. With better nutrition all the year round, the herds grew and to accommodate their growing flocks, herders extended their seasonal round to more distant pastures. Ultimately, the seasonal pastoralists abandoned settled life for full-time transhumant nomadism – an adaptation that the settlement pattern and archaeological data described here would suggest occurred between the *Terminal Lapui* and *Early Banesh* periods. While the existing archaeological record is not sufficiently detailed to offer clear evidence of such a process (Petrie *et al.* 2009: 189; Alizadeh 2010: 360), it seems a plausible scenario.

There are at least two advantages that accrue from a fully nomadic pastoral economy. First, herding produces high-quality food and valuable fibre from animals that feed and replicate themselves. Second, it creates the ultimate form of mobile wealth – a product that transports itself from pasture to market. In a system of seasonally transhumant mobile pastoralism, animals could be moved on their own feet from the highlands where they were born and raised to the lowlands where they could be sold. With a viable market for highland animals and animal products in lowland Mesopotamia, the surplus wool, milk, and animals produced by transhumant pastoralism could be transformed into the kind of portable wealth – worked metals, exotic stones and shells, elegantly sculpted vessels, and other crafted objects – evident in the *Banesh* deposits at Tal-e Malyan.

With their animals and animal products, the nomadic pastoralists would have the kind of wealth that could be used to acquire the goods and services that a city the size of Tal-e Malyan could provide, and the heads of the herding groups would have the incentive to establish residences and build productive, storage, and administrative facilities at this nexus of their migration route. These are Sumner's tribal khans, and this is potentially the system they exploited to gain and maintain their wealth and power.

Arguments for the presence of full-time nomadic pastoralists practising long-distance transhumance in the *Banesh* period are not universally accepted. In particular, Potts (2008) has emphasised that the ethnographically known pattern of Qashqai, Bakhtiyari, and Luri style nomadism is a post-Seljuk phenomenon and should not be used as a model for earlier times. Instead, he suggests that throughout Iranian prehistory agricultural villages and towns managed their herds "in a pattern of vertical transhumance that did not entail large-scale migrations by mobile pastoralists of the Qashqā'i sort" (Potts 2008: 206). Shepherds may have taken village flocks on seasonal visits to highland or lowland pastures, he indicates, but such movements need not have involved large segments of the population and certainly do not require the assumption of full-time pastoral nomadism. I agree that we need to be cautious in applying modern models to ancient societies. In the *Banesh* period situation discussed here, however, I do not believe a model like Potts's can explain the *Early Banesh* site cluster phenomenon, the excess ceramic production capacity of Tal-e Qarib, the apparent rapid growth of *Middle Banesh* Tal-e Malyan, the presence of a *Middle Banesh* city with no surrounding population sustaining the city or requiring a city's services, or the *Late Banesh* construction of Tal-e Malyan's massive city wall. A model assuming full-time nomadic pastoralism fits these data far more closely than a model of non-migratory seasonal pastoralism.

While the *Late Banesh* settlement system is very much like that of the *Middle Banesh*, the internal structure of Tal-e Malyan is notably different. The settled area within the site is considerably smaller, and an enormous wall has been built around the entire settlement. In addition, the *Late Banesh* occupation at Tal-e Malyan seems to be concentrated along the inside of the city wall rather than grouped into a series of separate clusters. The evidence for the distribution and extent of *Late Banesh* occupation at Tal-e Malyan is considerably less secure than for the *Middle Banesh* city, but the general differences between the two periods are evident.

The settlement pattern data give no indication that the *Late Banesh* subsistence economy is any different from what has been proposed for the previous era, but the discovery of ceramics in *Late Banesh* deposits at Tal-e Malyan, which were apparently produced in the neighbourhood of Ram Hormuz, indicates that people were indeed moving between the lowlands and highlands during this era, and adds physical evidence that is consistent with the proposition that, during the *Late Banesh*, the KRB may have been one nexus in a system of long-distance seasonally transhumant pastoral nomadism.[5]

The construction of the Tal-e Malyan city wall, however, implies that the political situation during the *Late Banesh* had changed dramatically. The wall transformed the city from a cluster of similar-sized but separate occupations surrounded by moderately sized fortifications into a single entity isolated from the surrounding countryside by a massive city wall. As Sumner pointed out, the wall indicates that the individual or group controlling the city had the power to mobilise the labour necessary to carry out this prodigious project, but it also suggests that the inhabitants of the city felt endangered by some external population. The settlement survey data, however, do not reveal any settlement in the KRB that might threaten a city the size of Tal-e Malyan, and no known settlement outside the KRB seems large enough and close enough to have been of serious concern. A large nomadic population, however, could have been threatening enough to persuade the people of the city that they needed the kind of serious protection that the *Late Banesh* city wall would offer.

One scenario for these changes would be that one khan or lineage had become paramount in the city, but could not extend this dominance to the mobile population. The city appears to have still played an important role for the tribes, but the relationship between the settled and nomadic elements of the *Proto-Elamite* population had become more competitive. The disappearance of urban settlement in the KRB during the *Banesh-Kaftari Transition* implies that the processes marked by the construction of the *Late Banesh* city wall represented the beginning of the end for the *Proto-Elamite* hegemony that had built the city of Tal-e Malyan.

Conclusions

Reconstructing economic behaviour and socio-political organisation from settlement data is a speculative endeavour, particularly when the data are neither as clear nor as complete as could be desired. It will not be surprising, therefore, if readers remain sceptical of some of the interpretations I have suggested. Nevertheless, I believe that the postulated appearance of full-time seasonally transhumant pastoral nomadism during *Early Banesh* times in the KRB offers the most parsimonious explanation for the archaeological information available for this era and this region. Although the argument I have made in this paper is essentially based on circumstantial

evidence, it is more than a "just-so story". In addition, there are several lines of independent evidence that are consistent with or supportive of the general picture presented here. I was of course aware of that evidence when writing this paper, so nothing mentioned here can be considered an independent test of the reconstructions I have presented on the basis of the settlement pattern data. Nevertheless, the following information should be taken into account when evaluating the strengths and weaknesses of the picture of *Proto-Elamite* society offered here.

First, declining proportions of juniper in the archaeobotanical material from Tal-e Malyan indicate a general deforestation of the valley floor between the *Middle Banesh* and the *Kaftari* (Miller 1985: 14–15). Such environmental degradation would not be expected if the population of the KRB during the *Late Banesh* and the *Banesh-Kaftari Transition* was as limited as the settlement data would indicate, but deforestation would not be surprising if the region was being utilised by pastoral nomads during the post-*Middle Banesh* occupation of the KRB. Miller (2010) also argues, on the basis of the apparent increase in nut-bearing trees and decline in both juniper and faster-growing species between the *Late Banesh* and *Kaftari* occupations at Tal-e Malyan, that nomadic peoples were present in the KRB during the *Banesh-Kaftari Transition* and that they were actively managing the woodlands in a way that left a permanent mark on the landscape.

Second, counts of animal bones identifiable by species from *Banesh* deposits from Tal-e Malyan (Zeder 1991: table 24) indicate that sheep and goat accounted for 98% of the bones from *Middle Banesh* levels and 99% of the bones from *Late Banesh* strata. These represent the highest percentage of ovicaprid remains of any late fourth-/early third-millennium BC site in south-western Iran (Mashkour 2009) and are noticeably higher than the later *Kaftari* era proportion of sheep and goat bones at Tal-e Malyan, i.e. 88% (Zeder 1991: table 41). These data are certainly consistent with a system where meat was a significant part of the Tal-e Malyan diet and where the residents of Tal-e Malyan acquired much if not all of their meat from non-resident pastoralists. Curiously, the ratios of goat to sheep show a steady decline during the *Banesh* sequence at Tal-e Malyan, from 2.6:1 for TUV Level 3, 2.1:1 for both ABC and TUV Level 2, and 1.2:1 for *Late Banesh* Level TUV 1 (Zeder 1991: table 26 and p. 140). Female goats are better milk-producers than female sheep (Dahl 2005: 94–97), so this pattern might reflect a change in herd management from strategies favouring milk production to strategies favouring wool and meat. Zeder and Blackman (2003: 128–29) have also observed that the osteological assemblages from the ABC and TUV excavations, which show the residents of ABC consuming meatier cuts of animals than the people living at TUV, are consistent with architecturally indicated differences in status between the two areas of the site and with a pattern of more direct access to live animals at TUV than at ABC.

Third, the reconstructions presented here are in general comparable to chronological changes in settlement patterns in other parts of the *Proto-Elamite* region. There is a general de-settlement at Susa and in the Susiana Plain from the *Middle Uruk* to the *Susa 3* (Johnson 1987; Alden 1987). In the Ram Hormuz Plain settled area declines from *Late Uruk* to *Proto-Elamite*, and after the *Proto-Elamite* period the plain is abandoned until early in the second millennium (Wright and Carter 2003; Alizadeh, in press). A similar pattern is evident in the small intermontane valleys of the southern Zagros during the same time span (Wright 1987). In the Mamasani region, as in the KRB, there is a steady decline in the number of sites from the *Lapui* to the *Banesh*, and the small numbers of diagnostic *Banesh* sherds at a significant number of Mamasani region *Banesh* sites also replicates the pattern observed in the KRB (Zeidi *et al.* 2009: 154–55; McCall 2009: 313–26).

The *Proto-Elamite* cultural assemblage also demonstrates close parallels between the KRB and lowland Iran during the late fourth to early third millennium BC. *Banesh* and *Susa 3* ceramics in the KRB, the Mamasani region, and the Susiana Plain are similar in both general and specific ways. Similarities in the style and iconography of glyptic art (Pittman 2003) and the presence in both the KRB and Susiana Plain of *Proto-Elamite* tablets that often seem to deal with animals and animal products (Dahl 2005) reinforce the notion that during the *Proto-Elamite* era the KRB and Susiana regions were inhabited by members of a single extended cultural community with a subsistence economy based on full-time seasonally transhumant nomadic pastoralism.

Finally, the *Banesh* period settlement patterns observed in the KRB and the socio-economic system proposed in accordance with that settlement data fit closely with theoretical models and archaeological reconstructions proposed for the development and functioning of transhumant pastoralist societies in both the central (Abdi 2003) and southern Zagros (Alizadeh 2003, 2006, 2008, 2010) regions of Iran (but *cf.* Potts 2008). The KRB settlement data imply an extended period of de-settlement during the *Banesh* period and are also, particularly during the *Early* and *Late Banesh* phases, consistent in several intriguing ways with the model of "non-uniform complexity" proposed for pastoral societies in Kazakhstan and the Margiana Oasis (Frachetti 2009: 29, 39). The economic and political system proposed here is also consistent with a range of models relating to the dualities of nomad/village, pastoral/agricultural, and mountains/ lowlands that feature so prominently in discussions of ancient Iranian societies.

Zeder and Blackman (2003: 138) argue that they see signs of "multiple levels of administrative hierarchy" in the internal differentiation observed in *Banesh*-era Tal-e Malyan, and say these indicate that Tal-e Malyan "served as the urban focus of an early state". Looking at the same data, I see nothing incompatible with a socio-political system based on lineage affiliations, with no evidence of centralised administration and no hierarchical control of information processing and decision-making. Of particular interest are Blackman's INAA data on unfired clay sealings, which show that the contemporaneous residents of TUV and ABC used separate sources of sealing clay. Although he cautions that this "does not necessarily mean…that these two sectors of the site functioned as independent autonomous economic units" (Zeder and Blackman 2003: 136), his data are completely compatible with the notion that these areas of Tal-e Malyan were occupied by different lineage groups operating autonomously within a shared socio-economic system.

In short, I do not see *Banesh*-era society as an early state. To me, the settlement pattern in the Kur River Basin suggests a socio-political system like that proposed by Sumner. While I am cognizant of scholarly concerns about using historical terminology to label ancient social phenomena (Garthwaite 2010), I see Tal-e Malyan as a place where a handful of tribal lineages lived in a collection of physically separate and more or less independent town-sized settlements. The tribal leaders – Sumner's "khans" – independently managed the needs of their separate lineages while also supporting groups of specialists who produced goods and services that could be exchanged within and between lineages as well as between settled and nomadic populations. Each settlement in the *Middle Banesh* city produced agricultural foodstuffs for, and procured meat from, the pastoral groups of their lineage while the khans engaged in what Sumner artfully described as "the serious business of dynastic intrigue and political manoeuvring."

The yearly round of these tribal leaders with their extended households and retainers, I suggest, was the same as that of their pastoralist kin. In spring, they arrived with the herds after a long journey from lowland areas like the Susiana Plain or Ram Hormuz near the Persian Gulf. They greeted relatives who had been left to watch over the winter crops and closed-up buildings at Tal-e Malyan, unsealed the locked doors and closed jars, and checked the contents of their storerooms against the numbers recorded on their tablets. Then, they settled in for the summer. Wheat and barley were harvested; kilns filled and fired. When locally available grazing grew scarce, the herds were moved to pastures further up the valley of the Kur River and further into the highlands. In the city, buildings were repaired, wool dyed and woven, tools forged, grapes harvested, and portable items manufactured using materials acquired through trade or along the course of the annual migration. In the autumn the nomads and their herds gathered at the city and, reunited with their settled kin, began a vigorous round of feasting, squabbling, trading, negotiating, arranging marriages, and adjudicating conflicts. The fields were ploughed and planted with winter wheat and barley. Then, after provisioning themselves for the long journey, the majority of the city's residents closed their buildings, said farewell to their overwintering relatives, and left for the lowlands with their nomad kin and those kinsfolk's flocks. There, at Susa and in encampments on the Susiana and other scattered plains and valleys near the edges of the Persian Gulf, they settled in for the winter and began the business of trading their sheep and goats for goods produced by the urban societies of Mesopotamia. And when the spring pastures of the lowlands began to turn brown, they set off with their flocks for the Kur River Basin.

In this scenario, the khans of Anshan were the khans of Susa. The *Banesh*-era residents of the KRB were the same people as the *Susa 3*-era residents of the Susiana Plain, using stylistically similar and functionally equivalent pottery and sharing an idiosyncratic writing system. This pastoral society found urban-scale settlements useful at the geographical ends of their migratory round, but they had no need for a state-level system of centralised control. When, during the span of the *Late Banesh*, Tal-e Malyan and its khans no longer served the needs of the tribes that had maintained them, or when external circumstances weakened the economic system that had sustained strong tribal leaders and a large central place, the city fell into disrepair and was largely abandoned.

The implications of Sumner's argument that *Proto-Elamite* society was based on mobile pastoralism, and this paper's development of that hypothesis, extend widely. It makes questions about whether various elements of the *Proto-Elamite* cultural assemblage originated in Susa or the Kur River Basin irrelevant. In valleys along the migration routes, we might expect INAA or ICP-MS analyses to find ceramics with non-local compositional signatures more commonly on un-mounded campsites along talus slopes than on centrally located mounds. With the *Proto-Elamite* writing system, if the signs denoting "owners" or "households" (Dahl 2005) indicate lineages and infixes identify individuals, it could explain why the same "owner/household" signs would be found on tablets from different sites and of different ages (Dittmann 1986, but cf. Damerow and Englund 1989: 16) as well as clarifying the relationship between tablets from different sites and relating to diverse topics – i.e. herding, labour, field management, and cereal production (Dahl *et al.*, this volume). Tablets at Tal-e Malyan and Susa might also refer to goods that

were stored at those sites during the seasons when their owners were away rather than goods that were being distributed or exchanged. The presence of large mobile populations offers a potential explanation for how settled population could have grown as rapidly as the archaeological evidence implies between the *Early* and *Middle Banesh* phases, and how the same kind of rapid growth in a settled area could have occurred in the KRB at the beginning of the *Kaftari* era in the late third millennium BC. Parallels between the geographical range proposed for *Proto-Elamite* pastoral nomads and the general extent of later *Elamite* polities may even argue in favour of ethnic and linguistic linkages between the earlier and later societies, making the designation "Proto-Elamite" for the early writing system more accurate and more insightful than sceptical scholars have argued (e.g. Potts 1999: 71–79). It is my hope that the settlement pattern data and broader interpretations presented in this paper in support of Sumner's hypotheses will encourage consideration of proposals like these, and lead to new insights on the nature and development of *Proto-Elamite* society in south-western Iran.

Notes

1   Indeed, in discussing the ideas Sumner presented in this paper, one prominent scholar of Iranian prehistory dismissed his suggestions as "highly speculative and impossible to verify" (Potts 1999: 81).

2   Geoff Emberling, Naomi Miller, Chris Thornton, Lloyd Weeks, and Henry Wright read and commented on this paper at various stages of the project, and their thoughtful suggestions and well-considered advice led to substantial improvements in my analysis and interpretation. I am also extremely grateful to Cameron Petrie for his detailed editing and cogent criticisms. The most substantive contributions to the paper, however, came from Bill Sumner, who in the last years of his life read every draft of this paper. These comments and criticisms allowed me to eliminate a number of errors and improve many aspects of my analysis.

3   A subsequent INAA testing programme, examining some 550 samples of ceramics from the KRB, is presently under way, and until the results of this study are analysed, the patterns indicated by the comparison of materials from Geser, Abu Fanduweh, and *Late Banesh* Malyan should be considered as awaiting confirmation.

4   The chronology of my proposal, however, differs from the mid-fifth-millennium BC chronology for the appearance of mobile pastoralism advocated by Alizadeh (2006: 94–97; 2008: 198–201).

5   Alden *et al.* (in press) discuss three possible mechanisms that might underlie the movement of ceramic vessels from Tal-e Geser to Tal-e Malyan. The vessels may have been part of the personal equipment of migrants, merchants, or nomads travelling from lowlands to highlands; the vessels may have been containers for trade goods such as oils, seeds, or exotic foodstuffs; or the vessels may have been moved from place to place for symbolic or social reasons, perhaps as tribute or as

physical signifiers of social relationships. It is our hope that the larger INAA study of KRB pottery mentioned in note 3 will allow us to reject one or more of these possible explanations.

Bibliography

Abdi, K. 2001. "Malyan 1999", *Iran* 39: 73–98.

Abdi, K. 2003. "The early development of pastoralism in the Central Zagros mountains", *Journal of World Prehistory* 17 (4): 395–448.

Abdi, K., Nokandeh, G., Azadi, A., Biglari, F., Heydari, S., Farmani, D., Rezaii, A. and Mashkour, M. 2002. "Tuwah Khoshkeh: a Middle Chalcolithic mobile pastoralist campsite in the Islamabad Plain, west Central Zagros mountains, Iran", *Iran* 40: 43–74.

Adams, R. and Nissen, H. 1972. *The Uruk Countryside: The Natural Setting of Urban Societies*, University of Chicago Press, Chicago.

Alden, J. R. n.d. The Early Banesh Period in Iran: Results of a Test Excavation at Tal-I Kureh, MS on file in the Malyan Excavation Archives, prepared in 1978.

Alden, J. R. 1979. *Regional Economic Organization in Banesh Period Iran*, unpublished Ph.D. dissertation, Department of Anthropology, University of Michigan, Ann Arbor.

Alden, J. R. 1982. "Marketplace Exchange as Indirect Distribution: An Iranian Example", in Ericson, J. and Earle, T. (eds), *Contexts for Prehistoric Exchange*, Academic, New York: 83–101.

Alden, J. R. 1987. "The Susa III Period", in Hole, F. (ed.), *The Archaeology of Western Iran*, Smithsonian Institution, Washington DC: 157–70.

Alden, J. R. 2003. "Excavations at Tal-e Kureh. Appendix D", in Sumner, W. M. (ed.), *Malyan Excavation Reports, Volume III: Proto-Elamite Civilization in the Land of Anshan*, University of Pennsylvania Museum, Philadelphia: 187–98.

Alden, J. R. in preparation. "Chapter 4: Stratigraphy and Ceramics" in Alden, J. R. (ed.), *Anshan in the 2nd Millennium BC: The GHI Excavations at Tal-e Malyan, Iran*, Malyan Excavation Reports, vol. IV, University of Pennsylvania Museum, Philadelphia.

Alden, J. R, Minc, L. and Alizadeh, A. in press. "INAA analysis of ceramics from three Iranian sites: trace element signatures and evidence for ceramic exchange as seen from Tal-e Geser. Appendix A", in Alizadeh, A. (ed.), *Ancient Settlement Patterns and Cultures in the Ram Hormuz Plain, Southwestern Iran*, Oriental Institute, Chicago.

Alden, J. R, Abdi, K., Azadi, A., Beckman, G. and Pittman, H. 2005. "Fars Archaeological Project 2004: Excavation at Tal-e Malyan", *Iran* 43: 39–47.

Alizadeh, A. 2003. "Some observations based on the nomadic character of Fars prehistoric cultural development", in Miller and Abdi 2003: 83–97.

Alizadeh, A. 2006. *The Origins of State Organizations in Prehistoric Highland Fars, Southern Iran: Excavations at Tall-e Bakun*, vol. 128, Oriental Institute Publications, Chicago.

Alizadeh, A. 2008. "Archaeology and the question of mobile pastoralism in Late Prehistory", in Barnard, H. and Wendrich, W. Z. (eds), *The Archaeology of Mobility: Old World and New World Nomadism*, Cotsen Institute of Archaeology, Los Angeles: 78–114.

Alizadeh, A. 2010. "The rise of the highland Elamite state in southwestern Iran: 'enclosed' or enclosing nomadism?" *Current Anthropology* 51: 353–83.

Alizadeh, A. in press. *Ancient Settlement Patterns and Cultures in the Ram Hormuz Plain, Southwestern Iran*, Oriental Institute, Chicago.

Alizadeh, A., Kouchoukos, N., Wilkinson, T. J., Bauer, A. and Mashkour, M. 2004. "Human-environment interactions on the Upper Khuzestan Plains, southwest Iran: recent investigations", *Paléorient* 30 (1): 69–88.

Beck, L. 1991. *Nomad: A Year in the Life of a Qashqa'i Tribesman in Iran*, University of California Press, Berkeley.

Beck, L. 2003. "Qashqa'i nomadic pastoralists and their use of land", in Miller and Abdi 2003: 289–304.

Dahl, J. 2005. "Animal husbandry in Susa during the Proto-Elamite period", *Studi Micenei ed Egeo-Anatolici* 47: 81–134.

Damerow, P. and Englund, R. 1989. *The Proto-Elamite Texts from Tepe Yahya*, The American School of Prehistoric Research, Bulletin 39, Cambridge MA.

Dittmann, R. 1986. "Seals, sealings and tablets", in Finkbeiner, U. and Röllig, W. (eds), *Gamdat Nasr: Period or Regional Style?* Ludwig Reichert, Wiesbaden: 332–66.

Frachetti, M. D. 2009. "Bronze Age societies of the Eurasian steppe", in Hanks, B. K. and Linduff, K.M. (eds.), *Social Complexity in Prehistoric Eurasia: Monuments, Metals, and Mobility*, Cambridge University Press, Cambridge: 19–46.

Garthwaite, G. 2010. "Comment on Alizadeh 2010", *Current Anthropology* 51: 377–78.

Jacobs, L. K. 1980. *Darvazeh Tepe and the Iranian Highlands in the Second Millennium BC*, unpublished PhD dissertation, University of Oregon, Portland.

Johnson, G. A. 1987. "The changing organization of Uruk administration on the Susiana Plain", in Hole, F. (ed.), *The Archaeology of Western Iran*, Smithsonian Institution, Washington DC: 107–39.

McCall, B. 2009. *The Mamasani Archaeological Survey: long term settlement patterns in the Mamasani district of the Zagros Mountains, Fars Province, Iran*, unpublished Ph.D. dissertation, Department of Archaeology, University of Sydney.

Mashkour, M. 2009. "Subsistence and zoology", paper presented at the *Ancient Iran and its Neighbours* conference in Cambridge, 26–28 June 2009.

Miller, N. F. 1982. *Economy and Environment of Malyan, a Third Millennium BC Urban Center in Southern Iran*, unpublished Ph.D. dissertation, Department of Anthropology, University of Michigan, Ann Arbor.

Miller, N. F. 1985. "Paleoethnobotanical evidence for deforestation in ancient Iran: a case study of urban Malyan", *Journal of Ethnobiology* 5: 1–19

Miller, N. F. 2010. "Plants, animals and people: the eternal triangle", paper presented at the *7th International Congress for the Archaeology of the Ancient Near East*, 12–16 April, 2010, London.

Miller, N. F. and Abdi, K. eds 2003. *Yeki bud, yeki nabud: Essays on the Archaeology of Iran In Honor of William M. Sumner*, Cotsen Institute of Archaeology, Los Angeles.

Miller, N. F. and Sumner, W. M. 2004. "The Banesh-Kaftari interface: the view from Operation H5, Malyan (Corrected)", *Iran* 42: 77–89.

Nicholas, I. 1990. *The Proto-Elamite Settlement at TUV*, Malyan Excavation Reports, vol. I, University of Pennsylvania Museum, Philadelphia.

Pittman, H. 2003. "Proto-Elamite glyptic art from Operation ABC", in Sumner, W. M. (ed.), *Malyan Excavation Reports, Volume III: Proto-Elamite Civilization in the Land of Anshan*, University of Pennsylvania Museum, Philadelphia: 107–08.

Petrie, C. A., Weeks, L. R., Potts, D. T. and Roustaei, K. 2009. "Perspectives on the cultural sequence of Mamasani", in Potts, D. T., Roustaei, K., Petrie, C. A. and Weeks, L. R. (eds), *The Mamasani Archaeological Project Stage One*, BAR International Series 2044, Archaeopress, Oxford: 169–96.

Potts, D. T. 1999. *The Archaeology of Elam: Formation and Transformation of an Ancient Iranian State*, Cambridge World Archaeology Series, Cambridge University Press, Cambridge

Potts, D. T. 2008. "Review of Alizadeh, A. et al. The origins of state organizations in prehistoric highland Fars, southern Iran. Excavations at Tall-e Bakun (Oriental Institute Publications Vol. 128)", *Bibliotheca Orientalis* LXV.1–2: 195–206.

Stolper, M. W. 1985. "Proto-Elamite Texts from Tall-i Malyan", *Kadmos* 24 (2): 1–12.

Sumner, W. M. n.d. *Settlement History of the Kur River Basin, Iran, and An Archaeological Gazetteer*, unpublished MS, June 2009.

Sumner, W. M. 1972. *Cultural Development in the Kur River Basin, Iran: An Archaeological Analysis of Settlement Patterns*, unpublished Ph.D. dissertation, Department of Anthropology, University of Pennsylvania, Philadelphia.

Sumner, W. M. 1985. "The Proto-Elamite city wall at Tal-e Malyan", *Iran* 23: 153–61.

Sumner, W. M. 1986. "Proto-Elamite Civilization in Fars", in Finkbeiner, U. and Röllig, W. (eds), *Gamdat Nasr: Period or Regional Style?* Ludwig Reichert, Wiesbaden: 199–211.

Sumner, W. M. 1988. "Prelude to proto-Elamite Anshan: the Lapui Phase", *IA* 23: 23–43.

Sumner, W. M. 1989. "Anshan in the Kaftari phase: patterns of settlement and land use", in Meyer, L. and Haerinck, E. (eds), *Archaeologia Iranica et Orientalis: Miscellanea in Honorem Louis Vanden Berghe*, Peeters Presse, Gent: 135–61.

Sumner, W. M. 2003. *Early Urban Life in the Land of Anshan: Excavations at Tal-e Malyan in the Highlands of Iran*, Malyan Excavation Reports, vol. III, University of Pennsylvania Museum, Philadelphia.

Sumner, W. M. 2005. "A Few Good Sherds", in "A View From the High Road: A Symposium in Honor of T. Cuyler Young, Jr", *Bulletin of the Canadian Society for Mesopotamian Studies* 40: 19–22.

Wright, H. T. 1987. "The Susiana hinterlands during the era of primary state formation", in Hole, F. (ed.), *The Archaeology of Western Iran*, Smithsonian Institution, Washington DC: 141–55.

Wright, H. T. and Carter, E. 2003. "Archaeological Survey on the Western Ram Hormuz Plain, 1969", in Miller and Abdi 2003: 60–82.

Wright, H. T. and Johnson, G. 1975. "Population, exchange, and early state formation in southwestern Iran", *American Anthropologist* 77: 267–89.

Zeder, M. A. 1991. *Feeding Cities: Specialized Animal Economy in the Ancient Near East*, Smithsonian Institution, Washington DC/London.

Zeder, M. A. and Blackman, M. J. 2003. "Economy and administration at Banesh Malyan: exploring the potential of faunal and chemical data for understanding state process", in Miller and Abdi 2003: 121–39.

Zeidi, M., McCall, B. and Khosrowzadeh, A. 2009. "Survey of Dasht-e Rostam-e Yek and Dasht-e Rostam-e Do", in Potts, D. T., Roustaei, K., Petrie, C. A. and Weeks, L. R. (eds), *The Mamasani Archaeological Project Stage One*, BAR International Series 2044, Archaeopress, Oxford: 147–68.

13. *MAHTOUTABAD I* (KONAR SANDAL SOUTH, JIROFT): PRELIMINARY EVIDENCE OF OCCUPATION OF A HALIL RUD SITE IN THE EARLY FOURTH MILLENNIUM BC

Massimo Vidale and François Desset

Introduction

Rescue excavations carried out from 2006 to 2009 at the site of the plundered graveyard of Mahtoutabad (near Konar Sandal South), revealed the remains of three successive settlements dating to the fourth millennium BC. The earliest phase of occupation, *Mahtoutabad I*, lies above the virgin soil, at a depth of about 3.5–4 m below the present surface and was radiocarbon dated to the late fifth–early fourth millennium BC. The second phase, *Mahtoutabad II*, above the remains of the first settlement, is represented by a thick series of sediments that are attributed, on archaeological considerations, to the last centuries of the first half of the fourth millennium BC. The occupation labelled *Mahtoutabad III*, limited to secondary deposits in a restricted area of the site, is distinguished by ceramics that are linked, on stylistic-morphological grounds, to the *Middle* and *Late Uruk*-related pottery assemblages of the central-eastern Iranian Plateau. *Mahtoutabad IV*, finally, is the large cemetery of the third millennium BC. This paper briefly describes the stratigraphy of the site, identifying some crucial information on the third-millennium graveyard. It then focuses on the archaeological record of the earliest phase, *Mahtoutabad I*, and discusses its cultural links with contemporary ceramic assemblages in the same general geographic area.

In contrast to some of the more intensively explored regions of Iran, the south-east has seen relatively limited investigation. Following Aurel Stein's (1937) initial discovery of various major sites (e.g. Shahr-i Sokhta), the 1960s and 1970s saw excavations and surveys carried out in various regions including the Bard Sir (Tal-e Iblis; Caldwell 1967), Sistan (Shahr-i Sokhta; Tosi 1968), Shah-Maran and Daulatabad (Prickett 1986), Soghun (Tepe Yahya; Lamberg-Karlovsky 1970; Beale 1986; Potts 2001), and Shahdad (Hakemi 1997). Many of these regions, however, are considerable distances apart and there are numerous areas that have not been explored intensively (Fig. 13.1). More recent archaeological investigation in the Halil Rud region highlights the importance of south-eastern Iran during the third millennium BC (e.g. Madjidzadeh 2008). This contribution will mainly present what we now know about the Halil Rud region in the early fourth millennium BC, in light of the preliminary finds at Mahtoutabad, which was undoubtedly one of the main burial grounds of the nearby third-millennium BC urban centre of Konar Sandal South.

The state of research on the Halil Rud

Initially discovered by Stein (1937), the site complex of Konar Sandal (Fig. 13.2) became very famous in 2002/2003, after news of the plundering of the Halil Rud graveyards and the recovery of many stolen antiquities spread throughout the archaeological scene and made a deep impact on the media (e.g. Madjidzadeh 2003a, 2003b, 2003c; Amiet 2002; Forest 2003; Pittman 2003; Perrot 2003; Perrot and Madjidzadeh 2003, 2004, 2005, 2006; Covington 2004; Lamberg-Karlovsky 2004; Lawler 2004, 2010; Cultural Heritage News Agency 2006). Information that

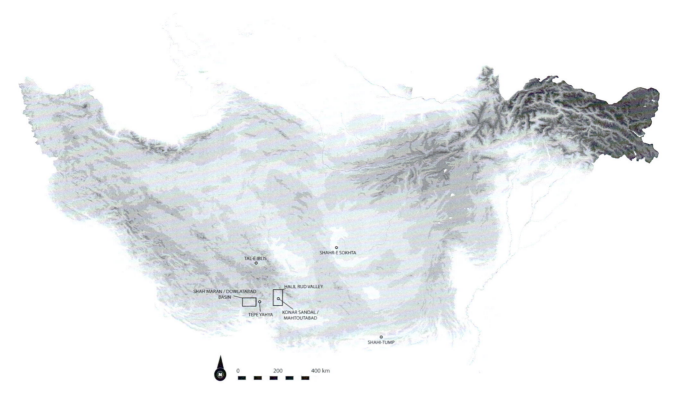

Figure 13.1. Schematic map of Iran with the location of the Halil Rud valley (F. Desset).

Figure 13.2. The area of the Konar Sandal sites, with the location of the Mahtoutabad looted site (F. Desset).

circulated from 2003 onwards was poor and biased but the sudden and unexpected discovery strongly suggested – although indirectly – that the Halil valley was the core of the production and probably of the distribution of the already famous so-called "intercultural style/*série ancienne*" carved chlorite artefacts (see Miroschedji 1973; Kohl 1975, 1978, 2001; Pottier 1984; Amiet 1986; Lamberg-Karlovsky 1988; Pittman 1990; Zarins 1978; Aruz 2003).

The consequences of the discovery of the Halil Rud valley archaeological sites are manifold. First, Tepe Yahya, the only ascertained manufacturing centre of these artefacts (Lamberg-Karlovsky 1970, 1988; Kohl 2001), is more likely to be interpreted as only one of the many possible locations where manufacturing was performed, near the still poorly known chlorite mining areas of the Kerman region.

Second, the sites of the Halil Rud valley now appear as important markets for such goods, as they seem to have been required en masse for the funerals of local elites (see below), and were not simply specialised suppliers for western demand. Labels such as "intercultural" or "trans-Elamite style" should thus be abandoned and we should rather refer to the specific style of the "Halil Rud culture" and, perhaps even more importantly, to its evolution in time.

Third, the label of "secondary state formation" (Kohl 2009) frequently applied to the Bronze Age social evolution of this part of south-eastern Iran should be at least quarantined, given the very initial stage of local scientific surveys and the reliable reports from the macro-region of hundreds of newly discovered prehistoric sites. The list of new sites includes an unbroken sequence from the late Neolithic and Chalcolithic (in the northern mountainous stretches of the Halil valley) and the Bronze Age, down to the Iron Age (unpublished materials and reports shown to the authors by Nader Soleimani). The hypothesis of an autochthonous civilisation needs to be substantiated, however, by further field research. In fact, to date topographic information is very partial, the results of local surveys have not yet been published, and the real extent and full archaeological sequence of the Konar Sandal site complex and its surroundings are still elusive.

Nonetheless, recent contributions are shedding important light on this early urban core area. These include an updated preliminary study of the human geography of the Halil Rud valley (Fouache 2009; Fouache *et al.* 2005), a largely factual preliminary report on the first seasons of excavation at the Konar Sandal sites (Madjidzadeh 2008), and a substantial volume in Farsi (Madjidzadeh 2004; at present being translated into English) entirely dedicated to the preliminary results of Madjidzadeh's project. This volume contains many specialist papers on the excavated architecture, ceramic and lithic studies, geomorphology, archaeo-zoology, and archaeo-

botany that positively anchor the third-millennium BC site of Konar Sandal South to the archaeology of contemporaneous cultures and civilisations.

Other efforts have identified relationships between the ceramic industries of the Halil Rud valley and the Arabian Peninsula (Potts 2005), wrestled with the extraordinary iconography of the chlorite artefacts (Perrot 2003, 2008; Perrot and Madjidzadeh 2003, 2004, 2005, 2006; Winkelmann 2005), and considered the surprising find of four tablets with an unknown writing system (Basello 2006; Madjidzadeh 2012; Desset in press). On the basis of this growing evidence, Steinkeller (1982, 2012) has proposed that the Halil Rud valley probably had a central role in Marhashi, a frequently quoted eastern polity in Mesopotamian texts (*contra* Francfort and Tremblay 2010, who would rather locate Marhashi in the Oxus region).

History of the excavations at Mahtoutabad: Trenches I–V

In 2004, Massimo Vidale was appointed by Youssef Madjidzadeh to direct the excavation of the first test trenches at Mahtoutabad. Funding was provided by IsIAO, Rome, the Italian Ministry for Foreign Affairs (MAE), and the Halil Rud Archaeological Research Project (HARP). Our first campaign at Mahtoutabad took place from January to February 2006, the second between November 2006 and February 2007, with the final phase being carried out under Iranian direction. At the end of November 2006, Trench I was enlarged on the north side with an additional exposure of 20 × 10 m (Trench IV; see Fig. 13.5). Here, in January– February 2007 Ali Daneshi unearthed part of the earliest deposits so far identified at Mahtoutabad. Excavation was then halted for two years.

When François Desset joined the team in January 2008, the workers were on strike for higher pay and it was impossible to excavate, so we took the opportunity of mapping the site in detail with a total station. The fourth and for the moment most recent campaign took place in January 2009, when Vidale was asked by Hassan Fazeli Nashli, then Director of the Iranian Centre for Archaeological Research, to continue the excavation in collaboration with Nader Soleimani of the Kerman Miras Farangi. Expenses for these final seasons were shared by the Italian and Iranian teams. At the time, the excavations at KSS had been suspended for lack of proper funding, and the small trenches excavated at the cemetery were the only active operation in the region.

The last season was quite successful, as we completed the excavation of the northern sector of Trench I, where we finally ascertained that the earliest deposits belonged to a single, large *Mahtoutabad I* semi-subterranean structure, and finally located the only undisturbed third-millennium BC (*Mahtoutabad IV*) burial ever found in this cemetery, which was situated in a collapsed catacomb-like grave similar to those well-known at Shahr-i Sokhta.

Mahtoutabad IV: the third-millennium graveyard

The geomorphology of the alluvial plain of Konar Sandal and its mountainous borders has been comprehensively described by Fouache *et al.* (2005) and Fouache (2009). The cemetery of Mahtoutabad (28°27′20″ N; 57°47′26″ E) lies about 1.4 km south-east of the Konar Sandal North Tappeh and 1.3 km northeast of the Konar Sandal South Tappeh (hereafter KSS) (Fig. 13.2).

Today, the surface of Mahtoutabad, around the area affected by the looting pits, shows the signs of recently abandoned cultivations, including old, washed-off ploughed fields and small irrigation furrows, which are situated in a residual landscape with low shrubs, tamarisks and, on the riverbanks, thick reeds. The uppermost alluvial layers in the cemetery site can only be generically ascribed to late proto-historic, historic, and more recent times. They were exploited for agricultural activities, as shown by the wavy ploughing interface recorded in the top of the section (see Fig. 13.7). Here, the large robbing pit at right and the earthen piles nearby are the dumps of the mass looting of 2001.

The graveyard, which is now completely ransacked (Fig. 13.3), was undoubtedly used by the Konar Sandal urban community, although perhaps only for a short period of time during the second half of the third millennium BC. It grew on the bank of the Halil River, which probably flowed west of the ancient burial ground (Fouache *et al.* 2005). The site's topography and the materials abandoned by the looters near their shafts suggest that the richest burials were those placed on the most elevated part of the burial ground. The natural bank, at the time, might have risen 2 m or more above the surrounding floodplain, and this would have been enough to protect the graves from the most immediate risks of flooding. The trampling surface of the graveyard, *Mahtoutabad IV*, is marked by layer 110, a 15–20 cm-thick horizontal layer that contained a certain amount of broken bowls and small jars of the mid-third millennium BC. We were able to ascertain that the pits and disturbances presumably linked to the graves were actually cut from this horizon.

The bank in which the graves were dug was formed by thick and very compact layers of locally derived light brown silt, including lenses of sand and occasional layers of coarse gravel. It gradually slopes eastwards, towards the present bed of the Halil. At some point in the past, the area was intensively flooded and the bank was entirely sealed by new alluvial layers.

Nothing was visible on the surface before a

Figure 13.3. A general view of the site of Mahtoutabad showing its very disturbed surface (photo M. Vidale).

ruinous flood in spring 2001 cut through the ancient riverbank and most probably brought to light the first graves and their treasures. This event is marked on the surface by a 10 cm-thick layer of loose, dark grey sand that is visible across an area of several hectares. This sand is still easily recognisable below the piles of earthen debris left by the looters during their months of repeated digging. The fact that no less than three major superimposed phases of occupation were actually invisible on the surface emphasises how arbitrary quantitative estimates of settlement and demographic trends of a region can be unless they are accompanied by geomorphological analysis to map the alluvial covering process and a strategy of sub-surface testing.

While tunnelling for antiquities at a depth of 3–4 m below the present surface, the local farmers came across archaeological layers rich in painted and unpainted ceramics. These sherds, often decorated with highly visible patterns and colours, were later ascribed to *Mahtoutabad I*, the earliest phase of occupation at the site so far discovered. Widely scattered on the surface by looting, these unmistakable sherds could easily be mapped and show that this early settlement extended for about 1.5 ha (Fig. 13.4).

A surface survey of the site in January 2008 also allowed us to delimit the extent of the third-millennium BC graveyard: for this purpose we

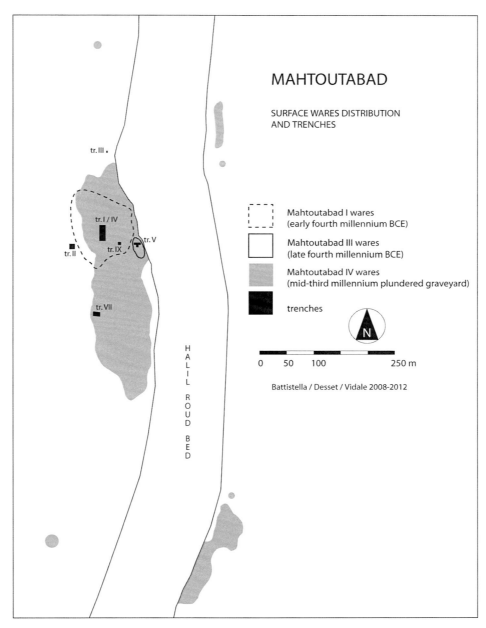

Figure 13.4. Map of Mahtoutabad, showing the location of the excavated trenches, the original extent of the graveyard, and the probable limits of the Mahtoutabad I *and* Mahtoutabad III *local deposits (E. Battistella, F. Desset, and M. Vidale).*

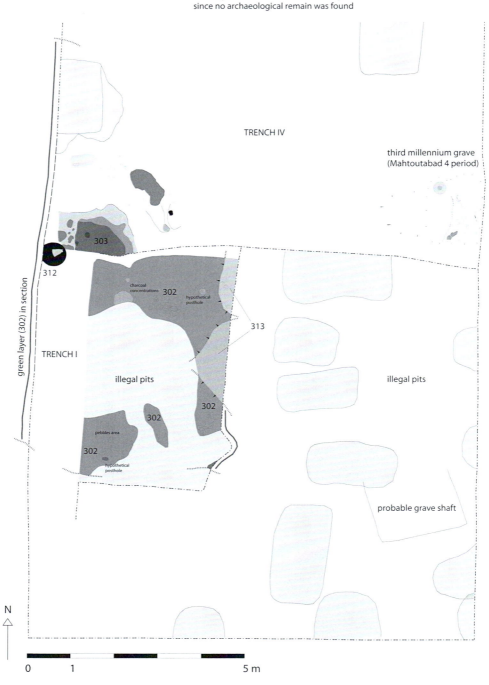

the northern part of the excavation is not represented
since no archaeological remain was found

TRENCH IV

third millennium grave
(Mahtoutabad 4 period)

green layer (302) in section

303

312

charcoal
concentrations   302

hypothetical
posthole

313

TRENCH I

illegal pits

illegal pits

302

302

pebbles area

302

hypothetical
posthole

probable grave shaft

N

0   1   5 m

Figure 13.5. Mahtoutabad, 2006–2009: map of Trench I with the northern extension dug in winter 2006 (Trench IV), but regularly excavated in January 2009. The light grey areas are the pits excavated by looters. The darker areas show the location of the disturbed green floor of the Oval Hut; the only undisturbed third-millennium BC grave so far located in the cemetery was found immediately to the east (F. Desset).

mapped the pits that had large third-millennium BC sherds with fresh fractures dumped nearby. By our calculation, the cemetery measured approximately 400 × 150 m (Fig. 13.4), not less than 6 ha. It probably also extended to the opposite side of the present bed of the Halil, which cut through the graveyard at a later time. Using a very conservative estimate of two graves for every 100 m², we calculate that at least 1000 graves

were looted at Mahtoutabad. As our main operation showed (Trenches I/IV) in the core of the cemetery, however, there were nine robbing pits or more per 100 m², and most of these had evidently hit a grave (Fig. 13.5). Although it is unlikely that there was an even distribution of graves within the cemetery, the total number of destroyed graves might originally have been almost double.

Feeling as though we were walking in the footsteps of Flinders Petrie at Abydos, we spent two seasons mapping and collecting artefacts on the disturbed surface (e.g. pottery, beads, inlay pieces, and metal objects and fragments), often excavating and systematically sieving the looting debris. On this basis, we were able to identify a small cluster of very rich graves containing copper weapons; hundreds of lapis lazuli, turquoise, and gold micro-beads; and dozens of chlorite and copper vessels that had been plundered in the south-western edge of the cemetery which, as stated above, is the most elevated part of the site.

While the results exceed the scope of this paper and will be published in the final report, it is important to stress that in this way we recovered an abundance of small fragments of carved chlorite vessels broken *in situ* and lost by the robbers. They display the majority of the most important Halil patterns (basket weave, embricated design, door pattern, snakes, date palms, scorpions). We also found many tiny inlay pieces (in mother-of-pearl, white limestone, turquoise, and red limestone) that had fallen from these vessels when they were stolen. Although recovered from disturbed contexts at the mouth of and inside the pits, these objects were associated to Emir grey wares and other distinctive third-millennium BC ceramic types, and scientifically demonstrate beyond any reasonable doubt that this cemetery is one of the sources of the mass of chlorite artefacts lost to the market; they also positively link the cemetery to the mid-third-millennium BC contexts excavated at KSS Tappeh, where carved chlorite artefacts with the same motifs were found in primary stratigraphic contexts (Madjidzadeh 2008).

Ultimately, the results show how misleading and one-sided it is to insist on treating the Halil Rud discovery, with all its problems, as a confused and dubious "Jiroft question" (e.g. Muscarella 2005, 2009). At present it seems more urgent and relevant to learn what the KSS sites are, rather than what "Jiroft" is not.

Mahtoutabad III

On the surface we recovered a large assemblage of *Mahtoutabad III* (Uruk-related) material in Trench V (Fig. 13.4), near the river (this settlement phase is not represented in the sequence of Trench I – see below). In 2007 and 2009 we dug a surface measuring in total about 100 m², with the 2009 excavations being directed by Nader Soleimani. These ceramics were in a secondary context of deposition, embedded in alluvial layers alternating with thin aeolian layers. The stratigraphy suggested a period of drought, suddenly interrupted by two or three flood episodes. No architectural remains were observed in the excavated area, but many vessels were complete or almost complete, suggesting that the materials had been eroded in a nearby location.

The pottery assemblage includes hundreds of sherds of bevel-rim bowls and coarse low-sided trays, flowerpots, globular jars with combed shoulder and staff-like handles, a few tall jars or bottles with downward-bent shoulder spouts, and three sherds of biconical vessels with nose-like lugs on the shoulder. There were also three fragments of terracotta sickles of unmistakable western fashion. Painted fragments (2–3% of the total) were limited to a set of small fine pots and truncated cone-shaped bowls stylistically similar to some contemporary assemblages of south-eastern Iran. The same deposits also contained several fragments of jar stoppers of unbaked clay (two with seal impressions) and two fragments of two different large weights in travertine, suggesting the performance of administrative activities. As no carbon survived in the flood layers, and the animal bones found had no surviving protein content, stylistic comparisons would place *Mahtoutabad III* to the mid- to late fourth millennium BC. Details and implications of this assemblage – the easternmost of this type so far found on the plateau – will be discussed in another report (Desset and Vidale, in preparation).

Mahtoutabad II

This settlement phase is represented by a sequence of horizontal layers extending below the third-millennium graveyard in its northern extension for about 2–3 ha, with a maximum thickness of 1.1 m. These layers appear to have been gradually deposited as a series of open-air trampling surfaces, rich in small-sized potsherds with a few smaller bones and lithics (see below). No architectural feature was uncovered in the excavated area. The *Mahtoutabad II* pottery has no apparent link or similarity with the *Mahtoutabad III* Uruk-related assemblage, a fact that obviously enough retouches on the old question of its "intrusive" nature across the Iranian Plateau. The repertoire of *Mahtoutabad II* pottery forms and decoration closely corresponds to many *Aliabad* ware specimens originally published as Iblis IV in Caldwell 1967. The *Mahtoutabad II* layers contain, among the most recognisable forms, tall conical footed vases with sturdy walls and thick ring feet; bowls and larger hemispherical basins with rims underlined by a deep groove; and small globular jars with short vertical rims. The rather coarse vessels are made combining coil building, probably moulding, and wheel throwing; the external surfaces are frequently heavily trimmed with the use of vertical movements. The painted decoration (recorded in about 15% of the sherds) is dark brown on buff, but many sherds show bichrome or even three-chrome patterns (variously combining black, light reddish brown, and white or greenish white). The motifs are rather simple: vertical hatched and wavy bands, concentric festoons (often filled with white dots), and lozenges, always traced with thick brushes. The patterns are rather irregular and freely occupy the outer and inner surface of the vessels. The pottery, as a rule, is well fired in oxidising or partially oxidising conditions, resulting in buff or pink-coloured pastes.

The pottery found in the *Mahtoutabad II* layers is clearly an evolution and from a technical viewpoint, a simplification of the earlier *Mahtoutabad I* wares (see below). Unfortunately, the study of this material is still at a very preliminary stage and we cannot include a detailed description; the rest of the article focuses on the evidence of the earliest occupation phase, *Mahtoutabad I*.

Figure 13.6. Mahtoutabad: a general view of Trench I during excavation, winter 2006–2007. The Mahtoutabad I *levels were exposed in the deepest test trench, at the top, at a depth of about 4 m from the surface (photo M. Vidale).*

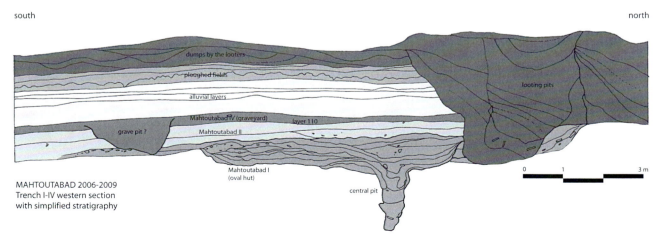

Figure 13.7. The western north–south section of Trenches I–IV, showing the sequence of the Mahtoutabad I *(Oval Hut), II, and IV (the third-millennium BC graveyard) occupation phases. The sequence is overlain by alluvial layers due to later floods and by the signs of later, possibly recent, agricultural activities. Finally the section shows a large pit and the debris piled up by the grave looters in 2001 (M. Vidale and F. Desset).*

Mahtoutabad I

Trench I was dug in the centre of the cemetery to explore its stratigraphy (Fig. 13.5), find the context of the sherds predating the third-millennium BC graves, and ascertain whether anything was left of the burials so extensively impacted by the robbing pits (Figs 13.6 and 13.7). The trench measured 11 m (east–west) × 10 m (north–south). In the first two seasons, we dug through the *Mahtoutabad II* layers, until we reached the early fourth-millennium BC layers at a depth of 3.5–4 m below the present surface, in a limited strip of 10 × 1 m along the western side (Fig. 13.7, upper right wall). The ceramic transition from *Mahtoutabad II* to *I* was gradual but evident. For example, the lowermost layers of the *Mahtoutabad II* settlement were excavated with artificial cuts 10 cm thick and as we went deeper we observed a constant increase of painted decoration, from about 15% of the *Mahtoutabad II* series to about 35% on top of the *Mahtoutabad I* filling. The narrow exposure on the west side of Trench I uncovered a green clay layer with a deep conical pit lined with silty clay in the centre, containing a number of well-preserved vessels and lithic tools.

Between November 2006 and January 2007 Ali Daneshi cleared a wide extension immediately north of Trench I in our absence (labelled Trench IV). He found that the green clay layer was actually the northern part of a large arc-shaped floor supporting fireplaces and abundant pottery, among which large sherds of storage jars, apparently dumped and crushed *in situ*. The area enclosed in Trench I was further dug in the last season (2009), reopening the eastern part of Trench I. At the end of January 2009 we had thus exposed at different times about half of what may be interpreted as an oval green-coloured floor (layer 302 in Fig. 13.5) studded with dumped artefacts and large bones, which belongs to a single large semi-subterranean structure, not less than 9.5 m long (from north to south) and possibly 8 m wide if the western unexcavated part is symmetrical (Fig. 13.5).

We labelled this structure, somewhat optimistically, the "Oval Hut" (sometimes expediently referred to as the "green layer" due to its very bright colour) but in fact, pits and tunnels have severely damaged its integrity, to the point that our reconstructions are partially conjectural. The deep clay-lined pit (feature 312 in Fig. 13.5), at least in its first stage of construction, might have been the seat of a large central supporting pole. Later, the post was removed and the central hole might have been temporarily used as a storage pit, because when its basal filling was further explored, we found other large pottery fragments, two complete conical vessels, and a large lozenge-shaped artefact in unbaked clay of unknown function.

The stratigraphic sequence of Trenches I–IV is illustrated in the western section illustrated in Figure 13.7. It shows that the cavity (feature 312) of the semi-subterranean Oval Hut (*Mahtoutabad I*) was originally lined at the edges with fine green silt. Its original depth would have been 0.8–1 m below its surrounding level. While the Hut or its cavity was still in use, the central pit and the floor were gradually filled with superimposed trampling surfaces, alternating with small-scale silty colluvial deposits and local floor restorations. In the northern side of the Hut's floor, a raised bench, made of fine greyish clay and probably supported by a series of small vertical logs, was related to these surfaces but is not represented in the Figure 13.7 section. At least three fireplaces were used, probably at different periods, in various areas of the hut.

Mahtoutabad I: *the pottery*

A preliminary inspection of the pottery from the filling levels in the Oval Hut shows that the most common forms can be attributed to four groups as follows: 1. truncated cone-shaped basins, large basins, and cylindrical jars; 2. sub-globular restricted jars and pots; 3. hemispherical bowls; and 4. conical footed vases (Fig. 13.8). The first two groups are distinguished by one or more horizontal ridges running below the mouth and belong to the ceramic class labelled "ridged ware" in the Tal-e Iblis report (Chase *et al.* 1967a: 182, 184); the other two belong to a type of fine painted ware which is reported and preliminarily described here for the first time.

1. *Basins, large basins* and *cylindrical jars* (Figs 13.8–13.10). These open vessels were made on a potter's wheel or similar device, by pressing and joining series of coils, which are visible in the rough unmodified external surfaces. In contrast, the interior frequently shows rotating marks. Basins and bowls, and the lower parts of jars, were thus assembled inside large open moulds, as indicated by sandy or dry clayey exterior surfaces and patterns of cracks, while the interior was smoothed with regular movements. The rim protruded from the mouth of the mould and often received one or more applied parallel ridges (hence ridged ware). The coarse incised line that runs below the rims of similar forms in the subsequent *Mahtoutabad II* pottery are a simplified version of the same ridges. The ceramic body is yellowish to pale brown (5YR 7/3 to 10YR 7/4). Large basins or open-mouthed cylindrical jars (from 60–80 cm and larger) were painted on the exterior with broad horizontal or oblique bands (e.g. Fig. 13.9), grey or dark reddish brown (10YR 5/1, 5YR 3/5), turning to olive (5Y 5/3) on the frequent over-fired specimens.

2. *Sub-globular restricted jars*, medium-sized and sometimes very large (Figs 13.8, 13.11), were fashioned with strips or horizontal slabs of clay (for the largest storage containers) or coils (for restricted pots), while the vessels were rotated on a slow wheel. Sub-globular restricted pots were then

HEMISPHERICAL BOWLS CONICAL FOOTED VASES SUBGLOBULAR RESTRICTED JARS

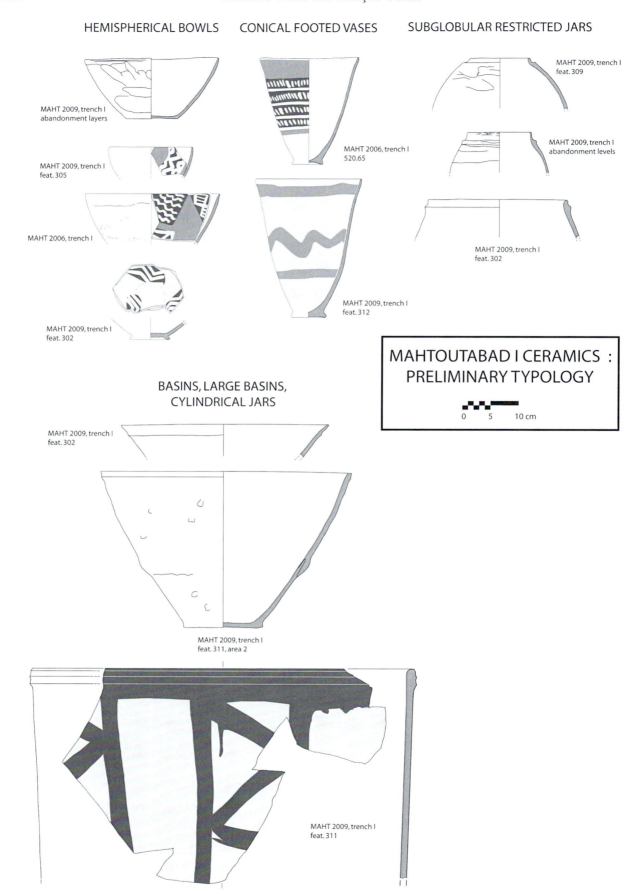

MAHTOUTABAD I CERAMICS :
PRELIMINARY TYPOLOGY

0   5   10 cm

Figure 13.8. Mahtoutabad I *preliminary ceramic typology (drawings R. Micheli, E. Battistella, F. Desset, and M. Vidale).*

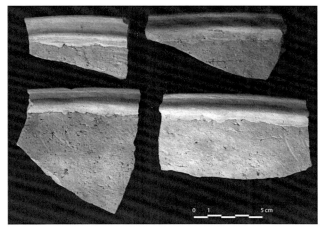

Figure 13.9. Mahtoutabad I: examples of ridged ware open bowls and basins (photo M. Vidale).

Figure 13.10. Mahtoutabad I, *ridged ware: a rim sherd of a large sub-cylindrical jar or basin externally painted with broad vertical and oblique lines (photo M. Vidale).*

Figure 13.11. Mahtoutabad I: *from the disturbed floor of the Oval Hut. A small- to medium-sized globular restricted pot painted with thick circles (photo M. Vidale).*

Figure 13.12. Mahtoutabad I: *an example of a hemispherical bowl, found in the filling of the central pit of the Oval Hut (photo M. Vidale).*

Figure 13.13. Mahtoutabad I: *three conical footed vases painted in white over black and brown-red backgrounds, found in the filling of the central pit of the Oval Hut (photo M. Vidale).*

Figure 13.14. Mahtoutabad I: *sherds of conical footed vases showing various geometrical designs (photo F. Desset).*

trimmed, but not turned, at the base with a blade-like tool. The exterior was often painted with thick circles (e.g. medium-sized specimens in Fig. 13.11). The ceramic body is whitish (10YR 8/2) to very pale brown (10YR 8/3), the pigments approximating grey-olive shadows (10YR 5/1 to 5Y 4/3).

3. *Hemispherical bowls* (Figs 13.8, 13.12) were carefully fashioned by joining coils thinned and shaped on the potter's wheel. The outer surface was trimmed after partial drying with secure vertical movements, making the walls much thinner. They often bear a ring-foot that was fashioned on the bottom of the vessel while it was upturned on the potter's wheel. Painted decoration involved the application of black, white, and red pigments that resulted in brightly contrasting patterns, as in the fourth group. The ceramic body's colour varies from pink (5YR 8/3, 7/3) to light reddish brown (5YR 6/3). The black bands are defined in the Munsell code as shadows of dark grey, dark reddish grey, or reddish grey (5YR 4/1, 4/2, 5/2); the pigments of the designs are white (5Y 8/1, 8/2) to pale yellow (5Y 8/4), while the red slip is a uniform yellowish red (5YR 5/6).

4. *Conical footed vases* (Figs 13.8, 13.13–13.15) are fine, elegant vessels, clearly ancestral to the sturdy, less curated conical footed vases of *Mahtoutabad II*. They were made with the same forming sequence (coil building and thinning on the potter's wheel; partial drying; vertical trimming; upturning and centring on the wheel; wheel-fashioning of the ring foot) and painting with the same pigments and techniques used for hemispherical bowls. Some

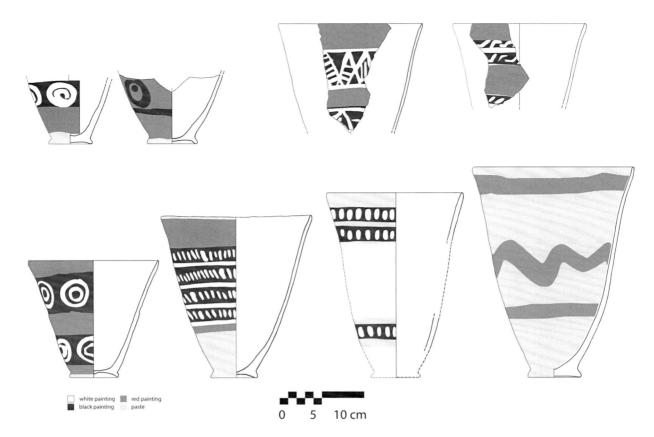

Figure 13.15. Mahtoutabad I *ceramics, including several examples of conical footed vessels painted in white over black and red backgrounds (drawings R. Micheli, E. Battistella, and M. Vidale).*

conical footed vases, moreover, were more simply painted in brown over a plain buff paste. In the three-colours technique (black, red, and white), the chromatic contrast creates interesting visual patterns, thanks also to a geometric repertory so far estimated to about 60 basic design elements (e.g. plain, stepped and wavy lines, fish-bone designs, meanders, dots and segments, stars, lozenges, triangles, circles, spirals, and many others; Figs 13.14–13.15).

From a technical viewpoint, the creation of permanent pigments with such contrasting colours in a kiln demands skill and many manufacturing hours. According to our preliminary studies, no less than three different stages of firing were involved, including the inversion of the atmosphere within the kiln (Vidale *et al.*, ongoing research). Such technology probably depended on the experience and skill of a long-established tradition, although the evidence for this has not yet been found in the Halil Rud valley. In fact, we are dealing with a very efficient, standardised manufacturing technology variously combining coiling, moulding, trimming, wheel forming, and an excellent control of the firing atmospheres which doubtless required well-designed kilns. It is possible that hemispherical bowls and conical footed vases, so

similar in form and decoration, were used to present and consume solid and liquid substances in the same dining contexts.

This attractive polychrome ware and its industry may have played an important role in technological exchange and more generally in the east–west interaction between the south-eastern margin of the Iranian Plateau and Baluchistan. In fact, it has been found in the Shah Maran-Daulatabad basin (Prickett 1986: fig. III.11.B, E, F, and I) while more recently, a small number of unmistakable sherds painted red, black, and white with the same designs were found at Shah-i Tump (Period IIIa), in the Pakistani Makran, in contexts preliminarily dated to the second half of the fourth millennium BC (Mutin 2007, this volume).

Conical footed vases generically resemble the tall conical vessels or beakers of northern Baluchistan (Pakistan) of the *Kechi-Beg* polychrome style (second half of the fourth millennium BC; see Jarrige *et al.* 1995) and the abundant production of similar vessels (fourth millennium BC) at sites in Pakistani Makran (Mutin 2007; Didier 2007), sometimes bearing similar white and red designs.

Finally, it is also important to mention that in the *Mahtoutabad I* assemblage we also recovered what appear to be a number of *Lapui* plain red ware sherds, quite different from the rest of the assemblage. *Lapui* red ware is usually attributed in Fars to the first half of the fourth millennium BC (Kur River Basin and Mamasani; Sumner 1988; Potts *et al.* 2009: 9; Petrie *et al.* 2009: 174–75), although it has been noted that *Lapui*-like wares have also been observed at Tepe Yahya and Tal-e Iblis (Beale 1986; Sumner 1988: 28–29; Petrie 2011, 2013; Mutin, this volume).

Other artefacts and industries

Obviously enough, what we excavated is too little, partial, and damaged for us to say much about the architectural forms and use of the settlement. Nonetheless, as noted above three fireplaces, which were possibly used in different events, were found on the floor of the structure. The nearby dumping of bovine bones (*Bos* sp.; M. Mashkour, personal communication), of broken large coarse chaff-tempered pans, and large of storage jars smashed *in situ* that can be refitted, suggests that domestic activities were being carried out.

Along the edges of the Oval Hut and on its floor, we recovered substantial amounts of light green frothy and fragile slag fragments. XRD analysis showed the presence of quartz, feldspars, diopside, cuprite (in two out of three samples), and traces of calcite. Feldspars and diopside, which are probably high-temperature products, and cuprite (Cu_2O) all point to copper metallurgy. Together with these glassy slags, we collected some thick chaff-tempered wall fragments or linings of small- to medium-sized ovens. There were also pieces of cylinder-like bars that might have been parts of suspended grids from a kiln.

On the occupation layers above the floors of the Oval Hut, we also found the vitrified fragment of a ceramic mould used for casting copper bars. Nearby was a cuprous alloy object, potentially a casting, which fitted exactly in the cavity of the mould. XRD analysis of its slagged surface reveals – besides quartz, diopside, feldspars, and calcite – the presence of cerussite (lead carbonate, $PbCO_3$), suggesting that copper could have been alloyed with lead. These artefacts, exported with the permission of ICAR for archaeometric study, were analysed by Christopher P. Thornton and Thilo Rehren in the Wolfson Archaeological Science Laboratory at the UCL Institute of Archaeology (complete report to be published in the final excavation volume).

The mould was made with a poorly levigated ceramic with heavy chaff temper containing a significant amount of angular quartz grains and iron oxide inclusions to ensure thermal expandability. Its slagged end contains copper and copper-sulphide prills in a cuprite-rich glassy matrix. In the bar-like ingot, XRF found a greater than 93 wt% Cu as well as ~1 wt% Pb and >0.5 wt% As. In sum, Thornton and Rehren conclude that while the metallurgical remains require further analysis, it is clear that the smelting

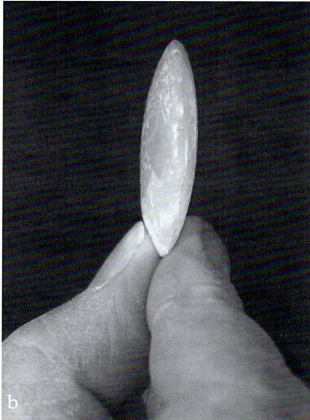

Figure 13.16/a. Mahtoutabad I: *fragments of finished and unfinished alabaster vessels and the lens-shaped white agate polisher (lower right) found by Ali Daneshi in January 2007 in the northern extension of the Oval Hut. The smaller triangular sherd left of the polisher is clearly unfinished (photo M. Vidale); b.* Mahtoutabad I: *lateral view of the white agate tool used to give the alabaster vessels their final polish (photo M. Vidale).*

of copper sulphides occurred somewhere on site, probably in copper refining, as did casting in moulds (possibly performed in the Oval Hut or nearby). The ores used appear to have contained minor amounts of lead and arsenic, which would have produced a useful alloy for casting.

The floor also contained fragments of finished and unfinished stone vessels and a unique lens-shaped white agate polisher, which indicates that alabaster

Table 13.1. Calibrated radiocarbon dates from Mahtoutabad I layers.

Sample number	Radiocarbon age BP	Calibrated range BC (2 sigma)	Probability
LTL 4244A	5284 ± 45	4240–3990 BC	95%
LTL 4240A	5038 ± 40	3960–3710 BC	95%
LTL 4239A	4805 ± 45	3700–3380 BC	95%
LTL 4241A	4745 ± 45	3640–3370 BC	95%

Table 13.2. Calibrated radiocarbon dates for Iblis IV.

Sample number	Radiocarbon age BP	Calibrated range BC (2 sigma)	Probability
P-927 (end of *Iblis III*)	5570 ± 60	4540–4330 BC	95%
P-928 (early *Iblis IV*)	5430 ± 60	4440–4050 BC	95%
P-929 (end of *Iblis IV*)	4680 ± 60	3640–3350 BC	95%

Table 13.3. Archaeological and chronological correlation between the archaeological sequences of Tal-e Iblis and Mahtoutabad, Trench I.

4540-4330 BC	**Iblis III**		**Mahtoutabad I** (white painted on brown background)	4240-3990 BC 3960-3710 BC 3700-3380 BC 3640-3370 BC
	stratigraphic continuity			
4440-4050 BC	**Iblis IV** : early Aliabad (without any Middle / Late Uruk related material)	same ceramic	**Mahtoutabad II** (red/brown painted on light past/slip)	
3640-3350 BC	**Iblis IV** : Aliabad (local and Middle / Late Uruk related material)			
			Mahtoutabad III (only Middle / Late Uruk related material)	

vessels were polished *in situ* (Fig. 13.16/a–b). Within the Oval Hut and its fillings, there were some unretouched chert flakes, probably debitage, but no formal tools. Several scrapers made from retouched ceramic sherds found during excavation were also an important component of the local tool kits, although their precise function remains unclear.[1]

Other small finds include a piece of a thick stone mortar of a peculiar yellow jasper breccia, two limestone beads, and several unbaked clay artefacts, among which a bull figurine and two biconical beads. In short, it appears that the inhabitants of the *Mahtoutabad I* Oval Hut were involved in small-scale metallurgical activities, the production of alabaster vessels, the knapping of chert, and in one or more unknown processing activities involving the manufacture and use of scrapers or choppers made by

flaking large potsherds.[2] Thus far, there is no record of administrative activities in the form of tokens, seals, or seal impressions.

Absolute dating

Four radiocarbon dates were obtained from charcoal gathered from *Mahtoutabad I* layers. The samples were processed at the AMS facility of CEDAD, University of Lecce (Italy) and have been calibrated using OxCal 4.1.3 (Table 13.1).[3]

The dates for *Mahtoutabad I* match the stratigraphy well. Apparently, there was a short chronological gap, perhaps a local abandonment, between the green layers of the first floor (LTL 4240A, 3960–3710 BC) and the layers just above (LTL 4239A and LTL 4241A, around 3700–3370 BC).

Mahtoutabad and Tal-e Iblis

Period IV at Tal-e Iblis was chronologically framed by three radiocarbon dates collected during the initial excavations: P-927 (end of *Iblis III*), P-928 ("early *Iblis IV*", layer characterised by both *Dasghar/Iblis III* and *Aliabad/Iblis IV* types), and P-929 ("end of *Iblis IV*").[4] These dates have been recalibrated using OxCal 4.1.3 (Table 13.2):

In the Iblis IV ceramic assemblage the excavators distinguished several ceramic types: *Aliabad* painted, *Aliabad* bichrome (black and red, brown and green, black and green), *Aliabad* plain, *Aliabad* brushed, and *Aliabad* ridged (Chase *et al.* 1967a: 182–88, figs 21–28). These wares frequently had a pinkish paste and were painted with different colours: black, brown, red, and green. Some bevel-rim bowls, shoulder spouts, and flowerpots were also reported (e.g. Chase *et al.* 1967a: figs 26, 29, 39–40).

The material (ceramic) transition between *Iblis III* and *Iblis IV* shows no apparent major cultural gap like that seen between *Iblis IV* and *Iblis V*. Several *Iblis III* types seem to occur during *Iblis IV* as well, such as *Dasghar* painted ware, which is perhaps an early stage of *Aliabad* painted ware. Area C at Tal-e Iblis is quite important for understanding *Iblis IV* and its transition with *Iblis III*. There, an "*Early Aliabad* layer" was actually observed between *Iblis III* and *Iblis IV*, occupying the lowermost 55 cm of a 170 cm-thick *Iblis IV* layer. Bevel-rim bowls and other shapes related to the *Middle–Late Uruk* horizon were not present in this *Early Aliabad* layer and appeared only afterwards, in the upper layers of the *Aliabad* occupation (Caldwell 1967: 23–25, 36–38; Chase *et al.* 1967b: 79; 1967a: 180–88).

The ceramic shapes most recurrent at *Mahtoutabad I* and *Iblis IV* are actually rather similar, and often *Mahtoutabad I* and *Iblis IV* vessels also present the same painted designs (e.g. Caldwell 1967: figs 21, 23; Sarraf 1981: figs 30.339–30.343, 31.347, 33.361–33.365, 34.366–33.371). As far as the original black and white illustrations allow us to judge (Caldwell 1967; Sarraf 1981), however, there is no ceramic with white designs painted on a black/dark background in *Iblis IV*, but only black/red painted motifs on light paste wares (Table 13.3).

The extant radiocarbon dates suggest that *Iblis IV* spans almost a millennium – but such a range is likely to be too imprecise – and their reliability is unclear. Nonetheless, the new datings for *Mahtoutabad I* fall within the broad time span of *Iblis IV*. In spite of its distinctive ceramic identity, *Mahtoutabad I* might therefore be at least partially contemporaneous with the earliest *Aliabad* layers at Tal-e Iblis. Our *Mahtoutabad II* material also matches the assemblage, but for the complete absence of bevel-rim bowls (see Potts 2009 for a recent review) and the other *Middle/ Late Uruk*-related forms that were exclusively found in large amounts in Trench V (*Mahtoutabad III*). In

fact, the *Aliabad* ware found above and consequently later than the *Mahtoutabad I* layers in Trench I – i.e. the *Mahtoutabad II* material – has good parallels with Caldwell's *Early Aliabad* material.

Thus, two different material assemblages may be at least partially contemporaneous: the very beginning of *Iblis IV* and *Mahtoutabad I*; while two similar material assemblages in two different regions, *Early Iblis IV* and *Mahtoutabad II*, might not be strictly contemporaneous. This phenomenon might be explained by a relatively slow diffusion process from the Bardsir region, where *Aliabad*-like wares are particularly abundant (see Sajjadi 1987), to the Halil Rud valley. Caution, further excavations, and more dates are required to address these points properly.

Conclusions

At present, the main achievement of Trench I, with the find of its *Mahtoutabad I* levels, is the discovery of an early occupation phase that could be dated to the late fifth/early fourth millennium BC. Together with the limited evidence of *Mahtoutabad II* potsherds recently identified in the deepest layers so far unearthed at the foot of the KSS mound (Madjidzadeh 2008), and our *Mahtoutabad III* materials, the evidence shows that the area was occupied (continuously or not, and in which type of settlements, we do not know) for the better part of the fourth millennium BC. In this light, the impressive outburst of the Halil Rud culture in the mid-third millennium BC should no longer necessarily be considered a rapid "secondary" effect of external processes (e.g. Kohl 2009), but could be an outgrowth of a local developmental trajectory.

Although there is still much to learn, from the point of view of manufacturing techniques, forms, and decoration the *Mahtoutabad I* pottery appears to be ancestral to the later *Aliabad* material, and it is probable that the culture or cultures that made these wares were active in the development of social complexity in the core of the Halil valley. The production of these ceramic wares might have been restricted to the southern part of Kerman (Halil Rud valley and Shah Maran/Daulatabad basin; only three sherds, at present, have been found in Shah-i Tump in Pakistani Makran). This new, deeply original and highly sophisticated ceramic production process capable of producing whitish designs on dark-red backgrounds, adds to the repertory of the high-quality ceramics of the fourth millennium BC that are known to have existed on the eastern borders of the Iranian plateau. Even at a first technical glance, it fully deserves to be considered an important element of what may be called "the millennium of technical complexity" (Chris Thornton, personal communication).

Acknowledgements

We are extremely grateful to Youssef Madjidzadeh for the opportunity of working at Mahtoutabad, a very disturbed but quite crucial archaeological site, and for his important suggestions. Many thanks are also due to Hassan Fazeli Nashli, Mrs Javadi, and all the colleagues of the Miras Farangi of Kerman, for their invaluable support of the project, and particularly to Nader Soleimani and Ali Daneshi, who generously helped us in the field for four seasons. On the Italian side Enrico Battistella, Roberto Micheli, Elisa Masioli, and Elisa Cortesi also worked in the field and made substantial input to the work. We would like to acknowledge the continuous scientific exchange with Profs C.C. Lamberg-Karlovsky and Holly Pittman, who have helped us to put many difficult questions in the right perspective.

Notes

1. Such objects had already been reported in Tal-e Iblis (Chase *et al.* 1967a: 165, fig. 34/1, fig. 35/7–8, fig. 45/4), in older layers (Tal-e Iblis I and II periods), Tepe Sabz (Mehmeh phase; Hole *et al.* 1969: 211), Tepe Djaffarabad I–III (end of the fifth/beginning of the fourth millennium BC; Dollfus 1971: 30), Tepe Bendebal (Dollfus 1983: 154), and Tol-e Baši (*Bakun* phase; fifth millennium BC; Pollock *et al.* 2010: 198).

2. About 100 m north of Trench I, within the extent of the *Mahtoutabad I* settlement, the looters uncovered a dozen blades and flakes of chert or chalcedony and five fragments of lapis lazuli, among which two blocklets bearing the distinctive marginal groove of the reduction technique originally described at Shahr-e Sokhta (Tosi and Piperno 1973). The single rim fragment of an unfinished chlorite vessel was found in similar secondary contexts. Massimo Vidale thinks that these stone-working indicators most probably date back to the fourth millennium BC, but their context prevents their inclusion in the present discussion. They will be published and discussed in the final report.

3. We would like to acknowledge the invaluable and generous help of Lucio Calcagnile, Gianluca Quarta, and the whole team of CEDAD.

4. Caldwell 1967: 23, 36 and Voigt and Dyson 1992 vol. 2: 131 for the original BP dates.

Bibliography

Amiet, P. 1986. *L'âge des échanges inter-iraniens, 3500–1700 avant .J-C.*, Notes et documents des Musées de France 11, Éditions de la réunion des musées nationaux, Paris.

Amiet, P. 2002. "Review of Madjidzadeh, 2003a", *Revue d'Assyriologie et d'Archéologie Orientale* 96/1: 95–96.

Aruz, J. 2003. ed. *Art of the first cities, the third millennium BC, from the Mediterranean to the Indus*, The Metropolitan Museum of Art, New York.

Basello, G. P. 2006. *The Tablet from Konar Sandal B (Jiroft)*, www.elamit.net, accessed on 7 November 2006.

Beale, T. W. 1986. *Excavations at Tepe Yahya, Iran, 1967– 1975, The Early Periods*, American School of Prehistoric Research, Bulletin 38, Peabody Museum, Harvard University, Cambridge MA.

Caldwell, J. R. 1967. *Excavations at Tal-i Iblis*. Illinois State Museum Preliminary reports No. 9, Illinois State Museum Society, Springfield.

Chase, D. W., Caldwell, J. R and Fehervari, G. 1967a. "The Iblis sequence and the exploration of excavation A, C and E", in Caldwell, J. R. (ed.), *Investigations at Tal-i Iblis*, Illinois State Museum Preliminary reports No. 9, Illinois State Museum Society, Springfield: 111–201.

Chase, D. W., Fehervari, G. and Caldwell, J. R. 1967b. "Reconnaissances in the Bard Sir valley", in Caldwell, J. R. (ed.), *Investigations at Tal-i Iblis*, Illinois State Museum Preliminary reports No. 9, Illinois State Museum Society, Springfield: 73–107.

Covington, R. 2004. "What was Jiroft?", *Saudi Aramco World*, September/October: 2–11.

Cultural Heritage News Agency. 2006. *Discovery of the Main Part of Kenar Sandal's Ziggurat, Latest Archaeological News from Iran*, http://iranarch.blogspot.com/2006/02/discovery-of-main-part-of-kenar.html, accessed on 25 February 2006.

Desset, F. in press. "A new writing system discovered in 3rd millennium BCE Iran: the Konar Sandal 'geometric' tablets", *IA* 49.

Desset, F. and Vidale, M. 2013. "Mahtoutabad III (province of Kerman, Iran), the easternmost evidence of an 'Uruk-related' material assemblage." *Iran* 51: PAGES

Didier, A. 2007. *Archéologie des confins indo-iraniens: Étude de la production céramique du Kech-Makran (Pakistan) dans la première moitié du IIIe millénaire av. J.-C.*, unpublished Ph.D. thesis, Université Paris 1 – Panthéon-Sorbonne, UFR 03, Histoire de l'Art et Archéologie.

Dollfus, G. 1971. "Les fouilles à Djaffarabad", *CDAFI* 1: 17–161.

Dollfus, G. 1983. "Tepe Bendebal", *CDAFI* 13: 133–275.

Forest, J. D. 2003. «La Mésopotamie et les échanges à longue distance aux IV et III millénaires», *Dossiers d'Archéologie* 287: 126–34.

Fouache, E. 2009. "Jiroft ii. Human geography and environment", *EIr*, www.iranica.com, accessed on 2 July 2010.

Fouache, A., Garçon, D., Rousset, D., Senechal, G. E and Madjidzadeh, Y. 2005. "La Vallée de l'Halil Roud (Région de Jiroft, Iran): Étude géoarchéologique, méthodologie et résultats préliminaires», *Paléorient* 31 (2): 107–22.

Francfort, H. P. and Tremblay, X. 2010. "Marhashi et la civilisation de l'Oxus", *IA* 45: 51–224.

Hakemi, A. 1997. *Shahdad, Archaeological Excavations of a Bronze Age Center in Iran*, IsMEO, Rome.

Hole, F., Flannery, K. V. and Neely, J. A. 1969. *Prehistory and human ecology of the Deh Luran plain, an early village sequence from Khuzistan, Iran*, Memoirs of the Museum of Anthropology, University of Michigan, No. 1, Ann Arbor.

Jarrige, C., Jarrige, J.-F., Meadow, R. H. and Quivron, G. (eds), 1995. *Mehrgarh: Field Reports 1974–1985 From Neolithic Times to the Indus Civilization*, The Department of Culture and Tourism, Sindh, Karachi.

Kohl, P. L. 1975. "Carved chlorite vessels: a trade in finished commodities in the mid-third millennium", *Expedition* 18 (1): 18–31.

Kohl, P. L. 1978. "The balance of trade in southwestern Asia in the mid-third millennium B.C.", *Current Anthropology* 19: 463–92.

Kohl, P. L. 2001. "Reflections on the production of chlorite at Tepe Yahya: 25 years later", in Beale, T. W., *Excavations at Tepe Yahya, Iran 1967–1975. The Third Millennium*, Bulletin of the American School of Prehistoric Research 45, Peabody Museum of Archaeology and Ethnology Harvard University, Cambridge MA: 209–30.

Kohl, P. L. 2009. *The Making of Bronze Age Eurasia*, CUP, Cambridge.

Lamberg-Karlovsky, C. C. 1970. *Excavations at Tepe Yahya, Iran, 1967–1969, Progress Report I*, Bulletin of the American School of Prehistoric Research 27, Peabody Museum of Archaeology and Ethnology Harvard University, Cambridge MA.

Lamberg-Karlovsky, C. C. 1988. "The 'Intercultural Style' carved vessels", *IA* 23: 45–95.

Lamberg-Karlovsky, C. C. 2004. "New centers of complexity in the Iranian Bronze Age", *The Review of Archaeology*: 5–10.

Lawler, A. 2004. "Rocking the cradle", *Smithsonian* May: 41–48.

Lawler, A. 2010. "The New Bronze Age", *Archaeology* January-February: 53–66.

Madjidzadeh, Y. 2003a. *Jiroft: The Earliest Oriental Civilization*, ICHO, Tehran.

Madjidzadeh, Y. 2003b. "La découverte de Jiroft", *Dossiers d'Archéologie* 287: 19–26.

Madjidzadeh, Y. 2003c. "La première campagne de fouilles à Jiroft", *Dossiers d'Archéologie* 287: 65–75.

Madjidzadeh, Y. 2004. ed. *First International Conference of Archaeological Research in Jiroft. The Halil Rud Civilization*, Cultural Heritage, Handicrafts & Tourism Organization of Kerman Province, Tehran (in Farsi).

Madjidzadeh, Y. with a contribution by Pittman, H. 2008. "Excavations at Konar Sandal in the region of Jiroft in the Halil Basin: first preliminary report (2002–2008)", *Iran* 46: 69–103.

Madjidzadeh, Y. 2012. "Jiroft tablets and the origin of the linear Elamite writing system", in Osada, T. and Witzel, M. (eds), *Cultural relations between the Indus and the Iranian plateau during the third millennium BCE; Indus project, Institute for humanities and nature, June 7–8, 2008*, Harvard oriental series, opera minor vol. 7, Department of Sanskrit and Indian Studies, Harvard University, Cambridge MA.

Miroschedji, P. de. 1973. "Vases et objets en stéatite susiens du Musée du Louvre", *CDAFI* 3: 9–42.

Muscarella, O. W. 2005. "Jiroft and 'Jiroft-Aratta'", *Bulletin of the Asia Institute* 15: 173–98.

Muscarella, O. W. 2009. "Jiroft iii. General survey of the excavations", *EIr*, www.iranica.com accessed on 2 July 2010.

Mutin, B. 2007. *Contribution à l'étude du peuplement des confins indo-iraniens au Chalcolithique: Caractérisation de la production céramique des Périodes II and IIIa du Makran pakistanais (4ème millénaire avant J.-C.*, unpublished Ph.D. thesis, Université Paris 1 – Panthéon-Sorbonne, UFR 03, Histoire de l'Art et Archéologie.

Perrot, J. 2003. "L'iconographie de Jiroft", *Dossiers d'Archéologie* 287: 97–113.

Perrot, J. 2008. "Iconography of chlorite artefacts", *EIr*, www.iranica.com accessed on 2 July 2010.

Perrot, J. and Madjidzadeh, Y. 2003. "Découvertes récentes à Jiroft (sud du plateau Iranien)", *Comptes Rendus de l'Académie des Inscriptions et Belles Lettres*: 1087–1102.

Perrot, J. and Madjidzadeh, Y. 2004. "Récentes découvertes à Jiroft (Iran): Résultats de la campagne de fouilles, 2004», *Comptes Rendus de l'Académie des Inscriptions et Belles Lettres*: 1105–20.

Perrot, J. and Madjidzadeh, Y. 2005. "L'iconographie des vases et objets en chlorite de Jiroft (Iran)", *Paléorient* 31 (2): 123–52.

Perrot, J. and Madjidzadeh, Y. 2006. "À travers l'ornementation des vases et objets en chlorite de Jiroft", *Paléorient* 32 (1): 99–112.

Petrie, C. A. 2011. "'Culture', innovation and interaction across southern Iran from the Neolithic to the Bronze Age (6500–3000 BC)", in Roberts, B. and Vander Linden, M. (eds), *Investigating archaeological cultures: Material culture, variability and transmission*, Springer, New York: 151–82.

Petrie C. A. 2013. "The Chalcolithic of south Iran", *Oxford Handbook of Iranian Archaeology*, OUP, Oxford: 120–157.

Petrie, C. A., Weeks, L. R., Potts, D. T. and Roustaei, K. 2009. "Perspectives on the cultural sequence of Mamasani", in Potts, D. T., Roustaei, K., Petrie, C. A. and Weeks, L. R. (eds), *The Mamasani Archaeological Project, Stage One: A Report on the First Two Seasons of the ICAR-University of Sydney Expedition to the Mamasani District, Fars Province, Iran*, Archaeopress, Oxford: 169–96.

Pittman, H. 1990. "Steatite or chlorite handled weights", in von Bothmer, D. (ed.), *Glories of the Past: Ancient Art from the Shelby White and Leon Levy Collection*, Yale University Press, New York: 41–43.

Pittman, H. 2003. "La culture du Halil Roud", *Dossiers d'Archéologie* 287: 78–87.

Pollock, S., Bernbeck, R. and Abdi, K. eds 2010. *The 2003 Excavations at Tol-e Bashi, Iran; Social Life in a Neolithic Village*, Archäologie in Iran und Turan 10, Verlag Philipp von Zabern, Mainz.

Pottier, M-H. 1984. *Matériel funéraire de la Bactriane méridionale de l'Âge du Bronze*, ERC, Paris.

Potts, D. T. 2001. *Excavations at Tepe Yahya, Iran 1967–1975. The Third Millennium*, Bulletin of the American School of Prehistoric Research 45, Peabody Museum of Archaeology and Ethnology Harvard University, Cambridge MA.

Potts, D. T. 2005. "In the beginning: Marhashi and the origins of Magan's ceramic industry in the third millennium BC", *Arabian Archaeology and Epigraphy* 16 (1): 67–78.

Potts, D. T. 2009. "Bevel-rim bowls and bakeries: evidence and explanations from Iran and the Indo-Iranian borderlands", *JCS* 61: 1–23.

Potts, D. T., Roustaei, K., Weeks, L. R. and Petrie, C. A. 2009. "The Mamasani district and the archaeology of southwestern Iran", in Potts, D.T., Roustaei, K., Petrie, C. A. and Weeks, L. R. (eds), *The Mamasani Archaeological Project, Stage One: A Report on the First Two Seasons of the ICAR-University of Sydney Expedition to the Mamasani District, Fars Province, Iran*, Archaeopress, Oxford: 1–16.

Prickett, M. 1986. *Man, Land and Water: Settlement Distribution and the Development of Irrigation Agriculture in the Upper Rud-i Gushk Drainage, Southeastern Iran*, unpublished Ph.D. dissertation, Harvard University.

Sajjadi, S. M. S. 1987. "Prehistoric settlements in the Bardsir plain, south-eastern Iran", *East and West* 37: 11–129.

Sarraf, M. R. 1981. *Die Keramik von Tell-i Iblis und ihre zeiltiche und räumliche Beziehung zu den anderen iranischen und mesopotamischen Kulturen*, Archäologische Mitteilungen aus Iran Ergänzungsband 7, DAI, Berlin.

Stein, A. 1937. *Archaeological Reconnaissances in Northwestern India and Southeastern Iran*, Macmillan and Co, London.

Steinkeller, P. 1982. "The question of Marhashi: a contribution to the historical geography of Iran in the third millennium B.C.", *Zeitschrift für Assyriologie und Voderasiatische Archäologie* 72 (2): 237–64.

Steinkeller, P. 2012. "New light on Marhashi and its contacts with Makkan and Babylonia", *Aux marges de l'archéologie. Hommage à Serge Cleuziou,* Giraud, J. and Gernez, G. (eds), Travaux de la Maison René-Ginouvés 16, De Boccard: 261–274.

Sumner, W. M. 1988. "Prelude to proto-elamite Anshan: the Lapui phase", *IA* 23: 23–43.

Tosi, M. 1968. "Excavations at Shahr-i Sokhta, a Chalcolithic Settlement in the Iranian Sistan, Preliminary Report on the first Campaign, October–December 1967", *East and West* 18: 9–66.

Tosi, M. and Piperno, M. 1973. "Lithic technology behind the ancient lapis lazuli trade", *Expedition* 16: 15–23.

Voigt, M. M. and Dyson Jr., R. H. 1992. "The Chronology of Iran, ca. 8000–2000 B.C.", in Ehrich, R. W. (ed.), *Chronologies in Old World Archaeology* (third edition), 2 vols, University of Chicago Press, Chicago/London: 122–78 (vol. 1), 125–53 (vol. 2).

Winkelmann, S. 2005. "Deciphering the Intercultural Style?" in Franke-Vogt, U. and Weisshaar, H-J. (eds.), *South Asian Archaeology 2003*, Linden Soft, Bonn: 185–97.

Zarins, Y. 1978. "Typological studies in Saudi Arabia archaeology: steatite vessels in the Riyadh Museum", *Atlatl* 2.iiia: 65–93.

14. CERAMIC TRADITIONS AND INTERACTIONS ON THE SOUTH-EASTERN IRANIAN PLATEAU DURING THE FOURTH MILLENNIUM BC

Benjamin Mutin

Introduction

This contribution discusses various factors relating to the ceramics of south-eastern Iran and Pakistani Kech-Makran (south-western Pakistani Baluchistan) that date from the fourth millennium BC to the early third millennium BC (Fig. 14.1).[1] Although a number of ancient sites of Kech-Makran had been visited and investigated earlier (e.g. Mockler 1877; Stein 1931; Field 1959; Dales and Lipo 1992), recent fieldworks conducted by the French mission directed by Roland Besenval and Vincent Marcon[2] have exposed a range of new materials and have established a reliable chronology for this region for the proto-historic periods. The research presented here has been supplemented by the results from a recent study of some Chalcolithic ceramics collected by Aurel Stein (1937) in the south-eastern Iranian province of Seistan and Baluchistan, mostly from the Bampur Valley. These collections are now held by the Peabody Museum of Archaeology and Ethnology (hereafter PMAE).[3] On the basis of the analysis of the French and Stein materials and utilising previous studies of ceramics recovered in south-eastern Iran, an attempt is made here to reconstruct the distributions of some of the main ceramic products and to present some important stages of the interregional relations seen from the ceramics across the south-easternmost areas of the Iranian Plateau during the fourth and early third millennia BC. In spite of several uncertainties, the ceramics tend to delineate distinct regions that increasingly interacted throughout this period, while they also maintained their own specificities. The ceramics are indicative of the significance of the local and interregional processes on the south-

eastern Iranian Plateau within the broader context of increasing long-range interactions and complexity observed during the fourth and third millennia BC on the Iranian Plateau as a whole.

First half of the fourth millennium BC

Kech-Makran **Miri** *ware*

In Pakistani Makran, the first half of the fourth millennium BC is referred to as *Kech-Makran Period II* (Table 14.1), and represents the first appearance of pottery in this region. The oldest phase of occupation so far found in the Kech Valley, at Miri Qalat, has been assigned to *Period I* (Fig. 14.1), and dates to the end of the fifth millennium BC.[4] The cultural material of *Period I* is primarily comprised of a lithic industry and bone awls, while very few sherds have been found, suggesting that there was no formal ceramic industry (Besenval 1994: 81; 2005: 1–4). At Shahi-Tump, the quantities of sherds reported show that ceramic vessels were absent in the oldest levels, and quite rare in the first occupations datable to *Period II*, before they came to be produced and used on a larger scale later in that period. The main ceramic type in *Period II – Miri* ware – is a fine, painted ware that includes several types of forms in buff-, tan-, and grey-coloured clay (Fig. 14.2/1–14.2/21). Decoration is mostly comprised of geometric designs, although a stylised ibex is also a common motif. These vessels were made by coiling (Fig. 14.3) and were then shaped and smoothed, most likely on a rotating device. Some show evidence that they were stacked during the firing, which enabled the production of grey ware (Besenval 1994: 82, fig. 6.2).

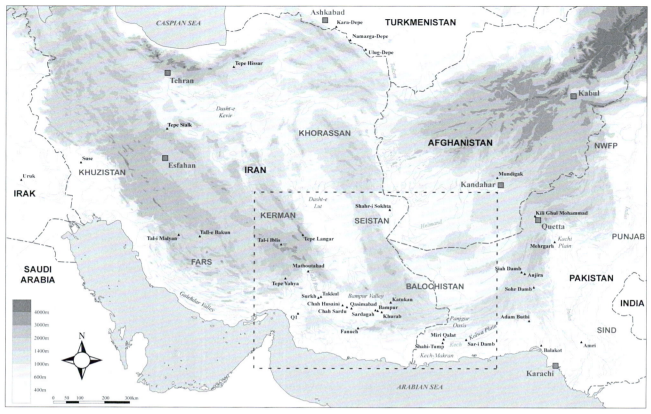

Figure 14.1. Map of Middle Asia showing the location of the areas and sites primarily considered in this paper (map B. Mutin).

Associated with *Miri* ware in *Period II* is a basket ware (Fig. 14.2/22–14.2/23) and a coarse ware (Fig. 14.2/24). Basket ware is a well-known production method that consists of moulding vessels inside baskets. This method occurred during the fifth millennium BC in eastern Pakistani Baluchistan such as at Mehrgarh (Vandiver 1995) and continued to be used until the third millennium BC in the Indo-Iranian borderlands (Mutin 2006).

Fragments of *Miri* ware were found on the surface of at least six and probably nine sites visited by Besenval in Pakistani Makran (Mutin 2007). Materials similar to *Miri* ware were also identified within the assemblage collected by Stein in 1932 at Qasimabad in the Bampur Valley and in the vicinity of Fanuch, located farther to the south (Fig. 14.4, collection of the PMAE). Chah Husaini, a site in the Bampur Valley, also produced some material that resembles *Miri* ware, and this will be discussed below. On the basis of the current evidence, although it is thin, the production and distribution of *Miri* ware seems to have been spread over an area of about 400 km from east to west (Fig. 14.8). Generally speaking, this ware shows a broad resemblance to Chalcolithic materials from the Iranian Plateau, while analogies with the ceramics from eastern Pakistani Baluchistan appear minor. The best comparative material comes from Kerman, particularly certain vessels of *Aliabad*

ware from Tal-i Iblis (*Period IV*; Chase *et al.* 1967a: 75–79; 1967b: 182–98) and, to a lesser extent, among the fine, painted ceramics from Tepe Yahya *Periods VI–V* (i.e. black-on-buff ware, black-on-red ware, and *Soghun* ware datable to the mid- to late fifth and the first half of the fourth millennia BC; Beale and Lamberg-Karlovsky 1986: 11, 47–55, 58–80) (Fig. 14.5).[5] Nevertheless, these similarities only relate to certain types of forms and decorations, and many other vessel forms and decorations from Makran find no parallel in Kerman. Furthermore, while *Miri* ware was built by coiling, Sequential Slab Construction was the primary building technique of the ceramics found at Tepe Yahya, Mehrgarh (Kachi Plain, Pakistan), and as far west as the Central Zagros from the Neolithic period (Vandiver 1986, 1987, 1995). I would argue that in the future coiling will most likely be identified in southeastern Iran. So far, however, the nearest evidence for ceramics built by coiling is in Fars, where vessels showing signs of this technique date to the Neolithic period (Bernbeck 2010: 67), and in Turkmenistan in the fifth millennium BC (Dupont-Delaleuf 2010). Some *Aliabad* ware vessels show that they were built using coils, but they relate closely to some of the goblets recovered in Pakistani Makran dating not to *Period II*, but to the succeeding *Period IIIa*. Thus, for now, *Miri* ware shows characteristics isolated enough during the first half of the fourth millennium BC to argue that this

Table 14.1. Chronological chart of southern Middle Asia and Mesopotamia during the fourth millennium BC. The chronologies of some of these areas are not yet totally clarified and this chart should be considered a rough guide.

Date B.C.	Southern Mesopotamia	Susiana	Fars	Kerman — Tepe Yahya	Kerman — Tal-i Iblis	Kech-Makran	Eastern Pakistani Baluchistan — Mehrgarh	Eastern Pakistani Baluchistan — Sohr Damb
5000	Ubaid 3	Late Middle Susiana		Yahya VII				
4500	Ubaid 4	Late Susiana 1	Bakun	Yahya VI	Iblis 0?	Period I	Period III	
4000	(Ubaid 5)	Late Susiana 2 / Susa I		Yahya VC / Yahya VB / Yahya VA	Iblis I–II	Period II		
3500	Uruk	Uruk	Lapui	Gap	Iblis III–V			Period I
3000	Jemdet Nasr	Proto-Elamite	Banesh	Yahya IVC Proto-Elamite	Iblis VI	Period IIIa	Periods IV–VI	Period II

type of ware represented a separate ceramic tradition belonging to the south-eastern Iranian Plateau. It gives evidence for a certain degree of achievement that does not agree with the ceramics one would expect to see in the first steps of pottery making as they were observed at Mehrgarh and at Tepe Yahya (Vandiver 1986, 1995). As no older ceramic was found in Makran, one would thus envisage that the emergence of *Miri* ware involved the knowledge of skilled potters from the surrounding areas where pottery was known earlier, while incorporating elements (such as the iconography?) of a tradition whose roots are probably to be found in the previous local aceramic period. Although direct technical connections are lacking, most of the evidence points towards the west with regard to the roots of *Miri* ware. Nevertheless, the presence of basket ware during *Period II* in Makran tends to imply connections towards the north-east, in eastern Pakistani Baluchistan, where this type of ceramic occurred first (Mutin 2006). It is also notable that baskets made by coiling were found at Mehrgarh during the Neolithic period, including examples in burials (Jarrige *et al.* 1995: 336, fig. 7.7).

Kerman black-on-buff ware, black-on-red ware, and Lapui ware

Soghun ware from Tepe Yahya seems mostly datable to the mid- to late fifth millennium BC so that it was probably anterior to *Miri* ware. Indeed, *Soghun* ware was found mostly in *Periods VI* and *VC* at Tepe Yahya. A few sherds of *Ubaid*-related style were found in *Period VI*, while the earliest examples of black-on-buff ware, recovered from *Period VC*, are considered imports from Fars, related to the fifth millennium BC *Bakun* ceramic tradition (Beale and Lamberg-Karlovsky 1986: 58–67, 87–88). Uncalibrated radiocarbon dates for *Periods VI* and *VC* range between 3900 and 3700 BC (Beale and Lamberg-Karlovsky 1986: 10, 13, table 2.2), but the calibrated radiocarbon dates provided by Prickett (1986a: 217) and the ceramic parallels place those periods within the mid- to late fifth millennium BC. Recalibration of two radiocarbon dates from *Period VIB* and one from *Period VB* (Beale and Lamberg-Karlovsky 1986: 12, table 2.1) using OxCal v4.1.7 (Bronk Ramsey 2009; r:5 Atmospheric data from Reimer *et al.* 2009) provided calibrated BC

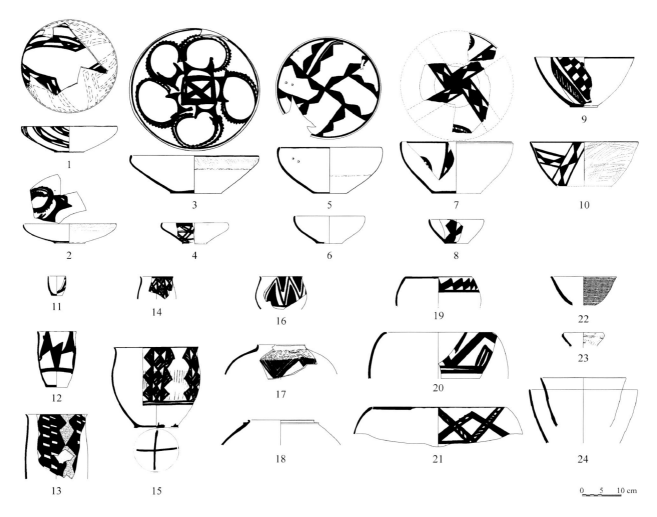

Figure 14.2. Ceramic assemblage of Kech-Makran Period II *(© MAFM).*

dates ranging between *c.* 4800 and 4000 BC for the *VIB* dates and between the last quarter of the fifth and the first quarter of the fourth millennia BC for the *VB* date.[6] Black-on-buff ware is then thought to have been produced locally starting during *Period VB*, and it continued to be used into *Period VA*. Black-on-buff ware is replaced by black-on-red ware from *Period VA*, which basically appears to have continued the same tradition into a red fabric (Beale and Lamberg-Karlovsky 1986: 67–80). While uncalibrated dates place these periods between 3700 and 3300 BC (Beale and Lamberg-Karlovsky 1986: 10, 13, table 2.2), Prickett (1986a: 217) situated *Periods VB* and *VA* between the mid-fifth and initial fourth millennia BC. These two chronologies agree on the fact that black-on-buff ware and black-on-red ware were at a minimum partly contemporaneous with *Miri* ware within the first half of the fourth millennium BC. As noted above, a date from *Period VB* recalibrated here agrees with a dating situated between the late fifth and the early fourth millennia BC, while two dates from *Period VA* recalibrated using the same software

and calibration are cal. BC between *c.* 4250 and 3600 BC.[7] This is also corroborated by the presence of *Lapui* ware, a burnished ware that was identified from *Period VI* to *Phase VA.2* (rarely in *Period VI* and *Phase VA.1* and commonly in *Periods VC* to *Phase VA.2*) (Beale and Lamberg-Karlovsky 1986: 55–58, 87). *Lapui* ware is characteristic of Fars essentially from the early- to mid-fourth millennium BC, although it was probably present in this province in a few numbers since the end of the fifth millennium BC *Bakun* period (Petrie *et al.* 2009: 171). Although this ware seems to have appeared and disappeared in Kerman earlier than in Fars (Petrie 2011, 2013), it seems likely that some of the examples found in *Periods VC* to *VA* overlapped chronologically with *Miri* ware within the first half of the fourth millennium BC. As discussed below there is also evidence that indicates that *Miri* ware was also partly contemporary with some ceramic products posterior to Tepe Yahya *Period VA*, including *Aliabad* ware. Although this scheme appears to be consistent, it is important to note that the radiocarbon dates from the early periods of Tal-i Iblis (*Periods I* and *II*) that

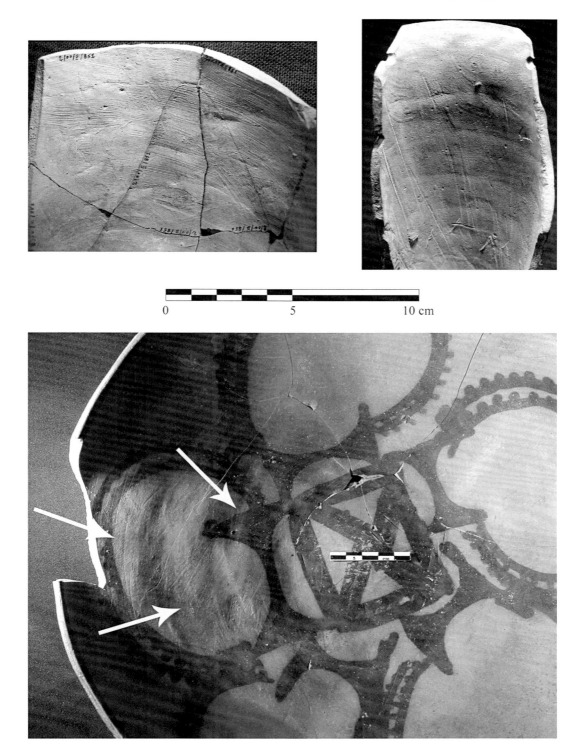

Figure 14.3. Miri *ware from Kech-Makran* Period II: *photographs showing the coiling. The arrows indicate coils (© MAFM).*

contained ceramics equivalent to black-on-buff ware, black-on-red ware, and *Lapui* ware are essentially older. The dates of *Iblis I* and *II* available in Voigt and Dyson (1992: 131, table 2), recalibrated using the same software and calibration method as that indicated above, are placed within the fifth millennium BC, with some dates even situated within the first half of the fifth millennium BC.[8]

In addition to Tepe Yahya, *Lapui* ware was also found at Tal-i Iblis (*Periods I–II*) and relations with Fars at this site are also indicated by *Bard Sir* painted ware which is equivalent to black-on-buff ware, the earliest examples of which are considered imports from this province (Beale and Lamberg-Karlovsky 1986: 86–89; Chase *et al.* 1967b: 152–54; Caldwell 1968: 179). *Lapui* ware has not been attested so far east of

Tump-i Qasimabad   Fanuch

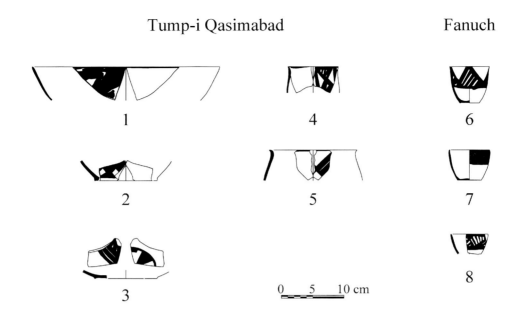

Figure 14.4. Miri *ware-related vessels from Qasimabad (nos. 1–5) and Fanuch (nos. 6–8).*

Tal-i Iblis: *Aliabad ware*

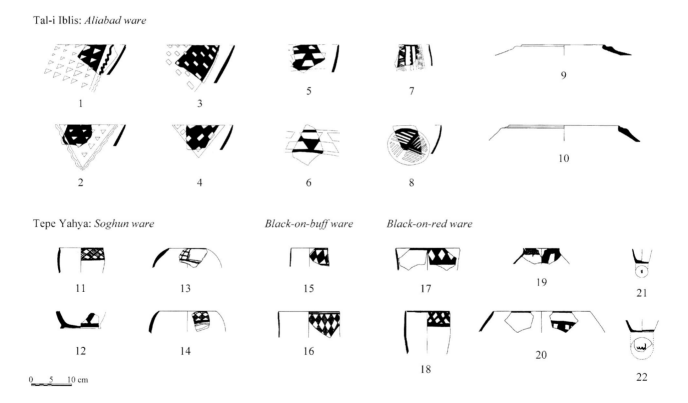

Tepe Yahya: *Soghun ware*   *Black-on-buff ware*   *Black-on-red ware*

Figure 14.5. Aliabad *ware from Tal-i Iblis (nos. 1–10 after Sarraf 1981: figs 17/190, 189; 15/173, 176; 13/161, 160; 23/265; 33/361; 48/154, 153); Soghun ware, black-on-buff ware, and black-on-red ware from Tepe Yahya (nos. 11–22 after Beale and Lamberg-Karlovsky 1986: figs 4.13n; 4.12f; 4.15b, d; 4.20k, w; 4.30o, e, h, r; 4.36w; 4.37jj).*

Kerman, while vessels similar to black-on-buff ware were found in the Bampur Valley at Chah Husaini and at Qala-i Sardagah (Fig. 14.6/1–14.6/4), and the distribution of black-on-red ware extended over 500 km from north to south and 475 km from east to west in south-eastern Iran. This zone included Tal-e Iblis, where black-on-red ware is equivalent to *Iblis* painted ware from *Iblis II*, the Bampur Valley, and a site near the Persian Gulf (Q1; Beale and Lamberg-Karlovsky 1986: 8, 85–89). Thus, east of Kerman, it seems that black-on-buff ware, black-on-red ware, and *Miri* ware were the earliest ceramics and the main products of the south-easternmost coastal areas of the Iranian Plateau starting from the fourth millennium BC.[9] The distribution of these wares overlapped in the Bampur Valley (Fig. 14.8), but it is important to note that the site of Chah Husaini, located in this valley, also provided other types of ceramics that appear to have been contemporary with them.

Chah Husaini wares

Stein (1937: 126–31) conducted soundings at the ancient site of Chah Husaini in 1932, and most of the collected material that is held by the PMAE relates closely to black-on-buff ware and black-on-red ware (Fig. 14.6). Among the collection, however, are a small number of sherds that relate to two other kinds of buff to tan fine, painted ware (Stein 1937: 129–30; Lamberg-Karlovsky and Schmandt-Besserat 1977: 130–32), which we propose to label *Husaini* monochrome ware and *Husaini* polychrome ware (Fig. 14.7). *Husaini* monochrome ware shows features

roughly comparable to the Chalcolithic ceramics of the south-eastern Iranian Plateau; including some that seem close to *Miri* ware (Fig. 14.7/4–14.7/6). *Husaini* monochrome ware also includes distinctive carinated pots and decorations that do not find any good parallels (Fig. 14.7/1–14.7/3), although certain types of black-on-buff ware and black-on-red ware are carinated, and carinated vessels were in use as early as the Neolithic period in Kerman (Beale and Lamberg-Karlovsky 1986: figs 4.4i, 4.20i, z, cc, 4.27, 4.30g; Evett 1967: 206, fig. 1.1). On the other hand, carinations are not observed in Makran. *Husaini* polychrome ware is characterised by a unique style of decoration mostly painted in black and red (Fig. 14.7/7–14.7/9). Good parallels are lacking for *Husaini* polychrome ware, with the exception of one goblet from Tepe Yahya *Periods IVC–IVB6* (Fig. 14.7/10). Also, black painted over a red slip or field is observed on some types of black-on-red ware (Beale and Lamberg-Karlovsky 1986: 78). Some *Husaini* monochrome ware and *Husaini* polychrome ware vessels might have been built using coils, but only further analysis will make it possible to determine whether that is in fact true. Although most of the fragments held by the PMAE come from the surface of Chah Husaini, the terse descriptions about the archaeological contexts and materials offered by Stein (1937: 126–31) might indicate that the *Husaini* wares and black-on-red ware were roughly contemporaneous. Furthermore, the features and relationships of the *Husaini* monochrome and *Husaini* polychrome wares agree with a dating situated within the fourth millennium BC. Nevertheless, this site is definitely worthy of further investigation and, for

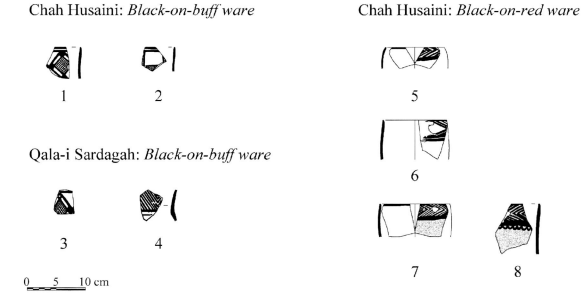

Chah Husaini: *Black-on-buff ware*

1   2

Qala-i Sardagah: *Black-on-buff ware*

3   4

0   5   10 cm

Chah Husaini: *Black-on-red ware*

5

6

7   8

Figure 14.6. Ceramics from Chah Husaini (black-on-buff ware and black-on-red ware: nos. 1–2, 5–8) and from Qala-i Sardagah (black-on-buff ware: nos. 3–4).

Chah Sardu   Takkul

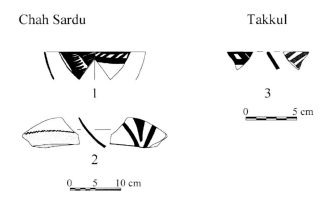

Figure 14.10. Early Shahi-Tump *ware-related vessels from Chah Sardu (nos. 1–2) and Takkul (no. 3).*

in Makran. Several types of ceramics collected by Prickett in the Rud-i Gushk (Kerman) show traits very similar to those of the conical goblets from Makran. Among them is a "straight-sided coiled slab cup" (Prickett 1986b: 1432–56). Some of these vessels were found associated with *Iblis IV/V* materials, and in the Bard Sir Plain some are included within the overarching definition of *Aliabad* ware, which dates to Tal-i Iblis *Period IV* (Fig. 14.11/5–14.11/6; Chase *et al.* 1967a: 75–79). These types of ceramics were rare in the excavated areas at Tepe Yahya, but a few similar materials were found in layers below the *Proto-Elamite* building of *Period IVC* (Prickett 1986b: 450–51; Potts and Lamberg-Karlovsky 2001: 198). Materials that resemble *Aliabad* ware or the related material from Kech-Makran were also identified within the assemblage collected by Stein in the Bampur Valley at Chah Sardu, Qasimabad, and Chah Husaini; and possibly near Fanuch and at Takkul (collection of the PMAE; Fig. 14.11/7–14.11/10), although one should remain cautious vis-à-vis the chronological position of these materials. At Tal-e Iblis, the *Iblis IV* assemblage also contained bevel-rim bowls, low-sided trays, and shoulder spouts similar to materials of the *Uruk* period in Mesopotamia and south-western Iran and which also resemble elements of the assemblage of the *Proto-Elamite* occupation of Tepe Yahya *Period IVC* (*Phases IVC2–IVB6*). Chase *et al.* (1967b: 182–97; Caldwell 1967: 36–37; 1968: 179, 182) considered these vessel types to be a minor component of the *Iblis IV* assemblage, and noted that in one earlier context, no such material was found associated with the *Iblis IV* assemblage. *Aliabad* vessels and materials related to *Late Uruk-Jemdet Nasr* periods have been recovered at Matoutabad in the Halil Rud (Vidale and Desset, this volume). The contexts of those two assemblages, defined as *Matoutabad II* and *III* respectively, are unfortunately not connected stratigraphically (Madjidzadeh 2008: 90–91, fig. 21; Vidale and Desset, this volume).

Alden (1982: 616) has pointed out the association of *Proto-Elamite* materials and *Aliabad* ware at Tal-e Iblis, and argued for full or partial contemporaneity between *Aliabad* ware and *Period IVC* at Tepe Yahya. Prickett (1986b: 449–52) and Beale and Lamberg-Karlovsky (1986: 86) considered this ware to be roughly contemporaneous with the end of Tepe Yahya *Period VA* and coincident with a gap between *Period VA* and the beginning of *Period IVC*. Uncalibrated radiocarbon dates at Tepe Yahya place the end of *Period VA* around 3300 BC (Beale and Lamberg-Karlovsky 1986: 11, 13, table 2.2), whereas Prickett (1986a: 217) placed a calibrated end for this period in the initial fourth millennium BC and *Iblis IV/V* (posterior to *Yahya VA* and anterior to *Yahya IVC*) in the first half of the fourth millennium BC. As seen above, the lower limits of two dates from *Period VA* at Tepe Yahya recalibrated here are situated around 3700 and 3600 BC. Caldwell (1967: 23–24, fig. 2, 36; 1968: 179) set the beginning of *Aliabad* ware and *Iblis IV* around the middle or at the end of the first half of the fourth millennium BC and provided a date of *c.* 3646 ± 59 BC for an occupation defined as early *Period IV*. Three dates from *Iblis III* and *IV* available in Voigt and Dyson (1992: 131, table 2), including the one cited by Caldwell (P-928), were recalibrated using OxCal v4.1.7 (Bronk Ramsey 2009; r:5 Atmospheric data from Reimer *et al.* 2009), and showed that two of the calibrated BC dates place within the second half of the fifth millennium BC and one date is situated around the mid-fourth millennium BC[11] (see also Vidale and Desset, this volume). *Iblis IV* followed *Iblis III* whose ceramic assemblage was defined as the *Dashgar* complex. In the initial publication, the *Iblis III* assemblage was envisaged as a prelude of *Iblis IV Aliabad* ware, and continued into this period (Caldwell 1967: 36). *Iblis III* followed *Iblis II* whose ceramics are equivalent to *Yahya VA* (black-on-red ware), as indicated above.

In Makran, the best comparative material for *Aliabad* ware is conical goblets that are mostly represented from *Period IIIa*, although several sherds very similar to *Aliabad* ware were found in the upper layers of *Period II* at Shahi-Tump and one should not rule out the connections between some ceramics of *Period II Miri* ware and some types of *Aliabad* ware indicated above. The pottery of *Iblis III* and its relationships to *Miri* ware may also merit further investigation. As indicated above, *Period II Miri* ware seems to have been partly contemporary with black-on-buff ware and black-on-red ware of *Yahya VA* and *Iblis II*. *Yahya VA* is thought to have ended during the first half of the fourth millennium BC (calibrated) while the following, *Proto-Elamite*, occupation at Tepe Yahya (*Phases IVC2–IVB6*) started in the last quarter of the fourth millennium BC (*c.* 3100–2800 BC; Lamberg-Karlovsky 2001: 270). While there are clear ceramic parallels between Kerman and Pakistani Makran in early *Period IIIa*, in the shape of conical goblets, there

Shahi-Tump   Tal-i Iblis

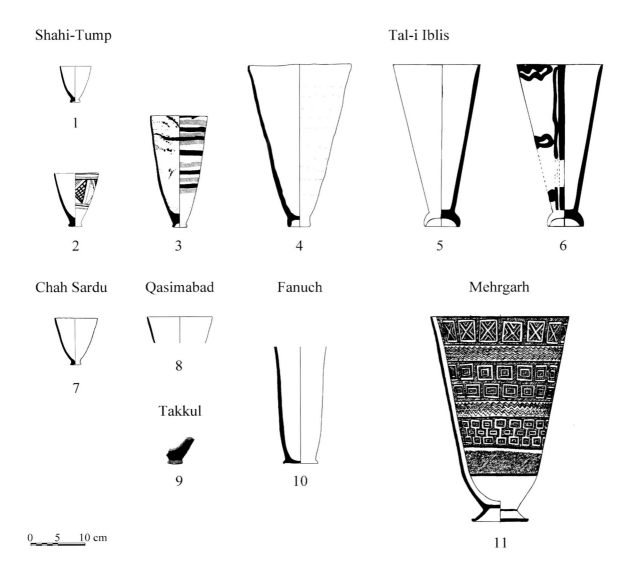

Chah Sardu   Qasimabad   Fanuch   Mehrgarh

Takkul

0   5   10 cm

Figure 14.11. Conical goblets from Shahi-Tump (nos. 1–4 ©MAFM); Aliabad ware from Tal-e Iblis (nos. 5–6 after Sarraf 1981: figs 48/145; 26/292); Aliabad ware-related vessels from Chah Sardu and Qasimabad (nos. 7–8), Takkul (no. 9 after Stein 1937: pl. XX Tak.16), and Fanuch (no. 10); and Kechi Beg ware from Mehrgarh (no. 11 after Jarrige C. et al. 1995: fig. 4.14a).

are also, in *Period II*, elements that connect this period to *Aliabad* ware. One may thus envision a chronological overlap between the end of *Period II* in Kech-Makran and the beginning of *Aliabad* ware and *Iblis III/IV* in Kerman in the second quarter of the fourth millennium BC; and the *Aliabad* phenomenon started to spread up to Kech-Makran mostly in the second half of the fourth millennium BC, starting with early *Period IIIa* (Fig. 14.14). This, however, remains a hypothesis. The *Aliabad* phenomenon needs more investigation in terms of chronology; only one of the three dates from Tal-i Iblis *Periods III* and *IV* agree with a dating overlapping with the mid-fourth millennium BC, while chronological variants of *Aliabad* ware are for now difficult to assess. The differences observed between the assemblages may indicate that regional variants

existed as well, as we are by and large comparing sequences at sites that are often considerable distances apart. The research conducted by Vidale and Desset (this volume) at Matoutabad will certainly shed essential new light upon this type of production. More generally speaking, in spite of some chronological uncertainties, one may propose at present that, around the middle of the fourth millennium BC, the ceramics of the south-eastern Iranian Plateau are indicative of a very broad phenomenon characterised by the production and use of conical forms with bichrome and trichrome decorations. This phenomenon is even represented in eastern Pakistani Baluchistan (e.g. Mehrgarh *Period IV*: 3600–3400 BC, Fig. 14.11/11; and Sohr-Damb *Period I*, Franke-Vogt 2005a: fig. 8a), but was the *Husaini* polychrome ware part of it?

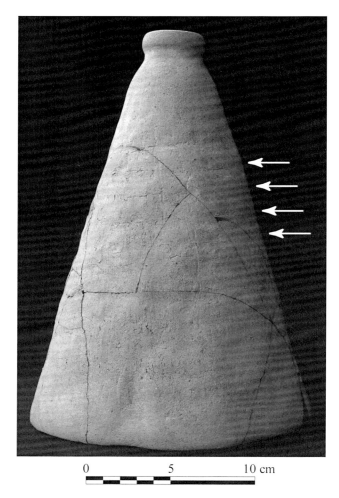

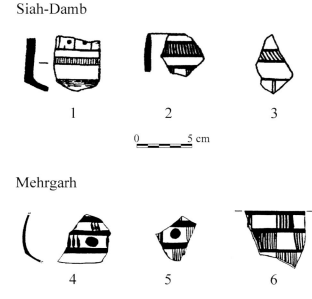

not to scale

Figure 14.13. Togau *ware from Siah-Damb (no. 1–3 after de Cardi 1965: figs 14/24; 13/9, 7) and Mehrgarh (no. 4–6 after Samzun 1988: fig. XXIX nos. 286, 284, 283).*

Figure 14.12. Conical goblet from Kech-Makran early Period IIIa: *photograph showing the coiling. The arrows indicate coils (© MAFM).*

Iblis IV is followed by *Iblis V*, a period not defined from excavations, which indicates ceramic continuation of *Iblis IV* (Caldwell 1967: 37; 1968: 179). Materials of *Iblis IV/V* have not been recovered so far at Tepe Yahya and, according to the sequence from Tal-e Iblis, it seems that those materials appeared after *Yahya VA* (*Iblis II*), were contemporary with the gap that followed at Tepe Yahya (*Iblis III* to *Iblis V*), and ceased being used before the *Proto-Elamite* occupation of *Yahya IVC*. During this gap, *Uruk*-related elements appeared in Kerman at both Tal-i Iblis and Matoutabad. Relations towards the west were also attested in contexts assigned to the following *Period VI* at Tal-i Iblis and by the *Proto-Elamite* settlement at Tepe Yahya. In Pakistani Makran, the cessation in the use of ceramics connected to *Aliabad* ware is not totally clarified. They no longer seem to be represented, however, when ceramics that one may connect to *Yahya IVC* appear in the sequence of Miri Qalat.

Eastern Pakistani Baluchistan wares

Although they are rare at that time, clear evidence for ceramic relations between the south-eastern Iranian Plateau and eastern Pakistani Baluchistan are given by a few types that were found associated with early *Shahi-Tump* ware in burials in Makran at Shahi-Tump and Miri Qalat (Fig. 14.9/16). These vessels display decoration related to the examples of *Togau* ware found at *Mehrgarh III* (Jarrige C. *et al.* 1995: 19), *Anjira III, Siah-Damb II i–ii* (de Cardi 1965), and *Sohr-Damb I* (Franke 2008: 654–56) (Figs 14.13 and 14.14). Such connections with fine ceramic types farther to the east were not observed during Kech-Makran *Period II*, and the recent discoveries made at Sohr-Damb would situate the beginning of *Sohr-Damb I* around 4000/3800 BC or perhaps more likely even later (Franke-Vogt 2000; Görsdorf and Franke-Vogt 2007: 703). Eastern-related ceramics then appeared more numerous in the levels located above these burials at Miri Qalat. These levels are discussed below.

End of the fourth millennium BC – early third millennium BC

Kech-Makran late Shahi-Tump *ware* – Yahya IVC–IVB6 – Shahr-i Sokhta I

In Pakistani Makran, the ceramic vessels produced during the second phase of *Period IIIa* include a fine, painted ware linked to early *Shahi-Tump* ware, although several changes can be noted in terms of

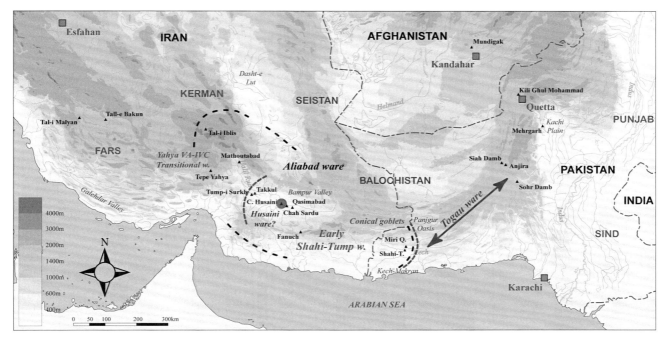

Figure 14.14. Map showing provisional reconstructions of the distributions of the main ceramic products on the south-eastern Iranian Plateau from around the middle of the fourth millennium BC: Aliabad *ware and* Aliabad *ware-related vessels; "Yahya VA-IVC Transitional wares"; early* Shahi-Tump *ware; Husaini wares (?); and* Togau *ware (map B. Mutin).*

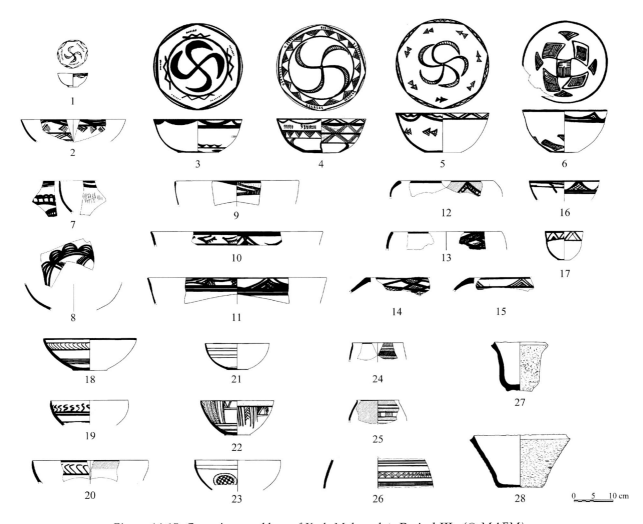

Figure 14.15. Ceramic assemblage of Kech-Makran late Period IIIa (© MAFM).

profiles and decoration (Fig. 14.15/1–14.15/17). The materials of this phase correspond to most of the funerary ceramics recovered by Stein (1931: 100) in the south-eastern part of Shahi-Tump. Based on his descriptions and illustrations, it is clear that most of these vessels show significant differences compared to the ceramics found by the French mission at the same site farther to the north-west in Trench II. Stein's bowls are, for example, mostly decorated using the swastika motif (Stein 1931: pls. XV–XVI). Miri Qalat seems to give stratigraphic grounds for the stylistic differences between the Stein and French material, although evidence is rare and comes from heavily weathered levels. Ceramics related to the assemblage recovered by Stein at Shahi-Tump were found at Miri Qalat in Trench IX, mostly in Levels VI–II. These levels sealed by architecture the burials of Level VII, which contained materials close to the assemblage found by the French expedition at Shahi-Tump in Trench II. Thus, most of the Stein materials may be considered as being more recent. Ceramics that relate to late *Shahi-Tump* ware were collected by Besenval on other sites in Makran (Mutin 2007), and by Stein (1931: pl. l.III, J.D.9, J.D.14, S.P.1, S.P.6) in the Panjgur Oasis, located north of the Kech Valley; in the Bampur Valley at Katukan; and at Fanuch (identified in the collection of the PMAE; Fig. 14.16/6–14.16/9). Also located in the Bampur Valley, Khurab provided a few comparative examples, including two sherds collected on the surface (Fig. 14.16/11–14.16/12) and two vessels recovered in one burial (Lamberg-Karlovsky and Schmandt-Besserat 1977: 125–30, fig. 6.14–6.15). The swastika painted on one of the Khurab funerary vessel is made using curved lines instead of curved bands usually observed among the Stein assemblage from Shahi-Tump (Fig. 14.16/10). The other materials associated with the collection from Khurab are more recent and this may indicate that the usage of curved lines instead of curved bands for the representation of the swastika corresponds to a later evolution of this type of decoration that is also observed in Makran in *Period IIIb* (*c*. 2800–2600 BC; Didier 2007, vol. II: fig. 108). It should also be noted that certain other traits that are observed on late *Shahi-Tump* ware are also attested later in Makran (in *Period IIIb*) and at Tepe Bampur, including friezes filled with triangles with curved sides (Fig. 14.15/6, 10–11, 15–16) (de Cardi 1970: figs 18.22, 18.35, 22.142). Although they are not numerous, good parallels for late *Shahi-Tump* ware have been identified in Tepe Yahya *Period IVC–IVB6* contexts (Fig. 14.16/2–14.16/5). More parallels can also be found at Shahr-i Sokhta (Seistan) in burials of *Period I* (dated to *c*. 3200–2800 BC, Fig. 14.16/1) (Salvatori and Tosi 2005: 284–85; Sajjadi 2003: 51), which consists of the earliest occupation so far found in Seistan. There are also indications of technical connections. For example, coiling is attested at Shahr-i Sokhta (Courty and Roux 1995; Laneri and Di Pilato 2000:

528–29), and it is seen at Tepe Yahya, starting with *Period IVC*, while it was not attested before (Vandiver 1986). The definition of late *Shahi-Tump* ware is at present preliminary. One may envisage that this ware represented a phenomenon spread over a wide part of the south-eastern Iranian Plateau, including Kerman, Seistan and Baluchistan, and Pakistani Makran. It seems rare farther to the west and farther to the east beyond the south-easternmost mountain ranges of the Iranian Plateau (Fig. 14.19). Some differences may be observed between the examples found in Kerman, Seistan and Baluchistan, and Pakistani Makran. We are, however, dealing with very few elements, and hence it is difficult to assess whether these differences result from chronological or regional discrepancies within a larger ceramic complex.

With regard to late *Shahi-Tump* ware, one should also remember the pioneering work conducted by Rita Wright (1984, 1989, 2002) on the painted grey wares of the Indo-Iranian borderlands. One of the results of her research was to make stylistic and geographical distinctions between *Faiz Mohammad* ware mostly found in north-eastern Pakistani Baluchistan, and *Emir* grey ware found at Shahr-i Sokhta and in the Bampur Valley (Wright 1984). Moreover, apart from the actual exchange of some ceramics from Pakistani Baluchistan to Seistan, she also demonstrated that the grey ware technology developed first in the Kachi area before it spread to Seistan (Wright 1984). *Emir* grey ware as Wright (1984: 124–44) defined it includes materials that share traits with late *Shahi-Tump* ware, while others find comparative materials in Makran in *Period IIIb* (Besenval 2005: 6). Should one envisage a transfer of technology towards Makran as well? Successive exchanges of technical knowledge seem to characterise the Indo-Iranian borderlands during the fourth millennium BC, so it seems consistent to envisage that potters from north-eastern Pakistani Baluchistan and Makran might have exchanged technological knowledge in the case of the grey ware of the late fourth–early third millennium BC. *Periods II–IIIa* in Makran, however, provide evidence for the early appearance and gradual development of grey wares within a local ceramic tradition that started in the early fourth millennium BC and continued into the third millennium BC. This offers a new south-western Pakistani outlook on the development of the grey wares in the Indo-Iranian borderlands and on the Iranian Plateau in general. The style of the fine, painted grey (but not only) ceramics associated with late *Period IIIa* in Makran, Tepe Yahya *Periods IVC2–IVB6*, and *Shahr-i Sokhta I* corresponds to a specific stage, situated around 3000 BC, within this development. This stage is also indicative of a widespread cultural phenomenon. Other cultural dynamics were also present on the south-eastern Iranian Plateau within the same chronological bracket.

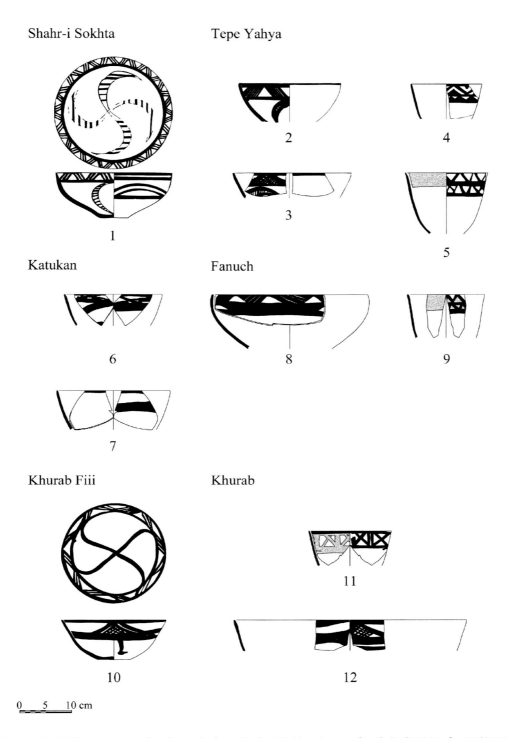

Shahr-i Sokhta

Tepe Yahya

Katukan

Fanuch

Khurab Fiii

Khurab

0   5   10 cm

Figure 14.16. Late Shahi-Tump ware-related vessels from Shahr-i Sokhta (no. 1 after Sajjadi 2003: fig. 26/1713.7); Tepe Yahya (nos. 2–5; no. 2 after Potts and Lamberg-Karlovsky 2001: fig. 3.7I; no. 3 after Beale 1986: fig. 4.39e; no. 4 after Potts and Lamberg-Karlovsky 2001: fig. 1.18B); Katukan (nos. 6–7); Fanuch (nos. 8–9); and Khurab (nos. 11–12). Vessel no. 10 is probably more recent.

Proto-Elamite–*Banesh materials*

At Tepe Yahya, the building of *Period IVC* (*Phases IVC2–IVB6*) is well known for its architecture and numerous materials that relate closely to the *Proto-Elamite* sphere generally and particularly the *Middle Banesh* period in Fars datable from the last quarter of the fourth into the early third millennium BC. The ceramics include jars comparable to the *Jemdet Nasr* and *Banesh* jars, bevel-rim bowls, and low-sided trays. *Proto-Elamite-* and/or *Uruk*-related materials were also recovered at Tal-i Iblis *IV–VI* (Chase *et al.* 1967b: 188–97), partly associated with *Aliabad* ware in *Period*

IV, and they have also been recovered from *Period III* at Mathoutabad (Vidale and Desset, this volume). In Seistan, the *Shahr-i Sokhta I* assemblage includes jars that have a few analogies (ear-lugs) with *Jemdet Nasr* jars, as well as a single tablet and seals related to the *Proto-Elamite* assemblage (Lamberg-Karlovsky and Tosi 1973: figs 16–18, 139–40; Amiet and Tosi 1978: fig. 16). *Proto-Elamite*-related materials are rare farther to the east, with the exception of a jar found in *Mundigak III.6* (southern Afghanistan), which was compared with the *Jemdet Nasr* jars (Jarrige J-F. 1987). A small number of bevel-rim bowls have also been found at Miri Qalat in Trench IX in Levels V and III, above the burials of early *Period IIIa* (Fig. 14.15/27–14.15/28; Besenval 1997a: 207–08, fig. 18; 1997b: 19).

Burnished ware

Another type of ware – burnished ware – was well represented at Tepe Yahya *Periods IVC–IVB* (Potts and Lamberg-Karlovsky 2001: fig. 1.28). Two sherds of burnished ware were found at Shahr-i Sokhta in *Period I, Phase 10* (Fig. 14.17). These burnished vessels find broad comparison with material from sites located south-east of the Caspian Sea such as Tepe Hissar (Schmidt 1937: 112–16), and as far afield as Mesopotamia and the Oman peninsula (see Didier and Méry 2012), although the comparative materials may date to later periods too. Nonetheless, no burnished ware was found at that time in Pakistani Makran where streak-burnished ware occurred only during *Period IIIc* (2600–2500 BC; Besenval 1997b: 24). With regard to the development of the surface treatment that consists of burnishing the vessels, apart from the northern comparisons, one should probably also consider a southern Iranian predecessor that is

attested since the late fifth and early fourth millennia BC in Fars and in Kerman: *Lapui* ware.

Eastern Pakistani Baluchistan wares

Numerous vessels that show linkages to ceramics from eastern Pakistani Baluchistan were found at Miri Qalat in the upper layers of Trenches III and IV and in Trench IX in Levels VI–III above the burials of early *Period IIIa* (Fig. 14.15/18–14.15/26). They include vessels related to the *Togau* ware "with hooks" and monochrome and bichrome ceramics similar to vessels dating mostly to the second half of the fourth millennium BC and into the early third millennium BC found at *Mehrgarh III–VII, Anjira III–IV, Siah-Damb II i–iii, Sohr-Damb I–II, Amri IA*, and *Balakot I* (Fig. 14.18; Besenval, 1997a: 206–08; 1997b: 19–20; de Cardi 1965; Franke-Vogt 2005c: 97–99).[12] Besenval (1997a: 207) even noted that *Togau* ware vessels decorated with hooks dominated the assemblage of Level VI in Trench IX. Recent excavations at Sohr-Damb have, however, showed that the dating of some of these wares need reappraisal (Franke 2008: 654–62). At this last site, *Togau* ware seems to come to an end at the end of *Period I*, while *Nal* ware appeared in *Period II* (Franke-Vogt 2005a: 67, 70). *Period II* is dated to *c.* 3100–2700 BC (Görsdorf and Franke-Vogt 2007: 705), although it may still be envisaged that this period started a little bit earlier. *Togau* ware with hooks appears to have been popular: it was not only reported from the Quetta region, but also as far as the Las Bela Plain to the south and from the Indus Valley to the Iranian border to the east, including the Rakhshan Valley and the Panjgur Oasis, north of the Kech Valley (de Cardi 1983: 42 fig. 5, 43; Stein 1931: pl. II no. Kar.b.1, Kar.1, pl. III no. Gar. 1).

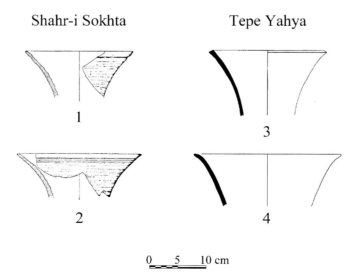

Shahr-i Sokhta   Tepe Yahya

Figure 14.17. Burnished ware from Shahr-i Sokhta (nos. 1–2 after Amiet and Tosi 1978: fig. 3) and Tepe Yahya.

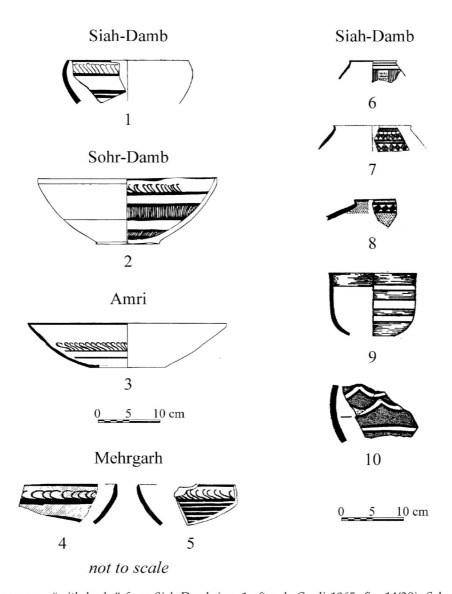

Figure 14.18. Togau *ware "with hooks" from Siah-Damb (no. 1 after de Cardi 1965: fig. 14/20), Sohr-Damb (no. 2 after Franke-Vogt 2005b: fig. 27), Amri (no. 3 after Casal 1964, vol. II: fig. 39/7), and Mehrgarh (nos. 4–5 after Samzun 1988: fig. LVIII nos. 647, 650); ceramics from Siah-Damb (nos. 6–10 after de Cardi 1965: figs 17A8; 15/59; 11/7, 15, 9).*

Farther to the north, some vessels of buff ware recovered at Shahr-i Sokhta in *Period I* find parallels both with materials from southern Turkmenistan (*Namazga III*) and with *Quetta* ware, a ware found mostly in north-eastern Pakistani Baluchistan and in southern Afghanistan. *Nal* ware was also found at Shahr-i Sokhta in *Periods I* and *II* (Amiet and Tosi 1978: 21–23), while one sherd that has parallels with *Nal* pottery was mentioned at Tepe Yahya in *Period VA* (Lamberg-Karlovsky 1970: 95). One may, however, consider that this last example was probably located originally in a more recent context in *Periods IVC–IVB*. Indeed, *Nal* ware was produced in eastern Pakistani Baluchistan mostly between the end of the fourth and the beginning of the third millennium BC, between

c. 3200/3100 and 2700 BC according to the dates from Sohr-Damb *Period II*, and was one of several regional variants of a widespread polychrome tradition at this time. Furthermore, the dates of *Shahr-i Sokhta I* and *II*, where *Nal* ware was found, are partly situated within the same chronological bracket (Salvatori and Tosi 2005: 285–86).

Materials related to north-eastern Pakistani Baluchistan were at that time also attested in south-eastern Pakistan (Amri, Balakot; Franke-Vogt 2005c) and as far as Tajikistan (Sarazm; Lyonnet 1996: 59–60) (Fig. 14.19), but with the exception of the single *Nal*-related sherd from Tepe Yahya, they seem rare to the west beyond the south-easternmost mountain ranges of the Iranian Plateau.

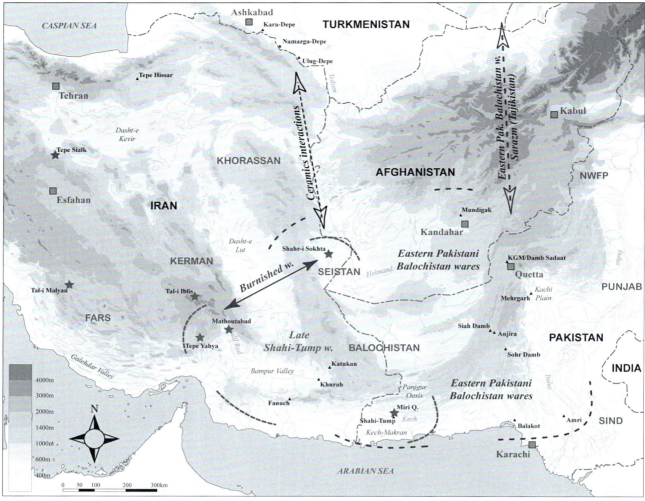

Figure 14.19. Map showing provisional reconstructions of the distributions of the main ceramic products on the south-eastern Iranian Plateau and in the Indo-Iranian borderlands from the end of the fourth to the early third millennium BC: late Shahi-Tump *ware and late* Shahi-Tump *ware-related vessels; burnished ware; and eastern Pakistani Baluchistan wares. The stars locate sites with* Uruk *and* Proto-Elamite *materials (map B. Mutin).*

Conclusion

Ceramics are attested from the seventh and sixth millennia BC in several regions of Middle Asia, including Kerman, Fars, and north-eastern Pakistani Baluchistan (Mehrgarh), but the distribution of ceramic technology is very variable. For example, in coastal Fars the earliest ceramics date to the fifth millennium BC and were recovered near the Persian Gulf in the Galehdar Valley (Askari Chaverdi *et al.* 2008). The fifth millennium BC also saw the development of fine, painted ceramics at the occupations of Fars, Kerman, and north-eastern Pakistani Baluchistan. Conversely, with the exception of Pakistani Makran, no occupation prior to the fourth millennium BC has been found in the area to the east of the Strait of Hormuz up to the province of Sind in Pakistan. Sites such as Balakot and Amri were first occupied only during the second half or by the end

of the fourth millennium BC (Franke-Vogt 2005c: 101; Casal 1964, vol. 1: 27, 29, 58). Farther to north, the site of Adam Buthi was occupied from the middle of the fourth millennium BC, while *Period I* at Sohr-Damb started around 4000/3800 BC or perhaps even later (Franke-Vogt 2000; Görsdorf and Franke-Vogt 2007: 703). Future fieldwork has the potential to change this situation, and different types of parameters such as massive alluvial deposits and sea-level changes may also be responsible for the absence of sites in some areas, as evidence in Makran shows that this inland region was inhabited during the fifth millennium BC. Furthermore, the marine shells observed at Tepe Yahya and at Mehrgarh from the Neolithic period onwards provide evidence for contacts with the coastal areas (Kenoyer 1995; Beale and Lamberg-Karlovsky 1986: 167–79), and potentially indicate that the coastal areas were occupied at that time. There is an absence of pottery, however, during *Period I* in the Kech Valley, dated to the late fifth millennium BC. In terms of ceramic production, compared to the north-eastern and north-western areas this period might thus be envisaged as a local "late" *aceramic horizon*. Besenval (1997b: 11) has previously pointed out the thick deposits and rarity of pottery at Sar-i Damb, a site located east of the Kech Valley (see Fig. 14.1). Excavations at this site have the potential to support this hypothesis, while other future fieldwork in south-eastern Iran will tell us whether or not the situation was the same farther to the west.

Starting mostly with the fourth millennium BC, the distributions of the different styles of ceramics tend to delineate several areas and are indicative of a successive series of interactions that included the south-easternmost areas of the Iranian Plateau. The oldest wares found in the Bampur Valley are similar to the ceramics found in Kerman during the first half of the fourth millennium BC and perhaps the end of the fifth millennium BC (black-on-buff ware and black-on-red ware, Fig. 14.8), and there are also indications of stylistic relationships between Kerman and Fars (e.g. early black-on-buff ware and *Lapui* ware). The origin of *Miri* ware in Kech-Makran needs more investigation, but this ware seems to share more resemblances with the ceramics of the Iranian Plateau in general than with those of the rest of Pakistan, although one cannot rule out the possible role of potters from the north-eastern areas of Pakistani Baluchistan in the emergence of pottery in Makran. Vessels similar to *Miri* ware were also identified in the Bampur Valley. Thus, the distributions of the Kerman wares and of *Miri* ware tend to show that the south-easternmost areas of the Iranian Plateau were dominated by two main ceramic traditions during the first half of the fourth millennium BC, with the former being distributed and/or produced in Kerman and the Bampur Valley and the latter in the Bampur Valley and Kech-Makran.[13]

In the succeeding period, starting around the middle of the fourth millennium BC or slightly before, early *Shahi-Tump* ware, found both in the Bampur Valley and Kech-Makran, indicates continuous ties between the two regions, while *Aliabad* ware, a product best identified in Kerman, has analogies with materials found as far as Kech-Makran (Fig. 14.14). On the other hand, there are fewer parallels with the ceramic products of Fars than before, although the earliest *Uruk*-related elements may have appeared in Kerman during this period. In the east, fine, painted ceramics related to those seen in eastern Pakistani Baluchistan started being used farther to the west in Kech-Makran. Then, the assemblages dating to the end of the fourth and into the early third millennium BC reflect a broader phenomenon of increasing interactions that is observed from Mesopotamia to southern Central Asia. Ceramics related to late *Shahi-Tump* ware are represented over a large portion of the south-eastern Iranian Plateau. At the same time, materials characteristic of the *Proto-Elamite* phenomenon are attested on the south-eastern Iranian Plateau and were in use contemporaneously with fine ceramics related to the eastern Pakistani Baluchistan traditions that seem to be progressively more numerous in this area (Fig. 14.19).[14] Other dynamics that seem to have penetrated the south-eastern Iranian Plateau in the same period are indicated by burnished ware found at Tepe Yahya and Shahr-i Sokhta and the ceramics with analogies to assemblages of southern Turkmenistan and north-eastern Pakistani Baluchistan found at the latter.

There are a range of questions related to the distribution, chronological position, and stylistic evolution of the various ceramic wares of the fourth millennium BC in south-eastern Iran that need further investigation. The interactions observed on the south-eastern Iranian Plateau during the fourth millennium BC need refining, especially in terms of the directions of influence and the types of interactive processes, in order to gain more insight into the nature of the social relations involved. Furthermore, fabrics analysis and quantitative data, if available, would give further insight into these interactions. At a minimum, the current data provide evidence for the existence of separate ceramic traditions and interregional interactions that could result in the sharing of technical knowledge, the use of similar approaches to vessel forms and decorations,[15] and in the movement of materials from one area to another. What does this mean in the context of the Iranian Plateau during the fourth millennium BC, which is characterised by an increasing complexity as seen in the development of new organisational structures and increasing long-range interactions? The fact that this paper deals only with ceramics does not enable us to offer an accurate and complete proposal on the processes that were involved in the developments of the fourth millennium BC of this region. Ethnographic examples have shown that one cannot make a direct association between ceramic types and ethnicity (e.g. Dietler and Herbich 1994). Nevertheless, it would inappropriate not to consider the areas that the distributions of the different types of ceramics tend to delineate on the south-eastern Iranian Plateau. Although the contours of these areas need to be refined, the assemblages being used in each of them show their own characteristics and indicate at the same time the existence of several separate interregional cultural relationships throughout the fourth millennium BC; some are based on pre-existent ones, while some are new.

The developments that took place on the Iranian Plateau during the fourth millennium BC and especially those of the end of the fourth and the early third millennia BC have often been envisaged with a primary focus on the trade and relationships with Mesopotamia (e.g. Algaze 1993; *cf.* Petrie, this volume: Introduction), although other types of dynamics have been underscored in south-eastern Iran and in its eastern neighbouring areas (e.g. Lamberg-Karlovsky and Tosi 1973). It would be misleading to ignore the *Uruk/Proto-Elamite* component on the south-eastern Iranian Plateau and, before that, the relationships between the buff painted wares and *Lapui* ware of Kerman and Fars. It would also be misleading to ignore the probable long-range interactions that traversed the Iranian Plateau during the fourth millennium BC. Even at sites that provide strong evidence for westwards-oriented long-range relationships, such as Tepe Yahya and Shahr-i Sokhta, assemblages show that these relations were only part of a system that clearly integrated other local and interregional dynamics. The ceramic styles of the south-eastern Iranian Plateau in this period indicate that their bearers were also involved within a set of cultural dynamics disconnected from those of western Iran and Mesopotamia. Those dynamics appear mostly as the result of internal processes within this area. In *Rethinking World-Systems*, Gil Stein (1999: 43) reviewed world-systems theory and noted, "[...] we need to consider alternative models that do not assume a priori external dynamics, core dominance, and the causal primary of long-distance interaction". It would be very questionable to offer here, from a single ceramics-based comparative analysis, any model explaining the situation on the south-eastern Iranian Plateau during the fourth millennium BC. At present, however, one may note that the south-eastern Iranian Plateau offers another example of a "periphery" of the Mesopotamian-western Iranian "centre" that acted as a core for multiple dynamics.

Whatever political and economic structures were impacting on pottery production and use on the south-eastern Iranian Plateau during the fourth millennium BC, the pots tend to be indicative of long-span cultural boundaries with fluctuations, and perhaps punctual breaks in some cases and long-span interregional relations. Kerman shared elements with western Iran, particularly Fars, that are attested by early black-on-buff ware, *Lapui* ware, and then *Uruk* and *Proto-Elamite* components, but those elements are rarer or absent east of Kerman, and this province was also continuously embedded within its own regional traditions and separate relationships oriented to the south-east.

In terms of ceramics, the Bampur Valley appears as an area embedded both within dynamics shared with Kerman and within dynamics shared with Kech-Makran, and it tends to represent a sort of ceramic crossroads for most of the fourth millennium BC, although it was not impermeable to larger phenomena

such as *Aliabad* ware and late *Shahi-Tump* ware. To the east the ceramic tradition, well attested in Kech-Makran from *Periods II* to *IIIa* (and which continued into *Period IIIb*) and identified in south-eastern Iran, has not been identified so far east of the Kolwa Plain in Pakistan. This ceramic boundary was penetrated from the east by traditions that originated in eastern Pakistani Baluchistan, especially starting with the mid- to late fourth millennium BC, but this did not prevent the populations of Kech-Makran from maintaining their own ceramic tradition. From the late fourth millennium BC the presence of this tradition (in the shape of late *Shahi-Tump* ware) in Seistan in the foundation period of Shahr-i Sokhta and at Tepe Yahya, informs us of its importance on the south-eastern Iranian Plateau at a time when numerous other separate cultural dynamics seem to have appeared in this area.

The ceramics of the fourth millennium BC on the south-eastern Iranian Plateau are indicative of the fact that an additional important set of local and interregional dynamics existed in this part of the Iranian Plateau. They complement the broader picture of the Iranian Plateau and its neighbours at that time, which tends to emerge as a multi-cultural frame and highlight the importance of long-span traditions. This reinforces the postulate that, in general, local and interregional processes are probably a key to understanding the developments towards – and the sustainability and probably the collapse of – the greater complexity and long-range interactions (which they most likely facilitated) in the context of the fourth millennium BC and probably also later on the Iranian Plateau and its neighbours.

Acknowledgements

This paper reports some results from a Ph.D. dissertation (Mutin 2007) and I would like to pay tribute to my supervisor Serge Cleuziou (†) and to thank Jean-François Jarrige, president of the jury committee, Roland Besenval, Sophie Méry, and Maurizio Tosi, members of the jury committee, and the UMR 9993 CNRS. At Harvard University, my work was supervised by Karl Lamberg-Karlovsky and Richard Meadow at the time of the conference. I would like to express my gratitude to them for their comments and reviews of this paper and for their support during my stay at Harvard. Also, many thanks are due to Patricia Capone, Susan Haskell, and the staff of the Peabody Museum who greatly facilitated the studies of the collection. This research was funded by the generosity of the Shelby White–Leon Levy Program for Archaeological Publications. Finally, many thanks to Cameron Petrie for the invitation to the conference that was both studious and welcoming.

Notes

1 This paper reports some results from a Ph.D. dissertation (Mutin 2007), which was devoted to the study of ceramics recovered in Pakistani Makran.

2 Mission Archéologique Française au Makran (MAFM), UMR 9993 CNRS.

3 The study of these materials was facilitated by a post-doctoral affiliation with the Department of Anthropology of Harvard University and with the kind permission of the PMAE.

4 Two calibrated dates assigned to *Period I* and one assigned to *Period I/II* from Miri Qalat fall within the late fifth and early fourth millennia BC (Besenval 1997b: 34 n. 28). Recalibration of these dates using OxCal v4.1.7 (Bronk Ramsey 2009; r:5 Atmospheric data from Reimer *et al.* 2009) has provided similar results: Gif-9340 (*Period I*): 4045–3713 BC (95.4%); Gif-9339 (*Period I*): 4257–3818 BC (95.4%); and Gif-9345 (*Period I/II*): 4321–3815 BC (95.4%). With the exception of one date that is much later, the radiocarbon dates from contexts assigned to *Period II* at Miri Qalat are essentially situated within the first half of the fourth millennium BC (Besenval 1997b: 34 n. 37). Recalibration of these dates using OxCal v4.1.7 has provided essentially the same results: Gif-8505: 3961–3700 BC (95.4%); Gif-8506: 3944–3646 BC (95.4%); Gif-8507: 4039–3656 BC (95.4%); Gif-8508: 4224–3653 BC (95.3%); Gif-8509: 3692–3372 BC (95.3%); Gif-8499: 3694–3381 BC (95.3%); Gif-8500: 3331–2885 BC (95.4%); and Gif-8503: 3944–3638 BC (95.4%).

5 *Soghun* ware was recovered mostly during *Period VI*. Black-on-buff ware was common mostly during *Periods VB–VA.2*, while black-on-red ware was found mostly in *VA.2–1* contexts (Beale and Lamberg-Karlovsky 1986). As discussed below, *Aliabad* ware probably started to be produced during the first half of the fourth millennium BC and continued to exist into the second half of the fourth millennium BC.

6 GX 1728: 4792–4075 BC (95.4%); GX 1737: 4777–4045 BC (95.4%); and Beta 6476: 4333–3715 BC (95.4%).

7 Beta 6480: 4243–3708 BC (95.4%) and Beta 6560: 4223–3639 BC (95.5%). The bracket of a third one is situated between *c.* 5200 and 3800 BC: WSU 872: 5205–3797 BC (95.4%).

8 P-924: 4716–4372 BC (95.4%); Gx-866: 4954–4246 BC (95.4%); Gx-868: 4520–4004 BC (95.4%); Gx-863: 5040–4333 BC (95.4%); Gx-867: 5474–4771 BC (95.4%); Gx-869: 5468–4848 BC (95.3%); Gx-865: 5207–4405 BC (95.3%); Gx-864: 5196–4842 (95.4%); P-925: 4929–4548 BC (95.4%); and P-926: 4906–4543 BC (95.4%).

9 And perhaps from the late fifth millennium BC for some elements of black-on-buff ware.

10 Four calibrated radiocarbon dates from *Period IIIa* contexts at Miri Qalat are essentially situated within the second half of the fourth millennium BC, with limits at *c.* 3700 and 2900 BC (Besenval 1997b: 35 n. 50). Recalibration of these dates using OxCal v4.1.7 has provided the same results: Gif-10055 (*Period IIIa*): 3505–3031 BC (95.4%); Gif-10058 (*Period IIIa*): 3692–3380 BC (95.4%); Gif-10062 (*Period IIIa*): 3336–2906 BC (95.4%); and Gif-10059 (originally assigned to *Period IIIb*): 3483–3031 BC (95.4%).

11 P-927 (Iblis III): 4532–4331 BC (95.4%); P-928 (Iblis IV): 4440–4055 BC (95.3%); and P-929 (Iblis IV): 3634–3358 BC (95.4%).

12 Franke notes that the "Balochi" types are rarer at Amri.

13 Although the *Husaini* wares show that the situation was probably more complicated, and *Aliabad* ware and the material of *Iblis III/IV* in general probably partly overlapped with *Miri* ware in the second quarter of the fourth millennium BC.

14 This is shown by *Togau* ware with hooks (and other wares) identified in Kech-Makran and the Panjgur Oasis, which, according to the sequence excavated at Sohr-Damb, dates to before *c.* 3200 or 3100 BC, and *Nal*-related materials, which according to the same sequence, overlap with the end of the fourth and the first centuries of the third millennium BC.

15 For example, the bowls with swastika in burials in Seistan and Makran and perhaps the conical goblets.

Bibliography

Alden, J. R. 1982. "Trade and politics in Proto-Elamite Iran", *Current Anthropology* 23 (6): 613–640.

Algaze, G. 1993. *The Uruk World System: The dynamics of expansion of early Mesopotamian civilization*, the University of Chicago Press, Chicago.

Amiet, P. and Tosi, M. 1978. "Phase 10 at Shahr-i Sohkta. Excavations in Square XDV and The Late 4th Millennium B.C. Assemblage of Seistan", *EW* 28 (1–4): 9–32.

Askari Chaverdi, A., Petrie, C. A. and Taylor, H. 2008. "Early Villages on the Persian Gulf littoral: Revisiting Tol-e Pir and the Galehdar Valley", *Iran* 46: 21–42.

Beale, T. W. and Lamberg-Karlovsky, C. C. eds 1986. *Excavations at Tepe Yahya, Iran 1967–1975. The Early Periods*, American School of Prehistoric Research Bulletin, Vol. 38, Peabody Museum of Archaeology and Ethnology, Cambridge, MA.

Bernbeck, R. 2010. "The Neolithic pottery", in Pollock, S., Bernbeck, R. and Abdi, K. (eds), *The 2003 Excavations at Tol-e Baši, Iran. Social Life in a Neolithic Village*, Archäologie in Turan and Iran 10, Philipp von Zabern, Mainz: 65–151.

Besenval, R. 1994. "The 1992–1993 field-seasons at Miri Qalat: new contributions to the chronology of protohistoric settlement in Pakistani Makran", in Parpola, A. and Koskikallio, P. (eds), *South Asian Archaeology, 1993*, Suomalainen Tiedeakatemia, Helsinki, Vol. 1: 81–91.

Besenval, R. 1997a. "The chronology of ancient occupation in Makran: results of the 1994 season at Miri Qalat, Pakistan Makran", in Allchin, F. R. and Allchin, B. (eds), *South Asian Archaeology, 1995*, Oxford and IBH Publishing Co. Pvt. Ltd, Vol. 1, New Delhi: 199–216.

Besenval, R. 1997b. "Entre le Sud-Est iranien et la plaine de l'Indus: le Kech-Makran. Recherches archéologiques sur le peuplement ancien d'une marche des confins indo-iraniens", *Arts Asiatiques* 52: 5–36.

Besenval, R. 2000. "New data from the chronology of the Protohistory of Kech-Makran (Pakistan) from Miri Qalat 1996 and Shahi Tump 1997 Field Season", in Taddei, M. and De Marco, G. (eds), *South Asian Archaeology, 1997*, Istituto Italiano per l'Afriaca e l'Oriente, Vol. 1, Rome: 161–87.

Besenval, R. 2005. "Chronology of protohistoric Kech-Makran", in Jarrige, C. and Lefèvre, V. (eds), *South Asian Archaeology, 2001*, ERC, Vol. 1, Paris: 1–9.

Bronk Ramsey, C. 2009. "Bayesian analysis of radiocarbon dates", *Radiocarbon* 51 (1): 337–360.

Caldwell, J. R. ed. 1967. *Investigations at Tal-i Iblis*, Illinois State Museum Preliminary Reports, Vol. 9, Illinois State Museum Society, Springfield.

Caldwell, J. R. 1968. "Pottery and Cultural History on the Iranian Plateau", *JNES* 27 (3): 178–83.

Casal, J-M. 1964. *Fouilles d'Amri*, Klincksiek, Paris.

Chase, D. W., Fehervari, G. and Caldwell, J. R. 1967a. "Reconnaissances in the Bard Sir Valley", in Caldwell, J. R. (ed.), *Investigations at Tal-i Iblis*, Illinois State Museum Preliminary Reports, Vol. 9, Illinois State Museum Society, Springfield: 73–107.

Chase, D. W., Caldwell, J. R. and Fehervari, I. 1967b. "The Iblis sequence and the exploration of excavation areas A, C, and E", in Caldwell, J. R. (ed.), *Investigations at Tal-i Iblis*, Illinois State Museum Preliminary Reports, Vol. 9, Illinois State Museum Society, Springfield: 111–201.

Courty, M-A., and Roux, V. 1995. "Identification of wheel throwing on the basis of ceramic surface features and microfabrics", *Journal of Archaeological Science* 22: 17–50.

Dales, G. F. and Lipo, C. P. 1992. *Explorations on the Makran Coast, Pakistan. A Search for Paradise*, Contributions of the Archaeological Research Facility, Vol. 50, University of California, Berkeley.

de Cardi, B. 1965. "Excavations and reconnaissance in Kalat, West Pakistan. The prehistoric sequence in the Surab region", *Pakistan Archaeology* 2: 86–182.

de Cardi, B. 1970. *Excavations at Bampur, a third millennium settlement in Persian Baluchistan, 1966*, Anthropological Papers of the American Museum of Natural History, New York, Vol. 51 (3): 233–355.

de Cardi, B. 1983. *Archaeological Surveys in Baluchistan, 1948 and 1957*, Institute of Archaeology Occasional Publication 8, University of London, London.

Didier, A. 2007. *Archéologie des confins indo-iraniens: Étude de la production céramique du Kech-Makran (Pakistan) dans la première moitié du IIIe millénaire av. J.-C.*, unpublished Ph.D. thesis, Université de Paris 1 Panthéon-Sorbonne.

Didier, A. and Méry, S. 2012. "Les premières céramiques fines grises d'Asie moyenne aux IVe et IIIe millénaires», in Lefèvre, V. (ed.), *De l'Archéologie au musée. Mélanges offerts à Jean-François Jarrige*, Brepols, Turnhout: 177–92.

Dietler, M. and Herbich, I. 1994. "Ceramics an ethnic identity: ethnoarchaeological observations on the distribution of pottery styles and the relationship between the social contexts of production and consumption", in Audouze, F. and Binder, D. (eds), *Terre cuite et Société. La céramique, document technique, économique, culturel*, Actes des XIVe rencontres internationales d'archéologie et d'histoire d'Antibes, Éditions APDCA, Juan-les-Pins: 459–72.

Dupont-Delaleuf, A. 2010. "Les chaînes opératoires de la céramique d'Ulug-Dépé (Turkménistan). Du Chalcolithique moyen à la période achéménide", *Les Nouvelles de l'Archéologie* 119: 47–51.

Evett, D. 1967. "Artifacts and architecture of the Iblis I Period: areas D, F, and G", in Caldwell, J. R. (ed.), *Investigations at Tal-i Iblis*, Illinois State Museum Preliminary Reports, Vol. 9, Illinois State Museum Society, Springfield: 202–55.

Field, H. 1959. *An Anthropological Reconnaissance in West Pakistan, 1955*, Peabody Museum of Archaeology and Ethnology, Cambridge, MA.

Franke, U. 2008. "Baluchistan and the Borderlands", *Encyclopedia of Archaeology*, Vol. 1: 651–70.

Franke-Vogt, U. 2000. *The Archaeology of Southeastern Balochistan*, http://www.harappa.com/baluch/e4.html, accessed 18/01/2013.

Franke-Vogt, U. 2005a. "Excavations at Sohr Damb/Nal: results of the 2002 and 2004 seasons", in Franke-Vogt, U. and Weisshaar, H. J. (eds), *South Asian Archaeology, 2003*, Vol. 1, Deutsches Archäologisches Institut, Aachen/Bonn: 63–76.

Franke-Vogt, U. 2005b. "Sohr Damb/Nal, Baluchistan, Pakistan Ergebnisse der Grabungen 2001, 2002 und 2004", *AMI* 35–36 (2003–2004): 83–141.

Franke-Vogt, U. 2005c. "Balakot Period I: A review of its stratigraphy, cultural sequence and date", in Jarrige, C. and Lefèvre, V. (eds), *South Asian Archaeology, 2001*, ERC, Vol. 1, Paris: 95–103.

Görsdorf, J. and Franke-Vogt, U. 2007. "Implications of radiocarbon dates from Sohr Damb/Nal, Balochistan", *Radiocarbon* 49 (2): 703–12.

Jarrige, C., Jarrige, J-F., Meadow, R. H. and Quivron, G. 1995. *Mehrgarh. Field Reports 1974–1985. From Neolithic times to the Indus Civilization*, Department of Culture and Tourism of Sindh (Pakistan) in Collaboration with the French Ministry of Foreign Affairs, Karachi.

Jarrige, J-F. 1987. "Une jarre polychrome à tenon perforé de Mundigak", in Gnoli, G. and Lanciotti, L. (eds), *Orientalia Iosephi Tucci Memoriae Dicata*, IsMEO, Rome: 661–66.

Kenoyer, J. M. 1995. "Shell trade and shell working during the Neolithic and Early Chalcolithic at Mehrgarh, Pakistan", in Jarrige, C., Jarrige, J-F., Meadow, R. H. and Quivron, G. (eds), *Mehrgarh. Field Reports 1974–1985. From Neolithic times to the Indus Civilization*, Department of Culture and Tourism of Sindh (Pakistan) in Collaboration with the French Ministry of Foreign Affairs, Karachi: 566–81.

Lamberg-Karlovsky, C. C. 1970. *Excavations at Tepe Yahya, Iran 1967–1969. Progress Report I*, American School of Prehistoric Research Bulletin, Vol. 27, Peabody Museum of Archaeology and Ethnology, Cambridge, MA.

Lamberg-Karlovsky, C. C. and Schmandt-Besserat, D. 1977. "An Evaluation of the Bampur, Khurab and Chah Husseini collections in the Peabody Museum and relations with Tepe Yahya", in Levine, L. and Young Jr., T. C. (eds), *Mountains and Lowlands: Essays in the Archaeology of Greater Mesopotamia*, Bibliotheca Mesopotamica, Vol. 7, Malibu: 113–34.

Lamberg-Karlovsky, C. C. and Tosi, M. 1973. "Shahr-i Sokhta and Tepe Yahya: tracks on the earliest history of the Iranian Plateau", *EW* 23 (1–2): 21–57.

Lamberg-Karlovsky, C. C. 2001. "Afterword – Excavations at Tepe Yahya: reconstructing the past", in Potts, D. T. and Lamberg-Karlovsky, C. C. eds 2001. *Excavations at Tepe Yahya, Iran. The Third Millennium*, American School of Prehistoric Research Bulletin, Vol. 45, Peabody Museum of Archaeology and Ethnology, Cambridge, MA: 269–280.

Laneri, N. and Di Pilato, S. 2000. "Searching for the Archaeological Evidence of Wheel-Throwing at Ebla, Susa and Shahr-i Sokhta", in Taddei, M. and De Marco, G. (eds), *South Asian Archaeology, 1997*, Istituto Italiano per l'Afriaca e l'Oriente, Rome: 521–40.

Lyonnet, B. 1996. *Sarazm (Tadjikistan) Céramiques (Chalcolithique et Bronze Ancien)*, Mémoires de la Mission Archéologique Française en Asie Centrale, Tome VII, Editions de Boccard, Paris.

Madjidzadeh, Y. 2008. "Excavations at Konar Sandal in the region of Jiroft in the Halil Basin: first preliminary report (2002–2008)", *Iran* 46: 69–103.

Mockler, E. 1877. "On ruins in Makran", *JRAS* IX (New Series): 121–34.

Mutin, B. 2006. "La Basket Ware, une production céramique originale de la Protohistoire des confins indo-iraniens", *Paléorient* 32 (2): 175–93.

Mutin, B. 2007. *Contribution à l'étude du peuplement des confins indo-iraniens au Chalcolithique : Caractérisation de la production céramique des périodes II et IIIa du Makran pakistanais (IVe millénaire av. J.-C.)*, unpublished Ph.D. thesis, Université de Paris 1 Panthéon-Sorbonne.

Petrie, C. A. 2011. "'Culture', innovation and interaction across southern Iran from the Neolithic to the Bronze Age (6500–3000 BC)", in Roberts, B. and Vander Linden, M. (eds), *Investigating Archaeological Cultures: material culture, variability and transmission*, Springer, New York: 151–82.

Petrie, C. A. 2013. "The Chalcolithic of south Iran", *Oxford Handbook of Iranian Archaeology*, OUP, Oxford: 120–57.

Petrie, C. A., Weeks, L. R., Potts, D. T. and Roustaei, K. 2009. "Perspectives on the cultural sequence of Mamasani", in Potts, D. T, Roustaei, K., Petrie, C. A. and Weeks, L. R. (eds), *The Mamasani Archaeological Project, Stage One: A Report on the First Two Seasons of the ICAR-University of Sydney Expedition to the Mamasani District, Fars Province, Iran*, Archaeopress, Oxford: 169–96.

Potts, D. T. and Lamberg-Karlovsky, C. C. eds 2001. *Excavations at Tepe Yahya, Iran. The Third Millennium*, American School of Prehistoric Research Bulletin, Vol. 45, Peabody Museum of Archaeology and Ethnology, Cambridge, MA.

Prickett, M. E. 1986a. "Settlement during the early periods", in Beale, T. W. and Lamberg-Karlovsky, C. C. (eds), *Excavations at Tepe Yahya, Iran 1967–1975. The Early Periods*, American School of Prehistoric Research Bulletin, Vol. 38, Cambridge, Peabody Museum of Archaeology and Ethnology, Cambridge, MA: 215–46.

Prickett, M. E. 1986b. *Man, Land and* Ware*: Settlement Distribution and the Development of Irrigation Agriculture in the Upper Rud-i Gushk Drainage, Southeastern-Iran*, unpublished Ph.D. thesis, Harvard University, U.M.I. Dissertation Information Service.

Reimer, P. J., Baillie, M. G. L., Bard, E., Bayliss, A., Beck, J. W., Blackwell, P. G., Bronk Ramsey, C., Buck, C. E., Burr, G. S., Edwards, R. L., Friedrich, M., Grootes, P. M., Guilderson, T. P., Hajdas, I., Heaton, T. J., Hogg, A. G., Hughen, K. A., Kaiser, K. F., Kromer, B., McCormac, F. G., Manning, S. W., Reimer, R. W., Richards, D. A., Southon, J. R., Talamo, S., Turney, C. S. M., van der Plicht, J. and Weyhenmeyer, C. E. 2009. "IntCal09 and Marine09 radiocarbon age calibration curves, 0–50,000 years cal BP", *Radiocarbon* 51 (4): 1111–150.

Sajjadi, S. M. S. 2003. "Excavations at Shahr-i Sokhta. First Preliminary Report on the Excavations of the Graveyard, 1997–2000", *Iran* 41: 21–97.

Salvatori, S. and Tosi, M. 2005. "Shahr-i Sokhta Revised Sequence", in Jarrige, C. and Lefèvre, V. (eds), *South Asian Archaeology, 2001*, ERC, Vol. 1, Paris: 281–92.

Samzun, A. 1988. Étude *des développements économiques, sociaux et commerciaux vers 4000 avant notre ère au Baluchistan et dans les régions frontières du sous-continent indien. Un examen de la culture matérielle du site de Mehrgarh (période III) au Pakistan*, unpublished Ph.D. thesis, Université de Paris 1 Panthéon-Sorbonne.

Sarraf, M. R. 1981. *Die Keramik von Tell-i Iblis und Ihre zeitliche und räumliche Beziehungen zu den anderen iranischen und mesopotamischen Kuulturen*, AMI, Ergänzungsband 7, Dietrich Reimer Verlag, Berlin.

Schmidt, E. F. 1937. *Excavations at Tepe Hissar, Damgham*, University Museum, Philadelphia.

Stein, G. 1999. *Rethinking world-systems: Diasporas, colonies and interaction in Uruk Mesopotamia*, University of Arizona Press, Tucson.

Stein, M. A. 1931. *An Archaeological Tour in Gedrosia*, Memoirs of the Archaeological Survey of India, Vol. 38, Archaeological Survey of India, Calcutta.

Stein, M. A. 1937. *Archaeological Reconnaissances in the North-Western India and South-Eastern Iran*, McMillan and Sons, London.

Vandiver, P. 1986. "The production technology of earthenware ceramics, 4900–2800 B.C.", in Beale, T. W. and Lamberg-Karlovsky, C. C. (eds), *Excavations at Tepe Yahya, Iran 1967–1975. The Early Periods*, American School of Prehistoric Research Bulletin, Vol. 38, Peabody Museum of Archaeology and Ethnology, Cambridge, MA: 91–100.

Vandiver, P. 1987. "Sequential Slab Construction; a conservative Asiatic ceramic tradition, ca. 7000–3000 B.C.", *Paléorient* 13 (2): 9–35.

Vandiver, P. 1995. "The production technology of early pottery at Mehrgarh", in Jarrige, C., Jarrige, J-F., Meadow, R. H. and Quivron, G. (eds), *Mehrgarh. Field Reports 1974–1985. From Neolithic times to the Indus Civilization*, Department of Culture and Tourism of Sindh (Pakistan) in Collaboration with the French Ministry of Foreign Affairs, Karachi: 648–61.

Voigt, M. M. and Dyson, R. H. 1992. "Chronology of Iran, ca. 8000–2000 B.C.", in Ehrich, R. W. (ed.), *Chronologies of Old World Archaeology*, Vol. 1, University of Chicago Press, Chicago: 122–78.

Wright, R. P. 1984. *Technology, Style and Craft Specialization: Spheres of Interaction and Exchange in the Indo-Iranian Borderlands, Third Millennium B.C.*, unpublished Ph.D. thesis, Harvard University, U.M.I. Dissertation Information Service.

Wright, R. P. 1989. "New tracks on ancient frontiers: Ceramic technology on the Indo-Iranian Borderlands", in Lamberg-Karlovsky, C. C. (ed.), *Archaeological Thought in America*, Cambridge University Press, Cambridge: 268–79.

Wright, R. P. 2002. "Revisiting interaction spheres – social boundaries and technologies on inner and outermost frontiers", *IA* 37: 403–17.

15. IRANIAN METALLURGY OF THE FOURTH MILLENNIUM BC IN ITS WIDER TECHNOLOGICAL AND CULTURAL CONTEXTS

Lloyd Weeks

Introduction

The fourth millennium BC in Iran is crucial for our understanding of the development of the extractive metallurgy of copper, lead, and silver. The origins of metal smelting technologies can be traced locally back to the fifth millennium BC and are related to an even earlier utilisation of native metals at *Neolithic* sites across Iran. Several studies have demonstrated Iran's significance for our understanding of the earliest alloying of arsenical copper and the eventual adoption of tin-bronze in the period from the late fifth through to the early third millennium BC. From a metallurgical perspective, the Iranian evidence is critical for characterising the development of extractive metallurgy and alloying across south-west Asia and neighbouring regions. From a socio-economic perspective, the development of early metallurgy in Iran has been linked to the rise and expansion of complex societies within Iran and in neighbouring Mesopotamia.

This paper reviews the major metallurgical developments that can be tracked across fourth-millennium BC Iran, and places these developments within the broader technological and cultural contexts of *Chalcolithic* western Asia. Particular attention is paid to similarities in the development of early metal smelting and the production of copper, copper alloys, lead, silver, and gold in the highland zones to the north and east of Mesopotamia. These similarities, and the cultural contacts they might represent, are discussed from archaeological, anthropological, and historical perspectives, focusing on mechanisms of technology transfer within and between social groups. The paper concludes with a consideration of the evidence for independent metallurgical developments in wider western Asia alongside an evaluation of the possible effects of increased cultural contact and human mobility beginning in the *Ubaid* period and peaking with the "*Uruk* phenomenon" of the fourth millennium BC.

Overview of research

The subject of prehistoric Iranian metallurgy has received significant (if insufficient) academic attention and good reviews of research up to the end of the twentieth century have been provided by Pigott (1999a, 1999b). Research undertaken since then, however, has transformed our understanding of early Iranian metallurgy, especially extractive metallurgy, and its archaeological chronology, particularly at sites like Ghabristan (Fazeli *et al.* 2004, 2005) and Tepe Hissar (Thornton, this volume). In particular, this paper benefits greatly from recent work undertaken by the joint Iranian-German projects at Arisman, Veshnoveh, and elsewhere (Vatandoust *et al.* 2011; Pernicka 2004; Chegini *et al.* 2004; Stöllner 2004, 2005) and by the study (and restudy) of metallurgical residues and artefacts from sites such as Tal-i Iblis (Frame 2004, 2012; Pigott and Lechtman 2003), Tappeh Sialk (Schreiner *et al.* 2003; Schreiner in Weeks 2008), Tepe Yahya (Thornton *et al.* 2002; Thornton and Lamberg-Karlovsky 2004; Thornton 2010), Godin Tepe (Frame in Weeks 2008; Frame 2010), Tepe Hissar (Thornton in Weeks 2008; Thornton and Rehren 2009; Thornton *et al.* 2009), and the *Early Bronze Age* graveyards of the central western Zagros (Fleming *et al.* 2005; Begemann *et al.* 2008). An excellent review of many aspects of this recent research can be found in Thornton (2009).

Iranian metallurgy before the fourth millennium BC

Iran has a long history of metal use that can be traced as early as the aceramic *Neolithic* period. Early metal finds at sites such as Ali Kosh and Chogha Sefid in Deh Luran, Tol-e Nurabad, Tall-e Mushki, Tall-e Jari in Fars, and Tappeh Sialk on the Iranian plateau, represent the use of native copper (Smith 1969; Hole 1977: 245; Fukai *et al.* 1973). The exploitation of this raw material seems to have lasted for millennia, and it continued to be used alongside the earliest smelted copper into the fourth millennium BC at sites such as Tepe Yahya (Thornton *et al.* 2002; Thornton and Lamberg-Karlovsky 2004). While initial explanations for the source of this material focused on the famous native copper sources of Talmessi/Meskani near Anarak (Smith 1969; Heskel and Lamberg-Karlovsky 1980), recent reconsiderations have noted the lack of evidence for early exploitation of these sites. Thornton's re-analysis of the native copper artefacts from Tepe Yahya (e.g. Thornton 2010) does not posit Talmessi/Meskani as a potential source, and Pernicka (2004) has suggested that the importance of Talmessi/Meskani for early Iranian metallurgy has been overestimated. Nevertheless, the exploitation of these famous plateau sources *does* seem to be indicated by recent lead isotope analyses of native copper artefacts from *Neolithic* Fars, from Tappeh Sialk I, and from Tal-i Iblis (Weeks 2008; Begemann and Schmitt-Strecker 2009: table A2). It should be acknowledged, however, that there are alternative native copper sources in Iran (e.g. Nezafati *et al.* 2005, 2008) that remain little investigated in comparison to Talmessi/Meskani and whose compositional and isotopic characteristics remain entirely unknown.

At present, the earliest known evidence for extractive metallurgy comes from the site of Tal-i Iblis in south-east Iran, where a large number of crucible fragments and simple fire pits dated to *Iblis Periods I* and *II* were excavated in the 1960s (Caldwell 1968). Radiocarbon dates and ceramic parallels indicate that these deposits date to the early to mid-fifth millennium BC. Elsewhere, the site of Cheshmeh Ali on the Iranian Plateau has produced a single crucible sherd suggesting that copper smelting was being carried out in the fifth millennium BC (Matthews and Fazeli 2004: 65), and an as yet unanalysed collection of metallurgical debris from Seh Gabi in the central western Zagros may represent the remains of late fifth-millennium BC metal extraction (Frame in Weeks 2008: 342). Recent analyses of *Iblis I* crucibles have demonstrated that they could and did function as reaction vessels for copper smelting (Frame 2004, 2012). The copper ores smelted at Tal-i Iblis (carbonates, sulfides, arsenates, and chlorides; Pigott and Lechtman 2003: 294–95) seem to have been carbonate-hosted, and there are numerous possible sources within 50–100 km of the site (Frame 2004,

2012). The copper produced contained significant impurities of arsenic, up to several wt percent in analysed prills from smelting crucibles (Frame 2004, 2012), although the few analysed copper artefacts from fifth-millennium BC contexts at Tal-e Iblis itself are of very pure copper (Pigott and Lechtman 2003). Earlier investigators (e.g. Heskel and Lamberg-Karlovsky 1980) highlighted the possible role of the copper arsenides algodonite (Cu_6As) and domeykite (Cu_3As) from Anarak/Talmessi in the earliest production of arsenical copper in Iran. The evidence from Tal-i Iblis for the smelting of arsenic-rich copper, however, focuses attention on alternative production processes and the widespread occurrence of arsenic-bearing ores in the region (Pigott in Weeks 2008: 341–42; contra Heskel and Lamberg-Karlovsky 1980).

The smelting of copper in the fifth millennium BC is also tentatively supported by analyses of finished artefacts at sites across Iran. While artefacts from *Iblis I* and *II* are of very pure copper that could feasibly be regarded as either melted native copper or very pure smelted copper, increases in the trace/minor element concentrations of arsenic, antimony, silver, nickel and lead in fifth-millennium BC artefacts from other sites such as Tepe Yahya (*Periods VIA* and *VA/B*) (Thornton 2010; Thornton *et al.* 2002), Tang-e Bolaghi sites DB73 and DB131 (Helwing and Seyedin 2010; Weeks *et al.*, in preparation), Tepe Hissar (*Period IA–B*) (Pigott *et al.* 1982: table 3) and Susa (*Period I*) (Malfoy and Menu 1987) suggest the presence of smelted metal. Significantly, metallographic studies of artefacts from *Iblis I* and *II* (Pigott and Lechtman 2003: 302 ff.), Yahya VI (Thornton 2010), and *Bakun* period sites in the Tang-e Bolaghi (Weeks *et al.*, in preparation), clearly indicate the ability to create artefacts by casting – a fundamental change from the *Neolithic* fabrication of native copper artefacts, which seems never to have incorporated melting.

Iranian metallurgy in the fourth millennium BC

Lead, silver, and gold

The fourth millennium BC witnesses a dramatic expansion in the evidence for extractive metallurgy in Iran and the widespread use of copper-base alloys alongside lead, silver, and gold. Evidence for the smelting of lead in the mid- to late fourth millennium BC consists of a lead ingot and several small lead pieces from Area C (*Proto-Elamite*) at Arisman (Helwing 2011a: 271–72, figs. 88, 96), as well as the large amount of litharge from the site (see below). In addition, lead slags (and copper-lead slags) were found at Hissar II (Pigott 1989; Thornton in Weeks 2008: 338), lead artefacts and scrap at Banesh Tal-e Malyan (Sumner 2003: 65–66), lead artefacts and copper-lead alloys in Susa (*Period II/III*) (Tallon

1987: i, 318; Malfoy and Menu 1987; Benoit 2004), and copper-lead alloys at Tepe Yahya (Thornton in Weeks 2008: 339).

Silver is a potential by-product of the smelting of argentiferous lead, and by the mid-fourth millennium BC large-scale production of silver by cupellation from lead was undertaken at Arisman in Area B (*Silk III$_{6-7}$* period) and elsewhere (Helwing 2011a: 265; 2011b: 524; Pernicka *et al.* 2011: 663–74), with contemporary examples of this technology found at Tappeh Sialk (Pernicka 2004) and possibly at Tepe Hissar (Tosi 1989). Lead isotope analyses indicate that the argentiferous lead processed at Arisman and Sialk came from Nakhlak on the central Plateau (Pernicka 2004: fig. 8). As there is no evidence for lead slags at Arisman or Sialk at this time, however – only for litharge cakes from cupellation – it is uncertain whether lead smelting was undertaken at these sites, or whether lead was smelted elsewhere and the resulting silver-rich metallic lead transported to Arisman and Tappeh Sialk for cupellation. Silver artefacts are reported from fourth-millennium BC contexts at Susa, Arisman, Tappeh Sialk, and Tepe Hissar (Benoit 2004; Stöllner 2005; Kohlmeyer 1994: 42; Roustaei 2004: 226; Helwing 2011a). The loci of production for such artefacts, most of which represent very high-quality craftsmanship, remain unknown, although Stöllner (2005: 194–95) has tentatively suggested that they were produced in the highlands.

Gold finds are much rarer than those of silver, but are recorded from Susa *Period II* (Acropole Lev. 17), from Arisman Area B in *Silk III$_{6-7}$* contexts (Helwing 2011a: 272 and fig. 50), Sialk *Period IV$_1$*, Hissar *Period II*, Iblis *Period IV* (Chase *et al.* 1967: 188, fig. 38.11) and from *Banesh* period Tal-e Malyan (Tallon 1987: 318–20; Sumner 2003: fig. 43). The sources of this metal remain unknown, although there are gold deposits in Iran at a number of locations with evidence for pre-modern (if not clearly prehistoric) exploitation (Momenzadeh 2004: 18 and fig. 7; Stöllner 2004: 54–55).

Copper smelting

Copper smelting of increasing sophistication and scale can be documented at a number of Iranian sites over the course of the fourth millennium BC. These sites are found in most metal-rich areas of Iran, including Tal-i Iblis *Periods III* and *IV* (Caldwell 1968; Frame 2012), Tappeh Sialk *Periods III$_{6-7}$* and *IV$_1$* (Schreiner *et al.* 2003; Schreiner in Weeks 2008), Tepe Hissar *Period II* (Pigott 1989; Thornton *et al.* 2009; Thornton and Rehren 2009), Tepe Ghabristan *Period II* (Majidzadeh 1979), and Arisman and earlier sites in its vicinity, such as Qaleh Gusheh (Chegini *et al.* 2004; Vatandoust *et al.* 2011). Extractive metallurgy seems also to have taken place in the central and southern Zagros in the early fourth millennium BC

at sites such as Seh Gabi (Levine 1975; Frame 2010), Godin Tepe *Period VI–1* (Frame 2010), and Banesh Tal-e Malyan (Pigott *et al.* 2003; Nicholas 1990). Although the specifics of smelting operations differed at each site, in part due to variations in locally available ores, all the early to mid-fourth-millennium BC plateau sites demonstrate a developed crucible-based smelting technology. This technology seems to have commonly, if not consistently, produced copper with impurities of up to several percent arsenic and lead and minor concentrations of Ag, Ni, Sb, and Fe (e.g. Malfoy and Menu 1987: tables E and G; Berthoud and Francaix 1980).

It is unfortunate that some of the most important metallurgical assemblages from Iran, most especially that from Tepe Ghabristan, have never been studied in detail. Nevertheless, the Arisman sequence is well analysed and instructive: early *Silk III$_{6-7}$* metallurgical operations in Area B utilised crucibles with a pierced base very similar to those found at contemporary Ghabristan, although Helwing (2011a: 262) indicates that these were most likely used for the smelting and casting of artefacts. Other crucible types recorded at the site show slag encrustations and were certainly used for smelting in simple pits in the mid-fourth millennium BC (Helwing 2011b: 525). Later crucibles exhibit the addition of a sealed and airtight clay lid (Helwing 2011a: 263). They are most commonly associated with the later fourth-millennium BC furnace fragments found in Slagheap D, and the earliest intact (and repeatedly reused) copper smelting furnace in Iran found in Slagheap A, dated to the *Silk IV$_1$* period (Steiniger 2011). The move to furnace smelting at Arisman in the *Proto-Elamite* period is regarded by Helwing (2011b: 528) as evidence of expanded copper production on an "industrial scale". Additional evidence for the development of furnace smelting in Iran at this time comes from several other sites. Slags that appear to have been tapped from furnaces are reported by the late fourth millennium BC from Hissar *Period II* (Thornton 2009; Pigott 1989), and a possible furnace wall fragment is reported from *Middle Banesh* Tal-e Malyan (Nicholas 1990: pl. 25a).

At Arisman, Areas B and C (mid-fourth to early third millennium BC) produced numerous moulds for ingots, flat axes, and a double axe (Helwing 2011a), and comparable casting moulds have been recorded from Tepe Ghabristan (Majidzadeh 1979), late fourth-millennium BC Tepe Hissar (Pigott 1989; figs. 5–8; Howard 1989: 60–61), and *Banesh* period Tal-e Malyan (Nicholas 1990: pl. 25b–d). The shapes of these moulds can be paralleled, for example, in metal artefacts from Susa *II/III* (Benoit 2004; Helwing 2011b: 527), *Protoliterate* Chogha Mish (Delougaz and Kantor 1996: pl. 29), and further afield in Mesopotamia (Helwing 2011a: 268), suggesting the widespread trade of Iranian copper-base metal.

The expansion in copper-base metal smelting in the fourth millennium BC on the Iranian Plateau is reflected in an increase in the use of copper-base artefacts at settlement sites. Susa, although having an important and substantial metal assemblage already in the late fifth to early fourth millennium BC (Susa I), has produced a significant assemblage of metal artefacts from late *Period II* and *Period III* (Tallon 1987). Metal was extremely rare at Chogha Mish in Khuzestan until the mid-fourth millennium BC, when *Uruk*-related deposits produced a "fair number" of artefacts (*c.* 20 in total; Delougaz and Kantor 1996: 105, pls. 29, 128). Alizadeh (2009: 89) also mentions a "large number of objects" from the East Area excavations at Chogha Mish, although their date is unspecified (*Protoliterate* remains were prominent in this area of the site). The Chogha Mish assemblage consists predominantly of small items, although one large (*c.* 600 g) flat copper-base axe/adze was recovered. While copper working (and perhaps smelting) appears to have been taking place in the central western Zagros by the late fifth or early fourth millennium BC (Godin VII levels at Seh Gabi; Levine 1975), copper-base artefacts appear at Godin Tepe only from *Period VI–1* (Frame 2010). In south-east Iran, there is an increase in the number of copper-base artefacts recorded from Tepe Yahya in *Period VB–VA*, i.e. from *c.* 3700–3300 BC (Heskel and Lamberg-Karlovsky 1986: 209).

Copper alloys

The fourth millennium BC is also critical for the development of copper-base alloys including arsenical copper, leaded copper, and possibly tin-bronze. Most significantly, by the end of the fourth millennium BC, there is some evidence for the intentional (if uncontrolled) production of arsenic-rich materials for deliberate alloying purposes. This includes atypical "brown stained… arsenide-rich" slags from Arisman (Pernicka in Weeks 2008; see also Pernicka *et al.* 2011: 652), but is seen most clearly at Hissar in *Period II*, where Thornton *et al.* (2009) have identified arsenic-rich "speiss slags" attesting to the production of Fe-As speiss. This material could have been used for the controlled production of arsenical copper. The possible intentional production of arsenical copper finds parallels in the analysed artefacts from Susa, where a distinct rise in the proportion (and As content) of arsenical copper in the assemblage is seen in *Periods II/IIIA* (Malfoy and Menu 1987: table A).

The early *Bronze Age* cemeteries of Luristan, Mir Khair, and Kalleh Nisar date from the *Jemdet Nasr* to *Early Dynastic I* periods and have revealed a small but not insignificant number of copper-base artefacts. All of the five analysed artefacts from Kalleh Nisar Area AI have proved to be of tin-bronze with 3.5–14.8% Sn

(Fleming *et al.* 2005: 36). If they date to the original construction and use of the tombs, these are among the earliest tin-bronzes in south-west Asia, and it is interesting to consider their relationship to the recently investigated tin-copper deposits of nearby Deh Hosein (Nezafati *et al.* 2006, 2009a). Having previously appeared to be a region without consistent tin-bronze use until the late third or early second millennium BC (Pigott 1999a), the central Zagros may in fact have played a role in the origins of tin-bronze production. Pigott (2009: 371) has noted, however, that these tombs show evidence of reuse as late as the second millennium BC, meaning that the tin-bronzes cannot be attributed with certainty to the late fourth or early third millennium BC.

Mining

Unfortunately, there is almost no direct evidence regarding the mining of copper, silver, lead, gold, or tin in prehistoric Iran, which represents a major lacuna in our understanding of the indigenous development of metallurgy. As discussed by Momenzadeh (2004), Stöllner (2004, 2005, 2011), Pernicka (2004), Berthoud (1975), Nezafati *et al.* (2008, 2009b), and others a large number of ore deposits show evidence of "ancient" workings, but no mines have yet been clearly dated to the fifth or fourth millennia BC. Although this lack of evidence is almost certainly the result of limited field research at mining sites, even some of the best known and largest copper deposits of Iran, such as those of Anarak/Talmessi, lack clear evidence for prehistoric exploitation, leading to the suggestion that they may not in fact have been exploited in antiquity (Pernicka 2004). Stollner (2005: 205) emphasises that the "sporadic and small-dimensioned exploitation" of copper deposits like Veshnaveh and other prehistoric sites makes their discovery difficult, as has the widespread destruction of ancient mining evidence by large-scale modern mining operations.

At present, the earliest direct evidence comes from the famous site of Veshnaveh, south of Qom on the Iranian plateau, where mining activities have been radiocarbon dated predominantly to the late third and early second millennium BC, although an early third-millennium BC radiocarbon date was also obtained (Stöllner 2005: fig. 14; Stöllner *et al.* 2011). Similarly, the workings at the Cu-Sn-Au deposits of Deh Hosein, consisting of more than 75 large ellipsoidal depressions (up to 70 × 50 m in area and 15 m deep), have thus far been dated no earlier than the second quarter of the second millennium BC (Nezafati *et al.* 2009a).

In some instances, however, indirect evidence from analyses of copper ores and slags on archaeological sites and from Pb-isotope analyses of archaeological and geological specimens has been able to suggest the exploitation of specific mines or mining regions in the fourth millennium BC. Analyses of slags from Tepe Hissar, for example, have suggested that steatite-hosted arsenic-bearing ores were the source of some of the smelted ores, suggesting that the nearby deposits at Taknar (or possibly Kuh-e Zar) were exploited in the fourth millennium BC (Thornton *et al.* 2009). Such a pattern supports the general observation made by Stöllner (2005: 192) that prehistoric Iranian metal extraction sites relied predominantly on local mineral resources, counteracting earlier models in which Talmessi/ Meskani were seen to supply metal and ores to prehistoric sites across Iran (Heskel and Lamberg-Karlovsky 1980; cf. Pigott 1999b: 112–13).

The lead isotope evidence for the exploitation of specific Iranian copper sources is more problematic, largely due to the limited (if increasing) lead isotope database of ores, processing debris, raw metal, and artefacts from prehistoric Iran. In general, the existing lead isotope studies have highlighted the complexity of copper ore exploitation patterns in fourth-millennium BC Iran, suggesting the use of multiple ore sources at individual smelting sites such as Arisman and Tappeh Sialk. Potential source areas for the Arisman raw material were difficult to identify isotopically, although the site of Baqoroq (aka Bagh Ghorogh; Pernicka 2004: fig. 8) and other sources near Nakhlak on the Central Plateau exhibit the most isotopic matches with material from the site, and it has been stated that "if one assumes there was only one major ore source that supplied the smelters of Arismān, then Anārak is clearly the most likely candidate" (Pernicka *et al.* 2011: 675, fig. 45). The Arisman lead isotope analyses suggest that local ores in the Karkas Mountains thus far analysed provided only a small proportion of the copper ores used at the site (Pernicka *et al.* 2011). A similar situation is recorded at Tappeh Sialk, where isotopic evidence and information on the gangue associated with the smelted ores allows the nearby mines of Veshnaveh to be ruled out as a source (Schreiner *et al.* 2003: 22), although there are isotopic matches between Tappeh Sialk slags and other local ores from the Karkas Mountains (Pernicka 2004: fig. 6).

With regard to tin sources, lead isotope analyses of ores from Deh Hosein indicate some matches with possible early tin-bronze artefacts from Luristan. This raises the possibility that Deh Hosein may have supplied some of the tin (or tin-bronze) used in the region in the late fourth/early third millennium BC (Nezafati *et al.* 2008: 84). The results of isotopic analyses seem clearer in regard to the exploitation of lead and silver. Very good (if not conclusive) indirect evidence for fourth-millennium BC mining of lead from Nakhlak on the Central Plateau is provided by the aforementioned lead isotope analyses of litharge cakes from Arisman and Sialk (Pernicka *et al.* 2011: fig. 41; Pernicka 2004: fig. 8).

Fourth-millennium BC Iranian metallurgy in its wider technological context

It is interesting to consider the evidence for early metallurgy in Iran in comparison to contemporary source areas for copper, lead, and silver to the north and west (Transcaucasia and Anatolia) and east (western Pakistan and Central Asia). Perspectives on the technological comparisons that can be drawn between these regions vary greatly: while some scholars highlight regional technological differences (e.g. Yener 2000), others recognise, for example, potentially significant long-term similarities in the development of metallurgy across highland Anatolia and parts of Iran (Chernykh 1992; Chernykh *et al.* 2002; Avilova 2008; see also Pigott 1999b).

Both perspectives are important. Yener's (2000) discussion is concerned primarily with the problems of the core/periphery dichotomy often used to characterise highland-lowland interactions. Such a theoretical stance is particularly problematic when applied to technologies like metallurgy that were greatly advanced in the highland source regions relative to contemporary lowland sites, irrespective of variations in political complexity (see also Kohl 1987). This point is extremely well developed in an Iranian context by Thornton (2009). Detailed archaeometallurgical reconstructions of metal extraction and working technologies have allowed for various idiosyncrasies in the development of Iranian metallurgy to be highlighted and characterised (e.g. Thornton 2010, 2009; Thornton and Lamberg-Karlovsky 2004; Frame 2010). Such studies display a developed theoretical perspective usually founded in the idea of "technological style" (Lechtman 1977; see also Killick 2004), i.e. the recognition that every stage of a technological process incorporates conscious and sub-conscious values, ideas, and choices that are socially constructed, and that the detailed study of the products and residues of technological systems can provide insights into the individuals and societies that produced them. Studies such as those mentioned above examine Iranian metallurgical traditions in their own terms, and continue a tradition of research aimed at characterising Iran's unique metallurgical development that was first seriously attempted by Heskel (1982; Heskel and Lamberg-Karlovsky 1980). There is no doubt that such approaches take us closer to the individual craftspeople who are the ultimate subject of archaeological research, and highlight the embeddedness (technological, economic, political, and social) of metallurgical production.

Nevertheless, Iran and neighbouring regions of Asia show many noteworthy examples of synchronous technological developments: a common origin and expansion of a crucible-based copper smelting technology from at least the early fifth millennium BC; diversification of the metal types that were exploited during the fourth millennium BC, encompassing the widespread exploitation of copper, lead, silver, and gold; the adoption of larger reaction vessels (furnaces) in the fourth millennium BC; and the establishment of arsenical copper industries by the mid- to late fourth millennium BC.

The comparisons are clearest with Anatolia, where crucible metallurgy becomes commonplace in the fifth and fourth millennia BC, as best attested at the numerous sites of the Altınova region including Tepecik, Tülintepe, Norşuntepe, Korucutepe, and Değirmentepe (Yalçın 2000: 23). The possible adoption of bowl furnaces for smelting copper is evidenced at Haçınebi in the fourth millennium BC (e.g. Özbal *et al.* 1999, although crucible remains are also reported from the site and may have been used within the bowl furnaces) and there is evidence for large-scale copper smelting using larger reaction vessels (with diameters up to 20 cm, as indicated by the size of slag remains) in the mid- to late fourth millennium at Murgul in north-east Turkey (Wagner and Öztunali 2000: 47).

Anatolia also parallels Iran in the fourth-millennium BC expansion of the exploitation of lead and the production of silver by cupellation. Silver artefacts become common in the fourth millennium BC in Anatolia, seen for example in large numbers in the graves of Koructepe in Altınova (Yakar 2002: 16–17; Yalçın 2000), and in the late fourth millennium BC silver artefacts and silver-copper alloys from Arslantepe (Hauptmann *et al.* 2002; Yakar 2002: 19–20). Pb-silver smelting slags and litharge are reported from the early fourth millennium BC at Fatmalı Kalecik in south-east Turkey and litharge and Pb-slags are said to occur at Arslantepe in the late fourth millennium BC (Hess *et al.* 1998: 57). Such finds are contemporary with the litharge recorded from the *Late Uruk* colony at Habuba Kabira (Kohlmeyer 1994; Pernicka *et al.* 1998). Gold is rarer than silver or lead, but nevertheless recorded at sites including late fourth-millennium BC Arslantepe (Yakar 2002: 20; Yalçın 2000: 23, 26). Finally, arsenical copper industries are established in Anatolia by the later fourth millennium BC at many (but not all) sites (e.g. Hauptmann *et al.* 2002; Yalçın 2000: 26; Chernykh *et al.* 2002; Chernykh 1992: fig. 49).

Similarities can also be seen between Iranian metallurgical traditions and those further to the east. This is visible, for example, in the dramatic expansion of arsenical copper use in Baluchistan during the fourth millennium BC and the concurrent appearance of lead and gold (Mille in Weeks 2008: 336). In fourth-millennium BC Baluchistan, lead was used alone and alloyed with copper for the process of creating lost-wax castings as seen in the "leopards weight" from Shahi-Tump (Mille *et al.* 2004, 2005). The first use of gold in the early Chalcolithic period at Mehrgarh is paralleled by the early occurrences at Susa, Tappeh Sialk, Tepe Hissar, and Tal-e Malyan noted above. In Central Asia, analyses by Terekhova

(1981: 317) indicated the use of copper, lead, gold, and silver, alongside copper-lead alloys and a dramatic expansion in the use of arsenical copper in the late fourth/early third millennium BC (*Namazga III* period). More recent studies of material from the site of Ilgynly-Depe in the Kopet Dagh piedmont push the use of lead, silver, and gold as early as the mid-fourth millennium BC (*Namazga II* period; Bonora and Vidale, this volume). The discovery of litharge from silver cupellation in surface deposits at Ilgynly-Depe (Salvatori *et al.* 2009) parallels the litharge from the near-contemporary sites of Arisman, Habuba Kabira, Fatmalı-Kalecik, and Arslantepe mentioned above.

Metallurgical "provinces" and technology transfer

One of the most explicit discussions of linkages within and between prehistoric metallurgical systems has been provided by E. N. Chernykh (1992), who used data on artefact typology, fabrication techniques, and composition to define a series of metallurgical/ metalworking "foci", "zones", and "provinces" (in increasing geographical scale) across Eurasia. More recent publications (e.g. Chernykh *et al.* 2002; Avilova 2008) have expanded the discussion of material from the Near East and suggested that parts of Iran and what might be termed greater Mesopotamia were incorporated into the so-called "Circumpontic Metallurgical Province" by the fourth millennium BC. In addition, Pigott (1999b: 107) has made a preliminary attempt, based on Chernykh's models, to define a separate metallurgical province centred on Iran in the *Chalcolithic* period.

Technological transfers across social and cultural boundaries are a fundamental component of such models, as the reconstructed metallurgical provinces are larger than even the largest prehistoric communities or archaeological "cultures". Chernykh noted that the provinces depended upon both horizontal technology transfer through intercultural contacts and vertical technology transfer through the inheritance of traditional techniques (Chernykh 1992: 9–10). His explanations for the formation of metallurgical provinces, however, generally relied upon migrations and cultural replacement (Chernykh 1992: 299).

While believing strongly in the existence of his reconstructed foci, centres, and provinces, Chernykh (1992: 296) recognised the difficulty of explaining their formation, and in this matter he is not alone. A review of the publications in the recent issues of the *Journal of World Prehistory* (2009, vol. 22 issues 1 and 2) devoted to early metallurgy provides a series of relevant examples of similar problems to those faced by Chernykh. Dorothy Hosler echoes Chernykh's comments by stating that, "documenting 'technology transfer' or the introduction of technology by one non-literate ancient people to another, has to be one of the most complex issues an archaeologist can face" (Hosler 2009: 209–10).

The difficulty in explaining such processes derives at least in part from the nature of technological knowledge and its transmission, which place restrictions on explanatory models. In the first instance, technological knowledge is both complex and probably limited to certain members or components of a society, a general pattern that is supported by ethnographic evidence. As Ottaway (2001: 95) writes:

"The skill of smelting had to be learnt painstakingly and transmission of accurate knowledge was probably carefully guarded...Indeed, the full knowledge was probably kept by the main smelter, who would surround the technique with magic and taboos, thus deepening the feeling of mystification which surrounded the smelt, excluding outsiders and keeping them in ignorance of the skills and techniques."

Secondly, as discussed by Pfaffenberger (1992: 507–09) and Schiffer (2008: 107–08), technologies generally do not consist of discrete ideas that can be expressed or learned verbally. Rather, they are skill sets representing embodied experiences acquired through long observation and practice. Schiffer (2008: 108) notes that "technoscience is not passed from artisan to artisan as a discrete package of ideas; rather, it merely inheres in technological practice and is replicated along with the technology."

Thirdly, technologies were understood through culturally specific (emic) classificatory systems involving myth and ritual, and depended for their adoption and reproduction on a wider set of technological, cultural, and economic conditions that we might call, following Pfaffenberger (1992), a "socio-technical system". The origins and development of metallurgy thus depended upon the "complex heterogeneous linkage of knowledge, ritual, artifacts, techniques, and activity" (Pfaffenberger 1992: 508) within specific cultural contexts, and metallurgical activities thus produced not only goods, but also power and meaning (Pfaffenberger 1992: 502).

Mechanisms for cross-cultural technology transfer

These considerations highlight the cultural specificity of complex technological knowledge systems such as extractive metallurgy. Significantly, they suggest that the transfer of technological knowledge is unlikely to have involved only the verbal transmission of information, or the visual examination of new artefact and alloy types. As noted by Moorey (2001: 2):

"Manufactured goods had travelled widely in the Near East and Egypt since time immemorial, whether as gifts, booty, or traded items; but to what extent had they ever

made craftsmen conversant with new techniques of manufacture and production? This way fresh designs, novel decoration and previously unknown raw materials might well have been transmitted, but not the means of manufacture and the usually well-guarded secrets of craftsmanship."

Rather, for technological transfer to have been successful, the craftspeople who produced these new kinds of metals, alloys, and artefacts must have met and interacted more closely. Consequently, there appear to be more mechanisms that facilitate horizontal, vertical, and oblique technology transfer *within* groups than *between* groups, an observation supported by ethnographic studies of the teaching and learning of technical knowledge. Some of these mechanisms include: transmission within families; learning through participation in activities where labour is recruited from across the community; learning through structured apprenticeships within larger kinship affiliations; and transmission through changes of residence with marriage (e.g. David and Kramer 2001). It is clear that such mechanisms for technological transmission were commonplace in the communities and cultures of fourth millennium BC south-western Asia.

In contrast, the evidence for cross-cultural technology transfer in the fourth millennium BC is much less robust. As discussed in detail below, opportunities for technology transfer *between* societies include exogamy across cultural/linguistic boundaries and the movement of craftspeople voluntarily or by force (e.g. itinerant or nomadic craftspeople, prisoners of war, or skilled artisans exchanged between royal houses).

The change of residence associated with exogamous marriage across linguistic boundaries provides opportunities for detailed and prolonged technological learning and cross-cultural transmission. Other factors, such as the concentration of specific craft skills within endogamous caste-like social groups that cross community and cultural boundaries, may also play a role. The relationship between technological transmission, marriage traditions, and caste-like social structures is clearly sketched in an ethnographic example provided by David and Kramer (2001: 215), who note:

"Other factors reinforce homogeneity in material culture, most notably the smith-potter caste among the southwestern montagnards. Caste members are disproportionately responsible for the production of material culture, including metal goods and ceramics... Because they are so few in number...they intermarry more frequently across community and language lines than do farmers, and, as divorce is quite common, a potter is likely to practice at several communities during her lifetime. Male smiths change residence less often but are regarded as important resources who are likely to be encouraged, in the past sometimes forcibly, to relocate to communities lacking their services."

Henry Wright (2001: 138–39) has suggested that similar processes may have developed in the *Uruk* world with increasing craft specialisation. The problem of course, as with all ethnographic observations, is determining the archaeological correlates of such social configurations in order to demonstrate that similar traditions existed in the past.

Historical and ethnographic studies provide some examples of mobile craftspeople, and itinerant smiths have played a role in some of the most famous archaeological reconstructions of prehistoric technology transfer (e.g. Childe 1930). Historical and ethnographic examples, however, suggest that there are limits to the actual mobility and the geographical scale of movements by such individuals or groups (Rowlands 1971: 214) and some scholars argue that there were no itinerant craftspeople in the ancient Near East before the first millennium BC (Zaccagnini 1983: 258). Moorey (2001: 11), although noting that the movement of craftsmen and specialists is mentioned as early as the Mari archives in the nineteenth century BC, similarly recognises that truly nomadic "travelling tinkers" are much harder to identify from historical or archaeological evidence. In any instance, it is in no way clear that the evidence from the second millennium BC can be projected backwards to explain technology transfer in the fourth millennium BC. Moreover, it is unlikely that travelling craftspeople could or would have provided the teaching/apprenticeship contexts fundamental to technological learning.

It has also been argued that nomadic or seasonally transhumant groups played a role in cultural transmission of technologies. Numerous scholars have discussed the possible existence of mobile pastoralist communities in Iran in the fifth and fourth millennia BC (e.g. Alizadeh 2006, 2008, 2010; Sumner 1988; Abdi 2003), although disagreements exist over the nature, scale, and significance of mobility at this time (see Potts 2008 for a review). Abdi (2003: 435–36) has argued that *Chalcolithic* nomadic groups distributed the products of their own ceramic pyrotechnology in the western Zagros, as well as playing a more general role in the diffusion of craft products, resources, and stylistic ideas between highland and lowland regions. Tonoike (2009) has similarly implicated nomadic pastoralists in the spread of Dalma pottery in the north-western and central Zagros, as early as the sixth millennium BC. For later periods, Stöllner (2005: 203) has suggested that the Veshnaveh copper mines were exploited by nomadic groups in the second millennium BC, based on the lack of nearby contemporary settlements. The few possible prehistoric nomadic sites in Iran that have been excavated, however, have not produced evidence for pyrotechnology (Abdi 2003; Alizadeh 2009), and the available evidence for metallurgical production in fourth-millennium BC Iran is concentrated within sedentary settlements, although

the existing archaeological record is undoubtedly biased towards larger sedentary sites. Moreover, the mechanisms through which detailed technological knowledge could/might pass between members of nomadic and sedentary communities are unclear. Co-residence for a significant portion of the year – perhaps several months – would seem to be required for the appropriate learning contexts to have existed. Tonoike's (2009: 152–60, 170) discussion of mobility and Dalma ceramic technology focused on the close kinship relations between ethnographically known mobile and settled groups in the Zagros, emphasising the significance of forms of village-based seasonal migration that might well have entailed substantial periods of co-habitation. Nevertheless, the possible role of mobile groups in technology transfer in fourth-millennium BC Iran remains uncertain.

Finally, the "forced" relocation of craftspeople can be considered. The exchange of skilled craftsmen between royal houses is abundantly documented in the eastern Mediterranean and the Near East from the later second millennium BC (Moorey 2001). Although this is a clear and viable means by which technological knowledge was transferred between cultures, such practices seem to have depended on a world so different from the fourth millennium BC that they cannot reasonably be used to explain prehistoric technology transfer at that time. In contrast, the capture of skilled craftsmen as prisoners of war is known historically from the mid-third millennium BC. An example of direct relevance to the transfer of metallurgical knowledge comes from the Lugalbanda Epic (Black *et al.* 1998: lines 410–12), where Inanna offers advice to Lugalbanda to aid Enmerkar in his battle against the ruler of Aratta, saying: "If he carries off from the city its worked metal and smiths, if he carries off its worked stones and its stonemasons, if he renews the city and settles it, all the moulds of Aratta will be his". *Uruk*-period iconography and texts support the notion of violence and conflict as a component of social action in the fourth millennium BC, and the existence in Mesopotamia of captive workers who probably represent prisoners of war (e.g. Pittman, this volume: figs. 16.5/e–h, 16.13/b; Algaze 2001: 36). The extent to which such conflicts were local or long-distance, however, is unclear (Rothman 2001a: 354), and the possibility of craftspeople being captured and relocated from highland metallurgical source areas is unknown. Nevertheless, if military activities and conquests did indeed take place, the movement of prisoners of war provides a possible context for cross-cultural technology transfer through the forcible relocation of craftspeople.

To summarise, although "cultures" are far from impermeable barriers to technological transfer (e.g. Kohl 2008; David and Kramer 2001), the nature of technological learning appears to offer many more opportunities for technological transmission within communities and societies than between them (e.g. Tehrani and Collard 2009: 295). One implication of this view is that the spread of technologies depended, to a significant extent, on the geographical dispersal of their practitioners through processes such as migration, nomadism, or exogamy. The fact that theories of metallurgical development incorporating movement of groups or individual craftspeople have been proffered by scholars with theoretical positions as diverse as Childe (1930), Chernykh (1992), Roberts *et al.* (2009), and Amzallag (2009) is at least in part a reflection of the specific dynamics of technology transfer. Nevertheless, claims continue to be made for the independent invention of metallurgy in different parts of the Old World (e.g. Radivojević *et al.* 2010), and even scholars favouring cultural transmission as the major mode of metallurgical innovation recognise the role of independent innovations in shaping local and regional metallurgical systems. The competing/complementary roles of cultural transmission and independent innovation in the development of fourth-millennium metallurgy in Iran and wider western Asia are considered below.

Fourth-millennium BC polymetallurgies: homologous and analogous change in the *Uruk* world

The synchronous rise of polymetallism appears to be a fundamental characteristic of *Chalcolithic* western Asia. Most explanations of this phenomenon have suggested that these parallel developments depended on the transmission (i.e. diffusion) of metallurgical technology across regions and between cultures, albeit with local innovations (e.g. Wertime 1973; Roberts *et al.* 2009). In discussing cultural transmission, VanPool (2008: 192–93) has argued that the principle of parsimony can be used as a criterion to differentiate between homologous traits (those that reflect shared ancestry) and analogous traits (those that reflect the independent development of similar attributes). Parsimony has been used to support arguments for the diffusion of technology in numerous debates on early metallurgy: for example, in their recent discussion of early Eurasian metallurgy, Roberts *et al.* (2009: 1014) state that, "given the virtually synchronous appearance of copper smelting throughout Southwest Asia and Southeast Europe, a single central region of invention is far more probable than many parallel independent discoveries".

In general, the argument from parsimony for the spread of metallurgy through cultural transmission is persuasive. Moreover, there is no doubt that the "*Uruk* phenomenon", however it might be debated in its specifics, facilitated homologous technological change. By integrating regional socio-economic systems into broader spheres of cultural interaction over a vast geographical area, the mobility of individuals and groups was substantially enhanced, as was the possibility of the transfer of knowledge and ideas.

Arguments from parsimony, however, can never attain deductive certainty. Firstly, there is nothing inherent in the technology of metal extraction to suggest it could not have been invented independently at a number of times and places within the Old World. The independent development of metallurgy in the New World is an oft-cited and unimpeachable case in support of this position. Secondly, assessing the similarity of extractive metal industries is complicated by the limitations on smelting parameters imposed by physics, chemistry, mineralogy, and pyrotechnology. This means that extractive industries that *do not* share a technological ancestry might be expected to show some technical similarities, whereas some homologously related industries might be expected to show differences based on, for example, adaptations to locally available ore sources. Thirdly and most importantly, synchronicity of change does not necessarily imply homologous developments through technology transfer. This is because simultaneous but analogous change could be either coincidental or engendered in separate regions by the synchronous influence of external forces.

Thus, I would like to conclude this paper by briefly considering a complementary explanation for the widespread adoption of polymetallurgy in fourth-millennium BC south-western Asia: that there were forces acting to promote independent, analogous (i.e. "convergent") metallurgical developments. In particular, I consider the empirical nature of early metallurgy and the role of "experiments" in generating change and innovation, as well as the possibility that incorporation into increasingly broad spheres of cultural interaction in the fifth and especially the fourth millennium BC, promoted parallel technological developments in both Anatolia and Iran without the necessity of any direct technology transfer between these two metallurgical source regions. At a general level, such convergences are recognised as being an important, if complex and understudied, component of many technological systems (Eerckens and Lipo 2007: 243–44; Tehrani and Collard 2009: 296).

The first aspect I would like to consider revolves around the willingness of early metallurgists to experiment with raw materials and technological processes. In one of the most famous reviews of the early development of metallurgy in the Old World, Theodore Wertime (1973) suggested that metallurgical advances occurred through an essentially rational process of experimentation influenced by pre-existing knowledge of materials, the geological co-occurrence of metallic ores, the diffusion of ideas between regions and related technologies, and socio-political change. Although the "rationality" of early metallurgical developments has been questioned (Budd and

Taylor 1995), Wertime is not alone in recognising the propensity of early metallurgists to experiment (e.g. Ottaway 2001: 93), and in a recent paper Helwing (2009: 215) has suggested that experimentation was a characteristic of the early third-millennium BC metallurgy of Lurestan. Such "experiments" should not be confused with models of modern, Western scientific research that would indeed be anachronistic in a prehistoric context. Nevertheless, consciously and empirically manipulating raw materials is a fundamental human behaviour, acting as a pervasive motor for technological change both in response to external influences and in their absence (e.g. Schiffer 2008: 110; Stone 2008: 158). Experimentation and empiricism were in fact the reasons why technology could develop for millions of years before the rise of modern science (Basalla 1988: 27). Even elaborate technologies such as metallurgy, embedded within complex emic explanatory systems and ritual behaviours, are open to change through the empirical manipulation of materials (Killick 2001: 490). As David and Kramer (2001: 347) have noted, "it is a common misconception that ritual has the effect of fossilizing technological procedures. Ethnoarchaeologists have shown that this is not the case and that ritual and technical innovation may go hand in hand."

Arguments for the omnipresent "curiosity" and empirical nature of early metallurgists have underlain a series of models of the development of metallurgy that incorporate elements of geological determinism. Most explicitly, Charles (1980) saw the development of early metallurgy as a mirror of the slow expansion of early mining down through the zones of an idealised weathered copper deposit (cf. Killick 2001: 487–88). Similarly, Wertime (1973: 881) emphasised the importance of ore geology for the development of polymetallism. In essence, such arguments posit that early metallurgists in widely separated areas, when faced with similar raw materials, were likely to experiment empirically with the parameters of their technology in ways that led to the discovery of a similar range of metals and alloys.

The criticisms of geological determinism as a general explanatory framework for early metallurgy are many and justified, as such models simply cannot explain the distinct paths of metallurgical development seen in different regions of the Old World (Killick 2001: 488). Nevertheless, one can argue that fourth millennium BC metallurgists in Iran and Anatolia were empirically manipulating (experimenting with) a similar range of polymetallic ores using comparable pyrotechnologies. The metallurgical innovations of the fourth millennium BC, especially the expansion in the range of known metals and alloys, can be seen as a result of the application of relatively new pyrotechnologies to a wider range of raw materials; and a merging and recombination of ideas that is fundamental to most

real-world processes of innovation (Eerckens and Lipo 2005: 320). It is certainly feasible – if unproven – that such processes of innovation could have occurred independently.

Secondly, I would like to highlight the fact that communities in fifth and especially fourth millennium BC Iran and Anatolia were also being influenced by similar cultural forces and affected by the widespread adoption of new ideologies. Specifically, it is likely that parallel or convergent technological developments in these two metallurgical source regions were promoted by their incorporation into the *Uruk* world (Rothman 2001b; Algaze 2005) and, possibly, the preceding *Ubaid* "interaction sphere" (Carter and Philip 2010; Stein 2010). The nature and extent of cross-cultural interactions in the *Ubaid* period are difficult to reconstruct, and fall outside the primary period of concern for this volume. There is no doubt, however, that various material indices attest to links between groups that are otherwise politically and culturally distinct in the fifth millennium BC, which may have impacted on the concurrent development of metal technologies. The case is easier to make for the fourth millennium BC, however, when metal use became much more widespread throughout south-west Asia and especially in southern Mesopotamia (Algaze 2008: 74–77) and when copper artefacts that seem to have been produced on the Iranian Plateau at sites such as Arisman begin to appear in lowland Susiana and, by the late fourth millennium, the Hamrin region and northern Mesopotamia (Helwing 2011b).

Characterisations of the "*Uruk* phenomenon" are many and varied, and there is no consensus on major issues, including the extent to which there was a physical movement of people (i.e. southern Mesopotamian "colonists"); the active management of the process from one or more centres in the southern alluvium; the nature of relations with indigenous groups; the role of demand for imports in "resource-poor" southern Mesopotamia; the nature and volume of exchange; the extent of warfare and repression; the correlation (if any) with regional developments in social complexity, etc. (see papers in Rothman 2001b). In more general terms, however, both the *Uruk* phenomenon and the preceding "*Ubaid* expansion" can be regarded as interaction spheres defined by expanding sets of ideologies and material behaviours, albeit expansions which are best treated as entirely separate and distinct phenomena (cf. Carter and Philip 2010: 11). Following Gosden (2004: 45), the *Uruk* phenomenon represented the "differentiation of an 'elite' culture throughout the region which gave a new shape to desire, ambition and aspiration". Similar concepts can be found in the work of other scholars examining cultural connections in the *Uruk* world: Sherratt and Sherratt (2001: 25) argue that the material signatures of the *Uruk* phenomenon reflect "an expanding set of consumption patterns and regimes of value", whereas Kohl (2008) regards developments in south-west Asia in the fourth–second millennia BC as a reflection of the adoption of "shared social fields". Significantly, these shared social fields are seen by Kohl (2008: 504) as promoting analogous change and cultural convergence. A more recent publication (Jennings 2011) regards the *Uruk* period as representing a prehistoric example of globalisation, with consequent implications for the movements of people and ideas.

The *Uruk* phenomenon may thus have provided a cultural context that positively promoted (independent) technological innovations in metallurgy. As outlined above, technological inventions depend for their widespread adoption on the development (or existence) of a wider socio-technical system in which they can be understood and employed as markers and makers of power and meaning. Metals, especially precious metals such as silver and gold, found ready acceptance in the socio-technical systems of *Uruk* Mesopotamia and its neighbours, as markers of status and as a basic material component of the exchange systems linking fourth-millennium BC south-west Asia. In attempting to situate discussions of technological change in this broader cultural context, Sherratt and Sherratt (2001: 27) have suggested that certain contexts favoured a "technological dialectic" between the urban heartlands of Mesopotamia and neighbouring areas with specific technological expertise, such as extractive metallurgy. Likewise, Schiffer's (2008: 109–10) discussion of stimulated variation suggests that the metallurgical developments in fourth-millennium BC south-western Asia were not random, but probably stimulated by the immediate selective contexts of metallurgy within newly restructured and hierarchically differentiated societies. If incorporation into the *Uruk* world provided the social context for the innovations of fourth-millennium BC metallurgy, then these innovations could have developed independently in the various metallurgical source regions of the *Uruk* world.

The development of metallurgy in fourth-millennium BC Iran was promoted and shaped by its cultural and technological contexts. The possibility of direct technological transfers between communities and across cultural boundaries was dramatically enhanced by the formation and expansion of the *Uruk* interaction sphere, which promoted culture contact as well as individual and group mobility. Such processes may have provided appropriate contexts in which crafts could be effectively shared and learned across traditional geographical boundaries and social groups. In addition, however, Iranian metallurgy was almost certainly affected by the less tangible aspects of the *Uruk* phenomenon, particularly new ideologies of consumption and social relationships and the contexts they provided for the development of novel technologies and materials that served in social differentiation and integration. In other words,

the expansion of the *Uruk* interaction sphere favoured technological change not only through increased inter-cultural transmission, but also represented the widespread adoption of a new socio-technical system that would have promoted parallel metallurgical innovations.

I would like to end with a note of caution, however. Due to the relative volume of publications and fieldwork and the lingering power exerted by the early complex societies of Mesopotamia on the archaeological imagination, it is very easy to over-emphasise the significance of the *Uruk* phenomenon for the development of Iranian metallurgy. That inter-cultural connections across Greater Mesopotamia were *not* the sole factor in the spread or development of fourth millennium BC metal technologies in Iran is indicated by the concurrent appearance of polymetallurgies in areas such as Baluchistan and Central Asia that were situated on the periphery or entirely outside the normally accepted boundaries of the *Uruk* world. These examples suggest that our explanations must not be limited to the operation of one putative interaction sphere. Rather, the cultural interactions of people and groups within fourth-millennium BC Iran were complex and multi-directional and defy simple modelling. Nevertheless, we are left with a clear example of the necessary synergies of archaeological research in addressing these difficult issues: elucidating the technological connections that linked Greater Iran offers the potential to improve our understanding of cross-cultural interactions, while broader archaeological studies of these interactions can help to characterise and clarify the social contexts in which such technological transfers took place.

Bibliography

Abdi, K. 2003. "The early development of pastoralism in the central Zagros Mountains", *Journal of World Prehistory* 17 (4): 395–448.

Algaze, G. 2001. "The prehistory of imperialism: the case of Uruk period Mesopotamia", in Rothman, M. S. (ed.), *Uruk Mesopotamia & its neighbors: cross-cultural interactions in the era of state formation*, School of American Research Press, Sante Fe: 27–84.

Algaze, G. 2005. *The Uruk world system: the dynamics of expansion of early Mesopotamian Civilization*, University of Chicago Press, Chicago.

Algaze, G. 2008. *Ancient Mesopotamia at the Dawn of Civilization: The Evolution of an Urban Landscape*, University of Chicago Press, Chicago.

Alizadeh, A. 2006. *The Origins of State Organizations in Prehistoric Highland Fars, Southern Iran*, Oriental Institute Publications 128, Chicago.

Alizadeh, A. 2008. *Chogha Mish II. The Development of a Prehistoric Regional Center in Lowland Susiana, Southwest Iran: Final Report on the Last Six Seasons of Excavations 1972–1978*, Oriental Institute Publications 130, Chicago.

Alizadeh, A. 2010. "The rise of the highland Elamite state in southwestern Iran 'Enclosed' or Enclosing Nomadism?", *Current Anthropology* 51 (3): 353–83.

Amzallag, N. 2009. "From metallurgy to Bronze Age Civilizations: the Synthetic Theory", *AJA* 113 (4): 497–519.

Avilova, L. 2008. "Regional Models of metal production in western Asia in the Chalcolithic, Early and Middle Bronze Ages", *Trabajos de Prehistoria* 65: 73–91.

Basalla, G. 1988. *The Evolution of Technology*, Cambridge University Press, Cambridge.

Begemann, F. and Schmitt-Strecker, S. 2009. "Über das frühe Kupfer Mesopotamiens", *IA* 43: 1–45.

Begemann, F., Haerinck, E., Overlaet, B., Schmitt-Strecker, S. and Tallon, F. 2008. "An Archaeo-Metallurgical Study of the Early and Middle Bronze Age in Luristan, Iran", *IA* 43: 1–66.

Benoit, A. 2004. "Susa", in Stöllner *et al.* 2004: 178–93.

Berthoud, T. 1975. Étude *sur la Métallurgie Iranienne aux IVè–IIIè Millénaires. Prospection en Iran en 1975. Rapport,* Commissariat à l'Énergie Atomique, Laboratoire de Recherche des Musées de France.

Berthoud, T. and Francaix, J. 1980. *Contribution* à l'Étude *de la Métallurgie de Suse aux IVème et IIIème Millénaires,* Centre d'Études Nucléaires de Fontenay-aux-Roses, Commissariat a l'Énergie Atomique Rapport CEA-R-5033.

Black, J. A., Cunningham, G., Fluckiger-Hawker, E., Robson, E. and Zólyomi, G. 1998–. *The Electronic Text Corpus of Sumerian Literature* (http://www-etcsl.orient.ox.ac.uk/), Oxford, accessed May 2010.

Budd, P. and Taylor, T. 1995. "The faerie smith meets the bronze industry: magic versus science in the interpretation of prehistoric metal-making", *World Archaeology* 27: 133–43.

Caldwell, J. 1968. *Investigations at Tal-i-Iblis*. Illinois State Museum preliminary reports no. 9, Illinois State Museum Society, Springfield.

Carter, R. and Philip, G. 2010. "Deconstructing the Ubaid", in Carter, R. and Philip, G. (eds), *The Ubaid and Beyond: Exploring the transmission of culture in the developed prehistoric societies of the Middle East*, University of Chicago Oriental Institute Publications, Chicago: 1–22.

Charles, J. A. 1980. "The coming of copper and copper-base alloys and iron: a metallurgical sequence", in Wertime, T. A. and Muhly, J. D. (eds), *The Coming of the Age of Iron*, Yale University Press, New Haven: 151–82.

Chase, D. W., Caldwell, J. R. and Feheravi, I. 1967. "The Iblis sequence and the exploration of excavation Areas A, C, and E", in Caldwell, J. R. (ed.), *Investigations at Tal-i Iblis*, Illinois State Museum, Springfield: 111–201.

Chegini, N., Helwing, B., Parzinger, H. and Vatandoust, A. 2004. "A prehistoric industrial settlement on the Iranian Plateau – research at Arisman", in Stöllner *et al.* 2004: 210–17.

Chernykh, E. N. 1992. *Ancient Metallurgy in the USSR: The Early Metal Age*, trans. Wright, S., Cambridge University Press, New York.

Chernykh, E. N., Avilova, L. I. and Orlovskaya, L. B. 2002. "Metallurgy of the Circumpontic area: from unity to disintegration", in Yalçin, Ü. (ed.), *Anatolian Metal II*, Der Anschnitt Beiheft 15, Deutsches Bergbau-Museum, Bochum: 83–100.

Childe, V. G. 1930. *The Bronze Age*, Cambridge University Press, Cambridge.

David, N. and Kramer, C. 2001. *Ethnoarchaeology in Action*, Cambridge University Press, Cambridge.

Delougaz, P. and Kantor, H. J. 1996. *Chogha Mish. Volume I, The first five seasons of excavations, 1961–1971*, ed. Alizadeh, A., Oriental Institute Publications vol. 101, Oriental Institute of the University of Chicago, Chicago.

Eerckens, J. W. and Lipo, C. P. 2005. "Cultural transmission, copying errors, and the generation of variation in material culture and the archaeological record", *Journal of Anthropological Archaeology* 24: 316–34.

Eerckens, J. W. and Lipo, C. P. 2007. "Cultural transmission theory and the archaeological record: providing context to understanding variation and temporal changes in material culture", *Journal of Archaeological Research* 15: 239–74.

Fazeli, H., Coningham, R. A. E. and Batt. C. M. 2004. "Cheshmeh-Ali revisited: towards an absolute dating of the Late Neolithic and Chalcolithic of Iran's Tehran Plain", *Iran* 42: 13–23.

Fazeli, H., Wong, E. H. and Potts, D. T. 2005. "The Qazvin Plain revisited: a reappraisal of the chronology of northwestern Central Plateau Iran, in the 6th to the 4th millennium BC", *Ancient Near Eastern Studies* 42: 4–82.

Fleming, S. J., Pigott, V. C., Swann, C. P. and Nash, S. K. 2005. "Bronze in Luristan: Preliminary Analytical evidence from copper/bronze artifacts excavated by the Belgian Mission in Iran", *IA* 40: 35–64.

Frame, L. D. 2004. *Investigations at Tal-i Iblis: Evidence for Copper Smelting During the Chalcolithic Period*, unpublished B.Sc. dissertation, Dept. of Materials Science and Engineering, Massachusetts Institute of Technology.

Frame, L. D. 2010. "Metallurgical investigations at Godin Tepe, Iran, Part I: the metal finds", *Journal of Archaeological Science* 37 (7): 1700–15.

Frame, L. D. 2012. "Reconstructing ancient technologies: Chalcolithic crucible smelting at Tal-i Iblis, Iran", in Jett, P., McCarthy, B., and Douglas, J. G. (eds), *Scientific Research on Ancient Asian Metallurgy: Proceedings of the Fifth Forbes Symposium at the Freer Gallery of Art*, Archetype, London: 183–204.

Fukai, S., Horiuchi, K. and Matsutani, T. 1973. *Marv-Dasht III: The Excavation at Tall-i-Mushki 1965*, Archaeological Expedition Reports 14, Institute of Oriental Culture of the University of Tokyo, Tokyo University Iraq-Iran.

Gosden, C. 2004. *Archaeology and Colonialism: Cultural Contact from 5000 BC to the Present*, Cambridge University Press, Cambridge.

Hauptmann, A., Begemann, F., Schmitt-Strecker, S. and Palmieri, A. 2002. "Chemical Composition and Lead Isotopy of Metal Objects from the 'Royal' Tomb and Other Related Finds at Arslantepe, Eastern Anatolia", *Paléorient* 28 (2): 43–69.

Helwing, B. 2009. "Rethinking the tin mountains: patterns of usage and circulation of tin in greater Iran from the 4th to the 1st millennium BC", *TÜBA-AR* 12: 209–21.

Helwing, B. 2011a."The small finds from Arisman", in Vatandoust *et al.* 2011: 254–327.

Helwing, B. 2011b. "Conclusions: The Arisman copper production in a wider context", in Vatandoust *et al.* 2011: 523–31.

Heskel, D. L. 1982. "A model for the adoption of metallurgy in the ancient Middle East", *Current Anthropology* 24 (3): 362–66.

Heskel, D. and Lamberg-Karlovsky, C. C. 1980. "An alternative sequence for the development of metallurgy: Tepe Yahya, Iran", in Wertime, T. A. and Muhly, J. D.

(eds), *The Coming of the Age of Iron,* Yale University Press, New Haven: 229–66.

Heskel, D. L. and Lamberg-Karlovsky, C. C. 1986. "Metallurgical Technology", in Beale, T. (ed.), *Excavations at Tepe Yahya, Iran 1967–1975: The Early Periods,* American School of Prehistoric Research Bulletin 38, Peabody Museum of Archaeology and Ethnology, Cambridge, MA: 207–14.

Hess, K., Hauptmann, A., Wright, H. T. and Whallon, R. 1998. "Evidence of fourth millennium BC silver production at Fatmali-Kalecik, East Anatolia", in Rehren, Th., Hauptmann, A. and Muhly, J. D. (eds), *Metallurgica Antiqua: In Honour of Hans-Gert Bachmann and Robert Maddin,* Der Anschnitt Beiheft 8, Deutsches Bergbau-Museum, Bochum: 57–68.

Hole, F. 1977. *Studies in the Archaeological History of the Deh Luran Plain: The Excavation at Chagha Sefid,* Memoirs of the Museum of Anthropology, University of Michigan 9, Museum of Anthropology, University of Michigan, Ann Arbor.

Hosler, D. 2009. "West Mexican Metallurgy: Revisited and Revised", *Journal of World Prehistory* 22 (3): 185–212.

Howard, S. M. 1989. "The stratigraphic sequence of the main mound at Tappeh Hesār, 1976", in Dyson, R. H. and Howard, S. M. (eds), *Tappeh Hesār: Reports of the Restudy Project, 1976,* Monografie di Mesopotamia 2, Casa editrice Le Lettere, Florence: 55–68.

Jennings, J. 2011. *Globalizations and the Ancient World,* Cambridge University Press, Cambridge.

Killick, D. 2001. "Science, speculation and the origins of extractive metallurgy", in Brothwell, D. and Pollard, A. M. (eds), *Handbook of Archaeological Sciences,* Wiley, Chichester: 483–92.

Killick, D. 2004. "Social Constructionist Approaches to the Study of Technology", *World Archaeology* 36 (4): 571–78.

Kohl, P. L. 1987. The ancient economy, transferable technologies and the Bronze Age world-system: a view from the northeastern frontier of the ancient Near East", in Rowlands, M. J., Larsen, M. and Kristiansen, K. (eds), *Centre and Periphery in the Ancient World,* Cambridge University Press, Cambridge: 13–24.

Kohl, P. L. 2008. "Shared social fields: evolutionary convergence in prehistory and contemporary practice", *American Anthropologist* 100 (4): 495–506.

Kohlmeyer, K. 1994. "Zur fruhen Geschichte von Blei und Silber", in Wartke, R. (ed.), *Handwerk und Technologie im Alten Orient,* Philip von Zabern, Mainz: 41–48.

Lechtman, H. 1977. "Style in Technology: Some Early Thoughts", in Lechtman, H. and Merrill, R. (eds), *Material Culture: Styles, Organization, and Dynamics of Technology,* West Publishing, St Paul: 3–20.

Levine, L. D. 1975. "The excavations at Seh Gabi", in Bagherzadeh, F. (ed.), *3rd Symposium on Archaeological Research in Iran,* Iranian Center for Archaeological Research, Tehran.

Majidzadeh, Y. 1979. "An early prehistoric coppersmith workshop at Tepe Ghabristan", in *Akten Des VII Internationalen Kongresses Fur Iranische Kunst Und Archaologie,* Archaologische Mitteilungen aus Iran, suppl. 6, Dietrich Reimer Verlag, Berlin: 82–92.

Malfoy, J-M. and Menu, M. 1987. "La Métallurgie du cuivre à Suse aux IVe et IIIe millénaires: Analyses en laboratoire", in Tallon, F. (ed.), *Métallurgie Susienne I: De la fondation de Suse au XVIIIe avant J.-C.,* Notes et Documents des Musées de France 15, Louvre Museum Dept. of Oriental Antiquities, Paris.

Matthews, R. and Fazeli, H. 2004. "Copper and complexity: Iran and Mesopotamia in the fourth millennium B.C.", *Iran* 42: 61–75.

Mille, B., Besenval, R. and Bourgarit, D. 2004. "Early 'lost-wax casting' in Baluchistan (Pakistan): the 'Leopards Weight' from Shahi-Tump", in Stöllner *et al.* 2004: 274–81.

Mille, B., Bourgarit, D. and Besenval, R. 2005. "Metallurgical studies of the 'Leopards Weight' from Shahi-Tump (Pakistan)", in Jarrige, C. and Lefèvre, V. (eds), *South Asian Archaeology 2001,* Éditions Recherche sur les Civilisations, Paris: 237–44.

Momenzadeh, M. 2004. "Metallic mineral resources of Iran, mined in ancient times. A brief review", in Stöllner *et al.* 2004: 8–21.

Moorey, P. R. S. 2001. "The mobility of artisans and opportunities for technology transfer between western Asia and Egypt in the Late Bronze Age", in Shortland, A. J. (ed.), *The Social Context of Technological Change: Egypt and the Near East, 1650–1550 BC,* Oxbow Books, Oxford: 1–14.

Nezafati, N., Momenzadeh, M. and Pernicka, E. 2005. "Darhand copper occurrence: an example of Michigan-type native copper deposits in central Iran", in Mao, J. and Bierlein, F. P. (eds), *Mineral Deposit Research: Meeting the Global Challenge,* Springer, Berlin: 165–166.

Nezafati, N., Pernicka, E. and Momenzadeh, M. 2006. Ancient tin: old question and a new answer", *Antiquity* 80 (308): Project Gallery.

Nezafati, N., Pernicka, E. and Momenzadeh, M. 2008. "Iranian ore deposits and their role in the development of the ancient cultures", in Yalçin, Ü. (ed.), *Anatolian Metal IV,* Der Anschnitt Beiheft 21, Deutsches Bergbau-Museum, Bochum: 77–90.

Nezafati, N., Pernicka, E. and Momenzadeh, M. 2009a. "Introduction of the Deh Hosein ancient tin-copper mine, western Iran: evidence from geology, archaeology, geochemistry and lead isotope data", *TÜBA-AR* 12: 223–36.

Nezafati, N., Pernicka, E. and Momenzadeh, M. 2009b. "Iranian ore deposits and their role in the development of the ancient cultures", in Yalçin, U. (ed.), *Anatolian Metal IV,* Deutsches Bergbau-Museum, Bochum: 77–90.

Nicholas, I. M. 1990. *The Proto-Elamite Settlement at TUV,* Malyan excavation reports vol. 1, University Museum monograph 69, University Museum of Archaeology and Anthropology, Pennsylvania.

Ottaway, B. S. 2001."Innovation, production and specialization in early prehistoric copper metallurgy", *European Journal of Archaeology* 4: 87–112.

Özbal, H., Adriaens, A. M. and Earl, B. 1999. "Hacinebi metal production and exchange", *Paléorient* 25 (1): 57–65.

Pernicka, E. 2004. "Copper and silver in Arisman and Tappeh Sialk and the early metallurgy in Iran", in Stöllner *et al.* 2004: 232–39.

Pernicka, E., Rehren, Th. and Schmitt-Strecker, S. 1998. "Late Uruk silver production by cupellation at Habuba Kabira, Syria", in Rehren, Th., Hauptmann, A. and Muhly, J. D. (eds), *Metallurgica Antiqua: In Honour of Hans-Gert Bachmann and Robert Maddin,* Der Anschnitt Beiheft 8, Deutsches Bergbau-Museum, Bochum: 123–34.

Lloyd Weeks

Pernicka, E., Momenzadeh, M., Vatandoust, A., Adam, K., Böhme, M., Hezarkhani, Z., Nezafati, N., Schreiner, M. and Winterholler, B. 2011. "Archaeometallurgical research on the western Central Iranian Plateau", in Vatandoust *et al.* 2011: 633–87.

Pfaffenberger, B. 1992. "Social anthropology of technology", *Annual Review of Anthropology* 21: 491–516.

Pigott, V. C. 1989. "Archaeo-metallurgical investigations at Bronze Age Tappeh Hesār, 1976", in Dyson, R. H. and Howard, S. M. (eds), *Tappeh Hesār: Reports of the Restudy Project, 1976*, Monografie di Mesopotamia 2, Casa editrice Le Lettere, Florence: 25–34.

Pigott, V. C. 1999a. "The development of metal production on the Iranian Plateau: an archaeometallurgical perspective", in Pigott, V. C. (ed.), *The Archaeometallurgy of the Asian Old World*, University Museum monograph 89, University Museum symposium series vol. 7, MASCA research papers in science and archaeology vol. 16, University Museum, University of Pennsylvania, Philadelphia: 73–106.

Pigott, V. C. 1999b. "A heartland of metallurgy: Neolithic/Chalcolithic metallurgical origins on the Iranian Plateau", in Hauptmann, A., Pernicka, E., Rehren, T. and Yalçin, Ü. (eds), *The Beginnings of Metallurgy*, Der Anschnitt Beiheft 9, Deutsches Bergbau-Museum, Bochum: 107–20.

Pigott, V. C. 2009. "'Luristan Bronzes' and the development of metallurgy in the west-central Zagros, Iran", in Kienlin, T. L. and Roberts, B. W. (eds), *Metals and Societies: Studies in Honour of Barbara S. Ottaway*, Verlag Dr. Rudolf Habelt, Bonn: 369–82.

Pigott, V. C. and Lechtman, H. 2003. "Chalcolithic copper-based metallurgy on the Iranian Plateau: a new look at old evidence from Tal-i Iblis", in Potts, T., Roaf, M. and Stein, D. (eds), *Culture Through Objects: Ancient Near Eastern Studies in Honour of P.R.S. Moorey*, Griffith Institute, Oxford: 291–312.

Pigott, V. C., Howard, S. M. and Epstein, S. M. 1982. "Pyrotechnology and culture change at Bronze Age Tepe Hissar (Iran)", in Wertime, T. A. and Wertime, S. F. (eds), *Early Pyrotechnology: The Evolution of the First Fire-Using Industries*, Smithsonian Institution, Washington, DC: 215–36.

Pigott, V. C., Rogers, H. C. and Nash, S. K. 2003. "Archaeometallurgical investigations at Malyan: Banesh period finds from ABC and TUV", in Sumner, W. M. (ed.), *Early Urban Life in the Land of Anshan: Excavations at Tal-e Malyan in the Highlands of Iran*, University Museum Monographs no. 117, University of Pennsylvania Museum of Archaeology and Anthropology, Philadelphia: 94–102.

Potts, D. T. 2008. Review of A. Alizadeh (2006), *Bib Or* LXV (1–2): 196–206.

Roberts, B. W., Thornton, C. P. and Pigott, V. C. 2009 "The development of metallurgy in Eurasia", *Antiquity* 83: 1012–22.

Radivojević, M., Rehren, Th., Pernicka, E., Šljivar, D., Brauns, M. and Borić, D. 2010. "On the origins of extractive metallurgy: new evidence from Europe", *Journal of Archaeological Science* 37: 2775–2787.

Rothman, M. S. 2001a. "The Tigris piedmont, eastern Jazira, and highland western Iran in the fourth millennium B.C.", in Rothman, M. S. (ed.), *Uruk Mesopotamia & its Neighbours: Cross-Cultural interactions in the era of state formation*, School of American Research Press, Sante Fe: 349–402.

Rothman, M. S. ed. 2001b. *Uruk Mesopotamia & its Neighbours: Cross-Cultural interactions in the era of state formation*, School of American Research Press, Sante Fe.

Roustaei, K. 2004. "Tappeh Hesār: a major manufacturing centre at the Central Plateau", in Stöllner *et al.* 2004: 222–31.

Rowlands, M. J. 1971. "The archaeological interpretation of prehistoric metalworking", *World Archaeology* 3 (2): 210–24.

Salvatori, S., Vidale, M., Guida, G. and Masioli, E. 2009. "Ilgynly-Depe (Turkmenistan) and the 4th millennium BC metallurgy of Central Asia", *Paléorient* 35: 47–67.

Schiffer, M. B. 2008. "Transmission processes: a behavioural perspective" in O'Brien, M.J. (ed.), *Cultural Transmission and Archaeology: Issues and Case Studies*, Society for American Archaeology, Washington, DC: 102–11.

Schreiner, M., Heimann, R. B. and Pernicka, E. 2003. "Mineralogical and geochemical investigations into prehistoric smelting slags from Tepe Sialk/central Iran", in Shamirzadi, S. M. (ed.), *The Silversmiths of Sialk*, Iranian Center for Archaeological Research, Tehran: 13–24.

Sherratt, A. and Sherratt, S. 2001 "Technological change in the East Mediterranean Bronze Age: capital, resources and marketing", in Shortland, A. J. (ed.), *The social context of technological change: Egypt and the Near East, 1650–1550 BC*, Oxbow Books, Oxford: 15–38.

Smith, C. S. 1969. "Analysis of the copper bead from Ali Kosh," in Hole, F., Flannery, K. V. and Neely, J. A. (eds), *Prehistory and Human Ecology of the Deh Luran Plain: An Early Village Sequence from Khuzistan, Iran*, University of Michigan, Ann Arbor: 427–28.

Stein, G. 2010. "Local identities and interaction spheres: Modeling regional variation in the Ubaid horizon", in Carter, R. and Philip, G. (eds), *The Ubaid and Beyond: Exploring the transmission of culture in the developed prehistoric societies of the Middle East*, University of Chicago Oriental Institute Publications, Chicago: 23–44.

Steiniger, D. 2011. "Excavations in the slagheaps in Arisman", in Vatandoust *et al.* 2011: 69–99.

Stöllner, T. 2004. "Prehistoric and ancient ore-mining in Iran", in Stöllner *et al.* 2004: 44–63.

Stöllner, T. 2005. "Early mining and metallurgy on the Iranian Plateau", in Yalçin, Ü. (ed.), *Anatolian Metal III*, Der Anschnitt Beiheft 18, Deutsches Bergbau-Museum, Bochum: 191–208.

Stöllner, T. 2011. "Archaeological survey of ancient mines on the western Central Iranian Plateau", in Vatandoust *et al.* 2011: 621–30.

Stöllner, T., Mireskandari, M. and Roustaie, K. 2011. "Mining archaeology in Iran – investigations at Vešnāve", in Vatandoust *et al.* 2011: 535–608.

Stöllner, T., Slotta, R. and Vatandoust, A. eds 2004. *Persiens Antike Pracht*, Deutsches Bergbau-Museum, Bochum.

Stone, T. 2008. "Social innovation and transformation during the process of aggregation", in O'Brien, M. J. (ed.), *Cultural Transmission and Archaeology: Issues and Case Studies*, Society for American Archaeology, Washington, DC: 158–63.

Sumner, W. M. 1988. "Prelude to Proto-Elamite Anshan: The Lapui Phase", *IA* 23: 23–44.

Sumner, W. M. 2003. *Early Urban Life in the Land of Anshan: Excavations at Tal-e Malyan in the Highlands of Iran*, University Museum Monograph 117, University of Pennsylvania Museum of Archaeology and Anthropology, Philadelphia.

Tallon, F. 1987. *Métallurgie Susienne I: De la fondation de Suse au XVIIIe avant J.-C.*, Notes et Documents des Musées de France 15, Louvre Museum Dept. of Oriental Antiquities, Paris.

Tehrani, J. J. and Collard, M. 2009. "On the relationship between interindividual cultural transmission and population-level cultural diversity: a case study of weaving in Iranian tribal populations", *Evolution and Human Behavior* 30: 286–300.

Terekhova, N. N. 1981. "The history of metalworking production among the ancient agriculturalists of southern Turkmenia", in Kohl, P. L. (ed.), *The Bronze Age Civilization of Central Asia: Recent Soviet Discoveries*, M.E. Sharpe, Armonk, NY: 315–24.

Thornton, C. P. 2009. "The emergence of complex metallurgy on the Iranian Plateau: escaping the Levantine paradigm", *Journal of World Prehistory* 22 (3): 301–27.

Thornton, C. P. 2010. "The rise of arsenical copper in southeastern Iran", *IA* 45: 31–50.

Thornton, C. P. and Lamberg-Karlovsky, C. C. 2004. "A new look at the prehistoric metallurgy of Southeastern Iran", *Iran* 42: 61–76.

Thornton, C. P. and Rehren, Th. 2009. "A truly refractory crucible from fourth millennium Tepe Hissar, Northeast Iran", *Journal of Archaeological Science* 36 (12): 2700–12.

Thornton, C. P., Rehren, Th. and Pigott, V. C. 2009. "The production of speiss (iron arsenide) during the Early Bronze Age in Iran", *Journal of Archaeological Science* 36 (2): 308–16.

Thornton, C. P., Lamberg-Karlovsky, C. C., Liezers, M. and Young, S. M. M. 2002. "On pins and needles: tracing the evolution of copper-base alloying at Tepe Yahya, Iran, via ICP-MS analysis of common-place items", *Journal of Archaeological Science* 29 (12): 1451–60.

Tonoike, Y. 2009. *Beyond Style: Petrographic analysis of Dalma ceramics in two regions of Iran*, unpublished Ph.D. dissertation, Yale University.

Tosi, M. 1989. "The distribution of industrial debris on the surface of Tappeh Hesār as an indication of activity areas", in Dyson, R. H. and Howard, S. M. (eds), *Tappeh Hesār: Reports of the Restudy Project, 1976*, Monografie di Mesopotamia 2, Casa editrice Le Lettere, Florence: 13–24.

VanPool, C. S. 2008. "Agents and cultural transmission", in O'Brien, M. J. (ed.), *Cultural Transmission and Archaeology: Issues and Case Studies*, Society for American Archaeology, Washington, DC: 190–200.

Vatandoust, A., Parzinger, H. and Helwing, B. 2011. *Early Mining and Metallurgy on the Western Central Iranian Plateau: The first five years of work*. Archäologie in Iran und Turan Band 9, Philipp von Zabern, Mainz.

Wagner, G. A. and Öztunali, Ö. 2000. "Prehistoric copper sources in Turkey", in Yalçin, Ü. (ed.), *Anatolian Metal I*, Der Anschnitt Beiheft 13, Deutsches Bergbau-Museum, Bochum: 31–68.

Weeks, L. R. 2008. "The 2007 early Iranian metallurgy workshop at the University of Nottingham", *Iran* 46: 335–45.

Weeks, L. *et al.* in preparation. Analyses of 5th millennium BC copper artefacts from Tang-e Bolaghi, Iran.

Wertime, T. A. 1973. "The beginnings of metallurgy: a new look", *Science* 182 (4115): 875–87.

Wright, H. T. 2001. "Cultural Action in the Uruk world", in Rothman, M. S. (ed.), *Uruk Mesopotamia & its neighbors: cross-cultural interactions in the era of state formation*, School of American Research Press, Sante Fe: 123–48.

Yakar, J. 2002. "East Anatolian metallurgy in the fourth and third millennia BC: some remarks", in Yalçin, Ü. (ed.), *Anatolian Metal II*, Der Anschnitt Beiheft 15, Deutsches Bergbau-Museum, Bochum: 15–26.

Yalçin, Ü. 2000. "Anfänge der Metallverwendung in Anatolien", in Yalçin, Ü. (ed.), *Anatolian Metal I*, Der Anschnitt Beiheft 13, Deutsches Bergbau-Museum, Bochum: 17–30.

Yener, K. A. 2000. *The Domestication of Metals: The Rise of Complex Metal Industries in Anatolia*, Brill, Boston.

Zaccagnini, C. 1983. "Patterns of mobility among ancient Near Eastern craftsmen", *JNES* 42 (4): 245–64.

16. IMAGERY IN ADMINISTRATIVE CONTEXT: SUSIANA AND THE WEST IN THE FOURTH MILLENNIUM BC

Holly Pittman

Introduction

Over the past three decades, archaeologists have focused considerable attention on the fourth millennium BC, when proto-urban societies first emerged in the Tigris and Euphrates drainage basin. Excavation has revealed much about the complex nature of this process, which involved not only large centres in southern (and also northern) Mesopotamia, but also engaged, affected, and transformed much of the piedmont zone embraced by the Zagros and Taurus Mountains. The forces that led to this profound transformation of human society are understood to be at their basis economic, involving strategies of agricultural production and animal husbandry, organisation of labour, and access to differentially distributed raw materials (Algaze 1993, 2005; Rothman [ed.] 2001; Butterlin 2003). As a result of a considerable range of archaeological research, we now have substantial evidence for the extent of this process both in space and time, and much energy has gone into using it to understand this profound transformation.

For historical reasons, this period of transformation is known under the rubric "*Uruk* period" because its material correlates were first identified and systematically investigated almost 100 years ago at the large site of Uruk/Warka in southern Iraq (e.g. Nissen 2002). The enormous size of the site, the shockingly monumental character of its fourth-millennium architecture and, most importantly, the discovery there of the earliest written documents led to the early conclusion that Uruk was not a normal type-site, but was indeed the actual centre that drove and controlled the profound transformation of society toward urban complexity (Algaze 1993, 2005; Rothman [ed.] 2001; Butterlin 2003). The diagnostic forms of material culture associated with this period (in particular ceramics, artistic imagery, and proto-cuneiform signs) were assumed to have originated in southern Mesopotamia, or in the case of writing and imagery, at the site of Uruk itself, and when found abroad were understood to be a material manifestation of contact with the southern Mesopotamian centre (e.g. Algaze 1993, 2005).

Since the 1980s this origin narrative has been subjected to intense scrutiny that has produced important new and re-examined old data. Behind this work is the intellectual quest to understand this period of profound transformation on its own terms. What happened, where did it happen, and why? Gradually a consensus has emerged that this was a long, gradual process that saw a radical reorganisation of human labour and society (Rothman [ed.] 2001; Butterlin 2003). In the ongoing debate, the relations between southern Mesopotamia as represented by Uruk and its neighbours to the north-west have received the most attention because new excavations produced findings that contributed directly to the debate (Rothman [ed.] 2001; Butterlin 2003). Uruk's relations with the east, especially the region of Susiana, have received less intense examination in the recent debates (Pittman 2001), a problem that the conference and current volume seek to address.

The study by Louis Le Breton (1957) of the material from the poorly stratified excavations at Susa systematically established that, during the fourth millennium BC, Susa and Uruk shared a complex assemblage of material culture that he called *Susa B*. During the 1960–1970s, excavations under the direction of J. Perrot gave stratigraphic precision to Le Breton's seriation. Alain Le Brun (1971, 1978a,

1978b, 1979, 1985, 1999) led the excavations of the sounding in *Acropole I* producing a well-stratified and essentially unbroken sequence for *Susa Periods A, B,* and *C,* spanning the fifth to the early third millennia BC. These periods were designated *Susa I, II,* and *III* to differentiate them from Le Breton's seriated alphabetic sequence. Other excavations at the site over the years by both French and American archaeologists also give structure to the uncontrolled results of the earlier excavations (see also Wright, this volume; Dahl *et al.,* this volume). Although general contemporaneity with developments in Mesopotamia was always recognised, a systematic effort to link the ceramic sequences of the two proximate but independent regions represented by Susa and Uruk was first undertaken by R. Dittmann (1986a). More recently P. Butterlin (2003) has reconsidered this material, offering refinements to Dittmann's cross-dating of the Uruk and Susa sequences. Both of these studies propose that a shared ceramic assemblage can be established with confidence linking Uruk/*Eanna XII* and Susa *Acropole I Levels 24–23.* By *Eanna VII* and Susa *Acropole I.20,* both southern Mesopotamia and Susiana represented at Susa, Sharafabad (Wright *et al.* 1980), and Farukabad (Wright 1981) shared a common ceramic assemblage that is defined as the *Middle Uruk* (see Wright, this volume). It is followed in *Eanna Levels VI–IV* and *Acropole I Levels 19–17* as *Late Uruk A* and *B* following Dittmann's terminology (1986a; see also Wright, this volume).

To date, there is little consensus on the nature of the relationship that is reflected in this shared ceramic assemblage between the southern Mesopotamian alluvium and Susiana during this period. Some conclude that *Uruk* presence in Susiana was the result of early colonisation of the region by people from southern Mesopotamia (Algaze 1993, 2005), while others describe the relationship as one of co-evolution between the two contiguous regions (Butterlin 2003). Whatever the economic forces that led to the mass-production of bevel-rim bowls as well as the other diagnostic markers of the period, they pressed equally on the communities of both regions (Butterlin 2003). It has been argued that Uruk did not directly dominate Susiana militarily, economically, or politically (Potts 1999). Rather, the two regions shared a material culture that reflects both close relations and largely identical life-ways. In fact, the label "Uruk" has come to be associated with both assemblages (i.e. ceramics, imagery, administrative documents) leading to the unarticulated assumption that all material proxies of this period originated at the site of Uruk. This assumption has, I believe, led to conclusions that I will reconsider here. In addition to the profound changes that mark the *Uruk* ceramic repertory, equally radical changes occurred in the physical residue of economic administration. It is commonplace to observe that at the very end of the long *Uruk* period, demands for an ever more robust administrative system led to the cognitive breakthrough underlying the invention of writing: the linking of spoken utterance to visible marks. There is no debate about where this remarkable intellectual achievement took place. The weight of accumulating evidence repeatedly confirms that writing was invented within the administrative environment of Uruk. Writing, however, was but one (admittedly huge) step in the evolution of the symbolic technology of economic administration that had been in use for a very long time and which saw an increasing intensification and elaboration over the last centuries before writing's invention. Like pottery, a radical transformation can be observed in the domain of image-making during the *Uruk* period, which like writing, was founded on a cognitive breakthrough that grasped and exploited in new ways the potential of non-verbal, representational, and abstract images to store and convey information vital to the functioning of an increasingly complex society (e.g. Damerow 2006).

While there is a sizeable body of proto-literate texts that provide insight into the use of images to convey information (e.g. Englund 1994; Englund and Nissen 2001, 2005), such images are preserved to us most abundantly in the residue of administrative activities in the form of impressions of engraved seals (cylinders and, to a lesser degree, stamps) made on clay documents while still damp enough to retain their engraved imagery. It is remarkable that at virtually every site producing *Uruk* pottery, at least in the lowlands, evidence for economic activity in the form of seal impressions is also found. It would appear that the system that employed standardised bowls also needed imagery to administer their proper deployment. Wherever found, the images carved on the seals from *Uruk* contexts share certain fundamental stylistic and iconographic features that allow us easily to categorise them as "Uruk" as distinguished from "local" products (Pittman 1999). As such, these images are used by scholars, often without reflection, as markers of contact or interaction with or influence from the "centre" of the *Uruk* phenomenon – that is to say, southern Mesopotamia in general and Uruk in particular. The general nature of the repertory of imagery is well understood for the *Uruk* period, but little effort has been made to reveal temporal or regional variety within a seemingly undifferentiated universe whose evolution and character is shared across the vast temporal and physical expanse of the Uruk culture (Amiet 1980; Pittman 1994a, 1994b, 2001).

Glyptic art, an integral tool of the administrative system during the fourth millennium BC, receives considerable attention in studies of this period, as part of the administrative system and, as importantly, because of its naturalistic character the images are used as "illustrations" of the kinds of social actors and activities that were current and relevant to the administrative domain. Of the several attempts to understand the semiotic system of the seal imagery carried on *Uruk*-period administrative documents, the most comprehensive are those undertaken by Brandes (1979, 1986) for Uruk and Dittmann (1986b) for Susa (also see Pittman 1994b).

My emphasis here, however, is not on the precise meaning of the imagery within the context of a site or an administrative system. Rather, through a comparative treatment of seal imagery, I will investigate the homo-/heterogeneity that can be detected within the imagery and style through time and across space during the *Uruk* horizon (*c.* 3800–3200 BC). In particular, I am interested in distinguishing Susiana from the west. This comparison reveals that while remarkable homogeneity can be observed in general stylistic features of this period, each region employs a different mix of themes that may reflect the types of economic activity that were subject to management through the use of the administrative toolkit. Furthermore, this examination argues that, on the basis of current evidence, the characteristic *Uruk* imagery was first developed and found its richest expression in Susiana. By the end of the *Uruk* period, the imagery was deeply entrenched in the administration of Uruk where it continued to evolve into the proto-historic *Jemdet Nasr* and early *Early Dynastic I* periods. Importantly, this continuity was *not* maintained in Susiana, where during the last phase of the *Late Uruk*, new imagery rendered in new styles was developed by new actors to meet new administrative needs. This divergence coincides precisely with the moment of the invention of writing (proto-cuneiform) at Uruk and the subsequent (or simultaneous) development of an independent script (*Proto-Elamite*), probably in Susiana. Is this a coincidence?

That such a comparative study has not been done is due in large part to the fact that until recently too much of the available material was not easily accessible. With the magisterial publication by Boehmer (1999) of the stratified glyptic evidence from the earliest levels at Uruk, the comprehensive presentation of the tablets and their seal impressions from Uruk (Englund 1994; Englund and Nissen 2001, 2005), and the recent publication of several crucial items of glyptic from the *Acropole I* sounding at Susa (Le Brun 1999; Butterlin 2003), it is possible to undertake a regional comparative study of the *Uruk* glyptic. It is appropriate to locate such a study within a volume that seeks to reconsider Iran's role in the developments of the fourth millennium BC, because it is indeed in Susiana that we have by far the deepest and broadest bodies of glyptic art for the entire span of the period. It must be noted here that no comparable body of evidence of administrative activity for the *Terminal Ubaid, Early* and *Middle Uruk* periods is

known in southern Mesopotamia. While these early phases have been defined ceramically through small-scale soundings at Uruk and Nippur, more excavation is needed to confirm the conclusion that glyptic art was not used systematically in southern Mesopotamia until the late *Middle Uruk* period and that it did not originate locally but was derived from earlier practices documented in the lowland and piedmont zones to the east and north.

Within the scope of a single article it is not possible to discuss and illustrate such a comparison in all its detail. Rather I present here a systematic but schematic comparison that allows an overview of the subject. My interest is to highlight the variation that is present in the corpus from Susiana when compared to that from Uruk. Furthermore, I seek to identify more precisely the so-called "interregional motifs" (cf. Dittmann 1986b) that appear in glyptic art and are shared across regions, perhaps similar in their common usage to that which is often assumed for the bevel-rim bowl. Within this context we can see that there is in fact a large number of such "interregional motifs," all of which first appear in Susiana. As is true of any comparative study, one that examines imagery used in administration across sites and regions is fraught with challenges. The data sets from the various sites are not comparable either in the nature of their deposit or in the manner of their retrieval. There are also problems caused by a lack of absolute dates from many excavations, and the existence of a large plateau in the radiocarbon calibration curve that spans the critical period from *c.* 3400–2900 BC (Dahl *et al.*, this volume; Petrie in press). With these constraints, establishing contemporaneity between regions can quickly slide into circular reasoning. Furthermore, determining which, if any, images were made by seals manufactured outside the site in which they were found must also be considered. If cross-dating between regions can be convincingly established through ceramic parallels, however, and if the assumption is made that all seal imagery was salient in some way within the administration in which it was *used* (as distinguished from the presence of actual seals which could have been imported), then it is my conviction that such a comparison can in fact reveal real differences and provide grounds for establishing the importance of Susiana in relation to the developments in the west during the fourth millennium BC.

The data

From southern Mesopotamia, the only glyptic material of the *Uruk* period having secure (if tertiary) provenance comes from the site of Uruk itself. There are approximately 84 individual images of seals that can be assigned with confidence to the *Uruk* period, all of them from the excavations either in the Eanna or the Anu precincts (Boehmer 1994, 1999, 2001, 2005). As recently summarised by Butterlin (2003: 286–97), the stratigraphy of the early phases at Uruk is notoriously complex and has been subjected to reanalysis on at least two occasions (Sürenhagen 1986, 1987, 1999; Eichmann 1989). Most of the administrative evidence including the seal impressions was found in, at best, secondary or more commonly tertiary contexts that allow us to establish only a *terminus ante quem* (e.g. see Nissen 2002). Little of a secure relative sequence can be established on the basis of stratigraphy. For this reason, I have for the most part followed the level assignments of Boehmer (1999) in this discussion without critical analysis. Except when noted, the discrepancy between Boehmer and Sürenhagen or Eichmann is not directly relevant to this discussion. Apart from a few poorly controlled levels at Anu (discussed in more detail below), and the context near the Steinstiftgebäude that produced a cache of seal-impressed hollow clay balls (also discussed in more detail below), the earliest stratified context that produced glyptic art is *Level V* in Eanna, followed by *Level IVc*, *Level IVb*, and *Level IVa*. It is only in *Eanna Level IVa* that the use of numerical, numero-ideographic, and proto-cuneiform tablets is established. Material from *Uruk III/Jemdet Nasr* contexts at Uruk is not included in my analysis, although as alluded to above, it is certainly relevant to the end of this story through its unbroken continuity with earlier conventions.

The archaeological situation in Susiana is much better. There are four *Uruk*-period sites that have produced seal imagery. As at Uruk, virtually all of this material comes to us in the form of impressions rather than seals. Although often fragmentary, this mode of preservation nevertheless allows us to have greater confidence of date and relevance, since administrative residue is not likely to be preserved beyond the context of its salience except through tertiary dump situations such as exist in Uruk/Eanna. There are two types of contexts at Susa. Forty-two images come from primary (or secondary) stratigraphic contexts of the *Acropole I* sounding (Le Brun 1971, 1978a, 1985). Unlike the tertiary foundational deposits of monumental official buildings at Uruk, the sealings found in the *Acropole I* sounding are in most instances associated with domestic architecture. A greater number of images (257) are carried on administrative devices retrieved through poorly controlled early excavations at Susa, and most of them have been published by Delaporte (1920) and/or Amiet (1972). In addition, Chogha Mish produced approximately 138 seal images carried on impressions of the *Uruk* period (Delougaz and Kantor 1996). Although there is little internal stratigraphic control for this material, the form of the administrative devices and the iconography and style of the glyptic establishes a clear chronological link to *Acropole I.19–18*, i.e. *Late Uruk A*. Chogha Mish was abandoned before the cultural transformation that can be observed

in *Acropole I.17*. Sharafabad produced 12 images from good *Middle Uruk* context (Wright *et al.* 1980), and Farukabad produced two or three also from *Middle Uruk* contexts (Wright 1981).

In stark contrast to the situation in Uruk, an uninterrupted sequence of development of glyptic imagery is preserved in the *Acropole I* sounding. Beginning in the *Susa A/Susa I* period of *Level I.27*, stamp seals are in use. Beginning with *Level I.21*, almost every level in the sounding produced glyptic art (primarily as sealings, but also including a few fragments of seals) giving us remarkably fine control for the internal development of the sequence (Le Brun 1971, 1999; Le Brun and Vallat 1978; Butterlin 2003). This well-controlled sequence allows us to seriate, with caution, the poorly controlled finds from elsewhere at Susa and incorporate them into the discussion. Dittmann (1986b) did this in his study of the iconography from Susa, and a similar approach has been used to seriate the *Proto-Elamite* tablets by Dahl *et al.* (this volume).

Using both seriated and stratified glyptic comparanda from Susiana, Boehmer (1999) proposed a hypothetical correlation between *Eanna Levels VIII–IV* at Uruk and *Levels 22–17* in the *Acropole I* sounding. Levels in the *Anu* sequence at Uruk that might be cross-dated to the *Middle Uruk* period produced only stamp seals (Boehmer 1999). A question that will remain outstanding until there is further excavation is whether there ever existed a comparably robust production and administrative use of cylinder seals at Uruk during the *Middle Uruk* phase, or as I believe to be more likely, was glyptic art an administrative tool that was introduced during that period into southern Mesopotamian from its eastern neighbours.

Prolegomena

While *Uruk* glyptic is dominated by the cylinder seal, it is useful to begin this comparison with a brief characterisation of the earlier stamp-seal tradition. While virtually absent in southern Mesopotamia in the *Halaf* and *Ubaid* horizons, stamp seals were in continual use in Susiana as early as the sixth millennium BC where they are abundantly documented at Jaffarabad and Jowi (Dollfus 1977; Pittman 2001). By the *Terminal Susa A* period around the turn of the fourth millennium BC, stamp-seal imagery is well documented at Susa among both the stratified and unstratified material. Their interest for this discussion comes from the fact that these early images lie, thematically and iconographically, at the beginning of the *Uruk* tradition.

In his discussion of the transition from *Ubaid* to *Early Uruk* ceramics at Uruk and Susa, Butterlin (2003) observes a gradual development in the ceramics at Susa, which for him stands in stark contrast to the abrupt appearance of new *Uruk* ceramic types in *Uruk/*

Eanna Level XII. He argues from this observation that there is no indication that the *Uruk* culture arrives at Susa from outside, but rather that it is a gradual internal evolution towards a new phase in diagnostic material culture. A similar argument can be proposed for the evolution of the glyptic imagery and indeed for the practices of administration more generally. The combination of unstratified administrative material with the evidence from the very small exposure in these early levels of the *Acropole I* sounding allows us to observe a gradual and continuous evolution of imagery at Susa, where perhaps by *Level I.21* and certainly by *Level I.20*, a new glyptic form, the cylinder seal, appears together with an image repertory that builds directly on the imagery familiar from the preceding *Susa A/Susa I* (Le Brun 1999). After an apparently slow beginning, there occurs an explosion of imagery in the *Middle* and especially *Late Uruk A* periods that plays a central role in the increasingly complex administrative practices.

The stamp seals found in *Acropole I Levels 27, 25,* and *23* (Fig. 16.1/a.i–iv) assist in the dating of some unstratified examples from Susa to the *Ubaid* and *Terminal Ubaid* phases, increasing the pool of images current in the pre-*Uruk* period. As Pierre Amiet (1972: 37) has repeatedly pointed out, many of the images carried on those stamp seals foreshadow the imagery of the later *Uruk* period. He drew special attention to the shaman-like figures wearing patterned skirts and animal headdresses (Fig. 16.1/b.i–v), comparing them to the later "priest king of Uruk". In addition, other *Uruk* themes have their origins in the earlier stamp-seal tradition, including the master of animals (Fig. 16.1/b.iii), narrative representation of ritual scenes (Fig. 16.1/b.iv,v), snakes and snake twists (Fig. 16.1/b.vi,vii), caprids (Fig. 16.1/b.viii), felines, bulls, (Fig. 16/1b.ix) and sign-like forms (cross) (Fig. 16.1/b.x). Indeed, the main thematic category of the *Late Uruk* missing in these early stamps is the various scenes of workers, although in contemporary stamp seals from Tepe Gawra scenes of workers (Fig. 16.1/c.i–vii) are clearly depicted (Pittman 2001). While outside the purview of this comparative exercise, it is relevant that the administrative functions of seals in the *Susa A/I* period also continue into the *Uruk* period (Amiet 1997). This long tradition of glyptic art as a tool of economic administration stands in contrast (notwithstanding the caveat given above) to the evidence from Uruk (or anywhere in southern Mesopotamia) where there is very little evidence for the administrative use of seals before the *Late Uruk* period (e.g. Porada *et al.* 1992: 97; Amiet 1992: 97).

Acropole I Level 21 has been variously assigned on the basis of ceramics to the end of the *Early Uruk* phase (Le Brun 1971, 1978b) or to the beginning of the *Middle Uruk* (Dittmann 1986a; Butterlin 2003). In addition to the cylinder seal (Fig. 16.2/a) that is tentatively associated with *Level I.21*, Le Brun (1999)

published a drawing of a square stamp seal that can be securely placed in that level (Fig. 16.2/b). In the same brief note, Le Brun (1999) also presented a drawing of a seal-impressed clay tag from *Level I.20* which provides the earliest securely stratified evidence for the administrative use of cylinder seals at Susa (Fig. 16.3/a). While sparse, the publication of actual images of the administrative material found in these *Early/Middle Uruk* levels allows us to describe with greater precision the early stages of imagery in administration, augmenting them through a judicious selection drawn from the unstratified material.

Uruk beginnings in Susiana: drilled and baggy imagery at Susa *Acropole I.20,* Sharafabad, and Farukabad

With *Acropole I.20* we have our first secure evidence for the use of cylinder seals as an administrative tool at Susa. Although the single stratified impression showing a heroic master of snakes is fragmentary, its drilled "baggy" style is clear (Fig. 16.3/a) and closely comparable to impressions from the excavations of the *Middle Uruk* pit at the small site of Tepe Sharafabad (Fig. 16.3/b.i–xii) (Wright *et al.* 1980). Combined with this image, the nine or 10 images from Tepe Sharafabad allow us securely to differentiate an important early transitional phase that stands near the introduction of the administrative practices that define the *Uruk* period. From a ceramically equivalent date, Tepe Farukabad produced a seal-impressed hollow clay ball (Fig. 16.3/c.i) as well as a bone stamp seal in the shape of a crouching humanoid (Fig. 16.3/c.ii) (Wright 1981). We can extend the evidence for this phase further using the poorly controlled material from Susa, which includes three impressions of stamp seals (Fig. 16.3/d.i–iii), one pair of stamp seal and cylinder seal impressed on a single clay ball (Fig. 16.3/d.iv,v), under a dozen stamp seals (e.g. Fig. 16.3/d.vi–xiii), and at least one cylinder seal (Fig. 16.3/d.xiv).

How long the baggy style persisted in stamps and cylinders is difficult to say. Two administrative stages in which the drilled-style seals were used can be posited. The first, described above, is seen at Tepe Sharafabad where only clay cups and counters but no seal-impressed hollow clay balls or fusiform tags were found. In a second stage not yet identified stratigraphically, but which fits with the scant evidence from *Acropole I Level 20*, hollow clay balls first appear apparently developed from the hemispherical cups to hold together allotments of counters and tokens securely enclosed by a surface marked with cylinder and occasionally stamp seals. A small number of such hollow clay balls impressed with drilled- or baggy-style images are known among the unstratified material from Susa which compare closely with the one published seal impression from *Acropole I.20* (Fig. 16.3/e.i–vi).

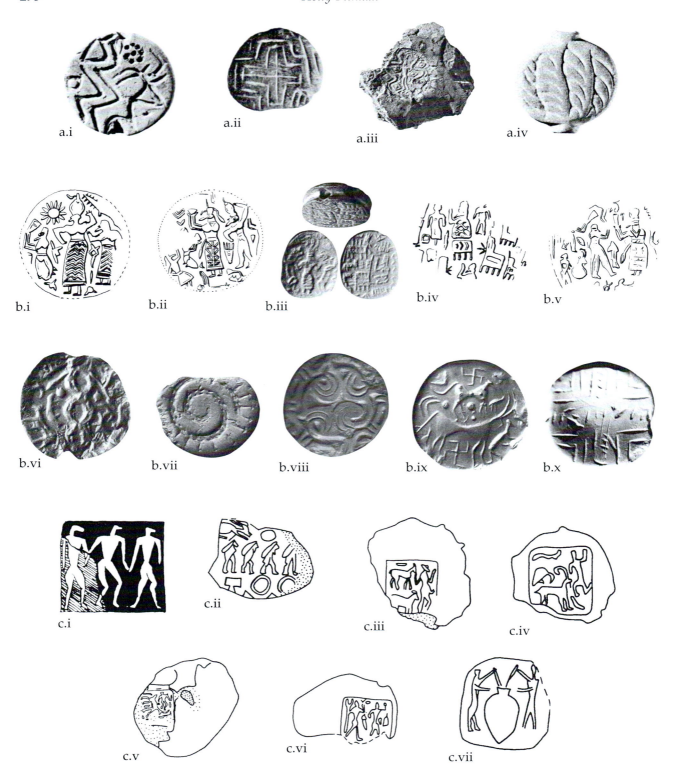

Figure 16.1. Stamp seals from a: Susa Acropole I.27, 25, and 23; b. Susa unstratified; c. Tepe Gawra. Image references: a.i. Susa Acropole I.27. Le Brun 1971: pl. 22:7; a.ii. Susa Acropole I.25. Le Brun 1971: pl. 22:11; a.iii. Susa Acropole I.25. Le Brun 1971: pl. 22:6; a.iv. Susa Acropole I.23. Le Brun 1971: pl. 22:10; b.i. Susa. Amiet 1972: pl. 2:231; b.ii. Susa. Amiet 1972: pl. 2:230; b.iii. Susa. Amiet 1972: pl. 49:222; b.iv. Susa. Amiet 1972: pl. 2:228; b.v. Susa. Amiet 1972: pl. 2:229; b.vi. Susa. Amiet 1972: pl. 47:190 bis; b.vii. Susa. Amiet 1972: pl. 47: 193; b.viii. Susa. Amiet 1972: pl. 53: 292; b.ix. Susa. Amiet 1972: pl. 45:143; b.x. Susa. Amiet 1972: pl. 47:197; c.i. Gawra Well, Level XIII. Tobler 1950: pl. 163:92; c.ii. Gawra Phase XIA, Level XIA/B. Rothman 2002: pl. 38:993; c.iii. Gawra Level XII, White Building. Rothman 2002: pl. 24:434; c.iv. Gawra West Trench, Level XIA/B. Rothman 2002: pl. 37:1068; c.v. Gawra Round House, Level XIA/B. Rothman 2002: pl. 40:1026; c.vi. Gawra Phase XA, Level XI/XA. Rothman 2002: pl. 38:1019; c.vii. Gawra Phase XIA, Level XIA/B. Rothman 2002: pl. 49:1843.

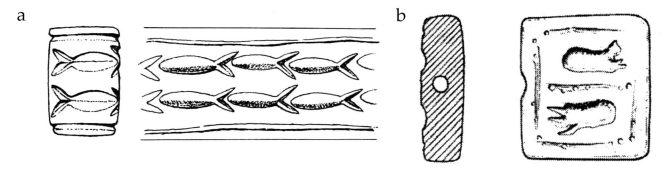

Figure 16.2. Cylinder and stamp seals from Acropole I.21. *Image references: a. Susa* Acropole I.21. *Le Brun 1971: fig. 43:10; b. Susa* Acropole I.21. *Le Brun 1999: fig. 1a.*

Most of the themes found in glyptic iconography of the *Late Uruk* phase in Susiana originate in the *Middle Uruk* drilled/baggy phase. For example, at both Tepe Sharafabad and Susa scenes of workers, conspicuously absent in the *Terminal Ubaid*, appear for the first time: seated workers manipulate vessels (Fig. 16.3/b.vii); processions of figures associated with commodities (Fig. 16.3/e.i–iii; rows of quadrupeds probably representing domesticated herds of sheep that are often accompanied by images of squatting humans (Fig. 16.3/e.iv–vi). Conflict or coercion between humans, a distinctive if uncommon theme in the *Late Uruk* repertory that appears most frequently in *Eanna V*, is also clearly recorded on a baggy-style stamp seal from Susa in which a large human figure wearing upturned shoes threatens a squatting worker with a club (Fig. 16.3/d.ix). A fragmentary impression preserves another example of the same scene (Fig. 16.3/d.i). As a paramount figure, this image, together with the hero mastering snakes from *Acropole I.20*, prefigures the *Late Uruk* priest-king who appears (rarely) in Susiana and with greater proportional frequency at Uruk itself. An early representation of the "administrative transaction" (Pittman 1993) that is so common in the *Late Uruk* seal imagery of Susiana (see below Fig. 16.17) is rendered on a drilled stamp (Fig. 16.3/d.viii). Significantly, *none* of these scenes are imported from the west (i.e. southern Mesopotamia). Rather, they clearly have their origins within the administrative system of the pre-writing *Uruk* phase in Susiana. When they do appear in the west, if any influence is to be inferred, this evidence establishes that these themes originated in the east in Susiana, and were subsequently adopted in the west.

Among the imagery of this baggy phase, there are two additional images that are significant for our review here. One from Susa shows a bear acting as a human, which is a distinctive iconographic conceit that finds its full expression in the post-*Uruk*/*Proto-Elamite* period (Fig. 16.3/d.iv). Amiet (1980) long ago identified the *Late Uruk* forerunners of this hallmark *Proto-Elamite* feature at Susa, but its presence among

the original imagery of the *Middle Uruk* phase at Susa allows us firmly to establish a distinctly "Iranian" component to the imagery in this early phase, which is never seen in the west. Another distinctly Iranian image is the combination of feline and bird into an imaginary creature (Fig. 16.3/e.vi). Surely this *Mischwesen*, which first appears in *Late Uruk Eanna Level IVa* as the lion-headed Anzu bird, has its conceptual origins in the baggy-style glyptic art of *Middle Uruk* Susiana where it continued to be an important element in the glyptic repertory throughout the *Uruk* period.

In southern Mesopotamia at Uruk, this phase of the drilled-style seals is not represented among the impressions on administrative documents. Its presence is indicated, however, by two large cylinder seals (Fig. 16.4/a,b). The first, a purely drilled-style seal (Fig. 16.4/a), was found completely out of context (Boehmer 1999: 113) while the second, a baggy-style seal (Fig. 16.4/b), was found associated with the Kleinfundeschicht beneath the White Temple on the Anu Ziggurat (Boehmer 1999). The relative dating of the White Temple of the Anu Ziggurat as earlier than *Eanna V* is based solely on the stylistic criterion of the glyptic, making it impossible to argue independently for an early date for either this seal or for the unique seal-impressed tablets (e.g. Fig. 16.4/c) found in the White Temple (Boehmer 1999: 81). From its style, the first, large seal showing a worker squatting among three registers of animals (Fig. 16.4/a) belongs to the phase represented by Tepe Sharafabad, while the cylinder from the Kleinfundeschicht at Anu (Fig. 16.4/b) (Boehmer 1999: 81), depicting two baggy figures in a field of snakes, is equivalent to impressions on hollow clay balls from Susa that can be associated with *Level I.20* (Fig. 16.3/e.i–vi). Since both of these seals are unique at Uruk and since there is no evidence that seals of either type were ever used in local administration at Uruk it is, in my estimation, likely that both of these seals originated in Susiana and were exported to the west where they were gathered and kept by elites, together with other

a

b.i b.ii b.iii b.iv b.v b.vi

b.vii b.viii b.ix b.x b.xi b.xii

c.i c.ii

d.i d.ii d.iii d.iv d.v

d.vi d.vii d.viii d.ix d.x d.xi

d.xii d.xiii d.xiv

e.i e.ii e.iii

e.iv e.v e.vi

exotic objects. Finally, more than a dozen gypsum tablets found in the White Temple are impressed by a single cylinder seal (Fig. 16.4/c) that finds no exact comparison either at Uruk or in Susiana. The relative date of the White Temple is continuously debated, and is based primarily on the "early" appearance of the unique seal impressed on the tablets. One close comparison for this unusual seal comes from a fragmentary seal impression from a *Middle Uruk* level at Hamoukar (Fig. 16.4/d). There does seem to be a consensus that the White Temple is earlier than *Eanna Level IV*.

Additional evidence for the administrative salience of this glyptic phase comes from Tell Brak in the Jezira where in Area TW13 a large cylinder carrying drilled figures, including a walking bear, was found together with diagnostic *Middle Uruk* pottery (Fig. 16.4/e) (Oates and Oates 1993). There is no other evidence for administrative activity in Area TW13, although administrative activity dated to the *Middle Uruk* period is present in another area of the site – Area HS1 (Matthews *et al.* 1994). There, seal impressions carrying images of a procession of figures (Fig. 16.4/f.i,ii) found together with *Middle Uruk* pottery, find close parallels to the procession scenes from Tepe Sharafabad (Matthews *et al.* 1994). From the photograph it would appear that this impression belongs to the second stage of drilled/baggy development when the drillings are mitigated by further working. As at Susa and Sharafabad, both examples can be dated on the basis of their associated ceramics to the *Middle Uruk* phase.

In the light of evidence provided by Le Brun about the glyptic of *Acropole I Levels 21, 20,* and *19,* Boehmer's assignment of the baggy style to *Acropole I.22–20* can be accepted if we equate the evidence from Tepe Sharafabad to *Acropole I Levels 22–21*. What cannot be accepted without further evidence, however, is Boehmer's (1999) suggestion that this phase of glyptic art existed at Uruk in levels equivalent to *Eanna levels VIII–VI*. As reviewed above, there is no securely

stratified evidence to support this claim. The three items that might belong to this *Middle Uruk* phase (Fig. 16.4/a,b,c) all come from levels that are dated by comparisons to glyptic from Susiana. What is obvious in any case is that unlike at Susa, there is no evidence for the administrative use of seals in the *Middle Uruk* phase at Uruk (with the unique exception of the gypsum tablets from the White Temple, depending on the dating). It is only with *Eanna V* that we can begin to evaluate the similarities and differences in the glyptic corpus between the west and Susiana. Boehmer (1999: 3–9) suggests a cross-dating of *Acropole I.19* to *Eanna V*. Given the homogeneity of *Acropole I Level 19–18* (Le Brun 1978a: 117), a combination of those levels provides a coherent stratigraphic context to compare to the rich glyptic evidence now available from *Eanna V* and *IVb*.

Late Uruk A

Uruk Eanna V–IVB

Impressed on a variety of clay closing devices, the iconography of the cylinder seal impressions of *Eanna V* is limited to two narrative themes involving humans (Fig. 16.5/a–i), large animal files (Fig. 16.5/j–l), heraldic lions with commodities (Fig. 16.5/m), and heraldic lions mastered by a human (Fig. 16.5/n). Two impressions show vessels with textiles (Fig. 16.5/o, p), while another shows a vessel with textiles together with a lion and bull attack scene (Fig. 16.5/q). The narrative themes include two processions of naked men carrying commodities (Fig. 16.5/a), one towards a temple (Fig. 16.5/b); a priest-king, female, and temple (Fig. 16.5/c); a ritual with snakes and temple (Fig. 16.5/d); three scenes of *coercion* (Fig. 16.5/e–g); and two more showing the priest-king receiving prisoners (Fig. 16.5/h–i). In *Eanna IVb* the master of animals (Fig. 16.6/a), felines often with commodities (Fig. 16.6/b.i–iv), and large animal files (Fig. 16.6/c.i–iii), continue. Two new iconographic elements appear in *Eanna*

Figure 16.3. Images of stamp and cylinder seals of Middle Uruk *Phase from: a. Susa Acropole I.20; b. Sharafabad pit; c. Farukhabad; d–e. unstratified contexts at Susa. Image references: a. Susa. Acropole I.20. Le Brun 1999: fig. 1b; b.i. Uruk Pit Sharafabad. Wright* et al. *1980: 279: fig. 6:2; b.ii. Uruk Pit Sharafabad. Wright* et al. *1980: 279: fig. 6:3; b.iii. Uruk Pit Sharafabad. Wright* et al. *1980: 279: fig. 6:5; b.iv. Uruk Pit Sharafabad. Wright* et al. *1980: 279: fig. 6:6; b.v. Uruk Pit Sharafabad. Wright* et al. *1980: 279: fig. 6:7; b.vi. Uruk Pit Sharafabad. Wright* et al. *1980: 279: fig. 6:8; b.vii. Uruk Pit Sharafabad. Wright* et al. *1980: 279: fig. 6:9; b.viii. Uruk Pit Sharafabad. Wright* et al. *1980: 279: fig. 6:4; b.ix. Uruk Pit Sharafabad. Wright* et al. *1980: 279: fig. 6:11; b.x. Uruk Pit Sharafabad. Wright* et al. *1980: 279: fig. 6:10; b.xi. Uruk Pit Sharafabad. Wright* et al. *1980: 279: fig. 6:12; b.xii. Uruk Pit Sharafabad. Wright* et al. *1980: 279: fig. 6:1; c.i. Farukabad. Wright 1981: fig. 29d; c.ii. Farukabad. Wright 1981: fig. 29d; d.i. Susa. Amiet 1972: pl. 3:455; d.ii. Susa. Amiet 1972: pl. 3:452; d.iii. Susa. Amiet 1972: pl. 4:462; d.iv. Susa. Amiet 1972: pl. 4:457; d.v. Susa. Amiet 1972: pl. 12:580; d.vi. Susa. Amiet 1972: pl. 60:448; d.vii. Susa. Amiet 1972: pl. 60:449; d.viii. Susa. Amiet 1972: pl. 60:453; d.ix. Susa. Amiet 1972: pl. 60:454; d.x. Susa. Amiet 1972: pl. 60:447; d.xi. Susa. Amiet 1972: pl. 60:442; d.xii. Susa. Amiet 1972: pl. 60:444; d.xiii. Susa. Amiet 1972: pl. 60:443; d.xvi. Susa. Amiet 1972: pl. 91:762; e.i. Susa. Amiet 1972: pl. 13:598; e.ii. Susa Amiet 1972: pl. 17: 678; e.iii. Susa. Amiet 1972: pl. 10:565; e.iv. Susa. Amiet 1972: pl. 10:563; e.v. Susa. Amiet 1972: pl. 10:552; e.vi. Susa. Amiet 1972: pl. 12:581.*

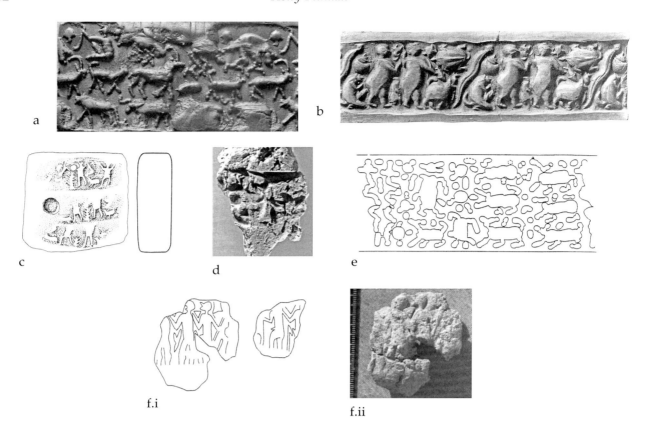

Figure 16.4. Images of drilled- and baggy-style figures on a–b. two seals from Uruk, and contemporaneous seal impressions from c. the White Temple in the Anu Ziggurat (stamped gypsum); d. Hamoukar; e–f. Tell Brak. Image references: a. Boehmer 1999: tf. 104, 61c; b. Boehmer 1999: Abb. 76a; c. Uruk, Anu, White Temple. Boehmer 1999: Abb. 93,1b; d. Hamoukar. Reichel 2002: 42: fig. 8; e. Tell Brak TW Phase 13. Oates and Oates 1993: 177, fig. 31; f.i. Tell Brak HS1, level 4. Felli 2003: fig. 4.26:20,21; f.ii. Tell Brak HS1, level 4. Felli 2003: fig. 4.14.

IVb: caprids with commodities (Fig. 16.6/d.i–vi) and confronted felines with intertwined necks (Fig. 16.6/e). In addition, sixteen hollow clay balls (in 26 pieces) were found in a cache close to the Steinstiftgebäude in a context that Boehmer associates with *Eanna IVb* (Boehmer 1999: 104–05), and they all carry seal images. Seven carry impressions (Fig. 16.7/a.i–vii) showing horned quadrupeds; one shows animal combat (Fig. 16.7/b); one shows rampant heraldic felines (Fig. 16.7/c); two show snake interlace (Fig. 16.7/e.i–ii); one shows a master of animals (Fig. 16.7/f) in an impression similar to the one found in *Acropole I.19* (see above); two show impressions of temple facades (Fig. 16.7/g); and two show processions of men carrying commodities (Fig. 16.7/h.i, ii).

Susa Acropole I Levels 19–18 *and Chogha Mish*

All of the themes present at Uruk in contexts assigned to *Eanna V* and *IVb* are documented among the abundant seal images from Susa that can be equated to *Acropole I Levels 19–18* and from Chogha Mish. Significantly, in addition to those themes, there are many more themes from Susiana that are not found at Uruk.

To judge from the one published seal impression (Butterlin 2003: 306, photo 19), by *Acropole I.19*, the imagery rendered in the drilled or baggy styles had evolved into a more complex stage that used smaller more carefully articulated figures made through a controlled combination of drilling and engraving (Fig. 16.8). This stylistic distinction between *Levels I.20* and *I.19* marks the beginning of the *Late Uruk* phase in glyptic art. No architecture was found in the small area of the *Acropole I* sounding that could be cleared in *Level I.19*. It is followed by a large exposure in *Level I.18* that is subdivided into four architectural sub-phases (Le Brun 1978b). Given the coherence of the ceramic and administrative evidence from these two levels, it is useful to follow Dittmann (1986b) in combining *Acropole I Levels 19* and *18*, to define the *Late Uruk A* administrative phase at Susa. The administrative toolkit expands in *Acropole I.18C* to include a particular type of squarish tablet usually having a lenticular section (Fig. 16.9). The obverse side of these tablets is always seal-impressed and has

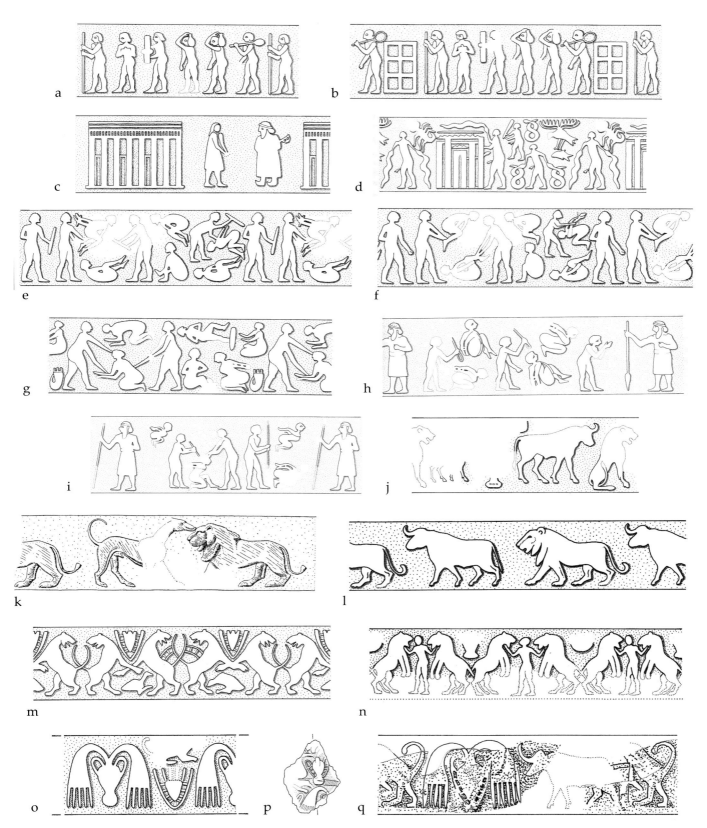

Figure 16.5. Cylinder seal impressions from Eanna V showing: a–i. humans; j–l. large animal files; m. heraldic lions with commodities; n. heraldic lions mastered by a human; p,o. vessels with textiles; q. a vessel with textile together with a lion and bull attack scene. Image references: a. Uruk. Eanna V. Boehmer 1999: tf. 3, Nr. 1A-E; b. Uruk. Eanna V. Boehmer 1999: tf. 7, Nr. 2A-X; c. Uruk. Eanna V. Boehmer 1999: tf. 35, Nr. 10A-L'; d. Uruk. Eanna V. Boehmer 1999: tf. 41, Nr. 13A-W; e. Uruk. Eanna V. Boehmer 1999: tf. 20, Nr. 5 A-G; f. Uruk. Eanna V. Boehmer 1999: tf. 22 Nr. 6C-E; g: Uruk. Eanna V. Boehmer 1999: tf. 26, Nr.9A-H; h. Uruk. Eanna V. Boehmer 1999: tf. 17, Nr. 4A-L; i. Uruk. Eanna V. Boehmer 1999: tf. 12, Nr. 3A-E; j. Uruk. Eanna V. Boehmer 1999: tf. 49, Nr. 19A-G; k. Uruk. Eanna V. Boehmer 1999: tf, 50, Nr. 21c; l. Uruk. Eanna V. Boehmer 1999: tf. 75, Nr. 22A-G'''; m: Uruk. Eanna V. Boehmer 1999: tf. 46, Nr. 17A-N; n: Uruk. Eanna V. Boehmer 1999: tf. 42, Nr. 14A-D; o. Uruk. Eanna V. Boehmer 1999: tf. 77, Nr. 25A-C;p. Uruk. Eanna V. Boehmer 1999: tf 78,b, Nr. 27; q. Uruk. Eanna V. Boehmer 1999: tf. 76, Nr. 23 A-C.

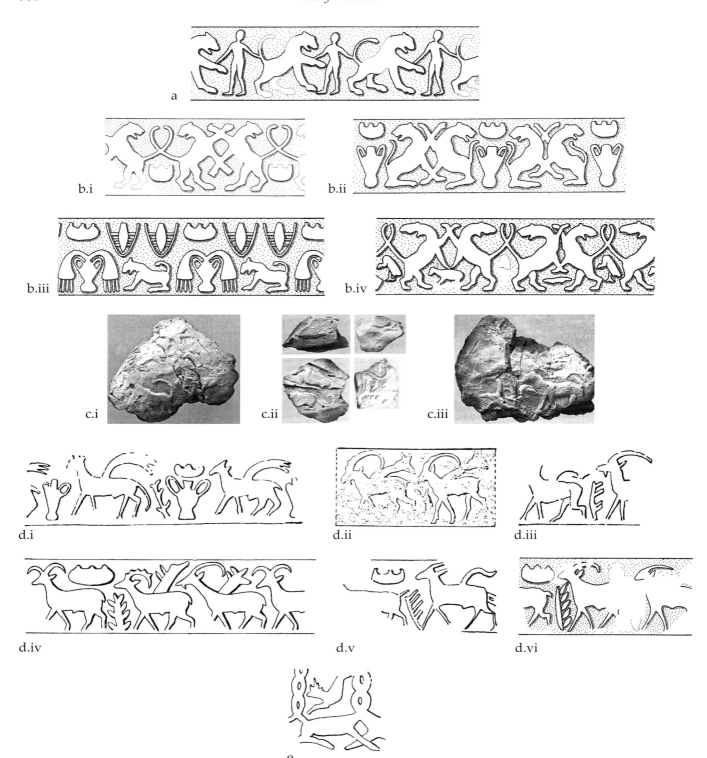

Figure 16.6. Cylinder seal impressions from Eanna IVb *showing: a. master of animals; b.i–iv. felines with commodities; c.i–iii. large animal files; d.i–vi. caprids with commodities; e. confronted felines with intertwined necks. Image references: a. Uruk. Eanna IVB. Boehmer 1999: Abb. 26A-K; b.i. Uruk. Eanna IVB. Boehmer 1999: Abb. 28A-G; b.ii. Uruk. Eanna IVB. Boehmer 1999: Abb. 29A-N; b.iii. Uruk. Eanna IVB. Boehmer 1999: Abb. 33a-b; b.iv. Uruk. Eanna IVB. Boehmer 1999: Abb. 27A-Q; c.i. Uruk. Eanna IVB. Boehmer 1999: Abb. 30; c.ii. Uruk. Eanna IVB. Boehmer 1999: Abb. 31A, B, C; c.iii. Uruk. Eanna IVB. Boehmer 1999: Abb. 32; d.i. Uruk. Eanna IVB. Boehmer 1999: Abb. 35A-G; d.ii. Uruk. Eanna IVB. Boehmer 1999: Abb. 39b; d.iii. Uruk. Eanna IVB. Boehmer 1999: Abb. 37; d.iv. Uruk. Eanna IVB. Boehmer 1999: Abb. 38A-C; d.v. Uruk. Eanna IVB. Boehmer 1999: Abb. 36, 2A-B; d.vi. Uruk. Eanna IVB. Boehmer 1999: Abb. 36,1b; e. Uruk. Eanna IVB. Boehmer 1999: Abb. 34, 1A-B.*

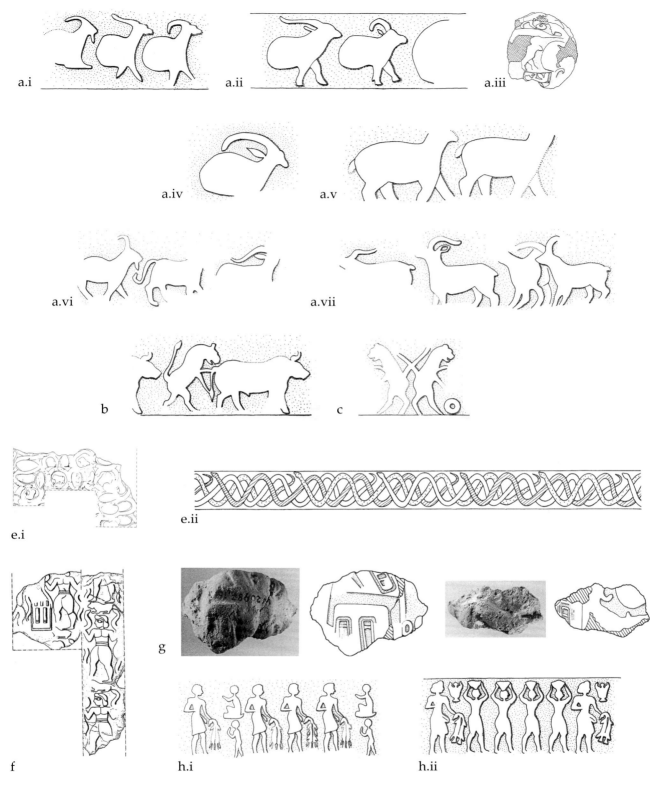

Figure 16.7. Hollow clay balls from cache close to the Steinstiftgebäude equated by Boehmer to Eanna IVb, showing: a.i-vii. horned quadrupeds; b. animal combat; c. rampant heraldic felines; e.i–ii. snake interlace; f. master of animals; g. temple facades; h.i-ii. processions of men carrying commodities. Image references: a.i. Uruk. Boehmer 1999: tf. 79, Nr. 28a-c; a.ii. Uruk, Boehmer 1999: tf. 81, Nr. 30a-l; a.iii. Uruk. Boehmer 1999: tf. 81, Nr. 30l; a.iv. Uruk. Boehmer 1999: tf. 82, Nr. 32a-e; a.v. Uruk. Boehmer 1999: tf. 83, Nr. 33a-f; a.vi. Uruk. Boehmer 1999: tf. 89, Nr. 39a-h; a.vii. Uruk. Boehmer 1999: tf. 85, Nr. 34a-m; b. Uruk. Boehmer 1999: tf. 88, Nr. 41a-d; c. Uruk. Boehmer 1999: tf. 88, Nr. 42 a-b; e.i. Uruk. Boehmer 1999: tf. 91, Nr. 45A; e.ii. Uruk. Boehmer 1999: tf. 89, Nr. 43i; f. Uruk. Boehmer 1999: tf. 95, Nr. 48i; g. Uruk. Boehmer 1999: tf. 100 Nr. 54a-d; h.i. Uruk. Boehmer 1999: tf. 96, Nr. 49a-d; h.ii. Uruk. Boehmer 1999: tf. 99, Nr. 50a-m.

Figure 16.8. More carefully articulated figures made through a controlled combination of drilling and engraving from Susa Acropole I.19. Image reference: Susa. Acropole I.19. Butterlin 2003: 306: photo 19.

Figure 16.9. Lenticular tablet from Susa Acropole I.18C. Image reference: Susa Acropole I.18. Le Brun and Vallat 1978: fig. 4,2.

both long and circular marks along the edges, which are thought to represent numbers. These tablets were used in combination with hollow clay balls, ovoid tags, and clay closing devices all impressed with seals, often the same ones (Fig. 16.10). As Le Brun and Vallat (1978) have shown, taken together this is residue of a coherent, highly integrated administrative system closely comparable to that found at Chogha Mish (Delougaz and Kantor 1996). When the evidence for the range of themes from *Acropole I* is combined with Chogha Mish (Fig. 16.11) and the unstratified evidence from Susa, we have a very large corpus of imagery originating in Susiana that can be compared with that from southern Mesopotamia. Not only has the style of the imagery evolved from the baggy stage, but also the iconography now expands to express in remarkable detail the hallmark theme of *Late Uruk A* glyptic at Susa, workers engaged in various production activities.

In an ambitious and important article, Dittmann (1986b) undertook to grasp the semiotic logic and administrative function of the seal imagery within the closed system of *Late Uruk A* at Susa. He identified numerous themes and came to the reasonable conclusion that the imagery on these early documents was not meant solely to identify the administrative responsibility of individuals, but rather it served most often to represent distinct institutional players identified through iconography within a hierarchically organised administration. Dittmann (1986b) sees at Susa a three- or four-tiered hierarchy that is differentiated through the subject matter of the imagery. Top-tier subjects include the image of a paramount ruler, warriors, monumental structures with or without storage activities, and heraldic compositions. Middle-tier players are identified by iconic representations of their domain of responsibility (transportation, herding, manufacturing, etc.).

Dittmann (1986b) made the assumption that all of the seals used at Susa were indeed made at Susa and that the imagery on them was immediately relevant to the economic concerns of that community. He identified a small number of images as "interregional"

Figure 16.10. Seals of various types impressed on various document types from Acropole I.18. *Image references: a. Susa. Acropole I.18. Le Brun and Vallat 1978: fig. 5,1; b. Susa. Acropole I.18. Le Brun and Vallat 1978: fig. 7,1; c. Susa. Acropole I.18. Le Brun and Vallat 1978: fig. 6,11; d. Susa. Acropole I.18. Le Brun and Vallat 1978: fig. 5,2; e. Susa. Acropole I.18. Le Brun and Vallat 1978: fig. 6,13; f. Susa. Acropole I.18. Le Brun and Vallat 1978: fig. 7,3; g. Susa. Acropole I.18. Le Brun and Vallat 1978: fig. 6,12; h. Susa. Acropole I.18. Le Brun and Vallat 1978: fig. 7,2; i. Susa. Acropole I.18. Le Brun and Vallat 1978: fig. 6,6; j.i; j.ii Susa. Acropole I.18. Le Brun and Vallat 1978: fig. 6,8; 6,10; k. Susa. Acropole I.18. Le Brun and Vallat 1978: fig. 6,9; l. Susa. Acropole I.18. Le Brun and Vallat 1978: fig. 6,7; m. Susa. Acropole I.18. Le Brun and Vallat 1978: fig. 7,8; n. Susa. Acropole I.18. Le Brun and Vallat 1978: fig. 7,7; o. Susa. Acropole I.18. Le Brun and Vallat 1978: fig. 6,5; p. Susa. Acropole I.18. Le Brun and Vallat 1978: fig. 6,4; q. Susa. Acropole I.18. Le Brun and Vallat 1978: fig. 6,1; r. Susa. Acropole I.18. Le Brun and Vallat 1978: fig. 5,9; s. Susa. Acropole I.18. Le Brun and Vallat 1978: fig. 7,5; t. Susa. Acropole I.18. Le Brun and Vallat 1978: fig. 7,6; u. Susa. Acropole I.18. Le Brun and Vallat 1978: fig. 7,4; v. Susa. Acropole I.18. Le Brun and Vallat 1978: fig. 5,5; w. Susa. Acropole I.18. Le Brun and Vallat 1978: fig. 5,7; x. Susa. Acropole I.18. Le Brun and Vallat 1978: fig. 5,6; y. Susa. Acropole I.18. Le Brun and Vallat 1978: fig. 5,10; z. Susa. Acropole I.18. Le Brun and Vallat 1978: fig. 5,8; aa. Susa. Acropole I.18. Le Brun and Vallat 1978: fig. 5,4; bb. Susa. Acropole I.18. Le Brun and Vallat 1978: fig. 5,3.*

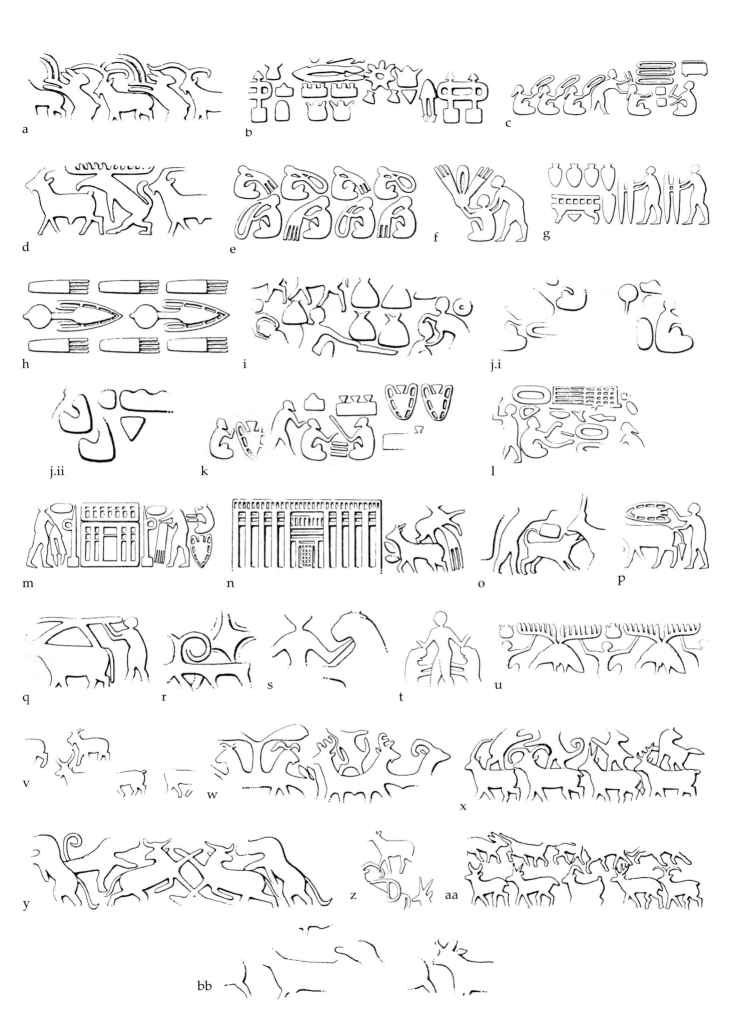

a

b

c

d

e

f

g

h

i

j.i

j.ii

k

l

m

n

o

p

q

r

s

t

u

v

w

x

y

z

aa

bb

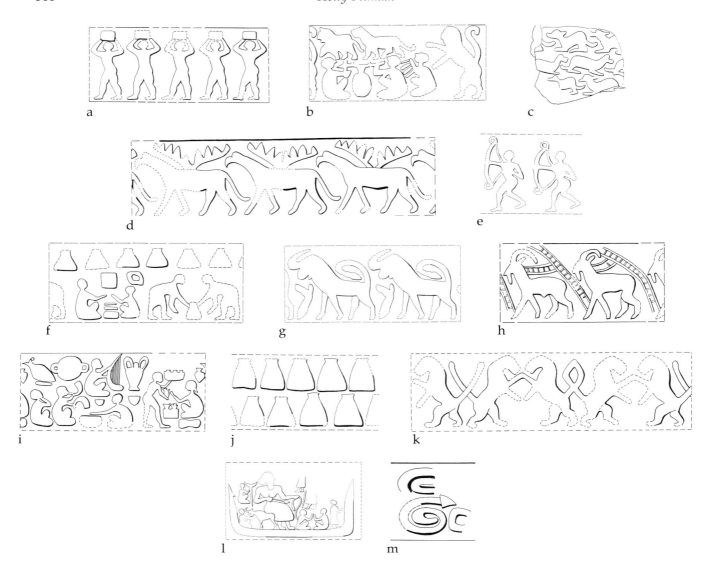

Figure 16.11. Seals of various types impressed on various document types from Chogha Mish. Image references: a. Chogha Mish. Delougaz and Kantor 1996: pl. 152F; b. Chogha Mish. Delougaz and Kantor 1996: pl. 147F; c. Chogha Mish. Delougaz and Kantor 1996: pl. 138E; d. Chogha Mish. Delougaz and Kantor 1996: pl. 136C; e. Chogha Mish. Delougaz and Kantor 1996: pl. 150D; f. Chogha Mish. Delougaz and Kantor 1996: pl. 148D; g. Chogha Mish. Delougaz and Kantor 1996: pl. 136F; h. Chogha Mish. Delougaz and Kantor 1996: pl. 143B; i. Chogha Mish. Delougaz and Kantor 1996: pl. 155A; j. Chogha Mish. Delougaz and Kantor 1996: pl. 149C; k. Chogha Mish. Delougaz and Kantor 1996: pl. 141C; l. Chogha Mish. Delougaz and Kantor 1996: pl. 151B; m. Chogha Mish. Delougaz and Kantor 1996: pl. 142C.

observing that they occur not only at Susa but also at Uruk, Habuba Kabira, and Jebel Aruda (Dittmann 1986b: 336). Inexplicably, he included in this category only caprid animal files with commodities (Fig. 16.12/a.i–vi) and snake-necked felines heraldically composed (Fig. 16.12/b.i-iv). While those two themes are indeed shared (unevenly) across these sites, there are in fact a much larger number of shared images that should be considered in a comparison that attempts to differentiate "interregional" from regional *Uruk* iconographies and to detect possible trajectories of interaction.

Indeed, as Boehmer (1999) illustrates (but does not explicitly discuss), virtually all of the images found in *Eanna V–IVb* can be included in the "interregional" category as they are found not only at Susa and Chogha Mish, but also frequently at *Uruk* period sites in the Middle Euphrates and Jezira. Processions of nude males carrying commodities (Fig. 16.13/a.i, ii), perhaps towards a structure, are known at Susa, beginning in the baggy phase (i.e. *Acropole I.20*) and continuing into the later phase (i.e. *Acropole I.19–18*), and are also common at Chogha Mish (Fig. 16.13/a. iii). In the upper Euphrates region such processions

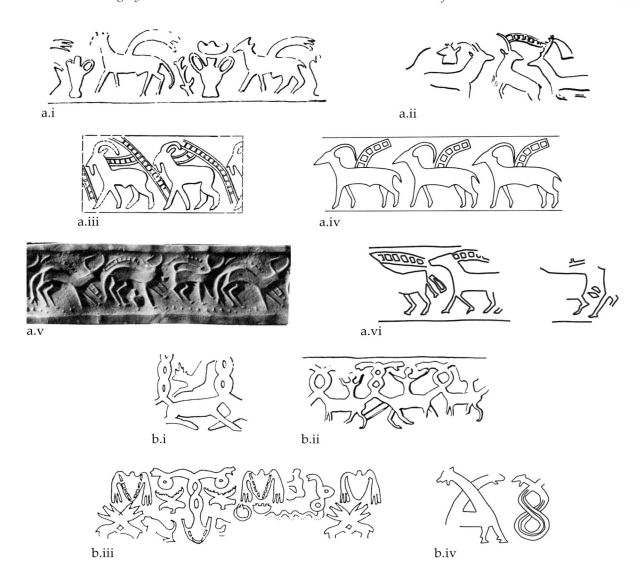

Figure 16.12. "Interregional motifs" as characterised by Dittmann, including: a. caprid animal files with commodities; b. snake-necked felines heraldically composed. Image references: a.i. Uruk. Boehmer 1999: Abb. 35A–G; a.ii. Susa. Amiet 1972: pl. 8:528; a.iii. Chogha Mish. Delougaz and Kantor 1996: pl. 143B; a.iv. Jebel Aruda. van Driel 1983: 39, n.5.; a.v. Habuba Kabira. Hammade 1994: 27, no. 289; a.vi. Tell Brak. TW level 12. 10278. unpublished drawing by author; b.i. Uruk. Boehmer 1999: Abb 34,1 A–B; b.ii. Susa. Amiet 1972: pl. 5. 475; b.iii. Habuba Kabira. Boehmer 1999: Abb. 117d; b.iv. Tell Brak TW level 12. 10172/TB 19068. Unpublished drawing by author.

are known from Jebel Aruda (Fig. 16.13/a.iv), Habuba Kabira (Fig. 16.13/a.v), Sheik Hassan (Fig. 16.13/a.vi), Hacınebi (Fig. 16.13/a.vii), and Tell Brak (Fig. 16.13/a.viii). Scenes of warfare are rare outside Uruk (Fig. 16.13/b.i), although they are certainly present at Susa (Fig. 16.13/b.ii), Chogha Mish (Fig. 16.13/b.iii), and Habuba Kabira (Fig. 16.13/b.iv). Compositions of heraldic animals, especially felines, appear at almost every site (Fig. 16.13/c.i–vii), as do compositions of animals with commodities or human handlers (Fig. 16.13/d.i–v), scenes of master of animals are limited to Uruk and Susiana (Fig. 16.13/e.i–iii), while files of large, sculptural felines and bulls (Fig. 16.13/f.i–vi), and rows of handled vessels with textiles emerging from their mouths (Fig. 16.13/g.i–vi) are widely distributed. Even the image of the priest-king is seen at Uruk (Fig. 16.13/h.i) but is also distributed far and wide, including Susa (Fig. 16.13/h.ii), Chogha Mish (Fig. 16.13/h.iii), Habuba Kabira (Fig. 16.13/h.iv), and Tell Brak (Fig. 16.13/h.v), though it always appears in very small numbers. In addition to the shared imagery carried on clay sealings or numerical tablets, the seal-impressed hollow clay balls found in a cache in *Eanna IVb* (as noted above, Fig. 16.6) carry

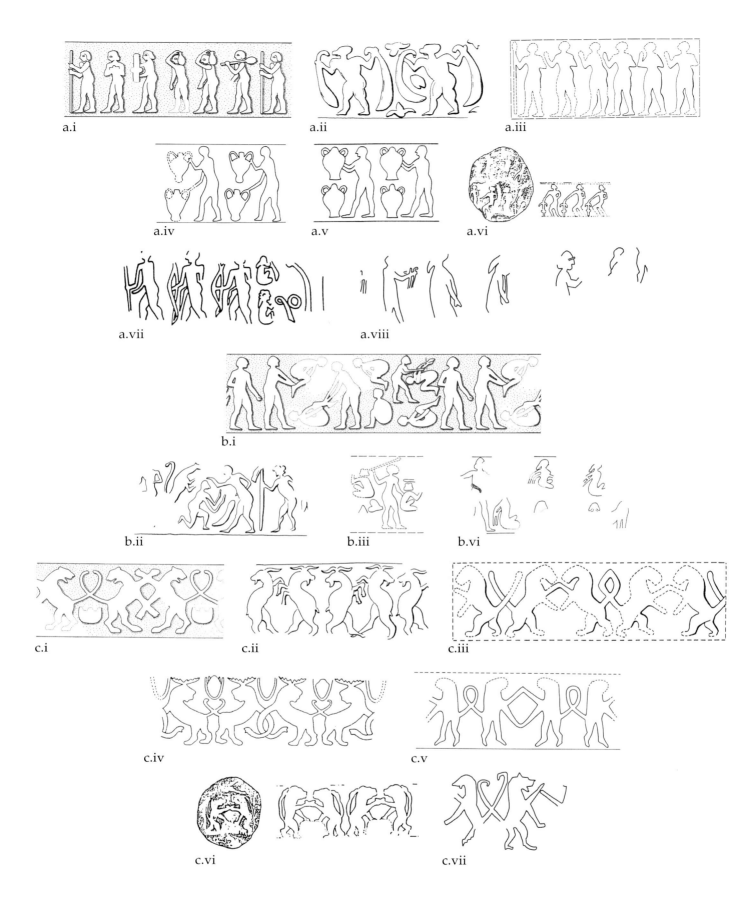

Figure 16.13. Expanded "Interregional motifs" from various sites (full caption on page 312).

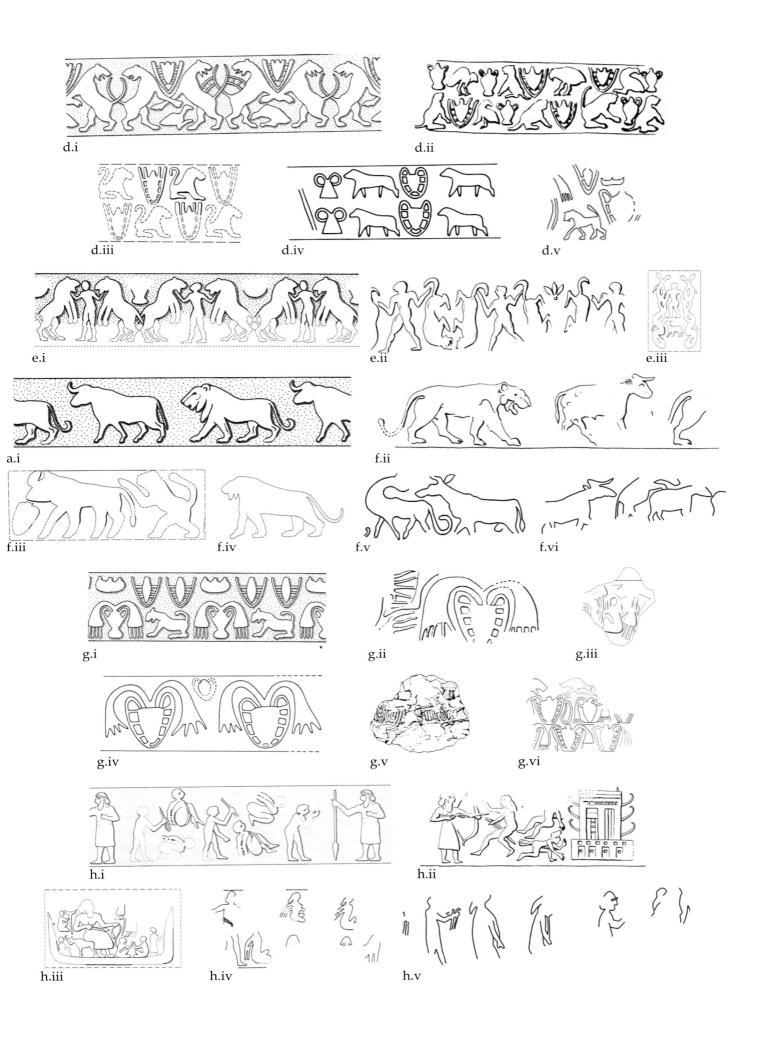

d.i

d.ii

d.iii

d.iv

d.v

e.i

e.ii

e.iii

a.i

f.ii

f.iii

f.iv

f.v

f.vi

g.i

g.ii

g.iii

g.iv

g.v

g.vi

h.i

h.ii

h.iii

h.iv

h.v

Figure 16.13. Expanded "Interregional motifs" from various sites showing: a.i–viii. procession of nude males carrying commodities; b.i–vi. warfare; c.i–vii. heraldic animals; d.i–v. animals with commodities; e.i–iii. master of animals; f.i–vi. files of large, sculptural felines and bulls; g.i–vi. rows of handled vessels with textiles emerging from their mouths; h.i–v. the priest-king. Image references: a.i. Uruk. Boehmer 1999: tf. 3, Nr. 1A-E; a.ii. Susa. Amiet 1972: pl. 13, 598; a.iii. Chogha Mish. Delougaz and Kantor 1996: pl. 152 A; a.iv. Jebel Aruda. van Driel 1983: pl. 45, 19a; a.v. Habuba Kabira. Strommenger 1980: 62 abb. 55; a.vi. Sheik Hassan. Boese 1995: 104, Abb. 8 c; a.vii. Hacınebi. Pittman 1999: 49, fig. 3,5; a.viii. Tell Brak. TW level 12. 10245. Unpublished, drawing by author; b.i. Uruk. Boehmer 1999: tf. 22 Nr. 6A-E; b.ii. Susa. Amiet 1972: pl. 19, 701; b.iii. Chogha Mish. Delougaz and Kantor 1996: pl. 150F; b.iv. Habuba Kabira. Boehmer 1999: Abb. 122h; c.i. Uruk. Boehmer 1999: Abb 28A-G; c.ii. Susa. Amiet 1972: pl. 4, 464; c.iii. Chogha Mish. Delougaz and Kantor 1996: pl. 141 C; c.iv. Habuba Kabira: TK; c.v. Jebel Aruda. van Driel 1983: 52, n. 32; c.vi. Sheik Hassan. Boese 1995: 104, fig. 8 d; c.vii. Tell Brak. TW level 12. 10203 TB 19074. Unpublished drawing by author; d.i. Uruk. Boehmer 1999: tf. 46, Nr. 17A-N; d.ii. Susa. Amiet 1972: pl. 8, 536; d.iii. Chogha Mish. Delougaz and Kantor 1996: pl. 147A; d.iv. Jebel Aruda. van Driel 1983: 42, n. 15; d.v. Tell Brak. TW level 12. 10049 TB 19032. Unpublished drawing by author; e.i. Uruk. Boehmer 1999: tf. 42, Nr. 14A-D; e.ii. Susa. Amiet 1972: pl. 13, 597; e.iii. Chogha Mish. Delougaz and Kantor 1996: pl. 158A; f.i. Uruk. Boehmer 1999: tf. 75, Nr. 22 A-G'''; f.ii. Susa. Amiet 1972: pl. 6, 493; f.iii. Chogha Mish. Delougaz and Kantor 1996: pl. 139D; f.iv. Jebel Aruda. van Driel 1983: 49, n. 26; f.v. Hacinebi. Pittman 1999: 49, fig. 3,4; f.vi. Tell Brak. TW level 12. 12015 TB 21071. Unpublished drawing by author; g.i. Uruk. Boehmer 1999: Abb 33 a-b; g.ii. Susa. Amiet 1972: pl 15, 633; g.iii. Chogha Mish. Delougaz and Kantor 1996:147B; g.iv. Jebel Aruda. van Driel 1983: 48, n. 24; g.v. Tell Qannas. Boehmer 1999: Abb. 24t; g.vi. Tell Brak. Boehmer 1999: Abb. 24u; h.i. Uruk. Boehmer 1999: tf. 17, Nr. 4A-L; h.ii. Susa. Amiet 1972: pl. 18, 695; h.iii. Chogha Mish. Delougaz and Kantor 1996: pl. 151 B; h.iv. Habuba Kabira. Boehmer 1999: Abb. 122h; h.v. Tell Brak. TW level 12. 10245. Unpublished drawing by author.

seal imagery (rows of caprids; heraldic felines; animal combat; human processions; master of animals) that is so closely paralleled at both Susa and Chogha Mish that Boehmer (1999) suggested that these documents might have been imported from Susiana. This attractive suggestion, however, is not supported by the results of neutron activation analysis, which indicates that hollow clay balls from Uruk (Margareta van Ess, personal communication) and the one from Hacınebi (Blackman 1999) were all made from clays local to each site. From the current evidence, we can thus conclude that while themes are differentially distributed, *all* of the seal imagery found at *Eanna V* and *IVb* belongs to an "interregional" repertory. Indeed, it is only in Susiana that both great diversity and regional specificity of imagery can be seen.

It is impossible in the *Eanna V* and *IVb* material to differentiate administrative patterns of use among the seal images. At Susa and Chogha Mish, however, all but one of these "interregional" images are found across functions and are most frequently impressed on administrative documents, such as fusiform tags, hollow clay balls, or early numerical tablets. The one theme that is only impressed (with one exception [Amiet 1972: no. 511]) on container sealings and not on documents is the caprid associated with the fringed textile (Fig. 16.12/a.i–vi). In Dittmann's hierarchy this theme is at the lowest level in the administrative ranking, denoting pastoral activities connected with textile production. It is possible that the kind of labour and product associated with the caprid and textile was not subject to the same accounting procedures as the manufacturing of

goods or the movement of grain. The commonality of use that excludes documents in favour of control of storage could reflect the distinct character of pastoral production, rather than a lower position in a hierarchy of administrators.

Other themes at Susa *Acropole I: Levels 19–18* and Chogha Mish

Because Dittmann's treatment of the administrative function of the iconography of Susa is comprehensive, for this study it is useful simply to emphasise that in addition to the "interregional" themes present at Uruk, there exists a large thematic category of workers that appears in numerous examples only in *Late Uruk A* at Susa and Chogha Mish. Apart from porters and warriors, only two or three examples of a seated worker are documented from Eanna. As the survey below will show, the theme is equally rare at sites in the Middle Euphrates and the Jezira.

Worker images

The theme that dominates the imagery at Susa, Chogha Mish, and Tepe Sharafabad during the *Middle* and *Late Uruk A* phases is variations on the image of the worker. Dittmann (1986b) treats these images as denoting sectors of the administered economic activity. The level of detail, the coherence, and the legibility of these images make these scenes the easiest to "decode", providing a visual window into the economic activities subject to administrative controls.

Worker seated – manufacturing scene

In various scenes, the worker is shown either seated usually on the ground, with one knee raised (Fig. 16.14). Seated workers are known through impressions at every *Uruk* site with glyptic, but they are rare except at Susa and Chogha Mish, where workers are shown engaged with jars of various shapes (Fig. 16.14/a) or with textiles or leather (Fig. 16.14/b). The workers can be female, denoted by a pigtail and a dress (Fig. 16.14/c), or male, shown bald and naked. These seals are often schematic and are closely related to the drilled-style seals that were early on associated exclusively with the *Jamdet Nasr* period because so many of them were found at that site (Mackay 1931). Susa has a number of actual seals showing pigtailed ladies with pots (Fig. 16.14/d), but never with textiles. At Chogha Mish several pigtailed lady seals are impressed on sealings.

In contrast to more than 100 images of workers known at Susa and Chogha Mish, at Uruk only three images of workers are known. One of the hollow clay balls is impressed with a stamp seal showing a single kneeling worker (Fig. 16.15/a.i). A second is carried on an impression of a cylinder seal on a tablet from *Eanna Level IVa* (Fig. 16.15/a.ii), and the third is found together with a procession of males carrying leather also on a hollow clay ball (Fig. 16.15/a.iii). At Tell Brak one seal preserved in many impressions shows females and males with textiles and jars (Fig. 16.15/b); at Habuba Kabira two impressions and five drilled-style seals carry images of workers (Fig. 16.15/c.i–vii); at Jebel Aruda four impressions preserve images of kneeling workers manipulating with pots or vegetation (Fig. 16.15/d.i–iv); at Sheik Hassan a hollow clay ball is impressed with workers with vessels (Fig. 16.15/e); and at Hacınebi two fragmentary impressions, perhaps from the same seal, show workers (Fig. 16.15/ f.i–ii).

Workers at granary

Granary scenes are concentrated in Susiana (Fig. 16.16/a, b). Susa has the most variety among the 14 granary scenes, including ones showing men filling sacks of grain and loading the grain into the domical granary (Fig. 16.16/a.i–xiv). In several examples, the scene of administration (see below) indicates that accounting is taking place in the context of grain distribution or storage (e.g. Fig. 16.16/a.i–iii). In one elaborate scene, a combat between heroes and felines separated by a snake twist is located next to a granary (Fig. 16.16/a.ix). At Chogha Mish a smaller number (four) showing similar diversity are documented (Fig. 16.16/b.i–iv). The only examples documented outside of Susiana were found at at Hacınebi Tepe (Fig. 16.16/c.i, ii).

Administrative activity

The same distribution holds for another distinctive *Uruk*-period glyptic theme, the representation of the act of administration. In a separate article I drew together the evidence for the interpretation of these distinctive scenes as administration (Pittman 1993). Significantly, I believe, it is known at Susa in multiple industries including textile and leather production, granary work, animal husbandry, and vessel manufacture (Fig. 16.17/a–r). Like many other scenes, it is carried over into the *Proto-Elamite* glyptic imagery, showing again the continuity of the Iranian elements through time (Pittman 1993). Chogha Mish has five scenes of administration, two of which are clearly associated with grain and granaries (Fig. 16.17/s–w). Outside Susiana, only Hacınebi has produced a fragmentary example of what may be an administrative scene (Fig. 16.15/f.i).

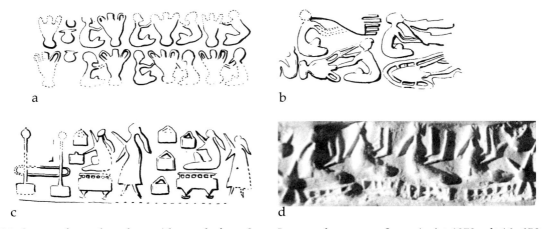

a   b

c   d

Figure 16.14. Scenes of seated workers with vessels from Susa. Image references: a. Susa. Amiet 1972: pl. 16, 650; b. Susa. Amiet 1972: pl. 15, 642; c. Susa. Amiet 1972: pl. 17, 674; d. Susa. Amiet 1972: pl. 90, 728.

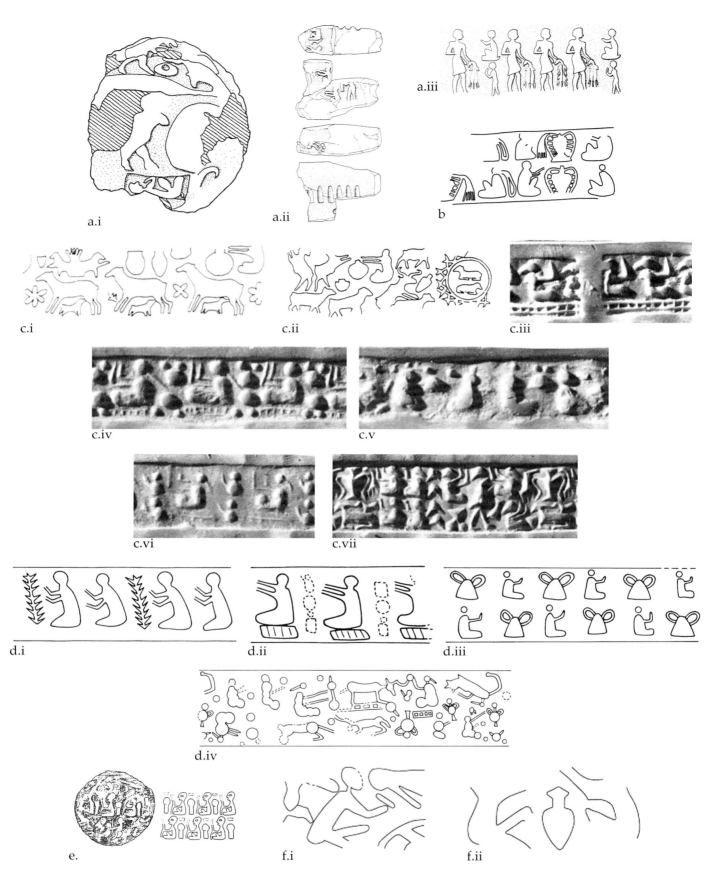

a.i a.ii a.iii b

c.i c.ii c.iii

c.iv c.v

c.vi c.vii

d.i d.ii d.iii

d.iv

e. f.i f.ii

Figure 16.15. Scenes of seated workers from: a. Uruk; b. Tell Brak; c. Habuba Kabira; d. Jebel Aruda; e. Sheik Hassan; f. Hacınebi. Image references: a.i. Uruk. Boehmer 1999: tf. 81, Nr. 30l; a.ii. Uruk. Boehmer 1999: Abb 63 a-d; a.iii. Uruk. Boehmer 1999: tf. 96. Nr. 49 a-d; b. Tell Brak. TW level 12. 10130 TB 19052. Unpublished drawing by author; c.i. Habuba Kabira. Boehmer 1999: Abb XIX; c.ii. Habuba Kabira. Boehmer 1999: Abb 117e; c.iii. Habuba Kabira. Hammade 1994: 31, n. 298; c.iv. Habuba Kabira. Hammade 1994: 32, n. 300; c.v. Habuba Kabira. Hammade 1994: 33, n. 299; c.vi. Habuba Kabira. Hammade 1994: 33, n. 301; c.vii. Habuba Kabira. Hammade 1994: 33, n. 302 ; d.i. Jebel Aruda. van Driel 1983: 46, no. 21; d.ii. Jebel Aruda. van Driel 1983: 47, no. 22; d.iii. Jebel Aruda. van Driel 1983: 47, no. 23; d.iv. Jebel Aruda. van Driel 1983: p 36, no. 2; e. Sheik Hassan. Boese 1995: 104. Abb. 8b; f.i-ii. Hacinebi, unpublished drawings by author.

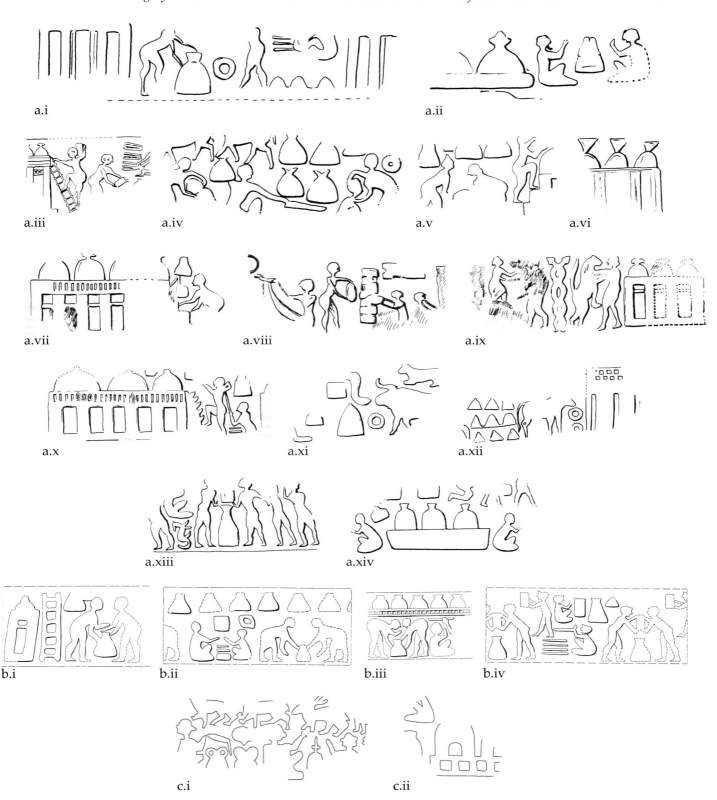

Figure 16.16. Scenes of granaries from: a.i–xiv. Susa; b.i–iv; c. i–ii. Hacınebi. Image references: Image references: a.i. Susa. Amiet 1972: pl. 16, 657; a.ii. Susa. Amiet 1972: pl. 16, 656; a.iii. Susa. Amiet 1972: pl. 16, 663; a.iv. Susa. Acropole I.18. Le Brun and Vallat 1978: fig. 6,6; a.v. Susa. Amiet 1972: pl. 16, 662; a.vi. Susa. Amiet 1972: pl. 16,658; a.vii. Susa. Amiet 1972: pl. 16, 661; a.viii. Susa. Amiet 1972: pl. 17, 669; a.ix. Susa. Amiet 1972: pl. 16, 659; a.x. Susa. Amiet 1972: pl. 16, 660; a.xi. Susa. Amiet 1972: pl. 16, 653; a.xii. Susa. Amiet 1972: pl. 16 652; a.xiii. Susa. Amiet 1972: pl. 16, 655; a.xiv. Susa. Acropole I.17B. Le Brun 1978: fig. 10,2; b.i. Chogha Mish. Delougaz and Kantor 1996: pl. 149 A; b.ii. Chogha Mish. Delougaz and Kantor 1996: pl. 148 D; b.iii. Chogha Mish. Delougaz and Kantor 1996: pl. 149 B; b.iv. Chogha Mish. Delougaz and Kantor 1996: pl. 148 B; c.i. Hacınebi/ Pittman 1999: 49 fig. 3,8; c.ii. Hacınebi. Pittman 1999: 49. fig. 3,7.

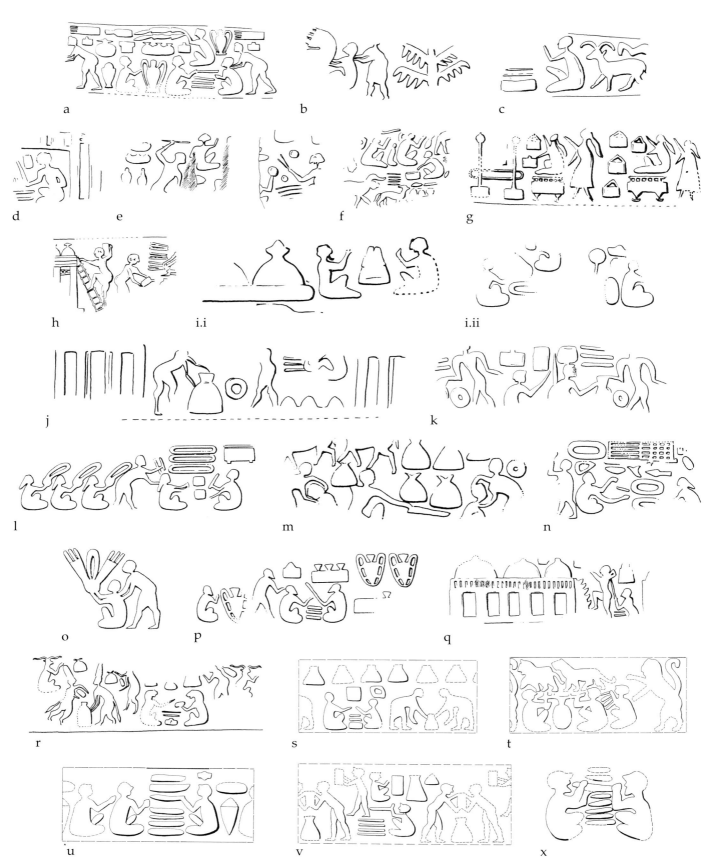

Figure 16.17. Scenes of workers and administration from Susa a–r; Chogah Mish; s–x. Image references: a. Susa. Amiet 1972: pl. 15, 646; b. Susa. Amiet 1972: pl. 15, 647; c. Susa. Amiet 1972: pl. 11, 575; d. Susa. Amiet 1972: pl. 15, 639; e. Susa. Amiet 1972: pl. 17, 664; f. Susa. Amiet 1972: pl. 15, 637; g. Susa. Amiet 1972: pl. 17, 674; h. Susa. Amiet 1972: pl. 16, 663; i.i. Susa. Amiet 1972: pl. 16, 656; i.ii. Susa. Acropole I:18. Le Brun and Vallat 1978: fig. 6,8; j. Susa. Amiet 1972: pl. 16, 657; k. Susa. Amiet 1972: pl. 16, 654; l. Susa. Acropole I.18. Le Brun and Vallat 1978: fig. 6,11; m. Susa. Acropole I.18. Le Brun and Vallat 1978: fig.6,6; n. Susa. Acropole I.18. Le Brun and Vallat 1978: fig. 6,7; o. Susa. Acropole I.18. Le Brun and Vallat 1978: fig. 7,3; p. Susa. Acropole I.18. Le Brun and Vallat 1978: fig. 6,9; q. Susa. Amiet 1972: pl. 16, 660; r. Susa. Amiet 1972: pl. 17, 680; s. Chogha Mish. Delougaz and Kantor 1996: pl. 148D; t. Chogha Mish. Delougaz and Kantor 1996: pl. 147F; u. Chogha Mish. Delougaz and Kantor 1996: pl. 148A; v. Chogha Mish. Delougaz and Kantor 1996: pl. 148B; x. Chogha Mish. Delougaz and Kantor 1996: pl. 148E.

Workers Seated – with animals (herding)

Also common in Susiana is the worker seated on the ground with one knee up among domesticated animals, probably depicting the animal husbandry sector of the economy. This theme has a far more narrow distribution, however. Only one example comes from the *Acropole I* sounding (Fig. 16.18/a.i), which can be combined with less than 10 images from the unstratified material from Susa (Fig. 16.18/a.ii–ix). Two additional scenes (Fig. 16.18/a.x–xi) show animals associated with a scene of administration, certainly a different moment in the economic process. At

Chogha Mish, two scenes show humans with animals in the field, and two show animals together with administration (Fig. 16.18/b.i–iv). It is significant that all of the animal groups are mixed and can combine various types of caprids with boars, bovids, and even felines. Furthermore, herding dogs, identified by their upward curled tails, often accompany the human minder (Fig. 16.18/a.v). Outside Susiana, one example of a seated worker with animals is recorded at Tell Brak (Fig. 16.19/a) and another from Habuba Kabira (Fig. 16.19/b).

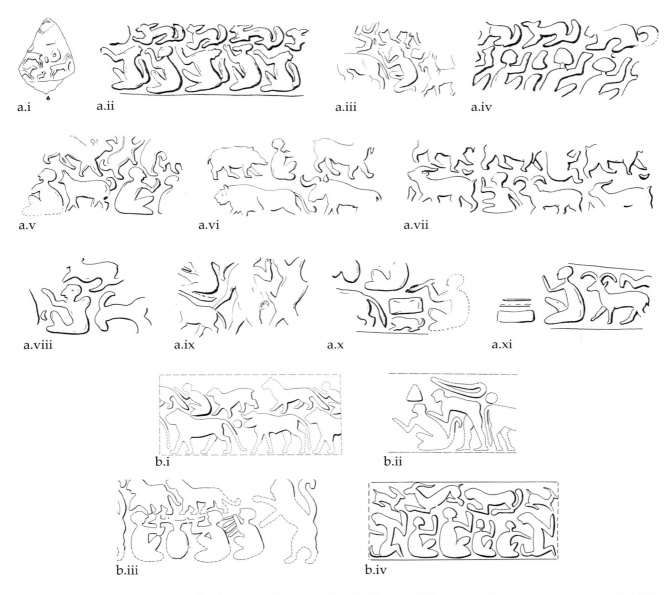

Figure 16.18. Scenes of workers and animals from Susa a.i–xi; b.i–iv Chogha Mish. Image references: a.i. Susa. Acropole I.17A. Le Brun 1971: fig. 44,6; a.ii. Susa. Amiet 1972: pl. 11, 565; a.iii. Susa. Amiet 1972: pl.11, 572; a.iv. Susa. Amiet 1972: pl. 10, 562; a.v. Susa. Amiet 1972: pl. 11, 570; a.vi. Susa. Amiet 1972: pl. 9, 549; a.vii. Susa. Amiet 1972: pl. 10, 552; a.viii. Susa. Amiet 1972: pl. 11, 566; a.ix. Susa. Amiet 1972: pl. 13, 594; a.x. Susa. Amiet 1972: pl. 11, 571; a.xi. Susa. Amiet 1972: pl. 11, 575; b.i. Chogha Mish. Delougaz and Kantor 1996: pl. 137 C; b.ii. Chogha Mish. Delougaz and Kantor 1996: pl. 147D; b.iii. Chogha Mish. Delougaz and Kantor 1996. pl. 147F; b.iv. Chogha Mish. Delougaz and Kantor 1996. pl. 138H.

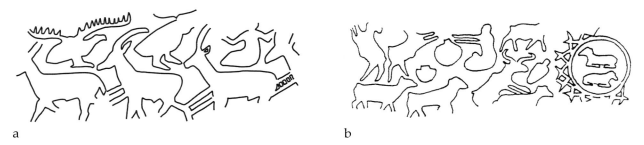

Figure 16.19. Scenes of workers and animals from a. Tell Brak and b. Habuba Kabira. Image references: a. Tell Brak. TW level 12. 10030 TB 19029. Unpublished drawing by author; b. Habuba Kabira. Boehmer 1999: Abb. 117e.

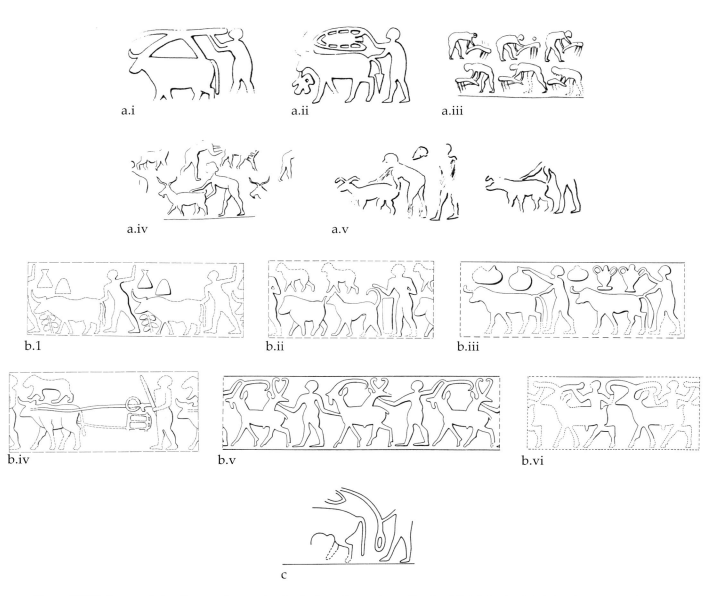

Figure 16.20. Scenes of standing workers and animals from Susa a.ic–v; Chogha Mish b.i–vi c. Jebel Aruda. Image references: a.i. Susa. Acropole I.18. Le Brun and Vallat 1978: fig. 6,1; a.ii. Susa. Acropole I.18. Le Brun and Vallat 1978: fig. 6,4; a.iii. Susa. Amiet 1972: pl. 14, 621; a.iv. Susa. Amiet 1972: pl.14, 614; a.v. Susa. Amiet 1972: pl. 14, 613; b.i. Chogha Mish. Delougaz and Kantor 1996: pl. 145A; b.ii. Chogha Mish. Delougaz and Kantor 1996: pl. 146A; b.iii. Chogha Mish. Delougaz and Kantor 1996: pl. 145B; b.iv. Chogha Mish. Delougaz and Kantor 1996: pl. 146B; b.v. Chogha Mish. Delougaz and Kantor 1996: pl. 145C; b.vi. Chogha Mish. Delougaz and Kantor 1996: pl. 145D; c. Jebel Aruda. van Driel 1983: 55, no. 39.

Standing workers in agricultural or herding scenes.

A smaller group of impressions show men hoeing, ploughing, milking, or birthing (Susa: Fig. 16.20/a.i–v; Chogha Mish: Fig. 16.20/b.i-vi,). Closely similar scenes are found only at Jebel Aruda (Fig. 16.20/c) among the *Uruk* glyptic from other sites.

It is hard to believe that the virtual absence at Uruk of the large category of worker imagery discussed above is simply an accident of retrieval. It would seem rather that during *Eanna V* and *IVb* cylinder seals were used in Mesopotamia to control different economic sectors than was the case in Susiana. To judge from the images, emphasis in Susiana is on production of commodities, while in Mesopotamia the emphasis is more on the movement of goods to an institution and on the activities surrounding the control of a workforce that was ultimately under the supervision of the paramount ruler. The frequent appearance of rampant wild animals in a heraldic formation at Uruk, Susa, Chogha Mish, Tell Brak, Sheik Hassan, Jebel Aruda, and Habuba Kabira is difficult to interpret, but following Dittmann (1986b: 337, 441), it may refer (at least at Susa) to an industrial economic unit. Unresolved is whether the heraldic imagery of rampant animals, for example, had the same exact meaning at all sites. If this were the case, it would suggest a highly integrated economic system across a huge geographic zone. It seems more likely that while the general semantic domain of such formal imagery might have been comparable or equivalent at each site, the specific institution or entity of reference was not trans-regional, but rather was local to each administrative universe.

The case of the bird-feline monster

Apart from the worker scenes, another theme that is essentially confined to Susiana is the bird-feline monster, common at Susa in *Acropole I.19–18* phase (Fig. 16.21/a.i–vi) and at Chogha Mish (Fig. 16.21/b.i–v). One example of this creature appears at Tell Qannas (Fig. 16.21/c). A different version of this distinctive image appears in *Eanna IVa*, twice on tablets (Fig. 16.22/a–b) and once in the form of the distinctive lion-headed Anuz bird on sealings (Fig. 16.22/c). Even more narrowly restricted to Susa is the continuation from the *Middle Uruk* baggy style into the *Late Uruk A* period of the strictly Iranian conceit of animals acting as humans (Fig. 16.23/a–f).

Late Uruk B and the beginning of the separation between southern Mesopotamia and Susiana

The very end of the *Late Uruk* period, when proto-cuneiform writing first appears at Uruk, marks the beginning of the profound divergence in the glyptic art between Susiana and Uruk. In both regions new themes appear. At Uruk these new images are entirely within the iconographic and stylistic conventions that we have seen develop since the *Middle Uruk* period. In Susiana, however, these *Late Uruk* themes and stylistic conventions begin to be replaced by what are clearly forerunners of images typical of *Susa III*, the *Proto-Elamite* phase. It is at this moment that all of the *Uruk*-related sites in the north-west were, like Chogha Mish, abandoned and when at several sites in Iran the new *Acropole I.17* administrative practices appeared.

Numerical tablets and the development of proto-cuneiform

Over the past 25 years, a team led by Hans Nissen, Robert Englund, and their collaborators have published in standardised drawings all of the proto-cuneiform tablets found in *Eanna IVa*. Among the approximately 5000 tablets, only one (or two) of the early numerical types known from *Acropole I.18* is known (Fig. 16.9). There are, however, about 40 numerical and numero-ideographic tablets (20 of which are seal-impressed) sharing both shape and general format with the new tablet shape introduced into the administrative toolkit at Susa in *Acropole I Level 17*. The remainder of the tablets from Uruk belong to the first phase of proto-cuneiform script, tablets of the *Eanna IVa* type (Englund 1998).

The lack of archaeological control for the tablets retrieved from Uruk is well known (e.g. Nissen 2002), and has forced epigraphers to organise their understanding of the development of the script according to formal features without reference to securely stratified provenance. In his review of the early stages of the evolution of writing Englund (1998: 50, note 98) states:

> "Until all tablets are published, and more examples from the north are unearthed, it will be difficult to state with confidence whether a preliminary categorization of these texts into early and late formats is justified. As a working hypothesis, it seems that the numerical tablets from Syria and northern Mesopotamia were of a more primitive form than most exemplars from Susiana and Uruk."

Englund here refers to the ("primitive") numerical tablet type known from Susa *Acropole I.18* (Fig. 16.9); 10 examples from the controlled excavations, plus an additional 20 examples from among the unstratified material), Habuba Kibira (15), and Jebel Aruda (nine), which stratigraphically precede the later numero-ideographic tablets. Because he does not acknowledge that this chronological sequence is clearly documented in the stratigraphy of *Acropole I*, however, Englund misses the relationship between regions that the distribution of this tablet type might reflect. In the next sentence Englund (1998: 50, note 98) goes on to observe:

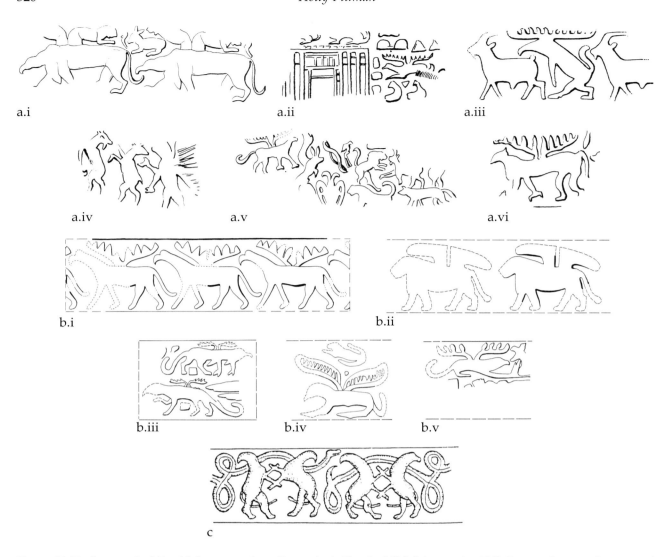

a.i

a.ii

a.iii

a.iv   a.v

a.vi

b.i   b.ii

b.iii   b.iv   b.v

c

Figure 16.21. Scenes of a feline bird creature from Susa a.i–vi, Chogha Mish b.i–v, and c. Tell Qannas. Image references: a.i. Susa. Amiet 1972: pl. 12, 581; a.ii. Susa. Amiet 1972: pl. 18, 692A; a.iii. Susa. Acropole I.18. Le Brun and Vallat 1978: fig. 5,2; a.iv. Susa. Amiet 1972: pl. 12, 586; a.v. Susa. Amiet 1972: pl. 12, 585; a.vi. Susa. Amiet 1972: pl. 12, 587; b.i. Chogha Mish. Delougaz and Kantor 1996: pl. 136C; b.ii. Chogha Mish. Delougaz and Kantor 1996: pl. 136D; b.iii. Chogha Mish. Delougaz and Kantor 1996: pl. 138G; b.iv. Chogha Mish. Delougaz and Kantor 1996: pl. 136E; b.v. Chogha Mish. Delougaz and Kantor 1996: pl. 138F; c. Tell Qannas. Boehmer 1999: Abb. 111D.

"This primitive form, attested at all sites (including an exact parallel to the Syrian documents from Uruk recently published by J. Reade, "An Early Warka Tablet," FS Strommenger [Munich 1992] 177–179 + pl. 79 [and ATU 5, pl. 121; see there p 17+26]) is characterized by a more rounded format, earlier seal motifs, and often numerical notations impressed along the edge of the tablets; note also the fact that the early tablets from Jebel Aruda…contained notations which were not in accordance with bundling rules attested both in later numerical tablets from Susa and Uruk, and in Uruk IVa period tablets from Uruk. The later [numero-ideographic] tablets were flatter, cushion-shaped, contained more structured numerical notations and later seal motifs. *This diachronic typology suggests that Late Uruk influence from southern Babylonia broke off earlier in the north than in Persia*" (my emphasis).

What Englund implies by this statement is that *both* the "primitive" numerical tablets (of the type best attested in *Acropole I Level 18* and *17B*) and the later numerical and numero-ideographic forms (known from *Acropole I.17B* and *17X/Ax* as well as other sites; see below) *a priori* must have developed first at Uruk and then appeared at other sites through the agency of "Late Uruk influence from southern Babylonia". We are left to conclude that he assumes that all things "Uruk" at Jebel Aruda, Habuba Kabira, and Susa/Chogha Mish derive from "Uruk influence from southern Babylonia," including the "primitive" tablet format. Given the virtual absence of the "primitive" tablet type at Uruk (one or two examples), and its robust and well-stratified presence at Susa and Chogha Mish, however, Englund's

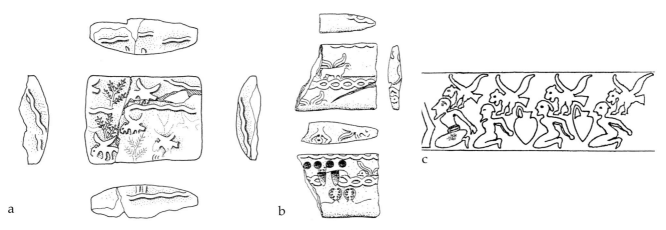

Figure 16.22. Scenes of a feline bird from Uruk. Image references: a. Uruk. Boehmer 2001: pl. 99: Nr. 13; b. Uruk. Boehmer 1999: 114, fnt 371; Abb. 105a; c. Uurk. Boehmer 1999. Abb 64A–D.

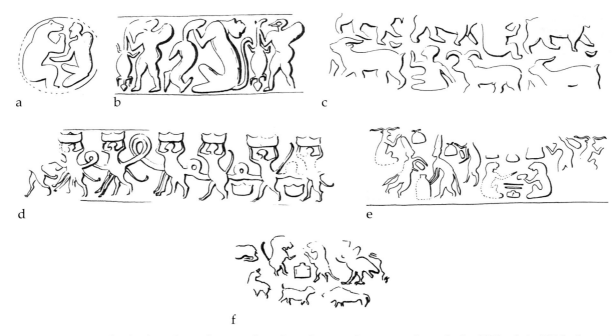

Figure 16.23. Scenes of animals acting as humans from Susa. Image references: a. Susa. Amiet 1972: pl. 4, 457; b. Susa. Amiet 1972: pl. 11, 567; c. Susa. Amiet 1972: pl. 10, 552; d. Susa. Amiet 1972: pl. 17, 679; e. Susa. Amiet 1972: pl. 17, 680; f. Susa. Amiet 1972: pl. 17, 681.

conclusion concerning its place of origin seems biased. As Le Brun and Vallat (1978) have argued, it is obvious that the "primitive" numerical tablet type developed alongside the hollow clay balls and fusiform tags that accompany it in the administrative system of Susiana. While it is possible that there was a still undocumented parallel development at Uruk, it must be acknowledged that we have yet to see any convincing evidence for it. On the basis of current evidence, it would rather be more accurate to say that this diachronic typology suggests that *Late Uruk* influence from Susiana broke off earlier

than the invention of proto-cuneiform writing proper at Uruk.

While it would be rash, without further evidence from Uruk, to give unquestionable priority to Susiana in the development of the pre-writing stages of the administrative system, it is at least clear that to date there is no incontrovertible evidence for "Late Uruk influence from southern Babylonia", but rather at best there was a parallel development in administrative technology in both Susiana and Uruk that may have begun as early as the *Early Uruk*. Furthermore, it is false to say that, "the Late Uruk influence from southern Babylonia broke off earlier in the north than in Persia". Rather, what we see is a collapse of the *Late Uruk* influence (which could have come from *either* Susiana or Uruk on the basis of the artefact assemblages) in the north-west and at Chogha Mish at some point before *Eanna IVa*. Susa is not abandoned, but at that moment of transformation in the final stage of the *Late Uruk* period, its administrative material culture displays an apparently rapid and independent evolution toward a new and distinct cultural phase (i.e. the *Proto-Elamite*) at a time essentially equivalent to the appearance of the first script at Uruk. Significantly, we see this new cultural phase expressed first and most clearly in the glyptic art, which begins to diverge from the glyptic of the earlier levels in *Acropole I.17*. This evolutionary trajectory stands in clear contrast to what happens to the *Late Uruk* visual language at Eanna where it continues an unbroken expansion into *Level IVa*.

Seal imagery from Eanna IVa

About half of the numerical and numero-ideographic tablets from Uruk are sealed, which is a far higher proportion than the dozen or so of the hundreds of tablets inscribed with *Eanna IVa* cuneiform script, suggesting that the adoption of script also saw a change in sealing practices (see also Dahl *et al.*, this volume). Unlike the earlier "primitive" numerical tablets, which are often (but not always) impressed only on the obverse, the numerical and numero-ideographic tablets are generally impressed on all of their surfaces before numbers and signs were added. Twenty-five different seals can be identified impressed on the numerical and numeric ideographic tablets from Uruk (Boehmer 1994, 1999, 2001, 2005). In at least one instance the same seal impresses both a numerical tablet and one with both numbers and signs, which allows us to be confident that both types of recording media are in use within the lifetime of one actor. There is, however, no overlap between seals impressed on these numerical type tablets and those carrying full-blown proto-cuneiform inscriptions in the *Eanna IVa* script, which, given the lack of any kind of stratigraphic control, would be the only way for us to be certain that all three tablets types were being used contemporaneously.

The seals impressed on the numerical and numero-ideographic tablets all continue in the iconographic and stylistic traditions seen in the earlier seal impressions of *Eanna Levels V* and *IVb* (Fig. 16.24). Three show animal combat scenes between felines and dogs or boars (Fig. 16.24/a–c); three show double register animals (Fig. 16.24/c–e); one shows addorsed bulls on top of a mountain with foliage (Fig. 16.24/f) while another shows calves emerging from a bier (Fig. 16.24/g). Heraldic compositions of rampant felines, confronted felines with intertwined necks, and felines rampant on a mountain are present (Fig. 16.24/h–j). A bovid is impressed on a fragmentary example, as is the facade of a temple (Fig. 16.24/k–l). As mentioned above, both the bird-feline image and the earliest image of an Anzu bird appear (Fig. 16.24/m), surely inspired from the earlier feline/bird *Mischwesen* of Susiana. Among the representations of humans, the priest-king is now shown in many more aspects than previously: as hunter; in the marshes with boar and dogs; in a boat approaching a temple; carrying a bow; holding the reins in a sledge (Fig. 16.24/n–r). Male figures are shown in procession (Fig. 16.24/s) and among bows placed horizontally (Fig. 16.24/t). One tablet carries impressions of seated and standing workers, a theme so common in Susiana and unique to this example in Uruk (Fig. 16.24/s). Another fragment is impressed with an image of vessels having textiles emerging from the mouth (Fig. 16.24/v), the first seen in *Eanna V*.

Impressed on tablets with proto-cuneiform script of the *Uruk IVa* type are 13 additional seals that include a ploughing scene (Fig. 16.25/a.i), unique at Uruk and closely comparable to a scene from Chogha Mish; and a herd associated with a bier (Fig. 16.25/a.ii), which is a scene that is never attested in Susiana. A new theme that appears is a compartmented snake interlace with single or double birds of prey (Fig. 16.25/a.iii–v), and another is a frontal monster figure mastering quadrupeds above a snake interlace (Fig. 16.25/a.vi). Four other proto-cuneiform tablets carry fragmentary impressions that seem to depict humans (Fig. 16.25/a.vii–xii). Impressed on sealings associated with *Eanna Level IVa* tablets are heraldic caprids and confronted felines with intertwined necks (Fig. 16.25/b.i–iii); single and double registers of animal files (Fig. 16.25/b.iv–v); compartmented interlace with winged

Figure 16.24. Seal impressions on numerical and/or numero-ideographic tablets found in Eanna Iva. *Image references: a. Uruk. Boehmer 1994: pl. 124h, Nr. 1; b. Uruk. Boehmer 1994: pl. 127h, Nr. 2; c. Uruk. Boehmer 1994: pl. 131, Nr. 7; d. Uruk. Boehmer 1994: pl. 135o, Nr. 8; e. Uruk. Boehmer 1994: pl. 128b, Nr. 3; f. Uruk. Boehmer 1994: pl. 129e, Nr. 4; g. Uruk. Boehmer 2001: tf. 96, Nr. 7 ; h. Uruk. Boehmer 1994: pl. 129f, Nr. 5; i. Uruk. Boehmer 2005: tf. 94, Nr. 9a-c; j. Uruk. Boehmer 2005: tf. 95, Nr. 11; k. Uruk. Boehmer 1994: pl. 138, Nr. 14; l. Uruk. Boehmer 2005: tf. 93, Nr. 6 A,B; m. Uruk. Boehmer 2001: tf. 99, Nr. 13a; n. Uruk. Boehmer 2001: tf. 97, Nr. 9; o. Uruk. Boehmer 1994: pl. 140a, Nr. 17; p. Uruk. Boehmer 2001: tf. 95, Nr. 1A-B; q. Uruk. Boehmer 2001: tf. 95, Nr. 2; r. Uruk. Boehmer 1994: pl. 140c, Nr. 18; s. Uruk. Boehmer 2005: tf. 93, Nr. 5; t. Uruk. Boehmer 2001. tf. 97, Nr. 10A-B; u. Uruk. Boehmer 1994: pl. 141, Nr. 19; v. Uruk. Boehmer 2001: tf. 99, Nr. 14.*

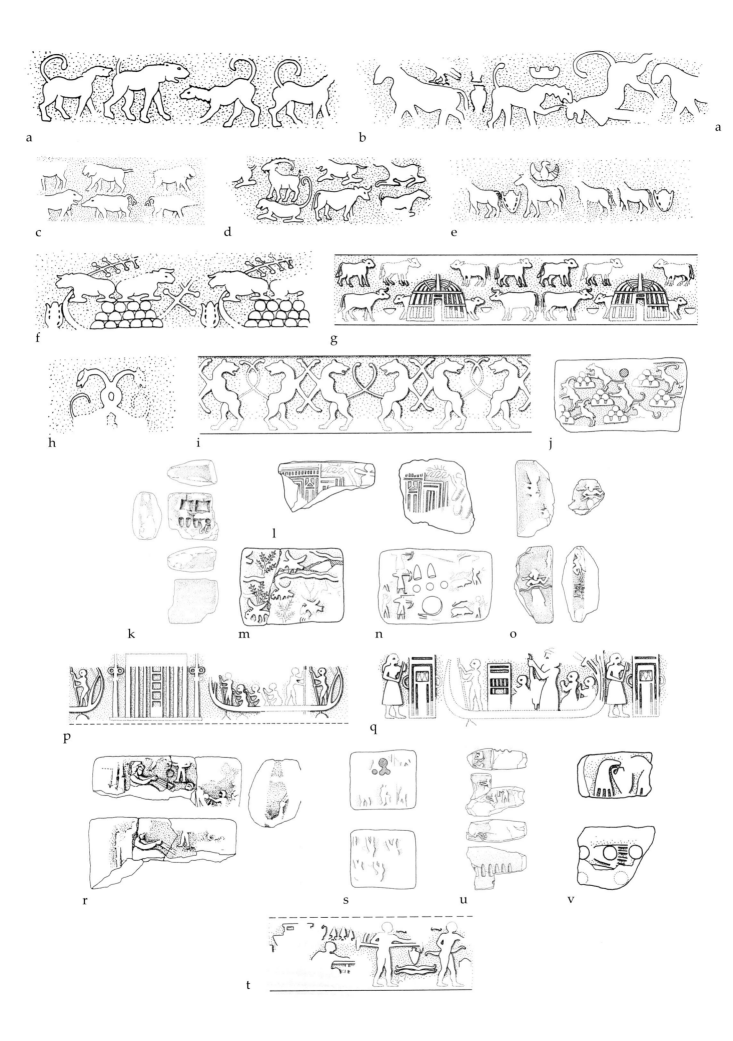

a

b

a

c

d

e

f

g

h

i

j

k

l

m

n

o

p

q

r

s

u

v

t

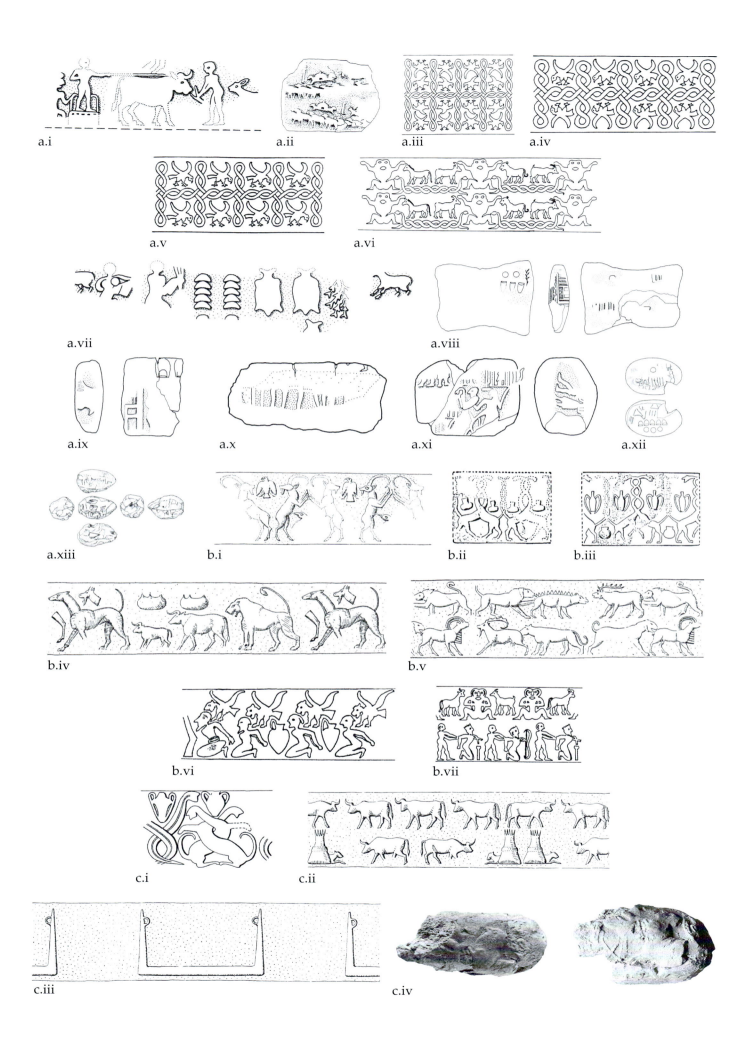

a.i

a.ii

a.iii

a.iv

a.v

a.vi

a.vii

a.viii

a.ix

a.x

a.xi

a.xii

a.xiii

b.i

b.ii

b.iii

b.iv

b.v

b.vi

b.vii

c.i

c.ii

c.iii

c.iv

Figure 16.25. Seal impressions on Uruk IVa-type tablets a.i–xiv. Eanna IVa or from Heidelberg collection; b.i–vii: scenes on sealings associated with Eanna IVa; c. scenes on sealings from levels in Anu equated to Eanna IVa. Image references: a.i. Uruk. Boehmer 2001: pl. 98, Nr. 11; a.ii. Uruk. Boehmer 1994: pl. 136, Nr. 9; a.iii. Uruk. Boehmer 1999: Abb 68, 3-5a-h (variant 4); a.iv. Uruk. Boehmer 1999: Abb 68, 3a-k (variant 3); a.v. Uruk. Boehmer 1999: Abb. 68, 2 A-F (variant 2); a.vi. Uruk. Boehmer 1999: Abb. 66 a-f; a.vii. Uruk. Boehmer 2001: pl. 98, Nr. 12; a.viii. Uruk. Boehmer 2001: pl. 96, Nr. 3; a.ix. Uruk. Boehmer 2001: pl. 96, Nr. 6; a.x. Uruk. Boehmer 2005: pl. 95, Nr. 14; a.xi. Uruk. Boehmer 2005: tf. 92, Nr. 3; a.xii. Uruk. Boehmer 2005: tf. 92, Nr. 2; a.xiii. Uruk. Boehmer 1994: pl. 136, Nr. 10; b.i. Uruk Eanna IVa Boehmer 1999: Abb. 60b; b.ii. Uruk Eanna IVa Boehmer 1999: Abb. 57; b.iii. Uruk Eanna IVa Boehmer 1999: Abb. 58c; b.iv. Uruk Eanna IVa Boehmer 1999: Abb. 48A-N; b.v. Uruk Eanna IVa Boehmer 1999: Abb. 52; b.vi. Uruk Eanna IVa Boehmer 1999: Abb. 64 A-D; b.vii. Uruk Eanna IVa Boehmer 1999: Abb. 65 A-C; c.i. Uruk, Anu Ziggurat. Boehmer 1999: Abb. 88 A-B; c.ii. Uruk, Anu Ziggurat. Boehmer 1999: Abb. 89 A-E; c.iii. Uruk, Anu Ziggurat. Boehmer 1999: Abb. 91 A-M; c.iv. Uruk, Anu Ziggurat. Boehmer 1999: Abb. 92a ,b.

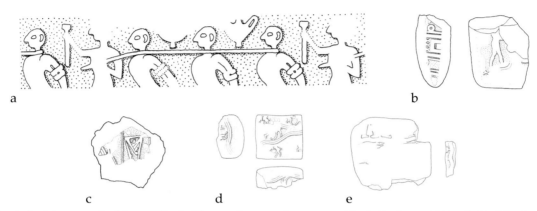

Figure 16.26. Seal-impressed tablets of Uruk III type. Image references: a. Uruk. Boehmer 2005: pl. 92, Nr. 1a-d; b. Uruk. Boehmer 2005: pl. 93, Nr. 4; c. Uruk. Boehmer 2005: pl. 93, Nr. 7; d. Uruk. Boehmer 2005: pl. 94, Nr. 10; e. Uruk. Boehmer 2005: pl. 95, Nr. 13.

birds of prey; kneeling prisoners dominated by Anzu birds in flight (Fig. 16.25/b.vi); and another frontal monster above a register of prisoners (Fig. 16.25/b.vii). From the area associated with the Anu ziggurat are four more impressions that probably belong to this phase (Fig. 16.25/c.i–iv).

While a few of these images can be compared to images from Acropole I Levels 18 or 17, many of them are elaborations on themes rendered in the modelled style typical of the "classic" Uruk glyptic art familiar from Eanna V and IVb. They are a testimony to the strength of a tradition that is firmly established, gradually evolves from its earliest attestation in Eanna V into the Jemdet Nasr phase of Uruk III (Fig. 16.26/a–e), a trend that is even more clearly manifest on the seal impressed tablets from Jemdet Nasr (Matthews 1993) and even continues into the early part of the Early Dynastic I period as attested in the Seal Impression Strata at Ur (Fig. 16.27/a–h).

Seal imagery from Susa Acropole I.17B, 17A, and the hypothetical 17X/Ax

In Acropole I.17 a different character appears in the administrative material. "Primitive" numerical tablets

of the Level I.18 type continue in diminished numbers. Three examples (Fig. 16.28/a–c) were found in Level I.17B together with a tag and a fragment of a hollow clay ball all impressed with seals (Fig. 16.28/d–e) that find close parallels in Acropole I.18. In addition to these document types that were falling out of use, 14 whole and fragmentary examples of a new shape of tablet were recovered in Level 17, six of which were seal-impressed. Vallat called this new shape of tablet a "coussinet bombe" (Le Brun and Vallat 1978), using a term that Amiet applied to similarly shaped examples from among the unstratified material from Susa (see Dahl et al., this volume). This new shape of tablet is the same as that of the numerical and numero-ideographic tablets found in Eanna IVa. It is often, but not always, impressed with one (or rarely more) cylinder seal on all its surfaces before it is impressed with numbers. The numbers are no longer placed along the edges of the tablet but are usually centred on the obverse. The reverse and the edge can also carry numerical impressions. Dahl (2005: 82) offers a tentative suggestion that the numero-ideographic tablets from Uruk and Iran can be differentiated on the basis of the arrangement of the numbers in relation to the non-numerical notation. In Mesopotamia

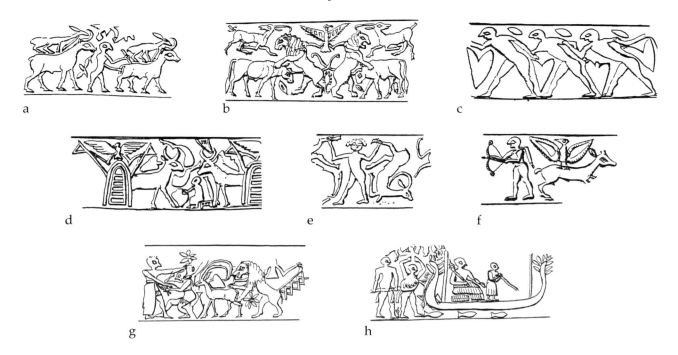

Figure 16.27. Seal imagery from Early Dynastic I *Seal Impression Strata Ur. Image references: a. Ur. SIS 4. Legrain 1936: pl. 16:308; b. Ur. SIS 4. Pit W. SIS 4-5. Legrain 1936: pl. 11:217; c. Ur. Pit Z. SIS 4-5. Pit W. SIS 4-5. Legrain 1936: pl. 17:329; d. Ur. Pit W. SIS 4-5. Legrain 1936: pl. 18:349; e. Ur. Pit W. SIS 4-5. Legrain 1936: pl. 15:294; f. Ur. SIS 4. Legrain 1936: pl. 15:288; g. Ur. Pit W. SIS 4-5. Legrain 1936: pl. 15:297; h. Ur. Pit Z. SIS 4-6. Legrain 1936: pl. 16:300.*

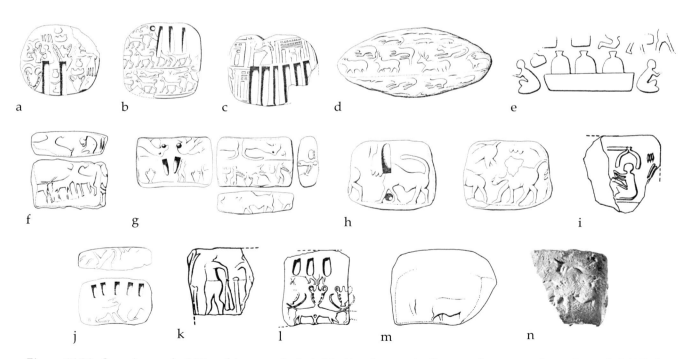

Figure 16.28. Susa Acropole I.17 *seal-impressed administrative documents. Image references: a. Susa. Acropole I.17B. Le Brun 1978a: fig. 8,5; b. Susa. Acropole I.17B. Le Brun 1978a: fig. 9,4; c. Susa. Acropole I.17B. Le Brun 1978a: fig. 9,3; d. Susa. Acropole I.17B. Le Brun 1978a: fig. 10,1; e. Susa. Acropole I.17B. Le Brun 1978a: fig. 10,2; f. Susa. Acropole I.17B. Le Brun 1971: fig. 44,8; g. Susa. Acropole I.17B Le Brun 1978a: fig. 8,6; h. Susa. Acropole I.17B. Le Brun 1978a: fig.8,1; i. Susa. Acropole I.17B Le Brun 1971: fig.44,7; j. Susa. Acropole I.17B. Le Brun 1978a: fig. 9,2; k. Susa. Acropole I.17B. Le Brun 1971: fig. 44,12; l. Susa. Acropole I.17A. Le Brun 1971: fig. 44,1; m. Susa. Acropole I.17B. Le Brun 1971: fig. 44,15; n. Susa. Acropole I.17A. Le Brun 1971: pl. 23,5.*

the number generally precedes the non-numerical notation, while in Iran the numerical notation follows the non-numeric notation. This observation can be augmented by the distinct regional character of the glyptic art carried by this particular tablet type. At Uruk, as seen above, the glyptic art is closely similar in theme and style to that carried in other formats (sealings, hollow clay balls, inscribed tablets) while at Susa, as will be illustrated in detail below, the glyptic impressed on these numerical-ideographic tablets can have a thematic and stylistic character that is distinct from that seen in *Acropole I: 19–18*.

Taken as a whole, the glyptic of *Level I.17* shows a similar transitional character to that seen in the

document types. Seal images that belong to the earlier *Level I.18* traditions are impressed on both types of tablet (Fig. 16.28/a–c, f–n). While the style of these images is consistent with earlier *Uruk* images, however, the depiction of the worker is diminished, replaced by a strong preference for animal themes. It is on both the sealings and the actual seals from *Level I.17* that entirely new imagery is introduced, which foreshadows what will becomes typical in *Acropole I.16* when the first tablets inscribed with *Proto-Elamite* signs appear. These new images include the patterns of the glazed steatite style (hourglass) (Fig. 16.29/p); geometric patterns (Fig. 16.29/o, r); an archer hunting (Fig. 16.29/n); and frontal-faced owls with signs (Fig.

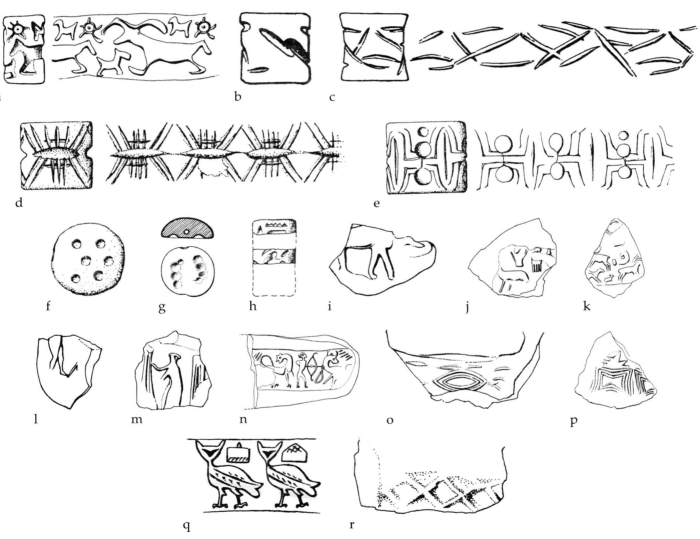

Figure 16.29. *Susa* Acropole I.17 *seals and sealings. Image references: a. Susa. Acropole I.17B. Le Brun 1971: fig. 44,5; b. Susa. Acropole I.17B. Le Brun 1971: fig. 44, 13; c. Susa. Acropole I.17B. Le Brun 1971: fig. 44, 11; d. Susa. Acropole I.17B. Le Brun 1978a: fig. 8,4; e. Susa. Acropole I.17B. Le Brun 1978a: fig. 9,1; f. Susa. Acropole I.17B. Le Brun 1978a: fig 8,2; g. Susa. Acropole I.17B. Le Brun 1971: fig. 44,17; h. Susa. Acropole I.17B. Le Brun 1978a: fig. 8,3; i. Susa. Acropole I.17B. Le Brun 1971: fig. 44,16; j. Susa. Acropole I.17A. Le Brun 1971: fig 44,10; k. Susa. Acropole I.17A. Le Brun 1971: fig 44,6; l. Susa. Acropole I.17B. Le Brun 1971: fig. 44,14; m. Susa. Acropole I.17B. Le Brun 1971: fig. 44,9; n. Susa. Acropole I.17B. Le Brun 1971: fig. 44,2; o. Susa. Acropole I.17B. Le Brun 1971: fig. 44,20; p. Susa. Acropole I.17B. Le Brun 1971: fig. 44,18; q. Susa. Acropole I.17B. Le Brun 1971: fig. 44,3; r. Susa. Acropole I.17A. Le Brun 1971: fig. 44,19.*

16.29/q). Additionally, for the first time since *Level I.21*, actual seals were found in *Level I.17*, including three geometric images (Fig. 16.29/b, c, d);; a repeating scorpion (Fig. 16.29/e); and a burnt steatite seal carrying an image of a horned animal carved with flat rather than modelled forms and a dotted circle (Fig. 16.29/a), which are both stylistic features of later Iranian glyptic. To judge from this evidence, it is clear that during *Acropole I.17* access to administrative and sealing technology was expanding to include a new type of actor in the administration, who was represented by a new visual language consisting of geometric patterns, new animal forms, and new material substrate for seals, namely burnt or glazed steatite. The fact that both types of numerical tablet found in *Level 17* are sealed with more "traditional" styles indicates that we are at the beginning of this shift in, or expansion of, administrative participation. This will change to include the new actors in the next, reconstructed phase.

In his publication of the unstratified material from Susa, which appeared before the *Acropole I* sounding confirmed Le Breton's seriation, Amiet (1972) identified a group of about 10 tablets that were impressed with numbers and sometimes also carried one or two incised signs that he concluded were earlier than the "classic" *Proto-Elamite* tablets and later than the *Uruk*-period administrative documents and seal impressions. After the *Acropole I* excavations revealed a stratigraphic sequence, and following others, Dittmann (1986a) proposed to intercalate a missing level of occupation of some undetermined length between *Acropole I.17A* and the beginning of *Acropole I.16*. He called this hypothetical level *Acropole I.17X/Ax*. It is to this phase that he assigned on typological grounds material from the poorly controlled French excavations. In 1986, Amiet further commented on his transitional tablets, linking them to the *Level 17X/Ax* proposed by Dittmann (see also Dahl *et al.*, this volume).

When examining the sealings and tablets from Susa during several research trips to the Louvre museum in the mid-1980s, I identified about 12 more seal-impressed numerical or numero-ideographic tablets that can be added to Amiet's group (Fig. 16.30). At least some of these tablets can be placed in *Level I.17X/Ax* rather than *Level I.17* because they carry a few incised ideographic signs in addition to impressions of numbers. It is certainly possible, however, that as at Uruk the numerical and numero-ideographic tablets from Susa were contemporary, as there is one instance in which the same seal impresses both numerical and numero-ideographic tablets. What matters here is that whatever their internal chronology, these tablets are no earlier than *Level I.17* and are certainly earlier than the *Proto-Elamite* tablets found in *Level I.16*, so their attribution to *Level I.17X/Ax* is appropriate. That they are precursors to *Proto-Elamite* rather than proto-cuneiform is confirmed by Dahl's criterion cited above (2005: 82; also Dahl *et al.*, this volume) that unlike proto-cuneiform, when present the ideographic sign(s) precedes the numbers on these tablets.

Certain features of the imagery of the seals impressed on these numero-ideographic tablets anticipate features typical in the *Proto-Elamite* period. Most obvious is the emphasis on the theme of horned animals but, with the notable absence of the caprids with textiles or fences in the field, is shared with the seal-impressed tablets from *Level I.17*. New is the appearance of geometric seal impressions on the tablets (Fig. 16.30/c.vi, d.i–ii, f.iv) a type of seal design that shows up in *Level I.17* only among the sealings and not on the tablets. Also new and anticipating features of the *Proto-Elamite* period, are scenes of larger and smaller animals (Fig. 16.30/b.i–iii, c.iv, e.ii), a pictorial effect that Amiet (1986) suggests is meant to denote perspective; highly elaborated animal horns and body hair (Fig. 16.30/b.iii); an eye as a drilled depression with a central dot (Fig. 16.30/e.iii); a drilled dot surrounded by drillings (Fig. 16.30/d.iii); a cross (Fig. 16.30/e.ii identical to *Proto-Elamite* sign M) in the field; the highly exaggerated modelling of an animal body (Fig. 16.30/d.vii, f.iii) ; the theme of a naked archer hunting animals (Fig. 16.30/b.v–vi, c.v, d.v) – as distinct from the priest-king as hunter).

It is potentially very significant that this new phase of administrative practice is not only documented in Susiana at Susa, but also appears at Godin Tepe, Tappeh Sialk, and Tepe Sofalin (see Rothman, this volume; Helwing, this volume; Fazeli this volume; Matthews, this volume). The presence at these sites of this new phase of administrative material both in the form of numerical and numero-ideographic tablets and as cylinder seals in the new style indicates, as suggested by Weiss and Young (1975), that a new line of interaction, exclusive of Uruk and focused only on Susa had begun, one that would expand both north and east during the following *Proto-Elamite* period.

Seal imagery from Godin Tepe

Found in two rooms of the building complex of Godin Tepe *Level VI:1* were a few sealings, and 38 complete and four fragmentary tablets that are comparable in shape to the new tablet type of *Acropole I.17* (Hallo n.d.; see Rothman, this volume; Matthews, this volume). Twenty-two of these were impressed with seals, 11 of which are at least partially legible (Fig. 16.31). All of the tablets are impressed with numbers on one or both sides and frequently carry numbers as well as seal impressions along the edges. One tablet is incised with a single sign, making this group typologically equivalent to *Acropole I.17X/Ax* (Fig. 16.31/a). That it is "Iranian" and not "Mesopotamian" is confirmed by the placement of the ideographic sign before rather than after the numbers (see Dahl *et al.*, this volume).

It is notable that the seal imagery impressed on the tablets is closely comparable to that carried on the tablets from *Acropole I.17*, meaning that there is a mix of images that look back to the *Acropole I.18* themes of animal files; feline on its haunch (Fig. 16.31/a); rampant felines with tails crossed (Fig. 16.31/c); and vessel surrounded by netting (Fig. 16.31/b). Three sealings, however, are closely linked to the new seal styles seen in *Acropole I.17*. These themes include the archer hunting (Fig. 16.31/d) and dotted circles in the field (Fig. 16.31/e). One image combines early imagery of the rampant felines with intertwined tails with an undulating plant element (Fig. 16.31/f) that is entirely foreign in the *Late Uruk* seal imagery, but is common among the later *Proto-Elamite* images. These new elements are augmented, as was true in *Acropole I.17*, by the two actual seals found at Godin Tepe, one in the building with the tablets and the other in a brick of *Godin Level IV*. Both seals belong squarely to the emerging tradition of the *Proto-Elamite* (Pittman 2001, 2011). In sum, certainly the glyptic and arguably the entire administrative assemblage from Godin Tepe can best be situated within the emerging tradition of the *Proto-Elamite* (contra Matthews, this volume), and should be treated as evidence for direct contact between the lowland communities of Susa and people at the strategically located highland sites such as Godin Tepe and Tappeh Sialk.

Seal imagery from Tappeh Sialk

In his reanalysis of the stratigraphy of Tappeh Sialk *Period IV*, Amiet (1985) identified two stages: *Sialk IV₁* produced seal impressions on clay sealings as well as on numerical and numero-ideographic tablets; and *Sialk IV₂* produced one tablet inscribed with full-blown *Proto-Elamite* script. Amiet (1985) equated the earlier material with *Acropole I.17X/Ax*. The administrative material of that phase consists of 17 numerical and numero-ideographic tablets, two of which were impressed with cylinders, one with a file of horned animals (Fig. 16.32/a), and the other a composition with two registers, including felines, horned animals, and a bird griffin (Fig. 16.32/b). Ten fragments of sealings (Fig. 16.32/c) were also retrieved, all impressed with animal files, several having the distinctive central drilling surrounded by drillings familiar at both Godin Tepe and Susa. Also following the pattern of Susa *Acropole I.17* and *Godin VI:1*, the administrative toolkit from *Sialk IV₁* includes actual seals (Fig. 16.32/d) as well as sealings and tablets. One of the seals showing felines and a figure manipulating a vessel could have derived from *Acropole I.18*, whereas two others carry animals files and the Iranian dotted circle, two are geometric, and one is a horned animal with vegetation, features of later *Proto-Elamite* glyptic art that are prefigured in this transitional phase.

The evidence from Tappeh Sialk and Godin Tepe is only a glimpse of the earliest stages of the evolution of the *Proto-Elamite* in Iran. Bits of evidence are among the early materials from Nineveh, including a fragment of a seal-impressed numerical tablet and seal impressions (Fig. 16.33) (Collon and Reade 1983). The still unpublished finds from Tepe Sofalin will provide us with further evidence for this phase. To the east, at Tal-e Malyan, in the next to lowest level of Operation ABC (*BL 4A*), this phase is documented through the presence of two cylinder seals as well as a very fragmentary impression of an animal file (Fig. 16.34/a–b) which are paralleled in the glyptic of both Godin and *Acropole I.17X/Ax*.

Conclusion

The goal of this survey has been to detail the relations as reflected in the glyptic art between Susiana and the west during the *Late Uruk* period. Several features of that relationship can be drawn from this review, and while confirmation awaits further excavations at Uruk, the glyptic confirms what Butterlin (2003) observed through the ceramics. Namely, that the transition from the *Late Ubaid* to *Early Uruk* is a smooth evolution at Susa that suggests no influence from the west. Whatever the similarities between southern Mesopotamian and Susiana, they cannot be interpreted as simply a reflection of influence, or invasion or colonisation by Uruk. By the *Middle Uruk* period in Susiana the earliest evidence for what becomes a highly complex administrative system is found in the form of sealings, clay cups, and the earliest cylinder seals cut with baggy-style images. These images, preserved at Tepe Sharafabad as sealings and at Susa as seals, depict the core theme of the *Uruk* period in Susiana, namely the image of workers. This phase in glyptic development is missing at Uruk, which is surprising since the relevant levels have been revealed at least through a number of small soundings. By the early part of the *Late Uruk* in Susiana, this administrative assemblage develops into a highly integrated, complex semiotic system involving various types of documents, imagery carried on seals, and numbers. This phase is also clearly present in southern Mesopotamia, where a relatively more restricted version of the same administrative toolkit was in use.

While waiting for more robust data, the minimum conclusion that can be drawn is that the development of what is usually referred to as the *Uruk* culture in Susiana is an internally coherent local development. There is no evidence for outside influence for any element of the administrative system, including both the document types and the imagery carried on the seals. The most conservative interpretation of this situation is that there was a millennium-long period of parallel cultural evolution in southern Mesopotamia

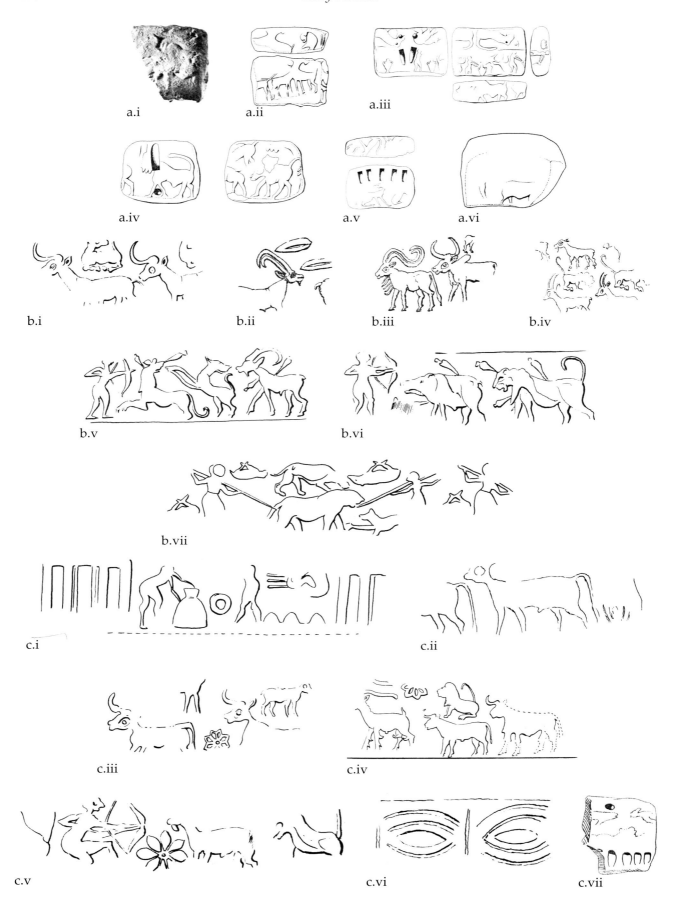

a.i a.ii a.iii

a.iv a.v a.vi

b.i b.ii b.iii b.iv

b.v b.vi

b.vii

c.i c.ii

c.iii c.iv

c.v c.vi c.vii

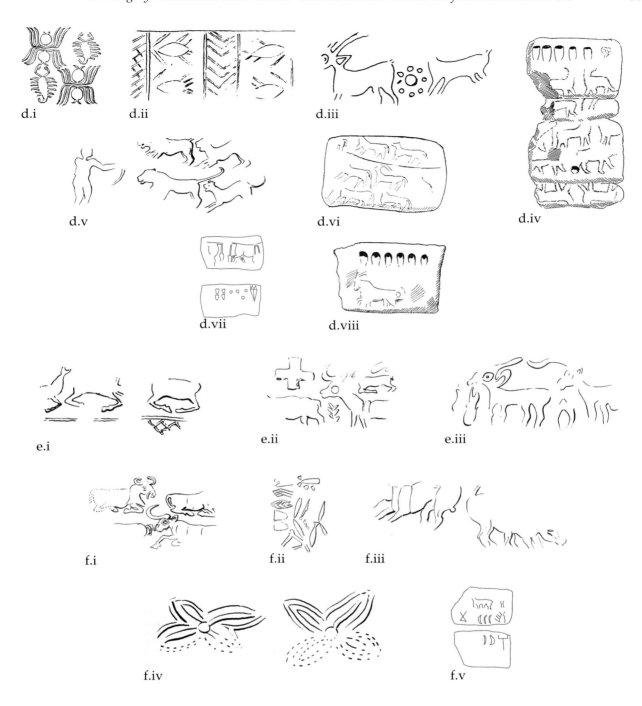

Figure 16.30. Seal-impressed numerical and numeric-ideographic tablets from Susa. Image references: a.i. Susa. Acropole I.17A. Le Brun 1971: pl. 23, 5; a.ii. Susa. Acropole I.17B le Brun 1971: fig. 44,8; a.iii. Susa. Acropole I.17B. Le Brun 1978: fig. 8,6; a.iv. Susa. Acropole I.17B. Le Brun 1978: fig. 8,1; a.v. Susa. Acropole I.17B. Le Brun 1978: fig. 9,2; a.vi. Susa. Acropole I.17B. Le Brun 1971: fig. 44,15; b.i. Susa. Amiet 1972: pl. 21, 928.; b.ii. Susa. Legrain 1921: pl. 8, 131; b.iii. Susa. Legrain 1921: pl. 8, 137; b.iv. Susa. Amiet 1972: pl. 21, 927; b.v. Susa. Amiet 1972: pl. 13, 606; b.vi. Susa. Amiet 1972: pl. 13, 600; b.vii. Susa. Amiet 1972: pl. 13, 605; c.i. Susa. Amiet 1972: pl. 16, 657; c.ii. Susa Amiet 1972: pl. 194, 2319; c.iii. Susa Amiet 1972: pl. 21, 926; c.iv. Susa Amiet 1980: pl. 33, 522; c.v. Susa Amiet 1972: pl.13, 602; c.vi. Susa Amiet 1972: pl. 194, 2320; c.vii. Susa. Scheil 1923: pl. 37, 261; d.i. Susa. Legrain 1921: pl. 28, 71; d.ii Susa Amiet 1972: pl 194, 2321; d.iii. Susa. Amiet 1972: pl 194, 2318; d.iv. Susa. Scheil 1923: pl. 4, 176 ; d.v. Susa. Amiet 1972: pl. 13, 604; d.vi. Susa. Scheil 1935: pl. 50, 453; d.vii. Susa. SB 6960 unpublished drawing by author; d.viii. Susa. Scheil 1923: pl. 2, 11; e.i. Susa. Amiet 1972: pl. 21, 931; e.ii. Susa Amiet 1972: pl. 21, 929; e.iii. Susa Amiet 1972: pl. 21, 925; f.i. Susa Amiet 1972: pl. 24, 988; f.ii. Susa. Legrain 1921: pl. 3, 52; f.iii. Susa. Amiet 1972: pl. 23, 969; f.iv. Susa. Amiet 1972: pl. 26, 1121; f.v. Susa. Sb 6364. Unpublished drawing by author.

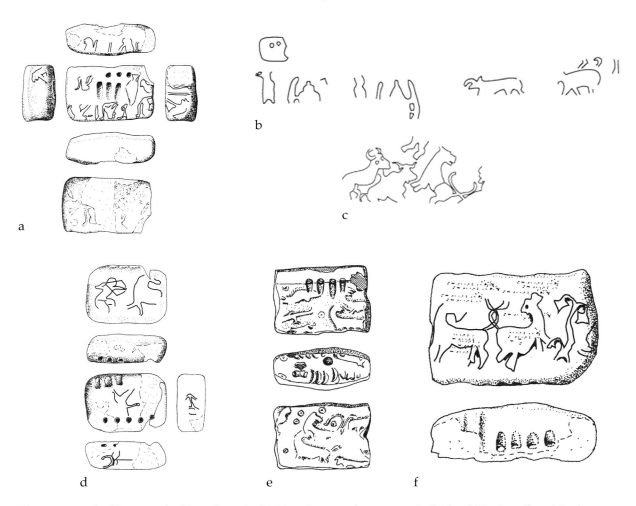

Figure 16.31. Seal impressed tablets from Godin Tepe. Image references: a. Godin level VI. Gopnik and Rothman 2011: fig. 4.43c Gd 73-295; b. Godin level VI. Gd73-161; c. Godin level VI. Gd 73-323; d. Godin level VI. Gopnik and Rothman 2011: fig. 4.43c Gd 73-320; e. Godin level VI. Gopnik and Rothman 2011: fig. 4.43b Gd 73-64; f. Godin level VI. Gopnik and Rothman 2011: fig. 4.43b Gd 73-153.

and neighbouring Susiana that reflected a period of intense contact between Mesopotamia and Susiana. The most radical interpretation would be that the material forms that define *Uruk* administrative culture, before the invention of writing at Uruk in *Eanna IVa*, were borrowed from Susiana by southern Mesopotamia.

By the end of the fourth millennium BC, the institutions and life-ways reflected by the *Uruk* material culture had become deeply embedded in southern Mesopotamia. This is particularly true of the symbolic forms, proto-writing, and imagery that go on to become foundational for the millennia of development that followed. In particular, imagery of kingship seen in *Eanna IVa* expresses *in toto* the multifaceted nature of that institution until the collapse of the Mesopotamian tradition in the middle of the first millennium BC. To judge from the administrative evidence, Susiana, on the other hand, does not follow that cultural trajectory, but instead takes a new direction, expressed administratively

through new visual imagery and for a short while a new script to convey its distinct cultural identity, which has been designated variously as *Susa III, Susa C,* or *Proto-Elamite*.

While there is no question that the administrative and textual material reflects a human community that is culturally distinct from the Sumerians of southern Mesopotamia, precisely whom this cultural phase (i.e. the *Proto-Elamite*) represents is more difficult to know. Amiet (1979) long ago argued that these new elements are the residue of powerful influence from the highlands surrounding the Susiana lowland. While this may be true, there is until now little from the highland that would support the notion that there was a burgeoning centre from which such influence emanated (see Alden, this volume). Amiet (1979) and others (e.g. Alden 1982) have previously suggested that Fars is the homeland of this new cultural element. This conclusion seems to be based on the presence of *Proto-Elamites* at Tal-e Malyan, and on the fact that in the second millennium BC Fars became the highland

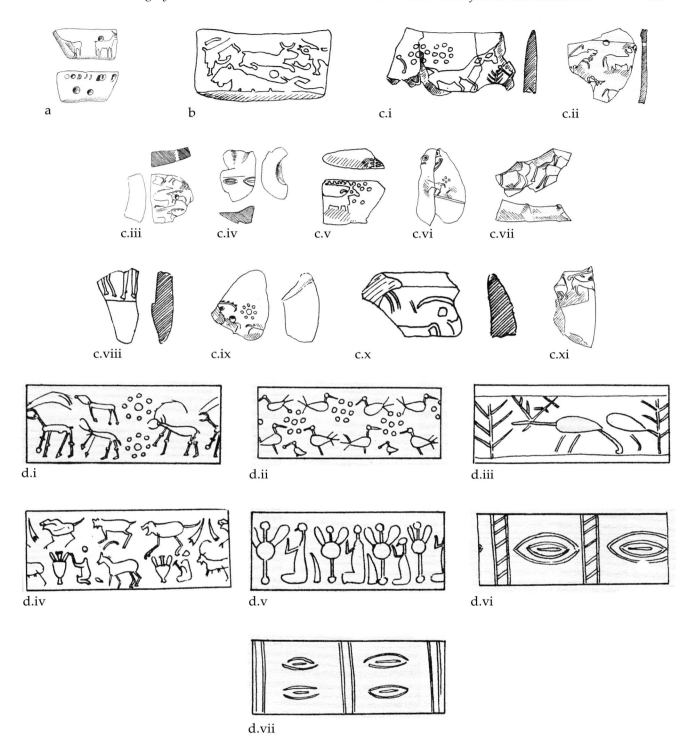

Figure 16.32. Seal impressions from Tappeh Sialk (Period IVa). Image references: a. Sialk level IVA. Ghirshman 1938: pl. 93, S. 1627; b. Sialk level IVA. Ghirshman 1938: pl. 93, S. 1628; c.i. Sialk level IVA. Ghirshman 1938: pl. 94, S. 1634; c.ii. Sialk level IVA. Ghirshman 1938: pl. 94, S, 1633; c.iii. Sialk level IVA. Ghirshman 1938: pl. 94, S. 1613; c.iv. Sialk level IVA. Ghirshman 1938: pl. 94, S, 1609; c.v. Sialk level IVA. Ghirshman 1938: pl. 94, S. 1610; c.vi. Sialk level IVA. Ghirshman 1938: pl. 94, S. 1612; c.vii. Sialk level IVA. Ghirshman 1938: pl. 94, S. 1633; c.viii. Sialk level IVA. Ghirshman 1938: pl. 94, S. 1634; c.ix. Sialk level IVA. Ghirshman 1938: pl. 94, S. 1614; c.x. Sialk level IVA. Ghirshman 1938: pl. 94, S. 1610; c.xi. Sialk level IVA. Ghirshman 1938: pl. 94, S, 1611; d.i. Sialk level IVA. Ghirshman 1938: pl. 94, S. 48; d.ii. Sialk level IVA. Ghirshman 1938: pl. 94, S, 25; d.iii. Sialk level IVA. Ghirshman 1938: pl. 94, S. 54; d.iv. Sialk level IVA. Ghirshman 1938: pl. 94, S. 79; d.v. Sialk level IVA. Ghirshman 1938: pl. 94, S. 89; d.vi. Sialk level IVA. Ghirshman 1938: pl. 94, S. 506; d.vii. Sialk level IVA. Ghirshman 1938: pl. 94, S. 42.

capital of the *Middle Elamite* polity, but nothing from within the administrative sector in the earlier *Bakun* or intervening *Lapui* phases supports this idea. The strongly geometric patterns of *Bakun* and *Lapui* glyptic (see Sardari, this volume) disappear by the mid- to late fourth millennium BC to be replaced at the end of the fourth millennium BC by the new cultural elements that evolve into the classic *Proto-Elamite*, and which is so coherently expressed in the building exposed in Operation ABC at Tal-e Malyan. To judge from the glyptic, the cultural element that develops into the *Proto-Elamite* has more in common with the stamp-seal traditions of the *Uruk* period in the Zagros Mountains where horned animals, felines, snakes, and the horned demon are at home.

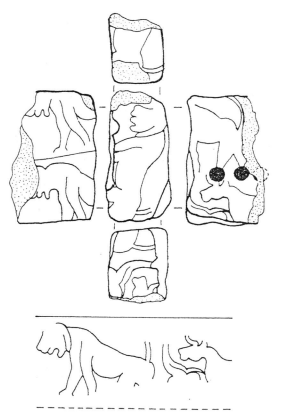

Figure 16.33. Seal impression from Nineveh. Image reference: Nineveh. Collon and Reade 1983: fig. 1.

An alternative interpretation is to see the gradual change from *Late Uruk A* to *B* as an internal one in Susiana, reflecting local adaptation to what were apparently profound challenges to the *Late Uruk* life-way that led to the destruction of Chogha Mish, the depopulation of the plain surrounding Susa, and the abandonment of *Late Uruk*-related communities along the Euphrates and in the Jezira. Establishing connections with communities in the Zagros Mountains, at Godin Tepe, along the route to the north at Tappeh Sialk and Tepe Sofalin, and also towards the east at Tal-e Malyan and Tepe Yahya, suggests that Susian relations with the outside world no longer focused on the west but focused towards the Iranian highlands both to the north and to the east.

Too often our interpretation of the early history of the ancient Near East is influenced by patterns discernible in later periods when we have a stronger grasp of intercultural dynamics. When it comes to the early periods, our Mesopotamia-centric view assumes a default position that cannot allow either the autonomy or indeed active influence of Iran in its dealings with its literate (and therefore superior) neighbour. The assumption has always been that the surrounding areas were by definition continuously under the intellectual, economic, and political sway of the powerful institutions of the Sumerians, Akkadians, Babylonians, and Assyrians. By the time we reach a period in the middle of the third millennium BC we have historical documents that spell out in words the relationship of Susiana with the west. While always a neighbour, however, Susiana and Susa are only rarely completely dominated by Mesopotamia. More often, Susiana is uniquely the closest point of contact for a competing cultural entity that was organised as a confederacy rather than a kingdom through the long years of the third millennium BC (see Potts 1999). While our knowledge of that world is still dim in the extreme, we know enough to anticipate that Iran was a full partner in the enormous cultural strides of the third millennium BC, whose foundations were undoubtedly laid in the productive synergy of the fourth-millennium BC period of social transformation.

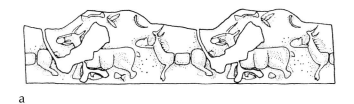

a   b

Figure 16.34. Seals from Tal-e Malyan BL.4A. Image references: a. Tal-i Malyan ABC level 4. Sumner 2003: fig. 44a; b. Tal-i Malyan ABC level 4. Sumner 2003: fig. 44b.

Bibliography

Algaze, G. 1993. *The Uruk World System – The Dynamics of Expansion of Early Mesopotamian Civilisation*, 1st edition, University of Chicago Press, Chicago.

Algaze, G. 2005. *The Uruk World System – The Dynamics of Expansion of Early Mesopotamian Civilisation*, 2nd revised edition, University of Chicago Press, Chicago.

Alden, J. R. 1982. "Trade and Politics in Proto-Elamite Iran", *Current Anthropology* 23 (6): 613–40.

Amiet P. 1972. *Glyptique susienne*, MDP 43, Geuthner, Paris.

Amiet, P. 1979. "Archaeological discontinuity and ethnicity duality in Elam", *Antiquity* 53: 195–204.

Amiet, P. 1980. *La glyptique mésopotamienne archaïque*, CNRS, Paris.

Amiet, P. 1985. "La période IV de Tepe Sialk reconsidérée", in Huot, J. L., Yon, M. and Calvet, Y. (eds), *De l'Indus aux Balkans: Recueil à la Mémoire de Jean Deshayes*, ERC, Paris: 293–312.

Amiet, P. 1986. *L'âge des échanges inter-iraniens, 3500–1700 avant J.-C.*, Éditions de la Réunion des Musées Nationaux, Paris.

Amiet, P. 1997. "L'utilisation des sceaux en Iran élamite," *Res Orientalis* 10: 11–21.

Blackman, J. 1999. "Chemical characterization of local Anatolian and Uruk style sealing clays from Hacinebi", *Paléorient* 25: 50–56.

Boehmer, R. M. 1994. "Die Siegelabrollungen auf den archaischen Tafeln der Frühen Uruk-Kamgagnen," in Englund, R. K. (ed.), *Archaic Administrative Texts from Uruk. The Early Campaigns*, Ausgrabungen der Deutschen Forschungemeinschaft in Uruk-Warka Band 17, Archaische Text aus Uruk Band 5, Von Zabern, Berlin: 25–28.

Boehmer, R. M. 1999. *Uruk: früheste Siegelabrollung*, Ausgrabungen in Uruk-Warka Endberichte Band 24, P. von Zabern, Mainz-am-Rhein.

Boehmer, R. M. 2001. "Die Siegelabrollungen auf den archaischen Tafeln der Heidelberger Sammlung", in Englund, R. K and Nissen, H. J. (eds), *Archaische Verwaltungstexte aus Uruk Die Heidelberger Sammlung*, Ausgrabungen der Deutschen Forschungemeinschaft in Uruk-Warka Band 17, Archaische Text aus Uruk Band 7, Mann, Berlin: 11–13.

Boehmer, R. M. 2005. "Die Siegelabrollungen auf den archaischen Tafeln der VAM-Sammlung II", in Englund, R. K and Nissen, H. J. (eds), *Archaische Verwaltungstexte aus Uruk. Vorderasiatisches Museum II*, Ausgrabungen der Deutschen Forschungemeneinschaft in Uruk-Warka Band 16, Archaische Text aus Uruk Band 6, Mann, Berlin: 11–13.

Boese, J. 1995. *Ausgrabungen in Tell Sheikh Hassan I. Vorläufige Berichte über die Grabungskampagnen 1984–1990 und 1992–1994*. Saarbrucker Druckerei und Verlag, Saarbrucken.

Brandes, M. 1979. *Siegelabrollungen aus den archaischen Bauschuchten in Uruk-Warka*, Freiburg Altorientalischen Studien, vol. 3, Steiner, Weisbaden.

Brandes, M. 1986. "Commerative Seals?", in Kelly-Buccelatti, M. (ed.) in collaboration with Matthiae, P. and van Loon, M., *Insight Through Images: Studies in Honor of Edith Porada*, Bibliotheca Mesopotamica 21, Malibu: 51–56.

Butterlin, P. 2003. *Les temps proto-urbains de Mésopotamie: Contacts et acculturation à l'époque d'Uruk au Moyen-Orient*, CNRS Éditions, Paris.

Collon, D. and Reade, J. E. 1983. "Archaic *Nineveh*", *Baghdader Mitteilungen* 14: 33–34.

Dahl, J. 2005. "Animal husbandry in Susa during the proto-Elamite period," *SMEA* (*Studi Micenei ed Egeo-Anatolici*) 47: 81–134.

Damerow, P. 2006. "The origins of writing as a problem of historical epistemology", *Cuneiform Digital Library Journal* (1): 1–10. [http://cdli.ucla.edu/pubs/cdlj/2006/cdlj2006_001.pdf], accessed 02 December 2012.

Delaporte, L. 1920. *Catalogue des cylindres, cachets, et pierres gravées de style oriental du musée du Louvre* vol. 1, Fouilles et missions, Paris.

Delougaz, P. and Kantor, H. 1996. *Chogha Mish: the First Five Seasons of Excavations 1961–1971*, ed. Alizadeh, A., Oriental Institute Publications 101, University of Chicago Press, Chicago.

Dittmann, R. 1986a. *Betrachtungen zur Frühzeit des Südwest-Iran, Regionale Entwicklungen vom 6. bis zum frühen 3. vorchristlichen Jahrtausend*, Dietrich Reimer, Berlin.

Dittmann, R. 1986b. "Seals, sealing and tablets", in Finkbeiner, U. and Röllig, W. (eds), *Jamdet Nasr: Period or Regional Style?* Beiheft zum Tübinger Atlas des Vorderen Orient, Band 62, Wiesbaden: 332–66.

Dollfus, G. 1977. "Djaffarabad 1972–74, périodes I et II", *CDAFI* 5: 11–120.

Eichmann, R. 1989. *Uruk, die Stratigraphie, Grabungen 1912–1977 in den Berichen Eanna und Anu-Ziggurat*, Ausgrabungen in Uruk-Warka Endberichte (AUWE 3), 2 vols., P. von Zabern, Mainz.

Englund, R. K. 1994. *Archaic Administrative Texts from Uruk. The Early Campaigns*, Ausgrabungen der Deutschen Forschungemeinschaft in Uruk-Warka Band 17, Archaische Text aus Uruk Band 5, Mann, Berlin.

Englund, R. K. 1998. "Texts from the Late Uruk period", in Bauer, J., Englund, R. K. and Krebernik, M. (eds), *Mesopotamien: Späturuk-Zeit und Frühdynastische Zeit*, Orbis Biblicus et Orientalis 160/1, Universitätsverlag Freiburg Schweiz Vandenhoeck & Ruprecht, Göttingen: 15–233.

Englund, R. K and Nissen, H. J. 2001. *Archaische Verwaltungstexte aus Uruk Die Heidelberger Sammlung*, Ausgrabungen der Deutschen Forschungemeinschaft in Uruk-Warka Band 17, Archaische Text aus Uruk Band 7, Mann, Berlin.

Englund, R. K and Nissen, H. J. 2005. *Archaische Verwaltungstexte aus Uruk. Vorderasiatisches Museum II*, Ausgrabungen der Deutschen Forschungemeneinschaft in Uruk-Warka Band 16, Archaische Text aus Uruk Band 6, Mann, Berlin.

Felli, C. 2003. "Developing complexity, early to mid-fourth millennium investigations: the Northern Middle Uruk Period," in Matthews, R. (ed.) *Excavations at Tell Brak 4: Exploring an Upper Mesopotamian Regional Centre, 1994–96*, McDonald Institute Monographs. Cambridge: 53–95.

Ghirshman, R. 1938. *Fouilles de Sialk près de Kashan 1933, 1934, 1937*, Geuthner, Paris.

Gopnik, H. and Rothman, M. eds 2011. *On the High Road: The History of Godin Tepe, Iran*, Royal Ontario Museum/Mazda Press, Toronto.

Hallo, W. n.d. "Godin Tepe: the Inscriptions", unpublished paper written at the request of T. Cuyler Young.

Hammade, H. 1994. *Cylinder Seals from the Collections of the Aleppo Museum, Syrian Arab Republic, Volume 2, Seals of known provenance*, BAR International Series 597, Oxford.

Le Breton, L. 1957. "The early periods at Susa, Mesopotamian relations", *Iraq* 19: 79–124.

Le Brun, A. 1971. "Recherches stratigraphiques à l'acropole de Suse, 1969–1971», *CDAFI* 1: 163–216.

Le Brun, A. 1978a. "La glyptique du niveau 17 B de l'Acropole de Suse, campagne 1978", *CDAFI* 8: 61–80.

Le Brun, A. 1978b. "Suse, chantier de l'acropole l", *Paléorient* 4: 177–92.

Le Brun, A. 1979. "Le niveau 17 B de l'acropole de Suse, campagne de 1972", *CDAFI* 9: 57–154.

Le Brun, A. 1985. "Le niveau 18 de l'acropole de Suse. Mémoire d'argile, mémoires du temps», *Paléorient* 11 (2): 31–36.

Le Brun, A. 1999. "Hacınebi et Suse", *Paléorient* 25 (1): 139–40.

Le Brun, A. and Vallat, F. 1978. "L'origine de l'écriture à Suse", *CDAFI* 8: 11–60.

Legrain, L 1921. *Empreintes de cachets élamites*, Mémoires de la Mission archéologique de Perse, Volume 16, Paris.

Legrain, L. 1936. *Archaic seal impressions*. Ur excavations, vol. 3. Oxford University Press.

Mackay, E. 1931. *Report on Excavations at Jemdet Nasr, Iraq*, Field Museum of Natural History Anthropology Memoirs, vol. 1, no. 3, Chicago.

Matthews, R., Matthews, W. and McDonald, H. 1994. "Excavations at Tell Brak, 1994", *Iraq* 56: 177–94.

Matthews, R. 1993. *Cities, Seals and Writing: Archaic Seal Impressions from Jemdet Nasr and Ur*, MSVO 2, Berlin.

Nissen, H. J. 2002. "Uruk: key site of the period and key site of the problem", in Postgate, J. N. (ed.), *Artefacts of Complexity: Tracking the Uruk in the Near East*, British School of Archaeology in Iraq, CUP, Cambridge: 1–16.

Oates, D. and Oates, J. 1993. "Excavations at Tell Brak 1992–93", *Iraq* 55: 155–99.

Petrie, C. A. in press. "Iran and Uruk Mesopotamia: chronologies and connections in the 4th millennium BC", in McMahon, A., Crawford, H. and Postgate, J. N. (eds), *Preludes to Urbanism: Studies in the Late Chalcolithic of Mesopotamia in Honour of Joan Oates*, McDonald Institute Monographs, Cambridge.

Pittman, H. 1993. "Pictures of an administration: the Late Uruk scribe at work", in Frangipane, M., Hauptmann, H., Liverani, M., Matthiae, P. and Mellink, M. (eds), *Between the Rivers and over the Mountains: Archeologica Anatolica et Mesopotamica Alba Palmieri dedicata*, La Sapienza, Rome: 235–45.

Pittman, H. 1994a. *The Glazed Steatite Glyptic Style, the Structure and Function of an Image System in the Administration of Proto literate Mesopotamia*, Dietrich Reimer Verlag, Berlin.

Pittman, H. 1994b, "Towards an understanding of the role of glyptic imagery in the administrative systems of protoliterate greater Mesopotamia", in Ferioli, P., Fiandra, E., Fissore, G. G. and Frangipane, M. (eds), *Archives Before Writing, Proceedings of the International Colloquium Oriolo Romano, October 23–25, 1991, Turin*, Pubblicazioni del Centro Internazionale di Ricerche Archeologiche e Storiche, Rome: 177–200.

Pittman, H. 1999. "Administrative evidence from Hacınebi Tepe: an essay on the local and the colonial", *Paléorient* 25 (1): 43–50.

Pittman, H. 2001. "Mesopotamian intraregional relations reflected through glyptic evidence in Late Chalcolithic 1–5 Periods", in Rothman, M. S. (ed.), *Uruk Mesopotamia and its Neighbors: Cross-cultural Interactions and their Consequences in the Era of State Formation*, School of American Research, Santa Fe: 403–44.

Pittman, H. 2011. "The Seals of Godin VI", in Gopnik, H. and Rothman, M. (eds), *On the High Road: The History of Godin Tepe, Iran*, Royal Ontario Museum/Mazda Press, Toronto: 113–15.

Porada, E., Hansen, D. P., Dunham, S. and Babcock, S. 1992. "Mesopotamia" in Ehrich, R. W. (ed.), *Chronologies in Old World Archaeology*, (3rd edition), University of Chicago Press, Chicago: 77–90.

Potts, D. 1999. *The Archaeology of Elam: Formation and Transformation of an Ancient Iranian State*, CUP, Cambridge.

Reichel, C. 2002. "Administrative Complexity in Syria during the 4th Millennium B.C. – the Seals and Sealings from Tell Hamoukar" *Akkadica* 123:35–56.

Rothman, M. 2002. *Tepe Gawra: The Evolution of a Small, Prehistoric Center in Northern Iraq*, University of Pennsylvania Museum of Archaeology and Anthropology, Philadelphia.

Rothman, M. (ed.), 2001. *Uruk Mesopotamia and Its Neighbours*, SAR Press, Santa Fe.

Scheil, V. 1923. *Textes de comptabilité proto-Elamites (nouvelle série)*, Mémoires de la Mission Archéologique de Perse, volume 17. Paris.

Scheil, V. 1935. *Textes de comptabilité proto-Elamites (troisiéme série)*, Mémoires de la Mission Archéologique de Perse, volume 26, Paris.

Strommenger, E. 1980. *Habuba Kabira: enie Stadt vor 5000 Jahren: Ausgrabungen der Deutschen Orient-Gesellschaft am Euphrat in Habuba Kabira, Syrien*, Philipe von Zabern, Mainz am Rhein.

Sumner, W. M. 2003. *Early Urban Life in the Land of Anshan: Excavations at Tal-e Malyan in the Highlands of Iran*, University of Pennsylvania Museum of Archaeology and Anthropology, Philadelphia.

Sürenhagen, D. 1986. "Archaische Keramik aus Uruk Warka. Erster teil: Die Keramik der Schichten XVI–VI aus der Sondagen "Tiefschnitt" und Sagengraben in Eanna", *Baghdader Mitteilungen* 17: 7–95.

Sürenhagen, D. 1987. "Archaische Keramik aus Uruk Warka", *Baghdader Mitteilungen* 18: 1–92.

Sürenhagen, D. 1999. *Untersuchungen zur relativen Chronologie Babyloniens und angrenzender Gebiete von der ausgehenden "Ubaidzeit bis zum Beginn der Frühdynastische II-Zeit, I. Studien zur Chronostratigraphie der Südbabylonischen Stadtruinen von Uruk und Ur*, Heidelberger Studien zum alten Orient Band 8, Heidelberger Orientverlag, Heidelberg.

Tobler, A. 1950. *Excavations at Tepe Gawra, Level IX–XX. Vol II*, University of Pennsylvania Press, Philadelphia.

Van Driel, G. 1983. "Seals and Sealings from Jebel Aruda 1974–1978", *Akkadica* 33: 34–62.

Weiss, H. and Young Jr., T. C. 1975. "The merchants of Susa, Godin V and plateau-lowland relations in the late fourth millennium B.C.", *Iran* 13: 1–17.

Wright, H. 1981. *An Early Town on the Deh Luran Plain. Excavations at Tepe Farukahbad*, Memoirs of the Museum of Anthropology 13, University of Michigan, Ann Arbor.

Wright, H. T., Miller, N. and Redding, R. 1980. "Time and process in an Uruk rural center», in Barrelet, M. T. (ed.), *L'archéologie de l'Iraq du début de l'époque néolithique à 333 avant notre ère: perspectives et limites de l'interprétation anthropologique des documents*, Colloque international du centre national de la recherche scientifique, Éditions du Centre national de la recherche scientifique, Paris: 265–84.

17. THE POWER OF WRITING: ADMINISTRATIVE ACTIVITY AT GODIN TEPE, CENTRAL ZAGROS, IN THE LATER FOURTH MILLENNIUM BC

Roger Matthews

Introduction

The power of writing lies in its ability to communicate through time and space by the systematic materialisation of information into durable substance. Much of our knowledge of ancient Mesopotamia and many parts of the ancient Near East derives from the fact that they wrote on clay, which is a very durable substance when fired. Socio-economic developments in lower Mesopotamia during the mid- to late fourth millennium BC provide the context for the origin and early stages of writing in the so-called proto-cuneiform tradition (Englund 1998; Glassner 2000; Cooper 2004). Algaze (2008: 135–39) has recently considered how the development of written methods of accounting and accountability is intimately connected with an increase in "interpersonal interactions" during the emergence of urban civilisation in Mesopotamia in the fourth millennium BC (see also Nissen 2002: 11–15). In particular, writing enabled the transmission of information among a range of participants enmeshed in the webs of control that evolved in early urban societies, including the scribes themselves, overseeing bureaucrats, and also contemporary and future generations of formally trained scribes and clerks. The complexities of early writing, with its initial use of some 900 signs (Englund 1998: 68; 2004: 140; Cooper 2004: 78), at the same time facilitated communication within specially trained cadres of professionals while ensuring obfuscation and exclusion to those not appropriately trained. The ability to write, in other words, was not for everyone but was reserved for those engaged in the implementation of "technologies of power" (Mann 1986) that characterised early state formation. While these developments are reasonably well addressed, if not fully understood, for the core area of state formation in later fourth-millennium BC Lower Mesopotamia,[1] there has been less focus on situating more peripheral occurrences of early writing, such as Iran, within an appropriate socio-political context.

In an overview study Cooper (2004: 94) has argued that, while the appearance of writing may generally be viewed as an answer to "problems raised by complexity", there are exceptions to this pattern whereby either apparently complex societies do not develop writing, or writing does occur but without clear evidence for increasing social complexity. Cooper suggests that the study of these exceptional circumstances may assist us to "understand better what needs writing arises to fulfil". The present study takes up this challenge by examining a small corpus of tablets and associated administrative artefacts dating to the later fourth millennium BC from Godin Tepe (*Period VI.1*), a settlement located in the mountains of central-western Iran, several hundred kilometres to the north-east of the mega-site of Uruk (Fig. 17.1).

This article attempts to situate the material evidence of administrative activities from Godin Tepe within a broad context of socio-economic developments in this period, including the issue of highland-lowland relations during the later fourth millennium BC. We suggest that, contrary to the excavators' interpretations (e.g. Weiss and Young 1975: 14), the administrative evidence from Godin Tepe *Period VI:1* (previously designated *Godin V*) does not directly relate to long-distance trade activities, but rather is closely tied to the management, arguably by a non-local cadre, of the local rural economy. In addressing the question

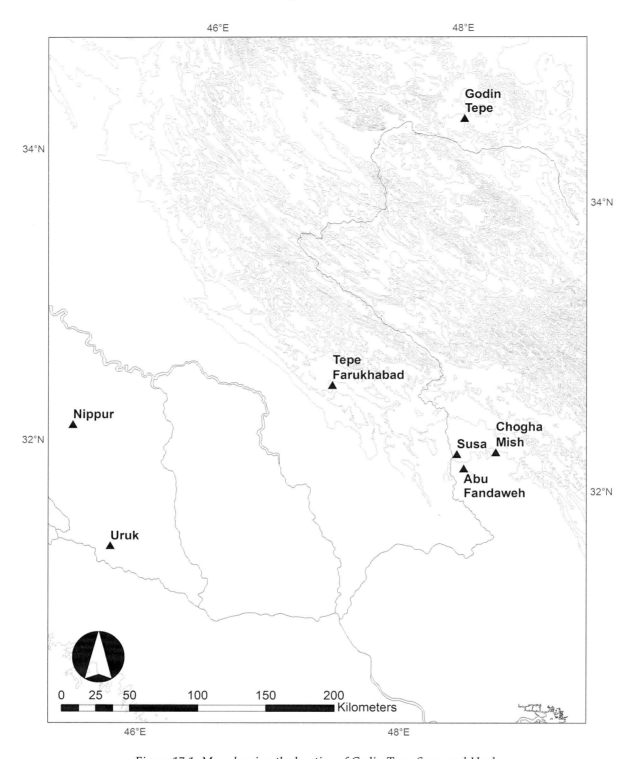

Figure 17.1. Map showing the location of Godin Tepe, Susa, and Uruk.

of the needs that writing arises to fulfil, we associate the appearance of proto-textual materials at Godin with the exercise of power by certain individuals over others, within a specific context that is both locally situated in time and space and a component of a much broader, inter-connected world that reaches across substantial temporal and spatial distance.

Godin Tepe: location and exploration

Godin Tepe is one of the most important archaeological sites of western Iran (Young 1986; Badler 2002; Rothman and Badler 2011; Rothman, this volume) (Fig. 17.2). The entire mound covers 15 ha in extent and rises to 30 m above the surrounding plain, with three distinct areas: the Outer Town, the Citadel,

Figure 17.2. View of Godin Tepe in 2007 with the walls of Period VI:1 *Oval Enclosure visible, looking north.*

and the Upper Citadel. Occupation at the site spans periods from around 4500 BC to approximately the eighth century BC, when the Citadel mound was crowned by a spectacular fortified Median manor house and associated structures.

Godin Tepe owes its importance and its long history of occupation to its location. It sits in the Kangavar valley, one of a series of connected valleys along the upper reaches of the Gamas Ab River, within the Central Zagros mountain region. This valley system is linked to others to its east and west to form the Great Khorasan or High Road, which connects the lowlands of Mesopotamia with the uplands of Iran. Prior to the foundation of the town of Kangavar, Godin Tepe was the main staging post for travel along this route, as it lay in a position to control traffic through a bottleneck in one of the most significant natural route ways of the ancient Near East.

The strategic significance of the location of Godin Tepe becomes apparent in light of the diverse distribution of natural resources across the Near East (Algaze 1993; Matthews and Fazeli 2004). Highland Iran is rich in metals such as copper, silver, and lead as well as other materials such as excellent building timber. In the fourth millennium BC and earlier it also provided access to much-desired commodities such as lapis lazuli, and subsequently also carnelian and probably tin from further east. Lowland Mesopotamia, by contrast, lacked these and other minerals, but instead hosted a natural wealth in the form of fertile soils and good water for irrigation, which, if intensively exploited, could support dense populations of people living in large cities such as Uruk, as began to happen in the course of the fourth millennium BC (e.g. Algaze 2008). Much archaeological and textual evidence from both regions over long periods of time illuminates the rich history of interaction between these lowland and highland regions of the ancient Near East (e.g. Potts 1999: 85ff.).

Godin Tepe came to archaeological attention during a multi-period survey of the region in 1961 by T. Cuyler Young, carried out as an offshoot of the Hasanlu project. Excavations commenced in 1965 and continued at two-year intervals until 1973. As later levels were excavated and removed, access to the earlier levels, especially on the Citadel, became easier and by the end of fieldwork there were extensive exposures of these earlier phases. Two Progress Reports were published by the Royal Ontario

Museum (Young 1969; Young and Levine 1974), and there have been several synthetic articles on particular aspects of the site's archaeology in subsequent years (e.g. Weiss and Young 1975; Young 1986; Badler 1995; 2002). More recently a renewed programme of publication of the Godin Tepe excavations has been successfully pursued to completion in book and website form (Gopnik and Rothman 2011).[2]

Godin *Period VI:1*: main characteristics

Arguably the most important phase of late prehistoric occupation at Godin Tepe was *Period VI:1*, which was marked by the establishment of what has been called an Oval Enclosure on the highest point of the mound (Rothman and Badler 2011; Rothman, this volume). *Godin VI:1* occupation was attested over the entire Citadel and almost all the Outer Town (Badler 2002: 82). Valid doubts have been raised (Edens 2002: 32), however, about the assumed contemporaneity of occupation between the Citadel and the Outer Town, based as it is on the presence in both areas of bevel-rim bowls and trays. More diagnostic ceramic types, with Lower Mesopotamian affiliations, occur principally on the Citadel and, as Edens (2002: 36) argues, it may be that the Outer Town settlement is older than the Citadel settlement and may already have been abandoned by the time the *Period VI:1* compound was built and occupied. The fact that *Godin VI:1* was originally labelled *Godin V* and only recently redefined as a sub-phase of *Period VI*, further underlines the ongoing uncertainty with regard to the site's internal relative chronology.

In any case, *Godin VI:1* dates to the last third of the fourth millennium BC, with radiocarbon dates spanning *c.* 3630–3020 BC for the middle phase of *Period VI:1* and 3350–2700 BC for the last phase of *Period VI:1* (Dyson 1987: 666–67; Wright and Rupley 2001; Badler 2002: 82; Rothman and Badler 2011: 82–85). In total, *Period VI:1* remains were exposed over an area of 550 m² in the Deep Sounding (DS) on the Upper Citadel, and in an operation of about 165 m² at the west base of the Citadel Mound in a trench called the Brick Kiln Cut (BKC; Badler 2002: 79). In BKC the *Period VI:1* house walls only slightly modified those of the *Period VI:2* buildings underneath, with much evidence for continuity. In the DS, by contrast, the layout and architecture of *Period VI:1*, the Oval Enclosure, indicates that there was a major reorganisation and reconstruction of buildings at this highest point of the entire site, even though there is no evidence for a chronological gap between *Periods VI:2* and *VI:1*.

Within *Period VI:1* on the Citadel there are three distinct phases (Badler 2002: 82–83), the earliest comprising an architectural layout not related to the Oval Enclosure. The middle phase sees the construction and first use of the Oval Enclosure, while in the late phase dividing walls were constructed and there is an apparent change in function of several rooms on the Citadel, with a new emphasis on craft and wine production and no evidence for the administrative activity so well attested in the middle phase of *Period VI:1* (Badler 2002: 83). The late phase of *Period VI:1* shows a lessening of *Uruk* influence in the ceramics and the appearance of examples of Transcaucasian wares. This article is concerned with the middle phase of *Period VI:1*, which is the original phase of the Oval Enclosure, and the locus of all the finds relevant to this study (Badler 2002: 82; Rothman and Badler 2011: 95ff.).

The architecture of *Period VI:1* on the Citadel is highly distinctive (Fig. 17.3), being dominated by an Oval Enclosure, within which series of courts, open spaces, and rooms are arranged across an area of about 33 × 25 m (Rothman and Badler 2011; Rothman, this volume). As noted by Rothman elsewhere in this volume, entrance to the Oval was through room 4 at the south, itself connected directly to rooms 5 and 3 to west and east. Room 5, with its hearth, is interpreted as a guardroom, while room 3 contained administrative artefacts, as discussed below. In its original layout court 1 was an extensive open space. Rooms 14–21 form a monumental building, with room 18 at its core. Room 18 has niches, double doors in its north wall, and double windows, with sills at waist height facing onto the main court, area 1. On the basis of brick sizes and hearth types, Badler (2002: 84–85) argues that the *Uruk*-style architecture of *Period VI:1* was constructed by local villagers using traditional methods rather than by foreign, *Uruk*, immigrant labourers.

Jars with grape product residue were found in rooms 18 and 20. Seven clay stoppers were found in *Period VI:1*, some with seal impressions but not in primary contexts, so they could well have fitted these vessels. Other evidence for the production and consumption of beverages includes funnels and lids mostly found in room 2, where a grape-based drink, perhaps wine, was being made, as attested by organic residue analysis (Badler 1995). Badler (1995; 2002: 89) suggests that wine may have been a major commodity for export from the highland zone to the cities of the lowlands. Rooms 10, 12, and 13 have no trace of domestic activity, and there is evidence for craft activity in room 12, including bone tools and spindle whorls.

Room 6 is an independent structure, which closely resembles the main room (room 18) of the monumental structure to the north. On the east side of the Oval only parts of another large structure were exposed, rooms 22 and 23, the former accessible directly from court 1. Charred roof beams lay on the floor of this room, and charred remains of legumes and grains were found here too. It is important to note the small size of the excavated Oval Enclosure relative to the

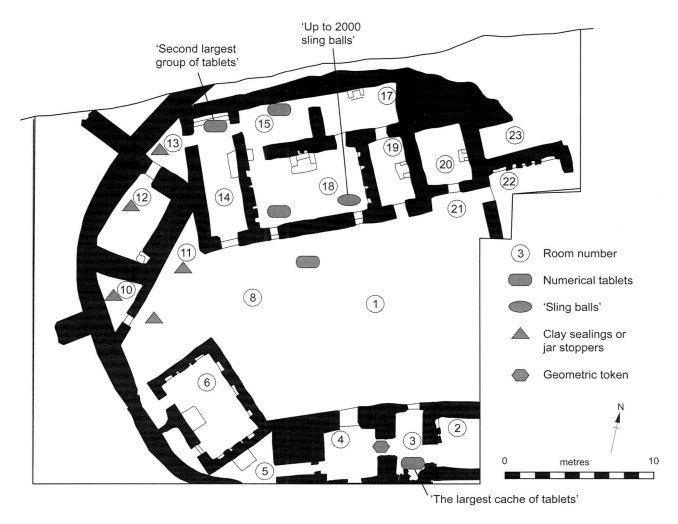

'Up to 2000 sling balls'

'Second largest group of tablets'

'The largest cache of tablets'

③	Room number
	Numerical tablets
	'Sling balls'
▲	Clay sealings or jar stoppers
⬡	Geometric token

N

0 metres 10

Figure 17.3. Godin Tepe, plan of Period VI:1, *middle phase, showing the distribution of administrative artefacts (according to Weiss and Young 1975).*

potential overall area of the mound in this period. There is every possibility of significant additional architecture, perhaps even further oval enclosures, contemporary with the one exposed in the DS, but for these levels to be reached, massive amounts of deposits from later periods would first need to be excavated.

The pottery of *Period VI:1* is not the focus of this paper and has been well studied by Badler (1995, 2002; also Rothman and Badler 2011: 121–33). Suffice to say that it is characterised by a bipartite assemblage that in many respects continues the local traditions attested in earlier occupation at the site, but in other regards contains newly attested forms and decorative techniques that have strong parallels in late fourth-millennium BC assemblages of Lower Mesopotamia, as found at Uruk, Susa, and elsewhere. This continues a trend from *Godin VI:2* (Badler 1995, 2002; Rothman and Badler 2011), which is also seen elsewhere in the highlands of Iran at sites like Tappeh Sialk and Arisman (Helwing, this volume). In the Oval Enclosure

the pottery is split roughly 70:30 between these two assemblages, while in the BKC area the split is 80:20, with the local style predominant in both cases. Badler (2002: 87) has made a stimulating case for the absence of *Uruk*-style cooking vessels as indicating the use of highland local cooking practices and she goes further, employing also the evidence of spindle whorls, to suggest that local women were doing the cooking and spinning, while a small number of foreign men resided in the Oval Enclosure. Neutron activation analysis of ceramics and other clay objects by James Blackman (2011: 111–12) supports the interpretation that much of the material, including some copies of *Uruk*-style vessels, was locally made, but a significant number of the *Godin VI:1* ceramics analysed, including many in the *Uruk* style, are compositionally distinct and may have been made from distinct local sources or imported from other locales. Edens's (2002) study of chipped stone tools from Godin Tepe stresses that the lithics of the *Period VI:1* Oval Enclosure conform fully with the pre-existing lithic traditions of the site,

Table 17.1. Room-by-room distribution of administrative artefacts in the Period VI:1 *Oval Enclosure. W & Y = Weiss and Young 1975; R & B = Rothman and Badler 2011; S-B 1981 = Schmandt-Besserat 1981; S-B 1992 = Schmandt-Besserat 1992.*

Room	Object No.	Object	Publication figure reference
1	T292	Tablet	W & Y: 5.1; S-B 1981: 1 (obv); S-B 1992: 90 (rev); S-B 1992: 113 (obv)
1	CS210	Cylinder seal	W & Y: 5.8
1	CS260	Cylinder seal	W & Y: 5.7
2	T279	Tablet	
2	S280	Sealing	
S of 2	T317	Tablet	
S of 2	S327	Sealing	
3	T286	Tablet	W & Y: 4.6; S-B 1992: 81
3	T288	Tablet	
3	T289	Tablet	R & B: 4.40.6
3	T290	Tablet	W & Y: 4.3; S-B 1992: 89 (mistakenly labelled Gd 73.19 in caption)
3	T291	Tablet	S-B 1992: 84
3	T294	Tablet	R & B: 4.39.4; S-B 1992: 92 (rev)
3	T298	Tablet	
3	T299	Tablet	
3	T319	Tablet	
3	T321	Tablet	
3	S330	Sealing	
3	S331	Sealing	
3	No no.	Clay cone	
4	No no.	>100 clay balls	
8	No no.	>10 clay balls	
10	T285	Tablet	
10	T296	Tablet	
10	S329	Sealing	W & Y: 5.6
10	No no.	>100 clay balls	
11	T273	Tablet	
11	T274	Tablet	
11	T293	Tablet	R & B: 4.40.11
11	T320	Tablet	W & Y: 4.4
11	T323	Tablet	
11	T324	Tablet	
11	T325	Tablet	
11	S326	Sealing	
12	S252	Sealing	R & B: 4.41.3
12	S269	Sealing	R & B: 4.41.4
12	S355	Sealing	
12	No no.	>10 clay balls	
14 (bin)	T154	Tablet	
14 (bin)	T155	Tablet	
14 (bin)	T156	Tablet	
14 (bin)	T157	Tablet	
14 (bin)	T158	Tablet	
14 (bin)	T159	Tablet	
14 (bin)	T160	Tablet	

Room	Object No.	Object	Publication figure reference
14 (bin)	T161	Tablet	R & B: 4.40.4
14 (bin)	T318	Tablet	
14 (bin)	T322	Tablet	
15	T53	Tablet	
15	T54	Tablet	W & Y: 4.1
15	T61	Tablet	R & B: 4.39.1 (obv); R & B: 4.39.2 (rev)
15	T153	Tablet	W & Y: 5.5
15	T162	Tablet	
18	T64	Tablet	W & Y: 4.5; S-B 1992: 80
18	T295	Tablet	W & Y: 4.2; S-B 1992: 115 (obv)
18	T297	Tablet	
18	No no.	1759 clay balls	
19	No no.	Clay cone	
20	No no.	>10 clay balls	
22	T415	Tablet	
22	No no	>10 clay balls	

suggesting that chipped stone tools, at least, were made and used by local inhabitants in the practice of agriculture and other activities, which he argued was perhaps under the control of "a small number of foreigners" (Edens 2002: 41).

Administrative technology: types of artefacts and spatial distribution

Let us examine the nature and spatial distribution across the *Period VI:1* Oval Enclosure of artefacts of administrative activity. The plan and table here (Fig. 17.3; Table 17.1) reveal what we learn about artefact distribution from the published reports and articles, principally Weiss and Young 1975, while the input of Rothman and Badler's more recent work is illustrated in Figure 17.4. By combining the information in Figure 17.4 and Table 17.1 we begin to see a rich and detailed picture of object distribution and association across the Oval Enclosure in this phase. The significance of the Godin Tepe administrative evidence should not be underestimated, relatively sparse as it is. It comprises one of the most informative sets of archaeological contexts for early administrative activity from anywhere in the ancient Near East, with great potential for approaching issues of how tablets, seals, and tokens were used, stored, and disposed of within specific architectural contexts. This potential is especially significant in light of the considerable difficulties in contextualising material finds of early writing at some of the major broadly contemporary sites of the late fourth/early third millennia BC, including Uruk (Englund 1998; Nissen 2002), Susa (Le Brun and Vallat 1978; Dahl *et al.*, this volume), and Jemdet Nasr (Matthews 2002), where it remains

impossible to make more than broad generalisations, either because of the secondary and tertiary nature of the deposits containing the tablets or because of the poor standards of excavation and recording.

In all, 43 tablets or tablet fragments were found in *Godin VI:1*, of which 27 are more or less complete. Of these, nine are published in drawings by Weiss and Young (1975: figs. 4–5), while a few others are illustrated in Gopnik and Rothman (2011) as part of a short overview by Hallo (2011: 116–18). Published depictions of the tablets are summarised in Table 17.1. There is still no exhaustive tablet-by-tablet treatment and analysis of this important early corpus, either as regards the impressed signs or the cylinder seal impressions on many of the tablets (see Dahl *et al.*, this volume; Pittman, this volume). Thirty-nine of the Godin tablets do feature on the CDLI web resource (http://cdli.ucla.edu/), but only early illustrations are available and there is no commentary. A full study will require renewed examination of the tablets themselves, which are housed in the National Museum of Iran, Tehran.

Twenty-six of the Godin tablets are numerical, one of them with numerical signs plus a single pictographic sign, and one tablet is blank. Of the 27 complete tablets, 10 have seal impressions from cylinder seals. Of the 16 tablet fragments, 10 have numerical signs and two of these also have cylinder seal impressions (Weiss and Young 1975: 11). Furthermore, one fragment without signs has a cylinder seal impression. Thus of a total of 43 tablets and tablet fragments, 13 – or 30% – have seal impressions. By comparison, of 44 published Susa numerical tablets, at least 27 – or 61% – have seal impressions (Matthews 1993: 27). As with other proto-cuneiform tablet assemblages (Matthews

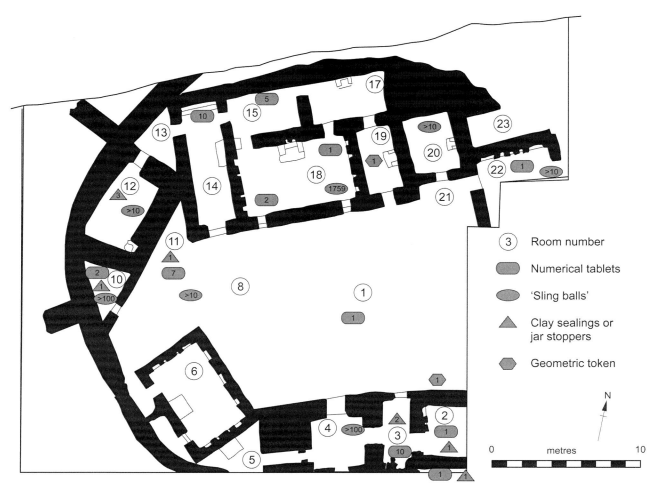

Figure 17.4. Godin Tepe, plan of Period VI:1, *middle phase, showing the distribution of administrative artefacts (according to Rothman and Badler 2011).*

1993), the sealing-inscribing sequence at *Godin VI:1* appears to be sealing first, inscribing second, with the seal impression thus acting in the role of letterhead or general designation of authority, rather than validation of specific written content.

Numerical tablets have a broad distribution in the later fourth millennium BC, at sites including Uruk, Susa, Chogha Mish, Khafajah, Habuba Kabira, and Jebel Aruda (Englund 1998: 50), as well as Tappeh Sialk (*Period IV₁*) and Tepe Sofalin in highland Iran (see Dahl *et al.*, this volume). The physical shape of the *Godin VI:1* tablets is strongly similar to contemporary numerical tablets from Susa *Acropole 17* (Amiet 1997: 18), Tappeh Sialk (*Period IV₁*), and Tepe Sofalin (Dahl *et al.*, this volume). It is notable that on at least one of the Godin Tepe tablets there are indications of the use of the shaft of the stylus to make lines of case separation (e.g. T286), which has been proposed as typical of the pre-ideographic phase of writing (Englund 1998: 52; Glassner 2000: 150), and is indeed otherwise restricted to numerical texts from both Uruk (script stage *IVa*) and Susa *Acropole 17* (Englund 2004: 126).

Of the total of 43 tablets and tablet fragments, Weiss and Young (1975: 3) informed us that "the largest cache of tablets and tablet fragments was found in the strange stepped niches" at the southern end of room 3, indicating its function as an active filing room. We now know that this cache constitutes 10 tablets (Rothman and Badler 2011: fig. 4.24; see Table 17.1). The proximity of room 3 to the only known entrance to the Oval Enclosure is noteworthy. This complex of rooms can be defined as a liminal zone between the outside and the inside, and we may start to wonder about the possible meaning of the tablets in these terms.

Another room specifically cited as containing tablet fragments is room 14, which at its northern extremity has "a bin or storage slot in which were found several apparently discarded tablet fragments" (Weiss and Young 1975: 3), also described as "the second largest group" of tablets (Weiss and Young 1975: 8), now known to be also 10 tablets (Rothman and Badler 2011: fig. 4.24; see Table 17.1). This end of room 14 is immediately adjacent to room 13, one of a suite of storerooms along the western edge of the Oval complex. Again it is noteworthy that the tablets here occur at an architecturally and functionally distinct liminal or transitional zone, where storage and craft activity are adjacent to formal architecture. Again we might surmise that the role of the tablets is here to record, mediate, and control the activities taking place between these two zones. We should also note that all the tablets found in this bin were fragmentary and may have been discarded in the bin either as temporary refuse or perhaps for later recycling. They are likely to have recorded commodities moving in and out of the storage rooms to the west of room 14.

According to Weiss and Young (1975: 8) "several" tablets were also found in rooms 15 and 18 of the monumental structure, and we know that tablets and tablet fragments were recovered from "several other rooms and in the courtyard", but none were recovered from room 6 or the exposure in the BKC. Almost all recovered tablets and fragments were either lying directly on floors or in debris immediately above floors, and all were of unbaked clay. The presence of a tablet blank indicates local manufacture and use of tablets. The find locations of 41 of the 43 tablets and fragments are listed in Table 17.1.

As to glyptic evidence from *Godin VI:1*, in addition to the 13 seal-impressed tablets, four sealed jar stoppers, two cylinder seals and a seal blank were found (Weiss and Young 1975: 11–13; Pittman 2011). One cylinder seal, Gd 73-210, was found in a *Period IV* mud brick but all other glyptic and sealing finds were from good *Period VI:1* contexts. Some unsealed clay sealing fragments were also found and "the majority of sealings and sealing fragments, both seal impressed and plain, came from in and around rooms 10, 12 and 13 and from areas 9 and 11 in the courtyard" (Weiss and Young 1975: 11), suggesting that these rooms were used for storing commodities within vessels that were stopped with clay sealings. No sealed clay bullae were found anywhere in *Godin VI:1* and no glyptic materials at all were found in the BKC.

The iconographies of the actual seals and of the seal impressions from *Godin Period VI:1* are quite different. The *Godin VI:1* cylinder seal impressions on tablets include design elements such as archers and two-handled vessels, and the best comparanda are from *Susa Ca/b* and *Susa Ccc*, equivalent to *Acropole 17* (Amiet 1972), as well as from *Late Uruk* levels at Uruk (Pittman 2011: 114). Seated lions, standards, drilled circles, rearward-looking lions, stylised trees, and bulls all have good parallels at Susa *Acropole 17* and also at Chogha Mish and Uruk. The two actual seals were recovered from area 1 and iconographically are in an early *Proto-Elamite* style (Pittman 2001, 2011: 114). Drilled circles, radial stars, wild goats, and bulls in distinctive style all resemble elements of the glazed steatite style and *Proto-Elamite* motifs (Pittman 1997, 2011). These iconographic elements do not occur on the seal impressions on the tablets and sealings from

Godin VI:1. This mismatch between the iconographies of actual seals as against seal impressions from the same site is a common, but poorly understood, feature of glyptic from late fourth-millennium BC sites across Mesopotamia and beyond (Matthews 1993: 17–18).

There were also five geometric tokens found in *Godin VI:1*, one a pierced cone from a doorway between rooms 3 and 4 (Gopnik and Rothman 2011: 97). Englund has proposed (2004: 127) that some of the so-called "complex tokens", as defined by Schmandt-Besserat (1992), might represent fractions of units within a numerical system for ceramic vessels containing ghee or butter oil, but on available evidence it is not possible to determine the significance of the Godin Tepe tokens in this regard.

In addition, in *Period VI:1* "up to 2000 clay sling balls" were found in the south-east corner of room 18, close to the window opening onto area 1. Badler (2002: 83) suggested that the windows were used to distribute objects to the enclave's foreign residents or local workmen. It is notable that there is also a lot of evidence for carbonised food remains in room 18, especially lentils and barley, which were no doubt kept in the numerous large jars found in this room. Beer residue has been identified in the base of a large open-mouthed jar from room 18, and wine may also have been distributed from here (Badler 1995). Varying quantities of clay sling balls are noted by Rothman and Badler (2011: fig. 4.23) as coming from rooms 4, 8, 10, 12, 18, 20, and 22, as indicated on Figure 17.4.

The nature of administrative activity at Godin Tepe

Weiss and Young's (1975) interpretation of *Godin VI:1*, based partly on glyptic comparanda, saw the site as an intrusive base for merchants from Susa protecting their interests in the region and beyond, by building and occupying an enclosure on the summit of Godin Tepe. They thus interpreted *Godin VI:1* as a trading post supported by a local farming community, possibly controlling trade along the Khorasan High Road. They suggested that the tablets found at the site might be records of such trade, perhaps of goods destined for Susa, and they posit lapis lazuli as being a likely commodity. Young (1986) later suggested that the intrusive merchants might be from Sumer rather than Susa, on the basis of parallels in pottery and other items, while Weiss (2003: 606) more recently sees *Godin VI:1* as "an extension of irrigation agriculture Diyala settlement" rather than connected to dry-farming Khuzestan.

Badler (2002) discussed *Middle Uruk* south Mesopotamian parallels in pottery from *Godin VI:2* and suggested that contacts already existed prior to *Godin VI:1*. Earlier fourth-millennium BC interactions between Mesopotamia and highland Iran are supported by finds of copper-bronze objects in *Godin VI:2* as evidence for trade and expertise in metals, also well attested in the earlier fourth millennium BC at sites on the Qazvin plain, and at Tappeh Sialk (Matthews and Fazeli 2004) and Arisman (Helwing, this volume; also Weeks, this volume). Badler (2002) mentions imported materials in the middle phase of *Godin Period VI:1* – metal pins, needles, a spearhead, stone beads, a mace head, and imported bitumen. The late phase of *Period VI:1* shows a lessening of *Uruk* influence on the ceramics and an increase in the Transcaucasian wares that become ubiquitous in *Period IV* (Badler 2002: 83; Rothman 2011).

There can be little doubt that the location of Godin Tepe is closely related to trade between the highland and lowland zones, but it is hard to see how the numerical tablets fit into such a trade network, and there is little evidence in the earliest writing from Uruk itself or from other sites for concerns with such exotic materials in the texts. The earliest texts deal with more mundane matters such as administration of flocks of animals, labour gangs, and allocations of fields (Englund 1998).

Let us consider the evidence from the *Godin VI:1* tablets themselves, or at least from the sample already published by Weiss and Young and briefly treated by Rothman and Badler (2011) and Hallo (2011). Four different numerical signs appear on the Godin Tepe tablets: wedges and dots, both made with the same stylus, fingernail-impressed crescents, and paired, joined dots, and these are all familiar from proto-cuneiform and *Proto-Elamite* tablets (Englund 1998; 2004).

A single *Godin VI:1* tablet, T295 from room 18 (Fig. 17.5), has been classed as numero-ideographic (Englund 1998: 51, fig. 16, 214–15; 2004: 126–27; Cooper 2004: 74–76), in that it displays numerical signs and a seal impression alongside a single pictographic sign, in this case a collared jar similar to an *Uruk IV* sign, DUG$_b$, which is not present in *Proto-Elamite* texts. This sign represents a container of sheep/goat dairy produce (milk fat, ghee) and is counted sexagesimally, as widely attested at Uruk (Englund 1998: 56). Previous identifications of the sign as representing a beer jar (Badler 2000: 48) do not fit with the sign's usage at Uruk (Englund 2004: 148). In the Godin Tepe case, a fine-pointed stylus has been used to incise the lines that comprise the ideogram DUG$_b$, and this was arguably the same thin stylus used to impress the linear dividing lines attested on at least one of the Godin Tepe tablets (e.g. 73–286).

The archaic texts from Uruk employ five basic numerical systems (Englund 1998), elaborated upon in an "irrationally exuberant" manner (Cooper 2004: 78) into at least 13 groups of counting systems (Potts 1999: 59–60). The basic systems are the sexagesimal, bisexagesimal, grain (ŠE) capacity system, area

(GAN2, "field") system, and the poorly understood EN system (Englund 1998: 118). Further counting systems include those employed for timekeeping and for liquid measures, combining elements of the basic numerical systems with ideographic components. Of the 13 numerical systems attested at Uruk, only three occur on contemporary proto-cuneiform texts at Susa (*Susa II*): the sexagesimal, bisexagesimal, and ŠE systems (Potts 1999: 60).

The sexagesimal system of notation (1-10-60-600-3600-36000) is used at Uruk and Susa for counting discrete objects including animals and people, animal products, dried fish, fruits, tools, stone and wooden objects, and containers (of beer, dairy products) (Englund 1998: 120; Potts 1999: 60). The specific form of the DUG$_b$ sign on the Godin tablet, with the collar of the pot depicted as a hybrid between a triangle (the *Uruk IV* form) and a rectangle (the *Uruk III* form) (Englund 1998: 168, fig. 60), may be purely fortuitous or may indicate the very late *Uruk IV* date of the text, which agrees with other chronological indicators for material from *Godin VI:1*.

Tablet T295 accounts for 33 units/jars of ghee. Studies of dairy metrology at Uruk by Green (1980) and Englund (1991; 1998: 169) suggest that the unit DUG$_b$ represents a yearly amount of dairy produce from one or two animals, at about 8 l per jar. The *Godin VI:1* tablet thus appears to record the receipt or disbursement of a total of 33 × 8 jars = 264 l of ghee from a herd or herds of between 33 and 66 milk animals over a period of one year. As to the type of vessel represented by the DUG$_b$ sign, Englund (1998: 159, fig. 54) has proposed the large collared vessel

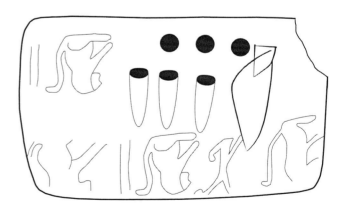

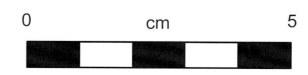

Figure 17.5. Tablet T295 (after Weiss and Young 1975: fig. 4.2).

with tapering base depicted in the *Early Dynastic* milking frieze from Tell al-Ubaid, which compares well with classic *Late Uruk* collared jars with tapering base ("torpedo-shaped", van Driel 2002: 201) found at many sites across the Near East, but not apparently at Godin Tepe itself (Badler 2002: 87; Rothman and Badler 2011: fig. 4.22). It is likely that at least some of the fragmented pots found in room 18 served a role within the system of storage and recording attested by the tablets and sealings.

The presence at Godin Tepe of this single numero-ideographic tablet is highly significant in view of Englund's identification of this type of tablet as a "missing link between numerical notations, which according to context imply an ideographic meaning, for instance a grain notation, and the mixed notations of numerical signs and ideograms which mark the inception of proto-cuneiform" (Englund 1998: 53). Similar numero-ideographic tablets have been found in what have been referred to as Susa *Acropole I Levels 17A* "contact" and *17X/Ax*, which immediately precede level 16 with its earliest *Proto-Elamite* tablets (Le Brun and Vallat 1978; Englund 1998: 56; Potts 1999: 63; Dahl 2009: 23; see Dahl *et al.*, this volume). This link, together with the numerical tablets, enables us to situate the *Godin VI:1* tablets and glyptic within a sharply defined and brief chronological span *c.* 3300–3200 BC (Englund 2004: 122), culminating in "the last direct contact between Persia and southern Babylonia" (Englund 1998: 215). In short, Godin Tepe tablet T295 hovers on the boundary between counting and writing. The presence of numero-ideographic tablets at Susa and Godin Tepe, but not in other Uruk-impacted regions such as Upper Mesopotamia and southern Anatolia (but see Simonetti 2007 for a single tablet from Arslantepe with incised sign), suggests a deeper and possibly slightly more extended interaction between Lower Mesopotamia and western Iran than with other regions of the Uruk world (Algaze 1993; Potts 1999; Cooper 2004: 74–75).

Others of the published Godin Tepe texts have evidence for the ŠE system of counting. At Uruk and Susa the ŠE system is always used to count capacities of grain, most commonly barley, and this was probably the commodity being counted and recorded in most of the Godin Tepe tablets. Therefore, at most two of the 13 *Uruk* numerical systems appear to be attested at Godin: sexagesimal, as the ghee text reveals, plus the ŠE system for grain, namely two of the three systems used at Susa. We thus have a tripartite hierarchy of complexity suggested by the quantity of numerical systems alone: 13 systems at Uruk, three at Susa, two at Godin Tepe. At both Susa and Godin, there does not appear to have been an importation of the complete package of accounting methods already in development at Uruk by this time, but rather a considered utilisation of only those parts of the system needed to administer affairs within their

particular socio-economic contexts. As Potts (1999: 61) puts it, "many more different types of things needed to be counted at Uruk than at Susa" and also presumably at Godin Tepe.

We might ask why were people counting and recording often rather modest amounts of certain types of agricultural produce at Godin Tepe in this period? One clue lies in the context of many of the tablets in room 3 – next to the only entrance to the Oval and a liminal boundary zone – hinting that they concern interactions between people settled or working in the Oval and people living outside the Oval. What might these interactions have been? By analogy with contemporary texts from Uruk, the likeliest sorts of activities requiring textual verification and accounting would include the passing of flocks of sheep and goat to the control of shepherds operating on the surrounding landscape, and the movement of specific commodities, such as dairy products, pulses, grain, beer, wine, oils, and suchlike from outside to inside the Oval, which are likely also to have been under the control of the sealings attested in the Oval Enclosure.

All these commodities are attested in the archaeological evidence from the site itself. The seal impressions on the numerical tablets potentially identify individuals within the Oval Enclosure whose flocks were being sent out to pasture, for example, or whose storerooms were receiving specified amounts of agricultural produce. Both parties to the agreement have to be able only to recognise the images and agree on the numbers impressed on the soft clay. This may explain the common occurrence of tablets at the gateway into the Oval Enclosure, where commodities and produce would be counted and the tablets cancelled (by breaking?) and/or filed in an office, in this case the niches cut into the south wall of room 3. This interpretation conforms to Schmandt-Besserat's (1992: 178–79) observation of the concentration of tokens and numerical tablets at gates and entrances in later fourth-millennium BC levels at Habuba Kabira and Uruk. Furthermore, Nissen (2002: 12) has pointed out that the role of proto-cuneiform writing at Uruk was "only to keep track of what entered the stores and what left them", and not to show any concern with ultimate origins or destinations of commodities. It is thus highly probable that writing at Godin Tepe was also limited to the specific concern of receipt into, and/or disbursement from, storage facilities.

These activities were part of the management of domestic economy and have little to do with the organisation of long-distance trade, although of course they may relate to the issue of provisions to traders passing through the site. The use of this simple yet distinctive system of domestic management at Godin Tepe argues for the presence of at least a small group of Uruk-origin people at the site who had a good familiarity with this system of accounting, which they applied within their new environment. I argue that the occupants of the *Godin VI:1* Oval were engaged in an attempt "to integrate economically related activities under a single organizational structure" (Algaze 2008: 131), as part of a system of administration devised and applied at Uruk in order to control large-scale movements of multiple commodities across multiple socio-economic levels. These "technologies of power" (Mann 1986) evolved within the context of large-scale, trans-regional interactions centring on the emergence of truly urban communities on the Lower Mesopotamian plain, an episode within which sites such as Godin Tepe played an integral part.

As to the use of seals and sealings within the administrative system at Godin Tepe, we do not possess the sort of rich contextual information that has enabled such meticulous reconstruction of activity at, above all, Arslantepe in the later fourth millennium BC (Frangipane 2007), with secure associations between pots, jar stoppers, sealings, and a small group of ovoid blank tablets, one with incised sign (Simonetti 2007: 154). Nevertheless, we may posit that seals and sealings were employed at Godin Tepe alongside numerical and numero-ideographic tablets in an integrated system of control over the receipt and disbursement of specific commodities to and from storage facilities within the Oval Enclosure.

What are we to make of the clay "sling balls" found in large quantities in room 18 and in smaller numbers elsewhere in the Oval? These are sometimes interpreted as evidence of military activity, as in the case of the Syrian site of Hamoukar where thousands of clay sling balls of fourth-millennium BC date have been recovered (Reichel 2009), and this interpretation has indeed been suggested for the Godin Tepe examples (Badler 2011: 99–100). Their distribution at Godin Tepe is, however, distinctive (Fig. 17.4): a very large assemblage (1759) in the south-east corner of room 18, significant numbers in the entrance chamber to the Oval, room 4, and the storeroom, space 10, and smaller numbers in rooms 12, 20, and 22. As with the tablets and sealings, with which they almost always co-occur at Godin Tepe, the clay balls are located in distinctive spaces where activities are measured, counted, and recorded.

One argument is that in the *Godin VI:1* case, the clay balls may be blanks for clay sealings or tablets, as suggested with some reservations by Damerow and Englund (1989: 62) for the similar objects found also in a corner of a room in the *Proto-Elamite* building at Tepe Yahya, dating to the late fourth millennium BC. They may also have served in some unidentified way as simple counting devices (of numbers of sheep/goat being consigned to or received from herders?) within the overall administrative operation, while being suitable at the same time for sling ammunition as and when required.

The broader context of *Godin VI:1*

There are other large *Uruk*-period sites in the valleys west of Godin Tepe along the High Road, including the Mahi Dasht and Shahabad valleys (Goff 1971; Henrickson 1994) and many have sherds from bevel-rim bowls. These sites are situated strategically along the great natural route way connecting the highlands and the lowlands, and may indicate trade in goods and commodities between these two very different zones, no doubt facilitated by the use of domesticated donkeys as pack animals, as attested at the *Late Uruk* site of Rubeidheh at the Iraqi end of the High Road in the Hamrin region and elsewhere (Henrickson 1994: 95; Algaze 2008: 140–42). While direct material evidence for such trade is largely lacking, it is likely that metals, above all copper, played an important part in these interactions, and that highland Iran as a resource-rich region had a significant role to play in this long-lasting interaction (Algaze 1993, 2005); Matthews and Fazeli 2004; Helwing, this volume; Weeks, this volume). A recent study of the distribution of bevel-rim bowls across Iran (Potts 2009), however, urges caution in seeing the bowls as evidence for Mesopotamian contacts. Potts (2009: 13) prefers to divorce much of the Iranian bevel-rim bowl evidence from the rich Mesopotamian indications for their use in a coordinated system of ration disbursement, instead viewing the Iranian evidence as indicative of a burgeoning "taste for leavened bread" baked within these distinctive bowls.

It is worth considering the clear connections between the material culture of *Godin VI:1*, as encountered at Godin Tepe and other sites in Iran, and that of the immediately subsequent *Proto-Elamite* phase, potentially spanning the period *c.* 3300–2900 BC (for dating of the *Proto-Elamite* period, see Abdi 2003: 140; Englund 2004: 143; Dahl *et al.*, this volume). These connections are apparent in the glyptic (Pittman 1997, 2001, 2011) and also, as Damerow and Englund (1989), Englund (2004), and Potts (1999: 75–77) have made clear, in certain recurrent features in the structure and content of texts from both the *Late Uruk* and *Proto-Elamite* periods, including use of the ŠE counting system and continued use of the stylus shank to define columns of text (Englund 2004: 104, 126–27). These links suggest a collaboration during *Susa Period II* of a few *Uruk* individuals with local elite elements who in *Susa III*, the *Proto-Elamite* phase, maintain some aspects of that collaboration even after the incomers have left or been thrown out, while developing their own script and other material culture attributes in distinctive ways. The spread of *Proto-Elamite* texts across Iran strongly echoes but also expands the distribution of the preceding *Susa II* or *Late Uruk* contacts. It may therefore be that *Proto-Elamite* communities were doing roughly the same things as the *Susa II/Late Uruk* people in highland Iran, namely concerning themselves with long-distance interactions in cherished commodities while managing local economies through simple but distinctive bureaucratic means, involving a mix of inducement and coercion, reward and penalty. As Lamberg-Karlovsky (1989) phrases it, "The proto-Elamite phenomenon results from the assimilation by the proto-Elamites of the earlier Uruk social technology."

This point is supported also by a parallel shift, in both Lower Mesopotamia and Iran, in sealing practices in the late fourth/early third millennia BC, away from sealing tablets to sealing container and door sealings, as richly attested in assemblages from many sites in both broad regions (Dittmann 1986; Matthews 1993; Pittman 1997). A decline in the practice of sealing *Early Dynastic I* tablets in Mesopotamia, attested only by the corpus from Ur, which lacks any seal impressions, is matched by a marked decline in the practice of sealing *Proto-Elamite* tablets as compared to earlier *Susa II/Uruk*-style tablets in Iran. Broadly, sealing on *Susa II*-period tablets in Iran varies between 30–60% of tablets, site by site, but for *Proto-Elamite* tablets, the sealed percentage drops to 12%, just as we see a massive increase in the use of seals on door and container sealings, as attested at Susa, Tal-e Malyan, and other sites (Matthews 1993: 26–27 summarises all the evidence; see also Dittmann 1986; Pittman 1997). This structural shift in sealing practices in both regions, despite major script divergence, suggests a degree of convergence in terms of the use of seals within proto-literate administrative practices: the increasing capacity of written signs rendering redundant most instances of seal use (Dittmann 1986).

Proto-Elamite societies in late fourth-/early third-millennium BC Iran thus maintained a structure and system of control and interaction across much of the region that retained some elements of the preceding *Uruk* phenomenon, alone among the regions of the Near East affected by that phenomenon before that system collapsed too. The Godin Tepe case study may be compared with the contemporary situation at Arslantepe in south-east Anatolia, at the northern limits of *Uruk* impact (Frangipane 2007). As at *Godin VI:1*, the ceramic and glyptic evidence in *Level VIA* at Arslantepe indicates some degree of engagement with Lower Mesopotamia but with significant continuity of already well-developed local traditions in style and manufacture. Nevertheless, as at *Godin VI:1*, there is arguable evidence for *Uruk* impact on bureaucratic practice, most notably in the form of five small clay lenticular tablets, only one of which bears a single incised sign, taken to suggest "either that some Uruk officials/scribes went to work at Arslantepe, and these five tablets were left behind by them, or, more plausibly, that the local administrative structure had acquired embryonic techniques of notation at the end of the fourth millennium BC" (Simonetti 2007:

155–56). The distinctive nature of the single Arslantepe incised sign, not quite matched by any one sign in the *Uruk* proto-cuneiform sign-list, and incised on the tablet when dry rather than wet (thus against all *Uruk* scribal practice), underlines the special character of Arslantepe's cultural trajectory in this, as in other, periods of its history.

Finally, to return to the challenge posed by Cooper (2004) and set out at the beginning of this paper, what do we learn about the connections between early writing and social complexity from the Godin Tepe case study? The first question must be, what needs did writing arise to fulfil at Godin Tepe? The site is small (at least that part of it known to have been occupied by the Oval Enclosure) and the quantities of commodities are small and could have been managed with a few tokens, seals, and sealings, if they needed managing at all. Writing at Godin Tepe does not appear to have been an answer to "problems raised by complexity" (Cooper 2004: 94). Rather, we interpret the *Godin VI:1* administrative apparatus as the conscious deployment of a technology of power, a tool of domination by a small elite group exercising their skills and expert knowledge in a local, rural environment, a system "imposed on the local population by Babylonian accountants" (Englund 2004: 128). Just as *Uruk*-inspired architects coerced local builders into constructing Lower Mesopotamian style buildings within the Oval Enclosure, itself delimited by a surrounding wall which provided strictly controlled access to those buildings, so did *Uruk*-trained bureaucrats attempt to construct the mindsets of local peoples under their administrative control. These thoughts rejoin us with Algaze's (2008: 138) sober quote from Levi-Strauss: "the primary function of writing, as a means of communication, is to facilitate the enslavement of other human beings."

One hint of this specific aspect of writing at Godin Tepe, as interface between those "in the know" and those not, may show itself in the seal impression on tablet T295 (Fig. 17.5). As one looks at the tablet as it would be held in the hand for inscribing, the seal impression is upside down, and thus atypical of the orientation of seal impressions on proto-cuneiform tablets generally (Matthews 1993: 26), and on numerical and numero-ideographic tablets specifically (Englund 2004: fig. 5.18). The separation of text and image in terms of orientation is likely to be deliberate and significant. One explanation is that, while holding the clay tablet, the scribe-administrator is displaying to the reader – who may be standing facing the scribe across the window in the south-west corner of room 18 where T295 was found – not the content of the text (including the sole pictogram) but the depiction of the seal impression. In other words, the external viewer of the tablet is allowed to "read" the seal impression, which would have conveyed accepted meanings of authority, but is assumed not able to, or not allowed to, read the content of the text. If correct, such an interpretation further illustrates the divide that is likely to have existed at *Godin VI:1* between those who exercised technologies of power and those upon whom they were exercised.

Notes

1 See Nissen 2002, however, for increasing scepticism about the security of interpretations based solely on the evidence from Uruk itself.

2 I originally prepared the substance of this paper for a conference in Kermanshah in 2006, before learning of the renewed programme of publication led by Mitchell Rothman and Hilary Gopnik (Gopnik and Rothman 2011). Mitchell was kind enough to send me copies of draft chapters of the volume prior to its publication, for which I am very grateful. From this paper's point of view, the main asset is the ability to place individual tablets, and a few sealings, into the rooms where they were found, as listed in Table 17.1 and illustrated in Figure 17.4 here.

Bibliography

Abdi, K. 2003. "From écriture to civilization. Changing paradigms of proto-Elamite archaeology", in Miller, N. F. and Abdi, K. (eds), *Yeki Bud, Yeki Nabud. Essays on the Archaeology of Iran in Honor of William M. Sumner*, Cotsen Institute of Archaeology, Los Angeles: 140–51.

Algaze, G. 1993. *The Uruk World System*, 1st edition, University of Chicago Press, Chicago.

Algaze, G. 2005. *The Uruk World System*, 2nd revised edition, University of Chicago Press, Chicago.

Algaze, G. 2008. *Ancient Mesopotamia at the Dawn of Civilization. The Evolution of an Urban Landscape*, University of Chicago Press, Chicago.

Amiet, P. 1972. *Glyptique susienne des origines à l'époque des Perses Achéménides*, (Mémoires de la Délégation Archéologique en Iran 43), Paul Geuthner, Paris.

Amiet, P. 1997. "L'utilisation des sceaux en Iran élamite", in Gyselen, R. (ed.), *Sceaux d'Orient et leur emploi*, Groupe pour l'Étude de la Civilisation du Moyen-Orient, Bures-sur-Yvette: 11–21.

Badler, V. R. 1995. "The archaeological evidence for winemaking, distribution and consumption at proto-historic Godin Tepe, Iran", in McGovern, P. E., Fleming, S. J. and Katz, S. (eds), *The Origins and Ancient History of Wine*, Gordon and Breach, New York: 45–56.

Badler, V. R. 2000. "The dregs of civilisation: 5000 year-old wine and beer residues from Godin Tepe, Iran", *Bulletin of the Canadian Society for Mesopotamian Studies* 35: 48–56.

Badler, V. R. 2002. "A chronology of Uruk artefacts from Godin Tepe in central western Iran and implications for the interrelationships between the local and foreign cultures", in Postgate, J. N. (ed.), *Artefacts of Complexity. Tracking the Uruk in the Near East*, British School of Archaeology in Iraq, London: 79–109.

Badler, V. R. 2011. "The function of the clay balls from the Godin VI Oval Compound", in Gopnik and Rothman 2011: 99–100.

Blackman, J. 2011. "Chemical characterization of Godin Period VI ceramics by instrumental neutron activation analysis", in Gopnik and Rothman 2011: 111–12.

Cooper, J. S. 2004. "Babylonian beginnings: the origin of the cuneiform writing system in comparative perspective", in Houston, S. D. (ed.), *The First Writing. Script Invention as History and Process*, Cambridge University Press, Cambridge: 71–99.

Dahl, J. L. 2009. "Early writing in Iran: a reappraisal", *Iran* 47: 23–31.

Damerow, P. and Englund, R. K. 1989. *The Proto-Elamite Texts from Tepe Yahya*, American School of Prehistoric Research Bulletin 39, Peabody Museum, Harvard University, Cambridge, MA.

Dittmann, R. 1986. "Seals, sealings and tablets: thoughts on the changing pattern of administrative control from the Late Uruk to the proto-Elamite period at Susa", in Finkbeiner, U. and Röllig, W. (eds), *Ǧamdat Nasr: Period or Regional Style?*, Ludwig Reichert, Wiesbaden: 332–66.

Dyson Jr., R. H. 1987. "The relative and absolute chronology of Hissar II and the proto-Elamite horizon of northern Iran", in Aurenche, O., Evin, J. and Hours, F. (eds), *Chronologies du Proche Orient – Chronologies in the Near East. Relative Chronologies and Absolute Chronology 16,000–4,000 B.P.*, BAR International Series 379 (i–ii), Archaeopress, Oxford: 647–80.

Edens, C. 2002. "Small things forgotten? Continuity amidst change at Godin Tepe", *IA* 37: 31–46.

Englund, R. K. 1991. "Archaic dairy metrology", *Iraq* 53: 101–04.

Englund, R. K. 1998. "Texts from the late Uruk period", in Bauer, J., Englund, R. K. and Krebernik, M. (eds), *Mesopotamien: Späturuk-Zeit und Frühdynastische Zeit*, Freiburg University, Göttingen: 13–233.

Englund, R. K. 2004. "The state of decipherment of proto-Elamite", in Houston, S. D. (ed.), *The First Writing. Script Invention as History and Process*, Cambridge University Press, Cambridge: 100–49.

Frangipane, M. ed. 2007. *Arslantepe Cretulae. An Early Centralised Administrative System Before Writing*, University of Rome "La Sapienza", Rome.

Glassner, J-J. 2000. *Écrire à Sumer. L'invention du cunéiforme*, Seuil, Paris.

Goff, C. 1971. "Luristan before the Iron Age", *Iran* 9: 131–52.

Gopnik, H. and Rothman, M. S. eds 2011. *On the High Road. The History of Godin Tepe, Iran*, Royal Ontario Museum/ Mazda Publishers, Costa Mesa.

Green, M. W. 1980. "Animal husbandry at Uruk in the archaic period", *JNES* 39: 1–35.

Hallo, W. 2011. "The Godin Period VI tablets", in Gopnik and Rothman 2011: 116–18.

Henrickson, E. F. 1994. "The outer limits: settlement and economic strategies in the central Zagros highlands during the Uruk era", in Stein, G. and Rothman, M. S. (eds), *Chiefdoms and Early States in the Near East. The Organizational Dynamics of Complexity*, Prehistory Press, Madison: 85–102.

Lamberg-Karlosvky, C. C. 1989. "Introduction", in Damerow, P. and Englund, R. K. (eds), *The Proto-Elamite Texts from Tepe Yahya*, American School of Prehistoric Research Bulletin 39, Peabody Museum, Harvard University, Cambridge, MA: v–xiii.

Le Brun, A. and Vallat, F. 1978. "L'origine de l'écriture à Suse", *CDAFI* 8: 11–59.

Mann, M. 1986. *The Sources of Social Power*, vol. 1, Cambridge University Press, Cambridge.

Matthews, R. 1993. *Cities, Seals and Writing: Archaic Seal Impressions from Jemdet Nasr and Ur*, (Materialien zu den frühen Schriftzeugnissen des vorderen Orients 2), Gebr. Mann, Berlin.

Matthews, R. 2002. *Secrets of the Dark Mound. Jemdet Nasr 1926–1928*, British School of Archaeology in Iraq, Warminster.

Matthews, R. and Fazeli, H. 2004. "Copper and complexity: Iran and Mesopotamia in the fourth millennium BC", *Iran* 42: 61–75.

Nissen, H. J. 2002. "Uruk: key site of the period and key site of the problem", in Postgate, J. N. (ed.), *Artefacts of Complexity: Tracking the Uruk in the Near East*, British School of Archaeology in Iraq, Warminster: 1–16.

Pittman, H. 1997. "The administrative function of glyptic art in proto-Elamite Iran: a survey of the evidence", in Gyselen, R. (ed.), *Sceaux d'Orient et leur emploi*, Groupe pour l'Étude de la Civilisation du Moyen-Orient, Bures-sur-Yvette: 133–61.

Pittman, H. 2001. "Mesopotamian intraregional relations reflected through glyptic evidence in the Late Chalcolithic 1–5 periods", in Rothman, M. S. (ed.), *Uruk Mesopotamia and Its Neighbors*, School of American Research Press, Santa Fe: 403–43.

Pittman, H. 2011. "The seals of Godin Period VI", in Gopnik and Rothman 2011: 113–15.

Potts, D. T. 1999. *The Archaeology of Elam. Formation and Transformation of an Ancient Iranian State*, Cambridge University Press, Cambridge.

Potts, D. T. 2009. "Bevel-rim bowls and bakeries: evidence and explanations from Iran and the Indo-Iranian borderlands", *JCS* 61: 1–23.

Reichel, C. 2009. "Hamoukar", *Oriental Institute 2008–2009 Annual Report*, Oriental Institute, Chicago: 77–87.

Rothman, M. S. 2011. "Migration and resettlement: Godin Period IV", in Gopnik and Rothman 2011: 139–206.

Rothman, M. S. and Badler, V. 2011. "Contact and development in Godin Period VI", in Gopnik and Rothman 2011: 67–138.

Schmandt-Besserat, D. 1981. "Decipherment of the earliest tablets", *Science* 211: 283–85.

Schmandt-Besserat, D. 1992. *Before Writing*. Vol. 1. *From Counting to Cuneiform*, University of Texas Press, Austin.

Simonetti, C. 2007. "Small clay tablets, one with an incised sign", in Frangipane, M. (ed.), *Arslantepe Cretulae. An Early Centralised Administrative System Before Writing*, University of Rome "La Sapienza", Rome: 153–57.

van Driel, G. 2002. "Jebel Aruda: variations on a Late Uruk domestic theme", in Postgate, J. N. (ed.), *Artefacts of Complexity: Tracking the Uruk in the Near East*, British School of Archaeology in Iraq, Warminster: 191–205.

Weiss, H. 2003. "Ninevite 5 periods and processes", in Rova, E. and Weiss, H. (eds), *The Origins of North Mesopotamian Civilization: Ninevite 5 Chronology, Economy, Society*, (Subartu 9), Brepols, Turnhout: 593–624.

Weiss, H. and Young Jr., T. C. 1975. "The merchants of Susa. Godin V and plateau-lowland relations in the late fourth millennium B.C.", *Iran* 13: 1–17.

Wright, H. T. and Rupley, E. S. A. 2001. "Calibrated radiocarbon age determinations of Uruk-related assemblages", in Rothman, M. S. (ed.), *Uruk Mesopotamia and Its Neighbors*, School of American Research Press, Santa Fe: 85–122.

Young Jr., T. C. 1969. *The Godin Tepe Excavations: First Progress Report*, Royal Ontario Museum, Toronto.

Young Jr., T. C. 1986. "Godin Tepe period VI/V and central western Iran at the end of the fourth millennium", in Finkbeiner, U. and Röllig, W. (eds), *Ǧamdat Nasr: Period or Regional Style?*, Ludwig Reichert, Wiesbaden: 212–28.

Young Jr., T. C. and Levine, L. D. 1974. *The Godin Project: Second Progress Report*, Royal Ontario Museum, Toronto.

18. CHRONOLOGICAL PARAMETERS OF THE EARLIEST WRITING SYSTEM IN IRAN

Jacob L. Dahl, Cameron A. Petrie and Daniel T. Potts

Introduction

Although it is possible to reconstruct a general outline of the events leading up to the invention of writing (Englund 1998; Damerow 2006; Dahl 2009), the absolute and to some extent relative dates of the different evolutionary steps involved are still very much a point of discussion. The absolute date of the earliest inscribed objects from the ancient Near East is far from being only a question of "firsts". Rather, the date has relevance for our understanding of the spread of technologies and knowledge in a global setting.

Proto-Elamite (hereafter *P-E*), the topic of the present paper, plays an important role in the study of the invention and spread of writing, as it is one of the few early writing systems with a proven dependency (Damerow and Englund 1989). Moreover, *P-E* occupies a place in time and space which could link other seemingly indigenous writing systems to the Mesopotamian invention of writing (Damerow 2006). *P-E* was a highly specialised notational system, however, used by people who shared some cultural bonds, and it is therefore unlikely that it could have been transferred between culturally distinct groups without undergoing very significant adaptation.

In addition to the proto-cuneiform texts of *Uruk IV/III* type from Uruk, Jamdat Nasr, Tell Uqair, and Tell Asmar (Englund 1996: 7–19), *P-E* or *Susa III*-type texts from Iran constitute a second important collection of documents displaying some of the earliest evidence of administrative record-keeping known from the ancient Near East. Compared to the *Uruk* texts, however, which have been the subject of renewed, intensive study (following Falkenstein's original publication of 1936) by the Berlin and UCLA group (ATU 2–6 etc.), *P-E* documents have received far less attention. Since P. Meriggi's studies of the 1970s (1971, 1974a, 1974b), only a few scholars have

seriously engaged with the *P-E* material (e.g. Stolper 1985; Damerow and Englund 1989; Dahl 2002, 2005b; Vallat 2003; Englund 2004).

Ongoing study of the *P-E* texts by one of us (Dahl) suggested that it was possible to document the internal evolution of the *P-E* writing system, a process which need not have been protracted, but which could have occurred very quickly over the course of a number of "scribal generations".[1] As this evolution had a chronological dimension, it therefore became obvious that, rather than approaching this topic from a purely palaeographic or typological perspective (e.g. using tablet shape, contents or other variables inherent in the texts themselves as criteria), the archaeological contexts of the *P-E* texts should be re-examined in order to determine whether micro-stratigraphic or chronological differentiation existed within the corpus which corresponded with or contradicted the presumed evolution of the texts themselves. In addition, the available radiocarbon dates from all relevant sites and contexts had to be recalibrated in order to determine whether any internal chronological refinements suggested themselves, which might help reconstruct an evolutionary sequence within the *P-E* text corpus. Furthermore, the particular problems of the calibration curve in the late fourth millennium BC had to be taken into consideration. Consequently, the second and third authors (Petrie and Potts) joined forces with the first author in order to interrogate the stratigraphic and radiocarbon sources as an adjunct to the texts themselves. This paper summarises the results of our collaboration.

The corpus

Currently, *P-E* texts are known from eight sites: Susa, Tal-e Ghazir, Tal-e Malyan, Tappeh Sialk, Tepe Ozbaki, Tepe Yahya, Shahr-e Sokhta, and Tepe Sofalin (see Dahl *et al.,* 2012) near Tehran (Fig. 18.1). *P-E*

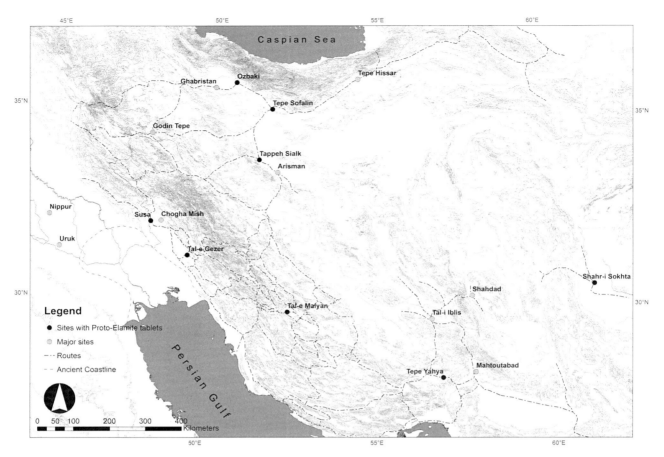

Figure 18.1. Map of Iran and neighbouring areas showing the location of sites with P-E texts.

tablets have also been reported from Godin Tepe, Tepe Hissar,[2] and most recently Jiroft, but none of the published objects from these sites are in fact *P-E*. The Godin Tepe tablets are all *Uruk*-style tablets (*Uruk V*, perhaps early *Uruk IV*; see also Rothman, this volume; Matthews, this volume); the Tepe Hissar objects are tablets with cuneiform signs; and the Jiroft finds are much later and belong to an entirely different category altogether (Linear Elamite) (see Dahl 2009).[3]

In the following sections, the find spots of the individual corpora of *P-E* texts will be discussed. This will be followed by a discussion of the radiocarbon dates from each site. The sites will be presented in a specific geographical order, starting at Susa, introducing the sites along a transect to the north-east, and then returning to Khuzestan and following a transect to the south-east.

Susa

Location: 32° 11' 19.32'' N 48° 15' 01.83'' E

Texts: *c*. 1557 as follows: 198 (Scheil 1905) + 490 (Scheil 1923) + 655 (Scheil 1935) + 50 (de Mecquenem 1949) + 15 (de Mecquenem 1956) + 20 (Vallat 1971) + 129 (unpublished tablets and fragments in the Louvre, to be published by Dahl).[4]

Contexts: Susa has been the object of extensive excavations by English, French, and Iranian archaeologists since the mid-nineteenth century. The vast majority of the *P-E* tablets from Susa were found during the pre-World War II French excavations, when almost no stratigraphic information was recorded.[5] The reinvestigation of the Acropole mound by A. Le Brun (1971), however, afforded scholars a second look at the fourth-millennium BC stratigraphic sequence of Susa. During the course of four seasons of excavation (winter 1968/1969, January–March 1970, January–February 1971 and 1977), a series of 27 architectural/stratigraphic levels was excavated (*Acropole I.1–27*; see Fig. 18.2).

Although *Acropole I.18* was originally represented by a *c*. 60 cm-thick series of deposits and floors containing no architecture,[6] the 1977 excavations of an expanded area (160 m²) revealed a multi-roomed complex of domestic mud-brick architecture (Le Brun and Vallat 1978: 11, figs 1–2) with the same orientation as the rooms found in the higher levels (Fig. 18.3/a–c; *Acropole I.17B–14B*; cf. Le Brun 1971: figs 33–34 for plans of levels 17b, 16, 15, and 14b). Slight modifications to the fabric of the building allowed the excavators to identify four architectural sub-phases. While the earliest of these (1) was not

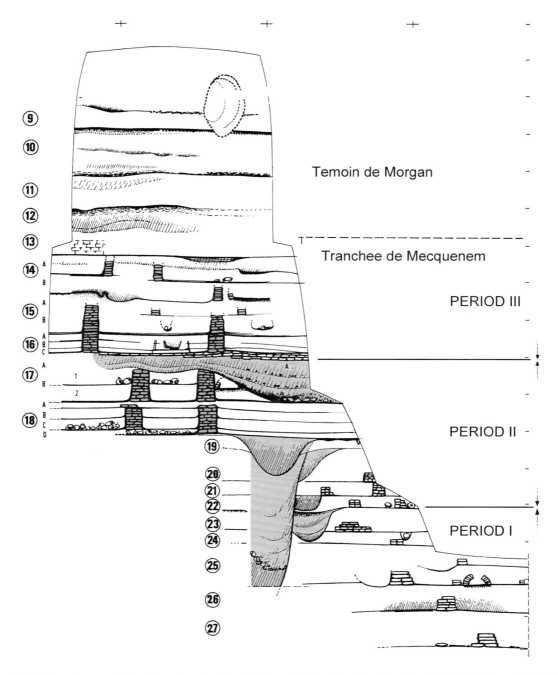

Figure 18.2. Susa Acropole I section showing the stratigraphic location of various levels (after Le Brun 1978: fig. 29).

fully excavated, the next level (2) contained seven, and the one above that (3) contained four numerical tablets, the earliest attested in stratigraphic context in the *Acropole I* sounding (Le Brun and Vallat 1978: fig. 4 and pl. 4).[7]

The subsequent phase (*Acropole I.17*; Fig. 18.3/b) contained a similar, though less well-preserved, arrangement of domestic mud-brick architecture called *Level 17B* (Le Brun 1971: fig. 33 top), which had three distinct occupation surfaces that contained two tablets with numerical signs (Le Brun 1971: figs 43.8–9 and 44.8). This was in turn covered by

a thick deposit of striated layers of debris, without architecture, called *Level 17A*, which contained a further six numerical tablets (Le Brun 1971: figs 43.4–7 and 44.1).

The first *P-E* tablets found in the *Acropole I* sounding appeared in what Vallat referred to as "au contact 17A–16" without any further explanation (Vallat 1971: 237), nor was this concept explicated further by Le Brun.[8] The expression "au contact" may be rendered in English as "at the contact (point)" or "interface". If we refer solely to the schematic section (Fig. 18.2), then surely texts found at the contact point of *Levels*

Figure 18.3. Susa Acropole I, *a) plans of Level 18; b) Level 17B; c) Level 16C (after Le Brun 1978: figs 31, 33 and 35).*

17 and *16* should have appeared immediately beneath the lowest floor in *Level 16C*, presumably in a context which, at the time, was impossible to attribute with complete certainty to either *Levels 17A* or *16C*. Three of the four tablets that Vallat attributed to "au contact 17A–16"[9] (S.1237.1, 1241.9 and 1241.5), however, appear on Le Brun's initial plan of *Level 17B* (Le Brun 1971: fig. 33 upper, to the east and west of an erosion gully in the south-western part of the plan; see Fig. 18.3/b), but not on the subsequent publication of the plan of *Level 17B* after the trench was extended (Le Brun 1978: fig. 33). No indication is given of their elevation, but if the *Level 17A* deposits underlie these *P-E* tablets – as would seem to be implied by the notion of having been discovered in the contact zone between *Levels 17A* and *16* – it is rather odd to illustrate them on a plan of *Level 17B*, where all the other texts shown are clearly of the numerical rather than the *P-E* type. In fact, much of the confusion surrounding the provenance of these three *P-E* texts was clarified in an unpublished lecture given by A. Le Brun at the Jamdat Nasr symposium held in Tübingen in 1983. As Dittmann relates, "The famous 'contact 16–17' which could be misunderstood as being a zone between layer 17A and 16, is in fact unstratified material from an adjacent step of the old excavations of de Mecquenem at the Témoins de Morgan. The tablets having been labeled to come from this 'contact' should therefore be considered as being out of stratigraphic context (personal communication from A. Le Brun)" (Dittmann 1986: 171, n. 1). We must therefore assume that the three *P-E* tablets shown on Le Brun's initial plan of *Level 17B* were displayed there simply to indicate their find spot, as there was no plan of "au contact 17A–16". The plan of the extended trench may have been an attempt to remove any confusion with regard to the context of these tablets.

Contrary to some statements (e.g. Dyson 1987: 648), the orientation of the mud-brick architecture in *Level 16C* does not differ from that of *Level 17B* (Fig. 18.3/c; cf. Le Brun 1971: fig. 33 top showing 17B, and bottom showing 16), despite the presence of the *Level 17A* debris layers. Nonetheless, the *Level 17A* debris was, in places, covered by baked brick paving that is clearly visible in section, and on top of which wall 728 was built. Thus, even if the orientation was similar, the stratigraphic separation of *Levels 17A* and *16C* was clear.[10] Le Brun, moreover, noted clear differences in the ceramic assemblage between *Levels 17B/17A* and *Level 16C*, particularly the disappearance of high cylindrical jars and nose-lug jars with incised decoration, and the appearance of wheel-turned, footed goblets, and trays with rounded, everted rims (Le Brun 1971: 192; cf. Dyson 1987: 648).

The nature and duration of the transition in the writing system, architecture, and ceramics are, however, unclear. Scholars have expressed differing views on whether the changes were sudden or gradual, and whether a period of abandonment might have occurred between *Levels 17B* and *16C*.[11] Certainly the ample quantity and variety of finds from *Level 17A* would seem to argue against a complete abandonment of the site, despite the absence of standing architecture.[12] Moreover, given the fact that level *18* seemed at first to lack architecture, until excavations were shifted in 1977 to an area where mud-brick remains similar to those found in *Levels 17B, 16, 15,* and *14B* were discovered, it would be unwise to suggest, on the basis of the *Acropole I.17A* deposits alone, that there was no occupation on the Acropole at that time. Nevertheless, whether the time elapsed between *Levels 17A* and *16C* was brief or not, the appearance of *P-E* tablets in *Level 16C* suggests that a period of transition may have taken place between the use of numerical and the appearance of *P-E* tablets (Le Brun 1971: 210). Consequently, Le Brun and Vallat (1978: 31) hypothesised that there may have been a transitional phase elsewhere on the site associated with the first steps in the development of *P-E* that was not attested in the Acropole sounding, and termed it *Acropole I.17X* (or *I.17Ax;* Dittman 1986: 186).

There were clearly multiple phases of occupation at Susa characterised by the use of *P-E* texts. Room 707 in *Level 16,* and the areas to the east and west of it, are shown in the schematic section as having three distinct floors (Le Brun 1971: fig. 32). In addition, Le Brun wrote of "trois occupations successives, marquées par des aménagements nouveaux" (Le Brun 1971: 189). *P-E* tablets were found in *Levels 16C* and *16A.* The schematic section of *Levels 27* to *13,* however, shows very clearly that two walls which stood throughout all three sub-phases (distinguished by separate floors) of *Level 16* – 732[13] and 728 – also continued to stand in *Level 15B* and *15A,* albeit with new numbers (689 and 681 according to the section, 689 and 688 according to the plan). It is true that an ashy green surface covered most of the excavated area of *Level 15B* and separated *Levels 16A* and *15B,* but there can be no doubt that only a relatively short amount of time can have elapsed between these phases since the same mud-brick walls were in use in both. A small number of *P-E* tablets was also found in *Levels 15B, 15A,* and *14B.*

Based on a consideration of tablets, seals, and ceramics, R. Dittmann divided the Acropole *Levels 16–11* as follows: *PE. 1 = Levels 16–15B;*[14] *PE. 2a = Levels 15A–14B; PE. 2b? = Levels 14A–13;* and *PE. 3 = Level 11?* (Dittmann 1986: table 1). Given the selectivity involved in the initial publication of the ceramics from the Acropole sounding, however, it is questionable whether, on the basis of the preliminary reports, such divisions can be sustained.

Tappeh Sialk, South Mound

Location: 33° 57' 53.38'' N 51° 23' 38.25'' E

Texts: 7? (S.28, S.1620, S.1623, S.1624, S.1626, S.1630, S.1621?) (Ghirshman 1934, 1938).

Contexts: Tappeh Sialk is located near the modern city of Kashan on the Iranian Central Plateau. The *Sialk IV* deposits on the South Mound contained distinctive ceramic forms such as low and tall bevel-rim bowls, low-sided trays, and drooping and straight spouted jars (Ghirshman 1938: 58–71, pls. XXVI–XXXI, LXXXVIII–XCV; Amiet 1985). On the basis of the cultural material and architectural remains, *Period IV* was divided into two phases (IV_1 and IV_2) dating to the mid- to late fourth millennium BC (Dyson 1987: 661; Voigt and Dyson 1992: 168). The mud-brick structures and associated deposits of *Sialk IV_1* included numerical tablets comparable to the late *Susa II* tablets from *Acropole I.17B* (Voigt and Dyson 1992: 168), and the *Sialk IV_1* ceramics correlate best with those of *Acropole I.17A–B* (Dittman 1986: 184–85) and Godin Tepe *Period VI:1* (Dyson 1987: 661ff.; Voigt and Dyson 1992: 168; contra Helwing 2005: 42). *Sialk IV_2* comprised disturbed deposits above the *Sialk IV_1* walls (Ghirshman 1938: 58–61; Voigt and Dyson 1992: 168).

In 1933, during the excavation of the *Sialk IV_2* deposits in *Chantier I,* a relatively well-bounded stratum at 1–1.30 m depth beneath the surface was discovered, which contained bevel-rim bowls (e.g. Ghirshman 1938: S.20), two jars of Jamdat Nasr affinity, and a *P-E* text (S.28; Ghirshman 1938: pls. XXXI:1, XCII). P. Amiet considered this the only true *P-E* text recovered at Tappeh Sialk (Amiet 1985: 296),[15] and further noted that an apparently sterile lens, *c.* 70 cm thick, separated "les témoins de l'époque d'Uruk de ceux parmi lesquels gisait l'unique tablette proto-élamite" (Amiet 1985: 312). In contrast, Weiss and Young (1975: 11) noted (following Ghirsman 1938: 67), "The eighteen numerical notation tablets and fragments from *Sialk IV_1* include five with Proto-Elamite signs". In fact, one of these texts (S.1631) has only numerical signs: the sign on the reverse that made Weiss and Young include it among the *Proto-Elamite* tablets is in fact either a scribal design (see Dahl 2012), as also suggested by Ghirsman, or a seal impression. Apart from S.28, the Tappeh Sialk texts have clumsily drawn signs (Damerow and Englund 1989: 2, n. 6; Dittman 1986: 184–86) and some scholars have suggested that they represent the elusive *Acropole I.17X* developmental phase (but see the remarks above on the unstratified nature of those texts) of *P-E* writing (e.g. Dyson 1987: 663). There are no radiocarbon dates available from the South Mound of Tappeh Sialk.

Tepe Ozbaki

Location: 35° 59′ 51.99′′ N 50° 32′ 43.54′′ E

Texts: one (Madjidzadeh n.d.; Vallat 2003).

Contexts: the site of Tepe Ozbaki consists of one large mound surrounded by nine small mounds in the area of Ozbaki, in northern Iran, and excavations were undertaken in 1998–2000 and again in 2006 (Madjidzadeh 2001: 141; 2003). Although the other contemporaneous material is still awaiting publication, one *P-E* tablet fragment (here called Ozbaki 1) was found during the excavations of one of the low mounds next to what may tentatively be termed the "Acropolis" (Madjidzadeh 2001: 145). There are no radiocarbon dates available for Tepe Ozbaki.

Tepe Sofalin

Location: 35° 18′ 58′′ N 51° 44′ 06′′ E

Texts: many reported; 12 prepared for publication (Dahl *et al.*, 2012).

Contexts: the site of Tepe Sofalin lies in the eastern part of the Ray plain of the north Central Iranian plateau, approximately 35 km south-east of Tehran. The site is situated at a strategically important location, where the east–west routes across the northern part of the Central Plateau meet those running north–south along its western edge. It is also notable that the site sits adjacent to a large alluvial fan, and such environments are known to have been important for settlements based on agriculture from the Neolithic onwards across a large area of the ancient Near East and western South Asia (e.g. Petrie and Thomas 2012). Limited excavations were conducted between 2006–09, and in area H14 a collection of *P-E* tablets was recovered together with tablet blanks, cylinder sealings, bevel-rim bowls, and bichrome pottery (Hessari and Akbari 2007). Very little information about the stratigraphic context of the finds is available, but the *P-E* tablets appear to have been dumped together with a range of earlier administrative artefacts, including a sealed bulla, several numerical tablets, and as many as 3000 sealings. The sealings in particular show close similarity with material from Susa.

Tal-e Ghazir

Location: 31° 21′ 27.39″ N 49° 25′ 1.11″ E

Texts: one (Whitcomb 1971: 37, pl. XIA = Tl 2.0, G-20, CA 27921).

Contexts: the complex of mounds known as Tal-e Ghazir is one of the most important sites on the Ram Hormuz Plain. Mound A was excavated in 1948 and 1949, revealing a sequence probably beginning in the late fifth and continuing throughout the fourth and into the early third millennium BC, with second-millennium BC and Islamic occupation preserved in the upper levels (Caldwell 1971: 348–55; also Whitcomb 1971). A single *P-E* tablet was recovered in Mound A, in Trench I, below levels containing Elamite material of second-millennium BC date (Caldwell 1971: 348; Whitcomb 1971: 11, 64, 105, pl. XI.A). At present, there are no radiocarbon dates available for Tal-e Ghazir, but the original excavations are being prepared for publication by Abbas Alizadeh.

Tal-e Malyan

Location: 30° 00′ 40.04′′ N 52° 24′ 27.70′′ E

Texts: 32 tablets and fragments (only partially published in Stolper 1985).

Contexts: Tal-e Malyan has extensive and well-dated occupation from the *Middle Banesh* period in two main areas, Operation ABC, which was situated at the edge of a large mound that dominates the north of the site, and Operation TUV, which was situated atop a low mound in the south-east corner of the site (Sumner 1988: fig. 1; 2003: fig. 4; Alden, this volume: fig. 12.2). The hypothesised period of transition from the *Susa II* to *Susa III* phases (i.e. *Acropole I.17X*), appears to be contemporary with the *Early Middle Banesh* phase (Operation ABC levels 4B–5 and Operation TUV level 3B), while *Acropole I.16–14b* appears to be contemporary with the *Late Middle Banesh* phase (Operation ABC levels 2–4A, Operation TUV levels 2–3A) (Sumner 2003: 53, table 12; Voigt and Dyson 1992: 141; Alden, this volume). *Building Level (BL) III* in Operation ABC comprised a monumental building decorated with wall paintings that contained *P-E* tablets and cylinder seals (Fig. 18.4; Sumner 1988: 309; 2003: 27–34). A solitary *P-E* text was also recovered from *BL 4A* (stratum 13A), but none were found in the limited exposures of *BL 4B* and *5* (Fig. 18.4; Sumner 1988: 308; 2003: Appendix A, mf 1690). Additional texts were recovered from *BL 2–3A* in Operation TUV, but none were recovered from *BL 3B* (Fig. 18.4; Sumner 1988: 310; Nicholas 1990). It is notable that no numerical tablets were recovered at Tal-e Malyan, although the existence of *Middle Banesh*-period occupation levels without *P-E* tablets suggests that occupation at the site began before *P-E* was being used in the highlands.

Tepe Yahya

Location: 28° 20′ N 56° 52′ E

Texts: 26 (Damerow and Englund 1989).

Contexts: Tepe Yahya is located in the Soghun Valley in Kerman province, slightly north of the mid-point between the Iranian coast on the Straits of Hormuz and Kerman city. *P-E* tablets were excavated during the 1970, 1971, and 1975 seasons, in and around the

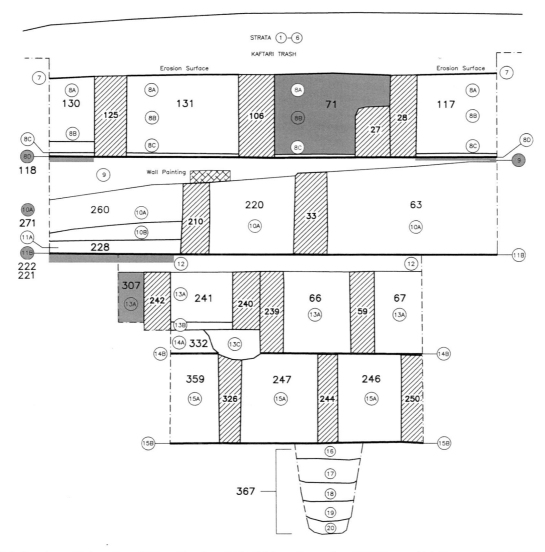

Figure 18.4. Stratigraphic location of P-E *tablets from Tal-e Malyan Operation ABC (Strata 13A [feature 307], 11B [features 211, 222], 10A [feature 271], 9 [?], 8D [feature 118], 8B [features 71, 118, 128] highlighted in grey) (after Sumner 2003: Figure 6).*

so-called *Period IVC* building (Fig. 18.5; Damerow and Englund 1989: fig. 1; Potts 2001). Within Room 1b of the building, texts TY 7, 9, and 10 were found on a higher floor than TY 11, 14, 15, 17, 18, 19, 20 and 21 (Fig. 18.5; cf. the situation at Tal-e Malyan). Otherwise, there is no obvious stratification of the texts, and all seem to be archaeologically contemporary. Tepe Yahya was not occupied in the period immediately prior to construction of the *Period IVC* building (*Period VA*; Potts 2001: 199–202). The layout and construction of this building has been described as "Western", as it has parallels with buildings exposed in Susa *Acropole 18* and later fourth-millennium BC levels (Potts 2001: 10; also Beale and Carter 1983), and the reoccupation of the site following its earlier abandonment appears to have been a foreign initiative, potentially emanating from Susa (Lamberg-Karlovsky 1978; Potts 2001: 198).

Shahr-e Sokhta

Location: 30° 35′ 20.19″ N 61° 19′ 19.20″ E

Texts: one (Amiet and Tosi 1978: figs 16 and 31, cat. 22; photo in Salvatori *et al.* 2001: 36).

Contexts: Shahr-e Sokhta is located in Iranian Seistan. During the seventh season of excavations, on 31 October 1975 a single *P-E* tablet was found in cut 12 in square XDV, an area of domestic architecture (Fig. 18.6; Amiet and Tosi 1978: 24). The tablet was "found at the very top of layer 14", a stratum described as "fine-textured earth with pottery, sealings and animal bones interspersed with sporadic lenses of dung. The *P-E* tablet was found just below 13b in cut 12, *c.* 0.08 m. from the eastern wall of CCXCI" (Amiet and Tosi 1978: 20), a partially excavated room. A photograph and line drawing of the inscribed face of the tablet

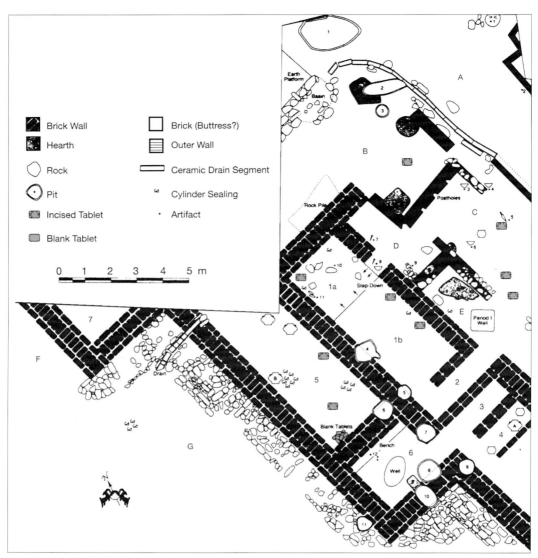

Figure 18.5. Tepe Yahya, plan of the Period IVC *building showing the location of the* P-E *tablets highlighted in grey (after Potts 2001: Figure 1.1).*

(the reverse bore "obliterated impressions", i.e. seal impressions), made by P. Meriggi, were published and the tablet was described as "roughly rectangular, pillow-shaped, with straight sides, as is recurrent at Susa 16–13. It was made out of a lump-free clod of greenish clay" (Amiet and Tosi 1978: 24). The dimensions published were "H. 0.036 m, w. sup. 0.046 m, w. inf. 0.54 m, th. 0.0165 m" (Amiet and Tosi 1978: 31).

Overview of the radiocarbon evidence

The radiocarbon dates from the sites discussed above are of variable quantity and quality. It is not our intention here to resort to proxy data from sites without *P-E* texts that are relatable to the sites just described on the basis of ceramic parallels. While contemporary sites with well-stratified radiocarbon dates do exist (e.g. Tol-e Nurabad and Tol-e Spid), the evidence from them is circumstantial at best so long

as they cannot be unequivocally linked with *P-E* texts.

The absolute dating of Susa itself is problematic. Although Le Brun's excavations on the Acropole yielded tablets in well-excavated contexts, they were relatively few in number. Although samples for dating were collected, only one sample from the *Acropole I* sequence has been published. Other samples come from the Apadana and *Acropole II*. Unfortunately all of these samples are problematic for various reasons, and with only one exception, they date before 3350 BC (Fig. 18.7).

Of the sites with *P-E* tablets reviewed above, *Middle Banesh* Tal-e Malyan is undoubtedly the most interesting since tablets found in Operations ABC and TUV were clearly discovered in a series of internally differentiated building levels, some of which are directly dated by radiocarbon (Sumner 2003: table 13; also Voigt and Dyson 1992 II: 131). With a few exceptions, however, virtually all of these determinations span the period between 3300 and

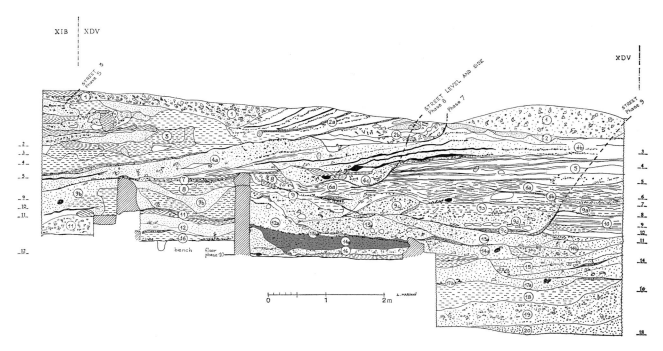

Figure 18.6. Shahr-e Sokhta, the deposit where the single P-E tablet was recovered is highlighted in grey (after Amiet and Tosi 1978: Figure X).

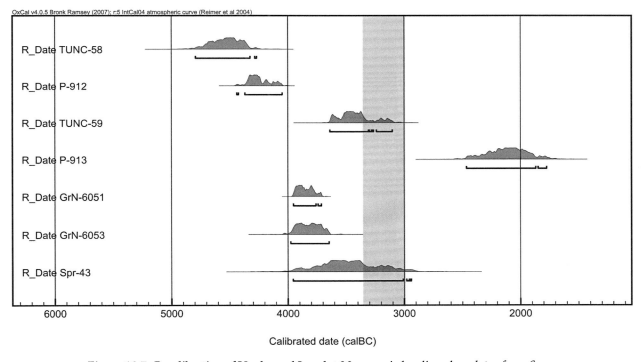

Figure 18.7. Recalibration of Uruk- and Jemdat Nasr-period radiocarbon dates from Susa.

3000 BC (Fig. 18.8). Two of the dates from *Tal-e Malyan* Operation ABC come from *BL 4A* (stratum 13A), which contained only one *P-E* tablet (Sumner 1988: 308; 2003). Although these dates are stratigraphically earlier than those from *BL 3*, all of the determinations from both phases fall within the 3300 to 3000 BC range, although it should be noted that they typically have relatively large standard deviations of between 50 and 280 years. Wright (1985) used the dates from Tal-e Malyan to suggest that some part of the *Jamdat Nasr* period dates to *c.* 3200 BC.

The significance of, and problems associated with, the *c.* 3300–3000 BC time span become clearer when we look at the determinations from Godin

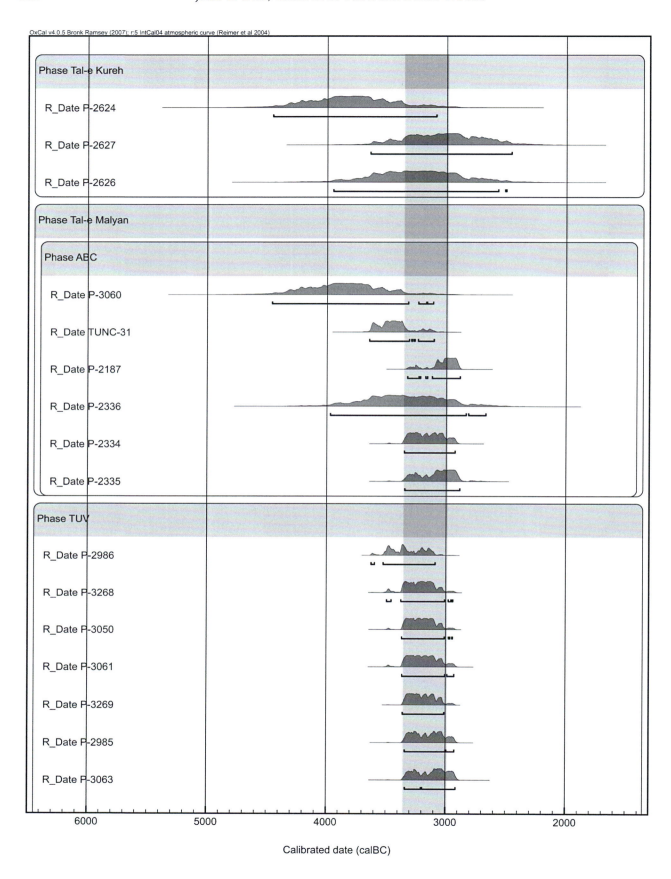

OxCal v4.0.5 Bronk Ramsey (2007); r:5 IntCal04 atmospheric curve (Reimer et al 2004)

Figure 18.8. Recalibration of radiocarbon dates from Tal-e Kureh and Tal-e Malyan (Areas ABC and TUV).

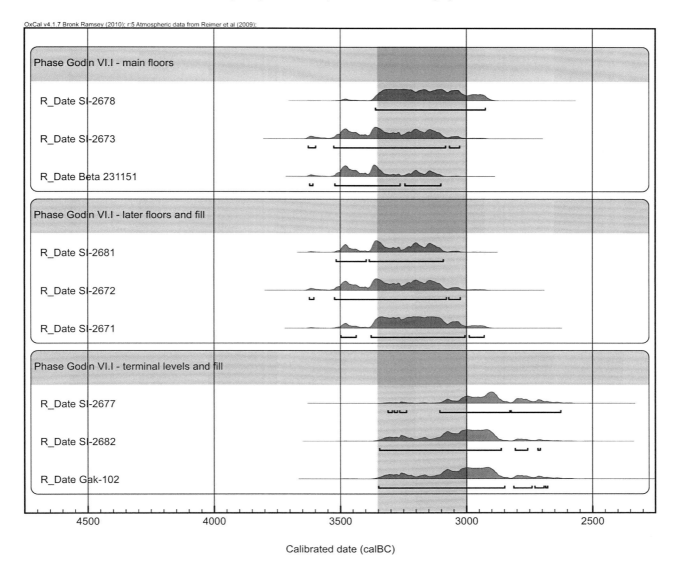

Figure 18.9. Recalibration of radiocarbon dates from Godin Tepe Period VI:1.

Tepe. Although the ceramic assemblage in the Oval Enclosure (*Godin VI:1*) has strong correlations with the *Acropole I.17* material (Weiss and Young 1975; Badler 2002; Rothman and Badler 2011; Rothman, this volume; Matthews, this volume), the absolute radiocarbon dates, which have been recalibrated by Wright and Rupley (2001), Rothman and Badler (2011: table 4.2), and us (Fig. 18.9) suggest that *Godin VI:1* was at least partially contemporary with the *Middle Banesh* phases at Tal-e Malyan (Wright and Rupley 2001: fig. 3.1–3.3, 3.7–3.8). They also suggest that the *Godin VI:1* structures were occupied for much longer than previously assumed (Helwing 2005: 44; Petrie, in press). In fact, what have been referred to as the "terminal" dates from *Godin VI:1* (Dyson 1987: table 2; Rothman and Badler 2011: table 4.2) appear to post-date, at least partly, the latest *Middle Banesh* determinations from Tal-e Malyan (cf. Fig. 18.8). Our comprehension of the absolute chronology of *Godin*

VI:1 is hampered by the fact that samples were not collected systematically throughout the stratigraphic sequence, and none of the available radiocarbon determinations are of particularly high precision. This means that it is unreliable to refine the dates from *Godin VI:1* using Bayesian statistical approaches (contra Rothman and Badler 2011: 84).

This cursory look at the absolute dates from Tal-e Malyan and Godin Tepe suggests that the *Susa II/III Transition*, potentially attested at *Godin VI:1*, and the *Middle Banesh* phase, attested at Tal-e Malyan, were more or less contemporary. However, a glance at the relevant section of the radiocarbon calibration curve shows that there is a significant plateau spanning the period between *c.* 3400 and 2900 BC, which also includes an area of *reversal* where the slope of the curve is inverted, meaning that dates that calibrate between 3350–3200 BC appear to have *younger* calibrated ranges than dates that fall between

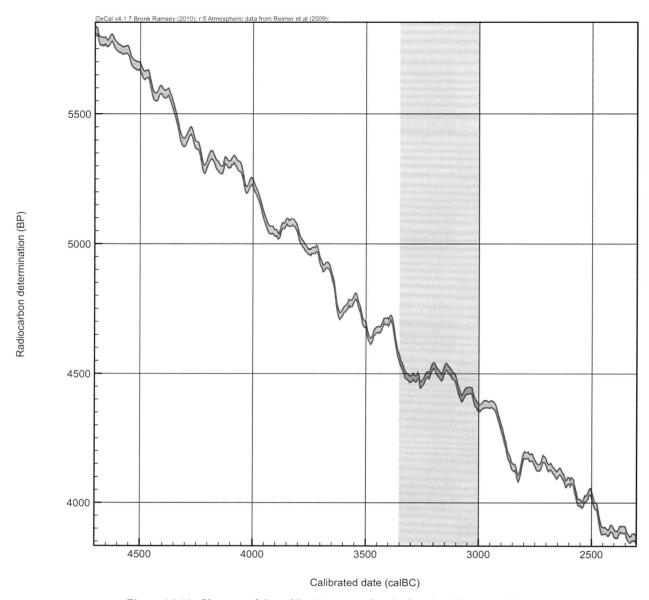

Figure 18.10. Close-up of the calibration curve for the fourth millennium BC.

3200–3100 BC (Fig. 18.10). The existence and impact of plateaus in the radiocarbon calibration curve have been noted with respect to the period between 12000 and 5000 BC in the Near East (Aurenche *et al.* 2001: 1199, fig. 9) and the late fourth-millennium BC plateau has been the subject of discussion in European archaeology (e.g. Raetzel-Fabian 2001: Abb. 1). Wright (1985: 96–97) has previously drawn attention to "perturbations in atmospheric carbon 14" during this period, but apart from this the plateau has not found its way into discussions of the fourth-millennium BC chronology of the ancient Near East (e.g. Wright and Rupley 2001; see Petrie, in press). In effect, a calibration plateau concertinas dates that might be chronologically discrete and makes them appear to have the same probability range.

The importance and deleterious impact of this plateau cannot be overstated. With a range that spans the period from *c.* 3400 to 2900 BC, it coincides with the projected date ranges for the *Late Uruk* and *Jamdat Nasr* periods in Mesopotamia, the *Susa II/Late Uruk* (*Acropole I.22–18*), the *Susa II/III Transition* (*Acropole I.17–17X/17Ax*) and the *Susa III/Proto-Elamite* (*Acropole I.16–14B*) occupations at Susa, *Godin VI:1, Sialk* $IV_{1-}IV_{2'}$ *Period IVC2* at Tepe Yahya, and the entirety of the *Middle Banesh* occupation at Tal-e Malyan and other sites in Fars (Petrie, in press/2013). On the face of it, the plateau in the calibration curve suggests that there was not a complete chronological separation of the *Late Uruk* and *Proto-Elamite* phenomena. This obviously contradicts prevailing views based on ceramic and glyptic comparanda (e.g. Alden 1982; Dittman 1986; Sumner 1986, 1988; Potts 1999; Helwing 2005: 41).[16]

Nor is the situation helped by the large measurement errors for some of the dates from older excavations, particularly Tal-e Malyan, Tepe Yahya, and Godin Tepe. These factors are unavoidable limitations of radiocarbon dating, which is susceptible to atmospheric variation in radiocarbon. One way to deal with the calibration plateau decisively would be to establish well-dated, local chronologies with high-precision radiocarbon assays collected from well-stratified sites, including dates from before, after, and across the plateau. Only then will it be possible to use Bayesian-based calibration analysis to incorporate prior information about the relative ordering of the dates based on stratigraphy to improve the posterior probabilities of the radiocarbon determinations (Buck *et al.* 1996) and, it is hoped, isolate sub-periods of development (Petrie, in press).

For the time being, however, there is no real alternative but to work on refining our relative chronological correlations. Although conventional chronological indices such as ceramics and cylinder seals are as imprecise in absolute terms as the radiocarbon dates from the late fourth millennium BC reviewed above, the *P-E* texts themselves offer us an opportunity to circumvent the opacity of the calibration plateau by using tablet format, writing conventions, and sign forms as criteria for the construction of an internal chronology of the development of *P-E* writing. Moreover, if the texts from *P-E* sites in Iran can be segregated into chronological sub-groups, these may serve as a proxy

for a refined chronology of late fourth-millennium BC Iran that is superior to both calibrated radiocarbon dates and relative ceramic chronologies.

The *Proto-Elamite* tablets

As should be clear from the site-by-site discussion above, the largest corpus of published *P-E* texts, by several orders of magnitude, comes from Susa. Consequently, much of the discussion that follows will be based on that corpus. With the exception of two possible metro-mathematical school tablets (J. Friberg, personal communication), *P-E* was used exclusively to write administrative documents. Thus far, the following topics are attested in the *P-E* corpus: animal husbandry (e.g. herd accounts, production records, etc., with a noticeable dearth of records relating to cattle herding); labour texts (e.g. inventories, ration disbursements, etc., perhaps occasionally recording the names of workers and overseers); field texts (e.g. ploughing records and yield accounts); and cereal production (e.g. beer and bread accounts).

Tablet format

Proto-Elamite tablet format seems to be independent of content, and tablets can be divided into three major groups according to their physical shape (Fig. 18.11/a–d):

Format Group 1 (Fig. 18.11/a) – thick, oblong tablets which often appear to be clumsily written. The text

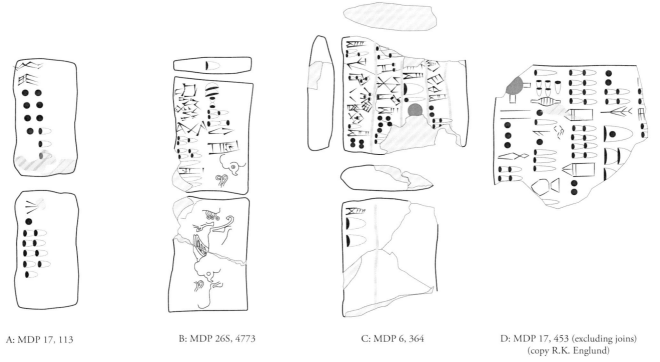

A: MDP 17, 113   B: MDP 26S, 4773   C: MDP 6, 364   D: MDP 17, 453 (excluding joins)
                                                                                                          (copy R.K. Englund)

Figure 18.11. Examples of the three P-E tablet Format Groups.

is placed randomly on the surface of the tablet, often with only one entry per surface. Thus, the semantic structure of the entries is much less sophisticated than on tablets of *Group 2* and *2sub*. Although no *Group 1* tablets were found in the *Acropole I* sounding, and as such are known only from the earlier Susa excavations, their style of writing and simple semantic structure would suggest that these are among the earliest examples of *P-E* writing known (Sb 22219; Sb 22233; Sb 22235; Sb 22244; Sb 22296, etc.).

Format Group 2 (Fig. 18.11/b) – generally thin and rectangular, "Standard" *P-E* tablets. The long side of the tablet is always parallel to the direction of the text, according to the original direction of writing.[17] Most of the standard *P-E* tablets are ruled using the edge of a thin stylus (Fig. 18.11/b). In some cases the ruling is slanted towards the right. Un-ruled tablets may represent a chronologically earlier sub-group that preceded ruled tablets. Standard texts consist of a header and one or more entries, which may be totalled. They are written in an in-line style, not in visual hierarchies as is the case with the proto-cuneiform texts from Mesopotamia (Englund 2004: fig. 5.3b). The first two *P-E* tablets found by de Morgan (Sb 15221 and Sb 15227 published in MDP 2; cf. Dahl 2005b: 84), and essentially all of the early finds published in MDP 6 and MDP 26 belong to this type. In addition, *Group 2* tablets were found in *Acropole I.16c–14b* (*16c*: S.ACR 1018.1, 1067.1, 929.1, 964.1; *15b*: S.ACR 736.1, 733.1; *15a*: S.ACR 710.1, 838.1, 482.1; *14b*: S.ACR 316.1, 316.2; *16–15b contact*: S.ACR 845.1).

Format Group 2sub (Fig. 18.11/c) – "cushion" or pillow-shaped tablets with a highly developed internal structure. These texts are always ruled. One tablet belonging to *Group 2sub* was found during stratified excavations at Susa (S.ACR 316.2, cf. Sb 22221 and Sb 22238 found during de Morgan's excavations).

Format Group x (Fig. 18.11/d) – very large, flat, and thick tablets (Sb 22616; Sb 22608; Sb 21888+22597+22587 (?); Sb 22602; Sb 22601; Sb 22600; Sb 22599, all published in MDP 17). Although these presumably belong to an early group, this cannot be proved since none were found in stratified contexts (perhaps S.ACR 1237.1 belongs to this group, but it was found in the problematic "au contact 17A–16" (see above), and may very well belong to any of the levels above, i.e. *Levels 16c–14*). This group is as yet poorly understood.

Signary

The *P-E* signary is characterised by an apparent lack of standardisation (Dahl 2002; 2005a: §3.1 and 5.3; building on Damerow 1999: 10 and 12, reprinted as Damerow 2006: §8.1–2 and §8.5) as demonstrated by the expanding number of unique signs documented in successive text publications (Dahl 2005b: 86; cf.

Farmer *et al.* 2004: 36–37). As such, *P-E* was probably ill-suited as a communication system (Damerow 2006). Some speech coding, reflected in the growing complexity of sign-strings, the introduction of poly-valency, and a more restricted signary may be present in certain (late) texts (Dahl 2009). An investigation of the signary may help to divide the texts into separate chronological groups.

Primary semantic differentiation (Fig. 18.12)

The primary semantic distinction in *P-E* is between numerical and non-numerical signs. The principal reason we are able to distinguish between these two categories is the fact that most of the numerical systems used and almost all of the numerical signs were directly borrowed from the slightly older proto-cuneiform writing system (Damerow and Englund 1989: 27–28; Friberg 1978–79: 12–36, 41–42), pointing to close contact with southern Mesopotamia during the formative period of writing's invention in Iran (Englund 2004: 122–27).

Primary graphic differentiation

The primary graphic distinction in *P-E* is between concrete and abstract signs, i.e. signs which resemble what they stand for, and signs with no apparent visual similarity to the object they represent (Fig. 18.13). It is not always easy to apply this criterion since certain concrete signs are never used to represent the object they graphically represent (Dahl 2005b: fig. 11), and since some seemingly abstract signs may in fact be graphically correct representations of objects. *P-E* is noteworthy for its high number of abstract signs.

Semantic subdivisions: object signs

Semantically, we can further subdivide the non-numerical signs into object and non-object signs (Fig. 18.14). Finally, the non-object signs can be divided into simple owner signs and signs used to qualify owners in a complex way.

Object signs are those signs that are directly qualified by a numerical notation. Many of the object signs in Mesopotamian proto-cuneiform texts can be deciphered thanks to their pictographic quality, or by using their known value in the later Sumerian cuneiform writing system. The same methods cannot be used to decipher object signs in *P-E*, because *P-E* object signs are often very abstract and because *P-E* was not followed by a successor system (Dahl 2009). Object signs in *P-E* may be described as:

- direct loans from Mesopotamian proto-cuneiform;
- signs which belong to a common pool of signs used in both Mesopotamia and Iran;
- "natural" signs;
- indigenous signs.

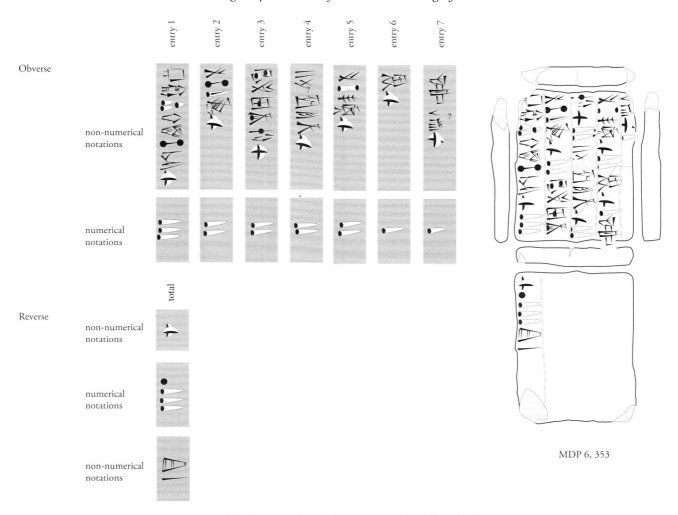

Figure 18.12. Example of primary semantic differentiation.

Owner signs

Non-numerical, non-object signs (Fig. 18.15) can be divided into two groups:

•signs representing an owner (understood in the broadest sense as an individual, a temple or family household, a clan or any other socio-economic unit);
•signs qualifying an owner by combining one or more signs in a complex way (restricted to *Group 2* and *2sub* tablets).

The signs used to describe owners show a graphical evolution and a distributional pattern which may reflect certain social organisational paradigms specific to this period (see also Dahl 2005b: 111; 2012).

Restricted signaries

Longer strings of signs in the primary entries can be broken down and shown to consist of an object segment and a non-object segment (followed by a numerical notation qualifying the object) (Fig. 18.16).

The non-object segment is sometimes made up of signs belonging to two different signaries, designated *Restricted Signary 1* and *2*. The signs belonging to *Restricted Signary 1* can be used independently as signs for owners or objects, and are therefore believed to represent titles, or something comparable. The signs belonging to *Restricted Signary 2* are believed to be some sort of pseudo- or quasi-syllabary and comprise, according to our most recent count, *c.* 100 signs occurring mostly in groups of 2, 3, or 4. A few of these signs also have a concrete meaning (object or owner value), suggesting that limited polyvalence had been introduced at some point. When both are present, a sign or short string of signs from *Restricted Signary 1* precedes a string of signs belonging to *Restricted Signary 2*.

The *Susa* tablet sequence

As we have seen, *P-E* tablets vary with respect to tablet shape, placement of text on the surface, structure of text, and signary. Can we use these parameters to

signs with no clear graphical referent   signs with clear graphical referent

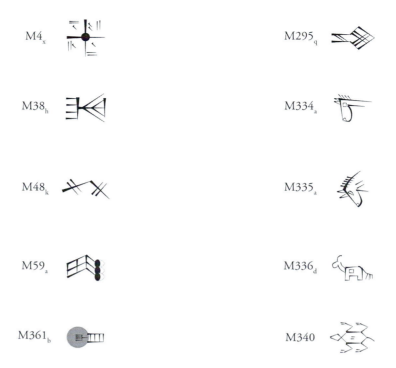

Figure 18.13. Example of primary graphic differentiation.

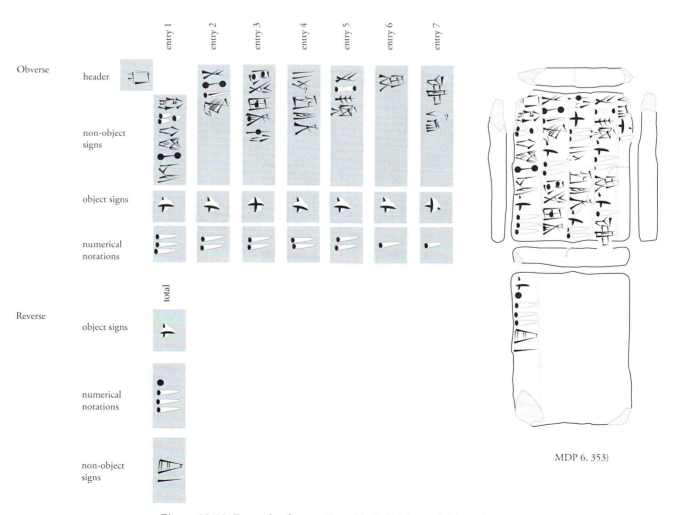

Figure 18.14. Example of semantic subject divisions of object signs.

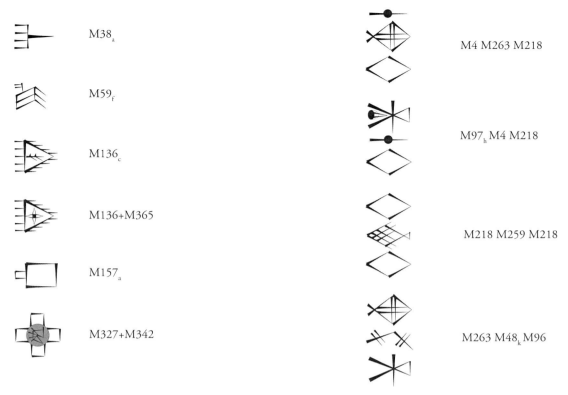

signs representing an owner
through a one-to-one correspondance with an emblem(?)

M38ₐ

M59f

M136c

M136+M365

M157ₐ

M327+M342

signs representing an owner
by combining syllabic value(?) signs in short strings

M4 M263 M218

M97h M4 M218

M218 M259 M218

M263 M48k M96

Figure 18.15. Examples of owner signs.

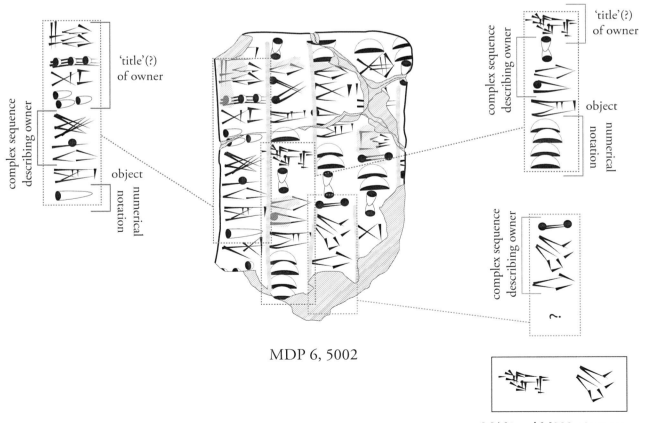

'title'(?)
of owner

complex sequence
describing owner

object

numerical
notation

'title'(?)
of owner

complex sequence
describing owner

object

numerical
notation

complex sequence
describing owner

?

MDP 6, 5002

M461 and M332d signs are
graphical representations of animals

Figure 18.16. Examples of restricted signaries.

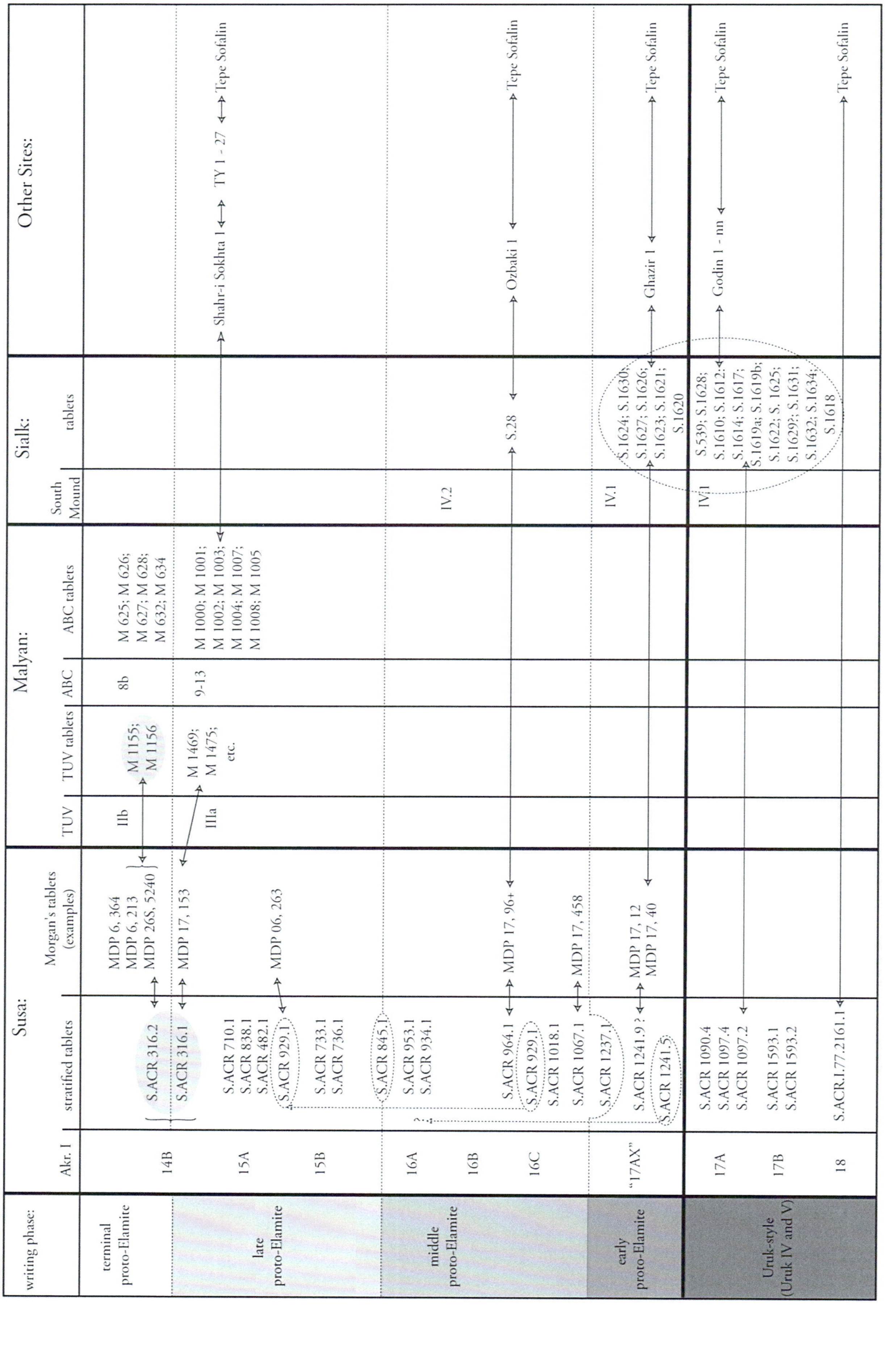

writing phase	Akr. I	Susa: stratified tablets	Susa: Morgan's tablets (examples)	Malyan: TUV	Malyan: TUV tablets	Malyan: ABC	Malyan: ABC tablets	Sialk: South Mound	Sialk: tablets	Other Sites:
terminal proto-Elamite	14B	S.ACR 316.2 S.ACR 316.1	MDP 6, 364 MDP 6, 213 MDP 26S, 5240 MDP 17, 153	IIb IIIa	M 1155; M 1156 M 1469; M 1475; etc.	8b 9–13	M 625; M 626; M 627; M 628; M 632; M 634 M 1000; M 1001; M 1002; M 1003; M 1004; M 1007; M 1008; M 1005			Shahr-i Sokhta 1 ↔ TY 1–27 ↔ Tepe Sofalin
late proto-Elamite	15A	S.ACR 710.1 S.ACR 838.1 S.ACR 482.1 S.ACR 929.1	MDP 06, 263							
late proto-Elamite	15B	S.ACR 733.1 S.ACR 736.1								
middle proto-Elamite	16A	S.ACR 845.1 S.ACR 953.1 S.ACR 934.1								
middle proto-Elamite	16B		MDP 17, 96+					IV.2	S.28	Ozbaki 1 ↔ Tepe Sofalin
middle proto-Elamite	16C	S.ACR 964.1 S.ACR 929.1 S.ACR 1018.1 S.ACR 1067.1	MDP 17, 458							
early proto-Elamite	"17AX"	S.ACR 1237.1 S.ACR 1241.9 ? S.ACR 1241.5	MDP 17, 12 MDP 17, 40					IV.1	S.1624; S.1630; S.1627; S.1626; S.1623; S.1621; S.1620	Ghazir 1 ↔ Tepe Sofalin
Uruk-style (Uruk IV and V)	17A	S.ACR 1090.4 S.ACR 1097.4 S.ACR 1097.2						IV1	S.539; S.1628; S.1610; S.1612; S.1614; S.1617; S.1619a; S.1619b; S.1622; S.1625; S.1629; S.1631; S.1632; S.1634; S.1618	Godin 1 – nn ↔ Tepe Sofalin
Uruk-style (Uruk IV and V)	17B	S.ACR 1593.1 S.ACR 1593.2								
Uruk-style (Uruk IV and V)	18	S.ACR.I.77.2161.1								Tepe Sofalin

Figure 18.17. The tablet sequence from Susa and the chronological relationships of other tablet groups.

establish a relative chronology for the *P-E* tablets? Intuitively, we can suggest that the structure of the entries will have become increasingly complex over time. Examples to the contrary exist in the history of writing (Houston *et al.* 2003: 458ff.), however. Furthermore, polyvalence tends to develop over time, and generations of scribal training tend to make scripts more coherent. The relative chronology of the *P-E* corpus presented in this paper is summarised in Figure 18.17.

The content of most *Format Group 1* tablets consists of owner signs – described with one sign, or a sign-cluster – and object and numerical signs. These texts contain a very high number of singletons, a feature perhaps related to the development of the writing system.[18] Some, but not all, *Format Group 1* tablets have a header. None have entries with sub-entries (see below and Fig. 18.17). All have the same physical format, and the text is placed in the same non-linear way on the surface of the tablet. *Format Group 1* tablets form a coherent group but unfortunately none were ever found in a stratified context at Susa.

In contrast, texts of *Format Group 2* describe owners with longer strings of signs that can often be separated into two groups: one belonging to *Restricted Signary 1*, and one belonging to *Restricted Signary 2*. The text on tablets from *Format Groups 2* and *2sub* is often organised neatly in lines across the surface of the tablet, sometimes marked with the ruling of a stylus. Some *Format Group 2* and *2sub* texts have a rather complex format with entries and sub-entries (Sb 15100; Sb 22215; Scheil 1935: n. 312 etc.) approaching the complexity of *Uruk III/Jamdat Nasr* texts (see Fig. 18.17). Most *Group 2* and *2sub* texts have a header. Based on the distribution of signs between the two signaries, we can suggest that limited polyvalence (e.g. "the sign x which is a graphical representation of the object y is used to represent the sound z") had been developed in the texts on *Format Group 2* and *2sub* tablets (see Fig. 18.11B). Signs with the same semantic properties found on *Format Group 1* and *Format Group 2* and *2sub* tablets show a graphical development from simple to more complex (see Fig. 18.18).

Although no *Format Group 1* tablets were found in stratigraphic context at Susa, circumstantial evidence from the old excavations suggests that they originated from levels below those containing *Format Group 2* and *2sub* tablets. The tablets from Susa were initially published soon after their discovery. This means that the later they were excavated and published, the deeper in the site they were found. Thus, we can suggest that *Format Group 1* tablets were indeed found in layers below those containing *Format Group 2* tablets because none were published in MDP 6 (or MDP 26S) – which contained the tablets from the first seasons of work at Susa and appeared in 1905 – and the first examples did not appear in print until the publication of MDP 17 in 1923.

All of the other indicators outlined above suggest that *Format Group 1* tablets are older than *Format Group 2* and *2sub* tablets. *Format Group 2sub* tablets are also likely to be younger than *Format Group 2* tablets. Within *Format Group 2* tablets we may also be able to distinguish, on a text-to-text basis, between early and late using the same parameters as outlined above.

The Susa tablets can thus be divided into four main groups: *Uruk*-style (numerical tablets, numero-ideographic tablets, and bullae), with which we have not concerned ourselves here; followed by early (*Format Group 1*), middle (*Format Group 2*), and late (*Format Group 2sub*) *P-E* tablets.[19] *Format Group x* tablets remain difficult to place, but may tentatively be considered older than *Format Group 2* and younger than *Format Group 1*.

Regional *P-E*

Is it possible to align texts from other sites with this chronology? In the following discussion we shall look at two groups of tablets, one (*Content Group A*) consisting of tablets from Susa recovered during both the stratified excavations of Le Brun (1971, 1978; Le Brun and Vallat 1978) and the excavations of de Morgan, as well as Tepe Ozbaki and Tappeh Sialk; and the other (*Content Group B*) from Susa that were recovered during the excavations by de Morgan, and also Tal-e Malyan.

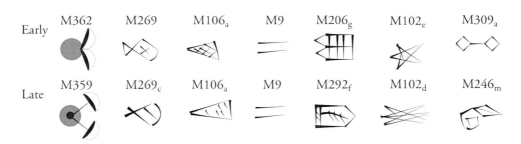

Figure 18.18. Examples of signs showing graphical development.

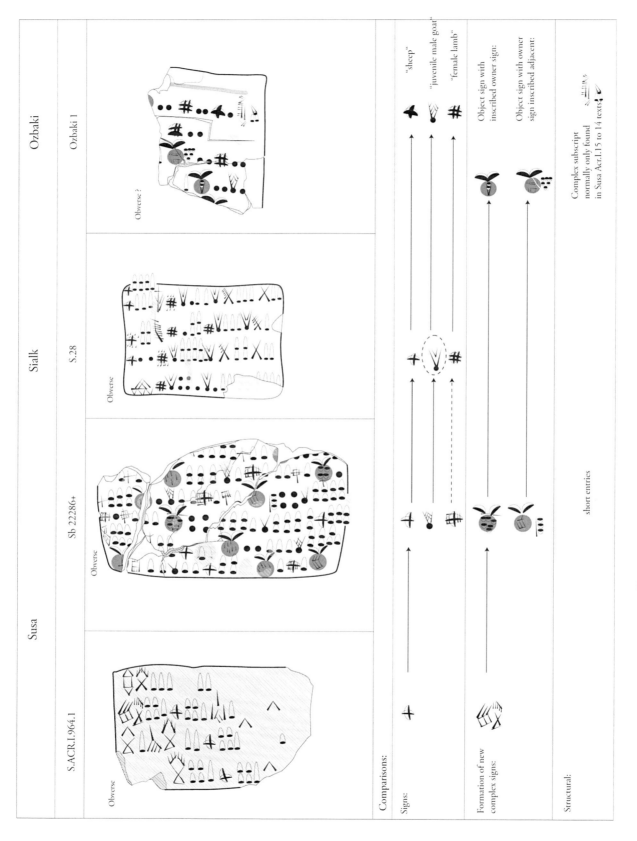

Figure 18.19. Examples of Content Group A from Susa and Ozbaki.

Content Group A *(Sb 22286+, S.ACR 964.1, S. 28, and Ozbaki 1)*

The four texts dealt with below all have related content (Fig. 18.19). Two of them (Sb 22286+ and S.ACR 964.1) are from Susa, one from the old and one from the more recent excavations. The other two texts are from Tappeh Sialk (S.28) and Tepe Ozbaki.

Sb 22286+[20] was published by V. Scheil in MDP 17. It is an account of *c.* 14 herds of sheep and goat, each of which is made up of male and female adult and juvenile animals of both species. The owners are described with complex graphemes, sometimes inscribed into the first sign for a counted animal – the sign for a nanny-goat (M362) – or placed next to it.[21] The text has no header, and the entries continue on the reverse, seemingly without giving a total. It is not ruled, and the organising principle is unclear since the largest herd is not mentioned first. This tablet is closely related to two tablets listing the production of butter-oil, cheese, and other products from the same herds.[22] All three tablets are flat and rectangular, and sealed with the same seal depicting goats.

S.ACR 964.1 was found in *Level 16c* (square H-6 room 711) in the *Acropole I* sounding, the earliest phase in which *P-E* tablets were recovered in well-stratified context (Le Brun 1971). This is an account of several herds of sheep and the production of ghee obtained from them. At least one of the owners is identified by an owner sign (M59) which is also attested on Sb 22286+.[23] The text does not appear to have a header, and is unruled. The tablet is flat and rectangular.

S.28 is the only complete *P-E* tablet from Tappeh Sialk and as noted above, it was found in a context assigned to *Sialk IV₂*.[24] It is an account of one or more herds of animals. The text seems to have a header, but the sign in question (a variant of M134) may simply qualify the first entry rather than act as a header for the entire text.[25] The total, written on the reverse, is divided into two parts, corresponding to entries 1–12 and 13–16 of the main text.[26]

Ozbaki 1 is an account of several herds of sheep and goat.[27] Only the lower left-hand corner of the tablet is preserved. We can distinguish at least two owners (entries 3′ and 6′), each described with a complex grapheme analogous to those found in comparable herding texts from Susa (see above; also Dahl 2005a). The owner sign in entry 3′ was formed by inscribing an otherwise unknown sign into the sign for a nanny goat (M362). The owner in entry 6′ is described with a complex grapheme, which can be analysed as the nanny-goat sign (M362) inscribed with an unknown sign, juxtaposed with a common Susa sign for a high-ranking official (M386).[28] As none of the Susa accounts comparable to this have a subscript, the last two signs of Ozbaki 1 remain enigmatic.[29]

A number of features link these four texts. All, including S.28 and Ozbaki 1, are concerned with sheep and goat herding; the texts share many signs; the creation/formation of new signs and derived signs is identical in all four texts (hatching and addition of signs to create semantic variants); the tablet format is identical (except perhaps the use of line-ruling in Ozbaki 1); and the structure of the texts is similar (except perhaps the subscript in Ozbaki 1).

Each of the texts also displays idiosyncrasies which can perhaps be interpreted as local features. Some of the object signs in S.28 and Ozbaki 1 are unattested in the Susa signary. One of these (M346_d), a graphic doubling of the standard sign for an adult sheep in *P-E* (M346), is found in both S.28 and Ozbaki 1. It can be classified as a semantically and graphically derived form of M346. Due to its position in the texts it can be suggested that this modification relates to the age of the animal. This would be analogous to the way primary and derived signs for sheep and goat are formed in the Susa text Sb 22286+.[30] Nevertheless, both S.28 and Ozbaki 1 belong squarely within the *P-E* epigraphic tradition. All of the signs that are native to S.28 and Ozbaki 1 can be classified as derived forms of similar graphically derived forms attested at Susa. In addition, the complex graphemes appear just as they do in the Susa texts. In fact, the complex graphemes concerning herded animals in Ozbaki 1 are entirely analogous to those found at Susa, and M59, one of the owner signs in S.28, occurs at Susa with the same semantic property (Sb 06310).

It may therefore be concluded that, regardless of the local terminology for certain semantically derived signs for sheep and goat, as well as independent, but typologically similarly constructed owner signs, both the Tepe Ozbaki tablet (Ozbaki 1) and the tablet from Tappeh Sialk (S.28) appear to be contemporaneous with the stratigraphically excavated Susa tablet S.ACR 964.1, which came from the second or middle phase *P-E* deposits in the *Acropole I* sounding (*Level 16c*), and with texts from de Morgan's excavations such as Sb 22286+. It is therefore likely that this group is mid-*P-E* in date (Fig. 18.17).

Content group B *(M1155, Sb 15166 and Sb 15242)*

Let us now turn to the texts from Tal-e Malyan (Fig. 18.20). These are by far the most complex *P-E* texts found outside Susa. Stratigraphically, Tal-e Malyan M1155 and M1156, both of which come from Operation TUV *BL IIB* are the latest and, in many respects, the most important texts from Tal-e Malyan. Both texts are rectangular and rather thick and pillow-shaped, and are also ruled and sealed with stamp seals. On both texts the stamp sealings are found in the same locations where cylinder seals are found on Susa tablets (i.e. on the blank space of the reverse, see Dahl 2012). As such these two Tal-e Malyan texts resemble Susa texts that were classified as belonging to *Format Group 2sub*. Both are presumably lists of workers attached to persons or institutions. The

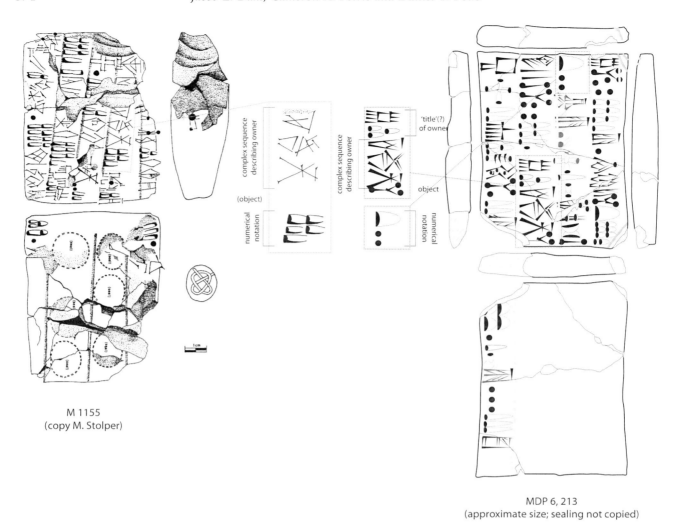

M 1155
(copy M. Stolper)

MDP 6, 213
(approximate size; sealing not copied)

Figure 18.20. Examples of Content Group A from Susa and Tal-e Malyan.

persons or institutions in M 1155 are described with rather lengthy strings that all fit the common pattern for long *P-E* strings in the Susa material.

A string such as entry 7 on the obverse of M1155 (M38$_f^?$ M146$^?$ [x] M110$_a$ M242$_b$ M96, 5N$_1$) can be successfully split into three parts, according to the principles of semantic structure discussed above. Whereas the numerical notation, 5N$_1$, can be quickly isolated, the qualified object must be inferred from the global structure of the text: the first entry, as well as the total on the reverse, indicates that this is M388. It was left out of all the other primary entries, a well-attested phenomenon in both *P-E* and proto-cuneiform texts. M388 is part of the first section of the strings in a majority of the entries in our text, but is absent in entry 7. The extant signs at the beginning of entry 7 (M38$_f^?$ M146$^?$) can be classified as belonging to *Restricted Signary 1*. The remaining three signs (M110$_a$ M242$_b$ M96) are common signs belonging to *Restricted Signary 2* and appear in at least four texts at Susa. In all four cases the context is very similar to that of the Malyan text M 1155:

Sb 15166 entry 6: M207$_a$ M388 M110$_a$ M242$_b$ M96 M376, 1N$_{34}$ 3N$_{14}$

Scheil 1935: no. 250 entry 2: x x M110$_b$ M242$_b$ M96, 1N$_1$

Sb 15323 entry 7: M110$_a$ M242$_b^{?!}$ M96 x , 1N1

Sb 15242 entry 4: M305 M388 M110 M242$_b$ M96 [...], [...] The first two signs (M305 M388) on Sb 15242 occur more than 50 times in the Susa corpus in the same capacity as found here. All of these, except perhaps Sb 15242, are thin rectangular tablets. Sb 15166 is sealed with a cylinder seal on the reverse. Sb 15242 is a fragment of a large squarish tablet, probably not belonging to *Format Group x*. Thus none of these tablets belong to *Format Group 2sub*.

In summary, it appears that certain texts from Tal-e Malyan exhibit a structure, content, and signary which are virtually indistinguishable from that of the later Susa texts (those from *Acropole I.15b–14b*). The only significant difference in administrative practices between the two sites is the use of stamp seals at Tal-e Malyan as compared to the exclusive use of cylinder seals at Susa. Further links with

stratified texts from *Acropole I.15b–14b* (S.ACR 316.1, S.ACR 733.1, and S.ACR 482.1) allow us, with great certainty, to map the Tal-e Malyan texts onto the Susa sequence established above. In both cases, the texts are among the very latest discovered at each site, suggesting that Tal-e Malyan TUV *BL 2B* and Susa *Acropole I.15b–14b* are palaeographically (and archaeologically?) contemporary (Fig. 18.17).

Conclusions

This paper has attempted to assess the full range of available chronological information related to the various *P-E* text corpora from Susa, Tappeh Sialk, Tepe Ozbaki, Tepe Sofalin, Tal-e Ghazir, Tal-e Malyan, Tepe Yahya, and Shahr-e Sokhta. One of the primary aims of this study has been to document the internal evolution of the *P-E* writing system and to use stratigraphic, absolute dating, and palaeographic evidence to establish the chronology of that evolution. Unfortunately, most of the currently known *P-E* texts come from the largely unstratified excavations at Susa that were conducted in the early twentieth century. The analysis of the stratigraphic and radiocarbon dating evidence relevant to the smaller number of well-excavated texts has, however, made it clear that there are a number of significant problems with the available contextual data and the associated absolute dates. The existence of a substantial plateau in the radiocarbon calibration curve has been highlighted as a major impediment to understanding the absolute chronology of the fourth millennium BC, which in turn hinders our understanding of the socio-economic dynamics of the ancient Near East at that time. Many of the extant problems of absolute chronology will only be resolved through renewed excavations targeting specific chronological problems.

The detailed analysis of the format, structure, content, and signary of the *P-E* tablets from Susa and various other sites has, however, shown that it is possible to differentiate early, middle, and late *P-E* texts. One significant outcome of this study has been to show that there appears to be a complex spatial distribution of both *Format* and *Content Groups* (see Fig. 18.17). For instance, *Format Group 1* and *2* as exemplified by *Content Group A* tablets (which date to the early and middle *P-E* phases), only appear at Susa, Tal-e Ghazir, Tepe Sialk, Tepe Ozbaki, and Tepe Sofalin, suggesting an early geographical trajectory that linked Susiana to the north-central Iranian Plateau. In contrast, the *Format Group 2, 2sub* and *x*, and *Content Group B* tablets, which date to the late *P-E* phases appear at Susa, Tal-e Malyan, Tepe Yahya, Shahr-e Sokhta, and Tepe Sofalin, suggesting a later trajectory that linked Susiana to the southern Zagros and eastern Iran, although the Sofalin evidence suggests that the link to the north Central Plateau continued.

Both trajectories reveal the critical role of Susa in the development and proliferation of the *P-E* writing system. This conforms well to Potts's (1999: 81–82) proposal that the *P-E* corpus might be better referred to as the "Susa III writing system".

While this paper has shown the relationship between elements of tablet format and signary, it has not commented overtly on the rationale behind the spread of this early Iranian writing system. Analysis of the documents and the raw materials from which they were made at sites like Tal-e Malyan and Tepe Yahya have emphasised that the texts relate to local-scale economic affairs and appear to have been made from local clays (e.g. Damerow and Englund 1989; Zeder and Blackman 2003; also Potts 1999: 81–83). Despite earlier claims to the contrary (e.g. Lamberg-Karlovsky 1978), it is unlikely that these texts reflect the economic integration of the entire Iranian Plateau and its littoral, but precisely what the widespread adoption of the *P-E* writing system represents is unclear, and is beyond the scope of this contribution. Many other papers in this volume have speculated on the reasons underlying the spread of the *P-E* writing system (see Helwing, this volume; Fazeli, this volume; Alden, this volume), but as the final chapter of this volume shows, there are limits to what can be said without a more robust body of evidence (Petrie, this volume: Conclusion).

One thing we can comment on specifically here is the chronological scope of the *P-E* writing system. In the introduction to this paper, reference was made to "scribal generations", which it can be argued correspond to the training, active career, and perhaps teaching period of individual scribes and their students. It is our contention that visible developments in signary, tablet shape, and writing conventions may have emerged in the course of just a few years or decades, and it is entirely possible that the entire *P-E* corpus was produced within the span of a small number of scribal generations. We have clear evidence for the relatively rapid development, evolution, dispersal, and adoption of a sophisticated administrative writing system, and while it was clearly in use across multiple, stratigraphic phases of occupation at several sites (e.g. Susa, Tal-e Malyan), it is also clear that it ceased to be used relatively quickly. The significance of this is unclear, but it is probable that the *P-E* writing system was in the hands of a very small number of practitioners who lost power and/or influence.

Notes
1   As used here the term "scribal generation" corresponds to the training, active career, and perhaps teaching period of individual scribes and their students. In our opinion, visible developments in signary, tablet shape, and writing conventions may have emerged in the course of just a few years or decades. Relatively compressed archaeological stratigraphy

with distinctive floor levels and buildings or deposits containing tablets may not necessarily represent centuries of occupation, but rather much shorter time spans, equivalent to "scribal generations".

2   It is important to note that R. H. Dyson Jr. never claimed that any of the so-called clay tags or labels from Tepe Hissar were inscribed with *P-E* signs.

3   Transliterations, meta-data, and supplementary visual documentation of all tablets discussed in this article are available on the CDLI (http://cdli.ucla.edu); s.v. the tablet IDs given in the text (where possible, museum numbers or primary publication).

4   Several fragmentary tablets have also been recovered at Susa in excavations directed by Mirabeddin Kaboli (ICAR). These are illustrated without further commentary in Anonymous 2001.

5   Indeed, in some cases statements contained in the published reports concerning find circumstances are contradicted by the contexts of *P-E* tablets found during later stratified excavations (Dahl 2005b). According to V. Scheil, many of the tablets he published were found in several large lots (Scheil 1923: i).

6   Described as "une succession de sols d'occupation creusés de foyers, de trous de piquets et de fosses larges et profondes qui descendent jusqu'au niveau de la couche 26" and dominated by bevel-rim bowls (Le Brun 1971: 177). For a schematic section showing this clearly, see Le Brun 1971: fig. 32.

7   At the time of writing, the earliest level (1) was not fully excavated and Le Brun and Vallat (1978: 12) foreshadowed the possibility that tablets might be found in it. No tablets were found in the latest *Acropole I.18* sub-phase (4).

8   Le Brun (1971: 210) merely referred to "les tablettes trouvées au contact des couches 17/16" without any further clarification as to what this meant precisely.

9   The legend to the drawings of these texts (Vallat 1971: fig. 43.1–3) gives the context less precisely as "contact 16–17" rather than "au contact 17A–16".

10   This consistency of orientation, in spite of the presence of the *Level 17A* deposits that lack architecture, could easily be explained if, in the areas around the sounding, standing architecture remained visible and in use. This would necessarily have constrained the builders of the *Level 16C* architecture to follow a similar orientation, one that replicated the no longer visible building complex in *Level 17B*.

11   Thus Le Brun and Vallat (1978: 31) wrote, "On remarque, en effet, à l'Acropole, un hiatus entre ces deux couches". In our opinion, this would only be correct if level *Level 17A* was effectively sterile, but this was not the case, as the archaeological finds from *Level 17A* published in Le Brun 1971 clearly show. These included tablets (Le Brun 1971: figs 43.4–7 and 44.1), cylinder sealings (1971: fig. 44.4, 6, 9, 14, 19 and 20), a stamp seal (1971: fig. 44.17), pottery (1971: figs 45.2, 6–9, 11, 13 and 14; 46.4, 6–14, 16 and 17; 47.1, 3–4, 6, 8–10 and 12; 48.1–9 and 15; 49.3–7, 9–10 and 12; 50.9–11; 51.2–6 and 8–11; 52.5; 53.1), stone objects (1971: figs 54.6 and 11; 55.2; 56.7; and 57.18–19), stone vessels or vessel fragments (1971: fig. 55.6, 9–11, 13 and 14), terracotta (1971: figs 56.3–4 and 16; and 57.7, 15 and 21–24), flint (1971: fig. 56.18), copper (1971: fig. 57.1–3 and 5) and bone (1971: fig. 57.8–11 and 16).

12   According to Canal (1978) the *haute terrasse* was finally abandoned at this point. Steve and Gasche (1971) identified an erosion layer of roughly this date on the surface of the ruined *Acropole* (MDP 46: 10, plan 2, coupe c, plan 7, coupe 4), suggesting the abandonment of some parts of the site. On the other hand, the fact that the earliest evidence of occupation in the *Ville Royale* encountered by E. Carter dates to the *P-E/Susa III* period and *ED I* may imply that, while some areas of the site were being abandoned, others were being settled.

13   The number 782 on the section (Le Brun 1971: fig. 32) is incorrect. According to the plan of level 16 (Le Brun 1971: fig. 33, lower), this should read 732.

14   The architectural continuity just noted between *Levels 16, 15B* and *15A* is another argument in favour of grouping them together.

15   Thus, he described it once as "tablette restée unique" and further as "l'unique tablette proto-élamite", and he used it to define the chronology of the stratum in which it was found. In 1934 Ghirshman excavated an extension of *Chantier I*, known as IP, where he came upon a "couche de tablettes proto-élamites", but Amiet considered the first (and stratigraphically highest, hence chronologically latest) tablet discovered here, S.539, to be a "tablette-coussin de l'époque d'Uruk" (Amiet 1985: 305). Finally in 1937, at a depth of 4.5–5 m, Hardy excavated some private houses which contained "la série de tablettes presque exclusivement numérales...très semblables à celles de Godin Tépé et de Suse 17" (Amiet 1985: 306).

16   This plateau does not just have significance for late fourth-millennium BC sites in Iran. As a means of situating the Iranian dates into a wider regional context, it is also instructive to compare the dates from these Zagros sites with those from Greater Mesopotamia. Not only do the radiocarbon dates from *Godin VI:1* appear to be virtually identical if not later than those from the *Middle Banesh* deposits at Tal-e Malyan, but both sets of determinations appear to predate the determinations from Jebel Aruda, Hassek 5B, Habuba Kabira, and Arslantepe VIA (Fig. 18.10; also Wright and Rupley 2001: figs 3.1–3.3). This has dramatic implications for models of the *Uruk expansion* that need to be addressed – particularly the date and motivation of the major phase of colonisation that saw the establishment of Habuba Kabira/Jebel Aruda. Johnson's (1989: 607) so-called "refugee proposition" may have a stronger chronological basis than was initially apparent, and the evidence of similar linear measurement systems at Tepe Yahya, Eridu, and Habuba Kabira (Beale and Carter 1983) may in fact be completely contemporaneous.

17   In publications *P-E* tablets are conventionally turned 90° counter-clockwise to conform with the standards in Assyriology.

18   See Damerow 2006, who connected the decreasing number of singletons in proto-cuneiform with the emerging standardisation aided by lexical texts, but note that a re-evaluation of the results in Dahl 2002, taking the relative date of the tablets into consideration, did not show any significant reduction in the number of singletons and noted the lack of any lexical tradition in *Proto-Elamite*.

19 cf. Dittman's PE 1, PE 2a, and PE 2b periods (Dittman 1986: tables 1–2 and 4).

20 cf. Dahl 2005b: 99–106 for a description of this text and the two related production accounts Sb 22276 and Sb 06353.

21 This way of forming complex graphemes was discussed first in Dahl 2005a and later in Dahl 2005b.

22 Sb 22276 and Sb 6353.

23 For reasons which are not clear the owner signs are placed next to the object sign resembling ghee (M269$_a$), rather than the object sign for sheep (M346). Since neither of these objects signs leaves any room for inscribing the owner sign, the owner sign is placed next to the object sign it qualifies.

24 cf. Ghirsman 1934: 115ff.; 1938: pls. 31.1 and 92.

25 This may be compared with the header of Sb 22354, a fragment of a herding account from Susa. It is possible to suggest that a sign like M387 preceded *M134. This kind of complex header is well known at Susa.

26 The second section of the total as well as the primary entries are further qualified by the sign M124, a sign commonly used at Susa for a specific worker category.

27 An image of Ozbaki 1 was originally published in a Farsi-language journal of the Iranian Cultural Heritage Organization (Madjidzadeh n.d.) and later republished by F. Vallat (2003). The copy published here (Fig. 18.19) is based on that photograph.

28 Transliterated on the CDLI as M362xX+M386. It is, however, possible that nothing was intentionally inscribed inside M362, but that the surface of the tablet was slightly disturbed.

29 Subscripts are found primarily in particular tablet groups (such as the "plough-team" texts discussed by Damerow and Englund [1989: 27, n. 88 and 57, n. 159]) presumably dating to the very latest phases of the use of *P-E*. Subscripts are of course well known from Uruk texts.

30 A few other graphically unique signs are found in S.28 as well, e.g. a hatched version of M346 not attested in Susa, and a seemingly indigenous variant of M6.

Bibliography

Alden, J. R. 1982. "Trade and Politics in Proto-Elamite Iran", *Current Anthropology* 23 (6): 613–40.

Amiet, P. 1985. "La période IV de Tépé Sialk reconsidérée", in Huot, J-L., Yon, M. and Calvet, Y. (eds), *De l'Indus aux Balkans, Recueil Jean Deshayes*, Éditions Recherche sur les civilisations, Paris: 293–312.

Amiet, P. and Tosi, M. 1978. "Phase 10 at Shahr-i Sokhta: excavations in Square XDV and the late 4th millennium B.C. assemblage of Sīstān", *East and West* 28: 9–31.

Anonymous. 2001. *Les recherches archéologiques françaises en Iran, 20 octobre au 21 novembre 2001*, Institut Français de Recherche en Iran, Musée National d'Iran, Tehran, Musée du Louvre: 159–60, nos. 77–79.

Aurenche, O., Galet, P., Régagnon-Caroline, E. and Évin, J. 2001. "Proto-Neolithic and Neolithic cultures in the Middle East – the birth of agriculture, livestock raising, and ceramics: a calibrated 14C chronology 12500–5500 cal BC", *Radiocarbon* 43 (3): 1191–1202.

Badler, V. R. 2002. "A Chronology of Uruk Artefacts from Godin Tepe in Central Western Iran and Its Implications for the Interrelationships Between the Local and Foreign Cultures", in Postgate, J. N. (ed.), *Artefacts of Complexity: Tracking the Uruk in the Near East*, British School of Archaeology in Iraq, Aris and Philips, Oxford: 79–110.

Beale, T. W. and Carter, 1983. "On the track of the Yahya large Kuš: evidence for architectural planning in the period IVC complex at Tepe Yahya", *Paléorient* 9: 81–88.

Buck, C. E., Cavanagh, W. G. and Litton, C. D. 1996. *Bayesian Approach to Interpreting Archaeological Data*, John Wiley and Sons, Chichester.

Canal, D. 1978. "La haute terrsse de l'Acropole de Suse", *Paléorient* 4: 169–76.

Caldwell, J. R. 1971. "Ghazir, Tell-I", *Reallexikon der Assyriologie* 3: 348–55.

Dahl, J. L. 2002. "Proto-Elamite sign frequencies", *Cuneiform Digital Library Bulletin* 2002/1: 1–3.

Dahl, J. L. 2005a. "Animal husbandry in Susa during the Proto-Elamite period", *Studi Micenei ed Egeo-Anatolici* 47: 81–134.

Dahl, J. L. 2005b. "Complex graphemes in Proto-Elamite", *Cuneiform Digital Library Journal* 2005/3: 1–15.

Dahl, J. L. 2009. "Early writing in Iran: a reappraisal", *Iran* 47: 23–32.

Dahl, J. L. 2012. "The marks of early writing", *Iran* 50: 1–12.

Dahl, J. L., Hessari, M. and Yousefi Zoshk, R. 2012. "The Proto-Elamite tablets from Tape Sofalin", *Iranian Journal of Archaeological Studies* 2.1: 57–73.

Damerow, P. 2006. "The origins of writing as a problem of historical epistemology", *Cuneiform Digital Library Journal*, 2006, http://cdli.ucla.edu/pubs/cdlj/2006/cdlj2006_001.pdf accessed 23 December 2012.

Damerow, P. and Englund, R.K. 1989. *The Proto-Elamite texts from Tepe Yahya*, Peabody Museum of Archaeology and Ethnology, Harvard University, Cambridge, MA.

Dittmann, R. 1986. "Susa in the Proto-Elamite period and annotations on the painted pottery of Proto-Elamite Khuzestan", in Finkbeiner, U. and Röllig, W. (eds), *Ğamdat Naṣr: Period or regional style?*, TAVO Beiheft B 62, Wiesbaden: 171–98.

Dyson, R. H. Jr, 1987. "The relative and absolute chronology of Hissar II and the Proto-Elamite horizon of Northern Iran", in Aurenche, O., Evin, J. and Hours, F. (eds), *Chronologies in the Near East: Relative Chronologies and Absolute Chronology 16,000–4,000 B.P.*, BAR International Series 379 (ii), Archaeopress, Oxford: 647–78.

Englund, R. K. 1996. *Proto-cuneiform texts from diverse collections*, MSVO 4, Berlin.

Englund, R. K. 1998. "Texts from the Late Uruk Period", in Attinger, P. and Wäfler, M. (eds), *Spätururk–Zeit und frühdynastische Zeit*, OBO 160/1, Göttingen: 15–233.

Englund, R. K. 2004. "The state of decipherment of Proto-Elamite", in Houston, S.D. (ed.), *The First Writing; Script Invention as History and Process*, CUP, Cambridge: 100–49.

Falkenstein, A. 1936. *Archaische Texte aus Uruk*, ATU 1, Gebr. Mann Verlag, Berlin.

Farmer, S., Sproat, R. and Witzel, M. 2004. "The collapse of the Indus-script thesis: the myth of a literate Harappan Civilization", *Electronic Journal of Vedic Studies* 11–2 (13 Dec. 2004): 19–57.

Friberg, J. 1978–79. *The Third Millennium Roots of Babylonian Mathematics, I–II*, University of Göteborg, Department of Mathematics, Göteborg.

Ghirshman, R. 1934. "Une tablette proto-élamite du Plateau iranien», *RA* 31: 115–19.

Ghirshman, R. 1938. *Fouilles de Sialk près de Kashan*, Geuthner, Paris.

Helwing, B. 2005. "Early complexity in highland Iran: recent archaeological research into the Chalcolithic of Iran", *TÜBA-AR* VIII: 39–60.

Hessari, M. and Akbari, H. 2007. "The preliminary report of the excavation campaign in Tape Sofalin, Pishva", *Archaeological Reports* 7: 167–200 (in Persian).

Houston, S. D. 2004. *The First Writing: Script Invention as History and Process*, Cambridge University Press, Cambridge.

Johnson, G. A. 1989. "Late Uruk in Greater Mesopotamia: expansion or collapse?", *Origini* 14: 595–611.

Lamberg-Karlovsky, C. C. 1978. "The Proto–Elamites of the Iranian plateau", *Antiquity* 52: 114–20.

Le Brun, A. 1971. "Recherches stratigraphiques à l'Acropole de Suse, 1969–1971", *CDAFI* 1: 163–216.

Le Brun, A. 1978. "Le niveau 17B de l'Acropole de Suse (campagne de 1972)", *CDAFI* 9: 57–154.

Le Brun, A. and Vallat, F. 1978. "L'origine de l'écriture à Suse", *CDAFI* 8: 11–59.

Madjidzadeh, Y. n.d. *Ozbaki*, Iranian Center for Archaeological Research, Tehran.

Madjidzadeh, Y. 2001. *The Ancient Ozbaki Site, Savoudjbolaqh, Iran*, Pishin Pajoh Cultural Center, Tehran.

Madjidzadeh, Y. 2003. *The Third Season of Excavations at Ozbaki*, Iranian Center for Archaeological Research and Iranian Cultural Heritage Organisation, Tehran.

Mecquenem, R. de. 1949. *Epigraphie proto–élamite*, MDP 31, E. Leroux, Paris.

Mecquenem, R. de. 1956. "Notes protoélamites", *RA* 50: 200–204.

Meriggi, P. 1971. *La scrittura proto-elamica. Parte Iª: La scrittura e il contenuto die testi*, Accademia Nazionale die Lincei, Rome.

Meriggi, P. 1974a. *La scrittura proto-elamica. Parte Iª: Catalogo die segni*, Accademia Nazionale die Lincei, Rome.

Meriggi, P. 1974b. *La scrittura proto-elamica. Parte Iª: Testi*, Accademia Nazionale die Lincei, Rome.

Nicholas, I. 1990. *The Proto-Elamite Settlement at TUV*, Malyan Excavation Reports, vol. I, University of Pennsylvania Museum, Philadelphia.

Petrie, C. A. in press. "Iran and *Uruk* Mesopotamia: chronologies and connections in the 4th millennium BC", in McMahon, A., Crawford, H. and Postgate, J. N., *Preludes to Urbanism in the Ancient Near East: A Conference in honour of Joan Oates*, McDonald Institute Monographs, Cambridge.

Petrie, C. A. and Thomas, K. D. 2012. "The topographic and environmental context of the earliest village sites in western South Asia", *Antiquity* 86 (334): 1055–67.

Potts, D. T. 1999. *The Archaeology of Elam: Formation and Transformation of an Ancient Iranian State*, CUP, Cambridge.

Potts, D. T., 2001. *Excavations at Tepe Yahya, Iran 1967–1975: The Third Millennium*, American School of Prehistoric Research Bulletin, 45, Peabody Museum of Archaeology and Ethnology, Harvard University, Cambridge (MA).

Raetzel-Fabian, D., 2001. „Anmerkungen zur Interpretation von 14C-Daten", in Czebrezuk, J. and Müller, J. (eds), *Die absolute Chronologie in Mitteleuropa 3000–2000 v. Chr*, Poznań Bamberg Rahden, Westphalia: 11–23.

Rothman, M. S. and Badler, V. 2011. "Contact and development in Godin Period VI", in Gopnik, H. and Rothman, M. (eds), *On the High Road: The History of Godin Tepe, Iran*, Royal Ontario Museum/Mazda Press, Toronto: 67–137.

Salvatori, S., Tosi, M. and Vidale. M. 2001. "Crocevia dell'Asia. L'Iran orientale e l'evoluzione delle civiltà protostoriche ad oriente della Mesopotamia", in Gramiccia, A. (ed.), *Antica Persia, I Tresori del Museo Nazionale di Tehran e la Ricerca Italiana en Iran*, Edizioni de Luca Rome: 32–37.

Scheil, V. 1905. *Documents archaïques en écriture proto–élamite*, MDP 6, E. Leroux, Paris.

Scheil, V. 1923. *Textes de comptabilité proto–élamites*, MDP 17, E. Leroux, Paris.

Scheil, V. 1935. *Texte de comptabilité*, MDP 26, E. Leroux, Paris.

Steve, M.-J. and Gasche, H. 1971. *L'Acropole de Suse*, MDP 46, E. Leroux, Paris and Leiden.

Stolper, M. W. 1985. "Proto-Elamite texts from Tall-i Malyan", *Kadmos* 24: 1–12.

Sumner, W. M. 1986. "Proto-Elamite civilisation in Fars", in Finkbeiner, U. and Rollig, W. (eds), *Gamdat Nasr: Period of Regional Style?*, Beihefte zom Tubinger Atlas des Vorderern Orients 62, Ludwig Reichert, Wiesbaden: 199–211.

Sumner, W. M. 1988. "Maljan, Tall-e (Anšan)", *Reallexikon der Assyriologie* 7: 306–20.

Sumner, W. M. 2003. *Early Urban Life in the Land of Anshan: Excavations at Tal-e Malyan in the Highlands of Iran*, Malyan Excavations Reports III, University Museum Monograph, 113, University of Pennsylvania Museum of Archaeology and Anthropology, Pennsylvania.

Vallat, F. 1971. "Les documents epigraphiques de l'Acropole (1969–1971)", *CDAFI* 1: 235–45.

Vallat, F. 2003. "Un fragment de tablette proto-élamite découvert à Ozbaki, au nord-ouest de Téhéran", *Akkadica* 124: 229–31.

Voigt, M. and Dyson Jr., R. H. 1992. "Chronology of Iran, ca. 8000–2000 B.C.", in Ehrich, R. W. (ed.), *Chronologies of Old World Archaeology*, I & II, Chicago University Press, Chicago: 122–78; 125–53.

Waddington, C. H. 1974. "Horse brands of the Mongolians: a system of signs in a nomadic culture", *American Ethnologist* 1: 471–88.

Weiss, H. and Young Jr., T. C. 1975. "The merchants of Susa: Godin V and plateau-lowland relations in the late fourth millennium B.C.", *Iran* 13: 1–18.

Whitcomb, D. S. 1971. *The Proto-Elamite period at Tall-i Ghazir, Iran*, unpublished B.A. thesis, University of Georgia, Athens.

Wright, H. T., 1985. "Problems of absolute chronology in protohistoric Mesopotamia", *Paléorient* 6: 93–98.

Wright, H. T. and Rupley, E. S. A. 2001. "Calibrated radiocarbon age determinations of Uruk-related assemblages", in Rothman, M. S. (ed.), *Uruk Mesopotamia and Its Neighbors*: Cross Cultural Interactions in the Era of State Formation, School of American Research Press, Santa Fe (NM): 85–122.

Zeder, M. A. and Blackman, M. J. 2003. "Economy and administration at Banesh Malyan: exploring the potential of faunal and chemical data for understanding state process", in Miller, N. F. and Abdi, K. (eds), *Yeki bud, yeki nabud: Essays on the Archaeology of Iran In Honor of William M. Sumner*, Cotsen Institute of Archaeology, Los Angeles: 121–39.

19. SCALES, DIFFERENCE, AND MOBILITY

Susan Pollock

This paper concentrates on underlying conceptual issues that link many of the contributions in this volume. In doing so, my goal is to draw out some of the themes that are explicitly raised in these contributions as well as others that remain under the surface, but which play a significant role in the approaches adopted and interpretations reached by the authors. I will also mention a few matters that are not broached in these papers but which should, to my mind, play a role in further research on the fourth millennium BC in Iran and surrounding regions.

Regional variation

In a volume entitled *Ancient Iran and its Neighbours*, it is worth posing the question at the outset, whether the notions of "Iran" or "its neighbours" are indeed useful categorisations. In what respect are contemporary political boundaries appropriate ways to think about the ancient past? Of course, any examination of the past must set some kinds of geographical as well as chronological limits, and modern political boundaries often shape research histories in significant ways. The inclusion of Iran's neighbours in the volume's title is a clear attempt to avoid letting modern geography become a straitjacket. Yet the focus of the papers is principally on those sites and regions that fall within the present-day borders of Iran (a primary exception is the contribution by Bonora and Vidale). While on the one hand the focus on Iran seeks to displace the overwhelming emphasis on Mesopotamia as the font of all major historical developments, replacing one geographic entity with another carries with it some of the same problems: categories mould thoughts, including the questions that are appropriate to ask and the answers that are judged to be acceptable. While none of the authors allows modern borders simply to dictate the limits of her or his investigations, the point nonetheless requires emphasis: modern

political entities and borders should not structure our thinking about the past, as they tend to lead to the reification of arbitrary divisions in our research. That said, a striking feature of many of the papers in this volume is the emphasis on variation rather than uniformity among regions, in particular in the forms of political organisation and their developments over the course of the fourth millennium BC. This perspective is to be applauded, coming as it does on the heels of a relatively long period in archaeology in which the emphasis has been on supra-regional comparisons that have tended to underplay (local) differences in favour of (regional and interregional) similarities.

Alden, for example, aims to understand fourth-millennium BC developments in the Kur River Basin in a way that avoids imposing a "one-size-fits-all" model of state development derived from south-western Iran and Mesopotamia (e.g. Wright and Johnson 1975; Wright 1998; Johnson 1973, 1980). He adopts Sumner's (1986) position that mobile pastoralism, organised along tribal lines, may have been a significant structuring element of society, which in turn produced a distinctive form of political organisation. Regardless of whether one accepts the specific arguments brought to bear by Alden and Sumner, the insistence on significant differences in the political developments in southern highland Iran in comparison to Mesopotamia takes an important step away from the heavily Mesopotamia-centric tendencies in western Asian archaeology, which have resulted in something of a blindness to the possibility of other historical trajectories.

In a related fashion Bonora and Vidale argue that the Kopet Dag region of southern Turkmenistan should not be considered, as has historically been the case, a "passive recipient of cultural innovation", but rather an integral and leading partner in a south-western Asian cultural interaction sphere. In this way they draw attention to the active role played in historical trajectories by people in all regions, effectively dissolving the clear-cut distinction between centre and periphery. At the same time, the notion of a geographically and temporally extensive "cultural interaction sphere" (Lamberg-Karlovsky and Tosi 1973), risks becoming a kind of "black box" into which unspecified forms of interactions and sociocultural, political, and economic relations are placed. Other ways of thinking about such complex relationships, for example notions of hybridity (cf. Feldman 2006), offer alternatives for conceptualising and examining large-scale cultural connections.

Mobility

Following the pioneering work of William Sumner (1972) in the Kur River Basin and Henry Wright (1987) and Allen Zagarell (1982) in the highland Zagros valleys, the importance of mobile populations has been emphasised in the archaeological literature on Iran. Many discussions of mobility have been fuelled by comparisons, both direct and indirect, to ethnographic and historical information on nomads in recent times (e.g. Abdi 2003; Mashkour 2003; Alizadeh 2008). The principal arguments for using modern nomads as ethnographic parallels rest on the assumption of a constant geographic situation between past and present, approximately similar environmental conditions, and often technology as well (cf. Ascher 1961). In drawing such analogies, however, we risk ignoring the vast economic, political, and social changes that have occurred in the region since the fourth millennium BC. I would therefore argue that such projections should be treated as possibilities to be critically investigated rather than taken over wholesale (see also Bernbeck 2008; Potts 2010).

A welcome element in the contributions to this volume is a general understanding that mobility consists of more than just nomadism. Transhumance is one important alternative, with the precise forms varying in terms of timing, distance, and the segments of a community that moved or stayed behind. In his paper on the Kur River Basin in the fourth millennium BC, Alden argues that significant parts of Tal-e Malyan were occupied only seasonally in *Middle Banesh* times. His logic is that the site grew quite rapidly and, coupled with limits on agricultural productivity in Tal-e Malyan's sustaining area, it is likely that it was "supported by and providing non-agricultural goods and services to a large non-resident population of non-settled people….". The restricted possibilities for farming led to an emphasis on trade, craft production, and political activity. In this case, as in Sumner's argument cited by several authors, greater mobility is said to be a direct outcome of low or declining agricultural productivity, a reaction

to particular conditions rather than a positive or desired step of its own. Fazeli *et al.* are appropriately cautious in assuming that a substantial break in the settlement record during the *Late Chalcolithic* period on the Tehran and Qazvin Plains can be equated with transhumance. They point to climate change, environmental catastrophes, and economic crisis as probable grounds for the adoption of more mobile ways of life.

While all of these potential reasons can and should be considered, one should not exclude the possibility that mobile ways of life were in some cases preferred for social and cultural reasons. In other words, while we may consider a (largely) sedentary way of life desirable, this need not always and everywhere have been the case. Furthermore, mobility is not limited to pastoral nomadism or transhumance. As has been increasingly discussed in the literature on the Late Neolithic in western Asia, mobility is not restricted to the medium term (seasonal and annual movements), but rather may take place on a shorter basis (e.g. daily) or over longer time scales, as when communities move to a new settlement once or more in a generation (Bernbeck 2008). An example of this latter form of mobility is illustrated in the paper by Petrie *et al.* on Tol-e Spid, where successive occupations and reoccupations in *Lapui* times were separated by layers of destruction by fire or levelling of the previous settlement. Little time seems to have elapsed between one settlement and the next. Elsewhere, Henry Wright has proposed that the widespread similarity among *Late Uruk* ceramics over vast areas might be due to the movement of a specific segment of the population – potters – rather than necessarily to the wholesale migrations of communities or colonies (Wright 2001: 134–35; see also Petrie 2011).

Interpretations of material culture similarities and differences

The interpretation of similarities and differences in material culture is a bread-and-butter issue in archaeology. It is therefore surprising that in this regard archaeologists have generally tended to rely on a host of unexamined assumptions, which often lack the sophistication one would expect for such a central issue. In recent years this has begun to change, thanks in part to the rebirth of interests in material objects and materiality in anthropology more generally (Meskell 2004; Miller 2005; Pollock and Bernbeck 2011).

The authors in this volume draw on an array of assumptions, occasionally explicit but more often implicit, concerning the identification and especially the interpretation of similarities and differences in archaeological material. In his discussion of the *Early* and *Middle Uruk* periods in Fars and Khuzestan, Wright considers "broader questions of trans-regional interaction", primarily in terms of similarities in domestic crafts and ceramics, with attention to vessel forms, decoration, wares, and forming technologies. On grounds of the near absence of similarities in these craft-based elements, he argues that there were few contacts or relations between the two areas during these times. Although not made explicit, this argument is predicated on the idea that interactions among groups invariably result in the exchange or imitation of elements of material culture. While this may indeed be a likely outcome of interactions, whether sustained or episodic, it is perhaps well to keep in mind the implications of Barth's pioneering work (1969; see also Stark 1998) demonstrating that frequent interactions may also result in a clearer marking of borders via differences in material accoutrements. In this regard it is crucial to consider the kinds of interactions that took place and their material consequences rather than simply their presence or absence.

In Rothman's paper, as in many discussions of the *Uruk* period in Mesopotamia (e.g. Algaze 1993, 2008), interactions are presumed to imply (material) exchange relations and to be visible in terms of pottery styles, among other material traits. Rothman suggests that one of the two major themes of research on the fourth millennium BC has been "the nature of interactions across the region, specifically how exchange relationships affected the evolutionary trajectories of societies....". Exchange becomes the assumed motor driving similarities in material culture, unless proved otherwise (for a related argument, see Matthews, this volume). In the particular case of Godin Tepe, Rothman argues that if the locations where *Uruk* pottery has been found in the Zagros highlands are mapped, one sees a pattern that follows one of the well-known routes out of the lowlands up the Diyala River into the Mahidasht plain, and from there into the Kangavar region (and Godin Tepe). The immediate assumption would, therefore, be the movement of people – as traders, for example – from lowland Mesopotamia into the Zagros highlands. Neutron activation analyses, however, have shown that these "Uruk" pots were made with local clay, which – in this case – requires a modification of the assumption of exchange of goods, in this case pots, in order to take into account the possibility of local copying of *Uruk* ceramics.

In a similar fashion, Thornton *et al.* seek to understand why, with rare exceptions, neither *Late Uruk* nor *Proto-Elamite* material culture is found at Tepe Hissar. They turn to explanations involving trade and political authority: either merchants were uninterested in what the inhabitants of Tepe Hissar had to offer, or the political powers in their home cities were unable to exert authority over this distance; but one must ask once again whether political supremacy and trade are the only bases for such interactions.

Moreover, it seems that pots (or their absence) are assumed to demonstrate cultural connections (or lack thereof), but not lapis lazuli, which was present in large quantities at Tepe Hissar in the late fourth millennium "despite limited cultural connections." This suggests an implicit evaluation of the meaning of pottery vessels versus lapis lazuli, the rationale for which needs to be made explicit.

Rather than relying solely on explanations based on contacts and interactions, Petrie *et al.* note the importance of shifts in key technologies in leading to observed material changes. For example, in *Lapui* times the introduction of the slow wheel led to the appearance of "refined" rim forms and regular vessel openings, while in the *Middle Banesh* period, the use of the fast wheel and moulds resulted in a shift toward greater simplicity and efficiency of production. These were not newly introduced and previously unknown technologies, but rather "the result of cultural responses to changing socio-economic requirements" (J. Blackman 1989, as cited in Petrie *et al.*, this volume). This argument has the salutary effect of putting the explanation of observed changes in material culture in the realm of (partly) intentional human actions, rather than a result of nebulous "contact" or "interaction".

In his paper Sardari remarks that despite the striking difference in ceramics between the *Bakun* and *Lapui* periods in Fars, there are important similarities in settlement patterns, subsistence, management mechanisms (presumably administrative devices and their use), weaving technologies, etc. These in turn point to continuities in socio-economic systems from the fifth to the fourth millennium BC. His astute observation points to a balance between continuity and change that can and should be the subject of investigation. In this way, he moves away from the all-too-common tendency to reify the periodisations we produce on the basis of a limited range of material categories, in particular pottery and seals.

A closely related issue is the role of practice in our archaeological thinking, that is, an emphasis on the doing of things, rather than on static end products. Although not framed in these terms, Sardari's comparison of the *Bakun* and *Lapui* periods points in this direction, as he considers the ways in which things were used – for weaving, administration, subsistence, etc. – rather than simply what objects such as pottery looked like. In a discussion of lowland *Uruk* influences on Iranian traditions in the earlier fourth millennium BC, Helwing contends that the adoption of *Uruk*-related ceramic forms as well as other objects (seals, tokens) on the Iranian central plateau did not significantly impact those communities, whereas in the Iranian (Zagros) highlands, impact seems to have been inversely related to the distance from the Mesopotamian lowlands. Although the question of how impact is assessed remains somewhat vague,

Helwing also notes that the use of seals and tokens as well as other objects, and not simply their appearance, offer relevant information for such a judgment.

I would argue that we need to pursue in more detail the question of how we identify similarities and differences in archaeological materials and to what we attribute them. More specifically, such enquiry should lead to examinations of the ways in which the typically broad-brush, coarse-scale changes we observe (e.g. changes in ceramic styles or technologies, demographic shifts, settlement patterns) were produced by the small-scale practices of people, rather than simply imposed from top down or assumed to be automatically adopted as the result of, for example, "contact." The concept of political economy, in which the nexus of production, exchange and consumption is a focus of research, is a direction that could be usefully expanded. While political economy can be investigated in other fashions, it lends itself well to being combined with attention to practice and therefore serves as a way to integrate studies of the everyday and small-scale with the large-scale sphere of top-down decisions and structures. For example, Thornton *et al.* mention the ubiquitous presence of chaff-tempered trays in certain periods at Tepe Hissar. In addition to being chronological or cultural markers, what might the presence of these trays tell us about food preparation practices? How were they used, what were the social and technical contexts of their production, and what does such information offer in terms of other ways of thinking about the meaning of material culture similarities and differences?

Who were those people?

A final topic in these papers on which I would like briefly to comment is the focus, mostly implicit, on the question, "who were those people?" One can pose such a question about people in the past (or present) in many different ways, that is, with many different expectations regarding the possible answers.

In the context of the Godin Oval, Rothman asks whether the complex was occupied by foreigners or by local people, but how exactly foreigners or local people are defined remains less clear. Rather than taking these to be static, clearly bounded categories that are marked by specific forms of material culture, I would argue that an emphasis on practices would be more productive: how did different kinds of people use objects to carry out particular tasks? Were, for example, the bevel-rim bowls and other types of *Uruk*-like pottery in the highlands used in the same ways as in the lowlands (Potts 2009)? And what does that tell us about who the people

were who made and/or used the vessels? Much as we would like it to be, the answer to this question is not as simple or straightforward as "foreign" or "local" would suggest, as post-colonial studies and concerns with hybridity have shown (Liebmann and Rizvi 2008).

In the context of his discussion of the *Proto-Elamite* period in the Kur River Basin, Alden proposes that the "khans" of Susa were also the "khans" of Anshan. He bases his contention on the existence of a tribal, mobile pastoral society in which people engaged in a yearly round that took them from the lowlands to the highlands and back. Even accepting the argument for mobility, however, can we answer the question of explicit political identity archaeologically? Is it appropriate to speak of "khans" in the distant past (Garthwaite 2010)? Are these kinds of identity-related issues that equate modern categories with assumed classifications in the past really the most interesting questions to ask of our archaeological material?

What's missing?

I end my commentary with a mention of one theme that is, with a few exceptions, missing in these papers but that I consider to be an important direction for future research: a perspective that takes seriously the small scale of intra-community differences. In addition to a research focus on overarching structures and large-scale processes (e.g. the development of states or other forms of socio-political complexity), there needs to be an emphasis on the practices of daily life, the distinctions among households, neighbourhoods, genders, classes, and so on. Such an approach entails taking people seriously – as actors and makers of history, in both a theoretical and practical way. From this perspective regional comparisons and large-scale political and economic structures as well as their implications cannot be adequately comprehended without incorporating the small scale and taking into consideration the dialectical relations between the small scale of daily life and the "global" level of political, economic, and other structures (Pollock and Bernbeck 2010; Pollock 2013). While it may be objected that existing data do not provide the necessary resolution to address micro-scales and the questions about practices and subjectivities associated with them, I would turn the argument around: it is not only a matter of what we can answer right now but also of the questions and research directions that can be proposed. Without formulating new questions it is unlikely that the necessary methods will be developed and adapted or the appropriate data collected to allow us to propose answers to them.

Bibliography

Abdi, K. 2003. "The early development of pastoralism in the Central Zagros Mountains", *Journal of World Prehistory* 17: 395–448.

Algaze, G. 1993. *The Uruk World System: The Dynamics of Expansion of Early Mesopotamian Civilization*, University of Chicago Press, Chicago.

Algaze, G. 2008. *Ancient Mesopotamia at the Dawn of Civilization: The Evolution of an Urban Landscape*, University of Chicago Press, Chicago.

Alizadeh, A. 2008. "Archaeology and the question of mobile pastoralism in late prehistory", in Barnard, H. and Wendrich, W. (eds), *The Archaeology of Mobility: Nomads in the Old and in the New World*, Cotsen Institute of Archaeology Publications, Los Angeles: 78–114.

Ascher, R. 1961. "Analogy in archaeological interpretation", *Southwestern Journal of Anthropology* 17: 317–25.

Barth, F. ed. 1969. *Ethnic Groups and Boundaries: The Social Organization of Cultural Difference*, Universitetsforlaget, Oslo.

Bernbeck, R. 2008. "An archaeology of multisited communities", in Barnard, H. and Wendrich, W. (eds), *The Archaeology of Mobility: Nomads in the Old and in the New World*, Cotsen Institute of Archaeology Publications, Los Angeles: 43–77.

Feldman, M. 2006. *Diplomacy by Design: Luxury Arts and an "International Style" in the Ancient Near East, 1400–1200 BC*, University of Chicago Press, Chicago.

Garthwaite, G. 2010. Comment on Abbas Alizadeh's "The rise of the highland Elamite state in southwestern Iran: 'enclosed' or enclosing nomadism?", *Current Anthropology* 51: 377–78.

Johnson, G. 1973. *Local Exchange and Early State Development in Southwestern Iran*, Anthropological Papers 51, University of Michigan Museum of Anthropology, Ann Arbor.

Johnson, G. 1980. "Spatial organization of Early Uruk settlement systems", in Barrelet, M-T. (ed.), *L'archéologie de l'Iraq du début de l'époque néolithique à 333 avant notre ère*, Centre National de la Recherche Scientifique, Paris: 233–63.

Lamberg-Karlovsky, C. C. and Tosi, M. 1973. "Shahr-i Sokhta and Tepe Yahya: tracks on the earliest history of the Iranian Plateau", *East and West* 23: 21–58.

Liebmann, M. and Rizvi, U. eds 2008. *Archaeology and the Postcolonial Critique*, Altamira, Lanham, MD.

Mashkour, M. 2003. "Tracing ancient 'nomads': isotopic research on the origins of vertical 'transhumance' in the Zagros Region", *Nomadic Peoples* 7 (2): 36–47.

Meskell, L. 2004. *Object Worlds in Ancient Egypt: Material Biographies Past and Present*, Berg, Oxford and New York.

Miller, D. ed. 2005. *Materiality*, Duke University Press, Durham and London.

Petrie, C. 2011. "'Culture', innovation and interaction across southern Iran from the Neolithic to the Bronze Age (*c.* 6500–3000 BC)", in Roberts, B. W. and Vander Linden, M. (eds), *Investigating Archaeological Cultures: Material Culture, Variability, and Transmission*, Springer, New York: 151–82.

Pollock, S. 2013. "Commensality, public spheres and Handlungsräume in ancient Mesopotamia", in Robb, J. and Pauketat, T. (eds), *Big Histories, Human Lives: Tackling Issues of Scale in Archaeology*, School of Advanced Research, Santa Fe: 145-170.

Pollock, S. and Bernbeck, R. 2010. "Neolithic worlds at Tol-e Baši", in Pollock, S., Bernbeck, R. and Abdi, K. (eds), *The 2003 Excavations at Tol-e Baši, Iran: Social Life in a Neolithic Village*, Archäologie in Iran und Turan 10, Philipp von Zabern, Mainz: 274–87.

Pollock, S. and Bernbeck, R. 2011. "An archaeology of categorization and categories in archaeology", *Paléorient* 36 (1): 37–47. (Thematic issue "Social Development in the 6th and 5th Millennia BCE (Turkey, Iran and Southern Levant)," coordinated by Susanne Kerner).

Potts, D. 2009. "Bevel-rim bowls and bakeries: evidence and explanations from Iran and the Indo-Iranian borderlands", *JCS* 61: 1–23.

Potts, D. 2010. "Nomadismus in Iran von der Frühzeit bis in die Moderne. Eine Untersuchung sowohl aus archäologischer als auch historischer Sicht", 5, Thomsen-Vorlesung, *Eurasia Antiqua* 16: 1–19.

Stark, M. ed. 1998. *The Archaeology of Social Boundaries*, Smithsonian Institution Press, Washington, DC.

Sumner, W. 1972. *Cultural Development in the Kur River Basin, Iran. An Archaeological Analysis of Settlement Patterns*, Ph.D. dissertation, University of Pennsylvania, UMI/Pro Quest, Ann Arbor.

Sumner, W. 1986. "Proto-Elamite civilization in Fars", in Finkbeiner, U. and Röllig, W. (eds), *Ğamdat Nasr: Period or Regional Style?* TAVO Beiheft 62, Reichert, Wiesbaden: 199–211.

Wright, H. T. 1987. "The Susiana hinterlands during the era of primary state formation", in Hole, F. (ed.), *The Archaeology of Western Iran: Settlement and Society From Prehistory to the Islamic Conquest*, Smithsonian Institution Press, Washington, DC: 141–55.

Wright, H. T. 1998. "Uruk states in southwestern Iran", in Feinman, G. and Marcus, J. (eds), *Archaic States*, Santa Fe, School of American Research Press: 173–97.

Wright, H. T. 2001. "Cultural action in the Uruk world", in Rothman, M.S. (ed.), *Uruk Mesopotamia and Its Neighbours*, School of American Research, Santa Fe: 123–47.

Wright, H. T. and Johnson, G. 1975. "Population, exchange, and early state formation in southwestern Iran", *American Anthropologist* 77: 267–89.

Zagarell, A. 1982. *The Prehistory of the Northeast Bahtiyārī Mountains, Iran. The Rise of a Highland Way of Life*, Reichert, Wiesbaden.

20 ANCIENT IRAN AND ITS NEIGHBOURS: EMERGING PARADIGMS AND FUTURE DIRECTIONS

Cameron A. Petrie

Introduction

The papers in this volume consolidate and dramatically expand our understanding of the archaeological evidence of the Iranian Plateau and its mountain and piedmont zones during the fourth millennium BC, and also highlight the limitations of our current state of knowledge. As a whole, the volume examines a range of spatial, temporal, and thematic elements and importantly, it presents and discusses the evidence from the Iranian Plateau on its own terms. It is perhaps to be expected that some periods and themes have seen more focus than others, while some parts of the greater Iranian Plateau are discussed in a more cursory fashion. This volume, nonetheless, provides the most comprehensive evaluation yet assembled of the archaeology of the greater Iranian Plateau, and the interaction between Iran and its neighbouring regions during this critical period of socio-economic and political transformation.

The various papers of this volume do not present a consensus view regarding a number of major questions that challenge our understanding of this protracted period, either as they relate to the Iranian Plateau itself or to the greater region. This closing chapter will synthesise the significant conclusions drawn in the various papers, delineate the emerging paradigms that shape our current understanding of the fourth millennium BC in Iran, and outline an agenda for future research on this period.

The introduction paid particular attention to the various interpretations of the interactive processes taking place during the two major phases of local development and long-range contact and interaction: the *Uruk* and *Proto-Elamite* periods. Assessment of the prior investigation of both of these periods revealed several issues worthy of further discussion.

Firstly, most broad-scale explanatory models addressing the *Uruk* period have focused on *Uruk*-related settlements in Iran and have lacked consideration of the local non-*Uruk* contexts. This lack is at least partly because a reflexive assessment of the broad-scale interactive processes, looking from Iran, has previously been wanting. A similar pattern is evident for the *Proto-Elamite* phase, where the assessment of large (or at least "important") sites and broader dynamics has tended to overshadow small-scale interactions and local processes and the degree to which local agents may have been opting into broader developments. The local dynamics in the mid- to late fourth millennium BC were derived from longer-term processes that developed during the earlier fourth millennium BC, the fifth, or even the sixth millennium BC.

Secondly, the interpretation of the situation in Iran during much of the fourth millennium BC has lacked the richness and level of nuance that is now available for south-east Turkey and north-east Syria. This disparity is at least partly due to a lack of long-term excavation projects in Iran. It was noted in the introduction that the privileged distribution of desirable raw materials in the highlands of the Iranian Plateau would have meant that the constituent regions possessed a material advantage that had the potential to be harnessed as a fundamental source of economic power. It is also clear that the inhabitants of the highlands possessed the technological knowledge to exploit these resources, particularly copper, the use of which had been developing since the fifth millennium BC. Nevertheless, whether this potential for economic power was actually realised before the late fourth millennium BC is debatable. It is also not entirely evident how this potential for economic power impacted on local developments and interaction between populations in the highlands, and between those groups and the inhabitants of the neighbouring regions. These dynamics are important for understanding not only the *Late Uruk* and *Proto-Elamite* periods, but the early to mid-fourth millennium BC as well.

At the end of the introductory chapter a range of broad themes was outlined, which have been addressed in varying degrees by the subsequent papers. These are as follows:

• Environment, landscape, and spatial scale
• Chronology and issues of temporal scale
• Local developments and regional diversity
• Technology and transmission
• Long- and short-range interaction and manifestations of trade
• Power, control, negotiation, conflict, and violence

The synthesis that follows will draw information from relevant papers to explore these themes, critically review and contextualise the conclusions made in the various papers, and highlight areas of consensus and disagreement. This will be followed by some concluding remarks and thoughts about future agendas. Where authors are named but citations are not provided, the author's contribution to this volume is the source.

Environment, landscape, and spatial scale

Variation in climate, geography, environment, and vegetation

The greater Iranian Plateau is marked by a considerable degree of spatial and chronological variation in climate, geography, environment, and vegetation (Petrie; Wright; Rothman; Petrie *et al.*; Sardari; Alden; see also Appendix A; Appendix B). The fourth millennium BC sits at a key period of climatic transition between the early Holocene "optimum" climate and the present late Holocene climate state that is marked by a weakened monsoon and other changes to global climate and weather patterns (Jones *et al.*). Despite its size, there is only a limited number of climate proxy records for the Iranian Plateau at present (e.g. Urmia, Zeribar, and Mirabad), and Jones *et al.* caution against extrapolation of what are essentially local proxy sequences across such a geographically and climatically diverse landscape. Fortunately, lakes with considerable potential are present in various areas (e.g. Muharlou and Parishan), so a more detailed and nuanced understanding of climate dynamics and variation across the plateau and through time will develop in due course.

There is a growing body of evidence for geomorphological processes and tectonics on the Iranian Plateau, and two elements are notable. The recent evidence for sea-level variation in the Persian Gulf during the Holocene (e.g. Heyvaert 2007; Heyvaert and Baeteman 2007; Hritz and Pournelle, in press; see Jones *et al.*) is particularly significant for highlighting the likelihood that Khuzestan and southern Mesopotamia were largely separated by the swamps, permanent fresh- and saltwater marshes, lagoons, estuaries, tidal flats, and coastal sabkhas of the combined Euphrates-Tigris-Karun delta during the fourth millennium BC (Sanlaville 2003: 97–99, figs 1, 5; Pournelle 2003: figs 17, 29–30, 46, 76, 89, 91; Hritz and Pournelle, in press; Pournelle and Algaze, in press). Such a situation has a range of implications for the nature and means of interaction between the populations of Khuzestan and southern Mesopotamia. For instance, it has long been supposed that one of the major lowland overland routes would have been via Deh Luran (e.g. Wright 1981; Neely and Wright 1994), and this is now virtually confirmed. Nevertheless, it is important to consider whether the presence of water limited or enhanced movement, particularly between Susa and Uruk, as the potential for water transport should not be underestimated (cf. Algaze 2008: 53–62). There is also evidence of the influence of tectonic activity in various parts of the Zagros range. The evidence of fourth-millennium BC earthquakes at Tol-e Spid in Mamasani (Petrie *et al.*; Berberian *et al.*, in press) and at Tappeh Sialk (Berberian *et al.* 2012) highlights the diverse range of environmental factors that had the potential to impact on human populations.

Varied environments and the dynamics of human settlement

Although there are gaps, there is now information available about the nature and distribution of human settlement in a wide range of environments across the greater Iranian Plateau during the fourth millennium BC. The geography and to some extent, the environment and vegetation, of these regions are fundamentally different to those of the alluvial plains of Mesopotamia, Central Asia, and South Asia, particularly in terms of the possibilities of scale for human settlement. The smaller plains, valleys, and basins of the plateau and its piedmonts provide more limited opportunities for extensive and intensive settlement, constraining and facilitating specific types of behaviour (Petrie; also Petrie *et al.* 2009). During the fourth millennium BC all these regions would have been traversed on foot or with the use of pack animals and simple wheeled vehicles (Sherratt 1997; Wright 2001), and the topography and passes that constrained the routes via which people and ideas moved would also have facilitated networks of communication, interaction, and trade.

The highland and lowland zones, particularly in south-western Iran, have traditionally been viewed as being both geographically and culturally dichotomous (e.g. Alden; Amiet 1979; Alizadeh 2010). It is more fruitful and appropriate to view the highlands and lowlands of the south-west as complementary environments linked by interaction networks (Hopper and Wilkinson), which were not limited to the south-west but extended across other parts of the plateau (Petrie *et al.*). Iran in the fourth millennium BC, therefore, might best be seen as a contiguous landscape connected by routes that channelled and facilitated interaction across a series of interconnected cultural, material, and conceptual networks.

Attempts to reconstruct long-term settlement trajectories usually assume that the extant data sets are representative (e.g. Sumner 1990; de Miroschedji 2003), but various factors suggest that the current settlement data are biased because of coverage and factors such as variable sedimentation. The reconstructed patterns of prehistoric settlement should thus be seen as a minimal count (Hopper and Wilkinson). The degree to which the visible patterns reflect actual changes in settlement dynamics remains unclear, and it is not yet possible to assess population dynamics for the whole of the Iranian Plateau in the *longue durée*. Nevertheless, peaks in population occur at different points in time in Khuzestan, the Kur River Basin, and Mesopotamia, and Hopper and Wilkinson (cf. Adams 1981: 60) emphasise that the apparently massive increase in settled population in southern Mesopotamia at the end of the fourth millennium BC would have required a combination of population growth, immigration, and/or sedentarisation of mobile populations. The implication is that there was considerable potential for population flux, both between regions, including movement between Iran and Mesopotamia (Hopper and Wilkinson; also Johnson 1989), and between different subsistence groups within any region (urban, rural, and mobile; Hopper and Wilkinson; cf. Adams 1966: 58). The workability of such a reconstruction implies that these groups were linked by complex physical, cultural, social, and political networks and that relations were fluid enough to permit the movement of people to fill deficits in other sectors/regions (Hopper and Wilkinson). The social, economic, political, climatic, and/or environmental mechanisms impacting on or resulting from processes such as population flux largely remain open for discussion, and it is important to remember that such dynamics carry the potential for conflict within and between communities (cf. Wright; see below).

There has been a tendency to draw ethnographic analogies with the behaviour of nomads and/or mobile groups to frame explanations of several of these dynamics throughout late prehistory (Petrie), and reference to such groups appears in several papers here (e.g. Wright; Alden; also Weeks). Hopper and Wilkinson (cf. Alizadeh 2010: 372) mention the possibility that "desettlement" took place during the late fourth millennium BC, when a large portion of a given population did not leave a region but shifted to a life of pastoral nomadism. While this option is compelling and can be supported with a range of ethnographic examples, Hopper and Wilkinson rightly note that it would fit only some of the circumstances indicated in the population trends. For instance, it is difficult to see how it would be possible to have both desettlement *and* large-scale population movements leading to the intensification of settlement in southern Mesopotamia during the later fourth and early third millennium BC. For a period like the fourth millennium BC, when there is evidence of long-range contacts, it is absolutely essential that the appropriate geographical scale be considered.

Plants, animals, and humans

As for the *'Ubaid* period (Kohl 1992; Weeks *et al.* 2010: 267–68), consideration of the evidence and implications for bioarchaeological remains in the *Uruk* and *Proto-Elamite* periods across the greater Iranian Plateau is still lacking, as analysis of plants and animals is relatively limited. Thankfully this situation is constantly improving. While populations were by and large fed by wheat, barley, sheep, goat, and cattle-based agriculture and pastoralism (e.g. Wright; Rothman; Fazeli *et al.*; Bonora and Vidale; Petrie *et al.*; Sardari; Alden), it is the proportional exploitation of domesticated and wild animal and plant species that will provide insights into the nuances of local and regional subsistence patterns. Much of this work is still being undertaken and will clarify discussion of potential shifts in subsistence strategies during the fourth millennium BC (see below).

Chronology and issues of temporal scale

The current state of knowledge of the archaeology of the fourth millennium BC in Iran is heavily dependent on a number of excavations that were carried out with relatively limited attention to stratigraphy and/or the systematic documentation of artefact and sample find spots (Petrie; Wright; Rothman). There are thus few, if any, reliable radiocarbon dates from several sites of critical importance (e.g. Susa, Wright and Rupley 2001; cf. Petrie, in press, in preparation) and substantial numbers of relatively poor-quality radiocarbon dates from other sites whose precision cannot be improved (e.g. Godin Tepe, Tal-e Malyan, Tepe Yahya). Thankfully, a number of reconsideration projects have obtained new datable material from several sites excavated in the early to mid-twentieth century (e.g. Cheshme Ali, Fazeli *et al.* 2004; Tappeh Sialk, Nokhandeh 2010; Tepe Hissar, Thornton *et al.*), while new excavations are incorporating methods designed to obtain precise absolute dates (e.g. Helwing 2011a; Fazeli *et al.*; Petrie *et al.*; Sardari). There are also initiatives compiling all the known absolute and relative dates from the late fourth and early third millennium BC and using Bayesian-based calibration to constrain the chronological range of individual periods in different parts of the ancient Near East, including western Iran (cf. Petrie, in preparation).

Potentially the most problematic factor impacting upon the absolute dating of the late fourth millennium BC is the extended plateau in the radiocarbon calibration curve from *c.* 3350 to 2900 BC (Dahl *et al.*; also Petrie, in press, in preparation). As Dahl *et al.* note (also Petrie, in press, in preparation), this span coincides with the projected dates for the *Late Uruk* and *Jemdat Nasr* periods in Mesopotamia, the *Susa II/Late Uruk* (*Acropole I.22–18*), the *Susa II/III Transition* (*Acropole I.17–17X/17Ax*) and the *Susa III/ Proto-Elamite* (*Acropole I.16–14B*) occupations at Susa, *Godin VI:1, Sialk IV₁–IV₂, Period IVC2* at Tepe Yahya, and the entirety of the *Middle Banesh* occupation at Tal-e Malyan and other sites in Fars. This chronological span is critical for understanding early urbanism, administration, and writing, and our ability accurately to date these processes is therefore acutely hampered. Thornton *et al.*'s work at Tepe Hissar has shown that it is possible to create clear, statistically robust chronological sequences, which can be sharpened through Bayesian statistical methods, but this requires long sequences of dates from individual sites that bracket the period of interest, and such sequences of dates are not available for most sites. The stark reality is that without more reliable absolute dating evidence for the whole of the fourth millennium BC at sites that contain appropriate evidence, we must continue to rely on relative comparandae to establish chronological and cultural correlations.

Local developments and regional diversity

It has long been apparent that there is regional diversity in the cultural assemblages of the early to mid-fourth millennium BC across the greater Iranian Plateau (e.g. McCown 1942; Voigt and Dyson 1992).[1] This situation is, however, not unique and diversity in material culture was also evident in much of the fifth millennium BC (e.g. Weeks *et al.* 2010; Helwing 2013; Petrie 2013b), and persisted into the later fourth millennium BC. In fact, many of the papers in this volume show that there was more underlying regional diversity than similarity in Iran throughout the fourth millennium BC. Nonetheless, the populations of different regions were not isolated, and there is evidence for the movement of material through exchange and trade and the sharing of technological knowledge across the plateau. These processes intensified in the mid- to late fourth millennium

BC, suggesting an increase in interdependence and "entanglement" between distant populations (see below).

Pollock prudently notes that most of the papers in this volume make assumptions that the use of similar material culture or technological processes directly reflects interaction between groups – essentially a variant of "pots equals people" culture historicism. Human behaviour is considerably more variable than this and interaction may see the reinforcement of differences, thus it is imperative that interpretations are suitably nuanced and open to a range of possibilities.

Khuzestan

Excavations and surveys have revealed a coherent cultural sequence for Susiana and Deh Luran in the fourth millennium BC that displays evidence of continual long-term contact with southern Mesopotamia (Wright). The appearance of similar material culture in both regions – initially canonical pottery types and subsequently a range of administrative paraphernalia – suggests that interaction involved the sharing of material culture and technology over several centuries. It has long been accepted that Mesopotamia had primacy in this relationship, and that the initial appearance of this material in Susiana is indicative of the movement of Mesopotamian populations, although the nature of this movement is debated (e.g. Algaze 1993 [2005]; Potts 1999: 57–58; Alizadeh 2010). It is now certain that the alluvial plains of Susiana and southern Mesopotamia were separated by a range of water features during the fourth millennium BC (see above). Given this geographical separation, it is worth reconsidering whether the developments in Susiana were the result of population movement from Mesopotamia or of local processes that were related to, yet distinct from, those occurring in Mesopotamia. To consider this, the nuances of the evidence from the two regions must be examined to assess whether it implies formal linkage, interdependence, or even independence.

Wright has long claimed that what was ostensibly an independent state based at Susa developed in Susiana during the *Early* and *Middle Uruk* periods (see also Johnson 1973, 1987; Wright 1987, 1994, 1998; Wright and Johnson 1975; Wright *et al.* 1975). In this volume Pittman reiterates that the clearest evidence for the sequential development of the canonical *Uruk*-period ceramic and glyptic assemblages comes from Susa and Susiana (cf. Butterlin 2003), and notes that there is no evidence of obvious precursors for these elements in the current evidence from Uruk.[2] She also argues that the glyptic, numerical tablets, and numero-ideographic tablets evince parallel developments in Susiana and at Uruk, with phases of interconnectedness and independence, suggesting that Susiana and Mesopotamia saw related yet independent development during the *Uruk* period (Pittman). This is not a new proposal and it has been contested in the past (e.g. Nissen 1985; Potts 1999: 59), but criticism of the arguments for parallel development largely centres on the fundamental differences in scale between the size and number of the centres in southern Mesopotamia and those in Susiana (e.g. Algaze, Appendix B, also Nissen 1985; Algaze 2008). Yet scale need not be a direct analogue for levels of complexity. The estimated population of Mesopotamia in the *Early Uruk* period is believed to have been about twice that of the northern Susiana Plain (Wright; Pollock 1999: 52–75, table 3.1), but the occupied area in Mesopotamia is considerably more than twice as large as Susiana, suggesting that occupation in Khuzestan was denser. It is not impossible that there was an equivalent need for administrative structures in both regions.

Pittman suggests that the proposed dynamic of independent development culminated in the appearance of proto-literate texts and administration at Uruk and *Proto-Elamite/Susa III* texts and administration at Susa. In terms of understanding the *Proto-Elamite* phenomenon, it is notable that the *Proto-Elamite* period occupation at Susa is characterised by indications of influence from the highlands, with the pottery usually being described as "*Banesh*-related" (Wright; Helwing; Alden; also Alden 1982, 1987), although there is some continuity of forms that appear in the *Uruk* period. The *Proto-Elamite* phenomenon, at least as it appears in Susiana, is thus potentially the culmination of a sequence of local developments combined with influence from the highlands. If realistic, these reconstructions have significant implications for our understanding of both the *Uruk* and *Proto-Elamite* phenomena (see below).

The Central Western Zagros

Several excavated settlements in the intermontane valleys of the Central Western Zagros, which are large "by Persian standards" (<10 ha; e.g. Baba Jan, Tepe Giyan, and Godin Tepe), display a distinctive material culture throughout the fifth and fourth millennia BC (*Middle* and *Late Chalcolithic*; Goff 1971: 139–46; Henrickson E. F. 1983, 1989, 1994; Voigt and Dyson 1992). The ceramic assemblage in use during the mid- to late fourth millennium BC (*Godin VI*) is found in Kangavar, Hamadan, Islamabad, Malayer, Nehavand, the Mahidasht, and Hulailan and includes painted wares and a mixture of lowland and local/highland undecorated forms (Rothman; Henrickson E.F. 1994; Abdi 2003b). The significance of this distribution pattern has not yet been articulated beyond its potential relationship to trade routes (Rothman; Matthews; Algaze 1993 [2005]).

The *Godin VI* occupation at Godin Tepe is usually discussed in terms of the construction of the Oval compound, the potential relationship of this enclosure with Mesopotamia and/or Susa, and the site's relation to trade (e.g. Rothman; Matthews; Weiss and Young 1975; Algaze 1993 [2005], 2008). The construction of the Oval is one phase of a long-term sequence of contact with Mesopotamia, as seen by the gradual shift towards the use of lowland/*Uruk* pottery production techniques and vessels during *Godin VI.2*, before extant buildings were enclosed by the Oval compound in *Godin VI.1* (Rothman; also Rothman and Badler 2011). The significance of the Godin Tepe Oval has been debated since its discovery, and it typically continues to be regarded as a colony from either Mesopotamia (e.g. Matthews; Algaze 1993 [2005], 2008: 131; Stein 1999; Gosden 2004) or Susiana (Weiss and Young 1975). The presence of *Uruk* vessel types is taken to reflect the presence of lowlanders and the existence of control structures, but this demonstrates the interpretative problems highlighted by Pollock. The interpretation of the Oval and the *Period VI.1* deposits at Godin Tepe in general risk being circular because of the assumption about the site's role in trading activities and the lack of reflection about the meaning behind the patterns of material culture present. It is important to consider the degree to which local and non-local people can be differentiated on the basis of material culture. The lowland forms found in the Godin Oval display local elements, local cooking pots were utilised, and all of the pottery from the site appears to have been made from local clay, which Rothman argues provides insufficient evidence that "southerners" actually inhabited the Godin Oval. In his view, it was not an outpost of a southern city, but the inhabitants were "a group with at least co-ordinating authority" over the local population (cf. Arslantepe). This interpretation is not free of problems, as it makes assumptions about identity because ceramics were locally produced. It is worth considering how we should interpret the production of ostensibly "non-local" pottery types by local potters. Does it imply emulation by locals, elites, or otherwise? Is it misleading to suggest that non-local people would only make use of pottery produced non-locally?

Some of the difficultly in interpreting the Oval compound comes from the assumption that the *raison d'être* for Godin Tepe is trade (cf. Rothman; Matthews). In fact, trade is still regarded as the key factor in the *Uruk*-period dynamics throughout Kangavar despite the evidence for local ceramic production and the local administration of activities. Even if Godin Tepe is not an outpost, it is viewed as a key player in the transport of highland goods and materials to the lowlands. Algaze (Appendix B) has nonetheless noted that the evidence for trade and, more importantly, the nature of the trading relationships throughout the Central

Western Zagros are largely inferential. The degree to which the presence of *Uruk*-influenced material culture reflects dominance, influence, or emulation remains open to interpretation.

The Central Plateau

There is a degree of cultural variability between the southern, northern, and north-eastern zones of the Iranian Central Plateau. During the early fourth millennium BC, the south Central Plateau was occupied by village-based communities using a painted ceramic repertoire (*Sialk III*) derived from local fifth-millennium BC precursors that were distinct from, yet related to, those of the Central Western Zagros (Helwing). The excavated settlements with *Sialk III* occupation (Tappeh Sialk, Arisman) show few signs of socio-economic differentiation in architecture or burial practices in the early to mid-fourth millennium BC (Helwing). By the mid-fourth millennium BC (*Sialk III$_{6-7}$*) there is evidence for what Helwing describes as "selective borrowing" of specific lowland pottery types, potentially as a result of contact with the lowlands related to the production of metals at these highland sites. There is thus evidence for some form of contact, but its significance is not obvious. Helwing argues that there is no evidence of influence on the internal organisation of the *Sialk III$_{6-7}$* communities, but the appearance of lowland ceramics may simply reflect the spread of lowland innovations in ceramic production into the Central Plateau and/or influence on culinary practices (cf. Potts 2009). The significance of the appearance of numerical tablets at Tappeh Sialk (*IV$_1$*) is unclear. Helwing notes that the subsequent *Proto-Elamite* phase of occupation at Arisman is distinct from that of the *Sialk III$_{6-7}$* phase, with change in architectural design and materials, ceramic production technology, and the scale of metal production. The surrounding landscape was also largely abandoned, suggesting that the *Proto-Elamite* phase marks a point of socio-economic transformation (Helwing).

The northern part of the Central Plateau is not entirely dissimilar to the southern part, but the orientation of its geography is different and this is at least partly reflected in the material culture of the inhabitants. Fazeli *et al.* note that during the early fourth millennium BC (the local *Middle* and *Late Chalcolithic* periods), most settlements of the north Central Plateau display cultural material similar to that used in north-eastern Iran, whereas this affiliation shifts to the Central Western Zagros and north-western Iran after 3400 BC. Examples of bevel-rim bowls and conical cups are known from the early excavations at Ghabristan (Qazvin Plain) (Majidzadeh 1981: 146; Voigt and Dyson 1992: 167), and there is evidence of *Proto-Elamite/Sialk IV* period occupation at Tepe Sofalin (Tehran Plain), including

a large corpus of administrative material made up of a clay bulla, a possible *Uruk/Susa II* tablet, and numerous *Proto-Elamite* tablets (Fazeli *et al.*; Dahl *et al.*; also Hessari and Akbari 2007; Hessari 2011; Dahl *et al.* 2012). Fazeli *et al.* argue that ranked societies appeared on the north Central Plateau during the fifth and continued into the fourth millennium BC. Drawing on the evidence from Tepe Hissar, Thornton *et al.* point out that the north-east of Iran has long been an important "divided" frontier zone, which is reflected in differences in the material culture in the adjacent regions. Unfortunately our comprehension of the significance of these dynamics remains relatively simplistic. During the latter half of the fourth millennium BC Tepe Hissar maintains a very distinctive material assemblage, which is different to that associated with the *Uruk* and *Proto-Elamite* phenomena (Thornton *et al.*). Chaff-tempered trays – characteristic of both the *Uruk* and *Proto-Elamite* phases – are present, perhaps suggesting some type of culinary impact from the west (Thornton *et al.*), but the absence of bevel-rim bowls is notable. Metal and bead production (particularly lapis) became large-scale and centrally organised, leading to increased prosperity at the settlement and socio-economic differentiation (cf. Helwing). Thornton *et al.* suggest that the apparent "rejection" of *Proto-Elamite* influence may reflect a conscious move to preserve local political independence in the face of the growth of *Proto-Elamite* interaction in other areas, although this assumes that the *Proto-Elamite* phenomenon involves the imposition of political control.

The Kopet Dag and south Central Asia

The piedmonts, plains, and oases along the northern edge of the Kopet Dag are situated where the Iranian Plateau proper meets the plains of Central Asia. The *Middle Chalcolithic* (mid- to late fourth millennium BC) is marked by the growth of modest sized urban centres with gates and walls, developed craft activities (exploiting turquoise and lapis lazuli), incipient administration, and signs of social stratification in architecture and burials (Bonora and Vidale). There are links between the Kopet Dag piedmont, the regions of Iran, and areas further to the west in the *Neolithic* period (e.g. Harris 2010; Weeks 2013). There are no overt indications of contact with areas of Iran beyond the northern plateau in the fourth millennium BC, although it was via the Kopet Dag piedmont or Khurasan that lapis lazuli most likely moved to the west (Petrie; cf. Wilkinson T. C. 2012). There are, however, various pieces of material evidence (figurines, small clay cones and balls, and handled weights or *gyr*) that indicate links between the Kopet Dag and settlements at the easternmost edge of the plateau in the north-west frontier of South Asia (Bonora and Vidale; cf. Knox *et al.* 2010).

Although the Kopet Dag piedmont and the oases to its east are ostensibly one "region", there is evidence of diversity in cultural behaviour in the western, central, and south-eastern zones (Bonora and Vidale). At several sites there were wealthy child burials that contained copper and bone artefacts, providing indications of a developing socio-economic hierarchy (Bonora and Vidale). The piedmonts and oases of south Central Asia thus appear to be engaging in their own form of early complexity in the fourth millennium BC distinctive to that being practised on most of the Iranian Plateau. Contact with the plateau is, however, indicated by the movement of semi-precious stones, and the use of a red-slipped ware said to be akin to *Lapui* red-slipped ware has been found at central zone sites (Bonora and Vidale; see below).

Fars

In general, the cultural material of Fars in the early fourth millennium BC is broadly similar, and distinct from that in Khuzestan, the Central Western Zagros, and also the Central Plateau (Wright; Rothman; Helwing). While also distinct from that of the southeast, there are connections, primarily via the use of similar potting techniques.

There is considerable variation in the *Lapui* period settlements and settlement dynamics in different parts of Fars (Petrie *et al.*; Sardari). It is also evident that the composition of the *Lapui* ceramic assemblage changed over time (Petrie *et al.*), although continuation in the use of the *Bakun*-style administrative paraphernalia potentially indicates a degree of continuity of the late fifth-millennium BC economic structure into the early to mid-fourth millennium BC (Sardari). The appearance of lowland vessel forms at highland sites in the mid-fourth millennium BC, particularly bevel-rim bowls at Tal-e Kureh, Tol-e Spid, Tol-e Nurabad, suggests that there was contact between the lowlands and the southern highlands during this period, but its nature and motivation are largely unknown (Petrie *et al.*). During the late fourth millennium BC, the inhabitants of Fars were a part of the *Proto-Elamite/Banesh* cultural milieu, and *Banesh* material culture was being used in the Kur River Basin and Mamasani. The degree to which this material characterised the entire region is unknown, however, as there are no contemporary excavated sites in other areas of Fars (Petrie *et al.*).

Sumner (1986, 1988a, 1988b, 1990, 1994, 2003; also de Miroschedji 2003) argued that the Kur River Basin saw a long-term trend of increase in settlement density during the fifth and then progressive decline during the fourth millennium BC, and attributed this trajectory to the transformation of a *Bakun*-period irrigation-based subsistence economy into – by the *Banesh* period – one based on pastoral nomadism (cf. Alden). Alden suggests that this major transformation

began properly during the *Early Banesh* period, when the western part of the Kur River Basin was dominated by two or three major settlement clusters, which were the size of small towns and inhabited by lineage or kin groups living close to, but spatially separated from, each other. Dominance shifted completely to the Tal-e Malyan settlement cluster in the *Middle Banesh* phase, and walls may have been built around individual areas. The density of settlement reduced in the *Late Banesh* period, but the local settlement system continued and a larger wall was built around Tal-e Malyan, incorporating a large uninhabited area (Alden; also Sumner 1985).[3] The area within this wall has not been examined, but it was presumably built in response to a threat (perceived or real), and Alden suggests that this may have been from a large nomadic population. This implies that the relationship between the settled and nomadic proportions of the population had changed dramatically during the mid- to late fourth millennium BC (see below).

The excavations at Tol-e Spid and Tol-e Nurabad emphasise that *Banesh*-period Fars was not characterised by a homogeneous material assemblage, as there are indications that potting techniques and wares used at Mamasani were not being used in the Kur River Basin. Moreover, the inhabitants in Mamasani may not have been making use of the entire *Banesh* material assemblage, as no texts have been found and the *Banesh* ceramics seen at Tol-e Spid and Tol-e Nurabad are distinct both from those in the Kur River Basin and from each other (Petrie *et al.*). These factors indicate that the inhabitants were making choices about what and what not to adopt; and perhaps that the *Banesh/Proto-Elamite* assemblage was not a homogeneous "set" of material that was adopted and/or used everywhere (Petrie *et al.*).

The south-east

The distribution of distinctive combinations of ceramic technological and decorative style suggests that a range of different interactive dynamics was in operation in south-eastern Iran throughout the fourth millennium BC (Mutin). As noted above, the ceramic assemblages of the early fourth millennium BC in Kerman display some connections to Fars (e.g. *Bakun* and *Lapui*-type material; Mutin 2012; also Beale 1986; Petrie 2011, 2013b; Petrie *et al.*), and also connections to material seen elsewhere in south-eastern Iran, Kech-Makran, and eastern Baluchistan (Mutin 2012). Such patterns continue in the mid- to late fourth millennium BC, but the decorated wares appear across larger distribution zones. It has long been known that *Aliabad* wares were found at Tal-i Iblis in period IV deposits together with examples of various *Uruk/Proto-Elamite* style vessels (e.g. bevel-rim bowls, low-sided trays, shoulder spouts) (Chase *et al.*

1967), but the stratigraphic relationship between the two assemblages has been unclear and they remain poorly dated. The recent excavations at Mahtoutabad in the Halil Rud show that there was a developmental sequence of *Aliabad* ware during *Mahtoutabad I–II* that preceded the appearance of various "lowland"/*Uruk* or perhaps *Proto-Elamite* forms in *Mahtoutabad III* (Vidale and Desset; Desset *et al.* 2013). The occupation at Tepe Yahya in *Period IVC* also has evidence of links to other *Proto-Elamite* settlements to the west, and with the Kech-Makran and Shahr-i Sokhta.

While the relative correspondence between the cultural assemblages in south-eastern Iran is becoming clearer, there are still problems with the dating of the various sequences, so it is not yet possible to establish whether specific ware types were being used at the same time in different regions, or whether particular ware types were used during specific periods. While *Yahya IVC* corresponds to the *Proto-Elamite* period and potentially a late phase of that period, it is not yet certain that *Iblis IV* and *Mahtoutabad III* can be correlated directly with the *Late Uruk* and/or the *Proto-Elamite* periods because there is a lack of good-quality absolute dates.

The north-west frontier of South Asia

One substantial gap in the coverage of the archaeology of the greater Iranian Plateau presented in this volume is its extreme east, which comprises modern Afghanistan and the borderland areas of Afghanistan and Pakistan where the plateau meets the piedmonts and plains of the South Asian subcontinent. While the archaeology and associated cultural dynamics of the area to the south-east of the plateau (Mutin) and the comparable evidence from the piedmonts to the north of the plateau have been discussed (Bonora and Vidale), the areas of northern Baluchistan, Khyber Pakhtunkhwa, and Afghanistan have only been mentioned tangentially. Our knowledge of the interactive dynamics in the area between northern Baluchistan and Central Asia has been enhanced through the publication of the surveys and excavations carried out in southern Khyber Pakhtunkhwa by the Bannu Archaeology Project between 1986 and 2001 (Petrie 2010). Archaeological fieldwork in Afghanistan, however, has been extremely limited since the late 1970s and the work that has been conducted has largely involved rescue excavations and issues of preservation and consolidation. It has long been known that north-eastern Afghanistan was the major source of ancient lapis lazuli, and that abundant tin sources are present in central Afghanistan. New insights into the archaeology of this region in the fourth millennium BC will only be forthcoming when it is possible to conduct systematic rather than opportunistic surveys and excavations.

Technology and transmission

A range of technological developments took place during the fourth millennium BC, and the transmission of these developments lies at the heart of the overarching discussions about the interactive dynamics of this period throughout western Asia. Understanding these dynamics on the Iranian Plateau is essential for interpreting the *Proto-Elamite* phenomenon and the relationships between Iran and Mesopotamia in the *Uruk* period.

Algaze's (2008: 64–92, 127–39) *Uruk*-period "ideational" technologies or "technologies of the intellect" (cf. Goody 2000) include changes in the organisation and techniques of producing pottery and metals and in the processes of administration. A similar set of technological developments spread across the Iranian Plateau in the *Proto-Elamite* period, and these are undoubtedly related yet distinct "technologies of the intellect", whose appearance suggests that there was some emulation and adaptation of *Uruk* practices (cf. Helwing). With this in mind, it is important to consider the degree to which the fourth millennium BC was a period of transformation on the Iranian Plateau as a whole and the underlying question of whether the local developmental processes were independent of, or influenced by, the dynamics of southern Mesopotamia.

Pottery

The move towards mass production and standardisation of pottery vessels (and potentially their contents) was a dramatic shift in the organisation and execution of ceramic production. In Mesopotamia bevel-rim bowls have long been regarded as standardised vessel forms, and although they have traditionally been interpreted as ration containers (e.g. Nissen 1988; Nissen *et al.* 1993), other functions have been proposed (cf. Millard 1988; Potts 2009; Goulder 2010; Rothman). The appearance of *Uruk*/lowland vessel forms is not simply indicative of "influence" in a culinary or any other sense, but also indicates the spread of specific potting techniques. While bevel-rim bowls and trays are easy to produce, knowledge of the forming processes must have been shared for their basic shape to be so consistent across such a vast area. During the *Proto-Elamite* period a number of mass-produced types also appear to have developed in the highlands (e.g. chaff-tempered goblets; Alden), undoubtedly fulfilling local socio-economic needs. We do not know what these chaff-tempered goblets were used for, but they were found in enormous quantities at Tal-e Qarib (Alden); they are notably infrequent at other *Banesh/Proto-Elamite* sites (Tol-e Spid and Tol-e Nurabad, Petrie *et al.*; Tepe Yahya, Potts 2001: 8, fig. 1.13; Arisman, Helwing 2011b).

While much has been made of the widespread distribution of *Uruk* and *Proto-Elamite* ceramic forms in highland contexts, the adoption of this material does not follow a consistent pattern. There are differences in the types of decoration on the four-lugged jars that appear in different areas (e.g. incision at Uruk, Susa, and Godin Tepe; painting at Arisman, Tal-e Malyan, and Mahtoutabad), and types such as the low-sided trays, flowerpots, and the *Banesh* chaff-tempered goblets do not appear everywhere. Such patterns suggest that the adoption, incorporation, and use of these vessel forms were in the hands of the local populations in each area.

In addition to the dispersal of lowland influences on highland ceramic repertoires, there were interesting dynamics in other areas of the plateau. The most distinctive is the evidence from south-western, south-eastern, and northern Iran for the use of fine red-slipped wares that potentially resembles the *Lapui* pottery seen in Fars (see Thornton *et al.*, Petrie *et al.*; Mutin; Vidale and Desset; also Petrie 2011, 2013b). If the material is actually comparable, the widespread appearance of similar approaches to vessel forming and decoration across the plateau in the early fourth millennium BC suggests that the sharing of technological knowledge was independent of any lowland interaction or influence. Such dynamics thus suggest the existence of mechanisms via which innovations in ceramic production technology and decoration of the mid- to late fourth millennium BC might have moved without the need for influence to be "driven" from the lowlands.

Metals

There are changes in various aspects of metals production on the Iranian Plateau during the fourth millennium BC, although whether these changes reflect local developments or shifts in market demand is presently unknown. Most notably, the range of metals being produced expands beyond native copper to include arsenical copper, silver, lead, and gold. In the *Proto-Elamite* period Arisman also sees changes from crucible to furnace smelting, and from the production of elaborate cast shaft-hole axes to more straightforward flat axes. Helwing (also 2011c, 2011d) attributes this to a shift towards industrial scale copper production, although the impetus for this shift is still unclear.

The key debate in understanding the rise of poly-metallurgy across western Asia in the fourth millennium BC is whether there was one centre of technological development from which the knowledge radiated, or multiple centres engaging in synchronous developments. There is evidence that production of metals took place in several locations across the Iranian Plateau, and while there is significant regional variation in the specific technological processes, there

are also technological parallels between the practices in Iran and contemporaneous processes in Anatolia, eastern Baluchistan, and Central Asia (Weeks; see below).

Administration

Although stamp seals and counting systems had become relatively sophisticated in the fifth millennium BC (e.g. Schmandt-Besserat 1992; Root 2005), the fourth millennium BC saw the transformation of these nascent technologies, culminating in the creation of two distinct yet related early writing systems: the proto-writing system that developed at Uruk, and the *Proto-Elamite/Susa III* writing system (e.g. Nissen 1988, 2002; Nissen *et al.* 1993; Damerow and Englund 1989; Englund 1998). The latter appears to have developed at Susa and was then dispersed to other settlements scattered across the Iranian Plateau (Pittman; Dahl *et al.*; also Potts 1999: 71–79, 81–83).

The administrative innovations that took place at Uruk and Susa during the fourth millennium BC have long been a subject of interest and, as noted above, Pittman queries the primacy of southern Mesopotamia in the development of these new technologies. She suggests that at the very least Uruk and Susiana witnessed a parallel development, including phases of shared influence and independent elaboration (cf. Butterlin 2003). She actually goes so far as to argue that Susa was the source of many of the innovations (Pittman; cf. Porada *et al.* 1992; Amiet 1980).[4]

There is a divergence of the Uruk and Susiana glyptic iconography at the end of the fourth millennium BC (*Jemdet Nasr/Susa III*; Pittman). The glyptic from the last *Late Uruk* phase attested at Susa (*Acropole I.17*) develops out of the earlier Susiana tradition and begins to pre-empt the motifs and styles seen in *Proto-Elamite* glyptic, and the numero-ideographic tablets at Uruk and Susa order signs and numbers in different ways (Dahl 2005). Pittman suggests that the differences in iconography between Uruk and Susa glyptic in the *Middle Uruk* and the early part of the *Late Uruk* period reflect differences in the types of economic activities at both centres. It is notable that the comparable tablets from Godin Tepe and Tappeh Sialk utilise the Susa format and thus relate to Susa and the emerging *Proto-Elamite* tradition (Pittman; Pittman 2001, 2011; contra Matthews; see Petrie, in press).

A range of factors suggests that *Proto-Elamite* is related to, yet derivative from, the proto-writing system developed at Uruk (Dahl *et al.*; also Damerow and Englund 1989). There are, however, aspects that indicate that the two systems were distinct, for instance *Proto-Elamite* includes a decimal counting system that is not attested at Uruk (Dahl *et al.*; also Englund 1998). The distribution of *Proto-Elamite* texts was also considerably more widespread than *Uruk IV* proto-cuneiform, being found at sites distributed throughout western Iran and also across the south and south-east (Dahl *et al.*; cf. Potts 1977; Lamberg-Karlovsky 1978; Alden 1982; Damerow and Englund 1989). As Potts (1999: 81–82; also Dahl *et al.*) has observed, Susa has the largest number and most complex tablets as well as the longest sequence of occupation related to the development of the *Uruk*-related numerical and *Proto-Elamite* writing systems, and it is thus likely to be the settlement where the latter originated. It is significant, however, that the numerical, numero-ideographic, and/or proto-literate material from Godin Tepe (Rothman; Matthews), Tal-e Malyan, and Tepe Yahya document local-scale economic affairs (Damerow and Englund 1989), suggesting that these tablets do not indicate the economic integration of the entire Iranian Plateau (contra Lamberg-Karlovsky 1978; Alden 1982). Dahl *et al.* (Fig. 18.17) demonstrate that there were at least three, and possibly four, phases in the development of *Proto-Elamite* and these phases appear to have been marked by different spatial dynamics, with an early geographic trajectory linking Susa with Tal-e Ghazir and sites on the north Central Plateau (Tappeh Sialk and Ozbaki) and a later trajectory linking Susa with Tal-e Malyan, Tepe Yahya, and Shahr-i Sokhta. It is notable that there are indications of connections to Tepe Sofalin in the north Central Plateau in both phases (Dahl *et al.*).

Measurement systems

Multiple numerical systems were developed in the earliest phases of proto-writing (Friberg 1994), and Susa only has three of the thirteen numerical systems that have been attested at Uruk (Potts 1999: 65). The presence of similar number systems at Susa should not be surprising considering the similarities between the glyptic and other administrative paraphernalia at the two sites. That only some of the numbering systems appear at Susa might also be expected; as Potts (1999: 65) points out, there are obvious differences in the size and almost certainly the administrative requirements between Uruk and Susa. The introduction of three numerical systems might be the result of one scribe being brought in to Susa from Uruk for specific purposes. It is also not impossible that more straightforward numerical systems were first developed at Susa and were then adopted at Uruk, where they proliferated and became more complex to suit more elaborate requirements. Irrespective of the point of origin of the numerical systems, the counting and measurement systems were certainly being shared across considerable distances and between different populations.

The evidence for numerical systems also draws attention to the evidence for the sharing of a specific unit of linear measurement, and its application to the construction of particular buildings in different parts of the ancient Near East. Beale and Carter (1986) observed specific similarities between construction techniques and proportions of room size used at the *Period IVC* building at Tepe Yahya, and those seen at the Hofhaus H and Werkstatt W at Habuba Kabira, and Temples VII and VI at Eridu, which they describe as a standardised unit of linear measurement (the "Yahya large kuš" = 72 cm) that was used in a "design code". Although not as evident as at Tepe Yahya, it is possible that elements of this unit and design code were used to lay out the regular-shaped rooms exposed at Arisman Area C (see Chegini *et al.* 2011: figs 7–10), and Tal-e Malyan ABC BLs 5, 4 and 3 (see Sumner 2003: figs 8–12), although this will only be demonstrated through a formal analysis. Similar exposures of architecture were made in the Susa *Acropole I* and the Godin Tepe Oval compound excavations, but in these instances the wall stubs were not cleaned and published in such a way that any underlying units of measurement could be reconstructed. Thus there are potentially also influences on measurement systems, architectural plans, and construction methods that were also dispersed and shared.

Transmission

At present we know little about the way that knowledge related to ceramic and metal production and administrative and measurement systems was shared on the plateau. Although speaking specifically about metallurgy, Weeks reminds us that technologies involve sets of skills that must be learned through observation and practice, and successful transfer of such technological knowledge requires close interaction between craftspeople. In the Iranian context, it is likely that from the *Neolithic* onwards successful sharing of specialised knowledge may have ranged from the handing down and sharing of knowledge between practitioners within families through to processes like exogamy, the voluntary or forced movement of itinerant craftspeople or even the movement of entire groups, which would facilitate the sharing of knowledge between populations in different regions (Weeks *et al.* 2006: 20ff.; 2010: 265; Petrie 2011: 169). Technology might also have been in the hands of caste-like social groups that crossed cultural boundaries (Weeks).

It is notable that the four different categories of evidence discussed here are each marked by different *patterns* of transmission, although there are undoubtedly underlying similarities in the *processes* of transmission. There is considerable evidence for between-group modes of ceramic technology transfer, although the degree to which the various vessel types at different settlements were being produced through the replication of the same technological style has not yet been explored. In contrast, there is less overt evidence for between-group modes of metallurgical technology transfer, but similar technological developments occurred in different parts of Iran and also in neighbouring regions (Weeks). Weeks notes that the evidence for metallurgy is found within sedentary sites, thus the role of mobile groups in metallurgical technology transfer is uncertain.

In contrast to the evidence for metallurgy, *Proto-Elamite* writing appears to have developed at Susa and to have then dispersed from there, and almost certainly only involved a small number of scribes (Dahl *et al.*; Appendices A and B). It is likely that scribal training in these early stages was limited to an extremely small group, possibly even one family, and that knowledge of the system was potentially passed down from father to son (Appendix B). The similarities in various aspects of the *Proto-Elamite* writing system that appear across such large distances (e.g. owner signs; cf. Dahl *et al.*) suggest that scribes who had been trained in the system may have been despatched from Susa to far-flung locations. At present we do not yet understand the rationale behind this pattern or the practicalities of its execution, but we have evidence for within-group transfer of knowledge and then direct dispersal of that knowledge, presumably through the movement of individuals. The knowledge of writing was not widespread at any one settlement, and if we are seeing the whole process of the development and dispersal of *Proto-Elamite* writing taking place over a small number of scribal generations (cf. Dahl *et al.*), the collapse of the system might be a result of the opportunities for transmission of the administrative knowledge being too tightly constricted and thus vulnerable to changes of whim or to strife. If *Uruk*-style proto-writing and *Proto-Elamite* tablets are thought of as a technology, and more specifically a "technology of power" (Mann 1986), then we may be able to get closer to comprehending the latter's spread and to understanding its ultimate disappearance (see below). It is interesting to note that there are sites with *Proto-Elamite* material culture that have not produced texts, but it is unclear whether this is due to the chance nature of archaeological discovery or because texts were not used everywhere.

Of the four categories, it is the knowledge of the standardised unit of linear measurement and its associated "design code" that is perhaps the hardest to explain. Elements of the design code are probably related to specific construction techniques, but the unit of measurement was potentially one of the many numerical and measurement systems being used in Mesopotamia and on the Iranian Plateau at this time. It is likely that the knowledge of the system was somehow related to the administrative and writing systems, and we might expect to see texts at sites where we see the design code in place. Our comprehension is complicated by the fact that

the best parallels come from sites in the *Uruk* and *Proto-Elamite* worlds.

Weeks suggests that the early metallurgical experimentation at various centres is potentially due to communities across western Asia being linked by a broad-scale interaction sphere (cf. Caldwell 1968), or a shared social field (cf. Kohl 2008). While this may be true, it is the mechanisms through which these interaction spheres or shared social fields operated that require further investigation. The interactive dynamics fostered by the *Uruk* and *Proto-Elamite* phenomena may well have promoted independent but analogous metallurgical developments (Weeks), but there are nuances to this process that need to be disaggregated (see below).

Long- and short-range interactions and manifestations of trade

There is evidence for long-range exchange and trade throughout the ancient Near East from the aceramic *Neolithic* onwards, with down-the-line trade and exchange in obsidian (Renfrew 1975, 1977), lapis lazuli (from the '*Ubaid* period; Herrmann 1968; Majidzadeh 1982), and objects made from native copper (Weeks 2012, 2013). Although there has been considerable focus on the importance of trade between Iran and Mesopotamia, it is important to remember that there was also trade within and between regions throughout the greater Iranian Plateau. Movement between some regions must have been at least partly seasonal due to the constraints imposed by altitude and weather (see Figs 1.1a–1.1b).

Algaze (2008: 156) has argued that trade was the key transformative agent for the development of early Sumerian urban societies, and for him it was not the product of complexity but was potentially the key driver in the process. In the initial formulation of his *Uruk* World System model, Algaze (1993 [2005]) also saw trade as the factor that motivated the development of complexity in peripheral regions, and although this has been challenged in relation to the types of interaction between southern Mesopotamia and the regions to the north (e.g. Stein 1999), the impact of *Uruk* contact within highland Iran has been under-theorised. The evidence presented in this volume makes it possible to update our assessment of the relationship between long-range interactions across the plateau and local developments throughout the fourth millennium BC, and the way that these processes relate to developments in the neighbouring regions.

Resources

It is well known that the particular geological and environmental conditions of the greater Iranian Plateau offer a range of natural resources including stone, metal, and wood, which are not available on the alluvial plains of Mesopotamia, the Indus, and Central Asia (Petrie; Rothman; Weeks; Matthews; cf. Potts 1999: tables 2.6, 2.9). These resources are regarded as the key motivation for lowland interest in highland areas, and the routes via which these resources are believed to have moved are used to explain the distribution of lowland material in the uplands (Rothman; Matthews; also Algaze 1993 [2005], 2008; Matthews and Fazeli 2004).

The chronological evidence suggests that lowland contact with the highland zones of the Iranian Plateau was related to the acquisition of products made using extant technology. There is evidence for precocious metallurgical technology at a number of different centres from the late fifth millennium BC onwards (e.g. Tal-i Iblis, Tappeh Sialk, Tepe Yahya, Ghabristan; see Weeks 2012) preceding any direct contact with the lowlands of either Susiana or Mesopotamia. It is possible that lowland/highland contact might still have been a driver for the further socio-economic developments seen on the plateau during the later fourth millennium BC, as indicated by the changes in metal production at Arisman.

Evidence for the use of lapis in lowland Mesopotamia during the fourth millennium BC is relatively limited (e.g. Herrmann 1968: 29–33), which contrasts with the abundant evidence for lapis production and consumption in the early to mid-third millennium BC. Lapis and turquoise are both present at sites along the Kopet Dag piedmont and Tepe Hissar, but they are not abundant materials elsewhere on the plateau (see Tal-e Malyan, Sumner 2003; Tepe Yahya, Potts 2001). Thus, exotic materials were moving, but the quantity of material and the importance of this trade and exchange for the parties at both ends are still largely unknown.

Routes, impact, and implications

Detecting trade in exotics is dependent upon the material that is being moved. Where perishable materials were being exchanged for durable exotics, half of the trading system will be archaeologically invisible. The trade of lapis lazuli is relatively obvious as there is one major source area and the material is readily recognisable at its destination, no matter what type of object it has been turned into. Reconstructing the specifics of copper distribution networks is inherently more difficult. While there is a limited number of spatially distinct ore sources, and at lowland settlements there are shaft-hole axes similar in style to those produced in the highlands (e.g. Susa; Helwing 2005), moulds are known from more than one highland site (e.g. Ghabristan and Arisman; Helwing), and the material can be reshaped (potentially many times) at its point of consumption. It is thus not self-evident where particular copper

objects originated. Analysis of artefacts to identify metal technology and sources has the potential to inform discussions of metal production and trade networks, but little such work has been carried out. The same is true for gold, silver, and lead, so Algaze's comments about the inferential nature of trade (Appendix B) continue to hold.

Rothman argues that the Central Western Zagros is not simple to traverse, and suggests that the physical constraints may have impacted upon the types of material that were exchanged and traded. To him metals, ores, wool, and semi-precious stones would have been more practical than large wine jugs and wooden logs (Rothman), although all of these types of material were actually moved from the highlands to the lowlands (Potts 1999). It is often stated that the "high road" through the Central Western Zagros was a major route throughout prehistory, and the other major route of passage into the highlands was via the south-west through regions like Mamasani and the Kur River Basin. The precise routes by which copper and lapis lazuli made their way to the west are, however, not known. It is important to emphasise that the routes through the Central Western and south-western Zagros were not single roads or tracks, but broader corridors made up of a range of different possible routes (cf. Potts 2004). Specific routes may have been favoured at different times, but it is likely that the potential for one particular settlement to dominate one or other route was far more limited than is usually claimed.

The presence of both lapis and turquoise at sites along the Kopet Dag piedmont and at Tepe Hissar, suggests that at least one route probably skirted the piedmont before ascending onto the plateau and following routes across the Central Plateau before descending through the Zagros. There are also routes that ascend the plateau via Khorasan. As noted in the introduction, a least cost path analysis has shown that a land route following the Caspian coast is the most straightforward, but it would be informative to establish how the least cost path modelling would be affected by the inclusion of Tepe Hissar as a node through which the material must pass. Until the entire Zagros Range is investigated, it will be impossible to confirm whether one route or many were preferred for penetrating the Zagros.

Although Mesopotamia is usually regarded as the ultimate destination for the prized trade goods coming from the highlands, the specific destination for this material within Mesopotamia potentially affected the routes that were used and the networks that were accessed. If one corridor was used extensively, then goods were perhaps redistributed once they reached the lowlands. One lowland centre or place might thus have controlled supply. Despite the size dominance of Uruk in the later fourth millennium BC, it was still only one of several substantial centres on the Mesopotamian alluvium (Adams 1981: 60ff, figs 12–13; Pollock 1999; 2001: figs 6.3–6.4), and the degree to which these centres were operating independently or in some sort of coalition in this period is unclear. It is possible that Susa was a hub via which much of the contact with highland Iran passed, and it was undoubtedly also an independent source of demand for trade goods. It is not yet possible properly to investigate the details of these trading networks relationships with the clarity that would enable us to unravel this dynamic process, but it is important to identify where the existing models might be oversimplified.

Power, control, negotiation, conflict, and violence

The fourth millennium BC saw a major transformation in the manifestation and demonstration of elite power over, and control of, the ancient Near East. We have a limited understanding of the socio-economics of south Mesopotamia in the early fourth millennium BC (cf. Algaze 2008: 164–65), but the institutionalisation of socio-economic hierarchies, major building programmes, and the iconography of leadership at Uruk during the mid- to late fourth millennium BC suggest that there was a step-change in the level and scale of elite power and control. There were similar transformations in northern Mesopotamia (Tell Brak) and Susiana (Susa), although there was variation in terms of their development and scale, suggesting that we are faced with more than one trajectory of increasing complexity in the greater region.

The appearance of ostensibly Mesopotamian and/or Susian material culture at settlements along trade routes and close to sources of raw materials has prompted models, counter-models, and ongoing debate about the nature of contact implied by this pattern of evidence and its *raison d'être*. Our understanding of the broad-scale dynamics of the mid- to late fourth millennium BC continues to revolve around the question of whether the appearance of lowland material culture represents colonisation, trade, and/or emulation (cf. Rothman 2001b). Given that each of these options deals with the manner in which cultural influence was exerted, it is also important to consider processes such as "domination", "acquiescence", "resistance", "co-existence", "assimilation", and "adaptation". The initial formulation of the *Uruk* World System advocated the existence of an asymmetrical core-periphery relationship (Algaze 1993 [2005]), but did not focus particular attention on the types of post-colonial responses that might have occurred at local scales. It is important to consider the possibility that there was resistance to lowland influence, and that conflict and violence may also have played a role (see Appendix A; Appendix B). Both are shown on

the *Uruk*-period seal impressions from Uruk, Susa, Chogha Mish, and Habuba Kabira (Pittman).

When considering the nature of lowland cultural influence in Iran during the mid- to late fourth millennium BC, the Godin Tepe Oval is the most obvious case to assess. It presents a very distinctive combination of cultural material preserved within an enclosure that has been widely utilised in discussions of the *Uruk* phenomenon (e.g. Algaze 1993 [2005]; Stein 1999; Gosden 2004), and continues to elicit differing interpretations (Rothman; Matthews). Godin Tepe is Algaze's (1993 [2005], 2008) archetypal outpost of southern Mesopotamia that sits at a "choke point" on a main Central Zagros intermontane route (cf. Matthews). This model is a type of "push" dynamic that was mentioned at several points during the conference (Helwing, Algaze in Appendix B). Godin Tepe was a local centre that has evidence for contact with the lowlands, and this is believed to be related to trade (Rothman; Algaze 1993 [2005]; Stein 1999), although there are no stocks of lapis lazuli, turquoise, or copper present and there is no evidence of their transhipment. For Rothman, the lowland affiliation of the seals from the Oval suggests that there was a specific relationship between "local" coordinators and "foreign" traders/administrators, and there might have been lowlanders present to negotiate the terms of trade and to mark destinations. The ways that "local" and "foreign" agents negotiated these trade and administration relationships is, however, unknown and a range of possible scenarios might be posited to explain the process.

The pre-Oval *Godin VI.2* deposits contain a limited number of lowland vessel forms, whereas the Oval sees an increase in the quantity and range of lowland material, including seals and tablets, although this material is deeply embedded in a local context. This evidence may indicate the creation of a lowland outpost (Algaze 1993 [2005]; Matthews) and interaction between highland elites and lowland intermediaries (Rothman), but it is not at all certain that the presence of lowland material indicates the presence of lowlanders. The administrative evidence from Godin Tepe might relate to the management of the local rural economy by a non-local cadre (Matthews), but this interpretation is not definitively supported by the other categories of material culture. That there was contact between Kangavar and Susa (seals, tablets; cf. Pittman) is almost incontrovertible, but it is feasible that the elites of Godin Tepe were adopting lowland material culture and a lowland system of power, in the form of administrative technology – potentially "buying in" elements of a lowland administration system. This would be a type of "pull" dynamic, which was also mentioned several times during the conference (Helwing, Algaze in Appendix B). As Algaze notes (Appendix B), these "push" and "pull" dynamics might have been operating simultaneously.

It is the dynamics behind the distribution of these "technologies of power" (cf. Mann 1986; Matthews) that are perhaps the critical component for understanding both the *Uruk* and *Proto-Elamite* phenomena. In each instance where *Proto-Elamite/Susa III* texts have been identified in the highlands, the proto-writing system was used for the management of the local rural economy (Damerow and Englund 1989), which seems to work against the possibility that the *Proto-Elamite* phenomenon represents the formal economic integration of the entire Iranian Plateau (Lamberg-Karlovsky 1978; Alden 1982). If the widespread use of the writing system does not indicate economic integration the question is, what does it signify? The nature of the *Proto-Elamite* script is such that its use seems to have been in the hands of a small number of individuals, who appear to have been trained either in or by people from Susa, thus the presence of the script may well indicate the presence of lowlanders. Their presence, however, might actually be evidence of local elites across the plateau "buying in" a specific lowland "technology of power".

We are still left with questions when it comes to comprehending the reception of these new technologies at a local scale. We are not yet able to differentiate adoption from acquiescence or resistance. We can see the assimilation and/or adaptation of lowland material into local highland assemblages, but other than the use of *Proto-Elamite/Susa III* script, the degree to which this represents the actual presence of lowlanders is unknown. In the conference discussions it was noted that there is an absence of overt evidence for conflict and violence in fourth-millennium Iran (Appendix B), which either reflects the nature of the process of interaction or the unpredictability of archaeological excavation. There was certainly potential for conflict, and Johnson (1973, 1989) suggested that the *Late Uruk* in Susiana was marked by conflict between Susa and Chogha Mish, and that such dynamics might have produced elite and adherent refugees, who might appear as colonists in other areas. Wright finds it hard to believe that the pattern of abandonment and resettlement at Susa between the *Late Uruk* and *Proto-Elamite* phases was driven by anything other than conflict between very different highland and lowland polities, although direct evidence for this is lacking.

There is evidence for conflict elsewhere, and the recent evidence from Tell Brak (McMahon *et al.* 2011; McMahon, in press) and Hamoukar (Reichel 2006; Lawler 2006; al-Kuntar and Abu Jayyab, in press) provides incontrovertible evidence for violence in the fourth millennium BC. The latest assessment of the stratigraphy at Uruk suggests that the large fortification walls there date to the Early Dynastic period (Nissen 2002, 2013), but there is evidence for fourth-millennium BC fortifications at Hamoukar (Lawler 2006; Ur 2010; al-Kuntar and Abu Jayyab, in press), Habuba Kabira (Strommenger 1980), Hacınebi (Stein *et al.* 1996), and Godin Tepe (Rothman; Rothman and Badler 2011); Godin Tepe also has abundant evidence for the storage of unfired clay sling balls (Rothman; Matthews; Rothman and Badler 2011). At Tell Brak, the violence appears to have been as a result of local strife rather than long-distance aggression, although the latter cannot be ruled out. We know that from the third millennium BC onwards, interaction between the populations of the greater Iranian Plateau and those of Mesopotamia involved considerable hostility (Potts 1999). It is particularly notable that Susiana and particularly Susa (i.e. lowland Elam) were engaged in recurrent phases of hostility with the cities and states of southern Mesopotamia during this time (cf. Amiet 1979), which were themselves constantly engaged in conflict.

De- and/or reconstructing explanatory models

This volume has presented a range of evidence that makes it possible to consider the archaeology of the Iranian Plateau during the fourth millennium BC in a more reflexive manner, akin to the approach used for the archaeology of north-eastern Syria and south-eastern Turkey (cf. Stein 1999; Rothman 2001a). Ideally this will facilitate a reassessment of various models that have been developed to explain the interactive dynamics that operated during different phases of the fourth millennium BC, but there are inevitable limitations.

Various overarching models of interaction have been put forward both here and elsewhere to encapsulate the dynamics of different phases of the fourth millennium BC, including "interaction spheres", "world systems", "distance parity", "trade diasporas", "shared cultural milieus", "shared social fields", "metallurgical provinces", and to these might also be added "interaction networks", "peer polity interaction", and many others. While it is imperative to build models and speculate about possible processes, it is important to acknowledge where they have limitations, seek the evidence that might overcome these limitations, and be prepared to reject or adapt them when they are no longer suitable. It is also essential that our thinking does not atrophy and that we do not accept that what was outlined as a "model" is the infallible "truth". The final sections of this chapter will move the debate forward by drawing attention to a number of specific dynamics and emerging views.

Although there has been considerable progress in re-evaluating the processes of local development and long-distance contact in Syria and Turkey during the fourth millennium BC, the lack of similar research on Iran has meant that understanding of a fundamental component of the *Uruk* world has remained stagnant.

The recent surge in new work and the reassessment of older work inevitably goes some way to redressing the balance. Our initial understanding of the *Proto-Elamite* phenomenon was actually based on an extremely small number of excavations spread across the large expanse of Iran, so explanatory models were unavoidably tenuous. The most recent phase of research has, however, identified settlements in different areas and variation that was not previously evident, emphasising that the *Proto-Elamite* period will only be understood properly with due consideration of the entire Iranian Plateau.

The Uruk *phenomenon*

There are several key elements relating to the *Uruk* period that are deserving of reconsideration. Firstly, it is potentially fruitful conceptually to decouple Susa and Susiana from southern Mesopotamia, or at least from Uruk and its hinterland. While there are developmental similarities between these two regions during the fourth millennium BC, there are sufficient differences for them to be regarded as distinct entities. Secondly, several papers in this volume encourage us to reorient the way in which we conceive lowland interaction with the highlands of Iran during the fourth millennium BC. It is important to consider the possibility that much of the "lowland" interaction with the Iranian Plateau might have been via Susa – it might thus be more correct to speak of "lowland" rather than "*Uruk*" contact, as has been adopted in this conclusion. Thirdly, we should reassess the degree to which lowland/highland interaction was based on the acquisition of raw materials and finished products. Although there was evidence of long-range trade and the sharing of technological knowledge during the fourth millennium BC, much of the evidence is inferential (cf. Algaze, Appendix B).

Pittman's proposal that Susa witnessed a parallel and potentially precocious development of early administrative technology is compelling, but the poor quality of the stratigraphic evidence from Uruk means that it is currently impossible to prove whether one site had chronological primacy. Potts (1999: 59–65) suggests that Susa does not see a contemporary development of the technology, but that the technology is "received". Nevertheless, the differences in the physical proportions of the tablets, the arrangement of the numerical and non-numerical signs, the types of numerical systems being used (Dahl *et al.*; also Potts 1999: 63–65; Dahl 2005), and the subjects of glyptic iconography at Uruk and Susa (Pittman), all suggest that distinctive systems were used to suit the different local contexts. There *are* differences in the size of the two sites and the ways that they have been excavated, but it is certainly valid to question whether Uruk deserves the position of primacy that it is given.

The degree to which long-distance trade networks were controlled, monitored, or even exploited by elites or other groups within south Mesopotamian cities is also open to interpretation, and it is important to reassess the degree to which lowland material culture penetrated into highland regions. In addition to the Oval compound at Godin Tepe (Rothman; Matthews), lowland/*Late Uruk* material is also evident at settlements on the Central Plateau (Tappeh Sialk and Arisman) and at various locations throughout the southern Zagros (Tol-e Nurabad, Tol-e Spid, Tal-e Kureh), although in many of these areas there are only a small number of *Uruk*/lowland vessel forms or material. At some of these settlements, the appearance of lowland vessel forms may simply reflect the movement of lowland potters or their craft techniques rather than entire communities (Wright; cf. Petrie 2011).

The excavations at Tepe Sofalin and Mahtoutabad prompt reconsideration of the nature of lowland penetration further into the plateau. In addition to the extensive collection of *Proto-Elamite* administrative documents at Tepe Sofalin, *Late Uruk*-styled bullae and a numerical tablet have also been reported (Hessari and Akbari 2007; Hessari 2011; Dahl *et al.* 2012), which have only otherwise been found in Iran at Susa. What this find signifies will only become evident when the material and the excavations are fully published. Tepe Sofalin sits at a point on the Central Plateau where the north–south routes meet those extending east–west, thereby fitting with Algaze's model of settlements being placed at strategic locations, but it is very isolated from Susa and/or southern Mesopotamia. Mahtoutabad is also isolated, being situated in the Halil Rud, which is actually further east than the Bard-Sir and other areas of the south-east that have known copper sources and sites with evidence for early metal processing (Tal-i Iblis and Tepe Yahya). It is evident that the inhabitants of the Halil Rud engaged in a range of craft-production activities and interacted widely with the other regions of south-eastern Iran throughout the fourth millennium BC, but during the mid- to late fourth millennium BC they must also have been interacting with the *Uruk* and/or *Proto-Elamite* worlds (Vidale and Desset; cf. Desset *et al.* 2013). This provides a provocative nuance to the prevailing models for interaction across the plateau being land-based (Algaze 1993 [2005], 2008; Rothman). The quantity of "intrusive" material at *Mahtoutabad III* is much greater than that seen at any of the other sites in the intervening highland zone. It is notable that the Halil Rud has straightforward access to the northern coast of the Persian Gulf, although the distance is still around 200 km as the crow flies. As noted in the introduction (Petrie), the fourth millennium BC saw a decline of interaction between Mesopotamia and the Persian Gulf and the current evidence suggests that overland routes were used for trade and communication in preference to the water route. We know nothing, however, about the fourth-millennium BC occupation on the northern coast of the Persian Gulf, and it is not impossible that important settlements existed there. The evidence in the Halil Rud for *Uruk*-period contact with a nebulous west, therefore, opens up the interesting possibility that there was contact and interaction with Mesopotamia and/or Susiana via the northern Persian Gulf during the mid- to late fourth millennium BC. Future surveys should focus on establishing the nature of fifth-, fourth-, and third-millennium BC occupation along this coastline.

The extent of the *Uruk*-period *oikoumenê*, as perceived from the lowlands, is unknown and realistically is dependent upon the degree to which lowland centres were in control of the supply of material imported from the highlands. The significance of lowland vessel forms in the highlands is equivocal, so the degree to which the population of Susiana was intimate with the highlanders of Fars is unknown. It is also not yet apparent how Mahtoutabad fits into this pattern. The most obvious indications of direct contact with the lowlands in the *Uruk* period are found at sites in the Central Western Zagros (Godin Tepe) and on the Central Plateau (Tappeh Sialk, perhaps Tepe Sofalin), which have evidence of lowland administrative material, although the presence of this material might be explained by both "push" and "pull" dynamics. Whether this implies a shift from down-the-line trade to some form of directed market system is unclear.

In Weeks's view, the *Uruk* phenomenon is but one interaction sphere operating in ancient Western Asia generally, but also specifically on the Iranian Plateau. The evidence from the north Central Plateau and south-eastern Iran also highlights the importance of interactive dynamics that operated in different directions. The populations around Tepe Hissar and the areas to its east appear to have been interacting closely with those in the Gorgan and Kopet Dag regions (Thornton *et al.*), and there are indications of contact with populations living in Kerman, the Bampur Valley, Seistan, western Baluchistan, and beyond (Mutin; Vidale and Desset). The lowlands of Susiana and Mesopotamia are unlikely to have been *the* core around which all other dynamics on the plateau revolved. As amply demonstrated by the papers presented in this volume, the Iranian Plateau and its mountains and piedmonts form a zone over which populations interacted throughout the fourth millennium BC and both before and afterwards. The greater Iranian Plateau and its neighbours are thus characterised by the operation of multiple overlapping dynamics of interaction that develop, flourish, and then deteriorate. Beyond the patterns of cultural behaviour, it is the landscape that has the potential to shape the types of interactions that take place across it.

The **Proto-Elamite** *phenomenon*

The prevailing view is that *Proto-Elamite* occupation appears roughly concurrently over a large area and shares uniform architecture, pottery, and administrative artefacts (Lamberg-Karlovsky 1978; Alden 1982; Nissen 2001; Helwing 2005). Elements of this are true, but *Proto-Elamite* material culture is always nested within a local material context that continues to show regional variation (Potts 2004). There is also an interesting but poorly understood chronological dimension to the *Proto-Elamite* texts, which indicates that there might be more nuances to the process than previously believed (Dahl *et al.*).

Helwing (2005) has argued that the appearance of *Proto-Elamite* material culture was a gradual process that culminated in the rise of a distinctive highland political entity based in substantial urban centres with large-scale administrative buildings. This should perhaps be qualified in the sense that these buildings are large relative to other buildings in Iran, but not relative to the contemporaneous buildings in Mesopotamia (cf. Goff 1971, see above). As Helwing notes, the evidence exposed at Uruk has shaped our expectations for what an urban centre should look like, but urban centres took many forms (McMahon 2013). How the *Proto-Elamite* population of Susiana was constituted and how it interacted with the populations of the highlands is not entirely clear. Amiet (1979) and Alden (1982) have suggested that Fars was the home of the *Proto-Elamites*, but as Potts (1999; also Pittman) outlines, it is only in Susiana that we have the development of the administrative technologies that are the hallmark of the *Proto-Elamites*. Furthermore, Dahl *et al.* show that it is at sites on the northern part of the plateau that we see the earliest types of *Proto-Elamite* tablets. The indications of contact between Susa and Godin Tepe (*IV.1*) and Tappeh Sialk (*IV$_1$*) suggest that there was an increase of interaction with the populations of the highland zone at the end of the *Late Uruk* period, which may reflect a reorientation of Susian relations. This dynamic may well have coalesced into the *Proto-Elamite* phenomenon (cf. Petrie, in press).

Helwing argues that the *Proto-Elamite* was preceded by a widespread disruption in occupation at all of the excavated sites, including Susa, Tappeh Sialk, Arisman, and possibly Tol-e Spid, while sites such as Tal-e Malyan and Tepe Yahya show signs of new occupation or reoccupation after a hiatus, as potentially do Mahtoutabad and Tal-i Iblis. With this in mind, Helwing speculates that the pre-*Proto-Elamite* communities of the greater Iranian Plateau engaged in indirect contact with the lowland *Uruk* world (including Susa), and following a short-term collapse of the *Uruk*-dynamic, the plateau communities saw a significant increase in complexity and in her view emulated the lowland form of complexity. The "*Uruk* model" was thus known to the highland communities through previous contacts and was emulated when a vacuum occurred in the lowlands, resulting in the elites of the highlands exerting their authority (Helwing). Helwing refers to them as "new elites", implying that there had not been elites on the central plateau earlier. This model presupposes that there were no highland elites, rather than there being a change in the way that elites exerted their authority. In Helwing's view the shift in lowland power allowed or perhaps facilitated an opportunistic increase in complexity, as marked by indications of more specialised labour, administration, and differentiation in burial goods.

The evidence for a break in occupation is not consistent across the Iranian plateau. There was a displacement of the occupied area at Arisman and the establishment of a new settlement using a different and distinctive form of architecture (Helwing). Tepe Yahya was reoccupied after a period of abandonment with a similarly new and distinctive form of architecture (Mutin; Potts 2001; Mutin and Lamberg-Karlovsky, in preparation). At Susa there was a gap in the *Acropole I* sequence, but not elsewhere on the Acropole (Dahl *et al.* discussion, Appendix A), and the evidence for interruptions at sites such as Tappeh Sialk, Tal-e Malyan, Tol-e Spid, and Tol-e Nurabad is equivocal, and poorly characterised in each instance. At present, the evidence of a disruption is at least partially a result of the nature of the investigations.

Unfortunately there may be too few excavated sites in Fars adequately to understand the later fourth millennium BC in this region, and this is in fact a lesson that should be considered across the remainder of the plateau. The question "how representative is the available evidence?" is one that deserves to be considered constantly. On balance, the evidence suggests that the highland regions of southern Iran were not linked as a homogeneous "cultural unit" during the late fourth millennium BC (Petrie *et al.*). Although there is evidence for the "sharing" of material culture between regions, all of this material was used in a local context.

Petrie *et al.* suggest that the widespread distribution of particular types of ceramics may be indicative of culinary influence, which would have been negotiated in different ways by the populations of different regions. They also suggest that the dispersal of this highly distinctive material culture and its incorporation into a range of locally distinct material assemblages may have been a veneer of influence of varying "thicknesses" or even "layers" in different regions. The concept of a veneer is not drastically different from the horizon style that Potts (1977) and Abdi (2003a) have spoken of, but what this veneer signifies still remains an open question. One way to move the debate forward is perhaps to stop thinking of the *Proto-Elamite* material assemblage as a "package". There is variation in the types of *Proto-*

Elamite ceramic vessels that appear at different sites, and this material is found with different combinations of local material in different regions. The reasons behind the adoption of specific ceramic vessel forms are likely to be variable and moreover, might not be the same reasons why *Proto-Elamite* writing and administrative tools were adopted. It is notable that *Proto-Elamite* writing has not been recovered from all the sites that have produced *Proto-Elamite* material culture. What is not yet known is whether the absence of tablets at sites like Arisman and Tol-e Nurabad is indicative of a real pattern or is a symptom of the scale of the excavations and the luck of the excavators. If we think about *Proto-Elamite* writing and administrative paraphernalia as a range of associated technologies of power, then it is possible that they were adopted by local elites. It is of course possible that foreign elites might be in control of particular locations – carrying out local scale administration and using locally produced pottery – but, as noted above in the discussion of Godin Tepe, it is important to re-evaluate the assumptions upon which we base our interpretations.

It is interesting to see that there are limits to the range of *Proto-Elamite* material culture. As Bonora and Vidale note, the piedmonts, plains, and oases of southern Central Asia are outside the influence of the *Proto-Elamite* interaction sphere, and they suggest that the *Proto-Elamite* phenomenon "clashed" with the highly structured and different social world of the north-east. As Thornton *et al.* show, the extent of *Proto-Elamite* influence did not even extend as far to the north-east as Tepe Hissar, which suggests that there was no clash of culture with the inhabitants of Central Asia. In fact, to the best of our knowledge, Tepe Sofalin is the settlement with *Proto-Elamite* material culture that is closest to Tepe Hissar, perhaps indicating that the *Proto-Elamite* dynamic was primarily orientated in a north-western to south-eastern direction, largely following the alignment of the Zagros Mountains. This orientation conforms to the natural advantages for passage and mobility afforded by the Zagros ridges. It is the lowland evidence from Susa that is most anomalous in this pattern.

We are not yet in a position to explain why the *Proto-Elamite* structure, whatever it is, breaks down. Several things change, the most obvious being that *Proto-Elamite* writing is abandoned. This may represent the rejection of a technology and perhaps also a structure of power, but it might also be because transmission of administrative knowledge was too tightly constricted and thus vulnerable (see above).

Nomadism versus mobility: are we entangled in terminology?

In all of these debates, we are faced with the fact that ancient populations interacted with each other over great distances. Thus mobility is a key factor, but questions remain about how mobility is manifested. The role of nomads throughout Iranian prehistory has long been debated (e.g. Hole 1974; Wright 1987). Claims that nomadic groups played a key role in all the major phases of socio-economic and political transformation in south-western Iran (e.g. Alizadeh 2003, 2006, 2008, 2010) contrast with varying levels of scepticism about the suitability of such models and questions about the degree to which nomads are detectable in the archaeological record (e.g. Potts 2008, in press; Weeks 2010; Weeks *et al.* 2010; Petrie 2011). The role and potential power of nomadic populations in Iran during the fourth millennium BC remains a major point of contention (compare Hopper and Wilkinson; Wright; Alden with Petrie *et al.*; Weeks; Pollock; also Appendix A; Appendix B). The two sides to the debate are largely separated by the degree to which the scholars concerned are willing to build speculative models using an inductive approach. While such models should be considered, it is important to acknowledge that some key categories of evidence are either open to interpretation or are lacking substantive data. It is prudent to review these data and point out potential issues that result from an often opaque use of terminology.

There have been numerous claims that there were dramatic shifts in settlement trajectories and subsistence practices during the fourth millennium BC, and these have often been used to argue for a shift towards mobile pastoralism during this period (e.g. Hopper and Wilkinson; Alden; also Sumner 1986, 1988a; Alizadeh 2010). In this volume, the most detailed consideration of the role of nomads is Alden's assessment of the fourth-millennium BC settlement in the Kur River Basin, and its arguments serve as useful prompting for a discussion of nomads and mobility.

The necessity of resorting to a "nomadic pastoralist explanation" to explain the *Banesh* dynamics largely comes from the need to identify a "missing" component of the population. In addition to progressive changes in settlement systems between the *Lapui* and *Early Banesh* periods and the spatial patterning of the settlement clusters, Alden's claim that there must be an additional non-settled component to the population is based on the discovery of enormous chaff-tempered goblet waster piles at Tal-e Qarib. Alden's careful calculations show that each individual at the known *Early Banesh* settlement sites might have had up to five goblets per year for 200 years. He proposes that considerably more of these vessels were being produced than the known settled population of the Kur River Basin could consume, and thus speculates that an otherwise invisible mobile pastoralist portion of the population used these vessels. While compelling, this hypothesis neglects to consider the function of the goblets. The quality of these vessels and the

quantity of wasters suggests that the goblets were extremely disposable. If this is the case, five, ten, or more goblets per person per year might not be an unreasonable number. Populations may have used such vessels in regular feasting activities. It is perhaps telling that no mobile pastoralist explanation has ever been proposed for the similarly massive quantities of bevel-rim bowls (*c.* 250,000 fragments) found at *Uruk*-period Chogha Mish (Delougaz and Kantor 1996: 49). Further insights into the use of disposable vessels come from modern South Asia where a wide variety of mass-produced ceramic vessels are used for tea, yoghurt, and other products and then thrown away after one use. Such behaviours should certainly be considered for explaining the large-scale pottery dumps, although until residue analysis is used to establish what the goblets held, it is perhaps unwise to ascribe specific functions to these vessels.

A fundamental challenge in assessing the bioarchaeological record as a whole is encapsulated by Miller and Kimiaie's observation (2006: 107, 113) that because the available samples come primarily from settled communities, they are unlikely directly to address the question of nomadic pastoralism. It is thus arguable whether we are yet in a position critically to assess the specific models of socio-economic transformations in approaches to subsistence.

The fact that the faunal data available for the Kur River Basin, and Iran more generally, are by no means comprehensive and that the available information is open to more than one interpretation, is also a constraint. *Banesh*-period Tal-e Malyan certainly does have a high proportional use of caprids; Zeder (1991: table 24) documented very high percentages (98–99%) of caprid exploitation in the *Middle Banesh* period, and only slightly lower percentages for the *Late Banesh* period. These data have been taken as evidence of a mobile pastoral subsistence economy, at least in relation to animal exploitation (cf. Alden; Sumner 1986), yet there are no comparable data from the *Lapui* and *Early Banesh* periods in the Kur River Basin that could confirm whether these proportions actually represent a dramatic shift. It is possible to compare different bone assemblages to show that there was some intensification in the use of sheep or goat in this period, but if the data from Tol-e Spid and Tal-e Malyan are compared there is only a shift from 80 to 98% between the *Lapui* and *Banesh* periods (Zeder 1991; Mashkour 2009), which is hardly a revolutionary change. Furthermore, in her conference presentation Mashkour (2009) highlighted the fact that caprids dominate animal bone assemblages throughout late prehistory on the plateau. For example, at Tol-e Nurabad, caprids make up over 90% of the *Neolithic* bone assemblage (Mashkour 2009).

Identifying patterns of pastoralism and/or nomadism in the archaeological record is particularly difficult, and Zeder (1991: 161) has noted, "it is practically impossible on the basis of faunal data to establish whether caprids were raised locally or were the products of mobile pastoral specialists." Thus we do not yet know how far the animals that were exploited at Tal-e Malyan had been moved, and whether they were moved in vertical or horizontal patterns of transhumance. So far, the methods needed definitively to discriminate a generalised agro-pastoral economy from one that has specialised farmers and (long-distance) herders (e.g. stable isotope analysis; cf. Mashkour *et al.* 2005; Mashkour 2009) have not been used on archaeological samples from anywhere on the Iranian Plateau.

As with the archaeozoological data, there are limitations to discussing the archaeobotanical materials of the greater Iranian Plateau during the fourth millennium BC. Domesticated cereals (primarily barley [*Hordeum vulgare*] and wheat [*Triticum dicoccum* and *Triticum monococcum*]) played a major role in the agricultural economy of the sites that have had botanical remains analysed (e.g. Miller 1982, 1985; Tengberg 2004). In addition to the primary cereal crops, archaeobotany can also reveal much about the variable exploitation of fruits, wild species, and wood species (Tengberg, Appendix B). These species are likely to be much more sensitive to local environmental conditions and particular subsistence strategies, and they have the potential to play a critical role in differentiating an agro-pastoral economy from a grazing one, but there will still be a problem because samples are obtained from sedentary settlements. Thus, the available bioarchaeological evidence does not provide any definitive evidence for dramatic shifts in the patterns of plant and animal subsistence during the fourth millennium BC.

One problem with the conception of nomads being agents in various explanatory scenarios comes from concomitant social interpretations that come with the nomad label, that is, the involvement of tribes and tribal confederations (see Rowton 1974: 2). It is this particular element for which evidence from archaeology is lacking. In many respects Alden's identification of site clusters is a very important step towards identifying possible loci of socio-economic differentiation within *Banesh* settlements in the Kur River Basin, but the possibility that this pattern indicated the presence of tribal lineages is just one plausible scenario. In many regions throughout the Old World, including ancient Mesopotamia (McMahon 2013) and the Indus Civilisation (Petrie 2013a), early cities were often polycentric and comprised multiple zones dominated by various elite groups that were broadly equal in terms of socio-economic status, competed with each other and interacted in complex ways. These dynamics suggest the existence of heterarchical relationships within individual settlements, which need not be constituted as competing tribal lineages.

While the capacity for transhumance should not be denied, it is the degree to which the transhumant elements of the populations held the reins of power that is a key component to the arguments presented by Sumner (1986), Alizadeh (2006, 2010), and Alden. Alizadeh (2006) has proposed that the primary source of power lay with the mobile pastoralist khans from the *Bakun* period onwards, whereas Sumner (1986) and Alden both favour a *Banesh*-period date for the rise of nomadic power on the back of a fully nomadic pastoral economy. The Kur River Basin, and specifically Tal-e Malyan, is regarded as one nexus in this system, which Alden does not regard as a state. Instead, he argues for a society comprised of a number of tribal lineages that lived in a collection of physically separate independent towns in close proximity to each other. Specialists produced goods and services that could be exchanged within and between lineages as well as between settled and nomadic populations (Alden). Pollock, however, questions whether it is appropriate to speak of "khans" in the distant past primarily on the basis of whether or not such classifications are really the most interesting questions to ask of the archaeological material. Perhaps most importantly, it is important that we do not become beguiled by the "archaeopoetry" (Alizadeh 2006: 26) of the nomad hypothesis and that we remain open to a range of interpretations.

The proposal that the inhabitants of Tal-e Malyan were at least partly made up of the tribal khans in charge of a fully nomadic pastoral economy serves to perpetuate the division of the archaeology of south-western Iran into a highland/lowland dichotomy. Alden characterises all of south-western Iran (at least Khuzestan and western Fars) as an extended cultural community with a subsistence economy based on full-time seasonally transhumant nomadic pastoralism. In many ways this provides an explanation for the *Proto-Elamite* dynamics in this particular region, but other regions need to be considered, particularly when it comes to understanding the *Proto-Elamite* phenomenon as a whole. For instance, Tal-e Geser in Ram Hormuz is a substantial mound site with a multiple phase of occupation during the fourth millennium BC, and further up into the highlands there is also evidence for continued settlement in the Mamasani region throughout the fourth millennium BC. Any suggestion about the possibility that tribal khans may have been moving their herds between the highlands and lowlands must consider how those populations interacted with the populations of regions such as Mamasani and Ram Hormuz. In fact, there is evidence that suggests links between Susiana and the Kur River Basin and other areas, both those that have been investigated and those that have not. There is a real possibility that populations were mobile across much larger distances than have hitherto been considered, and this should force us to consider the entirety of the Iranian Plateau as a zone across which populations interacted throughout the fourth millennium BC. Whether populations were nomadic pastoralists or simply included mobile and/or migratory components is open to question, and we need to explore ways of explaining mobility throughout prehistory without resorting to nomads as a default.

A key problem in the discussion of the role of nomads may lie in a misperception in the use of the term. In his most recent synthesis, Alizadeh (2010) builds a model that sees the nomadic pastoralists in late prehistory as living in sedentary communities at each end of an annual or sub-annual migration route and engaging in farming as and when required. This is quite different to the Oxford English Dictionary (OED) definition of nomad as "a member of a people that travels from place to place to find fresh pasture for its animals, and has no permanent home", and it is this discrepancy that lies at the core of some of the criticism of the application of the nomad analogy to various stages of Iranian later prehistory (e.g. Potts 2008). The OED definition fits what could perhaps best be described as true nomadism (Sadr 1991), which implies a symbiosis between a specialised sedentary agricultural population and specialised nomadic populations living in tents that move as appropriate and occupy no fixed abode. Alizadeh (2010) reformulates Rowton's (1974) term "enclosed nomadism" and coins the phrase "enclosing nomadism" to describe the nomadic populations that he sees as surrounding the urban centres rather than occupying the interstices between them, and this reconstruction is broadly followed by Alden. The situation outlined by Alizadeh for south-western Iran is, however, fundamentally different to the OED definition, and implies that while herds were being moved over admittedly long distances, they were generally moving between more or less fixed seasonal pastures, and herders were potentially living in settlements and practising opportunistic agriculture.

In a paper focusing on the Central Western Zagros, Abdi (2003b) identifies a broad spectrum of variation in the degrees to which populations are mobile. Alden speaks of dualities (e.g. "nomad/village", "pastoral/ agricultural", "mountains/lowlands"), but these dualities potentially should not be taken to represent hard and fast differences in the ancient populations: the same population or portions of it could well have engaged in sedentism and mobility, agriculture and pastoralism. As Hopper and Wilkinson note, the highlands and lowlands are actually continuous and contiguous rather than a dichotomy. In the final discussion of the *Ancient Iran and Its Neighbours* conference (Appendix C), Mitchell Rothman was discussing the Trans-Caucasus and made the point that while "we are not talking about pastoral nomads and we are not talking about pastoral farmers, we

are talking about some of their modality", that is, the modes of behaviour that nomads use. There is actually limited concrete evidence for the existence of nomadic populations in late prehistory, and a lack of direct evidence for the annual migration of large proportions of the highland population. It is thus perhaps more appropriate to continue speaking of transhumant agro-pastoralists.

Options for the future

This volume is far from the last word on the archaeology of the fourth millennium BC in Iran. There are several areas where further work is required. These include the spatial coverage of the available evidence and the application of new fieldwork and analytical methods to current and future data sets. Perhaps most importantly in the conceptual sphere, we must understand where our interpretative approaches and frameworks need to develop and incorporate influences from a broader theoretical canvas.

Spatial coverage and methods

There are many areas on the plateau where only a basic awareness of the archaeological record exists, and many other areas that have not yet been investigated systematically. There is now new and ongoing research in various regions, however, which has the potential to fill a number of gaps in our knowledge and ultimately revolutionise our understanding of different aspects of the archaeology of the fourth millennium BC. The authors and editor of this volume hope that it will ultimately be superseded when more comprehensive fieldwork produces new evidence that challenges our current understandings.

There are a number of gaps in the coverage of the archaeology of the greater Iranian Plateau, which has been presented in this volume. This is primarily a result of several confounding factors. Firstly, there are regions that have not yet been surveyed systematically, including various intermontane valleys throughout the Zagros. Secondly, while there has been an increase in regional survey throughout Iran, much of this material remains unpublished and there is no consolidated database that records which areas have been surveyed and which have not. There are also problems of coverage caused by the modern political situation, which have meant that our knowledge of the archaeology of several regions has not progressed for decades. There are obvious steps that can be taken to address these issues, and strategies for future question-oriented research can readily be formulated.

Wright makes a number of specific recommendations about future research (new surface and geoarchaeological surveys, new excavations including horizontal exposures, absolute dating, and new technical studies). These suggestions fit neatly with changing archaeological agendas in advocating investigations of peripheral areas and ephemeral sites, evidence for environment and climate, as well as making maximal use of the expanding and diversifying range of archaeological science methods (e.g. micromorphology, isotopes, phytoliths, DNA, etc.). As noted above, one area that needs attention is absolute dating, as there are a number of specific issues that will only be resolved by the dating of new samples and the application of Bayesian approaches to calibration (Dahl *et al.*; Wright and Rupley 2001; Petrie, in press).

Suitably scaled approaches to the survey data are clearly essential, but our knowledge of settlement distribution in south-western Iran is not yet paralleled across the plateau. The gaps in our knowledge and the problems with regional chronologies noted by Hopper and Wilkinson mean that there are inevitable limitations in the degree to which definitive answers can be proposed. There is, however, a range of extant (e.g. de Miroschedji 1972; Prickett 1986) and new (e.g. Moghaddam and Miri 2003, 2007; McCall 2009; Moghaddam 2012) survey data sets available for both the south-west and elsewhere in Iran. It would be judicious to integrate all of these data into an overarching *longue durée* analysis of settlement dynamics across the greater Iranian Plateau and in the neighbouring regions.

New conceptual approaches

Algaze (Appendix B) asks whether we can conceptualise urbanism in Susiana and elsewhere in Iran in local terms. If we consider Pittman's suggestions, then the local developments at Susa during the fourth millennium BC should be considered much more carefully than they have been previously. Pollock urges us to investigate how we identify similarities and differences in archaeological materials and to what we attribute them, particularly with how broad-scale changes were the product of small-scale practices and behaviour. Pollock advocates investigating the small-scale intra-community distinctions within settlements – the details of household and neighbourhood life ways – as it is these elements that underpin large-scale political and economic structures. These types of conceptual developments must be followed up if we are to further our knowledge of this critical period.

The term "interaction sphere" has long been used to discuss the interactive dynamics operating across the Iranian Plateau (e.g. Caldwell 1968), and it is mentioned in several papers here (e.g. Weeks; Appendix B). This term largely focuses on perceived interaction between people – based on the presence of specific types of material culture – and lacks the capacity to define the degree, orientation, and intensity of contact and interaction between different groups. In contrast, the developing concept of "interaction networks" creates the opportunity to discuss socio-economic factors, as well as relationships suggested by material culture and, perhaps most critically, geography (cf. Knappett 2011, 2013).

As populations became more engaged with their material world, and increased in socio-economic complexity in such a way that exotic and elite artefacts were desired, then populations became increasingly "entangled" with one another (i.e. within groups and between groups), just as they became "entangled" with their material world (cf. Hodder 2012). It is likely that this process led to the development of long-term "networks of entanglement", where continued and intensified interactions that began through the movement of people, trade and exchange of goods and raw materials, and transfer of technological knowledge, evolved into mutual dependency. It could be argued that the *Uruk* and *Proto-Elamite* phenomena represent the culminations of such long-term "networks of entanglement".

Perhaps the most interesting questions relate to the reasons why these networks change, break down, and reformulate. Networks inevitably operated at different scales, from micro- to macro-, and over time these networks would have had different levels of intensity and orientation, evolving with the rise and fall of different nexuses of power. The greater Iranian Plateau is a landscape that facilitates the creation of interaction networks having specific orientation and foci, but there are patterns of connectivity that are evident at different times throughout the fourth millennium BC, and these patterns transform in subsequent periods. By thinking in terms of networks, it is possible to make use of tools such as geographical information systems and agent-based modelling to model relationships and processes (e.g. MASS Simulation project; cf. Wright, Appendix B). Such approaches are capable of incorporating the new work that will inevitably be conducted in the various unexplored or under-explored regions of the greater plateau and will provide a solid basis from which to improve our understanding of the archaeology of the Iranian Plateau during the fourth millennium BC.

We now have significantly more information about Iran in the fourth millennium BC than ever before. The papers in this volume have shown, however, that the evidence is open to different interpretations and that there are still a number of methodological, theoretical, and practical limitations to gaining an improved understanding of this critical period. There are perhaps more questions posed here than answers given, but if nothing else, this volume highlights where to look for more data and further answers, and the types of new approaches that should be used to improve our comprehension of familiar questions. The inability to be definitive is at least partly methodological in that limitations are imposed by the way that sites have been investigated and cultural material has been recovered, analysed, interpreted, and published. These issues are compounded by the traditional focus on intrusive material rather than on entire assemblages of material culture in their broader regional context.

Perhaps the greatest challenge presented by the study of Iran in the fourth millennium BC is that of geographic scale. Although attempting to understand the vast region between the plains of Mesopotamia to those of western South Asia across an entire millennium is not presently possible, the papers in this volume have incontrovertibly demonstrated that a focus on any one part of Iran during the fourth millennium BC will inevitably be too narrow to address processes of change adequately. The leitmotif of the archaeology of fourth-millennium BC Iran is not particular types of pottery or particular writing systems, but the broader networks of entanglement that linked the populations across the plateau, and which in turn demand a broad-scale regional archaeological perspective.

Notes
1   Although Iran was largely a culturally fragmented landscape where populations differed in both material culture and life ways (Helwing), it is important to acknowledge that they all engaged in variations of wheat, barley, sheep, goat, and cattle-based agriculture and pastoralism with at least a degree of sedentism.
2   It is important to note that even though the early pottery sequence from Uruk has been reanalysed, the published *Uruk*-period sequence is unreliable and not representative (Nissen 2002; Butterlin 2003: 286–97). The Uruk and Susa sequences are thus not strictly comparable.
3   The Tal-e Malyan city wall surrounding the entire settled area was certainly in place during the *Late Banesh* period (Sumner 1985) but may have been built at the end of the *Middle Banesh*; it appears to have replaced the walls that surrounded individual areas at Tal-e Malyan earlier in the *Middle Banesh* period (Alden).
4   Most of the administrative evidence from Uruk, including the inscribed tablets, comes from poorly stratified contexts, and although glyptic is attested from *Eanna Level V*, numerical, numero-ideographic, and proto-literate tablets are only known from *Eanna Level IVa* (Pittman). The *Acropole I* sequence at Susa begins with stamp seals (*Level I.27–22*), and then from *Level I.21–20* onwards cylinder seal glyptic is evident (Pittman). Pittman notes that while *Eanna Levels VIII–IV* are believed to correlate to *Acropole I.22–17*, only stamp seals were recovered from the extremely limited excavations of *Middle Uruk* levels in the Anu sequence, suggesting that at present there is no overt evidence for the development of cylinder seal technology at Uruk during the *Middle Uruk* phase.

Bibliography

Abdi, K. 2003a. "From Écriture to Civilisation: Changing Paradigms of Proto-Elamite Archaeology", in Miller, N. F. and Abdi, K. (eds), *Yeki bud, yeki nabud: Essays on the Archaeology of Iran in Honor of William M. Sumner*, 48, Cotsen Institute of Archaeology, University of California, Los Angeles: 140–51.
Abdi, K. 2003b. "The Early Development of Pastoralism in the Central Zagros Mountains", *Journal of World Prehistory* 17.4: 395–448.
Adams, R. M. 1966. *The Evolution of Urban Society*, Aldine Publishing Company, Chicago.
Adams, R. M. 1981. *Heartland of Cities: Surveys of Ancient Settlement and Land Use on the Central Floodplain of the Euphrates*, University of Chicago Press, Chicago.
Alden, J. R. 1982. "Marketplace Exchange as Indirect Distribution: An Iranian Example", in Ericson, J. and Earle, T. (eds), *Contexts for Prehistoric Exchange*, Academic, New York: 83–101.
Alden, J. R. 1987. "The Susa III period", in Hole, F. (ed.), *The Archaeology of Western Iran: Settlement and Society from Prehistory to the Islamic Conquest*, Smithsonian Institution Press, Washington DC: 157–70.
Algaze, G. 1993. *The Uruk World System: The Dynamics of Expansion of Early Mesopotamian Civilisation*, 1st edition, University of Chicago Press, Chicago.
Algaze, G. 2005. *The Uruk World System: The Dynamics of Expansion of Early Mesopotamian Civilisation*, 2nd revised edition, University of Chicago Press, Chicago.
Algaze, G. 2008. *Ancient Mesopotamia at the Dawn of Civilisation: The Evolution of an Urban Landscape*, University of Chicago Press, Chicago.
Alizadeh, A. 2003. "Some Observations Based on the Nomadic Character of Fars Prehistoric Cultural Development", in Miller, N.F. and Abdi, K. (eds), *Yeki bud, yeki nabud: Essays on the Archaeology of Iran in Honor of William M. Sumner*, Cotsen Institute of Archaeology, University of California, Los Angeles: 83–97.
Alizadeh, A. 2006. *The Origins of State Organizations in Prehistoric Highland Fars, Southern Iran*, Oriental Institute Publications 128, Chicago.
Alizadeh, A. 2008. *Chogha Mish II. The Development of a Prehistoric Regional Center in Lowland Susiana, Southwest Iran: Final Report on the Last Six Seasons of Excavations 1972–1978*, Oriental Institute Publications 130, Chicago.
Alizadeh, A. 2010. "The rise of the highland Elamite state in southwestern Iran 'Enclosed' or Enclosing Nomadism?", *Current Anthropology* 51/3: 353–83.
Amiet, P. 1979. "Archaeological discontinuity and ethnicity duality in Elam", *Antiquity* 53: 195–204.
Amiet, P. 1980. *La glyptique mésopotamienne archaïque*, CNRS, Paris.
Beale, T. W. 1986. *Excavations at Tepe Yahya, Iran 1967–1976: The Early Periods*, American School of Prehistoric Research Bulletin, Volume 38, Peabody Museum of Archaeology and Ethnology, Cambridge, MA.
Beale, T. W. and Carter, S. M. 1986. "On the track of the Yahya large kuš: evidence for architectural planning in the Period IVC complex at Tepe Yahya", *Paléorient* 9/1: 81–88.
Berberian, M., Malek Shahmirzādi, S., Nokandeh, J. and Djamāli, M. 2012. "Archaeoseismicity and environmental crises at the Sialk mounds, Central Iranian Plateau, since

the Early Neolithic", *Journal of Archaeological Science* 39/9: 2845–58.

Berberian, M., Petrie, C. A., Potts, D. T., Asgari Chaverdi, A. *et al.* in press. "Archaeoseismicity of the mounds and monuments along the Kāzerun fault (western Zagros, SW Iranian Plateau) since the Chalcolithic period", *IA* 49: 1–81.

Butterlin, P. 2003. *Les Temps Proto-Urbains de Mésopotamie*, CNRS Éditions, Paris.

Caldwell, J. R. 1968. "Pottery and the Cultural History of the Iranian Plateau", *JNES* 27: 178–83.

Chase, D. W., Caldwell, J. R. and Fehérvári, I. 1967. "The Iblis Sequence and the exploration of excavation areas A, C and E", in Caldwell, J. R. (ed.), *Investigations at Tal-i Iblis*, Illinois State Museum Preliminary Reports 9, Springfield: 111–201.

Chegini, N. N., Fahimi, H. and Helwing, B. 2011. "Excavations in Arisman, Area C", in Vatandoust *et al.* 2011: 40–68.

Dahl, J. L. 2005. "Animal husbandry in Susa during the proto-Elamite period," *SMEA (Studi Micenei ed Egeo-Anatolici)* 47: 81–134.

Dahl, J. L., Hessari, M. and Yousefi Zoshk, R. 2012. "The Proto-Elamite tablets from Tape Sofalin", *Iranian Journal of Archaeological Studies* 2/1: 57–73.

Damerow, P. and Englund, R. K. 1989. *The Proto-Elamite texts from Tepe Yahya*, Peabody Museum of Archaeology and Ethnology, Harvard University, Cambridge, MA.

Delougaz, P. and Kantor, H. J. 1996. *Chogha Mish Volume 1: The First Five Seasons of Excavations 1961–1971*, (ed. Alizadeh, A.), Oriental Institute Publications 101, Chicago.

Desset, F., Vidale, M. and Alidadi Soleimani, N. 2013. "Mahtoutabad III (Province of Kerman, Iran): an "Uruk-related" material assemblage in eastern Iran", *Iran* 51: 17–55.

Englund, R. K. 1998. "Texts from the Late Uruk Period", in Attinger, P. and Wäfler, M. (eds), *Späturuk–Zeit und frühdynastische Zeit*, OBO 160/1, Göttingen: 15–233.

Fazeli, N. H., Coningham, R. A. E. and Batt, C. M. 2004. "Cheshmeh-Ali revisited: towards an absolute dating of the Late Neolithic and Chalcolithic of Iran's Tehran Plain", *Iran* 42: 13–23.

Friberg, J. 1994. "Preliterate counting and accounting in the Middle East", *Orientalistische Literaturzeitung* 89: 477–502.

Goff, C. 1971. "Luristan before the Iron Age", *Iran* 9: 131–52.

Goody, J. 2000. *The Power of the Written Tradition*, Smithsonian Institution Press, Washington DC.

Gosden, C. 2004. *Archaeology and Colonialism*, Cambridge University Press, Cambridge.

Goulder, J. 2010. "Administrators' bread: an experiment-based re-assessment of the functional and cultural role of the Uruk bevel-rim bowl", *Antiquity* 84: 351–62.

Harris, D. R. 2010. *Origins of Agriculture in Western Central Asia: An Environmental-Archaeological Study*, University of Pennsylvania Museum of Archaeology and Anthropology, Philadelphia.

Helwing, B. 2005. "Early complexity in highland Iran: recent archaeological research into the Chalcolithic of Iran", *TÜBA-AR* 8: 39–60.

Helwing, B. 2011a. "Archaeological comments on the radiocarbon datings", in Vatandoust *et al.* 2011: 374–75.

Helwing, B. 2011b, "Proto-Elamite pottery from areas A, C, D and E", in Vatandoust *et al.* 2011: 194–251.

Helwing, B. 2011c. "The small finds from Arisman", in Vatandoust *et al.* 2011: 254–327.

Helwing, B. 2011d. "Conclusions: The Arisman copper production in a wider context", in Vatandoust *et al.* 2011: 523–31.

Helwing, B. 2013. "The Chalcolithic of northern Iran", in Potts, D. T. (ed.), *Oxford Handbook of Iranian Archaeology*, Oxford University Press, Oxford: 79–92.

Henrickson, E. F. 1983. *Ceramic Styles and Cultural Interaction in the Early and Middle Chalcolithic of the Central Zagros*, Ph.D. dissertation, Department of Anthropology, University of Toronto, University Microfilms, Ann Arbor.

Henrickson, E. F. 1989. "Ceramic evidence for cultural interaction between the 'Ubaid tradition and the Central Western Zagros Highlands, western Iran", in Henrickson, E. F. and Thuesen, I. (eds), *Upon this Foundation: The 'Ubaid Reconsidered*, Carsten Niebuhr Institute of Ancient Near Eastern Studies 9, Museum Tusculanum Press, Copenhagen: 369–403.

Henrickson, E. F. 1994. "The outer limits: settlement and economic strategies in the Central Zagros Highlands during the Uruk Era", in Stein, G. and Rothman, M. (eds), *Chiefdoms and Early States in the Near East: the Organizational Dynamics of Complexity*, Prehistory Press, Madison: 85–102.

Herrmann, G. 1968. "Lapis lazuli: the early phases of its trade", *Iraq* 30/1: 21–57.

Hessari, M. 2011. "New evidence of the emergence of complex societies on the central Iranian plateau", *Iranian Journal of Archaeological Studies* 1/2: 35–48.

Hessari, M. and Akbari, H. 2007. "The preliminary excavation report on Sofalin mound in Pishva", *The 9th Annual Congress [meeting] of the Iranian Archaeologists, Volume 1*, Iranian Cultural Heritage, Tourism and Handicraft Organization, Tehran: 131–64.

Heyvaert, V. M. A. 2007. *Fluvial Sedimentation, Sea-level History and Anthropogenic Impact in the Great Mesopotamian plain: A new Holocene Record*, unpublished Ph.D. thesis, Vrije Universiteit Brussel, Brussels.

Heyvaert, V. M. A. and Baeteman, C. 2007. "Holocene sedimentary evolution and palaeocoastlines of the Lower Khuzestan plain (southwest Iran)", *Marine Geology* 224: 83–108.

Hodder, I. 2012. *Entangled: An Archaeology of the Relationships between Humans and Things*, Wiley-Blackwell, Oxford.

Hole, F. 1974. "Tepe Tūlā'ī: an early campsite in Khuzistan, Iran", *Paléorient* 2/2: 219–37.

Hritz, C. and Pournelle, J. in press. "Feeding history: deltaic resilience, inherited practice, and millennial-scale sustainability in an urbanized landscape" in Goldstein, D. (ed.), *From Field to Table: Historical Ecology of Regional Subsistence Strategies*, University of South Carolina Press, Columbia.

Johnson, G. A. 1973. *Local Exchange and Early State Development in Southwestern Iran*, Archaeological Papers, 51, Museum of Anthropology, University of Michigan, Ann Arbor.

Johnson, G. A. 1987. "The changing organisation of Uruk administration on the Susiana Plain", in Hole, F. (ed.), *The Archaeology of Western Iran: Settlement and Society from Prehistory to the Islamic Conquest*, Smithsonian Institution Press, Washington DC: 107–39.

Johnson, G. A. 1989. "Late Uruk in greater Mesopotamia: expansion or collapse?", *Origini* 14: 595–611.

Knappett, C. 2011. *An Archaeology of Interaction: Network Perspectives on Material Culture and Society*, Oxford University Press, Oxford.

Knappett, C. 2013. (ed.). *Network Analysis in Archaeology: New Approaches to Regional Interaction*, Oxford University Press, Oxford.

Knox, J. R., Thomas, K. D., Khan, F. and Petrie, C. A. 2010. "Small finds from Sheri Khan Tarakai", in Petrie, C. A. (ed.), *Sheri Khan Tarakai and early village life in the borderlands of north-west Pakistan*, Bannu Archaeological Project Monographs, Volume 1, Oxbow Books, Oxford: 211–303.

Kohl, P. L. 1992. "Review of 'Upon this Foundation – the 'Ubaid Reconsidered'", (eds Henrickson, E. F. and Thuesen, I.), Museum Tusculanum Press, Copenhagen", *American Antiquity* 57: 371–71.

Kohl, P. L. 2008. "Shared social fields: evolutionary convergence in prehistory and contemporary practice", *American Anthropologist* 100/4: 495–506.

al-Kuntar, S. and Abu Jayyab, A. K. in press. "The Political Economy of the Upper Khabur in the Late Chalcolithic 1–2: Ceramic mass-production, standardisation and specialisation", in McMahon, A., Crawford, H. and Postgate, J. N. (eds), *Preludes to Urbanism: Studies in the Late Chalcolithic of Mesopotamia in Honour of Joan Oates*, McDonald Institute Monographs, Cambridge.

Lamberg-Karlovsky, C. C. 1978. "The Proto-Elamites on the Iranian Plateau", *Antiquity* 52: 114–20.

Lawler, A. 2006. "North versus south, Mesopotamian style," *Science* 312: 1458–63.

McCall, B. 2009. *The Mamasani Archaeological Survey: long term settlement patterns in the Mamasani district of the Zagros Mountains, Fars Province, Iran*, unpublished Ph.D. dissertation, Department of Archaeology, University of Sydney.

McCown, D. E. 1942. *The Comparative Stratigraphy of Early Iran*, Studies in Ancient Oriental Civilisation 23, University of Chicago Press, Chicago.

McMahon, A. M. 2013. "Mesopotamia", in Clark, P. (ed.), *The Oxford Handbook of Cities in World History*, OUP, Oxford: 31–48.

McMahon, A. M. in press. "State warfare and pre-state violent conflict: battle's aftermath at Late Chalcolithic Tell Brak", in McMahon, A., Crawford, H. and Postgate, J. N. (eds), *Preludes to Urbanism: Studies in the Late Chalcolithic of Mesopotamia in Honour of Joan Oates*, McDonald Institute Monographs, Cambridge.

McMahon, A. M., Sołtysiak, A. and Weber, J. 2011. "Late Chalcolithic mass graves at Tell Brak, Syria, and violent conflict during the growth of early city-states", *JFA* 36/3: 201–20.

Majidzadeh, Y. 1981. "Sialk III and the pottery sequence at Tepe Ghabristan, the coherence of the cultures of the Central Iranian Plateau", *Iran* 19: 141–46.

Majidzadeh, Y. 1982. "Lapis lazuli and the Great Khorasan Road", *Paléorient* 8/1: 59–69.

Mann, M. 1986. *The Sources of Social Power*, Vol. 1, Cambridge University Press, Cambridge.

Mashkour, M. 2009. "Subsistence economies in south-western Iran c. fourth millennium BC viewed from archaeozoology: the state of the question", unpublished paper presented at the *Ancient Iran and Its Neighbours Conference*, McDonald Institute, Cambridge, 26–28 June 2009.

Mashkour, M., Bocherens, H. and Moussa, I. 2005. "Long distance movement of sheep and goats of Bakhtiari nomads tracked with intra-tooth variations of stable isotopes (13C and 18O)", in Davies, J., Fabiš, M., Mainland, I., Richards, M. and Thomas, R. (eds), *Diet and Health in Past Animal Populations: Current Research and Future Directions*, Oxbow Books, Oxford: 113–24.

Matthews, R. and Fazeli, H. 2004. "Copper and complexity: Iran and Mesopotamia in the fourth millennium B.C.", *Iran* 42: 61–75.

Millard, A. R. 1988. "The bevelled-rim bowls: their purpose and significance", *Iraq* 50: 49–57.

Miller, N. F. 1982. *Economy and Environment of Malyan, a Third Millennium BC Urban Center in Southern Iran*, unpublished Ph.D. dissertation, Department of Anthropology, University of Michigan, Ann Arbor.

Miller, N. F. 1985. "Paleoethnobotanical evidence for deforestation in ancient Iran: a case study of urban Malyan", *Journal of Ethnobiology* 5: 1–19.

Miller, N. F. and Kimiaie, M. 2006. "Some plant remains from the 2004 excavations of Tall-e Mushki, Tall-e Jari A and B, and Tall-e Bakun A and B", in Alizadeh, A. *The Origins of State Organizations in Prehistoric Highland Fars, Southern Iran, Excavations at Tall-e Bakun*, Oriental Institute Publication 120, Chicago: 107–18.

Miroschedji, P. de 1972. "Prospections Archéologiques dans les valées de Fasa et de Darab (rapport préliminaire)", in Bagherzadeh, F. (ed.), *Proceedings of the 1st Annual Symposium on Archaeological Research in Iran*, Iranian Centre for Archaeological Research, Tehran: 1–7.

Miroschedji, P. de 2003. "Susa and the Highlands: Major Trends in the History of Elamite Civilisation", in Miller, N. F. and Abdi, K. (eds), *Yeki bud, yeki nabud: Essays on the Archaeology of Iran in Honor of William M. Sumner*, Cotsen Institute of Archaeology Monograph No. 48, Cotsen Institute of Archaeology, Los Angeles: 17–38.

Moghaddam, A. 2012. *Later Village Period Settlement Development in the Karun River Basin, Upper Khuzestan Plain, Greater Susiana, Iran*, BAR S2347, Archaeopress, Oxford.

Moghaddam, A. and Miri, N. 2003. "Archaeological surveys in the 'Eastern Corridor', south-western Iran", *Iran* 41: 23–55.

Moghaddam, A. and Miri, N. 2007. "Archaeological research in the Mianab Plain of lowland Susiana, south-western Iran", *Iran* 45: 99–137.

Mutin, B. 2012. "Cultural dynamics in southern Middle-Asia in the fifth and fourth millennia BC: a reconstruction based on ceramic traditions", *Paléorient* 38/1–2: 159–84.

Mutin, B. and Lamberg-Karlovsky, C. C. in preparation. *The Proto-Elamite Settlement and Its Neighbors: Tepe Yahya Period IVC*, ASPR, Brill, Leiden.

Neely, J. A. and Wright, H. T. 1994. *Early Settlement and Irrigation on the Deh Luran Plain: Village and Early State Societies in South-western Iran*, Technical Report of the University of Michigan Museum of Anthropology No. 26, Ann Arbor.

Nissen, H. J. 1985. "Problems of the Uruk-period in Susiana, viewed from Uruk", *Paléorient* 11/2: 39–40.

Nissen, H. J. 1988. *The Early History of the Ancient Near East, 9000–2000 BC*, University of Chicago, Chicago.

Nissen, H. J. 2001. "Cultural and political networks in the ancient Near East during the fourth and third millennia B.C.", in Rothman 2001a: 149–79.

Nissen, H. J. 2002. "Uruk: key site of the period and key site of the problem", in Postgate, J. N. (ed.), *Artefacts of Complexity: Tracking the Uruk in the Ancient Near East*, British School of Archaeology in Iraq, Cambridge University Press, Cambridge: 1–16.

Nissen, H. J. 2013. "Anfänge und frühe Entwicklung der Stadt Uruk", in Crusemann, N., van Ess, M., Hilgert, M. and Salje, B. (eds), *Uruk – 5000 Jahre Megacity*, Publikation der Reiss-Enghorn-Museen, Band 58, IMHOF, Berlin: 107–14.

Nissen, H. J., Damerow, P. and Englund, R. K. 1993. *Archaic Bookkeeping: Writing and Techniques of Economic Administration in the Ancient Near East*, University of Chicago Press, Chicago.

Nokandeh, G. 2010. *Neue Untersuchungen zur Sialk III-Periode im zentraliranischen Hochland: auf der Grundlage der Ergebnisse des, Sialk Reconsideration Project*, unpublished Ph.D. dissertation, Verlag im Internet GmbH, Berlin.

Petrie, C. A. (ed.). 2010. *Sheri Khan Tarakai and early village life in the borderlands of north-west Pakistan*, Bannu Archaeological Project Monographs – Volume 1, Oxbow Books, Oxford.

Petrie, C. A. 2011. "'Culture', innovation and interaction across southern Iran from the Neolithic to the Bronze Age (6500–3000 BC)", in Roberts, B. and Vander Linden, M. (eds), *Investigating Archaeological Cultures: material culture, variability and transmission*, Springer, New York: 151–82.

Petrie, C. A. 2013a. "South Asia", in Clark, P. (ed.), *The Oxford Handbook of Cities in World History*, OUP, Oxford: 83–104.

Petrie, C. A. 2013b. "The Chalcolithic of south Iran", in Potts, D. T. (ed.), *Oxford Handbook of Iranian Archaeology*, Oxford University Press, Oxford: 121–59.

Petrie, C. A. in press. "Iran and Uruk Mesopotamia: chronologies and connections in the 4th millennium BC", in McMahon, A., Crawford, H. and Postgate, J. N. (eds), *Preludes to Urbanism: Studies in the Late Chalcolithic of Mesopotamia in Honour of Joan Oates*, McDonald Institute Monographs, Cambridge.

Petrie, C. A. in preparation. "Radiocarbon", in Helwing, B. (ed.), *Associated Regional Chronologies for the Ancient Near East and the Eastern Mediterranean: Western Iran*, Turnhout.

Petrie, C. A., Weeks, L. R., Potts, D. T. and Roustaei, K. 2009. "Perspectives on the Cultural Sequence of Mamasani", in Potts, D. T., Roustaei K., Petrie, C. A. and Weeks, L. R. (eds), *The Mamasani Archaeological Project Stage One: A report on the first two seasons of the ICAR – University of Sydney Joint Expedition to the Mamasani District, Fars Province, Iran*, 2nd edition, BAR International Series 2044, Archaeopress, Oxford: 169–96.

Pittman, H. 2001. "Mesopotamian intraregional relations reflected through glyptic evidence in Late Chalcolithic 1–5 Periods", in Rothman 2001a: 403–44.

Pittman, H. 2011. "The Seals of Godin VI", in Gopnik, H. and Rothman, M. (eds), *On the High Road: The History of Godin Tepe, Iran*, Royal Ontario Museum/Mazda Press, Toronto: 113–15.

Pollock, S. M. 1999. *Ancient Mesopotamia: The Eden that Never Was*, Cambridge University Press, Cambridge.

Pollock, S. M. 2001. "The Uruk period in southern Mesopotamia", in Rothman 2001a: 181–231.

Porada, E., Hansen, D. P., Dunham, S. and Babcock, S. 1992. "Mesopotamia" in Ehrich, R. W. (ed.), *Chronologies in Old World Archaeology*, (3rd edition), University of Chicago Press, Chicago: 77–90.

Potts, D. T. 1977. "Tepe Yahya and the end of the 4th millennium on the Iranian Plateau", in Deshayes, J. (ed.), *Le Plateau Iranien et l'Asie Centrale des origines à la conquête islamique*, Centre National de la Recherche Scientifique, Paris: 23–31.

Potts, D. T. 1999. *The Archaeology of Elam: Formation and Transformation of an Ancient Iranian State*, Cambridge World Archaeology, Cambridge University Press, Cambridge.

Potts, D. T. 2001. *Excavations at Tepe Yahya, Iran 1967–1975: The Third Millennium*, American School of Prehistoric Research Bulletin, 45, Peabody Museum of Archaeology and Ethnology, Harvard University, Cambridge.

Potts, D. T. 2004. "The Uruk Explosion: more heat than light?", *The Review of Archaeology* 25/2: 19–28.

Potts, D.T. 2008. "Review of Alizadeh, A. 2006. *The Origins of State Organizations in Prehistoric Highland Fars, Southern Iran*, Oriental Institute Publications 128, Chicago", *Bib Or* 65/1–2: 196–206.

Potts, D. T. 2009. "Bevel-rim bowls and bakeries: Evidence and explanations from Iran and the Indo-Iranian Borderlands", *JCS* 61/1: 1–23.

Potts, D.T. in press. *Nomadism in Iran: From Antiquity to the Modern Era*, Oxford University Press, Oxford.

Pournelle, J. R. 2003. *Marshland of Cities: Deltaic Landscapes and the Evolution of Early Mesopotamian Civilization*, Ph.D. dissertation, UC San Diego.

Pournelle, J. R. and Algaze, G. in press. "Travels in Edin: deltaic resilience and early urbanism in Greater Mesopotamia", in McMahon, A., Crawford, H. and Postgate, J. N. (eds), *Preludes to Urbanism: Studies in the Late Chalcolithic of Mesopotamia in Honour of Joan Oates*, McDonald Institute Monographs, Cambridge.

Prickett, M. 1986. *Man, Land and Water: Settlement Distribution and the Development of Irrigation Agriculture in the Upper Rud-I Gushk Drainage, Southeastern Iran*, Ph.D. dissertation, Department of Anthropology, Harvard University.

Reichel, C. 2006. "Urbanism and warfare – the 2005 Hamoukar, Syria, excavations", *Oriental Institute News and Notes*: 1–11.

Renfrew, C. 1975. "Trade as action at a distance: questions of integration and communication", in Sabloff, J. A. and Lamberg-Karlovsky, C. C. (eds), *Ancient Civilisation and Trade*, School of American Research, Albuquerque: 3–59.

Renfrew, C. 1977. "Alternative models for exchange and spatial distribution", in Earle, T. and Ericson, J. (eds), *Exchange Systems in Prehistory*, Academic Press, New York: 71–90.

Root, M. C. 2005. (ed.). *This Fertile Land: Signs + Symbols in the Early Arts of Iran and Iraq*, Kelsey Museum Publication 3, Ann Arbor, Michigan.

Rothman, M. S. (ed.). 2001a. *Uruk Mesopotamia and Its Neighbours: Cross-Cultural Interactions in the Era of State Formation*, SAR Press, Santa Fe.

Rothman, M. S. 2001b. "The local and the regional: an introduction", in Rothman 2001a: 3–26.

Rothman, M. S. and Badler, V. 2011. "Contact and development in Godin Period VI", in Gopnik, H. and Rothman, M. (eds), *On the High Road: The History of Godin Tepe, Iran*, Royal Ontario Museum/Mazda Press, Toronto: 67–137.

Rowton, M. 1974. "Enclosed nomadism", *Journal of the Economic and Social History of the Orient* 17.1: 1–30.

Sadr, K. 1991. *Nomads and States: The Development of Nomadism in Ancient Northeast Africa*, University of Pennsylvania Press, Pennsylvania.

Sanlaville, P. 2003. "The deltaic complex of the lower Mesopotamian plain and its evolution through millennia," in Nicholson, E. and Clark, P. (eds), *The Iraqi Marshlands*, Politico's Publishing, London: 133–50.

Schmandt-Besserat, D. 1992. *How Writing Came About*, University of Texas Press, Austin.

Sherratt, A. 1997. *Economy and Society in Prehistoric Europe*, Edinburgh University Press, Edinburgh.

Stein, G. R. 1999. *Rethinking World-Systems: Diasporas, Colonies, and Interaction in Uruk Mesopotamia*, University of Arizona Press, Tuscon.

Stein, G. R., Bernbeck, R., Coursey, C., McMahon *et al.* 1996. "Uruk colonies and Anatolian communities: an interim report on the 1992093 excavations at Hacınebi, Turkey", *AJA* 100: 205–60.

Strommenger, E. 1980. *Habuba Kabira, eine Stadt vor 5000 Jahren*, von Zabern, Mainz.

Sumner, W. M. 1985. "The Proto-Elamite city wall at Tal-i Malyan", *Iran* 23: 153–61.

Sumner, W. M. 1986. "Proto-Elamite Civilisation in Fars", in Finkbeiner, U. and Röllig, W. (eds), Ğamdat *Naṣr: Period or Regional Style? Papers given at a Symposium Held in Tübingen, November 1983*, Beihelfte zum Tubinger Atlas des Vorderen Irients, Reihe B. (Geisteswissenschaften) Nr. 62, Dr. Ludwig Reichert Verlag, Wiesbaden: 199–211.

Sumner, W. M. 1988a. "Prelude to Proto-Elamite Anshan: the Lapui Phase", *IA* 23: 23–44.

Sumner, W. M. 1988b. "Maljan, Tall-e (Anšan)", *Reallexikon der Assyriologie* 7: 306–20.

Sumner, W. M. 1990. "Full-Coverage Regional Archaeological Survey in the Near East: An Example from Iran", in Fish, S. K. and Kowalewski, S. A. (eds), *The Archaeology of Regions: A Case for Full-Coverage Survey*, Smithsonian Series in Archaeological Inquiry, Smithsonian Institution Press, Washington D.C.: 87–115.

Sumner, W. M. 1994. "The Evolution of Tribal Society in the Southern Zagros Mountains, Iran", in Stein, G. and Rothman, M. S. (eds), *Chiefdoms and Early States in the Near East: the Organizational Dynamics of Complexity*, Prehistory Press, Monographs in World Archaeology, Madison: 47–65.

Sumner, W. M. 2003. *Early Urban Life in the Land of Anshan: Excavations at Tal-e Malyan in the Highlands of Iran*, Malyan Excavations Reports III, University Museum Monograph 113, University of Pennsylvania Museum of Archaeology and Anthropology, Pennsylvania.

Tengberg, M. 2004. "Archaeobotanical analysis at Tepe Sialk: results from the 2003/04 season", in Malek Shahmirzadeh, S. (ed.), *The Potters of Sialk*, Sialk Reconsideration Project Report 3, Archaeological Report Monograph Series 5, Iranian Center for Archaeological Research, Tehran: 25–32.

Ur, J. 2010. *Urbanism and Cultural Landscapes in Northeastern Syria: The Tell Hamoukar Survey, 1999–2001*, Tell Hamoukar Volume 1, OIP 137, Oriental Institute, University of Chicago.

Vatandoust, A., Parzinger, H. and Helwing, B. (eds). 2011. *Early mining and metallurgy on the Central Iranian Plateau.*

Report on the first five years of research of the Joint Iranian-German Research Project, Archäologie in Iran und Turan 9, Philip von Zabern, Mainz-am-Rhein.

Voigt, M. and Dyson Jr., R. H. 1992. "Chronology of Iran, ca. 8000–2000 B.C.", in Ehrich, R. W. (ed.), *Chronologies of Old World Archaeology*, Vols. I–II, Chicago, Chicago University Press: 122–78; 125–53.

Weeks, L. R. 2010. "Reviews of Abbas Alizadeh, *Chogha Mish, Volume 2: The Development of a Prehistoric Regional Center in Lowland Susiana, Southwestern Iran. Final Report on the Last Six Seasons of Excavations, 1972–1978*, Oriental Institute Publications 130, Chicago", *AMIT* 42: 309–13.

Weeks, L. R. 2012. "Metallurgy", in Potts, D. T. (ed.), *A Companion to the Archaeology of the Ancient Near East*, Oxford, Wiley-Blackwells: 295–316.

Weeks, L. R. 2013. "The development and expansion of a Neolithic way of life", in Potts, D. T. (ed.), *Oxford Handbook of Iranian Archaeology*, Oxford University Press, Oxford: 49–75.

Weeks, L. R., Petrie, C. A. and Potts, D. T. 2010. "'Ubaid-related-related? The 'black-on-buff' ceramic traditions of highland southwest Iran", in Carter, R. A. and Philip, G. (eds), *Beyond the 'Ubaid, Transformation and Integration in the Late Prehistoric Societies of the Middle East*, Studies in Ancient Oriental Civilization Series, Oriental Institute of the University of Chicago, Chicago: 247–78.

Weeks, L. R., Alizadeh, K., Niakan, L., Alamdari, K. *et al.* 2006. "The Neolithic settlement of highland SW Iran: new evidence from the Mamasani District", *Iran* 44: 1–31.

Weiss, H. and Young, T. C. 1975. "The Merchants of Susa Godin V and Plateau-Lowland Relations in the Late Fourth Millennium B.C.", *Iran* 13: 1–17.

Wilkinson, T. C. 2012. *Tying the Threads of Eurasia: Trans-Regional Routes and Material Flows in Eastern Anatolia and Western Central Asia, c. 3000–1500 BC*, unpublished Ph.D. dissertation, Department of Archaeology, University of Sheffield.

Wright, H. T. (ed.). 1981. *An Early Town on the Deh Luran Plain: Excavations at Tepe Farukhabad*, Memoir No. 13, Museum of Anthropology, University of Michigan, Ann Arbor.

Wright, H. T. 1987. "The Susiana hinterlands during the era of primary state formation," in Hole, F. (ed.), *Archaeological Perspectives on Western Iran*, Smithsonian Institution Press, Washington: 141–55.

Wright, H. T. 1994. "Pre-state political formations", in Stein, G. and Rothman, M. (eds), *Chiefdoms and Early States in the Near East*, Prehistory Press, Madison: 67–84. [Reprinted with corrections from Earle, T.K. (ed.), 1982. *The Evolution of Complex Societies: The Harry Hojier Lectures for 1982*, Undena Press, Malibu].

Wright, H. T. 1998. "Uruk states in southwestern Iran", in Feinman, G. M. and Marcus, J. (eds), *Archaic States*, SAR, San Diego: 173–97.

Wright, H. T. 2001. "Cultural action in the Uruk world", in Rothman 2001a: 123–47.

Wright, H. T. and Johnson, G. A. 1975. "Population, exchange, and early state formation in southwestern Iran", *American Anthropologist* 77: 267–89.

Wright, H.T. and Rupley, E.S.A. 2001. "Calibrated radiocarbon age determinations of Uruk-related assemblages", in Rothman 2001a: 85–122.

Wright, H. T., Neely, J. A., Johnson, G. A. and Speth, J. D. 1975. "Early fourth millennium developments in southwestern Iran", *Iran* 13: 129–47.

Zeder, M. A. 1991. *Feeding Cities: Specialized Animal Economy in the Ancient Near East*, Smithsonian Institution Press, Washington.

APPENDIX A: TRANSCRIPT OF CONFERENCE PAPER QUESTION SESSIONS

Paper 02 – Matthew Jones (MJ) *et al.*

David Wengrow: Some archaeologists have talked of a localised climactic downturn in the Persian Gulf. I think Hans Wilkman talks about the "dark millennium" in the fourth millennium BC. But that didn't seem to feature in your review here. I wondered if you could talk about how it might fit your assessment or not.

MJ: Sorry, I haven't heard of the work. I've never seen any of the actual data or anything to support a millennium-long climate event that is particularly grim at that time. It is actually right at the beginning of this massive transition. It might have been grim compared to what had come before, because we went from what is called the climatic optimum, but whether it was an optimum for people everywhere is another issue. You went from the fourth millennium to the first millennium where things have changed. And the effect on people would have depended on the speed of that change. In some places it seems to have been pretty quick, like within the mediaeval, and if people experienced that they would have suffered because they wouldn't have had any history of this new environment to live in.

David Wengrow: It seems to correlate with a sort of widespread desertion of sites along one coast of the gulf.

Tony Wilkinson: I think one of the issues with the dark millennium is that a lot of the communities are affected by that, because there is a dearth in sites during that period, they were mobile pastoralists for at least part of their cycle and mobile pastoralists are going to respond much more quickly to any climate downturn than sedentary groups. Of course, this comes back to the big question, to what degree are there mobile pastoralists? Are these communities

responding in a similar way, or is it a complex group of sedentary and mobile groups responding in that complex way? The comment I was going to make is that I am glad you made the point about how complex these physical systems are, because in fact there is a tendency for archaeologists to think that we have complex human systems so that the physical systems are all simple. But it's complex on both sides and that is what makes the correlations so damn complex!

Henry Wright: It appears from your image of Mamasani that the Fahliyan River in Dasht-e Rustam Yek was captured and Dasht-e Rustam Do then became dry and the elevations work out, as I understand it. Why do you think that steam capture occurred?

MJ: I couldn't say. There is just no evidence to back up any guess. I mean the whole area is active tectonically all the way through and there is work being done to the south.

Cameron Petrie: In terms of the locations of archaeological sites Tol-e Spid is sitting on the modern course of a stream and it lies on the direct course of the river if it was actually going straight. There isn't much to say as we haven't had a chance to do the geomorphology.

Henry Wright: OK, thank you.

Editor's note: for more information on tectonic activity in Mamasani please see Petrie *et al.* this volume, and also Berberian *et al.* in press.

Reference

Berberian, M., Petrie, C. A., Potts, D. T., Asgari Chaverdi, A., Dusting, A., Ghāssemi, P., Noruzi, R., Sardari Zarchi, A. and Weeks, L. in press. "Archaeoseismicity of the mounds and monuments along the Kāzerun fault (western Zagros, SW Iranian Plateau) since the Chalcolithic period", *IA 49*.

Paper 03 – Kristen Hopper (KH) and Tony Wilkinson (TW)

Christopher Thornton: How do you come up with numbers for population density? What is the formula for that? Not in detail, but is it through mortuary, settlement?

KH: I think a lot of ethnographic studies have been done where they looked at densities of households and settlements and they came up with certain figures that are generally applied, 100 or 200 people per hectare, but that obviously masks a lot of variability. So what we are trying to do is show the amount of settled area per square kilometre of survey region and we will hopefully not go too far in terms of (interrupted).

Guillermo Algaze: It doesn't matter if it is 100 or 200 or 900 people, what matters is the relative trend, so it increases and increases, whether synchronous or not.

TW: What messes things up of course is if you get one period with very dense indications of settlement and another period where you get much sparser settlement. You can sometimes see that from the actual settlement record where sites become extensive over a fairly large area. But the fundamental data that we are looking at is aggregate settlement in hectares through time and that's a simpler one of course; this is something that Kristin mentioned which needs to be emphasised: the chronological periods. And as soon as you change the chronology then the Dewar calculations also change. And the chronologies are changing. We are going to hear a lot about chronologies and therefore a lot of the relative changes; a lot of the relative trends will change when the chronology changes and that is a key thing one has to be aware of when looking at these long-term trends.

Cameron Petrie: I was quite interested in what are effectively "blocks" that appear in the presentation of the Kur River Basin settlement data because each individual period is essentially treated homogonously, whereas there were obviously many more nuances and sub-phases. If you look at the Gregory Johnson data he identifies much more variability in terms of material within shorter periods. But you said you are dealing with the parts of the fourth millennium BC that have got more detailed chronology, so there are more nuances to the settlement density numbers.

TW: Personally I think that when you look at relatively short periods of time, say a millennium, and you are looking at little differences, all of those differences will change after a few years once you get a new set of data points in. So I think that what we were really interested in was very long-term trends. Particularly – and this is something that interested Greg Johnson and Bob Adams – this huge dip that Kristin showed in the *Susa III* period and the very *Late Uruk*, which is of course at the time when Uruk is growing. If you

look at it within the general picture I think that still does hold. The question is, will it still hold at the end of this conference?

Reinhard Bernbeck: I find the interpretation of these very large-scale patterns already at the outset, equilibristic. If you take the model that you showed at the end, like population reservoirs and things like that you produce historiographic *deux ex machina*, what is not there you fill up with nomads. What I would like to see is a clear method to estimate mobile populations for specific time periods and unless we have that we are just arguing with evidence *ex negativo*.

TW: I think the problem with the entire mobile argument is that by generalising, what we are doing is putting a conceptual framework out there. My problem, my own problem, is that really I find it difficult when people are simply arguing "right I have an event here and I produce a mechanism to explain it", and I think by drawing a larger conceptual framework we are at least able to conceptualise the issue. We are not able to explain it in any depth. I think that we are a long, long way from being able to quantify the mobile population. I think it is such a long way off that I would rather deal with the more conceptual narrative. That's not an answer, but it's a response.

John Alden: I was really pleased that you pointed out that the *Susa III* population minimum might reflect alluviation of sites in the northern plains. The *Susa III* settlements do all tend to be really low and flat, at least the ones that I found, with small areas, and I think that is a perfectly valid point.

TW: When we were building up this talk the very interesting area around Tell Brak in northern Mesopotamia came to mind – there you get this incredible expansion of settlements around Tell Brak. It is very low. Some of it is actually in pits. And if that existed around Choga Mish or Susa there is no way that you would see it. So these irrigation settlements are very important.

Susan Pollock: I wanted to come back to your point about "long term" and what constitutes "short term/ long term" and so on. Just as you said, I think quite rightly, if the chronology is revised then one has to revise the calculations one makes using Dewar's model and so on, and potentially overturn some of the kinds of things that you are seeing right now. Isn't it really of huge importance how you define "long term", because you can smooth out all that variation if you look long-term enough and you can create far more variation if and when we are capable of making chronologies that have higher and higher resolutions? So the scale within which you're working and looking seems to me has a huge effect on the overall trends you see.

TW: Yes, absolutely.

Susan Pollock: So how do you define your scale?

TW: Well I think it's a matter of revisiting these questions and I think the notion of sensitivity analysis, where you put in a different set of chronological scales at a later date then run the calculations again; the sort of stuff that Nick Kouchoukous was doing, and what you and Reinhard have actually done for southern Mesopotamia as well. One just needs to keep refining the models, refining the data, and the actual chronological scales. It would be interesting to see whether a sensitivity study of that sort completely removes that *Susa III/Late Uruk* dip. That's the sort of thing that I think we will eventually be able to discuss.

Guillermo Algaze: No, that dip is there.

TW: Well, we've had sites by democracy and vote on them, but I think we have to do even more sensitivity studies. We are not just looking at data as truth; we are looking at data that needs to be reinvestigated through time.

Cameron Petrie: You mention the irrigation sediments and I know you did it sometimes in Mesopotamia, so I am wondering whether you did any coring on and off sites within Khuzestan to see the level of alluvial sediments around particular settlements near Susa, as opposed to what's going on at Chogha Mish for example?

TW: No, we didn't have enough time. It is something that we were going to do. We were there for two or three weeks and it was going to be part of the longer-term project and some of the interpretations that I just brought out are new interpretations, because I went back to my notebooks and looked at the original soil maps and realised there were significant differences. The only trouble is that it would be bloody difficult to actually make interpretations of irrigation soils from coring anyway. You can do it, but on the other hand, I put a little very subtle description in the *Paléorient* (Alizadeh *et al.* 2007) article in recognition of that soil, but it is tricky.

Cameron Petrie: I was actually talking about looking at the edges of sites. The impact of alluviation is something we have noticed in Mamasani. Sites that look like they are 2 ha in size on the surface are probably much, much larger because of the alluviation around them. So the other half of my question was about the types of "sites" that are being buried by these alluvial soils. Presumably the ones that we've got preserved are the ones that are bigger mounds.

TW: Yes.

Cameron Petrie: So we are potentially losing the "nomad" sites, and/or the smaller/single period village sites.

TW: But we could also be losing 40 ha of extensive settlements with buildings. I mean, a site like Habuba Kabira could be buried and completely obscured. These are the parameters that we are dealing with. We need to be a little more explicit about these processes. It is not just alluviation from rivers. Irrigation deposits are very significant and it is interesting that these are coming from the earliest soil surveys but not the later soil surveys. So you've got to use a variety of interpretive data sets.

Henry Wright: I can answer your question. I have quantified 25 1 x 2 m cuts down to the late Pleistocene and I offer them to you.

TW: Great, we can discuss that afterwards.

Reference

Alizadeh, A., Kouchoukos, N., Wilkinson, T. J., Bauer, A. M. and Mashkour, M. 2004. "Human-environment interactions on the upper Khuzestan plains, southwest Iran: recent investigations", *Paléorient* 30(1): 69–88.

Paper 04 – Henry Wright

John Alden: You say that seasonal, transhumant, full-time, nomadic specialisation occurred in the fourth millennium BC?

Henry Wright: You have two questions: one is an economic question (OBSCURED) really quite important. I think Kamyar (Abdi)'s evidence from Islamabad showing a gradual development of increasingly large territories is going to be found in other areas. This research has to be repeated in other areas and he has to publish his material fully. But when did major nomad secondary linage systems with political clout appear? I think probably in the *Late Uruk*: I don't see any evidence for that kind of site from any of the advantageous discovery sites in the nomad regions in the high valleys. I'd love to see more survey in places like Charmahal va Bakhtiari to really verify that. I think it needs to be done and people are interested in that now.

Paper 05 – Mitchell Rothman (MR)

Barbara Helwing: You put out this table showing us that the (*Godin*) *VI.1* is after 3300 BC. The local pottery that you show is exactly like unpainted *Sialk III* so I think that phase should be a bit older.

MR: I think it is possible. We've done some more carbon samples, but again we have the same problem: are they from reliable places? And we get a very wide scatter of dates. They tend to be of a later era. They tend to push it even into the 2900s.

Cameron Petrie: That's a calibration issue.

MR: I know. I'm not saying it is easy to solve. Again I'd love to hear about it because I'm not settled. This is what we have been able to give you. This is what we have.

Lloyd Weeks: Mitchell, what you're talking about essentially is a kind of post-colonial explanation for what is happening at Godin; Chris Gosden has written a book where he looks at archaeology and colonialism and he takes the *Uruk* phenomenon as one of his case studies. I was wondering if his ideas influenced yours, or his theories about colonialism in a shared cultural milieu? That's the phrase he uses.

MR: Well, I have to admit that I haven't read it so I guess it didn't.

Lloyd Weeks: He has a lot of similar ideas to what you are saying and certainly focuses on a bottom up approach to understanding some of these issues and looking more at interactive processes.

MR: Well, that is certainly the way I would like to see things.

Reinhard Bernbeck: I would not characterise your approach as being bottom up except that you enter the middle level when you say you need to take into consideration agency and such like. You talk about the local power holders, rather than those who are at the bottom; and the question I would have is how can they, even in such a system, – Kangavar is a relatively small valley – get people to stay in place? If you think of someone like Antonio Newbury, he would say evasion subterfuge is the easiest thing to adopt to get out of the grips of these people who try to build up a local power centre. I would push the question even further and ask how are they able to set up a system that keeps other people locally in check and where are they?

MR: I won't make something up because I really haven't thought about it, but it is a worthwhile point. Again in the book (Gopnik and Rothman 2011) we try to look at it much more long-term – actually, from the *Middle Chalcolithic* – as a sort of a progression upwards. My guess would be that it has to do with certain kinds of products and certain kinds of technologies, but again we just don't have enough of Godin to give a broad picture, which is why I keep pushing for the idea of broad horizontal excavation because what we are seeing, if I am correct, is a sort of focal centre of the region. But as for what is happening in the rest of the system, we just don't have a clue.

Guillermo Algaze: The answer to the question of how you keep the peasants in place so they actually work for you is very simple. It is a combination of coercion and giving them something that they need. You give them something they require in order to marry off their wives, something they require so their children can become men, or another initiation rite. So essentially they get access to a wider world and

between that and hitting them over the head they tend to stay in place.

Henry Wright: I was impressed by the distributions that you had, the maps for *Godin VI.1*. I saw some parallels to Arslan Tepe which I have never seen before until I saw these plans, the structure of the XIV–XIX – Complex 1, with its windows rather than doors. There are a couple of hundred of these large structures from different periods: the *Middle Susiana* period building at Choga Mish also with a lot of flint working, storage jars, clay sealing materials, but not really sealings. I wonder if we are seeing either the activity of a big family as per Roger (Matthews) or some kind of community building where the officials or the lineage heads are concerned with group storage, work allocation, and so on.

MR: I think you are very likely right that Arslan Tepe had a . . .

Henry Wright: You have 5000 seals to actually test.

MR: We certainly do have enough in comparison. How are we really going to figure this out in the first place? I think we have to be very clear, I'll be looking at cases and coming up with criteria. What I do explicitly say in the book is "OK, how does Godin, given what we know, given all the problems with it, given the limits actually of what we have: how does that fit if we are looking at Arslan Tepe as a model? How does it look if we are looking at Kurban as a model? How does it look if we are looking at Habuba Kabira as a model?" and so on and so forth. What are the similar patterns that we can see that are going to tell us how these different places are responding to their local conditions and to this contact? – which was something that I think really was happening with an outside world. I came down feeling that Arslan Tepe was a great model for Godin in many ways and certainly just as it is not a colony in my estimation, I don't think Godin was either, and that was very influential. When they finally started to survey around the site we could see a little bit better what the valley looks like. Even that is starting to look much more like Arslan Tepe than like Susiana. Again this is an argument built on fairly shifting sands and I am well aware of that, but it is what we have and it makes logical sense if you try to do it in a structured, comparative way. I am hoping that Roger (Matthews) will give us a new perspective and I will be proved wrong. But again, based on what we have, that's what seems, to me, a logical conclusion. I have only given you a little piece of the argument.

Reference

Gopnik, H. and Rothman, M. 2011. *On the High Road: The History of Godin Tepe, Iran*, Royal Ontario Museum/ Mazda Press, Toronto.

Paper 06 - Barbara Helwing (BH)

Holly Pittman: Can you differentiate *Sialk IV*$_1$ and *IV*$_2$ in your Area C? You're not doing that, or is it all *IV*$_1$?

BH: I think the burials are *IV*$_2$ and the settlement is *IV*$_1$. The problem is with these washed-away burials. The pottery from burials is washed into the bones so no matter how carefully we excavated . . .

Holly Pittman: So you have all the types mixed. The other thing I would say is that you don't want to include the chlorite in your discussion about this horizon because that is something that really starts in *Yahya IVB*, it doesn't start before, so I would take that out.

BH: OK.

Guillermo Algaze: You mentioned that you didn't know the size of the *Proto-Elamite* settlement, but do you have a ballpark estimate about how big this well-built, well-planned *Proto-Elamite* settlement may have been?

BH: No. If I am honest, I must say no, because, if you look at the topographical map you can see that this span (indicates distance) is about 1 km and you can see that this area is on something like an elevation. So we started just by chance in an area where we had 1.5 m of cultural layers, but when we extended the trench by another 10 m², then we only had 40 cm left. So I have no means to tell precisely how big the site was.

Cameron Petrie: I wanted to ask about the construction methods. There is a paper that Tom Beale published in *Paléorient* in the 1980s (Beale and Carter 1983) where he noticed that there were similarities between proportions of brick sizes and the measurement ratios of room sizes and other things. He noticed a similarity between the building at *IVC* at Tepe Yahya and the architecture at Habuba Kabira. I wondered whether you had had a chance to do anything like that.

BH: I can do, but I haven't yet.

Cameron Petrie: I can't remember exactly the way it had been worked out, but it was something to do with the size of the bricks and the way that you arranged them. You picked up pairs of bricks and that was a brick wall width…is that right?

Holly Pittman: That's right…

BH: So at Arisman the construction technique is usually to have one brick laid this way and on the next layer you have two bricks laid lengthwise. And the slightly thicker walls have one and a half.

Cameron Petrie: That sounds quite similar.

Holly Pittman: That's the same pattern.

Cameron Petrie: So it is possible that there is a construction system that's shared between builders at Habuba Kabira, Arisman and Tepe Yahya.

BH: So as a conclusion, I started to think that maybe it is not all this technology that we were after at the beginning that makes the changes, but it's the changes in social organisation; this urban background that allows people to have the time and maybe also the security to develop these things like furnace smelting. It is the hen and the egg problem. It's an interconnected process; huge-scale metallurgy always starts with the urban site.

John Alden: I looked at the pictures of the environment and I have to ask this question. Are they simply doing mining and smelting there or are they producing their own foods? Is there food coming in and was this perhaps a seasonal working settlement?

BH: I don't have much information on the botany of the site. I have some information on the animal bones – there is just the normal range of sheep and goats, but there is also some cattle, which is a bit surprising given that this is now an all arid environment. But there must have been at least riverine or oasis-like spots where cattle could be grazed. Marjan isn't here but she would have asked "did metallurgy have an impact on the environment?" – which was one of our starting hypotheses. What we can prove from the botanical analysis is that it was always like this. These people did not cut down forests because there were no forests in the first place and the wood that they used in their furnaces is *artemisia* that you find all along the fringe of the desert. And it apparently makes a good wood.

Henry Wright: You illustrated one jar with a sharp shoulder and a buff black paint and nose lugs from site C, is that from a burial or is that from a house context?

BH: I guess it is from a burial. It's from the very first year of excavation.

Henry Wright: There is, as you know, one like this from Jemdet Nasr and there is another one from a sealed tomb in Kunji cave (Emberling *et al.* 2002). Is this unique at Jemdet Nasr, that single vessel, or are there more?

Roger Matthews: There are sherds from other ones. It is interesting your distribution map of flat axes, there is one of those from Jemdet Nasr itself – excavated in 1920s – which is identical to the ones you've shown in your slides.

BH: I think we even analysed that one.

Roger Matthews: Right.

BH: The silver pendant, for example, Kunji cave also has a silver pendant.

Henry Wright: Yes. This is not, maybe, *Jemdet Nasr* but intrusive into the *Jemdet Nasr* from something from the Pusht-i Kuh.

Massimo Vidale: What about other things? Do we have much evidence for precious-stone processing there, lapis lazuli for example?

BH: No, nothing. What I did not mention is that many other things change when we come to this urban site in the second millennium BC. We have a total change in the lithics from formally having large blades to a sort of *ad hoc* industry. But there are no borers, nothing that you would expect to reuse for the production of beads.

Massimo Vidale: That's interesting. We should also consider these types of absences and perhaps that sites were specialised more than we thought.

Lloyd Weeks: Given that there is no evidence for precious-stone processing, what do you think about the beautiful silver inlay artefact that was found in Arisman, do you think that was produced at Arisman or do you think it was produced in a different settlement?

BH: This pendant travelled to Bochum for the exhibition 4–5 years ago and when they put it under the microscope – they had the Susa examples there as well – they said that they both look as though they are from one workshop. But they couldn't determine which one.

References

Beale, T. W. and Carter, S. M. 1983. "On the track of the Yahya large Kuš: evidence for architectural planning in the period IVC complex at Tepe Yahya", *Paléorient* 9: 81–88.

Emberling, G., Robb, J. E., Speth, J. D. and Wright, H. T. 2002. "Kunji cave: Early Bronze Age burials in Luristan", *IA* 37: 47–104.

Paper 08 – Christopher P. Thornton (CT)

Lloyd Weeks: Beautiful chronology, very delightful to see it extend right through the end of the late fourth millennium BC. You incorporated the radiocarbon into your discussion and at the start of the conference Cameron highlighted the problem with the plateau at the end of the fourth millennium and I noticed you've got that period in your dates – you started around 3100 and I wondered how you managed to discriminate the beginning and end of those phases.

CT: The radiocarbon dates are actually listed in the abstract so feel free to go through them and challenge me on this. Part of that comes from Dyson. Stratigraphically there are some that are earlier and some that are later; therefore you can divide the dates accordingly. I know that there is a wonderful statistical method that Oxford uses that I would love to understand but I have no ability to. Basically you can use that stratigraphic information to improve the resolution of the date. Our dates actually do cluster

a little earlier and a little later in that period. So, as I said, these are very rough dates, and I'm just trying to get 100/200-year slots. Remember also that these levels are single architectural phases. They are 80 cm to 1 m in depth. So the idea that they lasted for 200 year is, I think, very difficult to sustain. But I am trying to push these ranges down because, certainly Barbara has had to deal with the *Hissar II* sequence: *c.* 3800 to 2800 is *Hissar II* and you sort of go 'harrumph'. I'm doing my best.

Cameron Petrie: I think Lloyd's comment was meant to be a compliment because of the way of working through and combining the stratigraphy and the radiocarbon. I've sort of worked through that for the paper that will be presented on texts (Dahl *et al.*, this volume)

CT: It's the only way and it works. I wish I had the ability. If anyone in this room would like to play with those radiocarbon dates and give me a statistical understanding…

Cameron Petrie: I'll show you!

Barbara Helwing: Taking up this comparison between the Hissar region and the area to the south-west of the desert, as you know I have tried this comparison between *Hissar II* and Arisman once. There are many things that show that they are really oriented in different directions. There is the type of pottery kilns and so on. But it's still noticeable that at Arisman you have a certain amount of grey ware, and I would like to connect this grey ware with the Hissar and Gorgan grey ware.

CT: I think that is an interesting point. It would be interesting to look at those because of course the grey wares that are coming from Qasvin and *Ghabristan III* are quite different and you know this pottery, so I am sure you are right. But there are grey wares at Shahr-i Sokhta I, which I feel fairly confident are probably coming from this region. They are rare but they are probably coming down. There are also a few bits and bobs in here which seem to be imported. Like I said there is the Hissar-type stuff out in Sarazm, so Hissar is doing a lot of exporting of culture, but the inhabitants themselves seem to be very insular. There is nothing at Hissar that looks really imported, except for the Gorgan stuff, there's influenced stuff definitely – all the Sialk stuff from the *Hissar I* to *II* transition – but it's a very strange phenomenon.

Marjan Mashkour: You didn't talk at all about the salvage excavations of '95, why?

CT: Yagmai's work.

Marjan Mashkour: Yes.

CT: There is not much for me to say. Your work has been the only work that I have been able to access.

Marjan Mashkour: But did you have any contact with them?

CT: I tried.

Marjan Mashkour: I know it is tough, but I think I was there not two years ago when there was a conference, nothing came out of it. Nothing was shown.

CT: As you know he has had some family tragedies and has left the field; he was at the Hissar conference and I tried to speak to him but he didn't really want to talk. The stuff coming out of his work that I find the most interesting is that they have those tablets with cuneiform but those are probably early second millennium BC.

Marjan Mashkour: Yes. Glassner has read them, but he didn't publish them.

CT: And Kourosh Roustaei has done various soundings around Hissar looking at the extent of the site, but really his work, which has just been published, is much more interesting in that it shows an *Iron Age II* period at Hissar, which we didn't know about and which is not on the mound itself but sort of around it. For those interested in the third millennium BC, the Hissar third- into early second-millennium BC sequence is really not understood and I am hoping that in the future it becomes something that we can deal with. It is becoming quite clear that the top of the mound has probably been very severely eroded because a number of things that Schmidt found at the very top of the sequence correlate very well with early to mid-second-millennium BC ceramic forms. For those of you who know Jean Deshayes work, he argued that Tureng Tepe went later than Hissar because of certain ceramic forms. We actually do have those forms, but they were all in that top stuff that was just melt of erosion. The Iranians have done work there and I don't have access to Yagmai's stuff unfortunately.

Paper 10 – Cameron Petrie *et al.*

Susan Pollock: When you showed your satellite patterns maps for *Bakun*, *Lapui*, and *Banesh*, you said that there was movement between settlements despite the fact that you have this incredible continuity of numbers. How much movement between settlements? Is there continuous occupation in some and movement in others or is this a wholesale movement?

Cameron Petrie: This is the focus of a Ph.D. that was finished a few months ago that I have not read in detail. One of the problems that we face – and this is actually something that I commented on as a result of Kristen and Tony's work – is that particularly with this period our understanding is based on long blocks of time. So when I showed the *Bakun* period, the distribution map that has been put together here is showing all of the *Bakun* sites. Bernadette McCall,

who did the analysis, has attempted to break up the occupation into *Early*, *Middle*, and *Late*, but I don't have the ability to show that here. I think the problem that we have is that we also have an abundance of sherds that we cannot attribute to any particular sub-phase.

You can see in each of these periods there appears to be continuity of occupation of Dasht-e Rustam Do and I am fairly certain that is because of the abundant water resources in that area. And we have *Bakun* settlements in the middle of the Dasht-e Rustam Yek, but you can see there are several sites here. Bernadette was partially measuring the importance of individual sites based on the abundance of pottery rather than issues of area, so there are certainly nuances that could be brought out further. But you can see that in Dasht-e Rustam Do we've got a small group of *Bakun* sites, then we've got one *Lapui* site, and then we've got several *Banesh* sites. And if we look at Dasht-e Rustam Yek we can sort of see there are several sites located in different zones of the plain. But there is actually direct continuity between the *Bakun* period and the *Lapui* period occupations at some sites and this is quite interesting. You have a more or less similar pattern in the *Banesh* period – continuity and some change – we lose one of the sites up here but we gain one here. And we are probably talking about a displacement of a settlement of about 3 or 4 km.

Guillermo Algaze: It is a question perhaps not for now but for later, you keep on having bevel-rim bowls isolated in assemblages here and the same thing happens all over the place all the way over to Makran, and also across northern Iraq and Syria. At some point we should ask, obviously in addition to some evidence of contact, what else are they doing there? Why only that particular type? Whether we want to address this now or not, is up to you.

Cameron Petrie: I am more than happy to make a brief comment now. I think one of the interesting things is that from the evidence that we have from these Mamasani sites bevel-rim bowls were found at tiny 2 ha village sites, and from what I understand, some of the earlier sites where bevel-rim bowls are found in the Kur River Basin are equally small. None of the sites in the Mamasani region are particularly massive. Tol-e Nurabad is only a 4 ha site at this point so we are not necessarily dealing with some sort of redistributive colony that is being controlled in some manner. So my first instinct is that it is some sort of culinary component that spread. And people are more than welcome to completely disagree with me. Exactly what culinary component, I am not sure – perhaps bread moulds. There are a range of options and possibilities, but it is clear that we have this very specific vessel form and it is very widespread.

Guillermo Algaze: This is a question, not a statement. Is it widespread only along lines of communication or is it widespread everywhere? In other words if you are working in a valley that is pretty isolated and not on the route to someplace else, would there be bevel-rim bowls there?

Cameron Petrie: Well, according to Kamyar Abdi's work in the Islamabad plain, they found bevel-rim bowls in a cave.

Henry Wright: A teeny, weeny little cave, 1 m wide and 2 m long.

Cameron Petrie: Yes. That is just one example. I don't know whether we can answer the question that you asked because I have the feeling we are only looking at the sites along those routes. We are not looking at all at the odd little in-between areas.

Lloyd Weeks: Everyone is on the way to somewhere else.

David Wengrow: You mentioned that you hadn't gotten to the bottom of these trenches. Am I right in saying the earliest cultural material that you have from anywhere in this region is fifth millennium BC?

Cameron Petrie: No. Lloyd can tell you more about it, but the site at Tol-e Nurabad has a 5 m-deep sequence of ceramic *Neolithic* occupation. There is apparently no aceramic *Neolithic*, but we've only got to the bottom in one part of the site. We have occupation from *c.* 6200 or 6000 BC that is more or less continuous at any one of the sites right up to the *Achaemenid* period. However, if you look at the radiocarbon dates in the book outside you will see that there are actually several gaps in our excavated sequence. We don't have a continuous sequence. I imagine if we keep looking at enough sites we might end up finding occupation in all of the periods. What it does suggest is that there was continuous occupation in this particular zone but the people are moving around within the zone as and when necessary. My suspicion is that Mamasani is a relatively stable and nice place to live as opposed to parts higher up into the mountains and lower down, but I will ask the environmentalists and they will probably disagree completely.

Matthew Jones: No, I think it was.

Vanessa Heyvaert: I have one question. It seems you have got an alluvial fan.

Cameron Petrie: Yes there is a massive alluvial fan adjacent to Tol-e Spid.

Vanessa Heyvaert: So when did it start to grow, your alluvial fan?

Cameron Petrie: I think this fan has been gradually burying Tol-e Spid since the *Neolithic* period. Interestingly enough we have historic period sites sitting on the fan. We don't have any prehistoric sites on the fan, but Tol-e Spid is sitting right on the edge of the fan as it is today preserved. The interesting thing is that Tol-e Spid is at least buried by 5 or 4 m of alluvium, probably from this fan.

Vanessa Heyvaert: So they didn't protect themselves against the water from the fan?

Cameron Petrie: We can't tell as we've only dug this little, tiny trench. The other interesting fact is that Tol-e Spid is located on the edge of the fan, which is obviously getting affected by annual rainfall and water flow, and we also have a perennial spring that flows right past the site and is actually directed past the site today. Tol-e Spid appears to benefit from two different types of water supply.

Mitchell Rothman: I wanted to make a comment on bevel-rim bowls. I think that in the context of Uruk or Susa, they certainly were part of a redistributed system. But I think the advantage of bevel-rim bowls is that they are so low-tech. Its simple, any idiot can make them. You just take a glob of the right sort of stuff, put it on your fingers, hollow them out, and do a quick curve so it's sort of like Tupperware. You don't need a potter, you don't need talent. You don't need a great kiln. Basically it is a very simple technology. Just in the way we are finding that much of the 'Ubaid stuff isn't so much distribution of a style, per se, but it's the distribution of a certain technology of making them that makes that style almost logical. You might find it in places like this; of course it would be in a small place because it's sort of a cheap and dirty piece of technology.

Cameron Petrie: I agree with you in one respect, but not in another. It might be simple, but it is not just going to appear spontaneously in the highlands, it has to get there through some mechanism or for a reason. Presumably somebody who knew how to make a bevel-rim bowl had to show the people in Mamasani either through making one for them or teaching them how to make one. But the interesting thing is that from our excavations they are never abundant. They always appear in very, very small numbers. Even in the *Banesh* period they are not abundant. That may well be a bias due to the size of the exposures.

Lloyd Weeks: I don't know if our trenches are entirely representative of the site or the region.

Cameron Petrie: I agree.

Lloyd Weeks: We dug a fair bit of *Banesh* material at Tol-e Nurabad but didn't find a single low-sided tray, but a fair few bevel-rim bowls, whereas you've got both. So the small trenches are also skewing our picture somewhat.

Henry Wright: Were you legally obliged to dig these smaller trenches? Is this part of your survey permit or do you just not have any money?

Lloyd Weeks: We just wanted to learn the pottery from the region in a quick way and one way is to dig 25 m of stratigraphy.

Henry Wright: I hope you will expand.

Cameron Petrie: It is very logical to open up Tol-e Spid to much more extensive excavation. One problem is that the trench is actually located up against a 14 m-high section and a big abandoned building. The building is about 3 m away from the sounding. We basically know where the fourth-millennium BC occupation is, but it is just very hard to get to. That is one of the reasons we haven't done any more digging there since 2007. Other parts of the site have third-, second- and first-millennium BC occupation. The fact that the fourth-millennium BC material is so deep means that it is going to take a really massive investiture of time and money to get the early material out. The geoarchaeologists are probably shuddering at the quality of the stratigraphy. We haven't taken micromorphological samples, but Tol-e Spid is ripe for it.

Henry Wright: Regarding the learning curve on making a bevel-rim bowl, I can teach you to make a bevel-rim bowl in two minutes. It is really easy.

Lloyd Weeks: Maybe we can do that after the end of the workshop.

Cameron Petrie: Take home bevel-rim hats!

Henry Wright: All we need is some horse manure.

Lloyd Weeks: Perhaps we could find some mounted police for that?

Paper 11 – Alireza Sardari

Christopher Thornton: Is the assumption here that *Lapui* and *Bakun* are not chronological differences, but they may be regional differences that overlap?

Cameron Petrie: They have very clear evidence in the sounding that there is *Early*, *Middle*, and *Late Bakun* and then *Lapui* on top of that.

Henry Wright: Did he say what the later occupation at the site was?

Cameron Petrie: Alireza mentioned that it was *Achaemenid*, or historical/*Achaemenid*, which presumably means that there was a big gap in the occupation. To come back to Chris's question, to the best of my knowledge, the only site that has any evidence for any inter-digitation of the *Lapui* and *Bakun* is the *AV* levels at Bakun A. Otherwise the phases appear to be one on top of the other. It is possible that the transition exists at Tol-e Spid, but we haven't got down far enough.

Christopher Thornton: Those seals and sealings were straight out of *Bakun*. They show absolutely no difference – the seals anyway.

Cameron Petrie: When I was shown this I was astonished and delighted that they had found them.

Roger Matthews: Can you zoom in on those in any way? You can't really see anything.

Cameron Petrie: I think in some ways Chris is right, they are *Bakun*-esque, they are geometric, and there are various different geometric shapes. I haven't actually asked Alireza whether there is a spatial correlation between the seals and the sealings.

Christopher Thornton: That star-shaped seal does look very finely cut, it looks too finely cut to be a ceramic seal. But maybe I'm making assumptions. It looks like a metal compartmented seal from the third millennium BC that you can see on Shahdad pottery.

Cameron Petrie: This one looks to be ceramic, these two are stone.

Lloyd Weeks: The seal on the left also has a matching sealing.

Mitchell Rothman: They are also jar sealings.

Christopher Thornton: Jars and bags. It looks like a stone seal.

Cameron Petrie: One of the interesting things that strikes me is that there are no *Lapui* period sites in the Kur River Basin that are higher than about 2 or 3 m. As far as I can tell from the Sumner report they are all small flat sites.

Henry Wright: There is one big one.

Cameron Petrie: Do you remember where?

Barbara Helwing: Alizadeh writes that he has some sites that are 7 ha in size.

Cameron Petrie: In the *Lapui* period? There are big *Bakun*-period sites recorded.

Barbara Helwing: I think before.

Cameron Petrie: I am mostly thinking of the differences within Fars. We have these very large mound sites in Mamasani and places in the northern part of Fars, but most of the tells in the Kur River Basin are not 10 m high. There are some, but there seems to be variability within Fars in the nature of occupation at certain types of sites.

John Alden: The higher mounds appear to be in the southern and eastern portions.

Cameron Petrie: Yes, Tall-e Shogha, for example, is a great big site, but it is much later.

Henry Wright: I have a question about the section. In the middle of the *Lapui* period there is a nice wall in brown brick that is sitting on a solid layer of brick. The Japanese reported solid platforms of brick at Tal-e Gap and it is quite common in *Late Susiana* for special buildings, temples and so on. I have never heard it reported for late fifth- or early fourth-millennium BC material anywhere. Did you see this? Do you think it is a solid layer of brick?

Cameron Petrie: I have only seen that photograph. I haven't actually seen any of the architecture from this trench. It is a 2 x 2 m sounding that goes straight down to a depth of 12 m. It is astonishing – there are no steps.

François Desset: Did they hit virgin soil?

Cameron Petrie: Yes, apparently they hit the virgin soil, but they also went so far down they hit water, which may have been due to the rising water table because of the dam. As far as I know they are planning to submit a paper on the *Bakun* deposits to *Iranica Antiqua* when they get their radiocarbon dates. I am very thankful to Alireza to have put the paper together and also to send it in at this time. I think that it's a very important site, and not everyone knows about it.

Paper 12 – John Alden (JA)

Christopher Thornton: I have long been struck by the fact that there are a number of parallels between what happens at Tepe Hissar and what happens at Tal-e Malyan. Two obviously extremely different sites on different scales, and I will just throw this out there. Maurer Trinkaus's Damghan (1981) survey found that in the fifth millennium BC you have randomly distributed small sites. In the fourth millennium BC you have one site and it is big and you have two or three tiny sites with *Hissar II* ceramics on them. So you have the urbanisation, if I can use that term very loosely.

Guillermo Algaze: How big is Hissar?

Christopher Thornton: 12 ha, tiny. Tiny for the Mesopotamian sense, but for the Daghan region, it's enormous.

JA: But complete agglomeration of the population.

Christopher Thornton: Correct. At least that is the theory. Hissar is in fact a cluster of mounds with very distinct identities: South Hill vs. The Twins vs. North Flat, Trader Hill vs. Red Hill, there is some erosion between them so there is some linkage. However, it is pretty clear that they weren't one big site, that they were a cluster of mounds. I've written in my work on metallurgy that we have this difference in production between the domestic main mound and the industrial South Hill – the South Hill that has these tablets. You have at Tal-e Malyan the ABC/TUV difference that Vincent Piggot has written about, which is exactly the same, looking at parallels. And then in the early third millennium BC in the *Hissar IIIA* period you have this quasi-collapse, where there are people around but there doesn't seem to be any settlement at the main site, which then picks up again at the end of the third millennium BC. So I was just throwing that out to the group, it is just really interesting that you talk of these clusters at Malyan.

JA: I'm not willing to say that they reflect the same process, but I am perfectly willing to let you say that.

Christopher Thornton: I just want to throw the observation out there.

Guillermo Algaze: If Jason Ur was sitting here, he would comment on this. I wonder about these so-called *Middle* and *Late Banesh* clustering patterns in terms of the urban form of the Malyan and the earlier process that takes place at Brak, which also appears to be something along these lines. The processes are distinct but the material evidence is not all that dissimilar. Having said that, may I remind everybody that while we have no archaeological evidence, we have textual evidence that Warka was at least two separate settlements into one, maybe more – twin settlements are not all that unusual in early Mesopotamian urbanism.

Jane McIntosh: Have you any data on what was happening in the rest of your walled area? Could it, for example, be used for penning animals?

JA: It could very well. And again, given the license to speculate, it almost certainly was during the *Late Banesh*. There are a series of distributional features in *Late Banesh* ceramics that indicate that most of the settlement was alongside the edge of that city wall. It's the ideal kind of pattern if you are going to come in and deal with the head of your lineage plus the head of all the lineages. You want to bring some of your sheep and goats, you've got a huge enclosure to put them in and protect them. Nomads do that in modern times: they come in and camp in the remains of Malyan. So, yes, I'm very much in agreement with the suggestion that this could have been a place where animals were penned. Perhaps at the beginning of a season, in preparation for migration down to the lowlands or when people moved between the lowlands into the highlands, this might be the place where they came first and then spread out into the valley, utilised the grasslands for grazing during the summer months, and then went back to the homelands in winter. Winter in the Kur River Basin can be pretty miserable. It is cold, wet, and dark.

Lloyd Weeks: Sounds like England!

Cameron Petrie: I find the issue of nomads very troubling. Abbas Alizadeh has written about it extensively, and he has often said it is an idea or concept that is difficult to prove. I think in some respects we are going to constantly be faced with this issue of actually proving the nomadic component. For example, you mentioned the *Banesh* sheep/goat ratio and it wasn't exactly clear to me until Marjan presented her big chronological chart, but it seems to me that from the *Neolithic* the same pattern exists. So you've got the fact that the sheep/goat dominate through most of Fars throughout prehistory. And it didn't strike me that there was a major point of change. To use the example from Tol-e Spid, in the

Banesh period we actually had less sheep/goat than the *Lapui* period. Proportionally, this is a tiny sample, so it is always going to be difficult to prove anything using that site, but it is interesting.

JA: I saw that and I thought "hmmm".

Cameron Petrie: I wonder whether the sheep/goat ratio indicates a specific sort of pastoral economy. Can we tell whether we have nomads or long-range pastoralists? I think there is a range of options.

Another thing I wanted to ask: you suggested you've got khans moving from highlands to lowlands, and this is something you probably know better than anyone else, but exactly how similar is the *Proto-Elamite* pottery from Malyan and the pottery from Susa? I know that there are a lot of similar forms, but are we talking about the same vessel types or are they subtly distinct?

JA: Shared elements, obvious parallels, but when you handle them, not the same. The *Late Banesh* ceramics that I found have lowland signatures, found at Malyan, and are visually distinct from the *Late Banesh* material that has the Malyan signatures. And to get back to the point, why don't we have ceramics from the highlands in Ram Hormuz? My feeling is that the settlement patterns, the use of the settlements, and the use of the occupations are very different. Malyan has a big enclosure, and you are absolutely right, people come into the enclosure. People come from the lowlands with their animals and their pottery, so finding broken pottery within the enclosure at Malyan from the lowlands makes perfect sense. I think that probably the pattern in Ram Hormuz is different. I think that people come from the highlands to the lowlands. They camp along the edges of the valley, the talus slopes, the relatively well-watered areas, the areas where there is no conflict between the settled population and the transhumant population. And my suspicion is that if we are to find highland ceramics in the lowlands, we are not going to find it in the centre – because people are not coming into the centre – we are going to find it around the fringes. The ceramics we have available right now from the University of Chicago material are all from the excavation at Tell-e Gezer so they are from the central site. And my hypothesis, which is pretty self-serving, I admit, would be that we are not looking in the correct place to find ceramics that have been produced in the highlands and have been moved by transhumant nomad populations into the lowlands.

Jane McIntosh: Would you necessarily carry the pottery around? If you've got highland occupation, lowland population, why not leave your pottery at home and use local pottery when you get there?

JA: Certainly not – I mean you would never carry the big storage jars. Most of these, and this is one of the curious things about the *Late Banesh* ceramic

assemblage, it really tends to be small jars. There is a real preponderance if you look at the collections and if you look at the Sumner material, the things that are distinctively *Late Banesh* tend to be the small painted vessels; they tend to be very well fired, almost vitrified. I think these are tough little jars that people are using to store things with and carry them up and down; using them to cook things in. I don't know. You wouldn't move too much, but modern nomad populations move quite a bit. I am not going to argue that *Banesh* period nomadism is the same as what we see ethnographically. But yes, I think you move a small number. I can't argue with the data. I do believe that those are lowland-produced ceramics that are turning up in the highlands. Whether they were filled with goods that were being traded, you can make that argument. There are a lot of alternative explanations, but it is data that needs to be explained.

References

Maurer Trinkaus, K., 1981. "Pre-Islamic settlement and land use in Damghan, northeast Iran," *IA* 18: 119–44.

Paper 13 - Massimo Vidale (MV) and François Desset

John Alden: Quick first impression: it does not look like *Banesh*.

MV: OK. It is different. Thank you.

John Alden: There are lots of similarities, but in terms of exact parallels, the assemblage, no.

MV: It is not exactly, yes, thanks.

Henry Wright: Agreed and it's almost exactly like *Susa Acropole 17*. I can go through every sherd and show you.

MV: *17*, you say *18/17* or just *17*?

Henry Wright: Late *18*, let's say *18/17*.

MV: Personally I found a lot of comparisons with Chogha Mish also in these types of sherds. I would just like to make one more comment. We have seen in *Mahtoutabad I* that there are a lot of craft materials. When we move to the *Uruk* assemblage in later periods there is little craft, almost nothing. We found only two moulds. There is very little chert and no evidence of any processing of any exotic material. This may be related to the formation process of this deposit because this deposit was washed, but still it is peculiar that the representation of craft in the second assemblage, when we should have a major involvement in the trade of commodities, is very little. But I will keep cautious about this because of the nature of the assemblage.

Guillermo Algaze: Is it at all possible that your *Mahtoutabad I* and *Mahtoutabad III* levels are actually contemporary and not different periods?

MV: No. I would say no, because I didn't find a single piece of a bevel-rim bowl in the other trench. They would be somehow mixed, at least one. So it seems that *Mahtoutabad I* and *II* are before the bevel-rim bowls. This would be my guess. Unfortunately we did not find a single piece of carbon and this is probably because the level was flooded away, which would have happened a lot.

Barbara Helwing: Do you have any idea where the obsidian comes from?

MV: No. It is a sickle blade of obsidian. An old one; because it was oblique in this way.

Christopher Thornton: Is it very high-quality obsidian?

MV: No, it is not high-quality obsidian. It is very average.

Christopher Thornton: Because the high-quality stuff really goes out of use and a lot of stuff people call high-quality obsidian is actually slag. You could check it.

MV: OK. No, it is bad quality, it is almost grey.

Christopher Thornton: The local Iranian stuff is pretty bad-quality obsidian.

Roger Matthews: Quick comment about the culture. You don't seem to have some of the types that appear in southern Mesopotamia as characterising exclusively *Jemdat Nasr*. That is the solid stands, the certain type of spout with the thumb push in it, and one or two other types. It looks purely *Late Uruk* to me, very *Late Uruk*.

Paper 14 – Benjamin Mutin (BM)

Cameron Petrie: I thought it was very interesting the way you were laying together the technological similarities and the decorative similarities. It strikes me that there is a lot of interconnection and sharing of technological knowledge between ceramic producers and it is going in different directions. I think it is very nice to see that there is technological innovation going from east to west.

BM: Yes, and there were probably more examples of this.

Cameron Petrie: Even though you had a lot of evidence for coiling and other things, it seems that still within your group there is some regional variation – even though some similarities in the decorative styles are still distinctive, would you agree? In some of the more black-on-buff decoration you were showing, there was a similar "grammar" in the way they were constructing the motifs, but it seemed as though what was happening in Baluchistan was just a little bit different.

BM: That's the problem. There are indeed several similarities between the assemblages found in south-eastern Iran and the Indo-Iranian borderlands. *Miri* ware defined in Kech-Makran shows resemblances (some forms and decorations) with materials found in Kerman. At the same time, this type of production has traits in terms of decorations and forms that are not observed elsewhere. Furthermore, contrary to the other ceramic products of the south-eastern Iranian Plateau (although this will probably change in the future), *Miri* ware was built using coils. The differences relating to forms, decorations, and technique have led us to define *Miri* ware as a separate ceramic tradition of the south-eastern Iranian Plateau. Nevertheless, its relationships to some other ceramics of this area should not be discarded and this ware still fits well within the Iranian ceramic sphere seen as a whole. In the case of *Miri* ware, one should also remember that its development was probably linked originally in some ways to the traditions that existed before on the south-eastern Iranian Plateau. The answer to the question of whether the wares of the south-eastern Iranian Plateau in the fourth millennium BC corresponded to regional variations of a larger ceramic complex or to separate traditions depends on the scale we use to look at them. In detail, *Miri* ware cannot be confused with black-on-buff ware or black-on-red ware, while certain decorations of some *Miri* ware and some *Aliabad* ware vessels seen only from publications may be confused. There are, however, enough differences to envisage two separate groups, although a more detailed comparative analysis of the relations between *Miri* ware and *Iblis III* and *IV* ceramics in general would probably be fruitful. Although the influences from certain regions on other regions on the south-eastern Iranian Plateau should not be discarded, I think we should envisage for now that separate ceramic groups existed at that time, until more material is excavated between Kerman and Kech-Makran and the chronology is refined. The periods that followed *Miri* ware give evidence for the presence of multiple separate ceramic traditions in this area, with regions characterised by one type of product more than the other, but again, long-distance similarities have also been noticed across the regions bearing distinct styles.

Barbara Helwing: Just a question about technology. For the *Miri* ware and for the subsequent ware you showed pictures where you have on the surface some sort of geometric incision. Can you specify how this appears?

BM: These marks – the parallel incisions you mentioned – probably result from smoothing the outside surface of the vessels using a ribbing tool (such as a spatula or paddle for example), while the vessel was being rotated. But instead of being fluid, these marks indicate that parts of the smoothing were jerky. The marks are usually observed in a short series of several parallel, spaced examples. They probably correspond to intermittent impacts of the ribbing tool on the surface of the vessel, while the spaces between them represent the moments when the tool was not in contact with the surface. This type of mark is well observed in Pakistani Makran on fine ceramics dated to the fourth and third millennia BC. They are also attested for instance on the fine ceramics from Shahr-i Sokhta found from *Periods I* and *II* (labelled *Emir grey* ware), on the fine ceramics with relations to Kech-Makran (late *Shahi-Tump* ware) found in *Yahya IVC*, and in eastern Pakistani Baluchistan (*Faiz Mohammed* ware).

Massimo Vidale: This is what you find in *Emir grey, Faiz Mohammed*, but nobody has ever studied it for this type of trace.

Barbara Helwing: It looks like a paddle/anvil, which I know from a totally different place. These paddles always have stripes so that they don't stick to the pot.

Massimo Vidale: I have a comment. I'm going to tell everybody that you have destroyed the theory of Pamela Vandiver, and she is going to eat you alive. She will not believe me because I believe that there is a lot of coiling going on since the *Neolithic* and this has simply not been recognised or published, and now you have presented it.

BM: Contrary to what Pamela Vandiver argued (1987), it seems that there is indeed more and more evidence for coiling during the *Neolithic* and *Chalcolithic* periods, including in Kech-Makran, but also in several other areas of Middle Asia. You agree with me?

Massimo Vidale: Yes.

BM: I have your support, then.

John Alden: One question. You do have bevel-rim bowls. Do you have any of the flat trays?

BM: I was not digging at Miri Qalat when the bevel-rim bowls were found, but I know that only five fragments of such bowls were recovered. The excavation was small so maybe there were more at Miri Qalat, and maybe there were also low-sided trays, but they didn't find any.

Cameron Petrie: And the chronology suggests that it is definitely late fourth millennium BC rather than early third millennium BC?

BM: For this?

Cameron Petrie: Yes, bevel-rim bowl contexts.

BM: Yes. The fragments were found in *Levels V* and *III* in Trench IX at Miri Qalat. Calibrated radiocarbon dates for these levels and one date from the level below them (*Level VI*) are essentially situated within the second half of the fourth millennium BC, with the exception of one date whose lower limit is *c.* 2900 BC. Some of the ceramics found in those levels have styles that are found within the second half of the fourth

millennium BC in the Indo-Iranian borderlands. However, the comparative chronologies such as those of Tepe Yahya and Shahr-i Sokhta overlap with the beginning of the third millennium BC. So, I would say yes, but would also stay cautious for now.

References

Vandiver, P. 1987. "Sequential Slab Construction; A Conservative Southwest Asiatic Ceramic Tradition, ca. 7000–3000 B.C.", *Paléorient* 13: 9–35.

Paper 15 – Lloyd Weeks (LW)

Massimo Vidale: This was a very long presentation, but it was a perfect introduction to whatever we might want to discuss and I think many of us will have questions. I would like to know your opinion on something. You discussed all these different models, possibilities, different approaches to understanding these problems of cultural diffusion, evolution, and so on. We are seeing in the mid-fourth millennium BC that everyone started to refine lead and silver. Might this be related to the so-called *Uruk* expansion? And then, can we think that many communities of the Iranian Plateau are returning to silver when they realise it is a very good medium for making goods for the exchange network, as we know from the literary texts. Silver becomes a very strong medium for measuring wealth in any kind of commercial transaction. A model like this, how would you fit it in with the ideas that you have put out so far?

LW: I think that there is undoubtedly influence on technological processes from the broader cultural context. There can't be an *Uruk* selection of silver as an important material unless it is already being produced and we know that there is lead produced in very early periods right back into the fifth millennium BC; so there is a long-standing tradition of production of these materials which does extend into the fourth millennium BC. Linking that with *Uruk* expansion or demand for materials from particular sources is where it gets complicated of course, but also where it gets interesting as well. In this case I think we have to look closely at the internal dynamics of change as well as external demand for any particular product. That is not much of an answer, I know, but it is maybe something we could debate at the end of the session.

Susan Pollock: I really like your discussion at the end when you are thinking about how these technologies are transferred. I wonder if you can say anything about some of the internal developments. For example, you made an important point about the development of smelting and so on at different points in time, but what are some of the social implications of the change in technology in the context in which it happens? Never mind the technological transfer, but what does it mean to move towards a smelting technology as opposed to cold hammering in terms of social relations?

LW: Right. That's a very good and very broad question. Can I possibly defer on answering that, but rather contribute to our general discussion at the end of the session? Because I think it is central to stuff which Barbara also wants to talk about with regards to Arisman, where we have this change in a mode of production documented clearly and which Chris I am sure would also weigh in on from the perspective of Hissar; and as I would probably summarise their work, I'd like to leave it to them to talk about some of these issues. So, apologies.

Vanessa Haevaert: I have an environmental question. Have you looked at the impact of the growth of metallurgy and the effects on environment, especially on wood and forests?

LW: That is a perennial issue in archaeometallurgy and early smelting operations. There tend to be two schools: those that say in all instances that you can see massive environment degradation, and then there are those that say that is massive over-simplification; that in fact, it depends on a case-by-case basis. In these specific instances I don't know if there has been a clear relation of the location of smelting operations and their effects on potentially environmental aspects. Again Barbara may like to talk more on that in the context of Arisman. I don't know of any specific environmental factor that has been brought into this.

John Alden: Working with arsenical coppers and especially cupellation of lead to produce silver are really nasty processes. Is this showing up in the skeletal remains? I mean I don't expect to find data, I'm wondering about it.

LW: The potential certainly exists to find trace element levels, enriched trace element levels for arsenic and lead in the skeletal remains of metal workers, but there have been no analyses to my knowledge.

Christopher Thornton: There was one project in the Levant, an *Early Bronze Age* site. It was interesting: at the site they were smelting copper arsenic and they had burials. We don't know if they were the people smelting, of course, but they had burials and there was no trace that they could find, which led them to argue about the smelters being upwind from it so it was all blowing away from the site, i.e. that the smelters were aware of the dangers.

LW: It is all very complicated because there are some examples where arsenic levels have been found in skeletal remains, but the argument is that it could be from microbial contamination in the burial environment rather than pre-deposition. So it is very difficult to illustrate.

John Alden: Are the lead objects that you are finding depleted in silver? That is, are they smelted: heating it up and steaming off the oxide of the silver nodule and then resmelting the lead oxide to make it into metallic lead?

LW: I don't think so. It doesn't seem so, there is so little litharge at this site that I don't think it's been reprocessed into lead and we certainly would be able to pick it up because the lead levels are roughly 100 parts per million for lead that has been resmelted from litharge. And we would expect there to be substantially higher silver levels in lead which hadn't gone through that process.

Christopher Thornton: Also litharge is not just a skimming thing. The lead oxide is absorbed into a ceramic or into a fuel ash so it is actually a very complex mixture of ceramic clays and ash with lead oxide. I don't think you could reprocess it to create ore, to create metal again. I think there would have to be different processes.

LW: It is documented in much later periods.

Roger Matthews: I think that one of the frameworks in which we have to think, to cover in particular your last three points there, is the ideological framework. Because if one has a shared ideology in which certain practices have to be undertaken – for example the production of particular paraphernalia for cultic practices or the construction of cultic statues in a particular way with particular materials by particular craftspeople – then that kind of framework encourages all of the three things you've got there: the rewarding of particular capabilities and attributes through skills and materials, the spread of ideas rapidly and uniformly across huge regions. I really think this kind of phenomenon needs explaining, even if we can't get at the substance of ideology within a framework that has that as its major component.

Guillermo Algaze: Well, what about a shared ideology about how you express rank?

Roger Matthews: Absolutely, as an example of something that involves and encourages particular abilities and use of technical materials for very specific purposes.

LW: Yes I agree. And with these last three points I attempted to bring the technology in the ideological realm and I think that is the only mechanism through which we'll really be able to explain some of these characteristics which we see, archaeologically at least.

Paper 16 – Holly Pittman (HP)

Jacob Dahl: I would like to concentrate on two questions and comments since the talk that Cameron and Dan Potts *in absentia* will give later that will give a rather different view but following the same lines of argumentation. Two points where I would differ in opinion. One: why would you carry a bulla from Susa to Hacınebi? A bulla would record whatever you need for a couple of weeks to survive.

HP: I really don't think so. The fact is that Jim Blackman did the analysis and it is identical to analyses that he has done of material from Susa.

Jacob Dahl: Yes, but sand and clay have flowed those river for thousands of years. They did a test up there in Hacınebi, but similar sediments could have been washed down from somewhere else etc.

HP: No, that is not how neutron activation works.

Jacob Dahl: OK, that is my view on this, but I think one of the problems with this is that we have to define what these documents are and the only reason there is that it could be carried simply out of curiosity. Something that is bizarre and we take with us. My concern is that these are entirely local administrations. They cannot be read by people who do not belong to the system, who don't understand this system.

HP: Well, except that if we look at the material from Hacınebi, from Brak, from Sheikh Hassan, from Susa, right, they are clearly all working with the same basic practices.

Jacob Dahl: No, we don't know that, because we have not enough evidence.

HP: But typologically?

Jacob Dahl: We do not have enough material to say statistically that they actually had the same organisational belonging, because these bullae have not been open, for example. So we cannot say that it's exactly the same system. One could say that about the decimal system or a sexagesimal system.

HP: All you are saying is true. But . . .

Jacob Dahl: Anyway I do not know enough about the testing of these things. But I will make one point on something that I know something about and that is the *Proto-Elamite* texts. To my knowledge, the majority of the texts you mention as being *Acropole I.17*, *16 a* and *b*, in particular the very famous text with the onagers, which I sort of re-edited in an article in 2005, and which is clearly from the same level as the texts found in *Acropole I.16 a-b*. So the one up in the column there is *16 a–b* and a couple of other ones. The point of that is that we have many texts that look like they are numerical, that look to be early, because they are a different level of administration. You will find numerical texts from almost all periods of Mesopotamian history. But numerical can be either a chronological grouping or it can be a typological place in the administration and that makes these analyses very dangerous to make, to my mind.

HP: Well this one is stratified. Do you accept that?

Jacob Dahl: Well, yes but I will also prove that with *Uruk IVa*. I would say that is an *Uruk* text.

HP: All right, but it's stratified in *IVa*.

Jacob Dahl: The two texts down, lower, to the right I would say are probably *16 a–b.*

HP: Yes, well…

Joan Oates: Can I just intervene. Are there any stratified *Uruk* texts?

Jacob Dahl: At Uruk?

HP: No.

Jacob Dahl: There is a long tradition and a lot of internal arguments about how to divide them into *IVa* and *IVb* and *III*. And unless you want to throw out 80 years of scholarship on *Uruk* texts I think we should go with that.

Joan Oates: I'm not throwing out, I'm only saying that writing in Mesopotamia has a much longer history that is reflected by a single deposit of rubbish that is put in its current place simply as fill for a large building. So we have no stratification.

Jacob Dahl: We have no stratification of the *Uruk* texts.

Joan Oates: And that includes tablets that are very simple like the numerical tablets, and more complex ones.

Jacob Dahl: They all come from the same pit at *Uruk III/IVa* and *IVb*, in the same pit with texts with only numerical signs. They can be and are in some cases proved to be *Uruk III* and *IVa* and *IVb*.

Joan Oates: I am not saying that they are not contemporary. All I am saying is that we have a deposit that in itself has no secure stratification.

HP: And we are not talking about Uruk here, we are talking about Susa and you don't have any seal impressions like this at Uruk.

Joan Oates: But since I stuck my oar in, could I just say I am not disagreeing with you and Boehmer at all, but it is true that if you describe Susa *Acropole I.17* as not an *Urukian* corpus, you are carrying . . .

HP: I'm not saying it's not, it is half and half. This is a transitional period.

Joan Oates: The other side of my question is the fact that has just been established I hope, that we have no stratification in southern Mesopotamia at this point and that we have no earlier material from Warka. And what other site has given us any early material in south Mesopotamia?

HP: Zero.

Joan Oates: So there is a sort of psychological contradiction between talking about Uruk from Susa and Susa as *Urukian*?

HP: Well as I said, Boehmer's response to that is that enough work has been done, so that if there was data, we would have it. I agree.

Joan Oates: I'm not so sure.

HP: I mean I'm not so sure about the fact that we are not missing stuff.

Joan Oates: I'm not disagreeing; I am just saying that you do have a big gap from a real excavation in southern Mesopotamia.

HP: A huge gap. But I would like to see us do neutron activation analysis on those bullae from Warka.

John Alden: I was going to say that the key question is, "why were they carrying this bulla?" I don't think that you can deny that they carried it. I think that the neutron activation signatures must stand, Blackman is good at what he does.

Jacob Dahl: (Obscured)

John Alden: But you know, I've never checked his particular analysis or the identification, but "why carry this one pound ball?" is a good question.

Jacob Dahl: We are making an enormous thing out of this bulla that to them was simply a little thing; they did some calculations with a couple of sheep coming in and out.

John Alden: Then why is a foreign piece of clay…

Wendy Matthews: Someone is watching his sheep while he is away.

John Alden: I don't know.

Barbara Helwing: Different topic about the origin of the patterns and the dismissal of *Bakun*. I wonder if it would be useful to look also at the pottery decoration?

Cameron Petrie: This is the most elaborate figurative decoration in highland Iran.

Barbara Helwing: And see the images of these animals that carry stuff on their back,. And as you know this was all painted in the Zagros, they emphasise animal decoration and I think it would be good not to keep to the glyptic, but . . .

HP: And the Susa pottery at the same time. And certainly some of the signs, the cross and that sort of thing are forms that we see carried on.

Barbara Helwing: I think you can trace them back to this kind of ware.

Guillermo Algaze: A couple of very quick points. In addition to Joan's point about the lack of stratification

of the *Uruk* materials which Boehmer seems to completely ignore . . .

HP: No, those seal impressions are stratified; it's the tablets that are unstratified.

Joan Oates: There is nothing stratified at Uruk before the *Jemdat Nasr*.

HP: Right, right.

Guillermo Algaze: My recollection from Nissen is that only a minute portion – he suggested 10% of the total amount of sealings from Uruk – has actually been published and that includes the Boehmer publication, in which case we probably know more of the sealings from Susa than we do from Uruk.

HP: Well Boehmer says that he published everything and that is why it took so long…

Jacob Dahl: I think it's pretty certain that there are lots of drawers that have not been catalogued.

HP: Well he didn't publish *Uruk III*. I have those pictures, *III* is not published, but he says that he published all the material.

Guillermo Algaze: In 2001 Nissen essentially said that it is only 10% that has been published.

HP: OK.

Jacob Dahl: That is not the same information.

Guillermo Algaze: So we may actually know relatively more about Susa than we do about Uruk.

HP: Right, right.

Christopher Thornton: First off, a quick thing, unrelated. Holly, is it true that the sort of picture that you came to that was interesting is that the glyptic in southern Mesopotamia seems to be very much of the same style – very homogeneous. Not homogeneous, but you see the same types of styles. And that what you see at Susa is a huge variety of different things, and they are all sealings…

HP: No, there are lots of seals…

Christopher Thornton: But of the different styles, I mean you had one that was like a bubble-stamped seal; there is a huge variety. There are seals as well. I think that's very interesting.

HP: That is also true of the *Proto-Elamite*. That within the corpus of what you can call *Proto-Elamite* there is a tremendous variety which is workshop-based or…

Christopher Thornton: Probably regional-based, thinking of Iran…

HP: Yes, maybe. But it is much more various, much less homogeneous as a corpus.

Henry Wright: Just being a devil's advocate, I'm struck that we have one small region in Mesopotamia with one 40 ha site (Susa) that has this seemingly vast influence on the north, when lower Mesopotamia proper has 10 or 15 cities, more than 100 ha probably. I understand your argument; I just find it historically questionable based on present knowledge of the masses of people in the two areas.

Christopher Thornton: You're talking about a technological, or a glyptic dominance…

Henry Wright: That is meaningful material that is moving, reflecting some sort of cultural information, not just technology.

HP: I think we can't know if Boehmer is right that these balls from Uruk come from Susa and therefore are the…

Henry Wright: A great deal of could be resolved if somebody could do a comparable neutron activation analysis.

HP: We just need to get Jim (Blackman) to do it.

Jacob Dahl: Can I just say that before anyone starts doing a survey of the clay, can we just open a bulla? The majority of these bullae have not been opened yet, which is why we still don't know what is being recorded. The clarity is not there, what we want to see is small incisions on the tokens.

HP: I am totally in favour of that.

Joan Oates: There are problems with that. They don't add up.

HP: They usually don't add up!

Wendy Matthews: Instead of doing destructive neutron activation, which is an elemental analysis, you can do non-destructive portable XRF, you can just take the equipment to the museum.

Cameron Petrie: Any sort of compositional analysis would be better than nothing.

Paper 17 – Roger Matthews (RM)

Jacob Dahl: I agree with almost everything, but just want to add a few points to the date of the export or import of writing from southern Mesopotamia to Iran. I count more numerical systems – I think we now count 40 with the 'divide systems' within Mesopotamia.

RM: 40?

Jacob Dahl: I think so and 10 in Susa, and still only two in Godin. Notably there is one system that they invented at Susa and that is the decimal system; that of course has not been imported into lower Mesopotamia, which would have happened if the direction had been that way. One should think about this.

Massimo Vidale: So we have 10 different systems in Susa?

Jacob Dahl: Yes. I can't remember exactly, but about 10.

Guillermo Algaze: I wondered if you or anyone in the room has any more information on these two new sites near Tehran? (Tepe Sofalin and Shoqali)

Massimo Vidale: I have been there.

RM: Yes, you were there a few days ago?

Guillermo Algaze: So what exactly are these materials? Massimo Vidale: I did not see the materials, I saw the site.

RM: You've been there, I've seen the materials. Jacob has handled the materials.

Jacob Dahl: I asked if I could show the texts here, but the excavators weren't happy for that to happen.

Guillermo Algaze: Can you tell us about them?

Jacob Dahl: It's almost all standard *Proto-Elamite*. They have what they believe is an *Uruk*-period numeric tablet, but I suspect that it's simply one of the tablets with only numerical signs – it conforms otherwise to early or standard *Proto-Elamite*.

Christopher Thornton: The tablets were all found in one pit, correct?

Jacob Dahl: Yes, they were there with something like 1200 sealings, but the most fantastic thing they found is sealings that have drawings of signs. So they are not signs but drawings by somebody who couldn't write.

RM: Including the "hairy triangle" sign.

Jacob Dahl: Yes, it's incredible.

RM: Signs scratched on sealings.

Holly Pittman: They have those at Susa. You have the drawing of both pictures and signs?

Jacob Dahl: But that place has a very interesting role because the sign is found on the tablets. It's not a sign from the writing system but rather like a pot mark. It is used instead of a seal.

Guillermo Algaze: And the material culture that accompanied these tablets was what?

RM: Red-on-black painted *Proto-Elamite* pottery but, …

Christopher Thornton: There are two sites, but the site we were at…it was all *Uruk*-related. I mean not even *Sialk IV* type, all *Uruk*-related.

RM: So was that Sofalin?

Christopher Thornton: We were at Sofalin. They are right next to each other.

Guillermo Algaze: Are the tablets and the *Uruk*-related pottery from the same site or the same levels?

Jacob Dahl: The tablets were from Sofalin.

Christopher Thornton: So we were at the right site. So everything was on the surface, we found trays.

Guillermo Algaze: That is *Proto-Elamite*.

Massimo Vidale: No surviving jars.

Christopher Thornton: Roger, do you remember the paper that Youseffi gave on sealings?
RM: Yes. They were extraordinary.

Christopher Thornton: They were extraordinary sealings. At the time that we were looking at them we were saying they looked earlier rather than later, right? They looked like Susa *Acropole I.16*?

RM: Well, they looked as if they covered quite a spread to me, because some of them were fully developed piedmont style, others looked earlier.

Holly Pittman: Were there classic *Proto-Elamite* seals?

RM: In a particular twist there were animals in human positions. There was a lion holding a staff, a bow in its left hand.

Holly Pittman: There was an impression of one. There was an exhibition of all that material in Tehran while I was there and there was a seal that was certainly a classic *Proto-Elamite* seal impression.

Jacob Dahl: I have ONLY seen classic *Proto-Elamite* and *Jemdat Nasr* style from what they have sent me. It's all been that kind of stuff.

Cameron Petrie: They presented a paper in Ram Hormuz in December 2009 and they just showed tablets and no stratigraphy or site plans or anything like that.

RM: I don't think that they have found any architecture.

Massimo Vidale: The other information is that it is definitely an industrial site. It is full of a very rough native industry…it looks *Acheulean* with…

RM: *Acheulean*!?

Massimo Vidale: Its very, very rough, but. . .

RM: But definitely *Proto-Elamite*.

François Desset: Perhaps quite a stupid question, the 2000 sling balls? Could they be preparation for tablets?

Benjamin Mutin: Could the sling balls be a preparation for tablets? I was sort of hinting at that without committing myself.

Henry Wright: Too small.

Cameron Petrie: Are they, were they fired?

Mitchell Rothman: If it's a sling ball, that is one of the distinguishing features of it. If you want to use it as a weapon you never fire it because the firing will actually make it lighter so you want it to be wet and heavy. In fact in some later Sumerian and even Assyrian texts it talks about heavy clay, because you don't want to bake them, you want them to go and cause damage and then break.

Massimo Vidale: And they will dry if there are more than 1000 together.

Joan Oates: We had some in an industrial village near Tell Brak and they were in a bag in the corner of the room. They were obviously being used for the clay in the room.

Mitchell Rothman: And I think you can distinguish that. One of the interesting things I've found from reading Willem Floor's *Traditional Crafts in Qajar Iran* (2003) is that one of the typical things they used for bobbins were things that looked like little clay footballs and they tied them on the thread; and at Tepe Gawra there were almost no sling balls, but we think that a lot of them were either blanks for sealings or probably bobbins because of where they were found and what they were found with; but none of them were of that shape and none of them were of that weight. So I think that it is certainly possible and I argued that with Virginia Badler for months, but she sort of won.

John Alden: I've got a specific question, from what you said, Roger. We have two concentrations of tablets, one by the entrance and one at the back by the largest room, and you made the very interesting suggestion that they might be recording materials as they passed through the door. I wondered – and you might not have the data to answer this – are there more blank tablets or sealed tablets without numbers by the door and more tablets with numbers back in the niche, which would agree with your functional analysis?

RM: I haven't worked that out actually, but we probably can.

Mitchell Rothman: Oh yes, we know that, I'm just trying to remember. I know that a number of the blanks were in the trash. I don't believe that there were any blanks in the north building.

RM: That's the next stage in the process.

References

Floor, W. 2003. *Traditional Crafts in Qajar Iran, 1800–1925*, Mazda Publishers, Los Angeles.

Paper 18 – Jacob L. Dahl (JD), Cameron Petrie (CP) and Dan Potts

CP: I wanted to say one thing to finish off the paper. Without a doubt the most important site that we need to pay attention to in order to resolve things about the

Proto-Elamite tablets and their chronology is Susa. I think Susa is the only site where we are actually going to solve this problem. Unfortunately at the moment we can't do much. Speaking with Henry earlier, he mentioned that samples were collected, more samples collected for radiocarbon dating?

Henry Wright: The idea was to take all the samples out at the same time so that Alain's (LeBrun) samples and my samples from *Acropole III* were aggregated into one box. And that year it was thought that things would be rather difficult, and we had better bring them out next year. And that was the last year. I don't think samples that have been sitting in plastic bags for 30 years should be run. I think there is a need to do a cleaning of the sections and to take new samples.

CP: I think the typological work is really interesting, but the key thing we need to answer this question and the dating problem at the end of the fourth millennium BC, is a long sequence of dates from stratified levels. I don't know whether *Acropole I* is going to solve the problem because we have the discontinuity. There is the critical issue of the discontinuity between *I.17* and *I.16*, which we can answer with a handful of radiocarbon dates very quickly. But the problem is going to be that the radiocarbon dates are going to fall probably exactly in this plateau period. It's almost as if we need micro-stratigraphic information with radiocarbon dates from almost every single occupational surface.

Henry Wright: If you will allow us to use different excavations, if Susa becomes possible in the future, which some day it will be, if the problem is solvable with different excavations. There is a part of Susa where Jean Perrot dug in the first season he visited, when Father Steve was still in charge. There he found an intermediate phase apparently, judging from the sherds. Secondly, the problems that you see in the lower levels – around *I.20* and *I.19* – with pits is not a problem with *Acropole III*, which has a continuous sequence.

JD: Of course any of what you said is a very simplified part of the larger project; for example all the tablets published in MDP 26, not MDP 26 supplement, appear to have come from a different part of Acropole by the Chateau and appear to be slightly older than *2A* and *2B* and actually fall between *2B* and *2A*, but they also seem to be dealing with other things. So the problem is, of course, dealing with an undeciphered writing system, with undeciphered language also, found mostly without context.

Holly Pittman: And why do you think they are slightly earlier or slightly later, what are the criteria?

JD: Well the problem with these texts is that they were the ones, you probably know, that stayed in Iran, so there is the added problem with the credibility.

Those that were published were published using the sample there or whatever. This means that there is an element of judgement involved, and according to the drawings, there is some variation in the sign forms. Structure-wise, it looks a little older than what I call *2B* here, so it would be in between *Middle* and *Late*.

Holly Pittman: Do you have a list of all the tablets and what you think the dates are?
JD: I have put some of the information in the standard catalogue of *Proto-Elamite* tablets, which is the catalogue that is online through the CDLI. So if I haven't done it, it will happen, and you will be able to search for *Early*, *Late Proto-Elamite* and get a sample of all of them and have a look at them.

Guillermo Algaze: You have a sequence of three signs that you were interpreting as a name, which appear at both Susa and Malyan. What are the political or social conclusions you draw from that? Are we discussing…

JD: This is horrible. It's like finding a shipwreck and not having the money to get it out. I don't have the time to look at it. I think that they must belong to the same group, or at least a whole range of occupants.

Guillermo Algaze: But the group or an individual? I mean, is it the name of a person?

JD: Well, more than one individual could have the same name. But the fact that they – not so much this particular string – formed complex graphemes in entirely the same way, used the same kind of simple stroke for indicating ownership and so on, and then they invented this way of writing who they are and we find the same designations. It is a very complex way to do it. And we find that in most places. That's only what I think.

Guillermo Algaze: I'm sorry I don't quite get it. You think this is the name of a person or the name of an institution?

JD: No, I think it is a person. He is called whatever these symbols translate to.

Guillermo Algaze: But it is the same person.

JD: I don't think it is the same person, because I think it is a low-level person, it's a worker.

CP: So is it a scribe for example?

JD: Essentially you are asking whether Hansen in Minnesota and Hansen in Germany are Danes?

John Alden: Could it be the name of a lineage?

JD: Yes, yes, possibly. Realistically it is undeciphered, so you can think what you want! It seems to be an ABB BBA kind of name, so one could potentially move ahead. But we are not nearly far enough along with filtering the sign list, this will take years.

John Alden: Do you have good photographs of all the Malyan material?

JD: Yes.

Holly Pittman: Because we don't.

JD: We put all the photos that Stolper gave me online immediately.

Holly Pittman: I'm of course thinking about linking what I've been doing with what you've been doing and clearly it is the pillow-shaped tablets that are at issue.

JD: What I called pillow-shaped tablets is different from what you did, I think.

Holly Pittman: Well I am just wondering whether you illustrated for us what you call a pillow-shaped tablet?

JD: No, because I have no photo of it. I think it makes no sense to give you a hand copy, it looks exactly like the others. They actually look like little pillows, little neat pillows, they are very fat, and . . .

Holly Pittman: But they have two or three or four truly *Proto-Elamite* signs?

JD: In long strings, if you look at it you'd think it looks like cuneiform.

Holly Pittman: Except for that one I showed, all of the others were either just numerical or had one sign. So I think that group can still stay in the period that is equal to *Acropole I.17*. That's what I am trying to figure out. Where do you put those?

JD: I have no real *Proto-Elamite* tablets in *Acropole I.17*, but I hypothesise this: I agree with the fact that it must be an earlier level than *Acropole I.16c*. It must be somewhere. Susa must have been something earlier than *Acropole I.16c*.

Holly Pittman: Yes, I agree with that.

JD: But those are my *Group 1* or oblong, they are always very dark, they have 1 and 3 signs.

Holly Pittman: Yes and they have very light seal impressions on them, oftentimes you can barely even see it.

JD: That is possible, but I am not a seal specialist.

Holly Pittman: Right. I have pictures of all of them so we should look at them together. I'm curious because I was allowed to photograph everything.

JD: OK, but I was allowed to photograph for my own use and I don't find that particularly interesting. If I have a photo and I can't share it with you, I would prefer not to have it. Sometimes I make a hard decision that if I can't put it online I will not take the photo.

Holly Pittman: I used the photographs that I took. They didn't say that I couldn't use them.

JD: I did not agree with the distinctions you made between the tablets. I thought that the majority of tablets you showed to be *Acropole I.17* were in fact *Acropole I.16*.

Holly Pittman: Fine…or *Acropole I.17x*?

JD: No I think really *Acropole I.16*.

Holly Pittman: So the tablet that's in *Acropole I.17* that is oblong.

JD: There is no tablet with *Proto-Elamite* signs that is in *Acropole I.17*.

Holly Pittman: There is a numerical tablet in *Acropole I.17* that is oblong.

JD: The only way you can distinguish between a numerical tablet from…a numerical ideographic tablet (as Englund termed them): from the intermediate phase between Susa and Uruk is the order of the objects and the count, so at Susa you always have the object that you count before the numeric notation, whereas at Uruk you always have the number signs before the object that you count. Which is what makes me think that your Godin tablet may be written by someone who later became a *Proto-Elamite* person, because he puts his non-numerical sign before the numeric notation. We are speaking of one or two examples, and that is what is so incredibly difficult.

Holly Pittman: What are these tablets that have no signs that are at Godin for example?

JD: We also have clear texts from this period that have only numerical signs. These are signs, for example only for calculations of the area of a field with some of these horrible texts with lots of little dots around the area, the edges, and so on. So, just as you probably do when you have to calculate your budget, you have a little piece of scrap paper when you do the numbers.

Holly Pittman: Yes, I understand the type that you are talking about, but the type that I was showing are identical to the ones at Godin, which we all agree are of that early phase.

Mitchell Rothman: Why do they write? Why do they bother with accounts at all? Writing the tablets at all?

JD: Two points on that. First of all, when humans invent something new they start playing. And that is the first thing we see at Uruk. As soon as they invent writing they start playing with it. What do they do? They start trying to calculate with the number 7 which is notoriously difficult in the 6 decimal system. And they start making up signs that have no relevance. It is really a deep part of who we are. We start playing when we invent a new toy. So that is part of the reason why we write. But the other is that it is a very effective system of control. If you can say "it is written", you have power. I think you can control people and goods. I think they very quickly found out that this was a good way to control people. Let's not forget that it comes at the end of a long tradition of a recording system, just not permanently, or maybe permanent for briefer periods. Maybe they had tokens in little sacks before they put them in bulla. Who knows? But we do know that they recorded this for long periods before they started inventing writing. They would sit with counting boards and make quick calculations. And it just all comes together with the *Uruk* bullae, when they actually put it into the bulla and sealed them. But we probably lose a lot of other methods of administration when that happens; as was pointed out with the disappearance of seals – of course we can now start writing who these people are so you don't need those seals. At least that was the theory of Damerow and Nissen.

CP: You show us a chronological development, which is potentially being controlled by the scribes doing it. Do you have a sense of how long that might take?

JD: Yes and no. So what you would do in that case is you start to measure the signs, which is what all epigraphers should do when they go to a place with these early texts, because they will be able to detect the different scribes and so on. I started doing that, but it gets a bit tedious after a while. It gets especially tedious with the new populations of *Proto-Elamite* texts because there are very, very few scribes. At least they had the same styli – perhaps they inherited them. There is one styli I found at Yahya, a silver styli. If we combine that with what we know of other periods in Mesopotamia it changes very, very quickly. These periods look like grand periods, but I think the entire thing is only a few generations. In fact I think what is the most interesting is that it spreads and peaks rapidly and then just disappears entirely.

Holly Pittman: Like 150 years?

JD: That depends where you want to start. The early periods probably take longer than the later ones, so that it takes you a long time to muddle around with it before you get the hang of it. So from Susa *Acropole I.16b* I would say that it is only two or three generations.

Roger Matthews: It is also very striking how long it is before writing reappears again.

JD: In Iran? It is amazing!

CP: I was talking to Karl Lamberg-Karlovsky and he described it as the rejection of an invention, which is an interesting way to think about it. It's not being rejected automatically because writing is spreading and being used for some time, and then falling out of use. There is a parallel in the Indus as well, in terms of the use of the Indus signs: it starts, exists for a time, and then stops.

JD: I think we have to forget the romantic idea of novels and letters because this is not what this is. This is a system to control your workers, your goats, and so on. So maybe people, when this system starts

falling down, might be happy! "We're not going to touch this stuff again!"

Guillermo Algaze: So there is nothing in the *Proto-Elamite* corpus – and I know you can't read them – that would be equivalent to a lexical list?

JD: I would have talked about that in a longer talk, but there is only so much time. *Proto-Elamite* is exclusively administrative except for two possible metro-mathematical texts. Grune Friberg, a mathematician, points out that these two texts have very long sequences of numbers that keep getting larger. Apart from those two small tablets it is all administration, no lexical lists. Very, very frustrating; and therefore no standardisation of signs throughout the entire period. So we have this ever-growing corpus of signs. As I said, there seems to be more singletons in the *Group 1* texts: the Ghazir, Sialk, and Malyan texts. I haven't been able to do a statistical analysis. I did one statistical analysis of an entire *Proto-Elamite* sign repertoire and showed the typical situation of a very large number of singletons and 20 signs repeating again and again and again. It is very difficult to split up the corpus and do the same, but I think there are more singletons in the early texts.

Susan Pollock: I just want to pick up on the remark you made before – I think this is a very interesting potential point – not just that people stop writing but maybe the people who are being controlled through this writing system essentially wouldn't accept it any more to the point where it falls apart. Because it strikes me that we always say that writing allows us to recall things, to materialise memory and so on, but of course in contexts where people don't rely on writing or don't rely on writing so heavily, there is a huge lore of wisdom or knowledge etc. that is passed down, typically through elders, wise people, and so on, whose authority may or may not be questioned. So we question things that are not written down, or the equivalent, but that doesn't necessarily mean everything which is not written down is always subject to question. It seems to me that it raises the very interesting point of what it means to start controlling people through these kinds of technologies, or not. In this case where it then stops for some time, what is actually happening there, is quite intriguing.

JD: I agree: it's very exciting. In fact those kinds of questions are exactly what we should be looking at.

CP: When I first looked at your table I thought there was some kind of pattern and I'm not sure if it's real or whether it is me making it up. Is it correct to say that Susa is like a hinge? You show two different trajectories and according to your chronological tables, there is a separation.

JD: It is interesting that it is far easier to show a comparison between Susa, Sialk, Ozbaki, and maybe even Sofalin than it is to show, for example Ozbaki, Sialk, and Yahya. It just is easier. It comes more naturally when you look for similarities. And likewise, it is much easier including the similarities with the one text from Ghazir, which means you can only say so much; but it is easier to show the same correlations between Susa, Malyan, and Yahya than it would be between Malyan and Sialk. How much one can read into that is difficult. I would hope that they find even more tablets and I think they should go back to Ozbuki also. If I end up getting photos of all the text from Sofalin it would be interesting to isolate all the particular names of owners, special cycles that only appeared in this extension and, vice versa, in this extension. My initial hypothesis would be that is what we are looking at. That if there is any connection it goes through Susa.

Holly Pittman: Are any of the Sofalin tablets seal-impressed?

JD: Yes there are some beautiful seals…fantastic seals…

Holly Pittman: On the tablets?

JD: On the tablets. One of them has this animal with a large neck that makes a circle. I gave a talk in London and some students said "it's a dragon" or a devil I think. So yes we have seals and very fantastic seals. There is more new stuff in the seals than in the texts themselves. So they were very disappointed when I said that they were just texts about sheep and goat and barley. But who were the people, what were their names?

Roger Matthews: Somebody did tell me in Tehran last week that there were actually 50 *Proto-Elamite* texts from Ozbaki.

JD: Really? Well you know I heard last year…

Roger Matthews: There were…there were 50 excavated.

JD: I was told that north of the mountains, north of Tehran a lot of – about 50 – tablets were found a couple of years ago, but they were in such bad shape that they deteriorated. But 50 tablets more would be very nice.

APPENDIX B: TRANSCRIPT OF CONFERENCE DISCUSSION SESSIONS

COMMENTS AND DISCUSSION LED BY
GUILLERMO ALGAZE

Guillermo Algaze: I want to bring up three points, not necessarily so we can solve them today – I doubt that anyone will solve them soon, but we need to be thinking about them. My points, probably not surprisingly, deal with the neighbours rather than with Iran. There are a number of specialists here and we are focusing more and more on Iran, but I would like to put out three themes that in a sense connect with the first three papers that we heard this morning (Hopper and Wilkinson; Wright; Rothman). The first theme that I would like to put out there for people to think about, whether we discuss it now or not, is the theme of "Greater Mesopotamia". We have talked about interconnections. We are talking about Iran. But to what degree is Iran a proper unit of study? Or should we think in broader units of study, something that we might want, or not, to call "Greater Mesopotamia". To my knowledge, or at least in my opinion, the paper that Hopper and Wilkinson gave this morning focused on one of the most important points of this conference and that has to do with the long-distance articulation of the processes in those regions. Particularly in cases of urbanism, which tends to be a fairly swift and massive process, and in many ways we could argue that it is not understandable in local terms, it is only understandable as a trans-regional or interregional sense. And we could perhaps look at urbanism in southern Mesopotamia and its impact in Iran, at least in south-western Iran and quite possibly areas further a field, much as we can look at urbanism in, say, the Khabur area and its impact on Anatolia and the Tigris basin. Can we conceptualise these things in local terms? That is something that I think we should be certainly talking about. I have opinions about this, but I want people to think about it.

The second issue that I want to raise is the issue of scale. We are talking about processes that take place in Iran, or about processes that take place elsewhere in "Greater Mesopotamia". Right now it should be very clear that I am one of those that believe that we can only look at this in a trans-regional sense, but that doesn't mean that it is the same everywhere, that there aren't any substantial differences. A point raised a number of times today is that we have to focus on the differences. One of the differences that I would like us to focus on at some point in this conference is the issue of scale. Is what is happening in the very different sub-regions of Iran comparable in scale to other comparable processes elsewhere? If not, why not, and what are the differences?

The third subject again is related – it is the issue of Iranian development. To what degree was this an indigenous process or was this more probably a process that can only be understood as part of a network relationship with other societies? To give you only a very brief idea of how my own thoughts about this are trending, Henry mentioned this morning that there this tension between models that try to explain the creeping "Mesopotamisation", were that to be a word, of the Susiana Plain in the fourth millennium BC, models that try to explain it as a case of diffusion or as a case of very strong interaction, versus models that tend to see it as an issue of colonisation, but I wonder whether we need to look at these as mutually exclusive. Could this be evolutionarily connected? In other words, what starts as a process of intense interaction and diffusion ends up later on as a process of migration and colonisation, whatever this word may mean in this context. As you know, these ways of looking at the world are not black and white and we might want to look at them as connected in an evolutionary sense.

So those are the three general topics that I see particularly in the first three papers that were

436

presented. I think at some point sooner or later, and particularly in this conference, we must certainly address them. Does anybody want to start? Are any of these issues that anybody wants to address?

Wendy Matthews: Looking at Godin Tepe and your idea of us looking at different scales: Virginia Badler's work looking at the scale of hearths and spindle whorls showed that there's very much a local continuity going on; and also if you look at the local pottery which Mitchell showed us today, there are connections between this local pottery – some of the carinated cups or the red slip wares – and northern Mesopotamian sites like Mohammed Arab al Kheran; a different scale will give us slightly different pictures of the interconnectivity.

Guillermo Algaze: The issue of scale is also related. Henry made a comment that really struck me like a slap in the face because I never looked at it in that way: the similarities between Godin and Arslan Tepe. But again, there would be substantial differences in scale between those two sites.

Mitchell Rothman: Jim Blackman and I did a study on LC1, late fifth-/early fourth-millennium pottery types, the so-called "sprig-ware" and the finer impressed ware. We were actually quite shocked to find how extensive the littoral movement was, not just the ideas but the physical objects were moving in the area of the northern Euphrates all the way into the Khabur, earlier than anybody would have thought. So when we talk about movement of goods and movement of things or ideas, we need to be very careful and be really specific about what are we talking about. So for example, if we are talking about people or about cooking practices we might want to spend a little more time on cooking ware, which I know is very ugly and usually not very interesting, but I think that's extremely important, probably in certain ways more important that a lot of middle-level sorts of containers, jars, etc. Let's be really specific at looking at different categories within our big categories and really try to figure out their utility, their place within society.

Guillermo Algaze: Why do some things move and other things not?

Mitchell Rothman: Yes, why do some things move and others don't, because clearly that happened. And what is it about the nature of interaction, what is it about the nature of supply and demand of certain kinds of things? And how does that change over a longer span of time because you can't say "every time a cooking pot moves its 'this'" – maybe in one period it means something and in another period it doesn't necessarily. Think of woks. It sounds like a stupid example but it's not. It's really not. It comes with a certain kind of cuisine, but people are also making hamburgers with them. And so you have to be really careful about the introduction of new ideas

vs. development *in situ* of those ideas. Comparing how in different places the *in situ* development might take different directions. So what I was trying to say this morning is that I think there's a lot that we just haven't done, that we could do. But it means we have to be really specific about what it is we are looking for and what is the likely need. Our last speaker (Marjan Mashkour) has the great advantage of science. We probably don't all have similar evidence. But that doesn't mean we still don't have ways of really establishing criteria and then following those criteria as they pan out over a long period of time. I think we haven't done much of that. We've been very general; we talk about pottery as if it is just this lump of things. But it's not realistic. It's a lot of different things. Playing into what moves and what doesn't move; what's adopted and what isn't adopted; what stays etc., and that has a whole bunch of different kinds of meanings. That's what I am playing with for the Trans-Caucasians. The people living at Khirbet Kerak probably never saw the Trans-Caucasians. They were surrounded by other people, probably for hundreds of years, who had much more sophisticated pottery, who had all sorts of different types of potters. Why the devil are they keeping this pretty simple, ugly pottery for all these hundreds of years? What is it about the nature of that one element that is truly working? Rafi Greenberg (Tel Aviv University) is doing a really interesting petrographic study. He is looking at the designs of these types and comparing them to the soils; how do certain soils indicate that different types are moving differentially, in different directions over different spans of geography? And can we look within this monolithic corpus? As certain aspects, certain motifs, certain things that move independently when we are looking at a potter. And I think that our ideas will not come to fruition until we get a lot more specific about what we are looking for and what the meaning of the patterns we are going to see is going to be about.

Reinhard Bernbeck: I just have a comment on what you said and maybe also in the talks generally. You talked about scale and largely you meant spatial scale, but of course there is also temporal scale, and thinking about the talks, at best it's either long-term or very short-term, the seasonal yearly scale. And of course, in terms of temporal scale one should also imagine whether there are rhythms, certainly on the scale of the conjunction – what Hodell calls conjunction – like 70 years, 100 years, or something where you might have changes that are repetitive rather than just linear and then you forget them.

Guillermo Algaze: Any other points?

Roger Matthews: I just want to make a point about the maps and how the maps we use and the maps we show in our talks and how publishing our books

Holly Pittman: Well it may be a very long…If in fact we are missing these early levels at Uruk and they are all there, we are missing a very long substrate where in fact it isn't just the elite, we are missing a whole middle class as well which participates in something that starts with the *Early Uruk*. Right?

Guillermo Algaze: Yes. We definitely have more data for the *Early Uruk* period coming out of settlement survey analysis, if Nissen is correct that the *Uruk* sequence is not to be trusted anytime before level 5 in the sequence. We have a lot more from settlement survey data than we have excavated data for the earlier part of, say, 500 years.

Susan Pollock: And if I could add, I don't know if that is the direction your question was going, Holly, southern Mesopotamia consists of more than the site of Uruk.

David Wengrow: I was just wanting to come back to the more general issue that Susan raised about technology and the spread of technology. It seemed to me that where you have – unfortunately the guy who talked about painted pottery just walked out – a paper about painted pottery, you have another paper about metals, and another paper about modes of communication and recording – these things don't generally develop in isolation, but the change in methods of recording is going to place certain new demands on the material world. And one of the striking things about proto-cuneiform is this correspondence we have between, for example, standardisation of ceramic container forms and quantification of certain kinds of goods where you may even have direct correspondences, sometimes, between a sign form for a vessel and a vessel one finds on an archaeological site. Now part of what strikes me as an interesting contrast with Iran is that we seem to have the continuity of the painted wares in a lot of these areas, which strikingly drop out of the Mesopotamian picture, which Cameron and I were discussing yesterday. I am sure this is telling us something extremely important. I am not quite sure what that is but it's a good starting point. And then if one looks at that in relation to what Jacob is talking about with these tablets, one question I would like to put to him is, what about things such as vessel forms, these kinds of correspondences that have been hypothesised for proto-cuneiform, between written signs and objects? Are there any grounds for those kinds of comparisons in your material?

Jacob Dahl: I don't think that has been studied. Whether it can be done, I don't know, but it is very interesting that some of the distinct types of pottery that I've been sitting here looking at, appears closely matched by signs in the writing system. For example, the one with the spout, the spouted vessel, you have a *Proto-Elamite* sign that is very similar to that. And the ones that are like this with the double band, you

have a sign that is exactly like that. And bear in mind that we don't have any signs for body parts in *Proto-Elamite* as you have in proto-cuneiform.

Mitchell Rothman: I also wonder that we don't look more at the use and disposal of objects. One of the things that strikes me, we talk about administration as if we all know what we are talking about, but if you really look at the profession of supposed administrative artefacts or administrative technology, the way that they are treated, not only in their use but in their finished use, is really critical. I remember when I did cuneiform, I was reading about good old Hammurabi. He says very specifically that they have this archive that included all the land deeds, all sorts of facts about how much yield a particular field had in a certain year. They were writing not simply for a temporary record. They were writing for a permanent source of knowledge that they could then use. One of the things that struck me so strongly about the Arslan tepe system, is they were not simply marking these things, but for some period of time – and we don't really know how long, but I suspect a fairly short time – they were auditing. Now I am hardly an expert on cuneiform and early proto-literate stuff, but certainly from Godin they seem to get the tablets and then just dispose of them. To what degree does the way these objects are used and then disposed of tell me about the nature of the system that they were used for? Because we tend to have such a clear idea of what administration means, what these things mean, we don't tend to ask questions like that, which I think are just full of incredible meaning and incredible information, but we just glance over it. Maybe the reason they stopped is in fact that they weren't getting the information from the tablets that they needed and they couldn't see their way to the next stage. I don't know, but no one asks that question, and I think it's really important.

Susan Pollock: There are a lot of people who want to respond, but if I could just say something beforehand. I would respond immediately and say this is not relevant only to tablets and administrative items, but to anything.

Mitchell Rothman: I meant that. But I was thinking about the tablets.

Wendy Matthews: I just wanted to build on that. I think a contextual approach is that we need to look at what segments of society are participating in these different social networks. And also what context – is it a burial context that is deemed important to do it? Or a particular exchange of food? – and all of that. I think building on that is a contextual approach where we can understand what contexts and things have meaning and who was engaging in that.

David Wengrow: I think maybe there is an indirect lesson in the paper yesterday by Marjan Mashkour, who went up into the highlands of Iran and asked the locals to give her some goats. One of her problems was how to know if these people are telling the truth – "I have asked for some goat and they are telling me that the goat has gone up the mountain". I actually think that this question has a very big bearing on the origins of writing, because it is precisely these questions of trust. In a sense what we are really talking about is that – I think it is generally accepted now in these early writing systems – language is a relatively small part of what is actually being put down on the clay or whatever. We are really talking about changing relationships between people and animals and things and commodities, and in that sense, again I just ask, why is there this lack of correspondence between these very far-flung exchange networks and the systems of recording that seem to be only concerned with the local, what's going on, on the spot? To me there is something very intriguing about that. There must be a relationship.

Jacob Dahl: I have a theory of what is going on, it's probably completely wrong, but . . . during the *Early Uruk* period, the expansive period, there is so much influx of goods, you get so much, you grab so much, that you don't have to write it down.

David Wengrow: So you DON'T have to write it down?

Jacob Dahl: No, because you've got enough. And during the *Late Uruk* period when the system contracts, you start notating.

Guillermo Algaze: But we know nothing about what is coming in and out in the *Early Uruk* period.

Jacob Dahl: As always, it's a theory based…that is what appears to be happening in the *Ur III* period. We have very few tablets from the early days of the kings when they go out and beat down the Elamites continuously. And in the very last period when it seems to contract, they write everything down. They even write about what they scraped off the furniture in the royal household, writing about the gold that can be used and so on. So that was just a theory.

Christopher Thornton: Following from what David said, I've always wondered about these funny colonies, especially in Iran, the Godin Oval and the *Yahya IVC*. There is really no sign of bloodshed, there is no sign of any sort of violence whatsoever. I don't think anywhere in the *Uruk* expansion you have really strong signs of violence, do you?

Anonymous: Well, you have Hamoukar evidence, which can be interpreted in either direction. The question is, "who did it"?

Christopher Thornton: But in the Iranian context there is not and in fact Barbara's (Helwing) work has shown that there is even a transition into it.

Guillermo Algaze: But that is perfectly explainable. The lack of violence actually makes sense. Particularly in times of initial context when you are meeting another who is really, really different and who is really, really prestigious, then you acquiesce.

Christopher Thornton: Yes and no, but have you met the nomads in the highlands of Iran? They are not fuzzy cuddly people, really. And my only thought, I'm just throwing this out there, following what David said about trust and this sort of thing. What if they conquered with bureaucracy? What if these weird people showed up and they just wanted to start writing how many goats you had. You might acquiesce to that; as you are saying, you might just go, "OK, I have 50".

Roger Matthews: Well it really does depend on power, doesn't it? If you have power, you can do it. If you don't you have to be sure that people have a stake in what you are doing…that they get some benefit from it, whether it is from more efficient management of their land, access to materials.

Guillermo Algaze: And the weirder you are the easier it is.

Roger Matthews: It is either inducement or coercion and coercion means real power.

Christopher Thornton: And the creation of these separating things like the Oval wall and the Yahya compound. They are as much to keep people out as to keep yourself in and separate from the community. More than just a symbolic power, but it could also just be a cultural variant.

Roger Matthews: Another thing we should keep in mind. At all of these sites we only have samples of the situation. At Godin for example, although the Oval is a relatively large area, you could fit several more Ovals on that site. Or you could have a completely different local community that is not buying into that assemblage of artefacts.

Susan Pollock: One thing I would add here too is that I think when we are talking about what writing means, we are forgetting that we have these millennia of various kinds of mnemonic devices, some of them potentially administrative devices and systems that precede writing. So it's not like nobody has ever counted anything before and materialised it through anything from tokens or iconography. The other thing I would say, I always find these discussions about what it would be like when someone showed up at Godin a little worrying, because we make it seem like nobody knew anyone else was living anywhere until the *Uruk* period or until the now *Middle Uruk* period, or however we want to date it. And while clearly there may have been movements of people that went beyond in scope and in magnitude before the *Uruk* period, to think that someone in the highlands of Iran had never seen anybody from lowland Mesopotamia in life, I'm not sure that that's something we can justify.

Guillermo Algaze: But counters are magical. It is really esoteric knowledge. And not only them, but all the other organisational innovations that may have been brought.

Susan Pollock: Yes, that is certainly the case.

Cameron Petrie: I wonder if we are missing something in the sense that everyone that has been talking about the tablets has been talking about the fact that we are always dealing with local administration – so we are dealing with local administration at Godin. But why is that of interest to somebody in Susa, I wonder? My question is, are we talking about colonisation or are we actually talking about the selling or buying into a system of power?

Roger Matthews: I don't believe it is colonisation.

Cameron Petrie: There were words such as the arrival of *Uruk* people and things like that used. So why is there always somebody possibly moving? It is just a question: is there perhaps a structure of power, a structure of control that is moving?

Mitchell Rothman: It doesn't necessarily have to do with power. They've got something I want, the guys up on the hills they have this copper stuff, they have all of these things.

Cameron Petrie: But Godin doesn't have the copper stuff, the copper stuff is coming from much further into the highlands or on the plateau.

Mitchell Rothman: Godin has some of the copper. And again, is it passing through? It could be 300 miles away but if it is going to come down the Diyala it is going to pass Godin, and Godin is guarding the gate. So they might very well, but you want to know…

Guillermo Algaze: There is a question right there…

Mitchell Rothman: If you want something. And part of the problem with the old system, which was a down-the-line system or some sort of local exchange system, is that it is very episodic. It is very unreliable. You can't tell how much is coming. You can't tell who is going to get it. It's a very unstructured system. If the *Uruk expansion* means anything, you're creating structure and you are creating a system whereby you can both determine amounts and direct certain amounts in certain very specific directions. And that is why I was basically coming back to Godin with the southern thing with Susa. I don't think they controlled Godin. I don't think they necessarily lived in any numbers at Godin, but I think they *were* involved in some way in influencing the fact that stuff was going to come in certain reliable numbers in their direction. And then the question is, how do you do that? And it is not necessarily power per se. It is not necessarily "I'm going to beat you up and look more

glorious and therefore you are just going to acquiesce up in this mountain where I could kill you any time I want". They have to find other means. It might be what they give them. It might be some sort of way for potential leaders to get some sort of bump. We really don't know. We have distractible scattered theories, but we really don't know. But if we start with a simple idea "you've got what I want, I want to get it at a certain clip because my whole production system is dependent on the fact that I am going to get this stuff" and I am not going to be able to say "oh sorry, we have nothing to produce this week", then that becomes a whole different, clearer question: how is this going to happen? And it is not just going to happen one way across this entire span; they are very different circumstances to start with. So it seems to me what we want to do – and that's why I was saying let's not talk about the system per se – let's assume the system and then talk individually about how the system worked if you are at Hacınebi. How did the system work if you're at Sialk? How did the system work? Because it is not necessarily the same everywhere.

Cameron Petrie: I am not doubting the question. I guess the thing I am wondering is: are others buying into the system? For example, we find sites that don't have the Godin Oval. In Mamasani something like this may be there, but based on our excavations we don't have anything big. In the middle of the fourth millennium we have handfuls of bevel-rim bowls and that's it. Everything else is local. This is along the main route through the southern Zagros. So what might be going on there? This is presumably well in advance of what is going on at Godin. So I am just wondering about the sort of local buy-in to this. The material moving can't just be there without a process. That is just my point. I am trying to understand the negotiation situation.

Susan Pollock: I think we have a long-time question in the back, Jane?

Jane McIntosh: I know the political situation is very different in the early second millennium BC, but I am surprised that no one is trying to use the Assyrian trade in Anatolia as at least some way of seeing the kinds of things that might be happening. So there, the records are by the Assyrian merchants for what they are doing. They are for internal consumption, if you like. So couldn't the *Proto-Elamite* records be what the *Proto-Elamite* traders were doing to manage the stuff that they are getting in, without actually involving the local people at all in the writing? And there you've got negotiated ways of retaining all the things you want by making arrangements with the local people in power, but also with other people who wish to trade. So there is the whole complexity of information that I think could give some insight at least into the kinds of things that might be happening, obviously in a different political context in the fourth millennium BC.

Wendy Matthews: One possible model is that it's the local elite who are engaging in the trade and actually moving and travelling and ensuring that the local economy continues normally through writing. In other words, it is the local management that is being ensured, perhaps while they are away, through the texts, basically as a guarantee in their absence. Building on that, they are the merchants who are going off to do this.

Christopher Thornton: You are talking about the local elite?

Wendy Matthews: Yes, I don't see why you have to bring in these other people. They are just local elites engaging with this international network.

Guillermo Algaze: But the local elites are not going to go all the way down to lowland Mesopotamia. You need to have some sort of intermediary, but your point is very well taken. Why do it yourself when the locals are already doing it and all you need to do is co-opt them to make sure that, as Mitchell said, it comes in your direction rather than your competitors'.

Barbara Helwing: There are several points that I am thinking about. Since my very first talk to an academic audience, I have argued against the "Uruk expansion", it's a big topic that has been discussed a lot elsewhere. However, one point I want to raise is that I think that we tend to think that there is Uruk, or whatever it is around Uruk, forcing something from the people outside – in a way it is a push situation. But I think maybe we have to turn around the perspective and think there is nothing that people want to learn from there, but that they go, they see, and they take it home as an idea. If you take a diachronic view from, say, the end of the *'Ubaid* period, where you see an increase in competition between growing centres, such as in northern Syria – we have this at Brak, and Hamoukar is another example. So just saying "competition" is of course imprecise, but pushing this further would mean that we have to consider issues like warfare in this whole process. I think we are generally almost against militaristic scenarios, but we have all these seals with rows of captives, and we talk about slaves. So what about, let's say forceful population accumulations for a certain period. People who are displaced and working for other people. And then maybe we see some people finally going back and taking some ideas with them. For example when we are in a diaspora, and working in Iran, we are not able to drink a beer in the evenings. We might then go and take the *ghaliyun* (water pipe), and after two months of this habit we go home, and we bring the *ghaliyun* home. We wouldn't necessarily even use it, but this is just an example of the type of thing that could have happened. Also, except for administration that is forcing things on people, I think

there are many more levels that we have to consider and we have avoided some big aspects.

Susan Pollock: If I could just add one thing to that, I think we also have to remember as we are talking about administration, administrative systems, and texts, which we certainly know for parts of northern Mesopotamia now, whatever we are going to call this – and I am not fond of the "Uruk expansion" either – but this goes back well before *Late Uruk* at this point. It goes back to something *Middle Urukian* long before we have writing, so we can't think of these things as going totally hand in hand.

Roger Matthews: Also as a general point, the past 30 years or so have shown just how varied and different these relationships are between different parts of the Middle East in the second half of the fourth millennium, and that is extremely exciting and interesting. Things are very specific, region by region. But what is also striking and I think needs more study, is the way that this process collapses in different parts of the Middle East at different paces and in different trajectories. Iran has a very specific trajectory of its own as things are collapsing. It clearly sheds some material cultural attributes but it retains others, and it retains structures that transcend changes in scripts and other attributes uniquely in regions of the ancient Near East. So that is a really striking pattern: continuity of structures and activities in the face of change in material culture attributes.

Susan Pollock: And also even that we talk about the fact that something is collapsing, which I know Hans Nissen always rejects: he says that if we look at this from the point of view of Uruk, nothing is collapsing. That this is also a part of the perspective that we take on this whole phenomenon at the moment. First we see it as a collapse of something.

Salaam al-Kuntar: I might say something about the exchange partnership. If it's like the whole *Uruk* stuff, from the start they had an exchange partnership with the north. Northern Mesopotamia also had exchange partnerships, maybe with Anatolia before the southerners even came. So how homogeneous were these exchange relations? Were all the southerners one part and the northerners another, or was there some northern/southern partnership, in the north of course? How does that work?

Guillermo Algaze: Differently. In some places they took over lock, stock and barrel – Habuba for example. Other places there may have been a few people there: Hacınebi and maybe Godin but it's not clear there. So essentially the mode of interaction will depend on the nature of the pre-existing societies. The more complex the pre-existing society, the more it will be done through intermediaries. The less complex, the more it will be done by something that could be called an implantation. But your point is very well taken. I have no idea whether there were *Uruk* people sitting at Godin. There is no question in my mind that there is a tremendous amount of contact. But how the contact is mediated, I don't know. Are there *Uruk* people at Hassek (Huyuk)? I have no idea. Are there *Uruk* people at Habuba? – there I would say of course. So clearly there is an expansion. We can argue about the specific sites, we can argue about the nature of the expansion in specific areas: the degree of peripheral agency and all of that will vary – there is a tremendous degree of variability. But the system does have some hierarchy. You don't see a material culture from the north sitting in Uruk. You see material culture from southern Mesopotamia sitting in various configurations across the north.

Barbara Helwing: That is exactly the point where I would like to, instead of having this push idea, to have a pull factor.

Guillermo Algaze: And the pull is the more complex. The more indigenous trade that existed, the more complex the society that handled the trade, the more likely it is that they will head specifically in that direction. If there is such a thing as an "Uruk expansion", it probably went in the direction of those that already controlled the trade and those that were already, to some degree, complex. And in some cases they may have taken them over by violence. In others they simply managed to redirect that trade or some portion of that trade depending on the nature of the societies that existed. But there is a pull factor. There is a very important pull factor.

Mitchell Rothman: Why wouldn't you say at the end of the process that it was simply the locals taking over the system before the collapse? It is therefore not a collapse. As much metal, more metal, came into Mesopotamia after the fourth millennium BC than before it.

Guillermo Algaze: It is not an issue of how much trade flows; it is an issue of who controls the trade and the terms of the trade.

Mitchell Rothman: Well, it is not a collapse if the same partners simply . . .

Guillermo Algaze: No, of course it is not. Trade does not collapse as specific *Uruk* sites withdraw.

Mitchell Rothman: Yes, but that is not a collapse of the system. It is a collapse of certain . . .

Guillermo Algaze: Well, it is the collapse of the *Uruk* implantation system. It is not a collapse of trade at all.

Lloyd Weeks: I don't know if I really want to say this. I'm going to regret it afterwards, but is there anything that we draw, any structural parallels to be drawn, from the *Uruk* expansion and the *'Ubaid* expansion which happened 1000 years before that?

Barbara Helwing: Is there an *'Ubaid* expansion?

Lloyd Weeks: Well, there was a question mark after that in the title of a recent book I believe (Carter and Phillip 2010), but it's not necessarily the fourth millennium where we see a wide spread of material culture over a very large and otherwise culturally separate part of the Middle East.

Mitchell Rothman: Go to the *Neolithic*.

Lloyd Weeks: Well, exactly. Should we talk about periods where this doesn't happen as strange rather than where it does happen as unusual? I think I am not really helping the debate at all by raising that point because it is too big an issue, but there are similarities to be drawn between those two processes.

Mitchell Rothman: I think that the difference is that in the fourth millennium, there is a different kind of pattern. It is not simply cultural contact. There has been cultural contact since the *Palaeolithic*. The question is the nature of it, the extent of it, and the terms of it. And I think what Guillermo's whole theory was about is the nature of this contact; yes, there was certainly cultural interchange during the *'Ubaid* although it is looking less and less like a controlled thing, and more like a spread of technology, which we are assuming means something that maybe it doesn't.

Lloyd Weeks: But isn't that what we are arguing now in the *Uruk* controlled situation? Or is it something more than . . .

Mitchell Rothman: Well, we are. The basic question is that there is something fundamental that is happening in the fourth millennium than hadn't happened before. And then it would change afterwards as well. So what is the nature? Yes, it pays to look at the *'Ubaid* almost as a contrast rather than a simple repetition. Is it just difference in scale or is it difference in kind? If it is not difference in kind than we are wasting a lot of time.

David Wengrow: We've forgotten about Iran.

Massimo Vidale: For the Indus civilisation, when we go to the last century of the third millennium BC we have a similar situation. We have colonies of people in Gujarat for example and you have the Indus people living in separate compounds, in walled compounds. And I think that there was an attempt to control the local resources because we see stockpiles of stones, stockpiles of shells. We have also the capability of control and the know-how of craft production. We have kilns for faience that you find within the compounds where the Indus people were living and separating themselves from the local population, which seems to use a different type of ceramics and eat different food. This is clearly being seen at sites like Bagasra and so on. So my question to you – I am not really aware of the details of this "Uruk expansion" problem – but do you have anything comparable, which really speaks of the control of the resources as we have from the Indus civilisation at the end of the late third millennium BC?

Mitchell Rothman: That is basically Guillermo's argument.

Guillermo Algaze: Well, the evidence for control is entirely indirect. Initially, I was wondering why these sites were in non-random positions, why they were located near junctures of communication? That implied indirectly some attempt to, I don't know if control is the right word, but redirect or tap into trade; but the bottom line is, we have no evidence. That is to say there is no way of quantifying the influx of materials into the south. *Uruk* sites have not been excavated in that manner. For that matter, there are assumptions about what trade items might have been given in return. Later on it was textiles, so why not say it is textiles in the fourth millennium BC? Is there evidence for that? It is all indirect. These sites are not in a small remote valley of Iran, they are usually in valleys that are across major arteries of communication. This is the same with their positions along rivers in northern Mesopotamia. And from location one can infer motivation, but there is no real proof.

Massimo Vidale: There is no real proof for the trade towards the location of the resources. That's what came up in discussion before, it is automatically . . .

Guillermo Algaze: Again, you only go to the resource areas when you have to exploit them yourself. That is very expensive. Ideally, you just settle at a strategic location and let the locals come and trade with you. That is the most efficient way of doing things.

Massimo Vidale: Well, the Indus people did it differently. They really went near the resources, the strategic points where they could extract the shell . . .

Guillermo Algaze: Again, that just means that the locals were not well-organised enough to extract those resources.

Massimo Vidale: It is a possibility.

Guillermo Algaze: So, again, the strategy of contact will depend directly on the nature of the pre-existing society.

Massimo Vidale: I agree.

Guillermo Algaze: But there are some strategies that complex societies follow – you can maximise efficiency by getting the locals to cooperate as opposed to actually having to impose your will on them, which is expensive. If you have to send in the army, if you have to send in the miners, you've already lost.

Massimo Vidale: You could use ideology, not necessarily the army . . .

Guillermo Algaze: Yes.

Massimo Vidale: Ideology would be more efficient.

Guillermo Algaze: Absolutely. Why would the locals want to deal with you? If you have something that they think they want, and that could be, I don't know, that you are closer to the gods, or your gods are more powerful.

Massimo Vidale: You dress in blue for example.

David Wengrow: On the Harappan comparison – although they are not contemporaneous I think it is very instructive for the *Uruk* and also with regard to what might be different with Iran. Daniel Miller made this interesting observation in 1985 I think, about the Harappan expansion and about the extent to which material culture becomes standardised, even from the smallest site to Mohenjo Daro. Even down to the exact measurements.

Massimo Vidale: The statement about homogeneity is a bit over-simplified.

David Wengrow: Well, it was 1985.

Massimo Vidale: Now we know there was a lot of variation.

David Wengrow: OK, but in the scheme of things it's a standardised world compared to what came before and after. And I think we have seen similar arguments here about mud-brick sizes from Tepe Yahya and Habuba Kabira. And again it seems to me that Iran is interestingly different in this respect. We don't seem to be seeing – at least in ceramics – the same kind of rigid levelling out and standardising of material relationships. I'm not quite sure what that implies, but it must imply something.

Guillermo Algaze: Where in Iran? Because in Susiana you do, but up in the highlands you don't.

David Wengrow: I'm sorry. I'm talking now about the *Proto-Elamite* network.

Guillermo Algaze: Yes, in the highlands you don't and that tells you something about how many people are in contact.

David Wengrow: I'm sure it is to do with scale.

Guillermo Algaze: . . . and the strategy of contact.

Jacob Dahl: There is certainly standardisation going on during this period, we see it in the seals, used across the entire area where *Proto-Elamite* is used, the lack of depictions of humans, or even humans depicted by animals, and so forth.

David Wengrow: Standardisation, but it doesn't seem to be the same as what we are talking about with Harappa or Uruk, where it's standardisation and a kind of – what is the right word? – a sort of sparseness, an emptying out of any kind of visual expression.

Cameron Petrie: Before we end, I just wanted to bring up one last thing, and this is drawing on what Holly was saying – this, in a way, bifurcation that seems to be happening in *Acropole 17*. And it strikes me that there is something about Iran, there is something about Susa. We have been talking about Uruk, and are we actually making a mistake by talking about Susa and Uruk together? I know yesterday we talked very clearly, and it is quite obvious that we have massive urbanism in southern Mesopotamia at a number of sites, and that what happens in Iran is different. One of the things that came out today is that there were very explicit connections between the glyptic at Susa and the glyptic at Godin, for example. I wonder, should we think of Godin being a Mesopotamia thing or should we think about it being a Khuzestan thing, or is there no difference?

Holly Pittman: Well, that is one of the questions I'm investigating.

Cameron Petrie: The reason I'm asking that question is, I think one of things about the *Uruk* debate that is sometimes dropped off is the *Proto-Elamite* bit that comes immediately after it and the structure of that, which made use of the same landscape.

Holly Pittman: Which is always there, somehow, I mean at least by *Acropole I.17*, it is there. If Guillermo is right that we've got this overlay somehow by *17*, that overlay is beginning to break down…

John Alden: You're speaking exclusively of Susa?

Holly Pittman: Yes.

John Alden: OK. You're not making a statement about the *Proto-Elamite*?

Holly Pittman: No, no, no. But I think another thing we need to think about is the *Proto-Elamite* parallel phenomenon. Is it an expansion that is coming out? I mean, we are not even talking about the *Proto-Elamite*, I guess we don't want to go into the third millennium BC.

Cameron Petrie: I don't mind! But I don't think the *Proto-Elamite* is third-millennium. It doesn't have to be.

Holly Pittman: Does it follow the same form and that's why the writing system is so similar throughout? Or do we have the development of writing at Yahya, at Malyan, at Sofalin all independently – obviously not?

Cameron Petrie: No.

Holly Pittman: Right.

Jacob Dahl: I think there can be little doubt that the system was invented at Susa, for a number of reasons such as complexity of texts, size of the recorded administration and so on.

Holly Pittman: And people are going out, scribes are going out. Or are scribes training people? How are they transmitting such a coherent system?

Lloyd Weeks: How do you learn to write? How long does it take?

Jacob Dahl: You sit next to your brother when you are a child, it is apprentice-knowledge.

Lloyd Weeks: Well, if you are in Godin your older brother is probably not at Susa and if he is, then that is the interesting thing about systems…

Jacob Dahl: Godin really is pre-writing. I think we have to separate pre-writing, proto-writing, and writing. Pre-writing is the counters, the bullae, the seals – and all kinds of other things that you would help you store information. Maybe proto-writing starts with the texts that have one non-numerical sign. Godin has proto-writing, it has pre-writing tools of a most elaborate kind. However, it is still a long way from "real" writing, like *Proto-Elamite*.

Jenny Marshall: Not everyone is writing so you wouldn't necessarily learn it from your brother. It was presumably almost like a craft or a trade, I would imagine, where you would be apprenticed into it.

Jacob Dahl: Yes, we don't know it from this period but we know it from other periods – your father is a scribe, therefore you are a scribe, so somebody must have moved I would guess.

Cameron Petrie: So according to the evidence that Guillermo brought up before, these signs seen at three sites: are they names, are they lineages? At the least they are showing connectivity.

Jacob Dahl: Sure, very close.

Cameron Petrie: So somebody has got to be moving.

Guillermo Algaze: Two models – they are not necessarily mutually exclusive, they could both coexist. Let's, for the sake of argument, call one the "Uruk expansion model", the colonial, entirely hierarchical – in Barbara's terms it would be called the "push" model. There is the other model, it is the "pull" model, the Hamoukar model. Essentially, you have a bunch of indigenous societies that compete against each other, share some sort of general ideology, iconography, and are in constant contact with each other, but are entirely independent and there is no control. These models are not mutually exclusive. Reality is very complex.

Susan Pollock: We also have a tendency to be talking about these big chunks of either cities or regions or whatever but of course, as a number of people have pointed out, there are a lot of people with a variety of different interests. So when we talk about people moving or people wanting things from other places, I think we have to start working towards also being more specific about these groups of people and accept that there is going to be internal conflicts of interest within places like Susa, and Uruk, and Godin, and so on.

Mitchell Rothman: I also think we need to look at different possibilities for the way mobility works. I've been talking to Tony Sagona for a long time about the Trans-Caucasus and the presence of pastoral nomads. We are both coming to the conclusion that we are not talking about pastoral nomads and we are not talking about pastoral farmers, we are talking about some of their modality. My best analogy is the Romani of Europe. They actually move as clans. They maintain their own identity. They have their own kinship structures. And they have specialities – they move into communities and have special technical knowledge.

Salaam al-Kuntar: That is what happened with the Assyrian invasion, they moved the entire clan, families, everything. It never was individuals.

Mitchell Rothman: Right, and so there are other modalities as well of how people move, when they move, and the size of the units that move. To me, what I was hearing this morning about these craftsmen sort of walking around, I thought "oh great, this guy from Godin is going to walk into Uruk and say 'hey, can I make some pots'?" – this struck me as a little scary and implausible. But if you come in as a group, and I don't mean necessarily big, we are just talking about 50 to 100 people, you come in as a group and ask to settle and start this negotiation over what you have that we want, what we have that you want. That is a whole different model of how this might work without, necessarily, pastoral nomads who tend to stay in the same place. They tend not to move as a mass to a whole new place. They tend to drive within their own territory because they move within it but they tend to maintain themselves. The Bakhtiari don't say "we are going to become something else. We are just going to move ourselves as a whole". That is not how they work. So nomads might be a bad model for what we are talking about.

Roger Matthews: If you look historically, one of the great impetuses for moving is actually religion, and the gods actually tell people they have to move or their prophets tell people that they have to move. Of course we can't really get at this in previous periods, but I think it is something that we should think about. One could come up with a religiously driven interpretation for Godin Tepe and pretty much any site that you care to name. Pilgrims, or the drive to obtain materials that must be used in constructing cult statues, for example, is interesting. There is an impetus and one can of course say there is an ideology that goes with it that hides or transmutes all sorts of power relations. These are things that are very, very hard to get at, but if we look for historical analogies of that kind . . .

Mitchell Rothman: Well, to some degree. But let us say that the idea of ideological takeover is the case. My god is more powerful than your god. Wouldn't you expect to see all the features of religion in the place that is being influenced, adopted? And that is certainly what happened in the European model with the spread of Christianity. Yes, my god is stronger and by the way I am going to kill you anyway. But then you saw churches, you didn't see them being "I'm so impressed with you Christians and therefore I am going to stay a pagan". No, they actually adopt. So shouldn't we see the development – if it's ideological or religious – the adoption of southern Mesopotamian temples, infrastructure, statuary? If that is what they are doing there would be signs.

Guillermo Algaze: Don't forget that the lord of Aratta had a temple to Inanna.

Mitchell Rothman: It is not that it is invisible, because we do have signs of religion. And if that is the means by which you are co-opting people, or converting them, they should be adopting it.

Roger Matthews: I am not sure the evidence speaks either way on that point.

Mitchell Rothman: Well it could be, but you should see adoption of those things.

Holly Pittman: They may not actually have to explain why they want to be up there. The motive is to get special woods for the arms of the god, but they are not intending to proselytise. They just want to get this special wood that they were told they needed to get. So they go and install themselves in a place. That could work that way.

Guillermo Algaze: And we have different groups and different motives. Half of the conquistadores wanted to loot and the other half wanted to save souls, and they did both.

References

Amiet, P. 1979. "Archaeological discontinuity and ethnicity duality in Elam", *Antiquity* 53: 195–204.

Carter, R. A and Philip, G. eds 2010. *Beyond the 'Ubaid, Transformation and Integration in the Late Prehistoric Societies of the Middle East*, Studies in Ancient Oriental Civilization Series, Oriental Institute, University of Chicago, Chicago.

SUMMATION AND DISCUSSION LED BY CAMERON PETRIE

Cameron Petrie: At the outset I was interested in exploring a range of issues, and in some respects the sessions were arranged to reflect these themes, but there was variation in scope and approach. We had discussions on elements of landscape and the environment, and many other papers also discussed these issues. We explored ideas of local development and also the nature of regional diversity in Iran. The nature of long-range interactions and the unspoken component, that is the idea of trade, is very critical. There is an aspect of technology but this needs to be thought of in terms of technology, style, and perhaps put into the context of the phrase that Lloyd (Weeks) mentioned, this idea of an age of experimentation.

Lloyd Weeks: I stole it from Barbara (Helwing).

Cameron Petrie: That's OK, it's a time-honoured tradition. I would also like us to use this session to talk about issues of chronology and review the various explanatory models. At the beginning I highlighted the geographical variety of Iran and its relationship to its surrounding areas. I think this was something that has come out in many papers. One of the things that I was quite interested to see, for example – and I also highlighted these geographical regions and drew blobs on the map and actually drew a "happy little blob" around Tepe Hissar, not quite knowing what that would do – it was very nice to see that Chris (Thornton) had two nice bars on the map which suggested there was some type of socio-cultural boundary at various periods and times. I would like us to discuss that element further. This idea of routes and pathways and connectivity I think is going to underlie a lot of what we discuss. We've actually talked quite a bit about the *Proto-Elamite* phenomenon in terms of evidence, but we haven't necessarily talked about it in terms of explanations and models, and I think we probably need to think a little bit about what's going on there. That has the potential to work in both the local and long range, and other sorts of elements as well. We had several papers that dealt with metal exploitation, metal technology, and metallurgical provinces. Barbara's distribution map showed the distribution of certain categories of cast axes, which appear to have been produced on the Central Plateau. So this fits into the idea of technologies, style, and trade redistribution.

There has been quite a bit of discussion about ceramic technologies and ceramic production. Also the theme that struck me – being someone who is very interested in this – is the massive amount of variety and the different types of technological developments that seem to be taking place in different areas and how these are shared and not shared. For example, the effective disappearance of decoration during the *Lapui* period, or between the *Bakun* and the *Lapui*. We see a similar yet distinct phenomenon on the Susa plain as well. Perhaps the discussion of models of interaction can frame how we discuss things, or perhaps general issues of trajectories in contact, interaction, and communication.

We might also consider the possibility that there was some sort of separation between Susa and lowland Mesopotamia, and whether or not that's actually real. Before the conference I was happily drawing nice little lines indicating connections across the Plateau and all the way to Baluchistan, and I think it is very reassuring to see that we should be thinking about the arrows going in both directions. One thing that is very important not to forget is that we have a trajectory coming across the southern Plateau from east to west and also connections up into Central Asia.

Christopher Thornton: Cameron, can I just throw in there the possibility of the sea route, the costal route? Especially when you talk about Baluchistan/Makran. I just find it difficult to believe that they were hiking over Baluchistan.

Cameron Petrie: Certainly. I did want to point out that, despite what we have been able to cover in the last two and a half days, we lack coverage of certain things. We lack coverage of the costal evidence because this coast has not been surveyed properly. We lack information about Shahr-i Sokhta because no one has been here talking about it. Due to some mis-communication we don't have any papers about Central Asia. I wasn't able to get in contact with some of the French people soon enough, and Alan LeBrun wasn't able to come to talk about the excavations at Susa.

While I would like for us to talk about issues as far as we can, I am also going to pursue other people to fill in some of these gaps as best we can so that the resulting "volume" that we will hopefully end up with will get us somewhere.

I have written out a list of themes that we can talk about, some of which are themes that relate very much to what I initially put forward, and I've added manifestations of trade which is related very much to long-range interactions, though I felt that it was worthwhile making a differentiation. I call them parameters, and that is not necessarily the right word, but I think there are a number of different issues and factors that we need to consider – and these were brought up by Guillermo – various issues which he outlined in his summation, and also things Susan and others brought up in their comments.

There is very much an issue of time generally; not just chronology, but also this issue of deep time and long-range connectivity. I think it is all too easy to forget the fact that people have been moving around back and forth across the Iranian Plateau for millennia before the fourth millennium, and I think that we are talking about long-term interactive relationships.

And we've got issues of scale both in space and in time which I think are important. Understanding the nature of the interaction that is happening, particularly the idea of transmission. What things are transmitted, what things aren't transmitted, what these patterns might mean – issues of power, control, and negotiation. How these relationships were manifested, whether we see the *Uruk expansion* or not, and how these processes were negotiated with specific regions and areas, specific populations in certain areas. And also something that Barbara commented on quite specifically: where we might often have the relatively peaceful arrival of a group from outside, there should also be consideration of the possibility for aggressive reaction to this. The evidence for violence and conflict is something we do need to consider.

And then perhaps lastly, as this is maybe something that is underlying everything, we need to remember that we are dealing with flawed data sets in many respects, so we need to think about what we need to do to try and resolve those issues. I don't want to talk too much more, and I'm not wedded to the idea of following these themes in order, but maybe we can start with issues of environment and landscape because they have underpinned a lot of things that we are dealing with. Maybe if some of the people who presented papers on the themes could offer reflections they might have had on the basis of other papers and the like and that will get us started. Would anyone like to make any comments? Matthew, I'm not deliberately looking at you . . .

Matthew Jones: I can make a couple of comments. To start with a more general comment, we could think about why people were or were not moving – I'm not sure anyone actually mentioned climate or environment as reasons why people actually moved. This could actually be either a push or a pull factor, and this is something we have to think about. Clearly we don't have the data or the spatial data coverage to answer that, but it is something that is testable if we can get the data. Maybe some of those other possibilities are less testable. This spatial coverage should not just be lateral but also vertical. One of the things that we have tried to do in Mamasani is get climate records from different elevations because these climate changes are not necessarily just spatial, they can be vertical, and what we need to do is look at change in high altitude as well as low altitude at a site, because this is clearly something that, for people moving up and down, would have an impact.

My second major point is half a plea as well. It's the idea of trying to use the archaeological sites themselves as a palaeoclimate archive and I think there is a lot of information that people get that can be used in a palaeoenvironmental way or a palaeoclimatic way that maybe isn't used in that way at the moment. There is a very nice paper that was published last year based in Syria using the delta ^{13}C values from the radiocarbon dates as a palaeoenvironmental proxy. We have some really nice long stratigraphically coherent sets of radiocarbon dates from quite a few sites now and if we can get the delta ^{13}C data we can start to look at trends. This is one thing I would like to work on in the future. Also things like snail shells and the like that are often found on sites. I know that we have them in Mamasani, and I know that other people have them, but they haven't actually been mentioned. We find them living in the environment today, we know where they are living, we can do geochemistry and test them and they can be used as a palaeoclimatic archive.

Mitchell Rothman: And there are other animals too. Gerbils, it turns out, are very sensitive to wetness and humidity.

Matthew Jones: It is not just the species changes, but what we can do with them with some of the more destructive analyses, focusing on the teeth and isotope…

Henry Wright: What can you do with freshwater bivalves? We save those more frequently than snails.

Matthew Jones: If we can find them – even if we can't – but especially if we find them living today, we do isotope and chemistry analysis on where they are living today, we compare that to the signatures from ancient samples and if the water has changed, if the climate has changed the waters they are living in, that will be picked up. If they are big enough you can look at seasonality like you can in teeth and all these kinds of things, so they can give you quite a lot.

Henry Wright: I am told by an oncologist that because of pollution, of herbicide and pesticide use, that the molluscan fauna of the entire Euphrates system has been reduced by about 80%. It is down to 20% of what it was in the 1950s.

Matthew Jones: I can imagine.

Henry Wright: That just means that there are a lot of proxies, a lot of control back-up studies that cannot be done.

Matthew Jones: But some can be done. I mean the ones. . .all the snails that we find in Mamasani on the site, for example. There is a very limited species distribution and we found the same species living in the area today.

Henry Wright: At Mamasani you probably don't have this chemical pollution problem.

Matthew Jones: But I would still say that using the snails you can look at trends and at variability and even if you don't, you might find the same species somewhere else. We use what we have. And they are always taken; they are always put away in the box.

Henry Wright: That is the point, I have tons.

Matthew Jones: They can be used and we have the material.

Vanessa Haevaert: I've got another question. You've got all those settlement distribution maps. I had the same idea about the need to integrate the environmental factors. Whenever you have an interrelationship with the past environment and you are producing distribution maps of settlements. For example, in your area you have this big fan and under the fan you are going to be losing settlements.

Cameron Petrie: Definitely.

Vanessa Heyvaert: So you start to compare…you've lost one settlement on one side over there. In the next period you only have five settlements, so you should also take into account the environmental factors. It is something that was missing here during this workshop. And also I was missing the influence of humans on the environment and the opposite, the influence of the environment on humans, so the interactions between both is something that was not focused on during this workshop. I think it is quite important. It is not only environment to humans but also humans to environment.

I know it is a big job and you will say we do not have the data to have an idea about past environments with the settlement patterns, but most of you use GIS and you use remote-sensing images, so you can easily start to map all the different palaeo-channels for example. Then you have already acquired an idea of which kind of channels you had in the past. You have already acquired a small idea about what happens. And then on a second level you can basically re-evaluate archaeological sites. Take some geomorphologists who can go every year, let them have a look around.

Cameron Petrie: We only managed to get one geomorphologist into the field for about eight days and that was all.

Vanessa Heyvaert: It needs to be for six weeks or something.

Cameron Petrie: I agree with your point. I thought Tony Wilkinson dealt with a lot of these issues. It was a very broad overarching paper, focusing on Susiana and mentioning things in the Kur River Basin. John Alden covered a lot about the settlement dynamics of the Kur River Basin, but wasn't necessarily incorporating the geomorphological evidence, so there wasn't the sort of integration you are talking about. There has been quite a lot of discussion about the relationship between environmental degradation and settlement distribution and things in the Kur

River Basin. But that's right, we have not covered it explicitly.

Vanessa Heyvaert: For Mesopotamia there are some very nice examples where some major sites were abandoned because of a shift in the river. So it is very important to start taking such things into account, and also historical sources, tablets, texts from tablets, we've got to take into account everything. It's not only geology, it's not only the archaeological excavation, but everything around it.

Cameron Petrie: Karl Lamberg-Karlovsky was going to talk about the landscape of Daulatabad and other things and I think this would have been very interesting because this is a unique landscape from the fifth and fourth millennia.

Massimo Vidale: In Seistan lots of things are open now. The Iranians are surveying and they found around 1600 sites from the prehistoric and historic periods. It still remains a mystery why settlement started there in the late fourth millennium BC. We don't have anything before, and it is such a favourable region for agriculture. All the possible shifts of rivers should be reinvestigated with a new methodology, and so on.

Cameron Petrie: Absolutely.

Massimo Vidale: It is an incredible laboratory for any sort of hypothesis given the preservation of botanical and other types of material, so we are really waiting for something to happen there.

Cameron Petrie: While the environment is one very important parameter to consider, we are generally faced with limitations and there is a lot that can be done with GIS and Google Earth for example. Henry has been playing with Google Earth.

Massimo Vidale: We really have to intensify the collaboration with Iranians because they are working a lot, they have a lot of young people who come here and get new ideas and go back to Iran. Without this type of input we will always have separated boxes, here and there.

Cameron Petrie: Yes, I agree. Eta did you want to say something?

Margareta Tengberg: Yes, on the environmental impact. That is often very important and we don't know very much about those areas, even though it is almost certain that in the fourth millennium the societies probably had quite a big impact on the environment. And, in fact, from an archaeobotanical point of view, for example, you can see that there is a big difference between the fourth millennium and now, of course, but you can see the progressive impact on the environment only when you have a quantity of data and you can measure, and that is very rare. Up till now we have just had a few sites where we have counts and systematic sampling and such things. And it is absolutely necessary to measure and even to detect the said data: the impact on the environment. Which is there from woodcutting, herding, and also irrigation practices and such things, which are probably very important. And what Vanessa talked about also, the changing of river courses, which was apparently often human-induced, even in older periods.

Vanessa Heyvaert: It is clear for northern Mesopotamia and also for the south, avulsion has been the main force in the shift of the Tigris and Euphrates. People have started to study it based on historical and older texts, and then it got into the geological community and it seems that avulsion is one of the major processes. If you look at the Karun Basin there must have been a lot of shifts and changes of watercourses. The area is very dynamic.

Cameron Petrie: I think that probably the whole of the Zagros was as well, there must be so many dynamic processes operating. It is pretty easy for me to draw lines on the map that show modern passes, but some of these passes may not have existed 7000 or 5000 years ago.

Anonymous: Walking around the lower Khuzestan plain, it looks like it is a very stable plain, nothing is happening, you can't see anything. But in the past it was very dynamic, it's possible when you are on your site and you think OK, this is a very nice stable environment, people must have liked to live here, but in the fourth millennium if may have been a very dynamic and difficult environment.

Massimo Vidale: You have seen how strong the impact on the river in Fars was, would that type of exploitation of an acid erosion facilitate changes in the belts of the river?

Margareta Tengberg: Yes because it is binding the sediment. Yes, it is probably an indicator.

Vanessa Heyvaert: You've got it also in Rhineland in the Netherlands, a correlation between woodcutting and the shifting of rivers.

Margareta Tengberg: On the subsistence economies, especially from the bioarchaeological data, in fact what strikes me after listening to all the different presentations is that the data both Marjan and I have from archaeozoology and archaeobotany are quite homogeneous. We see barley and wheat for the archaeobotany and caprini for the archaeozoology. So the subsistence economies are very homogeneous for big areas and also long periods, and we don't have these clear period limits at all. There are some specific characteristics for this period compared to the *Neolithic* and then compared to the *Bronze Age*, but there is no clear limit in the cultural periods. We are working now in the path of time, you might say, and we can't see. Also it is perhaps more difficult

to see exchanges which are more easily seen in the material culture. The subsistence economy is much more conservative and much more homogeneous and cross-cultural, it doesn't seem to be very linked to culture, at least the species that are used. And then the precise practices are probably different between the different cultures, which we don't know very well yet because we haven't studied these things in detail. We need many more studies. So what is very positive is that more and more specialists – and Iranian specialists – are training in this discipline so there will be a multiplication of studies.

Christopher Thornton: Quick question. Your comment about the wheat and barley and the caprines, is this a pan-Middle Eastern and South Asian thing? I mean, does it go all the way to the Indus and the Mediterranean?

Margareta Tengberg: It is a bit different…

Massimo Vidale: There is an emphasis on bovines in the Indus.

Christopher Thornton: Can you hypothesise about boundaries for this homogeneous behaviour?

Margareta Tengberg: What you can say is that wheat and barley is common across the whole world, but there are different species in different regions – small differences – but I think there are some quite big differences that we have problems characterising right now. It is the difference in varieties in cultivars. You can see it in the different morphotypes, special types of cereals in one area, and it is not really determined morphologically, and yet it should be possible to be more precise on the variability.

Henry Wright: I have a question. Archaeozoologists have made some progress with determining trade in animals, animals coming up and down with nomads and so on, using trace elements. Early studies by Zeder weren't really followed up. Then recent work with stable isotopes we have heard about from Marjan and that seems to be doable. The problem is getting the reference samples that can best be done by local people. But I heard a rumour that Gordon Hillman was trying to do this with grains, that he was trying to take carbonised grains and find trace elements that indicated what was being traded around different parts of Anatolia. Not Gordon, but his students were working on it. And I never heard any results from this. This was about five years ago. You've not heard of this?

Margareta Tengberg: No, not at all.

Henry Wright: Do you think it is insane?

Margareta Tengberg: Probably not! They have started using isotopes, but more to detect environmental degradations. That could be very interesting in this area on cereals for example, on irrigation, on ecological conditions and such. And this is also something that hasn't been done at all in these areas.

Henry Wright: I have a comment for just about everyone here, Mitchell don't go away quite yet. In the American south-west, the problem is recognised that the relationship between farmers and the environment is on an annual basis and we have to do something about the alternation of wet and dry years. Whether they are three-year droughts or five-year droughts and it can be done with tree rings. The south-west of the US has the oldest developed tree ring sequence in the world. We have the beginning of a tree ring sequence now for parts of Anatolia thanks to Arslan Tepe. And I think I am told by the tree ring people and the climatologists that once we get it going for Anatolia it will extend right across Iran. And that these bad years and wet years and dry years may quite highly correlate across this vast region, but we have to bring them the wood. So, Mitchell, you some wood at one of those houses in Godin.

Mitchell Rothman: We did, and we went through everything, everything, but unfortunately they weren't thinking about any of that stuff and they let it all crumble. The biggest piece we have is like that and it wasn't cross-sectional. So had there been anything, believe me we would have done something.

Henry Wright: Ring analysis will work with tiny pieces of stuff, if you've got juniper or something like that.

Mitchell Rothman: I had Naomi (Miller) look at it and she didn't think there was.

Henry Wright: Well.

Wendy Matthews: I just wanted to say that at the ICAR Symposium in December, dendrochronology and tree rings were employed as one of the key areas that many Iranians are looking to expand, so it's possible that it will come on in the future.

Barbara Helwing: These are people working on dendrochronology in Iran, they are not archaeologists, they are in the Kharaj geology department. And they are more into just studying climate events, they are not concerned with cultural history at all.

Margareta Tengberg: The problem on the archaeological site is that you always have almost very small fragments and you don't have enough tree rings to fit it in the reference sequence. They recommend at least 40 layers.

Wendy Matthews: 50.

Margareta Tengberg: 40/50.

Barbara Helwing: And not being poplar or anything like that, it is what people would use for building.

Margareta Tengberg: Poplar is fast-growing. There is another problem – specific for the south-east for example, for the southern regions. They are not temperate. I mean the Halil Rud, the Makran and southern Khuzistan – there are no clearings. It is difficult.

Matthew Jones: There might have been once upon a time. We don't know throughout the south. Today there is no permanent water south of where we are working – from Mamasani towards the areas of Siraf – but in the past, I am sure that these were permanent bodies.

Margareta Tengberg: But for the periods we are discussing, I mean the second half of the Holocene, we have the same sort of subtropical climate as we have today.

Matthew Jones: We are almost in a transition in the fourth millennium. Not far before that but maybe into the fourth millennium.

Margareta Tengberg: Yes. I suppose we had acacia in some places – and there are subtropical species in the charcoal. So the climate was not that different, according to the charcoal.

Vanessa Heyvaert: To change the topic completely towards the Mesopotamian area. Are you doing provenance studies on your sherds?

Cameron Petrie: In Mesopotamia?

Vanessa Heyvaert: Are you analysing which product from which kinds of clays, and where they were excavated?

Henry Wright: There was a vast project run by Roman Mansura Minders who had done more than 10,000 thin sections of referencing in lower Mesopotamia. She was the one that was able to identify the *Jemdat Nasr* pottery from Abu Dhabi as being specifically from the Babylon Kish area. Because you could break up parts of Mesopotamia but not specific sites.

Massimo Vidale: Sophie Méry's done a lot of work with that in Oman, so she is quite aware. Rita Wright and Jim Blackman are sitting on quite a lot of information.

Christopher Thornton: What happened to all the data or all her thin sections?

Henry Wright: I believe she has it in Oxford. I'm not sure.

Massimo Vidale: So there was a lot of work going on, but it was never coordinated.

Christopher Thornton: There is a lot of recent stuff that came out of northern Mesopotamia. Chicago had two people, Ph.D.s, on cooking and ceramics specifically. They had one that was looking at cooking wares and what was getting traded and not fine wares. Fine wares were produced locally but cooking wares were not, because it was so technologically difficult to get really good cooking wares, those were being traded because they were specialised.

Cameron Petrie: Well, we just nicely segued from environment into pottery! I am happy to make that change, but one comment I wanted to make about the compositional analysis, for example, is that John presented some results from neutron activation. I presented some results from ICP and they are not compatible. In some respects that's because the elements that are measured are different and the techniques are different. As Massimo implied, we need much more integration in terms of the programmes that might be attempted, specifically if we are looking at bigger-picture questions. We don't necessarily need to talk about pottery too much, but it would be good to talk through the relevant ideas and then we can move on to ideas on technology.

Massimo Vidale: Can I talk about this idea of frontiers…technological frontiers? I very much liked Chris's observations and I would like to add something that I have been concerned with over the last year or so. It really does not concern the third millennium or the fourth millennium specifically, which I am working on more now. We have considered Shahr-i Sokhta, which is a very strange site. There we had a lot of terracotta cakes, which are typical Indus artefacts that are never found at other sites across the Iranian Plateau – we don't have one, we have about 40. And at Indus sites we have hundreds of these things. But they are modified according to the local technology. We have stamps and impressions in them and in Indus sites it shows that they were used in a different way. We just finished a paper that is coming out in the next issue of *Paléorient*, which is dealing with interactions between Shahr-i Sokhta and this area, and you will see how permeable this site is. Also without major trade, without having many commodities coming up and down, but a trickle of artefacts coming from the Indus region, bowls from the first part of the third millennium and the second part of the third millennium. And we might even add some production of Indus fired steatite beads with Indus technology at Shahr-i Sokhta. While at Tepe Hissar there is a totally different industry, a different technological approach to the manufacture of basically the same object: small steatite beads. So I believe we have another boundary there and this is a frontier that is very interesting. Another one…

Cameron Petrie: So let's clarify that. You are suggesting that the same types of objects are being produced but with a different technological approach so we've got similar style, different type of technology…

Massimo Vidale: Yes, it is a similar style, but made in a different way. The same as was mentioned yesterday, for the white on polychrome ceramics – in the Indus version it is made with talc and when we move to the Halil Rud civilisation it is made with a different type of rock. And we have complex firing technologies to overcome the problem of producing this material.

Cameron Petrie: But they try to produce something…

Massimo Vidale: Oh they do they same thing, you know, white on ceramics; it's not easy to get the white colour on ceramics. In the Indus area they did it with talc and then with Halil Rud they did it in a different way. So these are interesting barriers of the same type, besides metallurgy. And then another important barrier concerns the diffusion of zebu cattle, which probably started in the fifth or fourth millennium BC. I am sorry that Marjan is not here but she was mentioning that they might have identified some form of hybridisation between the Iranian cattle for the fourth millennium BC.

Cameron Petrie: Where was this? She didn't specify.

Massimo Vidale: Anyhow we have a lot of zebu iconography in south-eastern Iran so that is another very, very important aspect of change in cultural systems. So these are the frontiers that I have picked up that enter into the picture.

Cameron Petrie: There is something that I noticed from the *Neolithic* onwards – across southern Iran there appear to be periods of innovation which spread. This is specifically in ceramic production technology. And the thing that became clear is that these innovations would spread over certain distances and it wasn't necessarily all happening in one continuous movement. But it seems that in some respects technology moved, but local regional differentiation was maintained. I found that balance quite interesting. It is obviously due to some socio-cultural reasons.

Christopher Thornton: Maybe what Caldwell called the interaction sphere. That was the whole point, the shared technology or shared culture, but regional differences.

Cameron Petrie: Yes, and I think that is something that is very robust within… I just wonder if there is a relationship between the environmentally deterministic components. Is there something about the nature of the Iranian plateau that does this or is it just something else? I don't know. But it was interesting for me because I was initially focusing on the western end of the Plateau and getting as far as Tepe Yahya, but then seeing Benjamin's information about ceramic production in Baluchistan and how that was almost like the eastern end of the pattern. Pamela Vandiver proposed that on the Iranian Plateau sequential slab production spread across this massive area and was used for a long period of time.

Massimo Vidale: This is a very simple system for looking at vessels. I do not know how much I believe that. In the assemblages that Pamela was working with there was a lot of sequential slab construction, but I am really sceptical that coiling is really so rare, in fact I have personally seen a lot of evidence of coiling at least in the late *Neolithic*, so I think we should probably be ready for a more composite pattern of variation and innovation. I've been working with Fazeli with material from the Tepe Pardis excavation, and personally I think I have positive evidence of the introduction of the first wheel around 5000 BC.

Salaam al-Kuntar: When?

Massimo Vidale: 5000.

Salaam al-Kuntar: This is the fast wheel? This is very interesting because in northern Mesopotamia, it doesn't look like there is any clear evidence for the fast wheel before.

Massimo Vidale: I think we have to compare results of the same technical applications. I have seen this through X-rays, through various types of X-rays, and we probably should use X-ray imagery to discuss this, otherwise we are on personal impressions and so on. I believe in X-rays. I was told to use this technique by Pamela Vandiver and I always found that it is a very powerful technique. So probably she might disagree with my conclusions now. But . . .

Christopher Thornton: She is pretty relaxed in her old age.

Massimo Vidale: I am not very confident with this concept that once you have this potter's wheel, it will run fast or slow as you like, but once you have it I think you can exploit the centrifugal force on it, so this process is probably less gradual – a punctuated process.

Cameron Petrie: Punctuated I think is the right word. That is my catchphrase.

Massimo Vidale: They introduced the network of rotating devices that included the rotating devices of the wheel for transportation – the potter's wheel – and I've also considered the possibility that some form of turning on a radius was introduced at a very early moment. This is completely open to new research and more results. So these forms of innovation are very important, but I think we really need to draw more evidence before discussing this. But we should be prepared to change many ideas. Traditional ideas.

Cameron Petrie: I agree.

Massimo Vidale: And this is also true for moulding. They have a lot of elements of the pottery from Mahtoutabad and they made extensive use of moulds.

This idea that in the late fourth millennium you see the start of mass production of the bevel-rim bowls and this is technological innovation, is false. This principle of moulding is much more ancient, you have had this technology since… The problem in this case is the result.

Cameron Petrie: That is a very interesting observation.

Lloyd Weeks: On the general idea of technology. The things I was trying to get across in my presentation and which I think we have excellent parallels with in the archaeobotanical evidence that Eta was discussing – we look at a number of differences in material culture and other things that seem to characterise the *Proto-Elamite* period and other periods, and we tend to draw boundaries between these things. But when we look at other categories of material culture, evidence for archaeobotany and so forth, what we are seeing is long-term similarities in developmental processes, which continue underneath what seem to be comparatively rapid political changes. We tend to think of major change being associated with periods that come up but there is a whole lot of continuity going on when we start to look at technological aspects and aspects of archaeobotany, which we somehow also need to incorporate into these models, given the perspective of these different kinds of approach and areas, in some ways the different perspectives into the overall character of what is going on in the fourth millennium.

Margareta Tengberg: Some materials were adapted and for some there are no changes.

Lloyd Weeks: I think it can take us some way towards understanding what processes were actually going on when we can see changes in the archaeological record. Who was involved in those changes? What segments of the society or what proportion of society? These are the kinds of questions we should be dealing with. Looking at when they are unique or when they co-vary or don't co-vary. It gets very complicated.

Cameron Petrie: Lloyd, your presentation alluded to this example of metallurgy where we are dealing with quite a specific bracket of technological knowledge and that technology is effectively being shared between small groups of people. Is that right?

Lloyd Weeks: Well, that's one potential explanation – this very broad similarity demands an explanation. The explanation is either that it is shared, or that it is developing independently and then converging, or some combination of the two.

Cameron Petrie: It is important that we remember the balance: we've got the people who are doing the producing and those are the people who are using the objects. I think the producers can innovate as much as they like, but unless everyone is willing to go along with what they are producing it isn't necessarily going to continue. I was asking Jacob before whether he would consider the *Proto-Elamite* texts as falling under the heading of technology. I think in some respects it's a specific administrative technology. One of the things that was interesting, and this is relating a little bit to something that Karl Lamberg-Karlovsky has mentioned: in Mesopotamia you have this sort of administrative technology and you have an apparent long-term continuum, whereas in the Iranian plateau you have an administrative technology that is used, and then apparently it stops.

Jacob Dahl: I would make a slight differentiation between the early stuff, the pre-writing, and the proto-writing systems. Pre-writing, bullae, and numerical tablets and so on, can presumably be taken over as an administrative tool without belonging to the cuneiform group, but maybe the systems that develop out of that – the *Uruk III* and the *Proto-Elamite* – might be more specific to one culture. They may not be so much only a technology, but also actually some sort of activity.

Henry Wright: How many cubic metres of deposit have actually been excavated that date between 2900 and 2300 BC?

Jacob Dahl: Of course for those periods, Susa has been completely cleaned and they looked for tablets.

Henry Wright: But you had 1200 guys with railroad picks.

Jacob Dahl: The tablets are what they came for. So those excavations cover it, at least for texts written on permanent materials.

Roger Matthews: You have these similar very long gaps in writing in Anatolia, for instance.

Jacob Dahl: And in Mesopotamia, in fact.

Roger Matthews: After the Hittite collapse you don't have serious writing for at least 300 years and even then it's far sparser.

Henry Wright: There was another gap in Iran from 1300 to 800 BC, but this cannot have been total because when they came back again they were writing Elamite, not too different from what they had used 500 years before. Somewhere – we just haven't found the site – it was going on.

Jacob Dahl: Well, what happens continuously in Mesopotamia was that there were long gaps and they pick up thing again – although there has been a long gap, things continue.

Henry Wright: Would somebody care to comment on the tablets that have been found at Konar Sandal, or can we not talk about that?

François Desset: First of all I think you saw the details in the CDLI site, yes? There is a problem with the dating of this tablet. Perhaps it could be dated around 2400 BC.

Massimo Vidale: 2300 BC, probably later according to the pottery that I have seen.

François Desset: OK, so the second part of the third millennium; but first of all, from my point of view, I think this is a new type of writing. There is also *Linear Elamite*, which is also linked with texts from Susa. So it doesn't really bridge the gap between the *Proto-Elamite* complex and the *Linear Elamite* one, which we know in Susa, because there is nothing *Proto-Elamite* in the Konar Sandal texts. So we have a new writing, we have *Linear Elamite I*. I think it must make us very modest about what we know, because we excavated in Iran for 100 years with the French in Susa and they quite recently discovered a new writing.

Henry Wright: What is out there?

Christopher Thornton: Jacob will have a very different opinion on this.

Jacob Dahl: If you show these objects to any specialist of writing they would do what we all have done, that is to start counting the signs. And there are not more than 90 signs altogether, and only nine different signs. So you have nine signs repeated 10 times each.

Christopher Thornton: You are talking about the fronts?

Massimo Vidale: Do you agree, François, with this?

Jacob Dahl: There is nothing to agree on – I mean they are circles and triangles and lines.

Massimo Vidale: That is how you count them. There are some variations. I am not really deep into the material…

Jacob Dahl: You will agree?

François Desset: Say it again clearly.

Jacob Dahl: 96 signs all together but there are only 9 different ones shown about 10 times each. On one of them – on the brown one.

François Desset: The biggest one?

Jacob Dahl: And that is just a statistical impossibility. That cannot represent writing. That is just impossible. You can't have a system like that which represents speech or codes information of an advanced nature that works like that. So the problem is that on the back of two of them you have what looks like very good *Linear Elamite*. That is a bit of a problem. So in my opinion you have to put this into a completely different context. The context is that you have limited use of writing, which is the *Linear Elamite* stuff. And then on the other side these triangles and squares, that is completely different, and which is not writing as we understand it. A manual perhaps for steps or things you do when you perform a cultic ritual or something like that; and subsequently something that we would probably never find any more of – you will find a couple of examples of it, and that is all.

Massimo Vidale: I understand your point of view, but when the zoologist for the first time saw a platypus, they said it was an impossibility. It cannot be a mammal, it cannot be a bird, so this animal is a fake.

Jacob Dahl: Humans are fantastic and ingenious, but craziness is in human nature as well, luckily. To me this looks like someone who is looking at stars and recording down that sort of information, not a real writing system.

Massimo Vidale: It is entirely possible, but I think we should just wait for excavations to go on…

Roger Matthews: If I could say a word about zebu…

Cameron Petrie: Please! Zebu save us.

Roger Matthews: A few years ago I spent some time looking at zebu and how they were represented iconographically in the record across the Near East. I published an article in *Antiquity* in which I tried to associate representations of the zebu with climactic episodes of aridification at the end of the third and second millennium. I don't think that I was particularly successful, but anyway I think it is an interesting idea. The trouble with zebu is that while they are very clear in pictorial representations, they are very difficult to detect archaeozoologically. You essentially need a couple of the spine bones: the humps are distinctive of zebu. Otherwise it could just be a small cow. They are extremely difficult to identify and therefore they are very under-represented in our surviving assemblages.

Massimo Vidale: What about genetics?

Roger Matthews: There have been genetic studies done on zebu.

Christopher Thornton: Recently they have been doing a lot I think.

Roger Matthews: Yes, that is right…and associating it with domestication of cattle in various different places, and detecting a common ancestor for zebu and non-zebu cattle.

Massimo Vidale: If I am not wrong, they also date the introduction of the zebu to the eastern coast of Africa to a very early period – fourth millennium BC. Somebody brought these animals by ship to Africa.

Cameron Petrie: We are moving onto a form of mobility, which might take various forms that do not necessarily need to be exclusive of one another. Mobility of people, mobility of materials, animals and ideas, etc. I think that's a very important point, Roger, and we certainly do have evidence for the movement of these animals. But in my mind it is the structure and the nature of that which is quite interesting, because

I think this is one of the things that underpins the models of interaction, and the intensification or the centralisation of interaction.

Wendy Matthews: I just wanted to say about the seasonality of movement: Marjan has presented these wonderful case studies and ways forward through the teeth, but also looking at detecting who are pastoralists. It is possible to use geoarchaeology and micromorphology to see animal pens very easily in the field. We can do more of that. I want to use things like phytolith studies, and within the micromorphological thin sections as well, you can actually see what the animals were eating and thereby pick up potential seasonality and also charred plant materials. So that's a very important aspect, to be able to bring up seasonality, seasonality in middens, and other types of activities.

Massimo Vidale: Just to jump in, we need information on seasonality badly. We need it for craft production. All the issues of the part-time specialists versus full-time can only really be faced if we start to do microstratigraphic excavation and take pollens from micro-layers and try to understand the organisation by means of climatic indicators. This I believe is true for husbandry, it is true for craft production. We badly need this type of approach. Thank you for reminding me of this. I think this is really a key point, whatever we do.

Christopher Thornton: Wendy, for those of us who get rare access to sites, and are working on sites but don't have a soil micromorphologist on site, what do you recommend? For example, when you are excavating a floor. Should you just make a block and try to take it home with you? What do you recommend?

Wendy Matthews: Yes, you could recommend to the site director that you collect a series of blocks and you can always keep those on the site archive, on the site.

Christopher Thornton: Would you wrap them in plastic?

Wendy Matthews: We'd wrap them tightly in tissue and tape. Just kitchen roll and parcel tape that you can get anywhere. That's right.

Massimo Vidale: And how big should it be, for example for a floor to have meaningful samples?

Wendy Matthews: Well, a large thin section is 14 × 7 cm. I should post on my website how to collect samples.

Christopher Thornton: Well, Iranians, especially the young ones, are very interested. If they learned how easy it was – at least just to take the samples. And as there isn't a micromorphologist who is now working in Iran, this could be a whole new revolution for them and a very useful one.

Wendy Matthews: We are bringing someone to Reading next autumn term, so it should be possible to do this, and in our ICAR report from CZAP (Central Zagros Archaeology Project) we've put this methodology in, so it is all there. It's on a pdf on our website.

Massimo Vidale: I think for the *Uruk* period it is a tremendous example of what we should and could do.

Wendy Matthews: Another thing we are finding are probably human coprolites; Lisa Shillito is doing work on phytoliths and also organic resides. With GCMS you can see if they are human. It is a way of getting a diet, a short-term diet. Seasonality in the human diet as well, by what is turning up in these – whether they were consuming nuts.

Carla Lancelotti: Another easy thing to do, if you cannot manage to get blocks for micromorphology – and I am not saying that they give the same information – but just take loose soil for phytolith analysis. That requires a very small amount of soil: about 20 g is more than enough.

Christopher Thornton: From floors?

Carla Lancelotti: From whatever context where you are interested in understanding what was going on with plants generally.

Massimo Vidale: Would phytoliths be sensitive to seasonal variation as much as pollen would be?

Matthew Jones: That would be more than enough for pollen analysis as well.

Salaam al-Kuntar: Also, is it better to sample open courtyards?

Carla Lancelotti: It is not necessarily better…they will give you different information. The information will not only be on seasonality, but also the use of space in terms of plant use. If you think that some sort of activity related to plant processing was going on, either inside or outside, phytolith analysis would be perfect. And if you can get control samples, samples from outside the site, to get a clear idea what the vegetation around the site was, what was brought into the site, and what was left out.

Massimo Vidale: If they are multilayered, from a kiln, do we sample the ash?

Carla Lancelotti: Yes.

Massimo Vidale: This is very meaningful for seasonal variation.

Carla Lancelotti: It is. It can be meaningful. And also phytoliths are bigger than pollen so they move less into the sediment and they are more easily controlled in the stratigraphy.

Margareta Tengberg: There is one source of seasonality in the wild plant species: the fruit species that we have collected on most sites – pistachio, almond, and so on.

Cameron Petrie: I guess the other point in terms of specific archaeological recovery is that often we need to be able to differentiate these layers. We may be dealing with a palimpsest layer of reused floors – in some respects it depends on the nature of the occupation.

Margareta Tengberg: The context.

Cameron Petrie: Yes. In terms of methodology there seems to be quite a clear range of things that we could be doing, and emphasising the range and also the relevance to specific contexts is a very, very good idea.

Christopher Thornton: Sort of along these lines, we are talking about methodology now. We've talked a lot about these *Uruk* people, *Proto-Elamite* people, communities moving merchants, elites, traders, whatever. I think – and I know it's something Guillermo has thought of for many, many decades and I would love his opinion on this – we've identified the phenomenon now in Iran of the "*Proto-Elamite* expansion", but also something that looks maybe *Proto-Elamite* or connected to Mesopotamia, like Susa, which is what we are looking at here. The question is, what is the methodology that we can use to start answering questions as opposed to just pointing out phenomena? How do you solve the problem?

Guillermo Algaze: DNA.

Christopher Thornton: You think DNA? DNA is problematic.

Guillermo Algaze: As are many things.

Christopher Thornton: If we had burials that had just *Proto-Elamite* stuff in the burials, in a community like Godin or Yahya. It would be a fascinating thing. Otherwise I feel like we are just shooting in the dark.

Guillermo Algaze: It is just because we don't have the data; that would be a proper way of solving it.

Christopher Thornton: Right. In theory.

Lloyd Weeks: Ancient DNA is difficult. They have tried extracting it from burial contexts in the Mediterranean and they are pushing it back to the middle of the second millennium but beyond that, it is just too difficult.

Cameron Petrie: From what I am understanding from the people who do DNA in our department, they are actually often having trouble doing DNA from the seventeenth and eighteenth centuries, so while I think it is a route, we are not there yet.

Margareta Tengberg: Isotopes, stable isotopes.

Christopher Thornton: Again, we haven't identified a single *Proto-Elamite* person; do you know what I mean? There is not a single burial that I can think of that you would say. . .

Roger Matthews: "Well, I'm a Sumerian".

Guillermo Algaze: You can count the number of *Uruk* burials on the fingers of one hand.

Margareta Tengberg: Why do we not have more? Because we haven't been looking in the right places?

Cameron Petrie: We've got the traces of the people; we haven't got the people themselves.

Guillermo Algaze: Burial practice is also something that is a specific problem.

Cameron Petrie: I just remember doing a lot of reading about the *'Ubaid* period in Iran, there are about four *'Ubaid*-period burials I think, or fragmentary burials.

Roger Matthews: Even if we could get DNA evidence reliably from that period, it would be extremely mixed. It would be highly unlikely that we would get a distinctive imprint of an Elamite DNA signature . . .

Christopher Thornton: I am sure isotopes would be more helpful to differentiate between locals from imports.

Roger Matthews: But even then, it is likely to be mixed.

Margareta Tengberg: If you live in one place for a certain time…

Christopher Thornton: It can change your isotopic signature. There is a difference with the teeth! Baby isotopes!

Guillermo Algaze: Then again all of these things assume that we have lots of dead people, which we don't, so. . .

Christopher Thornton: Actually, the only place we have burials of that period as far as I know are at Sialk and places like Arslan. And then Hissar, but then you are out of the sphere apparently.

John Alden: From the outside everyone else's analytical method looks like it is going to be the solution and in your own analytical method you recognise that the problems are difficult.

Jenny Marshall: That is what I was going to say about DNA. The specialists, when you read through reports, are arguing amongst themselves and you have to come in and pick your pathway through it. As you were saying, it is someone else's method and you think, "oh, maybe it is OK", and the people themselves that are presenting it are arguing between themselves and they don't 100% agree with what they are saying.

Christopher Thornton: It is a good thing we are all in agreement!

John Alden: When we've looked at chronology we've got the same challenges. At one point I was talking about the stratified *Kaftari* period and Holly Pittman said, "you just do the stratification and I will give you the chronology" – from the iconographic and glyptic material. We've seen some really interesting diversions between what radiocarbon tells us, what pottery tells us, what iconography tells us, what textual analysis tells us. And it would be really nice to sort those out. That is a problem that we all have to address as a group.

Christopher Thornton: I think along those lines, I think we should throw out… I know that one of the things that Barbara has written – which I think is really brilliant – was her "Tracking the Proto-Elamites" paper from 2004. She points out something which we know but we need to constantly remember: that we are conflating different things that we all call *Proto-Elamite*. There are ceramics, there is a time period, there are texts, and there is iconography. Those are four distinct things, and they clearly have a coherence, . . . – it is this "Neolithic package" problem. There is a coherence, but are they contemporary and are they coming from the same direction? She argued, based on her radiocarbon dates, that what we call *Proto-Elamite* pottery is probably coming from the highlands to the lowlands. Right, it is earlier in Sialk than it is down in Susa. This is versus texts which seem to be happening earlier in the lowlands.

Jacob Dahl: How did she date Sialk? Has she dated it earlier than Susa based on radiocarbon or what?

Christopher Thornton: Yes, because *Sialk IV* was coming back to 3600/3500 BC.

Cameron Petrie: Radiocarbon dates. We don't have the radiocarbon dates from Susa, which creates problems.

Christopher Thornton: But it is a valid point. Whether it holds up is irrelevant.

Cameron Petrie: Even within the *Proto-Elamite* we are dealing with regional variety. That is part of the reason that I asked you, John, the question about the highland and lowland pottery – even though we might have this overarching *Proto-Elamite* thing, and there are things that we would identify as being *Proto-Elamite*, specifically the ceramics. However, there is actually a great deal of regional variety within the ceramics. There is a small amount of regional similarity, but there is a predominance of variation. Kamyar Abdi (2003) put out this idea that it should be described as "horizon style", which is interesting and useful in the sense that it covers bits and pieces of material, but I think it also assumes that there is a commonality.

Christopher Thornton: The interaction sphere idea, Caldwells's idea (1964), works better.

John Alden: Well, he's using horizons from the New World.

Cameron Petrie: Guillermo, would you like to say something?

Guillermo Algaze: It is a pity that Barbara (Helwing) isn't here as she mentioned the concept of a push and pull. Is there a *Proto-Elamite* expansion? Should we think in those terms? I don't have an opinion one way or the other on this point. Should we be talking in terms of an interaction sphere or a horizon style? Essentially we have seen the *Proto-Elamite* phenomenon. It occurs in many different places, but does it occur everywhere for the same reason? Are there any parallels between the so-called *Proto-Elamite expansion* and the *Uruk expansion*? This needs to be looked at. In the case of the *Uruk expansion* at least some have argued that there is actual movement of people. Should we consider the *Proto-Elamite expansion*, if there is such a thing, as a movement of Susians? As a movement of Malyanians? Or was it simply locals who were in interaction with Susians and Malyans, and saw a more prestigious culture which they started to emulate. Or is it a combination of both?

Christopher Thornton: Because at Yahya it is very clear you have a colony. You have something that comes in and is very intrusive. Whereas at Sialk you have a very strong transition from the pre-*Proto Elamite* into the *Proto-Elamite* periods, according to work at Arisman and Sialk and in terms of ceramic and stuff like this.

Margareta Tengberg: Check for fingerprints on the ceramics.

Cameron Petrie: I think one of your points, Chris, was quite interesting. What we have are these layers of evidence, in a way, and it tends to get put together in a package, but we actually have a chronological element to it. As Jacob was implying – the texts are coming at the end. If we think about the *Uruk* component, the texts were at the end. In some respects with the *Proto-Elamite*, what becomes *Proto-Elamite* sees the texts come at the end. Certainly at Malyan according to the stratigraphy we have this deep sequence, we've got Operation ABC, Levels 5 and 4 before you get to level 3 where all the tablets are.

John Alden: There are also tablets in Level 2.

Cameron Petrie: So there are actually several phases of things happening before the appearance of the tablets.

Jacob Dahl: You can of course explain that as the early archives were discarded, and what you have is the last of them because that is when they move away, and they leave everything on the floor. But since we do not know how they dealt with archives or how they dealt with their texts, it is very difficult to say.

Wendy Matthews: Something we can look at as archaeologists, because we are getting bound up in the concept of people – who is doing what and moving where – is practices and contexts. What spheres? I'm not talking about interaction spheres on a large scale, but small-scale within the sites. What were the spheres of life and practices that were being influenced? And which weren't? We can see it through our data.

Guillermo Algaze: We have to be very careful with the terminology that we use because by saying "spheres" we are implying a system of peers interacting on an equal basis, whereas by using terminology like "world systems" we are implying a hierarchy. These words all have hidden meanings so we have to be very, very careful with what we mean and which word we use.

Cameron Petrie: To come back to something from yesterday: Guillermo, when you gave your discussant presentation you talked about scales, and I thought it was very interesting to see John's observations about this; and Henry you talked about this as well. We've got this difference in scales. Certainly in between what is going on at Susa, for example, and what is going on in Uruk/Mesopotamia. Not just in Uruk but in southern Mesopotamia generally, we've apparently got an abundance of large urban sites. We don't really have this in Iran. Large urban sites at a maximum of 40 ha. Is that how big Susa gets in the fourth millennium? 40 ha, Malyan's 40 ha…

Guillermo Algaze: Yes, but Malyan is 40 ha later.

Cameron Petrie: True! And it is also 500 km away from Susa, so there are different parameters. I don't want to harp too much on the difference between Iran and Mesopotamia, but I think there is a fundamental difference between the possibilities of scale in Iran. We don't have this massive alluvium. There is a geographical difference. We have much smaller basins and plains that can be used in slightly different ways. That is why I wonder when we think about the *Late Uruk* period, say – and we often think about the material similarities between Susiana and the Susiana plain and Mesopotamia – I wonder how linked they are in a direct sense or whether at Uruk they are doing similar things with independence? And I wonder whether we can identify that.

Guillermo Algaze: Sure, what is the relationship between the two areas, is that what you are asking?

Cameron Petrie: Yes, and I know that Henry and Greg Johnson have these ideas of lowland states in Khuzistan. Essentially they exist as a more or less independent entity. That is why I was very interested in Vanessa's reconstruction of the coastline. I threw this to you the other day, Guillermo, this idea about boats. Possibly there is a large embayment separating Khuzistan from Mesopotamia.

Wendy Matthews: Or connecting…

Guillermo Algaze: YES, YES!

Cameron Petrie: Separating by water but…

Guillermo Algaze: Who wants to use a donkey when you can use a boat?

Henry Wright: I think what Vanessa's reconstruction shows is that you are not going to make sense of the first-millennium texts of the Assyrians, they were having trouble getting across the water. There was nothing there but water. They were having to thread their way through the sewers of Basra, the Shatt al-Arab, it was a straight shot for a sailboat. Bashime is not very far from Bushire, somewhere to the east of Bushire.

Cameron Petrie: Unfortunately Vanessa has left, which is disappointing! Tony's not here either. He knows the other side of the coast.

Henry Wright: Well, I am not sure we can apply what she has done yet to the fourth millennium. I'd love to!

John Alden: There is something that really has got lost here: I would like to say thank you to the people who are reanalysing data from other sites, to people who are working with Godin. Publishing Godin, publishing Mamasani. You are making a tremendous contribution and the more published material we have, the more everybody can work with these issues of how things are happening. So the long drudgerous process of doing this kind of basic publication like Mitchell has done for Godin, deserves a huge vote of thanks from everybody. And people like me who have publication responsibilities that aren't yet complete can feel guilty. Publication is a problem.

Guillermo Algaze: Let he who is free of guilt throw the first stone. For many of us this is a problem. Don't flog yourself.

Cameron Petrie: Unfortunately Barbara left before we could talk about this, but she mentioned it to me several times over dinner last night: this idea of conflict and violence. I think one of the things that came through in a lot of the discussion was that we were talking about 50 to 100 people who just came and settled in an area and started negotiating a relationship with these local inhabitants in the Godin district; and I wanted to point out that Barbara is convinced that none of this can happen without reaction, violent reaction. She wants us to remember the very visible evidence that we have from the sealings for captives and other things.

Lloyd Weeks: They also set up on top of the best mound, they took up a prominent location on the landscape, and their settlement was right on top.

Henry Wright: I think this relates to what John said about *Proto-Elamite* interaction between Anshan and

Susa. I've argued for a long time that this was a war. The reason for this is primarily because I take the best evidence for warfare to be the sudden abandonment of a region. And what has happened? If you look at all the little valleys that we have surveyed, Izeh and Ram Hormuz, you get *Middle Uruk* material all the way up to the Zagros. They are abandoned. You get *Late Uruk* material a little farther back. Suddenly, you have no people making the material culture at Zagros at all. You suddenly have settlements that are making *Proto-Elamite* material culture. And lo and behold this is the time when Chogha Mish is founded and eastern Khuzistan becomes a huge area, a lot of little villages, previously unoccupied in that part of Susiana. Now what you need is to take that kind of indirect argument away from some preliminary evidence; one of its problems is that Augusta MacMahon has evidence of a lot of people with their heads bashed in rotting in the dumps of Braq, which appears to be violence of some kind. It might be a lot of executions but it looks an awful lot like cleaning up a battleground to me. The sort of evidence that Clemens Reichel has from Hamoukar, late Hamoukar, with these sling balls in mass quantities – which Joan Oates is actually very dubious of because many of them are actually soft when they are thrown and you couldn't really do a lot of damage to somebody if they were hit with a blob of mud. Clemens's argument is that at the end of the battle the people of Hamoukar did not have time to dry their sling missiles, so they just threw them anyway.

Excavation evidence does not always tell you what we learn about violence from European sites because it is hard to burn a mud-brick building. The kinds of traces we look for of violence in other parts of the world with other types of architecture are harder to find in Mesopotamia, but not impossible. We clearly have evidence of a good solid sacking – *Chalcolithic* people when they sack each other, they don't do as thorough a job as Assurbanipal.

Roger Matthews: We do know that slaves feature very prominently in later texts and the easiest way to get slaves is to conquer somewhere and grab as many slaves as you can. Bob Englund has just published an article on the CDLI website where he is looking at the frequency of occurrences of slaves not just in *Late Uruk* texts but in all texts and following slave names – "The Smell of the Cage" it is called.

Margareta Tengberg: What about the metallurgy or the metal objects, arms and such things?

John Alden: Axes.

Lloyd Weeks: Yes, that is what Barbara was arguing when I was talking to her about the idea of shared metal typology across those regions and she said, "look at all those big weapons. If your enemy has one of those, you ought to get one of those." That is one logical reason you might see the spread of some types of large implements.

Margareta Tengberg: They are arms? That is known?

Lloyd Weeks: Not necessarily.

Christopher Thornton: I don't agree with that. I think that you don't really see spears and daggers coming in until the end of the third millennium BC. You do have daggers in the fourth millennium BC but they are rare. You have axes and you have mace heads, but not metal naturally – stone generally. Axes…to me those axes are very symbolic. I don't see them as being useful. I mean you hit someone over the head with an axe like that, you are going to do some serious damage, don't get me wrong, but I could do the same with the chair. I find those…I don't know if you disagree but…

Massimo Vidale: Well, in Mahtoutabad we have axes, spears, and daggers from one of the plundered graves.

Cameron Petrie: What period is this?

Massimo Vidale: 2400 BC – the third millennium.

Christopher Thornton: Yes, it is only in the third millennium when you get lots of daggers and spears.

Lloyd Weeks: What do you think of the Arslan Tepe material?

Christopher Thornton: It is very exceptional.

Guillermo Algaze: It is soft metal.

Christopher Thornton: It is very ceremonial, the silver blades.

Lloyd Weeks: But if someone is hitting you over the head with it many times?

Guillermo Algaze: It wouldn't survive hitting me over the head many times.

Christopher Thornton: Well, a dagger would be a thrusting weapon anyway. It wouldn't be used for really hitting someone over the head at that time. The point is that those things are very unusual. They are extremely unusual. The Maikop material that showed up in Iran, now dated to the mid-fourth millennium BC, that stuff is totally out of sequence with the Iranian material. That is why it is so clearly intrusive. But the Maikop people are producing lots of weapons, right? They are possibly a nomadic group, if I can say that, from the Caucasus. They seem to have a very violent culture. Very elaborate, but also very violent, and it is totally intrusive to the Iranian sequence. It looks very intrusive. The big objects of metal are hoes, shovels, things like that.

Cameron Petrie: So does that suggest that the Iranians weren't violent until the Maikop populations came? Or that they were using different types of weapons?

Christopher Thornton: I think that it is possibly on a different scale – that is what we are looking at: sling balls. Sling balls are the sort of thing where I stand on my hill and you stand on your hill and we rattle our sabres and throw our sling balls. I don't know if that is really warfare or skirmish. Tribal skirmish.
John Alden: It is absolutely warfare. Sling balls are deadly weapons.

Henry Wright: Read the article in *Scientific American* by Manfred Korfmann published about 25 years ago.

John Alden: There are Latin inscriptions on how you extract a sling pellet from a wounded person.

Christopher Thornton: But you are talking about actual sling balls that were made of lead by the Roman period. We are talking about big clumps of clay that can knock you senseless, but I doubt it could kill you without a very well aimed shot right to the temple.

John Alden: No, absolutely deadly. Read about the Spanish response – it is the primary weapon in the Andes.

Christopher Thornton: But are they stone or is it a clay sling ball?

John Alden: They throw stones, but listen, a hard piece of clay is as hard as a stone.

Wendy Matthews: Also if you're not finding burials, then you might not find the metal artefacts.

Christopher Thornton: We have burials.

Lloyd Weeks: The basic point about the functionality is well made.

Guillermo Algaze: This issue of conflict, I am all for conflict. I want to point out that conflict might be a secondary phase in the process of contact. The earliest contact may not be – particularly if there is a perceived ideological difference – violent. The violence may only start once there has been sustained contact between two cultures. At least in the Euphrates you don't find any presence of walls in the *Middle Uruk* sites, only the *Late Uruk* ones. So there may be a time lag between the onset of contact and the onset of conflict.

John Alden: Conflict can be invisible archaeologically. Major conquests – totally invisible – the archaeological record may or may not have clear evidence of it. Often it doesn't leave a trace – sometimes you get a burned city, sometimes you get nothing.

Henry Wright: Positive evidence means something in this case. Negative evidence is hard to do. We've missed a whole bunch of topics. We've just wandered into trade. I mean, once Guillermo brought the time lag up he was essentially telling us we should be talking about trade.

Lloyd Weeks: Can I make one last remark on the topic of violence and conflict before we move on? It seems like the distances and scales that we are talking about are hundreds and hundreds of kilometres. It is very difficult to get what you want through violence and conflict and maintain the threat of violence with such great distances. These systems are more likely to work when there is something to be had for both parties involved in the interaction rather than just being imposed from the top. So while violent conflict might have had a role in some of these systems, it might not necessarily have played the dominant role in maintaining the system at various times.

Henry Wright: This is the argument that I use against all classical definitions of the origin of states or societies. They use legal force to suppress violence and to suppress class conflict and so on. Those are states that don't work. Most states persuade people to do the right thing. I'm sorry that Reinhardt is gone, we'd have a nice fight about this. But certainly on the level of within the society or polity, what you say is true – intersociety as well.

John Alden: I would emphasise that in my opinion, violence disrupts trade and contact. It doesn't facilitate it, it prevents it. If you've got a lack of political control, you've got lack of social agreement. The exchange stops. Violence is a negative factor.

Guillermo Algaze: And moving armies over distances under primitive conditions is expensive.

Cameron Petrie: OK, can we combine the idea of interconnections and the idea of trade? We are talking about expansions of contact and in some respects we are talking about the pre-existence of networks. I wanted us to talk about this idea of the way trade is operating, and weather we are actually seeing a change in the way trade is operating in Iran. Can we identify it or is it something that we can only really identify through proxies? Chris, you talked a little bit about lapis and access to it, did you see change throughout the fourth millennium in any aspects?

Christopher Thornton: Well, it is limited to what I can say, but we know that Hissar was producing a huge amount of metal and doing a lot of lapis processing in the second half of the fourth millennium, which continues into the beginning of the third – somewhere around the end of this period we are all discussing – and then it ceases. In the earlier part of that, around 3600, it does not seem that there was lapis processing going on.

John Alden: When...what time?

Christopher Thornton: 3600/3500 BC. There was metal but there was no lapis being really seriously done. Those workshops that Tosi studied on the South Hill don't really take off until 3400/3300 BC. So it is within that radiocarbon plateau that you have all this big-scale production and it is clearly not production of finished objects – it's that middle-man production like you see at Shahr-i Sokhta in the third millennium BC.

Massimo Vidale: No I don't agree with that, it's later at Shahr-i Sokhta, 2550 BC, and there is no... I went through the whole thing – publishing everything.

Christopher Thornton: So you disagree with the ingot idea.

Massimo Vidale: No, no, no. I went through all the collection of about 5000 pieces. It is the manufacturing of small beads for internal consumption. The same three types that we find in the graves.

Christopher Thornton: Where at Hissar it is definitely not, because you have very little lapis in the graves and there are a lot of lapis wasters...

Massimo Vidale: There is a big chronological gap...

Christopher Thornton: Right, but my point is that Hissar, at least, is playing a role as a production station that is then sending stuff on. It is all happening in the same area of the site, the South Hill. It is being regulated with seals and with these non-tablet things and being shipped on. In my mind there is no question of that.

Cameron Petrie: But we lack...

Massimo Vidale: We lack the end of the chain.

Christopher Thornton: Yes, who is collecting it.

Cameron Petrie: We also lack the other signatures of contact with Godin or whoever else they were dealing with – from Hissar specifically.

Christopher Thornton: I will point out that the lapis, of course, is interesting because lapis is not commonly used in Iran in the fourth millennium BC. It appears in graves, but it is rare. Versus the fact that it appears in Mesopotamia more frequently and that is always the argument for it being shipped to Mesopotamia because it is just not commonly consumed.

Salaam al-Kuntar: But it is in northern Mesopotamia at Gawra, at the end of the Gawra phase. It had to have come through the Iranian Plateau.

Cameron Petrie: What about the issue of quantity? There seems to be a substantial quantity at Hissar. What were you about to say, Henry?

Henry Wright: There is this upper Mesopotamian early trade in lapis that was recognised years ago. But in lower Mesopotamia you don't get a lot of lapis until the very end of the *Uruk*, with the *Jemdat Nasr* and *Early Dynastic* etc.

Christopher Thornton: That is when Hissar is doing most . . .

Henry Wright: Very end of the *Uruk*...3200 BC?

Christopher Thornton: Yes, 3200 to 2900 BC.

Roger Matthews: Carnelian is the same. Carnelian really takes off in south Mesopotamia after 3000 BC.

Henry Wright: We have it a little earlier in Susiana: there, carnelian is common before lapis. Of course you can find carnelian not that far away. There is a source of carnelian near Tahiri.

Roger Matthews: There is not much *Late Uruk* carnelian in South Mesopotamia. More like *Early Dynastic I*.

Christopher Thornton: I will point out something, which for me is interesting and maybe you will find interesting. It seems that for the earlier stuff, around 3600–3400 BC, they are doing steatite bead production and steatite working at Hissar. Steatite is local at Hissar, and in the graves of that period you find steatite seals, and beads, and things. Then at the end of the fourth millennium BC they have shifted to working lapis and alabaster.

Cameron Petrie: Is there lapis earlier in the fourth millennium BC and then it intensifies, or is it a marked change?

Christopher Thornton: I don't know. They didn't have any evidence of it until later.

Guillermo Algaze: What are they getting in return? That is the question.

John Alden: Tablets.

[Laughter]

Cameron Petrie: Ah bureaucracy! I think Guillermo has raised a very important point. It has to go both ways. It can't all go in one direction.

Henry Wright: Harriet (Crawford) is no longer here, unfortunately, but she made this point.

François Desset: Of all the things they could get in return, we could perhaps use the texts, the Sumerian texts, such as those from Lagash. They are more recent of course, about the reign of Urukagina, but they seem to have been selling some agricultural products such as wheat, barley, and milk products.

Christopher Thornton: But they are not going to be sending those to Hissar, which is producing its own wheat and barley.

François Desset: OK, but we always miss the invisible.

Roger Matthews: Iran does currently import wheat from the United States.

François Desset: It is written in the texts.

Guillermo Algaze: And the lord of Aratta asks for wheat to be shipped, but wheat is simply too big and too bulky. It needs to be something more portable.

Jane MacIntosh: What about textiles? Marjan said the sheep weren't being kept for wool, didn't she? She said they were being kept for meat.

Henry Wright: We talked about that afterwards and she said that she understood that her data actually could be for fibres, goat hair, and wool and that you had to differentiate the sexes of the animals that were being saved into adulthood. She is just beginning to get those kinds of data.

Lloyd Weeks: There are a lot of spindle whorls.

Christopher Thornton: They are clearly producing their own textiles. Whether they were importing foreign elite-type textiles that have value because they were distant, that is obviously what we are considering.

Massimo Vidale: This is the branding argument; I believe there is some substance in that. This could be one solution, but I don't think we can really cover all the facts.

Guillermo Algaze: It need not be only one thing that is being exported.

Christopher Thornton: Just to finish the Hissar thing. I think that is also what makes it so interesting, that Hissar is not part of the *Proto-Elamite* world; because you can always argue at these *Proto-Elamite* sites that you have are elite-driven, they had a colony there, or it was just part of this ideology. Hissar was clearly – at least in its material culture – absolutely refusing to jump on the bandwagon and yet they played a pivotal role in this incredibly important trade in copper, lead, silver, and lapis, which is what they were exporting. I have no answer for that, I just think it is really interesting.

Margareta Tengberg: About agricultural products: I think agricultural products such as cereals could have been transported at some moments, but in a punctuated way because as you said they were producing them themselves. But other products, more cash products, like oil or sweet things perhaps?

François Desset: I would like to also add something about the transport of cereal and grain: we know from the *Neo-Assyrian* text that they were selling wheat. We also know that during the *Ur III* period, when the Sumerians were invaded, there was discussion of the transportation of grain. We can't show that people at Hissar were in direct contact with Mesopotamia, or that the people in the south were making trade with the people of Arisman, but I think we mustn't dismiss . . .

Guillermo Algaze: Yes, sure! The only thing I was dismissing was lowland/highland continued systematic trade in grain. But if you want to argue lowland/lowland trade in grain and then down-the-line uphill trade in other more valuable things, well that is not a problem.

John Alden: I'd like to suggest that one very valuable item for trade would be dye stuffs. And any vegetal species that are good producers of dyes would be wonderful to have. I would expect that dye stuffs would be a very valuable item of trade.

Margareta Tengberg: Probably, but they are not present in the archaeobotanical record so far. The problem is that we also have certain categories of plants that are very visible and over-represented and others that we hardly ever see. Perhaps they were there, but we don't find them because they were not in contact with fire. If they didn't burn by accident in a destruction . . .

Henry Wright: Chris Edens has made a good argument for animal-derived dye. (Obscured) blue dye and in a world with no dyes at all is better than nothing. Coming from the islands in the second-millennium Persian Gulf – a site that has got Qaleh ware. We have that same shell in Farukhabad in the *Early Dynastic I* for sure and a few in the *Late Uruk*, but it is always worked, which has always troubled me as you can imagine. To be moving a dye shell to the interior where it would stink pretty badly.

John Alden: The dye comes from the creature itself, the living body not the shell?

Henry Wright: Yes, the living body.

Massimo Vidale: Which species of shell?

Henry Wright: Open that up and let me check (opens parcel containing books).

Margareta Tengberg: They could have been trading wood perhaps. We have evidence from the third millennium BC, but not earlier.

Cameron Petrie: This is almost like a paradox – we have the texts relevant for administration and control in one sphere and then we have trade that is not at all referred to in the text.

Massimo Vidale: Lapis is a very precious material, at least for those in Mesopotamia.

Cameron Petrie: It seems to make sense that the lapis from Central Asia is going somewhere else. Where do you think the metal from Hissar is going? Which direction? You drew very clearly your . . .

Christopher Thornton: Yes, my little lines.

Cameron Petrie: The reason I am asking this is because it seems we have a large number of areas that are engaging in metal production. Hissar belongs to one cultural sphere. Ghabristan and Arisman possibly belong to another one, and then we've got Iblis.

Christopher Thornton: I think the metal at Hissar is probably being exported to Gorgan, where we have evidence of metal casing and -working, but absolutely no evidence of smelting. Of course you

are down there in the lowland plain nowhere near any sources. And obviously you have these very strong links, as I pointed out in my talk that happen in the *Sialk IV* period. So that, to me, is a very strong argument. And my feeling is – and this is totally off the record – the metal would be going to Central Asia; because they become desperately in need of metal – the *Namazga IV–V* periods become very complex, and also *Namazga III–IV*, and they have no copper sources nearby. They have their own sites, as I say, east of my little line, but not necessarily metal-producing sites. So I find it unlikely that they are exporting their metal to a place like Kashan where you have Arisman doing exactly the same technology. The technologies are identical. We compared them in Nottingham actually.

Cameron Petrie: To run the risk of simplifying things: can we say we have a clear relationship between Hissar and Central Asia?

Christopher Thornton: Well, as we talked about the lapis route, if there is a steady flow of…it tends to be pure copper and lead. It is probably silver and not lead that is being exported, but anyway, copper and silver, let's say, and there is a steady flow that needs to go through Godin and Gawra and all of this, and into Mesopotamia; it is possible that Arisman shoots it north and it goes out and Hissar shoots it south and it goes out.

Cameron Petrie: I was just wondering if it was possible that it was going in two different directions.

Christopher Thornton: It is possible but there is absolutely no evidence. That is purely hypothetical because we know that Central Asia has a lot of metal at that time. It is producing in the fourth millennium BC, at Ilgynly for example, but I am not sure about the late fourth millennium BC. I am not sure how many production sites we have there, in terms of metal production.

Massimo Vidale: There is a little bit near Yahya.

Christopher Thornton: But, for example, Altyn Tepe is like the Gorgan: it is doing metal casting and -working, but not much metal smelting. Ilgynly is an exception but unfortunately we didn't have a talk on that. At Ilgynly, the technology again looks very similar to Hissar and very similar to Arisman. So the products seem to be the same, even the technology seems to be the same, so it's a shared technological . . .

Cameron Petrie: Milieu?

Massimo Vidale: Milieu? Sphere. That is producing that same product again and again, in my opinion, and is producing it for export. Where to? Everywhere. I don't know.

Lloyd Weeks: I also raised the point that there are other areas of Iran that need copper, so it is not all going down to lowland Mesopotamia. Perhaps Malyan is another region, which could be added as a destination.

Christopher Thornton: Malyan does its own production.

John Alden: But certainly not smelting.

Lloyd Weeks: But there are other slags. We have talked about slags that have never been studied.

John Alden: This is a comment I had in a discussion with Barbara (Helwing). I said, if this is a smelting site wouldn't you expect a bunch of slag? Kiln rubble, furnace rubble, tuyères, etc., broken beakers everywhere? Oh yes, she said, everywhere. There is very, very little of that at Malyan and what there is, they are very small pieces. And we both agreed that these are signs perhaps of metalworking but not metal extraction. So I would say there is no metal extraction at Malyan.

Christopher Thornton: The ores in Iran are very complex and this nonsense you hear from the Levant about slag-less smelting, which can happen in the Levant because they have very clean ores. It does not happen in Iran, I am a firm believer in that. Maybe at Iblis when you are in the sixth/fifth millennium BC, but by the fourth millennium they are smelting extremely complex ores that produce a lot of slag.

Lloyd Weeks: Like the slag they are making at Hissar.

John Alden: Henry made a comment – I am going to go back to this – at one point in your paper on the *Uruk*, you talked about travelling craftsmen instead of travelling products. I think that is really a model . . .

Christopher Thornton: V. Gordon Childe.

Henry Wright: We have this very nice ethnographic work by François Zalouz about potters in Afghanistan that not only move from valley to valley, but make a different style for each valley.

Massimo Vidale: That is the problem with the moving craftsmen, they change their style…

Cameron Petrie: It is a decorative style or a technological style?

Christopher Thornton: A decorative style.

Massimo Vidale: All the current arguments were based upon technologies. You cannot recognise metallurgical provenances other than on the basis of the form of the object. You should do it on the technology.

John Alden: This is why your examination of ceramics is so important because it looks at the actual techniques used to produce it rather than the appearance of the finished object.

Massimo Vidale: A problem with itinerants is that they are going around supposedly with a lot of valuable ore. It is not really something you want to carry around for a long distance, all this metal, because as you know, this metal is wealth.

John Alden: It is also pretty heavy.

Massimo Vidale: I mean, it is also dangerous for their own security.

Christopher Thornton: They would not be carrying the metal around with them.

Lloyd Weeks: They would ask the customer to bring them the metal.

John Alden: If you had the tools and technology you could make the moulds or carry a small selection of moulds. You set up shop and you make a little furnace.

Guillermo Algaze: In the historic period some metals are held by palaces and are given out, very precisely, to the craftspeople. So local elites would hold the metals then give them out to craftspeople.

Massimo Vidale: And also the tools.

Lloyd Weeks: In an article about movements of people across the Middle East based largely on textual material, Carlos Zaganini says that it is unrealistic to believe that there are itinerate craftspeople before the *Bronze Age*.

Henry Wright: Who says this?

Lloyd Weeks: Zaganini.

Henry Wright: He's wrong. It is unreasonable to say this before the donkey becomes available to move those wheels and things around. This is as far as potters go.

Guillermo Algaze: Where is this article?

Lloyd Weeks: I don't have the reference. It's 1983 in *JAS*.

Margareta Tengberg: You can make a wheel wherever you go.

Henry Wright: People love their wheels: they are made of special wood.

Margareta Tengberg: Yes, but if they stay for several months?

Henry Wright: I wrote a long paper about this kind of thing in the *Uruk* and I don't want to get into it.

John Alden: Well, there is also the possibility that as an itinerate craftsman you have a cycle you go through. You go from A to B to C and you appear every six months and you do your work.

Christopher Thornton: I think something that is important is that by the time you get to the fourth millennium, the crafts are not simple crafts, right? They are not crafts in the way that you can find native copper and someone says "if you hit that you can bend it into a bead". These are very complex crafts, extremely complex crafts. More complex than anything you see in the second millennium in some locations. With this age of experimentation they are doing some absolutely mind-blowing stuff. So the idea that you don't have people who are really craftspeople, whether that is their total specialisation or whatever – but you have to have this knowledge and it is not knowledge that you can just casually pick up. In pottery it is the same, in metals it is the same. Lithics – I think the lithics are great...

Cameron Petrie: From what Jacob is saying, textual evidence...

Salaam Kuntaar: But can you talk about the exclusive skill, because in the text, like the *Ur III* texts, there is a lot of craft-production information. The value always went to the object. There is not much reference to the skill.

Christopher Thornton: But that is what I mean. In the *Ur III* period you are not looking at a lot of skill, you are not looking at incredible technological crafts. You are looking at mass production – "chuck it on the wheel, pull it up and take the next one" – from the fourth millennium BC where I think every single slag we look at is just so amazing. But I understand your point and I think that is the big difference.

Salaam Kuntaar: But that is not how it spread because there was not that much controlling technology. That kind of thing, it doesn't appear from the text.

Henry Wright: And technology control is internal to the castes and guild-like organisations, which we don't have in the text until the first millennium BC and then there is quite a bit of it.

Christopher Thornton: Surely they existed.

Massimo Vidale: The Indus is an interesting case: the Indus remains very complex until 2000 BC, the very end or something like that, but this is probably exactly...because they have a very caste- and guild-like organisation, but I think it is a peculiar case.

Cameron Petrie: We've covered a lot of the topics and a lot of other things, but some of the things we have been focusing on are intensely bottom-up. Focusing on microstratigraphy and various ways of solving problems. We have talked a bit about issues of trade. We haven't talked about everything that is up on the board, but I wonder if we can explore whether or not it is possible, . . . I think Guillermo is leaning towards the view that one model is not going to answer our questions.

Henry Wright: This is going to come as a shock, Guillermo. Having spent most of my life arguing for general models of trade, warfare, and state formation, I assert now that due to the level of detail – we have so many variables interacting in our thoughts; look at this conversation, the complicated discussion, movement, materials, and local processes, and regional processes – we can't confidently look for single massive explanations. We have a method now – unfortunately, the one person who has tried it recently isn't here and that is Tony Wilkinson – and it is agent-based modelling. Influenced strongly by modelling of many agents with different kinds of knowledge and interaction. He has done this for Beydar as an experiment with Tell Beydar, which is well documented archaeologically with survey and excavation and for which there is a lovely little collection of archival fragments. Not so many that you get confused – just enough to do something. He has done a number of papers on Beydar. It is called the MASS Simulation. Unfortunately the plug has been pulled on the money, so the innovation that Tony got started – I don't know if it is going to be continued at Chicago. I hope I am wrong, but this is something that can unite people who have general anthropologically based ideas, people with very specific ideas of historic interest. When you start this kind of model you are looking at specific systems in real historical context, you are trying to tickle it out variable by variable, and make a model in which your electronic agents are as close as you can build them to ancient Mesopotamians and Iranians. It is doable. You have to make a lot of assumptions right now to make these kinds of models. This does not involve sophisticated mathematical knowledge. It involves a poor graduate student, who comes from a programming background; a lot of the computer programs are now available, you can borrow them and you can almost always find money at universities that do this kind of thing because administrators like it. And I really think that rather than talk of general theories of the origins of states as we have done before, we are now talking about various types of modern very specific multi-variant models that enable us to see how forests interact with gross geomorphological processes, with climate, with weather, and obtaining minerals; and the ideological knowledge that underlies the demand for exotic materials that Roger brought up the other day and we haven't touched on since. There is a whole bunch of things that can be handled in these kinds of system models or historical models. That's all I want to say.

John Alden: Well, we've dealt with every one of those things.

Henry Wright: But you can't deal with them one by one.

Cameron Petrie: It would be nice if we could finish at 3; has anyone got anything more to say?

Henry Wright: Do you want to do a book?

Cameron Petrie: I absolutely want to do a book.

Lloyd Weeks: Can I just raise the issue of what happens after this workshop, because it seems that there are so many interesting interconnections that are being formed between people working on this issue. Questions like Matt has pointed out about the environmental usage that various archaeological samples can be put to… and questions about micromorphology. Is there some way of creating a communication space where we can start to ask these questions and build on the relations brought up by this workshop?

David Redhouse: You mean an email list?

Lloyd Weeks: Maybe an email list.

Cameron Petrie: I think spaces are notoriously difficult to look after, but I think mailing lists and discussion groups are less so.

Margareta Tengberg: A new workshop.

Cameron Petrie: More workshops are certainly…

Lloyd Weeks: When is the next one?

Cameron Petrie: We should ask Maurizio Tosi because he was talking about something next year. I don't know, we will see. But I think that having these things too close together doesn't get you anywhere because you end up reiterating the same ideas. We don't necessarily need 25 years between them, but I do think we need some time so the agenda can shape and reshape. But yes, I think we can think about it.

Christopher Thornton: It may be also interesting, thinking in the future – another fourth-millennium BC thing maybe in a few years, if you could think – Cameron especially – of some key questions. Not just theoretical questions that all of us could sit around for hours and discuss. Key issues in the material culture. Key issues in – we talked about the environmental data, the soil micromorphology, the key thing that we are trying to bring out… very practical things that we are trying to address. One thing I would throw into the mix, which I noticed from Ben's and Jerome's papers – who are both working in Pakistan – and Cameron, you are in Fars in south-western Iran: the *Yahya V* period has been dated in this conference between 4500 and 4000, I would date it 3500 to 3000. And it has been dated to 4000 to 3500. Why is that important? Because it is the link between what you are doing in Fars and what Ben is doing in Pakistan.

Cameron Petrie: Absolutely.

Christopher Thornton: And Mahtoutabad sits right in the middle of this area as well. And some little key things like that where people should be… I asked Ben while he was at Harvard, can he look at the *Yahya V* material, even just casually.

Ben Mutin: I tried but…

Christopher Thornton: But just casually. Look at the fabric, the technology – I would love to come

and look at it again and maybe I will come up and visit you and we will slog through it. Cameron, you and I had this argument back in Nottingham when you were putting *Lapui* so early and I said absolutely impossible, you are crazy. You have the radiocarbon dates to support it now, but what does that say about the *Lapui* at *Yahya VA*? These are fundamental material culture problems that we can actually formally address and clear up.

Cameron Petrie: In many ways I think we are lacking holistic pictures of Iran. We don't have a lot of attempts of really wrestling with Iran as a whole. We have things like the *Chronologies of Old World Archaeology* chapter (Voigt and Dyson 1992), which attempted to patch all these things together and draw all these links, but Iran is not really a topic that people attempt to take on. You get Dan's (Potts) Elam book (1999), which takes on a little corner. There is something there which I think we can move towards.

Margareta Tengberg: Thinking about illustrations, there was your map that everyone commented on with the valleys.

Cameron Petrie: That was fun to put together. One of the things that I would personally like to see more of is an integration of the Baluchistan, Central Asia, and Seistan material. I think unfortunately we haven't managed that here and we need to integrate it more into our thinking – what is going on in the bigger picture. Even in the discussion just now we talked about Hissar and Central Asia, but we didn't actually get to talk about South Asia much, other than zebu and other things Massimo brought up, and issues of the metallographic links and the ceramic technology. I certainly think there are more things to bring on and so that is why I hope that with the book we can achieve the things that we have not necessarily done here, and set out an agenda.

I just want to say thank you all so much for coming and sitting throughout the afternoon. We were trying to finish by lunch at 1pm, and now it is 3 and no one has complained about the fact that the papers have gone long. In my opinion, without exception, all the papers were interesting and almost all of them had new data or new interpretations of old data, so I really think we got somewhere. And I don't think we can ask for more than that.

References

Abdi, K. 2003. "From Écriture to Civilisation: Changing Paradigms of Proto-Elamite Archaeology", in Miller, N. F. and Abdi, K. (eds), *Yeki bud, yeki nabud: Essays on the Archaeology of Iran in Honor of William M. Sumner*, Cotsen Institute of Archaeology, University of California, Los Angeles: 140–51.

Caldwell, J. R. 1964. "Interaction spheres in prehistory", in Caldwell, J. R. and Hall, R. L. (eds), *Hopewellian Studies*, Scientific Papers, Illinois State Museum 12, Springfield, Illinois: 135–43.

Englund, R. 2009. "The smell of the cage" *CDLI* accessed 11/01/2013 www.cdli.ucla.edu/pubs/cdlj/2009/cdlj2009_004.html

Helwing, B. 2004. "Tracking the Proto-Elamite on the Central Iranian Plateau", in Malek Shahmirzadi, S. (ed.), *The potters of Sialk*, Sialk Reconsideration Project, Report 3, Iranian Cultural Heritage Organisation, Tehran: 45–58.

Korfmann, M. 1973. "The sling as a weapon", *Scientific American* 229 (4): 34–42.

Potts, D. T. 1999. *The Archaeology of Elam: Formation and Transformation of an Ancient Iranian State*, Cambridge World Archaeology Series, Cambridge University Press, Cambridge.

Voigt, M. and Dyson Jr., R. H. 1992. "Chronology of Iran, ca. 8000–2000 B.C.", in Ehrich, R. W. (ed.), *Chronologies of Old World Archaeology*, I & II, Chicago University Press, Chicago: 122–78; 125–53.